TH ASIA
L DIVISIONS,
PAL CITIES,
TERRAIN
200 300 400 500 Miles
00 400 500 Kilometers
Lhasa
Tsangpo
HIMALAYA MTS.
ARUNACHAL PRADESH
Thimphu
HUTAN
Itanagar
Brahmaputra
ASSAM
Guwahati
NAGALAND
NAGA HILLS
Chindwin
Kohima
KHASI HILLS
Shillong
MEGHALAYA
Sylhet
MANIPUR
Imphal
Dhaka
Agartala
TRIPURA
Aizawl
MIZORAM
MYANMAR
Comilla
Khulna
Chittagong
Mandalay
ARAKAN RANGE
Irrawaddy
Sitwe (Akyab)
ARAKAN COAST
Salween
O F
A L
ANDAMAN ISLANDS
Port Blair
ANDAMAN AND NICOBAR ISLANDS U.T.
NICOBAR ISLANDS
SUMATRA
INDONESIA

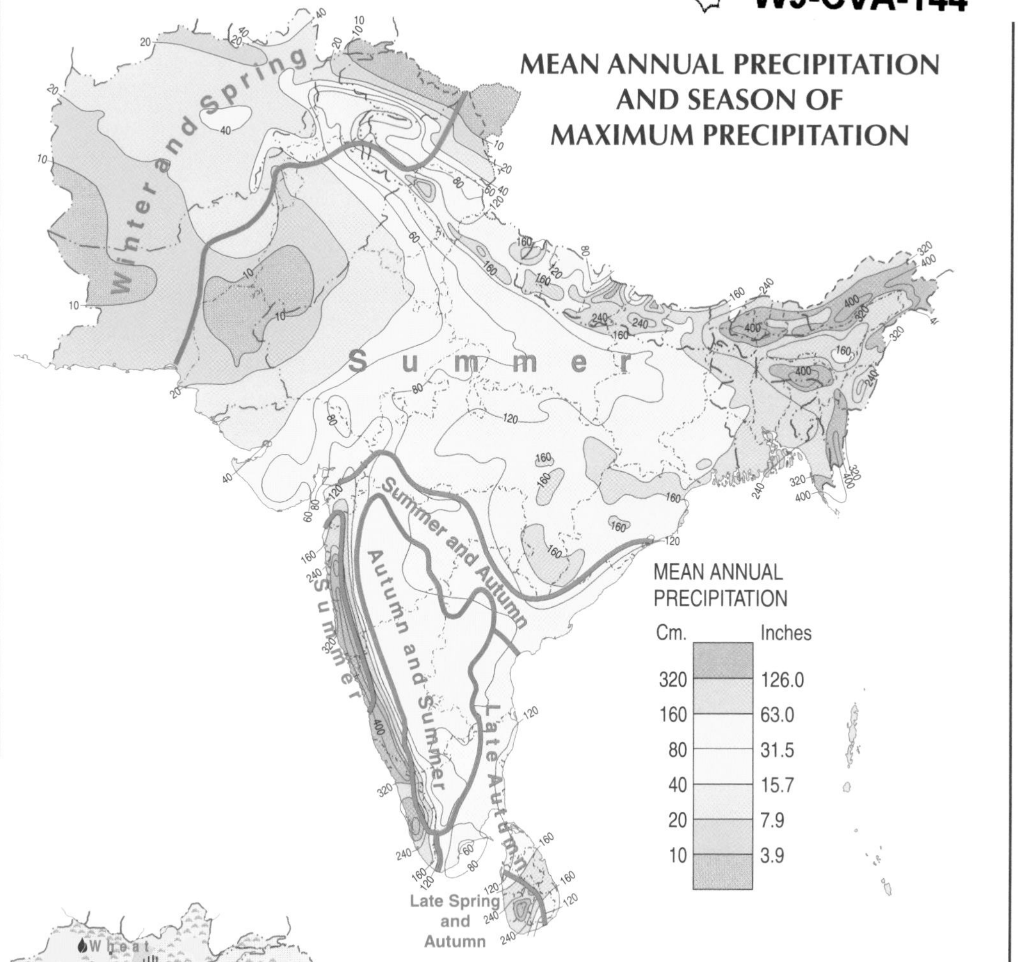
MEAN ANNUAL PRECIPITATION AND SEASON OF MAXIMUM PRECIPITATION
Winter and Spring
Summer
Summer and Autumn
Autumn and Summer
Late Autumn
Late Spring and Autumn
MEAN ANNUAL PRECIPITATION
Cm. Inches
320 126.0
160 63.0
80 31.5
40 15.7
20 7.9
10 3.9

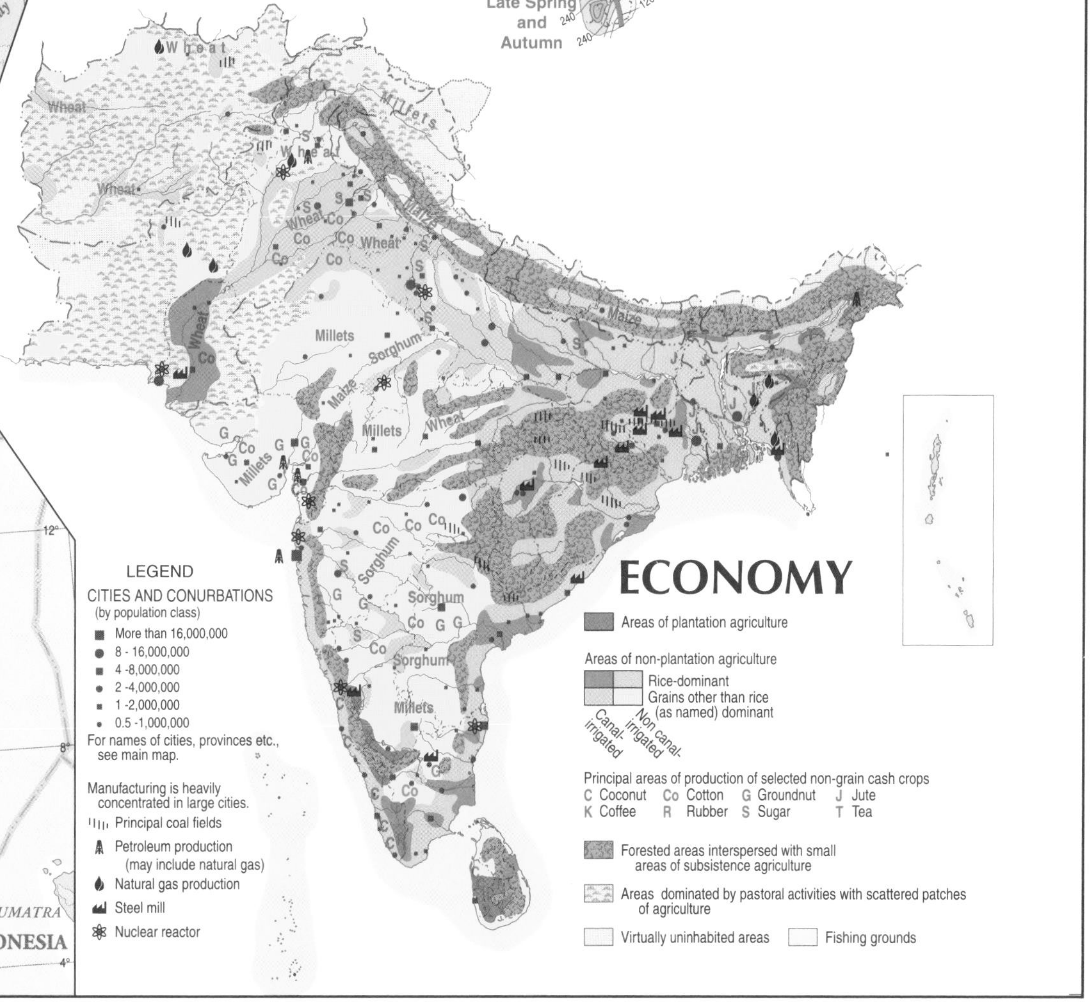
ECONOMY
Wheat
Millets
Maize
Sorghum
LEGEND
CITIES AND CONURBATIONS (by population class)
More than 16,000,000
8 - 16,000,000
4 -8,000,000
2 -4,000,000
1 -2,000,000
0.5 -1,000,000
For names of cities, provinces etc., see main map.
Manufacturing is heavily concentrated in large cities.
Principal coal fields
Petroleum production (may include natural gas)
Natural gas production
Steel mill
Nuclear reactor
Areas of plantation agriculture
Areas of non-plantation agriculture
Rice-dominant
Grains other than rice (as named) dominant
Canal-irrigated
Non canal-irrigated
Principal areas of production of selected non-grain cash crops
C Coconut Co Cotton G Groundnut J Jute
K Coffee R Rubber S Sugar T Tea
Forested areas interspersed with small areas of subsistence agriculture
Areas dominated by pastoral activities with scattered patches of agriculture
Virtually uninhabited areas
Fishing grounds

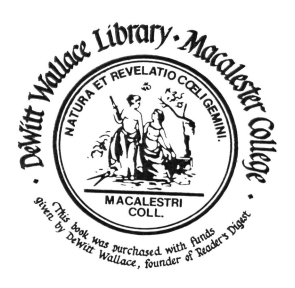

ENCYCLOPEDIA OF *India*

editorial board

ENCYCLOPEDIA OF *India*

VOLUME 3

K–R

Stanley Wolpert

Editor in Chief

CHARLES SCRIBNER'S SONS

An imprint of Thomson Gale, a part of The Thomson Corporation

THOMSON
GALE™

Detroit • New York • San Francisco • San Diego • New Haven, Conn. • Waterville, Maine • London • Munich

THOMSON
GALE

Encyclopedia of India

Stanley Wolpert, Editor in Chief

For more information, contact
Thomson Gale
27500 Drake Rd.
Farmington, Hills, MI 48331-3535
Or you can visit our Internet site at
http://www.gale.com

LIBRARY OF CONGRESS CATALOGING-IN-PUBLICATION DATA

Encyclopedia of India / Stanley A. Wolpert, editor in chief.
p. cm.
Includes bibliographical references and index.
ISBN 0-684-31349-9 (set hardcover : alk. paper)—ISBN 0-684-31350-2 (v. 1)—ISBN 0-684-31351-0 (v. 2)—ISBN 0-684-31352-9 (v. 3)—ISBN 0-684-31353-7 (v. 4)
1. India—Encyclopedias. I. Wolpert, Stanley A., 1927–
DS405.E556 2005
954'.003—dc22
2005019616

This title is also available as an e-book.
ISBN 0-684-31512-2
Contact your Thomson Gale representative for ordering information.

Printed in the United States of America
10 9 8 7 6 5 4 3 2 1

table of contents

list of maps

list of articles

KABIR ***(1440–1518), mystic poet.*** Although tradition states that Kabir was born in 1398 and lived to be 120 years old, he was born in 1440 and lived only until 1518. He is the most quoted poet, apart from Tulsidas (1532–1623), in India. He was a disciple of Ramananda (c. 1400–c. 1470), the Hindu mystic poet. Kabir was an illiterate Muslim weaver of Varanasi (Benares), although some say he was the son of a Brahman widow who was adopted by the childless Muslim *julaha* (low caste weaver) Niru and his wife. Kabir married Loi, and they had two children. His devotional poems and his devotion led many to follow him (*Kabirpanthis*), irrespective of their sectarian faith, in his love of God. He contributed to the *bhakti* tradition, and his conception of devotion to God as suffering may come from the Sufis; his integration of these elements with the *nath sampradaya* "lord" or "master" tradition, whereby a devotee followed a teacher, produced his distinctive religion.

Kabir preached that a simple union (*sahaja-yoga*), an emotional integration of the soul with God through personal devotion, could be achieved by all people, whether they were Hindus or Muslims ("I am not a Hindu, nor a Muslim am I"), or whether they were of high or low caste ("Now I have no caste, no creed"). He denounced the mullahs and the Muslim practice of bowing toward Mecca, and he criticized Hindu practices as well, condemning ritualistic and ascetic practices of the Brahmans and yogis. Accordingly, he was condemned by both. He satirized hypocrisy, greed, and violence, especially of the overtly religious. He preached *ahimsa* (nonviolence), and he believed that women were a hindrance to spiritual progress.

Kabir's simple songs of devotion to God, popularized through the song form, *sabda* or *pada*, were written in an unsophisticated Hindi that could be understood by the uneducated and that continues to inspire the masses of Hindus and Muslims in North India and in Pakistan and Bangladesh. He is said to have written thousands of couplets (*doha* or *sakhi*), love songs, and mystic poems. He was claimed by both Hindus and Muslims, and legend states that when he died at Maghar near Gorakhpur, his body turned to flowers; his Muslim followers buried half of them, and his Hindu followers cremated the other half. The Sikhs also adopted Kabir's works, and their holy book, the Granth Sahib, contains over five hundred of his verses. He is held by Sikhs in much the same kind of reverance as their ten Gurus. His work was collected in the Granth Sahib by Guru Arjan Dev in 1604, and in two other collections, the Kabir Granthavali and Bijak, the sacred book of the Kabir Panth, the Sikh sect devoted to Kabir's teachings.

Roger D. Long

See also **Bhakti; Sikhism**

BIBLIOGRAPHY

Hess, Linda, and Shukdeo Singh, eds. *The Bijak of Kabir.* New Delhi: Oxford University Press, 2002.

Keay, F. E. *Kabir and His Followers.* New Delhi: Aravali Books International, 1997.

Vaudeville, Charlotte. *A Weaver Named Kabir: Selected Verses with a Detailed Biographical and Historical Introduction.* New Delhi: Oxford University Press, 1993.

KALI. *See* **Devī.**

KĀLIDĀSA, ***fifth-century Indian dramatist and poet.*** Kālidāsa, considered to be the premier literary figure of the Sanskrit tradition, set the standard for classical Indian poetry and drama in his widely celebrated works. The poet's vibrantly evocative landscapes (particularly around the North Indian region of Ujjayinī), detailed urban settings, and apparent knowledge of court life suggest an association with Chandragupta II, who ruled most of North India from 375 to 415. Inscriptions at Aihole, praising the poet's abilities, clearly date his works to before 634, but more specific historical information is lacking.

Kālidāsa's literary legacy is based on seven surviving works. The *Meghadūta* (Cloud messenger) is a spellbinding lyrical tour de force in which a cloud is asked to voyage through a myth-laden landscape of India and carry a message to the protagonist's beloved. Two longer poems (*mahākāvyas*), derived from earlier epic sources, combine heroic narratives with breathtaking natural descriptions. The *Raghuvansha* (Lineage of Raghu) depicts the great solar race of warrior kings, into which Rāma, an incarnation of the Hindu god Vishnu, is born. The *Kumārasanbhava* (Birth of the war god Kumāra) narrates the divine emergence of the son of Shiva for the restoration of cosmic order.

Kālidāsa's plays, employing both Sanskrit and Prakrit languages, affirm profound levels of cosmic unity, reconciling life's inevitable conflicts through a union of the hero and heroine, echoing the ritual sacrifice of Vedic literatures. *Mālavikāgnimitra* (*Mālavikā and Agnimitra*), generally classified as a secular romance in which the characters are "invented" as opposed to being taken from epic sources, depicts the love between King Agnimitra and an exiled servant Mālavikā, who turns out to be a princess. *Vikramorvashīya* (Urvashī won by valor) retells the Vedic and epic legend of love between the mortal king Purūravas and the immortal nymph Urvashī and explores the sentiments of love in union and separation. The poet's best-known work, *Abhijñānashākuntala* (Shakuntalā and the ring of recollection), often referred to as *Shākuntala*, is also based on an epic narrative and is hence characterized as a heroic romance. It tells of King Dushyanta's fateful meeting with the daughter of a royal sage and a celestial nymph, Shakuntalā, in her adopted father's hermitage. Although the king marries her in secret, he is cursed to forget about the union until the ring he had given her is found in the belly of a fish. When the king's memory is restored, he reunites with Shakuntalā as the tension between desire (*kāma*) and duty (*dharma*) is reconciled through a blending of erotic and heroic sentiments. This elevated aesthetic mood, or *rasa*, in which divisions between the audience, actors, and author were said to dissolve, was the expressed goal of the literary work of art, and Kālidāsa's ability to inculcate the distilled and universalized emotional essence of *rasa* is unparalleled in the Sanskrit literary tradition. His rapt imagery, aesthetic sensitivity, and dazzling landscapes, infused with the presence of Shiva and the Goddess, reveal the divine presence in all things.

Rick Jarow

BIBLIOGRAPHY

Abhijñānashākuntala. Devanagari recension with commentary of Rāghavabhatta. 12th ed., edited by N. R. Acharya. Mumabai: Nirnaya Sagar Press, 1958.

Mālavikāgnimitra, edited by K. A. Subramania Iyer. New Delhi: Shitya Akademi, 1978.

Meghadūta, edited by S. K. De. Delhi: Sahitya Akademi, 1957.

Raghuvansha, with Mallinātha's commentary, ed. and trans. G. N. Nandargikar. Reprint, Delhi: Motilal Banarsidass, 1982.

SECONDARY SOURCES

Ānandavardhana. *The Dhvanyāloka of Ānandavardhana*. With the "Locana" of Abhinavagupta. Translated by Daniel H. H. Ingalls, Jeffrey Moussaieff Masson, and M. V. Partwardhan. Cambridge, Mass.: Harvard University Press, 1990.

Baumer, Rachel van M., and James R. Brandon, eds. *Sanskrit Drama in Performance*. Honolulu: University of Hawaii Press, 1981.

Dimock, Edward Cameron, et al. *The Literatures of India: An Introduction*. Chicago: University of Chicago Press, 1974.

Miller, Barbara Stoler, et al. *Theater of Memory: The Plays of Kālidāsa*. New York: Columbia University Press, 1984.

KĀMA SŪTRA Composed by Vātsyāyana Mallanāga, the Kāma Sūtra is a treatise on erotic love, deemed one of the three spheres of worldly life in ancient India. The dates of the author are uncertain, but evidence suggests he lived sometime in the third or fourth century of the common era, just before the inception of the great Gupta empire. The Kāma Sūtra is the earliest surviving text of the quasi-scientific genre of writing on the subject of erotic love known as *kāma shāstra* (the science of erotics). Though earlier works on the subject are no longer available, this genre became abundant in later times. The Kāma Sūtra has a thirteenth-century commentary, called *Jayamangala*, written by one Yashodhara.

Long viewed as a sort of Hindu parallel to the *Joy of Sex*, recent research suggests that the Kāma Sūtra is actually better seen in the context of the courtly and urban culture that emerged during Gupta times. The Kāma Sūtra is divided into seven books, each comprising two or more chapters. The first book sets out the lifestyle of the "man about town," or *nāgaraka*, a figure to whom most of the text is seemingly addressed. Vātsyāyana gives details about his daily routine, social engagements, household, potential female partners, and a vast list of arts (*kalās*) that he was to master as part of a courtly education. The second book, on sex itself, begins by dividing women and men up into a sexual typology (named famously after animals), based on size, endurance, and temperament. In subsequent chapters the author treats a variety of subjects, including embracing, kissing, nail scratching, biting, positions in intercourse, and oral sex, in a highly technical, often dry style. The third book advises a young man how to obtain a virgin for marriage, noting both more and less respectable methods, depending on his circumstances. It also discusses the manner in which a bride was to be sexually approached and "won over" on the days following the marriage. The fourth book discusses the conduct appropriate for married women, a profoundly complex subject given the fact that polygyny was widespread among the elite classes in early India. Vātsyāyana discusses the delicate protocol of the harem (Sanskrit, *antahpura*), where the master of the household met his wives and concubines on a daily basis, the dynamics of which were often complex, dangerous, and consequential for the maintenance of stability in the household. The fifth book discusses sex with other men's wives, a practice Vātsyāyana warns against in all but the most desperate circumstances, when a man simply cannot control his desires. Here the use of intermediaries, as well as secret liaisons with women of the *antahpura*, are discussed. The sixth book is addressed to courtesans, instructing them on how to seduce, cajole, extract money from, and even dispose of, potential patrons. The last book sets out esoteric formulas (magical and medicinal) for those who, for various reasons, were unable to follow the policy laid out in previous chapters. These formulas are mostly aimed at controlling noncompliant lovers or enhancing one's sexual prowess.

Daud Ali

See also **Devī; Hinduism (Dharma)**

BIBLIOGRAPHY

Bhattacharya, Narendra Nath. *History of Indian Erotic Literature*. Delhi: Munshiram Manoharlal, 1975.

Chakladar, H. C. *Social Life in Ancient India: A Study of Vatsyayana's Kamasutra*. 1929. Reprint, Kolkata: Susil Gupta, 1954.

Kamasutra. Translated by Wendy Doniger and Sudhir Kakar. Oxford: Clarendon, 2002.

Roy, Kumkum. "Unravelling the *Kamasutra*." In *A Question of Silence: The Sexual Economies of Modern India*, edited by Mary E. John and Janaki Nair. Delhi: Kali for Women, 1998.

KANPUR An industrial city in Uttar Pradesh, Kanpur (population 2.5 million in 2001) is located on the banks of the Ganges about 250 miles (400 kilometers) to the southeast of Delhi. Its old name, Kanhpur, is derived from one of the names of Krishna (Kanha). It was located in the heartland of the Mughal empire. In the eighteenth century, it was included in the territory under the control of the *nawāb*s of Oudh. In 1803 the *nawāb* of Oudh had to cede the southern part of his realm to the British, and Kanpur was at the center of this ceded territory. Unlike in Bengal, where the British introduced a permanent settlement of the land revenue, they subjected this newly acquired area to a stiffer revenue settlement. Many peasants lost their land as the British collectors auctioned it off for the slightest default in revenue payments. The peasants were forced to turn to cash crops, and the soil of this formerly fertile area was degraded within a few decades. For these reasons, many of the peasants of this area joined the "Mutiny" of 1857. Kanpur became a major center of resistance against the British in 1857 and was the scene of a massacre of British men, women, and children. Nana Saheb, the last Maratha *peshwa* of Pune, was banished to the old Bitur palace outside Kanpur, and seemed to be as innocuous a pensioner as the powerless Great Mughal in Delhi, but he joined the mutinous soldiers and took over the city, directing the massacre.

In 1872 Kanpur had only 123,000 inhabitants, but in subsequent decades it emerged as a major center of India's new cotton textile industry, started by British entrepreneurs, unlike the earlier mills in Bombay (Mumbai) and Ahmedabad, which were mostly owned by Indians. When the large Indian textile mills declined, the government of India tried to stimulate industrial growth in Kanpur by establishing one of the five great Indian Institutes of Technology (ITTs) in that city. The land was granted by the government of Uttar Pradesh, and the buildings were completed in 1963. An Indo-American program was launched in 1962, under which nine leading institutions in the United States helped provide equipment and training for ITT staff and students. At present, the Kanpur ITT has about 1,400 undergraduate and 850 postgraduate students and a faculty of 300, and Kanpur has become a center of India's technological revolution.

Dietmar Rothermund

BIBLIOGRAPHY

Mukherjee, Rudrangshu. *Spectre of Violence: The 1857 Kanpur Massacres*. New Delhi: Penguin, 1998.

Yalland, Zoe. *Traders and Nabobs: The British in Cawnpore, 1765–1857*. Wilton, U.K.: Russell, 1987.

———. *Boxwallahs: The British in Cawnpore, 1857–1901*. Norwich, U.K.: Russell, 1994.

KANVAYANA DYNASTY. *See* **History and Historiography.**

KARACHI The capital of Sind province in southern Pakistan, Karachi is the country's largest city and principal seaport, and it serves as a major center for commerce and industry. The city occupies an area of 228 square miles (591 sq. km), with a metropolitan region that covers around 560 square miles (1,450 sq. km). The population, according to a 1998 census, is approximately 9.8 million.

Karachi's recorded history extends over a period of approximately three hundred years. The area that became Karachi was until 1725 a mostly barren piece of land surrounded on three sides by the Arabian Sea. The city takes its name from Kalachi-jo-Kun, referring to the area's deep saline creeks and the presence of a fishing hamlet.

The British East India Company occupied Karachi in 1839, conquering the larger region of Sind in 1843. The city was made an administrative center and thereafter expanded rapidly. When Sind was incorporated into the Bombay presidency, Karachi became its district headquarters. Economically, as a major port for the British Raj, Karachi was linked to the cotton- and wheat-producing areas elsewhere in the subcontinent. In 1935 Sind was made a separate province, with Karachi as its capital.

Between August 1947 and April 1951 the open borders between India and Pakistan saw 8 million Muslims move to the newly independent state and 6 million non-Muslims flee in the other direction. Karachi, at the time Pakistan's capital, received large numbers of Muslim refugees, including educated arrivals who hoped to find government employment. The 1951 census identified close to 55 percent of the city's population, then more than 1 million, as Muhajirs—Urdu-speaking immigrants from India.

Karachi experienced further rapid growth over the next two decades with the arrival of migrants from the rural Sind, and from Pakistan's North-West Frontier (NWFP) and Punjab provinces. Ethnic Pathans from NWFP, mostly a working-class community, expanded squatter settlements and shantytowns constructed earlier by Muhajirs. Competition for scarce available resources among antagonistic ethnic groups resulted over the following decades in near political and social breakdown, and contributed to an often corrupt and ineffective city administration. The Muhajirs' major political organization, the Muhajir (later Muttehida) Qaumi Mahaz (MQM, or People's Movement), emerged, seeking enhanced political recognition in Sindh for the Urdu-speaking community, and it has since called for Karachi to become a separate province. MQM has contested elections and sought national influence in alliance with other parties. It has also resorted to violence and has been subjected to heavy-handed repression from federal authorities.

Ethnic troubles are not the only factor in Karachi's turbulent politics. Small arms were smuggled into the city during the anti-Communist jihad in Afghanistan during the 1980s, making more lethal the urban culture of violence. Afghan refugees settling in the city have been linked to the city's flourishing drug trade. Millions of Pakistanis have become addicts due to easy access to heroin.

Karachi nevertheless retains a special character and importance for Pakistan. It serves as the country's center for transportation, finance, commerce, and manufacturing. Most international trade reaching Pakistan and Afghanistan passes through the city's modern port, and it boasts a major new airport. Karachi has a large automobile assembly plant, an oil refinery, a steel mill, shipbuilding, and textile factories, and it is the center of the country's media and entertainment industries. Although the seat of the national government shifted to Islamabad in 1960, Karachi remains the most vibrant city in Pakistan and the nucleus of the internationally oriented sector of Pakistan's economy.

Marvin G. Weinbaum

BIBLIOGRAPHY

Baillie, Alexander F. *Kurrachee*. Karachi: Oxford University Press, 1997.

Hasan, Arif. "The Growth of a Metropolis." In *Karachi—Megacity of Our Times*, edited by H. Khuhro and A. Moorej. Karachi: Oxford University Press, 1997.

———. *Understanding Karachi: Planning and Reform for the Future*. Karachi: Oxford University Press, 1999.

KARAIKKĀL AMMAIYĀR ***(c. A.D. 550), mystic, early poet-saint of the*** **bhakti** ***movement.*** Karaikkāl Ammaiyār, or the Lady of Karaikkāl, was a mystic devoted to Shiva, the dancing lord of Tiruvālankādu, Tamil Nadu. As one of the earliest of the sixty-three *nayanārs* (Shiva saints) and a contemporary of Pūdam, the first *ālvār* (Vishnu saint), Karaikkāl Ammaiyār helped to usher in the Tamil *bhakti* (devotional) movement, which spread from this region across India. *Bhakti* saints represented the folk voices of many castes, and their hymns in the local languages proclaimed the supremacy of a personal love for God above priestly ritual. Although *bhakti* mystics did not overturn caste hierarchies, their cultural imprint on India has been profound.

Karaikkāl Ammaiyār's songs are among the earliest *bhakti* compositions for Shiva in the *prabandha* mode, which became popular among the medieval saints. The hymns and hagiographies of the *nayanārs* are recorded in the twelve Tirumurai, the scripture for the Tamil Shaiva Siddhanta school; Karaikkāl Ammaiyār's three long hymns are recorded in the eleventh Tirumurai. Her work is inspired by the literary styles of the classical Tamil Sangam era (1st–5th centuries) and the evocative tone of fifth-century early *bhakti* texts like Tirumurukārrupatai, a guide to god Murukan's sacred sites, and Paripātal, in praise of Murukan and Vishnu-Tirumāl. Karaikkāl Ammaiyār's three hymns are *Mūtta-tirup-patikañkal*, twenty-two verses in classical melodies; *Tiru-irattai-manimālai*, twenty verses of two alternating styles; and *Arputat-tiru-vantāti*, one hundred one verses in the *antāti* genre, a sonorous web of praises in which the last word of each verse is echoed in the next.

Unlike the ninth-century *bhakti* saint Āndāl, who resisted marriage on Earth for love of Vishnu, Karaikkāl Ammaiyār was married to a merchant when she was a young woman called Punitavati. The myth of her transformation from chaste wife to chaste yogi is recorded by the sage Sēkkilār in *Periya Purānam*, a thirteenth-century hagiography of the *nāyanārs*. One day, Punitavati's husband handed her two mangoes, which he had received as the gift from a sage. She fed a poor Shiva devotee with one fruit; and she magically produced more mangoes for her husband at mealtime by praying to Shiva. Frightened by this display of divine powers, her husband fled and remarried. On practicing severe yogic austerities, Punitavati came to be addressed as Karaikkāl Ammaiyār. In a rare example of reversed spousal roles, her husband returned to prostrate humbly at her feet. The myth highlights the auspicious power of both the chaste, faithful wife (*pativrata*) and the chaste yogi who renounces sensuality. This follows the Tamil tradition of the *pativrata* Kannaki, who is transformed from a meek wife to a powerful, semi-divine heroine in the Sangam epic, Shilappatikāram.

Karaikkāl Ammaiyār sang of her ironic, joyful bondage to Shiva, whose grace would free her from earthly bondage in the cycle of birth and death (*samsāra*). In another poem, she begs that Shiva at least grant her the boon of always remembering him. Sēkkilār states that Shiva respectfully addressed her as "Ammaiyār," or Mother, when she achieved enlightenment and *moksha*, or freedom from *saṃsāra*. A thirteenth-century Chola bronze provides a visual representation of the ghoulish yet gleeful yogi who described herself as a *pey* (ghost), "a female wraith of shriveled breasts, swollen veins, protruding eye-balls, white teeth, sunken stomach, fiery red hair, two protruding fangs," according to Sēkkilār (Vanmikanathan, p. 537). Frescoes depict her life on the walls of her modern shrine at Karaikkāl; and young women today offer mangoes to the icon of this venerable woman saint.

Sita Anantha Raman

See also **Bhakti**

BIBLIOGRAPHY

Cilappadikāram. *Ilañkōvatikāl Iyarrurruliya Cilappatikāram* (Ilango Adigāl's Cilapaddikāram, editor, P. V. Sōmasundaram). Chennai: Saiva Siddhānta Society, 1969.

Dehejia, Vidya, trans. *Āntāl and Her Path of Love: Poems of a Woman Saint from South India.* SUNY Series in Hindu Studies. Albany: State University of New York, 1990.

Harle, J. C. *Art and Architecture of the Indian Subcontinent.* Pelican History of Art Series. 2nd ed. New Haven, Conn.: Yale University Press, 1994.

Hart, George L., III. *The Poems of the Ancient Tamil: Their Milieu and Their Sanskrit Counterparts.* Berkeley: University of California Press, 1975.

Sastri, K. A. Nilkanta. *A History of South India: From Prehistoric Times to the Fall of Vijayanagar.* Delhi: Oxford University Press, 1975.

Shulman, David Dean. *Tamil Temple Myths: Sacrifice and Divine Marriage in the South Indian Saiva Tradition.* Princeton, N.J.: Princeton University Press.

Subramanian, K., ed. *Patinōnrān Tirumurai* (Eleventh Tirumurai). Saiva Siddhanta Math series. Srivaikuntam: Kumara Guruparan Sangam, 1972.

Vanmikanathan, G. *Periya Purānam: A Tamil Classic on the Great Saiva Saints of South India by Sekkizhaar.* Mylapore: Sri Ramakrishna Math, 1985.

Varadarajan, M. *A History of Tamil Literature.* New Delhi: Sahitya Akademi, 1988.

Yocum, Glenn. *Hymns to the Dancing Siva: A Study of Mānikkavācakar's Tiruvācakam.* New Delhi: Heritage Publishers, 1982.

Younger, Paul. *The Home of Dancing Sivan: The Traditions of the Hindu Temple in Citamparam.* New York: Oxford University Press, 1995.

KARGIL CONFLICT, THE In late April 1999, Indian soldiers patrolling along the Kashmir Line of Control (LOC) near the Indian town of Kargil were ambushed by unseen assailants who had occupied secret positions high atop frozen mountain peaks along the Great Himalayan Range. After several frantic weeks of confusion, Indian military and intelligence officers realized the intruders were not Kashmiri militants, as they initially had assumed, but in fact were well-trained troops from Pakistan's Northern Light Infantry (NLI), and that the infiltration was much larger and better organized than earlier believed. In response, the Indian government mounted a major military and diplomatic campaign to oust Pakistan's occupying forces. After two months of intense high-altitude fighting, during which each side suffered more than 1,000 casualties, Pakistan ordered its soldiers home, India regained its mountain posts along the LOC, and the conflict ended.

Although in the end no territory changed hands—as it had in the previous wars India and Pakistan fought in

1947–1948, 1965, and 1971—the Kargil conflict was a momentous event. Occurring just a year after India and Pakistan openly detonated nuclear explosives, this military engagement dispelled the conventional wisdom that nuclear-armed countries cannot fight one another. Like the only other direct military clash between nuclear weapons powers—the Sino-Soviet skirmishes over Zhenbao Island in the Ussuri River in the spring of 1969—the Kargil conflict did not come close to causing a nuclear war. However, it is now known that Indian troops were within days of opening another front across the LOC, an act that might have triggered a large-scale conventional war, which in turn might have led to the employment of nuclear weapons.

Several analysts from India and the United States consider Kargil to be the fourth Indo-Pakistani war. It probably is more accurate to view Kargil as a "conflict," or a "near war," as one Indian general put it. The scale and intensity of the fighting well exceeded even the high levels of peacetime violence typically experienced along the Kashmir Line of Control, where fierce artillery duels and ten-person-a-day body counts have been far too common. However, the military engagement in the spring and summer of 1999 was confined to a small section of mountainous terrain in Indian-held Kashmir; only a fraction of each side's soldiers and military arsenals were used; and both countries tried to reduce the risk of escalation by keeping their political and military objectives limited. Moreover, because about seven hundred Indian and Pakistani soldiers perished in the mountains near Kargil, this conflict did not meet the classical definition of war as an armed conflict with at least one thousand battlefield deaths.

Background

The Kargil intrusion is deeply rooted in India's long-standing dispute with Pakistan over the political status of Jammu and Kashmir. In late 1947, Maharaja Hari Singh, the ruler of semiautonomous Kashmir, delayed acceding to either of South Asia's newly independent countries, India or Pakistan, ignoring the rules of partition issued by the British viceroy, Lord Louis Mountbatten. Hari Singh's dreams of an independent Jammu and Kashmir were interrupted by a tribal rebellion near Poonch. With the assistance of Pakistan army officers, tribal *lashkars* (forces) from Pakistan's North-West Frontier province raided Kashmir, as they had done many times in the past, seeking glory and loot. India's new prime minister, Jawaharlal Nehru, sent in the Indian army to repulse these raiders, and India and Pakistan found themselves engaged in their first war within months of independence.

Kargil was a key battleground in the 1947–1948 war. In May 1948 a small force of Pakistan's Gilgit Scouts captured the high-altitude Zojila pass, the only strategic passage that links Srinagar with the Northern Areas and Leh on the Indian side of the LOC, and with it the surrounding towns of Kargil, Dras, and Skardu. Major General D. K. Palit, who was serving in a nearby Indian unit at Poonch, noted India's apprehension over this development: "As a result of the fall of Skardu and Kargil, the Valley of Kashmir was threatened from the north as well as the east; what is more, the only line of communication between Srinagar and Leh, over the Zojila and through Kargil, was disrupted. Failing rapid reinforcements, it would be only a matter of months before the enemy could walk into Leh" (Palit, p. 241). Kargil's strategic importance was as clear to the Indian government then as it is now.

India reacted immediately to this threat by sending a brigade-size force from Srinagar and Leh to retake Kargil and reopen the road. This episode is significant because the Gilgit Scouts eventually were incorporated into the NLI as part of Pakistan's Force Command Northern Areas (FCNA). These units remembered, through stories from previous generations and evidence retained in their archives, that they had captured the Kargil heights with a small, determined force. Second, it also is notable that India was unwilling to accept such an outcome and would retaliate forcefully to vacate any intrusion in this strategically important area—a crucial lesson. In the end, the fighting during what could be called the first Kargil conflict proved inconclusive. Pakistani and Indian forces reached a military stalemate, and a negotiated cease-fire line was codified in the Karachi Agreement of 1949.

Pakistanis generally believe that Hindu leaders have long oppressed the Muslim population of Jammu and Kashmir, and the questionable accession into the Indian union has denied the populace of their right to self-determination. They stress the United Nations (UN) Security Council's demand for a "free and impartial plebiscite," although other UN demands for "a cessation of the fighting" and the creation of "proper conditions" for such a vote to take place are generally overlooked. Pakistanis also consider the Indian government's refusal to grant Kashmir independence as proof that Indians ultimately do not accept the "two-nation theory," which is the raison d'être for Pakistan's creation and its continued existence.

Pakistan always has faced a larger, more populous, wealthier, and militarily more powerful neighbor in India. Pakistani defense planners have had great difficulty finding ways to compensate for these profound structural asymmetries. The sense of political and strategic necessity, when combined with a strong belief of moral righteousness, has justified the use of almost any means for the sake of liberating Kashmir and resisting Indian primacy on the subcontinent. As a result, the Pakistani army repeatedly has attempted daring and unconventional methods to wrest Kashmir from India by force and to liberate the Kashmiri Muslims from Indian rule—and it repeatedly has been stymied in these efforts. The 1999 Kargil operation was the latest failed attempt to seize the upper hand in South Asia's enduring rivalry.

Pakistan's Bold Plan

The Kargil operation was an audacious attempt to seize an opportunity of historic proportions. Pakistan's Kargil gambit can be seen as a logical—though perhaps extreme—continuation of its long-standing competitive policy with India. The Pakistani people view the Kashmiri cause as moral and just, and in 1999 Pakistani security planners continued a tradition of asymmetric strategies to circumvent India's conventional military advantages. A successful Kargil intrusion would have shown that Pakistani soldiers were willing to endure incredible hardships to support the Kashmiri struggle. It could have given a timely boost to a weakening insurgency inside Kashmir. And finally, if the plan succeeded, it could have forced India back to the negotiating table and given Islamabad greater leverage to resolve the Kashmir dispute on favorable terms once and for all.

In the winter of 1998–1999, Indian troops predictably vacated their high-altitude posts along the LOC as they retreated to winter positions—a normal measure taken by both Indian and Pakistani forces to reduce the strain on forces during the harsh winter months. Pakistani planners aimed to seize this unprotected territory to the maximum feasible limit, with an eye on interdicting National Highway 1A (NH-1A), the strategically important Indian road that runs between Srinagar and Leh. But the plan's boldness also made it dangerous and ultimately untenable. Its success would require hundreds of troops to infiltrate across the LOC without detection. After their inevitable discovery, these troops would have to fend off Indian counterattacks until the onset of snow the next winter, which would close the passes, halt military operations, and allow Pakistani infiltrators to harden their positions. This military fait accompli would have enabled Pakistan to redraw the LOC.

At remote posts in the higher altitude terrain along the LOC separating the portions of Kashmir that India and Pakistan possess, each side's forces would retreat to lower heights during the winter owing to the intense logistical and weather hazards associated with deploying troops during such conditions. After the creation of the cease-fire line (and subsequently the LOC), India and Pakistan tacitly allowed such winter retreats to occur without taking advantage of them, a norm consistent with the letter and spirit of the 1949 Karachi Agreement. Following India's military seizure of Siachen Glacier in northernmost Kashmir in 1984, however, both sides dramatically reduced the number of forward posts they would vacate during the harsh winter months. The loss of hundreds of square miles of territory around the Siachen Glacier was a deep scar for the Pakistan army, in particular the FCNA, which is tasked with its defense. So in the winter of 1998–1999, when Indian troops vacated their high-altitude posts in the area around Kargil, on the belief that invaders could not carry out any meaningful infiltration in such difficult terrain during inclimate weather, Pakistan was quick to mount, and then expand, its secret Kargil campaign.

The Kargil operation's planners seemed convinced that India would not expand the conflict elsewhere along the LOC or the international border, and that the world community would view the Kargil operation as part of the normal pattern of violence along the LOC, similar to India's daring occupation of the Siachen Glacier fifteen years before. While some of the Pakistani army's calculations were borne out by events, the faulty assumptions they made, when combined with tactical missteps on the ground, doomed the Kargil operation to failure. Perhaps most crucially, Kargil's planners failed to recognize the significance of the nuclear revolution. The international community could not endorse any attempt to use force to redraw international boundaries, even if they were disputed, and in particular would not permit what looked like the manipulation of nuclear escalation, even if that was not what Kargil's planners had in mind.

India's Political-Military Strategy

By the end of April 1999, Pakistan's intruding force had occupied about 130 posts in the Dras, Mushkoh, Kaksar, Batalik, and Chorbat-la sectors of northern Kashmir, covering an approximate area of 62 miles (100 kilometers) across the LOC and running 4–6 miles (7 to 10 kilometers) deep into the territory previously held by India. This far exceeded what is believed to be the Pakistani army's original plan to seize two dozen or so posts in a much smaller swathe of territory across the LOC. Some of the captured positions directly overlooked NH-1A, and put Pakistani troops in a position to interdict the strategically important road with artillery and long-range small arms fire.

The Indian army first learned about the intrusions in late April 1999. Initial Indian attempts to retrieve the heights, which were then thought to be held by Kashmiri militants, were easily rebuffed by Pakistan's well-trained and well-armed NLI soldiers. In fact, Indian troops experienced weeks of enemy fire without even seeing who was shooting at them, for the infiltrators were well hidden high atop the 13,000–18,000 foot-high (4,000–5,500-meter) mountain peaks. Indian officials gradually realized that circumstances were far more serious than they initially had assumed. Local commanders frantically began to maneuver their forces to contain the intruders and launched military patrols to determine the extent of the enemy intrusion. Because of poor intelligence, improper acclimatization of troops, a shortage of high-altitude equipment, and coordination difficulties, Indian troops suffered their heaviest casualties during this initial, frenetic phase of the military engagement.

The Indian armed forces launched a major counteroffensive, codenamed "Operation Vijay" (Victory), during the third week of May 1999. On 26 May, the Indian air force commenced air strikes in support of ground troops, vertically escalating the conflict. Indian troops simultaneously started mobilizing to war locations in other parts of the country, deploying forces along the India-Pakistan international border and elsewhere along the LOC. The Zojila pass opened in early May 1999, significantly earlier than normal. Pakistani defense planners had not counted on this development. The opening of Zojila facilitated India's induction of troops, supporting units, and logistics necessary for an effective counteroffensive. The Indian army achieved its first success on 13 June in the Dras subsector when they captured point 4590 at the Tololing Ridge after nearly three weeks of heavy fighting. This tactical victory was a turning point for the Indian counteroffensive, which the Indian army progressively built upon until the first week of July, when it had managed to recapture a significant portion of previously occupied territory.

As the Indian military reclaimed more territory, Pakistani prime minister Nawaz Sharif found himself under mounting international pressure to pull back Pakistani regular and irregular forces from the Indian side of the LOC. After a hastily arranged visit to Washington, D.C., over the Fourth of July holiday weekend, Prime Minister Sharif signed the Washington Declaration with U.S. president Bill Clinton and agreed to instruct Pakistani troops to vacate the captured territory. On 11 July, the Directors General Military Operations (DGMOs) of the Indian and Pakistani armies met at the Wagha checkpost, where the Pakistani DGMO consented to commence withdrawal by 11 July and complete it by 16 July, a date that later was extended until 18 July. Pakistanis insist that this cease-fire was not implemented in good faith, as Pakistani troops suffered heavy casualties throughout July. Indians counter that the use of force was authorized only to counter resistance or to attack positions that Pakistan still occupied after the cease-fire had expired. On 26 July 1999, the Indian DGMO declared at a press conference that all Pakistani intrusions had been vacated in and around the Kargil heights, thereby marking an official end to the conflict.

Was There a Risk of Nuclear War?

The Kargil conflict caused an especially high degree of alarm worldwide because it was the first major military engagement between two countries armed with nuclear weapons since the Sino-Soviet border clashes of 1969. Although no Indian or Pakistani nuclear weapons were actually deployed in 1999, and although previous Indo-Pakistani crises during the 1980s and early 1990s had occurred under the shadow of covert nuclear capabilities, the nuclear context of Kargil had three unprecedented effects on the strategic behavior of India, Pakistan, and outside parties, especially the United States. First, the achievement of mutual nuclear deterrence may have emboldened Pakistani military leaders to take assertive military action in Kashmir. Second, Indian officials believed that the nuclear revolution had fundamentally transformed the Indo-Pakistani competition, and thus reacted in a slow and confused manner to the infiltration. As Pakistan's military role became apparent, India responded with unexpected vigor, both militarily and rhetorically. Third, India's forceful response fed into the worst fears of the Clinton administration about nuclear escalation and spurred President Clinton to become personally involved in effecting Pakistan's withdrawal and preventing escalation to full-scale war. Pakistan ultimately misread the impact of nuclear weapons on Indian and American behavior, mistakenly believing that India would not expend sizable resources to restore the *status quo ante* and that any international intervention would freeze the ground situation to Pakistan's advantage.

These effects are striking because, prior to the Kargil infiltration, Indian and Pakistani elites viewed their nuclear capabilities as largely political, rather than military, tools, and assumed that they would stabilize their long-standing competition. Leaders of each country made assumptions about the impact that nuclear arsenals would have on the other side's behavior, but these assumptions were mutually contradictory, and ultimately failed to account for the attitudes and responses of the other side. As a result, nuclear weapons did not deter war. They did not cause the conflict, but they may have emboldened Pakistan to launch the Kargil operation, and they significantly heightened the alarm with which India, the United States, and other countries viewed Pakistan's intrusion.

The value of nuclear weapons as "cover" for the pursuit of Pakistani ambitions at lower levels of intensity was both recognized and publicly addressed prior to the conflict. Shortly before the intrusion was discovered, Pakistan chief of army staff general Pervez Musharraf announced that while nuclear weapons had dramatically changed the nature of war, "this, however, does not mean that conventional war has become obsolete. In fact conventional war will still remain the mode of conflict in any future conflagration with our traditional enemy" (Kargil Review Committee, p. 242). India's military leadership recognized this possibility, as did some intelligence analyses of Pakistani intentions. According to the Indian Kargil Review Committee report, as early as 1991 the Joint Intelligence Committee anticipated that Pakistan would use its nuclear capability to limit Indian conventional retaliation in the event of low-intensity conflict. On 10 February 1999, Indian chief of army staff general V. P. Malik declared, "Having crossed the nuclear threshold does not mean that a conventional war is out" (Cherian, "Political and Diplomatic Background"). While political elites were ruling out conventional war, within two months of each other, both army chiefs ruled conventional war back in.

Indian and Pakistani Nuclear Threats

Veiled and direct nuclear threats from a range of official and unofficial sources created a chilling backdrop to the fast-paced diplomatic interaction during the crisis, and not surprisingly added to the general confusion, raising the fears of military escalation. While leaders on both sides engaged in nuclear rhetoric, neither side directly threatened to use nuclear weapons and, judging by subsequent statements and actions, neither side feared the use of nuclear weapons by the other. However, observers in the United States and elsewhere were alarmed by the possibility that the limited conflict might escalate into a conventional war and then possibly to a nuclear exchange.

In late May, Pakistani foreign secretary Shamshad Ahmed made the most prominent nuclear statement of the conflict when he warned India that Pakistan could use "any weapon" to defend its territorial integrity ("Pakistan Warns It May Use Any Weapon"). This articulation is significant because Pakistani statements on nuclear doctrine usually focus on the use of nuclear weapons as a "last resort" when the survival of the state is at stake. It also took place quite early in the crisis—shortly after India had escalated the military situation by authorizing use of the Indian air force to conduct precision strikes against Pakistani positions on the Indian side of the LOC. This suggests that Pakistan was manipulating the nuclear threat, publicly setting a deliberately lowered nuclear threshold in an effort to spur international intervention and, as a consequence, to limit India's conventional response. Pakistani planners probably assumed that foreign intervention would freeze hostilities at an early stage of the crisis, leaving Pakistan in possession of at least some of its captured territory across the LOC and thereby enabling it to bargain over Kashmir from an advantageous position.

The Indian government-appointed Kargil Review Committee writes that, unlike Pakistan, India issued no nuclear threats. This statement is not entirely correct. Indian officials made nuclear threats in response to Pakistani statements. Indian leaders also issued several statements in June apparently intended for domestic audiences. Indian naval chief admiral Sushil Kumar stated that the Indian navy could both survive a nuclear attack and launch one in retaliation. Since the Indian navy had not taken custody of any nuclear weapons, this statement probably was intended to draw attention to the movement of elements of India's Eastern and Western fleets to strategic positions in the North Arabian Sea and also to position the Indian navy more favorably for future budget debates.

A 20 June 1999 editorial in the newspaper of the extremist Rashtriya Swayamsevak Sangh (RSS), affiliated with Prime Minister Atal Bihari Vajpayee's Bharatiya Janata Party (BJP), which led the coalition that ruled India at the time, urged the government to launch a nuclear strike on Pakistan. Given the close ideological and political connections between the RSS and the more militant members of the governing BJP coalition, Pakistani leaders could have interpreted this as an official statement. While it certainly did not reflect Prime Minister Vajpayee's views, these provocative statements by figures outside the actual decision-making loop complicated crisis management.

Pakistan also had its share of unsanctioned nuclear saber rattling, especially at the height of the crisis. As Prime Minister Nawaz Sharif prepared to travel to China and the United States to obtain support for Pakistan's position, his religious affairs minister, Raja Zafarul Haq, publicly warned that Pakistan could resort to the nuclear option to preserve Pakistani territory, sovereignty, or security. Minister Haq was not involved in Pakistan's nuclear command and control apparatus. This statement was uttered for domestic, or perhaps even personal, political reasons. Nonetheless, the international community viewed the remark with some alarm, and India responded emphatically to it. Prime Minister Vajpayee cautioned that India was prepared for all eventualities. According to the *Hindu*, "The Union Defence Minister, Mr. George Fernandes, said here today that Pakistan's threat of a full-fledged nuclear war should not be taken frivolously and that the country was prepared for any eventuality" ("India Ready for Any Eventuality"). National Security Adviser Brajesh Mishra added that India would not use nuclear weapons first, but that India was prepared in case "some lunatic tries to do something against us." ("India Prepared for Pakistan Nuclear Attack"). In this case, an apparently unofficial remark prompted a series of retaliatory statements by Indian officials at the highest level.

This rhetorical exchange during the Kargil crisis revealed a surprising lack of sophistication by India and Pakistan in nuclear diplomacy. Public statements in South Asia frequently are high on rhetoric and short on substance. In contrast to the U.S. and Soviet experiences, India and Pakistan had no history, organizational apparatus, or guidelines in sending nuclear signals. What occurred during the Kargil crisis was ad hoc, uncoordinated, and somewhat confused nuclear rhetoric. As a result, both sides took steps to tighten control over nuclear rhetoric in future crises.

Mysterious Nuclear Maneuvers

In addition to the ad hoc nuclear posturing, it has been reported that both sides increased nuclear readiness and may have made nuclear weapons available for actual employment. According to a report by a respected Indian journalist, nuclear warheads were readied, and delivery systems, including Mirage 2000 aircraft, short-range Prithvi missiles, and medium-ranged Agni missiles, were prepared for possible use. Nuclear weapons, according to this report, were placed at "Readiness State 3"—ready to be mated with delivery systems at short notice (Chengappa, 2000, p. 437). However, this claim has been discounted in Washington, Islamabad, and New Delhi. Moreover, no U.S. officials at the time mentioned it in any of their interviews or statements.

The most interesting postconflict testimony is that of Bruce Riedel, then-Special Assistant for Near East and South Asian Affairs at the U.S. National Security Council. According to a monograph he wrote in 2002, on 3 July 1999, U.S. intelligence detected "disturbing evidence that the Pakistanis were preparing their nuclear arsenals for possible deployment" (p. 5). According to Riedel, in a personal meeting with Prime Minister Sharif, President Clinton asked, "Did Sharif know his military was preparing their nuclear-tipped missiles?" Reportedly, Sharif responded only by saying "India was probably doing the same" (p. 7). While most observers discount this report, it apparently was confirmed by Indian chief of army staff general Sundarajan Padmanabhan, when he stated in early 2001 that Pakistan "activated one of its nuclear missile bases and had threatened India with a nuclear attack" (Chengappa, 2001). Pakistani authorities have been steadfast in their denials of moving missiles or preparing for a nuclear attack.

Although well-informed sources made the claims about Indian and Pakistani nuclear deployments, other evidence has not corroborated them. Moreover, they fly in the face of other, more official claims that no nuclear deployment took place. What some observers say could have occurred was that Pakistan dispersed its nuclear-capable missiles out of storage sites for defensive purposes—a development that could have been misinterpreted by intelligence agencies as an operational deployment. Similarly, others have not verified accounts that India heightened the readiness of its nuclear forces.

Because official spokespeople in Washington, Islamabad, and New Delhi have refused to say more, these claims about nuclear maneuvers must remain a mysterious backdrop to the Kargil conflict. However, it follows that any serious military crisis occurring in the future between India and Pakistan (or, for that matter, any other pair of nuclear states) probably will be accompanied by a great deal of confusion, controversy, and alarm over possible operational deployments. And this certainly will be the context in which the United States and other concerned parties will regard future Indo-Pakistani military crises.

Peter Lavoy

See also **Jammu and Kashmir; Kashmir; Nuclear Programs and Policies; Pakistan and India; Strategic Thought**

BIBLIOGRAPHY

Bammi, Y. M. *Kargil 1999: The Impregnable Conquered.* Noida, India: Gorkha Publishers, 2002.

Chengappa, Raj. *Weapons of Peace.* New Delhi: HarperCollins India, 2000.

———. "The Nuclear Shadow." *India Today*, 24 January 2001. Available at <http://www.indiatoday.com/webexclusive/columns/chengappa/20010124.html>

Cherian, John. "The Political and Diplomatic Background." *Frontline* 5 (June 1999). Available at <http://www.flonnet.com/fl1612/16120080.htm>

"India Prepared for Pakistan Nuclear Attack." *Financial Times Information*, 4 July 1999.

"India Ready for any Eventuality." *Hindu*, 1 July 1999.

Kargil Review Committee. *From Surprise to Reckoning: The Kargil Review Committee Report*. New Delhi: Sage Publications, 2000.

Mazari, Shireen M. *The Kargil Conflict 1999: Separating Fact from Fiction*. Islamabad: Institute of Strategic Studies, Islamabad, 2003.

Mehta, Ashok, and P. R. Chari, eds. *Kargil: The Tables Turned*. New Delhi: Manohar, 2001.

"Pakistan Warns It May Use Any Weapon in Defence." *Financial Times Information*, 31 May 1999.

Palit, Maj. Gen. D. K. *Jammu and Kashmir Arms: History of the J&K Rifles*. Dehra Dun: Palit & Dutt, 1972.

Qadir, Shaukat. "An Analysis of the Kargil Conflict 1999." *Journal of the Royal United Services Institution* 147, no. 2 (April 2002): 24–30.

Riedel, Bruce. *American Diplomacy and the 1999 Kargil Summit at Blair House*. Policy Paper Series 2002. Philadelphia: Center for the Advanced Study of India, 2002. Available at <http://www.sas.upenn.edu/casi/reports/RiedelPaper051302.htm>

Singh, Jasjit, ed. *Kargil 1999: Pakistan's Fourth War for Kashmir*. New Delhi: Institute for Defence Studies and Analyses, 1999.

Swami, Praveen. *The Kargil War*. New Delhi: LeftWord, 2000.

Talbott, Strobe. *Engaging India: Diplomacy, Democracy, and the Bomb*. Washington, D.C.: Brookings Institution Press, 2004.

Tellis, Ashley J., C. Christine Fair, and Jamison Jo Medby. *Conflict under the Nuclear Umbrella: Indian and Pakistani Lessons from the Kargil Crisis*. Santa Monica, Calif.: Rand, 2001.

"Warring Nations: India and Pakistan." *Straits Times Press* (Singapore), 5 July 1999.

KARMA. *See* **Upanishadic Philosophy.**

KARMA YOGA. *See* **Bhagavad Gītā.**

KARNATAKA A state in South India, Karnataka has an area of 74,051 square miles (191,791 square kilometers). In 2001 its population was 52.7 million. Its capital is Bangalore, and the language is Kannada, which belongs to the Dravidian family of languages. The name of the state means "highland," which refers to its Deccan plateau, though Karnataka also has a coastline of about 185 miles (300 kilometers). The state in its present form was established in 1956, but its name was changed from Mysore to Karnataka only in 1973. It consists of two areas: the former princely state of Mysore and the Kannada-speaking districts of the erstwhile Bombay presidency, which were merged with Mysore to form a unified linguistic state. The maharaja of Mysore had signed the treaty of accession to India immediately after the attainment of indepedence. The legislature of the Bombay presidency had decided as early as 1938 that the Kannada-speaking districts should be merged with a future linguistic state. There was a dispute concerning the Belgaum and Karwar districts later on, since they had a sizable Marathi-speaking population, but they remained in Karnataka.

The state has many ancient monuments. The Mauryan emperor Ashoka had some of his famous inscriptions installed there in the second century B.C. Later, this area became a stronghold of Jainism. The huge statue of a Jain Tīrthānkara at Sravanbelgola is an impressive example of this tradition. In the northwestern part of the state, the Chalukya dynasty of Badami (Vatapi) created several beautiful temples in the seventh and eighth centuries A.D., which were influenced by the style of the Northern Gupta dynasty. Pattadakal, one of these temple towns, has been recognized by the United Nations Educational, Scientific and Cultural Organization as a World Heritage site. In the twelfth and thirteenth centuries, the Hoysala dynasty established the beautiful temples of Belur and Halebid. From the fourteenth through the sixteenth centuries, the Vijayanagar empire dominated the region. Its capital, Vijayanagar, (City of Victory) is located near Hampi, about 185 miles (300 kilometers) north of Bangalore. Bijapur, in the northwestern part of the state, houses one of the most impressive monuments of Muslim architecture, Gol Gumbaz, the seventeenth-century mausoleum of Sultan Muhammad Adil Shah of Bijapur, which has the widest cupola in the world.

Karnataka is a stronghold of the Congress Party. It does not have a state party like its neighbors Tamil Nadu and Andhra Pradesh, though the Janata Party had played this role and ruled the state for some time after it had lost its importance as a national party. In the assembly elections of 2004, the Congress Party lost many seats while the Bharatiya Janata Party (BJP) captured 79 seats, an unprecedented party success in a southern state. Even though the BJP won the largest number of seats of any party in the assembly, the Congress Party (with only 64 seats) managed to form a new government with the help of other parties.

With the exception of Bangalore, Karnataka has no big industrial cities. There are only two other major urban centers in this state: Mysore and Hubli-Dharwar. The latter consists of two separate towns that have formed a joint municipal corporation. Dharwar is a university town, and Hubli is a major trading center. In addition, there are some important district towns, such as Belgaum, Bellary, and Mangalore. As far as per capita income is concerned, Karnataka is close to the national average.

Dietmar Rothermund

BIBLIOGRAPHY

Desai, P. B. *History of Karnataka*. Dharwar: Kannada Research Institute, 1970.

Diwakar, R. R. *Karnataka through the Ages: From Prehistoric Times to the Day of the Independence of India*. Bangalore: Government of Mysore, 1968.

Gururajachar, S. *Some Aspects of Economic and Social Life in Karnataka (AD 1000–1300)*. Mysore: Prasaranga, 1974.

KARTIKEYA. *See* **Shiva and Shaivism.**

KASHMIR Since the partition of India in 1947, the state of Jammu and Kashmir has remained a bone of contention between India and Pakistan, provoking three wars between the two countries. In 1989 a secessionist movement, supported by Pakistan, arose in the Valley of Kashmir, demanding freedom from India. The two countries hold irreconcilable positions on Kashmir. For Pakistan, the state of Jammu and Kashmir is a disputed territory, and its future should be determined through a plebiscite in conformity with a United Nations Security Council resolution; India considers the state an integral part of its territory. India builds its case on the legal accession of Jammu and Kashmir and on subsequent elections through which the people of Kashmir created their own constitution and their own successive civil governments.

Historical Background

The state of Jammu and Kashmir, with its three distinct regions of the Valley of Kashmir (predominantly Muslim and Kashmiri-speaking), Jammu (majority Dogri-speaking Hindus) and Ladakh (majority Ladakhi-speaking Buddhists), is a relatively recent political and geographical entity. Prior to the mid-nineteenth century, these three regions existed separately. In March 1846, under the terms of the Treaty of Amritsar, the British transferred the territories of Jammu, Kashmir, and Ladakh to Jammu's Raja Ghulab Singh. This transfer was in return for a payment by the raja to the British of 7.5 million rupees. Because of Britain's trade interests in Central Asia and its concerns over Russian expansion, the Jammu and Kashmir state was quickly integrated into princely British India. Until the partition of India in 1947, the state of Jammu and Kashmir remained under the rule of the Hindu Dogra rulers. After the death of Raja Ghulab Singh in 1856, the state was ruled by Maharaja Ranbir Singh (1856–1885), Maharaja Pratap Singh (1885–1925), and Maharaja Hari Singh (1925–1947).

As a result of British interventions in the Dogra rule, various administrative, constitutional, and educational reforms were introduced, the major beneficiaries of which were the Hindus, both from Jammu and the valley. They directly benefited from a new state-subject ordinance (1927) that restricted government employment exclusively to citizens of the state. Kashmiri Muslims, who constituted the vast masses of uneducated and exploited peasantry, remained largely untouched by these reforms. Muslim grievances first found a voice in 1931 when the Muslim Conference of Kashmir, under the leadership of Sheikh Mohammad Abdullah, launched a protest. In 1939 Abdullah was to transform the Muslim Conference into a mass-based secular, socialist nationalist movement against Dogra rule, called the National Conference. Sheikh Abdullah invoked the fourteenth-century Kashmiri historical and cultural concept of Kashmiriyat to unite both Hindus and Muslims in opposition

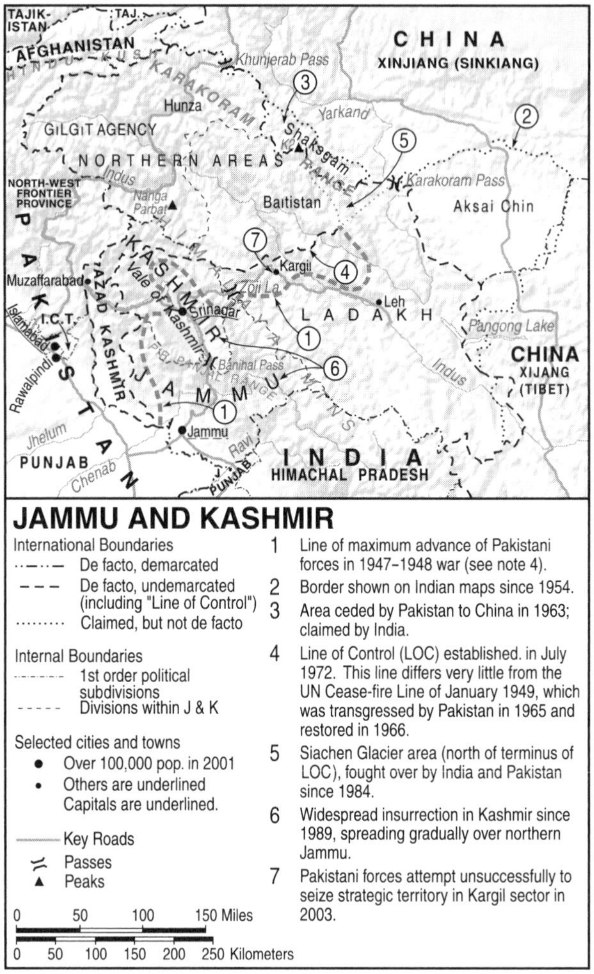

India's View of the Disputed Territory of Jammu and Kashmir

to Dogra rule. This indigenous concept of Kashmiriyat, while not excluding the presence and influence of religion, emphasizes syncretism and tolerance for all Kashmiri religions, differentiating both Kashmiri Hindus and Muslims from their counterparts elsewhere. The National Conference ushered in a new ideological agenda, underlined in the New Kashmir Manifesto, seeking constitutional reforms, a bill of rights, a national economic plan for eradicating poverty land reforms, and the right to self-determination. In 1946 the National Conference launched a "Quit Kashmir" movement against Dogra rule and received complete support from the Indian National Congress and its leadership.

After the British granted independence to India and Pakistan, Jammu and Kashmir was one of only three Princely States not to accede either India or Pakistan. In October 1947 the Pathan tribesmen of the North-West Frontier province of Pakistan invaded Kashmir. Unable to defend the state, Maharaja Hari Singh signed the

Instrument of Accession dated 26 October 1947 and requested India's military assistance to free the state from that tribal invasion. In accepting the offer of accession under special circumstances, Governor-General Lord Mountbatten informed the maharaja that the question of accession should be settled by a referendum to the people, once law and order was restored in Kashmir and the invaders had been pushed out. India's Prime Minister Jawaharlal Nehru confirmed the conditional acceptance of Kashmir's accession to India. The Indian army succeeded in driving the tribal invaders from some two-thirds of the state, which has remained under Indian jurisdiction, with the other third staying under Pakistan's control. Sheikh Abdullah headed the Emergency Administration in the state from its accession until March 1948.

India's Complaint to the United Nations

On 1 January 1948, under Article 35 of the Charter of the United Nations, the government of India lodged a complaint to the Security Council against Pakistani "aggression" against the people of Jammu and Kashmir. The complaint explained the circumstances leading to Hari Singh's accession of Kashmir to India and provided evidence of Pakistan's involvement in aiding the tribal invaders, who were still occupying a substantial portion of the state's territory. In April 1948, the Security Council set up the United Nations Commission for India and Pakistan (UNCIP). In the UNCIP Resolution of 13 August 1948, accepted by both India and Pakistan, both consented to a cease-fire, and to the withdrawal of Pakistani forces from the state of Jammu and Kashmir, to be followed by the withdrawal of the bulk of Indian forces in stages to be determined by the Commission. Part 3 of the resolution laid out a framework for a plebiscite in the state. Even though India's initial complaint of Pakistani aggression had been earlier verified as legitimate when UNCIP delegates, who had arrived in India in early July, observed that Pakistan had sent troops to the state of Jammu and Kashmir, the 13 August resolution put Pakistan on a par with India. Both were asked to withdraw their troops, which amounted to denying any legality to the accession treaty between the maharaja of Kashmir and India, making Kashmir a disputed territory until a plebiscite was conducted under peaceful and fair conditions. Initially, irresolvable difficulties over procedural matters led to the nonimplementation of both the original UNCIP resolution of August 1948, and the extended resolution of 5 January 1949, which sought demilitarization and the appointment of a plebiscite administrator. In the early 1950s, the domestic situation in the valley, combined with Pakistan's military alliance with the United States, led India to abandon its prior agreement to hold a plebiscite in Kashmir.

In response to a Hindu nationalist movement in Jammu calling for full integration of the state into India, Sheikh Abdullah began to support the idea of an independent Kashmir. In the Jammu region—where a majority of the population were Dogra Hindus, emotionally attached to the Dogra Rajput dynasty—the Praja Parishad Party, strongly linked to the RSS (Rashtriya Swayamsevak Sangh), began agitating in 1952 for complete accession and full integration of the state of Jammu and Kashmir to India. The movement received vocal support from the militant Indian Hindu party, Bharatiya Jan Sangh (BJS), and its leader Shyama Prasad Mookerjee. Though the movement lost momentum after Mookerjee's death in the Kashmir valley, its Hindu-chauvinistic demands made a powerful impact on Sheikh Abdullah's decision to call for a third option for the state: independence. In July 1953, the Working Committee of the National Conference, under the presidency of Abdullah, proposed four alternatives for the settlement of the Kashmir dispute: a plebiscite to choose among the three options of accession to India, accession to Pakistan, or independence; independence for the whole state; independence for the whole state with joint Indo-Pakistan control over foreign affairs; or the Dixon plan (partition of the state, with Jammu and Ladakh going to India, and independence for the Kashmir Valley). It is alleged that in a meeting with U.S. Senator Adlai Stevenson, the latter had encouraged the Kashmiri leader to repudiate accession to India and declare Kashmir independent. Although this report was repeatedly denied, Nehru became increasingly suspicious of U.S. intentions. On 9 August 1953, India arrested Abdullah and replaced him with Bakshi Ghulam Mohammad.

During 1954 and 1955, the United States signed three different military assistance agreements with Pakistan. In the absence of any resolution of the Kashmir problem, India viewed the U.S.–Pakistan military pacts as enhancing the military power of Pakistan, which could then be used against India. Although in February 1954, U.S. president Dwight D. Eisenhower tried to assure Prime Minister Nehru that the decision of the U.S. government to provide military assistance to Pakistan was not aimed against India, Nehru believed that U.S. support to Pakistan undermined the ability of the United Nations to realize a so-called impartial solution to the Kashmir problem.

Jammu and Kashmir's Constitutional Status within the Indian Federation

In January 1950 the Indian Constituent Assembly approved Article 370, outlining Jammu and Kashmir's political relationship with the Indian Union. Article 370 of the Indian Constitution was applied to the state under the "Constitution (Application to Jammu and Kashmir)

Order, 1950." This article, while restricting the central government's legislative power to the areas of foreign Affairs, defense, and communications, allowed the state government to legislate on all residuary issues. A subheading of this Article states that the constitutional provisions with respect to Jammu and Kashmir are temporary. At the time of the creation of the Indian Constitution, India remained firm on its offer of a plebiscite to the people of Kashmir. The Indian leadership, particularly Nehru, apparently had complete faith in the positive outcome of a plebiscite in Kashmir—an attitude that changed entirely in 1953. Article 370 also made provision for the revocation of the temporary constitutional arrangement.

In September 1951, elections to the Jammu and Kashmir Constituent Assembly were held, and in November 1951, the assembly was convened. In July 1952 the leaders of Jammu and Kashmir and India entered into the "Delhi Agreement," which laid out the basic principles and framework within which the Jammu and Kashmir Constituent Assembly would proceed with its work. The seven components of this agreement related to the application of the provisions of the Constitution of India to citizenship, fundamental rights, the emergency powers of the Indian president, the division of powers between the state and the central government, the abolition of Dogra rule, the retention of the state flag, and the acceptance of Urdu as the official language of the state. The Constitution of Jammu and Kashmir was proclaimed on 26 January 1957. Its special features included: provisions with regard to the citizenship of the people of Kashmir and their classification into a special category of "Permanent Residents"; the Directive Principles of State Policy, outlining the socialist agenda of the New Kashmir Manifesto of the National Conference Party; internal autonomy to the state in all powers except foreign affairs, defense, and communication; and a parliamentary system of government, with its elected head, Sadar-Riyasat, a Permanent Resident of the state. The constitution determined that the legislative assembly be composed of 100 members chosen through direct election, based on universal adult franchise. Out of these 100 seats, 25 were reserved for the territories of the state under the "occupation" of Pakistan.

The citizenship provisions in the new state constitution were closely guarded by the Kashmiri leadership so that nonresidents were disallowed to seek employment, to buy property, and to participate in elections. In the constitution, citizens of the state are defined as "all those people who were born and residing in the territories of the state, when it was founded by the Maharaja Gulab Singh in 1846, the people who settled in the state later but before 1885, the people who settled in the state under special permission before 1911, and the people who took permanent residence in the state and acquired immovable property under the 'Ijazat Nama Rules' before May 14, 1944" (Teng, Bhat, and Kaul, p. 210). Although in 1959, with the extension of the powers of the Election Commission of India to conduct and control elections in the state, a slow and steady integration of the state into the Indian union began, the state has remained protective of its citizenship requirements—an essential ingredient in strengthening the Kashmiri identity and maintaining its distinct status within the Indian federation.

The State's De Facto Integration within the Indian Union

The years 1957 to 1974 witnessed the extension of various entries in the Union and the Concurrent Lists of the Indian Constitution to the state of Jammu and Kashmir, with the approval of the state legislature. As all three governments in the state, under the respective leaderships of Bakshi Ghulam Mohammad, G. M. Sadiq, and Mir Kashim, existed with the approval of the Indian central government, the local legislature's approval was hardly problematic. The original Article 370, the first Presidential Order of 1950 and 1954, has been amended several times in order to make most of the provisions of the Indian Constitution applicable to Jammu and Kashmir. In 1956, Article 356, allowing the central government to impose President's Rule, and Article 357, empowering Parliament to confer upon the president the power of the state legislature, were applied to Jammu and Kashmir. The same year saw the changes in the designations of the head of state and the head of the government, respectively, from Sadar-i-Riyasat to governor and from premier to chief minister—bringing the state in line with other federal units in India. In 1967 the Jammu and Kashmir Representation of the People's Act was brought into conformity with the Central Law, enabling the Election Commission to appoint retired judges of the high courts of other states as members of the Election Tribunal. It also authorized the commission to interfere during the elections at the vote-counting stage in case of suspected irregularities. Articles 248, 249, and 250 of the Indian Constitution have been extended to the state so that the central government may legislate in matters of state jurisdiction. Under these constitutional provisions, the Indian Parliament would legislate on any matter not enumerated in the Union List. Article 248, in particular, gives extensive powers to the central government to interfere in state matters under the pretext of defending Indian sovereignty and preventing activities, including terrorist acts, directed against the territorial integrity of India, or causing insult to the Indian national flag, the Indian national anthem, and the Indian Constitution.

Patronage Politics and the Repression of Dissidence

During the period of Jammu and Kashmir's de facto integration into the Indian union, the state government employed the complementary strategies of patronage distribution and repression of democratic opposition. Through the use of large transfer payments from the central government (amounting to almost half of the state government revenues), the state expanded its governmental sector and became the largest employer. During the twenty-five years between 1964 and 1989, the public sector's share of economy more than doubled, from under 5 percent to 10 percent. This rapid expansion of the governmental sector becomes even more glaring when one realizes that the state paid negligible attention to the economic development of the region. The state leadership made only limited attempts to develop the region's manufacturing and industrial sectors. Consequently, rampant corruption prevailed within the state. Middle- and upper-middle-class Kashmiris took advantage of the expanded educational facilities, thus creating a massive burden on the state to accommodate the newly educated within governmental and state-supported institutions such as hospitals, schools, and social service institutions.

During the integration era, another significant characteristic of Kashmir politics was the leadership's determination to suppress political dissent. Whenever a dissident group tried to set up an opposition party, that group was either absorbed into the ruling party or simply outlawed. Until 1974 no effective opposition existed in the state. Any groups splintering from the dominant ruling party were quickly reabsorbed into it. The real opposition to Jammu and Kashmir's integrative politics was to come from two groups: the Plebiscite Front (formed by Sheikh Abdullah, and his close associate Mohammed Beg, after Abdullah's arrest in 1953) and the religious pro-Pakistan Jamait-i-Islami. Both groups served as significant avenues for those demanding self-determination for the people of Kashmir. The two groups were barred on and off by the ruling party from participating in the governing process. It is alleged that the Indian leadership viewed the emergence of an effective opposition as a threat to India's "national interests." As a result of limited public presence, the dissident groups remained ineffective in mobilizing the Muslim population of the valley toward their goal of holding a plebiscite. This was evident by their inability to take advantage of two significant political events in Kashmir, the "disappearance" of a holy relic in 1964 and the Pakistani armed infiltration into the valley in 1965. The Muslim population generally has a *dedar* (showing) of the holy relic (a hair from the prophet Muhammad's beard) after the Friday noon prayers at Srinagar's Hazrat Bal Mosque. Its disappearance in the winter of 1964 brought the Kashmir capital to a standstill. Daily processions went through the streets, with anger expressed at the Jammu and Kashmir state government. Religious tension was so high that the Kashmiri Hindus soon joined the Muslims in their mass protest. The government of India quickly got involved and sent an emissary, Lal Bahadur Shastri, to the valley to coordinate the recovery and the authentication process with the Central Investigative Agency and local religious leaders. Once it was found, Kashmir's Mirwaiz Maluvi Farooq authenticated the relic. The Indian government's sensitive handling of the dispute averted further crisis, and denied the dissident groups an opportunity to convert the Kashmiri Muslim population's religious outrage into anti-Indian sentiment.

In 1983, although the electoral success of opposition groups was not significant, managing as they did to win only one seat in the legislature, it provided impetus to several dissident factions to fight a united battle in the next elections. For the 1987 assembly elections, an eleven-party oppositional alliance, the Muslim United Front, was created. Despite the overwhelming popularity of the Front, the group won only four seats. There were widespread accusations of rigging of the elections, thus setting the stage for the birth of a violent secessionist movement in the valley in 1989.

The Secessionist Movement

A mass-based secessionist movement, accompanied by political insurgency, began in the Kashmir Valley in 1989. Its immediate catalyst was the rigging of the 1987 elections and the unpopular alliance between Kashmir's ruling party, the National Conference, and the India's Congress Party. Overnight, dozens of secessionist groups emerged in the valley, demanding sovereignty and freedom (*azadi*) from the Indian state. The two most prominent among these groups were the Jammu and Kashmir Liberation Front (JKLF), demanding unification of the Indian and Pakistani sides of Kashmir and seeking independence for all of Kashmir, and the Hizbul-Mujahideen, demanding an Islamic state and unification with Pakistan. Despite its killing of some Kashmiri Hindus in 1989 and 1990 (causing the departure of the small minority of Hindu Pandits from the valley), the JKLF claimed that its movement was essentially secular and that a unified Kashmir has room for both Hindus and Muslims. During the early stages of the movement, various Islamic fundamentalist groups failed to impose strict Islamic laws and customs, such as the compulsory veiling of Muslim women. This lack of adherence to the strict practices of Islam, as well as the popularity of the JKLF vision of freedom, led the Islamic secessionist groups to rethink their strategy. To maintain the movement's momentum and to unify several secessionist groups, an apex organization of more than thirty militant-nationalist groups, the Kul-Jammat-e-Hurriyat-e-Kashmir (All Kashmir Freedom Front), was formed in 1993.

Pakistan's involvement in Kashmir's secessionist movement goes beyond its claims of moral, political, and diplomatic support. During 1988 several secessionist leaders crossed the border into Pakistan-controlled Azad ("Free") Kashmir, received military training and weapons, and returned to the valley prepared for insurgency. By the end of 1989, the secessionist groups were successful in bringing about the total breakdown of the civil and administrative structures of the government. In 1990 the state of Jammu and Kashmir was brought under India's President's Rule with a massive occupation by the Indian armed forces. For the first three years of the movement, militant violence was accompanied by harsh repression by Indian armed security forces, inflicting serious human rights violations. With increased international pressure from human rights agencies, as well as Pakistan's continued support for the Kashmiri cause in various global forums, the Indian government took steps to discipline its security forces, setting up its own human rights watch agencies. India also began to reactivate the electoral process within the state, setting the stage for a return to civil government. Since 1996 two legislative elections and three parliamentary elections have taken place. With each election, voter participation has risen consistently, with the exception of a few urban-based constituencies in the valley. The valley's response to India's efforts to reactivate civil society can be attributed to three factors: a general fatigue of the population with the movement, the inability of the secessionist groups to deliver *azadi*, and the continued violence by both the secessionist groups and India's security forces. Consequently, the secessionist groups have come to be divided into two camps: the moderates who seek a peaceful solution to the Kashmir issue, and the extremists who continue to use violent means to promote their cause. The latter, which includes a small portion of the local Hizbul-Mujahideen cadres, is largely dominated by violent Pakistan-based and sponsored groups such as Lashkar-e-Taiba, Harkat-ul-Mujahideen, and Jaish-e-Mohammed. The Fidaʿiyyeen suicide attack is the newest and one of the more successful strategies adopted by these groups. The Kashmiri secessionist groups are now in the hands of the imported Islamic groups, sidelining the indigenous nationalist groups.

Since 1997 the Indian state has taken advantage of this situation and has adopted a dual strategy, on the one hand, to engage the moderate secessionist groups in dialogue, and on the other hand, to pursue the elimination of the militant leadership. Until 11 September 2001, the engagement of the moderates brought about limited successes. However, the events of 11 September and the resulting war on terror have been responsible for isolating the extremists and giving the moderates an opportunity to seek a peaceful solution to the Kashmir issue. The October 2002 attack on the Jammu and Kashmir Legislative Assembly and the December 2002 attack on the Indian Parliament by Pakistan-based militant groups have strengthened India's hand vis-à-vis Pakistan in convincing international public opinion that the Kashmir issue cannot be resolved without Pakistan's commitment to prevent its territory from being used for political insurgency in Kashmir.

In April 2003, during his visit to Kashmir, India's prime minister A. B. Vajpayee made a promise to the Muslim population of the valley to seek a peaceful solution to the Kashmir problem and to extend India's hand of friendship to Pakistan. In January 2004, following several confidence-building measures to reactivate relations between the two countries, which had become severely strained after the attack on India's Parliament, India and Pakistan set in motion a process of dialogue on several issues, including Kashmir. Meanwhile, the Indian central government and the Hurriyat leadership have begun a series of talk to seek a peaceful resolution to the Kashmir issue. While it appears that it might be difficult for India to convince Pakistan to abandon its claims to Kashmir and to accept India's solution of making the Line of Control the international border, from the Indian perspective there is greater hope of coming up with a reasonable solution, such as increased constitutional autonomy for the state of Jammu and Kashmir, which might satisfy the moderate secessionist groups within the valley.

Reeta Chowdhari Tremblay

See also **Jammu and Ladakh; Pakistan and India**

BIBLIOGRAPHY

Behera, Navnita Chadha. *State, Identity and Violence: Jammu and Kashmir and Ladakh.* New Delhi: Manohar, 2000.

Bose, Sumantra. *The Challenge of Kashmir: Democracy, Self-Determination, and a Just Peace.* New Delhi: Sage Publications, 1997.

Ganguly, Sumit. *The Crisis in Kashmir: Portents of War, Hopes of Peace.* Cambridge, U.K., and New York: Cambridge University Press, 1997.

Jha, Prem Shankar. *Kashmir, 1947: Rival Versions of History.* New Delhi: Oxford University Press, 1996.

Schofield, Victoria. *Kashmir in Conflict: India, Pakistan, and the Unfinished War.* London and New York: I. B. Tauris, 2000.

Teng, Mohan Krishen, Ram Krishen Bhat, and Santosh Kaul. *Kashmir: Constitutional History.* New Delhi: Light and Life Publishers, 1997.

Krishna Serenading Radha, c. 1730–1750. Watercolor and ink on paper. The Kashmir artistic tradition faced extinction during the political and religious upheaval of the fourteenth century, but had revived significantly by the eighteenth century, finding expression in the illuminations of manuscripts, horoscopes, folk art, almanacs, and individual paintings, with religious themes dominating. BENOY K. BEHL.

Thomas, Raju G. C., ed. *Perspectives on Kashmir: The Roots of Conflict in South Asia.* Boulder, Colo.: Westview Press, 1992.

Wirsing, Robert G. *Kashmir in the Shadow of War: Regional Rivalries in a Nuclear Age.* Armonk, N.Y.: M. E. Sharpe, 2003.

KASHMIR PAINTING Our understanding of the painting traditions of Kashmir is limited by a dearth of surviving evidence. Manuscript paintings dating prior to the seventeenth century are virtually unknown. In related media, the mural paintings at the sites of Alchi (Ladakh, western Tibet) are the only indicators of a previously existing Kashmiri style and its eastward dissemination. Moreover, the manuscript paintings from the eighteenth century onward are so varied in style—ranging from the heavily Persianized to the purely indigenous (often termed "folkish")—that it is not possible to identify a single style among these as characteristic of the region. An inversion of the interpretative paradigm, then, is perhaps more beneficial. Rather than perceiving Kashmiri painting to be a directionless and mediocre imitation of styles from the Islamic and Indic worlds, another perspective could be more productive: the wide and rich variety of painting styles evidenced in but two centuries of surviving examples demonstrates that Kashmiri painters were not only prolific, but that they also fruitfully incorporated the many stylistic strains reaching them through commercial and other conduits connecting the region with lower India, Central Asia, and the Near East.

The earlier Buddhist foundations at Alchi date to around the late twelfth or early thirteenth century. Like other such establishments, this complex also took advantage of its location on a hub of trade routes linking the region with Kashmir and Central Asia. Efforts to "purify" their Buddhist practices inspired Tibetan monks to visit learned counterparts in Kashmir, and to invite Kashmiri masters and artists eastward. Thus, the Sumtsek's mural paintings at Alchi evince a relationship to the decoratively intricate, jewel-colored, compositionally balanced works likely admired at Kashmiri courts. Moreover, Kashmir's—and western Tibet's—linkages with larger Indic traditions are also discernible here: the series panels, separated by classicizing columns, are reminiscent of Gandharan stupa drum plaques (2nd–4th centuries), while the repetitive patterning of some of the figures' textiles hearkens to the western Indian style of painting prevalent in North India between the twelfth and fifteenth centuries. Exceptions to the gap in small-scale painting before the seventeenth century are the rare manuscript covers. Manuscript covers provide evidence not only of the continuity of the hybrid Tibetan-Kashmiri style, but also of significant Buddhist patronage.

The 1719 *Shāhnāma-ye Firdausi* provides a point of comparison for undated manuscripts, and its illustrations show local adaptation of a Persianate style that probably originated in Shiraz. There is a spontaneity and expressiveness in the figures that becomes rote in later works. Reminders of Shirazi and Timurid painting in general include the intricate arabesques of the textiles. In addition, the landscape lacks depth and, other than the detailed shrubbery, is schematic in its undulating lines. The figures' features, however, are rooted in local tastes as expressed in Hill painting, particularly the large, well-defined eyes and facial profiles.

Together with the strong presence of Persian-influenced painting styles in Kashmir, pre-Mughal idioms were still alive among the Kashmiri painters. Indeed, illustrations of Indic texts are convincing examples of the vast range of styles used freely by the painters, regardless of the illustrations' contents. An image from a Bhāgavata Purāṇa of about 1750 shows a subtle amalgamation. Basohli elements, particularly the rounded facial profiles with prominent noses and large eyes, are brought together with identifiably "Sultanate" characteristics. Compositionally, the whole image is strongly reminiscent of the late fifteenth-century *Candāyana*'s depiction of Candā's flight with her lover Laur (Bharat Kala Bhavan, Banares [Varanasi]); meanwhile, the rendering of the striated domes and eaves, and the delicate color palate, are not unlike the Chhatrapati Shivaji Maharaj Vastu Sangrahalaya's (formerly known as the Prince of Wales Museum) *Candāyana* (c. 1525–1570).

The image that captures and quite possibly personifies the trajectory of Kashmiri painting through the nineteenth century is one of the Goddess. She is shown in her apotropaic aspect, with many arms and weapons; her eyes look confidently ahead. Her aspect is somewhat softened by the mythical thousand-petaled lotus on which she sits, gently radiating and forming a transition to the muted colors and delicate arabesques of the *shamsa*. The image as a whole is the perfect balance of the stylistic poles discernible in Kashmiri painting. The traditions inherited from the Islamic world are abbreviated in the neatly executed *shamsa*, which makes reference to manuscript illustration, a practice associated with (though not exclusive to) Islamic culture. Simultaneously, the Goddess is shown complete with all accoutrements, executed in a style representing the indigenous, "folkish" traditions abundantly evidenced in illustrations of Indic religious texts. The two styles represent the vast spectrum of creative resources available to Kashmiri painters throughout the common era.

Alka Patel

See also **Sculpture and Bronze Images from Kashmir**

BIBLIOGRAPHY

Goepper, Roger. *Alchi: Ladakh's Hidden Buddhist Sanctuary*. Boston: Shambhala Publications, 1996.

Goetz, Hermann. *Studies in the History and Art of Kashmir and the Indian Himalaya*. Wiesbaden, Germany: Otto Harrassowitz, 1969.

Goswamy, B. N., and Eberhard Fischer. *Pahari Masters: Court Painters of Northern India*. Zürich: Museum Rietberg, *Artibus Asiae Supplementum* 38, 1992.

Goswamy, Karuna. *Kashmiri Painting: Assimilation and Diffusion; Production and Patronage*. Shimla: Indian Institute of Advanced Study, 1998.

Khandalavala, Karl J., and Moti Chandra. *New Documents of Indian Painting: A Reappraisal*. Mumbai: Prince of Wales Museum of Bombay, 1969.

Losty, Jeremiah. *The Art of the Book in India*. London: British Library, 1982.

Pal, P., ed. *Art and Architecture of Ancient Kashmir*. Mumbai: Marg Publications, 1989.

KASHMIR SHAWLS Of the myriad varieties of textiles for which India was famous over much of Europe and Asia from at least the time of the Roman Empire, the Kashmir shawl stands out as the only woollen one. Although its precise origin is lost in a haze of myth and legend, it is safe to say that it grew out of a unique combination: a superlatively fine fiber plus the highly developed set of skills necessary to work the fiber. Or, as a nineteenth-century government report put it, "It is impossible not to admire the felicitous conjunction, in the same region, of a natural product so valuable and of workmen so artistic."

The raw material of the Kashmir shawl, known in the West as "cashmere," is called pashm in India, and the fabric woven from it pashmina. It is the warm soft undercoat grown by goats herded on the high-altitude plateaus of Tibet and Ladakh as protection against the bitter winter cold. Combed out by their herders at the onset of summer, for centuries the entire clip was sent down in a series of complex trading operations to Kashmir, the only place whose craftspeople had developed the skills necessary to process it. In the 1820s it was estimated that between 121,000–242,000 pounds (55,000–110,000 kilograms) a year reached Srinagar, to be made up into some 80,000 to

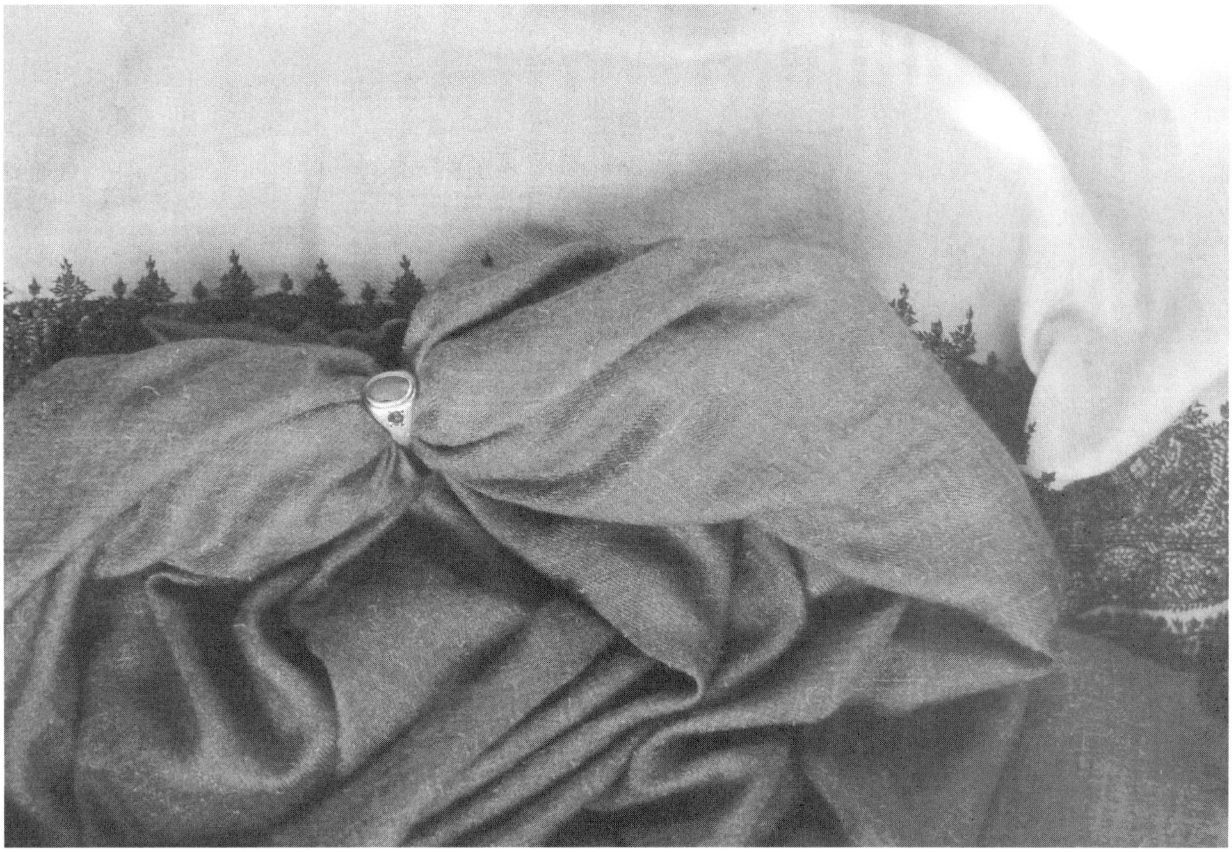

Pashmina Shawl. Between the sixteenth and eighteenth centuries, Kashmir or pashmina shawls were an essential element of the Indian royal and aristocratic lifestyle. In the late twentieth century they became a symbol of wealth in the West. JYOTI M. BANERJEE / FOTOMEDIA.

100,000 shawl pieces. The very finest shawls were woven from *toosh*, a similar but even finer material produced by the Tibetan antelope or *chiru*, an undomesticated species. Although the precious wool has always been procured by slaughtering the *chiru*, the amount consumed was negligible, probably less than 1,100 pounds (500 kilograms) a year, insufficient to make a dent in a population estimated in the millions. By the early twenty-first century, however, the situation had changed; wholesale slaughter in the late twentieth century brought the *chiru* population down to a few thousand. It is recognized as an endangered species, and trade in its products is banned.

Manufacture of Shawls

The transformation of the raw *pashm*, a mass of greasy fibers, into a fabric renowned for its fineness involved a series of processes. The shawl entrepreneur supplied the *pashm* in its raw state to women who, in the seclusion of their homes, undertook the painstaking and laborious task of removing the coarse outer hairs from the fleece; they then cleaned it with rice-flour paste, and spun it on wheels similar to those used everywhere in India. The skill of spinning such delicate fiber was passed down over generations from mother to daughter.

Meanwhile the entrepreneur had employed a pattern-drawer to design the pattern of the proposed fabric. The pattern was passed to a color-master who filled in the colors, and finally to a skilled scribe who reduced the colored pattern to a shorthand form known as *talim*, which enabled a complex pattern to be recorded on quite a small piece of paper. The dyer then dyed the spun yarn in the required colors. Other workers prepared the warp and fixed it to the loom; only then did the actual weaving begin.

The classic Kashmir shawl employs a weave technically known as 2:2 twill tapestry, which is unique to this product. Tapestry implies that the design is woven into the very structure of the fabric; the weft is inserted not by a shuttle, but by a series of small bobbins filled with various colored yarns. Depending on the complexity of the design, one line of the weft may involve dozens or scores of such insertions. In Kashmir the technique is known as *kani* or *tilikar*, referring to different names for the bobbins.

Tapestry is an ancient textile technique, practiced in different areas all over the world in a plain weave, in which the weft passes alternately over and under one warp-thread at a time. It was only in Kashmir, however—and to some extent in Iran—that shawl weavers used a twill weave for tapestry, in which the weft passes over and under two warp-threads at a time, the pairing of the warps changing with every line of the weft. It is presumed that this modification was adopted to minimize the strain on the delicate pashmina warp-threads. Fabrics woven in twill exhibit a characteristic very fine diagonal rib, which enlivens the finished pattern. The borders were often woven on a silk warp, to strengthen the shawl's edging, and sometimes on a separate loom, being attached to the main body, with almost invisible seams, by the *rafugar*, or needleworker.

The creation of intricate patterns in tapestry requires an extraordinary level of manual dexterity, though in the case of shawls this was exercised with no scope for creativity, rather in mechanical response to the instructions read out from the *talim* by the master weaver. The shawl weavers were bonded to their employers by a system of perpetual debt, paid barely enough to sustain them and, on top of that, were taxed to the limit by the government. The rooms where they worked were often dimly lit and badly ventilated, and it was said that a weaver could be distinguished by the pallor of his face, his sickly physique, and above all, his delicate hands.

Tapestry weaving is a highly laborious and time-consuming technique, and by the middle of the nineteenth century, as the designs became ever more elaborate, particularly fine shawls took months and even years to complete. Accordingly, the manufacturers adopted two distinct methods of speeding up production, both exploiting the skills of the *rafugar*. On the one hand, not only the borders, but also the main bodies of the shawls began to be woven in pieces—sometimes literally hundreds, for elaborate all-over patterns—using several looms. It was the *rafugar*'s job to join these with seams so fine that only the expert eye can discern them. The other method was to abandon the twill-tapestry technique altogether, the *rafugar*'s skill being applied to the creation of patterns by embroidery in silk on plain pashmina fabric.

The word "shawl" originally referred not so much to a garment as to a fabric, and the long shoulder mantle—in India originally worn by men—was only one of many varieties of shawl-goods. Shoulder mantles were woven in pairs, and often stitched together back-to-back; they were called *do-shala*. Square items, *qasaba* or *rumal*, were made for women's wear, and long narrow ones, *patka* or *shamla*, for men's sashes. Lengths of shawl fabric in all-over designs, *jamawar*, were intended to be tailored into men's coats *(jama)*. Apart from these four main categories, about twenty-five varieties of shawl-goods were produced, including turbans, stockings, horses' and elephants' saddlecloths, carpets, curtains and other kinds of hangings, bedspreads, and shrouds for tombs.

Shawl Design

The earliest extant shawl fragments, probably from the mid- to late seventeenth century, have the two ends decorated with a simple and elegant repeated design of single flowering plants—a favorite motif of Mughal decorative art from about the 1620s—enclosed in a floral meander. Gradually the single flower evolved into a bouquet, or a flowering bush *(buta)*, assuming a cone shape, typically with the topmost bloom inclined to one side. In the later eighteenth century the plain background acquired a sprinkling of small flowers; by the 1820s, as this grew denser and more elaborate, it necessitated an outline to emphasize the main motif. Thus emerged the quintessential theme of shawl design, the bent-tip *buta*, which later became known as the "paisley," after the town in Scotland whose weavers, in the mid-nineteenth century, cornered the British market for imitation Kashmir shawls. This perennially popular design motif, noticed on objects as diverse as nineteenth-century buckles in Cyprus and contemporary coffee mugs in Scotland, to say nothing of fabrics for all sorts of uses, may be regarded as Kashmir's gift to the world.

The bent-tip *buta* found expression in myriad forms, often incorporated into other design formats, of which the most common were flower-filled stripes—especially for *jamawar*—and roundels. Square shawls often had a large floral medallion in the center, with quarter-circles in the four corners. They are known as *chand-dar*, or moon shawls.

As the nineteenth century progressed, the patterns on the shawl's ornamented ends became increasingly complex, and also larger, often invading the central field entirely, leaving no empty space at all. At the same time, French manufacturers were adapting and developing Kashmiri design for their own Jacquard-woven shawls, while sending such modified designs to be made up in Kashmir. The resulting elaborate and fanciful shawls represented an astonishing degree of technical virtuosity. Today's embroidered shawls are made up in the whole gamut of traditional designs, modified only by the difference in technique.

History of the Kashmir Shawl

The earliest explicit documentation of the Kashmir shawl comes in the late sixteenth century in the *Ain-i-Akbari*, a comprehensive description of the Mughal empire in the time of the emperor Akbar. The *Ain*, however, is clearly referring to an already mature industry, which must have been flourishing for decades if not centuries. Kashmiri tradition attributes its origin to the great fifteenth-century sultan, Zain-ul-Abdin, who is said to have encouraged the immigration of textile workers from abroad, possibly from Iran and central Asia.

For over two centuries Kashmir shawls and shawl-goods were an essential element of the Indian royal and aristocratic lifestyle. Demand was such that by the middle of the eighteenth century there were said to be 40,000 shawl looms in and around Srinagar. In 1752 Kashmir was wrested from the Mughals by the Afghans, who ruled until 1819. They, and the Sikh and Dogra governments that followed, imposed such heavy taxes that in the 1820s the revenue to the state from the shawl-weaving industry was greater than that from all other sources combined. As a result of these exactions the number of looms fell, and those weavers who could escape from the serflike conditions under which they were employed emigrated to the Punjab and elsewhere in North India. Even so, according to a report in the early 1820s, at least 130,000 people were working in the industry, while the value of shawls exported was about 60 lakhs (6 million) rupees.

Shawls were commissioned in designs according to the demands of different markets. As well as plains India, many Asian countries also imported Kashmir shawl-goods from the seventeenth to the nineteenth century. They are mentioned in Ottoman customs records as early as 1624. *Jamawar* was popular in Iran, while both there and in the Ottoman Empire shawls were part of men's wear, worn as turbans, or around the waist as sashes. Even distant Egypt imported shawl-goods; they were admired by officers of Napoleon Bonaparte's army in 1798, some of them purchasing shawls to take home as gifts. The empress Josephine's passion for shawls set an enduring fashion in France. They had already entered the fashion scene in Britain around 1780, brought home by returning officers of the East India Company, and were regularly imported from the beginning of the nineteenth century. Over the next seventy years, export to Europe became the mainstay of the industry. At the same time, flourishing industries in "imitation Indian shawls" sprang up in both France and Great Britain; in fact, the Jacquard loom was invented as an attempt to reproduce the intricacies of Kashmir design by mechanical means.

Decline and revival. The decline of the *kani* shawl in the last decades of the nineteenth century is often attributed to changes in European fashion; but the story is more complex. Social and political shifts in India and elsewhere in Asia led to erosion of the luxurious lifestyles of elites; as they started to adopt Western fashions, the shawl became irrelevant. By the early twentieth century, reduction in demand had led to the almost complete disappearance of *kani* work. The industry was kept alive by increased production of embroidered shawls, which came to be considered an essential accessory to the winter wardrobe of middle-class women in north India.

Remarkably, however, in the early years of the twenty-first century there are indications of a purposeful revival of the *kani* shawl. The development of a wealthy business class in India, especially after the economic reforms of the 1990s, created a market for such highly priced luxury goods, in response to which some astute Kashmiri shawl-makers have initiated the resuscitation of almost extinct skills. Thus, despite political upheavals, Kashmir's craftspeople—the designer, the spinner, the plain weaver, the *rafugar* and now once again the *kani* weaver—continue to keep alive the region's tradition of manufacturing textiles of unparalleled delicacy and beauty.

Janet Rizvi

See also **Textiles: Early Painted and Printed**

BIBLIOGRAPHY

The classic text on the Kashmir shawl industry in the nineteenth century is the report by William Moorcroft; it was published in an abbreviated form in William Moorcroft and George Trebeck, *Travels in the Himalayan Provinces of Hindustan and the Panjab; in Ladakh and Kashmir; in Peshawar, Kabul, Kunduz and Bokhara, from 1819 to 1825* (2 vols., 1841; reprint, Karachi and New York: Oxford University Press, 1979). Unfortunately this edited version is neither comprehensive nor entirely accurate; serious students will want to go to Moorcroft's original text in the Moorcroft MSS in the Oriental and India Office Collection of the British Library in London: MSS Eur. E113 and D264. The nineteenth-century picture is updated in Charles Ellison Bates, *Gazetteer of Kashmir* (1873; reprint, New Delhi: Light and Life Publishers, 1980). Otherwise, most nineteenth-century travelers' accounts need to be treated with caution. There are however useful references for the pre-Moorcroft period in Jean Deloche, *Voyage en Inde du Comte de Modave 1773–1776* (Paris: Ecole française d'extrême-orient, 1971), and Mountstuart Elphinstone, *An Account of the Kingdom of Caubul* (London 1815). The best general modern study is still John Irwin, *The Kashmir Shawl* (London: Her Majesty's Stationery Office for the Victoria and Albert Museum, 1973). For detailed analysis of the evolution of design in Kashmir shawls, with numerous illustrations, consult Frank Ames, *The Kashmir Shawl and its Indo-French Influence* (Woodbridge, UK: The Antiques Collectors Club, 1986). For the technique of "patchwork" shawls, see Grace Beardsley, "Piecing in Twill Tapestry Shawls of Persia and Kashmir" in *Textiles as Primary Sources: Proceedings of the First Symposium of the Textile Society of America* (St. Paul, Minn.: Textile Society of America, 1988).

Jaya Jaitly, ed. *Crafts of Jammu, Kashmir and Ladakh* (Ahmedabad, Mapin Publishing, 1990) usefully puts the Kashmir shawl into the context of other woven textiles of the region, and its crafts in general; while Michelle Maskiell, "Consuming Kashmir: Shawls and Empires, 1500–2000" in *Journal of World History*, 13, (1) 2002, uses the Kashmir shawl as a peg on which to hang a trenchant critique of the imperialist appropriation of the skills and sensibilities of colonized peoples.

KASI (BANARES). *See* **Geography; Varanasi.**

KATHAK. *See* **Dance Forms.**

KATHAKALI. *See* **Dance Forms.**

KAYASTHS The Kayasth caste has been historically important in all three of its regional incarnations, in North India, Maharashtra, and Bengal. The Chitragupta Kayasths of North India, the Prabhu Kayasths of Maharashtra, and the Bengal Kayasths of Bengal, with mother tongues of Hindi, Marathi, and Bengali, respectively, fulfilled similar roles in their regional political systems. All three were "writing castes," traditionally serving the ruling powers as administrators and record keepers. Although there is a modern tendency to see the three regional divisions as part of a single caste, they did not historically intermarry, and when Kayasth is used alone, it usually means the North Indian or Chitragupta community.

Members of all three communities were noted for their adaptability. Their linguistic and administrative abilities gained them key places in service to various rulers, and the Chitragupta and Bengal communities in particular were noted for their early movement into service with the incoming Muslim rulers of North India. They learned Persian, Urdu, and even Arabic, and many Chitragupta Kayasths accompanied the Mughals to Rajputana and the Deccan, becoming significant intermediaries in these new regional administrative systems as well. One theory about the historical origin of the Kayasths postulates that the caste arose only in medieval times, formed by those who adapted themselves earliest to service with the new rulers.

In fact, this Kayasth caste is hard to place in the Brahmanical *varṇa* system, the four caste categories elaborated in post-Vedic Sanskrit literature. The men participated fully in the various Muslim and Mughal court cultures developing throughout India since medieval times. They typically learned Arabic, Persian, or Urdu from Muslim clerics and began their education with a *bismillah* ceremony, like Muslims in those days. Sometimes the men's names reflected their competence and membership in India's medieval bicultural synthesis: Iqbal Chand, Jehangir Pershad, or Mahbub Karan. However, in their domestic life the Kayasths subscribed to high caste Hindu regulations governing social intercourse and life-cycle rituals. Their marriage and death customs followed high caste Hindu models, and they maintained hereditary relations with specific Hindu service castes, Brahmans and barbers, for example.

Historical sources fail to link many medieval and modern castes to the Brahmanical four-*varṇa* system, yet attempts have been made, by Kayasths themselves or by the British Indian legal system at various times and places, to place Kayasths in one of the four *varṇa*s. The Kayasths have been considered either Brahmans because of their literacy and learning, Kshatriyas because they were closely linked to rulers (and, at least in the Deccan, often to military service as well), or Sudras because they deviated significantly from the orthodox practices enjoined upon the first three *varṇa*s (this last in a legal decision in British Bengal, but elsewhere as well, where Kayasths ate meat and drank wine).

The most common Kayasth myth of origin avoided this problem of *varṇa* classification by cleverly postulating the creation of a fifth *varṇa*, the Kayasths, to keep records concerning the other four. Brahma, they say, after creating the four *varṇa*s, created the first Kayasth, pen and inkpot in hand. This was Chitragupta, and his chief employment was for Yama, the god of death, recording the good and bad activities of all men. Chitragupta then had twelve sons by two wives, and the subcastes or endogamous divisions among the North Indian Kayasths are traced to these sons. The subcastes have patron deities, home areas, and nominal *gotra*s (exogamous divisions within the endogamous subcaste, a feature of Brahman caste organization); in reality, family distinctions, or *al*s, played important roles in marriage arrangements.

Members of an urban literate caste wherever they appear in India, the Kayasths seem to have always reflected a close association with the ruling power. This was true under the Mughals, when a number of outstanding Kayasths attained very high rank in the Mughal empire, and true under the British in British India, when Kayasths were among the first to learn English and continue their administrative service. It is true today in independent India's modern democracy; Lal Bahadur Shastri, prime minister of India from 1964 to 1966, was a Chitragupta Kayasth, and there have been other distinguished Kayasths in government service. In the past, Kayasths have sometimes been criticized for this adaptability, most often in connection with their service to the Mughals (it is said that they are like a cat on a wall, they can fall to either side), but Kayasths are not the only caste or caste cluster notable for its adaptability to ruling powers, and sometimes men said to be Kayasth are actually Khatri or Brahmo-Khatri, castes with similar names and traditions. In fact, Kayasths, like many other upwardly mobile individuals or castes in Indian history, exemplify flexibility and adaptability. They continue today to use their administrative and now professional capacities to integrate India's diverse communities.

Karen Leonard

See also **Caste System; Hyderabad**

Communist Party Leader E. K. Nayanar. The longest-serving chief minister of Kerala, Communist Party leader E. K. Nayanar before his death in 2004. The portraits of his idols (Marx, Engels, and Lenin) look on. INDIA TODAY.

BIBLIOGRAPHY

Kane, P. V. "The Kayasthas." *New Indian Antiquary* 1 (1929): 739–743.

Leonard, Karen. *Social History of an Indian Caste: The Kayasths of Hyderabad.* Berkeley: University of California Press, 1978.

Prasad, Munshi Kali. *The Kayastha Ethnology*. Lucknow, 1877.

Shastri, Pandit Raghuvara Mitthulal Shastri. "A Comprehensive Study into the Origin and Status of the Kayasthas." *Man in India* 11, no. 2 (1931): 116–159.

Varma, Gopi Nath Sinha. *A Peep into the Origin, Status and History of the Kayasthas*. 2 vols. Bareilly, 1929, 1935.

KERALA, COALITION POLITICS In parliamentary democracies, political parties constitute the most essential elements for a nation's successful functioning. In India, coalition politics came rather late, mainly because the omnibus Indian National Congress, the institutional vehicle that brought freedom to India, remained the multipolar party that ruled India's central government for three decades after independence. Non-Congress parties could not effectively organize coalition opposition to Congress at the national level prior to 1975. In Kerala state, however, soon after its formation in 1957, Congress lost to the Communist Party of India, elected with minority parties who supported its Left Democratic Front.

Between 1957 and 2003, there were twelve midterm elections to Kerala's state assembly. Of the eighteen state governments since 1957, only two were led by a single party, and both of these were short-lived. Congress led its own United Democratic Front coalition, which alternated in governing Kerala with the Left Democratic Front. The United Democratic Front government, led by Congress's A. K. Antony, has ruled the state since May 2001.

The Bharatiya Janata Party could not win even a single seat in Kerala's 140-member state assembly, or any of Kerala's 20 seats in the Lok Sabha (the lower house of India's Parliament) or its 9 seats in the Rajya Sabha (the upper house of India's Parliament).

Coalition politics in Kerala has built consensus among parties and public, and political discourse in Kerala is constantly energized through the dynamics of multiparty debates within the coalition framework. As in London's parliamentary democracy, Kerala's opposition is expected to play a constructive, responsible role. The Treasury Bench, on the other hand, estimates the potential of the rival front to come to power in the next election, thereby providing much-needed political stability and continuity. Viewed from this perspective, Kerala can serve as a model to most other Indian states, though forging an ideological unity is hardly possible in a democratic pluralist culture.

G. Gopa Kumar

See also **Kerala, Model of Development**

BIBLIOGRAPHY

Chander, N. Jose. *Coalition Politics: The Indian Experience.* New Delhi: Concept Publishers, 2004.

Gopa Kumar, G. *Regional Political Parties and State Politics.* New Delhi: Deep and Deep, 1986.

John John, Pariyarathu. *Coalition Governments in Kerala.* Trivandrum: Institute for the Study of Public Policy, 1983.

Nair, A. Balakrishnan. *Government and Politics of Kerala.* Thiruvananthapuram: Indira Publications, 1994.

Ramakrishnan Nair, R. *The Middle Class Rule in Kerala.* Tivandrum: Kerala Academy of Political Science, 1978.

———. *Social Structure and Political Developments in Kerala.* Trivandrum: Policy Studies Institute, 1978.

Thomas, E. J. *Coalition Game Politics in Kerala.* New Delhi: Intellectual Publishing House, 1985.

KERALA, MODEL OF DEVELOPMENT Modern Kerala formally emerged as a constituent state of the Indian Union on 1 November 1956, comprising three regions: Travancore, Cochin, and Malabar. The Linguistic Reorganization Committee, which recommended the reorganization of India's states based on the majority's common language, created modern Kerala as a state in which Malayalam was the unifying language. Kerala has 392 miles (631 kilometers) of narrow coast in India's southwest, facing the Arabian Sea. It occupies a narrow but fecund strip of land (1.5 percent of the total land area in the country), supporting 4.5 percent of the nation's population. Beautiful Kerala, called "God's own country," is one of the world's most popular tourist destinations.

Kerala, a model for other Indian states, has achieved social and educational development comparable to most Western nations; this achievement is not yet matched by industrial growth or economic development. Its excellent record in education, health, and land redistribution provides a unique case for arguing that the basis for true development is social and human, rather than economic.

As of 2003, Kerala enjoyed a literacy rate of over 90 percent, only slightly higher among males than females. Kerala pioneered equitable land reforms and elected India's first Communist state government by democratic means in 1957. The population growth rate in Kerala is the lowest in India (0.9 percent per annum), competing with China's near zero population growth rate. Population pressure on Kerala's meager land is very high, however, with 819 persons per square mile (the third highest in India). The low level of infant mortality (14 per thousand) is an indicator of the excellent health standards of the population, among both males and females. Life expectancy, averaging over 70 years for males and 75 for females, is the highest in India. The social status of Kerala's women is very high, supported by nuclear families, and Kerala has a high rate of females in the workforce. The state also recorded the lowest rate of child labor in the country. The younger population of Kerala is well trained in both software and hardware programming. Many people born in Kerala work in other parts of India, as well as in the Gulf countries, Europe, and North America. One in four Kerala households has received some of its income from the Gulf states since 1973. Of the total of some 40 million people born in Kerala, more than 8 million were living and working outside Kerala State in 2003.

However, Kerala's high levels of human development are not matched by industrial growth or generation of employment opportunities within the state. The economy became stagnant and nonproductive in many sectors, except tourism. Globalization policies had already affected its traditional industries, such as coir, hand-loomed textiles, and cashew nuts, thereby multiplying the number of unemployed in the state (25 percent in 2003, the highest in India). Nearly 4.2 million people were unemployed, and the proportion of nonworkers (including children, the elderly, and the disabled) in Kerala (68 percent) is higher than the national average (61 percent). The per capita income in Kerala, however, is estimated at 19,460 rupees, compared to 16,047 rupees at the national level.

All the villages and towns of Kerala are electrified and 91 percent of the rural habitations have access to potable water. According to the National Sample Survey, the population below the poverty line constituted only 12.5 percent, the lowest of any state in the country.

At the political level, Kerala has a healthy tradition of bipolar coalition politics in the backdrop of a multiparty system. The Indian National Congress and the Communist Party of India (Marxist) are the two leading parties. Smaller parties, like the Communist Party of India, the Indian Union Muslim League, the Kerala Congress (M), the Kerala Congress (J), and the Kerala Congress (B), compete for power in the coalitions. The State Legislature has 140 seats, besides 9 seats in Delhi's Rajya Sabha (the Upper "House of the States" in Parliament) and 20 seats in Lok Sabha (the Lower "House of the People").

Though in 2003 54 percent of Kerala's population were Hindus, it had the largest concentraton of Muslims (25 percent) after Jammu and Kashmir. It also had 20 percent Christians and a small but ancient Jewish minority.

Political History

The princely states of Travancore and Cochin were not under the direct control of Britain's paramount imperial power, but the Malabar region was part of the British Raj's Madras presidency. Historically, Travancore led the other regions in terms of social development. Its maharaja welcomed Christian missionaries, who established churches, schools, and colleges, offering a liberal Western education to the masses. The missionaries also pioneered the state's struggles against harsh Hindu practices, including untouchability and slavery. The struggle for responsible government in Travancore and the national freedom struggle in Malabar gave Kerala a galaxy of social and political leaders, known as the "four Ms": maharajas, missionaries, movements, and Marxists.

Kerala's Communist Party transformed itself into a powerful social democratic force, and adapted to India's parliamentary democratic framework. It headed seven coalition state governments, besides its own brief interlude of Communist rule, implementing land reforms and decentralization measures long before other states. High wages for workers and powerful trade unions were also contributions of the Communist Parties in Kerala.

The Kerala model of social development is unique in several respects. Its nearly egalitarian society, positive records in health, education, decentralization, and population planning, and its active coalition system of governing have made the state a vibrant civil society, transforming itself from traditional, ancient feudal roots. Kerala concentrated more on investing in its people rather than in markets. Human resources are the mainstay of its development.

G. Gopa Kumar

See also **Development Politics**

BIBLIOGRAPHY

Centre for Development Studies. *Poverty, Unemployment and Development Policy: A Case Study of Selected Issues with Reference to Kerala.* New York: United Nations, 1975.

Drèze, Jean, and Amartya Sen, eds. *Indian Development: Selected Regional Perspectives.* Delhi and New York: Oxford University Press, 1997.

Franke, Richard W., et al. *Kerala: Development through Radical Reform.* New Delhi: Promilla, 1994.

George, K. K. *Limits to Kerala Model of Development: An Analysis of Fiscal Crisis and Its Implications.* Thiruvananthapuram: Centre for Development Studies, 1993.

Government of Kerala. *Economic Review.* Thiruvananthapuram: State Planning Board, 2001.

Harilal, K. N., and K. J. Joseph. "Stagnation and Revival of Kerala Economy: An Open Economy Perspective." *Economic and Political Weekly* (7–13 June 2003).

Harris, John. *Depoliticising Development.* New Delhi: Left Word, 2003.

Isaac, Thomas T. M., and Richard W. Franke. *Local Democracy and Development.* New Delhi: Left Word, 2001.

Jeffrey, Robin. *Politics, Women, and Well Being: How Kerala Became a Model.* Houndmills, U.K.: Macmillan, 1992.

Parayil, Govindan. *Kerala: The Development Experience.* London and New York: Zed Books, 2000.

Prakash, B. A. "Gulf Migration and Its Economic Impact: The Kerala Experience." *Economic and Political Weekly* (12 December 1998).

Prakash, B. A., ed. *Kerala's Economy: Performance, Problems, Prospects.* New Delhi: Sage Publications, 1994.

Tornquist, Olle. *The Next Left? Democratisation and Attempts to Renew the Radical Political Development Project: The Case of Kerala.* Copenhagen: Nordic Institute of Asian Studies, 1995.

KERKAR, KESARBAI ***(1892–1977), Hindustani classical singer.*** Kesarbai Kerkar, who hailed from the state of Goa, was born into a community of professional singers. Her first tutelage was under Abdul Karim Khan of the Kirana Gharana (lineage) for a brief period. It was followed by intermittent study under Ramkrishnabuwa Vaze for a period of ten years. Barkatullah Khan, a leading sitar player of the early twentieth century, also tutored her in singing. She mastered the complex singing style of Alladiya Khan of the Jaipur-Attarauli Gharana, under whom she studied from 1921, training for at least eight hours a day.

Kesarbai sang with a broad and flawless "aa" (a musical utterance of the vowel "aa"), which invested her music with a unique luminosity. Her vigorous, weighty execution of double-stranded fast tonal patterns left listeners speechless with wonder. She could swoop from a high octave to a deep, resonant low octave, while retaining a remarkable uniformity of volume. Continuity of sound through amazing breath control was one of the principal tenets of her singing style, and this seemingly unending breath lent grandeur to her music. Fast tonal patterns woven into the rhythmic passages compelled the constant attention of the listener. Kesarbai won many national honors. Her recording of a *thumri* in Bharavi was selected by the U.S. National Aeronautics and Space Administration for inclusion in a collection of Earth's best music, which will be sent on the spaceship *Voyager*.

Amarendra Dhaneshwar

BIBLIOGRAPHY

Deodhar, B. R. *Pillars of Hindustani Music.* Mumbai: Popular Prakashan, 1993.

Haldankar, Shrikrishna. *Aesthetics of Agra and Jaipur Traditions.* Mumbai: Popular Prakashan, 2001.
Ranade, Ashok D. *On Music and Musicians of Hindoostan.* New Delhi: Promilla, 1984.

KESARI. *See* **Tata, Jamsetji N.**

KHAJURAHO Khajuraho, a medieval temple town, situated in the state of Madhya Pradesh in central India, preserves twenty-five magnificent Hindu and Jain temples. Known in inscriptions as "Kharjura-vahaka," it flourished between A.D. 900 and 1150 as the capital of the powerful Chandella Rajputs, who ruled the region called Jejakabhukti, now the Bundelkhand area in Madhya Pradesh and southern Uttar Pradesh. Surrounded by hills of the Vindhya Range, the original town extended over 8 square miles (21 sq. km) and contained, according to tradition, about eighty-five temples, built by the successive Chandella rulers, their ministers and merchants.

The Chandellas were originally local chieftains and feudatories of the imperial Pratihara monarchs of Kannauj, but by the middle of the tenth century they consolidated power and became independent rulers. The Chandella prince Yashovarman acquired the prestigious image of Vaikuntha-Vishnu from his Pratihara overlord, and he celebrated his victory by building a splendid temple (now called Lakshmana temple), the first in the elite Nagara style, at Khajuraho around 950. The Chandella kings encouraged poetry, drama, dance, and music. Two of the rulers were themselves poets. Above all, they were great sponsors of temple art. Under them Khajuraho became one of the most important temple towns of northern India. In 1022 the Muslim historian Alberuni mentioned "Kajuraha" as the capital of the Chandella kingdom. From the twelfth century, however, the Chandellas shifted their activities to the nearby town of Mahoba and the hill forts of Kalinjar and Ajaygadh, and consequently the temple building at Khajuraho lost momentum. Even so, it remained a religious center, important enough to attract the attention of the Arab traveller Ibn Battuta, who visited Khajuraho in 1335 to see its *jogis* (yogis, mendicants) and their magical feats. Thereafter, Khajuraho gradually slipped into oblivion.

Some five centuries later, Captain T. S. Burt, a British engineer, spotted the vanished temples amidst a jungle growth that had all but covered them, and he presented his colorful account to the Asiatic Society of Bengal in 1838. The local maharaja of Chhatarpur undertook extensive repair work on the temples between 1842 and

Vishvanatha Temple, Part of the Khajuraho Complex. The progressive ascent of the temple's numerous indentations and projections converges at the pinnacle, a soaring curvilinear spire. In the late twentieth and early tweny-first centuries, the temple, like others in the tenth-century complex, has provided the backdrop for dramatically lit, nighttime dance performances. AFP / GETTY IMAGES.

1847. Major General Alexander Cunningham, later the first director general of the Archaeological Survey of India (ASI), visited the site from 1852 onward and systematically described the temples in his ASI Reports. Khajuraho monuments have remained under the care and supervision of the ASI, which has identified eighteen mounds and has undertaken excavation of at least two. Today Khajuraho is a small village, serving the tourist trade with its fine hotels. It has three museums: the Archaeological Museum, the Jain Antiquities Museum, and the Tribal and Folk Art Museum. It can be approached by road from Jhansi (109 miles [175 km]) and Satna (73 miles [117 km]), and by air from Delhi, Varanasi, and Agra. Khajuraho was designated a World Heritage Site by the United Nations Educational, Scientific, and Cultural Organization in 1986.

The Temples

Of the twenty-five temples, eighteen are dedicated to the two main Hindu deities: ten to Vishnu, including his powerful composite form, Vaikuntha; and eight to Shiva. There is one temple dedicated to the sun god, one to the esoteric Yoginis (goddesses), and five to the Jain patriarchs of the Digambar sect. A colossal inscribed image of the seated Buddha was also found at this site, indicating the prevalence of Buddhism as well, though on a limited scale. An inscribed image of Hanuman attests to the worship of this monkey god. Khajuraho thus was a religious center where many cults flourished. A synthesis of cults is also indicated by a number of syncretistic icons that combine divinities, as well as by the presence of sculptures of Hindu divinities on Jain temples, and vice-versa. The Hindu religious systems of Khajuraho were Tantra-based but, unlike the skull-bearing Kapalika sect, were not extreme Tantric.

The temples are clustered in three zones. The western zone, located near the Shivasagar tank, is associated with the Chandella royal family, and it includes some of Khajuraho's most magnificent monuments: the Varaha shrine (c. 940); Lakshmana or Vaikuntha-Vishnu temple, built by King Yashovarman (consecrated in 954); Vishvanatha, built by King Dhangadeva (inscribed 999); Matangeshvara (c. 1000), originally a memorial shrine with a colossal lingam 8 feet (2.5 m) in height; and the Kandariya Mahadeva, possibly built by King Vidyadhara (c. 1030). The eastern zone comprises Jain temples built by merchants, most notably the Parshvanatha (c. 955), Ghantai (c. 970), and Adinatha (c. 1075). The southern zone includes the Chaturbhuja temple (c. 1100) with a majestic 9-foot-(5.6 m) tall icon of a unique form of Vishnu—some scholars believe it to represent the Dakshinamurti (Teacher) form of Siva—and the Duladeva temple (c. 1130), the latest in the series, built on a stellate plan. An open-air sanctuary, dedicated to the Sixty-four Yoginis (c. 900), is situated to the southwest of the Shivasagar tank, away from the main western group of temples.

Recent excavations by the Archaeological Survey of India at the Shatdhara mound in the northeastern zone have yielded early Chandella (pre-950) sculptures and architectural remains of a temple complex, affiliated to Vishnu (Dwarf incarnation). Excavations at the Bijamandala mound, in the southern zone, have exposed remains of an eleventh-century Vaidyanatha Shiva temple (112 ft [34 m] long), the largest discovered at the site.

Architectural features. Though affiliated with different religious sects, the temples have a cognate architectural style. Except for the early shrines of the Sixty-four Yoginis (c. 900), built of rough granite, and the Lalguan Mahadeva (c. 900–925) and Brahma (c. 925), constructed of both granite and sandstone, other temples from the middle of the tenth century are constructed of fine-grained sandstone in the Nagara style with its typical curvilinear spire over the sanctum. Unlike the Orissan temples in eastern India, which have their halls as separate structures, the Khajuraho temples are compact, integrated monuments consisting of four or five units: the cella or sanctum (*garbhagriha*), vestibule (*antarala*), large hall (*maha-mandapa*), hall (*mandapa*), and porch (*ardha-mandapa*). Four of the large temples are *sandhara;* that is, they have an inner ambulatory. Two of these, namely the Lakshmana and the Vishvanatha, are five-shrined (*panchayatana*), with subsidiary shrines in the four corners of the platform. Most of the temples are erected on the east-west axis and get the direct rays of the rising sun. They have no enclosure walls, as in the case of the South Indian and Orissan temples, but they have their own separate platforms to demarcate their sacred space.

The Khajuraho temples stand on a tall *jagati* (platform). They have three main divisions on elevation: basal story (*pitha*), wall (*jangha*), and the roof or spire (*shikhara*). The basal story consists of a series of ornamental moldings depicting rows of human activities (*narathara*), "masks of glory" (*kirtimukha*), and geometrical designs. The wall section is divided into two or three sculptural zones, consisting of figural sculptures—celestial maidens (*apsaras*), griffins (*vyalas*), couples (*mithunas*), and divinities. The numerous indentations and projections carried upward from the ground level to the superstructure of the temple produce a wonderful dramatic effect.

The architectural imagery of the Khajuraho temples helps us to conceive of the temple as a model of the cosmos. While the subordinate structures such as the porch and halls have pyramidal roofs, the sanctum is covered with a soaring curvilinear spire with graded peaks clustered around it. The architect creates the semblance of a mountain by emphasizing the progressive ascent of superstructures of the component units, converging at the pinnacle. Significantly, the inscriptions of Khajuraho compare the temple with Mount Kailasa, the abode of Shiva, and Mount Meru, the center of the universe. The Kandariya Mahadeva, 102 feet (31 m) high, mountainlike with its eighty-four minispires clinging to its central spire, is a masterpiece of Indian temple art.

The plan of the cella of the large temples (Lakshmana, Vishvanatha, Kandariya, Parshvanatha) resembles a three-dimensional *yantra* (geometric diagram), with the eight corners guarded by the regents of space (*dikpalas*). The three cardinal niches represent manifestations or incarnations of the main divinity enshrined in the sanctum. The iconic scheme is integrated with the religious cult of the temple.

Sculpture

Sculpture in the Khajuraho temples is harmoniously integrated with their architecture. The unified design of the temple, with its horizontal bands of sculpture, is perfectly balanced with the rising verticality of the building. Both the exteriors and interiors of the temples are lavishly carved. Ceilings are decorated with intricate geometric and floral designs. Pillar brackets bear sculptures of griffins alternating with maidens, standing under trees, carved in high relief. The sanctum doorway is decorated with conventional auspicious motifs: *mithunas* (couples), creepers, and dwarfs. It is guarded by *dvarapalas* (doorkeepers) and is "purified" by the river goddesses, Gaṅgā and Yamuna, sculpted in human form. Indeed, the profusion of figural sculptures is overwhelming. Cunningham counted 646 figures on the exterior and 226 in the interior of the Kandariya Mahadeva alone.

Style. The human body is depicted in sensuous charm in a variety of postures and attitudes. The figures are not muscular, as in Greek sculpture. The beauty of the human form is revealed from many angles through diaphanous clothes. Sculptors were adept at turning the figure around its axis. The figures of nymphs combine two views of the front and the back. Divinities smile softly and stand with languid grace. The measured elegance of the divine images, as well as the spontaneity and lyricism of the loving couples on the walls, is remarkable.

There are three phases in sculptural portrayal: prior to 950, in the excavated Shatdhara mound, revealing elements of the style prevalent in Kannauj and other sites of the Pratiharas overlords; c. 950–1100, in the principal temples starting with the Lakshmana up to the Chaturbhuja temple, with typical Chandella features such as serenity of expression, tight volumes, and full modeling of figures; c. 1100–1200, the style seen in the Duladeva temple (c. 1130), with sharp features, angular bodies, and heavy ornamentation, represented also in other late Chandella sites such as Jamsot, near Allahabad.

Several categories of sculptures are seen in temples, among which are divinities, sacred and mythic animals, celestial maidens, and secular themes, including erotic figures.

Divinities. Divine images consist of cult icons in the sanctum, generally standing formally in *sama-bhanga* (equipoise, or weight equally on two feet), and carved according to canonical formulae; and multiple manifestations of the principal deity in the cardinal and surrounding niches. Also present are the *dikpala*s (regents of space), Matrikas (Divine Mothers), *graha*s (planets), and numerous lesser divinities, demigods such as flying *vidyadhara*s, *gandharva*s (celestial musicians), and *gana*s (dwarfs) placed in different parts of the temple. There are hundreds of images of divinities holding manuscripts in hand, suggesting the importance of knowledge and learning. Several deities—Vishnu, Shiva, Surya, Devi, and Jinas—sit in yogic positions.

Sacred and mythic animals. There are carvings in the round of Nandi, Shiva's bull, and of Varaha, the boar incarnation of Vishnu. The zoomorphic icon of Varaha (c. 925), installed in the western complex of the site, is represented as a cosmic form, carrying more than 650 divinities of the Hindu pantheon carved in relief on its massive animal body. The *vyala*, a mythic composite animal, is seen in its many varieties, with faces of different animals and birds, combined with the body of a lion. Mythic aquatic creatures, *makara*s, decorate arches and niches.

Secular scenes. Warriors, dancers, musicians, hunting parties, sculptors at work, and royal figures are mainly sculpted in relief on the rows of the plinth, and in small niches of the superstructure. Men fighting a *vyala* or a lion is a favorite theme. Idealized portraits of a king and queen performing a ritual, carved in the round, are now in the site museum.

Erotic figures. It should be clarified that Khajuraho is neither synonymous with erotic sculpture nor do the temples illustrate the Indian handbook of love, the Kāma Sūtra, as is generally believed. Erotic themes constitute not even one-tenth of the total sculpture on the temples but have drawn undue attention. Erotic depiction was believed to be a good omen because it symbolized regeneration, and it was part of a larger tradition prevalent across India. As an auspicious and apotropaic motif, it is depicted on most temples of India—Hindu, Buddhist, Jain—built between 900 and 1300, and it is represented according to the sculptural canons of the region in which the temple is situated. Generally, however, the figures are small and placed in insignificant location. At Khajuraho, as in Orissan temples, erotic figures are placed, apart from several parts of the temple, conspicuously on the main wall. The sculptures are large in size and in graceful postures. Significantly, at Khajuraho the artists have made creative use of this already established theme, the conjunction of opposites, the union of the male and female principles, by placing it on the juncture walls (of *sandhara* temples) that link the hall for devotees and the sanctum of the divinity, to metaphorically convey something beyond the erotic. Though the surface meaning is erotic, a hidden meaning lies beneath, expressing a subtle yogic-philosophic concept—the goal of nonduality.

Maidens. *Apsara*s or *nayika*s appear on all temples of the Nagara style, whether Hindu or Jain. They are shown absorbed in various everyday activities, such as applying makeup, removing a thorn from the foot, writing a letter, or carrying a baby. One of the favorite motifs of Khajuraho artists is a woman undressing to throw a scorpion from her body, a poetic device that expressed a fertility theme. The *apsaras* of Khajuraho and other medieval temples are auspicious art motifs whose origins can be traced back to vegetation spirits (*yakshis*) and fertility figures of early Indian art at Sanchi, Bharhut, and Mathura. In fact, the architectural Vastu texts specifically ordain sculptures of female figures on temple walls.

Meaningful Form

The art of Khajuraho reflects the highly sophisticated and Sanskritized ethos of the Chandella court. Knowledge of Sanskrit and its grammar was highly appreciated by the elite. Sculptors were innovative in creating images with unique iconography, for instance, the god Sadashiva with four feet (*padas*), suggestive of (by way of a pun on the Sanskrit word *pada* = foot = part) the four parts (*padas*) of the Shaiva religious texts.

The architects of Khajuraho were learned in Shastric (textual) traditions, as inscriptions and designs in the temples testify. They place sculptures in architectural schemes not just to decorate temples or to fill space, but also to convey concepts of cosmological import. In the Lakshmana temple, for instance, the architect arranges collective images of planetary divinities (*grahas*) on the exterior plinth, as if encircling the temple, thereby projecting the concept of the temple as Mount Meru, the mythical mountain in the center of the universe, around which the planets revolve.

The most refined achievement of Khajuraho art, the Kandariya Mahadeva temple, embodies the symbolism of the *yantra* in the plan of its sanctum, the imagery of the cosmic mountain in its multiturreted spire, and a visual expression of the Shaiva metaphysical system in its iconic scheme. Shiva-*liṅga*, considered the sign of the unmanifest ultimate reality, is installed in the center of the sanctum, with graded manifestations of Shiva, emanations and subemanations, in the surrounding niches, as if radiating the power of the divinity enshrined within. The temple is an ordered whole in which images are part of an integrated scheme. The Khajuraho temples represent a creative moment in Indian art when artistic talent combined with religious aspirations to produce a meaningful form.

Devangana Desai

See also **Asiatic Societies of Bengal and Bombay**

BIBLIOGRAPHY

Burt, T. S. An account of his visit in *Journal of the Asiatic Society of Bengal*, VIII, 1839.

Cunningham, Alexander. *Archaeological Survey of India Reports*, Vols. II, VII, X, XXI. Simla-Calcutta, 1864–1885.

Desai, Devangana. *Erotic Sculpture of India: A Socio-Cultural Study*. 1975. Rev. ed., New Delhi: Munshiram Manoharlal, 1985.

———. "Temple as an Ordered Whole: The Iconic Scheme at Khajuraho." *Journal of the Asiatic Society of Bombay* 70 (1995): 38–58.

———. *The Religious Imagery of Khajuraho*. Mumbai: Franco-Indian Research, 1996.

———. *Khajuraho*. Monumental Legacy Series. New Delhi: Oxford University Press, 2000.

Deva, Krishna. "The Temples of Khajuraho in Central India." *Ancient India* Bulletin of ASI, no. 15 (1959): 43–65.

———. *Temples of Khajuraho*. 2 vols. New Delhi: ASI, 1990.

Meister, Michael. "Juncture and Conjunction: Punning and Temple Architecture." *Artibus Asiae* 41 (1979): 226–228.

Mitra, S. K. *The Early Rulers of Khajuraho*. Rev. ed., Delhi: Motilal Banarsidass, 1977.

Prakash, Vidya. *Khajuraho*: *A Study in the Cultural Conditions of Chandella Society*. Mumbai: Taraporevalas, 1967.

Zannas, E., and J. Auboyer. *Khajuraho*. The Hague: Mouton, 1960.

KHALSA. *See* **Sikhism.**

KHAN, ABDUL GHAFFAR ***(1890–1988), Pakhtun leader, opponent of partition, proponent of a Pakhtun state.*** Jailed for twelve years by the British and for fifteen years by Pakistani authorities, Abdul Ghaffar Khan, born in 1890 in Utmanzai in the North-West Frontier province (NWFP), remains a symbol of the values of nonviolence and Pakhtun dignity.

Ghaffar Khan's towering figure was often seen alongside Mahatma Gandhi's smaller frame, both faithfully adhering to *ahimsa* (nonviolence) and opposing the partition of India. "Badshah" Khan endured long prison terms and solitary confinements, and was admired as much for his fearlessness as for his principles. He did not hesitate to urge his male Pakhtun followers to acknowledge their harshness to women, or to urge all of South Asia's Hindus and Muslims to live in friendship.

Living on both sides of the boundary between the NWFP and Afghanistan and distributed among numerous tribes, the Pakhtuns were never wholly subdued by armed expeditions launched by the British, who divided Pakhtun territory into insulated "tribal" preserves governed by chiefs loyal to the British and "settled" districts directly run by Britons. Ghaffar Khan's uneducated father Behram Khan, belonging to the Muhammadzai tribe, possessed lands in the "settled" part—in Utmanzai and elsewhere in the fertile Charsadda valley, watered by the Indus and Kabul Rivers and also by canals built by the British.

Though British occupation had offended the Pakhtuns, Behram Khan sensed its longevity and saw its

Abdul Ghaffar Khan. Freedom fighter from the northwest provinces of India, Khan was the tireless advocate of Pakhtun autonomy and peaceful Muslim-Hindu coexistence. K. L. KAMAT / KAMAT'S POTPOURRI.

advantages, and sent his boys Abdul Jabbar and Abdul Ghaffar (Jabbar was older by eight years) first to a British-run municipal school and then to the Edwardes Mission School conducted by a Reverend Wigram. Ghaffar Khan would always say that he learned the service of fellow humans from Reverend Wigram.

In 1912 Ghaffar married Mehr Qandh of Rajjar village, near Utmanzai. Two years later he made an unsuccessful bid, in company with a few others, to set up a secret anti-British base in the village of Zagai in the tribal territory of the Mohmand Pakhtuns. By this time Ghaffar had come close to Haji Fazli Wahid of Turangzai, a leading Pakhtun foe of British rule. He also visited the nationalist Muslim center of Deoband in the United Provinces, and he started a school, free of British influence, in Utmanzai.

In 1915, after having given birth to two sons, Ghani and Wali, Mehr Qandh died of influenza. Five years later, Ghaffar Khan married Nambata, also from Rajjar, who gave birth to a boy, Ali, and a daughter, Mehr Taj, but died in 1924. Two of Ghaffar Khan's four children—Ghani, later a poet and painter of renown, and Mehr Taj—were sent to the West for their studies.

Ghaffar Khan advocated both Pakhtun reform and Pakhtun autonomy. In 1919 Mahatma Gandhi, who had returned four years previously from his long struggle for Indian rights in South Africa, called for a nationwide nonviolent protest against the repressive Rowlatt "Black" Acts. The anti-Rowlatt rally in Utmanzai that Ghaffar Khan organized and addressed on 6 April 1919 marked the beginning of his nonviolent struggle for Pakhtun and Indian independence. It would bring him bitter prison terms in 1919, 1922 to 1924, 1930 to 1931, 1931 to 1934, 1934 to 1935, and 1942 to 1945. In 1928 he launched the journal *Pakthun* and the following year his "Red Shirt" Khudai Khidmatgar (Serving Volunteers of God) movement, which included a political dimension.

Though most Khudai Khidmatgars were Muslims, the organization included Hindus, Sikhs, Christians, and Parsis. During the 1930s and the early 1940s, the volunteers added up to more than thirty thousand. Each took a pledge to eschew violence and revenge, and to reduce feuds in Pakhtun society. Ghaffar Khan's nonviolence was doubtless connected to his association with Gandhi, whom he first saw in 1920, but even more to his longing to rescue the Pakhtuns from the custom of *badal* (revenge) and to the violence of British reprisals.

One of the dramatic episodes during the India-wide campaigns of the 1930s occurred in Peshawar's Kissa Khwani Bazaar. On 23 April 1930, during a crackdown in which a number of Pathans were killed, soldiers of the Raj's Garhwal Rifles refused to obey their officer's order to fire at a crowd of unarmed Pathans. In 1934 the presidency of the All-India Congress was offered to Ghaffar Khan, who claimed inadequacy and declined the honor, wary perhaps of being drawn too deeply into non-Pakhtun affairs.

After elections for provincial power held in 1937 and again in 1946, the Khudai Khidmatgars, who had merged into the Indian National Congress, formed ministries in the NWFP, headed by Ghaffar Khan's older brother, Dr. Khan Sahib, as Abdul Jabbar was then called.

On philosophical as well as practical grounds, Ghaffar Khan opposed the Pakistan demand articulated from 1940 by the Muslim League. His tolerant Islam sanctioned Muslim-Hindu coexistence. Moreover, he feared for the future of Pakhtun culture in a Punjab-dominated Pakistan. Preferring a wider polity, he allied with the Congress until the spring of 1947, when the Congress accepted the subcontinent's partition. Feeling betrayed, Ghaffar Khan and his Khudai Khidmatgars left the Congress, boycotting the NWFP plebiscite (which went in Pakistan's favor), calling for a state of Pakhtunistan (land of the Pakhtuns). In the years that followed, when he and his followers were persecuted and imprisoned, Ghaffar

Khan repeatedly insisted that his Pakhtunistan would remain connected to Pakistan, but Pakistan's rulers considered him a secessionist. When not in prison he continued to advocate Pakhtun autonomy, nonviolence, and antipoverty policies. Some of his agenda was taken up by his son Wali Khan, who became the president of the National Awami Party that Ghaffar Khan helped found in the early 1950s.

From 1965 until his death, Ghaffar Khan divided his time between Pakistan and Afghanistan, where he wrote his autobiography and where, in the town of Jalalabad, he built a home. Visiting India in 1969, the centenary of Gandhi's birth, he spoke candidly about the vulnerability of India's Muslim minority and what he saw as India's rejection of nonviolence. In 1987 India honored him with its highest award, the Bharat Ratna.

Ghaffar Khan's death in a Peshawar hospital in 1988 was followed by an unprecedented procession of thousands of Pakhtuns accompanying his coffin across the Khyber Pass to Jalalabad, where, by his choice, he was buried.

Rajmohan Gandhi

BIBLIOGRAPHY

Banerjee, Mukulika. *The Pathan Unarmed.* New Delhi: Oxford University Press, 2001.

Caroe, Olaf. *The Pathans: 550 B.C.–A.D. 1957.* Karachi: Oxford University Press, 1983.

Desai, Mahadev. *Two Servants of God.* Delhi: Hindustan Times, 1935.

Dupree, Louis. *Afghanistan.* Princeton, N.J.: Princeton University Press, 1973.

Easwaran, Eknath. *Badshah Khan: A Man to Match His Mountains.* New Delhi: Penguin, 2001.

Gandhi, Rajmohan. *Ghaffar Khan: Nonviolent Badshah of the Pakhtuns.* New Delhi: Viking, 2004.

Khan, Abdul Ghaffar (as narrated to K. B. Narang). *My Life and Struggle.* Delhi: Hind Pocket Books, 1969.

Korejo, M. S. *The Frontier Gandhi: His Place in History.* Karachi: Oxford University Press, 1993.

KHAN, ALI AKBAR ***(1922–), musician and educator who helped popularize North Indian classical music in the second half of the twentieth century.*** The son of Allaudin Khan, Ali Akbar Khan was born in Shivpur, East Bengal, in 1922. He studied with his father (who also taught sitarist Ravi Shankar) in a context of royal patronage and experimentation. His professional career has included a diversity of roles, including court musician (to the Maharaja of Jodhpur), film composer (including *Devi* for Satyajit Ray), radio station music director, concert performer, and prolific teacher, and he has received numerous awards and honors. Khan, perhaps more than any other modern Indian classical musician, has demonstrated a flair and an interest for melding Indian sensibilities and Western materials.

Ali Akbar Khan's distinctive approach to the sarod, a North Indian lute, has emphasized original ideas, a rhythmic flair, and collaborative dynamics. His fluent melodic adeptness is evident in his creation of new *rāga*s from existing tunes and motifs as well as in his ability to draw new ideas from old *rāga*s. His performance style features a masterful control of rhythm and time and recognition of the drummer's art.

His Ali Akbar College of Music has two campuses—one in Kolkata and one in the San Francisco area—that have trained a new generation of performers and helped to educate the world about Indian music. More recently, in keeping with his previous musical experiments for film, he has explored cross-cultural musical idioms.

Gordon Thompson

BIBLIOGRAPHY

Khan, Ali Akbar, and George Ruckert. *Introduction to the Classical Music of North India.* St. Louis: East Bay Books, 1991.

"Khan, Ali Akbar." Available from <http://www.ammp.com/bio.html>

KHAN, LIAQUAT ALI ***(1895–1951), Pakistan's first prime minister (1947–1951).*** Muhammad Liaquat Ali Khan was born in Karnal, Punjab, India, on 1 October 1895. He was the second son of the *nawāb* of Karnal (his elder stepbrother, Sajjad, inherited the title). Liaquat received his early education at home, studying the Qurʾan and the Hadith and taking music lessons. He was fond of singing, dancing, and theater. Throughout his life he was known as an amiable and warmhearted person, though reserved. In 1910 he joined the Muhammadan Anglo-Oriental College school at Aligarh. Matriculating in 1915, he entered the college, and graduated in 1918. He was married to his cousin Jehangira Begum; their only child, a son, Wilayat, was born in 1919.

Liaquat entered Oxford University in 1920 as a "non-collegiate student," enrolling in Exeter College there the following year. He received his bachelor of arts in jurisprudence in August 1921. The following year he was called to the Bar from London's Inner Temple. He returned to India at the end of 1922 and enrolled as an advocate in Punjab's High Court. Independently wealthy, he did not practice law, instead devoting his life to politics and education, joining the Muslim League in 1923.

Liaquat Ali Khan. In May 1950 the principled Liaquat journeyed from Pakistan to solidify his country's relations with the United States. Here he addresses a New York City audience. His refusal to tolerate political corruption among his cabinet ministers is widely believed to have led to his assassination a year later. BETTMANN / CORBIS.

He stood, unsuccessfully, in 1923 for election to the Legislative Assembly of India for East Punjab. In 1926, however, he was elected to the Legislative council of the United Provinces, as an independent from Muzaffarnagar District, a Muslim constituency. In the council he founded his own political party, the Democratic Party. He was also one of the leading figures of the Uttar Pradesh Zamindars' Association, an organization devoted primarily to landlord interests. He had a very successful career in the Uttar Pradesh Legislative Council, being elected deputy speaker in 1931. In social matters he was liberal, speaking, for example, in favor of education for women; he was conservative, however, on fiscal issues. As a landholder he was concerned about agricultural issues and as a Muslim he was devoted to Muslim interests. He was no bigot, however; his second wife was a Christian, the educator and social reformer, Ra'ana Liaquat Ali Khan. They had two sons, Ashraf and Akber. In 1937 Liaquat was elected to the Legislative Assembly of the United Provinces.

In 1928 Liaquat was one of twenty-four Muslim League delegates chosen to attend India's All-Parties Convention to consider the Motilal Nehru Report on Constitutional Reforms. Mohammad Ali Jinnah was the Muslim League spokesman at the convention, and from that time Liaquat became his lifelong devoted follower. In 1933 Liaquat testified before the Joint Statutory Commission in London, where he again met Jinnah.

In April 1936 Jinnah, as president, asked Liaquat to become the general-secretary of the Muslim League. He was to hold that position until 1947, and he was to become Jinnah's most trusted lieutenant and political adviser. Liaquat was totally loyal, and Jinnah came to depend heavily upon him. In 1939, when Jinnah signed his last will and testament, he appointed Liaquat one of the executors and trustees of his estate. All of the organizational work involving the Muslim League's committees, conferences, and publications was handled by Liaquat, who spent long days working in the League office in Delhi, while continuing his legislative and educational responsibilities, serving as president of the Anglo-Arabic College in Delhi and as a member of the board of trustees of Aligarh University.

Liaquat was elected to the Legislative Assembly of India in 1941, joining Jinnah on the Muslim League bench there, serving as deputy leader of the League's parliamentary party. In Jinnah's absence Liaquat became the League's spokesman. He established the League's first newspaper, *Dawn*, as a weekly in 1941, and the following year turned it into a daily. In 1943, when Liaquat was reelected general secretary of the Muslim League, Jinnah called him "my right hand." In 1945 and 1946 Liaquat was Jinnah's chief associate at the two Simla summit conferences. In 1946 Jinnah nominated Liaquat to be the British viceroy's finance member and asked Liaquat to accompany him to London for constitutional talks with Prime Minister Clement Attlee. In 1947 Liaquat issued the controversial "Poor Man's Budget," and Governor-General Jinnah later appointed him prime minister of the new state of Pakistan.

As prime minister, Liaquat worked diligently to establish the country on a sound organizational footing, a task for which he was ideally suited. Until Jinnah's death on 11 September 1948, however, Liaquat was overshadowed by the towering figure of Jinnah, whose authority in Pakistan was supreme. From 1947, the issue that poisoned India-Pakistan relations and made an enormous impact on the political and military history of the country was the conflict over Kashmir, which had been given to India by its Hindu maharaja. Liaquat was successful in raising the issue of Kashmir at the Commonwealth Prime Ministers' conference in 1949. The same year he arranged for the passing of a Directive Principles Resolution, which established the basic principles of Pakistan's Constitution, which would later be promulgated. Liaquat made a successful trip to the United States in 1950, helping to establish a friendly and lasting relationship between the two countries.

Liaquat and the new government had to deal with several serious problems, including the settlement of millions of Muslim refugees from India; the setting up of a central government in Karachi almost from scratch, including the creation of a sound economic system; and the crisis over Kashmir, which immediately led to war between India and Pakistan. Only the Kashmir crisis was not solved within a short time, through herculean efforts by Liaquat and the government.

Liaquat was an exceedingly generous man, and when he migrated to Pakistan, he refused to accept any property in Pakistan in exchange for his landholdings in India. His property was all given to his first wife and their son. His refusal to tolerate political corruption among his cabinet ministers is thought to have led to his assassination at Rawalpindi on 16 October 1951, when he was shot at close range. His assassin, Said Akbar, an Afghan, was shot dead immediately by police, and no one was ever charged in what many believed was a conspiracy by members of his own government.

Roger D. Long

See also **All-India Muslim League; Jinnah, Mohammad Ali; Pakistan**

BIBLIOGRAPHY

Kazimi, Muhammad Reza. *Liaquat Ali Khan: His Life and Work.* Karachi: Oxford University Press, 2003.

Wolpert, Stanley. *Jinnah of Pakistan.* New York: Oxford University Press, 1984.

KHAN, VILAYAT ***(1924–2004), classical North Indian musician.*** Vilayat Hussain Khan's virtuosic sitar playing and international tours have helped to define Indian classical music, both in India and abroad, in the second half of the twentieth century. His family's musical tradition often describes itself as the Imdad Khan *gharānā*, after his renowned grandfather, although they also trace their lineage to the even more celebrated musician Tan Sen. Vilayat Khan studied with his father, Inayat Khan, until his death in 1938; he then continued his studies with his mother and her father, Bande Hasan Khan. The family tradition has emphasized the sitar and the *surbahār*, but Vilayat Khan's unique background (he had both instrumental and vocal teachers) has led him to integrate vocal devices and idioms into his performances. Indeed, a sitar performance by Vilayat Khan is likely to have a section in which he sings the principal melody. This *gāyakī ang* (singing style) approach to playing the sitar and *surbahār* marks both his performances and those of his brother, Imrat Khan, and now continues in the playing style of Vilayat Khan's son, Shujaat Khan.

Vilayat Khan's style of playing and his demeanor on stage hark back to the courtly origins of India's modern classical music. When Satyajit Ray sought someone to compose music and to direct the music sequences for his film about an aging aristocratic *zamindar* (*Jalsa Ghar;* The music room), he chose Vilayat Khan. Khan's recordings of the *rāg*s Yaman, Bhairavī, and Jaijaivanti are iconographic for many musicians; the recording of his duets with *shahnā'ī* virtuoso Bismillah Khan may be one of the most popular recordings of North Indian classical music. Also noteworthy are his illustrative examples for Jairazbhoy's *The Rāgs of North Indian Music* (1971) which serve as *rāga* references for many music scholars.

Gordon Thompson

BIBLIOGRAPHY

Jairazbhoy, Nazir. *The Rāgs of North Indian Music.* Middletown, Conn.: Wesleyan University Press, 1971.

Miner, Allyn. *Sitar and Sarod in the Eighteenth and Nineteenth Centuries.* Wilhelmshaven, Germany: F. Noetzel, 1993.

KHAYAL *Khayal* (Arabic-Persian, "lyric" or "imagination") is perhaps the most important vocal genre in the Hindustani *sangīt paddhati*, or musical tradition. The origins of *khayal* are often associated with the famous musician Amir Khusrau. (1253–1325).

The sultans of Jaunpur—notably Mohammad Sharqi (1401–1440) and Hussain Sarqi (r. 1458–1499), who were contemporaries of the Mughal emperor Babur—were patrons of musicians who developed *khayal.* In that era, the genre was "ornate and romantic," most popular with Muslim musicians, and reflected the growing dominance of Islamic power.

Khayal grew in importance in seventeenth-century Jaipur and found a prolific champion in Sadarang (Niyamat Khan), a musician in the court of Muhammad Shah (r. 1719–1748) and a descendant of Tansen. Sadarang was a *dhrupad* (he composed praise and/or Hindu devotional music) singer who apparently adopted the musical techniques of *qawwālī* (Sufi devotional music) musicians to create a genre that was both artistically sophisticated and a compelling vehicle for virtuosic performance. Because he and his nephew Adarang were officially *dhrupad* singers, the performance of this new genre was not part of their duties. However, others could perform *khayal,* especially if they were disciples, not in direct line with Sadarang and Adarang. *Khayal* thus offered a contrast to the more austere *dhrupad.*

Chronicles of the seventeenth-century Delhi-Agra rule of Shah Jahan (r. 1628–1658) mention *khayaliyās* (singers of *khayal*) among the royal performers. In eighteenth-century northern India, hereditary musicians consolidated their power by fostering musical knowledge within their families. The *khayaliyās* of the mid-eighteenth century came from families who specialized in either *dhrupad* or *qawwālī*. However, they came to focus increasingly on *khayal* as their primary performance medium. The earliest performers were primarily Muslim. During the nineteenth and twentieth centuries, performers further developed *khayal, and* this style of singing became the predominant vocal genre in the improvisatory system of North Indian music.

A full performance of *khayal* is organized of two main parts—*badā khayal* and *chotā khayal*—and each of these has at its core a musical theme, the *cīz* (Persian, "thing, idea"). The melodic structure of a *cīz* serves as the framework around which performers improvise. Sometimes, the melody is the framework upon which the singer creates elaborate melodic detail. At other times, the singer presents the *cīz* in a simple, unadorned form, contrasting the fixed composition with elaborate extemporizations.

In the *badā khayal* (Hindustani, "big" *khayal*), a singer performs in very slow tempo (*ati vilambit lay*). Tīntāl, Ektāl, and Jhūmrā are the most common *tāla*s (in 16, 12, and 14 beats respectively). The *badā khayal* also serves as a parallel to the *ālāp* (free-time melodic introduction) of *dhrupad* in that the performer has considerable rhythmic freedom. The tempo of the *badā khayal* slowed considerably in the twentieth century, notably through performances by Ustad Amir Khan.

The *cīz* consists of two parts: *sthā'ī* (composed in *mandra sthān* [lower octave] and the bottom half of the *madhya sthān* [middle octave]) and the *antarā* (composed in the upper half of the *madhya sthān* and the lower half of the *tār sthān* [upper octave]). The former is the more important, recurring regularly as a refrain, while the latter generally has more text content.

In the *badā khayal*, the *sthā'ī* and *antarā* imitate the structure of the *rāg ālāp* found in other South Asian forms. In the *badā khayal,* the singer often refers only briefly to the original *cīz*, singing just the *mukharā* (face) of the composition.

The *cīz* in the *chotā khayal* (Hindustani, "small" *khayal*) is in fast tempo (*drut lay*), commonly set in Tintal, and is more plain than in *badā khayal.* Here, the focus of the singer is on virtuosic extemporization, featuring fast melodic figures and difficult rhythmic elaborations.

Khayal texts can be of a variety of types, ranging from historic poems to contemporary creations by musicians or patrons. Their subjects can be advice, religious devotion, deities (e.g., Krishna), praise of patrons, or descriptions of seasons. Love, both divine and human, is a common theme.

Although the *badā khayal* replaces the *ālāp* of other forms in the Hindustani *sangīt paddhati*, some similarities remain. The *rūpak ālāpti* (Sanskrit, "shape" or "form" *ālāp*) is an *ālāp*-like section of the *badā khayal*, sung to the preexisting shape of the *cīz* and set metrically rather than in free time.

Most of the musical attention in *khayal* focuses on the various kinds of *tan*, fast melodic figures of a virtuosic nature. These commonly include *ākār tāns* (Hindustani, literally "to do 'a'"; elaborations in which the singer uses only the syllable "a"), *gamak tāns* (*gamak,* Hindustani, "syllable"; elaborations using a heavy glottal shake), and *bol tāns* (*bol,* Hindusani, "syllable"; elaborations intended to expand upon the meaning of the words of the text).

A number of these improvisations are common to both *khayal* and *dhrupad.* Examples include *bol bānt* (Hindustani, "syllable distribution"; the use of the *cīz bol*s for purposes of rhythmic play [*laykārī*], such as the creation of *tihā'ī*s using the text), *sārgam* (Hindustani, *sā-re-gā-mā*; elaborations using the mnemonic pitch syllables *sa-re-ga-ma*, etc.), and *nom-tom* (elaborations with a rhythmic pulse created through the use of syllables like "*nom*," "*tom*," and "*ta-ra-na*").

Gordon Thompson

BIBLIOGRAPHY

Wade, Bonnie. *Khayāl: Creativity within North India's Classical Music Tradition.* Cambridge, U.K. and New York: Cambridge University Press, 1985.

KHILAFAT MOVEMENT. *See* **Afghani, Jamal-ud-din; Gandhi, Mahatma M. K.**

KHUSRAU, AMIR ***(1253–1325), poet, writer, and musician.*** Amir Khusrau was born in Patiali, in the Braj-speaking Indo-Gangetic Plain, in 1253, the son of a central Asian, Turkic-speaking father and an Indian mother. Sometimes known as Amir Khusrau Dihlavi or Amir Khusrau-e-Dihlavi, Khusrau was the most important poet, writer, and musician of his age and the subject of much musical speculation. His poetry, both in Persian and Hindi, remains popular both for its imagery and as a source of musical settings. His riddles, like his poems, draw on the sound and meaning of words and continue to entertain readers. Some have credited Khusrau with the creation of specific melodies and rhythms, of instruments such as the sitār and the tabla, and even of genres such as *qawwālī* and *khayal.* Although most of these attributions are mythic, Khusrau was influential in the fusion of West Asian (particularly Persian) musical ideas with those of India. (Some confusion may exist because of the similarity of his name to that of Amir Khusrau Khan, an important eighteenth-century Delhi musician.) Khusrau was influenced by the Sufi teacher Khwaja Nizamuddin Auliya for whom music was an important mode of experiencing the divine.

Of the courts in which Amir Khusrau was known to have been active, that of Ala'-ud-Din Muhammad Khalji, sultan of Delhi (r. 1296–1326), proved to be particularly fertile ground for cultural exchange. The Muslim rulers of late thirteenth- and early fourteenth-century Delhi attempted to raise the prestige of their courts by patronizing scholars and artists as advisers and courtiers.

Rudyard Kipling. In his lifetime, as a firm believer in British imperialism, Kipling went from being the unofficial poet laureate of Great Britain to one of the most denounced writers in modern history. As his literary reputation declined, Kipling's work matured and by his death he had compiled one of the most diverse collections of poetry in the English language. HULTON-DEUTSCH COLLECTION / CORBIS.

Probably as a consequence of his role as a courtier, Khusrau studied and described many musical theories and performance practices of his era.

Gordon Thompson

BIBLIOGRAPHY

Miner, Allyn. *Sitar and Sarod in the Eighteenth and Nineteenth Centuries.* Wilhelmshaven, Germany: F. Noetzel, 1993.

KHYBER PASS. *See* **Baluchistan and the North-West Frontier; Geography.**

KIPLING, RUDYARD ***(1865–1936), British poet and novelist.*** Joseph Rudyard Kipling was Britain's greatest poet of the Raj. His works, including his "White Man's Burden" (1899) and *Kim* (1901), sought to extol the "virtues" of racial prejudice and imperial power. Born in India, where his father, John, worked as an architectural sculptor in the Bombay School of Art, Rudyard's first five years were carefree; but when shipped "home" to live with a mean-spirited "pious" family in Southsea, he suffered wretched "beatings and humiliations." His mother, Alice, returned from India in 1877 to rescue him from the tyranny of pious discipline, entering her brilliant son in the United Service College, Westwood Ho. Five years later, Kipling returned to India as a reporter, hired by Lahore's *Civil and Military Gazette*, for which he wrote *Departmental Ditties* (1886) and *Plain Tales from the Hills* (1888), as well as *Barrack-Room Ballads* (1892), which soon made his name and poetry more famous than any viceroy of India.

Nor was his fame limited to India, for in 1889, Kipling traveled to Japan and to the United States, living four years in Brattleboro, Vermont, where he wrote *The Light That Failed* (1891) and started his two *Jungle Books* (1894–1895), anticipating his later *Just So Stories for Little Children* (1902). Kipling believed so deeply in the virtues of British imperialism that he wrote his "White Man's Burden" to help Theodore Roosevelt persuade many doubting Americans to seize the Philippines in 1899.

Take up the White Man's burden—
Send forth the best ye breed—
Go bind your sons to exile
To serve your captives' need.

When World War I started, Kipling pushed his own sixteen-year-old son to a tragically early grave on the Western Front, pulling strings with friends at the War Office, to hustle underage John off to Loos, where he was killed after less than a month of bloody combat.

Take up the White Man's burden—
The savage wars of peace—
Fill full the mouth of Famine
and bid the sickness cease;
And when your goal is nearest
The end for others sought,
Watch Sloth and heathen Folly
Bring all your hope to nought.

For Kipling believed that it was, indeed, to "civilize" India's darkly "benighted natives," not to exploit and bully them, that thousands of "selfless servants" of the British Raj hefted their daily "burdens."

"And the end of the fight is a tombstone white, with the name of the late deceased," another of Kipling's popular poems reminded his comrades in the Great Game of shaking South India's "Trees" bare of their golden pagodas, and milking North India's sacred cows dry. "And the epitaph drear:/ 'A fool lies here who tried to hustle the East.'" Born to India though he was, Kipling's contempt for its "natives" was imbibed with his ayah's milk, even as Jallianwala Bagh Brigadier Dyer's was. As Kipling put it: "East is East, and West is West, and never the twain shall meet!" That was the theme as well of his novel *The Man Who Would Be King* (1899).

In 1907 Kipling won the Nobel Prize for literature. He started to write his autobiography, *Something of Myself*, but died in London, on 18 January 1936, before it was finished.

Stanley Wolpert

See also **British Impact**

BIBLIOGRAPHY

Kipling, Rudyard. *The Writings in Prose and Verse of Rudyard Kipling.* 12 vols. New York: Charles Scribner's Sons, 1898.

Maugham, W. Somerset. *Maugham's Choice of Kipling's Best.* Garden City, N.Y.: Doubleday, 1953.

KĪRTANA The Sanskrit word *kīrtana* (recital, glory) refers to the praise of God. The South Indian *kīrtana* is a simple song with a main theme or refrain (*pallavi*) and several stanzas (*charana*). Here, as in many other parts of the country, the *kīrtana* or *kīrtan* forms the basis for responsorial singing (*bhajana*). Under the guidance of an experienced singer (*kīrtanakār*), the practice of *nāma sankīrtana* (singing His praises) is conducive to ecstatic experiences, as described by Tyāgarāja in his piece "Intakannānandamēmi" (*rāga Bilahari*): "Is there any bliss greater than this—to deem it sufficient to dance, to sing divine music, to pray for His presence and to be in communion with him in mind . . . to become one with Him." (Raghavan).

With reference to a tripartite concert item in a South Indian concert, the term *kīrtana* is also used as a synonym for *kriti.* Wherever the *anupallavi* (middle section) is dispensed with, for instance in Tyāgarāja's invocations of the "divine names" of Vishnu (*divyanāma kīrtana*), the term *kīrtana* is used more appropriately. During a Karnatak concert, several *kīrtanas* and *kriti*s by famous as well as less-known composers are usually heard.

When Tanjāvūr came under Marāthā rule (late seventeenth to early nineteenth centuries), *harikathā*, the narration of stories (*kathā*) about Vishnu (*hari*), developed into a popular form of art and entertainment. The *Gītā Govinda*, Jayadēva's celebrated Sanskrit work (twelfth century), facilitated the spread of the cult of Krishna and Rādhā and inspired South Indian poet-musicians (*vāggēyakāra*) to explore its erotic symbolism through Telugu lyrics. While the concept of "classical" Karnatak music began to evolve, there was widespread appreciation for the vernacular lyrics of many devotional *bhakti* poets.

Shabad Kirtan at Nehru Park. Musicians and signers perform in a *kīrtana* concert at a park in New Delhi, 2003. AVINASH PASRICHA.

For Tyāgarāja, as for his father before him, the *Rāmāyaṇa* epic provided ideal role models in terms of righteousness and self-control. He and other learned musicians (*bhāgavatar*) refined their presentations of songs and stories for the purpose of expounding ideas derived from *advaita* (nondualist) philosophy, emphasizing the divine origin and destination of all human existence. Several poet-singers called for reforms and condemned social evils such as the caste system and ritualism. The time-honored literary motifs and musical techniques employed by these "saint-singers" of South India were consolidated and refined in the course of the eighteenth century, when artists from many parts of India were brought into contact with one another either through involuntary migration or in search of patronage.

As the court and temple establishments of Tamil Nadu promoted scholarship and the arts throughout history, the *kīrtana* evolved as a flexible musical form that could capture and convey the ideas and feelings of all sections of society in many different ways. In this sense, the *kīrtana* not only absorbed some of the elements from tradition (*sampradāya*) but effectively superseded older musical forms such as the medieval *prabandha*. Other genres—most notably the *kriti*, with its emphasis on musical refinement, and the *jāvali*, which is based on erotic lyrics—can therefore be traced back to the new type of *kīrtana* of South India.

*Kīrtana*s (Tamil *kīrtanai*) have enriched other branches of South India's performing arts. A case in point is the art of narrating and expounding religious stories in a musical context, known as *harikathā kālakshēpam*. This genre is traditionally presented by learned male performers (*bhāgavatar*), although at a later stage, several women became famous exponents in their own right. A close relationship among the various genres, including the dance music for *bharata nāṭyam*, *kuchipudi*, and *mōhiniyāttam*, and also for drama (*Mēlattūr bhāgavata mēlam*), has characterized all devotional poetry and music of South India since time immemorial. As a result, numerous poetic references to other artistic and literary genres are found in the lyrics of the *kīrtana* repertoire heard today, for instance the fast rhythmic passages (*sholkattu*), reminiscent of dance movements, contained in the songs of Ūttukādu Venkata Subba Ayyar (c. 1700–1765).

By way of endowing the patriotic sentiments of South India's educated classes with a religious dimension, the customary *kīrtana* has also contributed to the freedom struggle that led to India's independence in 1947. Through the lyrics of patriotic poets and social reformers like Bhāratiyar, elements from Karnatak music found their way into popular music, and other famous musicians and composers of the twentieth century introduced elements based on the *kīrtana* into radio, film, and television productions. The same applies to cross-cultural ventures variously described as *jugalbandi* (joint performances by Indian musicians) and fusion music outside India's borders.

The lyrics of several contemporary poets whose names are listed as "composers" are commonly presented during concerts without mentioning the names of the musicians who have composed the music. This is indicative of the prestige associated, even today, with the lyrics (*sāhitya*) rather than the melodic and rhythmical framework (*varnamettu*) of a song. The prevalence of such notions, not to mention the vast creative scope within Karnatak music, leaves many questions about the authenticity and integrity of the songs by most early composers unanswered. In the case of most "rediscoveries" of songs by composers who lived before the late nineteenth century, experienced musicians are widely believed to have demonstrated their compositional skills by providing suitable tunes and rhythms to existing lyrics. Ascribing one's art or knowledge to a revered personality of the distant past has long been a common practice in different fields of learning in India.

Ludwig Pesch

See also **Kriti; Music: South India**

BIBLIOGRAPHY

Allen, Matthew Harp. "Tales Tunes Tell: Deepening the Dialogue between Classical and Non-Classical in the Music of India." *Yearbook for Traditional Music (Journal of the International Council for Traditional Music)* 30 (1998): 22–52.

Raghavan, V. *Muttuswami Dikshitar*. Mumbai: National Centre for the Performing Arts, 1975.

———. *The Great Integrators: The Saint-Singers of India*. New Delhi: Publications Division, 1979.

———. "Introductory Thesis: Saint Tyagaraja." In *The Spiritual Heritage of Tyagaraja*. Chennai: Sri Ramakrishna Math, 1981.

———. *Tyāgarāja*. New Delhi: Sahitya Akademi, 1983.

Raghavan, V., ed. *Composers*. New Delhi: Publications Division, 1979.

Seetha, S. *Tanjore as a Seat of Music*. Chennai: University of Madras, 1981.

KOLKATA. *See* **Calcutta.**

KRISHNA. *See* **Hinduism (Dharma).**

KRISHNA IN INDIAN ART The origin and history of the myth of Krishna are complex. Over a period of a thousand years or more, many strands coalesced to form a predominant, multifaceted character called Krishna. Myths and legends associated with him pervade India's literature as well as its visual and performing arts. Concurrently, there are theological and liturgical works that interpenetrate into the aesthetic theories and artistic expressions.

The Bhāgavata Purāṇa consolidates the several myths into an impressive narrative, which has held the imagination of artists and devotees alike for a millennia or more. Jayadeva wrote a poem titled Gītā Govinda in the twelfth century, in which he introduced the character of Rādhā, a special beloved of Krishna. There was but a faint mention of her in the Bhāgavata Purāṇa. Jayadeva's poem gave a new twist to the perennial theme of Krishna and the *gopi*s (cowherdesses). From then on, a further coalescing of Krishna as Vishnu and of Rādhā as Sri and Lakshmī and Shakti (female energy personified) took place. Sculpture, painting, theater, music, and dance rely heavily on these principal literary sources of varying periods. In turn, theology and liturgy has been affected by them. Many theological schools evolved, known as *Sampradaya*s; each was a distinctive cult that incorporated the verbal, visual, and kinetic arts as an integral part of Krishna worship and ritual. The kernel of the myth of the baby child, adult king, and counselor was retained, but many modifications took place in India's regional literatures and in its visual and performing arts until the nineteenth century.

The Krishna Theme in Sculpture

The first examples of the Krishna theme in Indian sculpture belong to the Kushan period, during the first and second centuries A.D. The thematic context of these sculptures revolves around Krishna Vasudeva, not Krishna Gopala. There are, however, a few important exceptions. A relief in the Mathura Museum depicts Vasudeva carrying baby Krishna across the Jamuna River to the village of Gokula. Besides these, other Kushan sculptures depict Krishna-Vasudeva, of the Virshni lineage, along with his kinsmen, particularly Samkarsana Balarama, his elder brother, and sister Ekanamsa.

A clear change in emphasis begins with the Guptan period, fourth to sixth centuries, roughly A.D. 320–530. There are many more sculptures on the Krishna theme, especially in his aspect as Krishna Gopala of Braj. The Krishna Gopal theme becomes pervasive not only in Mathura and Rajasthan, but is equally popular in South

Painting of Young Krishna. Krishnalila remains a favorite theme of contemporary art schools in India. Here, painting of the young Krishna in his opulent palace. Image photographed c. 1925. BETTMANN / CORBIS.

India. While the Mandor and Osian panels are important evidence from Rajasthan, no less important are the Krishna life panels from South India, particularly Badami. All these belong to the fifth to seventh century.

From the tenth century onward begins another phase of medieval Indian sculpture. Several major temples were built in the north, south, west, and east. In many of them there are friezes portraying the episodes of Krishna's early life. Sometimes they are single panels, as in the Lakshman temple in Khajuraho, Madhya Pradesh. At other times there are continuous serialized depictions, as in the Hoysala period temples of Belur, Halebid, and Somanathpur in Karnataka. An elaborate visual panorama unfolds on these walls, almost like a painting scroll.

While friezes of continuous narration are one methodology, there is the other of equal importance. It is largely during this period that single images of Krishna appear both in stone and in bronze. The baby Krishna with a butter ball is popular among the Chola bronzes. Equally important and impressive are the bronzes of Krishna dancing on the serpent Kaliya, and Krishna as the flute player (Venugopala), and Krishna the dancer supreme. The South Indian bronzes, especially those of Chola, are outstanding for their artistic skill.

The Krishna theme appears on the wooden chariots of practically all parts of South India. There are intricate carvings on the different parts of the chariot, including the spokes of the wheels and the frame of the chariot seat. Krishna is depicted in the metal sculpture of Nepal. Some sculptures, especially of the dancing Krishna and Krishna with flute (Venugopala), display exquisite craftsmanship.

The Vishnupur temples of the eighteenth century of Bengal began to use the medium of terra-cotta. The brick and terra-cotta temples of Bengal belong to the last phase of the Indian architects' and sculptors' preoccupation with the Krishna theme.

The Krishna Theme in Indian Painting

The inspirations provided by the Bhāgavata Purāṇa gave rise also to devotional poetry in many Indian languages: Braja Bhasa in the north; Gujarati in the west; Tamil, Telugu, Malayalam, and Kannada in the south; and Bengali, Oriya, and Asamiya in the east. By the fifteenth century there was a vast body of poetry, which was not only the preserve of the elite or Sanskrit speaking, but was the language and literature of the high and the low, the affluent and the poor.

Painting, music, dance, and theater were the visual, aural, and kinetic counterparts of this powerful and pervasive movement. Any account of the Krishna theme in Indian painting has necessarily to recognize the rise of Vaishnavism, the popular *bhakti* movement, and the impact of the poetry of the *bhakti* poet-saints.

Evidence of the Krishna theme in Indian mural painting has to be traced to the magnificent large-scale depiction of the theme in South India, particularly Kerala. The Padmanabhapuram palace, the Mattancherry palace of Cochin (18th century), and the Padmanabhaswami temple (17th century) murals are striking examples of a distinctive style of painting that is analogous to the performing arts tradition of the region, particularly Kathakali.

However, by the fifteenth century and more particularly the sixteenth and seventeenth centuries, there was a prolific popularity of miniature paintings based on the Bhāgavata Purāṇa and the Gītā Govinda. Later, the poetry of Suradas, Keshavadasa, Bihari, and other poets became the backdrop or springboard for their pictorial visualization of the theme. The paintings have been considered as mere illustrations of the text. However, a closer analysis reveals that the painters employed a variety of means to create their own visual text, which did not literally follow the verbal text.

It is in the varied schools of Rajasthani painting that we encounter a major preoccupation with the Krishna theme. Indeed, besides portraits and a few other local legends, such as Dhola Maru, most Rajasthani painting, in all its schools and styles, revolves around Krishna. The Bhāgavata Purāṇa is central, but the Gītā Govinda is not far behind. A Muslim artist, Sahibdin, executed a Bhāgavata Purāṇa. Housed in the Bhandarkar Institute of Pune, it is an exquisite example of the Mewari school of Rajasthani painting. He also painted over two hundred leaves of the Gītā Govinda. He followed the poem canto by canto, verse by verse, and yet made his paintings as if to sing the songs of praise of Lord Krishna. The artistic excellence of these paintings is clear proof of the artist's deep immersion in the theme and his acquaintance if not subscription to the symbolic import of the meaning of the text he was interpreting.

While the Mewar school has other sets, the paintings of the schools of Bundi, Kotah, Bikaner, and Keshangarh, from the seventeenth to late eighteenth centuries, largely revolve around the Krishna theme. So far more than thirty sets of the Gītā Govinda alone have been identified. There are perhaps others. Their content and stylistic analysis is beyond the scope of this article. There are other Bhāgavata Purāṇa sets besides those of Mewar, including important sets from Malwa. The poet Surdas's work *Bhramar Gītā* is another favorite, and so is the *Rasikapriya* of Keshavadasa, on the love of Krishna and Radha.

Two developments should be noted. First, the Bhāgavata Purāṇa, especially canto 10 (*Dasamaskanda*), provides the basis of pictorially depicting the Krishna dance *rasa*. Second, the other childhood pranks or plays (*lila*) of the Gītā Govinda place Rādhā as a special *sakhi*, central to the theme. The theme of love in separation and union becomes the theme not only of the paintings illustrating the Gītā Govinda but also of others that revolve around the seasons, such as *Barahmasa* (the 12 seasons), and the paintings that revolve around the hero-heroine typologies (*Nayaka-Nayika*). While the *rasa* symbolizes the love of the human and the divine, Rādhā and Krishna begin to represent the yearning of the individual soul for the universal (*jivatma* and *paramatma*). This aspect is subsumed; even when explicit, these paintings appear amorous, sensuous, and profane, yet they are largely sacred and devotional in essence. The sensuous and spiritual become two levels of the same pictorial image.

Finally, there is another group of paintings, which are directly related to ritual. In the sixteenth and seventeenth centuries, Braj became the center of Krishna worship. This was the result of the overpowering influence of Saint Chaitanya (1485–1533), who was responsible for establishing through his followers a special type of Vaishnavism called Gaudiya Vaishnavism. Music, dance, and floor painting were integral to the ritual. All revolved around the couple Rādhā and Krishna. Also, a Vaishnava saint called Vallabhacharya came to Braj from South India, establishing a sect called the Vallabhacharya. An important temple was built in Rajasthan, and Krishna was worshiped as Sri Nathji. Cloth curtains were hung behind the "icon." These painted clothes, called *pichchavar*s, were many; the costume of the icon was changed according to the seasons and the cycle of the ritual calendar. The cloth paintings were also used as hangings. More than twenty-four iconographic types developed, each with its specific color and costume of Krishna, and the accompanying episode in his life.

No account of the Krishna theme in the visual arts would be complete without at least passing reference to the many folk forms of paintings still extant and flourishing in different parts of India. Among these are the Paithani paintings, so popular in Maharashtra and Karnataka. These paintings were used by itinerant bards who were reciters and singers of the epics. This style of painting is akin to the shadow puppets of the region. Profiles and extended eyes are prominent. The scenes of the epic battle of Kurukshetra, with Krishna as Arjuna's charioteer, are popular. The preoccupation of these painters was not with the Krishna of Braj; it was instead with the counselor of the Pandvas.

In Bihar, in the region called Mithila, women used to paint the mud walls of their homes, both outside and inside, on auspicious occasions. The depiction of Krishna and Rādhā in the inner chambers of young newlyweds was considered auspicious.

Concurrently, with the evolution of Kalighat paintings in Bengal, there was an equally significant movement in South India, spearheaded by the painter Raja Ravi Varma. Raja Ravi Varma's style of painting is deeply indebted to European naturalism. Indeed, it was this image of Krishna that became popular, largely through the oleographs that adorn the walls of domestic shrines in many Indian homes.

The myths and legends of Krishna have permeated contemporary Indian art in many ways. One modern Indian artist, Anjalie Ela Menon, captures the image of the child Krishna. Her medium, however, is modern: the Moreno glass of Italy. Of course, there is the extensive and popular world of Indian films, in which Krishna regularly appears.

The Krishna theme, as is obvious from even this brief and general survey, has for over two thousand years captured and enraptured the Indian psyche. Behind the phenomenon of a staggering diversity and distinctive regional, local, or individual and changing style, there is an unmistaken unity of vision and dependence upon the literary sources, in most if not all parts of India. The perennial and the ephemeral, the ancient, medieval, and modern move as if in tandem, not conflicting or negating, but building upon the received and given. The scope of improvization and variation within an ambit is vast. Perhaps this is the enigma of the Krishna theme, which has held the imagination of the ancient and continues to engage the contemporary and modern.

The Krishna Theme in the Performing Arts

As in the case of Indian miniature painting, the theater, music, and dance revolving around Krishna was a medieval phenomenon. Many forms that evolved were coeval with the evolution and development of the varied schools of Indian painting. The variety of the performance genres was as rich and extensive as the styles of Indian painting. Krishna theater forms and specific genres of music and dance are known to practically all parts of India. Each is distinctive in style and technique, yet there is an underlying unity of vision and purpose. A brief account of some will be given here, though not all genres of theater are still extant in India.

Important among these is the genre of theatrical performance known by the generic name *rasa lila* (the "play of *rasa*"). It is performed during specific seasons for particular occasions in the Braj area. From references in the literature, it is possible to say that the *rasa lila* performance in the precincts of the temple was well established by the time of Akbar. It has a complex history of development, and there are varying views among scholars. It may be more pertinent to restrict this account to a brief description of the contemporary performance of *rasa lila*.

The contemporary *rasa lila* of Vrindavana is the special domain of the *svamis* and the *gosvamis* (priests) who trace their family history back many generations, in most cases to the sixteenth century. The special organization of the contemporary performers of the *rasa lila* is popularly called the *rasadhari mandalis*. In all cases, the *rasa lila* demands a special stage. It is normally a circular platform of stone or concrete, 3 feet (.9 m) high. The symbolic significance of the circular stage is clear, for it recalls the descriptions of the *rasa mandala* (the round arena of the *rasa*) in the Shrimad Bhāgavata. On one end of the stage is a dais or platform called *rangamancha* (the stage of the dance) or a raised throne called the *simhasana*. All the scenes in which Rādhā and Krishna appear in their deified forms, and to which they return at the end, are performed on the raised back stage; other scenes suggesting the passage of time or change of location are performed on the lower stage. The performance is divided into two clear-cut portions: the *rasa* and the presentation of the *lila*s.

Throughout the performance, the objective is to emphasize the symbolism or the dual level on which the theatrical spectacle moves. The *rasa* is performed exclusively by child actors, as suggestive of happenings elsewhere, and at no point is there a realistic presentation of the theme. The nature of stylization and the techniques used are very different from those in epic dramatic forms, which revolve around the Mahābhārata theme. In the *lilas*, it is truly a play, a vision or glimpse with a mystical significance. A dreamlike lyrical form, swiftness of movement, and lightness of touch are characteristic.

The end of the *rasa* is the beginning of the *lila*s. There are enactments of the early life of Krishna that has been mentioned in the context of painting. Many literary sources are employed, which include the Bhāgavata Purāṇa as well as the poetry of the *ashtachhapa* school (eight poets of Braj of the 17th century). Night after night the life of Krishna as child, adolescent, and youth is re-created sequentially. Each night a new theme is presented. Popular among these is the famous *Govardhana lila*, in which Krishna lifts Mount Govardhana on his little finger, and the *chiraharan*, in which Krishna steals the clothes of the *gopi*s. Unlike the *rasa*, the *lila*s are presented more realistically, with actual earthen pots being broken and milk and butter strewn across the stage.

It was this *rasa lila* of Vrindavana that traveled to distant Manipur and Assam in the easternmost regions of India. It reached Assam without the character of Rādhā but in Manipur she was included. Vaishnavism entered the valley only in the sixteenth century, with Rangba (in A.D. 1568) the first king to be initiated. He was followed by Garib Nivas, who was the principal ruler instrumental in converting the valley inhabitants into Vaishnava *bhakta*s. The origin of the famous *rasa* dances is attributed to Rajarshi Bhagya Chandra Maharaj (1763–1798), who, along with Chandra Kirti (1850–1886), laid the foundations of classical Manipuri dance.

Among the most beautiful lyrical manifestations of this transformation of an earlier layer of Manipuri culture to Vaishnava culture is the *rasa lila*. Today it is easily the most highly intricate and refined form of dance-drama. The message of Chaitanya was taken to Manipur by a disciple, who introduced the tradition of community singing and dancing. In the fields and open spaces of Manipur, one can still regularly participate in dances that extol the name of Lord Krishna.

There are several types of *rasa lila* in Manipur. The *Basantrasa* (spring *rasa*) is performed at full moon in March, and the focus of the story is the union of Rādhā and Krishna after a painful separation. The *Kunjrasa* is lighter in spirit and is performed during the early autumn festival of Dussehra. It represents the daily life of Rādhā and Krishna, who are portrayed as ideal lovers, amusing themselves and revelling in a relationship unmarred by separation. The *Maharasa* is performed on a full moon in November–December and depicts the separation of the divine lovers.

The *Vishnu* and the Bhāgavata Purāṇa also traveled to Assam. In the course of time, through the genius of one man, Shankaradeva, a whole genre of theater was created around the Krishna theme. A poetic language called *Braja boli* was the vehicle of communication; the tool of their missionary zeal was a theatrical form, today called the *bhaona* or *ankia nata.* It continues to be performed in the monasteries of Assam, called *sattra*s.

Among the many important forms of dance and drama in South India, there are two widely known forms called Kathakali and Krishnattam. While it is impossible to elaborate on the history of these important forms, it should be pointed out that Krishnattam also emerged in Kerala as a result of the influence of the Bhāgavata and the Gītā Govinda. The two works transformed the earlier Shaivite traditions into Vaishnava theater. King Manavedan, who reigned in Kerala from 1655 to 1658, was a renowned poet and the author of a work titled *Krishnagiti.* He was also a great patron of the famous Guruvayur temple, which is today the most important center of the Krishna faith in the South. His work, the *Krishnagiti,* was deeply influenced by the Gītā Govinda, but is significantly different. Today it is performed in an eight-day serialized enactment in the precincts of the Guruvayur temple, by an all-male cast. Except in the performance of the *rasa krida* on the third night of the cycle of plays, little else is lyrical or romantic. The episodes are played throughout the night, and by morning the spectators are moved to an elated state of wonder and devotion. This dance-drama is confined to the precincts of the temple.

Kathakali, the related dance-drama of Kerala, moves into the open spaces. It is the same world of gods and demons, heroes and villains, but now the life of Krishna is based on the episodes from the epics, especially the Mahābhārata and the Rāmāyaṇa. The libretto is in Sanskrit or in Malayalam. It is sung and narrated; the dance is highly stylized, with a fully developed language of hand and facial gestures. Krishna appears in two roles, as the young brother of Balarama and as the warrior hero.

The poetry of the medieval poet-aints—whether of the south, north, east, or west, written in Tamil, Telugu, Kannada, Hindi, or Oriya as the base—has inspired great dancers in the solo classical dance forms recognized as Bharatanatyam, Odissi, and Kathak. The poetic line is set to a melody (*rāga*) and metrical cycle (*tala*). The verbal imagery is then interpreted through the movements and gestures and mime in endless permutations and combinations, depending upon the creative genius of the performer. Great dancers have kept large audiences spellbound by the presentation of a single verse or line. The dancer's ability to improvize and present variations is the test of both artistic skill and devotional and spiritual involvement. Other lyrics revolving around the child Krishna have inspired dancers to present memorable performances. The episode of the child Krishna eating mud and being reprimanded by Yashoda has been danced by one of India's greatest dancers, T. Bālasarasvati, who performed the piece for over four decades. Each time the cosmos was re-created through her mime, and the audience was transported to a mystical state, oblivious of time. Other great dancers have chosen verses from the Gītā Govinda, Surdas, Vidyapati, or the Ālvārs, and have transformed the stage into the universal Vrindavana of Krishna. The sacred and the profane, the romantic and the mystical, the poetic and the pictorial, the aural and the visual, the movement and the stillness of love in separation and in union, all come together in these performances of Krishna, the blue God, and Rādhā, the yellow heroine. The earth and the sky unite, the clouds pour rain through the sound of music, ankle bells, and speaking hands to re-create the vision of the blue God, eternal and ever new.

Kapila Vatsyayan

See also **Bhakti; Dance Forms: Kathakali; Miniatures: Bundi; Miniatures: Kotah; Miniatures: Marwar and Thikanas**

BIBLIOGRAPHY

Banerjee, Priyatosh. *The Life of Krishna in Indian Art.* New Delhi: Patiala House, 1978.

KRISHNAMURTI, JIDDU ***(1895–1986), spiritual figure and author.*** Admired by millions throughout the world for his philosophic wisdom, Jiddu Krishnamurti was hailed by India's Theosophical Society president, Annie Besant, as a "world master" and new "Messiah." Born in Madras (Chennai), Jiddu and his younger brother, Nityananda, were introduced by Charles Leadbeater to Besant at their Theosophical Society's headquarters in Adyar. She agreed that young Jiddu's "aura" was "divine" and sponsored his education and global travel, taking him with her first to London, and later to California, where she had a lovely home (Arya Vihara) built for him on the grounds of Theosophy's West Coast headquarters in Ojai's "Happy Valley." Jiddu returned to Ojai annually for most his life, but his frail brother died there in 1922, just a few years after they first arrived.

Krishnamurti was worshiped as Master of the Order of the Star of the East, founded by Besant a year after his initiation, "At the Feet of the Master," in 1911. The Order of the Star enrolled over 50,000 Theosophists, many of whom gathered annually at Adyar to hear their Master speak, believing him "divine," until 1929, when he shocked his followers by announcing "I am not the Messiah." Some disciples, refusing to accept him as a fellow mortal, considered his denial proof positive of his soul's "divine" character. From 1910 until his last year of life, Krishnamurti wrote and published over fifty books, mostly philosophical dialogues, recording views and ideas that emerged during his popular evening "talks," which were often filled with longer intervals of silence than speech. All of his books have been reprinted by the press of the Theosophical Society in Ojai, which keeps his writings and lectures in its fine library, and in print, with tens of millions of copies sold and still read the world over.

Most of Krishnamurti's works are dialogues, much like the ancient Upanishadic Vedanta texts that predate the common era, embodying the wisdom of Hindu sages' philosophic responses to questions posed by disciples seeking enlightenment. His answers were often pithy and paradoxical: "To know is to be ignorant, not to know is the beginning of wisdom." Or "Nobody can put you psychologically into prison. You are already there." And "It is truth that frees, not your effort to be free." Laughter, love, and silence were vital aspects of his philosophy. Shortly before his death he said: "If you don't know how to laugh and love . . . you're not quite a human being." Krishnamurti was one of India's greatest modern sages.

Stanley Wolpert

See also **Theosophical Society**

BIBLIOGRAPHY

Blau, Evelyne. *Krishnamurti: 100 Years.* New York: Stewart, Tabori, and Chang, 1995.

Krishnamurti, J. *The Awakening of Intelligence.* New York: Harper & Row, 1973.

———. *Krishnamurti's Notebook.* New York: Harper & Row, 1976.

———. *The Collected Works of J. Krishnamurti.* 17 vols. 1933–1967. Reprint, Dubuque, Iowa: Kendall-Hunt, 1991.

KRITI In South Indian or Karnatak music (*Karnataka sangītam*), the Sanskrit term *kriti* (work or composition) refers to a tripartite song with Sanskrit or vernacular lyrics. As most solo performers acquire their repertoire of *kriti*s from a *guru* belonging to a lineage of several teachers and disciples (*guru shishya parampara*), associating oneself with a well-established tradition (*sampradāya*) or personal style (*bāni*) remains a matter of prestige.

History

The term *kriti* is widely regarded as being synonymous with *kīrtana*, although some scholars make a distinction and reserve *kriti* for the more differentiated form of art music. Any simple devotional song is referred to as *kīrtana*, *pada*, or *dēvarnāma*. The sparing use of text in a *kriti* has resulted in a melismatic and expressive style. Many scholars believe that Tyāgarāja (1767–1847) was the composer who perfected the *kriti* form.

In the early twentieth century, the *kriti* became the main Karnatak concert item, as it provides all participants with ample scope for solo improvisations and spontaneous interaction. Until then, the creative aspect of art music (*manōdharma sangīta*) consisted mainly of formal and highly complicated elaborations of a single theme (*pallavi* or *rāgam tānam pallavi*).

With its mellifluous quality, Telugu continues to be the favorite Dravidian language for *kriti* lyrics. Tamil, the medium of the earliest *bhakti* poetry, has played a greater role since the Tamil music movement (Tamil Ishai) was institutionalized in the 1940s.

Structure

A *kriti* consists of three main themes: (1) an opening theme or refrain (*pallavi*, P, "sprouting"); (2) a secondary theme building on the *pallavi* (*anupallavi*, A); and (3) the concluding stanza, or several stanzas (*charanam*, C, "foot"). The typical arrangement of these *kriti* parts (*anga*) can be summarized as P-A-P-C-(A)-P. Any section may comprise several lines and repetitions. The three themes are often enriched with complex variations (*sangati*), either as intended by the composer or in the form of additions made by other musicians. Both the profusion and refinement of *sangati*s are regarded as the hallmark of Tyāgarāja's *kriti*s.

For his short *kriti*s, Dīkshitar employed a different format known as *samashti charana*, in which the *anupallavi* is omitted, much as in a *kīrtana*. Some of the *kriti*s of Shyāma Shāstri and Dīkshitar, and also those of several later composers, are characterized by the use of meaningless sol-fa syllables (*chittasvara*), each syllable representing the name of a note (*svara*). A less common but important variant is known as *svara sāhitya*, in which a composer amalgamates meaningless sol-fa syllables (*svara*) with meaningful syllables as part of the lyrics (*sāhitya*), usually as an extension of the *charanam*. Tyāgarāja did not normally employ such techniques, the notable exceptions being found in the *kriti*s popularly known as the five gems (*pancharatna*). Thus all the *chittasvara*s performed along with his pieces constitute additions made by others.

More than any other genre, the *kriti* facilitates the exploration of melodic and rhythmical intricacies. This important quality manifests itself in two ways, namely in the variations (*sangati*) provided by a composer, and in the optional solo improvisations (preludes and interludes) by concert musicians. A nonmetrical *rāga* exposition (*rāga ālāpana*) creates the appropriate mood (*rāga bhāva*) for a *kriti* in a manner that can be compared to the first part of a *rāgam tānam pallavi* performance. Sometimes the *kriti* that is presented as the highlight of a concert includes a *tānam* (a pulsating variant of the *rāga ālāpana*); then three more improvised sections are typically inserted in the *anupallavi* or *charanam* section before returning to the *pallavi* of the *kriti*: (1) *niraval* (filling up), which initially follows the distribution of the text syllables in order to heighten a particular mood; (2) several rounds of *kalpana svara* (decorative notes); and (3) *tani āvartana*, an extensive drum solo that concludes the main concert item. To establish their identity and discourage others from altering their songs, most *kriti* composers incorporate a seal (*mudrā*) toward the end of their lyrics, be it a pen name, their personal name, or that of their chosen deity (*ishtadēvatā*).

Themes

A *kriti* leads its listeners through a series of experiences that appeal to their artistic sensibilites as well as their innermost spiritual longings. In the *kriti*s composed by Tyāgarāja, Shyāma Shāstri, Muttusvāmi Dīkshitar, and many of their successors, the aim of art music has been transformed radically: they refused to entertain or eulogize a powerful patron (*narastuti*), traditionally a highly cultured person belonging to a royal dynasty, often credited with divine qualities. Instead they focused on songs that praise their personal deity (*ishta dēvatā*), for instance Srī Rāma, the divine king whose glory is described in most of Tyāgarāja's songs. Far from feeling intimidated by the grandeur he describes in such detail, Tyāgarāja even feels entitled to converse with God in rather familiar if not jocular terms, depending on the context of a song and his own disposition: "In *Brovabhāramā*, he asks if he is too much of a burden for Rama to bear and points out the huge burdens that the Lord had borne in the past, the mountain of Mandara and Govardhana on his back and palm, and the entire universe in his stomach" (Raghavan). In several songs, the saintly composer skillfully resorts to mocking praise (*nindāstuti*) and social satire with the help of succinct lyrics whose expression required a corresponding range of musical means. The Telugu is lyrical and minimal, possessing classical dignity and meaning.

Ludwig Pesch

See also **Kīrtana; Music: South India; Rāga**

BIBLIOGRAPHY

Jackson, William J. *Tyāgarāja: Life and Lyrics*. Chennai: Oxford University Press, 1991.

———. "Features of the Kriti: A Song Form Developed by Tyāgarāja." *Asian Music* 24, no. 1 (1992): 19–61.

———. *Songs of the Three Great South Indian Saints*. Delhi: Oxford University Press, 1998.

Parthasarathy, T. S. *Music Composers of India*. Chennai: C. P. Ramaswami Aiyar Foundation, 1982.

Raghavan. V. *The Spiritual Heritage of Tyagaraja*. Chennai: Sri Ramakrishna Math, 1981.

Seetha, S. *Tanjore as a Seat of Music*. Chennai: University of Madras, 1981.

KSHATRIYAS. *See* **Caste System.**

KUCHIPUDI. *See* **Dance Forms.**

KURUKSHETRA. *See* **Mahābharāta.**

KURUS. *See* **Vedic Aryan India.**

L

LADAKH. *See* **Jammu and Kashmir.**

LAKSHMĪ. *See* **Devī.**

LAND TENURE FROM 1800 TO 1947 The pattern of land tenure in India at the beginning of the nineteenth century was far from egalitarian. A substantial portion of India's agrarian population comprised a class of agricultural laborers who neither owned arable land nor held any customary rights to occupy and cultivate it. In South India, about 20 percent of the agricultural population, mainly Dalits and other low caste members, were employed by landowners to cultivate their land. In Bengal, also, there is considerable evidence that during early British rule, a system of agricultural labor prevailed. Landless agricultural laborers were reported to form about 20 percent of the agricultural population in Dinajpur in 1808, although the rate of the landless population was likely to be lower in some other regions, especially in eastern Bengal, where the majority of villagers were peasants cultivating their lands. In western India, while agricultural laborers were few in the Deccan, there was nevertheless a system of hereditary farm servants in some districts of Gujarat.

Those who either owned land or had customary rights to cultivate it were not homogeneous in the early decades of the nineteenth century. In the Tamil district of South India, a handful of village elites called *mirasidar*s, very often belonging to Brahman and other high castes, asserted their rights of ownership over the land of the entire village and controlled village affairs. Under them was a group of farmers who either held permanent rights to cultivate village land or were temporary tenants belonging to other villages. Under the *ryotwari* settlement system, the government recognized *mirasidar*s as the sole proprietors of land, dismissing tenants' rights completely. Only in villages where no *mirasidar* system existed were those villagers holding permanent occupancy rights recognized as landholders responsible for the payment of land revenue. In Bengal, under the *zamindari* settlement, *zamindar*s who had ruled a wide area covering a large number of villages were recognized as the proprietors of land, collecting rents from farmers (*ryot*s), paying only a small fraction of those revenues to the government. In some regions, like Dinajpur, in addition to a group of small peasants who cultivated their land mainly with family labor, there was a class of rich *ryot*s who held many acres of land, which they leased to sharecroppers. In North Indian districts, where a system of joint holding of village lands called *bhaichara* tenure was prevalent, shares of the holdings were unequally distributed, even by the 1820s.

Even though the aggregate result of changes in the size of landholdings appears negligible, the composition of each landholding-size group seems to have changed over time, hinting at transformations in village agrarian structure at least in some regions of India. In South India, some merchants, moneylenders, and other nonagricultural interests expanded their landed property and grew to be large landlords, who let their lands to tenants, whereas the previous large landholders of Brahman and other high caste origins gradually moved to urban areas and decreased their holdings in rural areas. The aggregate result of these mixed changes was that there was no substantial expansion of large landholdings. At the other end of the landholding scale, migration to overseas plantations provided landless agricultural laborers with a chance to emancipate themselves, and some among them acquired tiny pieces of land, whereas a new group of agricultural laborers appeared as a result of the dispossession of the landholdings of small peasants. A similar change in the composition of agricultural laborers has been reported for Bengal. A reduction in the number of landless laborers as a result of their migration to cities was witnessed in British Gujarat between 1911 and 1931. For the eastern part of Bengal, the occupancy *ryot*s seem to have disintegrated into village landlords and sharecroppers with no occupancy rights. Taking into account these different trends in landholding, sometimes counteracting one another, the process of the differentiation of landholding peasants may not be ruled out, and it may have been actually witnessed, at least in some regions.

Another change noticed in some areas of India was a decline in communal land tenure. In some regions, landholders collectively held village land, each owner holding only a share at the beginning of the nineteenth century. Such collective landholding was divided among shareholders over the next several decades. While the direct cause for this division was the government policy to settle land revenue on the individual holder for each plot of land, a gradual loosening of unity among landholders also contributed to this end.

Various factors contributed to these changes in land tenure. The impact of the commercialization of agriculture on the peasant classes was complex. It sometimes strengthened small peasants by providing a higher income, but often the growing fluctuation in prices led them to disintegrate into a group of richer peasants, who benefited from the fluctuation, and others who came under the grip of moneylenders and merchants. In general, it contributed to the expansion of landed property by the nonagricultural population, though the extent of such transfer differed by region. The trend among high-caste landowners to move to urban areas resulted in reducing their landownership, whereas the migration of laborers provided them with opportunities to purchase small pieces of land.

Jajmani System

In the 1930s, Willam H. Wiser found a system of hereditary obligations of payment and of occupational and ceremonial duties between two or more specific families of different castes in the same locality. Each member of the village service castes had his own client families to whom he was entitled and responsible to serve and who, for his service, gave some stipulated amount of remuneration. He called this dyadic type of relationship the *jajmani* system. The dominant view presupposed that the system was rather dominant before the nineteenth century but was gradually declining in the twentieth century.

Peter Mayer, however, questioned the presupposition and argued that the *jajmani* system is of recent origin and is essentially a feature of the Gangatic Plain. According to him, the system that prevailed widely in North India, at least until the second half of the nineteenth century, was one in which the artisans and others, like Chamars, had general obligations of service to the entire class of village landholders and were compensated for these services by all cultivators, either directly by payment at harvest time or indirectly through grants of village land.

Evidence from western India of the pre-colonial period provides an interesting case, indicating a mixture of collective and individual remunerations to service providers. Washermen served an entire village body and were rewarded for their services by the village as a whole. At the same time, they could get perquisites from individual peasants when they provided a specific service to them, indicating that there existed a dyadic and individual relationship between each service provider and each peasant, operating within the framework of the holistic system of dividing labor in a village. An 1811 report from South India describes a case in which the share of harvested grain to which servants of landholders were entitled was insufficient for their subsistence, so they were to receive further payments in grain by their masters until the total reached a stipulated amount. This also seems to indicate the existence of a dyadic relationship together with a collective form of remuneration.

Even if it would be an exaggeration to deny the existence of an individual and dyadic relationship between service providers and other villagers, there is no doubt that a holistic system of dividing labor predominated in pre-colonial India. The loosening of the village community in the nineteenth century surely weakened such a holistic system. The colonial land policy was generally to deny the collective landholding system that had prevailed in some regions of India, and it was reluctant to recognize revenue-free land having been granted to members of service castes, though the policies differed by region. As the result of the decline of the holistic remuneration system, the *jajmani* system gradually came to be the dominant form of remuneration in the course of time.

Haruka Yanagisawa

See also **Agricultural Wages, Labor, and Employment since 1757**

BIBLIOGRAPHY

Bose, Sugata. *Agrarian Bengal: Economy, Social Structure and Politics, 1919–1947*. Cambridge, U.K.: Cambridge University Press, 1986.

Guha, Sumit. "Agrarian Bengal, 1850–1947: Issues and Problems." *Studies in History* 11, no. 1 (1995): 119–142.

Kotani, Hiroyuki. *Western India in Historical Transition: Seventeenth to Early Twentieth Centuries*. New Delhi: Manohar, 2002.
Kumar, Dharma, ed. *The Cambridge Economic History of India*, vol. 2: *c. 1757–c. 1970*. Cambridge, U.K.: Cambridge University Press, 1983.
Mayer, Peter. "Inventing Village Tradition: The Late Nineteenth Century Origins of the North Indian 'Jajmani System.'" *Modern Asian Studies* 27, no. 2 (1993): 357–395.
Nakazato, Nariaki. *Agrarian System in Eastern Bengal, c. 1870–1910*. Kolkata: K. P. Bagchi, 1994.
Ray, Rajat, and Ratna Ray. "The Dynamics of Continuity in Rural Bengal under the British Imperium: A Study of Quasi-Stable Equilibrium in Underdeveloped Societies in a Changing World." *Indian Economic and Social History Review* 10, no. 2 (June 1973): 103–128.
Yanagisawa, Haruka. *A Century of Change: Caste and Irrigated Lands in Tamilnadu, 1860s–1970s*. New Delhi: Manohar, 1996.

LAND TENURE SINCE 1950 British rule established in India a system of intermediaries—called "landlords" by the British—who were to collect rent from the cultivators on behalf of the state and who would in turn receive a share of the revenue collected. Those intermediaries had largely controlled the land tenure system during India's pre-independence period, though the role of intermediaries varied across the country. The land tenure system of pre-independence India was broadly divided into three categories: the *zamindari* system, the *mahalwari* system, and the *ryotwari* system. In the first two categories, the intermediaries—*zamindar*s and village headmen, respectively—were responsible for the collection of rent from the cultivators; in the third category, there were no intermediaries, and cultivators paid the rent directly to the state. The control of intermediaries over land ownership and the tenure system led to exploitation of cultivators. In order to eliminate intermediaries and to pass on ownership rights to the actual cultivators, the process of land reforms was initiated after independence. The objective of land reforms was to abolish intermediaries and to bring changes in the revenue system that would be favorable to cultivators. Tenancy reforms were considered the most important component of land reforms, and many changes were effected in India's land tenure and revenue system.

Legislation of Land Tenure

First Five-Year Plan. Efforts to abolish the landlord system were actually enacted in the early 1950s with the *Zamindari* Abolition Act. India's Planning Commission introduced its national policy on tenancy regulation in its Five-Year Plans. The first proposition of the National Policy on tenancy reforms, as presented in the First Plan, recommended that large landowners be allowed to evict their tenants and to bring under personal cultivation land up to a ceiling limit to be prescribed by each state. It was further suggested that tenants of nonresumable land be given occupancy rights on payment of a price to be fixed as a multiple of the rental value of the land. The term "personal cultivation" was defined as cultivation by the owner or by other members of the family.

Though precise definitions were not provided for small and middle owner-cultivators, a distinction was made to consider "owners of land not exceeding a family holding as small owners." Land belonging to small and middle owners was divided into two categories: land under personal cultivation, and land leased to tenants at will. However, limited protection was envisaged for such tenants of landowners possessing land below the ceiling restriction. It was suggested that tenancy should be for five to ten years and should be renewable, and that the maximum rent payable should not exceed 20 to 25 percent of the gross produce.

Second Five-Year Plan. To provide effective protection for tenants and to bring a degree of uniformity across the states, the definition of "personal cultivation" was amended with three elements: risk of cultivation, personal supervision, and personal labor. It was suggested that the produce rent should be converted into cash rent and the maximum rent should be fixed as a multiple of land revenue. The Second Plan also suggested that tenants of nonresumable areas should be enabled to acquire ownership rights on purchase at a reasonable price. Further, the payment should be allowed in installments that might be fixed in such a way that the burden on the tenant did not exceed 20 to 25 percent of the gross produce.

Third and Fourth Five-Year Plans. Based on a review of the steps taken in the First and Second Plan periods, the Third Plan stated that the impact of tenancy legislation on the welfare of tenants had been less than expected. Hence, the Third Plan reiterated that the final goal should be to confer rights of ownership to as many tenants as possible. Though it was considered appropriate to confer the rights of ownership to tenants of nonresumable land of small holders, the Third Plan did not make any recommendation in this direction, but suggested that the states should study the problem and determine the suitable action in light of prevailing conditions. However, the condition of tenants did not improve, and remained precarious even after the Third Plan period. With a view to ensuring the security of tenure to tenants and subtenants, the Fourth Plan recommended measures such as "to declare all tenancies non-resumable and permanent except in the case of landowners working in defence services or with any disability." In the exceptional cases, the tenancy should be for a period of three years and subjected to renewal. Provisions were made for complete security of tenure in homestead lands where cultivators, agricultural laborers, and artisans had constructed their houses.

Fifth Five-Year Plan. The Fifth Plan contained the recommendations of a special task force for appraising the progress of problems of land reforms. Subsequently, the National Commission on Agriculture (NCA) in its report gave the following recommendations:

- In view of the prevailing land-man ratio, tenancy could not be banned completely until a large-scale transfer of the population from agricultural to non-agricultural sectors occurred.
- The NCA reiterated the provision of ownership rights for all tenants of land except the landowner of marginal holding and special cases. It further recommended that the price should be lower than the market price and the tenant should be provided with credit either by the state government or by financial institutions.
- The sharecroppers should also be recognized and recorded as tenants and should be bestowed with all due protection.

Sixth Five-Year Plan and After. Until the Sixth Plan period, many regulations were passed, but their implementation appeared lacking. In order to fulfill this goal, the Sixth Plan emphasized measures to ensure the effective implementation of the accepted policies. A time-bound schedule was given to the states to implement the measures of land reforms. It further recommended that the states in which legislative provisions for conferment of ownership rights on all tenants did not exist should immediately introduce appropriate legislative measures within one year (by 1981–1982). Even in the Seventh Plan period, the recommendation for appropriation of legislative measures by the states to secure the rights of tenants remained the major issue. Thus, the major legislations on land tenure were created in the first three Plans, and their implementation was given priority in the subsequent period.

Progress in the Implementation of Tenancy and Revenue Reforms

Progress of land reforms can be assessed in terms of three important aspects: regulation of rent, security of tenure, and conferment of ownership rights to tenants.

Regulation of rent. The rent paid by the tenants during the pre-independence period was exorbitant; it varied between 35 and 75 percent of gross produce throughout India. With the enactment of legislation for regulating the rent payable by the cultivators in the early 1950s, fair rent was fixed at 20 to 25 percent of the gross produce level in all the states except Punjab, Haryana, Jammu and Kashmir, Tamil Nadu, and the Andhra area of Andhra Pradesh. In these states, the rent payable by the tenants varied between 25 percent and 40 percent, depending on the available irrigation facilities. However, the effectiveness of fair rent was observed only for tenants who actually enjoyed security of tenure. As per the 1981 census, about 80 percent of the tenants were insecure. As a result, the majority of tenants could not derive benefit from the legislation on fair rent. Further, field studies conducted in Bihar, Orissa, and West Bengal during 1971 and 1972 indicated that though the Tenancy Act in these states fixed the maximum rent payable at 25 percent, most of the tenants, particularly sharecroppers, were paying 50 percent of gross produce.

On the other hand, the mode of payment was flexible, either by cash or kind or both, depending on the option of the tenant, in almost all states except in West Bengal and the Bombay area of Maharashtra. In the case of West Bengal only kind payment was allowed, while in the Bombay area only cash payment was allowed.

Security of tenure. Providing security of tenure was the second important legislation brought about during the first three Five-Year Plans. Legislation for security of tenure had three essential elements: ejection could not take place except in accordance with the provision of the law; land could be resumed by an owner, but only for personal cultivation; and in the event of resumption, the tenant was assured of a prescribed minimum area.

Tenancy laws were enacted in all states in accordance with the guidelines under this legislation, though their implementation varied widely across the states. Depending on the pattern of tenancy laws enacted, all the states can be broadly grouped into four categories: restricted leasing out to certain special and disabled categories (Andha Pradesh–Telenaga Area, Bihar, Karnataka, Madhya Pradesh, Uttar Pradesh, and Himachal Pradesh); no restrictions on leasing out (Andhra Pradesh–Andhra Area, Orissa, Rajasthan, Tamil Nadu, and West Bengal); leasing permitted but the tenant acquires rights to purchase land (Assam, Gujarat, Haryana, Maharashtra, and Punjab); and prohibition of lease (Jammu and Kashmir, Kerala, and Manipur). The NSS (National Sample Survey) reports suggested that despite the tenancy laws, concealed tenancy existed in almost all the states. Further, in the majority of states, sharecroppers were not explicitly recognized as tenants and thus were not protected under tenancy law. However, sharecroppers in West Bengal were provided with heritable rights on the leased land through Operation Bargha in 1971. The term "tenant" was reported to be wide enough to cover sharecroppers but not wide enough to provide tenancy security in the majority of states. In some states, like Punjab and Haryana, sharecroppers were recognized as hired laborers as defined under personal cultivation. Further, a recent study (Haque) on tenant reforms indicated that even after four decades of initiation of tenure reforms, secured tenancy exists only in the states of Gujarat, Maharashtra, Tamil Nadu, and West Bengal, and the flaws in the definition of personal cultivation have rendered tenancies insecure in all other states. In addition, security of tenure had also faced serious problems from the "voluntary surrender." Taking advantage of this clause, powerful landlords compelled their tenants to give up the tenancies on their own and thus evaded the tenancy laws. An important deficiency identified in this regard has been lack of proper land records in a majority of states. Security of tenancy can be ensured only when there are reliable and accurate records on tenancy.

Conferment of ownership rights to tenants. The third important component of tenancy legislation was the conferment of ownership rights to tenants. Despite repeated emphasis in the plan documents, only a few states, like West Bengal and Kerala, have passed legislation to confer rights of ownership to tenants. No estimate is available at a nationwide level, but some state-level evaluation studies have estimated the number of tenants and the extent of land entitled for conferment of ownership rights. A committee set up by the government of Maharashtra in 1968 for the evaluation of land reforms reported that only 375,000 of a total of 2,600,000 entitled tenants acquired ownership rights until the mid-1960s. The number was reported to have reached 1,118,000 during the 1980s. In the case of West Bengal, the inception of Operation Bargha in 1977 led to conferment of ownership rights to 1,500,000 sharecroppers covering about 2,700,000 acres (about 1,100,000 hectares) up to December 1998. In Karnataka, about 489,000 tenants have been conferred rights for nearly 4,500,000 acres (1,850,000 hectares) of land up to 31 July 2000. Further, in Gujarat, about 462,000 tenants were benefited from 2,400,000 acres (970,000 hectares) of land, and in Rajasthan, 199,000 tenants were benefited from 940,000 acres (382,000 hectares).

The Impact of Tenancy and Revenue Reforms

Agricultural productivity and growth. As the implementation of tenancy reforms coincided with a technological revolution, isolation of the specific impact of tenancy reforms on agricultural productivity and agricultural growth became a difficult task, particularly after the 1970s. However, some studies attempted to separate all the other effects and concluded that there was correlation between the growth in production and the progress of tenancy (Banerjee and Ghatak). Studies also indicated that it was the consolidation of management around tube well command areas that triggered the growth in West Bengal agriculture (Webster). It was also reported that Operation Bargha in West Bengal had led to changes such as greater social equity and self-confidence among the poor (Gazdar and Sengupta). Contrary to this, there were also arguments that Operation Bargha had not been successful in augmenting production and productivity on the sharecropped land due to the poor resource base (Pal). On the other hand, Haque opined that Operation Bargha and other land reform measures might not be solely responsible for rapid growth in agriculture in West Bengal but had led to indirect effects in the form of a changing rural power structure, accessibility to irrigation, and modern inputs.

Size of the farm. Apart from agricultural productivity, major changes in the pattern of owned and operated holdings, as per the latest agricultural census (1995–96) and NSS rounds, indicated that the proportion of landless agricultural households in the rural area had stabilized at around 11 to 12 percent. About 80 percent of the cultivators were reported as marginal (less than 2.5 acres, or 1 hectare) and small (2.5–5 acres, or 1–2 hectares), and their land holdings accounted for 36 percent of the total cultivated area in 1995–1996. Nearly 18 percent of cultivators owned semi-medium (5–10 acres, or 2–4 hectares) and medium (10–25 acres, or 4–10 hectares) holdings, which accounted for 49 percent of the total cultivated area in 1995–1996. However, the number and the area under large holdings (25 acres, or 10 hectares, and above) have been declining consistently.

The steady increase in the area under the marginal and small holdings group could be attributed to the legislative measures supplemented by market processes, but an increase in their number might be the result of an increase in population and lack of alternative employment opportunities in the rural areas.

Employment. There are no systematic studies to arrive at specific conclusions on changes in the pattern of employment induced by tenancy reforms over a period of time. The census data indicated a steady increase in agricultural laborers (from 21.8 percent in 1961 to 33.2 percent in 2001) as well as an increase in other workers (from 12.9 percent in 1961 to 22.9 percent in 2001).

The liberalization of tenancy has become the latest issue of debate, and many recent seminars have supported and recommended the same. According to a proposal of the Ministry of Rural Areas and Employment, the liberalization of tenancy, particularly in the less developed areas, would help in improving the access of the poor to land through the legalization of leasing. However, thus far no steps have been taken in this direction.

With the initiation of economic reforms and liberalization, agriculture has been moving toward commercialization. As a part of this trend, the practice of contract farming has been initiated by multinational companies, such as Pepsi Company and Hindustan Level Limited in Punjab. So far contract farming has been mostly informal and has taken place without any written agreement. However, an institutional mechanism is expected to help the small and marginal farmers to access the benefits of contract farming without compromising their ownership rights.

L. Thulasamma

See also **Agricultural Labor and Wages since 1950; Contract Farming**

BIBLIOGRAPHY

Appu, P. S. "Tenancy Reforms." Proceedings and Papers of the Seminar on Land Problems: A Project and Prospect. New Delhi: Planning Commission of India, 1989.

Banerjee, A. V., and M. Ghatak. "Empowerment and Efficiency: The Economics of Tenancy Reform." Working paper, Harvard University, 1995.

Behuria, N. C. *Land Reforms Legislation in India.* New Delhi: Vikas, 1997.

Dantawala, M. L., and C. H. Shah. *Evaluation of Land Reforms,* vol. 1. Mumbai: General Report, 1971.

Gazdar, Hariss, and Sunil Sengupta. *Agricultural Growth and Recent Trends in Well Being in Rural West Bengal in Sonar Bangla.* New Delhi: Sage Publications, 1999.

Haque, T. *Impact of Tenancy Reforms on Productivity Improvement and Socio-economic Status of Poor Tenants.* Policy Paper 13. New Delhi: NCAP, 2001.

Joshi, B. H. *An Analytical Approach to Problems of Indian Agriculture: A Theoretical and System Approach.* Delhi: B. R. Book Co., 1992.

Malaviya, H. D. *Land Reforms in India.* 2nd ed. New Delhi: All-India Congress Committee, 1955.

Pal, Sasanka. *Operation Barga and Its Impact on Tenancy Pattern and Productivity.* Hyderabad: NIRD, 1997.

Webster, Neil. *Panchayati Raj and the Decentralization of Development Planning in West Bengal.* Kolkata: K. P. Bagchi, 1992.

LANGUAGES AND SCRIPTS The Indian subcontinent has been a virtual laboratory of humanity, from its first settlement by modern humans while on their way to Australia and East Asia, some 50,000 years ago. The remnants of this founding population can still be found in genetics, linguistically in some of the "tribal" languages (Andamanese, Kusunda), and in various substrates. The initial settlement was followed by the immigration of speakers of diverse languages belonging to a number of major language families.

Languages

India's language families are, from north to south: Tibeto-Burmese, Indo-European (Iranian and Indo-Aryan), Khamti (Tai), Austro-Asiatic (Munda, Khasi), and Dravidian. There also are several isolates. Burushaski is regarded by some as the eastern extension of the Macro-Caucasian (Basque–N. Caucasian–Burushaski) family; Kusunda and Andamanese are perhaps linked to Indo-Pacific (Papuan, Tasmanian). In the past, many more languages must have been spoken, as the little studied substrates indicate. Substrates are found in Nahali, Tharu, Vedda, and even in Hindi, where some 30 percent of the agricultural terms are from an unknown source. The same seems to be true for many other North Indian languages; southern Indian substrates have hardly been touched as yet. In sum, South Asia was as linguistically diverse then as it is today.

Most South Asian languages now belong to the Indo-Aryan subgroup of the Indo-European language family that stretched, before the colonial period, from Iceland to Bengal and Sri Lanka. Speakers of Old Indo-Aryan (OIA) must have entered South Asia in the mid-second millennium B.C. OIA, beginning with the Vedic form of Sanskrit, is a close relative of Old Iranian, which has been preserved in some Old Persian inscriptions (519 B.C.) and in the Avesta, the sacred language of the Zoroastrians (Parsi). Dating the earliest OIA is difficult; however, the Vedic dialect that was brought into the Mitanni realm of northern Iraq/Syria (c. 1400 B.C.) is slightly more archaic than the oldest Vedic text in India, the Rig Veda. The early forms of Sanskrit show clear substrate influences, in part from the Bactria-Margiana Archaeological Complex (2400–1600 B.C.) and from the Hindu Kush–Pamir areas, all of which points, together with the Mitanni, to evidence of an influx of OIA speakers into South Asia from the northwest.

Other forms of OIA include middle and late Vedic; Classical Sanskrit, still a fully inflectional language like Greek and Latin, emerged from a conservative form of OIA. It was codified by the ingenious grammarian Pāṇini, who lived near Attock on the Indus (c. 400 B.C.). Vedic OIA was spoken from this area up to the borders of Bengal and also in western Madhya Pradesh and northern Maharashtra. In its classical form (Sanskrit) it expanded, as the language of the learned, all over South Asia and beyond, to Bali, Vietnam, and, with Buddhist missions, through Afghanistan into Central Asia, China, and Japan.

By the time of the Buddha (c. 400 B.C.) OIA had been supplanted as popular language by Middle Indo-Aryan (MIA); some MIA forms are occasionally visible in Vedic texts. The Buddha taught in MIA, though texts in his own eastern dialect have not been preserved; instead, they have come down in the western Pali variety of MIA. Fragments of Buddhist texts also survive in some more recent forms of MIA, as in the oldest Buddhist manuscripts from the first century A.D. The first datable testimony of MIA are the inscriptions of the emperor Ashoka (c. 250 B.C.) They are found, in various dialect forms, all over South Asia. They are, however, in Greek and Aramaic in western Afghanistan, and they are absent in the deep (Dravidian) south.

MIA differs from OIA by a number of phonetic and grammatical innovations, such as the assimilation of consonant groups and the restructuring of the verb system. MIA has heavily influenced the epic Sanskrit of the Mahābhārata and the Rāmāyaṇa. Around the beginning of the common era, several later Prakrit forms of MIA emerged that were used in classical Sanskrit dramas: Śaurasenī in the midlands, Māhārāstrī in southwest India, the little used "popular" Māgadhī in the east; further, the little known Paiśācī, the Ardha-Māgadhī preferred by the Jains, and the Gāndhārī of some Buddhist texts. For a millennium, Prakrit languages were used in inscriptions and poetry as well as in Jain texts, until they gradually gave way to early forms of New Indo-Aryan (NIA) during the latter part of the first millennium A.D. Further loss of grammatical endings is a characteristic of NIA; therefore, both the noun and verb systems were completely restructured, somewhat along the lines of the change from Latin to the Romance languages.

The earliest form of NIA is the Apabhraṃśa, preserved in quotes recorded by medieval writers and in the Buddhist stanzas in an eastern dialect. Most of the religious poets of the High Middle Ages used early NIA. Apabhraṃśa and its later form Avahaṭṭha developed into the modern NIA languages during the second millennium A.D. These languages can be divided into central languages (various forms of Hindi) and outlying ones, or into some eight separate subgroups: the conservative northwestern Dardic (such as Kalash, Khowar, Shina, Kashmiri); the partially conservative Pāhārī (in Himachal Pradesh, Uttarkhand, and Nepālī, which is spoken up to Sikkim, Bhutan, and Assam); the languages of the Punjab (Lahnda, Panjabi) and Sind, of western India (Gujarati, Marathi, with its Konkani dialect in Goa); the southernmost languages Sinhala (Sri Lanka) and Dhivehi (Maldives); the eastern group with Maithili and Magahi (Bihar), Bengali, Oriya, and Assamese. The large central part of North India is covered by various forms of Hindi. Next to the standard language, there are Bhrāj, the more divergent Bhojpuri, and Sadani, or Nimari in the South. Urdu is a variant of central NIA and virtually the same language as Hindi, though with much more Persian and Arabic vocabulary; it is written in a version of the Arabic script. Consequently, Pakistan and Kashmir use Urdu, and most states of North India, from Himachal Pradesh up to Andhra and West Bengal, use Hindi.

Kannada Stone Inscription. A stone inscription in the Kannada language near the town of Banavasi (in the Uttara Kannada district of Karnataka). In the early 1970s, archaeologists stumbled on a stone pillar (where this piece was unearthed) that shed light on the powerful Kadambas, who ruled Karnataka from A.D. 325. K. L. KAMAT / KAMAT'S POTPOURRI.

Compared to the dominance of NIA languages and their speakers, the Dravidian languages are by and large limited to South India, where Tamil, Malayalam, Telugu, Tulu, and Kannada are the dominant languages today. Its earliest forms are attested, from about 200 B.C. onward, in the Tamil inscriptions of Tamil Nadu and Kerala, and in the classical Tamil texts of the Sangam poems. The early inscriptions indicate influences from a lost proto-Kannada. The other Dravidian languages have been attested only hundreds of years later, and many "tribal" ones only over the past two hundred years. The time and exact location of the influx of Dravidian into the subcontinent is unclear, but there are clear remnants in topographical terms in Sind, Gujarat, and Maharashtra. These and early cultural influences on Dravidian all point westward: agricultural words came from Sumerian or Elamite, and some even from farther west. However, the language(s) of the Indus Civilization (2600–1900 B.C.) are uncertain, as its inscriptions cannot be read (if indeed they are a script). The supposed linguistic remnant of that time, modern Brahui in Baluchistan, however, is a late medieval immigrant from central India (as is Kurukh/Oraon and Malto in Jharkhand). Central India has also retained various Goṇḍī dialects, and South India, especially the Nilgiris (with Toda), has other "tribal" Dravidian languages. A conservative dialect of Tamil has been spoken in northern and northeastern Sri Lanka for many centuries and has considerably influenced the Indo-Aryan Sinhala.

Proto-Dravidian is an agglutinative language like its supposed relative, Uralic. It shares many areal features with Central, North, and Northeast Asia and, surprisingly, highland Ethiopia. Some scholars unite Dravidian and Indo-European, along with South Caucasian (Georgian), Afro-Asiatic (Semitic, Old Egyptian, Berber, etc.), Uralic, and Altaic (including Korean and Japanese) in a Nostratic superfamily or, according to a recent proposal, in Eurasiatic. The historical development of the Dravidian languages has been investigated only on a limited basis thus far, in spite of its importance both for the history of the subcontinent as well as for the little-studied southern influence on the literary and religious history of the North. There also has been an enormous influence of Dravidian on the northern languages, starting with certain parts of the oldest OIA text, the Rig Veda. While its earliest stages seem to lack Dravidian words, the text otherwise has a number of early Dravidian loans. Their amount increases throughout Vedic literature, and their impact continues until today, though most speakers of Sanskrit or NIA do not recognize that such words as daṇḍa (stick) are loans from Dravidian. Strong Dravidian influence is also seen in phonology, word formation, and syntax of OIA, MIA and NIA: we can therefore speak of a South Asian "linguistic area" (*sprachbund*). This linguistic area also includes the Munda languages.

Northern Munda is now spoken in eastern and also in western India (Korku, on the Tapti River). In the east, Santali (West Bengal, Jharkhand) and Mundari are the languages with the most speakers; however, Northern Munda (Kherwari) also includes Asuri, Ho, and so on; Central Munda includes Kharia, Juang, and others; and Southern Munda, spoken on the borders of Orissa and Andhra, includes Sora, Pareng, Gutob, and others. Munda itself is the western branch of Austro-Asiatic, which includes, inside India, also Khasi and War (Meghalaya) as well as Nicobar, and outside India, Mon-Khmer, the related Tai languages, and Vietnamese. Khamti (northern Tai) was the language of the medieval Ahom kingdom and still survives in northeastern Assam. Austro-Asiatic must once have been spoken in a much larger area of North India, as many prefixing loans (often closer to War-Khasi) survive in the Rig Veda. Proto-Munda, which has been reconstructed only over the past few decades, was a largely mono/bisyllabic language working with prefixes and infixes. Under the *sprachbund* influence of Indo-Aryan, it has shifted to a (largely) suffixing language, especially Northern Munda, which also has an enormous number of NIA loans. The largely uninvestigated Munda and War/Khasi languages (and their oral literatures) contain much that is important for the linguistic, religious, and cultural prehistory of the subcontinent. In the Jharkhand and Meghalaya states, at least Santali/Mundari and Khasi may be maintained, while many of the small tribal languages face quick extinction due to the pressure of neighboring NIA and Dravidian languages.

The northern rim of South Asia is occupied by Tibeto-Burmese languages that are linked to Chinese (Sino-Tibetan). Their early history in the subcontinent is unknown; however, even early Vedic texts speak of a mountain people, the Kirāta. The earliest documentation is found in place names and in the Licchavi inscriptions (Kathmandu Valley, c. A.D. 200–750), which also refer to the Kirāta. After A.D. 983, there are land sale inscriptions on palm leaf in early Newari, the dominant language of the Kathmandu Valley until the Gorkha conquest in 1768–1769, when NIA Nepālī became the offical language. Most other Tibeto-Burmese languages of the Himalayan belt have not left records until very recently. From west to east, they include among others: Magar, Gurung, Tamang, Rai, Limbu, Lepcha, Bodo, Naga, Meitei (in Manipur). In the northernmost Himalayan uplands, various forms of Tibetan are spoken, such as the archaic western dialect of Ladakh, the eastern one of the Sherpa, or the southern one of Bhutan (now the official language, Dzonkha). Early influence of Tibeto-Burmese on OIA can be discerned in the Vedas, such as the topographical names Kosi and Kosala, or the word for cooked rice (Hindi, *cawal*; Nepālī, *camal*).

The rest of the South Asian languages, whether remnants or substrates, have been recorded only over the past two centuries. Taken together, they open a wide vista of early relationships: westward to the Caucasus (seen in Burushaski, Dravidian), to Central Asia and beyond (Vedic Sanskrit, Indo-Iranian), Southeast Asia (origin of Munda, Khasi, Khamti), and Greater Tibet (Tibeto-Burmese). Even wider relationships emerge in the remnant languages and substrates (Kusunda with Andamanese/Papuan, Nahali with Ainu, which is now also evident in genetic data, i.e., sharing the early Y chromosome haplogroup IV videlicet D). The predominance of retroflex sounds found from the Hindu Kush east and southward perhaps was a feature of even the earliest substrates (as in Andamanese).

In spite of the great diversity of the prehistoric, ancient, and modern South Asian languages, it has been

Sanskrit Inscription. The Qutub Minar (a mosque in Delhi also known as Quwwatu'l Islam, "the might of Islam") was constructed using the components of the Hindu temples it replaced. In its courtyard stands this massive iron column that bears a Sanskrit inscription in Gupta script, paleographically assignable to the fourth century, a date also confirmed by the peculiar style of the column's capital. D. J. RAY / FOTOMEDIA.

the Vedic form of Sanskrit (still used in ritual) and especially Classical Sanskrit that have exercised a dominant influence on the languages of the subcontinent. Sanskrit has functioned as the language of administration, scholarly discourse, and religion, not unlike Latin in Europe. In spite of the dominant role of Persian in most of northern India after A.D. 1200–1500, Sanskrit remained the language even of some diplomatic and administrative contacts well into the British period. According to census figures (1991), some 45,000 people still claimed it as their (near-)native tongue. Like Latin and Greek in the West, Sanskrit continues to supply technical terms for administration (*rāṣṭrapati*, "president"; *antārāṣṭrīya*, "international") or technology (*ākāśvāṇī*, "radio"; *dūrdarśana*, "television"; *jala vidyut āyoga*, "hydel (or hydro-electric) project"). Sanskrit influence on the "officialese" of most modern languages is so strong that one jokes that one cannot listen to "the news in Hindi" but rather has to look for "the Hindi in the news." There is a stealthy Sanskritization of most South Asian languages.

However, since the British colonial period, and now with globalization, English has increasingly become the lingua franca, largely supplanting the official language, Hindi. South Asian English has developed into a distinct dialect with strong substrate influences, such as pronunciation of dentals (t, d, th) as retroflexes, a peculiar pitch intonation with partially misplaced accents, lack or hypercorrect insertion of the definite article, colloquial changes in the verbal system ("I am knowing this"), and an abundance of substrate words (*dacoit*, "bandit"; *godown*, "storage") and frequent code switching with the local language.

Scripts

The earliest scriptlike symbols of the subcontinent belong to the Harappan or Indus Valley Civilization (2600–1900 B.C.). They remain undeciphered, though they have been claimed to represent an early form of Dravidian, and though it is entirely uncertain whether

Dravidian was indeed spoken there and to what extent. The substrates in Vedic rather point to a number of Indus languages. In addition, there even is no consensus about the exact number of the Indus signs (400–600), as to their mutual combinations, and whether the signs represent an alphabet, a syllabo-logographic script, or no script at all. In spite of some regional differences, however, the signs are fairly well standardized throughout the large Harappan area (Pakistan, Punjab, Haryana, and Gujarat). Whether the symbols were used in trade or to indicate political dominance, they quickly disappeared when the Indus Valley Civilization disintegrated. Attempts to link these symbols with later scripts are doomed. Barring a decipherment, the Indus signs provide enough simple, often geometric forms that can be connected with any early script, or even with some potter's and mason's marks. Further, there is a millennia-long gap between the last Indus inscriptions (c. 1900 B.C.) and the first ones in later Indian scripts (under Emperor Ashoka, c. 250 B.C.).

The first writing in South Asia appears only after the impact of Persian domination of much of Pakistan (530 or 519–327 B.C.). Indeed, Karoṣṭhī, the earliest script of the northwestern subcontinent, is an Aramaic-based, rather cursive, Semitic-style alphabet. Aramaic was the language of administration in the Persian empire and even in some of Ashoka's inscriptions (in Kandahar and Taxila). Unlike all other Indian scripts, Kharoshthi is written from right to left. It is a true alphabet: all vowels that begin a syllable and all consonants are represented by individual signs, but vowel length is not marked. However, due to the abundance of a/ā sounds in MIA, postconsonantal a/ā are not written but are inherent in the consonant sign. All other postconsonantal vowels are marked by small diacritical signs above, below, or crossing the consonant sign in question. Certain consonant clusters are expressed by ligatures or special individual signs. Unlike Semitic alphabets such as Aramaic, the script therefore is well attuned to the Indian phonetic system. Kharoshthi is older than its sister script, Brahmi, and continued to be used until the third century A.D. in the northwest and in Central Asia (Xinjiang).

The other script used in Ashoka's inscriptions in the rest of India was Brahmi. It seems to have been derived from Semitic scripts (Aramaic, Kharoshthi), but it was completely reconfigured, perhaps under contemporary Greek (Hellenistic) influence, which would be plausible if Brahmi was indeed created under Ashoka. Like Kharoshthi, Brahmi perfectly fits the various contemporary MIA languages; however, it clearly was not designed for Sanskrit. Several Sanskrit phonemes or their allophones (such as ṛ, ṝ, ḥ) that are missing in MIA are not represented, and Sanskrit inscriptions begin only in the first century B.C. (Ayodhya, Mathura). Brahmi also lacks a method to mark the final vowel-less consonants of Sanskrit words, a feature that does not occur in MIA. As in Kharoshthi, short postconsonantal -a is not written but inherent in the consonant sign. However, long ā and all other postconsonantal vowels are marked by small diacritical signs above, below, and to the right of the consonant. Only superficially, this system may look like a mixture of an alphabet with a syllabary. With little variation, the system has been followed until today (except in the early Tamil Brahmi script). Consonant groups are mostly represented by writing a single consonant (in MIA), and later on by a ligature with one subscribed consonant below the other (for Sanskrit). The perfect match between MIA/Sanskrit phonemes and the script has often been explained as the influence of the well developed Vedic phonetic sciences and of Pāṇini's grammar. Indeed, Indian alphabets follow, unlike the Semitic ones, a strictly phonetic arrangement, beginning with vowels, then with the consonants arranged from their place of realization at the back of the mouth (velars) to the front (labials), followed by resonants and sibilants.

Recently, the finds of some small fragments of inscribed pot shards in Sri Lanka (and then in Tamil Nadu) have cast some doubt about the age of the Brahmi script. Various early dates have been claimed for the finds, all of which are pre-Ashoka. However, small pottery shard fragments can easily be transported through rat holes into lower archaeological levels. More finds are to be awaited. The Brahmi inscriptions must also be viewed in the context of early Tamil Brahmi used in southernmost India (Tamil Nadu and Kerala). Since the second century B.C., Brahmi has been used to write early Tamil, with four signs added for sounds restricted to Tamil. Other than in Ashokan Brahmi, a short postconsonantal -a and all other vowels were indicated by a diacritic, thus k+a, k+ā, k+i, and so forth. Thus, unlike in all other Indian scripts, double consonants could be written simply by doubling the sign. It is unclear whether this system was based on Ashokan Brahmi that was used in nearby Karnataka, Andhra, and Sri Lanka, or whether it went back to a lost early South Indian form. In sum, Brahmi was used, with little regional variation, all over South Asia, with the exception of the northwest (Kharoshthi). All later alphabets of South Asia (and most of Southeast Asia and Tibet) are derived from Ashokan Brahmi. Even the ordering of the native Japanese Kana syllabary is based on the Indian alphabetic order. During the first centuries A.D., the Brahmi script gradually developed nail-like extensions at the top of the letters (head markers) and, due to writing with ink on palm leaves, a more cursive form as well as some regional variations. A few letters were added that were necessary to write Sanskrit (ṅ, ḥ, intervocalic ḻ, allophones of ḥ, ẖ, h̆). A diacritic indicating vowel-less consonants was added, as well as increasingly more conjuncts (ligatures) for consonant groups (a system used until today). Also, an (invisible) square frame was gradually developed for all letters, which resulted in the squarish northern Gupta script (due to use of ink and pen, c. A.D. 300) and the more rounded southern variety (due to use of stylus for incising letters on palm leaf).

The intricacies of paleographical development cannot be traced here. However, the early split between northern and southern alphabets increased. The northern Gupta script developed, during the sixth century, into the angular Siddhamātrikā script that was widely used—even, due to the spread of Buddhism, in China and Japan (where it still survives as Siddham script). A subvariety emerged in the northwest: the early Śāradā script, used in Kashmir, Himachal Pradesh, Gandhara, Swat, and the Punjab, where modern Gurmukhi is a distant descendant. Śāradā slowly developed over the Middle Ages and was used in Kashmir by Brahmans well into the twentieth century. Another variety developed in the east: Eastern Nagari (or Proto-Bengali, Gauḍī). It took local forms in Bengal, Mithila, and in the Kathmandu Valley (Newari script with many attested subsequent forms: Bhujimol/Kuṭilā/Rañjanā, etc.) Modern Newari script is still used for ceremonial purposes. Early Bengali script developed, around 1400, into the Oriya script that favored, as in South India, round shapes of letters.

The mainstream Siddhamatrika developed, around A.D. 1000, into early Devanāgarī, with its typical horizontal top line (not maintained in all Siddhamatrika-derived scripts). It has been used in the central area, but also in Gujarat, where it was used by Jains and Brahmans well into the nineteenth century, when it developed its modern Gujarati forms separately. Devanāgarī has also been used in Maharashtra. In the middle ages, a somewhat variant form (Nandināgarī) was used in the southern Vijayanagara and Tanjore kingdoms. Due to the selection of Hindi as India's official language, the use of Nagari has spread to the Himalayas, Haryana, Rajasthan, Madhya Pradesh, Chattisgarh, Jharkhand, and Bihar. Sanskrit publications everywhere now use Devanāgarī, though Sanskrit, which has always been written in local scripts, is still written in local forms for local use.

In South India, scripts deviated at the same time as in the North. The Pallava script of Tamil Nadu (c. A.D. 500) also had a profound influence on the development of all Southeast Asian scripts. In Karnataka and Andhra, the rounded southern characters became almost fully closed, resulting in the modern Telugu-Kannada scripts. In the deep South, the Grantha script (for Sanskrit) and Tamil were developed from earlier southern scripts. They retain, to some extent, the less rounded forms of the late South Brahmi and Pallava scripts. Tamil has the shortest Indian alphabet, due to an ingenious system of writing only phonemes (neglecting predictable allophones, thus k [k, x]) and because of the lack of ligatures, as vowel-less consonants are marked with a superscripted dot/circle (*puḷḷi*). Thus, Tamil script has been easiest to learn, a feature of Tamil writing systems from the beginning. In the middle of the second millennium, Malayalam script was developed out of the Grantha script. The Sinhala script of Sri Lanka is another development of southern Brahmi script. It has been influenced by other medieval South Indian scripts while achieving its typical, rounded modern form.

The Siddhamatrika-derived Tibetan script, close to early Sharada, is used in Tibet and in the northernmost areas of the subcontinent, as well as for the national language of Bhutan (Dzongkha). The Limbu, Lepcha, and Meitei scripts are based on a version of the Tibetan script and were used for religious writings. One recently developed form of the Meitei script has been revived as the quasi-official script of Manipur.

All Indian scripts are unique and perfect adaptations to the Indian sound systems (phonemes, including some allophones). Most of them, however, remain unwieldy (even in computer use) due to their heavy reliance on individual ligatures for consonant clusters, by positioning Nagari i- before consonants, or due to the split up of the signs for medial -e-, -o- (Bengali, Orissa, southern alphabets). Similarly, the Arabic script used for Urdu and some regional languages (Khowar, Shina, Kashmiri) remains inadequate in expressing the complex vowel systems of NIA. One can only read the Urdu script well if one knows the words intended. However, in Bangladesh the Bengali alphabet (and many Sanskrit loanwords) have been retained. Persian language and script were widely used during the Middle Ages and in the early British colonial period, until Persian was replaced by English in 1835.

The English alphabet has been used since for a variety of goals, such as street signs or film advertisements. Some tribal languages (and Nepālī as used by the British army) have also been written in the Roman alphabet, though Devanāgarī has been introduced in many areas more recently. After independence, some had proposed to make a variety of the Roman alphabet the national script, but this idea did not take hold. The recent adaptations for computer use have given a further boost to South Asian alphabets, though the quick spread of computers has also substantially increased the use of the English language, which is still spoken by only a tiny minority of South Asians.

Michael Witzel

See also **Indus Valley Civilization; Literature; Vedic Aryan India**

BIBLIOGRAPHY

Anderson, G. D. S. "Recent Advances in Proto-Munda and Proto-Austroasiatic Reconstruction." Paper at the Third Round Table on the Ethnogenesis of South and Central Asia. Available at <http://www.fas.harvard.edu/%7Esanskrit/images/html_images/Andersonaamorph-rtf.pdf>

Benedict, P. K. *Sino-Tibetan: A Conspectus*. Cambridge, U.K.: Cambridge University Press, 1972.

Berger, H. *Die Burushaski-Sprache*. Wiesbaden: Harrassowitz, 1999.

Cardona, George. *Panini, His Work, and Its Traditions*. Delhi: Motilal Banarsidass 1988.

Emeneau, M. B. "India as a Linguistic Area." *Language* 32 (1956): 3–16.

———. *Dravidian Borrowings from Indo-Aryan*. Berkeley: University of California Press, 1962.

———. *Language and Linguistic Area: Essays, Selected and Introduced by Anwar S. Dil*. Stanford, Calif.: Stanford University Press, 1980.

———. *Toda Grammar and Texts*. Philadelphia: American Philosophical Society, 1984.

Farmer, S., R. Sprout, and M. Witzel. "The Collapse of the Indus-Script Thesis: The Myth of a Literate Harappan Civilization." *Electronic Journal of Vedic Studies* 11, no. 2 (2004): 19–57. Available at <http://users.primushost.com/~ india/ejvs/issues.html>

Hansson, G. *The Rai of Eastern Nepal, Ethnic and Linguistic Grouping: Findings of the Linguistic Survey of Nepal*. Kathmandu: Linguistic Survey of Nepal and Centre for Nepal and Asian Studies, Tribhuvan University, 1991.

Hart, G. L. *Poets of the Tamil Anthologies: Ancient Poems of Love and War*. Princeton, N.J.: Princeton University Press, 1979.

Hinüber, O. von. *Das ältere Mittelindisch im Überblick*. Vienna: Verlag der Æsterreichischen Akademie der Wissenschaften, 1986. 2nd rev. ed., 2001.

Hultzsch, E. *Inscriptions of Asoka*. Corpus inscriptionum Indicarum, vol. 1. Reprint, Delhi: Indological Book House, 1969.

Kölver, B., and U. Kölver. "On Newārī noun inflection." *Zentralasiatische Studien des Seminars für Sprach- und Kulturwissenschaft Zentralasiens der Universität Bonn* 9 (1975): 87–117.

———. "Classical Newārī verbal morphology." *Zentralasiatische Studien des Seminars für Sprach- und Kulturwissenschaft Zentralasiens der Universität Bonn* 12 (1978): 273–316.

Krishnamurti, B. *The Dravidian Languages*. Cambridge, U.K. and New York: Cambridge University Press, 2003.

Kuiper, F. B. J. "The Genesis of a Linguistic Area." *Indo-Iranian Journal* 10 (1967): 81–102.

Lubotsky, A. "The Indo-Iranian Substratum." In *Early Contacts between Uralic and Indo-European: Linguistic and Archaeological Considerations*, edited by C. Carpelan et al. Helsinki: Suomalais-Ugrilainen Seura, 2001.

Mahadevan, I. *Early Tamil Epigraphy: From the Earliest Times to the Sixth Century A.D.* Chennai: Cre-A; Cambridge, Mass.: Harvard University Press, 2003.

Masica, C. P. "Aryan and Non-Aryan Elements in North Indian Agriculture." In *Aryan and Non-Aryan in India*, edited by M. Deshpande and P. E. Hook. Ann Arbor: Center for South and Southeast Asian Studies, University of Michigan, 1979.

———. *The Indo-Aryan Languages*. Cambridge, U.K., and New York: Cambridge University Press, 1991.

Rajan, V.S. *A Reference Grammar of Classical Tamil Poetry: 150 B.C.–Pre-Fifth/Sixth Century A.D.* Philadelphia: American Philosophical Society, 1992.

Salomon, R. *Indian Epigraphy: A Guide to the Study of Inscriptions in Sanskrit, Prakrit, and the Other Indo-Aryan Languages*. New York: Oxford University Press, 1998.

———. *Ancient Buddhist Scrolls from Gāndhārī: The British Library Kharoṣṭhī Fragments*. London: British Library, 1999.

Sivaramamurti, C. "Indian Epigraphy and South Indian Scripts." *Bulletin of the Madras Government Museum*, New Series, General Section, 3, no. 4. Chennai: Government of Madras, 1948; reprint, 1966.

Steever, S. B., ed. *The Dravidian Languages*. London: Routledge, 1998.

Szemerényi, O. *Introduction to Indo-European Linguistics*. Oxford: Clarendon Press; New York: Oxford University Press, 1996.

Tagare, G. V. *Historical Grammar of Apabhramsa*. Poona: Deccan College Post-graduate and Research Institute, 1948.

Tulpule, S. G., and A. Feldhaus. *A Dictionary of Old Marathi*. Oxford: Oxford University Press, 2000.

Westhouse, P., T. Usher, M. Ruhlen, and W. S.-Y. Wang. "Kusunda: An Indo-Pacific Language in Nepal." *Proceedings of the National Academy of Sciences* (2004) 101: 5692–5695.

Witzel, M. "Tracing the Vedic Dialects." In *Dialectes dans les littératures indo-aryennes*, edited by Colette Caillat. Paris: Collège de France, 1989.

———. "Early Sources for South Asian Substrate Languages." *Mother Tongue*, October 1999.

———. "Linguistic Evidence for Cultural Exchange in Prehistoric Western Central Asia." *Sino-Platonic Papers* 129 (2003).

Zide, N. H. "Munda and Non-Munda Austroasiatic Languages." *Current Trends in Linguistics* 5 (1969): 411–430.

LANSDOWNE, LORD ***(1845–1927), fifth marquis of Lansdowne, viceroy of India (1888–1894).*** Henry Charles Keith Petty-Fitzmaurice, the fifth marquis of Lansdowne, was born into a powerful Anglo-Irish family closely associated with progressive Indian policy. His predecessors had sponsored Sanskrit and English education on the subcontinent. The "father of modern India," Ram Mohan Roy, was once a guest in the home in which Lansdowne was born. Charles "Clemency" Canning (viceroy, 1858–1862) was a close family friend. As a result, Lansdowne came to view his service as undersecretary for India (1880) and his assumption of Canning's former office as a family obligation.

Upon his arrival on the subcontinent, Lansdowne found that his predecessor Lord Dufferin had left him with an empty treasury, a constrained scheme for political reform, and a more active policy on India's northwestern frontier that had alienated the amir of Afghanistan and had unsettled relations with the peoples of that borderland. He soon encountered several new problems, including a bloody revolt in Manipur (1890–1891), an attempt by Parliament to slow the growth of indigenous Indian industry (1891) and a series of political debacles that he largely attributed to the Indian Civil Service's "lack of sympathy for those they ruled."

Believing that the rise of Indian nationalism was an inevitable by-product of British administration, Lansdowne legitimized the work of the Indian National Congress in an official circular (1890). His relations with Congress leaders were not always smooth, but Lansdowne never strayed far from his faith in India's political advancement. He overcame harsh Indian Civil Service opposition to his own expanded and more liberal version of Dufferin's Provincial Councils plan, which was passed into law as the Indian Councils Act of 1892. This act, a pale reflection of the more democratic legislation Lansdowne would have preferred, was cropped by the home government, and the viceroy had to settle for an indirect, rather than explicit mention of the right of Indians to elect their representatives. The act nonetheless became the foundation for India's further political development. As leader of the House of Lords in 1909, Lansdowne silenced opposition to the expansion of the 1892 legislation (the Morley-Minto Reforms) by George Curzon and other Tory officials. He also secured their acceptance of the appointment of an Indian to both the Council of India and the viceroy's Supreme Council.

Lansdowne was less fortunate in sustaining what was then thought to have been his greatest triumph in India: the making of the Durand Line (1893–1894). This demarcation of the Indo-Afghan border divided several indigenous communities between British India and Afghanistan, but was designed to both amicably settle a host of disputes with Afghan amir Abdor Rahman and provide a new footing for the defense of British India's northwestern borderlands. Immediately upon his return to England, Lansdowne urged home officials to create a North-West Frontier province that would be managed so as to secure the amir's good will and also win the support of the Pathans along the frontier by offering the latter the benefits of closer relations with the British, without threatening the political autonomy they cherished. Lansdowne was convinced that unless this change was made immediately, the frontier would soon erupt with catastrophic results. His concerns and advice were ignored, however, and the British military debacles in Chitral and the Tirah followed shortly thereafter.

Lansdowne deeply regretted the cost to India of these "little wars" for empire. This may explain his interest in India during his later service as secretary of war (1895–1900) and foreign secretary (1900–1906). While at the War Office, he testified before the Welby Commission in support of Gopal Krishna Gokhale's contention that India had long been wrongly charged for military expenditures made in defense of imperial, rather than Indian, interests.

Marc Jason Gilbert

See also **British Crown Raj**

BIBLIOGRAPHY

Gilbert, Marc Jason. "Lord Lansdowne in India." Ph.D. diss., University of California at Los Angeles, 1978.

———. "Lord Lansdowne and the Indian Factory Act of 1891: A Study in Indian Economic Nationalism and Proconsular Power." *Journal of Developing Areas* 16, no. 3: 357–372.

———. "The Manipur Disaster of 1891." In *Research on Bengal*, edited by Ray Langsten. East Lansing: Michigan State University, 1983.

Newton, Lord. *Lord Lansdowne*. London: John Murray, 1929.

LARGE-SCALE INDUSTRY, 1850–1950 The term "large-scale industry" refers to factories that combine at least three characteristics: use of machinery, employment of wage labor, and the application of regulatory measures such as the Factory Act or Disputes Act. These features were of recent origin in nineteenth-century India and, to a large extent, products of British colonial rule. In employment statistics, the units registered as "factories" under the Factory Act can be considered large-scale industry. In reality, the registered factories included a fair number of units that did not employ machinery, but with few exceptions, registered factories did possess the other two features.

Scale, Spread, and Composition

Employment in factories in British India increased from 317,000 in 1891 to 1,266,000 in 1938, or from 5 percent of industrial employment to 11 percent (it was 29 percent in 1991). The share of factories in real income generated by industry increased from about 15 percent in 1900 to 45 percent in 1947 (it was 55–60 percent in the mid-1990s). Factory employment in all princely states increased from 130,000 in 1921 to 299,000 in 1938.

Impressive as it was, the growth was an uneven one. Industries around Bombay (Mumbai) and Calcutta (Kolkata) accounted for about half of factory employment. Ahmedabad, Madras (Chennai), and Kanpur saw limited development of factories. In the interwar period, key resources such as capital, labor, knowledge, railway connection, and electric power were no longer concentrated, and industrialization began to spread. As much as 45 percent of factory employment in the early twentieth century was engaged in cotton and jute textiles. Other important groups included tobacco and leather. The share of chemicals, metals, and machinery was very small. Machinery and manufactured intermediate goods were still largely imported. From about World War I, a few bold industrial initiatives were taken, the Tata iron and steel venture being the most significant example.

Chronology

The first burst of investment in cotton and jute mills occurred in the third quarter of the nineteenth century. The capital came partly from foreign investment and partly from capital accumulated in the early-nineteenth-century trades in opium and cotton. The growth of India's trade with China after the British East India Company's monopoly in China trade ended (1834–1835) played an important role in the growth of mill enterprises. The U.S. Civil War (1861–1865), which cut off supplies of American cotton to Lancashire, created a boom in Indian cotton and large profits, part of which found its way into building cotton mills. A tea mania of a similar nature in Calcutta and a gold mania in Madras stimulated the local stock exchanges.

World War I was a landmark event. Massive excess demand for Indian goods developed, but at the same time, the flow of machinery, raw materials, spare parts, and chemicals normally imported from Britain or Germany stopped. The immediate impact of supply constraints was rapid inflation from which cotton, jute, and steel emerged as major gainers, though many other constituents of India's economy were heavy losers. Until the war, the British Raj had followed a hands-off policy with respect to Indian industries, and a buy-British policy with respect to all machines required for defense, railways, or administration. After the war, the government began to look toward local sources and became more open to promoting them. Three events that represent this shift in attitude are the establishment of the Indian Munitions Board (1918), the Indian Industrial Commission (1916–1918), and the Indian Fiscal Commission (1921–1922). All three bodies underscored the need to develop local capability, and endorsed the use of fiscal measures for that purpose. The Fiscal Commission sanctioned the use of protective tariffs for industrial promotion.

The interwar period saw rapid industrialization as well as mounting crises. Protective tariffs enabled dramatic growth in sugar, steel, cement, matches, paper and woolen textiles. Within older industries, such as cotton and jute mills, the period saw both the start of new firms in new locations as well as crises in old firms in old locations. Competition in textiles and steel was more intense in this period than before. In textiles, competition came from Japan and from many new mills that were started in small towns far from Bombay. The Indian nationalists convincingly argued that the rupee was an overvalued currency in the late 1920s. In steel, world capacity had advanced faster than demand. In jute, Indian capacity grew faster than world demand. The result in each case was low or fluctuating profits. Tariffs alone could not solve these problems. There were attempts to introduce new technology and management practices and to voluntarily restrict supplies.

The Great Depression thus came at a bad time for industries like steel, paper, sugar, cement, and jute. Yet turmoil in the financial market, caused by debt crisis and gold exports, led to a conversion of idle rural assets into industrial-commercial uses.

World War II again saw excess demand in the presence of supply constraints, and massive inflation. But Indian industry in 1939 was more diversified and better equipped to diversify than it had been in 1914.

Capital and management. Pioneers in modern industry came from communities that had specialized in trading and banking activities. On the west coast, the Parsis, Khojas, Bhatias, the Gujarati traders and bankers based in Ahmedabad, and the Bombay-based Baghdadi Jews were the early mill owners. Several of these communities had a history of collaboration with Europeans. Some had withdrawn from the maritime trade as European firms based in London took control of it. In Calcutta, and in North and South India, Europeans dominated import-export trade, banking and insurance, and eventually jute, engineering, mines, plantations, railways, power, and dockyards. Commodity trade, however, was not in European hands, but in the hands of Indian traders, chiefly the Marwaris. By the end of the interwar period, prominent Marwari firms in Calcutta had entered the jute industry, and on a smaller scale, sugar, paper, cement, construction, and share-broking. The European capitalists did not welcome this trend. Consequently, a schism opened in Calcutta's industrial-commercial world that took a toll when large European firms became targets of predatory takeovers shortly after independence.

Industrial capital was persistently scarce in India, and financial market institutions were undeveloped. The major government-backed Presidency Banks of the period did not supply long-term capital. Indian joint-stock banks were prone to bankruptcy. The informal money market served too narrow a clientele with too few instruments.

The British "managing agency system," wherein the owners of a company contracted its management to another firm for a fee was common in India since the nineteenth century. Principals and agents then belonged to a small network, but that situation changed when limited liability became popular beginning in the 1870s. The small shareholder could no longer monitor the managing agent, paving the way for mismanagement and fraud. Despite these problems, the system continued until 1970, in part because the agent facilitated loans and deposits. With the expansion of professional managers and the use of the "holding company" for control, the system became redundant.

Limits on industrialization. Large-scale industry entered the processing of natural resources, abundant and cheap in India, with knowledge imported from Britain. Machinery and intermediates did not develop to a comparable extent because Indian factories could more easily import than produce such things as electrical machinery, transport equipment, or heavy and fine chemicals. It could also import foreign technicians. India's import-dependence for technology and knowledge had weakened, however, by the mid-twentieth century. Significant changes came only after independence, with protection for the capital goods industries, and substantial government funding for higher and technical education.

Tirthankar Roy

See also **Economic Policy and Change, 1800–1947; Industrial Labor and Wages, 1800–1947; Small-Scale and Cottage Industry, 1800–1947**

BIBLIOGRAPHY

Bagchi, A. K. *Private Investment in India, 1900–1939.* Cambridge, U.K.: Cambridge University Press, 1972.

Morris, M. D. "The Growth of Large-Scale Industry to 1947." In *The Cambridge Economic History of India*, vol. 2: *c. 1757–1970*, edited by Dharma Kumar. Cambridge, U.K.: Cambridge University Press, 1983.

Ray, R. K., ed. *Entrepreneurship and Industry in India.* Delhi: Oxford University Press, 1994.

Roy, Tirthankar. *The Economic History of India, 1857–1947.* Delhi: Oxford University Press, 2000.

LEADERS, CHRISTIAN The Protestant Christian communities in South India can be traced back to the work of two German missionaries, George Bartholomeaus Ziegenbalg and Heinrich Pleutschau, of the Royal Danish Mission, at the Danish settlement of Tranquebar, in 1706. Missionaries of various societies from England and America later strengthened the Tranquebar community, so that by the end of the nineteenth century the South Indian Protestant missions were well coordinated, concentrating their energies on winning converts and establishing Christian churches. Christian doctrines, traditions, and institutions spawned by the missionary community were, of course, interpreted and appropriated by indigenous groups to fulfill their own needs and aspirations. While accepting the "new faith," the converts evolved their own agendas, which did not necessarily conform to that of the missionaries.

The interaction between the missionaries and the Indians among whom they worked set in motion unpredicted consequences. The earliest and the most fascinating account unfolded in rural Tirunelveli, where Robert Caldwell (1814–1891) achieved the largest conversion among the low caste Shanars, known today as Nadars. Caldwell, a missionary of unparalleled importance, left his imprint on almost every aspect of Tamil society. He established schools and churches, and evincing a keen interest in Indian culture and religion, learned several Indian languages. Caldwell's greatest impact was in education. He produced a number of works, most important of which were *The Tinnevelly Shanars: A Sketch of Their Religion and Their Moral Condition and Characteristics as a Caste* (1849) and *A Comparative Grammar of the Dravidian or South Indian Family of Languages* (1856).

Rankled by the derisive portrayal of Nadars in Caldwell's *The Tinnevelly Shanars* and the authoritarian behavior of the missionaries, Arumainayagam (also known as Sattampillai), a Nadar catechist, founded his Hindu Christian Church of Lord Jesus in 1857 at Prakasapuram in Tinnevelly district. Sattampillai (1824–1919) established the new church to subvert the missionary authority, developing a substantial critique of Western Christianity, which he claimed was corrupt and inauthentic. He also appropriated elements of Judaism for his new church, which he represented as the restoration of the original, pure form of Christianity, thus investing his adherents with a spiritual superiority. Sattampillai's Hindu Christian Church signaled the first wave of indigenization of Christianity.

Caldwell's magnum opus, *A Comparative Grammar of the Dravidian or South Indian Family of Languages*, was a pioneering philological work, constructing a new genealogy for South India's Dravidian languages and culture, as opposed to the Sanskritic languages and culture. It was appropriated by upper caste non-Brahman Hindus to forge a non-Brahman ideology to counter the socio-cultural and intellectual hegemony of the Brahmans in South India. Another notable missionary in the Tirunelveli district, G. U. Pope (1820–1907), a colleague of Caldwell, continued his philological tradition by translating Tamil literary works such as *Tirukural*, *Tiruvasagam*, and *Naladiar*, as well as publishing Tamil dictionaries and grammars, extolling the historic glories of Tamil culture. Pope's work helped to generate theories concerning the autonomy and purity of the Tamils, stimulating the revival of Tamil language and literature.

Indian nationalism's encounter with Christianity added another dimension to the story. Prominent among the Protestant missionaries in this regard was H. A. Popley (1868–1960), who supported Indian nationalism, openly expressing his solidarity on one occasion by unfurling the Indian National Congress flag next to the Union Jack on the roof of his bungalow during an official visit by the governor of Madras. Popley was keenly interested in traditional music and Tamil literature, and he was the first to set the Gospel hymnal to indigenous melodies. Influenced by Tamil forms of Hindu devotion, he was in the forefront of musical evangelism, assimilating traditional music and performing it during his Christian preaching. He prepared a *Hand Book of Musical Evangelism* to illustrate the adoption of Indian notation in his work. *The Music of India* is Popley's most celebrated work, which reveals the rich heritage of Indian musical culture. He translated the Tamil classic *Thirukural* into English and quoted from it profusely in his sermons.

Among the educated Christians of high social standing, John Lazarus, V. Chakkarai, and P. Chenchiah, prominent public figures in Madras, developed a deep awareness of Indian nationalism. John Lazarus (1849–1925) was a missionary and pastor of the Danish Mission Society in Madras and a firebrand of the Christian community there. Deeply concerned about the prospects and challenges confronting the Indian Christians, he was instrumental in founding the Madras Native Christian Association (1888), aimed at promoting the welfare of the Indian Christian community "by legitimate means" and furthering the political, social, moral, and intellectual advancement of its members. In 1890 he launched the *Christian Patriot*, an English weekly newspaper of "social and religious progress" in Madras. He was an ardent advocate of the National Church of India, which he tried to revive after the demise of its founder Dr. Pulney Andy. He exhorted Indian Christians to unify by shedding Western sectarianism and creating a united indigenous church in South India. Lazarus evinced keen interest in the Indian National Movement. He praised the Indian National Congress's role in creating a nation, and he made an appeal to the Christian community to spend "their time and strength and their means" for the welfare of the "Indian nation." A Tamil scholar, writer, and translator, he was involved in bringing to the fore the richness of Tamil literature and the great antiquity of the Tamil people. He made an intense study of Tamil, translating the grammatical work *Nannul* and part of the Tamil classic *Thirukural* into English. He also translated and published a corpus of ten thousand Tamil proverbs.

V. Chakkarai (1880–1958) converted to Christianity while a student at Madras Christian College, influenced by William Miller, principal of the college and a well-known Christian liberal, who joined Indians in their social reform initiatives. Graduating from Christian College in philosophy, Chakkarai completed his bachelor of law degree at Madras Law College in 1906. In 1907 he attended the Indian National Congress session at Surat and became a follower of the extremist leader B. G. Tilak. In 1917 he participated in the Home Rule Movement, and in 1920 he joined Mahatma Gandhi's movement. Active in the Indian National Congress, he was also an executive member of the Madras Presidency Association, a non-Brahman enclave within the Congress. As a member of the Madras Presidency Association, he favored reservation of electoral seats for non-Brahmans. In 1926 Chakkarai left the Congress, protesting against the practice of serving meals separately to Brahman and non-Brahman students at Shermadevi Gurukulam, a nationalist educational institution run by V. V. S. Aiyar.

One of the founding fathers of the trade union movement in India, Chakkarai served as president of the Madras Provincial Trade Union Congress from 1943 to 1958 and as president of the All-India Trade Union Congress from 1949 until his death in 1958. He was a Madras Municipal Corporation councillor for more than thirty years, between 1916 and 1948. He was elected mayor of Madras city in 1941 and was a member of the Madras Legislative Council from 1952 to 1958. Chakkarai's theological concerns centered on building an indigenous Christian theology. Along with P. Chenchiah, he was one of the founders of the Madras Christo Samaj (Christian Society), which worked for the Indianization of the church. A powerful orator, he was also a prolific writer; his theological quest was reflected in two of his works, *Jesus the Avatar* and *The Cross and Indian Thought*.

P. Chenchiah (1886–1959) converted to Christianity, along with his entire paternal family, in 1901. In 1906 he graduated from Madras Christian College, where he was influenced by William Miller. He obtained his degree in law in 1908 and began his legal career under veteran politician T. Prakasam, who later became the first chief minister of Andhra Pradesh. Qualifying himself for the master of law degree in 1913, he worked for a while as part-time professor at the Madras Law College. He practiced as an advocate, and from 1929 to 1941 served as chief judge of Pudukottai State High Court. He went to England in 1919 on a political mission to give evidence, as an Indian Christian, before the British Joint Parliamentary Committee in connection with the Montagu-Chelmsford Reforms. An ardent nationalist, he was also recognized as a stimulating thinker in conceptualizing an

Indian Christian theology and he was actively involved in the Christo Samaj.

Indigenization of Christianity was possible within the framework of the Indian church organization. Those who stood outside the church were concerned more about the nationalists' critique of Christianity than the anxieties of the Christian community, which was drawn largely from the lower castes. In this process of Indianization, they could function within a miniscule community of Christian intellectuals based on an estrangement with the Christian community and the church organization.

Vincent Kumaradoss

See also **Christian Impact on India, History of**

BIBLIOGRAPHY

Arooran, Nambi K. *Tamil Renaissance and Dravidian Nationalism, 1905–1944.* Madurai: Koodal Publishers, 1980.

Grafe, Hugald. *History of Christianity in India: Tamil Nadu in the Nineteenth and Twentieth Centuries*, vol. IV, part 2. Bangalore: Church History Association of India, 1990.

Houghton, Graham. *The Impoverishment of Dependency: The History of the Protestant Church in Madras, 1870–1920.* Chennai: Christian Literature Society, 1983.

Sundkler, Bengt. *Church of South India: The Movement towards Union, 1900–1947.* Rev. ed. London: Lutterworth Press, 1965.

Thangasamy, D. A. *The Theology of Chenchiah.* Bangalore: Christian Institute for the Study of Religion and Society, 1967.

Thomas, M. M. *The Acknowledged Christ of the Indian Renaissance.* Chennai: Christian Literature Society, 1991.

Thomas, P. T. *The Theology of Chakkarai.* Bangalore: Christian Institute for the Study of Religion and Society, 1968.

LEGAL SYSTEM. *See* **Judicial System, Modern.**

LIBERALIZATION, POLITICAL ECONOMY OF In July 1991, just a month after assuming power, and with India facing an acute balance-of-payments crisis, the government of Prime Minister P. V. Narasimha Rao announced a major reorientation of economic policy. Rao's finance minister, Dr. Manmohan Singh, quickly began lowering trade barriers, scaling back industrial regulation, and inviting in foreign investors. The gradual process of policy change, which came to be known generically as "liberalization" or "economic reform," was sustained until the Congress Party coalition lost power in 1996. Succeeding governments—of the left and right—have continued to steer India's economic policy toward a greater reliance on markets and increased exposure to the world economy.

Not every reform recommended by market-oriented economists, or proposed by the government itself, has been introduced. Almost a decade and a half after liberalization began, the long-promised "exit policy," to relax laws that restrict firms' ability to shed workers, had yet to be implemented. Reforms to India's agricultural economy also lagged behind, as did pledges to rein in government expenditure and privatize state-owned firms. India's import tariffs remained consistently higher than many had hoped for, and important controls on the movement of capital were retained.

Nevertheless, the shift of economic paradigm beginning in 1991 has been profound. Liberalization's radical implications emerged only slowly over time, as key policy reforms became rooted and new measures accumulated. Surely, this slippery-slope approach—hoping that early reforms would acquire a self-propelling momentum—helped to neutralize some of the political resistance to liberalization. Of considerable value to reformers was the widespread idea that the reforms were limited in scope, not permanent, and, most of all, were being introduced by prominent members of a political class that had seemingly no interest in shrinking a state to whose largesse they served as gatekeeper.

Indeed, in 1991, the new economic policies were greeted by many observers as yet another doomed attempt—one in a long line of half-hearted reform episodes dating at least to the mid-1960s—to fundamentally change India's *dirigiste* framework. Even so, for analytical purposes, it is helpful to treat the politics of these two processes—of initiating and then sustaining economic reform—separately.

The Politics of Initiation

The theoretical backdrop to the politics of economic reform was a widely held set of assumptions concerning the change-resistant qualities of Indian democracy. Powerful interest groups were thought to exercise a collective veto over any attempt to restructure the policy regime. Pranab Bardhan's model of the "dominant proprietary classes"—widely quoted during the late 1980s and early 1990s—was the classic statement of this view. The clout wielded by these groups appeared to have been demonstrated conclusively when attempts to reform the Indian economy—by Indira Gandhi during the early 1980s, and by Rajiv Gandhi later in the decade—faltered. In both cases, relatively modest policy initiatives were seen to have given way to politically inspired backtracking, or at least a failure to follow through with more far-reaching reforms. The lack of constancy was blamed on the influence of such powerful constituencies as subsidized farmers, protected industrialists, and rent-seeking bureaucrats, though some accounts highlighted ideological attachments as much as material incentives.

Much of the debate during and since 1991 focused on the role of the international financial institutions (IFIs), namely the World Bank and the International Monetary Fund (IMF), in provoking India to introduce a new, more radical wave of market-oriented reforms than had been contemplated during the 1980s. There were conditions—or "policy conditionalities"—attached to some of the loans that the Indian government received from the World Bank and the IMF at the height of the foreign-exchange crisis. The government's insistence on remaining vague about the nature of the agreements, and widespread awareness within India that conditionalities contained within such loans to other developing countries were in some cases draconian, fueled domestic political speculation that the new government had been forced to announce a wholesale change of policy orientation. Critics of the new wave of reforms argued that India was suffering only a short-term balance-of-payments crisis, not a fundamental economic catastrophe. Only IFI pressure, said the critics, could explain why a short-term crisis was met with such far-reaching policy reversals.

Another view, expressed at the time and bolstered considerably since then, was that India was not pushed by the IFIs into reforming, but that it jumped of its own volition. Montek Singh Ahluwalia, the chief official at the finance ministry during the early 1990s, subsequently argued that India's reform effort was "homegrown," a view also taken by scholars who have examined closely the sequencing of reform initiatives in such policy domains as financial markets and telecommunications regulation. During the mid-1980s, when India was not under direct pressure from the IFIs, decisions were taken to liberalize slowly in these and other areas, and government-appointed commissions had offered recommendations that subsequently formed the basis of government policy. From this perspective, the IFIs were by 1991 pushing at an open door, not one locked shut by interest groups fearful of losing their perquisites.

Others see the IFIs as an important element in the push toward reform, but as actors operating less through coercion and more through a process of modified persuasion. Devesh Kapur (2004) argues that remittances sent back home to India by its global diaspora include "social remittances," among which he classifies the knowledge and networks of India's large cadre of foreign-trained economists. Mitu Sengupta (2004) focuses on the key role played by economists of Indian origin who had previously spent time working in the World Bank and the IMF. There were indeed—in the 1980s, but particularly in the 1990s—a sizable number of high-profile "lateral entrants" to the upper echelons of India's extended economic bureaucracy, people who because of their expert knowledge and transnational professional networks were brought into the policy process, either as special advisors, as secretaries to government, or as economists running government-affiliated research institutes, like the National Council of Applied Economic Research, or working within bodies such as the Planning Commission. The lateral entrants brought with them an intangible clout due to their training and experience at elite institutions abroad. This cut both ways, of course, since some of their opponents charged them with being out of touch with Indian realities, or in the thrall of abstract models; others questioned their motives, claiming that plum jobs in Washington awaited them if they towed the IFI line while serving as government officials.

Sengupta takes a more nuanced, and plausible, position on this question. What secured these lateral entrants their positions was a widespread (and probably correct) perception among senior Indian political leaders that the lateral entrants were likely to be treated favorably by IFI representatives when arguing India's case for additional funding, better terms, and so forth. In other words, the lateral entrants would enter government largely due to their ability to act as external interlocutors, officials who could speak the language of the "Washington Consensus." They were like ambassadors to a foreign court. Even so, the internal influence of lateral entrants on policy debates was not expected to be great: after all, the politicians who appointed these lateral entrants could arrange for them to exit laterally as well. As it turned out, a number of these "official economists" proved politically deft, in some cases relying on privileged access to bank-conducted research studies in order to prevail in policy battles raging within the upper echelons of Indian officialdom.

The Politics of Sustainability

The second key question concerned the ability of India's reformers to overcome the daunting political obstacles facing them, whatever their motivation for initiating reforms in the first place. Rob Jenkins argued that the reorientation of India's development strategy could be characterized, to a considerable degree, as "reforming by stealth"—a process in which various tactical maneuvers were employed by governing elites. Based on a strategy of delay, key actors deliberately refrained from highlighting the longer-term implications of initial reform decisions. Narasimha Rao, after leaving office, said of effecting this kind of policy reversal: "What it really entails is a complete U-turn without seeming to be a U-turn."

Jenkins's explanation stressed three interrelated factors: the political skills of India's reformers, the fluid institutional environment within which they operated, and the incentives created by the initial policies employed to address the 1991 crisis. The institution of federalism, for instance, meant that politicians in the central government could pass the burden of fiscal reform to the states. Politicians in New Delhi could also rely on state governments to fall in line with the liberalizing ethos, regardless of their preferences: once the central government loosened restraints on private investors the states would be forced to compete for inward investment by reforming their own policy environments. Over time, federalism began to influence the nature of India's engagement with institutions of global governance. Several state governments entered into structural reform agreements with the World Bank. Moreover, states ruled by "regional" parties became points of leverage for regionally concentrated economic interests adversely affected by the central government's approach to the World Trade Organization (WTO). With a well-placed regional party advocating their case, such interests were sometimes able to exploit the fact that regional parties had become key elements in national coalition governments. Increasingly, a regional party's support for a national coalition government was conditioned upon policy favors from New Delhi that would help provincially important economic interests—including measures to cushion them from the effects of WTO agreements.

Another explanation for the political durability of India's reform program of the 1990s was offered by Ashutosh Varshney (1999), who claimed that the government had, during the first several years of reform, focused mainly on issues of little concern to India's masses, such as financial-sector reforms and trade policy. In other words, reform was politically durable only because India's was a skewed, cautious, version of reform. India's reformers had thus mastered the "elite politics" of reform, but had not tackled the "mass politics." The reformers had achieved what they had, moreover, only by relying on the enormous social cleavages—particularly in the rural sector—that impeded collective action among adversely affected constituencies. Ultimately, Varshney argued, India's reformers would need to devise a political discourse through which the idea of markets as a social instrument could be sold to a mass audience. The explanations offered by Jenkins and Varshney are not, however, fundamentally in contradiction. Jenkins argued that one of the three factors identified in his framework for understanding the politics of reform—the political skill to cloak policy change in the guise of continuity—is in fact one of the means by which India was able to prevent any reform decisions from entering mass politics. Rather than disagreeing on the nature of causal mechanisms, the difference between these two authors is that Varshney considers one of the variables fixed (the degree to which policy decisions enter mass politics), whereas Jenkins sees it as susceptible to the exercise of political skill.

Future Questions

The future research agenda in this field lies largely in sectoral studies, or in research that charts the political implications, rather than the political determinants, of policy choices. These will respond both to existing theories as well as to new challenges to the orthodoxy surrounding India's economic performance. Dani Rodrik and Arvind Subramanian (2004) represent one such challenge, arguing that whatever one thinks about the intensity (or political durability) of the reforms ushered in by Narasimha Rao and Manmohan Singh, the reformers of the 1990s had the distinct advantage of taking office at the end of a decade—the 1980s—during which India's long-term "Hindu rate of growth" (3–3.5 percent annually) had jumped to 5 percent and more. This performance during the 1980s was achieved, according to Rodrik and Subramanian, without fundamental reforms having been undertaken. It was a matter of government sending the correct signals to business interests at the beginning of the 1980s.

This could be interpreted to mean that India's 1980s growth performance relieved the Narasimha Rao government of the obligation to undertake, in 1991, the truly difficult (mass-affecting) reforms for which many analysts called. Another reading would be that the twenty-year time frame merely indicates how important is a gradual approach to achieving sustained reform.

Rob Jenkins

See also **Development Politics; Economic Reforms of 1991**

BIBLIOGRAPHY

Bardhan, Pranab. *The Political Economy of Development in India.* Oxford and New York: Oxford University Press, 1984 (rev. ed., 1998).

Echeverri-Gent, John. "Financial Globalization and India's Equity Market Reforms." In *The Politics of India's Next Generation of Economic Reforms*, edited by Rob Jenkins and Sunil Khilnani. Special Issue of *India Review* 3, no. 2 (November 2004): 306–332.

Harriss, John. "The State in Retreat: Why Has India Experienced Such Half-Hearted Liberalisation in the 1980s?" *IDS Bulletin* 18, no. 4 (1987): 31–38.

Jenkins, Rob. *Democratic Politics and Economic Reform in India.* Cambridge, U.K.: Cambridge University Press, 1999.

———. "How Federalism Influences India's Domestic Politics of WTO Engagement (And Is Itself Affected in the Process)." *Asian Survey* 43, no. 4 (2003): 598–621.

———. "Labor Policy and the Second Generation of Economic Reform in India." In *The Politics of India's Next*

Generation of Economic Reforms, edited by Rob Jenkins and Sunil Khilnani. Special Issue of *India Review* 3, no. 2 (November 2004): 333–363.
Kapur, Devesh. "Ideas and Economic Reforms in India: The Role of International Migration and the Indian Diaspora." In *The Politics of India's Next Generation of Economic Reforms*, edited by Rob Jenkins and Sunil Khilnani. Special Issue of *India Review* 3, no. 2 (November 2004): 364–384.
Kohli, Atul. "The Politics of Liberalisation in India." *World Development* 17, no. 3 (1989): 305–328.
———. *State Directed Development: Political Power and Industrialization in the Global Periphery.* Cambridge, U.K.: Cambridge University Press, 2004.
Mukherji, Rahul. "Managing Competition: Politics and the Building of Independent Regulatory Institutions." In *The Politics of India's Next Generation of Economic Reforms*, edited by Rob Jenkins and Sunil Khilnani. Special Issue of *India Review* 3, no. 2 (November 2004): 278–305.
Rodrik, Dani, and Arvind Subramanian. "From 'Hindu Growth' to Productivity Surge: The Mystery of the Indian Growth Transition." KSG Working Paper no. RWP04-13. Cambridge, Mass.: Harvard University, March 2004.
Sengupta, Mitu. "The Politics of Market Reform in India: The Fragile Basis of Paradigm Shift." Ph.D. diss., University of Toronto, 2004.
Varshney, Ashutosh. "Mass Politics or Elite Politics? India's Economic Reforms in Comparative Perspective." In *India in the Era of Economic Reforms*, edited by Jeffrey D. Sachs, Ashutosh Varshney, and Nirupam Bajpai. New Delhi: Oxford University Press, 1999.

LINLITHGOW, LORD ***(1887–1952), viceroy of India (1936–1943).*** Victor Alexander John Hope, second marquis of Linlithgow, was viceroy of India from 1936 through October 1943. A graduate of Eton, and a colonel in World War I, Lord Linlithgow chaired Parliament's Select Committee on Indian Constitutional Reform from 1933 to 1934. His committee's plan was adopted as the Government of India Act of 1935. Linlithgow went out to India a year later to implement that act, succeeding Lord Willingdon as viceroy. A Tory landlord and avid hunter, "Hopey," as friends called him, expanded the Council of India from seven to fifteen members by the end of his long tenure, hoping perhaps to foist an illusion of representative government on his Indian subjects, despite keeping India's most popular leaders of the Congress, especially Mahatma Gandhi and Jawaharlal Nehru, at bay or locked behind British bars. His hatred and distrust of Mahatma Gandhi was no less irrational than Winston Churchill's.

During World War II, Sir Stafford Cripps was sent to India on his famous mission to try to win wartime cooperation from the leaders of India's National Congress and of the Muslim League. He was authorized to offer India full dominion status after the war ended, though any province wishing to "opt out" of that dominion would be permitted to do so, thus implicitly conceding Mohammad Ali Jinnah's "Pakistan." Linlithgow so resented Cripps's private meetings with Nehru and Gandhi, as well as with Colonel Louis Johnson, Franklin Roosevelt's special emissary to India, that he angrily wired Prime Minister Churchill, undermining Cripps's negotiating power, forcing that one and only wartime Cabinet overture to India to collapse. Then, as soon as Gandhi attempted to launch a final *satyagraha* movement against the British Raj in August 1942, Linlithgow ordered Gandhi's predawn arrest, together with that of members of Congress's Working Committee, doomed to rust for the remaining years of the war behind British bars.

Like Churchill, Linlithgow preferred dealing with Muslim leaders, primarily Jinnah, the Muslim League's Quaid-i-Azam (Great Leader), than with any member of the Congress. The British Indian army remained heavily dependent on its Muslim and Sikh recruits. Linlithgow knew that as long as Jinnah's League remained strong, it would serve to contradict Congress's claim to represent "all" of India's population, not just its Hindu majority. Churchill and Linlithgow were not the only Tory leaders to play that Muslim "green card" in their political negotiations with Congress, but they were two of the most powerful.

Linlithgow was succeeded as viceroy by India's commander in chief, Field Marshal Lord Wavell. Linlithgow returned home to chair the Midland Bank, and also served as Lord High Commissioner of the Church of Scotland. He died during a bird shooting party on his vast estate in 1952.

Stanley Wolpert

See also **Gandhi, Mahatma M. K.; Government of India Act of 1935; Jinnah, Mohammad Ali; Wavell, Lord**

BIBLIOGRAPHY

Amery, L. S. *The Empire at Bay: The Leo Amery Diaries, 1929–1945*, edited by John Barnes and David Nicholson. London: Hutchinson, 1988.
Glendevon, John. *The Viceroy at Bay: Lord Linlithgow in India, 1939–1943.* London, 1971.
Mansergh, N., and E. W. R. Lumby, eds. *The Transfer of Power, 1942–7*, vols. I–IV. London: Her Majesty's Stationery Office, 1970–1973.
Wolpert, Stanley. *Jinnah of Pakistan.* New York and Oxford: Oxford University Press, 1984.
———. *Shameful Flight: The Last Years of the British Empire in India.* New York and Oxford: Oxford University Press, 2005.

LITERATURE

This entry consists of the following articles:

MODERN

Throughout its history, the literature of the Indian subcontinent has been characterized by an exuberant diversity of languages and has been enriched by ever-shifting dialogues among these languages and the regions and cultures they represent. The development of modern Indian literature in the second half of the nineteenth century was the result of such dialogues—between the English language, a colonial import that replaced Sanskrit and Persian as the medium of education, and the more than twenty regional languages of India, many with literary traditions stretching back a thousand years or more. In the nineteenth century, some Indian writers wrote in English, but the majority adapted European genres, such as the novel and the short story, to the "vernacular," regional languages, writing on modern themes and forging new literary languages and styles. The second half of the twentieth century saw the adoption of English as a major language for Indian fiction, and from the 1980s onward, Indian and South Asian writers in English have been leading figures on the global literary scene. Modern Indian literature mirrors the diversity and vibrancy of modern India. From its very beginnings, Indian fiction has offered—often more discerningly and more reliably than documentary sources—imaginative commentary on India's social and political realities, and on the negotiations of India's traditional cultures with the West and with the modern world.

The British Colonial Period to 1947

Modernity, the novel, and the nation. The rise of modern Indian literature in the nineteenth century reveals the complexity of India's encounter with colonialism, and of the country's entry into modernity. As early as 1835, the British colonial government had introduced English education for upper-class Indians, so that they could serve in the administration of the colony. With the establishment, in 1857, of universities in the three Presidencies of Madras (Chennai), Bombay (Mumbai), and Calcutta (Kolkata), a significant number of Indians gained access to European thought. The colonists had hoped that an English education would teach their Indian subjects Western values, and would wean them from what they considered pernicious ideas propagated by Indian religious and literary texts. British condemnation extended to the aesthetic of Indian literature as well. However, the creation of an English-educated upper middle class affected Indian literary production in ways that the colonial government could hardly have anticipated. The new education had brought with it the nineteenth-century European ideals of individualism, progress, and nationalism. Stung by British criticism of Indian society and literature, yet exhilarated by European Orientalist scholars' celebration of ancient Indian culture, Indians began writing in modern literary forms to represent new realities, but also to reimagine India's history, and to advocate for social and political change. And they wrote in the Indian languages, rather than in English. Prose fiction, marked by realism, linear narrative, and a focus on the individual, displaced the earlier Indian literary modes of myth and poetry, with their emphasis on ideal images and social types. Not surprisingly, the novel, a form whose development in Europe was linked with the rise of the middle class and the concept of the nation, became the principal genre of Indian literature in the last quarter of the nineteenth century. However, from the very beginning, Indian writers shaped the Western literary form to suit Indian linguistic, literary, and cultural sensibilities, drawing eclectically from the diverse literary traditions they had inherited, both classical and popular, in Sanskrit, Persian, and the regional languages.

The "Bengal Renaissance" in Calcutta, the British capital, was at the vanguard of the new literary and cultural movements. The pioneering writer Bankim Chandra Chatterji wrote Bengali novels on social reform and resistance to colonial rule. In *Bisha briksha* (1873; translated as *The Poison Tree*, 1884), Chatterji treated the plight of upper caste Hindu widows, who were forbidden to remarry. His *Rājsingha* (1881) was a fictional account of the glory of the Rajput chiefs, suggestive of the grandeur of Indian civilization; in *Ānanda Math* (1882; translated as *The Abbey of Bliss*, 1906), in the guise of a historical novel about an earlier period, he allegorized the violent overthrow of British rule in India. By 1885, the date of the founding of the Indian National Congress, an organization dedicated to economic and political reform, the ideals of nationalism and social justice had become the inspiration, not only for political activists, but also for Indian writers.

Many early Indian novelists dealt with social issues, and especially with controversies relating to the treatment of women in Indian society, the object of the most trenchant European criticism, and a sore point with Indians, both reformers and traditionalists. The early novels focused on the ways in which Indian women of the middle and upper classes were oppressed by the denial of personal freedom, education, and economic autonomy. The writers were also deeply engaged with the question of women's entry into the modern nation and public life, and the tremendous social upheavals these developments entailed. Chatterji's *Poison Tree*, Baba Padmanji's *Yamuna paryatan* (Yamuna's journey, 1857, in Marathi), and *Chokher bali* (1901, in Bengali; translated as *Binodini*, 1968) by Rabindranath Tagore, a great humanist and a towering figure in the history of modern Indian writing, were only three among a large number of novels focusing on the condition of widows. In *Indulekhā* (1889), the first novel written in Malayalam, Chandu Menon presented his eponymous heroine as the ideal "modern" woman. In *Ghare bāire* (1915, in Bengali; translated as *Home and the World*, 1919) Tagore criticized fanatic nationalism, while sympathetically portraying the dilemmas of women caught in the debate between tradition and modernity. In the 1880s and 1890s, publishing short stories that sensitively depicted the lives of ordinary villagers in East Bengal, the multifaceted Tagore introduced the short story genre to Bengali (e.g., *Chuti*, 1892; translated as *The Homecoming*, 1916) and to Indian literature.

Poetry and other genres. Departing from the archaizing cadences of the Bengali verse of the pioneering poet Michael Madhusudan Dutt (*Meghnādbadh*, 1861; translated as *The Slaying of Meghanada*, 2004), Tagore also pioneered a modern poetry for the Bengali language. In 1913 he was awarded the Nobel Prize for *Gītāñjali* (Song offering, 1912; translated as *Gitanjali*, 1916), a collection of his poems that he translated into English at the request of the poet W. B. Yeats. Tagore's many musical dramas (e.g., *Dāk-ghar*, 1912; translated as *The Post Office*, 1914) were performed at Santiniketan, the modern school he founded near Calcutta to nourish Indian culture and arts, and throughout India. Like her predecessor Toru Dutt, Sarojini Naidu, a Bengali by birth, wrote poetry in English. While Dutt died at a very young age, Naidu became a celebrated leader of India's freedom movement and published, in addition to several volumes of poetry on Indian culture and Indian women's lives (e.g., *The Golden Threshold*, 1905), speeches and essays in English. Modern poetry flourished in all the Indian languages, and grew to maturity in the middle years of the twentieth century. The Tamil writer Subramania Bharati's passionate poems espousing the cause of freedom from British rule are among the first examples of modern writing in the Tamil language. Other writers, such as the noted Hindi poets Sachidananda H. Vatsyayan ("Agyeya"), Suryakant Tripathi ("Nirala"), and Mahadevi Varma (a woman writer and winner of a major award from the Indian Academy of Letters), wrote poetry of a more introspective, personal character.

In the late nineteenth and early twentieth centuries, women from the rising Indian middle class became authors of fiction as well as nonfiction, especially memoirs and works centered on women's issues and social change. Celebrated examples include: *The High-Caste Hindu Woman* (1887, in English), reformist Pandita Ramabai's book about the condition of Hindu women; Rokeya Sakhawat Hossain's Bengali writings on the constraints of seclusion (*purdah*) on Muslim women (e.g., the collection of essays *Avarodhbasini* [1928–1930; translated as *Inside Seclusion*, 1981]); and Krupabai Satthianadhan's autobiographical novel *Saguna: A Story of Native Christian Life* (1894, in English). Tarabai Shinde argued for the superiority of women's character in her Marathi essay *Stri-purush tulna* (1882; translated as *A Comparison of Men and Women*, 1991); in *Sultana's Dream* (1905, in English), Rokeya Hossain imagined a utopian world in which women ruled benevolently and ushered in progress through scientific achievement.

Indian writing from World War I to 1947. Two movements influenced and stimulated Indian writing between World War I and II: the nonviolent movement toward freedom for India, led by Mahatma Gandhi, and the international Marxist-socialist movement advocating social justice for laborers, peasants, and the masses. Two great novels of social realism and critique of injustice were published in 1936: *Godān* (translated as *The Gift of a Cow*, 1968), the Hindi writer Premchand's epic novel of peasant life in North India; and the Bengali novelist Manik Bandyopadhyay's *Putul nācher itikathā* (translated as *The Puppet's Tale*, 1968), a novel about rural Bengal. By the 1930s and early 1940s, the short story had become a major genre in Indian literature, and Premchand and other writers of this generation are celebrated for their classic short stories on similar themes. Bibhuti Bhushan Banerjee's *Pather pānchālī* (1929, in Bengali; translated as *Song of the Road*, 1968), a classic evocation of a rural childhood, stands out as a novel in the humanistic tradition of Tagore.

The 1930s also saw the rise of the Indian novel in English. Raja Rao's *Kanthapura* (1938) was revolutionary, in terms of both theme (the involvement of Indian villagers in the Gandhian freedom movement) and style. Rao himself declared that he had written this novel not in the standard language and style of English fiction, but in an English reshaped to reflect the Kannada language speech of women in a South Indian village and the style of storytelling in the Sanskrit Purāṇas (mythological texts) and women's folktales. Mulk Raj Anand's English novels *Untouchable* (1935) and *Coolie* (1936), dealing with the injustice of caste and oppressive labor practices, are representative of the progressive stream in Indian writing in this period. R. K. Narayan, who began a long and illustrious literary career with the novel *Swami and His Friends* (1935), is an exception among the writers who flourished in the mid-1930s, since his novels focus on character and the flow of human life, rather than on larger social and political issues.

Autobiography as a genre gained in popularity during this period. Mahatma Gandhi's *An Autobiography: Or, The Story of My Experiments with Truth* was quickly translated from Gujarati into English (1929). Jawaharlal Nehru, Gandhi's disciple and the future prime minister of India, published his English autobiography in 1936 (*An Autobiography*). Nirad C. Chaudhuri's *The Autobiography of an Unknown Indian* (1951, in English) is second only to Gandhi's autobiography in fame.

Modern Indian Literature from Independence to the Twenty-first Century

Major themes and trends, 1947–1980s. The year 1947, in which India became free of British colonial rule, marks a watershed in the development of modern Indian literature. Independence impelled writers to grapple with the ideals and realities of post-colonial nationhood. On the one hand, there was the euphoria of freedom. On the other, the division of the Indian subcontinent into two separate nations, India and Pakistan, and the ensuing violence traumatized the Indian people. Through the years of the freedom movement, Hindus and Muslims had become increasingly divided on the issue of cultural-national identity, and the partition of India was accompanied and followed by great communal violence, especially on the new territorial borders, in the divided territories of Punjab and Bengal and in the disputed area of Kashmir. The agony of partition became a part of the experience and memory of the people of India and Pakistan, many of whom were uprooted from their home territories or suffered from the division of their families. Indian fiction from 1947 to the present reexamines India's recent past, both positive and negative aspects, explores the political and social problems and issues that have emerged in independent India, and comments on the changing Indian society in an era of increasing globalization and the migration of South Asians to Western countries.

In the years following independence, the humanistic and progressive trends represented by earlier writers such as Manik Bandyopadhyay and Mulk Raj Anand continued to flourish in fiction from every region in India. Examples include: U. R. Ananta Murthy's Kannada novel *Saṃskāra* (1965; translated as *Samskara: A Rite for a Dead Man*, 1976), a work about the decaying Brahman priestly community in a Karnataka village; the Hindi writer Shrilal Shukla's *Rāg Darbārī* (1968; translated as *Raag Darbari: A Novel*, 1992), a novel about politics in a North Indian provincial town; *Chemmeen* (Shrimp, 1956), Thakazhi Sivasankara Pillai's celebrated Malayalam novel about the fate of the individual in a fishing community in Kerala; and Vyankatesh Madgulkar's *Bangarvāḍī* (1955; translated as *The Village Had No Walls*, 1967), a Marathi novel about the shepherds of Maharashtra. Modern Indian drama often undertakes social and political critique. Marathi playwright Vijay Tendulkar directs mordant satire at Maharashtrian society in plays such as *Shāntatā, kort chālū āhe* (1967; translated as *Silence! The Court Is in Session*, 1978) and *Ghāshīrām Kotwāl* (Ghashiram the constable, 1972). Drama has also been the medium for avant-garde and experimental work such as Girish Karnad's Kannada plays *Hayavadana* (Horse-head, 1971), a meditation on reality and personal identity through a folktale, and *Nāgamandala* (1989; translated as *Play with a Cobra*, 1990) a play that illuminates the power of stories through its evocation of a folk ritual.

From the 1970s onward, activist and feminist women writers have become major voices in Indian fiction. In her Urdu short stories, written between the 1950s and 1970s (e.g., *Badan kī khushbū*, translated as "Scent of the Body" in 1994), Ismat Chughtai uses bold and direct language and vivid, detailed descriptions to depict the ironies and injustices of women's lives in Indian society, especially in Muslim circles in India. Mahasweta Devi, winner of the Indian government's Jnanpith award, combines social activism among tribals and other marginalized groups in eastern India with an extraordinary writing career. Creating an array of memorable characters in her powerful Bengali short stories and novels (e.g., *Stanadāyinī*, translated as *Breast-Giver*, 1988), Devi exposes with devastating clarity the convergences between the exploitation and subordination of women and the lower classes. Recent anthologies of fiction in translation, such as *Women Writing in India* (edited by S. Tharu and K. Lalita, 1990–1993), have helped make Indian women writers accessible to a wider audience.

The recent movement of Dalit ("oppressed") writing, in which men and women of marginalized and low caste communities write poetry and fiction about their own lives, communities, and points of view (e.g., the Marathi poems and essays by Namdeo Dhasal and others, in English translation, in *Untouchable!: Voices of the Dalit Liberation Movement*, edited by Barbara R. Joshi, 1986), is a significant development in modern Indian literature. Dalit writers have produced poetry and fiction in all of the Indian languages. Autobiography, with its power to document and bear witness to the struggles of the disenfranchised, is a major genre in Dalit writing (e.g., Vasant Moon, *Growing Up Untouchable in India: A Dalit Autobiography*, translated from the Marathi in 2000).

The partition of the Indian subcontinent is perhaps the single most persistent theme in Indian and Pakistani fiction since 1947, appearing in writing in English as well as in the regional languages. Khushwant Singh's *Train to Pakistan* (1956, in English) is one of the earliest novels to evoke the horrors of the violence that accompanied partition, while Saadat Hasan Manto, who lived first in India and then in Pakistan, bears witness in his eloquent Urdu short stories to the personal trauma of divided identities and the societal and national tragedies brought about by partition. Manto's most famous story is *Tobā Tek Singh* (translated in *Kingdom's End and Other Stories*, 1987), in which he depicts the dislocation of populations at partition as an absurd event viewed from the perspective of the inmates of a lunatic asylum. Indian writer Bhisham Sahni's Hindi novel *Tamas* (translated as *Darkness* in 1989), a chronicle of partition, was made into a film for Indian television. In the Pakistani woman writer Bapsi Sidhwa's gripping English novel *Cracking India* (published as *Ice-Candy Man*, 1988), we see the events of 1947 through the eyes of a little girl.

Indian writers in English: From the 1970s to the present. The most striking change in Indian literature from the 1970s onward is the accelerated rise of English as a major language for Indian literary endeavor. In the post-independence era India has produced a noteworthy body of poetry in English, by such figures as Nissim Ezekiel, Arun Kolatkar, Jayanta Mahapatra, and Arvind Krishna Mehrotra. Fiction, however, is the chosen vehicle of the majority of Indian writers in English, who apparently feel more at home in English than in any other literary language. The acclaim they have won, both among the increasingly cosmopolitan urban middle classes in today's India and among an international audience, attests to the fact that English is now firmly a part of the Indian literary landscape.

The earlier generation of Indian writers in English (often called "Indo-Anglian" writers) is represented above all by R. K. Narayan, who is celebrated for his humanism. Between the 1950s and 1980s, with the publication of more than twenty novels, including the celebrated *The Financial Expert* (1952), *The Man-eater of Malgudi* (1961), and *The Vendor of Sweets* (1967), Narayan became the preeminent Indian author in English. The idiosyncratic, likable characters in Narayan's novels, who live in the world of middle-class South India as seen through the author's ironic yet compassionate eyes, and the mythic town of Malgudi, created as the setting of his major fictional works, are well known throughout the world. Prominent among Narayan's contemporaries are the women writers Kamala Markandaya (*Nectar in a Sieve*, 1954) and Ruth Prawer Jhabwala (*Heat and Dust*, 1975). Anita Desai is another powerful voice in Indian English fiction of the 1970s and 1980s. In her finely crafted novels Desai explores the sensibilities of Indian men and women of the English-educated middle classes in the post-colonial era. Among her major novels are *Clear Light of Day* (1980), in which she portrays the relationship of siblings in a Delhi family against the background of partition, and *In Custody* (1984), a comedic yet profound treatment of the fate of Indo-Islamic Urdu poetry and aesthetics in post-independence India.

The publication of Salman Rushdie's *Midnight's Children* in 1980 marks a turning point, not only in the history of modern Indian literature, but in English fiction worldwide (the novel won the Booker Prize in 1981). This spectacular novel narrates the life and adventures of Saleem Sinai, a child of mysterious and contested parentage, who is born at midnight on 15 August 1947, the precise moment of India's birth as an independent nation, and who is thus "handcuffed to history"; through this narration, Rushdie offers remarkable insights into the problems of personal and national identity in post-colonial nations. As a South Asian author who had lived in India, Pakistan, and Britain, in 1980 Rushdie was uniquely positioned to interrogate the conception of nationality in the late twentieth century. Equally remarkable is the host of innovative stylistic features in the novel, including a highly original narrative style, a uniquely Rushdian magical realism, and an English that is effectively infused with words, phrases, and entire registers from Indian languages. Rushdie's other works include *Shame* (1983), a novel about Pakistan, and *The Moor's Last Sigh* (1995), in which his wonderfully inventive imagination and linguistic facility are fully in evidence.

Since *Midnight's Children*, a growing number of young Indian writers have written novels in which they explore the issues of national and transnational identity and history within the Indian context. In *A Fine Balance* (1996), a novel set in Bombay, Rohinton Mistry deals with the modern Indian politics of class and communalism in the setting of the "National Emergency" declared by Prime Minister Indira Gandhi in 1975. Upamanyu Chatterjee's *English, August: An Indian Novel* (1988) explores the cultural and political dilemmas of the young Indian bureaucrat; Vikram Seth's epic novel *A Suitable Boy* (1993) traces the history of a family in a fictional town in post-independence India. Among the most ambitious and innovative of these new authors is Amitav Ghosh, whose first novel, *The Circle of Reason* (1986), offers a bold new approach to the issue of cultural identity. In *The Shadow Lines* (1988), Ghosh simultaneously traces the histories of two families, one Indian and one British, and exposes the senselessness of the violence engendered by the division of the Indian state of Bengal, leading to the formation, in 1947, of East Pakistan and, in 1971, of Bangladesh. *The Shadow Lines* questions the validity of boundaries of all sorts, interpersonal as well as international.

The latest Indian author in English to achieve world renown is Arundhati Roy, whose *The God of Small Things* (1997) won the Booker Prize and has since been translated into a large number of world languages. In her novel, Roy makes masterful and original use of language, metaphor, and narrative style, both to evoke the deeply vulnerable

Arundhati Roy. With the new crop of Indian writers describing the experience of life in a post-colonial world, Indian writing in English has become a major phenomenon in world literature. In her acclaimed *The God of Small Things*, Arundhati Roy, photographed here, has made original use of language, metaphor, and narrative style to deliver a powerful critique of oppression. AMIT BHARGAVA / FOTOMEDIA.

emotional world of childhood and to deliver a savage critique of oppressive social institutions. Her powerful, crystalline images and musically resonant sentences have a haunting beauty, even as they convey a stunningly vivid sense of human emotion. Estha and Rahel (Roy's "dizygotic twin" protagonists), Sophie Mol (the cousin whose death transforms their life), and the love between the twins' mother Ammu and Velutha, the Paravan "untouchable," have become part of the cultural memory of communities as far apart as Finland and Thailand, and the small Kerala town of Ayemenem is now a familiar and beloved place the world over. With this new generation of Indian authors, who have written powerful novels about the experience of living in a post-colonial world, Indian writing in English has become a major phenomenon in world literature.

In the final decade of the twentieth century and the early years of the twenty-first, a new group of writers is becoming increasingly prominent among authors of fiction on themes related to India and South Asia. Variously identified as "diaspora writers," "Asian American writers," and so on, these are writers of Indian (or Sri Lankan, or Pakistani) origin who live abroad, or who have grown up outside South Asia, and who write about the conflicts and challenges of negotiating hybrid and transnational identities. An accomplished and pioneering writer in this group is Bharati Mukherjee, whose fiction ranges from the novel *The Tiger's Daughter* (1971), in which she portrays the cultural dilemmas of a young upper class Bengali woman who visits her family in Calcutta after marrying an American, to the short stories in the collection *The Middleman and Other Stories* (1988), in which she depicts both the exhilaration and the conflicts of the immigrant experience in the United States, portrayed through characters of varied class affiliation and national origin. Jhumpa Lahiri won acclaim (and a Pulitzer Prize in 2000) for the short stories she published in *The Interpreter of Maladies* (1999), in which she maps, with great restraint, and in spare, elegant prose, the delicate emotions and complex inner worlds of Indian immigrants. In *The Namesake* (2003), her first novel, Lahiri fulfills the promise of her earlier work, using the powerful trope of naming to illuminate the complexities of the immigrant experience of self, identity, and belonging. When her protagonists Ashima and Ashoke Ganguli, a traditional Bengali couple who have settled in Cambridge, Massachusetts, are forced by circumstances to bestow on their newborn son the improbable name of "Gogol," entire worlds are thrown out of balance, but wondrous epiphanies are also made possible.

Global fiction, global audiences: "Indian" writing today. The high visibility of Indian English authors in the global arena has prompted some critics to wonder whether English writing will deflect the world's attention from equally good writing in the Indian languages, and whether, within India itself, the rise of English might stifle literary production in the other languages. So far, however, Indian writers of every description, those who live abroad and those who live in India, those who write in English and those who write in the Indian languages, continue to produce vibrant works, and to command avid readerships. Within India, the Sahitya Akademi (India's national "Academy of Letters," established by the government in 1954), and private organizations such as Katha (Story), work diligently to promote the translation of contemporary regional language fiction from the original language to other Indian languages and English, and from English to Indian languages. With the rapid growth in travel, migration, and communication between India and the rest of the world, there is reason to believe that works from all the Indian languages will in time gain global circulation.

There are undeniably major differences in the concerns, approaches, and audiences of modern writing in English (especially by diaspora writers) and writing in the Indian languages. While the former is inevitably preoccupied with issues such as cultural identity and postcolonial hybridity, the latter is often focused on highly localized cultural experiences within the diverse, intensely particularized linguistic, cultural, and physical landscapes of India. And yet, perusal of the boldly conceived anthology of modern Indian writing (*The Vintage Book of Modern Indian Literature*, 2004), in which the writer Amit Chaudhuri has juxtaposed Indian English fiction and nonfiction with works in translation from the regional languages, reveals surprising and exciting linkages between the two categories of works. Both the Asian American writer Bharati Mukherjee, in the short story "The Tenant" (1988), and the Chennai (Madras)-based author Manjula Padmanabhan, in her English short story "Mrs. Ganapathy's Modest Triumph" (1996), are interested in a recurrent theme in South Asian fiction: single women and the Indian arranged marriage system. Ambai (C. S. Lakshmi)'s use of an innovative mix of realism and counter-realistic description in her Tamil short story "*Velippadu*" (1988; translated as *Gifts*, 1992) aligns her as much with Salman Rushdie as with any other writer, and the quality of her writing is evident even in translation. Neela Padmanabhan's Tamil novel *Talaimuraikal* (1968; translated as *The Generations*, 1972) exudes the very smell of the soil of a village in Nanjilnadu in South India; Manil Suri's *The Death of Vishnu* (2001, in English) and Rohinton Mistry's *A Fine Balance* (1996, in English) make the apartment houses, bustling streets, and the diverse inhabitants of intricate social networks in the modern city of Mumbai palpably real; and Pankaj Mishra's *The Romantics: A Novel* (2000, in English) breathes the atmosphere of the ancient Indian city of Benares and the River Ganges. More than 150 years after its inception, modern Indian literature seems to be alive and well, as productive and as irreducibly plural as ever, and English and the Indian languages appear to be engaged in a new series of conversations.

Indira Viswanathan Peterson

See also **Anand, Mulk Raj; Chatterji, Bankim Chandra; Chaudhuri, Nirad C.; Naidu, Sarojini; Narayan, R. K.; Tagore, Rabindranath**

BIBLIOGRAPHY

Bhalla, Alok. *Stories about the Partition of India*. Delhi: HarperCollins, 1994. A representative collection of short stories on the partition of India, by South Asian authors from India, Pakistan, and Bangladesh, in Urdu, Hindi, Punjabi, Bengali, and Marathi.

Chaudhuri, Amit. *The Vintage Book of Modern Indian Literature*. New York: Vintage Books, 2004. The best introduction to modern Indian writing in a historical context, from the beginnings to the present. In his thoughtful, critical introduction Chaudhuri points out the importance of reading modern Indian works in English and the Indian languages as a coherent, connected body of work. Selections include fiction, poetry, autobiography, and essays in English and in translation from the major Indian languages. The authors represented range from Rabindranath Tagore to Vikram Seth.

Joshi, Barbara R., ed. *Untouchable! Voices of the Dalit Liberation Movement*. Atlantic Highlands, N.J.: Zed Books, 1986. A landmark collection of fiction, poetry, essays and other writings by Dalit authors. Translation, mainly from Marathi, with a comprehensive introduction to the history of the Dalit movement.

Rushdie, Salman, and Elizabeth West, eds. *Mirrorwork: Fifty Years of Indian Writing, 1947–1997*. New York: H. Holt, 1997. Selections from writing from the postindependence era, in English, except for a story by Manto in translation from the Urdu.

Tharu, Susie, and K. Lalita. *Women Writing in India: 600 B.C. to the Present*. 2 vols. New York: Feminist Press at the City University of New York, 1991–1993. An original and comprehensive anthology of Indian women's writing from the beginnings to the present, mainly in translation from the Indian languages. Excellent contextual introductions and critical introductions to each author and her works.

HISTORICAL SURVEYS

Das, Sisir Kumar. *A History of Indian Literature*, vol. 8: *Western Impact: Indian Response, 1800–1910;* vol. 9: *Struggle for Freedom: Triumph and Tragedy, 1911–1956*. New Delhi: Sahitya Akademi, 1991. These two volumes treat modern Indian literature through the 1950s in the Sahitya Akademi's multivolume history of Indian literature.

Iyengar, K. R. Srinivasa. *Indian Writing in English*. London: Asia Publishing House, 1962. A critical survey of Indian writing in English through the late 1950s.

Naik, M. K. *A History of Indian English Literature*. New Delhi: Sahitya Akademi, 1982. A brief survey of Indian English writing to 1980.

CRITICAL STUDIES

Kanaganayakam, Chelvanayakam. *Counter-realism and Indo-Anglian Fiction*. Waterloo, Ontario: Wilfrid Laurier University Press, 2002. Kanaganayakam illuminates counterrealism as a stylistic strategy used by widely different Indian writers in English, such as R. K. Narayan and Salman Rushdie, to resist Eurocentric and colonialist literary histories and categorizations.

Mukherjee, Meenakshi. *The Twice Born Fiction: Themes and Techniques of the Indian Novel in English*. New Delhi: Heinemann, 1971.

———. *Realism and Reality: The Novel and Society in India*. Delhi: Oxford University Press, 1985.

———. *The Perishable Empire: Essays on Indian Writing in English*. New York: Oxford University Press, 2000. Mukherjee's three works constitute the best critical, historical studies of modern Indian fiction from the beginnings to the present. *Realism and Reality* traces the rise of the novel in India, and the interplay of English and the Indian languages in this development. *The Twice Born Fiction* is a nuanced study of the Indian novel in English in the first half of the twentieth century. In the essays in *The Perishable Empire*, Mukherjee discusses global Indian fiction of the late twentieth century in relation to national, colonial, post-colonial, and global politics.

Tamil

Tamil, the oldest of the Dravidian language group spoken in southern India, has a history dating back to the early centuries before the common era. The earliest Tamil literature to survive is known by later Tamil commentators from the seventh century as the poetry of the Caṅkam or "academy" of Madurai. This poetry is diverse, and it was organized into anthologies of different sizes some time after their composition. The Caṅkam literature is thematically divided into *akam*, "interior" love poems with anonymous characters, and *puram*, "exterior" poetry on war, the praise of kings, and other subjects. The Caṅkam poetry relies on a complex and highly conventional system of seasons, times, and landscapes to indicate different moods and situations. These conventions are laid out, inter alia, in the earliest grammar of the language, known as the *Tolkāppiyam*, composed perhaps in the first centuries of the common era.

The Caṅkam age, sometimes characterized as the "heroic" period of incipient state structures, gave way to a more established agrarian society of settled kingdoms, in which longer poems and didactic works were composed, between the third and sixth centuries A.D. The most famous of these were Iḷaṅkō Aṭikaḷ's "Tale of an Anklet," or *Cilappatikāram*, a long narrative and lyrical poem telling the story of the widow Kaṇṇaki, and the *Tirukkural*, a collection of gnomic verses on love, politics, and righteousness by Tiruvaḷḷuvar. Many works of this period were strongly influenced by the religions of Jainism and Buddhism. By the seventh century the Hindu cults of Shaivism and Vaishnavism gained widespread popularity through songs known as the *ālvār* and *nāyanmār*, composed by wandering saint devotees. Though these poems sometimes built on earlier Caṇkam poetic conventions, they tended for the most part to be composed in a simpler and more direct style, in keeping with the message of devotion to the Shiva or Vishnu. The hymns of the saints were collected and anthologized from the twelfth century, during the apogee of the famous Chola kingdom of Tanjavur (c. A.D. 950–1250). The Chola period saw numerous important literary innovations at court, which were heavily influenced by Sanskrit *kāvya*. The courts of the later Chola kings produced some of the most famous poems of the medieval period, like Kampan's *Irāmavatāram* (a Tamil version of the Rāmāyaṇa) and the courtly epic *Kaliṅkattupparaṇi*, by Cayaṅkoṇṭar. The *Kaliṅkattupparaṇi* formed one of a large number of new genres, called as a class *prapantam*. The *prapantam* literature formed the staple of literary accomplishment until as late as the nineteenth century, and acted as the umbrella under which a number of folk and courtly genres met during later medieval times.

From the late Chola period a rich commentarial and scholastic literature also emerged in a number of fields, including grammar, poetics, and theology. During the seventeenth and eighteenth centuries, under the Nāyaka kings of Madurai, Senji, and Tañjavur, northern languages, like Telugu, Marathi, Urdu, and Sanskrit, were often heavily patronized by the elites. The study of Tamil literature was confined almost entirely to Shaiva monasteries, or *maṭhas*. European missionary activity in the eighteenth and nineteenth centuries led to important new developments, chief of which was the proliferation of indigenous printing presses from 1835. Modern genres like novels, autobiographies, and essays, and newspaper writing became widespread throughout the nineteenth century. By the first decades of the twentieth century, a number of important writers had sparked a new public interest in Tamil literature and history, which became caught up in the anti-Brahman movement and organized Dravidian nationalism.

Daud Ali

See also **Chola Dynasty; Languages and Scripts**

BIBLIOGRAPHY

Parthasarathy, R., trans. *The Tale of an Anklet: An Epic of South India, the Cilappatikāram of Iḷāṅko Aṭikaḷ.* New York: Columbia University Press, 1993.

Peterson, Indira Viswanathan, trans. *Poems to Siva: The Hymns of the Tamil Saints.* Princeton, N.J.: Princeton University Press, 1981.

Ramanujan, A. K., trans. *Poems of Love and War: From the Eight Anthologies and Ten Long Poems of Classical Tamil.* New York: Columbia University Press, 1985.

Ramaswamy, Sumathi. *Passions of the Tongue: Language Devotion in Tamil India, 1891–1970.* Berkeley: University of California Press, 1997.

Zvelebil, Kamil. *The Smile of Murugan: On Tamil Literature of South India.* Leiden: E. J. Brill, 1973.

LODHI DYNASTY. *See* **Islam's Impact on India.**

LOK SABHA. *See* **Political System.**

LOVE STORIES The composition of full-length love stories in Indian literature can be traced back to the epic Mahābhārata, long before the beginning of the common era. The Mahābhārata narrates the stories of King Nala and Damayanti, and of King Dushyanta and Shakuntala,

Nineteenth-Century Painting by Ravi Varma. The painting recounts a scene from Mahakavi ("Great Poet") Kālidāsa's Abhijnana Shakuntalam, written in the fifth century A.D. It is the popular tale of the inconsolate Shakuntala who is destined to search endlessly for her lost husband Dushyanta until the gods restore his memory of her and their idyllic love. K. L. KAMAT / KAMAT'S POTPOURRI.

in detail; both tales acquired great popularity. Mahakavi ("Great Poet") Kālidāsa was the first to dedicate a full-length drama to the story of Dushyanta and Shakuntala in his *Abhijnana Shakuntalam*, written in the fifth century A.D. Subsequently a number of romantic tales were written either in the form of drama (*natakam*) or in the form of story (*akhyana*, or *Akhyayika, or Mahakavya*) in Sanskrit by writers like Bana, Bhavabhuti, Subandhu, and others, but these never captured the imagination of painters.

The practice of illustrating love stories, however, came into vogue with the development of Indian miniature painting from the sixteenth century onward. Moreover, these artists did not have to depend on Sanskrit compositions, as romantic literature had become available in local dialects, such as Apabhramsha, Hindi, and Avadhi. There is a vast literature in the Prakrit language, including *Tarangavai*, *Lilavai*, *Malayasundari Katha*, and others, and in Apabhramsha, including *Bhavisayatta* and *Nayakumara Chariyu*. These were illustrated particularly in Rajasthan and western India, but since these Jain compositions have heavy religious overtones, they are not looked upon as secular love stories.

The popularity of romantic literature in Avadhi can be attributed to the spread of Sufism after the fourteenth century, which uses the imagery of human love to symbolize the love of the soul for the Supreme. Love stories provided an excellent vehicle to communicate this philosophy to the elite as well as the masses and hence were often illustrated.

Love Stories Inspired by Sanskrit Literature

Abhijnana Shakuntalam. This famous drama in Sanskrit, by the legendary poet Kālidāsa, narrates the romance between King Dushyanta and Shakuntala, the adopted daughter of sage Kanva, who lived in a hermitage in the forest. King Dushyanta fell in love with Shakuntala at first sight, and they were married in a private ceremony, the king giving her his ring. Dushyanta then returned to his wife in his royal capital. Later, when Shakuntala went to his kingdom, pregnant with his child, she found to her dismay that he had forgotten her, for enroute to the palace she had lost his ring in a rushing stream. She suffered for years until one day the royal ring was recovered from a fisherman and returned to Dushyanta, restoring his memory of Shakuntala and their idyllic romance. The drama ends with a happy reunion. A beautifully illustrated Shakuntala manuscript, painted in the Nagpur region and dated 1789, as well as a series of paintings from Hindur, painted in the nineteenth century, are preserved in the collection of the National Museum in New Delhi.

Nala and Damayanti. Originally the story narrated in the Mahābhārata was rendered in the form of a Sanskrit *mahakavya* (epic poem), *Naishadhiya Charita*, by the famous poet Shri Harsha in the eighth century A.D. Subsequently several versions of the story were written in Apabhramsha, Hindi, and Deccani Hindi, centered around the love, separation, ordeals, and eventual reunion of King Nala and Damayanti. An Avadhi version of the story, titled *Nal Daman*, was written by Suradasa of Lucknow in 1637, and the *Nalaraya Davadanti Charita* was written by a Jain monk, Rishivardhanasuri, in Apabhramsha around 1465, illustrated in the popular Mughal style. The folios of these works are now scattered in several museums and private collections. *Nal Daman* has been a part of the repertoire of the artists of most schools of Indian miniatures. including Mughal, Rajasthani, Pahari, and late Mughal. A profusely illustrated manuscript of *Nal Daman*, written by Babulla in Deccani Hindi and preserved in Chhatrapati Shivaji Maharaj Museum of

Mumbai, is an exquisite example and is evidence of its popularity in the Deccan region as well.

Madhavanala Kamakandala Katha. The love story depicting the intense love affair between Madhava and Kamakandala was written in different forms of literature by various writers. The earliest version in Sanskrit is a story titled *Madhavanal Akhyana* by Anandadhara, believed to have been written in 1300. Jodh, the court poet of Emperor Akbar, wrote *Madhavanala Kamakandala Katha* in 1583. It was also composed in a *prabandha* form as *Madhavanala Kamandala Prabandha* by the poet Ganapati. This is a story of a vina (Indian lute) player Madhava and the court dancer Kamakandala, with overtones of the traditional concept of rebirth, in which Madhava was the incarnation of the love god Kama, and Kamakandala the incarnation of his wife Rati. The story, which ends in a happy union, was very popular in North India during the Mughal period. A beautiful illustrated manuscript in Sanskrit, painted in a horizontal format, datable to the seventeenth century, and now scattered in various museums, is one of the earliest illustrated manuscripts of this love story. It was later illustrated in the Deccani and the Pahari schools of painting as well.

Love Stories Inspired by Folklore and Legend

Dhola Maru. Composed around the fourteenth century, *Dhola Maru ra Doha* is the earliest love story written in Hindi that seems to be based on some folk legend. *Dhola Maru* by Kushalalabha, composed in 1560, and *Dhola Marawani* by the poet Kallol of Jodhpur, written in 1620, are the best known versions of this tale. Both tell the story of Dhola, who was engaged to Maravani at a young age but later was married to Malavani, the princess of Malwa. Maravani sent her emissaries, who narrated her lovelorn state to Dhola. He realized his folly and, mounting a camel, went to bring Maravani. The story ends with a happy union of Dhola and Maravani. Rajasthani artists delighted in painting colorfully attired Dhola and Maravani riding a beautifully decorated camel, against a plain desert background. Several illustrated manuscripts of *Dhola Maru* from the eighteenth and nineteenth centuries, all from Rajasthan, where it was particularly popular, are preserved in the libraries of Rajasthan as well as in other collections; a very colorful one is the *Dhola Maru* series of about 1820, now in the Maharaja of Jodhpur Palace Library in Jodhpur.

Madhumalati. Another story in which the hero and the heroine are incarnations of the god of love and his wife Rati is *Madhumalati.* The most popular version of this story was written in Avadhi by Chaturbhujadas in the first half of the sixteenth century. Madhu, the son of an important trader, fell in love with the princess Malati. There was a long period of separation, dejection, frustration, and ordeals, after which the hero and the heroine were united with the help of a friend. Profusely illustrated manuscripts of the work are available from Rajasthan, particularly notable ones being from Kota, painted in 1771, and from Mewar, painted sometime in the eighteenth century.

Wedding of Rāma and Sītā, Cloth Painting. Upon breaking a sacred bow, Rāma won the hand of Sītā, daughter of Janaka. This colorfully painted cloth depicts their festive wedding: They remain the world's quintessential lovers. AKHIL BAKSHI / FOTOMEDIA.

In addition to these love stories, there are others, such as *Adamant* by Lakshmansena, *Rosaria*, *Mainmast*, *Rope Mandarin*, and others, which, though popular as literature, do not seem to have been patronized by art lovers; no illustrated manuscripts of these have thus far come to light.

Love Stories Inspired by Sufi Philosophy

Around the mid-fourteenth century, Sufi poets in India started writing the *masnavis* (long narrative poems in rhyming couplets with a common meter) in Hindi or in the local dialects. Amir Khusrau (A.D. 1253–1325) was one of the great Indian Sufi poets of the time who is believed to have especially favored writing in Hindi. The Indian Sufi poets and writers based several compositions on the available resources in Indian as well as Persian literature and contemporary folklore. Besides the compositions in Hindi and local dialects, several original famous Persian love stories were also illustrated in India, the most notable being Nizami's *Laila Majnu*, *Khushrau-wa Shirin*, and *Yusuf-wa-Zulaikha*. A number of illustrated manuscripts were commissioned by Muslim patrons.

Emperor Akbar patronized illustrations of love stories and is thought to have commissioned illustrations of *Khamsa-e-Nizami* (Five poems of Nizami); *Raj Kunvar*, a Hindu romance of a prince who disguised himself as a mendicant and went through ordeals and adventures to win his beloved, written in Persian; *Duval Rani Khizr Khan* by Amir Khusrau, a Persian text narrating the tragic romance between Khijar Khan, the son of Ala'-ud-Din Muhammad Khalji, and a princess of Gujarat Duval; *Nal Daman*; and others. An extensively illustrated manuscript of *Raj Kunvar*, dated 1603–1604, is in the Chester Beaty Library in Dublin. *Duval Rani Khijar Khan*, illustrated in 1567, is in the collection of the National Museum of New Delhi.

Sufism concentrates on the agony and longing of the lovers and the beauty of the beloved as the reflection of divine beauty. In fact, the expression of love in Sufi poetry itself contains the seeds of pain and suffering that symbolize the hardships of the spiritual journey to attain ultimate union with God. The non-Sufi literature, on the other hand, is a combination of diverse sentiments and perspectives, including eroticism, conjugality, truthfulness, and devotion. The illustrations of the non-Sufi romances therefore illustrate the erotic aspect of the romance between hero and heroine, whereas the Sufi-based stories avoid directly erotic representation.

Laur-Chanda. One such popular love story, laced with Sufi ideology, was *Laur-Chanda* or *Chandayan*, written by Mulla Daud in the Avadhi dialect in 1380. Based on a Dhalmai folk tale, Laur-Chanda is a popular ballad of Uttar Pradesh, Bihar, Bengal, and central India, even today. The story narrates the romance of Laurak and Chanda and the hurdles they faced after their elopement. Illustrated copies of this manuscript were commissioned from the mid-fifteenth century, as evidenced by the manuscript of Laur Chanda in the Staat Bibliothek of Berlin, painted sometime between 1450 and 1470. It was a popular text for illustrations in the sixteenth century as well; two of these manuscripts are available, one preserved in the Chhatrapati Shivaji Maharaj Museum in Mumbai and the other in the John Rylands University Library of Manchester, England.

Mirgavat. Kutban wrote *Mirgavat* (*Mrigavati*) in Avadhi in 1504; it became popular in the early sixteenth century, when it was profusely illustrated. It is a story of romance between Prince Rajkunvar and Princess Mrigavati, incorporating adventures and fairy tales with episodes of romance, separation, longing, and final reunion.

Madhu Malati. A commonly illustrated Sufi poem, especially in the Rajasthani styles of painting, is *Madhu Malati*, written by Manjhan in 1545. This is another version of the *Madhumalati* by Chaturbhujdasa.

Sufism was thus gradually spreading its roots in India. The seventeenth century was particularly productive as far as the Sufi love stories are concerned. Some of the popular works of the time were *Kutb-Mushtari* and *Sabras* by Mulla Vajahi, *Saif-ul-mulk* or *Vadi-ul-Jamal* by Gavasi of Golkonda, *Chandrabadan Mahiyar* by Mukini of Bijapur, *Gulshan-e-ishq* by Nusarati, *Ysuf-wa-Zulaikha* by Hashmi of Bijapur, and *Kissa-e-Behram-wa Gulbadan* by Tawai of Golkonda. The works were often illustrated, especially in the Deccan.

Gushan-e-ishk. Composed sometime in the late seventeenth century by Muhammad Nusarat of Arcot, *Gulshan-e-ishq* is one of the most popular love stories in the Deccan. The poet was a court poet of the Bijapur sultan Ali Adil Shah II. *Gulshan-e-ishq*, also sometimes known as *Madhumalati*, narrates the story of Prince Manohar, the only son of king Surajbhan of the city Kanayagiri, and Princess Madhumalati. The earliest manuscript of *Gulshan-e-ishq* thus far known is dated 1669. It is preserved in the collection of the Salar Jung Museum, Hyderabad, which has a total of eight manuscripts of the same, copied and painted at different times.

Single Paintings Representing Love Stories

In addition to the illustrated manuscripts and series of illustrations that narrate these stories, there are some legends that were depicted by a single, particular visual composition incorporating the most significant episode of the story, serving as an iconographic representation of the story. These were the tales of the legendary lovers Baz Bahadur and Rupamati, Sohni and Mahiwal, and Sassi and Punnu.

Rupamati and Baz Bahadur. Bazid Khan (1531–1561), also known as Baz Bahadur (Brave Falcon), was the last king of Malwa; Rupamati was the daughter of a Rajput chieftain from Dharampur. Baz Bahadur saw Rupamati bathing in a pool in the forest and fell in love with her. Infuriated by this, Rupamati's father decided to poison her. However, Baz Bahadur rescued her and they eloped.

The story is illustrated either by depicting them riding horses or resting during their flight, as in a Mughal painting of the mid-seventeenth century in the Punjab Museum at Chandigarh and a Garhwal painting of the eighteenth century in a private collection at Ahmedabad. The theme was popular even in the Deccan area. The other type shows Rupamati climbing down the fort wall to elope with Baz Bahadur, who is waiting for her below, as seen in a Jaipur painting in the Chhatarapti Shivaji Maharaj Museum of Mumbai.

Sohni Mahiwal. Izzat Beg, later known as Mahiwal, was a merchant from Bukhara who settled in a city on the banks of the river Chenab. He fell in love with Sohni, a potter's daughter, but the family disapproved of the relationship. The tale ends with the death of Sohni, who drowns while crossing the river to meet Mahiwal. The last scene, depicting Sohni in midstream with her pot, is representative of the story. Several Pahari and Rajasthani paintings depict this scene; some of the outstanding ones include a Kangra painting of the late eighteenth century in the Bharat Kala Bhavan at Varanasi, a Bundi painting dated 1790 in the Kunwar Sangram Singh Museum of Jaipur, and one from Farrukhabad, painted around 1770, in the collection of Edwin Binney of Dublin.

Sassi Punnu. This folktale is well-known throughout Punjab. Sassi, because of an unhappy prophecy, was abandoned by her parents and was brought up by a Muslim washerwoman. She grew up to be a beautiful maiden. Punnu, son of a prosperous chief, fell in love with her, and they married secretly, much to the dismay of his parents, who carried him away while he was asleep. Sassi set out to look for Punnu, and after a misadventure, she died. Punnu met the same fate, and the two were united in death.

The illustration generally depicts Punnu being carried away on a camel while Sassi laments behind. A painting from the Kangra region, datable to the eighteenth century, poignantly depicts the lamentation of Sassi trailing behind the kidnapped Punnu. The Victoria and Albert Museum in London has a beautiful set of five paintings of this theme, painted at Siba around 1800.

Kalpana Desai
Vandana Prapanna

See also **Literature; Miniatures**

BIBLIOGRAPHY

Archer, W. G. *Indian Paintings from the Punjab Hills*, vol. I–II. Delhi: Oxford University Press, 1973.

Daljeet, P. C. Jain. *Shakuntala*. New Delhi: Aravali, 1998.

Ehnbom, J. Daniel. *Indian Miniatures: The Ehrenfield Collection*. New York: Hudson Hills Press, 1985.

Goswamy, B. N. *Essence of Indian Art*. San Francisco: Asian Art Museum, 1986.

Keith, A. Berriedale. *A History of Sanskrit Literature*. Oxford: Clarendon Press, 1928.

Losty, Jeremiah P. *The Art of the Book in India*. London: British Library, 1982.

Pandeya, Shyam Manohar. *Madhya Yugeen Premakhyana*. Allabahad: Mitra, n.d.

Randhawa, Mohinder Singh, and John Kenneth Galbraith. *Indian Painting: The Scene, Themes, and Legends*. Boston: Houghton Mifflin, 1968.

M

MACAULAY, THOMAS BABINGTON ***(1800–1859), British politician and writer.*** Thomas Babington Macaulay, brilliant historian of England, was the first law member of the British East India Company's Supreme Council in Calcutta (Kolkata; 1834–1837). A precocious genius, reading from age three, Macaulay started writing his compendium of "universal history" at seven. He took up residence at Trinity College, Cambridge, at eighteen, was called to the Bar from Gray's Inn at twenty-six, and entered the House of Commons at thirty. Four years later he left for India, joining the executive council of Governor-General William Bentinck as British India's first law member.

Macaulay compiled British India's Code of Criminal Procedure almost single-handed, as both of his original collaborators soon fell too ill to continue. His contempt for ancient Indian religious philosophy and literature—based on his total ignorance of both—led him to argue that "a single shelf" of "paltry abridgements" of works based on Western science was of much greater value to Indian students than the entire corpus of ancient India's "false" and "superstitious" Sanskrit Vedas, Brāhmaṇas, and epics. Lord Bentinck's Calcutta Council was so impressed with Macaulay's rhetoric that they voted against "wasting" any company funds allocated for higher education on "Oriental learning" for Indians, who were only to study "Western learning" in English. Indian civilization's richly wonderful cultural roots and scientific wisdom were thus left undiscovered by most of the brightest young Indians of the nineteenth century, who memorized works of John Milton, Geoffrey Chaucer, and William Shakespeare instead. Macaulay's goal, as he put it in his famed 1835 "Minute on Education," was "to form a class of persons, Indian in blood and colour, but English in taste, in opinions, in morals, and in intellect."

Though Macaulay sailed from Calcutta less than four years after he arrived there, his impact on India's educational future, as well as upon its entire legal system, was perhaps greater than that of any other nineteenth-century Englishman in the service of the East India Company. A year after returning home, he joined the British Cabinet as secretary of war (1839–1841), and was later appointed paymaster general (1846–1847). His health started to fail, however, so he devoted most of his last years of life to writing his monumental *History of England*, five volumes of which he finished before being honored by the Crown as Baron Macaulay of Rothley in 1857, the year Britain almost lost India, following the "Sepoy Mutiny" at Meerut in early May.

Stanley Wolpert

See also **British East India Company Raj; Educational Institutions and Philosophies, Traditional and Modern**

BIBLIOGRAPHY

Dharkar, C. D., ed. *Lord Macaulay's Legislative Minutes.* London and New York: Oxford University Press, 1946.

Macaulay, Thomas Babington. *History of England.* 5 vols. Boston: Crosby, Nichols, Lee and Co., 1861.

———. *Essays, Critical and Miscellaneous.* New York: D. Appleton, 1864.

Pinney, Thomas, ed. *The Letters of Thomas Babington Macaulay,* vol. 3: *Jan. 1834–August 1841.* London: Cambridge University Press, 1976.

Wolpert, Stanley. *A New History of India.* 7th ed. New York: Oxford University Press, 2003.

MĀDHAVIAH, A. ***(1872–1925), Tamil writer and proponent of women's rights.*** A. Mādhaviah was a modern Tamil humanist who championed women's rights through literature; he defined as well the contours of modern Tamil fiction. Mādhaviah used his literary talents to help change attitudes toward misogynistic customs, enhancing the humanism of Tamil society in colonial Madras (Chennai). In his short life of fifty-three years, he wrote over sixty Tamil and English novels, plays, biographies, essays, nonsectarian hymns, and translations. His brilliant critiques of the hypocrises of Hindus and Christians, Indians and Westerners won him a wide circle of admiring middle-class readers. Mādhaviah's writing helped to crystallize the intersecting identities of Tamil ethnicity and pan-Indian nationalism. He contributed patriotic English essays to the *Hindu* journal, and Tamil articles for the *Swadēsamitran* (Friend of independence). He edited two journals, *Tamil Nēsan* (Friend of the Tamils) and *Panchāmritam* (Nectar).

Born on 16 August 1872 to upper caste parents in the *brāhmana* village of Perunkulam near Tirunelvēli, he hated parochial caste exclusions, which he described in his later writings. He attended a local Tamil school, then studied English at a government high school in Pālayamkōttai, a Protestant missionary center. He contributed English poems to the Madras Christian College journal under the guidance of Reverend William Miller. Mādhaviah, a sharp critic of certain Hindu social and religious inequities, also attacked Christian proselytizing. Some chapters of his "Savitri Charitram" (Savitri's story) on upper caste women were first published in the journal *Viveka Chintamani*, and later rewritten as the novella *Muthumeenakshi* in 1903. It promoted widow remarriage, and criticized child marriage and marital rape. In 1898, his Tamil novel *Padmāvati Charitram* (Padmavati's story) was published, and it has been acclaimed as his greatest work. Its revelations of female illiteracy, male lust, and mercenary marriage customs startled its many readers. For thirty years, Mādhaviah worked as a Salt and Excise Department official, touring remote areas by day, returning to write late into the night by candlelight.

His Tamil writings include a semihistorical novel, *Vijaya Mārtāndan* (1903); the plays *Tirumalai Sētupati* (1910) and *Udayalan* (1918); *Siddhārthan* (1918) on the Buddha; *Rajamārthandam* (1919), a dramatization of his English novel *Lieutenant Panju* (1915–1916); the nonsectarian hymnal, *Podu Dharma Sangeeta Mañjari* (Collection of new hymnals for all) in 1914; and marriage songs, *Pudu Māthiri Kalyāna Pāttu* (1925). His English works include *Thillai Gōvindan: A Posthumous Autobiography* (1903); *Satyānanda* (1909) about an illegitimate Christian hero; *Clarinda* (1915) about a Brahman widow Christian convert; and *Thillai Govindan: A Miscellany* (1907). He retold Indian myths like *Mārkandēya* (1922), *The Story of the Rāmāyana* (1914), and *Nandā: The Pariah Who Overcame Caste* (1923), which became school texts. His humorous *Kusikar Kutti Kathai* (Kusikar's short stories) was published in 1924.

Inspired by Vēdanāyakam Pillai's use of Tamil fiction to promote change, Mādhaviah's literary realism made him the more effective reformer who skillfully cited Indian humanistic texts to promote Western social liberalism. He believed that one remained a slave by remaining silent in the teeth of injustice. As he never feared to speak out, he was often ostracized. He died of a heart attack while addressing the Madras University Senate, urging them to make Tamil a compulsory subject for the bachelor of arts degree. That resolution was finally passed sixty years later.

Sita Anantha Raman

See also **Madras; Women's Education**

BIBLIOGRAPHY

Nambi Arooran, K. *Tamil Renaissance and Dravidian Nationalism, 1905–1944.* Madurai: Koodal, 1980.
"Old Norms in New Bottles: Constructions of Gender and Ethnicity in the Early Tamil Novel." *Journal of Women's History* 12, no. 3 (Autumn 2000): 93–119.
Rajagautaman. *A. Madhaviah, 1872–1925* (in Tamil). Bangalore: Kavya, 1995.
Raman, Sita Anantha. *Getting Girls to School.* Calcutta: Stree, 1996.
Raman, Sita Anantha, and Vasantha Surya, trans. *A. Madhaviah: A Life and a Story.* Delhi: Oxford University Press, 2004.
Varadarajan, M. *A History of Tamil Literature.* Delhi: Sahitya Akademi, 1988.
Venkatachalapathy, A. R. "Domesticating the Novel: Society and Culture in Inter-War Tamil Nadu." *Indian Economic and Social History Review* 34, no. 1 (1977): 53–77.
Venkataraman, C. *A. Madhaviah* (in Tamil) Delhi: Sahitya Akademi, 1999.

MADRAS Madras was founded in 1639 by the British East India Company as their mercantile gateway to South India. The modern city grew from Fort St. George, named after the legendary "soldier of Christ" who was regarded as the special patron of British soldiers. Francis Day and Andrew Cogan, the East India Company factors, purchased approximately 2 square miles (5 square kilometers) of the sandy fishing village of Mandaraz (Chennaipattinam) from the local governor of the South Indian Vijayanagar kingdom. In time it was to grow into a metropolis of roughly 66 square miles (170 square kilometers) with a population of over 7 million, the fourth-largest city of modern India.

Before coming under British control, Madras, or Chennnaipaatinan—from which the city acquired its present Tamil name, Chennai—had been a popular trading port in the spice and cotton trade, frequented by Portuguese and Dutch merchants in the sixteenth and

View of Madras, Once the Hub for the East India Company. Here, part of the eighteenth-century Pantheon Complex, formerly an exclusive meeting place for wealthy British traders, that has since been transformed into a government museum, the National Art Gallery, and the Connemara Public Library. The stately pink edifice is a striking example of the fusion of styles that is often characteristic of Indian architecture. LINDSAY HEBBERD / CORBIS.

seventeenth centuries. Madras's primacy in maritime trade made it a contentious city among the European colonial powers. The French East India Company (Compagnie des Indes Orientales), founded in 1664, set up its headquarters a decade later at Pondicherry, about 85 miles (137 kilometers) south of Madras on the Coromandal coast. Thus ensued the Anglo-French rivalry for the control of the Carnatic kingdom, with its capital at Arcot on the Palar River, 65 miles (105 kilometers) southwest of Madras. Arcot played an important part in the Carnatic Wars that ensued between the French and British trading companies during the eighteenth century. Robert Clive, who later became governor of Bengal, captured Arcot from the French in 1751 with only a small force of about 500 British and Indian soldiers. This compelled the French to give up their siege of the British-held town of Trichinopoly (now Tiruchirappalli). The French and their Indian allies, numbering 10,000, then laid siege to Clive's forces in Arcot. Clive and his small army defeated the French. These and later victories broke French power in South India and gave the British a stronghold in that region. In 1780, Hyder Ali, the Muslim ruler of Mysore (modern Karnataka), conquered Arcot; however, in 1801, the British gained full control of the Carnatic region, including Arcot.

The British occupation notwithstanding, Madras retained its old traditions and rural ties: consequently, in spite of soaring population, the city has grown horizontally rather than vertically, retaining its rural character, its slow pace, and its traditional southern hospitality. The best British building effort is reflected in George Town. The strong and solid township contains many historical sites: Clive's Corner, Robert Clive's house; St. Mary's Church, inaugurated in 1680, the oldest Protestant church in the East; and the oldest British tombstones in India. Wellesley House was the residence of Governor-General Wellesley during his first active military duty. The legislative assembly and the secretariat of the Tamil Nadu government are built around what was Fort House, the home of the governors of Madras. The Fort Museum is a fine repository of artifacts dating back to the early

British period. On the site of Fort St. George's first Indian town, which once housed the first lighthouse, now stands the splendid Indo-Saracenic buildings of the High Court and the Law College. Near the college was an old British cemetery; all that is now left of it here are a couple of tombs, including one of David, son of Elihu Yale. Near the High Court building is the city's second lighthouse tower, and the highest point in the court building, which once housed the third lighthouse. George Town is a warren of straight and narrow intersecting streets that developed as Madras grew. Today, it is the crowded commercial hub of the city. In the northern part of the city are to be found more traditional eighteenth-century homes. Rajaji Salai (North Beach) Road separates George Town from the harbor and, along one side of it, starting with the earliest British commercial house, Parry's, are several of the major commercial institutions in Madras, dating back to the eighteenth and nineteenth centuries, including Bentinck's Building (the British Collectorate), once the home of the city's first Supreme Court.

Among more modern British constructions in Madras is the Ripon Building, home of the Madras Corporation, the oldest municipality in India. This splendid white domed building, built in 1913 in Indo-Saracenic architectural style, foreshadows the British vision of New Delhi, and is a part of a large municipal complex that also includes parks and gardens, Nehru Stadium, Victoria Public Hall, and Moore market, a fascinating shopper's paradise. Not far away are the College of Arts and Crafts and the imposing headquarters of the Southern Railway, built in stone. Once the exclusive meeting place for Englishmen and Europeans, the eighteenth-century Pantheon Complex has since developed into the Connemara Library, one of India's best examples of fusion between Rajput-Hindu Jaipur and Mughal architectures. The Government Museum is another impressive British building.

The economic liberalization of the 1990s that helped spawn commercial culture in India has produced in the city theme parks—such as Kishkinta, MGM Dizzy World (mimicking Disneyland), Vandalur Zoo, VGP Golden Beach Resort, Crocodile Bank, and Muttukadu Boat House—shopping malls, fast-food restaurants, and other architectural icons of modern consumerism. Madras has joined Bangalore and Mumbai in the race to become the premier Indian city in information technology, attracting young professionals from around the country. Like its presidency cousins, Mumbai and Kolkata, Madras's burgeoning population is pushing the city's infrastructure to its limits. The income disparity between the young professionals and the old residents has created myriad social problems. Much like the British attempt to build a modern city in their own image, this generation's attempts to transform the old culture have resulted in incompleteness. Madras, or Chennai, with its respect for tradition and its search for continuity with the past, could never become an Anglo-Indian city in the manner that Kolkata could subvert British rule, or Mumbai could become the financial center of post-colonial India. Modern Madras, correctly understood, shares with its contemporary condition an underlying connection with its cosmological Tamil past.

Ravi Kalia

See also **British East India Company Raj; Urbanism**

BIBLIOGRAPHY

Broeze, Frank, ed. *Gateways of Asia: Port Cities of Asia in the Thirteenth–Twentieth Centuries.* New York: Kegan Paul International, 1997.

Lawson, Sir Charles. *Memories of Madras.* London: S. Sonnenschein, 1905.

Ramaswami, N. S. *The Founding of Madras.* Madras: Orient Longman, 1977.

MADURAI Formerly called Madura, Madurai is the second-largest city in Tamil Nadu. It is located on the river Vaigai and is surrounded by the Anai (elephant), Naga (snake), and Pasu (cow) hills. Between the first and fifth centuries A.D. it was the capital of the Pandya dynasty when three dynasties—the Pandyas, the Cheras, and the Cholas—ruled South India. In the medieval period it was the capital of the medieval Pandyas (6th–10th centuries), and in the mid-sixteenth century it was the capital of the Nayaka dynasty, founded by Vishvanatha around 1529, which came to an end in 1736. In 1801 it came under control of the British. Madurai was most renowned for its Tamil academy (*sangam*, or *cankam*) from about the second century A.D. Over two thousand *sangam* poems are extant in nine anthologies written by some five hundred poets. In addition, the *Tolkappiyam* grammar tells us not only about the grammar of the early Tamil language but also a great deal about their social life, from their castes based on geographical location to their matriarchal succession. The city was occupied and sacked around 1310 by the Muslim Tughluqs from Delhi and for almost fifty years was a province of the Tughluq empire. It was rebuilt by the Nayakas, originally viceroys of Vijayanagar; its walls were demolished by the British in 1837 to allow for expansion. Madurai-Kamaraj University was established in 1966.

The heart of the old city was built by the Nayakas and corresponds to the classical Hindu square *mandala* oriented to the four cardinal directions. In the center is the great Minakshi Sundareshvara Temple (*koyil*) complex,

Minakshi, or Sundareshvara, Temple Complex in the Center of Madurai. Here, two of the complex's soaring towers, each approximately 160 feet (49 m) high, rise from solid granite bases, adorned with stucco figures of deities, mythical animals, and monsters painted in vivid colors. CHARLES & JOSETTE LENARS / CORBIS.

dedicated to the god Shiva and comprising two separate sanctuaries and twelve towered gateways (*gopuras*). Minakshi ("fish-shaped eyes," a metaphor for feminine beauty) is the goddess Devī or Shakti, a warrior queen, and Sundareshvara (beautiful lord) is her husband, the god Shiva; after their marriage they are depicted as monarchs. The god Vishnu, in Tamil mythology Shiva's brother-in-law, gave the bride away in marriage. The temple is usually known as the Minakshi Temple, after the local popularity and preeminence of the goddess. Coronation and marriage festivals about the two deities dominate the ritual life of the city. The Chittirai festival celebrates their coronation and marriage. A series of plays (*lila*s) are the main events of the Avani Mula festival, and in the Teppa Festival, the deities are portrayed as monarchs, placed on a raft, and pulled around the golden lily tank.

Roger D. Long

See also **Chola Dynasty; Literature, Tamil; Shiva and Shaivism**

BIBLIOGRAPHY

Balaram Iyer, T. G. S. *History and Description of Sri Meenakshi Temple*. 5th ed. Madurai: Sri Karthik Agency, 1988.

Devakunjari, D. *Madurai through the Ages: From the Earliest Times to 1801 A.D.* Chennai: Society for Archaeological and Epigraphical Research, 1979.

Mitchell, George, ed. *Temple Towns of Tamil Nadu*. Mumbai: Marg Publications, 1993.

Thapar, Romila. *Early India: From the Origins to A.D. 1300*. Berkeley: University of California Press, 2002.

MAGADHA One of sixteen major states (*mahajanapada*s, or "great tribal regions") in North India, stretching from Bengal to the North-West Frontier province between about 770 and 450 B.C., Magadha was one of the two most powerful. (The other was Kosala, the site of Ayodhya and Kashi and adjacent to the Buddha's home, Kapilavastu.) With its capital at Rajagriha (the King's House), a city surrounded by five hills that formed a natural defense, Magadha's prosperity depended on its fertile land, favoring the cultivation of rice, its forests, which provided timber and elephants, the mineral resources of the Barabar Hills, especially iron ore and copper, and control of the eastern Gangetic trade through its command of the trade on the river Ganges. Attacking east and south, Magadha incorporated its Bengali neighbor Anga, thereby controlling the ports in Bengal and trade from the east coast. Its most renowned rulers were Bimbisara (c. 555–493 B.C.) and his son Ajatasatru (c. 459 B.C.), who murdered his father to ascend the throne. Bimbisara was the great patron of the Buddha (c. 563–483 B.C.), who won him over, according to the Pali canon, by preventing a Brahman priest from sacrificing fifty of the king's goats. Another Buddhist text talks of Ajatasatru visiting the Buddha. If Buddhism and Jainism owe their creation and survival to the business classes—the Jain leader Vardhamana Mahavira (c. 540–468 B.C.) was also born and taught in the area—then Magadha is one of the most important sites in history.

Bimbisara adopted the catapult and the chariot, enabling him to dominate the region militarily. He also formed marriage alliances with neighboring states, including a marriage into the Kosala royal family. Bimbisara started a land revenue collection system, which his successors expanded. Each village headman (*gramani*) was responsible for collecting taxes, which were handed over to a set of officials responsible for their transport to Rajagriha. Wasteland, which came to be considered the property of the king, was cleared in the forest, further expanding revenue. The king's customary share was reflected in the term for the monarch, *shadbhagin* (one-sixth). Ajatasatru continued his father's policies but also founded the city of Pataligrama (later Pataliputra, then Patna) on the south bank of the Ganges, where it became an important source of revenue as it controlled the river trade.

After the death of Ajatasatru a number of ineffectual kings ruled over Magadha, and Sisunaga founded a new dynasty which in turn was ousted by the Nandas, whose vast armies may have caused Alexander the Great's Greek army to mutiny and to refuse to march farther east than the Punjab. Maghada, with its capital at Pataliputra, was also the site of the great Mauryan dynasty (4th–2nd century circa B.C.), and the state once again dominated all of North India and a great deal of the south as well. It declined in the early centuries A.D. but rose again under the Guptan dynasty in the fourth century. It was finally destroyed by Muslim invaders in the twelfth century but was refounded in 1541.

Roger D. Long

See also **Alexander the Great; Bimbisara; Buddhism in Ancient India; Guptan Empire; Jainism**

BIBLIOGRAPHY

Thapar, Romila. *Early India: From the Origins to A.D. 1300.* Berkeley: University of California Press, 2002.

MAHĀBHĀRATA The Mahābhārata describes itself as "sprung from the oceanic mind" (1.53.34) of its author Vyāsa, and to be his "entire thought" (1.1.23; 1.55.2) in a text of a hundred thousand couplets (1.56.13). Although no version reaches that number, when the Mahābhārata describes texts of that size it denotes the originary vastness (see 12.322.36). Indeed, the Mahābhārata mentions a "treatise" (*shāstra*) of 100,000 chapters (12.59.29) that undergoes four abridgments. To describe its magnitude, many cite a verse that claims, "Whatever is here may be found elsewhere; what is not here does not exist anywhere" (1.56.33; 18.5.38). Some take it to indicate that by the time the Mahābhārata reached its "extant" mass, it would have grown from oral origins into a massive "encyclopedia" that had agglutinated for centuries. Many such scholars also cite another verse in support of this theory, which says that Vyāsa "composed a Bhārata-collection (saṃhitā) of twenty-four thousand couplets without the subtales (*upākhyānair vinā*); so much is called Bhārata by the wise" (1.1.61). Although a hundred-thousand verse Bhārata is also mentioned (12.331.2), translators have tried to help the developmental argument along by adding that Vyāsa composed this shorter version "first" (van Buitenen, I, p. 22) or "originally" (Ganguli, I, p. 6). But the verse says nothing about anything coming first. Since "without" implies a subtraction, and since the passage describes Vyāsa's afterthoughts, the twenty-four thousand verse Bhārata would probably be a digest or abridgment (Shulman, p. 25) that knowers of the Mahābhārata could consult or cite for purposes of oral performance from a written text. Another passage tells that the divine seers once gathered to weigh the "Bhārata" on a scale against the four Vedas; when the "Bhārata" proved heavier in both size and weight, the seers dubbed it the "Mahābhārata" (1.1.208-9), thereby providing a double "etymology" (*nirukta*) for one and the same text. Yet despite nothing surviving of this shorter Bhārata, scholars have used it to argue for an originally oral bardic and heroic story that would have lacked not only subtales but frame stories (narratives that contextualize the main narrative), tales about the author both in the frames and elsewhere, didactic additions, and devotional passages with "divinized" heroes.

New developments have complicated this profile. These include the completion of the Pune Critical Edition, along with wider recognition of Mahābhārata's design; intertextual studies positioning the Mahābhārata in relation to both Indo-European and Indian texts;

Kamasan-Style Painting by Nyoman Mandra. The final episode of the *Mahābhārata,* the longest epic in world literature, in which the central character of Yudhishthira approaches paradise. As painted by the contemporary artist Nyoman Mandra, proponent of the highly stylized Kamasan school. LINDSAY HEBBERD / CORBIS.

genre study, including the history of *kāvya* (Sanskrit "poetry" composed according to classical aesthetic norms); and debate on the likely period of the Mahābhārata's composition in written form. Similar developments apply to the Rāmāyaṇa.

A signal result of the Pune Critical Edition of the Mahābhārata is its establishment of a textual "archetype." There remains debate as to whether this archetype takes us back to the text's first composition, or to a later redaction that would put a final stamp on centuries of cumulative growth. This essay favors the first option. In either case, this archetype includes a design of eighteen Books, or *parvan*s, nearly all of the epic's hundred "little books," or *upaparvan*s (the list of these at 1.2.30–70 problematically includes parts of the *Harivaṃsha* as the last two), its often adroit chapter (*adhyāya*) breaks, and its subtales, or *upākhyāna*s. The latter present a topic whose significance has yet to be appreciated.

The Whole and the Parts

As observed, the *upākhyāna*s are precisely the units mentioned as omitted in the "Bhārata." *Upākhyāna*s must first be considered among the multigenre terms by which the Mahābhārata characterizes itself and its components. The epic's two most frequent self-descriptions are "narrative" (*ākhyāna*) fourteen times and "history" (*itihāsa*) eight times. But it also twice calls itself a work of "ancient lore" (*purāṇa*), a "collection" (*saṃhitā*), a "fifth Veda," the "Veda that pertains to Kishna" (*Kārshṇa Veda*, probably referring to Vyāsa as Krishna Dvaipāyana), and a "great knowledge" (*mahaj-jñāna*). And once it calls itself a "story" (*kathā*), a "treatise" (*shāstra;* indeed, a *dharmashāstra*, *arthashāstra*, and *mokshashāstra* [1.56.21]), an *upanishad*, an "adventure" (*carita*), a "victory" (*jaya*), and, surprisingly, a "subtale" (*upakhyāna*: 1.2.236)! In addition, while not calling itself one, it is also a "dialogue" (*saṃvāda*), for it sustains the dialogical interlacing of each of its three dialogical frames, not to mention the multiple dialogues that the frame narrators and other narrators report.

Indeed, most of these terms are used doubly. The more "didactic" (*veda*, *saṃhitā*, *upanishad*, and *shāstra*) not only describe the Mahābhārata as a whole, but refer to sources outside of it that the epic's narrators cite as authoritative and sometimes quote in part or digest—particularly the many *shāstra*s, or "treatises," mentioned in Book 12. But the more "narrative" terms (*saṃvāda*, *ākhyāna*, *itihāsa*, *purāṇa*, *carita*, *kathā*, and *upākhyāna*) can also be cited as authoritative tales. In this way the Mahābhārata sustains itself as a multigenre work in both its multiple self-designations for the whole and in the interreferentiality between the whole and its parts. This contrasts with the Rāmāyaṇa, whose poet composes his work under the single-genre title of *kāvya* (poem). The Mahābhārata is not called a *kāvya* until a famous interpolation in which the god Brahmā appears to Vyāsa to pronounce on the genre question. Says Vyāsa, "I have created this highly venerated *kāvya* in which I have proclaimed the secret of the Vedas and other topics" (Pune Critical Edition 1, App. I, lines 13–14), to which Brahmā replies, "I know that since your birth you have truthfully given voice to the *brahman*. You have called this a *kāvya*, and therefore a *kāvya* it shall be. No poets (*kavayo*) are equal to the excellence of this *kāvya*" (lines 33–35). In a later interpolation, Brahmā then recommends that Gaṇesha be Vyāsa's scribe (1, App. I, from line 36).

One striking thing about the epic's self-descriptive "narrative" terms—that is, the terms themselves, even though the genres they describe all develop, change, and overlap by classical times—is that they are all but one

Vedic. Indeed, the Vedic resonances of three of them—*ākhyāna*, *itihāsa*, and *saṃvāda*—are so strong that a century ago they were at the heart of debates over an "*ākhyāna* theory" of the origins of Vedic poetry. But even *carita* (Rig Veda 1.110.2) and *kāvya* (Rig Veda 8.79.1) have Vedic usages. The one non-Vedic term is *upākhyāna*, which may have been given first life in the Mahābhārata.

To distinguish *upākhyāna* from *ākhyāna*, there would be an analogy between the usages of *ākhyāna: upākhyāna* and *parvan*: *upa-parvan*. In both cases, *upa-* implies "subordinate" and "lesser" (as in *upa-purāṇa* for the "lesser purāṇas"), and denotes ways of breaking the Mahābhārata down by terms that relate its whole to its parts. But *ākhyāna* and *upākhyāna* are also frequently used interchangeably (as are the other "narrative" terms mentioned above). Sometimes, especially in the *Parvasaṃgraha*—the "Summaries of the Books" that forms the epic's second *upaparvan*—it would seem that metrical fit decides which of the two terms was used (e.g., at 1.2.124–125). But the first usage of *ākhyāna* to self-describe a sub-narrative in passing may suggest a useful distinction. The first *ākhyāna* narrated in its entirety, "the great Āstīka *ākhyāna*" (1.13.4), is the oft-interrupted *āstīkaparvan* (1.13–53). Like the oft-interrupted Mahā-Bhārata-ākhyāna, it brims with substories of its own. It is delivered by the bard Ugrashravas to the seers of the Naimisha Forest as the main introductory piece to entertain that audience in the epic's outer frame. In contrast, *upākhyāna* designates major *uninterrupted* subtales told to rapt audiences usually composed of the epic's heroes and heroines, or, alternately, of one or another of its frame audiences.

There are sixty-seven narratives that the Mahābhārata calls *upākhyānas* in one or more of three contexts: in their traditional titles (which are usually mentioned in the colophons), in the *Parvasaṃgraha*, or in passing. Fifty-six of these are addressed to main heroes and heroines. Of these, forty-nine are told primarily to the eldest of the five Pāṇḍava brothers, Yudhisthṭhira; forty-eight of these to him and his five brothers together; and forty-four of these also to their wife-in-common Draupadī (all of these, once they are in the forest). On the Kaurava side, three are addressed to the chief villain Duryodhana and two to his great ally Karṇa, who is secretly the Pāṇḍavas' real eldest brother. Adding one narrated to the Pāṇḍavas' father Pāṇḍu by his wife Kuntī (the only *upākhyāna* spoken by a woman), which bears on the Pāṇḍavas' birth, and one addressed to Draupadī's father by Vyāsa that explains the legitimacay of their polyandrous marriage to her, one finds that all fifty-six concern the larger Pāṇḍava-Kaurava household to which all these listeners (if we can include the Pāṇḍavas' father-in-law) belong, and of which Yudhishṭira is clearly the chief listener. Of the rest, ten are told by Vyāsa's disciple Vaishampāyana to King Janamejaya, the Pāṇḍavas' great-grandson, as the chief listener of the epic's inner frame; and one is told by Ugrashravas to the Naimisha Forest sages who listen from the outer frame.

Another statistical approach to the *upākhyānas* is to think about volume and proportion. Taking the Mahābhārata's own numbers, on the face of it, if the epic has 100,000 couplets (1.56.13) and Vyāsa composed a version of it in 24,000 couplets "without the *upākhyānas*," the *upākhyānas* should constitute 76 percent of the whole. That proportion is nowhere near the present case. Calculating from the roughly 73,900 couplets in the Critical Edition (Van Nooten, p. 50; Brockington, p. 4), the full total for the sixty-seven *upākhyānas* is 10,521 couplets or 13.87 percent; and if one adds certain sequels to four of the *upākhyānas* totaling 780 verses to reach the most generous count of 11,031 verses, one could say that, at most, 14.93 percent of the Mahābhārata is composed of *upākhyāna* material. While we are nowhere near 76 percent, these proportions are not insignificant. Moreover, one can get a bit closer to 76 percent if one keeps in mind the interchangeability of the epic's terms for narrative units and calculates from the totality of its substory material. According to Barbara Gombach, "nearly fifty percent" of the Mahābhārata is "represented by ancillary stories," with Books 1, 3, 12, and 13 cited as the four in which "the stories cluster more densely" than in the other Books (2000, I, pp. 5 and 24). Gombach (I, pp. 194, 225) gives 68 percent for the ancillary stories in the *Shāntiparvan* (Book 12), which has fourteen *upākhyānas*; 65 percent for the *Anushāsanaparvan* (Book 13), with eleven *upākhyānas*; 55 percent for the *āraṇyakaparvan* (Book 3), with twenty-one *upākhyānas*; and 44 percent for the *ādiparvan* (Book 1), with eleven *upākhyānas*. Of other Books that contain more than one *upākhyāna*, the *āshvamedhika-* (Book 14) with two, *Shalya-* (Book 9) with two, and *Udyoga-parvan* (Book 5) with three are comprised of 54, 28, and 17 percent ancillary story material respectively—but still, nothing near 76 percent.

Fifty-seven of the sixty-seven *upākhyānas* thus appear in *parvans* 1, 3, 12, and 13 where "stories cluster" most densely. There are, however, two major differences in the ways that *upākhyānas* are presented in the two early Books from the two later ones. Whereas Books 1 and 3 provide multiple narrators for their thirty-two *upākhyānas*, all but three of the twenty-five *upākhyānas* in Books 12 and 13 are spoken by one narrator, Bhīshma. And whereas Books 1 and especially 3 show a tendency to cluster their *upākhyānas* (two in a row told by Vaishampāyana and three in a row by the Gandharva Chitraratha in Book 1; nine, five, and two in a row by *rishis* whom the Pāṇḍavas encounter while pilgrimaging in Book 3), in Bhīshma's run of 450 *adhyāyas* in Books 12 and 13, he tends to present his twenty-one *upākhyānas* there only intermittently. Yet there is one run, from the end of Book 12 through the first third of Book 13, where he concentrates nine of them. These two books run together the totality of Bhīshma's postwar instructions to Yudhishṭhira in four consecutive *upaparvans*, which James Fitzgerald calls "four large anthologies" (2004, pp. 79–80). Both books abound in dialogues (*saṃvādas*) and "ancient accounts" (*itihāsam purātanam*). Why then does Bhīshma start telling *upākhyānas*—or, perhaps better, resume telling them (he has already told the *Ambā* and *Vishva-Upākhyānas*)—only in the *Anushāsanaparvan*? This question will be taken up in the synopsis.

The *upākhyānas*' content should also be important. But they are too varied to summarize fruitfully. It does not seem possible to break the sixty-seven down by their primary personages into less than ten categories: seventeen about leading lights of the great Brahman lineages, fifteen about heroic kings of varied dynasties, eleven about animals (some divine), seven about gods and demons, four (including the first two) about early kings of the main dynasty, four about women, three about the inviolability of worthy Brahmans and hurdles to attaining that status, three about revelations concerning Krishna, two about current background to the epic's main events, and one about the Pāṇḍavas as part of the main story. From this, the only useful generalization would seem to be that all this content is represented as being of interest to the rapt audiences that listen these tales. But this leads to an important point. Regarding the most famous of all the Mahābhārata's *upākhyānas*, the *Nala-Upākhyāna*, Fitzgerald regards "Nala" and some other non-*upākhyāna* stories as "good examples of passages that do exhibit an inventive freedom suggestive of 'fiction'" (2003, p. 207). More pointedly, Gombach credits Madeleine Biardeau's study of "Nala" as a "case for regarding this *upākhyāna* as a story composed in and for the epic to deepen its symbolic resonances" (2000, I, p. 73). "Nala" is what Biardeau now calls one of Book 3's three "mirror stories" (2002, I, pp. 412–413): stories that reflect on their listeners' (the main heroes and heroine's) current trials. But once one admits that one story is composed to fit one or another feature of the epic's wider surroundings, the principle cannot be easily shut off, as shall often be implied in the synopsis.

In any case, to summarize the Mahābhārata, it should not be enough to tell its main story, especially with the suggestion that its main story would have been the original "Bhārata." Even though it must require shortcuts, one owes it to this grand text to attempt to block out the main story against the backdrop of its archetypal design, which includes its frame stories, *upaparvans*, *upākhyānas*, and the enigma of the author.

The Mahābhārata, Book by Book

Of the Mahābhārata's eighteen books, only the first nine and Books 12-14 will be summarized in any detail. That takes one to the end of the fighting of the Mahābhārata war and the last Books to include *upākhyānas*.

Book 1, the *ādi Parvan* or "Book of Beginnings," comprised of nineteen *upaparvans*, takes the first five to introduce the three frames: how Vyāsa recited the epic to his five Brahman disciples, first to his son Shuka and then to the other four, including Vaishampāyana (1.1.63); how Vaishampāyana recited it at Vyāsa's bidding to Janamejaya at his snake sacrifice so that he could hear the story of his ancestors; and how Ugrashravas, who overheard Vaishampāyana's narration, brought it to Shaunaka and the other seers of the Naimisha Forest. *Upaparvan* six, "The Descent of the First Generations," then takes one through the birth of Vyāsa (son of the seer Parāshara and the ferryboat girl Satyavatī) and the descent of the gods to rescue the goddess Earth (who seeks their aid in ridding her of oppressive demons) to an account of the origins of gods, demons, and other beings.

Upaparvan seven begins with the epic's first two *upākhyānas*, on *Shakuntalā* and *Yayāti*, to take us into the genealogy of the early Lunar Dynasty and down to the youths of the main heroes, with heightened attention given to the second generation before them: beginning with the third *upākhyāna* about Mahābhīsha, a royal sage residing in heaven whose boldness with the heavenly river Gaṅgā leads to their marriage on earth, he as King Shāntanu; Bhīshma's birth as their ninth and sole surviving son, and Gaṅgā's departure once Shāntanu asks why she drowned the first eight; Shāntanu's second marriage to Satyavatī, now a fisher-princess, upon her father's obtaining Bhīshma's double vow to renounce kingship and women, for which Shāntanu gives Bhīshma the boon to be able to choose his moment of death; Bhīshma's abduction of three sisters, two of whom become brides for Shāntanu and Satyavatī's second son, who dies soon after becoming king, leaving the two as widows, and the third, the unwedded Ambā, with thoughts of revenge against Bhīshma; Satyavatī's determination to save the line by getting the two widowed queens pregnant, first by asking Bhīshma, who refuses to break his vow of celibacy, and then, admitting her premarital affair, recalling her first son Vyāsa; Vyāsa's unions with the two widowed sisters, cursing the first to bear a blind son because she had closed her eyes at his hideous ascetic ugliness and the second to bear a pale son because she had blanched; the births of the blind Dhritarāshṭra, the pale Pāṇḍu, plus a third son, Vidura, sired with the first widow's low caste maidservant. The fourth *upākhyāna*, named after the sage Aṇimāndavya, then tells how Vidura came to suffer a low caste human birth because this sage cursed the god Dharma (lord of postmortem punishments and thus tantamount in this debut to Yama, god of the dead) to undergo such a birth after the sage learned that he had been impaled "unjustly" as Dharma's punishment for a childhood sin in his previous life. Then comes the marriage of Dhritarashṭra to Gāndhārī and the birth of their sons, the hundred Kauravas, incarnate demons headed by Duryodhana; the marriages of Pāṇḍu to Kuntī and Mādrī and, after Kuntī tells the eventually impotent Pāṇḍu *upākhyāna* five about a queen made pregnant by her husband Vyushitashva even after he was dead, she reveals the means that make possible the birth of the five Pāṇḍavas as sons of gods—Yudhishṭhira of Dharma, Bhīma of the Wind god, Arjuna of Indra (all sons of Kuntī), and the twins Nakula and Sahadeva sired by the Ashvin twins with Mādrī. The young cousins then begin their early lives up to their initiations in weapons, to which they are introduced, via Bhīshma, to the Brahman guru Droṇa, and continue on to the friendships and rivalries they form with others who receive Droṇa's martial training, notably Ashvatthāman (Droṇa's son) and Karṇa (born from Kuntī's premarital union with the Sun god), both of whom will ally with the Kauravas; and the Vrishṇis and Andhakas (1.122.46)—unnamed for now, but among whom one cannot exclude Krishna and Sātyaki who will join the Pāṇḍavas and Kritavarman who joins the Kauravas.

Upaparvans 8 to 11 then tell how the Pāndavas must hide in the forest after Duryodhana tries to kill them. There Bhīma marries a Rākshasī (demoness) who bears him a Rākshasa son, Ghaṭotkaca, who goes off with his mother to the wilds but remains available for filial tasks. At Vyāsa's prompting, the Pāṇḍavas then live in a village for a while disguised as Brahmans, and then, upon another appearance of Vyāsa, make their way to Pañcāla, where Vyāsa tells them they will meet their destined bride (1.157). On the way, the Gandharva Citraratha challenges Arjuna and is defeated, and upon being shown mercy by Yudhishṭhira, tells the Pāṇḍavas they are vulnerable without keeping a priest and holy fires, and then relates the *upākhyāna*s of Tapatī, Vasishtha, and Aurva—stories about one of their ancestresses and two Brahmans, which prepare them for forthcoming adventures while imparting some positive and negative information on sexuality. *Upaparvan* 12 then tells how the Pāṇḍavas, still disguised as Brahmans, marry Draupadī. Arjuna wins her in an archery contest, and then all five find the pretext to marry her jointly in some mistaken yet irreversible words of Kuntī. Both Krishna and Vyāsa sanction the marriage, the latter by telling Draupadī's father Drupada the ninth *upākhyāna* (so called in the *Parvasaṃgraha*) about the "Five Former Indras," which reveals that Draupadī is the goddess Shrī incarnate and that the Pāṇḍavas were all former husbands of hers as previous Indras, making the marriage virtually monogamous. After some amends are made between the two camps, and the Pāṇḍavas are given the Khāṇḍava Tract in which to found their own half of the kingdom (*upaparvans* 13–15), the seer Nārada arrives at their new capital, Indraprastha, to tell the tenth *upākhyāna* (so called in the *Parvasaṃgraha*) of "Sunda and Upasunda" about two demonic brothers who kill each other over a woman, thereby warning the Pāṇḍavas to regulate their time with Draupadī and providing them a reverse mirror story of their own situation (*upaparvan* 16)—and the very rule that will send Arjuna into a period of exile in which he will marry three other women, including Krishna's sister Subhadrā (*upaparvans* 17–18). Finally, *upaparvan* 19 tells how Arjuna and Krishna's burning of the Khāṇḍava Forest satisfies the fire god Agni and reveals their former identities as the great *rishi*s Nara and Nārāyaṇa. The conflagration clears the ground for the construction of Indraprastha, and leads into the narration of *upākhyāana* eleven about four precocious birds reminiscent of the Vedas, who escape the blaze.

Book 2, the *Sabhāparvan*, or "Book of the Assembly Hall(s)," takes seven of its nine *upaparvans* to tell how the great audience hall at Indraprastha was built; how Nārada convinced Yudhishṭhira to assert paramountcy there by performing a Rājasūya (royal consecration) sacrifice, and the obstacles that entailed—most notably, at Krishna's urging, the killing of Jarāsandha, a rival for paramountcy as king of Magadha who had forced Krishna's people to flee from Mathura to Dvārakā, and Krishna's killing of his obstreperous cousin Shishupāla. Its last two *upaparvans* then enter the epic's dark heart, describing events that occur in the Kaurava assembly hall at Hāstinapura: how Duryodhana, spurred to jealousy, plotted with his maternal uncle Shakuni to challenge Yudhishṭhira to a "friendly dice match"; how Shakuni, playing for Duryodhana, won everything, leaving Draupadī to be the last wager after Yudhishṭhira had bet himself; how Draupadī, knowing this, asked if Yudhishṭhira had bet himself before betting her, setting the court to debate this question as one of *dharma* while Yudhishṭhira, the son of Dharma, kept silent "as if he were mad"; how Duhshāsana, second oldest of the hundred Kauravas, tried to disrobe Draupadī, and was frustrated when Krishna miraculously multiplied her saris; how Dhritarāshṭra then terminated the unresolved debate by offering Draupadī three boons, of which she said two were enough: her husbands' freedom and the return of their weapons; how Duryodhana, grumbling at this result, invited the Pāṇḍavas to a return match with a one-throw winner-take-all stake—that the loser undertake twelve years of forest exile followed by one year incognito as the condition of recovering their half of the kingdom; and how, having lost again, the Pāṇḍavas made vows of revenge and departed with Draupadī for the forest.

Book 3, the *Araṇyakaparvan,* or "Book of Forest Teachings," then comprises sixteen *upaparvans* and tells twenty-one *upākhyānas*. After a transitional *upaparvan* 29, in which Krishna tells Book 3's first *upākhyāna*—the *Saubhavadha-Upākhyāna* (3.1–23)—to explain his absence from the dice match, the most notable *upaparvans* are the second through fourth and the last three. The first series tells of the Pāṇḍavas' forest-entering encounter with the monstrous Rākshasa Kirmīra, killed by Bhīma; Arjuna's encounter with Shiva on Mount Kailasa to obtain divine weapons; and Arjuna's further adventures in the heaven of his father Indra (*upaparvans* 30–32). Then, after many wanderings, the last three *upaparvans*, 42–44, tell how Draupadī was abducted by the Kauravas' brother-in-law Jayadratha, how Karṇa gave his natural-born golden armor and earrings to Indra in exchange for an "unfailing dart" that he can only use once, and how, in closing, Yudhishṭhira saved his brothers' lives by answering a *yaksha*'s (goblin's) questions (an *upākhyāna* according to the *Parvasaṃgraha*). Between these episodes, seers tell the Pāṇḍavas and Draupadī numerous stories, many billed as *upākhyānas*. Most are told to edify them on their pilgrim routes. Thus nine are told during the "Tour of the Sacred Fords" (*upaparvan* 33) to the group (minus Arjuna)—eight of these by their traveling companion, the seer Lomasha. The best known of these are the first three: the *Agastya-*, *Rishyashriṅga-*, and *Kārtavīrya-Upākhyānas*. And the next six are later narrated by the ageless sage Mārkaṇḍeya to the reassembled Pāṇḍavas and Draupadī in *upaparvan* 37.

But the second and last two *upākhyānas* stand out as what Biardeau calls "mirror stories": the *Nala-Upākhyāna*—the love story about Nala and Damayantī told by the seer Brihadashva while Arjuna is visiting Shiva and Indra, and Draupadī misses this favorite of her husbands; the *Rāma-Upakhyāna*, the Mahābhārata's main Rāma story focused on Sītā's abduction and told to all five Pāṇḍavas and Draupadī by Mārkaṇḍeya just after Draupadī's abduction; and the *Sāvitrī-Upākhyāna*—the story of a heroine who saved her husband from Yama, death, as told by Mārkaṇḍeya just after the *Rāma-Upākhyāna* when Yudhishṭhira asks, having already heard about Sītā (and perhaps slighting her), if there ever was a woman as devoted to her husband(s) as Draupadī. The book ends as it began with the encounter of a monster, who, appearing first as a speaking crane, for the moment "kills" the four youngest Pāṇḍavas by a lake where they have gone to slake their thirst. But whereas the first monster was a Rākshasa, this crane turns into a one-eyed *yaksha* before he reveals himself, after questioning Yudhisṭhira, to be Yudhishṭhira's father Dharma in disguise. Gratified at his son's subtle answers to his puzzling questions, Dharma revives Dharmarāja Yudhishṭhira's brothers and gives him the boon of "the heart of the dice"—something that had saved Nala in the *Nala-Upākhyāna* and is now a cue to Yudhishṭhira not only to remember that story but to disguise himself as a dice-master in Book 4.

Book 4, the *Virāṭaparvan* or "Book of Virāṭa," has four *upaparvans* (45–48). The first tells how Yudhishṭhira chooses the kingdom of Matsya (Fish) for the Pāṇḍavas and Draupadī's thirteenth year of living incognito, how each chooses a disguise, and how they fool the Matsya king Virāṭa with these topsy-turvy identities when they enter his capital: Yudhishṭhira as a Brahman dice-master, Bhīma a cook, Draupadī a chambermaid-hairdresser, Arjuna an impotent dance master dressed in skirts, and the twins as handlers of horses and cattle. The other three *upaparvans* tell how Bhīma kills Kīcaka, the Matsya queen's brother, who had abused Draupadī; how the effeminate looking Arjuna, first driving the young Matsya prince Uttara's chariot and then reversing charioteer/warrior roles with him, singlehandedly defeats a raid on the kingdom by the leading Kauravas; and how Arjuna refuses the thankful Virāṭa's offer of his daughter Uttarā to him in marriage and arranges instead that she marry his son with Subhadrā, Abhimanyu, an incarnation of the splendor of the moon, who is destined to carry the genealogical thread of the lunar dynasty forward to Janamejaya.

Book 5, the *Udyogaparvan* or "Book of the Effort," a book of surprising symmetries and asymmetries, comprises eleven *upaparvans*, the front nine of which occur as efforts are made by messengers from both sides to state terms for peace or war even while everyone prepares for the latter. The initial *Upaparvan* 49 also traces how both sides try to secure the alliance of certain asymmetrically mutual kinsmen. Arjuna and Duryodhana come to Dvārakā to seek aide from Krishna, Arjuna's mother's brother's son and also his wife Subhadrā's brother. Krishna says bafflingly that his relation to each is equal, but since he saw Arjuna first he gives him the first choice of two options: Krishna as a noncombatant charioteer, or a whole army division composed of Krishna's Gopā Nārāyaṇa warriors. Arjuna chooses Krishna, and Duryodhana departs content (5.7). Then Shalya, king of Madra and brother of the twins' mother Mādrī, sets out to join the Pāṇḍavas but has his mind turned after he finds elegant way-stations along his route prepared for him by Duryodhana. Traveling on, he tells Yudhishṭhira that he has just allied with Duryodhana, and Yudhishṭhira, foreseeing that Shalya will be Karṇa's charioteer, asks him to destroy Karṇa's confidence in combat. Telling Yudhishṭhira that even Indra had ups and downs, Shalya consoles him with Book 5's first *upākhyāna*, a cycle of three ultimately triumphant Indra stories called the *Indravijaya-Upākhyāna*. Before this *upaparvan* is over, the Pāṇḍavas have seven army divisions and the Kauravas eleven.

As negotiations continue through the next eight *upaparvans*, events come to center on the lengthy sixth, *upaparvan* 54, titled "The Coming of the Lord," in which Krishna as divine messenger comes as the Pāṇḍavas' last negotiator with the Kauravas while a host of celestial seers descends to watch the proceedings and tell stories: one of them an *upākhyāna* told as a warning to Duryodhana by by Rāma Jāmadagnya about how the arrogant King Dambhodbhava was humbled by Nara and Nārāyaṇa. When arbitrations break down, Duryodhana tries to capture Krishna, who displays a divine and heroic host emanating from his body while bestowing on some in the court the "divine eye" to see it. Then Krishna quits the court. *Upaparvan* 55 then begins with the beautiful scenes in which Karṇa, even learning that he is Kuntī's firstborn son, resists the double temptations offered by Krishna and Kuntī to break his friendship with Duryodhana and side with the Pāṇḍavas. The negotiations end in *upaparvan* 58 with a last abusive message delivered to the Pāṇḍavas by Shakuni's son Ulūka (Duryodhana's mother's brother's son, who thus has the same relation to Duryodhana that Krishna has to Arjuna). Then, after all the armies have gathered and their heroes been evaluated by Bhīshma, Book 5 closes with *upaparvan* 60, the *Ambā-Upākhyāna-Parvan*, most of which, from its beginning, comprises Book 5's third *upākhyāna*, the *Ambā-Upākhyāna*, in which Bhīshma tells Duryodhana how Ambā, determined to destroy him, came to be reborn as Draupadī's brother Shikhaṇḍin, and why he will not fight Shikhaṇḍin because he was formerly a woman. Book 5 thus has one *upākhyāna* in its first *upaparvan*, leaving its listener Yudhishṭhira with a fateful secret about Karṇa that will advantage Yudhishṭhira in the war, and another in its last *upaparvan* leaving its listener Duryodhana with a fateful secret about Bhīshma that will disadvantage Duryodhana in the war.

Books 6 through 9 span the war's actual fighting through eighteen days at Kurukshetra, the Field of the Kurus. Each of the four war books is named after the marshal who leads the Kaurava army and is slain by the book's end. Although various side- and background-narratives are told in these books, only five of them are called *upākhyā*.

Book 6, the *Bhāshmaparvan*, contains five *upaparvans* (60–64). In the first, on Bhīshma's consecration as marshal, Vyāsa gives the Kaurava court bard Saṃjaya the "divine eye" with which to see the war in its entirety and report on it to Dhritarāshṭra, and promises that Saṃjaya will survive the war to do so. Then, after two *upaparvans* on cosmological matters, the fourth (63) includes the Bhagavad Gītā: just before the war, Saṃjaya reports how Krishna tells Arjuna various legal, philosophical, and divinely ordained reasons why Arjuna cannot renounce his duty to fight, and provides the disciplines (*yogas*) whereby Arjuna can perform action without desire for its fruits. The bulk of Book 6 is then the "Parvan on the Death of Bhīshma" (64), which begins when Yudhishṭhira crosses the battlefield to take leave of his elders Bhīshma, Droṇa, the Brahman Kripa, and Shalya. Early in the fighting Bhīshma pauses to tell Duryodhana the *Vishva-Upākhyāna*, revealing mysteries about Krishna. After ten days of fighting, Bhīshma falls at the hands of Arjuna and Shikhaṇḍin. So filled with arrows that no part of his body touches the ground, Bhīshma makes this his "bed of arrows" and uses the boon his father gave him to postpone his death for fifty-eight days until the winter solstice.

Book 7, the *Droṇaparvan*, contains eight *upaparvans* (65–72) and covers the war's next five days. Its train of deaths is fraught with sacrificial symbolism and deepens a theological current, especially in an overture and coda that balance the mutual impact of Krishna and Shiva. Early in the first *upaparvan*, in what Gombach calls "a surprising turn" (2000, II, p. 174), Dhritarāshṭra composes himself to hear about the killing of Droṇa by recounting to Saṃjaya the "divine feats" of Krishna, including that he saw Krishna's theophany in his own court in Book 5. Then, as *Upaparvan* 66 takes us from the eleventh into the twelfth day of battle, a group of sworn warriors that includes Krishna's Gopa Nārāyaṇas detains Arjuna at the southern end of the battlefield while Droṇa attacks Yudhishṭhira. Later that same day, Arjuna directs Krishna toward King Bhagadatta of Prāgjyotisha, who uses mantras to change his elephant hook into a Vaishṇava weapon, which Krishna intercepts on his chest before it hits Arjuna, turning it into flowers.

Upaparvan 67 then describes day thirteen, in which the chief event is the entrapment and killing of Abhimanyu in a circular array from which Jayadratha, thanks to a boon from Shiva, is able to block his exit. Arjuna then vows to kill Jayadratha on day fourteen or commit suicide, and Krishna helps him fulfill this incautious vow just before sunset by making it seem the sun has already set: Jayadratha raises his head to look at the atmospherics and loses it (*upaparvans* 68–69). Fighting continues deep into the night, and Krishna connives to get Karṇa to exhaust the one-use "unfailing dart" he got from Indra. Krishna prods Ghaṭotkaca to use his prodigious night-fighting powers as a Rākshasa against Karṇa, drawing Karṇa to use up the dart. And at Ghaṭotkaca's titanic fall Krishna does a little dance of joy, explaining that the dart can no longer spell Arjuna's death (*upaparvan* 70). Then, on day fifteen, Droṇa is killed by Dhrishṭadyumna, another brother of Draupadī, after he lays down his weapons, convinced that Yudhishṭhira could not have lied when he told Droṇa that his son Ashvatthāman had been killed (*upaparvan* 71).

Upaparvan 72 then closes Book 7 with a kind of theological coda on Shiva. While the Pāṇḍava ranks betray shame and blame over the foul means used to kill Droṇa, Ashvatthāman vows revenge with a Nārāyaṇa weapon Droṇa had given him, which must never be used against anyone abandoning their chariots. Krishna gets everyone to dismount and the weapon is neutralized. After using up another weapon against Arjuna and Krishna, Ashvatthāman flees but suddenly sees Vyāsa standing before him. Vyāsa explains why the weapons failed: Arjuna and Krishna are the two eternal seers Nara and Nārāyaṇa. Moreover, Shiva and Krishna worship each other. Vyāsa also knows Ashvatthāman's previous lives in which he pleased Shiva and was his devotee. Ashvatthāman bows to Shiva and acknowledges Krishna. Vyāsa then "arrives by chance" before Arjuna, who questions him about the fiery being he has seen preceding him in battle and killing foes. Vyāsa reveals this to be Shiva, recites a hymn to him, and goes "as he came." As Gombach observes (2000, I, pp. 216–219), the *Droṇaparvan* is notable for its ancillary stories involving Shiva, of which there are two more (7.69.49–71; 119.1–28). Jayadratha's blocking of Abhimanyu is also enabled by a boon from Shiva.

Surprisingly, Book 8, the *Karṇaparvan*, is an *upaparvan* in itself, number 73. By the end of day fifteen the Kauravas regroup, and make Karṇa marshal that night. After minor skirmishes on day sixteen end with the Kauravas demoralized, Karṇa promises to kill Arjuna on the seventeenth, and Arjuna likewise promises Yudhishṭhira—by now obsessed about Karṇa—that he will kill Karṇa. Karṇa requests Shalya as his charioteer, since he regards Shalya as the only match for Krishna's charioteering, and Duryodhana tells Karṇa and Shalya an *upākhyāna* about how Brahmā came to be Shiva's charioteer in the conquest of Tripura, the "Triple City" of the demons. Shalya agrees, on the condition that he can say what he pleases, and engages Karṇa in a duel of insults that includes still another *upākhyāna* in which he compares Karṇa to a crow challenging a gander (probably as part of fulfilling his promise to Yudhishthira to undermine Karṇa's confidence). As the day wears on, Bhīma drinks Duhshāsana's blood, fulfilling a vow he had made at Draupadī's disrobing, and Arjuna, prompted by Krishna, finally beheads Karṇa at sunset.

Book 9, the *Shalyaparvan*, usually has four *upaparvans* (74–77). Shalya is quickly slain in *upaparvan* 74 by Yudhishṭhira, who marvelously changes from mild to fierce. Duryodhana rallies his forces briefly. But when he is unable to find his remaining allies, he tells Saṃjaya to tell his father he has entered a lake. He does this by solidifying the waters with his *māyā*, or power of illusion. This is the Dvaipāyana Lake (29.53) one that bears the name of the author.

Upaparvan 76 begins with Duryodhana recuperating in the lake. The three Kaurava survivors, Ashvatthāman, Kripa, and Kritavarman, learn his whereabouts and implore him to come out and renew the fight, which Duryodhana says he will do tomorrow. Some hunters overhear and tell the Pāṇḍavas. Krishna urges Yudhishṭhira to force Duryodhana out of the lake by counteracting Duryodhana's *māyā* with his own. But Yudhishṭhira, "as if smiling" (when dealing with Krishna, Yudhishṭhira, unlike Arjuna, tends to have a mind of his own), only scolds Duryodhana for retreating from battle. Duryodhana says he is resting and will come out to fight tomorrow, adding that, with his brothers gone, he has no desire to rule and would offer the earth to Yudhishṭhira. Boldly replying that Duryodhana no longer has the earth to offer, Yudhishthira goads him into making a challenge to duel one Pāṇḍava. And to Krishna's dismay, he also offers Duryodhana the choice of both foe and weapon. Duryodhana breaks up through the solidified waters shouldering his iron mace, and returns the challenge to the Pāṇḍavas to choose which one will fight him. Alarmed at the predicament, Krishna says Bhīma is the only possible choice, and that it will be Bhīma's might versus Duryodhana's skill. As the two begin to taunt each other, Krishna's brother Balarāma, who trained them both, has neared Kurukshetra on his forty-two-day pilgrimage up the Sarasvati River, and hurries to see the duel between his disciples. From this point, the rest of *upaparvan* 76 is a flashback in which Vaishampāyana describes the pilgrimage while supplying stories, including two *upākhyānas* (one so called only in passing, at 9.42.28) relevant to sites along the way.

Once Balarāma arrives, the narrative returns to Saṃjaya with *upaparvan* 77, "The Battle of the Bludgeons." When the going gets tough, Krishna prompts Arjuna to signal Bhīma to strike Duryodhana's thighs. Shattering both thighs and driving Duryodhana to the ground, the savagely indignant Bhīma also kicks his head with his left foot. Yudhishṭhira tells Bhīma to desist. Balarāma wants him punished for breaking the rules of mace-fighting. But Krishna tells Balarāma the Pāṇḍavas are "our natural friends" (59.13), reminds him of all the vows and debts that Bhīma has just fulfilled, and urges him to recall that "the Kali Age has arrived" (21). Seeing Krishna and the Pāṇḍavas celebrate, Duryodhana denounces Krishna for his dodgy tactics, and hearing Krishna rebuke him in turn, proclaims himself to have lived a glorious life—words met by a rain of celestial flowers. Krishna then justifies his tactics by the argument of divine precedence. While the Pāṇḍavas visit the forlorn Kaurava camp, Duryodhana sends a final message through Saṃjaya to his parents and his three surviving allies. When the three see him in his grim plight, Duryodhana asks Kripa to consecrate Ashvatthāman as his (fifth) marshal, and the three leave to hatch their plot.

Book 10, the *Sauptikaparvan* or "Book of the Night Raid," tells how Ashvatthāman (possessed by Shiva), Kripa, and Kritavarman massacre the sleeping remnant of the Pāṇḍava army in their camp, which the Pāṇḍavas have vacated at Krishna's recommendation. They kill all the remaining Matsyas and kinsmen of Draupadī, as well as her children. Book 11, the *Strīparvan* or "Book of the Women," treats the women's lamentations for the slain warriors.

Books 12, the *Shāntiparvan* or "Book of the Peace," begins to tell how Yudhishṭhira, beset by grief over all the warriors slain so that he could rule, is persuaded by his family, counselors (including Krishna, Nārada, and Vyāsa), and Bhīshma to give up his guiltridden aspirations to renunciation and accept his royal duties. In its early going, Krishna contributes three *upākhyāna*s. At the capital, he recites two in a row: first, a string of sixteen vignettes about ancient kings whose deaths were also lamented, and then a death-and-revival tale about a boy named "Excretor of Gold" that briefly lightens Yudhishṭhira's mood. On the way to joining Bhīshma at Kurukshetra, he then describes Rāma Jāmadagnya's twenty-one massacres of the Kshatriyas there, answering Yudhishṭhira's curiosity about how the warrior class kept regenerating. For the rest, ten *upākhyāna*s are dispersed through Bhīshma's multigenre instructions in the three anthologies on *Rājadharma*, "laws for kings," *Āpaddharma*, "law for times of distress," and *Mokshadharma*, "norms concerning liberation" (*upaparvan*s 84-86). Bhīshma's *Shāntiparvan upākhyāna*s are noteworthy for the long dryspells between them. There are never two in a row; in the *Mokshadharma* one finds intervals of as many as sixty-four (12.194-257) and seventy-six (12.264-339) *adhyāya*s between them. Yet there is a striking pattern. Four of these *upākhyāna*s confront the Dharma King Yudhishṭhira with "puzzle pieces" about *dharma* in which lead characters are either his own father, the god Dharma, in disguise, or figures who bear the word *dharman*/*dharma* in their names. Moreover, one such tale occurs as the last *upākhyāna* in each anthology. Thus Dharma himself appears disguised in the *Sumitra-Upākhyāna* or *Rishabha Gita* near the end of the *Rājadharma*; a magnificent crane bears the name Rājadharman in "The Story of the Ungrateful Brahman" (*Kritaghna-Upākhyāna*) that ends the *Āpaddharma*; and, after Dharma appears in another disguise in the *Jāpaka-Upākhyāna*, the *Mokshadharma*'s first *upākhyāna*, that sub-*parvan* ends with the story of a questioning Brahman named Dharmaraṇya, "Forest of Dharma," who, like Yudhishṭhira at this juncture, has questions about the best practice to pursue toward gaining heaven—which turns out to be eating only what is gleaned after grains and other food have been harvested (*Uñchavritti-Upākhyāna*). Since Book 3 ends with an episode (an *upākhyāna*, according to the *Parvasaṃgraha*) where Dharma appears disguised as a crane and a *yaksha*, it would appear that one strain of the epic's *upākhyāna*s carries a major subcurrent through such puzzle pieces, especially in that they frequently punctuate the ends of major units. Moreover, with one such story ending the *Shāntiparvan*, we have reached the juncture mentioned earlier where Bhīshma is launching his only concentrated stretch of *upākhyāna*s.

Book 13, the *Anushāsanaparvan* or "Book of the Further Instructions," begins with Bhīshma's fourth anthology: his closing instructions to Yudhishṭhira on *Dānadharma*, "the law of the gift" (*upaparvan* 87). Here we must consider Fitzgerald's hypothesis that the four anthologies demonstrate decreasing "tautness" and increasing relaxation as the result of "a progressive loosening of editorial integration" (2004, pp. 147–148) over centuries, from the second century B.C. down to the fourth-to-fifth century A.D. (p. 114). Fitzgerald's point is buttressed by the general impression scholars have had that the *Anushāsanaparvan* is loose and late. R. N. Dandekar, the Critical Edition editor of this last-to-be-completed *parvan*, perhaps puts it best:

> The scope and nature of the contents of this *parvan* were such that literally any topic under the sun could be broached and discussed in it. . . . This has resulted in poor Yudhishṭhira being represented as putting to his grandsire some of the most elementary questions—often without rhyme or reason. Not infrequently, these questions serve as mere excuses for introducing a legend or a doctrine fancied by the redactor, no matter if it has already occurred in an earlier part of the Epic, not once but several times (1966, xlvii).

No doubt Dandekar had the *Bhangāshvana-Upākhyāna* principally in mind, in which Yudhishṭhira, indeed quite out of the blue, asks, "In the act of coition, who derives the greater pleasure—man or woman" (13.12.1; Dandekar 1966, p. lix), and thereby launches Bhīshma into a tale that makes the case that the luckier ones are women. But Yudhishṭhira is hardly a simpleton. He is portrayed throughout as having an underlying guilelessness that sustains him. The four anthologies repeatedly reinforce this trope, but nowhere more pivotally than in the transition from Book 12 to 13, which marks Yudhishṭhira's revived interest in stories. He begins Book 13 stating that he is unable to regain peace of mind, even after Book 12, "out of the conviction that he alone had been responsible for the tragic catastrophe of the war," and that he feels "particularly unhappy at the pitiable condition" of Bhīshma (Dandekar 1966, pp. lvii–lviii). But once Bhīshma tells him the opening "Dialogue (*Saṃvāda*) Between Death, Gautamī, and Others," Yudhishṭhira replies, "O grandsire, wisest of men, you who are learned in all the treatises, I have listened to this great narrative (*ākhyāna*), O foremost of the intelligent. I desire to hear a little more narrated by you in connection with *dharma*, O king. You are able to narrate it to me. Tell me if any householder has ever succeeded in conquering Mrityu (Death) by the practice of *dharma*" (13.2.1-3). This appeal launches Book 13's first *upākhyāna*, the *Sudarshana-Upākhyāna*, on how, by following the "the law of treating guests" (*atithidharma*), Death may indeed be overcome, a tale that reveals that the divine guest through whom a householder can overcome Death by showing him full hospitality—even to the point of offering him his wife—is Dharma himself. This would be a clever, beautiful, and relieving revelation to Dharma's son Yudhishṭhira, who, just after hearing the *Mokshadharma* on "the norms of liberation," which he knows cannot really be for him if he is to rule, hears a story that points the way to understanding how he can still overcome death by cultivating the generosity of a gifting royal householder.

Why is Bhīshma unbottled at this juncture? Granted that the *Dānadharmaparvan* is relatively loose and likely late, to the point of including entries down to "the last moment," it need be no later than its literary unfolding within the Mahābhārata's primary archetypal design. The four anthologies get more and more relaxed from one to the next because the interlocutors do as well. In the *Dānadharma*, they are at last beginning to enjoy themselves, to put the war behind them, to treasure the dwindling light of leisure they still have to raise questions and delight in stories on the bank of the Gaṅgā before Gaṅgā's son Bhīshma puts his learned life behind him. Cutting away for Vaishampāyana to describe the scene to Janamejaya, we hear, amid praise of the Gaṅgā, how forty-five celestial seers arrive to tell stories (*kathās*) "related to Bhīshma" (13.27.10), stories that cheer one and all—even at the seers' parting, when Yudhishṭhira touches Bhīshma's feet with his head "at the end of a story (*kathānte*)" (13.27.17) and returns to his questioning, which leads Bhīshma to tell him the *Mataṅga-Upākhyāna*. This anticipatory theme of not ending at the end of a story, of keeping the story going with a new story, comes up again when Bhīshma winds up the *Vipula-Upākhyāna* by telling how Mārkaṇḍeya had formerly told it to him "in the interval of a story (*kathāntare*) on Gaṅgā's bank" (13.43.17). It is as if living in ongoing stories alongside the salvific river is a main current in Yudhishṭhira's atonement, and that after the relative dialogical stringency of the three anthologies of the *Shāntiparvan*, it is good to get back to *upākhyānas* in "The Book of the Further Instruction." This bears further on the matter raised by Dandekar of returning to stories "no matter if" they have "already occurred." When Bhīshma and Yudhishṭhira return to such stories—most notably the *Vishvāmitra-Upākhyāna* (13.3–4) with its familiar cast of revolving characters (Vishvāmitra, Vasishtha, Jamadagni, Rīma Jāmadagnya, etc.)—it is from a new and different angle and, as always with any story, from the pleasure of hearing it again.

Book 13 then closes with a short *upaparvan* 88, describing Bhīshma's final ascent to heaven from his bed of arrows, attended by has celestial mother Gaṅgā.

With Book 14, the *Āshvamedhikaparvan* or "Book of the Horse Sacrifice," Yudhishṭhira, grieving once again over Bhīshma's demise and his guilt over the war, agrees to perform a sin-cleansing Horse Sacrifice at Vyāsa and Krishna's bidding. While the Pāṇḍavas prepare for it, Krishna wants to see his people in Dvārakā, and on the way he meets the sage Uttaṅka for the multistoried *Uttaṅka-Upākhyāna*. Arjuna then has many adventures guarding the horse. But immediately upon the rite's completion an angry half-golden blue-eyed mongoose appears from his hole to disparage the grand ceremony as inferior to the practice of gleaning. With this incident comes the *Mahabharata*'s final *upākhāana*: this time a double puzzle story that reveals the mongoose to have been Dharma in disguise, and before that a mysterious guest who tested the anger of the *rishi* Jamadagni. It addresses the question of whether a king's giving to Brahmans and others in sacrifice is comparable to the gleaner's "pure gift" (*shuddha dāna*; 14.93.57), done with devotion and faith and without anger, to Dharma, that ever-demanding guest. Again, a major unit ends with an *upākhyāna* puzzle piece on this theme.

Book 15, the *Āshrāmavāsikaparvan*, or "Book of the Residence in the Hermitage," tells of the final days of the Pāṇḍavas' elders Dhritarāshṭra, Gāndhārī, Vidura, and Kuntī at a hermitage. Book 16, the *Mausalaparvan*, or "Book of the Iron Clubs," tells of the final days of Krishna's people in Dvārakā, including Krishna and Balarāma.

Book 17, the *Mahāprasthānikaparvan*, or "Book of the Great Departure," describes the final journey of the Pāṇḍavas and Draupadī. Book 18, the *Svargārohaṇaparvan*, or "Book of the Ascent to Heaven," describes how Yudhishṭhira gets to heaven in his own body after one last test by his father Dharma in the disguise of a dog, and what he finds in heaven and in hell, before he gets back to heaven.

The Essence of the Subtales

There is one other reference to the epic's *upākhyānas* that is yet to be plumbed. It occurs toward the end of Book 12 in the highly devotional *Nārāyaṇīya* (which includes the *upākhyāna* narrated by Ugrashravas to the

Naimisha Forest *rishis* about Vishnu's manifestation as the Horse's Head). This takes us back where we began: to the "oceanic mind" of the author, and also to the *Āstīkaparvan* substory called "The Churning of the Ocean" (1.15–17). One should also recall that Duryodhana finds his last relief in an otherwise unheard of Dvaipāyana Lake.

About one-third of the way through the *Nārāyaṇīya*, itself an eighteen-chapter epitome of the Mahābhārata (although the Critical Edition splits a chapter and makes it nineteen), Bhīshma says that the story he has just told Yudhishṭhira about Nārada's journey to "White Island" (*Shvetadvīpa*)—an island somewhere on the northern shore of the milky ocean—is a "narrative (*ākhyānam*) coming from a seer-based transmission (*ārsheyam pāramparyāgatam*) that should not be given" to anyone who is not a devotee of Vishnu (12.326.113), and, moreover, that it is the "essence" of all the "other *upākhyāna*s" he has transmitted:

> Of those hundreds of other virtuous subtales (*anyāni . . . upākhyānaśatāni . . . dharmyāndi*) that are heard from me, king, this is raised up (or extracted, ladled out: *uddhtaḥ*) as their essence (*sāro*); just as nectar was raised up by the gods and demons, having churned (the ocean), even so this nectar of story (*kathāmritam*) was formerly raised up by the sages. (12.326.114–115)

Hearing this, Yudhishṭhira and all the Pāṇḍavas become Nārāyana devotees. This suggests that one could count the "White Island" story as a sixty-eighth *upākhyāna*. More than that, Bhīshma holds that it is the essence of them all. He has also used *ākhyāna* and *upākhyāna* interchangeably with each other and with *kathā*, story. And when he speaks of the "hundreds of other virtuous *upākhyāna*s that are heard from me," he probably implies not only those he has just told Yudhishṭhira in the *Shāntiparvan*, but all the others he has told or will tell elsewhere, and those which have been recited by others, which Bhīshma, given his heavenly and earthly sources, would be likely to know.

Still within the *Nārāyaṇīya*, just after its next major narrative, Shaunaka (correcting the Critical Edition, which makes the speaker Vaishampāyana) says to the bard (*sauti*) Ugrashravas:

> O Sauti, very great is the narrative (*ākhyāna*) recited by you, having heard which, the sages are all gone to the highest wonder. . . . Surely having churned the supreme ocean of knowledge by this hundred thousand (verse) Bhārata narrative (*akhyāna*) with the churning of your thought—as butter from milk, as sandal from Mount Malaya, and as Āraṇyaka (forest instruction) from the Vedas, as nectar from herbs—so is this supreme nectar of story (*kathāmritam*) . . . raised up [as] spoken by you, which rests on the story (*kathā*) of Nārāyaṇa. (12.331.1–4)

Although Shaunaka commends Ugrashravas for "having churned the supreme ocean of knowledge by this hundred thousand (verse) *Bhārata-ākhyāna* with the churning of *your* thought" (that is, Ugrashravas's thought), we must remember that Ugrashravas is only said to be transmitting the Mahābhārata to the Naimisha Forest *rishis* as the "entire thought" of Vyāsa (1.1.23). This suggests that the full hundred thousand verses—with the *upākhyāna*s included—of the *Bhārata-ākhyāna* were churned first by Vyāsa before they were rechurned by Ugrashravas, with Vaishampāyana, their intermediary, having also delivered Vyāsa's "entire thought" (1.55.2) at Janamejaya's snake sacrifice, where Ugrashravas overheard it.

Then, still within the *Mokshadharma* anthology of the *Shāntiparvan*, before these two passages but leading up to the story of Shuka (12.310–320), there is a third passage that uses the same metaphor and similes. It occurs within Bhīshma's account of the lengthy instruction that Vyāsa gives to his firstborn son Shuka (12.224–246), who is not only one of Vyāsa's five disciples (Vaishampāyana being another) to have first heard the Mahābhārata from him, but the son who will obtain liberation before the Mahābhārata—despite Shuka's having heard it—can have fully happened. Says Vyāsa,

> Untraditional and unprecedented, the secret of all the Vedas, this treatise (*shāstra*), of which everyone can convince himself, is instruction for my son (*putrānuśāsanam*). By churning the wealth that is contained in all the narratives (*ākhyṅa*s) about *dharma* and all the narratives about truth, as also the ten thousand Rigvedic verses, this nectar has been raised—like butter from curds and fire from wood, as also the knowledge of the wise, even has this been raised for the sake of my son (*putrahetoḥ samuddhritam*). (12.238.13–15)

The churning metaphor thus finds Vyāsa at its bottom, since he would be the first to use it—before Bhīshma or Ugrashravas. Indeed, Shuka is born when Vyāsa sees a nymph and ejaculates his semen onto his churning fire-sticks (12.311.1-10). Vyāsa's instruction to Shuka would also be churned up from all the *ākhyānas*—presumably of the Mahābhārata, which would imply as well the *upākhyāna*s and likewise imply that this "treatise" for his son epitomizes the Mahābhārata itself. Shuka's agenda of seeking liberation (*moksha*) is set here, and he attains *moksha* toward the end of Book 12 as a boy, soon after he is born, and just before the *Nārāyaṇīya* and Bhīshma's grand run of *upākhyānas* from Book 12 into Book 13. Taking the passage literally, it seems to say that Vyāsa churned all the Mahābhārata's narratives about *dharma* and truth for the sake of Shuka'a liberation, the very thing that Yudhishṭhira, shortly after hearing that story, accepts that he must do without, while asking for further stories.

These churning passages are hightened reflections on at least two of the purposes of narrative within the Mahābhārata's overall grand design: that it all rests on Nārāyaṇa, and that its essence is liberating instruction on both truth and *dharma*. They would seem to reflect the exuberant overview from within on the part of those who were involved in the production of the earliest totality of this work.

Alf Hiltebeitel

See also **Rāmāyaṇa; Rāmāyaṇa and Mahābhārata Paintings**

BIBLIOGRAPHY

Biardeau, Madeleine. "Nala et Damayantī: Héros épiques." Part 1. *Indo-Iranian Journal* 27 (1984): 247–274.

———. "Nala et Damayantī: Héros épiques." Part 2. *Indo-Iranian Journal* 28 (1985): 1–34.

———. *Le Mahābhārata: Un récit fondateur du brahmanisme et son interprétation*. 2 vols. Paris: Éditions du Seuil, 2002.

Brockington, John L. *The Sanskrit Epics*. Handbuch der Orientalistik, Zweite Abteilung, Indien, vol. 12, edited by J. Bronkhorst. Leiden: E. J. Brill, 1998.

Dandekar, R. N, ed. *Anuśāsanaparvan*. Introduction and apparatus. Vol. 17 of *Mahābhārata: Critical Edition*, edited by V. S. Sukthankar et al. 24 vols. with *Harivaśa*. Poona: Bhandarkar Oriental Research Institute, 1966.

Fitzgerald, James L. "The Many Voices of the Mahābhārata." Review of Hiltebeitel, 2001. *Journal of the American Oriental Society* 123, no. 4 (2003): 803–818.

Fitzgerald, James L., trans. and ed. *The Mahābhārata*, vol. 7: 11, *The Book of the Women; 12, The Book of Peace, Part One*. Chicago: University of Chicago Press, 2004.

Ganguli, Kisari Mohan, trans., and Pratap Chandra Roy, pub. *The Mahabharata*. 1884–1896. Reprint, New Delhi: Munshiram Manoharlal, 1970.

Gombach, Barbara. "Ancillary Stories in the Sanskrit Mahābhārata." Ph.D. diss., 2 parts, Columbia University, 2000.

Hiltebeitel, Alf. *The Education of Yudhiṣṭhira: A Reader's Guide to the Education of the Dharma King*. Chicago: University of Chicago Press, 2001.

Shulman, David. *The Wisdom of Poets: Studies in Tamil, Telugu, and Sanskrit*. New Delhi: Oxford University Press, 2001.

van Buitenen, J. A. B. *The Mahābhārata* , vols. I: 1. *The Book of Beginnings;* II: 2. *The Book of the Assembly Hall;* 3. *The Book of the Forest;* III: 4. *The Book of Virata;* 5. *The Book of the Effort*. Chicago: University of Chicago Press, 1973, 1975, 1978.

Van Nooten, Barend A. *The Mahābhārata*. New York: Twayne Publishers, 1971.

MAHARASHTRA The name Maharashtra, meaning "the land of the Marathi-speaking people," appears to be derived from *Maharashtri*, an old form of Prakrit. Some scholars believe that it was the land of the *maharatthis* (great charioteers) while others consider the term to be a corruption of Maha Kantara (the Great Forest), a synonym for Dandakaranya of the Rāmāyaṇa.

The Land and Its People

The state of Maharashtra is located in the northwest and center of peninsular India, bounded by the Arabian Sea to the west, Gujarat and Madhya Pradesh to the north, Andhra Pradesh to the east, Karnataka and Goa to the south. In area (118,828 sq. mi., or 307,762 sq. km), the state ranks fourth below Uttar Pradesh, Rajasthan, and Madhya Pradesh, while in terms of population (96,752,000; 2001 estimate) it ranks third in the country, below Uttar Pradesh and Bihar. Maharashtra's physical features divide it into three distinct regions: the Konkan coast; the mountainous Sahyadri Range; and the "Desh" Deccan plateau. The Sahyadri Range, the physical backbone of Maharashtra, rises on an average to 3,280 feet (1,000 meters), with steep cliffs dropping westward to the coastal strip of Konkan; the hilltops, locally called the Ghatmatha, drop in steps eastward through a transitional area known as Mawal to the large Deccan plateau. Lying between the Arabian Sea and the Sahyadri Range is the Konkan, a narrow coastal lowland, barely 30 miles (48 km) wide, alternating between narrow, steep-sided valleys and low laterite plateaus. In the north, the Satpuda Range and the eastward extension of the Bhamragad-Chiroli-Gaikhuri ranges provide natural borders for the state, historically serving as a barrier to invasions from the north.

Maharashtra's Traditions

Maharashtra is proud of its three heritages and of its cosmopolitan capital, Mumbai. First, it is the land of the historic Marathas, who produced a great Indian hero, Shivaji, and built a power structure lasting more than 150 years, administering both directly and indirectly three-quarters of the subcontinent at the time of the British takeover. Second, predating Shivaji and continuing to date, is Maharashtra's nine-centuries-old *bhakti* tradition, a movement unifying masses, urban and rural, rich and poor. Third, it was in its capital, Mumbai (Bombay), that the Indian National Congress was born in 1885, and it was from the same venue that Mahatma Gandhi launched the historic "Quit India" movement in 1942. Mumbai, its capital since the birth of the state on 1 May 1960, is also regarded as the country's industrial and financial capital.

The power center during Shivaji's early days and throughout the period of the Peshwai (1714–1818) was Pune (120 miles [193 km] southeast of Mumbai), the

Lithograph of a Maharashtra Warrior. The story of Maharashtra is the story of the great seventeenth-century warrior Shivaji Maharaj who, surmounting monumental difficulties, encouraged a spirit of independence among his people that enabled them to withstand, for well over 150 years, all attempts to conquer them. FOTOMEDIA ARCHIVE.

heart of Maharashtra, which also produced the first major nonviolent challenge to British rule through the leadership of Bal Gangadhar Tilak and Gopal Krishna Gokhale, as well as the violent alternative provided by Vinayak Damodar Sawarkar, Chaphekar Brothers, and Vasudeo Balwant Phadke. The city also boasts an array of excellent academic institutions in diverse fields, leading the country in the study of archaeology, linguistics, anthropology, and Sanskrit. Its engineering and medical education facilities stand among the top ten in the country.

The *Bhakti* Cult

A great social leveler in Maharashtra has been the sustained popularity of the *bhakti* (devotion to Krishna) cult, with an unbroken tradition, at least for nine centuries, of pilgrimage to the temple of Vithoba at Pandharpur. Every year, several hundred thousand *warkari* devotees, from all ranks of society, walk scores of miles from different towns and villages all over the state to converge on the temple. Along the way and at the temple, they sing *bhajans* (devotional songs) composed by poet-saints from the thirteenth to the seventeenth centuries, and eat together, regardless of caste or economic status.

Leading the *bhakti* tradition in Maharashtra was Jnanadeva or Jnanesvara (1271–1296), who synthesized philosophy, mysticism, and poetry in his Marathi rendering of the Bhagavad Gītā, which is still widely read in Maharashtra. The tradition was continued by many saint-poets, notably Namdev (1270–1350), Chokhamela (c. fourteenth century), Eknatha (1533–1599), and the much-loved Tukaram (1598–1650), whose poetry marked the peak of the *bhakti* tradition. Ramdas (1608–1684), regarded as Shivaji's political and spiritual guru, also belonged to the same poet-saint tradition. All these saint-poets focused on Vithoba of Pandharpur, which became the devotional capital of Maharashtra.

Together, these poet-saints established a "spiritual democracy," bringing the philosophy of the Vedanta in simple terms to ordinary people, who were encouraged to disregard caste distinctions in a common devotion to the Divine. The *bhakti* and *warkari* traditions are basic to the understanding of Maharashtrian ethos communality, a sentiment that provided a common platform for the Maratha polity founded by Shivaji and that was continued through the eighteenth century by the Peshwas and the Pentarchy, whose members were drawn from different communities.

Brief Historical Account

Major parts of Maharashtra came under different dynasties, such as the Chalukyas of Badami in the sixth century A.D. and the Rashtrakutas in the eighth century. The most notable rulers were the Yadavas of Deogiri (later named Daulatabad) immediately preceding their defeat by the northern sultanate, first by Ala'-ud-Din Muhammad Khalji in 1307 and later by Muhammad bin Tughluq in 1327. The latter's peremptory orders for thousands of people to move from Delhi to Daulatabad, his "second" capital, incited rebellions. One such rebel, Hasan Gangu, established in 1347 an independent kingdom over the Deccan and named it Bahamani in honor of a Brahman who had treated him well while in adversity. The Bahamani dynasty lasted nearly two hundred years before it broke into its five components, centered respectively in Ahmednagar, Bijapur, Golkonda, Bidar, and Berar.

Barring a few exceptions, the rulers of the Bahamani dynasty as well as of its five successor states treated its majority Hindu population well, even taking some of them into service as noblemen and generals. Shivaji's grandfather, Maloji Bhosle, served in Ahmednagar; his son Shahaji served both the rulers of Ahmednagar and Bijapur.

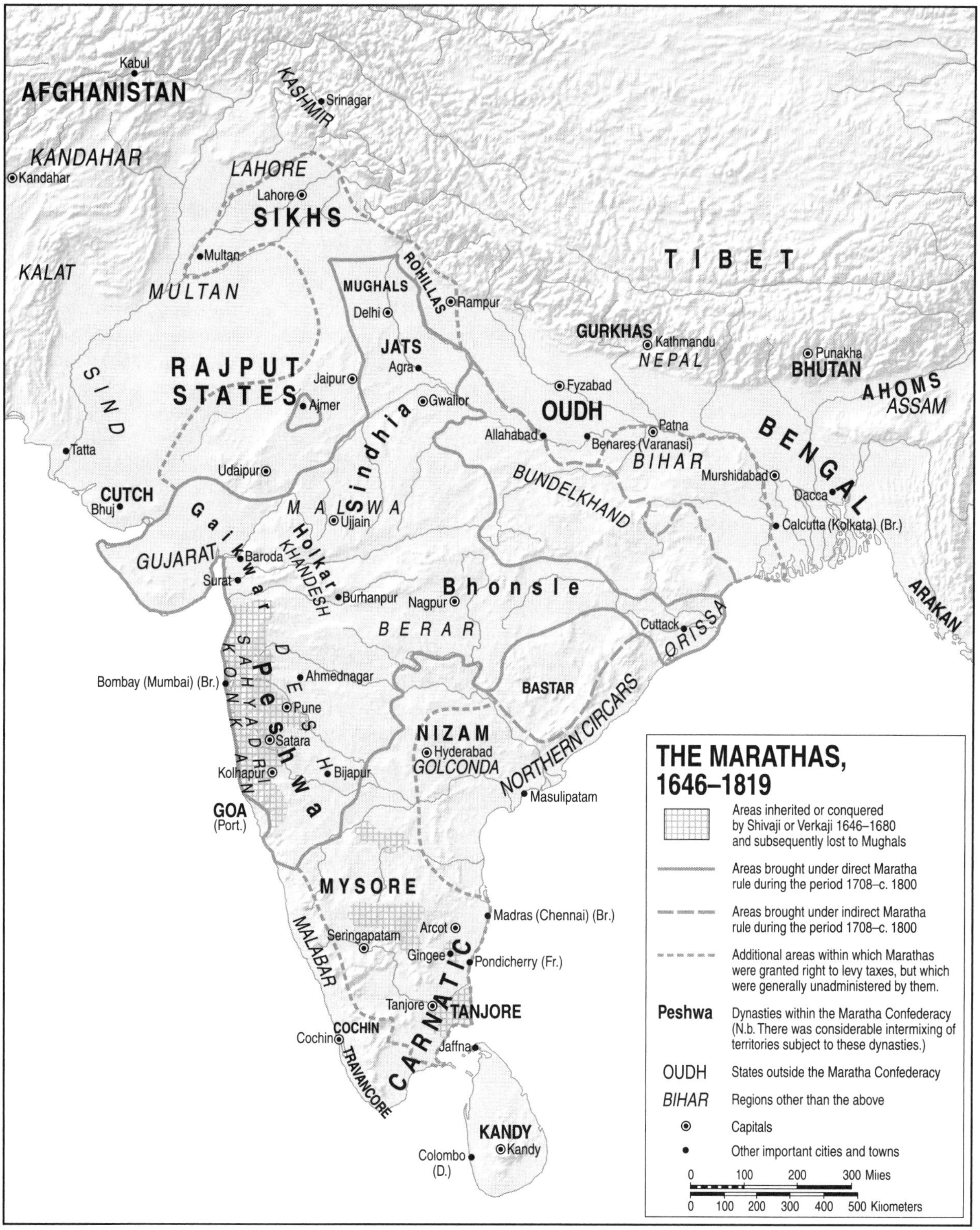

Shivaji's urge to establish an independent kingdom owed as much to his personal pride in freedom as his perception of the need to reestablish the tradition of religious tolerance so gravely disturbed by the reigning Adilshah of Bijapur and the Mughal emperor Aurangzeb. The latter's bid after Shivaji's death in 1680 to eliminate Maratha power only helped to reinforce Maratha protonationalism, which found a new manifestation and urge, under the Peshwas in the eighteenth century, to carry the Maratha flag to large swaths of territory in both north and central India.

D. R. SarDesai

See also **Bombay; Peshwai and Pentarchy**

BIBLIOGRAPHY

Deleury, G. A. *The Cult of Vithoba*. Poona: Deccan College, 1960.

Dikshit, K. R. *Maharashtra in Maps*. Mumbai: Maharashtra State Board for Literature and Culture, 1986.

Feldhaus, Anna. "Maharashtra as Holy Land: A Sectarian Tradition." *Bulletin of the School of Oriental and African Studies* 49 (1986): 532–548.

Ranade, R. D. *Mysticism in India: The Poet-Saints of Maharashtra*. Albany: State University of New York Press, 1983.

Wagle, N. K. *Countryside and Society in Maharashtra*. Toronto: Center for South Asia Studies, 1988.

———. "Hindu-Muslim Interaction in Medieval Maharashtra." In *Hinduism Reconsidered*, edited by G. D. Sontheimer and H. Kulke. New Delhi: Manohar, 1989.

MALDIVES AND BHUTAN, RELATIONS WITH With Maldives and Bhutan, India has evolved harmonious relations virtually free of bilateral problems. Since 1965, when the Maldives became independent, its relations with India have developed through close cooperation and mutual understanding. In 1976 the two countries reached an agreement to demarcate their maritime boundary. Considering that the atoll islands of Maldives are inherently weak and vulnerable, India has often promised to respect its independence, sovereignty, and territorial integrity. Maldives has reciprocated by respecting India's regional security sensitivities by, for example, refusing to lease its strategically important Gan Island to foreign powers during the cold war period. On its part, India remained responsive to the small state's security needs and provided prompt military assistance to foil a coup in 1988. During Prime Minister A. B. Vajpayee's visit to Male in September 2002, India offered to train and equip the Maldivian security forces in coastal defense.

India has extended a variety of economic and technical assistance, helping to develop infrastructure in Maldives. Its first project was a fish canning plant. In 1977 India set up the Maldivian airlines and modernized the country's only airport. Under the 1986 economic and technical cooperation agreement, India established a 200-bed general hospital, a nurse training center and a coronary unit and extended assistance in telecommunications, meteorology, and the preservation of ancient monuments. In January 1990 India helped Maldives establish an environmental program to arrest the greenhouse effect as well as a training program for civil servants in its foreign office. Over the years, India's assistance has increased to include information technology, tourism, and agriculture.

Similarly, India-Bhutan relations represent a rare case of harmony and friendship between two unequal states. Unlike Maldives, which has not had a friendship treaty with India, Bhutan's special relations are formalized by the treaty of perpetual peace and friendship signed on 8 August 1949. Clause 2 of the treaty is central to their relationship. It pertains to India's commitment to noninterference in the internal administration of Bhutan which, on its part, has agreed to be guided by the former's advice. On matters of defense, Bhutan has agreed to import its arms either from or through India. The treaty has established a bilateral free trade regime and includes provision for extradition of each other's citizens. It is a treaty in perpetuity unless terminated or modified by mutual consent. Bhutan has continued to adhere to the treaty provisions, notwithstanding some criticisms and unofficial demands for its revision.

Being a landlocked, underdeveloped country, Bhutan depends heavily on India for its economic support and development. India fully financed Bhutan's first two five-year plans, and subsequent plans received partial funding. India has undertaken several development projects, including the significant Chukha hydroelectric project at the cost of 2,440 million rupees (Rs. 244 crore). About 40 percent of Bhutan's external revenue is collected from the sale of electricity to India. Bhutan receives about 50 percent of the total Indian aid earmarked for the developing countries. India has provided over thirteen transit routes to Bhutan; trade with India constitutes about 70 percent of Bhutan's imports and 90 percent of its exports, though Bhutan is seeking to expand its commercial interactions with other countries. The five decades of India-Bhutan relations have been characterized by warmth and friendship.

Ponmoni Sahadevan

See also **South Asian Association for Regional Cooperation (SAARC)**

BIBLIOGRAPHY

Kohli, Manorama. *From Dependency to Interdependence: A Study of Indo-Bhutan Relations*. New Delhi: Vikas, 1993.

Phadnis, Urmila, and Ela Dutt Luithui. *Maldives: Winds of Change in an Atoll State*. New Delhi: South Asian, 1986.

MANDALA THEORY. *See* **Artha Shāstra.**

MANDAL COMMISSION REPORT On 20 December 1978 India's prime minister, Morarji Desai of the Janata Party, announced the formation of a second

Demonstration against the Mandal Commission Report. In August 1990, then Prime Minister V. P. Singh announced before Parliament his intention to implement the Mandal Commission's recommendations. Violent demonstrations soon broke out, especially in the North among the upper castes, who feared the commission's recommendations on advancing the socially and economically backward classes of India would reduce their access to higher education. INDIA TODAY.

Backward Classes Commission under chairman B. P. Mandal, a former member of Parliament. The commission's assignments were: to determine criteria for defining India's "socially and educationally backward classes"; to recommend steps to be taken for the advancement of those classes; to examine the desirability of reserving state- and central-government jobs for those classes; and to present a report to the president of India. On 31 December 1980 the Mandal Commission submitted its report to President N. S. Reddy, recommending ways to advance India's "socially and educationally backward classes."

Historical Background

Efforts to develop some version of affirmative action for India's "untouchables" and depressed classes began in various parts of British India during the nineteenth century. After India became independent in 1947, Dr. B. R. Ambedkar, spokesperson for India's "untouchables" and an architect of India's Constitution, made certain that the Constitution abolished "untouchability" and provided political and economic benefits for "scheduled castes" and "scheduled tribes." India's Constitution also authorized the state to make special provisions "for the advancement of any socially and educationally backward classes of citizens."

Since 1936, official lists ("schedules") had existed of India's castes and tribes that occupied a "degraded position in the Hindu social scheme." However, no official lists existed of India's "backward classes," that is, poor or otherwise disadvantaged groups that did not occupy a "degraded position in the Hindu social scheme." To address this deficiency, on 29 January 1953 the president of India appointed India's first Backward Classes Commission under Chairman Kaka Kalelkar. On 31 March 1955 the Kalelkar Commission submitted its report, including a list of 2,399 "backward" groups, 837 of which were considered "most backward," using caste as the major evidence of backwardness. The central government, fearing that the report's "caste test" would delay the ultimate creation of a casteless, classless society in India, rejected the recommendations of the Kalelkar Commission. From then until 1977, when the Janata

Party won India's national elections, the issue of determining nationwide criteria for "backward classes" remained effectively dormant.

Procedures and Recommendations

The Mandal Commission developed eleven indicators of social, educational, and economic backwardness. One indicator was being considered backward by other castes or classes. Other indicators included depending mainly on manual labor for livelihood and having an average value of family assets at least 25 percent below the state average. In addition to identifying backward classes among Hindus, the Mandal Commission identified backward classes among non-Hindus (e.g., Muslims, Sikhs, Christians, and Buddhists) if they had belonged to "untouchable" castes before they converted to a non-Hindu religion, or if Hindu castes with the same occupational names, such as *dhobi* (launderer), *lohar* (iron worker), *nai* (barber), or *teli* (oil presser), were considered backward.

In February 1980 the Mandal Commission conducted a nationwide socioeconomic field survey in which it gathered interview data from two villages and one urban block in 405 of the nation's 406 districts. The field survey data, combined with information from the 1961 census, various states' lists of their backward classes, and personal knowledge of Commission members and others, enabled the Mandal Commission to generate an all-India "other backward classes" (OBC) list of 3,743 castes and a more-underprivileged "depressed backward classes" list of 2,108 castes.

The Mandal Commission concluded that India's population consisted of approximately 16 percent non-Hindus, 17.5 percent Brahmans and "forward castes," 44 percent "other backward classes," and 22.5 percent scheduled castes and tribes. However, since the 16 percent non-Hindus presumably included approximately the same proportion of "other backward classes" as did the Hindus (i.e., another 8%), the total proportion of "other backward classes" (Hindu and non-Hindu) came to 52 percent (44% + 8%) of India's population.

The Mandal Commission would have recommended that 52 percent of central government posts be reserved for OBCs. However, the Supreme Court had already ruled that the total proportion of reservations under Articles 15(4) and 16(4) of the Constitution should be below 50 percent. Since the scheduled castes and scheduled tribes already accounted for 22.5 percent of India's population, only a little more than 27 percent of government posts could be reserved for backward classes without exceeding the below-50 percent limit. The Mandal Commission therefore recommended that 27 percent of central and state government jobs should be reserved for OBCs, and that the 27 percent figure should be applied to other "compensatory discrimination" or "compensatory protection" benefits, including those provided by universities and affiliated colleges.

On 7 August 1990 Prime Minister V. P. Singh, of the National Front coalition, announced to Parliament that he would implement the Mandal Commission's recommendations. Violent objections ensued, especially in northern India among the upper castes, who feared the commission's recommendations would reduce their access to higher education. Southern Indian responses to Prime Minister Singh's announcement were considerably milder. In several southern states the proportions of backward classes combined with scheduled castes and scheduled tribes had already approached 50 percent prior to the Mandal Commission's recommendations.

On 16 November 1992 the Supreme Court upheld the Mandal Commission's 27 percent quota for backward classes, as well as the principle that the combined scheduled-caste, scheduled-tribe, and backward-class beneficiaries should not exceed 50 percent of India's population. The Supreme Court also ruled that "caste" could be used to identify "backward classes" on condition the caste was socially backward as a whole, and that the "creamy layer" of the backward classes could not receive backward-class benefits. The "creamy layer" included children of constitutional office holders, class I and class II officers, professionals, owners of large agricultural farms, and those with annual incomes of over 100,000 rupees. In September 1993 Prime Minister Narasimha Rao, of the Congress Party, announced that he was prepared to implement the Mandal Commission recommendations. This time there was little public resistance.

Joseph W. Elder

See also **Ambedkar, B. R., and the Buddhist Dalits; Caste System; Dalits; Scheduled Tribes**

BIBLIOGRAPHY

Galanter, Marc. *Competing Equalities: Law and the Backward Classes in India*. Berkeley: University of California Press, 1984.

Government of India. *The Constitution of India, as Modified up to 15th April 1967*. Delhi: Manager of Publications, 1967.

Government of India. Backward Classes Commission (B. P. Mandal, Chairman). *Report of the Backward Classes Commission, First Part (Volumes I & II), 1980*. New Delhi: Controller of Publications, 1981.

Jaffrelot, Christophe. "The Subordinate Class Revolution." In *India Briefing: Quickening the Pace of Change*, edited by Alyssa Ayres and Philip Oldenburg. Armonk, N.Y.: M. E. Sharpe, 2002.

MANGESHKAR, LATA *(1929–), popular Indian vocalist.* India's greatest Bollywood "playback" singer, Lata Mangeshkar's voice is known to over four generations of Indian film fans, as she has lent her voice to countless screen heroines, enhancing the impact of their portrayals through her songs. Mangeshkar's home state is Goa, which has been home to many talented musicians, but she was born in Indore in Madhya Pradesh. Her father, Dinanath Mangeshkar, was a leading actor-singer of his generation. He owned a theater company, which staged musicals throughout the former Bombay Presidency. When Dinanath heard Lata correcting one of his students, who was not singing a phrase correctly, and also humming perfectly in tune with the *sarangi*, he decided to give her lessons. His life, however, was cut short by alcoholism.

Mangeshkar first appeared as a child actress in a few films. Her first song was for a Marathi film, *Kiti Hasal?*. Her first Hindi song, for the film *Aap ki Sewame*, was recorded in 1947. Since then, she has sung for over 200 music directors, 300 lyricists, and has done voice-overs for 100 male and 61 female performers. Mangeshkar had to struggle in the initial phase of her career, but by 1948 she became established as a "playback" singer, creating voice-overs for films, and soon rose to prominence.

Mangeshkar studied classical music under Aman Ali Khan of the Bhendi Bazar *gharana*. She also received guidance from Amanat Khan and Tulsidas Sharma and the composers Ghulam Hyder and Anil Biswas. Before her, the vocalist Noorjehan was the most sought-after "playback" singer. Noorjehan left for Pakistan, however, paving the way for Mangeshkar's rise, under the influence of Kundanlal Saigal. Her early songs reflect Noorjehan's vocal style, but Mangeshkar soon developed her own unique style.

Mangeshkar's voice is supple and velvety, its mellifluous quality enriching the lyrics of her songs. She is one of India's very few multilingual singers. Her most popular songs were from films made between 1947 and 1962, considered the golden age of Hindi film music. With melodies relegated to the background in later years, the quality of Indian movie music suffered an inevitable decline. Mangeshkar was awarded India's highest civilian honor, and the president of India nominated her as a member of Rajya Sabha, the upper house of India's Parliament.

Amarendra Dhaneshwar

BIBLIOGRAPHY

Bharatan, Raju. *Lata Mangeshkar: A Biography*. New Delhi: UBS Publishers, 1995.

Bhimani, Harish. *In Search of Lata Mangeshkar*. New Delhi: Indus, 1995.

MANIPUR A state in northeast India, Manipur has an area of 8,628 square miles (22,347 sq. km), and its population in 2001 was 2,388,634. Its capital is Imphal. Most of its people speak Manipuri, a Tibeto-Burman language. The name of the state means "jeweled place," and Manipur has been called the "jewel of India" because of the beauty of its green valleys and deep blue lakes, set on a highland plateau surrounded by jungle-covered hills that rise to elevations of 8,500 feet (2,590 m). Manipur, which has long been an integral part of India's history and culture, is mentioned in the epic Mahābhārata, the Purāṇas, and ancient Chinese texts. The game of polo, called *sogol kangiei* in Manipuri, is believed to have originated there. Manipuri dances, including its famous *ras lila*, are together considered one of the six major dance traditions of South Asia. It was also the site of bitter fighting against Japanese forces during World War II.

Manipuri polity has historically been controlled by the majority Hindu Methei people. Christian Nagas (25%) and Kukis (15%) and Muslim Pangals (7%) make up most of the remainder of the population. Ethnic rivalry, recurrent patricide and fratricide among its former traditional rulers, and their predilection for waging war with the powerful neighboring kingdom of Burma ensured that premodern Manipur was continually subject to threats both internal and external. Burmese forces occupied Manipur in 1819 until the Anglo-Burmese War of 1826 forced the invaders to waive their claims to the region. This step saved Manipur from certain absorption into the Burmese state, but also established a precedent for British control. What remained of its independence withered away after a series of assassinations, self-interested regents, and popular rebellions led the British government of India to repeatedly intervene in Manipuri affairs, usually at the behest of the ruling prince. The last of these debacles led to the Anglo-Manipuri War of 1891 and the formal assumption of British paramountcy in August of that year. Subsequent attempts by the British to force the pace of modernization in the state strained political relations between the increasingly Christian Naga and traditional Hindu Methei populations. It also poisoned center-state relations, which were further exacerbated in 1949, when Manipur was compelled to merge with newly independent India under unfavorable terms, which included the cession of the Kubaw Valley to Burma (present-day Myanmar). These tensions persisted after Manipur became a Union Territory in 1956 and a state on 21 January 1972, and increased thereafter due to political corruption and poorly conceived development policies emanating from Delhi, such as a *panchayati* reform program that acted to exclude women, long a force in modern Manipuri politics and society.

The early 1960s witnessed the emergence of an ethnically exclusive Methei nationalist movement, which opposed what they declared to be the Indian occupation of their land. A decade later, Naga political aspirations across the Northeast region of India included the incorporation of Naga districts in Manipur and elsewhere into a sovereign state of Nagaland. This angered the Methei population, but also attracted the wrath of the government of India. In 1980, in an effort to quash any secessionist ideas, the Indian authorities evoked the Armed Forces (Special Powers) Act of 1958 in support of counterinsurgency operations across the entire state. These operations not only added fuel to existing secessionist fires, but also sparked demand for an independent Kuki homeland. Since the mid-1980s, several of these competing movements joined to form the Manipuri People's Liberation Army (PLA) and other umbrella groups, though its members were and remain chiefly united only in their desire to break free of Indian control and act against the migration of Muslims and others into the state from Bangladesh and elsewhere.

However, continued malfeasance in the management of development funds and the brutality of the paramilitary Assam Rifles have helped to sustain these otherwise hopelessly splintered independence movements. All sections of the population were enraged at the Assam Rifles' arrest, torture, and murder of a thirty-two-year-old woman activist, Thangjam Manorama, on 11 July 2004. In response, the state government has sought to nullify the operation of the Armed Forces Act and has demanded that the Assam Rifles be withdrawn. Long-term unrest in the state has opened the door to drug lords, whose trade in heroin and other narcotics operates freely within this chaotic political environment.

Marc Jason Gilbert

See also **Burma; Ethnic Conflict; Insurgency and Terrorism; Nagas and Nagaland**

BIBLIOGRAPHY

Dena, Lal, ed. *History of Modern Manipur, 1826–1949.* New Delhi: Orbit Publishers, 1991.

Gilbert, Marc Jason. "The Manipur Disaster of 1891 and Indian Nationalism in Bengal: A Study in Rebellion and Revolution in the South Asian Context." In *Research on Bengal: Proceedings of the 1981 Bengal Studies Conference,* edited by Ray Langsten. East Lansing: Michigan State University Press, 1982.

Roy, Jyotirmoy. *History of Manipur.* 2nd rev. ed. Kolkata: East Light Bookhouse, 1973.

Tarapot, Phanjoubam. *Bleeding Manipur.* New Delhi: Har Anand Publication, 2003.

Thomas, C. Joshua, R. Gopalakrishnan, and R. K. Singh. *Constraints in Development of Manipur.* New Delhi: Regency Publications, 2001.

MANIPURI. *See* **Dance Forms.**

MANSABDARI SYSTEM. *See* **Akbar; Aurangzeb; History and Historiography.**

MANTRA. *See* **Hinduism (Dharma).**

MANU, LAWS OF. *See* **Dharma Shāstra.**

MARITIME COMMERCE, 1750–1947 India was an open economy for most of this period as controls over external transactions were confined to the two world wars and their aftermath, and the 1930s depression. Yet even at its height, India's foreign trade accounted only for a small proportion (15–17 percent) of its estimated national income. However, from the late nineteenth century, foreign trade affected the economy and people's livelihoods disproportionately because of its impact on money supply, and the colonial government's determination to collect India's external obligations, or the notorious "home charges," at any cost.

The story of India's foreign trade from 1750 to 1947 may be described most simply as its transformation from an exporter of fine handicraft manufactures, for which India was traditionally known, to an exporter of raw materials and an importer of cloth and other industrial manufactures. This transformation took place chiefly between 1815 and the 1870s. In the preceding decades India's external trade largely followed traditional patterns, while from the 1880s it resumed exporting manufactures in modest quantities. Changes in the external and domestic environments and the organization and financing of Indian trade also influenced the volume, composition, and structure of trade, and its overall impact on the economy.

1750–1815

Until the nineteenth century, India's great coastal trading regions—Bengal, the Coromandel coast, the Malabar coast, and Gujarat—were major nodes in a worldwide trading and financing network with dense concentrations in other parts of Asia. This network attracted diverse participants, from the large European companies to numerous indigenous traders, some of whose operations were equally diverse. Our knowledge of these networks and their activities remains incomplete, but it is clear that cotton textiles were the principal Indian export during this period. In 1811–1812 they accounted for a third of the estimated value of India's

Nineteenth-Century Print of Steam Vessel. The steam pilot vessel, the *Lady Fraser*, anchored in the Hoogly River. From 1871 to 1947, at the height of colonial rule, India's foreign trade witnessed a slow structural shift, with the staple exports of the past, such as opium and indigo, replaced by new commodities. SURVEY OF INDIA / AKHIL BAKSHI.

exports, followed by opium (about a quarter) and indigo (about a fifth). The share of cotton cloth would have been greater in earlier decades.

Indian trade was also geographically well distributed. Even for Bengal, where the British East India Company was predominant, the American share in imports was 23 percent between 1799 and 1804, exceeding by a small margin the share of imports recorded as having been shipped from London. In the mid- to late 1790s, when the American share was only 13 percent, imports from London made up only a fifth of Bengal's total imports, with other Asian ports accounting for over half. Though a bigger share of Bengal's exports went to Britain (about 35–40 percent) during the late 1790s and early 1800s, America and other ports, including those in Asia, accounted for 55 to 60 percent of the wares leaving the region.

The organization and financing of India's overseas trade during these decades witnessed the growing political and trading ascendancy of the British East India Company and the eclipse of all other European trading companies. Yet as late as 1790, trade carried or licensed by the British East India Company accounted for only about 40 percent of India's commerce with Europe. The East India Company's acquisition of the revenues of Bengal, after which its surpluses and servants' private profits displaced imports of bullion as the means to pay for Indian exports, marked a more profound transformation.

1815–1870

Striking evidence of the structural transformation of Indian exports during this period is offered by the sharp drop in the share of cotton textiles from about one-third in 1811 to less than 15 percent in 1815. By the 1870s this proportion had fallen below 3 percent. Raw cotton, on the other hand, expanded its share from about 5 percent in 1811 to 35 percent in 1870, the rise being particularly steep in the 1860s because of the U.S. Civil War. Indigo remained an important export in the first half of this period. Opium exports, principally to China, gained ground rapidly after the 1820s and emerged as India's largest single export by the mid-1830s. Britain's opium war with China further confirmed this status and helped maintain it through the next two decades.

The transformation of India's trading basket was mirrored in the composition of its imports. The share of cotton textiles rose from around 5 to 10 percent in 1820 to nearly 50 percent in 1870. Cotton twist and yarn was another major import, its share rising to about 13 percent by the 1870s as India's craft-weaving sector adapted to the challenge of industrial competition by switching to cheaper imported inputs.

The reversal of the trading relationship between India and Britain since 1815 was starkly reflected in the imbalance that developed between the sources of India's imports and the destinations of its exports. By the 1820s Britain's share of Indian imports had risen to over 60 percent. By 1870 this proportion stood at 80 percent. However, Britain now accounted for only about 45 percent of India's exports. India therefore ran a substantial trade deficit with Britain. However, it continued to run substantial trade surpluses overall. Only a small part of this was now liquidated by imports of treasure, the larger part (for example, more than 70 percent in 1828) being used to finance unilateral transfers to Britain. Until 1833 the latter were mainly the profits of the East India Company and private remittances of its officials. Thereafter, unilateral transfers comprised the British "home charges" that included, apart from private remittances by British officials and traders, service transfers, interest payments on railway and other loans from the 1860s, and British civil and military pensions.

Large opium exports to China were a major feature of Indian trade from 12 million rupees in 1820 to 143 million rupees in 1880 and transforming China into India's second-largest overseas customer. Britain, however, ran a large deficit with China because of its enormous imports of tea and silk. The opium trade thus formed the third side of the triangular pattern of settlements that enabled Britain in one stroke, as it were, to collect its tribute from India and liquidate its deficit with China.

1871–1947

During these decades India's trade witnessed a slow structural shift. Some staple exports of the past, such as opium and indigo, were replaced by new commodities, mainly raw jute, tea, and wheat, the last two each accounting for 10 percent of India's exports on the eve of World War II. A depreciating rupee, tied to silver until 1893, also stimulated the export of manufactures such as jute fabrics and cotton yarn and cloth. Assisted by the wartime disruption of Britain's staple export trade and the trade boom of the mid-1920s, exports of cotton cloth and jute goods expanded to account together for about 30 percent of Indian exports in the mid-1920s. Both of these exports, however, were hit hard by the global depression, during which primary or semiprocessed exports, such as raw cotton, hides and skins, seeds, and tea, reclaimed their former preeminence. Domestic industrialization had a more enduring effect, however, on the composition of imports. The share of cotton cloth declined steadily from a peak of 47 percent in 1871 to about 13 percent by the mid-1930s. Machinery also accounted for a growing share of imports on the eve of World War II.

Britain's importance to India's external trade declined steadily in the half century after 1871, its share of imports falling from 85 percent to 61 percent between these dates, before plummeting to 37 percent in 1939. Britain's share of Indian exports fell from 54 percent to 24 percent between 1871 and 1931. Britain's decline was offset by the rise of Japan and the United States as India's trade partners during the interwar years.

Trade and economic transformation. Between the 1870s and the 1940s, a modern global economy had emerged, which then suffered disruption and collapse in the wake of World War I and during the interwar depression. These decades witnessed the industrial transformation of many countries, notably the United States and Japan. India's economic and trading transformation was unimpressive, however, even by comparison with countries such as Australia and Brazil.

Viewed from the perspective of external trade and economic relations, India's lack of freedom to adopt tariffs until 1919, and restricted freedom thereafter, and Britain's enduring control of short-term macroeconomic instruments such as the exchange rate must count as key factors. The institutional transformation of the link between foreign trade, the monetary system, and the domestic economy after 1900, when remittance instruments sold in London replaced shipments of precious metals as the principal means of financing Indian trade, also retarded the development of India's financial system. The control that Britain thereby came to exercise over metallic flows to India was used to relieve the former's external financial needs in the 1920s and the 1930s, at the expense of growth and incomes in India. India's large gold exports in the 1930s, arising from rural economic distress, were viewed by economist John Maynard Keynes as a major factor in promoting Britain's swift recovery from the depression, while India's economy languished deeper in the slump.

G. Balachandran

See also **Trade Policy, 1800–1947**

BIBLIOGRAPHY

Balachandran, G. "Introduction." In *India and the World Economy*, edited by G. Balachandran. Delhi: Oxford University Press, 2003.

Chaudhuri, K. N. "Foreign Trade and Balance of Payments." In *Cambridge Economic History of India*, vol. 2: *c. 1757–c. 1970*, edited by Dharma Kumar. Cambridge, U.K., and New York: Cambridge University Press, 1983.

Prakash, Om. *The New Cambridge History of India*, vol. II.5: *European Commercial Enterprise in Pre-colonial India*. Cambridge, U.K., and New York: Cambridge University Press, 1998.

MARRIAGE LAWS. *See* **Caste System; Dharma Shāstra; Judicial System, Modern.**

MATHEMATICS. *See* **Āryabhatīya; Astronomy.**

MATHURA. *See* **Krishna in Indian Art; Vishnu and Avatāras.**

MAURYAN EMPIRE Arising in the kingdom of Magadha, the Mauryan empire (321–185 B.C.), with its capital Pataliputra (modern Patna), was the first imperial polity in South Asia. Under the able leadership of its founder, Chandragupta Maurya (r. 321–297 B.C.), and his successors Bindusāra (r. 297–272 B.C.) and Ashoka (r. 268–231 B.C.), the empire integrated several key regions of the subcontinent into a loosely structured but tightly drawn imperial network, and bequeathed a significant historical legacy to the subcontinent's history. The sources of Mauryan history include archaeological remains, Brahmanical and Buddhist textual sources, foreign travel accounts, and most importantly, the public edicts of Ashoka.

By the middle of first millennium B.C., a number of small polities called *mahājanapada*s had grown up along the Ganges. The more powerful of these at the time—the kingdoms of Kashi, Koshala, and Magadha, and the more distant Vrijji confederation—were clustered in the middle Gangetic Plain, which had seen extensive development in agriculture, intensive urbanization, and the rise of new religious movements like Buddhism and Jainism. By the beginning of the fifth century B.C., Magadha had gained the upper hand over its rivals through the leadership of the raja (king) Bimbisāra, whose line was eventually displaced by the Nanda dynasty at the beginning in the fourth century B.C. Nanda imperial ambitions might have brought them into conflict with the generals of Alexander the Great, who conquered the eastern provinces of the Achaemenid empire in northwestern India, but his usurpation by Chandragupta Maurya in 321 B.C. brought a swift end to Nanda rule.

With the Gangetic Plain largely under his dominion, Chandragupta pursued campaigns in central India and the northwest, where by the end of the fourth century B.C. he had gained territory from a Greek successor state ruled by Seleucus Nicator. An envoy of Seleucus, Megasthenes, visited the Mauryan empire and its capital at Pataliputra and left an account of it called *Indika*. Toward the end of his life, Chandragupta is said to have embraced the Jain faith, abdicated the throne, and migrated to Sravana Belgola in present-day Karnataka, where he fasted to death in Jain tradition. The events of the reign of Chandragupta's son, Bindusāra, are uncertain, but by the time that Ashoka inherited the kingdom in 268 B.C., the empire was considerably expanded. Knowledge of Ashoka's reign is drawn from a series of public edicts, which reveal the specific policies and vision of the emperor, and provide crucial information about Mauryan society. The edicts of the earlier half of his reign were carved on rock surfaces and distributed widely through the empire, while those toward the end were issued mostly in its Gangetic heartland and were inscribed on polished sandstone pillars, each surmounted with a finely carved animal capital. Most of the inscriptions were issued in the Prakrit language written in Brahmi scipt, but in the northwest some have been found in Greek and Aramaic, written in the Kharoshti script used in Iran. Ashoka extended the influence of the empire even farther than his forefathers, with the southernmost limits of his inscriptions being found in the lower Deccan. Sometime around 260 B.C., Ashoka conquered the region of Kalinga (present-day Orissa). The devastation wrought by his campagin so impressed him that he publicly expressed remorse in his thirteenth rock edict. Judging from this edict, Ashoka seems to have curtailed further wars of expansion and maintained cordial relations with neighboring polities, both within the subcontinent and beyond.

Many of Ashoka's edicts have a distinctly ethical dimension—enjoining his subjects to honor elders, show consideration to menials, refrain from hurting living beings, avoid needless ceremony, and most of all, follow *dharma* (right action, teaching). Many of these exhortations bear a distinctively Buddhist stamp, and indeed, Ashoka considered himself a lay convert to the faith and gave generously to its institutions. Perhaps as a concession to these principles, he deterred the performance of Vedic sacrifices that involved the killing of animals. In the Buddhist tradition, he became a legendary figure, being viewed as the paradigmatic Buddhist emperor, or *cakravartin*. The degree to which he actually propagated Buddhist doctrine, however, remains an open question,

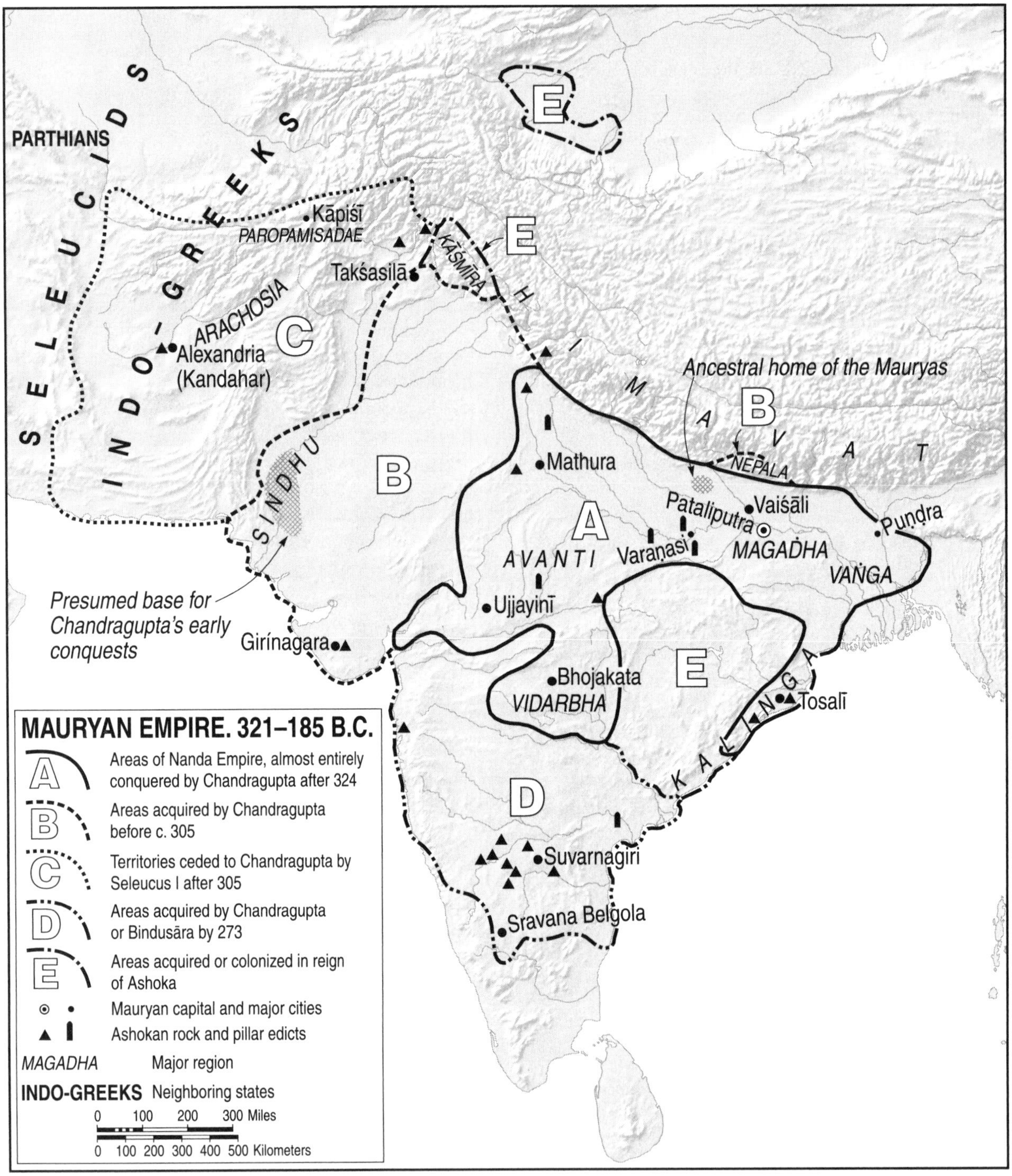

and it would seem that the *dharma* of his edicts did not refer to Buddhist doctrine as such but had a more general ethical sense. Yet the connection between Ashoka and Buddhism is undeniable, and it remains a fact that Buddhism grew into a powerful and influential religion, with imperial and universal ambitions, during the Mauryan period.

Regular agricultural revenues from the Gangetic heartland provided the basic wealth of the Mauryan empire, and punch-marked coins circulated as currency in certain sectors of the economy. Urban life continued to be important, with manufacturing and commerce forming an important source of individual and state wealth. Beyond inscriptions, another source used by scholars to understand the structure and functioning of the Mauryan empire is the *Artha Shāstra*, a treatise on government attributed to Chanakya (Kautilya), minister of Chandragupta. While the existing text was probably not compiled in Mauryan times, certain parts may be as early, and thus provide a normative perspective on Mauryan society and polity. Ashoka's edicts and the *Artha Shāstra*, read together, confirm that a set of regularized ministerial offices, service cadre, judges, and revenue assessors formed the core of the state apparatus. The inscriptions themselves mark the first widespread use of written records (after the undeciphered Indus Valley script). Assessing the structure of Mauryan polity from the evidence is more difficult. Until recently, historians tended to portray the Mauryan empire as a centrally organized, uniformly administered, bureaucratic polity. Recent work has suggested, however, that such an image, driven by modern theories of state, may not be correct. It has been argued that the Mauryan empire should be seen as a metropolitan hub (Magadha) linked to a number of core and peripheral "nodes." Cores and peripheries were not distinguished by geographical location, but by socioeconomic articulation. Core areas, typically represented by clusters of Ashokan inscriptions, were regions where the metropole significantly influenced local econony and society, while peripheral areas, less populated and developed, were largely incorporated for revenue extraction alone. Thus the empire was composed of a network of different local economies and social structures, linked through a relatively simple, but horizontal, imperial system. Although this system disintegrated not long after Ashoka's death in 231 B.C., the Mauryan empire—with its innovations in the technology of rule and its integration of economic networks—had a lasting effect on early India, acting as a catalyst for further economic and political development in many of the empire's core and peripheral regions.

Daud Ali

BIBLIOGRAPHY

Allchin, F. R. *The Archaeology of Early Historic India.* Cambridge, U.K.: Cambridge University Press, 1995.

Bongard-Levin, G. M. *Mauryan India.* New Delhi: Sterling, 1985.

Sharma, R. S. *Material Culture and Social Formations in Ancient India.* Delhi: Macmillan, 1983.

Sircar, D. C. *Inscriptions of Asoka.* Delhi: South Asia Books, 1998.

Thapar, Romila. *Asoka and the Decline of the Mauryas.* Delhi: Oxford University Press, 1973.

———. *From Lineage to State: Social Formations in the Mid-First Millennium B.C. in the Ganga Valley.* Delhi: Oxford University Press, 1984.

———. *The Mauryas Revisited.* Kolkata: K. P. Bagchi, 1987.

MEDIA With a population of over 1 billion, speaking eighteen officially recognized Indian languages and almost two hundred minor languages, it is not surprising that India has one of the largest media in the world. As literacy has increased from about 20 percent at the time of independence in 1947 to over 65 percent in 2005, the print media has expanded enormously to keep pace with rising literacy. Literacy in India is defined as the ability to read and understand a simple newspaper, and presumably a large portion of the adult literate population read the English or vernacular press. In 1950 there were 214 daily newspapers, with 44 in English and the rest in Indian languages. In 1990 the number of daily newspapers was 2,856, with 209 in English and 2,647 in indigenous languages. By 1993 India had 35,595 newspapers—of which 3,805 were dailies—and other periodicals. The audiovisual media, largely run by the government until liberalization in the 1990s, had long reached the hundreds of millions of illiterate people in the countryside. Large projected television screens were set up in earlier decades in the villages of India to provide mass access to the rural population.

Except for a brief period during the "National Emergency" of 1975–1977 declared by Prime Minister Indira Gandhi, the private Indian media has been free and independent, providing unshackled news and incisive analyses without fear of government retribution. Some of its limitations are not unlike those in Western countries, where corporations control the stock of the news media and where editors may use some discretion to avoid alienating corporate owners.

Newspapers

English-language newspapers. The pioneering English-language newspapers were started by the British in Bengal during the time of the British East India Company in the eighteenth century. The first of these was the *Bengal Gazette* in 1780, which mainly carried the news and social affairs of the British in Bengal. This was soon followed by the *India Gazette* and the *Calcutta Gazette*. As the empire took root in Madras and Bombay, the *Madras Courier* was published in 1785 and the *Bombay Herald* in 1789. The *Bengal Gazette*, the *Madras Courier*, and the *Bombay Herald* mainly carried official news of the British Raj in the Bengal, Madras, and Bombay presidencies. Some competition arose in Madras with the start of the *Madras Gazette* and the *India Herald*.

The establishment of the mainstream English-language Indian newspapers began from the mid-nineteenth century, founded by resident English entrepreneurs. *The Times of India* of Mumbai (Bombay) (initially the *Bombay Times and Journal of Commerce*) is the oldest of these, founded in 1838. The *Times of India* is published by India's largest media group, Bennett, Coleman and Company, now owned by an Indian conglomerate. It is published concurrently from six cities and has a circulation of about 650,000. Known as the Times Group, the company also publishes the *Economic Times*, *Navbharat Times* (in Hindi), and the *Maharashtra Times* (in Marathi).

The *Statesman* of Kolkata (Calcutta) began publication in 1875. It was the successor to *The Englishman*, founded in Calcutta in 1811. Until independence, it was owned and run by the British. The *Statesman* has been considered among the most independent and hard-hitting of the English-language daily newspapers of India. It was critical of the British during British rule, and has been highly critical of Indian governments, especially the previous Hindu nationalist government of the Bharatiya Janata Party. The *Hindu*, established in 1878 in Chennai (Madras), has arguably made claims to being the best of the English-language dailies in terms of the quality of its reporting and analyses. It claims to have a shared readership of 3 million. Its daily circulation is about 500,000.

The *Hindustan Times* of New Delhi, the first major newspaper that was not initiated by the British, was begun by a pioneering Indian newsman, Pothan Joseph, as the flagship newspaper of the Indian National Congress during the independence struggle. The *Hindustan* became its Hindi language partner later. Joseph subsequently established the *Dawn* in Karachi for the new state of Pakistan. He returned to India and published the *Deccan Herald* in Bangalore. The most widely distributed newspaper in India is the *Indian Express*, which has a daily circulation of 520,000 and is published in seventeen cities. There are also another half dozen English-language daily newspapers with circulations between 134,000 and 477,000, all competitive with one another.

Before independence, the content of the English-language newspapers was addressed to British residents and the rising English-speaking Indian elite. Today, these English-language print media are a highly secular and modern group of newspapers, their quality being comparable to the best in the Western world. They shape the attitudes of the Indian elite and the direction of Indian government policies.

Indian-language newspapers. The many Indian-language newspapers have large circulations, though usually on a statewide or citywide basis. With a daily circulation of 673,000, the Malayalam-language *Malayala Manorama* from Kerala has the largest circulation of any newspaper, but is read mainly in Kerala and its Malayalam-speaking diaspora. The Kerala population of 25 million is nearly 100 percent literate, hence the high readership. On the other hand, the Hindi-language *Dainik Jagran* has a circulation of 580,000, circulating mainly in Uttar Pradesh, which has a population of 140 million but a literacy rate of under 50 percent, and in New Delhi with a population of 8 million. The *Punjab Kesari* in Hindi sells in Punjab and New Delhi, with a daily circulation of 562,000. The *Anandabazar Patrika*, published in Kolkata in Bengali, has a daily circulation of 435,000. There are several smaller publications throughout India, the result of different voices demanding to be heard, and of Indian journalistic entrepreneurship. The combined circulation of India's newspapers and periodicals is more than 60 million, published daily in more than 90 languages.

Overall, there are four major publishing groups in India, each of which controls national and regional English-language and vernacular publications: the Times of India Group, the Indian Express Group, the Hindustan Times Group, and the Anandabazar Patrika Group.

News Agencies

Press Trust of India (PTI) and United News of India (UNI) are the two primary Indian news agencies. The former was created after it took over the operations of the Associated Press of India and the Indian operations of Reuters soon after independence in 1947. PTI is a non-profit cooperative of the Indian newspapers. UNI began its operations in 1961, though it was registered as a company in 1959. India has more than forty domestic news agencies, many with their own foreign correspondents. Many are the appendages of major newspapers, such as the Express News Service, the Times of India News Service, and the Hindustan Times News Service.

Audio-Visual Media

Until socialism was ended and economic liberalization policies were initiated in the early 1990s, the audio-visual media was owned and run by the government of India's Ministry of Information and Broadcasting. They included the national television network (Doordarshan) and the radio network, known as All-India Radio in English and Akashwani in Hindi. Their news reporting customarily presented the government's point of view. Complaints that these media supported the ruling government's candidates against opposition candidates during elections led to the introduction of the Indian Broadcasting Act in Parliament in 1990. The bill provided for the establishment of an autonomous corporation to run Doordarshan and All-India Radio. The corporation was to operate under a board of governors, in charge of appointments and policy, and a broadcasting council to respond to complaints. However, real change came in the early 1990s when television broadcasts were transmitted via satellite, effectively limiting the pro-government bias of the government-controlled electronic media. Today, BBC, CNN, CNBC, Pakistan TV, and other foreign television channels may be received in India.

In 1993 about 169 million people were estimated to have watched Indian television each week, and by 1994 it was reported that there were some 47 million households with televisions. There also is a growing selection of satellite transmission and cable services available. Star TV began broadcasting via satellite, bringing to India an array of Western television shows. Zee TV entered the market, offering competition to Star TV, whose prospects were then bolstered by billionaire Rupert Murdoch, who acquired the network in July 1993.

In response to international competition, Doordarshan started five new channels in 1993 and transformed its fare to more controversial news shows, soap operas, and coverage of high fashion. But only the new Metro channel of Doordarshan, which carries MTV music videos and other popular shows, survived in the face of public demands for more exciting Western fare.

Raju G. C. Thomas

BIBLIOGRAPHY

Brosius, Christiane, and Melissa Butcher, eds. *Image Journeys: Audio-Visual Media and Cultural Change in India.* New Delhi: Sage Publications, 1999.

Offredi, Mariola Offredi, ed. *Literature, Language and the Media in India.* Columbia, Mo.: South Asia Books, 1993.

Price, Monroe E., and Stefaan G. Verhulst, eds. *Broadcasting Reform in India: Media Law from a Global Perspective.* New Delhi: Oxford University Press, 2001.

Rao, N. Bhaskara, and G. N. S. Raghavan. *Social Effects of Mass Media in India.* Columbia, Mo.: South Asia Books, 1996.

MEDICAL SCIENCE EDUCATION India has multiple medical systems, including Āyurvedic, homeopathic, allopathic, and *unani;* the most widely practiced and accepted is the allopathic medical system. After finishing high school, students go straight into medical school, based on their achievement in high school and their rank on the medical college entrance exam. There are two main types of medical schools, state medical schools and federal schools; the state schools require residence within the state in order to be admitted. Recently, schools owned by trusts have developed, and admission to these schools is based on high school performance and the size of a monetary donation to the school.

The course leading to a degree in medicine is five and a half years long, which includes four and a half years of didactic training and one year of compulsory rotating internship in various major disciplines, as compared to United States, where students are admitted for four years of medical school after finishing undergraduate work. A significant number of Indian students, after receiving their bachelor's degree in medicine and surgery (M.B.B.S.), continue on to specialized training in their fields of interest. This training may vary from three to four years in length, with the end result being a doctorate of medicine (M.D.) or masters of surgery (M.S.), depending on the field of specialization. A small number of the physicians pursue further studies to obtain doctorate of medicine (D.M.) or master of churgury (M.Ch.) in a subspecialty of their choice, which may require another two to three years of training.

Medical training in India is predominantly based on the European system of education, which includes not only didactic lectures but also time spent with patients to interpret the physical symptoms and signs in a diagnostic fashion, despite limited resources for expensive laboratory and radiological studies. Teachers who train the prospective doctors must adhere to the very strict requirements laid down by the Medical Council of India.

India has 229 recognized medical schools, and 25,000 students pass through these colleges every year. After completing the compulsory rotating internship, these graduates are required to be registered with the State Medical Council or the Medical Council of India in order to practice in the country.

The science of healing the suffering through natural herbs is the basic principle of Āyurvedic medicine. Founded around 5000 B.C., Āyurvedic medicine is one of the oldest systems still in practice today. The physicians who practice Āyurvedic medicine are called *vaidyas*. Āyurveda is considered the "science of life," and its goal is physical, mental, social, and spiritual well-being. In 1916 the government of India decided to develop this ancient and indigenous system on a scientific basis and to increase its usefulness. The *vaidyas* are trained in special medical schools dedicated to this traditional form of medicine; their education is five and a half years long. After the completion of this study, the students are awarded a bachelor of Āyurvedic medicine and surgery (B.A.M.S.). There are 196 Āyurvedic medical colleges in India that provide not only a bachelor's education but postgraduate education as well.

Another system of medicine practiced in India is *unani* medicine. It was founded by the great Greek philosopher and physician Hippocrates (460–377 B.C.) and it was introduced to India in A.D. 1351 by the Arabs. It is based on the principles of earth, air, water, and fire, all of which have different temperaments—cold, hot, wet, and dry. A new temperament comes intp existence after the mixture and interaction of these four elements along the simple and compound organs of the body. This system of medicine believes in the promotion of health based on six essentials: atmospheric air, drink and food, sleep and wakefulness, excretion and retention, physical activity and rest, and mental activity and rest. The diseases are diagnosed with the help of a pulse and physical exam of urine and/or stools. The practitioners of this system of medicine are called *hakims*. India has thirty-three *unani* colleges and 19,685 practicing *unani* doctors. There are 177 hospitals dedicated to *unani* medicine, with a total bed count of 3,892.

The German physician Dr. Samuel Hahnemann founded the principles of India's fourth system of medicine, homeopathy, two hundred years ago. Its roots originate in the Greek words *homois* (minute dose) and *pathos* (suffering). It is based on the "law of cure," which claims that a compound given in large quantities to normal person may cause symptoms of a disease, but that same compound in minute amounts to an afflicted person may result in the cure of that disease. This minute dose of the compound acts as a triggering agent to stimulate and strengthen the existing defense mechanisms of the body. Compared to other systems of medicine, treatment is individualized under the homeopathic system and is unique to each person with the same disease. Homeopathy was brought to India in 1878, and by 2005 there were 124 five-year homeopathic medical schools in India. Nineteen of these colleges are maintained by the state and the others are privately owned. After the completion of graduate or postgraduate work, the student receives a bachelor of homeopathic medicine (B.H.M.S.) or a doctorate of homeopathic medicine (D.H.M.S.)

The Central Council of Indian Medicine oversees the standards of education and its practice in all of India's systems of medicine. A Central Council of Research has also been established, dedicated to all the disciplines, to promote advancement.

Deeptee Jain
Rajeev Jain, M.D.

See also **Health Care**

BIBLIOGRAPHY

Das, Bhagwan. *Fundamentals of Ayurvedic Medicine.* New Delhi: Konark Publishing, 1999.

Gupta, Giri Raj. *Social and Cultural Context of Medicine in India.* New Delhi: Advent Books, 1982.

Jaggi, O. P., ed. *Medicine in India: Modern Period.* New Delhi: Oxford University Press, 2001.

Kumar, Pragya. *Medical Education in India.* New Delhi: Deep & Deep Publishers, 1987.

Shanbag, Vivek. *A Beginner's Guide to Ayurvedic Medicine.* New York: McGraw-Hill, 1999.

Siddique, Mohammed Khalid. *State of Unani Medicine in India.* New Delhi: Ministry of Health and Family Welfare, Government of India, 1995.

Sindhu, Virendra. *Medical Colleges in India.* New Delhi: English Book Depot, 1971.

MEDICINE. *See* **Āyurveda.**

MEDIEVAL TEMPLE KINGDOMS The nearly eight-hundred-year span from the fall of the Gupta empire to the establishment of the Delhi Sultanate in the beginning of the thirteenth century has been a period of intense debate among historians of India. The sources for this period are extensive, comprising thousands of stone and copper plate inscriptions issued by scores of royal families and local lords; large numbers of religious, literary, and legal texts in both Sanskrit and regional languages; travelers' accounts in Arabic and Chinese; coins, monuments, and archaeological remains. In British colonial times, this period was judged to be one of "Hindu weakness," characterized by a bewildering array of petty dynastic houses engaged in constant internecine warfare—what one scholar called the "mutually repellent molecules" of Indian polity when not checked by a superior power. Until as late as the 1950s, the major concern of historians was simply to order the copious dynastic records into some sort of reliable political chronology. Since then, a number of more sophisticated cultural and social history perspectives have emerged.

One way to make sense of the diplomatic history of the royal houses of this period is the celebrated theory of the *rājamandala*, or "circle of kings," set out in the *Artha Shāstra*. According to this idea, the kingdoms of the subcontinent formed a great hierarchy of antagonisms and alliances, imagined as a vast set of concentric circles, at the center of which stood the ambitious king. A king seeking imperial status, signified by taking titles like *mahārājādhirāja* ("Great King over Kings"), sought to expand his sphere of influence by conducting wars of submission against contiguous kingdoms and by seeking alliance with those beyond their borders. While as a theory the *rājamandala* may explain the almost predictable diplomatic behaviors of kings during this period, it fails to capture the complexity of political relations on the ground. First, there was always more than one king (often there were several) who sought imperial status through such policies. This made the *rājamandala* in practice a highly complex, unstable, and multifocal structure. Second, the *rājamandala* was a theory of diplomacy rather than a theory of state. It tells us very little, in other words, about the structure and functioning of polity. All of the inscriptional evidence suggests that political conquest in these empires rarely entailed the direct annexation of territory; defeated kings were instead integrated into a loose imperial affiliative structure as underlords

Hoysaleshvara Temple, Halebid. The height of Hoysalan (or Karnatic) architecture survives in the form of the ornately carved double-shrine Hoysaleshvara Temple at Halebid, a city legendary for its former wealth and splendor. Laborers worked on its construction for some eighty years, beginning in 1121. The temple was never completed. CLAIRE ARNI.

(called *sāmantas*). They retained their ancestral territories and gained the protection of the imperial center, in return for tribute, military support, or service at court. Such imperial systems were most stable during periods of expansion and warfare, but tributary lords tended to assert their independence in times of either peace or imperial contraction.

As Gupta power in Gangetic and central India contracted at the beginning of the sixth century, a number of royal houses, some of whom had once been Gupta underlords, asserted independence and joined the Hūnas in vying for supremacy. Among these were the Maukharis of Kanauj, the Aulikāras of Mandasor, the Vardhanas of Sthānvīshvara, the Maitrakas of Valabhi, and the kings of Gauda, Vanga and Kāmarūpa. By the middle of the seventh century, the Vardhana king Hasha had annexed the neighboring kingdom of the Maukharis, with its prized city of the "Hump-backed Maiden," or Kanyākubja (Kanauj), and pursued an aggressive policy eastward against Gauda. Southward, the Chalukyas of Badāmi established themselves as the most powerful kings of the Deccan under the leadership of Pulakeshin II (r. 610–643), subduing many local kings like the Western Gangas, Kādambas, Bānas, and Alūpas—partly at the expense of the Pallava kings based farther south in Kānchi, who had earlier been dominant in the lower Deccan, but who from the sixth century were forced to turn southward for resources and allies. The Vardhanas of Kanauj, the Chalukyas of Badāmi, and the Pallavas of Kānchi thus formed three major foci in the overlapping hierarchies of the *rājamandala* system. This period set the pattern for the next six hundred years. By approximately 750, a new configuration had emerged, which saw three major imperial courts struggling for putative paramountcy: the Gurjara-Pratīhāras, an aristocratic clan with pastoral origins, who established a major empire from the city of Kanauj; the Rāshtrakūtas, a vassal house who defeated their overlords, the Chalukyas of Badāmi, in 757 to build a major empire in the Deccan and South India; and finally, the Pālas of Monghyr in eastern India, famous for their patronage of Buddhism, who rose to prominence in present-day Bihar and Bengal. Masudi, the Arab traveler who visited India in the tenth century, recognized these kings as the most powerful in the subcontinent. Their fortunes varied, and though regionally based, they spent great energy and resources in pursuing transregional imperial projects, assisted by their underlords.

In the latter half of the tenth century, a new crop of powerful dynasties rose to prominence. In North India, the Pratīhāra empire disintegrated into smaller kingdoms, some of whom claimed to be the "sons of kings," or *rajaputras*—the ancestors of the famous rajputs of the Sultanate and Mughal periods. The more powerful among these were the Chahāmānas of Ajayameru, the Gāhadvālas of Kāshi, the Chandellas of Kalanjara, the Kalachuris of Tripurī, and the Paramāras of Dhārā. A king from the last of these families, Shīyaka II, destroyed the Rāshtrakūta capital Mānyakheta in 973, and not long afterward, a former Rāshtrakūta vassal established a Chalukya kingdom based in the northern Deccan at Kalyāni, claiming links with the earlier Chalukyas. In South India, the Cholas overthrew the Pallavas of Kanchi, then underlords of the Rāshtrakūtas, and under the illustrious leadership of Rajaraja Chola (r. 985–1016) defeated the Pāndyas of Madurai to establish an empire in the south powerful enough to make its presence felt in Southeast Asia. After the success of Turkish armies on the northern Indian plains at the end of the twelfth century, and the establishment of the Sultanate of Delhi in the thirteenth, the political dynamics of northern India, and a century later of southern India as well, changed irreversibly.

The great majority of these kingdoms ascribed to the political ideologies, ritual programs, and historical worldviews of the theistic religions of Shaivism (the worshp of Shiva) and Vaishnavism (the worship of Vishnu), as they were embodied in cosmological "ancient tales," the Purāṇas, and ritual manuals called Āgamas and Saṃhitās. Though Shaivism and Vaishnavism had their origins in earlier times, it was during the post-Gupta period that they were transformed into powerful temple-based cults, gaining extensive royal patronage and dominating both rural and urban landscapes. This transformation was achieved in part by providing rulers with compelling new royal liturgies and imperial ideologies. The theistic cults largely dispensed with the older public Vedic fire-sacrifices like the *ashvamedha*, or horse sacrifice, and placed image worship in temples at the center of both public and private ritual. Temple building became a major preoccupation of Hindu rulers after the Gupta period, and dynasties like the Pallavas of Kanchi, Chalukyas of Badāmi, the Rāshtrakūtas of Mānyakheta, and the Cholas of Tanjavur built spectacular imperial temples and endowed them with large numbers of tax-free land holdings. Inside those temples were ritually established icons of Hindu gods and goddesses that were endowed with juristic personalities. Worship was governed by the ritual of *pūjā*, or "honoring." Unlike the distant divinities of the Vedic pantheon, to whom men dispatched offerings through the fire oblation, theistic ritual was based on a radically "immanent" and "emanative" conception of the divine. Vishnu and Shiva as cosmic overlords were thought to take many forms, both in the heavens and on the earth, to create, protect, and even destroy the cosmos. This theology had many implications for medieval life, but at the level of polity, it allowed kings to claim partial divinity (typically as an embodiment of Vishnu, the solar protector). Moreover, it provided kings with a rich language of imperial power. If the vast hierarchy of divine and human agencies was continuous with and mirrored the world of men, then it is perhaps not surprising that the language of sovereignty, the vocabulary of affiliation, and sumptuary palace routines of kings and gods were largely identical and reinforced one another.

The rise of dynastic kingdoms and temple cults in early medieval India overlay more complex social processes. Chief among these was the expansion of what one historian has called "state society," which saw the incorporation and transformation of relatively simple, clan- or kin-based societies into more economically specialized, socially differentiated, and ideologically elaborate social formations characterized by the existence of state apparati and an intellectual class largely freed from the strains of manual labor. The basis of these developments was an expanding agrarian economy—an expansion that saw tribal pastoralists, hunter-gatherers, and occasional agriculturalists transformed into settled, revenue-producing peasants. Historians have pointed out that the institution of the temple facilitated this long process of social and cultural integration by disseminating the values and ideologies of the elite (like devotion and submission to authority) among the lower orders as they were incorporated into caste society. Tribal and local gods were often absorbed into the prodigious pantheons of Vishnu and Shiva as lesser gods and local incarnations in the same way that tribal leaders could potentially convert their power into lordly status by taking on aristocratic norms. Despite these processes of dissemination and absorption, evidence suggests that the cultural change was multidirectional, as the persistence of tribal features in high caste pantheons and the spread of more egalitarian religious movements in the temple environment, which were hostile to landed interests, readily indicate.

Daud Ali

See also **Ashvamedha; Chola Dynasty; Guptan Empire; Harsha**

BIBLIOGRAPHY

Chattopadhyaya, B. D. *The Making of Early Medieval India.* Delhi: Oxford University Press, 1994.

Escheman, A., H. Kulke, and G. C. Tripathi, eds. *The Cult of Jagannatha and the Regional Tradition of Orissa*. Delhi: Manohar, 1986.

Inden, Ronald. "The Temple and the Hindu Chain of Being." *Purusartha* 8 (1985): 53–73.

Majumdar, R. C., ed. *Comprehensive History of India*, vol. III, pt. 1 (*300–985*). Mumbai: People's Publishing House, 1981.

Sharma, Ram Sharan. *Indian Feudalism: c. 300–1300*. 2nd ed. Delhi: Macmillan, 1980.

MEDITATION. *See* **Yoga.**

MEGHALAYA The "abode of clouds," Meghalaya is the wettest state in India. Also known as the Meghalaya Plateau or the Shillong Plateau, it lies between 450 and nearly 6,000 feet (137–1,829 m) above sea level. In the east of the state are the Jantia Hills; in the center, the West and East Khasi Hills; and in the west, the East and West Garo Hills. Over a dozen waterfalls grace the state, which is also subject to earthquakes; a major quake destroyed Shillong on 12 June 1897. In the west of the state in the South Garo Hills District is a vast tableland known as the "Land of Perpetual Winds," containing one of the richest areas of biodiversity in India. Known as the "Scotland of the East" for its resemblance to the Scottish Highlands, Meghalaya has one of the largest golf courses in Asia, the "Glen Eagle of the East," created in 1898. The capital, located in the east, is Shillong, 4,987 feet (1,520 m) above sea level, which is also the headquarters of a number of Indian military forces, including the Assam Rifles and the Eastern Air Command.

In the year 2000, the tribal Khasis, who call themselves Hynniewtrepsf (belonging to seven celestial families), and the tribal Jaintia made up 49 percent of the population of 2,175,000; the tribal Garos at 34 percent, Bengalis at 2.5 percent, and a variety of other ethnic groups, including Biharis, made up the rest of the population. Sixty-four percent of the population were Christian (most of the Khasis are Presbyterian or Roman Catholic, and the Garos are mostly Baptist), 17 percent animist, 15 percent Hindu, and 4 percent Muslim. The languages of the state are Khasi, Garo, and English. The tribals are said to have immigrated into the area before the common era and are of Mon-Khmer and Tibeto-Burman extraction. They are all matrilineal, and each tribe was formerly ruled by a raja. They practiced shifting cultivation. Rice cultivation continues to be the main agricultural occupation. Like all the tribals of the Northeast region, they celebrate the stages of the year with colorful dance festivals, which celebrate holidays originating in animistic practices, including the sacrifice of chickens and goats.

The British incorporated Assam into Bengal in 1838. The British occupied the Garo Hills in 1872, and Shillong became a hill station with a number of churches and cathedrals and Christian schools. They established a tribal district council, and Shillong became the capital of the Khasi and Jantia Hills District. In 1874, when the province of Assam was created and became a Chief Commissioner's Province, Shillong became its capital. In 1946 the Khasi-Jaintia Association was formed to demand a federation of the Khasi states, the same year the Hills Union called for a Hill State, and the Garo National Conference wanted a district administration with full political autonomy. This was the beginning of tribal political consciousness. In 1954 Shillong was made the capital of the North-East Frontier Agency. A number of political parties, including the Eastern Indian Tribal Union (1954), the All-Party Hill Leaders Conference (1960), and the Hill States People's Democratic Party (1968), were created to demand a separate state and to defend various tribal languages and interests. Meghalaya became an autonomous state within Assam on 2 April 1970, and it was inaugurated as a state of the Indian Union on 21 January 1972.

Roger D. Long

See also **Assam; Tribal Politics**

BIBLIOGRAPHY

Gurudev, S. *Anatomy of Revolt in the North East India*. New Delhi: Lancers Books, 1996.

Pakem, B., ed. *Regionalism in India: With Special Reference to North-East India.* New Delhi: Har-Anand Publications, 1993.

Phukon, Girin, and N. L Dutta, eds. *Politics of Identity and Nation Building in Northeast India*. New Delhi: South Asian Publishers, 1997.

MENON, V. K. KRISHNA *(1896–1974), Indian nationalist leader and politician.* Vengalil Krishnan Krishna Menon was a prominent Indian freedom fighter against British rule. With an intellectual orientation in common, Menon and Jawaharlal Nehru had forged a close friendship during the independence struggle. V. K. Krishna Menon was first appointed minister without portfolio (1952–1956) and then defense minister (April 1957–November 1962) in Prime Minister Nehru's government. During this time, Menon also served as leader of the Indian delegation to the United Nations (UN; 1952–1953 and 1954–1962).

He first gained international prominence in 1957 for an eight-hour improvised speech at the United Nations Security Council in defense of India's position on Kashmir. As leader of the Indian delegation, he was prominent in the negotiations that resolved the Korean War and the Suez crisis. In 1961 the West condemned India when, on Menon's advice to Nehru, Indian forces invaded Goa, seizing this colonial territory from the Portuguese in what was claimed to be a violation of the UN Charter on nonaggression and the resolution of disputes by peaceful means. A year later, Menon was pressured to resign as defense minister, following India's disastrous military defeat by Chinese forces along the Himalayan frontiers in October 1962. He was blamed for India's lack of military preparedness against China. Ironically, Prime Minister Nehru, the architect of Sino-Indian friendship, escaped blame.

Krishna Menon was born in Calicut, Cochin, now part of the state of Kerala, in 1896. He took an interest in the independence movement in the 1920s, first as an undergraduate student at Madras Presidency College, and then as a postgraduate law student at Madras Law College. As a law student he became associated with Annie Besant and her Home Rule Movement for India. Besant, impressed with the young Krishna Menon, sent him to England to study. In England he studied at the London School of Economics and at Lincoln's Inn, London, from where he was admitted to the English Bar as a barrister-in-law.

Menon founded the India League in London in 1928, and it became the center of Indian nationalist activities in England. The British Labour Party was impressed with his political skills and public oratory and made him one of its spokesmen. In 1934 he was elected to the London Muncipal Council from St. Pancras on a Labour ticket. He continued to be reelected from there until he became India's first high commissioner (ambassador) after India gained independence in 1947. During his time as a London councilman, Menon appeared as a barrister in several cases on behalf of London's poor. For his services, St. Pancras conferred on him the "Freedom of the Borough," an honor that until then had only been conferred on George Bernard Shaw. Menon also became a member of the Communist Party in London, an affiliation that plagued him later as a member of Nehru's Congress Party government. He was accused of excessive sympathy for China, blinding him to the threat from the north. Menon died in 1974 at the age of seventy-eight.

Raju G. C. Thomas

See also **China, Relations with; Nehru, Jawaharlal**

BIBLIOGRAPHY

Bakshi, S. R. *V. K. Krishna Menon: India and the Kashmir Problem*. New Delhi: South Asia Books, 1994.

George, T. J. S. *Krishna Menon: A Biography*. London: Jonathan Cape, 1964.

Kutty, V. K. Madhavan. *V. K. Krishna Menon*. New Delhi: Ministry of Information and Broadcasting, Government of India, 1998.

Ram, Janaki. *V. K. Krishna Menon*. New Delhi: Oxford University Press, 1997.

Varkey, K. T. *V. K. Krishna Menon and India's Foreign Policy*. New Delhi: Indian Publishers Distributors, 2002.

METALWARE There is an extremely long and highly developed tradition of metalworking in India and greater South Asia. Although the rich heritage of its sculptural manifestations and, to a lesser extent, coinage and jewelry are justly renowned, their equally sophisticated corollary artistic expressions of decorative metal vessels and containers, weaponry, and ritual objects are today much less known, rarely collected systematically by public institutions and scarcely studied by contemporary art historians. This lack of modern attention is curiously paradoxical because traditional handmade Indian metalware in particular was greatly admired during the Arts and Crafts Movement in England in the nineteenth century. This interest led to a prominent place for Indian metalware in many of the great international expositions and British Empire coronation celebrations held between 1851 and 1925. These exhibitions typically featured numerous examples of distinct geographical types of Indian metalware, with awards often bestowed for the best workmanship and design. Significant research on Indian metalware was also published in over a score of important articles, surveying its diverse regional forms and technical variations, that appeared in the *Journal of Indian Art and Industry* from 1886 to 1916. Conversely, for much of the remainder of the twentieth century and continuing into the twenty-first, the focus of most research on South Asian art switched from a media-based approach to a thematic one, centering on works of art and architecture affiliated with Buddhist, Hindu, Jain, or Islamic patronage and subject matter.

Early Material Evidence

Archaeological finds from the earliest periods of Indian protohistory attest to the existence of a well-developed tradition of metalworking. Excavations of the mature phase (c. 2600–1900 B.C.) of the Indus Valley Civilization, located in present-day Pakistan and northwestern India, have yielded copper, copper alloy (bronze), and silver vessels. No comparable gold examples have yet been discovered, but gold ornaments survive in considerable numbers. These early metal vessels replicate forms used widely for terra-cotta vessels, particularly cooking pots, water containers, and plate ware. They have been found primarily in burials and hoards, their preservation in this context certifying their high level of socioeconomic worth. After the decentralization and decline of the Indus Valley Civilization at the beginning of the second millennium B.C., extensive metalworking continued during the Late Bronze Age (c. 1700–1000 B.C.) in occupational communities dispersed primarily within the Ganges River valley and adjacent plains. Substantial hoards from this period have been discovered that contained a wide range of copper or copper alloy implements, weapons, and anthropomorphs (stylized human figures, perhaps of ritual significance). With the dawn of the Early Iron Age (c. 1200–1000 B.C.), iron weapons, tools, and domestic artifacts began to be produced and survive from a number of important archaeological sites throughout the Indian subcontinent. The Bronze Age and Iron Age evidence of Indian metalworking is well supported by contemporaneous literary references, which appear as early as the Rig Veda, approximately 1500 B.C.

Bejeweled Brass Samovar from Jaipur. From Jaipur, Rajasthan, rare seventeenth-century brass samovar inlaid with jewels. During the Mughal period, there was significant evolution in the technique and materials of Indian metalware, as enabled by the astounding wealth of the court. SUDHIR KASLIWAL.

Select Historical Masterpieces

In spite of the tragic fact that the vast majority of Indian decorative metalware and metal ritual objects created before the eighteenth century have not survived the ravages of time, warfare plunder, and the melting pot, sufficient isolated masterpieces survive, and myriad literary descriptions exist to create a compelling impression of what must have been a plethora of extraordinary artistic accomplishments.

One of the most accomplished examples of Indian metalware from the Early Historic period known to survive is the so-called Kulu Vase in the British Museum (OA 1880-22), which has been dated on stylistic grounds to the first century B.C. Once thought to be from Kulu in the Kangra District of the modern state of Himachal Pradesh, it is now known to have been found in a ruined monastery further north in Gondla in the Lahul and Spiti District. Made of bronze with a high tin content, the water vessel is fashioned in the traditional bulbous shape called a *lota*. The vessel is decorated on the shoulder and base with complex incised geometric designs, but its most remarkable feature is an elaborate procession engraved around the body. The highly detailed, sequential scenes present a king or prince performing a Buddhist religious ceremony and riding variously in a chariot, on an elephant, or on horseback. Several elegant females accompany the lead character. The engraving is exceptional not only for the artist's attention to detail and the lyrical grace of the stylized figures, but also for the sophisticated, subtle manipulation of the linear forms to accommodate the curved surface of the vase without betraying any hint of awkwardness or hesitation in draftsmanship.

The reigns of the imperial Guptas, who ruled the heartland of India from A.D. 319 to 484, and that of their contemporary southern neighbors, the royal Vakatakas (r. A.D. 275–518), are rightly regarded as among the pinnacles of cultural and artistic achievement in ancient India. Painting and sculpture reached extraordinary heights of development during this grand epoch, as evidenced by the famous late fifth-century murals at Ajanta in Maharashtra. A silver plate, now in the Cleveland Museum of Art (1972.71), is perhaps the finest extant example of the palatial decorative arts of this refined period. The plate is embellished with two registers depicting lively scenes of revelry. Each scene has a prominent male figure in the center, flanked by amorous females and male servants. The underside of the plate is decorated by a broad band of fluting surrounding a shallow foot, with a narrow band of elephants marching around the rim. The dense composition and rounded figural forms of this extraordinary silver plate stylistically resemble those found in the Ajanta paintings, which are important also for their pictorial documentation of contemporary metalware.

Indian metalware made during the medieval period (9th–15th centuries) perpetuated the superb aesthetic

> The cupp was of gould, sett all over with small turkyes [turquoise] and rubies, the cover of the same sett with great turquises, rubyes and emralds in woorks, and a dish suteable to sett the cupp upon. The valew I know not, because the stones are many of them small, and the greater, which are also many, are not all cleane, but they are in number about 2,000 and in gould about 20 oz.
>
> Sir Thomas Roe, *The Embassy of Sir Thomas Roe to India, 1615–19*, ed., Sir William Foster (London: Hakluyt Society, 1899; rev. ed., London: Oxford University Press, 1926), p. 225.

qualities of its ancient antecedents, but was also often distinguished by its complexity of design. The best surviving example of this more evolved stage of Indian metalware is a double-bodied ceremonial ewer dating from the early fourteenth century, which was found in a hoard in 1924 in Kollur in the Bijapur District of present-day Karnataka. It is now in the Chhatrapati Shivaji Maharaj Vastu Sangrahalaya, formerly called the Prince of Wales Museum of Western India, in Mumbai (Kollur, no. 200). The complex vessel has twin globular bodies, coupled together with a double concave bracket emblazoned with a leonine mask called a *kirttimukha* (face of glory). Each body is surmounted by a narrow neck and flared mouth, and each rests on a diamond-shaped pedestal foot graced with incised pipal (*Ficus religiosa*) leaf motifs. The dual vessel bodies are interconnected so that a single curvilinear spout with branchlike protrusions suffices for pouring.

The Mughal Period

During the Mughal period (1526–1858), northern Indian metalware was conceptually revitalized by a cross-fertilization of new vessel forms, types, and decoration introduced from the extensive panoply of Iranian and Central Asian Islamic metalware, and by the artistic inspiration of the reigning Mughal emperors themselves. Judging from the examples depicted in the oversize painted illustrations of the *Hamzanama* (The adventures of Hamza, created between 1556 and 1565), early Mughal metalware perpetuated Iranian and Central Asian metalware (and glassware) conventions of form and function. Its decoration consisted primarily of geometric designs, with stylized animal heads only occasionally serving as terminal and spout motifs. Soon, however, northern Indian metalware was transformed into a dynamic hybrid creation.

The exposure of the Mughal emperors to engravings in European herbal books and to the rich flora and fauna of the South Asian landscape, particularly the visit of the Mughal emperor Jahangir (r. 1605–1627) to the lush, flower-filled valleys of Kashmir in 1620, combined to engender a major artistic transformation in Indian metalware and its companion arts. Naturalistic flowering plants formally arranged against a plain background became the Mughal dynastic leitmotif, as exemplified on the Taj Mahal (1632–1643), and there was also an increased predilection for floral and animal imagery. In Mughal metalware, and the decorative arts in general, the ornamentation and often even the overall external shape of a vessel, container, weapon hilt, or other luxury object was typically derived from forms found in the natural world.

In addition to the artistic and conceptual developments that occurred in Indian metalware during the Mughal period, there was also a significant evolution in technique and costly materials that was enabled by the astounding wealth of the Mughal court. Gold and silver pouring and serving vessels made during the seventeenth century were particularly sumptuous, sometimes being inlaid with well over a thousand spectacular gemstones. These ornate Mughal palatial vessels are exceedingly rare today because most were stripped of their jewels and melted down for their cash value. The finest surviving examples are those looted from Delhi by the Iranian king Nadir Shah in 1739 and presented by his embassy in 1741 to Elizabeth Petrovna (reigned 1741–1762), daughter of Peter the Great of Russia. They are now in the Hermitage Museum in St. Petersburg, Russia. One of the most lavishly adorned of these vessels (V3-714) is a rose-water sprinkler made of gold with delicately chased floral and vegetal designs. Its surface is further enriched by the inlay of 40 diamonds, 1,439 rubies, and 509 emeralds. Mughal vessels of precious materials are often shown in contemporary paintings and are described in the journals and letters of seventeenth-century European travelers, such as Sir Thomas Roe, the English ambassador to Jahangir's court, who tells of being presented by the emperor in 1616 with a bejeweled golden cup.

Bidri-ware

During the Mughal period, a distinctive metalware tradition known as *bidri*-ware evolved in the Deccan region (south-central India). *Bidri*-ware was first made for temple use in the early fifteenth century in Bijapur in Karnataka, but an offer of full royal patronage by ʿAlaʾ al-Din Ahmad Bahmani II (reigned 1436–1458) soon lured its artisans to his kingdom in Bidar (whence its adjectival name) near Hyderabad in modern Andhra Pradesh. The production of *bidri*-ware flourished at Bidar and Hyderabad during the late sixteenth through nineteenth centuries, achieving its artistic zenith between 1650 and 1725. By the late eighteenth and nineteenth centuries, *bidri*-ware was also being produced at other Muslim courts in northern India, principally at Purnea in Bihar, Murshidabad in Bengal, and Lucknow in Uttar Pradesh.

Technique. *Bidri*-ware is made from a predominately zinc-based alloy, along with smaller amounts of lead, copper, and/or tin. Its technical process is complex and involves three metalworking specialists (metalsmith, engraver, and inlayer) and five manufacturing stages (casting, designing and engraving, inlaying, blackening, and polishing). *Bidri*-ware ornamentation is produced by means of several, often combined techniques: the inlay of sheets of precious metals (*tehnishan*) and single strands of wire (*tarkashin*), and the overlay of a sheet of silver with designs cut out in silhouette (*aftabi*). In the Deccan and eastern India, inlaid designs are rendered flush and burnished (*zarnishan*). In contrast, Lucknow *bidri*-ware often features designs in bold relief (*zarbuland*), in which the inlaid metals protrude slightly above the surface and are adorned with incised motifs or a thin overlay of gold or silver. Regardless of technique, silver was the favored metal used for inlaying *bidri*-ware in all of the major centers of production. The use of brass or brass mixed with gold as an inlay was confined to the Deccan and generally ceased around 1725.

Types of *Bidri*-ware. A broad spectrum of object types and forms were made in *bidri*-ware, including circular salvers (*thali*), octagonal plates (*tashtari*), water-pipe (hookah, *huqqa*) bases, containers (*pandan*) for prepared *pan* leaves (the popular Indian and Southeast Asian betel nut digestive), spittoons (*ugaldan*) necessary for disposing of the masticated betel nut remnants, candelabra (*shamadan*), and even furniture. A late eighteenth-century water-pipe base from Hyderabad, now in the Los Angeles County Museum of Art (M.2001.101), exemplifies the complexity of form and elegance of design found on the most accomplished *bidri*-ware. Its overlaid silver decoration consists principally of a meandering grape leaf and bunch motif.

Enameled Metalware

The use of enameled decoration (*minakari*) on Indian metalware is traditionally said to have begun in the late sixteenth century at Amber, near Jaipur in Rajasthan, when the Rajput ruler Man Singh (r. 1592–1614) reportedly established a royal enameling workshop with five Sikh enamelers brought from Lahore in the Punjab. This seems unlikely, however, considering that Man Singh is not regarded as an energetic patron of the arts, and no enameled metalware survives that can be attributed to Amber with certainty. The earliest historically plausible reference for Indian enameled metalware is during the rule of Emperor Akbar (r. 1556–1605), when enameling in the imperial ateliers was recorded by the official court chronicler, Abu'l-fazl ʿAllami, in his *A'in-i Akbari* (The institutes of Akbar). In the seventeenth and eighteenth centuries, additional knowledge of enameling techniques was imported by a number of European and Iranian goldsmiths and jewelers who are known to have been employed in various royal ateliers in India. By the nineteenth century, the production of enameled metalware had become widespread throughout South Asia. The leading centers were Delhi; Alwar, Bikaner, Nathdwara, and, especially, Jaipur in Rajasthan; Lucknow and Varanasi (Banaras) in Uttar Pradesh; Hyderabad in Andhra Pradesh; Kangra and Kulu in Himachal Pradesh; Kashmir; and Hyderabad and Multan in present-day Pakistan.

Almost all Indian enameled objects were created using the champlevé technique, which requires various stages of development: designs are engraved or ground into the surface of the metal; filled with a paste of powdered glass and the particular metallic oxide that would determine the desired brilliant enamel color; fired sequentially several times because of the different melting temperatures of the various enamel pastes; usually ground smooth; and polished. The cloisonné technique of separating areas of enameling with thin wire was only occasionally used. Enamel decoration was also simply painted onto the surface of the metal before firing. In early Mughal examples, the enamel is typically opaque, while in works created during and after the rule of Shah Jahan (r. 1628–1658), it is generally translucent. A particularly fine example of late eighteenth-century Lucknow enamel metalware is a brilliant hookah base, which is now in the Victoria and Albert Museum, London (IS 122-1886). Its distinctive blue and green enameling consists primarily of stylized poppy plants encircled by oval cartouches, with a twin border of a flowering vine.

"Ganga-Jumna" Metalware

Another important type of Indian metalware is known as "Ganga-Jumna" metalware. Its name is derived from the simultaneous use of two contrasting colors of metal, which symbolically refer to the two mighty rivers of North India: the Ganges (Ganga), considered light in color; and the Jumna (formerly called the Yamuna), thought to be dark. In the original and most costly Ganga-Jumna metalware, silver and gold were used to represent the two rivers. In most surviving examples, however, the less expensive metals of brass and copper or brass and bell-metal were used respectively to symbolize them. Ganga-Jumna metalware was once believed by Western scholars to be produced only in Varanasi, where the term is geographically appropriate. Yet, brass-and-copper vessels displaying engraved or inlaid inscriptions in South Indian languages and Hindu iconic decoration using South Indian figural styles prove that the distinctive two-tone metalware was also produced in the regions of Karnataka and Tamil Nadu, especially in Thanjavur (Tanjore). Regardless of origin, the two primary vessel types are the *lota* and the *chambu* (differentiated from the *lota* by its flattened spherical body, conical foot, constricted neck with ring molding, and wide-lipped mouth).

This brief survey skims only the surface of the deep well of Indian metalware. Numerous other important regional, temporal, ritual, secular, and folk traditions exist, such as the wide range of everyday brassware; the sophisticated silver metalware produced in the eighteenth century in Rajasthan and in Pune (Poona) in Maharashtra during the Maratha period; the Hindu "Swami" metalware of Thanjavur; the delicate silver filigree work of Cuttack in Orissa, Karimnagar in Andhra Pradesh, and Dacca (Dhaka) in modern Bangladesh; the European-influenced gold and silver metalware of Kutch in Gujarat; and the colonial-period silver of Kolkata (Calcutta) and Delhi.

Stephen Markel

BIBLIOGRAPHY

Agrawal, Yashodhara. "The Ganga-Jamuni Metal Ware of Banaras." In *Decorative Arts of India*, edited by M. L. Nigam. Hyderabad: Salar Jung Museum, 1987.

Chandra, Moti. "Ceremonial Utensils from Kollur." *Prince of Wales Museum Bulletin* 8 (1965): 1–7.

Errington, Elizabeth, and Joe Cribb, eds. *The Crossroads of Asia: Transformation in Image and Symbol in the Art of Ancient Afghanistan and Pakistan*. Cambridge, U.K.: Fitzwilliam Museum, 1992.

The Indian Heritage: Court Life and Arts under Mughal Rule. London: Victoria and Albert Museum, 1982.

Ivanov, Anatoli A., et al. *Oriental Jewellery: From the Collection of the Special Treasury, the State Hermitage Oriental Department*. Moscow: Art, 1984.

Jones, Owen. *The Grammar of Ornament*. 1856. Reprint, London: Studio Editions, 1986.

Kenoyer, Jonathan Mark. *Ancient Cities of the Indus Valley Civilization*. Karachi: Oxford University Press and American Institute of Pakistan Studies, 1998.

Lal, Krishna. *National Museum Collection: Bidri Ware*. New Delhi: National Museum, 1990.

Mahmud, Sayed Jafar. *Metal Technology in Medieval India*. Delhi: Daya Publishing House, 1988.

Mughal Silver Magnificence (XVI–XIXth C.). Brussels: Antalga, 1987.

Pal, Pratapaditya. *The Gupta Sculptural Tradition and Its Influence*. New York: Asia Society, 1978.

Sharma, Deo Prakash. *Newly Discovered Copper Hoard, Weapons of South Asia (c. 2800–1500 B.C.)*. Delhi: Bharatiya Kala Prakashan, 2002.

Stronge, Susan. *Bidri Ware: Inlaid Metalwork from India*. London: Victoria and Albert Museum, 1985.

Untracht, Oppi. *Traditional Jewelry of India*. New York: Harry N. Abrams, 1997.

Untracht, Oppi, et al. *Metal Marvels: South Asian Handworks*. Porvoo, Finland: Porvoo Museum, 1993.

Varney, R. J. "Enamelling in Rajasthan." *Roopa-Lekha* 29, nos. 1 and 2 (1958): 31–39.

Zebrowski, Mark. *Gold, Silver and Bronze from Mughal India*. London: Alexandria Press in association with Laurence King, 1997.

MILITARY INTERVENTIONS IN SOUTH ASIA From the standpoint of small South Asian states, the "India factor" in their security has both negative and positive connotations. India's large size and huge military power are considered the fundamental sources of their perception of potential danger. At the same time, India's centrality in the region, coupled with its capability to respond swiftly to an urgent call for assistance, is a positive feature. India has indeed rendered military assistance to Myanmar (then Burma), Nepal, Sri Lanka, and the Maldives, even though some of these countries have at times perceived India as a threat. India's security interests are integrated with those of the entire region; its neighbors' interests are closely linked to its own. If friendship with India is considered important for the security of its small neighbors, their internal political stability and independence remain vital factors in Indian security.

Indian military assistance has been rendered only upon the request of beleaguered South Asian states facing rebellion, insurrection, insurgency, or a coup d'état. States that sought Indian military assistance have been inherently weak, lacking sufficient military strength to defend their national interests. Decisions to commit Indian forces for security duties abroad were all taken by Indian Congress Party governments headed by three powerful prime ministers—Jawaharlal Nehru, Indira Gandhi, and Rajiv Gandhi—who belonged to the same family and pursued much the same foreign policy, with modifications to suit the changing international or regional situations. Nehru intended to make India the leader of Afro-Asia's third world; his daughter and grandson strove more to project India as the leader of South Asia. In this context they used the military as an instrument of diplomacy, projecting Indian power over South Asia. Though India readily extended military assistance during the cold war period, it has since grown more reluctant to undertake a security role. In 2000, for example, India did not consider Sri Lanka's request for military help. It also declined to accept a combat role against the Maoist insurgents in Nepal.

Early Instances of Military Involvement

Burma. Burma (now Myanmar) was the first to seek limited Indian military help in 1949, when the Anti-Fascist

Indian Peacekeeping Force (IPKF), in Sri Lanka. The IPKF arrive in Sri Lanka, July 1987. Part of the 70,000 troops dispatched there to enforce an accord reached by India and Sri Lanka to end the ethnic Tamil conflict in the latter nation. INDIA TODAY.

People's Freedom League government was threatened by a series of combined rebellions launched by the Communists and the Karen National Defense Organization, as well as by mutinies in the army. For Burma's Communists, who were excluded from power, the newly won "independence" seemed false, because Burma remained within the sphere of British power and influence. They wanted to create a Communist state through armed struggle. At the same time, the Karen ethnic group revolted against discriminatory treatment. Aggrieved over the denial of their right to secede from the union, which had been extended to the Shan and Kayah states, and the government's refusal to accept their boundary demands for a new Karen state, the Karens launched an armed secessionist movement. Simultaneously, other disgruntled minorities also revolted. The orgy of violence by the rebels pushed the entire nation into chaos. The Karen military rebels undermined the government so severely that it could control only the capital, Rangoon, and a few other cities. Burma badly needed external support to prevent its disintegration.

Nepal. In Nepal the level and intensity of rebel threat was much lower. Militant activities by K. I. Singh, a dissident Nepali Congress leader, helped by several criminal groups from 1951 to 1953, had caused political instability and lawlessness. Singh had mobilized Nepal's disgruntled Mukti Sena members against the Congress government's decision to share power with the autocratic Ranas, launching a nationwide reign of terror in 1951. In the same year, the separatist Kirantis living along Nepal's border with Tibet also refused to recognize the government's authority over the Eastern Hills. Singh, who was briefly jailed, escaped from prison on 11 July 1951 and declared himself local governor, seizing a government treasury. After his second escape from prison on 23 January 1952, he launched an attack on the capital, Kathmandu, with the help of 1,200 rebel soldiers, capturing the treasury, arsenal, broadcasting station, and airport. Nepal's communication links with India were disrupted. That revolt was crushed, but in April 1953, some 700 Nepalese rebels, led by Bhim Dutt Pant, attacked police stations and looted private property in Nepal's Western Terai region. Unable to crush the menace, the Kathmandu government sought Indian military assistance. India sent one battalion of its army and a constabulary force from Uttar Pradesh.

Sri Lanka. Insurrection and ethnic conflict had necessitated India's involvement in Sri Lanka twice, in 1971 and from 1987 to 1990. In April 1971, Sri Lanka faced a threat to the integrity of its polity when the Janatha Vimukthi Peramuna (JVP; the People's Liberation Front), a Sinhalese Buddhist youth movement with a strong ideological commitment to Marxism, launched an abortive insurrection to capture state power. It planned attacks on police stations and army camps, and hoped to abduct or kill the prime minister and capture the capital, Colombo. However, it was successful only in capturing a large number of police stations. The government lost control of over fifty major towns. To regain control and end the insurrection, Prime Minister Sirimavo Bandaranaike requested military assistance from many countries, including India. The second time, the need for military support arose in July 1987, when India and Sri Lanka signed a peace accord to end Sri Lanka's ethnic Tamil conflict. The accord itself made provision for India's military role. At the request of Sri Lankan president J. R. Jayewardene, Indian prime minister Rajiv Gandhi sent a contingent of the Indian Peacekeeping Force (IPKF), some 70,000 troops, to implement the accord. In fulfilling its obligations, India was obliged to wage a war against the Liberation Tigers of Tamil Eelam, a separatist militant group that rejected the autonomy solution offered by the accord.

Maldives. The Maldives were threatened by external mercenaries in November 1988, when a group of about 400 men, allegedly recruited by some disgruntled expatriate Maldivians, invaded the capital, Male, with the aim of overthrowing the regime headed by President Maumoon Abdul Gayoom. They stormed the presidential palace and easily took control of the government secretariat as well as radio and television stations. President Gayoom and some of his senior ministers took refuge at the headquarters of the National Security Service (a paramilitary force of 350 men in 1988, now increased to over 1,500); from there he appealed to India for military assistance. India sent three warships and some 1,600 paratroopers to secure the capital. Fortunately for the president, the mercenaries could not disrupt the atoll island nation's vital communication links, and India's timely intervention saved the Gayoom regime.

Motives and Results

Clearly, a combination of factors motivated India to undertake military roles in its neighborhood. In protecting the national interests of its distressed neighbors, India sought to promote regional stability, considering such political turmoil in neighboring states a threat to regional peace. In India's view, violence by the rebels in all these countries threatened democracy, whose maintenance has been a cardinal principle of India's South Asian policy. India has also remained opposed to the involvement of any extraregional powers in South Asia. By rendering military assistance to Burma and Nepal, India hoped to prevent Chinese intervention. Similarly, its unprecedented military role in Sri Lanka in the 1980s was designed to thwart President Jayewardene's attempts to become a strategic ally of the West (by, for instance, providing naval base facilities to the United States) and to prevent any further inroads by Pakistan and China. The 1987 peace accord also enforced India's dominant influence in matters of Sri Lanka's security.

As in Sri Lanka, where Indian military involvement was guided by its obligations under the accord, the Indo-Nepalese peace and friendship treaty of 1950 imposed specific obligations on India to protect Nepalese security. India's friendship with troubled neighboring regimes remained an important motivating factor. Leaders who were at the helm of affairs at the time of crisis in each country—Prime Minister U Nu (Burma), King Tribhuvan and Prime Minister Koirala (Nepal), Prime Minister Sirimavo Bandaranaike (Sri Lanka), and President Gayoom (Maldives)—all maintained friendly relations with the Indian leadership.

In some cases, India feared that violent developments among its neighbors would cause adverse effects on its own society and economy. For instance, the success of a Communist revolt in Nepal or the Karen ethnic movement in Burma might encourage or strengthen secessionist ethnic movements in northeast India. Prime Minister Nehru felt that Burma's disintegration would not only affect India's economic interests but would also endanger the lives of about 700,000 Indians living there.

Whatever little gains India's military interventions won, in most cases the benefits did not endure. After the rebellion in Burma, India was viewed as a trusted friend for some years, and on 7 July 1951, the two countries signed a friendship treaty valid for five years. Similarly, Nepal became openly pro-Indian for some years, and its leaders acknowledged India's importance to Nepal's economic development and security. Simultaneously, however, there existed a growing sense of discontent over India's frequent military involvement, which some opposition parties used to create a strong anti-Indian feeling. The Nepalese government leaders were condemned as puppets of India, and the opposition soon overthrew them. In Maldives, however, India's military help left a durable imprint of friendship. Expressing his government's deep appreciation and gratitude for Indian support,

President Gayoom disagreed with others' descriptions of India as a regional "hegemonic" power.

In Sri Lanka, on the other hand, the IPKF operations eventually turned into a costly politico-military affair, and by mid-1989, the presence of so many Indian troops became a divisive issue in bilateral relations. Sri Lanka demanded their withdrawal long before the assigned task of implementing the accord was achieved. In economic and military terms, India paid a heavy price: about 1,200 soldiers dead and 2,500 were injured, at a cost to India of about U.S.$180 million. Dismayed at the shabby treatment given their troops by the Sri Lankan government, the Indian government withdrew its forces in early 1990. Soon after, in March 1990, External Affairs Minister (later prime minister) I. K. Gujral declared that India would never again send troops to any neighboring country. Despite many changes in Delhi's government and leadership, this position has remained unchanged.

Ponmoni Sahadevan

See also **Burma; Maldives and Bhutan, Relations with; Nepal, Relations with; Sri Lanka, Relations with**

BIBLIOGRAPHY

Nehru, Jawaharlal. *India's Foreign Policy: Selected Speeches, September 1946–April 1961*. New Delhi: Ministry of Information and Broadcasting, 1974.

SECONDARY SOURCES

Gupta, Anirudha. *Politics in Nepal, 1950–1960*. Delhi: Kalinga, 1993.

Rohan, Gunaratna. *Sri Lanka: A Lost Revolution? The Inside Story of the JVP*. Kandy, Sri Lanka: Institute of Fundamental Studies, 1995.

Rose, Leo E. *Nepal: Strategy of Survival*. Mumbai: Oxford University Press, 1971.

Sardeshpande, Lt. Gen. S. C. *Assignment Jaffna*. New Delhi: Lancer, 1992.

Singh, Uma Shankar. *Burma and India, 1948–1962*. New Delhi: Oxford University Press and IBH, 1979.

Smith, Martin. *Burma: Insurgency and the Politics of Ethnicity*. London: Zed Books, 1999.

Wilson, A. Jeyaratnam. *The Break-up of Sri Lanka: The Sinhalese-Tamil Conflict*. London: C. Hurst, 1988.

MINIATURES

This entry consists of the following articles:

BIKANER

BUNDI

CENTRAL INDIA

HAREM SCENES

KISHANGARH

KOTAH

MARWAR AND THIKANAS

BIKANER

An important branch of the Rajput maharajas of the Rathod clan, under Rao Bikar, established the state of Bikaner in 1478 in the semibarren Thar Desert in northwest Rajasthan. Bikaner remained prominent under the imperial Mughals through the sixteenth and seventeenth centuries, and Bikaner painting, as well as other aspects of society, evinced a profound and sophisticated Mughal influence, to a greater extent than other schools of Rajput painting. Despite this impact, the Bikaner school lacked the liveliness and subtlety of the latter.

Royal archival day-to-day account diaries (*bahis*) and numerous inscriptions on Bikaner paintings make this one of the best documented of the Rajput schools. Inscriptions, mainly in the Marwari dialect but occasionally also in Persian script, reveal dates and artists' names and in some cases even the place of production and the occasions for which the works were commissioned. Evidently, there were interactions between visiting Muslim painters from neighboring Rajput states with local novices, who later adopted Islam and were called *ustas*. Political successes continued to draw more wealth, and painting flourished as well, attracting other Hindu and Jain painters.

Accomplished master artists, called *gajdhars* (or *sutrdhars*, "who hold a yardstick"), served as links between the patrons and their respective ateliers. In order to secure projects and their positions in court, they secured material, supervised the production of paintings, and disbursed stipends to other artists. They not only trained junior artists but also gave finishing individualized touches, which contributed to the style and trend of the traditional royal school.

Fewer than five hundred artists worked at the Bikaner court. They produced over fifteen thousand individual paintings and numerous illustrated manuscripts for the royal library, as well as *zananas*. Works were usually done on paper, but wood, hide, cloth, and ivory were also used. Surviving fine examples from the Bikaner Fort indicate that wall paintings, painted doors and furniture and even goddess statues (*Ganvar mata*, a form of Devī) were also painted by these artists. Modern postcard-size portraits of dignitaries as well as of Hindu divinities, especially Krishna with his flute, were produced as offerings to be presented on birthdays or after a death. Talented artists received high recognition and rewards, including money, land, and secure employment.

Bikaner Wall Painting. Inspired by contemporary events, Bikaner artists often delved into the pomp and circumstance of the royalty. AMIT PASRICHA.

The paintings delved into popular subjects, connected either with royalty or religious events, inspired by contemporary issues and by other Rajput and Mughal courts. The paintings depicted royal activities (male and female *durbār* scenes, amorous scenes), hunting and war expeditions, *Ragmala* sets depicting the modes of music, *Barahmasa* sets illustrating the twelve months of the year, and Krishna-*lila* and other purely religious compositions, such as the acclaimed *Vaikuntha Darsana* (Vision of Vishnu's paradise).

Typical of the school were dwarfed human figures with large heads, awkwardly proportioned, appearing to float in the air. Rajputi-style trees were placed in a Mughal landscape, which was highly finished but less expressive than other Raput styles. The male figures in the painting were inspired by the *shabih*s of the maharajas, but the females were more similar to the prototypes that were first introduced in Bikaner by the visiting master painter Ustad Ali Raza of Delhi (fl. 1645–1665).

Beginning from Raja Rai Singh (r. 1571–1612) to the first quarter of the seventeenth century, with the help of imperial *karkhana* and visiting imperial artists, Bikaner royal *karkhana* started producing Mughalized and Popular Mughal style works. Maharaja Karan Singh (r. 1631–1669) and Anup Singh (r. 1669–1698), both great connoisseurs of art, gave Bikaner painting its distinct character, that is, an artistic combination of Mughal elegance with a forceful Deccani palette, resulting in an aesthetic visual Rajput adaptation. This style, initiated by Ali Raza in the second half of the seventeenth century, became a trendsetter for local masters such as Usta Ruknuddin (fl. 1650–1700), Nathhu (fl. 1650–1695), Isa (fl. 1680–1715), and Rashid (fl. 1675–1695). Out of eight, two lineages of promising painters, named after their founders—Umrani and Lalani—found long-lasting patronage. Usta Ruknuddin, from the Umrani house, and his son Ibrahim (fl. 1675–1700) supervised extensive production during Anup Singh's reign. Themes were executed in great length, and a major production of a *Rasikpriya* series was accomplished, in which local Bikaner style was more or less crystallized; it continued to influence Bikaner painters for centuries.

Some of the masterpieces of this period include the *Vaikuntha Darshana* (Abode of Vishnu, c. 1650, Bharat Kala Bhavan, Banaras Hindu University, Varanasi) executed by the master painter Ali Raza; *Ladies' Party* (c. 1665), by Ruknuddin; and *Lady Looking into a Mirror* (1665) by Usta Natthu.

Influences of the Deccan and neighboring Rajput states of Jodhpur are evident in the works created during the period of Maharaha Sujan Singh (r. 1700–1736); here the approach was simple and direct. Following the existing trends, another set of *Rasikpriya*, under the supervision of painter Usta Nure (fl. 1646–1715), was produced. Human figures, trees, and architecture became slender and elongated, reminiscent of artistic trends during Aurangzeb's reign. Though some artists continued to prefer Ruknuddin's squarish faces, the majority followed Nure's preference for small oval faces. Until the third quarter of the century, human expressions remained lively, and landscape was well treated. However, compared to other Rajput schools, the compositions were less properly integrated.

The decline of the Mughals and political and matrimonial ties with Jaipur and Jodhpur witnessed another wave of pleasant interaction of local and neighboring artists during the reign of Maharaja Zorawar Singh (r. 1736–1745) and the first half of the reign of Maharaja Gaj Singh (r. 1746–1787). Jodhpuri influences dominated the prevalent conventional trends. Noteworthy, with its sinuous lines and delicate colors, is the portrait of *Zorawar Singh Hunting* (c. 1740, National Museum, New Delhi). Court master Usta Abu, son of Kasam, heavily inspired by Europeanized Mughal features, captured the grandeur of the court of Gaj Singh, who is said to have patronized over two hundred artists.

More artists arrived when further political and matrimonial ties with Jaipur were solicited during the period of Maharaja Surat Singh (r. 1827–1851). A new Bikaner hybrid style emerged with the coming together of the disintegrating Jaipur approach and the limping Bikaner style. Jaipur artists soon seized the prestige and landholdings of practicing painters such as Usta Abu, his son Ahmad (fl. 1804), and Ibrahim (fl. 1764). Crudely modeled figures, ornamental foliage and trees, and a preference for an unusal shade of acidic green characterize this new style. The technique seems to have been initiated by Usta Katiram of Jaipur (fl. 1815) and Gajdhar Sukharam and his son Balu (fl. 1754–1760).

The advent of the Company school of painting caused the further decline of the Bikaner school, as was the case throughout India. However, a small group of artists continued to work in the declining royal ateliers of Maharaja Sardar Singh (r. 1851–1872) and his successors.

Naval Krishna
Manu Krishna

BIBLIOGRAPHY

Goetz, H. *The Art and Architecture of Bikaner State.* Oxford: B. Cassirer, 1950.

Goswamy, B. N. *Painted Visions: The Goenka Collection of Indian Paintings.* New Delhi: Lalit Kala Akademi, 1999.

Krishna, N. "Bikaner Miniature Painting Workshops of Ruknuddin Ibrahim and Nathhu." *Lalit Kala* 21 (1985): 23–27.

Welch, S. C. *Gods, Thrones, and Peacocks.* New York: H. N. Abrams, 1965.

BUNDI

The state of Bundi in Rajasthan, formerly known as Haraoti, was the stronghold of the Hara Rajputs. It is surrounded by Jaipur and Tonk on the north, and the state of Mewar on the west. To the south lies the state of Kotah, where an identical style of painting prevailed. This entire region is mountainous, with fast-flowing rivers, dense forests and greenery. These natural physical features proved conducive to a picturesque landscape, which Bundi painters exploited to the fullest extent. The history of Bundi began in the era of Rao Surjan (r. A.D. 1554–1585), a vassal of Mewar, who after 1569 became a feudatory of the Mughals. The recently discovered Chunar Ragamala, dated to 1591, painted at Chunar near Banaras (Varanasi), provides conclusive evidence of the close relationship between the Mughal and the Bundi rulers. The Chunar Ragamala, apart from revealing some visual similarities between Mughal and Bundi painting, has a detailed colophon in Nastalique script, giving a date, place of execution, and a genealogy of painters, whose origins leads us to the period of the Mughal emperor Akbar (r. 1556–1605). Thus it stands to reason that early as well as late Bundi painting had been influenced by contemporary Mughal painting up to the nineteenth century.

As a result of the Vaishnava renaissance (in Rajasthan), which passionately captured the hearts of the Hindu masses with its doctrine of *bhakti* (devotion) to Vishnu and his *avatāra* Krishna, propagated by Vallabhacharya, various schools and styles of paintings sprang up, producing abundant devotional art. Authors and artists took great delight in writing about and painting themes of divine love, as in the Gītā Govinda of Jayadeva (c. 12th century), the Rasikapriya of Keshavadasa (c. 16th century), the Sur-Sagar of the blind poet Surdas, as well as the Dasama Skanda (tenth canto) of the Bhāgavata Purāṇa. Painters' repertoires also included sets of *Barahmasa* (pictorial descriptions of the Indian seasons) and the *Rāgamala* (pictorial renderings of the Indian musical modes in color), which became the favorite subjects Bundi and Kotah artists.

Apart from these devotional works of art, there were also many paintings of court life and outdoor activities, particularly hunting. Large *shikar* (hunting) scenes, music and dancing parties, and portraits of Bundi chiefs and their favorite animals, especially the elephant, became the stock and trade of the Bundi painters. They produced some exquisite studies of elephants in fury, engaged in intense battle, or escaping through narrow gateways. The taming of wild elephants has always been a subject of delight to Indian painters and patrons a like.

The discoveries of certain inscribed and dated paintings toward the middle of the seventeenth century helped to reconstruct a rough chronology of the development of Bundi style. Examples include: *Nobleman and the Lady Watching Pigeons*, Bundi, dated 1662; *Lovers in a Pavilion*, dated 1682, from the collection of the Bharat Kala Bhawan Banaras; and *Lovers Pointing to the Crescent Moon*, gift of the painter Mohan. All of these exhibit salient features of the school, which determine the definition of Bundi painting.

Female figures are tall, with narrow waists, having somewhat prominent noses and almond-shaped eyes. Their costumes consist of a *ghaghra*, a very high *choli*, and an *odhni*, and black tassels are attached to their wristlets and armlets. Men wear a long transparent *jama*, a long and narrow *patka*, and a *churidar paijama*. Mughal mannerisms, such as shading below the armpit, are also seen in many cases. A variety of turban types are depicted, among which the Khanjardar turban type (having a pointed top) invariably indicates nobility. Pictures are composed either in open courtyards or inside pavilions with lush green vegetation as a backdrop.

Bundi style also exhibits certain Deccani influences, due to close contacts with the Deccani ruler Rao Satrasal (r. 1631–1656), who was installed by Mughal emperor Shah Jahan as governor. Subsequently, there were many appointments of Bundi rulers in the Deccan, reinforcing the Deccani influence on Bundi style.

The eighteenth century witnessed a prolific production of portraiture on the one hand and depictions of the Krishna legend on the other. Most of the *Barahamasa* and *Ragamala* sets were produced by Bundi and Kotah painters during this period. Later Bundi paintings excel in certain prominent features, such as lush green vegetation with a variety of flowering vines and plants, evergreen plantains, and dramatic skies with grey, orange, and blue hues. Another peculiarity of Bundi painting is a cast shadow behind the faces and figures, highlighting the contours of the body. Nineteenth-century Bundi paintings developed a pale phase, in which artists preferred light hues and cool color notes, and there was an emphasis on outdoor scenes. The figures appear squat, and the cast shadows dominate. Toward the late nineteenth century there was a decline in the technique and quality of Bundi paintings, and folkish and pedestrian works were produced by undistinguished painters.

Shridhar Andhare

See also **Barahmasa; Rāgamālā**

BIBLIOGRAPHY

Barrett, Douglas, and Basil Gray. *Painting of India.* Cleveland: World Publishing, 1963.

Beach, Milo C. *Rajput Painting at Bundi and Kota.* Ascona: Artibus Asiae, 1974.

Chandra, Pramod. *Bundi Painting.* Mumbai: Lalit Kala Academi, 1959.

Central India

The art styles of Raghogarh, Malwa, and Bundelkhand define the Central Indian school of art. Central India, the Madhyadesh of the ancient scriptures, with no consistent geography, is almost an abstract concept, the unity of which may be discovered in its arts, architecture, culture, literature and language. In them and in performing arts, sculpture and religious and intellectual pursuits, Central India has a past receding to the Vedic days. As for the art of painting, it has the fifth–sixth century murals and Mandu, once the capital of Malwa, was one the earliest seats of miniature painting in India and the prime inspiration of the Rajasthani art style. Even the Mughal miniatures of Akbar's early days and the early art of Ahmednagar and Bijapur in Deccan borrow some of the features of Mandu art style.

Raghogarh

Raghogarh, an erstwhile small state of Central India, situated between Malwa, Rajasthan, and Bundelkhand, is little known for its art activity, though it has had a massive tradition of painting spreading over two hundred years. Its artists excelled both in portrait painting and the serialization of legends and mythological themes.

The patrons of these paintings, the Khichi rulers of Raghogarh—Raja Dhiraj Singh (r. 1697–1726), Vikramaditya Singh (r. 1730–1744), Balbhadra Singh (r. 1744–1770), and Balwant Singh (r. 1770–1797)—appear to have been quite moderate in their rule, political aspirations and personal lives. They believed in good relations with all, the Rajputs (of Jaipur and Mewar) and the Mughals. The Raghogarh paintings reflect these aspects of their patrons, as many of them portray their contemporary chieftains visiting Raghogarh.

Raghogarh artists produced a large number of paintings during this era, which began in 1697, when Raja Dhiraj Singh initiated the Khichi dynasty at Raghogarh. This prolific artistic output could not have been possible unless Raja Dhiraj Singh and his successors had promoted and patronized it. Portraiture seems to have been the primary passion of Khichis, as most of the best paintings, reported from Raghogarh, are portraits. It seems that the Khichis maintained a galaxy of painters who rendered paintings, which had suited their patrons' taste. They portrayed the royal family, their favorite men and women and their pets, as also rendered various traditional themes, such as *Rāga-Rāginīs*, the love legend of *Ūshā-Aniruddha*, and legends related to Hindu gods and goddesses, and several folk themes and important occasions, such as visits by kings and princes. The Raghogarh painters also rendered portraits of various Mughal emperors and Rajput princes. This they must have done to record their visits to Raghogarh, or to accord to them state's honour. These portraits have no lavish or luxurious backgrounds and are rendered with great simplicity. The Raghogarh artists abstained from glamorizing their subjects. They preferred painting on flat backgrounds with bright colors and red borders. They derive their excellence from the careful and graceful depiction of a figure's features, overall demeanor and style of clothes. The Khichis' patronage of the arts was one of the most important activities of their court.

The Raghogarh paintings have a distinctive character that distinguishes them from the paintings of any other school of Indian art. The Raghogarh painting style incorporates many attributes of the art styles of Rajasthan, Malwa, and Bundelkhand, though it has excellence of its own.

Malwa

Malwa, the heartland of Central India, has a great creative past. Its literary history began centuries before the common era, and that of painting around the fifth or sixth century A.D. The sixth-century wall paintings of Bagh caves in Malwa, in the tradition of Ajanta, bear testimony to its glorious past. The earliest miniature paintings at Malwa—the illustrations of the Jain Kalpa-Sūtrā, appear during the first phase of the medieval renaissance. The stylistic accomplishment of Kalpa-Sūtrā illustrations rendered at Mandu, the capital of Malwa, suggest that Mandu had by then assumed the position of one of the great centers of art in India. In 1401 A.D., Dilwar Khan, a descendant and the *subedar* (governor) of Mohammad Ghori, declared himself independent ruler of the region of Malwa. This period in the history of Malwa was full of turmoil. In 1405 Malwa fell into the hands of Hoshang Shah, a local Khalji Muslim. He made Mandu his capital, and under his patronage Indo-Islamic art and architecture flourished. The third Khalji ruler, Mahmud I, continued the tradition of his grandfather.

In 1540, after Sher Shah Sur defeated the Mughal emperor Humayun and captured all of his territories, including Malwa and Gujarat, he appointed Shiya Khan as governor of Malwa. Shiya Khan's son Bayazid, the well-known hero of the legend of Baz Bahadur and Rupamati, was also a great patron of arts and music. In 1555 he declared himself the independent ruler of Malwa. In 1562 Akbar defeated Baz Bahadur, and henceforth Malwa became a Mughal *subah* (province). In 1690 the Maratha ruler Peshwa Baji Rao entered Malwa and, in 1743, annexed it finally to Maratha state. Peshwa made formal grant of deputy governorship of Malwa in favor of Holkar and Scindhia, his two generals, who had rendered great help in conquering it. With this ended the Mughal hold over Malwa.

In Mandu, there already existed an earlier tradition of illustrating texts. *Niamatnama* (Book of delicacies) was illustrated during the first quarter of the fifteenth century. The dated Kalpa-Sūtrā of 1439, was also an early work of art. These texts were illuminated using fine combination of ultramarine, red, and gold colors. Later Malwa artists of the late sixteenth and early seventeenth centuries preferred a more fluid grouping in place of the tight geometrical compositions of earlier renderings. The style of luxuriant trees with swaying creepers creating a soft meandering rhythm, the use of vibrant colors, simplifications, and boldly primitive idioms for the depictions of plants and animal life are some of the main attributes of the Malwa paintings of this phase.

Though rendered at Mandu, Niamatnāmā and Kalpa-Sūtrā do not define Malwa style. Niamatnāmā represents the Islamic and Kalpa-Sūtrā the Jain style pursued alike in other parts of India. It was actually in Rāmāyaṇa, Rāgamālā, and Rasikapriyā illustrations of the period from 1630 to 1640 that Malwa discovered its stylistic distinction and its earliest examples. The Rāmāyaṇa paintings offer a rich background to the subsequent painters. Monkeys and demons add color to the epic. Similarly, the birds, rivers, ponds, and even the architecture appear as symbols, presenting attractive groups in their idealized and decorative forms. The achievement of these Rāmāyaṇa illustrations is their form of composition and arrangement of different episodes of the story. The musical instruments—*dolaka* (double or two-way drum), *shahnāi* (wind-blown musical pipe), and large cymbals—depicted in these paintings are still in common use in the Malwa region.

The Rāgamālā and Rasikapriyā paintings reflect deep influences of prior indigenous art traditions. Short *cholī* (blouse), striped *ghāgharās* (long skirt), *chākdār jāmā* (long gown with all four lower ends having angular formation), and the flat Akbarī turban are some of their special features. The Amaru-Sataka paintings of 1652 and the serializations of Puhakar's Rasavēli of 1660 depict emotional expressions of these love lyrics and represent the symbolic delineation of the *nāyikā bhēd* concept (the literary theory that classifies various heroines engaged in love) in color.

The Rāmāyaṇa series of 1634–1640, 1652, and 1660, the Amaru-Sataka of 1652, and the Rasavēli of 1660 represent various phases in the development of the Malwa school. Another significant set of Rāgamālā paintings painted in 1680 by the artist Madhodasa at Narsinghgarh, a centrally located small state in Malwa, represents a culmination of earlier traditions. These Rāgamālā paintings are known for their bright colors, lyrical draftsmanship, and careful rendering. The miniature series of the Bhāgavata Purāṇa of 1690–1700 is highly elaborate and is in exact adherence to the text. The primary themes of the Malwa artists were Hindu myths and legends. In illustrating such subjects, these paintings are very well defined, as also extremely elaborate and often imaginative. They frequently represent also the less significant aspects, events, themes, and characters of Indian mythology.

Malwa artists generally used bright red, purple, yellow, green, and blue colors, creating a harmonious, enamel-like effect. The delicately molded features of men and women formulate the model of ideal beauty. These paintings are simple but balanced, and at the same time have powerful compositions and are considered pure classical statement of Indian abstract principles.

Bundelkhand

Bundelkhand, forming the northern part of Madhya Pradesh, is a cultural region bounded by the river Yamuna in the north, the escarped ranges of the Vindhya plateau in the south, the river Chambal in the northwest, and the Panna-Ajaigarh ranges in the southeast. It is the state of Orchha, with its bifurcated state Datia, that primarily denotes the Bundelkhand school.

In A.D. 1531, Raja Rudra Pratap came across a panoramic site suitable for building his capital. He later laid there the foundation of his capital city, Orchha. His son Madhukar Shah (r. 1554–1592) was a great patron of arts, and the earliest art activity at Orchha in the form of wall painting is from his period. These murals, rendered primarily on the walls of Rajmahal, are endowed with miniature-like finesse and precision. The episodes from the Rāmāyaṇa and Krishna-lila as also various myths and legends are their main themes. They are broadly narrative in style, which constitutes a characteristic feature of the subsequent Bundelkhand miniatures.

Raja Bir Singh Ju Dev (r. 1605–1628), the most powerful grandson of Madhukar Shah, was a close ally of the Mughal emperor Jahangir (r. 1605–1627), who bestowed on him many honors, including a royal palaquin and a *mansabdārī* of seven thousand (the authority under which he could maintain an army of seven thousand soldiers). Bir Singh Ju Dev built at Orchha a palace known as Jahangirī Mahal, consisting of seven floors, for the state visit of Jahangir. The Jahangirī Mahal is one of the best examples of Indo-Islamic architectural style. The paintings that embellish the walls of this palace represent the second phase of Bundelā art. There is a significant shift from the earlier mythological themes to scenes of hunting, war, dance, and various floral designs and patterns. These wall paintings, with simple form and pronounced lines, largely influenced the theme and style of the subsequent miniature art of the region.

In 1626 Orchha was bifurcated into Orchha and Datia. Datia, the newly formed state, continued also the tradition of wall painting. The Datia's newly built Bir Singh palace was embellished with paintings on various themes and subjects, some of which, such as Rāgamālā, reflected the initial tradition of Orchha murals.

The miniatures from Datia too were more akin to the earlier mural tradition of Orchha. A set of miniatures in the collection of the National Museum, New Delhi, have great stylistic unity with the Orchha wall paintings serializing the story of Mahiravana, the son of King Ravana. This story is an offshoot of the Rāmāyaṇa. Both the random and the text illustrating paintings continued to depict the same myths, legends, and themes, as had the Orchha murals, but now to them were added portraits of rulers and themes like *nayikā bhēd*, and Bārahmāsā. Portraits formed the majority of these miniatures. In texts Keshavdas' Rasikpriyā and Matiram's Rasrāj were more prominent. The personality and the religious attitude of the rulers of Orchha and Datia added new dimensions to these mythological and religious themes. An outstanding work of art that was executed at Datia is its Rāmāyaṇa series rendered with great Mughal stylistic touch. It has inscriptions in Bundelī dialect on the reverse, which are translations from Valmiki's Sanskrit verses. These works not only bear eloquent testimony to the Bundelkhand's distinction as art style but also to its great contribution in the field of miniature paintings.

Bringing the art of portrait painting to new heights of popularity by infusing it with realism is one of the most notable contributions of this school. Portrait painting was a task that required great skill to create a realistic likeness, as there were no subsidiary or secondary objects, and the artists had to concentrate fully on a single figure. The Datia portraits, such as those of Raja Shatrujit-ju-Dev (r. 1762–1801), the eldest son of Raja Indrajit, achieved a new level of realism. These portraits of Raja Shatrujit represent him as a gallant and handsome prince. Dressed with elaborate care and in an imposing fashion, he is seen wearing a long *jāmā* and fine pearl jewelry. These paintings are intimate and real, with warm color tones. The Datia miniature painters of the eighteenth century blended facile craftsmanship with colorful ornamentation, putting their art of portraiture in a class by itself.

Despite the ethnic relationship with Rajasthan, Bundelkhand paintings have simpler compositions and are not overcrowded. Their episodes are complete in themselves, though sometimes compartmentalized, as in the Malwa and Mewar schools; their emphasis, however, is always on conveying a look of completeness. Ornate architecture, rich costumes, and gallant and handsome heroes engaged in the courtship of beautiful heroines form part of the poetry of the famous court poet Keshavdas of Orchha and are characteristics of Bundelkhand miniatures. The men invariably wear turbans crowned with a *kalagi* (crest), *jamas* (long gowns) painted with flowers, striped trousers, *kamarbandh* and slippers. The costumes of the women include the *choli* (blouse), transparent *odhani* (a cloak-type outer covering used by ladies), *ghagra* (a long skirt with large frill) and sari. They have besides beautiful pearl jewelry. These costumes are significantly shaded with lines. A rich color scheme with warmer tones, simple composition, and long eyes with sharp facial features are some of the important characteristics of Bundela paintings. The artists generally used coarse paper, locally known as Chattarpuri *kāgāz*, for their paintings.

Daljit Khare

See also **Ajanta; Jahangir; Rāgamālā; Rāmāyaṇa**

BIBLIOGRAPHY

Archer, W. G. *Central Indian Painting*. London: Faber and Faber, 1958.

Bajpai, K. D. *The Glory That Was Bundelkhand*. Mahendra Kumar Manav Felicitation Volume. Chhatarpur, 1986.

Bannerji, Adris. "Malwa School of Painting." *Roop Lekha* 32 (June 1960).

Bhattacharya, Asok K. *Technique of Indian Painting*. Kolkata: Saraswat Library, 1976.

Khandalavala, Karl J. "Leaves from Rajasthan." *Marg* 4, no. 3 (1950).

———. "Problems of Rajasthan Paintings: The Origin and Development of Rajasthan Painting." *Marg* 11, no. 2 (March 1958).

Khare, Daljit. *Immortal Miniatures*. New Delhi: Aravali Books International, 2002.

Khare, M. D., and Daljeet Khare. *Malwa through the Ages*. Bhopal, 1981.

———. *Splendour of Malwa Paintings*. New Delhi, Cosmo, 1983.

Krishna, Anand. *Malwa Painting*. Varanasi: Banaras Hindu University, 1968.

Nigam, M. L. *Cultural History of Bundelkhand*. Delhi: Sundeep, 1983.

Sircar, D. C. *Ancient Malwa and the Vikramaditya Tradition*. Delhi: Munshiram Manoharlal, 1969.

Skelton, Robert. "The Ni'mat Namah-A Landmark in Malwa Paintings." *Marg* 12, no. 3.

HAREM SCENES

The practice in India of having segregated accommodations for women is very old. Large residences of the wealthy and the titled always had a separate protected enclosure for women, known as the *antahpur*, or inner courtyard. Detailed descriptions of the *antahpur* abound in Sanskrit literature, especially in the dramas and epics. The Valmiki Rāmāyaṇa (1.5), describes the various buildings of the city of Ayodhya, including theaters, gardens, and sporting areas for females. The women, who generally resided on the top floors, were provided small windows (*gavāksha*), which gave them a glimpse of the outside world (Tulasi Rāmāyaṇa 1.224). When leaving on exile to the forest, Rāma says to his people, "Gaze upon Sita to your fill since you may look upon a royal lady only at the time of the *yajna* (sacrifice) and marriage, during a calamity and *vanagamana* (exile to the forest)" (*Pratimā Nātaka* by Bhasa, 1.29).

Cloistered they may have been, but the women enjoyed creative freedom, as reflected through the dramas of the period, which depict the heroine and other women as generally distinguished in the various performing arts. They play musical instruments like the vina and the flute, and are often artists and painters. Once a center of cultural activities, the *antahpur* was labeled *harem*, meaning a forbidden area with restricted entry, during the medieval period (Arabic, *harim;* Turkish, *harem*). Other names for it were *haramgarh*, *zanana* (from the Persian *zan*, meaning "women"), and *ranivas* (abode of queens). A velvet-lined cage for its women, the harem reflects the social structure of the male-dominated medieval society.

The trend of maintaining a large harem was set by the Delhi sultans, beginning in the late twelfth century in pre-Mughal India. Both the Mughal emperors and the Hindu rajas adopted the tradition. Fazal Abul writes in his *Ain-i-Akbari* about Akbar's harem: "His Majesty has made a large enclosure with fine buildings inside where he reposes. Though there are more than five thousand women, he has given to each a separate apartment. He has also divided them into sections, and keeps them attentive to their duties" (Abul, p. 46).

The size of the harem was a status symbol among kings. Along with the wives, all the other female members of the family—mothers, sisters, daughters—resided in the segregated area. The king's first wife was designated chief queen and was given accorded special privileges. Each queen was provided a special room and a staff of attendants.

At the next level came *kaniz*, or concubines, then *kanchanis*, or slaves of a higher rank, who provided entertainment like dance, drama, and music. Further down were *bandis*, who worked as maidservants. Women captured in war were also placed within this hierarchy. There was some upward mobility as well. A king could maintain relationships with any of the attendants. If a slave girl pleased the royal, she was given concubine status, with her own chamber and a high salary.

A governess and a chief eunuch supervised security. Eunuchs guarded the consorts so that they could not see or meet any man other than their husband. There were also female guards. The interiors were lavishly decorated, but the buildings were designed to preclude outside views. Gardens complete with flowering bushes and fountains were also incorporated into the royal harem. The only glimpses the women had of the outer world was through *jharokhas*, or roofed balconies located at great heights.

Niccolao Manucci, the Italian resident in the Mughal court who had a privileged access to the harem, described the miserable conditions of these women. He says, "The women, being shut up with this closeness and constantly watched, and having neither liberty nor occupation, think of nothing but adoring themselves and their minds dwell nothing but malice and lewdness" (Manucci, p. 352).

Nevertheless, there are notable cases in which the harem played a decisive and aggressive role in dynastic politics. The most notorious example is from the early life of Akbar, who was enthroned as a teenager. His wet nurse and foster mother Mahem Anega made her impress on politics by combating the ambitions of the young emperor's regent. Nur Jehan, consort of Akbar's son Jahangir, was entitled to signed *firmans*, or official orders. Neither were the princesses and queens illiterate. They had basic training in reading and writing and in the fine arts. Miniature paintings from Hyderabad and Golconda elaborately depict women writing, reading letters, and playing musical instruments.

Through Artists' Eyes

Royal memoirs, official records, and accounts by travelers and historians do provide some information on the harem, secret and guarded though it was. The subject fascinated artists, and the miniature paintings provide interesting glimpses of life in the women's quarters of the sixteenth to nineteenth centuries.

Earlier, the Delhi sultans, who possessed large harems, strangely did not favor it as a theme for their paintings. There are some scenes of women engaged in various activities in the inner chambers, but in design and decor they pale in comparison to the later lavish harem pictures of the Mughal era.

In the time of Akbar (r. 1556–1605), harem scenes were depicted as part of a biographical series. One painting in *Akbarnama* depicts the birth of Prince Salim in the Fatehpur Sikri palace harem. The subject was favored by painters of the post-Jahangir era and by the Rajasthani miniaturists, particularly of the Bundi and Thikana styles. Among the Pahari schools, mention must be made of the Guler style, particularly the paintings done in the time of King Govardhana Chand (r. 1741–1773), whose capital was Guler. Govardhana Chand was married to a Basohli princess, Balauria Rani, who is well represented in the paintings of this period. A painting in the collection of the Retberg Museum, Zürich, bears the inscription *Harem Patsah ki* (the king's harem). It may have been part of a series depicting various events in the women's quarters.

The Queen Prepares

Most commonly, the artists depict the king seated with his queen or concubine in a beautiful garden with fountains, drinking and enjoying music, with a range of women attendants at his service. Royal paraphernalia, such as perfume bottles, a betel nut box, goblets, and a rosewater sprinkler, all find their place within the scene, especially in the Thikana paintings. A eunuch stands guard. *A Ruler with his Zanana*, Jodhpur, Rajasthan, from the Maharaja Gaja Singhji Umed Bhavana Palace Jodhpur Collection, provides a good representation of the pavilion, garden, and their overall grandeur. The king seems to have the full harem in attendance.

Each night the king would select a particular queen of his thousand-odd wives to visit. The extensive preparations of the privileged queen to make it a memorable evening for the king was another favorite theme. Beautiful women prepare sandalwood paste, decorate the bed with flowers, dance and sing, and adorn themselves in pleasurable anticipation of the evening ahead. However, for every woman it was not a cherished moment. Some paintings show a eunuch or a female guard forcing a young girl to surrender to the king. One of the Malwa paintings from the Chhatrapati Shivaji Maharaj Vastu Sangrahalaya Collection depicts a eunuch forcing a young girl to have a drink so that she will be in no condition to resist.

Drinking and smoking were common practices among the royal women, especially during the Mughal period, to escape their loneliness. A well-dressed woman, looking despondent though surrounded by attendants and musicians, is another common theme of the miniatures. Drinking scenes depicted during and after the rule of Muhammad Shah are pointers to the decay in the court culture so carefully maintained by Akbar.

Other Subjects

Terrace party scenes are commonly depicted in the later Mughal and Deccani paintings. Bathing and sex scenes are in abundance, with the king and his partner inevitably surrounded by attendants and guards. In *By the Light of the Moon and Fireworks* (1740, Kishangarh School, Harvard University art museums, Arthur M. Sackler Museum, Cambridge) an elderly and drunk Mughal king is titillated by a beautiful young woman. He is almost lost among the many intoxicated ladies surrounding him, some of whom have taken lesbian partners. Among the women, the dark-skinned eunuch stands out.

Certain areas in the harem, such as the *rang mahal* and the *sheesh mahal*, whose walls were lined with mirrors and colored glass, were designated for various kinds of pleasurable activities. Some special rooms in some *zanana*s were decorated with paintings of erotic themes (for example, *Raja Shreenathji in the Zanana*, Thikana, Marwar, 18th century, Chhatrapati Shivaji Maharaj Vastu Sangrahalaya collection).

On very few occasions, the women were allowed to emerge from the palace doors. A visit to a religious place or a spiritual guru, hunting, playing polo, and hawking were some of these occasions. Women playing polo became the favorite theme of the Deccani paintings, especially those from Golconda. In quite a few paintings Chandbibi, the queen of Ahmednagar who bravely defended the Mughals in 1600, is shownplaying polo. Hawking was another favorite game of the Mughal queens, who enthusiastically adopted this Iranian sport, as did the Rajput queens. This theme is depicted in the Pahari miniatures, particularly those of Guler.

Playing *chaupar* (chess), buying jewelry, flying kites, and taming pigeons were some of the indoor activities depicted in paintings. A common subject painted by the Bundi school is a cat catching a pigeon or a parrot, with the agitated women trying to save the bird. Other paintings show the king enjoying festivals like Teej, Holi, and Gangaur with his queens. One of the beautiful illustrations of a king enoying the Teej festival, painted in 1770 in the Bundi style, is in the collection of Victoria and Albert Museum, London. In the same museum can also be seen a painting depicting *Maharana Chhatarsal of Kotah Celebrating the Festival of Gangaur*, painted at Kotah in 1870.

Painting by Hearsay

A large number of terrace party scenes showing the queen attending a musical concert were done during the later years of Muhammad Shah (r. 1719–1748). Due to the king's inability to govern, his wife Udham Bai became politically powerful. A very interesting painting by Meer Moran, in the collection of Edwin Benny, depicts women in European dress entertaining the queen, who sits authoritatively on a decorated *chowki* (throne). The inscription on the painting states that it was a New Year's gift to the queen in the twenty-third regnal year of Muhammad Shah, 1742.

How were these depictions of the forbidden areas painted? As male outsiders were not allowed inside the harem, it is likely that these paintings were based on eyewitness accounts, with information provided by one of the queen's attendants supplemented by the artist's imagination. And some of the artists were women. A famous artist of the Mughal period, for instance, was Safia Banu, who was well-known as a painter around 1620. Some women were also experts in the art of calligraphy.

Kalpana Desai
Vandana Prapanna

BIBLIOGRAPHY

Abul, Fazal. *The Ain-i-Akbari*. Vol. I. New Delhi: Oriental Books, 1977.

Chimono, Rosa Maria. *Life at Court in Rajasthan: Indian Miniatures from the 17th to the 18th Century*. Italy: Mario Luca G., 1985.

Desai, Vishakha N. *Life at Court: Art for India's Rulers, Sixteenth–Nineteenth Centuries*. Boston: Museum of Fine Arts, 1986.

Gupta, Kamala. *Social Status of Hindu Women in Northern India, 1206–1707 A.D.* New Delhi: Inter-India, 1987.

Kale, M. R., ed. *Pratimanatakam of Bhasa*. Delhi: Motilal Banarsidass, 1983.

Lal, K. S. *The Mughal Harem*. New Delhi: Aditya, 1988.

Manucci. *Storia*. Vol. II. London: John Murray. 1907.

Schimmel, Annemarie. *The Empire of the Great Mughals: History, Art, and Culture*. Oxford University Press, 2005.

Topsfield, Andrew. *Court Painting in Rajasthan*. Mumbai: Marg, 2000.

KISHANGARH

Bordered by the Rajput Rathor centers of Jodhpur and Jaipur, close to the sacred Lake Pushkar, Kishangarha was founded in 1609 by Maharaja Kishan Singh (r. 1609–1615). His descendant Rup Singh (r. 1643–1658) developed the state and supported its unique arts, as did Rai Singh (r. 1706–1748).

A synthesis of Mughal artistic idioms with the conventions of the provincial schools of Rajput Rathor in the eighteenth through the late nineteenth centuries gave birth to the brilliant school of Kishangarh painting, with its lyrical and delicate yet exaggerated treatment of human figures. Kishangarh landscapes, with their huge white palace backdrops, also reveal a distinct individuality, in contrast to those of the late Mughal and neighboring Rajput schools of Marwar, Jaipur, Bundi, Mewar, and

Malwa. Kishangarh paintings are specially dedicated to the Vaishnava *bhakti* (devotion), or the passionate love of Krishna and Rādhā, unlike other schools dominated by Brahman painters.

A new golden era of Kishangarh art began from the period of Maharaja Savant Singh (r. 1748–1758), who helped the Marathas fight against his brother Sardar Singh, forcing a partition of the state in 1755. Savant Singh's romance with a singer and concubine, Bani Thani, became a very popular subject of local paintings.

The artist Nihal Chand (1710–1782?), a *surdhaj* Brahman, started his artistic career at the age of fifteen. His palette consisted of rich reds, white, and greens, with a range of grays to black. He received training in the local styles from the masters, and he is thought to have initiated *bhakti* paintings in the Kishangarh school. The most famous among his (attributed) works is the *jharokha* bust portrait of Bani Thani, which incorporates all the unique qualities and exaggerated features of this school, such as the large curving eyes with arched eyebrows, pointed nose, and chin. His other notable work, *Godhuli vela* (The hour of cowdust), at the National Museum, New Delhi, depicts a tall blue-colored Krishna with an hourglass waist.

Based on the poetry of Nagari Das, the conventional three-tiered painting *Boat of Love* (National Museum, New Delhi, c. 1730–1735) depicts, against a late night background, finely rendered grand local palaces, lush greenery on the bank of a river, and stylized human figures (especially the haloed Krishna-Rādhā). The naturalistic treatments of cows in *Krishna Milking Cows* (National Museum, New Delhi) is reminiscent of late Mughal idioms.

Between 1755 and 1766, Kishangarh paintings flourished, including a small number of large-sized miniatures, among the most interesting works of the style. Sardar Singh (d. 1781) of Rupnagar, like his father Savant Singh, was a significant patron. Secular subjects, such as hunting, boating, and *darbar* scenes, emerged as common themes. The brilliant painter Amar Chand (1754–1812) succeeded Nihal Chand, working at both Rupnagar and Kishangarh. His *Moonlight Darbar of Sardar Singh* (c. 1764) is outstanding in size and workmanship, depicting monumental architecture and tiny human figures. His colleagues Joshi Sawai Ram and Suratram, his son Budhlal, and Surajmal (son of Nihal Chand) also enriched the atelier. Later Mughal styles were blended with local Krishangarh idioms. Other painters of the time, like Sitaram (another son of Nihal Chand), tried their best to follow Chand's idioms, but created disproportionate and unromantic figures, rendering female bust portraits or *darbar* and outdoor scenes. Bahadur Singh, a cousin of Savant Singh, evoked *vir ras* (valor) in Kishangarh paintings. The stiff figures delineated by Sitaram indicated his decline, yet he produced some new compositions, including scenes from the epic Rāmāyana. But his style was more rigid in form and his figures more angular.

Birad Singh (r. 1781–1788) stabilized Kishangarh's political situation. During the reigns of Rai Kalyan Singh (1797–1838), Mokham Singh (1838–1841), and Prithvi Singh (1840–1880), Kishangarh painting declined. Perhaps due to both the advent of the British Company school and the new medium of photography, the delicacy and lyrical quality of the earlier paintings was replaced by a static, harsh appearance. In modern times, some artists attempt to continue the style, using large panels and shading their figures, but one can hardly consider this an actual continuation of the unique Kishangarh style.

Naval Krishna
Manu Krishna

BIBLIOGRAPHY

Anand, M. R. *Album of Indian Paintings*. Delhi: Thomson Press, 1973.

Crill, Rosemary. *Marwar Painting*. Jodhpur: Mehrangarh Publishers, 2000.

Dickinson, Eric. "Kishangarh." *Marg* 11 (March 1958).

Dickinson, Eric, and Karl Khandalavala. *Kishangarh Painting*. New Delhi: Lalit Kala Akademi, 1959.

Randhawa, Mohindar Singh. *Indian Painting: The Scene, Themes and Legends*. Boston: Houghton Mifflin, 1968.

KOTAH

The state of Kotah, near Bundi, is located in the eastern part of Rajasthan, surrounded by Jaipur and Gwalior on the north, the state of Bundi to the west, the state of Udaipur on the south, and Rajgarh in the east. Like Bundi, Kotah enjoys extraordinary physical features. It has vast expanses of fertile land, sprawling mountain ranges, and river gorges covered with dense forests and abundant wildlife, including tigers. Its rich flora and fauna, reflected through its paintings, have made this state well known the world over.

Due to the close proximity of Kotah and Bundi, there is a uniformity of cultural traditions. Initially, Kotah style began as a simple variant of the Bundi idiom, so much so that in some of the early examples of paintings, the similarity of style, treatment of landscape, color schemes, and identical subject matter made it difficult even for scholars to differentiate between the two. Since the same dynastic family ruled the entire area, it was natural to find close contacts between states and artists.

Kotah, the land of the Hada Rajputs, was called Hadaoti, which comprised the old states of Bundi and

Kotah. Though Kotah began as an offshoot of Bundi in A.D. 1624, it surpassed Bundi in its economic and cultural progress. It was the fifth largest among the native states to enter the Indian Union in 1948. The antiquity of the Hada Rajputs goes back to A.D. 1241, to Rao Deva ("Rao" is the title of the Hada Rajputs), whose grandson Jaitsi pushed the Hadas across the Chambal River where Koteya, the chief of the Bhil tribes, ruled. After killing Koteya, Jaitsi offered his severed head to the construction of the citadel and the palace complex as a human sacrifice, and the town that grew around it was named Kotah.

According to some scholars, the earliest evidence of Bundi painting can be traced to an early *Ragamala* series painted at Chunar near Banaras in A.D. 1591. The painters of this series were Muslims who may have had some formal training at the Mughal atelier. It is apparent that Kotah artists may have treated these sets as a model, later developing (by about 1650) their own style, with certain elements borrowed from the nearby Mewar school. At the same time, a marked Deccani influence is also discernible in both schools, as the Hada rulers had campaigned in the Deccan from early Mughal rule until the end of Aurangzeb's reign in 1707.

A long genealogy of monarchs followed Kotah's first independent ruler, Rao Madho Singh (r. 1624–1640). Rao Jagat Singh (r. 1657–1684) deserves special mention; during his reign Kotah assumed an independent status as a school of painting. A few portrait studies, as well as the famous Kotah Bhāgavata, are attributed to this period. Maharao Durjan Sal (r. 1723–1756) and Maharao Ummed Singh (r. 1770–1819) were hunting enthusiasts, and *shikar* paintings (hunting scenes) became immensely popular during their reigns. The Kotah repository includes breathtaking hunting scenes from the Kotah palace collection.

The uniqueness of Kotah painting lies in its wonderful landscapes, which appear throughout its range of subjects, from mythological to political to social and genre paintings. Lush green vegetation, with a great variety of trees, plants, and vines, is depicted under a sky that is often filled with tumultuous rain clouds in hues of orange, grey, and blue. Large expanses of green undulating mounds, tall palms, and flowering shrubs and bushes, inhabited by colorful birds and animals, are the usual settings for the *Barahmasa* and *Ragamala* paintings. Architecture is limited to single- or double-storied buildings with prominent *chhajas* (weather sheds), windows and doors with rolled-up curtains, and floors overlaid with carpets. Men and women have flesh of an almost orange tint, with prominent stippling suggesting a cast shadow that highlights the contours of the face and body. Outdoor settings invariably have plantain groves, waterfronts with aquatic birds, and pairs of Saras cranes.

The upsurge of Vaishnavism in Rajasthan in the seventeenth century resulted in the production of a number of miniature paintings and manuscripts devoted to Krishna *bhakti* (devotion to Krishna). Popular poetic works like Bhāgavata Dashama Skanda (the tenth canto of the Bhāgavata Purāṇa), the *Gītā Govinda* of Jayadeva, and the *Rasikapriya* and the *Kavipriya* of Kashavadasa became favorite subjects of the Kotah painters, as did the *Rāgamālā* and the *Barahmasa*. Among these subjects, the *Barahmasa* (the depiction of 12 seasons indicating the responses of the divine couple, Rādhā and Krishna), painted against the background of seasonal flora and fauna and festival celebrations, particularly caught the eye of the Kotah painter. Two such complete sets are in the collection of the Chhatrapati Shivaji Maharaj Vastu Sangrahalaya (formerly known as the Prince of Wales of Museum) in Mumbai. The *Rāgamālā* (the pictorial representation of musical modes in color) were also appreciated by the masses and the elites alike.

In keeping with the Rajasthani tradition of maintaining an atelier or *karkhanas* (workshop) of painters, the Kotah rulers, impressed and influenced by the contemporary grandeur of the late Mughal emperors, encouraged portraiture and *darbar* (court) scenes on the one hand, and *shikar* (hunting) scenes on the other. Toward the end of the eighteenth century emerged some of the most astonishing elephant studies ever produced. The painting of Maharao Durjan Sal's elephant, *Kishnaprasad*, by Sheikh Taju, reveals a careful rendering of the contours of his dark and wrinkled body within a composition that dramatizes swift action; the elephant lifts a cheetah in his trunk, while the excited *mahavat* (driver) raises his *ankush* (an item of armor with a spearhead-like front) to control the elephant's fury. Tiger hunts in the jungles of Kotah were also among the favorite subjects of Kotah painters. *Maharao Ummed Singh I and His Chief Minister Zalim Singh Shooting Tigers*, attributed to Sheikh Taju, is one such breathtaking visual narrative.

The last known ruler of Kotah was Ram Singh II (r. 1827–1865). A king with nominal political authority, he was the last great patron of the arts. The political decline of Kotah during his time favored the development of painting to a great extent, as the king devoted all of his energy to religious festivities, court celebrations, and patronage of the arts. Fond of jewelry, clothing, hunts, the harem, and performances, his art collection included a large number of dated and inscribed drawings, as well as paintings using a peculiar green color imported from Germany of the nineteenth century. One such masterpiece, *Ram Singh II of Kotah and Companions Celebrating Holi*, inscribed with the name of Kishan Das, dated 1844, is now at the National Gallery of Victoria in Melbourne.

Shridhar Andhare

See also **Barahmasa; Rāgamālā**

BIBLIOGRAPHY

Singh, M. K. Brijraj. *The Kingdom That Was Kotah.* New Delhi: Lalit Kala Akademi, 1985.

Welch, Stuart Cary. *Gods, Kings, and Tigers: The Art of Kotah.* New York: Asia Society, 1997.

MARWAR AND THIKANAS

Marwar, a region in western Rajasthan, corresponds to Jodhpur state, formerly ruled by the Rathor dynasty of Rajputs. Other Rajput states founded by members of the same clan include Kishangarh and Bikaner. Marwar painting developed mainly in the court at Jodhpur, though subclans of the Rathors also held smaller territories (called *thikanas*) within Marwar, and some of these smaller courts also developed a distinctive local, *thikana* style.

Jodhpur was founded by Rao Jodha in 1459, but came under Mughal rule in 1570. The Jodhpur rulers married into the Mughal dynasty and were given appointments as military commanders of the Mughal army, in an attempt to ensure their loyalty. Their constant attendance at the Mughal court and their exposure to Mughal arts and culture is reflected in Marwar court art from the mid-seventeenth century onward. Mughal-inspired portraits and hunting scenes developed, however, alongside a parallel stream of traditional Hindu paintings, which were being produced at the Jodhpur court and in the *thikanas* during the same period.

The earliest surviving example of painting from the Marwar region is the so-called Pali *rāgamālā*. This charming set of thirty-seven paintings illustrating musical modes (*rāgas*) has a dated colophon, which states that it was painted at Pali in Marwar by Pandit Virji in 1623 for Sri Gopal Dasji and his son Bithal Das. The style of the paintings is related to that of Jain manuscript paintings and book covers from Rajasthan and Gujarat, but the style also contains elements of what has come to be known as the Early Rajput or Chaurapanchasika style. These elements include flat, boxlike architectural settings, a dark background that does not meet the top of the page but instead terminates in a jagged edge, strong colors, and bold decorative patterns, especially chevrons, checks, and stylized lotus petals.

Although the Pali set is the only securely datable evidence for painting in Marwar at this time, other undated manuscripts and dispersed pages confirm that this was not unique. The dispersed manuscript of the *Kathakalpataru*, for example, shows the same distinctive figures as does the Pali set, and may have been made for a Rajput patron, perhaps even Bithal Das. Unrelated *ragamala* pages dating from the first half of the seventeenth century also bear witness to the development of styles in Marwar as well as in neighboring Mewar (Udaipur).

While these very traditional themes and subjects dominated painting in Marwar at this time, Mughal forms, especially portraits, started to become popular from the middle of the seventeenth century under Maharaja Jaswant Singh (r. 1638–1678). Several very fine group portraits of Jaswant Singh and his nobles survive in the form of both drawings and finished paintings, dating from about the 1640s to 1660s, which show the extremely high quality attained by the Jodhpur artists, who must have been exposed to Mughal training. This emulation of Mughal forms would remain the basis of the Jodhpur court style until its demise in the mid-nineteenth century, and conventions such as the *jharokha* portrait, the group portrait, and the equestrian portrait all continued to play major roles.

After Maharaja Jaswant Singh's death in 1678, a succession dispute arose over the legitimacy of his posthumous son Ajit Singh. As a result, Jodhpur once again came under direct Mughal rule until the death of the emperor Aurangzeb in 1707, when Ajit Singh was able to reclaim his throne after nearly thrity years in hiding. Two paintings from his reign show that the Jodhpur artists were starting to move from the static portraits of the seventeenth century to adopt more ambitious compositions, and on a larger scale. One of these paintings, dated 1722, depicts a procession; the other is a hunting scene, dated 1718. In both, Ajit Singh is the center of attention, surrounded by courtiers and attendants who have already started to take on the distinctive appearance characteristic of eighteenth-century Marwar painting. Their large almond eyes, curling moustaches, and prominent noses recall the figures in the Pali *rāgamālā* and other early paintings, and there is also some influence from the neighboring state of Mewar, where Ajit Singh grew up in exile, and where he married a local princess. The earthy colors, dominated by yellow and green, and angular profiles that appear at this period continue to characterize painting in Marwar, and especially that of the *thikanas*, throughout the eighteenth century.

Several single paintings datable to around 1720 to 1730 are typical of this newly emerging Marwar style, in which Mughal traces are visible in the format (that of the group portrait, for example), while the palette of colors and the style of drawing are clearly far removed form the refined late Mughal style of the same period. Among the most characteristic of this type is the elegant portrait of a nobleman with a buck, now in the Chhatrapati Shivaji Maharaj Vastu Sangrahalaya (formerly known as the Prince of Wales of Museum), Mumbai; others are in the Victoria and Albert Museum, the British Museum, and private collections. Around this time, painting in the *thikanas* of Marwar also started to develop, and among the most active patrons of painting were the *thakurs* of Ghanerao, situated on the border of Marwar and Mewar. A fine group portrait of Thakur Pratap Singh of Ghanerao (r. 1714–1720) and his nobles, datable to around 1715 or 1720, shows the same earthy colors and sparse line as the portrait of the noble with a buck. Several portraits have survived of his successor, Thakur Padam Singh (r. 1720–1742). Probably the finest is a *darbar* (court) scene of the *thakur* with his nobles, sons, and officials ascribed to a Jodhpur artist named Chhajju and dated 1725, which is now in the Chhatrapati Shivaji Maharaj Vastu Sangrahalaya. Much of the work produced for Padam Singh and his successor Viram Dev (r. 1743–1778) has an undeniably "folky" feel, and was undoubtedly created by local artists rather than those (like Chhajju) who were connected to Jodhpur itself; they are still, however, very recognizably within the Marwar tradition (for example, a group portrait of Padam Singh and nobles by Manno, dated 1721, and a scene of Thakur Viram Dev worshiping at a Shiva shrine, from about 1745, both now in the Victoria & Albert Museum).

While this local style was developing in Jodhpur and the *thikana*s in the early eighteenth century, Maharaja Abhai Singh (r. 1724–1749) was commissioning some exceptionally fine paintings in pure Mughal style from a Delhi artist named Dalchand whom he employed in Jodhpur. Dalchand was the son of Bhawani Das, a renowned artist in Kishangarh, and elements of the Kishangarh style (for example, the exaggerated, curving lines of the horses, and of women's eyes) are also sometimes visible in Dalchand's work. Superb paintings by Dalchand from around 1725 include a large scene of Abhai Singh watching a nautch (a dance performance), an equestrian portrait of the maharaja with attendants (both still in Jodhpur), and two standing portraits of Abhai Singh with the poet Prithvi Raj (one dated 1727). Court paintings from Jodhpur of the mid-eighteenth century show Dalchand's influence in their formality and attention to detail. Abhai Singh's son and successor, Ram Singh, ruled for only two years (1749–1751), but left many highly distinctive portraits of himself and his nobles, wearing the toweringly tall turbans that were the fashion in Jodhpur in the mid-eighteenth century.

The next major phase in Marwar painting comes with the reign of Maharaja Man Singh (r. 1803–1843), the last period in which creative and innovative artists were at work in Jodhpur. After the murder of his Nath sect guru by discontented nobles in 1815, Man Singh became a virtual recluse, and in 1839 the British army took control of Jodhpur. In spite of what must have been a somewhat subdued atmosphere at court, many exuberant scenes of court life and festivities were produced during Man Singh's reign, including many large scenes showing the celebration of Holi and other festivals, and hedonistic scenes of Man Singh with his consorts in his gardens or at the hunt.

Man Singh also commissioned many sets of immense paintings to illustrate Hindu texts such as the Durgā Charitra, the Shiva Rahasya, the Shiva Purāṇa and the Rāmāyaṇa. Measuring between 47 inches (120 centimeters) and 53 inches (134 centimeters) in width, these huge sets range from 56 folios (the Durgā Charitra) to 109 (the Shiva Purāṇa) and are vibrantly colored and superbly painted and composed. Man Singh also commissioned sets of large paintings illustrating subjects relating to the Nath sect: the Siddh Siddhant, the Nath Purāṇa and the Nath Charitra. There are also hundreds of single paintings either of solitary Nath gurus, or of Man Singh paying homage to them.

Although Man Singh's successor Takhat Singh (r. 1843–1873) continued to patronize painting, employing several of the same artists who worked for Man Singh, the paintings produced during his reign were mostly stiff and unimaginative. This decline in artistic standards paved the way for the demise of painting in Jodhpur with the adoption of photography during the reign of its modernizing maharaja, Jaswant Singh II (r. 1873–1895).

Rosemary Crill

BIBLIOGRAPHY

Crill, Rosemary. *Marwar Painting: A History of the Jodhpur Style*. Mumbai: India Book House, 1999. Overview of painting in Marwar from the seventeenth to late nineteenth centuries; all major works illustrated.

———. "The Thakurs of Ghanerao as Patrons of Painting." In *Court Painting in Rajasthan*, edited by Andrew Topsfield. Mumbai: Marg Publications, 2000. Focuses on the major center for *thikana* painting in the eighteenth and nineteenth centuries.

Goetz, Hermann. "Marwar (with Some Paintings of Jodhpur from Kumar Sangram Singh)." *Marg* 11, no. 2 (1958): 42–49. Important early article on the subject.

MINTO, LORD *(1845–1914), viceroy of India (1905–1910).* Gilbert Elliot, the fourth earl of Minto, was viceroy of India from 1905 to 1910. Great-grandson of the first earl, who had been Whig governor-general of India from 1807 to 1813, Lord Minto served as governor-general of Canada from 1898 to 1904 before being sent to India by A. J. Balfour's Tory government. Though his name is historically linked to Secretary of State for India John Morley (as coauthors of the Morley-Minto Reforms), "Mr. Rolly" (Minto's nickname) was more interested in riding horses than in constitutional reforms.

Soon after Minto reached India, Balfour's Tory government was soundly defeated in the 1905 general elections in Britain by Henry Campbell-Bannerman's Liberals, bringing reform-minded John Morley to Whitehall as India's secretary of state. Imperial London's old palace guard feared, however, that recalling Viceroy Minto from India so soon after he had reached Calcutta (Kolkata), in the heart of recently partitioned, rebellious Bengal, might send a "dangerous" signal of "weakness" to India's National Congress leadership. They chose to leave India to suffer four years of harsh repression under Minto's inept governance, rather than immediately replacing him. Minto's predecessor, Lord Curzon, had left India following his October 1905 division of Bengal through its Bengali-speaking midland. This most provocative legacy was viewed by India's National Congress as "perfidious Albion's" plan to divide and rule with a vengeance.

Minto's own major legacy was to receive a delegation of thirty-five Muslim aristocrats, led by the Aga Khan, at his viceregal mansion in Simla on 1 October 1906, and to assure them that any "electoral representation" granted by any constitutional reform would "safeguard" their "Mohammedan community," giving them special weight and separate electorates. That promise, made from Minto's viceregal "throne," irrevocably committed British India to granting its Muslim minority a disproportionate number of separately elected representatives on every legislative council, central as well as provincial, from that time until the British left India divided in 1947. That single promise was, as one of Minto s officials so effusively told him, nothing less than "the pulling back of sixty-two million" Muslims from joining the "seditious opposition" of India's National Congress. Two months later, the All-India Muslim League held its first meeting in Dacca (Dhaka), capital of the newly created Muslim-majority province of Eastern Bengal and Assam. Forty-five years after that, the Muslim League's Dominion of Pakistan was born, carved out of Muslim-majority provinces of northern India.

Minto left India in 1910, when Morley, after appointing Liberal Viceroy Lord Hardinge to succeed Minto, left Whitehall. One of Hardinge's first acts was to propose the belated reunification of Bengal, announced by King George V at his coronation *durbar* in Delhi on 12 December 1911. But Minto's separatist legacy assured its second division in 1947, and along the very same line as the first; with the latter partition, what had been Eastern Bengal became East Pakistan (and after 1971, Bangladesh).

Stanley Wolpert

See also **All-India Muslim League; Bengal; British Crown Raj; Morley, John**

BIBLIOGRAPHY

Buchan, John. *Lord Minto: A Memoir.* London and New York: T. Nelson and Sons, 1924.

Das, M. N. *India under Morley and Minto: Politics behind Repression and Reforms.* London: George Allen and Unwin, 1964.

Minto, Mary, Countess of. *India, Minto and Morley, 1905–1910.* London: Macmillan, 1934.

Wasti, Syed Razi. *Lord Minto and the Indian Nationalist Movement, 1905 to 1910.* Oxford: Clarendon Press, 1964.

Wolpert, Stanley. *Morley and India, 1906–1910.* Berkeley and Los Angeles: University of California Press, 1967.

MĪRABAI ***(c. 1500–1545)*****, bhakti** ***saint and poet.*** Mīrabai is one of India's most popular *bhakti* saints, a Rajput princess who wrote fourteen hundred ecstatic *padas* (short devotional songs) to Krishna as Giridhar Gōpal, the divine cowherd who lifted a mountain to save his followers. Mīrabai composed hymns in Rajasthani; in the Hindi dialect of Braj Bhāsha, the language spoken in Mathura, Krishna's mythical birthplace; and in Gujarati, the language spoken in his mythical kingdom of Dwārakā. Her *padas* were sung, and her imprint on North Indian classical music is seen in the name of the *rāga* (melody) "Mīrabai ki Malhār." Mīrabai's sensuous verses highlight her divine lover's beauty, the agony of separation, and their beatific union. In one metaphor, Krishna's lips are like nectar, as sweet as curds; in another, her pain at separation is like the agony of a tree gnawed by insects. Despite her tone of intimacy with Krishna, her poems focus on her yearning for a surreal, sublime union, in contrast to Andal (6th century) and Akkamahadevi (12th century) who sometimes described their spiritual journey in sensual lyrics.

The Bhīl woman tasted them, plum after plum,
and found one she could offer him.
What kind of genteel breeding was this?
and hers was no ravishing beauty,
Her family was poor, her caste quite low,
her clothes a matter of rags,
Yet Ram took that fruit—that touched, spoiled fruit
for he knew that it stood for her love.
What sort of Vēda could she have learned?
But quick as a flash she mounted a chariot
And sped to heaven to swing on a swing,
tied by love to God.
You are the Lord who cares for the fallen;
rescue whoever loves as she did:
Let Mīra, your servant, safely cross over,
A cowherding Gōkul girl.

(Translated by John Stratton Hawley and Mark Juergensmeyer, in Susie Tharu and K. Lalitha, eds., *Women Writing in India: 600* B.C. *to the Present*, vol. 1, New York: Feminist Press, 1991.)

Painting of Mīrabai. With Krishna (here present as an apparition) never far from her heart, she was said to propagate *bhakti* (eternal devotion) through her music. RASHROTHAN PARISHAD / KAMAT'S POTPOURRI.

For Mīrabai, Vishnu was the Lord of the universe yet resided in the soul (*antarayāmin*). Inspired by the Bhāgavata Purāṇa like the other North Indian upper caste saints, Chaitanya (b. 1486), Sūrdās (sixteenth century), and Tulsidās (1532–1623), Mīrabai worshiped a God with attributes (*saguna bhakti*), using metaphors to revel in his names (*nāma*) and forms (*rūpa*). In contrast, working-class saints (*sants*) like Kabir, the fifteenth-century weaver, drew upon the Upanishadic vision of an "Unmanifest Being beyond attributes" (*nirguna*), encompassing the universe, yet uncontained by temple or icon. The difference between the two traditions lay only in the paths, as they shared an identical goal, that of spiritual knowledge and *moksha*, or freedom from the cycle of births and deaths (*saṃsāra*).

The earliest hagiography is dated 1712 as facts enriched by legends. Mīrabai's father was the powerful Rathor clan *rānā* (ruler) of Jodhpur (Marwar), and her family ruled Mērta near Ajmer. In 1516 they allied themselves politically with Chittōr (Mewar) by marrying Mīra to Bhōja Rājā, heir to the Sisōdia Rānā Sangha, who met the Mughal Babur in battle in 1527. Even as a girl, Mīrabai distanced herself from courtly preoccupations by visiting *sadhus* (renunciants) who gave her an image of Krishna, with whom she became enamored.

Declaring that Krishna was her true husband, Mīrabai rejected her husband's bed, and she remained childless. She sought *sadhus*, and danced in front of the temple, in direct opposition to patriarchal Rajput notions of chaste wives and clan loyalties. Tradition states that Bhōja Rājā first suspected her infidelity, but realized that her lover was divine. In any case, at his death, she repudiated widowhood and refused to become a *sati* who immolated herself on her husband's funeral pyre. Mīrabai describes his family's attempts to kill her, and her escape through Krishna's intercession. Their gift of a basket of snakes turned into a garland around her neck; when they sent her poison, it turned into ambrosia when she drank it. She appears to have left then for Dwārakā, but she was hounded by the powerful Rajput community. Mīrabai is believed to have finally disappeared into Krishna's image at a shrine.

Despite her acts of marital insubordination, some feminists suggest that Mīrabai was a conformist who reinforced the hierarchy between the genders by calling herself Krishna's *dāsi* (slave). Others point to her dismissal of Rajput paradigms for women, and of caste boundaries, as demonstrated by her poem in which she identifies with the low caste woman Sabari, who tasted plums before offering them to Lord Rāma.

Sita Anantha Raman

BIBLIOGRAPHY

Alston, A. J. *The Devotional Poems of Mirabai.* Delhi: Motilal Banarsidass, 1980.

Desai, Neera. "Women in the Bhakti Movement." *Samaya Shakti* 1, no. 2 (1983): 92–100.

Dingra, Baldoon, ed. and trans. *Songs of Meera: Lyrics in Ecstasy.* Delhi: Orient Paperbacks, 1977.

Harlan, Lindsey. *Religion and Rajput Women: The Ethic of Protection in Contemporary Narratives.* Berkeley: University of California, 1992.

Hawley, John Stratton, and Mark Juergensmeyer. *Songs of the Saints of India.* New York: Oxford University Press, 1988.

Jordens, J. T. F. "Medieval Hindu Devotionalism." In *A Cultural History of India*, edited by A. L. Basham, pp. 266–280. Oxford: Clarendon Press, 1975.

Macnicol, Margaret, ed. *Poems by Indian Women.* Heritage of India Series. London: Oxford University Press, 1928.

Mukta, Parita. *Upholding the Common Life: The Community of Mirabai.* Delhi: Oxford University Press, 1994.

Tharu, Susie, and K. Lalitha. *Women Writing in India: 600 B.C. to the Present*, vol. 1. New York: Feminist Press, 1991.

MISSIONARIES, CHRISTIAN. *See* **British Impact; Portuguese in India.**

MIZORAM One of the "Seven Sisters," Mizoram is one of seven small tribal states in the Northeast region of India. The picturesque capital of some 350,000 people, Aizawl, at 3,715 feet (1,132 m) above sea level, is built on tiers on the steep hillside. The twenty or so major hills of the state have an average altitude of some 2,600 feet (792 m). In the south is Mizoram's second-largest town, Lungleh, with about 140,000 people, and nearby is the "Phawngpui," the Blue Mountain, from which there is a breathtaking view of the Bay of Bengal. The heavy rains of the monsoon from May to September define the life of the state, allowing the cultivation of rice, which Mizos eat at least three times a day and with which they make the rice beer, *zu*, that plays an important role in their numerous dance festivals. The *cheraw*, or bamboo dance, the most popular and the most colorful Mizo dance, is performed using long pairs of horizontal staves that are tapped open and together in rhythmic beat as the dancers step in and out. It is a dance similar to those of parts of Southeast Asia. The *khuallam*, or dance for the guests, is performed by guests wearing the traditional Mizo cloth of black, red, green, and blue stripes wrapped around the shoulders.

The population of Mizoram, of over a dozen tribes, was by 2004 about 9 million people, most of whom are Christians. The state has the highest literacy rate in India, an average of about 90 percent for men and 86 percent for women. The Mizos, first known as Kukis, were part of the great wave of Mongolians who settled in Western Burma before moving on to northeastern India. The Lushais came later, and the area became known as the Lushai Hills. A tribal chief ruled the village. The Mizo code of ethics revolves around *tlawmngaihna*, hospitality and kindness and self-sacrifice for others, which young men learn while they live in a bachelor dormitory, or *zawlbuk*. In theory, the youngest son inherits all property, but in practice the inheritance is shared among all the sons. A bride price is paid by the groom, but the money is shared by the parents, elder sister, and paternal aunt in the bride's family, as a spirit of family and community well-being pervades Mizo society. Everyone who receives any bride price money is also responsible for the care of the bride. The care of widows and orphans is also a collective family responsibility.

In 1895 the British declared Mizo Hills as part of British India, and the Mizo Common People's Union, later known as the Mizo Union, was formed on 9 April 1946 to represent Mizo interests. The United Mizo Freedom Party demanded that the Lushai Hills join Burma on independence, but under the Indian Constitution the Lushai Hills Autonomous District Council came into being in 1952. In 1955 the Eastern India Union was formed of tribals in eastern India, the same year the Mizo Cultural Society was formed, with noted Mizo leader Pu Laldenga as its secretary. In 1959 the "Mautam famine" devastated the Mizo hills, and the Mizo Cultural Society became first the Mautam Front and then, in 1960, the Mizo National Famine Front, and finally, in 1961, the Mizo National Front. It initiated the widespread violence of the Mizo Insurgency of February 1966 and was outlawed the following year, but Laldenga and Prime Minsiter Rajiv Gandhi agreed on 20 February 1987 that Mizoram would become the twenty-third state of the Indian Union.

Roger D. Long

See also **Gandhi, Rajiv; Tribal Politics**

BIBLIOGRAPHY

Gurudev, S. *Anatomy of Revolt in the North East of India*. New Delhi: Lancers Books, 1996.

Pakem, B. *Regionalism in India: With Special Reference to North-East India*. New Delhi: Har-Anand Publications, 1993.

MODERN AND CONTEMPORARY ART Modernity in Indian art can be said to have begun at the end of the seventeenth century with the setting up of trading interests in Calcutta by the British East India Company. The British occupation of India swiftly replaced the indigenous miniature schools with naturalistic company painting, and institutions such as art salons and art schools generated a new breed of Indian elite painters who turned to oils and watercolors in a British style, though often with Indian subjects from myth, portraiture, or landscape.

Raja Ravi Verma (1848–1906) of Kerala was among the most popular of this first generation of Western-style painters. In sculpture, this phase was characterized by academic classicism as exemplified by G. K. Mhatre. Around the turn of the twentieth century, the nationalist (*swadeshi*) movement in Bengal spawned a new movement in art: the artist Abanindranath Tagore (1871–1951) and his students broke away from Western painting styles and self-consciously sought aesthetic standards and techniques rooted in Indian and Japanese traditions. This movement was also accompanied by and closely connected with the appearance of the discipline of Indian art history, largely the creation of British Orientalists and South Asian nationalists such as E. B. Havell (1861–1934) and Ananda Coomaraswamy (1877–1947).

M. F. Husain. Whatever the medium of his work—whether a painting or an installation—his is an art grounded in both the Hindu and Muslim cultures of village India. INDIA TODAY.

Later designated the "Bengal School," the fantasy-laden paintings of this movement served as a pervasive influence for many artists throughout India, as major practitioners of this school became heads of art pedagogical institutions by 1925. Particularly in Bengal, the Bengal School has been a major influence to recent times, due largely to the practices of the art school Kala Bhavan, at Rabindranath Tagore's educational center in Shantiniketan, where Abanindranath Tagore's foremost disciple Nandalal Bose (1882–1966) headed a progressive offshoot of this school. Nandalal Bose, along with his senior students and other teachers at Kala Bhavan, such as Benodebehari Mukherjee (1904–1980), Ramkinkar Baij (1906–1980), and Prosanto Roy (1908–1973), fashioned a contextual Bengali modernism that has left its enduring stamp on this region. As a sculptor, Baij's monumental groupings of tribal life opened the way for an indigenous vital expressionism in modern Indian sculpture.

Another institution founded by Gaganendranath and Abanindranath Tagore and prominent in the dissemination of Bengal School styles and ideas was the Calcutta-based Indian Society of Oriental Art, headed by Kshitindra Nath Majumdar. Two major sculptors to emerge from this school were Chintamoni Kar (b. 1915) and Meera Mukherjee (1923–1998). Taking after the Neo-Primitivism of Ramkinkar Baij, Meera Mukherjee adopted the tribal technique of Bastar lost-wax bell metal casting to create monumental single and multiple figure compositions of empathic tenderness taken from everyday life (*Boatman*, *Bauls*, etc.), myth (*Cosmic Dancer*, *Buddha*), or history (*Ashoka at Kalinga*).

Contemporary artists who can be seen as continuing in some way the legacy of the Bengal School include Ganesh Pyne (b. 1937), Ramananda Bandyopadhyay (b. 1936), Lalu Prosad Shaw (b. 1937), Suhas Roy (b. 1936), Sakti Burman (b. 1935), Biswarup Datta (b. 1951) and Anjan Chakrabarty (b. 1956). The most celebrated contemporary figure among these is Ganesh Pyne. Shy and reclusive by nature, Pyne's haunting fantasies draw viewers into surreal landscapes where history, reality and folklore intersect. Superb draftsmanship and very subtle washed color tonalities combine in his paintings to bring to life his worlds of magic.

The Bengal School's attempt at defining an Indian "national" style was not without contestation or alternate formulations; artists such as Abanindranath's brother Gaganendranath Tagore (1867–1938) and their uncle,

Anjolie Ela Menon. Menon before her work in 1995. Though the artist disdains facile categorization of her work, the human figure is prominent in much of it, as is an iconography of distance and loss. MATTHEW TITUS / FOTOMEDIA.

the famous poet Rabindranath Tagore (1861–1941), were among the earliest to embrace Western modernist idioms in their work. While Gaganendranath expressed a critical sensibility through his expressionistic cartoons and evoked magic worlds using a Cubist-influenced style, Rabindranath mined the inchoate forms of the subconscious in a mode reminiscent of German Expressionism. These two were also responsible for India's first exhibition of Western modernist painting, with a showing of Bauhaus artists in Calcutta in 1922. More grim versions of Gaganendranath's political and social satire may be seen in the paintings of some contemporary artists, like Paritosh Sen (b. 1918) and Chowdhury (b. 1939). The late 1920s and 1930s saw the gradual growth of other approaches towards Indian modernism. Jamini Roy (1917–1972) in Bengal adopted a decorative iconic style based on folk scrolls and the urban folk art of Kalighat, which became a powerful influence for later painters of Bengal. Artists like Dharmanarayan Dasgupta (1939–1998), Ramananda Bandyopadhyay (b. 1936), Biswarup Datta (b. 1951), and Paresh Maity (b. 1965) are among those who have assimilated this trend.

The 1940s

Amrita Sher-Gil (1913–1941), of half-Punjabi and half-Hungarian descent, was among the first twentieth-century Indian artists to be trained in Paris and to fashion a personal artistic style combining Paul Gaugin's Post-Impressionism with the frescos of Ajanta. The fact that the successive art movements of modern Europe drew on non-Western sources for inspiration is here mirrored in an Indian seeking affiliation with Western modernism. The recognition of modernity as a global phenomenon, emanating from Europe and producing forms of cultural critique with international applicability, becomes the basis for developing indigenous national or regional adaptations or reflections of these forms. A cross-cultural vocabulary thus comes into existence where, for instance, Henri Matisse finds a regional echo in Jamini Roy, and both artists can influence the contemporary adaptations of Paresh Maity.

This trend of looking westward for an international idiom gained momentum in the 1940s, along with an impending sense of India's national independence. A number of artists' collectives were organized in major cities such as Calcutta, Bombay, Delhi, and Madras. The Calcutta Artists' Group, founded in 1942, was among the earliest of these, with a number of its members expressing leftist sentiments and traveling to Paris for training. Gopal Ghose (1913–1980), Nirode Majumdar (1916–1982), Rathin Maitra (1913–1997), Paritosh Sen (b. 1918), and Govardhan Ash (1907–1996) were some of the prominent members of this group. Of these, it is the Post-Impressionistic lyricism of Gopal Ghose and the sharp political satire of Paritosh Sen that are perhaps the most memorable. The simultaneous rise to prominence of the Communist Party, along with the disaster of a manmade famine in Bengal in 1943, spawned a sterner strain of Marxist-inspired iconography, with artists like Zainul Abedin (1914–1976), Chittaprosad (1915–1978), and Somenath Hore (b. 1920). Hore is better known as a sculptor, his emaciated figures of oppressed and poverty-stricken life executed with striking originality.

Modernist ideals and tendencies similar to those of the Calcutta Group were behind the Progressive Painters' Association founded in Madras in 1944, the Progressive Artists' Group (PAG) in Bombay in 1947, and the Delhi Shilpi Chakra in Delhi in 1949. One of the painters of the Delhi Shilpi Chakra, Ramkumar (b. 1924), also trained in Paris, went on to become one of India's most celebrated painters of semiabstract landscape. Another prominent contemporary artist encouraged by the Delhi Shilpi Chakra, Satish Gujral (b. 1925), studied under David Alfaro Siqueiros in Mexico and developed a highly individual painterly idiom based on an expressionistic Surrealism. Another art institution, the Triveni Kala Sangam, was founded in New Delhi in 1951 and has fostered a new breed of prominent contemporary artists. At its inception, the art division of Triveni was headed by K. S. Kulkarni (1918–1994), a role currently filled by Rameshwar Broota (b. 1941). Some of Broota's students at Triveni who have earned international recognition are Vasundhara Tewari (b. 1955) and Surinder Kaur (b. 1955).

The Progressive Artists' Group (PAG) of Bombay, several of whose members have assumed iconic status in India's modernist canon, was the most vocal and assertive of the collectives of the 1940s. The founding members of this group were M. F. Husain (b. 1915), F. N. Souza (1924–2002), K. H. Ara (1913–1985), S. K. Bakre (b. 1920), H. A. Gade (b. 1917), and S. H. Raza (b. 1922). Powerfully instrumental in the rise to prominence of this group were three Germans, Rudy von Leyden, Walter Langhammer, and E. Schlesinger, who had immigrated to India after the rise of Nazism. The first two were art writers working for the English-language newspaper the *Times of India*. The third was a businessman-patron of the PAG. Also influential, as a teacher of contemporary art to several members of the PAG and other Bombay artists of this period, was S. B. Palsikar (1917–1984). The three most important painters of the PAG, Souza, Husain, and Raza, hail from minority religions of India, the first born a Roman Catholic and the other two Muslim, and each has staked a distinctive claim as a visual spokesman for a national modernism. Each of these has also been influential as a formative source for different directions of contemporary Indian art. Souza can be seen as the most individualistic of these artists, his paintings exerting powerful expressionistic distortions to landscapes and human forms, suggesting a sexuality intensified through repression. Husain, the most celebrated living Indian artist today, aligned himself from the beginning with a Nehruvian project of secular nation-building, and has woven eclectic modern myths from varied religious and popular sources in his works. Raza, beginning with abstraction, has settled into an experimentation with the mystical geometric forms of Tantra, a message of personal transformation that has gained increasing popularity since the 1960s. V. S. Gaitonde (1924–2001), another important artist, joined the PAG in 1950. Gaitonde's abstractions turned increasingly toward a minimalism of color and form dictated by the contemplative exigencies of Zen combined with textural and compositional affinities as varied as the works of Paul Klee and the miniatures of Basholi.

A number of the artists of this generation traveled to Europe to absorb firsthand the exciting legacy of the successive movements of modernism. Paritosh Sen of the Calcutta Group, Ramkumar of the Delhi Shilpi Chakra, and S. H. Raza of the Progressive Artists' Group traveled to Paris in the 1950s and came under the tutelage of André Lhote, an important figure in the dissemination of Cubism. Another Bombay-based artist who was influenced by Cubism in Paris was Jehangir Sabavala (b. 1922), who went on to distill his own essence of a monumental nomadic serenity from Synthetic Cubism. Souza moved to London in 1949. Another close associate of the PAG from Bombay, Tyeb Mehta (b. 1925), moved to London in 1959 and worked there until 1964, before returning to Bombay (Mumbai). Mehta's work extends a *Guernica*-like anguish into an exploration of existential angst expressed in mythical and spatial terms. Akbar Padamsee (b. 1928), also from the Sir J. J. School of Art in Bombay and a friend of the PAG, moved to Paris in 1951 and worked there until 1967. Padamsee, in his portraits and landscapes, combines an intellectual rigor with a burning sensitivity that expresses tenderness and pain.

The 1950s and 1960s

The 1950s and 1960s saw the consolidation of a rich and varied Indian modernism through the assimilation of the successive vocabularies of modernist movements of Europe and America into regional perceptions and ontologies. This was particularly fostered by the founding of regional centers of art headed by artists with articulate ideologies. The Baroda School of Art and the Madras College of Art are two such schools. The art division of the Maharaja Sayajirao University at Baroda, initiated by the lyrical Bengal School–derived modernism of the artist N. S. Bendre (1910–1990) and the sculptor Sankho Chaudhuri (b. 1916), developed an exciting artistic and art critical voice in the 1960s, veering away from internationalism and abstraction to figuration and regionalism. Two major artists of this school are Bhupen Khakkar (1934–2003) and Gulammohammed Sheikh (b. 1937), who eschewed prevailing canons both of Western modernism and a rural or traditional indigenism to open up an urban popular space for Indian modernism. Also seminal in this shift were the efforts of art critic Geeta Kapur. Other important artists to graduate from this school include G. R. Santosh (1929–1997), Himmat Shah (b. 1933), Jyoti Bhatt (b. 1934), and Ratan Parimoo (b. 1936). Among the sculptors from Baroda were students of Sankho Chaudhuri, such as Nagji Patel (b. 1937) and Balbir Katt (b. 1939). While Nagji Patel and Himmat Shah share a vocabulary of primitive naturalism, Balbir Katt chisels monumental stone sculptures, often with metaphysical themes. Mrinalini Mukherjee (b. 1949), daughter of artist Benodebehari Mukherjee, is another major sculptor from Baroda. She studied under K. G. Subramanium and makes massive shapes using fibers such as jute or hemp, emulating plant or human forms. Suspended from the ceiling or heaped on the floor, her knotted, twisted and twined three-dimensional forms have a textured organic quality, which is unique. The tradition of originality in sculpture has continued at Baroda; recent names to make a mark include Latika Katt (b. 1953), Dhruva Mistry (b. 1957), and G. Ravinder Reddy (b. 1956). Reddy's fiberglass realism emulates American Pop Art, while Mistry's cool surreal creations seem to have walked out of the paintings of Max Ernst.

Allied to the sculptural experimentations of the Baroda School in the 1960s are the works of two Bombay sculptors, Adi Davierwala and Piloo Pochkhanawala (1923–1986). Along with Raghav Kaneria of the Baroda School, these two Bombay sculptors turned to junk metal welding for their expression. Davierwala, who worked with wood in the 1950s creating heavy angular geometric forms, discovered a new vocabulary of shapes in junk metal, creating monumental sculptures which protrude and thrust into space while retaining a balanced stillness. Piloo Pochkhanawala experimented with a number of media and techniques in the 1960s and 1970s, including direct carving, cement and metal casting, finally settling on junk welding, using found forms. Her works highlight the texture and form of her materials and her technique and have tended to move away from solid modeling toward flattened forms that reach out into space. Amarnath Sehgal of Delhi is another important modern pioneer of metal sculpture. His assemblages of human forms are modulated with an eye to their expressive potential in describing social themes, often of inequity or cruelty, as in *Tyranny* or *The Tortured*.

The Madras School, among the early art institutions established by the British in India, underwent a transformation under the leadership of K. C. S. Paniker (1911–1977), who was also instrumental in the founding of an artists' village named Cholamandalam near Madras (Chennai). In his own work, Paniker utilized the geometric mystical symbols of Tantra, though with an intent more visual and aesthetic than spiritual. In doing this, he opened up a new direction for an indigenous form of modern abstraction, which fused the iconic and calligraphic visual aesthetics of artists such as Paul Klee with Indian folk and mystical meditative designs. This coincided with the enhanced interest and presentation in the 1960s of Tantric art by Ajit Mookherjee and others, leading to an important field of Indian abstract exploration, in which spiritual practices are brought together with pure visuality to engender internal transformations. This trend in art has been termed Neo-Tantra after the traveling exhibition of that name which toured Europe and North America in 1984–1986. In addition to S. H. Raza, mentioned above, other Neo-Tantric artists include G. R. Santosh (1929–1977), Biren De (b. 1926), and Sohan Qadri (b. 1932). Many younger contemporary artists, such as Biswarup Datta (b. 1951) and Amrita Banerji (b. 1965), also make use of visual metaphors taken from this direction, though not with any principled adhesion to the forms or ideas of Tantra. The influence of Neo-Tantra can also be seen fused with an American Op Art inspiration in the paintings of diasporic artist Anil Revri (b. 1956), who lives and works in Washington, D.C.

In sculpture, D. P. Roy Chowdhury (1899–1975), a Bengal School follower, was influential as a teacher at the Madras School. Though his own work emulated an Indian version of Rodinesque allegories, his students such as S. Dhanapal (1919–2002) branched off into original terra-cotta and metal figures. Extending Dhanapal's work, metal sculptures in repoussé resembling religious icons became the hallmark of P. V. Janakiraman (1930–1995), and this, in turn, became the basis for the welded shamanic figurines on sheet metal compositions created by S. Nandagopal (b. 1946).

The quest for a modern indigenism in the work of Paniker was paralleled by a number of other artists from different parts of India, such as K. G. Subramanyan (b. 1924), a student of Shantiniketan who later joined the faculty of the Baroda School, and J. Swaminathan (1928–1994), whose own paintings showed a mysticism similar to those of Paniker, drawing on Indian folk and tribal patterns as well as the iconic arrangements of Paul Klee. Swaminathan founded Group 1890 with a number of other artists, with the aim of expressing an immediacy based on regional and local experience. Artists affiliated with this movement include Laxma Goud (b. 1940) and Manjit Bawa (b. 1941). Thota Vaikuntham (b. 1942), a student of K. G. Subramanyan from the Baroda School, also exemplifies this form of indigenism.

Recent Developments

The acceptance of the visual vocabularies of Western modernism as an international affiliation for the global condition of modernity took a further step with the increased technological and economic integration of the world since the 1980s. This has led to diasporic Indian populations all over the world, who, rather than finding an international voice for a regional experience, are presented with the reverse dilemma of articulating global experiences in terms of a subjectivity often formed in India or under conditions of an Indian upbringing. Though several artists who have made their mark in India have gone on to reside abroad, like S. H. Raza (Paris), F. N. Souza (London and New York), and Sohan Qadri (Copenhagen), already mentioned here, a number of artists of Indian origin or upbringing have grown into prominence in the artistic milieu of the West. Anish

Kapoor (b. 1954) is a well-known sculptor from the United Kingdom. Natwar Bhavsar (b. 1934), another renowned artist, lives and works in New York. Bhavsar's cosmic abstractions and Anil Revri's focused optical meditations present a context-free internationalism, like that of Anish Kapoor—an important direction in diasporic art. However, another perspective on the diasporic experience is that presented by photographer and installation artist Allan DeSouza (b. 1958) of Los Angeles. DeSouza's work provides an intelligent social and psychological commentary on nation and identity, working from outside national boundaries to explore their effects on the human psyche.

Since the 1980s, a powerful body of art has been produced by contemporary artists focusing on gender issues. The homoerotic fantasies of Bhupen Khakkar or the feminist polemics of Nalini Malani (b. 1946), Arpana Caur (b. 1954), Arpita Singh (b. 1937), Gogi Saroj Pal (b. 1940), Nilima Sheikh (b. 1945), and others constitute a prominent direction of contemporary Indian art. Moreover, in keeping with contemporary art's revision of its own limits and functions throughout the world, photography, printmaking, video, computer, installation and performance art have gradually come to take center stage in India, displacing the primacy of painting and sculpture. The attempt to de-privilege the masculine spectatorial gaze from its vantage as viewer in context-less galleries or as the possessor of collections has led increasingly to the movement of art from the pictorial space of walls to more intimate and participatory social contexts. This may be interpreted as a movement from the modern to the postmodern in art, and, since the late 1980s, increasing numbers of Indian artists are presenting their ideas, interpretations, and social questions in these forms. Artists like Vivian Sundaram (b. 1943), Ranbir Kaleka (b. 1953), Subodh Gupta (b. 1964), and Sheela Gowda (b. 1957) have been at the vanguard of Indian installation art, producing some of the most exciting contemporary artworks of our time.

This however has not meant the extinction of painting as an art form. A number of artists have attempted to destabilize the conventional boundaries and viewing expectations of painting through the use of semiotic intertextuality and self-referentiality. Thus the diverse discourses of myth, fantasy, consumerism, and politics are often overlaid as coexisting pictorial signifiers offering a critical commentary on varied aspects of contemporary Indian lived experience. Atul Dodiya (b. 1959), Surendran Nair (b. 1956), and Anandajit Ray (b. 1965) are three prominent artists who have taken this direction. Atul Dodiya has moved from the play of memory using a faded photo-realism in the 1980s to a series of allegorical self-portraits locating himself critically at the intersection of myth and history since the 1990s. Surendran Nair, in an ironic variant of Tantric meditational anatomy, depicts the human body as a passive site of emblematic inscriptions or punctures effected by political and consumerist interests. Anandajit Ray splices science fiction, manga, anime and action movie images to create pop nightmare fictions of contemporary Indian life.

Other contemporary subversions of painterliness include emulation of and interplay with virtual reality and the hyper-modern. The canvases of Baiju Parthan (b. 1956) and Jitish Kallat (b. 1974), for example, are loaded with icons and hypertext depicting the human as a post-structural indefinable under the constructional impulses of new sciences and technologies and their political or commercial deployment as well as futuristic trans-technological scenarios. In the case of Parthan, the metaphor of cyberspace goes one step further through the exploration of the painted image alongside web-based virtual versions of the same. Nalini Malani, a senior woman artist, whose works transit between painting, performance, installation and collaboration, makes creative use of video projections in much of her work. Her themes focus on the inequalities and violences of gender, religion and class.

As with painting, the stand-alone aesthetic of traditional sculpture has also come to be questioned and replaced by a number of alternate or reconfigured objects. N. N. Rimzon (1957), for example, installs his sculptures within larger contexts often made of mass-produced objects to explore the dialectic between the spiritual and the socially unjust. A well-known work of his is *The Inner Voice*, where a nude male Tīrthānkara-like figure, symbolizing austerity and spiritual purity is placed iconically within a circle of swords, making a powerful, if ambiguous, visual statement on austerity and power, nonviolence and violence.

The decentering of the art gallery or museum as a viewing space and of patronage from the possessive intents of collectors has also led in the direction of site-specific installations and performance art. Site-specificity populates public spaces with objects which reference both the site and the viewer (user of the site) to create reflexive environments which bring submerged meanings of collective lived experience to light. These installations are often treated as events or performances which are durationally limited and thus cannot be bought or sold. Patronage here usually takes the form of sponsorship, often by the corporate sector. The Mumbai-based Kala Ghoda Association's Artfest 2000, for example, featured a number of installations scattered through public buildings in the precinct of Kala Ghoda, between 1 February and 14 February 2000. Titled "Making an Entrance," the project was conceptualized by art critic Ranjit Hoskote and included works by Jahangir Jani, Sudarshan Shetty, Kaushik Mukhopadhyay, Baiju Parthan, and Bharati Kapadia. According to the Kala Ghoda Association's web site, "The concept of 'Making an Entrance' has evolved from the perceived need to construct a new venue for art, an exhibition site that is neither gallery nor museum . . . [but] an unbound public space. Indeed, new viewing habits and practices may arise from such new viewing situations." Similarly, Vivan Sundaram used the lobby of the Victoria Memorial in Kolkata to present his 1998 installation *Journeys towards Freedom*. Here, the Victoria Memorial, a cultural and political landmark, is chosen for its sedimented memory of colonialism and nationalism and made the site for Sundaram's interpretations of political bondage and liberation.

Debashish Banerji

See also **Miniatures; Mughal Painting**

BIBLIOGRAPHY

Anand, Mulk Raj. *Amrita Sher-Gil.* New Delhi: National Gallery of Modern Art, 1989.

Appasamy, Jaya. *Abanindranath Tagore and the Art of his Times.* New Delhi: Lalit Kala Akademi, 1968.

———. *Introduction to Modern Indian Sculpture.* New Delhi: Indian Council for Cultural Relations, 1970.

Clark, John. *Modern Indian Art, Some Literature and Problematics.* Sydney: School of Asian Studies, University of Sydney, 1994.

Dalmia, Yashodhara. *The Making of Modern Indian Art: The Progressives.* New Delhi: Oxford University Press, 2001.

Guha-Thakurta, Tapati. *The Making of a New Indian Art.* Cambridge, U.K.: Cambridge University Press, 1992.

Herwitz, Daniel. *Husain.* Mumbai: Tata, 1988.

Kapur, Geeta. *Contemporary Indian Artsits.* New Delhi: Vikas, 1978.

———. *K. G. Subramanyan.* New Delhi: Lalit Kalal Akademi, 1987.

Mitter, Partha. *Art and Nationalism in Colonial India, 1850–1922.* Cambridge, U.K.: Cambridge University Press, 1994.

Mookerjee, Ajit. *Tantra Art: Its Philosophy and Physics.* New Delhi: Rupa, 1967.

Parimoo, Ratan. *The Paintings of the Three Tagores: Abanindranath, Gaganendranath, Rabindranath—A Comparative Study.* Baroda: University of Baroda,1973.

Said, Edward. *Orientalism.* New York: Pantheon, 1978.

———. *Culture and Imperialism.* New York: Knopf, 1993.

Sheikh, Gulammohammed, ed. *Contemporary Art in Baroda.* New Delhi: Tulika, 1997.

Sinha, Gayatri, ed. *Indian Art: An Overview.* New Delhi: Rupa, 2003.

Subramanyan, K. G. *The Living Tradition: Perspectives on Modern Indian Art.* Kolkata: Seagull Books, 1987.

Sundaram, V., et al., eds. *Amrita Sher-Gil.* Mumbai: Marg, 1972.

Tuli, Neville. *Indian Contemporary Painting.* New York: Abrams, 1998.

MOHENJO-DARO In 1922 Mohenjo-Daro was discovered by R. D. Banerji, two years after major excavations had begun at Harappa, some 366 miles (590 km) to the north. Numerous large-scale excavations were carried out at the site by John Marshall, Ernest Mackay, K. N. Dikshit, and other directors through the 1930s. Excavations were banned after excavations by George F. Dales in 1964, and only salvage excavation, surface surveys, and conservation projects have been allowed at the site in recent times. Located on the east side of the Indus River in the semiarid region of Sind province, Pakistan, this site was spared the looting of bricks that destroyed most sites in the Punjab. It is the largest and best-preserved urban center of the Indus civilization (2600–1900 B.C.), extending over 618 acres (250 hectares). Numerous mounded ruins rise up above the plain, while others are partly buried under the silts of the encroaching Indus River. The earliest levels of the site are inaccessible due to the high water table that is the result of modern irrigation canals. Pottery recovered from the deeply submerged levels are similar to pottery found at the nearby sites of Kot Diji and Amri, dating to around 3500 B.C. These discoveries suggest that Mohenjo-Daro has an earlier Kot Diji Phase occupation, like the site of Harappa. No cemetery area has been located at the site, though there have been reports of occasional chance burials discovered in the course of site conservation.

Most of the excavations at Mohenjo-Daro were focused in the uppermost levels of the site, which date to the last part of the Harappa Phase (c. 2200–1900 B.C.). The citadel mound on the west is the highest sector of the city and contains the famous Great Bath and so-called Granary as well as numerous other large buildings and impressive streets with covered drains. One portion of the citadel mound has not been excavated because it is covered by a Buddhist stupa dating to the Kushana period, circa 2nd century A.D. A massive mud-brick wall that had a large brick gateway in the southeast originally surrounded the citadel mound.

The other mounds of the city on the east are somewhat lower in height and have been referred to collectively as the "Lower Town," but in fact they form several distinct habitation areas set apart by massive mud-brick walls and platforms and wide streets. Additional suburbs are located further to the east and south. Each sector has numerous large brick houses that could have been the mansions of powerful merchants or landowners. No temples have been identified, though there is one building with a double staircase that may have had a ritual function.

Important crafts were carried out in different sectors of all the major mounds and include copper working, shell and ivory carving, and lapidary and stone tool production; in addition, many different types of furnaces

Excavation Site, Mohenjo-Daro. Mounds at the Mohenjo-Daro excavation site, discovered in 1922 and the subject of numerous digs in the 1930s. Located in present-day Pakistan, Mohenjo-Daro is home to the remains—some still to be unearthed—of the largest and best-preserved urban center of the Indus civilization. FOTOMEDIA ARCHIVE.

existed for the manufacture of terra-cotta pottery, stoneware bangles, glazed faience ornaments, and fired steatite beads. Seal-manufacturing workshops have been discovered in very restricted locations, indicating strong control of production. The variety of raw materials at the site demonstrates the vast trading networks that linked the city to distant resource areas.

Rare discoveries of gold and silver ornaments provide evidence of a class of wealthy merchants or landowners, similar to that seen at Harappa. At Mohenjo-Daro there are stone carvings of seated male figures that may represent some of the ancestral leaders of these communities. One of these fragmentary figures is called the "Priest-King," even though there is no evidence that either priests or kings ruled the city. This bearded sculpture wears a fillet around the head, an armband, and a cloak decorated with trefoil patterns that were originally filled with red pigment. Male and female human figurines as well as animal figurines were made of terra-cotta, bronze, faience, or even shell. Different styles of ornaments and headdresses on the human figures suggest that many different classes and diverse ethnic communities inhabited the city. The painted pottery of Mohenjo-Daro is similar to that seen at Harappa, but there is some regional variation that reinforces the distinct character of these two important cities.

At the end of the Harappa Phase, people using a slightly different type of pottery and new styles of geometric seals that did not have writing occupied Mohenjo-Daro. The transition from one culture to the next was gradual, as seen at Harappa, and there is no evidence for an Indo-Aryan invasion. The region around Mohenjo-Daro continued to be inhabited throughout the Early Historic period, and a modern village is located near the mound today.

Jonathan Mark Kenoyer

See also **Harappa; Indus Valley Civilization; Sind.**

BIBLIOGRAPHY

Jansen, Michael. *Mohenjo-Daro, City of Wells and Drains: Water Splendour 4500 Years Ago*. Bergisch Gladbach, Germany: Frontinus Society Publications, 1993.

———. "Mohenjo-Daro, Type Site of the Earliest Urbanization Process in South Asia: Ten Years of Research at Mohenjo-Daro, Pakistan, and an Attempt at a Synopsis." In *South Asian Archaeology 1993*, edited by A. Parpola and P. Koskikallio. Helsinki: Suomalainen Tiedeakatemia 1994.

Kenoyer, Jonathan Mark. *Ancient Cities of the Indus Valley Civilization*. Karachi: Oxford University Press, 1998.

Possehl, Gregory L. *The Indus Civilization: A Contemporary Perspective*. Walnut Creek, Calif.: AltaMira Press, 2002.

MOKSHA. *See* **Hinduism (Dharma).**

MONETARY POLICY FROM 1952 TO 1991

Indian monetary policy, as it was designed and implemented during the planning period of 1952 to 1991, with a heavy accent on government intervention, differed considerably from the normal concept of monetary policy in economic literature, which is identified with the regulation of quantity of money through indirect methods of changing the cost and availability of bank credit, rather than through direct methods of controlling its quantity. It was required to reconcile multiple objectives as embedded in India's first Five-Year Plan (1951–1956). The objectives were:

1. Price stability should be maintained.
2. Savings of the community should be mobilized, and its financial component (i.e., savings held in bank deposits, shares, etc.) should be steadily enlarged.
3. Savings so mobilized should be allocated to the sectors in accordance with national economic goals as set out in the country's Five-Year Plans.
4. The resource needs of the major sectors in the economy, that is, the public sector, should be met as a priority.

Little thought was, however, given to the mutual inconsistency of these objectives, desirable though they were. The goal of price stability often conflicted with meeting the resource needs of the public sector. In fact, channeling the resources to the public sector and the government undermined efforts to contain inflationary pressures. The mobilization of savings was admirably achieved, but savings so mobilized could not be allocated in an efficient manner to the sectors in accordance with plan priorities. In pursuing these goals, the Reserve Bank of India (RBI), a central bank, could not avoid a "mismatch between its responsibility to supervise and control the functioning of the monetary system on the one hand, and its authority to do so on the other" (RBI).

Monetary Policy Framework

Monetary policy under planning was formulated in rather a crude way by going through the following procedure. To begin with, a desirable level of supply of money was estimated on certain assumptions based partly on historical experience and partly on expectations about the movement of future economic events such as output growth and trends in prices; demand for money was assumed to grow in proportion to income growth. The magnitude of quantity of money so projected to match the demand for it was considered to be noninflationary. Working backward, using the balance sheet of the banking system, reserve money, that is, currency in circulation plus cash with banks and their deposits held with the RBI was calculated. It was the changes in the reserve money that the RBI targeted in order to ensure an appropriate level of bank credit both to the government and the private sector.

Monetary Policy Instruments

The RBI had recourse to the following instruments both for regulating the level of money and credit and for directing bank credit to the high-priority sectors of the Indian economy. These were: cash reserve ratio; open market operations; refinancing facilities from the RBI; administered interest rates; statutory liquidity ratio; and selective credit controls, known in economic literature as directed credit. The first three of these were used to regulate the reserve money changes, though the cash reserve ratio was more effective in the Indian conditions than the open market operations, or the refinancing facilities to neutralize the impact of reserve money changes on the credit operations of banks. This ratio was very high, at around 14 percent of deposits, entailing a heavy tax on the banking system, and for that reason it was difficult to make changes in it beyond a certain limit. Refinance facilities were not large enough to make a dent on reserve money variations. As regards the open market operations, they were employed more to "maintain a desired pattern of yields on government securities and generally to help the Government raise resources from the capital market" (RBI, 1985, pp. 262–263) than to bring about variation in the reserve money. Thus it became more a fiscal policy and less a monetary policy instrument.

India relied on the administered interest rate regime rather than on market mechanism to bring about the desired changes in interest rates. The RBI, through periodical issue of directives, fixed the minimum and maximum deposit and lending rates and maintained the return on government securities at a level consistent with that on banks' assets and liabilities. In addition, financial institutions of all types—provident funds, insurance companies, and so on—were guided by the government through the RBI as to how they should invest their funds. As a consequence, until the 1980s real interest rates, that is, money interest rates adjusted for changes in the wholesale price index, turned negative. There was, however, a welcome change after the mid-1980s, when the real interest rates turned positive, even when the administered interest rate regime system prevailed.

The statutory liquidity ratio, defined as the ratio of cash on hand of banks, net interbank balances, unencumbered government and government guaranteed securities, and gold to the total deposit liabilities was used to preempt bank resources for investment in government securities and away from the private sector. This ratio introduced a distortive element in the financial system inasmuch as the return on government securities was almost always lower, until 1990, than on bank loans. The height of this ratio at around 33 percent was also a serious disincentive to banks.

Selective credit controls were used to channelize credit flows to certain private sectors of the economy considered to be priority sectors. This instrument relied on setting margins, quantum of credit in terms of proportion of total credit and the interest rate subsidy. The proportion of such credit varied over the years, depending on the public policy objectives of the government, but generally accounted for around 40 percent of total bank credit. These credits turned out to be very costly as the default rate was very high. The accumulation of bad and doubtful debts, estimated to be roughly 25 to 30 percent of deposits, had virtually wiped out the entire capital base of several banks in 1989 and 1990.

Consequences

The monetary policy apparatus that evolved in the context of Indian planning made the RBI more a facilitator of fiscal policy with monetary intent rather than conventionally defined monetary authority. Given the institutional imperatives, as well as the exigencies of government finances, the RBI could only influence the operations of banks by stipulating and administering the cash reserves and statutory liquidity ratios, or adjusting floors and ceilings on interest rates charged by banks on their assets and liabilities, rather than by its perception of the monetary events and the practical precepts of central banking. Because of the obsessive preoccupation with government finances, the RBI had perforce to crowd out private sector investment, which should have been the main domain for the exercise of its monetary policy. It also became a helpless spectator for the growing public debt over time, which turned out to be one of the most destabilizing factors in the Indian economy since the mid-1980s. Only when the Indian economic policy changed radically after 1991 did the RBI come into its own to wield a monetary policy without fiscal apron strings.

Deena Khatkhate

See also **Monetary Policy since 1991; Reserve Bank of India, Evolution of**

BIBLIOGRAPHY

Government of India. Ministry of Finance. *Economic Survey.* New Delhi, 1988–1989, 1989–1990.

Khatkhate, Deena R. "National Economic Policies in India." In *National Economic Policies: Handbook of Comparative Economic Policies*, vol. 1, edited by Dominick Salvatore. New York: Greenwood Press, 1991.

———. "Indian Banking System: Restitution and Reform Sequencing." Report submitted to Government of India, New Delhi, 1993.

Reserve Bank of India. *Report of the Committee to Review the Working of the Monetary System (RCRWM).* Mumbai: Reserve Bank of India, 1985.

———. *Reports on Currency and Finance.* Mumbai: Reserve Bank of India, 1987–1988, 1988–1989.

MONETARY POLICY SINCE 1991 Monetary policy operations since 1991 reflect the responses of the Reserve Bank of India (RBI) to the challenges posed by the Indian economy's transformation from financial repression to a liberalized market orientation. Recent efforts to develop and integrate financial markets established a closer linkage of monetary management operations with internal debt management, exchange rate, and reserves management operations. The basic objective of monetary policy to maintain price stability and support growth by ensuring adequate flow of credit continued to be paramount, while its scope was broadened to encompass aspects of financial stability by maintaining orderly conditions in financial markets and achieving greater interest rate flexibility. Greater transparency has also been imparted through institutional mechanisms for internal coordination within the central bank and for external consultations.

With procedures increasingly shifting to market-based interventions, monetary policy operations have become primarily a process of managing liquidity on a day-to-day basis. These operations are, however, consistent with the overall policy announced in April and reviewed in October for every fiscal year. These announcements are considered useful as a framework for relevant measures, for capturing events affecting macroeconomic assessments including fiscal management and seasonal factors, and as a means of greater transparency, better communication, and an effective consultation process.

The period up to 1996–1997 reflected the challenges of macrostabilization and adjustment against the background of a high inflation rate, a difficult balance of payments situation, and massive draw down of foreign exchange reserves. The focus was on reining in inflationary pressures, and therefore a tight and cautious policy stance was taken. This period also saw far-reaching financial reforms, such as rationalization and liberalization of interest rates, greater autonomy for the central bank with elimination of automatic monetization of fiscal deficits, financial markets development and integration, and considerable easing of operational constraints on the financial system. The latter half of the 1990s and the early years of the new millennium represented a gradual phase of easing liquidity, softening interest rates reflecting the lowering of inflationary expectations, and further deepening of financial markets. This period also witnessed, however, a comparative slowdown in industrial and economic activity until 2003–2004, contributed by a variety of domestic and external shocks. Consequently, the focus was upon containing volatility in markets, particularly the foreign exchange market, strengthening reserves, and efficiently coordinating internal debt management with monetary operations.

A comparison of projections with actuals in respect to major monetary policy parameters, namely the growth rate, inflation rate, and M3 (broad money) reveals some interesting features (see Table 1).

During the period 1992–1993 to 1996–1997, since there was acceleration in economic activity due to easing of constraints, the growth projections were consistently underestimated; and actual inflation rates and M3 growth rates were mostly higher than the projections. During 1994–1995 and 1995–1996, the actual growth rates turned out to be higher than projections by about 2 percent. A very cautious and tight monetary policy stance was adopted in 1995–1996 to contain inflationary pressures. This was viewed by the market as a period of credit crunch, and the central bank had to defend its position very strongly by arguing that the credit growth was high enough. The inflation rate, which exceeded the projection in 1994–1995 by more than 3 percentage points at a double-digit level, was brought down by nearly 6 percentage points, to less than 5 percent in 1995–1996. The M3 growth was the lowest, at below 14 percent that year, and the ten-year gilt yield rate peaked to around 14 percent. There was practically no backtracking on the inflation front since then, and the inflation rate since 1995–1996 remained moderate throughout the period. The inflation projection has been brought down to less than 5 percent in the last two years. But, the economy consistently underperformed since 1997–1998, compared to projections. The softening of interest rates did not produce the 7 percent growth rate, the upper range of projections until 2000–2001. The success story of this period lies in the containment of inflation and inflationary expectations, substantial easing of interest rates, considerable strengthening of the external sector, reflected in a buildup of substantial foreign exchange reserves, deepening of financial markets, and the sharpening of debt and monetary management tools.

Since 1997 the bank rate, repo rate, and cash reserve ratio have been used more frequently to meet short-term monetary policy objectives in the light of the emerging domestic and external situations. Markets also perceive these changes as signals for movements in market rates of interest. Deposit and lending rates of banks also respond to these changes, though in varying degrees.

Open market operations, including repos operations under a Liquidity Adjustment Facility, combined with participation in primary issues of government securities serve the central bank to steer interest rates across the maturity spectrum, besides modulating volatility in government securities yields. This greatly helped effective monetary management, smooth debt management, and completion of the large borrowing program by the government. The daily repos operations lend considerable flexibility and leverage to the central bank in managing liquidity and the repo rate has gained prominence as a signaling instrument since 2001.

Institutional arrangements for monetary policy formulation had also undergone changes since 1997. An interdepartmental Financial Markets Committee now monitors developments in financial markets, reviews market developments with regard to both volume and rates in money, foreign exchange and government securities, and makes quick daily assessments of liquidity conditions for market interventions. The central bank also conducts resources management discussions with selected banks to get feedback on market perceptions for possible policy action. A Technical Advisory Committee on Money and Government Securities Markets has also been appointed, with representation from financial, banking, and academic communities to advise the central bank on new policy procedures.

Impact of Monetary Policy Operations: Some Key Indicators

From a macroeconomic perspective, there are key indicators that capture the impact of monetary policy operations since 1991. The interest rates in respect to call money and deposits in general have softened significantly after their peak in 1995–1996, though the bank lending rates showed some inflexibility, despite showing some decline (see Figure 1). As a result, alongside lower inflation rates, the real interest rate is perceived to be high. The effect of monetary policy, particularly on lending rates, is observed to be asymmetric, showing some downward stickiness.

TABLE 1

Major monetary policy parameters: Projections and actuals since 1991–1992

	Annual increases in percent								
	Real GDP			WPI threshold inflation			M3 (Broad money)		
Year (April–March)	P	A	A–P	P	A	A–P	P	A	A–P
1991–1992	4.0 (3.0)	1.3	−1.7	7.0	13.6	+6.6	14.0 (13.0)(1)	19.3	+5.3
1992–1993	3.5 (2)	5.1	+1.6	8.0	7.0	−1.0	11.0	14.8	+3.8
1993–1994	5.0	5.9	+0.9	— (3)	10.8	—	12.0 (14.0)	18.4	+6.4
1994–1995	N.A. (4) (5.5)	7.3	+1.8	7.2 (5) (6.8)	10.4	+3.2	14–15 (16)	22.4	+7.9
1995–1996	5.5 (well above 5.5)	7.3	+1.8	8.0	4.3	−3.7	15.5	13.6	−1.9
1996–1997	6.0	7.8	+1.8	6.0	5.4	−0.6	15.5-16.0	16.2	+0.5
1997–1998	6.0–7.0	4.8	−1.7	6.0	4.5	−1.5	15.0–15.5	18.0	+2.8
1998–1999	6.5–7.0 (6.0)	6.5	−0.25	5.0–6.0	5.2	−0.3	15.0–15.5	19.4	+4.2
1999–2000	6.0–7.0	6.1	−0.40	5.0	6.4	+1.4	15.5–16.0	14.6	−1.2
2000–2001	6.5–7.0 (6.0–6.5)	4.4	−2.35	4.5	5.5	+1.0	15.0	16.8	+1.8
2001–2002	6.0–6.5 (5.0–6.0)	5.6	−0.65	5.0	1.6	−3.4	14.5	14.2	−0.3
2002–2003	6.0–6.5 (5.0–5.5)	4.3	−1.95	4.0	6.5	+2.5	14.0	15.0	+1.0
2003–2004	6.0 (6.5–7.0) with an upward bias			5.0–5.5 (4.0–4.5)			14.0		

Notes: GDP=Gross Domestic Product; WPI=Wholesale Price Index; P=Projected; A=Actual. Figures given in parentheses are as reset in October Statements of Policy. Differences between Actual and Projected have been calculated with reference to April Statement and to the midpoint, where a range is indicated.
(1) Reset based on fresh information and acceleration in inflation rate to 8.9 percent up to 21 September 1991.
(2) Projection given in October statement.
(3) No projection for inflation given; some further moderation in inflation rate was indicated.
(4) No projection for growth rate was indicated in April; in October, an implicit rate was given.
(5) A reduction in inflation rate by 4 percentage points was envisaged.

SOURCE: Courtesy of author.

In contrast to domestic assets, the net foreign exchange assets have emerged as a significant contributing source of reserve money (see Figure 2).

The growth rates in both reserve money and broad money have been contained since 1998, and correspondingly, the price level remained stable and showed some decline (see Figure 3).

The money multiplier showed a secular increase, whereas the income velocity showed a similar decline (see Figure 4).

Some Key Issues in Perspective

While there is a growing consensus that central banks should have operational independence and concentrate on a single target, such as inflation, there is some sense of discomfort in India as to whether this will survive the test of time. This is particularly true as a result of a conflict between the goal of preventing future inflation, and avoiding a sharp downturn in industry. Under such circumstances, the reliance on mechanistic, simpler, and narrower rules restricting discretion or judgment does not appear feasible. The RBI is likely to pursue its multiple indicator approach for some time to come.

In the area of exchange rate management, a basic question is how much flexibility should be allowed. Based on the experience of many other countries, India has managed "floating" with no fixed rate targets. The rate is primarily determined by market forces, but India's foreign

FIGURE 1

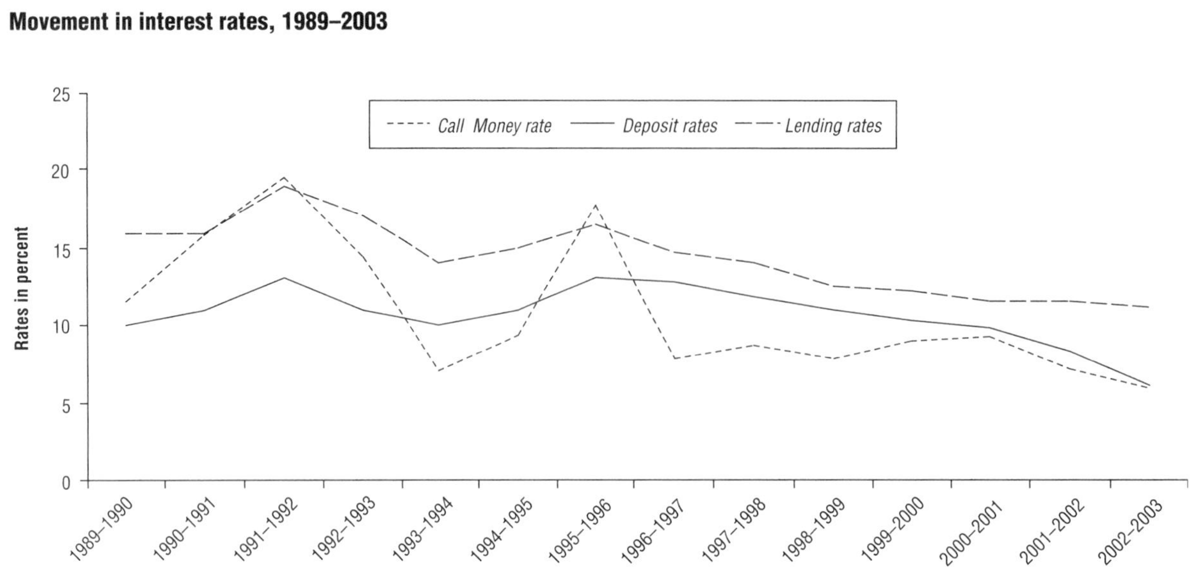

SOURCE: Courtesy of Balbir Kaur and Manjusha Mishra.

FIGURE 2

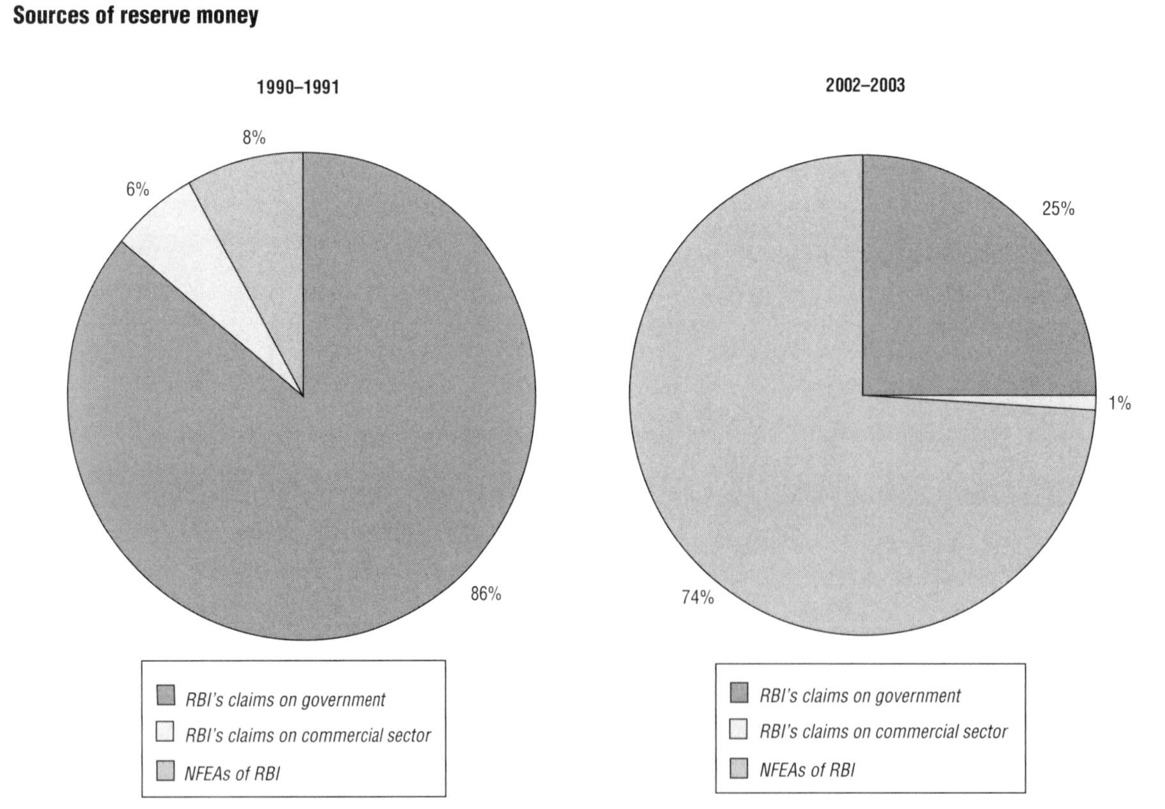

Note: RBI=Reserve Bank of India; NFEA=Net Foreign Exchange Assets.

SOURCE: Courtesy of Balbir Kaur and Manjusha Mishra.

FIGURE 3

Growth rates: Broad money, reserve money, gross domestic product (GDP), and wholesale price index (WPI)

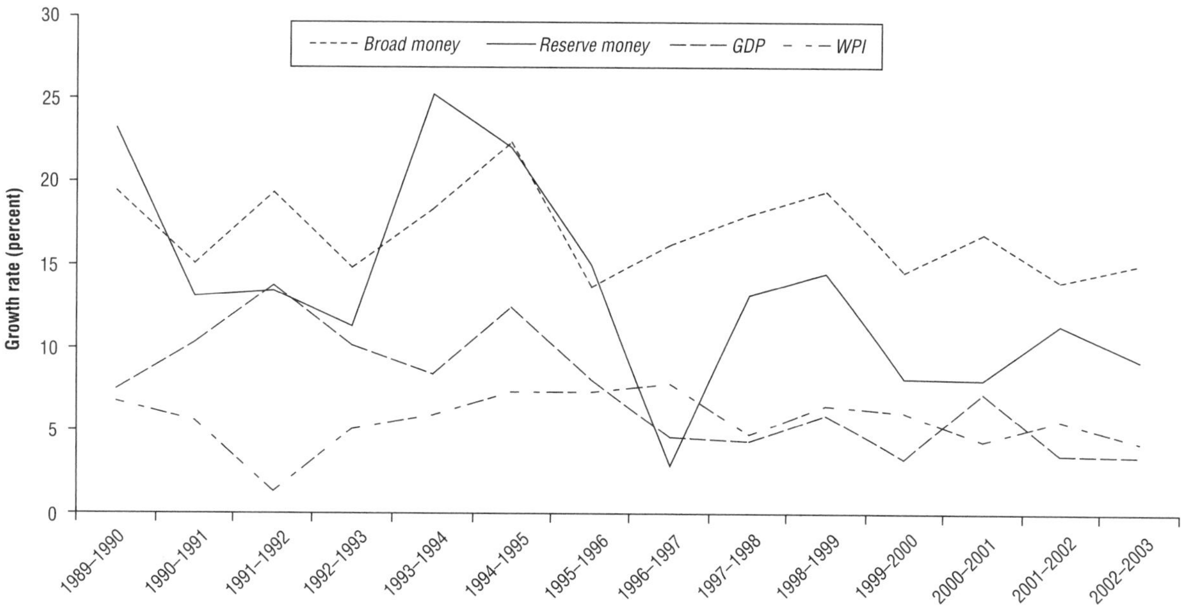

SOURCE: Courtesy of Balbir Kaur and Manjusha Mishra.

FIGURE 4

Select monetary ratios, 1989–2003

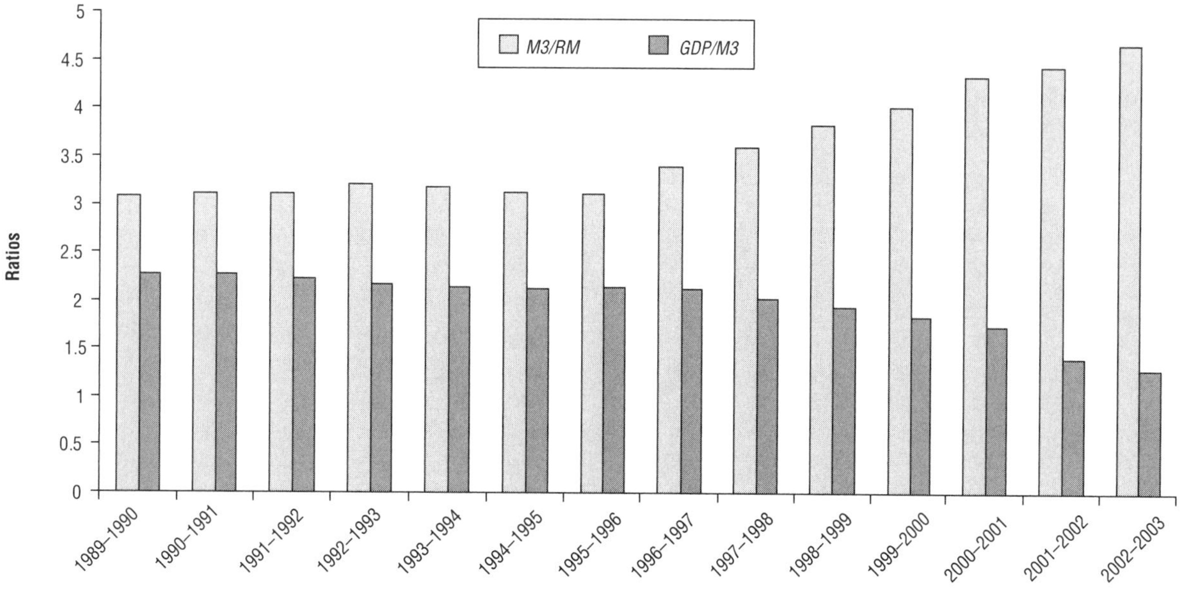

Note: M3=Broad money; RM=reserve money; GDP=gross domestic product.

SOURCE: Courtesy of Balbir Kaur and Manjusha Mishra.

exchange market being thin, the RBI intervenes in foreign exchange market to contain volatility and to maintain orderly market conditions.

Yet another issue dominating recent discussions of central bank autonomy is the separation of debt management and monetary management functions. The fundamental question is whether monetary policy can operate on an exclusive basis, outside fiscal constraints, before a sustainable level of fiscal deficit is attained. Integration of India's financial markets is yet to attain adequate depth before the central bank can completely withdraw from direct debt management. A Fiscal Responsibility and Budget Management Act was passed in 2003.

In the context of large capital inflows since the turn of the twenty-first century, questions about the adequacy of foreign exchange reserves and the sustainability of sterilizing such inflows have been raised. Limitations on instruments available for sterilization have recently been addressed by a Working Group. Its recommendations should enable the RBI to adequately shore up its capacity to sterilize large capital flows.

K. Sabapathy

See also **Balance of Payments; Debt Markets; Money and Foreign Exchange Markets**

BIBLIOGRAPHY

Government of India. *Report of the Committee on Banking Sector Reforms.* Delhi: GOI, 1998. (Chairman: M. Narasimham), (1998).

Kanagasabapathy, K. "Monetary Policy Underpinnings: A Perspective." *Economic and Political Weekly* 36, no. 4 (27 January 2001): 303–310.

Mohanty, Deepak, Sardar Amitava, and Prasad Abha. "Perspectives on Monetary Developments and Policy in India." *Reserve Bank of India Occasional Papers* 18, nos. 2–3 (1997): 225–277.

Rangarajan, C. "Issues on Monetary Management." Presidential address, 71st Annual Conference of the Indian Economic Association, Calcutta, 1988.

———. "Dimensions of Monetary Policy." In *Fifty Years of Central Banking: Governors Speak.* Mumbai: Reserve Bank of India, 1997.

Reddy, Venugopal Y. "Fiscal and Monetary Policy Interface: Recent Developments in India." *Reserve Bank of India Bulletin* 54, no. 11 (November 2000): 1257–1268.

———. "Government Budgets, Banking and Auditors, What Is New?" *Reserve Bank of India Bulletin* 54, no. 12 (December 2000): 1313–1322.

———. "Monetary Policy in India: Objectives, Instruments, Operating Procedures and Dilemmas." In *Monetary and Financial Sectors Reforms in India: A Central Bankers' Perspective*, edited by V. Reddy. New Delhi: UBS Publishers, 2000.

Reserve Bank of India. *Report of the Committee on Financial System.* Mumbai: RBI, 1991.

———. *Report of the Advisory Group on Transparency in Monetary and Financial Policies.* Mumbai: RBI, Standing Committee on International Financial Standards and Codes, 2000.

———. *Report of the Expert Committee to Review the System of Administered Interest Rates and Other Related Issues.* Mumbai: RBI, 2001.

Tarapore, S. S. "The Conduct of Monetary Policy: The Indian Experience." *Reserve Bank of India Bulletin* 50, nos. 1–2 (January/February 1996): 77–80.

MONEY AND CREDIT, 1858–1947 The singularity of India's monetary experience derives from the fact that India witnessed practically every type of monetary regime, passing successively from a silver standard to a managed inconvertible silver currency, then almost fortuitously to the gold exchange standard; subsequently to a paper standard, a gold bullion standard, and after 1931 to a sterling exchange standard. Also, India moved from a fixed fiduciary to a proportional reserve system without ever adopting the 100 percent reserve Currency Board system of the British colonies. There were no less than six high-powered official commissions of inquiry between 1893 and 1931, a number unmatched by any other country.

Monetary Standard

The major issues, which related to the exchange rate of the Indian rupee and the size and composition of India's currency cover, were hotly debated between the principal interest groups, namely, the British business community in India, the government of India, and the India Office in London under the secretary of state for India, and Indian public opinion, which was fractured by the rivalries between the regional financial centers, Calcutta, Bombay, and Madras.

The recent history of Indian currency falls into well-defined periods from 1835, when the silver rupee of 180 troy 11/12th fine was declared the sole legal tender. India was on a monometallic silver standard from 1835 to 1893, and a paper currency reserve with a maximum of 40 million rupees (Rs.) in government securities, the rest in silver coin and bullion, with provision for the inclusion of gold coin and bullion up to 25 percent. The period from 1893 to 1898 was one of transition because of the depreciation of the silver rupee, whose gold value had remained at fell from about 2s. since 1871, fell to 1s. (shilling) 2d. (pence) in 1892, precipitating the amendment of the Indian Coinage Act of 1879 and the Indian Paper Currency Act of 1882, following the recommendations of the 1892 Herschell Committee. The subsequent improvisations, following the recommendations of the Fowler Committee (1898) and the Act of 1899, resulted in an effective gold exchange standard, which was more economical than a gold standard and ensured practically

TABLE 1

Commercial bank deposits for selected dates, 1870–1946

(in millions of rupees)

	Presidency banks (1)	Others (2)	Exchange banks
1870	118	1	5
1921	726	802	752
1946	2,717	7,337	1,812

(1) Refers to Imperial Bank of India from 1921 onward.
(2) Banks with paid-up capital and reserves of Rs. 100,000 till 1945 and all categories for 1946.

SOURCE: Adapted from *Banking and Monetary Statistics of India*, Reserve Bank of India, Mumbai, 1954, Table 1, pp. 6–9.

TABLE 2

Bank failures at selected dates, 1913–1946

	Number of banks	Paid-up capital (thousands of rupees)
1913	12	3,154
1925	17	1,876
1939	117	2,491
1946	27	922

SOURCE: Compiled from *Banking and Monetary Statistics of India*, Reserve Bank of India, Mumbai, 1954, p. 279.

all the advantages of a gold currency. Nevertheless, proposals for gold coinage and a gold mint led to the appointment in 1913 of the Royal Commission, which broadly endorsed the existing standard. The extraordinary rise in the price of silver to about 89d. per ounce in February 1920 made it extremely difficult to maintain exchange stability. The British government therefore decided to raise the exchange rate in accordance with the silver price and appointed yet another committee in 1919 to make recommendations for a stable gold-exchange standard. Its report recommended stabilization of the rupee at 2s. gold, with a fixed exchange value for the rupee in terms of gold at 11.30016 g of fine gold. But the effort to maintain the rupee at 2s. gold failed, and with the return of sterling to gold in 1925 the rupee exchange rate fell back to 1s. 6d.

In 1926 the Hilton-Young Commission recommended: the creation of a gold bullion standard; an exchange rate of 1s. 6d. for the rupee; amalgamation of India's paper currency and gold standard reserves; and the creation of a central bank. Thus, the Currency Act of 1927 established a gold-bullion-and-sterling currency. But the rupee ratio of 1s. 6d., rather than a fairer 1s. 4d., provoked Indian public opinion and led to the heated ratio controversy in the following period (1927–1939). Following the British home government's decision to abandon the gold standard, the rupee was linked to sterling from 24 September 1931. The unchanged rupee-sterling ratio, however, led to a depreciation of the rupee in terms of gold and a rise in the price of gold in terms of rupees, which led to India's massive exports of gold over the next decade, a dramatic reversal of India's previous role as a perennial magnet for gold.

Commercial Banking

Since before 1860 there was no legal provision in India for limited liability, virtually all banks were started on the basis of unlimited liability, and until the Indian Companies Act (1913), which contained a few sections relating to joint-stock banks, there was no special legislation dealing with commercial banking. The amended Indian Companies Act of 1936 added many provisions relating to minimum capital, cash reserve requirements, and other operating conditions, but there was still no integrated statutory regulation of commercial banks in India until 1949. The main constituents of modern banking were: the quasi-official Presidency Banks of Bengal, Bombay, and Madras, which were amalgamated in 1921 into the Imperial Bank of India; the foreign-owned exchange banks; and the Indian joint stock banks, which played a marginal role in foreign exchange business and rural credit and specialized largely in short-term urban credit against conventional collateral. Bank failures occurred mostly because of individual imprudence and mismanagement and occurred in years when the system as a whole did not experience any exceptional stress; the failure rate was much higher among foreign-owned exchange banks.

Central Banking

The Royal Commission on Indian Finance and Currency (1913–1914) requested one of its members, J. M. Keynes, to prepare a scheme for a central Indian bank. It is particularly noteworthy that Keynes exhorted the framers of the Indian central bank's constitution to "put far from their minds all thoughts of the Bank of England" and to look to the state banks, especially those of Germany, or perhaps of Holland, for the "proper model." Ironically, when India did establish the Reserve Bank of India, it was modeled on the Bank of England under the influence of the then governor of the Bank of England, Montagu Norman. What finally emerged was the amalgamation of the three Presidency Banks into the Imperial Bank of India in 1921, as a commercial bank, but with the functions of banker to the government and manager of the public debt. Although there was no statutory provision, major commercial banks kept the bulk of their cash balances with the Imperial Bank, which also granted them liquidity credit and managed the clearing houses. But the note issue and foreign exchange were entrusted to the Finance Department of the government of India, until the Royal Commission on Indian Currency and Finance (1926) strongly recommended the creation of a full-fledged central bank, to be called the Reserve Bank of India.

The Reserve Bank of India was inaugurated on 1 April 1935, with a share capital of Rs. 50 million, divided into 500,000 fully paid-up shares of Rs. 100 each, subject to a maximum dividend of 6 percent. The first Indian Governor was C. D. Deshmukh, who assumed office in 1943.

The Reserve Bank of India in its initial phase had limited monetary powers. It was unable to activate the bank rate until about 1951, and its open market operations were largely net purchases in a narrow market. In its formative years (1935–1939), the Reserve Bank, in addition to promoting agricultural credit and acting as India's lender of last resort, was better able to coordinate the different segments of the money market, which resulted in a narrowing of seasonal and regional differentials in interest rates. The wartime phase (1939–1945) of the Reserve Bank was most notable for its well designed government borrowing program and the innovative technique of open market gold sales as an anti-inflationary device.

Anand Chandavarkar

See also **Balance of Payments; Fiscal System and Policy from 1858 to 1947**

BIBLIOGRAPHY

The following government reports are the basic primary sources useful alike for their evidence, analysis, and findings: India Currency (Herschell) Committee (1893); Indian Currency (Fowler) Committee (1898); Royal Commission (Chamberlain) on Indian Currency and Finance (1913–1914); Committee (Babington-Smith) on Indian Currency and Exchange (1919); Royal Commission (Hilton-Young) on Indian Currency and Finance (1926); Indian Central Banking Enquiry Committee (1931).

The primary statistical source is the *Banking and Monetary Statistics of India*, Reserve Bank of India, Bombay, 1954. A fascinating insider's account is *Central Banking in India* (A Retrospect) by Sir Chintaman D. Deshmukh, Poona: Gokhale Institute of Economics and Politics, 1948. A classic on the reform of the rupee and the pioneering case for a state bank for India is J. M. Keynes, *Indian Currency and Finance*, Collected Writings, vol. 1, London: Macmillan, 1971.

MONEY AND FOREIGN EXCHANGE MARKETS The Indian financial sector may be viewed as comprising the money, foreign exchange, capital, credit, debt, insurance, and derivatives markets. For India's monetary policy, "call/notice" money and "repo transactions" are most critical. Call/notice money consists of overnight money and money at short notice (i.e., up to 14 days). In the heavily regulated system of nationalized banking, directed credit, and the automatic monetization of government deficits that prevailed in India throughout the 1970s and 1980s, it was inevitable that this market remained narrow and undeveloped. Rate ceilings were also frequent in those days of volatile call money rates. The Chakravarty Committee (1985) and the Vaghul Committee (1987) suggested several measures for developing the Indian money market. Following these suggestions, extensive attempts were made to increase the number of money market participants. Currently India has two major types of entities participating in the call/notice market: (1) Banks (commercial and cooperative) and primary dealers acting as market makers. These are allowed to lend as well as to borrow; their total number is 112; and (2) All-India financial institutions, mutual funds, and insurance companies. These are permitted to operate as lenders only, and their number is 53. The average daily turnover in this market is now Rs. 12,000 crores (1 billion = 100 crores).

The Indian call/notice money market departs from international practice in not being a pure interbank market. The ease of transacting in the call/notice segment, especially the absence of documentation, has attracted non-bank participants, who often favor this funding channel over the repo channel. The fact that the call money rates are usually higher than the repo rate reinforces this tendency, non-bank institutions operating as lenders only. The strong presence of non-bank participants in the call/notice segment impedes the establishment of a risk-free short-term yield curve. Limits on non-bank activity in this segment have been imposed since May 2001.

Repo transaction represent an important stage in the evolution of the Indian money market, distinguished by the introduction of repos/ready forward contracts by the Reserve Bank of India in December 1992. A repo is essentially the sale of a security against immediate funds with a promise to repurchase the same at a predetermined date and price. The future repurchase price reflects the repo interest rate adjusted for the coupon interest earned on the security during the period of the repo. The repo interest rate is usually lower than the interbank loan rate, since the former represents collateralized lending against a high-grade security.

A stable framework for the repo system in India emerged by 1997, with two types of operations: interbank repos (covering banks, primary dealers, and select financial institutions); and Reserve Bank of India repos. In a typical interbank repo, the seller (a bank) might be attempting to meet an anticipated cash reserve ratio shortfall, while the buyer (also a bank) may be bridging a potential statutory liquidity ratio default. Banks also resort to repos as a hedge against interest rate volatility.

The Reserve Bank of India uses repo operations for day-to-day liquidity management via the so-called liquidity adjustment facility.

Foreign Exchange Market

The foreign exchange regime in India has undergone a number of vicissitudes since the collapse of the Bretton Woods Agreement in the early 1970s. In 1975 India's rupee was de-linked from Britain's pound sterling, and a managed exchange regime was put in place, based on a currency basket. In 1978 banks were allowed to engage in strictly controlled trading in foreign exchange. Following the balance of payments crisis in 1991, moves toward a greater role for markets in exchange rate determination were introduced in a series of important stages. The culmination of this process was marked by the rupee being made fully convertible on the current account on 20 August 1994, thereby paving the way for India to subscribe to Article VIII of the International Monetary Fund (IMF). Subsequent developments in the foreign exchange market have been driven by the recommendations of the Expert Group on Foreign Exchange Markets in India (1995) and the Committee on Capital Account Convertibility (1997).

Currently the Indian foreign exchange market is made up of three major segments: authorized dealers, numbering about one hundred, mainly foreign banks and large domestic banks; customers including foreign institutional investors, large domestic public sector units, and corporates; and the Reserve Bank of India.

Major transactions in the foreign exchange market arise from current account transactions of the balance of payments (imports, exports, and invisibles) as well as capital account transactions relating to foreign direct investment, portfolio investments (including American and Global Depository Receipts), external commercial borrowings and amortization, nonresident Indian deposits, external aid, and (since 1996) debt service repayments of the Indian government and the Indian Oil Corporation.

The forward market is an active segment of the foreign exchange market, with contracts permitted up to one year. The bulk of forward contracts, however, range from one-week to three-month maturity, with rollovers quite common. Since 1996 a number of far-reaching changes have been made in the foreign exchange market.

Two questions often raised in the context of the Indian foreign exchange market are about the prospects of capital account convertibility and the appropriate level of foreign exchange reserves. The Tarapore Committee (1997) laid out a detailed road map toward the goal of full convertibility over the three-year period from 1997 to 2000. Subsequent events, especially the Asian crisis, has made the Reserve Bank of India adopt a much more cautious stance.

The level of foreign exchange reserves in India in July 2004 was about $120 billion, and fears had been expressed by unofficial commentators that this level was excessively high. The Reserve Bank of India itself seems inclined to follow the rather loose guidelines set out under the so-called Guidotti Rule, or "liquidity at risk" factor, which relates reserve-adequacy to the foreseeable risks of financial crises, capital risk, and exchange market pressures that a country might face. Based on this consideration, the official line of the Reserve Bank of India seems to be that the current level of Indian reserves is adequate without being excessive.

Financial Markets and Monetary Policy

Since 1991 a two-way process was at work in India's financial markets, marked by the progressive removal of barriers to the flow of international funds, and the rolling back of rate and quantity restrictions in the various segments of the financial markets. Together, these have brought Indian financial markets closer to one another, as well as to their global counterparts. This has had fundamental consequences for the operation of Indian monetary policy. In particular, the maintenance of such increasing integration of India's financial markets has become an important monetary policy objective. The key guidepost of this market-oriented approach is a flexible multiple indicator (based on interest rates on a variety of financial assets together with some other macroeconomic variables) with open market operations as the major operating lever of monetary stimuli, and with the bank rate and the repo rate playing crucial roles as signaling devices.

To illustrate the current working of India's monetary policy, in a situation of excess demand for dollars in the foreign exchange market, leading to a surge in forward premia on expectations of rupee depreciation, if money market rates are lower than the forward premia, arbitrage opportunities exist for shifting funds from the money market (especially the call/notice segment), the government securities market, and the capital market. The Reserve Bank of India in these circumstances, could, of course, follow a passive wait-and-watch policy, allowing call rates to rise above the forward premia, and thus letting equilibrium restore itself. More likely, it may intervene actively in the foreign exchange market by selling dollars, depleting its reserves, encouraging nonresident Indian deposits (e.g., by reducing reserve requirements on such deposits), and discouraging exporters from delaying repatriation of proceeds.

Dilip M. Nachane

See also **Capital Market; Debt Markets; Monetary Policy since 1991**

BIBLIOGRAPHY

Greenspan, A. "Recent Trends in the Management of Foreign Exchange Reserves." *World Bank Conference on Recent Trends in Reserve Management.* Washington, D.C.: Federal Reserve Board, 1999.

Jalan, B. *Exchange Rate Management: An Emerging Consensus?* Mumbai: Reserve Bank of India, 2003.

Nautz, D. "How Auctions Reveal Information: A Case Study in German Repo Rates." *Journal of Money, Credit and Banking* 29, no. 1 (1997): 17–25.

Rangarajan, C. *Leading Issues in Monetary Policy.* New Delhi: Bookwell, 2002.

Reddy, Y. V. "Interest Rates in India: Status and Issues." *Reserve Bank of India Bulletin* 52, no. 7 (July 1998): 547–556.

———. "Parameters of Monetary Policy in India." *Reserve Bank of India Bulletin* 56, no. 2 (February 2002): 95–109.

Reserve Bank of India. *Committee to Review the Working of the Monetary System (Chakravarty Committee).* Mumbai: Reserve Bank of India, 1985.

———. *Working Group on the Money Market (Vaghul Committee).* Mumbai: Reserve Bank of India, 1987.

———. *Expert Working Group on Foreign Exchange Markets in India (Sodhani Committee).* Mumbai: Reserve Bank of India, 1995.

———. *Committee on Capital Account Convertibility (Tarapore Committee).* Mumbai: Reserve Bank of India, 1997.

———. *Committee on Banking Sector Reforms (Narasimham Committee-II).* Mumbai: Reserve Bank of India, 1998.

———. *Repurchase Agreements (Repos).* Mumbai: Reserve Bank of India, 1999.

Vasudevan, A. "Analytical Issues of Monetary Policy in Transition." *Reserve Bank of India Bulletin* 52, no. 1 (January 1998): 45–52.

MONSOON. *See* **Geography.**

MONTAGU, EDWIN S. *(1879–1924), secretary of state for India (1917–1922).* John Morley's Liberal protégé as undersecretary of state for India, Edwin S. Montagu served as secretary of state for India from 1917 to 1922, the only person of Jewish faith ever to hold that office. Calling himself "Oriental," Montagu was also the first secretary of state for India personally to venture East to tour the realm over which he presided, meeting with leaders of India's major nationalist parties, the Muslim League's M. A. Jinnah as well as Congress's Mahatma Gandhi. He was so impressed by Jinnah's eloquent brilliance that he considered it "a shame . . . so remarkable a man" could not become British India's viceroy. He underestimated Mahatma Gandhi, however, as "a pure visionary."

Montagu raised fervent Indian hopes and expectations of post–World War I independent Dominion status as Britain's reward for India's wartime cooperation and martial participation, when he announced from the floor of Britain's Parliament on 20 August 1917 that "the policy of His Majesty's Government . . . is that of the increasing association of Indians in every branch of the administration . . . with a view to the progressive realisation of responsible government in India." It certainly sounded hopeful to all factions within India's Congress and other parties, and only appropriate given the unstinting level of Indian forces, funds, and foods shipped off to the Western front and Mesopotamia. But the aftermath of 1918's Allied victory brought a plethora of disasters to India, first a million flu deaths, then bullets rather than free ballots in Punjab.

Montagu tried, nonetheless, to deliver some measure of political reform to India. The Government of India Act of 1919, also called the Montagu-Chelmsford Reforms, was hardly Dominion status, however. More elective seats were added to provincial and central government councils, and several more Indians were to be invited to join Viceroy Chelmsford's administrative council, but Congress felt so disappointed by the crumbs thrown to them—instead of the freedom they expected—that Gandhi led a mass boycott in protest, launching his first nationwide *satyagraha* (hold fast to the truth) against British extensions of martial "laws" in peacetime.

Stanley Wolpert

See also **Gandhi, Mahatma M. K.; Government of India Act of 1919; Jinnah, Mohammad Ali; Morley, John**

BIBLIOGRAPHY

Kaminsky, Arnold P. *The India Office, 1880–1910.* Westport, Conn.: Greenwood Press, 1986.

Strachey, G. L. *Characters and Commentaries.* 1933. Reprint, Westport, Conn.: Greenwood Press, 1971.

Wolpert, Stanley A. *Morley and India, 1906–1910.* Berkeley and Los Angeles: University of California Press, 1967.

MONUMENTS

This entry consists of the following articles:

Eastern India

Mughal

Southern India

Western India

Eastern India

To serve the needs of various religious sects, the architects of eastern India and Bangladesh built structural

Sun Temple in Konark, Orissa. The temple's entire complex was designed in the form of a huge chariot drawn by seven spirited horses on twelve pairs of exquisitely carved wheels, to symbolize the majestic stride of the sun god (Arka) and mark the culmination of Orissan architectural style. AMAR TALWAR / FOTOMEDIA.

monuments such as stupas, *caityagrihas*, monasteries, and temples. The stupas and *caityagrihas* were primarily for Buddhist worship, though evidence of stupas with Jain affiliation has been found. The monasteries were built for Brahmanical as well as Buddhist and Jain monks but, despite epigraphical references, no Brahmanical monasteries have yet been found. Temples were generally Brahmanical, sometimes Jain, but seldom Buddhist. Unable to withstand nature's fury, human indifference, and the fury of iconoclastic Turko-Afghan invaders, most of these monuments have disappeared, leaving many gaps in the history of their evolution.

Stupas and *Caityagrihas*

The Buddhist tradition affirms that the Licchavis of Vaishali had built many Buddhist stupas (mounds). Archaeological excavations at Vaishali (Bihar) led to the discovery of an earlier earthen core within a stupa that underwent successive enlargements. This earthen structure, containing a relic casket, is believed to be the stupa built by the Licchavis. Stupas built later are all in ruins. Presumably, as in other regions, eastern India's earliest stupas were large hemispherical domes, resting on circular drums, crowned by a parasol. Fragmentary remains, votive models, and sculptural depictions, dating from the seventh century A.D., indicate that over the centuries the stupa acquired an elongated shape by the addition of a square base, an increase in the height of the drum, and conversion of the crowning umbrella into a tapering row of flat discs. Sometimes a chapel, with an image of the Buddha in it, was provided at one or each of the four cardinal points of the stupa. Sites at which evidence of such stupas has been found include Nalanda in Bihar, Bharatpur in West Bengal, Paharpur, and Mainamati in Bangladesh, and Ratnagiri, Lalitgiri, and Udayagiri (Jajpur District) in Orissa.

A *caityagriha* was a Buddhist shrine, rectangular in plan with an apsidal back. A votive *caitya* (the other name of the stupa), within the apse, was the object of worship. Excavations have unearthed the foundations of two such *caityagrihas*, one at Lalitgiri and the other at Udayagiri (Jajpur District, Orissa).

Monasteries

Monastery architecture in eastern India began with a number of rock-hewn caves in the Barabar hills of Bihar. Donated by the Mauryan sovereigns (3rd century B.C.) to the Jain Ajivika ascetics, these caves are usually single-celled. Only two of them, Sudama and Lomasha Rishi, have double chambers. The facade of the Lomasha Rishi resembles the gabled front of a contemporary wooden house, suggesting a carpenter's hand in these rock constructions.

Kalinga rulers ofthe first century B.C. honeycombed the Udayagiri and Khandagiri hills near Bhubaneswar (Orissa) with caves excavated for Jain monks. Some of these caves have pillared verandas in front. Two caves, at Mancapuri and Ranigumpha, are double-storied and sculptured. In the arrangement of these caves, no systematic plan was followed.

The monastery architecture was systematized by the Buddhists. Known as *vihara* and *samgharama*, the monasteries had in common four rows of cells with continuous pillared corridors around an open rectangular court. Approach to the inner court was provided by a gate pavilion on one of the shorter sides. In the center of the rear row of cells was a sanctuary chamber, whose back side projected beyond the line of the monastery wall. Some of the monasteries, referred to as *mahavihara*s, attained fame as great centers of Buddhist learning. One of them, the Nalanda Mahavihara in Bihar, dating from the fifth century A.D., comprised a row of storied blocks, each in the usual plan of a monastery. Near the front of these blocks was a row of temples, each enshrining an image of the Buddha.

Deviating from the conventional plan of a monastery, the Somapura Mahavihara at Paharpur (Bangladesh) and a few others contained the sanctuary of a terraced plan in the center of the court, rather than the middle of the rear row of cells. In Orissa, the dwelling blocks of the monks, though following the general monastery pattern, sometimes had an imposing stupa outside as their principal object of worship. The Ratnagiri Mahavihara on the Ratnagiri hill was one such monastery.

Temples

A period of experiments with different forms marks the early phase of temple architecture of the region. The ruins of an apsidal Jain religious edifice of the first century B.C. have been discovered on the Udayagiri hill near Bhubaneswar. A temple of cylindrical shape, known as Maniyar Math, at Rajgir (Bihar) was raised on an earlier circular base, which may have been the foundation of a lost stupa. Now in a fragmentary condition, it once displayed fine stucco sculptures in the Guptan style of the fifth century A.D. A Kumrahar (Bihar) clay seal, bearing a second- or third-century A.D. inscription, depicts a Buddhist shrine with an arched facade and a pyramidal roof tower. That depiction may be the prerestoration Mahabodhi temple at Bodh Gaya (Bihar), or a temple of that type. An octagonal temple of Shiva, famous as Mundeshvari (a corruption of Mundeshvara) Shiva, stands on the hilltop at Ramgarh (Bihar). In its interior, four pillars on four corners of a raised dais support the flat ceiling. The roof of the temple has collapsed. If the year 30 inscribed on the foundation stone, discovered loose, refers to the Harsha era, the Mundeshvari may be ascribed to A.D. 636.

At about the beginning of the seventh century A.D., architects of eastern India introduced a few standardized temple styles, the most important of which was the one defined as *nagara* in Indian canonical literature. Its two distinguishing features were a cruciform ground plan and a curvilinear *shikhara* (towering roof). Found all over eastern India, the *nagara* temple style displayed regional variations in the course of its evolution, though without changing its basic characteristics.

In Bihar the emergence of the *nagara* style may be recognized in the *triratha* (three-wall) plan. Segments were produced upon the face of the temple wall, creating part of it on a more forward plane. Some walls were divided into three segments; other walls were divided into five (*panca-*) or seven (*sapta-*) segments; with three moldings (*vedibandha*) on the exterior wall, as on the older base of the modern Siddheshvaranatha temple on the Suryanka hill of the Barabar range. Reference to this temple is made in a seventh-century cave inscription found nearby. In course of time, the temple became *pancaratha*, as in the Narasimha temple at Gaya, and acquired a pillared *mukhashala* (forward hall) as demonstrated by the preserved core of the Sun temple at Dabthu. A roof cover in either instance is missing. In the succeeding years, the earlier *pancaratha* plan was continued, but a horizontal molding divided the part of the wall between the *vedibandha* and the entablature into two vertical halves. A curvilinear *sikhara* rose upon the temple. The *mukhasala* in front had balconied windows at the sides, and four interior pillars on four corners of a central platform. The dilapidated Shiva temple at Umga, while attesting to these developments, gives, in the summary treatment of its features, clear evidence of a decadent trend. This decadence only quickened in the following years.

The early *nagara* temples of Jharkhand were invariably built on a *triratha* plan. In elevation, the *bara* (perpendicular wall section) had three divisions: molded *vedibandha*, *jangha* (part of the wall between dado and entablature) with a niche on the *raha* (projected central *ratha*) and a recessed *baranda* (entablature). The *shikhara* upon the *bara* was divided into a number of *bhumis* (horizontal stages) by right-angled *bhumi-amalakas* (ribbed quoins). In the *mastaka* (set of members crowning the *shikhara*), the most conspicuous element was a large flattish *amalaka* (spheroid, ribbed at the edges). Representative examples of the period include the Durgā temple at Diuri and the Mahishasuramardini temple at Haradih. Sometime later the *pancaratha* plan was introduced. Other developments included the presence of Gaṅgā and Yamuna, two river goddesses, at the door flanks and *navagraha* (nine planets) panel on the door lintel. The Tanginath Shiva temple at Majhegaon is a shrine of this type. Now roofless, the temple appears, from its detached architectural parts lying about, to have once been covered by a curvilinear *shikhara* (tower) that supported a *mastaka* with a *kalasha* (pitcher) finial. Further development of the style is obscured by the absence of proper examples.

The extant *nagara* temples of Bengal were built either in stone or in bricks. The stone temples, now found only in West Bengal, are simple unpretentious structures. They began, as elsewhere, with a *triratha* plan, threefold division of the *bara*, curvilinear *shikhara*, and round *mastaka*. Of the three sections of the *bara*, the *vedibandha* was composed of three and sometimes four moldings, the *jangha* was plain except for a niche on the *raha*, and the *baranda* was indicated by a recessed frieze between two moldings. The *shikhara* had *bhumi* divisions by right-angled *bhumi-amalakas*. In the *mastaka*, the most prominent member was a large flattish *amalaka*. The two surviving examples of this early period, one Jain and the other Brahmanical, stand respectively at Charra and Tuisama. The developments in later temples showed an increase in the number of *vedibandha* moldings from an initial four to six, three pilasters in a row on the *kanika* (outermost *ratha* segment) in the *jangha* section, the occasional presence of *navagraha* panel on the door lintel, near-perpendicular rise of the *shikhara*, rounding off of the *bhumi-amalaka*s, and a vertical band of interlacing *caitya* arch (horseshoe-shaped arch motif) design on the *shikhara*. Temple numbers 16 (now lost) and 18 at Telkupi and a deserted temple at Banda are a few examples illustrating the different phases of these developments. In the succeeding years, elaboration of details continued, but with simultaneous decline of the style. Finally, the temple acquired a *saptaratha* plan, the number of moldings in the *vedibandha* rose at times to nine, the *jangha* became divided into upper and lower sections by a *bandhana* molding, and the protruding double cornice of the entablature sharply interrupted the free and flowing transition from the *bara* to the *shikhara*. The *bhumi-amalakas* disappeared from the *shikhara*, whose almost vertical ascent was awkwardly broken by a sharp inward, virtually straight-lined, bend near the top. In the *mastaka* upon the *shikhara*, the *amalaka* was disproportionately small and the *kalasha* finial narrow and tall. Among the temples showing those features, three are standing at Barakar. One of them is dated in Shaka 1382 (A.D. 1461).

In striking contrast to the simplicity of the stone temples, the few surviving brick temples of Bengal are remarkable for the splendor of their decorative embellishments. All of them belong to the *nagara* order. *Pancaratha* earlier and *saptaratha* later, they show a two-storied *jangha* with a *bandhana* running between, a double corniced *baranda*, and a vertical sequence of subdued *angashikharas* (miniature replicas of a temple) on the *shikhara*. The *bhumi-amalakas* in the earlier examples are right-angled, but those of later temples are round. Embellishments on stucco plaster display an amazing variety of elegant and graceful designs and motifs. Most remarkable of them is the stylized but exquisite and large *caitya* arch design that constitutes the central theme of the *shikhara* decoration. Two brick temples, now standing at Deulghata (West Bengal), are the finest specimens of the type.

Less affected by the iconoclastic frenzy of the early Muslim invaders, Orissa retains a series of temples representing the three principal stages of evolution of the *nagara* style of the region: early, transitional, and mature. The style lost its force once the mature phase was over.

Like other regions, the *deul*, the local name of the sanctum to distinguish it from its other adjuncts, was *triratha* in plan at the beginning. Its perpendicular wall section, *bara*, had a *vedibandha* (*pabhaga* in Orissa) of three (subsequently four) moldings, a *jangha* with a niche on each of its *ratha* facets, and a *baranda* composed of a recessed frieze between two moldings. The gently curved *shikhara* rose in *bhumi* stages, each *bhumi* being demarcated by a square *bhumi-amalaka*. The *mastaka*, when found complete, showed a *beki* (short cylindical neck), a flattened *amalaka*, a low *khapuri* (skull-like member), and a cylindrical (later *kalasha*) finial. The *deul*, though alone initially, was complemented sometime later by an oblong *mukhashala*. The niches on the *jangha* of the *deul* contained images of family members and manifestations of the deity enshrined. On the door lintel of the sanctum, a panel of eight *graha*s (planets) were carved. All the adornments, including the figure sculptures, were done in bas-relief. The Parashurameshvara at Bhubaneswar, the Kutaitundi at Khiching, and the Lingaraja at Bhawanipur are some of the temples bearing these features.

In the transitional period, the *deul* acquired a *pancaratha* plan, the *vedibandha* moldings increased to five, *nagastambha*s (pilasters entwined with human-headed snakes) appeared on the *jangha*, vertical bands of interlacing *caitya* arch designs textured the *shikhara*, and the door lintel of the sanctum bore a panel of nine *graha*s. Figure sculptures were shown in high relief. In a major development, a pyramidal roof of gradually receding tiers came to surmount the *mukhashala*, as in Bhadra *deuls* in Orissa. In later years, most of these features were included among the invariable characteristics of Orissan architecture. This transitional phase is represented at its best by the small but pretty Mukteshvara at Bhubaneswar. For its perfect proportions, graceful sculptural embellishments, delicate surface treatment, and unobtrusive decorative scheme, this exquisite little shrine ranks as the "gem of Orissan architecture."

In the fully evolved form of Orissan architecture, the principal features of the *deul* were *pancaratha* ground plan, fivefold division of the *bara*, lofty near-perpendicular *shikhara*, round *bhumi-amalakas*, rise of *angashikharas* in graded height on the *anuratha* (intermediate *ratha* facet between *raha* and *kanika*) of the *shikhara*, lion rampant on elephant projecting from each face of the *shikhara*, and *mastaka* composed of short *beki*, ponderous *amalaka*, emphatic *khapuri* and bulbous *kalasha*, and *dhvaja* (emblem of the deity enshrined). Images of the incarnations or family members of the installed divinity were contained by the central niches, and those of the eight *dikpala*s (guardian deities of the quarters) were housed by the subsidiary niches on the *jangha*. As a convention, the *navagraha*s were displayed on the door lintel. The entire temple complex, comprising the *deul*, the *mukhashala*, and sometimes a *natamandapa* (dancing hall) and a *bhogamandapa* (refractory hall) in the same axial length, was placed within a walled enclosure.

The majestic Lingaraja at Bhubaneswar embodies all the features specified above, in their most finished and perfect shape. The temple, surrounded by a massive wall, has four components: *deul*, *mukhashala* (commonly called *jagamohana*), *natamandapa*, and *bhogamandapa*, the last two being later additions. The *deul*, the principal member of the complex, is remarkable for the soaring verticality of its great tower. Subduing every detail of the temple to this vertical urge, the *shikhara* moves up in a rapid sweep to produce the effect of one continuous line on its profile. In this accent on the unbroken linear ascent of the *shikhara* profile, *rekha* (line), the local name of the *nagara deul* finds its ample justification. A masterpiece of Indian temple architecture, the Lingaraja stands as the model for all later temples of Orissa. An in situ inscription, dated A.D. 1114–1115, fixes the upper limit of its date.

The glorious tradition set by the Lingaraja was raised to a new height by the stupendous Sun temple at Konarak. In the novelty of its conception as a huge Sun chariot and the solemn grandeur of its masterfully executed sculptures, the temple, even in ruins, represents the supreme achievement of the Orissan architects.

D. R. Das

See also **Temple Types (Styles) of India**

BIBLIOGRAPHY

Das, D. R. "Early Temples of Chotanagpur (Bihar)." *Visvabharati Quarterly*, n.s., 3 (1992–1993): 218–236.

Dhaky, M. A., ed. *Encyclopaedia of Indian Temple Architecture*, vol. II, part 3. New Delhi: American Institute of Indian Studies and Indira Gandhi National Centre for the Arts, 1998.

Donaldson, Thomas F. *Hindu Temple Art of Orissa*. 3 vols. Leiden: E. J. Brill, 1985–1987.

Jamuar, B. K. *The Ancient Temples of Bihar*. New Delhi: Ramanand Vidya Bhawan, 1985.

Meister, Michael W., M. A. Dhaky, and Krishna Deva, eds. *Encyclopaedia of Indian Temple Architecture*, vol. II, parts 1–2. New Delhi: American Institute of Indian Studies and Princeton University Press, 1988–1991.

Mitra, Debala. *Buddhist Monuments*. Kolkata: Sishu Sahitya Samsad, 1971.

Panigrahi, Krishna Chandra. *Archaeological Remains of Bhubaneswar*. Mumbai: Orient Longmans, 1962.

Patil, D. R. *The Antiquarian Remains in Bihar*. Patna: Kashi Prasad Jayaswal Research Institute, 1963.

Saraswati, S. K. *Architecture of Bengal*. Kolkata: G. Bharadwaj, 1971.

MUGHAL

Babur (r. A.D. 1526–1530) who founded the Mughal rule in India also made a modest beginning of the architectural style that was developed by his successors, Akbar (r. 1556–1605) and Shah Jahan (r. 1628–1658).

Babur's Bagh-i-Gul Afshan (Flower-Scattering Garden) at Agra

Babur founded several terraced gardens at Agra, of which Bagh-i-Gul Afshan has survived intact. It is a vast garden, laid out in three descending terraces, on the bank of the river Jamuna. Water flowed through stone canals, cascades, and tanks, from one terrace to the other. Tree avenues and flower parterres were symmetrically laid out with these water courses. It was later renovated by Babur's great grandson Jahangir and renamed Bagh-i-Nur Afshan (1615–1619). Thus the concept of landscaping was introduced to the medieval architecture of India.

The Din-Panah, Sher-Mandal, and Qal'a-i-Kuhna Masjid, Old Fort Delhi (1533–1540; 1555)

The most ambitious architectural project of Humayun (r. 1530–1540; 1555–1556) was the building of Din-Panah (now called the Old Fort) on the river Jamuna at Delhi. Founded in 1533, its inner citadel with the three gateways; the Sher Mandal and Qal'a-i-Kuhna Masjid were completed by 1540. The gateways, built of red sandstone, have *jharokhas* (upper floor windows with their own pedestal, pillars, and roof) on the facade and *chhatris* (free standing pillared pavilions on the superstructure, roofed by a dome or cupola) on the superstructure. The Sher Mandal is an octagonal tower of red sandstone. The ground floor has closed alcoves. The upper floor alcoves are deeper, and four of them, on the cardinal sides, open into the interior, which is a square hall. Dados and spandrels have inlaid motifs. It is surmounted by an octagonal *chhatri*. Humayun was greatly interested in astronomy, and it was in this building that he died.

The Qal'a-i-Kuhna Masjid (the Mosque of the Old Fort), also built of red stone, has five bays and, correspondingly, five arches on the facade, which have a fringe of lotus buds. Wings are protected by slanting *chhajjas* (angled roof eaves) supported on upright brackets. The nave is roofed by a single dome, which is crowned by sheath of lotus petals, *amalaka* (myrobalan), and *kalash* finials. Multistoried octagonal towers are attached to its rear corners. Prominent *jharokhas* project on the side walls. Qur'anic (Arabic) inscriptions are carved on the *mihrab* arches. It seems to have been completed by Humayun after his restoration in 1555.

Humayun's Tomb at Delhi (c. 1560–1570)

Commissioned by Haji Begum (Bega Begum), Humayun's chief queen, and built during Akbar's early reign, it is the first monumental tomb of the imperial Mughals. It is planned in the center of the four-quartered garden (*chahar-bagh*) which had such pleasing water elements as stone canals, lotus tanks, lily ponds, and cascades, surrounded by the garden. The tomb building is square in plan, 156 feet (47.5 m), but its angles have been chamfered to give it an octagonal conformation. There is no minaret or tower at the corners of its plinth, and the absence of any flanking architectural member has left this grand mausoleum incomplete and isolated.

Each facade is composed of a central *iwan* (a large hall), containing a portal, flanked by wings that also have smaller central portals flanked first by blind ornamental double arches and then by double alcoves at the inclined angles, all in a two-storied arrangement. White and black marble has been used with red sandstone, and this simple color combination, more than its design, gives this tomb an exceedingly pleasing architectural effect. Its interior is composed of a central octagonal hall, octagonalized square rooms on the corners, and oblong portals on the sides, all interconnected through corridors. The tomb is roofed by a bulbous, double dome of white marble, flanked at the corners by red stone octagonal *chhatris*.

Agra Fort and the Bengali-Mahal (1565–73)

Akbar (r. 1556–1605) founded a fort of brick masonry and red sandstone at Agra in 1565. It was completed along with a large number of palatial mansions, also of red stone, in eight years. Situated on the bank of the river Jamuna, it is semicircular in plan, with its chord lying parallel to the course of the river. The massive enclosing walls are 70 feet (21.3 m) high and 30 feet (9.1 m) wide. Double ramparts have been provided with broad circular bastions at regular intervals. A deep moat (except on the river side) separates it from the mainland, from which it is accessible only by two drawbridges, attached to the Delhi Darwazah and the Akbar Darwazah. Of its four gateways, these two are monumental buildings. The former, completed in 1569, was the principal and ceremonial gate of the royal citadel. Protected by high bastions and ramparts with embrasures and loopholes, it has a crooked entrance with sharp curves and steep rises, rendering it impossible for the enemy to storm it. The inner archway had two life-size stone elephants on its sides, and it was therefore called Hathi-Pol (Elephant Gate). It has a four-storied elevation on the rear (eastern) side, in receding terraces, with living rooms, *dalans* (verandas), pavilions, and terraces. It has decorations in inlay and mosaic, stucco in arabesques, painting, glazed tiling, and, above all, stone carving in geometrical, animate, and *jali* (latticed) designs. The Akbar Darwazah (now called Amar Singh Gate) was similarly designed, though on a smaller scale and without the ostentations of the formal gateway.

Of other buildings of Akbar, in the fort, now only the Bengali Mahal has survived. It was also completed in 1569. At present, it is split into two complexes, Akbari Mahal and Jehangiri Mahal. Built of red sandstone, both are composed of such trabeated elements as pillars, brackets, lintels, beams, *chhajjas*, *jharokhas*, and *chhatris*. Besides a wide variety of flat ceilings, it also has some vaulted ceilings, built ingeniously by stone ribs and panels.

The western facade of these palaces had a uniform plan extending to about 430 feet (131 m), with two entrance portals and three towers, of which only one portal (*poli*) with two flanking towers, creating the western facade of the Jehangiri Mahal, has survived. It has, on its facade, a series of ornamental red stone arches with a white marble fringe of lotus buds, looking like silk tapestries or carpets hanging on the wall. Designs have also been inlaid on the portal, while its frieze has polychrome glazed tiles. Each palace is a complex arrangement of rooms and halls, corridors and galleries, *dalans* (verandas), terraces, and open courts—all grouped together in two stories around a large central quadrangle. Openings are protected by *chhajjas*, which are supported on exquisitely designed, three-tiered stone brackets, which give each facade a distinct personality.

Fatehpur Sikri and Its Monuments (1572–1585; 1601)

Akbar founded a large township at Fatehpur Sikri and he lived there from 1572 to 1585. Unlike Agra, which was an ancient habitat and grew by itself, Fatehpur Sikri was properly planned on three descending levels with three complexes: the mosque complex, the royal complex, and the public complex, respectively, in accordance with the slope of the ridge. All the buildings were so laid out as to have northern or eastern orientation, with perfect arrangement of drainage and water supply.

The Stone-cutters Mosque (c. 1562), situated in the mosque complex, is composed of simple pillars, arches, and a flat ceiling. Arches are built of stone slabs, and have no voussoirs. Qur'anic verses are carved upon them and also on the *mihrab* niche. The most distinctive feature of this small mosque, however, is the use of beautiful monolithic struts (serpentine brackets) on its facade to support the broad and slanting *chhajja*.

The Rang Mahal, situated nearby, is also an earlier building (c. 1565–1570). Originally it was a large, residential palace, of which only a single house with an inner court has survived. The interior is accessible by a crooked entrance to ensure *purdah* (segregation of women). *Dalan*s (verandas), rooms and *kotha*s (inner closed cells), composed of red stone pillars, brackets, *chhajja*s, and flat ceilings, are regularly disposed on all the four sides of the court, in two stories. All this gave an impression of open and airy spaces and ensured a comfortable living in this climate.

Founded by Sheikh Salim Chishti in 1564, the Jami Masjid of Fatehpur Sikri was completed by Akbar in 1571. The central court measures about 360 feet (110 m) by 439 feet (134 m). There are spacious *dalan*s (cloisters) of 38 feet (12 m) width on its eastern and northern sides. The *liwan* (sanctuary) on its western side measures 288 by 65 feet (87.8 x 19.8 m). It is divided into several sections. The central nave (*bahu*), which is 41 feet (12.5 m) square, is roofed by a single, high dome. Each wing is composed of a large colonnaded hall which has a square domed room in the middle, attached to the western wall. The *mihrab*s (arches of the western wall) have been gorgeously ornamented by inlaid mosaic of stone and glazed tiles, and carved and painted Qur'anic inscriptions. The side domes are supported on beautifully designed corbelled pendentives in the phase of transition, instead of vault, squinch, or stalactite.

The facade of the sanctuary has a deep central portal and an arcade on its either side. Arches are similarly ornamental and are protected by identical *chhajja*s supported on brackets. While there is one *chhatri* over each pillar of the *dalans*, arches of this facade each have an additional central *chhatri*, which gives an impression of profusion of *chhatri*s on the skyline. The Persian inscription in the central portal records its construction in 1571.

The stupendous Buland Darwazah, built in 1601 to commemorate Akbar's conquest of the Deccan, in place of the original southern gate of the Jami Masjid, is a complete momument with large halls, small chambers, passages, and stairways. Raised on a stepped platform 42 feet (12.8 m) high, it rises to a total height of 176 feet (53.6 m) above the road, with which it is connected by only a series of broad stairs, rendering its use as a gateway impossible. It measures 130 feet (39.6 m) across the front. The wings recede (offset) at a 135 degree angle, proportionately, giving the facade an exceedingly beautiful architectural effect. It is here, in fact, that the *iwan* formula has been most magnificently expressed in medieval art. *Chhatri*s of different denominations have been used on the superstructure.

The Tomb of Sheikh Salim Chishti is situated in the court of the Jami Masjid, facing the Buland Darwazah. It is a small but extremely beautiful white marble building, square in plan, measuring 48 feet (14.6 m) on each side, with an entrance porch attached to its southern side. The tomb chamber, roofed by a single dome has, on all sides, a spacious *dalan* (veranda), divided into square bays, spanned by corbelled slabs in *ksipta* (lantern) style and closed by exquisite *jali*s (latticed screens) of white marble. The broad slanting *chhajja*, which rotates on all external sides, is supported on gracefully designed monolithic struts, which look like carved ivory rather than chiseled marble. This feature bestows upon the tomb a distinct personality and impression. Qur'anic verses are carved on the porch entrance and on ornamental panels in the *dalan*. The tomb was completed in 1581, as is inscribed on the porch entrance. It was originally finished in red sandstone. Jehangir rebuilt its porch (portico), *dalan*, and dome with white marble between 1605 and 1607. Owing to its exquisite *jali*s and struts, the tomb is reckoned among the masterpieces of Mughal architecture.

The royal complex, situated at a little lower level, has the Raniwas (*harem*, seraglio) and some other buildings associated with Akbar's cultural activities. The Raniwas (wrongly called Jodhbai's Palace; 1569–1572) is the largest of Akbar's extant palaces at Fatehpur Sikri. It has double-storied residential suites, with *dalan*s, rooms, *kotha*s, and open terraces on all the four sides of the spacious inner court, which is approached through a crooked gateway and enclosed on all sides for strict *purdah* and security. Besides the open terraces, there are *chhatri*s, *chaukhandi*s, and *khaprel* (tiled) roofs on the upper floors, where the residents could spent their evenings pleasantly. Toilets are annexed on the southern side. A temple has also been provided.

The Mahal-i-Ilahi (1582; wrongly called Birbal's Palace), is a double-storied mansion built entirely of red sandstone of the finest quality. It has four square rooms, of equal size, measuring about 17 feet (5.1 m) on each side, open on all sides and interconnected by common doorways, and oblong porches on the north and south sides, on the ground plan. While rooms have flat ceilings, porches have triangular *chhappar* (hut) ceilings with pyramidal roofs on the first floor. A broad slanting *chhajja* supported on graceful three-tiered brackets protect it on all the external sides. They have been used dominantly and impart the building a distinctly ornate character. The two rooms on the first floor have domed ceilings made of ribs and panels, with *jharokha*s opening on the court. The domes were originally tiled. The most important feature of this palace, however, is the surface carving, in incised, low, and medium relief, with which it has been entirely ornamented in the interior as well as on the exterior, in a wide variety of designs, including arabesques, geometrical, and stylized florals. It was a formal building used by Akbar for the initiation ceremony of the Din-i-Ilahi.

The public complex has several palatial mansions arranged judiciously around a large, stone-paved court. The Khwabgah palace (1572) is situated on its southeastern segment, overlooking the magnificent Anup Talao. It is composed of several buildings: arched and colonnaded halls, open pillared *dalan*s, terraces, pavilions, and curtained passages, all built tastefully in red sandstone. The *hujrah* (room) of Anup Talao was ornately finished and was personally used by Akbar. The upper floor pavilion has *khaprel* (tiled) roofs on its verandas and figurative paintings in the interior, with Persian inscriptions in praise of this palace.

The Panch Mahal (1572–1575) is a rectangular building of five stories, open on all sides, composed of red sandstone pillars, with jalied (latticed) balustrades on the edges, or *chhajja*s and brackets, carved friezes, stairways, and flat ceilings. It is crowned by a square *chhatri*. Obviously, it dominates on elevation. Its stairs are on the western side, and it distinctly offsets toward the east, or the court, on which side is its facade. Akbar used this palace for daily worship of the rising sun and for showing himself, simultaneously, to his people, an indispensable function of the Mughal king.

On its northern side are situated the Record Office (1572–1575) composed of three oblong halls of equal size and the Ekastambha Prasada (1572–1575; the House of Unitary Pillar, wrongly called Diwan-i-Khas). The latter is a square building of red sandstone, measuring 43 feet (13.2 m) on each exterior side. The double-storied four facades are identical. Four *chhatri*s at the corners compose its superstructure. Its internal architecture is unique. The single-storied square hall measures nearly 29 feet (8.7 m) on each side. In its exact center is a huge column of red stone. It is square at base, octagonal on the shaft, and 16-sided and round above it, from which point rise 36 beautiful three-tiered brackets to support a circular platform above it. Four narrow bridges radiate diagonally toward the angles where they meet the inner balconies. The platform, bridges, and balconies are protected by latticed balustrades. The central column with its platform and bridges is certainly the raison d'être of this building. It is not functional but rather a symbolic monument, representing Akbar's belief in the "nitary pillar" concept of the sun.

The Diwan-i-ʿAm (Hall of Public Audience, 1572–1575) is spread on the eastern side of this court, at a lower level. It is a spacious oblong complex with a large court and raised pillared *dalan*s around it. In the middle of the western side is the Throne Pavilion. It has five openings made of pillars and brackets, with *jali* (latticed) screens separating the apartments. The most important feature of this pavilion is the *khaprel* (stone-tiled) roof over the veranda. It slopes gently from the frieze down to the capitals of the pillars and combines the effect of the *chhajja* and the superstructure. It is in this element that facade and superstructure are combined marvelously. The throne chamber faces east, the direction of the rising sun, in accordance with Akbar's faith. It may be noted that *dalan*s were not meant for actual use, but to provide an architectural accessory so that plain walls did not look monotonous. This feature was a constituent of the style used invariably with public buildings.

The Diwan-i-Khas (Hall of Private Audience, 1572–1585, wrongly called Daftar Khanah) is situated to the south of the Khwabgah. Planned with a court and pillared *dalan*s around it, it is composed of an oblong hall and a wide, spacious *dalan* (veranda) on east, north, and west sides, all connected by doorways. On the southern side, overlooking the ridge, are three openings and a central *jharokha*. This is thus an extremely open and airy building. It has a high *ladaodar* (wagon-vaulted) ceiling of stone ribs and panels. These features confirm that it was used as an assembly hall. The interior was originally painted with figurative subjects depicting contemporary life.

Tomb of Akbar, Sikandara Agra (1605–1612)

The tomb of Akbar at Sikandara Agra was built by his son Jahangir. It stands in the center of a vast enclosed garden divided into four quarters, on the Char-bagh plan, by causeways, of stone masonry, of 75 feet (22.9 m) width, with narrow water channels, tanks, and cascades. In the middle of each side is a monumental gate, the main one on the south side, the other three being ornamental only. The two-storied main gate on the south side is much larger and more ornately finished. It measures 137 feet

(41.9 m) east to west, 100 feet (30.5 m) north to south, and 75 feet (22.9 m) in height. Its north and south facades are identical, each having a colossal *iwan* (portal) 61 feet (18.6 m) in height and 44 feet (13.5 m) in width in the center, and double alcoves on the sides. The whole red stone exterior is finished in mosaic and inlay of multicolored stones, chiefly in geometrical designs. The spandrels of arches bear exquisite arabesque scrolls. Soffits of arches are painted in red and white. The most important feature of this gate is the use of four circular tapering minarets of white marble on the corners of the terrace which, along with the *chhatri*s, make up a wonderful superstructure.

The main tomb is square and has five receding stories. Each facade has a central *iwan* (portal) superimposed by an oblong eight-pillared *chhaparkhat* of white marble. Octagonal towers surmounted by *chhatris* are attached to the corners. The ground floor has spacious *dalan*s (veranda) of 22-foot (6.71-m) width. Four upper stories are composed of arched and pillared *dalan*s and superimposing *chhatri*s. There is no dome. The uppermost story is entirely built of white marble. The tomb has a large number of Persian inscriptions. Those on the main gate praise Jahangir and the tomb, and also give the date of its construction. The uppermost story has thirty-six Persian couplets, in praise of Akbar and on philosophical subjects.

Tomb of I'timad-ud-Daulah Agra (1622–1628)

Situated on the left bank of the Jamuna, it was built by Nur Jahan for her parents Mirza Ghiyath Beg, titled I'timad-ud Daulah, and Asmat Begum. It is also planned in the center of the *char-bagh*, as usual, with a beautiful garden setting and water elements. The white marble tomb is square in plan, with towers attached to the corners. These towers are octagonal but assume a circular form above the terrace and are surmounted by circular *chhatri*s. Each facade has three arches, the two on the sides closed by *jali*s, and protected by a *chhajja* and a balustrade. The interior is composed of a central square hall for cenotaphs, four oblong rooms on the sides and four square rooms on the corners, all interconnected by common doorways. It is essentially the typical *navagrha* (nine-house) plan of the Mughals. The building is not roofed by a dome, but by a square pavilion, having three arched openings on each side, and a pyramidal (*chaukhandi*) roof. The *chhatri*s of the towers combine impressively with this *barahdari* and make up an extremely beautiful superstructure.

Its exterior ornamentation by mosaic and inlay of multicolored natural stones in a wide variety of designs and motifs is the most important feature of its architecture. It is spread on almost every inch of the white marble surface with unprecedented lavishness, and the decorative aspect has superseded the structure in this tomb. It marks the transition from red stone to white marble, and also from carving to inlay and mosaic.

Shah Jahan's Palatial Mansions (1628–1640); Agra Fort

Soon after his accession to the throne, Shah Jahan (r. 1628–1658) commissioned the Diwan-i-Am of Agra Fort. Before it, the *durbār* (court) of public audience was held in a large tent. His Diwan-i-Am (1628–1635) is situated in a spacious quadrangle having arcaded *dalan*s (verandas) on all sides. It is a rectangular colonnaded open hall, three aisles deep, with nine bold, nine-cusped arches on the facade. Double columns have been used to support these massive arches, which are well proportioned. Though the construction is in red sandstone, the whole of it has been covered by white shell-plaster, giving the effect of white marble. Bays have flat ceilings. *Chhajja*, as usual, is supported on brackets, but there are no *chhatri*s on the superstructure. The throne chamber, in the middle of the eastern wall, is built of white marble and is exquisitely ornamented with inlaid stylized floral designs. It presides over the building functionally, as well as architecturally.

Shah Jahan did not like some of his grandfather Akbar's red sandstone palaces in Agra Fort and he ordered them to be rebuilt with white marble. The Muthamman Burj (Octagonal Tower) is the earliest of them. The spacious white marble pavilion surmounts the circular bastion, on the riverside, facing east, with five of its octagonal sides projecting forward. It is composed of pillars, brackets, lintels, *chhajja*s, and a beautiful *jharokha*—all of white marble. On its western side is a spacious *dalan* (veranda), which has a sunken water basin in the middle of its floor. Walls have graceful dados with stylized floral borders, and carved natural plant compositions in the center. Ceilings are flat. Exquisitely inlaid pillars, brackets, and lintels make up the three openings on the court side. Inlay art in stylized designs dominates the ornamentation of this building. An eight-pillared marble *chhatri* crowns it. It was here that Shah Jahan spent the years of his captivity (1658–1666) and died, in full view of the Taj Mahal.

Situated with the Jamuna on one side, and the Anguri Bagh garden, with its enchanting water devices, including a waterfall, on the other, the Khas Mahal (Arambagh; 1631–1640) is the most beautiful palace of Shah Jahan in Agra Fort. It is also built entirely of white marble. The interior is a spacious hall, on the river side, which has a three-aisle-deep *dalan*, with five nine-cusped arches on the facade, on its front. The hall was originally painted with stylized designs. A *chhajja* projects on the exterior, as usual. In its front is a large scalloped tank with fountains.

Its water flowed, through a waterfall, to the four-quartered Anguri Bagh, which is situated at a much lower level and provides the palace with a beautiful setting. On both sides of the palace, on the terrace, are oblong *bangladar* pavilions (with curved roof and *chhajja*) and open courts, secured by thin marble screens to ensure *purdah*. Though a regal building, it has been designed with abundant open spaces to facilitate cool breezes from the river, a pleasant garden front and landscapes, to ensure comfortable living in the hot climate of Agra.

The Diwan-i-Khas (1635) of Agra Fort was built of white marble. It consists of two halls, an outer pillared hall and an inner closed hall, both connected by archways. The outer hall, which is essentially a spacious *dalan* (veranda) has double pillars, supporting five nine-cusped arches on the facade, on the northern side, and three seven-cusped arches on eastern and western sides. These have been tastefully ornamented by inlaid and carved designs in low relief. A broad *chhajja*, supported on brackets, rotates on these three external sides. The palace has no superstructure. *Durbār* (court) was held in the outer hall. The inner hall, which was reserved for conducting important and confidential business, has alcoves in the southern wall, and raised seats with semisoffits on the eastern and western sides. *Jali*s (lattices) have also been used. The most important aspect of this palace, however, is its dados. Plant motifs are carved, in double rows, in the center, while a stylized vine design is inlaid in polychrome on the border. A Persian inscription distributed on twenty-eight oblong cartouches on the northern wall of the outer hall, dated in 1635, praise the king and the palace.

Red Fort Delhi and Its Palaces (1639–1648)

Shah Jahan transferred the formal capital from Agra to Delhi in 1638 and founded there a city, Shahjahanabad, and a citadel, the Red Fort, which were completed in nearly ten years (1639–1648). Palaces were built in the fort, where there was virgin space to lay out these buildings on a uniform plan. It has an octagonalized rectangular plan and measures 3,100 feet (944.9 m) north to south, 1,650 feet (493 m) east to west, and 75 feet (22.9 m) in height. Built of brick masonry, it is entirely finished in red sandstone. Its battlemented walls have the usual embrasures, machicolations, bastions, and a moat. The Lahori Gate on the west and Delhi Gate on the south are its main gates. The former has a covered market. The palaces are symmetrically laid out, with the Naubat Khanah (House of Ceremonial Music), Diwan-i-Am (Hall of Public Audience), and Rang Mahal (the Painted Palace) on the east-west axis, and the Rang Mahal, Shah Burj (the King's Tower), and Diwan-i-Khas (Hall of Private Audience) on the north-south axis, along the course of the Nahar-i-Bahisht (The Heavenly Canal), on a raised terraced. The gardens that originally connected the palaces have not survived.

The Diwan-i-Am was situated, originally, in a court of its own, with *dalan*s and gateways on all sides. They no longer exist. It is a three-aisle-deep, colonnaded hall with nine nine-cusped arches on the facade, built of red sandstone that was originally white plastered and polished to look like white marble. Overlooking the central bay is a white marble throne balcony in the eastern wall. It has a latticed balustrade in front and seats with pedestals on the sides. On its front, attached to it, is a beautiful white marble *bungla* (four-pillared pavilion with curved roof and *chhajja*), 12 by 9 feet (3.6 x 2.7 m) in size. Both the throne balcony and the *bungla* are gorgeously inlaid in a wide variety of floral and stylized designs. The back wall has, in addition, floral compositions with birds. On the top of it is the famous plaque depicting Orpheus playing to the animals. Essentially a Florentine work, this plaque was imported and placed here after Aurangzeb, sometime during the eighteenth or early nineteenth century.

The Rang Mahal, measuring 153 by 69 feet (46.79 x 21.11 m) is three aisles deep with five nine-cusped arches on the facade, thus having fifteen bays, each 20 feet (6.1 m) square, with a flat ceiling. But instead of pillars, piers have been used to support them. The whole interior was originally painted and gilded. On the river side are five window openings closed by *jali*s. The Nahar-i-Bahisht flowed through it in the middle, across its length, dividing it into two equal sections, as if the palace was pleasantly laid out on its two banks. In it, in the center of the building, exactly on the same axis as the throne chamber of the Diwan-i-Am, is a beautiful shallow marble basin sunk in the pavement. Designed as a lotus flower of 24 petals, it occupies the entire 20-foot (6.1 m) square side. It has a triple border with flowing curves. Floral and arabesques designs are inlaid in rare multicolored stones. When water rippled softly from the edges of the petals, it produced an optical illusion, and the petals appeared to rise and fall.

The Shah Burj, also known as Baithak, Khwabgah, Muthamman Burj and Khas Mahal, is a large palace complex, consisting of several *dalan*s and rooms, to serve as a full-fledged residential palace. The Nahar-i-Bahisht flows through it. Built entirely of white marble, it was profusely painted and gilded in stylized compositions. On the walls, overlooking the canal, are two Persian inscriptions, eulogizing the king and the palace, specifically the ethereal water devices. On its eastern side, overlooking the Jamuna, is attached the Muthamman Burj (Octagonal Tower), which was used by the king for appearing to the public.

The Diwan-i-Khas is situated on the same 4.5-foot (1.4 m) high terrace, overlooking the river, with the same

Nahar-i-Bahisht flowing through it. Originally, it also had its own court and arcaded *dalan*s, which have not survived. It is a rectangular colonnaded hall, built entirely of white marble. It measures 102 feet (31.1 m) north to south and 78 feet (23.8 m) east to west. Made up of 24 square and 8 oblong piers, it is 5 aisles deep, with 5 nine-cusped arches on the facade. Square piers have dados, with stylized vines on the border, and a natural plant composition in the center, both inlaid in multicolored stones. The remaining mural surface in the interior, including the ceiling, was originally painted and gilded. Riverside arches are closed by *jali*s. A broad, slanting *chhajja* protects it on the exterior. Four *chhatri*s on the corners of the roof make up a simple yet graceful superstructure.

Mosques of the Age of Shah Jahan (1628–1658)

Akbar (r. 1556–1605) and his son Jahangir (r. 1605–1627) built no public mosque at Agra, Lahore, or Delhi, the three metropolitan towns of the Mughal empire, and no private mosque in the forts of Agra and Lahore where they lived. It was left to Shah Jahan (r. 1628–1658), Jahangir's son, to commission mosques in these forts and the Red Fort Delhi, and also a large public Friday (Jami) mosque each in the cities of Agra and Delhi.

The small white-marble mosques—Mina Masjid (c. 1630) and Nagina Masjid (c. 1635) in Agra Fort; Moti Masjid in Lahore Fort (1630–1635); and Moti Masjid in Red Fort Delhi (c. 1658)—built by him were of a private nature and were attached to the royal harem. The last one is the most beautiful mosque of this class. Built entirely of pure white marble, it measures 40 by 30 feet (12.2 x 9.14 m) and is two aisles deep with a three-arched facade. Arches are engrailed. They are supported on square piers and are protected by a *chhajja*, which has no brackets. It is curved in the middle, above the central arch, and, correspondingly, the frieze is also curved. This *bangladar* (curved) feature gives prominence to the central part of the facade, as did the *iwan* portal. Like the Nagina Masjid, it also has triangular and vaulted ceilings, and three domes, which are fluted and are harmoniously set against the skyline. Combined with the mini-*chhatris*, which crown the pinnacles on all sides, they make up a marvelous superstructure. Called the Pearl Mosque, it ranks among the masterpieces of the Mughals.

The Jami Masjid of Agra (1644–1648) is a simple mosque of brick masonry finished in red sandstone with ornamental use of white marble. It stands on a high plinth, with the *liwan* (sanctuary) on the western side of the central court and *dalan*s (verandas) on three sides. The *dalan*s have seven-cusped arches supported on pillars, and are superimposed by square *chhatris*. The main eastern gate no longer exists. The side gates are also surmounted by *chhatri*s. The sanctuary is two aisles deep and is composed of extremely high, broad and massive arches supported on equally massive piers, all built of brick masonry that was plastered. Its facade has a broad *iwan* (portal) in the center and two smaller archways on either side. All these arches are plain. Square *chhatri*s have been used on the parapet of the facade. The sanctuary is roofed by three domes, which are somewhat flat and disproportionate. Octagonal towers, surmounted by *chhatri*s, are attached to the corners of the sanctuary and also to the eastern corners of the mosque. This profusion of *chhatri*s on the skyline make up, altogether, a gorgeous superstructure. The Persian inscription inlaid on its facade, along the *iwan* portal, records its completion in 1648, in five years, at the cost of 500,000 rupees.

The Moti Masjid (1647–1654) of Agra Fort is also built on a high plinth. Internally, it is built of pure white marble around the central court, which measures 154 feet (47 m) east-west by 158 feet (48.2 m) north-south. The *dalan*s are nearly 11 feet (3.3 m) wide and are composed of nine-cusped engrailed arches supported on typical Shahjahanian pillars having square bases, twelve-sided fluted shafts, and stalactite capitals, all of white marble. These are protected by *chhajja*s that do not have brackets. *Chhatris* are also absent, and these *dalan*s are crowned by a cresting. The main gate is on the river (eastern) side. Side gates are approached by double staircases. These gates are surmounted by *chhatris*. The sanctuary situated west of the court measures 159 by 56 feet (48.46 x 17.07 m) and is three aisles deep with an arcade of seven arches of equal dimensions on the facade. These arches are nine-cusped and are supported on massive square piers, all of white marble. Ornamentation by carved designs is minimal and the composition is plain and simple, yet graceful. Out of twenty-one bays of the sanctuary, only three have vaulted soffits (roofed by domes exteriorly), others have flat ceilings. The facade is protected by a *chhajja*, which also does not have brackets. Square *chhatris* have been placed on the parapet, one over each arch. Larger octagonal *chhatri*s have been used on all four corners of the sanctuary, and also on the two octagonal towers attached to the eastern corners of the mosque. Three bulbous domes, with the usual sheath of lotus petals and *kalash* finial, crown the sanctuary. The combination of these graceful forms of the *chhatris* and the domes on the skyline, in pure white marble, is incredibly beautiful. The Persian inscription inlaid on the facade, below the *chhajja*, records its construction in seven years (1647–1654) at the cost of 300,000 rupees.

The Jami Masjid of Shahjahanabad Delhi (1650–1656) is one of the largest and the finest mosques. It is built of red sandstone with liberal use of white marble. It stands on a plinth of 30 feet (9.1 m) height. This grand elevation enabled its three gateways, approached by a flight of stairs, to tower over its surroundings majestically. It is composed of an open court 328 feet (100 m) on each side, with a central tank, dalans on its three sides with a gateway in the middle of each one of them, and a sanctuary, which measures 200 by 90 feet (61 x 27.4 m) on the west. Its facade is composed of a central *iwan* portal with an arcade of five arches in each wing, and two lofty minarets 130 feet (39.6 m) high, crowned by *chhatris*, on the sides. Arches are cusped and are supported on white marble piers. There is only one *chhatri* on each wing, but there is no *chhajja*. The sanctuary has been ingeniously planned in the interior. The nave, roofed by the main dome, has a large *iwan* portal on its front. Each wing of the nave (along the western wall) is divided, by massive piers, into three sections: a square bay in the middle and two oblong bays on the sides. The square bay is roofed by a dome, while oblong bays have *chaukhandi* (pyramidal, wagon-vaulted) ceilings. Thus, there are three domed and four wagon-vaulted ceilings on the western section of the sanctuary. But this arrangement is not repeated on its front side, which has, on either side of the *iwan* portal, a *dalan* of five arches. Each *dalan* is a hall with a continuous ceiling. Thus, though externally it appears to be a two-aisled mosque with eleven bays, owing to eleven arches on the facade, in fact, it is only a single-aisled building with seven bays, alternatively oblong and square, having an *iwan* portal and two side *dalans* on its face. This is a unique design, representative of the genius of the Mughal architects, who could consistently organize space in a novel way. Ten oblong panels on the facade above the ten arches of the wings bear a long Persian panegyric in praise of the King Shah Jahan and the mosque. The *mihrab* arch bears Qur'anic verses. There is practically no ornamentation and its beautiful effect is essentially architectonic.

The Taj Mahal Agra (1631–1648)

Shah Jahan built this wonderful monument of love in the memory of his most beloved Queen Mumtaz Mahal, who died in 1631. Its site on the river Jamuna is ideal, environmentally as well as architecturally. The Taj was laid out in several descending terraces on a south-north axis, in accordance with the slope of the river bank. Beginning from the south side, a city, now called Tajganj, was founded with squares, markets, inns, and houses, obviously to support its institution. On the second terrace, at a lower level, is the main court, which has the main gate of the tomb, *dalan*s, annexes, and subsidiary buildings, providing a beautiful approach to the monument. The garden and the tomb are situated on the third terrace at a still lower level. As usual, it is an enclosed garden, divided into four quarters (*char-bagh*) by broad, stone canals which have fountains; double, stone-paved causeways, with the intervening cypress avenues in the middle; and flower parterres and tree avenues on the sides. Ornamental red stone buildings called Jal Mahal (Water Palace) are placed in the middle of east and west sides, to complete the architectural coherence. But the tomb building is not sited in the center of the garden, as was done in all earlier Mughal tombs. Instead, there is a raised lotus pond of white marble. The tomb is placed, on its north, just on the riverbank, in the middle of a rectangular red stone platform which measures nearly 971 feet (295.8 m) east to west and 365 feet (111.2 m) north to south, and is 4 feet (1.2 m) high from the garden and 42 feet (12.8 m) high from the river. It is flanked by a mosque on the west and Jam'at Khanah (Assembly Hall) on the east, with the garden lying at its feet. This was an innovation in the traditional *char-bagh* plan. The tomb stands in the background of a blank blue sky against which its white image silhouettes, almost magically. The sky changes its color every moment, and the Taj is always seen in this ever-changing setting, in a variety of tints and tones, and in innumerous moods and moments. The secret of its aesthetics lies in its novel layout, with the river on its one side and the garden on the other. The mosque and the Jam'at Khanah (also called Mehman Khanah) are identical, three-arched, three-domed, red stone buildings, with liberal use of white marble. It is noteworthy that each one of these annexes—the mosque, the Jam'at Khanah, the two Jal-Mahals, and the main gate—is a complete monument that can stand independently anywhere else, though here, each one stands beneath the architectural suzerainty of the Taj Mahal.

The mausoleum, built of brick masonry skeleton and finished entirely in white marble, stands in the middle of a square white marble plinth which measures 328 feet (100 m) on each side and 19 feet (5.8 m) in height from the red stone platform. It has four tapering circular minarets at the corners flanking the tomb building symmetrically. They are 132 feet (40.2 m) high, in three stories separated by balconies supported on brackets, and surmounted by octagonal *chhatris*. The tomb is, essentially, a square of 187 feet (57 m) on each side, but its angles have been chamfered to give it an octagonalized square plan. All facades are identical. Each one has a grand *iwan* (portal) in its center, practically occupying its whole height up to the parapet. It is flanked on both sides by double alcoves, one over the other, on a rectangular plan. Double alcoves given on the corners with a semioctagonal plan are distinctly visible from the gate. The *iwan* and alcove spandrels bear stylized arabesques, inlaid with multicolored natural stones on white marble. Portal dados have inlaid vines on the borders and carved natural plant compositions in the centers. Other mural surfaces are plain, giving a marked emphasis to this rare inlay ornament.

Taj Mahal. With its white marble and symmetry crisp against the background sky, the Taj Mahal rises almost magically. Built between 1631 and 1648 by Shah Jahan as a memorial, a "monument of love," for his beloved queen. FOTOMEDIA ARCHIVE.

Each section of the facade is demarcated by attached pilasters or miniature turrets which, beginning from the plinth level, rise above the parapet and are crowned by beautiful pinnacles with lotus buds and finials. A bulbous double dome with a broad, overspreading sheath of lotus petals and *kalash* finial (which originally measured 30.5 ft., or 9.3 m) majestically crowns the Taj. It rests on a high drum and rises to the total height of nearly 146 feet (44.4 m) from the base of the drum to the apex of the finial, and 285 feet (87 m) from the river level. Emphasis of its design is, obviously, on its elevation, in which its dome plays the decisive role. It is flanked on all four angles by four octagonal *chhatri*s placed at an extremely symmetrical distance from it. As a whole, it makes up an unbelievably gorgeous superstructure.

The interior plan has a central octagonal hall 58 feet (17.7 m) in diameter and 80 feet (24.4 m) in height, with four oblong rooms on the sides and four octagonal rooms on the corners, all interconnected by passages. This plan is repeated on the first floor, which overlooks the central cenotaph hall. Except for the entrance in the south portal, all arches are closed by marble screens, set with translucent glass to allow only a subdued light into the interior. The main cenotaph hall has been magnificently, though sparingly, ornamented. Spandrels of arches have inlaid stylized arabesque designs. The panels on the dados have beautiful floral compositions in high relief, with borders in inlaid stylized vine patterns. In each case, it is a beautiful *ghata-pallava* (vase and foliage) motif. An exquisitely finished marble *jali* screen (*jhajjhari*) with similar inlaid borders encloses the cenotaphs. Floral compositions have also been inlaid on the cenotaphs, which also bear Qur'anic verses. Chapters from the Qur'an have also been inscribed around the interior arches, on the *iwan* portals on all facades, on both sides of the main gate, and inside the mosque. There are short Persian inscriptions on the cenotaphs, recording the dates of the death of Mumtaz Mahal and Shah Jahan.

Completed in seventeen years in 1648, at the cost of 40 million rupees in an age when gold was sold at 15 rupees per tola (11.66 g), the Taj Mahal marks the zenith of Mughal architectural style; it is here that its idioms are perfected. Its site on the riverbank; its terraced layout with the garden setting; and above all, its wonderful design—with extremely harmonious and symmetrical placement of its components, ideal geometrical precision and proportions—have made it the most beautiful architectural work of the world, justifying the poetic definition "a resplendent immortal teardrop on the cheek of time" (Nath, *The Taj Mahal and Its Incarnation*, pp. 13–15).

R. Nath

See also **Agra; Akbar; Babur; Jahangir; Shah Jahan**

BIBLIOGRAPHY

Fergusson, James. *History of Indian and Eastern Architecture.* 1876. Rev. ed., London: J. Murray, 1910.

Havell, E. B. *Indian Architecture: Its Psychology, Structure and History.* 1913. Reprint, New Delhi: Chand, 1972.

Nath, R. . *The Immortal Taj Mahal.* Mumbai: D. B. Taraporevala, 1972.

———. *History of Decorative Art in Mughal Architecture.* Delhi: Motilal Banarsidass, 1976.

———. *Monuments of Delhi: A Historical Study.* English trans. of Sayyid Ahmed Khan's Urdu work, *Athar'al Sanadid.* New Delhi: Ambika, 1979.

———. *The Taj Mahal and Its Incarnation.* Jaipur: Historical Research Documentation Programme, 1985.

———. *Jharokha: An Illustrated Glossary of Indo-Muslim Architecture.* Jaipur: Historical Research Documentation Programme, 1986.

———. *Architecture of Fatehpur Sikri: Forms, Technisques, and Concepts.* Jaipur: Historical Research Documentation Programme, 1988.

———. *Agra and Its Monuments.* Agra: Historical Research Documentation Programme, 1997.

SOUTHERN INDIA

South Indian monuments of the premodern period represent two distinct regional styles of temple architecture: the Deccan style, which spread over the plateau of peninsular India; and the Dravida, or Tamil, style, which developed mainly in the Tamil region but which had a significant impact on the later phases of architecture in the Deccan and in Andhra Pradesh. The Deccan style in its early stage (6th–8th centuries A.D.) marks an initial attempt to use either the Nagara style or the Dravida style, but in its later stage develops into what may be called the Deccan style by combining some of the major elements of both. The main features of the Deccan style are a shrine with a *sikhara* (pyramidal roof), pillared halls, perforated stone screens, sloping roofs of passages around the shrine, and porches with sloping seat backs, all of which are evident in the later Deccan monuments of the eighth to the seventeenth centuries. The Dravida style evolved with a clear focus on the vertical ascent of the square shrine, or *vimāna*, with a pyramidal storied *sikhara* and a series of *mandapas* (columned halls) in an east-west alignment, enclosed by a *prākāra* (wall) with a rectangular entrance, or *gopura*. These two styles developed in the early medieval period (6th–12th centuries) in two phases, the twelfth century marking the apogee of both, together with their design and iconographic program. Their further elaboration took place in the period from the thirteenth to the seventeenth centuries. While in the first period the focus was mainly on the plan, design, and elevation of the architectural components (such as the shrine with its tower and the pillared halls aligned with it), the emphasis in the later period was on the horizontal magnification of the temple and its precincts, to serve the increasing ritual, festival requirements and iconographic developments. As the social and economic outreach of the temple expanded, so did the community's participation in its architectural expansion and in ritual worship. The temple's art and architecture served as the symbols of political authority as well as social and economic integration, thus becoming the focus of rural settlements and urban complexes.

Paṭṭadakal

Situated on the banks of the Malaprabha River, Paṭṭadakal is one of the three sites (Aihoḷe, Bādāmi, and Paṭṭadakal) with magnificent early Chalukya temples of the seventh and eighth centuries, built of gray-yellow sandstone, with several additions made during the Rashtrakuta period (9th–10th centuries). The Virūpāksha and Mallikārjuna complexes mark the culmination of the early Chalukya series.

Of the early Shiva temples (7th–8th centuries) with a rudimentary Nāgara plan (a pyramidal superstructure with curvilinear top), the ruined Galaganātha (7th century, reign of Vijayāditya) is the earliest of the Paṭṭadakal temples, similar to the early Chalukya temples in Ālampūr. Its tower is more sophisticated and refined in design than the others. Raised on a broad terrace, it follows the Deccan style in all its components. A marked feature of the Galaganātha temple is the eight-armed figure of Shiva in the *gavāksha* (windowlike projection/niche on the first tier). The Sangamesvara temple, patronized by Vijayāditya, has the usual plan of aligned structures of the Deccan style, while the Kāshivishvanātha temple combines a Nāgara *sikhara* with Dravida architectural motifs. The small Chandrashekhara temple is the only Rashtrakuta period structure within the same compound.

The Virūpāksha temple (A.D. 745), commissioned by Lokamahādevi, the chief queen of Vikramāditya II, to commemorate her husband's conquest of Kānchīpuram,

Avittathur Shiva Temple. Avittathur Shiva near Thrissur, Kerala, approximately a thousand years old. V. MUTHURAMAN / FOTOMEDIA.

is a grand complex with an entrance gateway, Nandi pavilion (a pillared structure for placing the *nandi* or bull), a porch, a *mandapa*, and a *liṅga* sanctuary, all aligned on an east-west axis with subsidiary shrines. It represents the climax of the early Chalukya series in terms of layout, exterior treatment, and sculptural décor. Its square pyramidal tower has three diminishing tiers or stories, a potlike finial, 57 feet (17.5 meters) above ground level, and a large *gavāksha* (a horseshoe-shaped window or niche for an icon or some decorative figure) in front with a dancing Shiva. Not only in its architectural aspects, which combine the Nāgara with Dravida elements, but also in its sculptural decoration, wall panels, column reliefs, and ceiling compositions, the temple surpasses in number and variety those found on any other religious monuments of the period; its rich repertoire of iconography includes a large number of Shiva and Vishnu and other deities, richly sculpted mythological narratives, and epic scenes from the Rāmāyaṇa and the Mahābhārata on the *mandapa* walls and columns, which are striking for their dynamic composition. Flying Mithuna couples (amorous couples usually shown in erotic postures) and lyrical figures of river goddesses on the sanctuary doorway, elaborate ceiling panels in the porches, and figures of musicians and dancers are other decorative features. The thirty-five panels on the outer walls, finished by different hands, along with the images in the minor shrines of Gaṇesha and Mahishāsuramardini, represent masterpieces of early Chalukya style. Ornamental parapets, perforated stone windows, porches and balconies, elephant torsos and lions, animal friezes and foliate devices provide a rich exterior.

The Mallikārjuna temple, built by Trailokyamahādevi, the younger queen of Vikramāditya II (Trailokeshvara), is a matching monument to Virūpāksha, and the two are laid out in unique diagonal formation. It is a smaller version, complete with its own walled compound, entrance gateways and subshrines, with a greater three-dimensional massing of volumes. Its iconographic scheme shows Shiva and Vishnu in various forms. The Kirātārjunīya story, the *Panchatantra*, and Rāmāyaṇa scenes are sculpted on the columns of the *mandapa*.

A short distance from the main group is the Pāpanātha temple, completed in the reign of Kirttivarman II (r. 634–645), in a mixed architectural style; Nāgara features mingle with Dravida elements like *kūḍus* (horseshoe-shaped windows) marking the cornice (*kapota*). The

Rāmāyaṇa reliefs of this temple represent the most complete cycle on any early Chalukya monument. This is the only temple with a pair of interconneting *mandapa*s, due to three succesive phases of construction.

The rich iconography of these temples shows a variety of Shaiva and Vaishnava forms in their interior and exterior, creating a rich repertoire of Purāṇic deities (the Hindu pantheon) and their mythology. Some distance west of the main group is the Jain temple, a well worked but somewhat austere structure, with a tower containing an upper chamber with a Dravida *kūṭa* roof. Its basement carries extraordinary life-sized torsos of elephants and *makara*s (crocodiles).

Belūr and Haḷebīḍ

Situated 25 miles (40 kilometers) northwest of Hassan in southern Karnataka, the Hoysaḷa temple of Chennakesava at Belūr, built in the reign of Vishnuvardnana in 1117 with a revolutionary design, represents the beginnings of a new tradition in architecture. The ground plan of the Hoysaḷa temples is stellate, or star-shaped, the one at Belūr being a half star for the main shrine, with a vestibule and an open *mandapa* (*navaranga*) in front, later closed with stone screens. It is a towerless *eka-kūṭa* shrine (a single shrine with a single story), measuring 34 feet (10.5 meters) corner to corner at its exterior. The length of the entire structure is 138 feet (42 meters), and the width of the open hall is 95 feet (29 meters). It is a *pancharatha* (a shrine that has five exterior projections) with Bhumija superstructures over the multiaedicular Nāgara shrines.

Standing on a 3.3-feet (1-meter) high platform, the whole temple is accessible through three flights of steps and three entrances, each flight flanked by miniature shrines with Nāgara roofs. The elevation has three main parts: the base, the wall surface, and the tower. The base is decorated with friezes of elephants, horses, and lions in horizontal rows, a forerunner of all other Hoysaḷa temples. In the *mandapa*, the perforated stone screens rise above the half pillars, resting on a parapet. *Madanika* (female) figures decorate the top of the pillars below the protruding *chadya* (eave) and are purely ornamental. The sculptured wealth is extraordinary, covering the surface from the base to the cornice (*kapota*), including mythological stories of Krishna and icons of Vishnu in various forms, with floral canopies. The interior has rich decorative carvings, especially the ceiling and the pillars. The large two-story wall shrines located in the middle have mixed Dravida and Nāgara elements, but without a Dravida or even a clear Nāgara structure

Haḷebīḍ (Dvārasamudra, the Hoysaḷa capital) is 9 miles (15 kilometers) northeast of Belūr. Here the temple design is innovative and introduces the typical Hoysaḷa style. Unequaled in size and extent, it is a double temple with a *dvikūṭa* Dravida *vimāna*, with both towers missing and with a half-star plan.Two open halls, linked together, have two additional shrines at the connection of the two. The pillars appear to be lathe turned. Facing the open halls are Nandi pavilions and a Sūrya shrine, all of which share a large platform following their outline. The ground plan is more detailed and schematic, with each *vimāna* measuring 26 feet (8 meters), the *vimāna* and the hall together 108 feet (33 meters) long, and the two halls 154 feet (47 meters) wide. Both *vimāna*s are *pancharatha* and have staggering projections and recessions, notably at the back, with six wall shrines. The temple has two entrances in front, and two lateral entrances to the open halls, all flanked by miniature Dravida shrines.

The base has eight lavishly sculptured friezes with horizontally arranged figures (elephants, horses, lions, and epics) and above, the wall surface has large images, representing almost the full Hindu pantheon and mythological scenes. The *antarāla* (vestibule) doorway decoration is equally rich, and the interior on the whole has decorative carvings on the ceiling and other surfaces. The decorative carvings have a fragile filigree effect, and no space is left uncarved. The Hoysaleshvara at Haḷebīḍ undoubtedly influenced the architecture of all later Hoysaḷa temples, of which the Somanāthapura triple shrine, with well preserved towers, pillared *navaranga*, base friezes, and decorative sculptures, is the best example.

Shravana Beḷgoḷa

The most celebrated Digambara Jain center in South India, Shravana Beḷgoḷa, in southern Karnataka, has a long history, starting from the Mauryan period to the present day. The early name of the town was Gommaṭapura, but after the twelfth century, the names Beḷgoḷa (white pond) and Jinanāthapura seem to have come into use, while the name Shravana Beḷgoḷa is not known before 1810. It has the largest number of Digambara Jain temples (33), located on two hills, known as Vindhyagiri/Indragiri (Doḍḍabeṭṭa/Pēr-Kaḷvappu) and Chandragiri (Chikkabeṭṭa/Kaḷvappu), and the surrounding areas. The monuments range in date from the ninth to the nineteenth century, but the most important ones were erected from the tenth through the fourteenth centuries under the Hoysaḷas and their subordinates, the Gangas, and under the Vijayanagara rulers of the fourteenth through seventeenth centuries. Its inscriptions number 579, the largest for a single center, although many of the early ones are *nisidhi* (memorial) inscriptions of those who followed the *sallekhaṇa*, or the ritual of death by fasting.

The chief monument is the famous Gommaṭa (Bāhubali) statue, the colossus within an open quadrangle on the Vindhyagiri. The statue is 58.8 feet (17.7 meters)

Durgā Temple. Dating to the late seventh or early eighth century, the Durgā Temple in Aihole, Karnataka. Dedicated to Vishnu and sitting atop a platform, the elaborately carved and decorated monument appears to be a Hindu adaptation of a Buddhist *chaitya* (great hall). FREDRIK ARVIDSSON.

high, the largest consecrated monolith anywhere in the world, and was commissioned by Chāmuṇḍarāya, the Ganga general of the Hoysaḷa kingdom, in 981. Endowed with a physiognomy that suggests an unmatched serenity, with half-closed eyes, the image re-creates a superhuman personality. An anthill at the base, with hissing snakes and a creeper that climbs the figure of Gommaṭa, are characteristic of a renouncer's stance, while a circular stone basin, called *lalita sarovara*, at the foot of the image, collects the ceremonial water, when the ceremonial bath (*abhisheka*) for the image is performed.

The Bhaṇḍara Basti (Chaturvimsati Tīrthānkara Basti), the largest temple of the complex, was consecrated in 1159. Along with the cloister around Bāhubali (Gommaṭa), it enshrines the images of the twenty-four Tīrthānkaras of Jainism. The ceilings of the cloister have carvings of the eight guardians of the directions, with Indra holding a pot to anoint the image of Bāhubali. While the Gommaṭa statue is of the Ganga style, nearly all other images in the Suttālaya are of the Hoysaḷa style. Subsequent renovations added a *gopura* (gateway) tower, a high walled outer enclosure, a pillared porch (*mukha maṇḍapa*), and an ornate doorway. The Sarasvatī *mandapa* in front was added by Mahāpradhāna Bukkarāya in 1527.

The small hill, Chandragiri-Chikkabeṭṭa (Kaḷbappu or Kaṭavapra), has 13 temples, 7 mandapas, 2 freestanding pillars, a crude enclosure on the top of the hill, and a few ponds. Tradition associates it with the migration of Jains from the north, led by Bhadrabāhu, accompanied by Chandragupta, the Mauryan king. The natural cavern, housing the footprint of Bhadrabāhu, has great sanctity and was converted into a temple after the eleventh century, with a porch added in the seventeenth century. The Chandragupta Basti, a small temple at the summit of the enclosure, enshrines Pārshvanātha, Kushmāṇḍini, and Padmāvati in three chambers opening from the vestibule. Its twelfth-century doorway, with stone screens on each side, carries the stories of Chandragupta and Bhadrabāhu in relief.

Of the several Jinalayas (Jain temples) on these two hills and the surrounding areas, the architecturally and historically significant ones are the Chāmuṇḍarāya Basti on the smaller hill and the Bhaṇḍara Basti on the larger hill, which are built of granite, while most of the others are in brick and mortar. The Akkaṇa Basti (A.D. 1181) in the town and the more ornate Shantīsvara Basti (A.D. 1200) in Jinanāthapura, both built in dark blue schist, are perfect specimens of the Hoysaḷa style. The reliefs of Tīrthānkaras, *yaksha*s (nature spirits), and other attendants in these temples are of considerable iconographic significance.

Archways and *mandapa*s, housing commemorative columns, were memorials, or *nisidhi*s, of Jain teachers and royal members. The Mahānavami *mandapa* of the twelfth century, on the larger hill, and the Nisidhi *mandapa* of the Rashtrakuta Indra IV (built in 982), and the Gangaraja *mandapa* (erected in 1120–1123) on the smaller hill, are such memorials. Historically important are the freestanding pavilions like the Tyāgada *kambha* (pillar of abandonment), of tenth-century Ganga workmanship, and the freestanding Yaksha pillar, both on the larger hill, the latter with an inscription of 1422, recording gifts made to Gommaṭa by Irugappa Daṇḍanāyaka, the Vijayanagara general. The Kuge Brahmadeva pillar of 974 is a fine specimen of Ganga workmanship, a commemorative column with a 113-line inscription giving a glowing account of King Mārasimha.

Jain *nisidhi* stones are numerous in the period from the sixth to the tenth centuries, but there was a significant decrease in *nisidhi*s and an increase in *basti*s, attracting pilgrims to the center from the tenth century. As a pilgrimage center, a large number of temples, ponds, and villages similar to the *agrahāra* (Brahman settlements) emerged.

Hampi

Hampi, or Vijayanagara, is one of the largest medieval cities in Asia. As the capital of the Vijayanagara rulers (14th–16th centuries), it is the earliest site with remains of both religious and secular (courtly) architecture. The remains of nearly 150 shrines and temples are found in the site, on the hills near the site, and in the valley. More important, the remains of a complex hydraulic system in the royal center reveal the importance given to irrigation and water supply under Vijayanagara.

The pre-Vijayanagara temples are located mostly in the hills (Rishyamukha, Hemakūṭa, Matanga, and Malyavanta) and date from the eighth to the thirteenth centuries, with some additional structures of the Vijayanagara period. They follow the Deccan style in general, but also include the Dravida type of *sikhara*, as in the Rashtrakuta temples of the tenth century. The Shaiva temples on the Hemakūṭa hill are of the Kadmaba-Nāgara style (10th–14th centuries). They are of the *dvikūṭa* (double shrine) and *trikūṭa* (triple shrine) variety, with niches of the Kalinga, Dravida, and Nāgara types. *Phāmsana* towers (pyramids of deeply cut tiers) appear over both Hindu and Jain temples of the Deccan style on the Hemakūṭa hill. The Jain *mānastambha* (ceremonial pillar) is an additional feature. The Kalinga-style *sikhara* with the stepped pyramidal form in diminishing tiers, is also common.

Other temples in the area and its suburbs (like Kamalāpura and Ānegondi), including the Jain temples, of the period from the fourteenth to sixteenth centuries, combine the Dravida *sikhara* with the Deccan style features of the pillared *mandapa*s, with rich carvings. The entrance *gopura* with a brick and mortar superstructure and with high *prākāra* (enclosure wall) emerged as the major Vijayanagara components.

The Vijayanagara temples in Hampi represent the Karnāṭa-Andhra style in three phases. The first two phases—the early Sangama phase of 1336–1404 and the second Sangama phase of 1404–1485—have temples that are modest in scale and decoration. A highly ornate sculptured idiom emerged with the Rāmachandra temple, and predominantly Dravida architectural components appear in the elevational treatment and columns. The third phase of the Karnata-Andhra style, under the Sāḷuvas and Tuḷuvas (1480–1570) was mainly inspired by Chola models. A coordinated layout of temple complexes as seen in the remodeling of the Virūpāksha temple under Krishna Deva Rāya (r. 1509–1529), became the paradigm for all subsequent architectural developments, showing further stylistic evolution in the *mandapa*s, as in the the Mahā *mandapa* of the Viṭṭhala temple (1534). Intricate decorative schemes on the *mandapa* ceilings became the hallmark of the Vijayanagara temples.

The single *prākāra* scheme, with *gopura*s on two sides, is the most popular. Yet more elaborate temple complexes, sometimes with double shrines, huge *mandapa*s, and multiple subsidiary shrines, contained within one or more rectangular *prākāra*s, and larger and more ornate *gopura*s, continued to evolve. A unique aspect of temple planning in this era is seen at the capital, where some temple complexes (Virūpāksha, Tiruvengalanātha, and Viṭṭhala) are provided with long colonnaded streets leading up to the main *gopura*s. The use of local granite was common in temple architecture, while statues, like the gigantic Narasimha monolith (22 feet [6.7 m] high) near the Krishna temple, were shaped out of gray-green schist.

The site of Hampi may be divided into the sacred and royal complexes, the royal complex also having a number of temples in and outside the fortified area. The Virūpāksha temple, dating from the seventh century A.D., was already an important religious center and became the focus of the sacred complex, housing the tutelary deity of Vijayanagara. Renovations and additions made it into a fairly large structure by the Vijayanagara period (by the 16th century). The temple has a Garbha *griha* (sanctuary), and three antechambers, a *sabhā mandapa* or *navaranga* (pillared hall for sacred congregations, rituals and discourses)

Interior of the Junagarh Fort in Bikaner, Rajasthan. Never captured in battle, the fort encloses a series of ornate stone palaces with lattice screens. Within its brightly painted rooms the maharajas ruled from 1589 until 1949. AMIT PASRICHA.

and *mukha mandapa* (front hall), pillared cloisters, entrances, and small shrines; the main entrance is the east *gopura* of nine stories, 173 feet [52.6 m] high. It combines Dravida features in its *sikhara* and plan, but carries distinct characteristics of the Deccan style in its *navaranga* with rich carvings of Shaiva themes, while the *mukha mandapa*, or *ranga mandapa*, has thirty-eight pillars, carved with scenes from the epics Rāmāyaṇa and Mahābhārata, and ceiling paintings, of which the sage Vidyāraṇya's procession is well known. Significant additions made in the Tuḷuva period are the *maharanga mandapa* (hall with highly decorative elements) and porches, and a one-hundred-columned hall, the *gopura*, and the painting on the ceiling of the *mahā mandapa* (outer hall).

The Hazāra Rāmachandra temple in the northwest. corner of the palace complex, built in the fifteenth century under Devarāya I, has the usual plan of a square sanctuary, a Dravida style *vimāna* with a storied *sikhara*, a *sabhāmandapa*, an eight-pillared porch, a *ranga mandapa*, and two antechambers. The *sabhāmandapa* has reliefs of Vaishnava themes, the Dasavatāra, and even Shaiva deities, Gaṇesha and Mahisamardini. The temple is a veritable picture gallery, as its outer walls are richly carved with bas-reliefs of the Rāmāyaṇa and Mahābhārata. The external face of the enclosure wall contains five friezes of a unique series of royal processional scenes—elephants, horses, soldiers, dancers and musicians, with royal figures within pavilions, depicted as if watching these parades. On the inner face of the wall, between the north and east gateways, are the panels of relief carvings of the entire story of the Rāmāyaṇa, repeated again on the outer walls of the *mandapa* of the principal shrine. The east-facing goddess shrine is situated north of the main temple. Under Krishna Deva Rāya, the Kalyāṇa *mandapa*, a high *prākāra* with two entrances, east and north, were added in 1521.

The Viṭṭhala temple (originally enshrining Viṭṭhala and Rukmiṇi), built on the south bank of Tungabhadra in the fourteenth and fifteenth centuries in the Tuḷuva period, has the usual plan with a *garbha griha*, *antarāla* (vestibule), *pradakshiṇā patha* around both, *sabhā mandapa* (*navaranga*), and *mahā mandapa*. To these were added several shrines, a high-walled *prākāra*, and gateways (east, north, and south), the whole complex measuring 500 feet X 310 feet (152.5 by 94.5 meters). The spacious *mukha mandapa* has fifty-six pillars, fashioned out of large blocks of granite, each forming a distinct sculpted group. Of particular interest are the clusters of delicately shaped columns, 4 or 5 feet (about 1.5 m) across, with animal motifs interposed between them, half natural and half mythical. With molded pedestals below and massive capitals above, these closely spaced columns have a bewildering intricacy. The pillars also contain large sculptures of deities, forms of Vishnu, and musicians and dancers. The *mandapa* has three entrances and is the finest example of religious architecture in Vijayanagara. The ornate basement of this *mandapa* has friezes of horses with attendants and miniature shrines housing images of the ten incarnations of Vishnu. There are the so-called musical pillars and *yāḷi* (a mythical monster) pillars, the latter being a favorite motif. The ceiling has elaborate lotus designs and other motifs. This structure stands out as a masterpiece of both Vijayanagara architectural technique and sculptural art. The Garuda shrine in the form of a chariot in front of this temple is an interesting and unusual structure as the only *vāhana*-shrine built like a chariot.

The Achyutarāya (Tiruvengalanātha) temple in the valley at Achyutapura enshrines Venkateṣa. Built in 1534, it has the usual plan, but with two *prākāra*s and a large Kalyāṇa *mandapa*, the main *gopura*s being those on the north and west.

Hampi has the earliest known secular architecture of South India in its remains of the royal center, including the palace complex, other courtly structures, and miltiary fortifications. Some of the structures with a definite ceremonial purpose are the great platform known as the Mahānavami *dibba*, the throne platform, and the hundred-columned audience hall. These seem to have had stone basements, probably with a wooden or brick superstructure. The annual royal festival of Mahānavami symbolized the imperial status of the Vijayanagara rulers, when all their subordinates and royal functionaries assembled at the capital to pay their tributes and homage to the king. The basements of the platforms preserve interesting moldings and a series of horizontal friezes of sculptured decoration consisting of floral and geometric devices, animals (elephants), and figures of human couples and dancers. The balustrades to the steps leading to the platforms are an interesting study in animal and mythical or hybrid creatures as decorative motifs.

More important are the Islamic-styled forms. These are the square water pavilion, which has a central basin constituing a square courtyard, around which is a corridor of twenty-four vaulted bays; two octagonal fountains, which have a central basin and arched entrances and pointed arched openings; the nine-domed structure, perhaps a reception hall; and the multidomed structure overlooking the approaches to the royal center. All of these show typical Deccani-Islamic features. The most monumental of all the Islamic–styled structures is the colossal building identified as the royal stable (for elephants). Apart from arched entrances, its eleven square chambers have domes of varying designs, with a ruined two-story structure in the middle of the roof. Another celebrated monument is the Lotus Mahal, a two-story pavilion, symmetrically laid out as a series of projecting squares to create thirteen bays and a staircase tower on the northeast. The superstructure consists of nine separate towers. It has a complex but impressive facade and a varied vaulting design.

Mahābalipuram (or Māmallapuram)

Māmallapuram (Kadal Mallai or Mallai), about 37 miles (59 kilometers) south of Chennai, is the famous seaport of the Pallavas, where the early phases of Dravida architecture evolved, as seen in the rock-cut caves, monoliths, and structural temples of the seventh century A.D. Narrative sculptures of epic and Purāṇic myths of great artistic merit also make this center aesthetically the most remarkable of the South Indian sites.

The caves, carved out of rock, are found mostly in the hill area. These are called *mandapa*s, because of their plan and design, which consists of a single or multiple cells with a pillared veranda in front or a pillared hall on the three sides of the cell. Of these, the most architecturally and sculpturally interesting are: the Ādi Varāha cave, with portraits of the royal family, in addition to powerful represention of the Varāha *avatāra* of Vishnu; the Varāha cave, with episodic narratives in dynamic compositions of the stories of Vāmana-Trivikrama *avatāra* and Varāha; the triple-shrined Mahishmardani cave, with huge panels of Vishnu as Anantasayi and Durgā (Mahishamardini) in combat with Mahishāsura; the Trimūrti cave, with three shrines for Shiva, Vishnu and Brahmā; and the Krishna *mandapa*, with a large relief composition of the Govardhana scene. Many such caves carry the characteristic features of a Dravida shrine, with a facade marking the tiers with rows of miniature *kūḍu*s, *shāla*s, and *panjara*s. The pillars invariably have the characteristic lion base, with multifaceted shafts and ornamental brackets. Sculptures of Gajalakshmi also form part of the panel decoration in the caves. The iconography of the caves is a fascinating study in the evolution of various forms of Shiva and Vishnu, drawn from Purāṇic mythology and depicted as per Āgamic tradition, predominantly the *avatāra*s of Vishnu and several forms of Shiva as metaphors for power and benevolence. The Somāskanda is perhaps the most important, symbolizing royalty, as it finds a prime position on the shrine's rear wall and is a composite icon evolved under the Pallavas.

The Panchapāṇḍava *ratha*s are freestanding monolithic shrines found in one group of five, with a few more scattered in the periphery. The Gaṇesha *ratha* at the southern end has a wagon-topped *sikhara* and is one of the finest monolithic temples, with a three-story, elaborately worked roof topped by nine vase-shaped finials; it is a precursor of the later *gopura*. The huge open-air rock sculpture, often described as Arjuna's Penance in the story of Kirātārjunīya, is carved on two large boulders with a narrow fissure between. The composition is bewildering in its variety, with gods, goddesses, celestial beings, wild animals, monkeys, and elelphants, and *nāga*s (hybrid serpents combining human and serpent forms). The cleft between the rocks, through which the river water (Gaṅgā) must have been shown as descending from the hill, would suggest that the theme of the huge rock relief may well be Bhagīratha's penance, which is supported by the presence of a four-armed Shiva and an emaciated man doing penance.

The Shore temple, built by Rājasimha, has two shrines, facing east and west, with a separate perambulatory for the east-facing, larger shrine. Both shrines house the relief of the Somāskanda group. Rampant lions, characterisitic of the Rājasimha temples, and sculptured panels are found on the exterior walls. Panels depicting scenes from the history of the Pallavas, as in the Vaikuṇṭha Perumāḷ temple, also lie scattered. Between the two Shaiva shrines is the reclining form of Vishnu, in a rock-cut oblong cell.

Kānchīpuram

Once ranked as one of India's seven most sacred cities, Kānchīpuram is on the banks of the Vēghavati River. As the Pallava capital, it had wide contacts with the Southeast Asian region, transmitting Indian civilization into Thailand, Cambodia, Java, and Vietnam. A major center of Sanskrit learning and culture, Kānchīpuram had a heterogenous tradition, representing Jain, Buddhist, Shaiva, and Vaishnava religions. It became a temple town with seventy-two temples, big and small, of which the most significant are those of the Pallava, Chola, and Vijayanagara periods. Several early shrines praised by the Shaiva and Vaishnava hymnal literature were built probably of brick and mortar, and were later rebuilt in stone or merely enlarged under the Cholas and Vijayanagara rulers.

Incessant temple building in stone began under the Pallavas. The Kailāsanātha (700–728), the first royal temple built by Rājasimha (r. 690–728) in the structural mode, is the most significant, both for its impressive architecture and iconography. The *vimāna* is a unique double-walled structure with three stories and with lateral and corner shrines attached to the main shrine. The shrine is preceded by an *antarāla* and *mandapa*, and the whole temple is surrounded by a series of small shrines along the cloistered enclosure, each with a single tiered roof. All of them, like the main *garbha griha*, enshrine a Somāskanda relief, a composite icon symbolically representing the royal family. The *liṅga* could well be a later addition or, together with the Somāskanda relief on the back wall, may stand for a conceptual equation between Shiva and the royal family. Another smaller shrine was added by Rājasimha's son Mahendravarman in front of the main shrine facing east and abutting the enclosure wall. Traces of mural paintings still remain in the shrines of the cloister.

The temple is a veritable treasure house of iconography, establishing Shiva as a major Purāṇic (Brahmanical Hindu) deity, central to the Āgamic form of temple worship. Vedic deities, such as Agni, Indra, Varuṇa, and Vāyu, become subsidiary or attendant divinities (*dikpālas*) to Shiva, who is here shown as Somāskanda. A variety of Shiva's forms are sculpted on the temple walls and the shrines, while Vishnu and Brahmā are shown in a subordinate position.

The Vaikuṇṭha Perumāḷ temple, built by Nandivarman II in the eighth century, is a different architectural experience. Its *vimāna* has three vertical sanctums and a *mandapa* in front. More interesting is the covered veranda, which runs along the enclosure wall, its pillars carved with lions facing inward. This corridor has a two-tiered sculpted history of the Pallava dynasty up to the accession of Nandivarman II Pallavamalla.The *vimāna* walls have sculpted panels signifying cosmography and Vishnu's Vyuhas (emanatory forms which are repetitions or a variety of a god's own godhead), *avatāra*s, and feats as related in the Bhāgavata Purāṇa and praised by the Vaishnava saint Tirumangai Alvar.

The Varadarāja temple on the southeast of the city also dates from Pallava times, although the present structure is not older than the Chola period. The sanctum of Vishnu in the inner *prākāra* is raised on a hill-like terrace and has a two-story oblong tower of the wagon vault type. The base or terrace has a low masonry sanctum fronted with a hall to signify a cave in the "hill," enshrining the icon of Narasimha as a yogi. The "hill" is encircled with a two-story cloistered veranda with colonnades, with a Chola style gateway on the west, the open courtyard within having shrines of Lakshmī and Sakti.

In the fourteenth century, a larger open courtyard was created, with an encircling wall to enclose the bathing tank and gardens; its western gateway was topped with a seven-story tower in the late Chola–Pāṇḍya style. The Vijayanagara rulers developed that area and built structures with minute carvings and embellishments, mostly in the early sixteenth century, including shrines for a Malayāḷa goddess and for Āṇḍaḷ. The fourth courtyard has a Kalyāṇa *mandapa* of 5,974 square feet (555 square meters) on a 6.6 feet (2-meter) carved plinth. Its ninety-six monolithic pillars have geometric designs, *yāḷis*, and rampant horses. This outer enclosure has on the east a slender 164 foot (50-meter) gateway of nine stories, topped with eleven vase finials.

The Kāmākshi temple, where the Kamakoṭi Pīṭha (Yantra-Shri Chakra) is believed to have been established by Adi Shankara in the ninth century A.D., was built probably in the eleventh century amid or replacing Buddhist structures. Its disoriented layout began in the fourteenth century, with the present Shri Chakra installed in the sixteenth century, along with a four-armed Lalita Kāmākshi. The Ēkāmranātha temple on the northwest of the city has a similar history; a small shrine of Pallava times was renovated and elaborated with several *prākāra*s and gateways under the Chola and Vijayanagara rulers.

Tanjāvūr

Tanjāvūr, 200 miles (322 kilometers) southwest of Chennai, on the southern bank of Vaḍāvāṟu, a distributary of the Veṇṇāṟu (Kaveri delta), was the capital of the Cholas, the Nayakas, and the Marāthas. The Brihadīshvara (Rājarājeshvara) temple complex is situated within the Sivaganaga "litle fort," surrounded by a moat on the west, north, and east, and the Grand Anicut (dam) canal on the south. The total area of the Sivaganga fort is over 45 acres (nearly 18 hectares), of which the temple itself covers 7 acres (2.85 hectares).

The Tanjāvūr temple is a stupendous imperial project, which marks the apogee of the Dravida style of architecture. The plan follows a ratio of 1:2 (790 feet east to west and 395 feet north to south), with a low two-story cloistered structure against the outer walls. This inner *prākāra* is further enclosed by another surrounding wall, which in turn is enclosed by a vast brick fortification known as the Sivaganga "little fort." Its imposing *vimāna* of thirteen tiers, rising to a height of over 200 feet (61 m), is a *sāndhāra prāsāda*, or double-walled structure, with a *māḍakkoyil*, a shrine on the terrace. The inner ambulatory between the two walls is well known for its Chola frescoes representing stories of the *bhakti* saints and iconographic forms of Shiva, including Naṭarāja, Tripuraāntaka, Dakshiṇamūrti, and others. The first story of the *vimāna* has a series of sculptures representing Shiva in various Bharata Natya poses.

In alignmant with the shrine are the *ardha mandapa* (front hall) with huge Dvārapālaka (doorkeeper of the god) images usually represented on either side of the entrances of the shrine, a *mahā mandapa*, and an entrance porch, all with plain pillars and no interior decoration. The exterior of the *vimāna* and the aligned structures are organized into niches flanked by pilasters, with different forms of Shiva and other deities (Tripuraāntaka occupying a special position, repeated on the second tier of the *vimāna* walls). The temple's iconographic program marks the most creative period in Chola art and in South Indian iconography.

The Rājarājeshvara represents a ceremonial complex, symbolizing Chola sovereignty through cosmic structures. The various aspects of the temple, including its architecture, sculpture, painting, and inscriptions, collectively provide an integrated view of this synthesising role. The temple had an impressive economic outreach under the Cholas. The architecture of the temple was planned and designed to represent the cosmos, in keeping with the Chola ideology, which equated the temple with the cosmos at one level and with territory at another level. Well conceived and majestic, the temple's architecture is the product of an imperial vision. The entire temple complex was designed to achieve a perfect balance between architecture and sculpture. The temple is conceived of as Dakshiṇamēru, or the axis of the universe, while the *dikpala* shrines, located at the cardinal points of the pillared cloister running on all four sides of the temple courtyard, complete its cosmic symbolism.

Chidambaram

Unique among the southern Dravida style temples, the Chidambaram Naṭarāja temple is a rare example of the coexistence of two shrines dedicated to both Shiva and Vishnu in a single (central) *prākāra* with a common *dvajastambha* (pillar which carries the god's flag). It developed into a major Shaiva pilgrimage center and as the symbol for the whole Shaiva community under the royal patronage of the Cholas from the tenth century, with Vishnu receding into the background.

Chidambaram (also known as Tillai, Perumbaṟṟappuliyūr, Puliyuṛ, and Chambalam) is the center for the worship of Naṭarāja, king of dancers, the Sabhanayaka. In Chidambaram, Shiva performed the cosmic dance

Gol Gumbad Mausoleum. Built in 1656, the Gol Gumbad in Bijapur, Karnataka. The acoustical system within this mausoleum (tomb of Mohammad Adil Shah) is no minor feat and it is thus often referred to as the "Whispering Dome." CLAIRE ARNI / FOTOMEDIA.

(*ānanda tāṇḍava*) to celebrate his victory over the ritualistic ascetics, representing the *panchakrityas* of creating, preserving, and destroying the visible universe. Among the five elements—earth, water, fire, wind, and ether—represented by the *linga*, the *ākasha* (ether) is manifest in Chidambaram's *linga* and hence invisible.

The temple, in fact, consists of five *sabhās* located in different *prākāras*. In the first is located the Chit *sabhā*, or Naṭarāja shrine, enshrining the *akasa linga* (ether), which is invisible, hence the Cidambara *rahasya* is represented by a string of *vilva* petals in gold, hung over the *prabhā*, with a black curtain of *ajnāna* over it. The shrine is believed to have been gilded by Pallava, Chola, and Pāṇḍya rulers. The Chit *sabhā* has wooden walls, its roof being supported by twenty-eight freestanding wooden pillars. The exterior of the Chit *sabhā* has a double colonnade of round columns of highly polished black stone. The original Tiru Mūlasthāna (main) shrine of Naṭarāja, facing east, is located in the second *prākāra* and is of the same style. This became secondary at the time of the temple's enlargement, to six times its original size under Kulottunga I (r. 1070–1112) and his successors.

The Edirambalam (Kanaka *sabhā*) was built opposite the Naṭarāja shrine within the first enclosure. The Kanaka *sabhā*, opposite the *dvajastambha*, is built in the form of a *tērkkoyil*, or wheeled chariot. The roof of the Kanaka *sabhā* is supported by eighteen wooden pillars, with copper-plated wooden doors between the pillars. They have rectangular, curvilinear roofs resembling that of the Draupadi *ratha* at Māmallapuram. The Chit *sabhā*, Kanaka *sabhā*, and Vishnu shrine of Govindarāja are the principal sanctums of the innermost enclosure.

The Deva *sabhā* is located within the second enclosure, where the *dīkshitars* who control the temple's worship and administration meet. In the second enclosure are located the shrines of the Vaishnava goddess Puṇḍarika Nacchiyār. The western gateway of this enclosure is called the Akaḷankan Tiruvāsal of Vikrama Chola.

The Raja *sabhā*, the thousand-pillared hall in the third *prākāra*, where the first exposition of the hagiographical work, the Periya Purāṇam, was held under Kulottunga II, is one of the most striking monuments in the temple. Measuring 194 feet by 331 feet (59 meters by 101 meters), it has huge pillars and brick vaulting with radiating arches. The *abhisheka* ceremony of Naṭarāja and Shivakāmasundari, the culminating session of the two great festivals, is held here. The hundred-pillared hall is is another *mandapa* located in this enclosure.

Under Vijayanagara, considerable remodeling occurred in the temple structure and administrative control with the restoration of the worship of Govindarāja. The four *gopuras*, each 138 feet (42 meters) high, have granite bases and brick and mortar superstructures. The western is the oldest, started by Vikrama Chola and completed by Kulottunga II (12th century). The southern *gopura* is of the period of Kopperunjinga and Sundara Pāṇḍya (13th century) The *gopura* on the north is of the period of Kulottunga II (12th century), of which the superstructure was begun by Krishna Deva Rāya and completed by Achyuta Deva. Beyond the *gopuras* are coconut groves and flower gardens. The *gopuras* are richly sculpted with forms of Shiva, the Navagrahas, and other celestial beings and sages, like Patanjali and Vyāghrapāda. Dance poses based on the *Nātya Shāstra* are carved on the doorways of each *gopura*, with labels in Grantha script.

Madurai

Madurai, on the Vaigai river, is one of the oldest Tamil cities, dating from the early centuries A.D. as the political center of the Pāṇḍyas down to medieval times, when Nayaka rule was established. It is also known as Tiru Ālavāy in Shaiva religious literature. The central core of the city was constructed mostly under the Nayakas, with the Mīnākshi temple as its focus. Mīnākshi is believed to be a Pāṇḍyan queen who married Shiva, from whom the Pāṇḍyas descended. Following the classical Hindu design of a square *mandala*, a grid with concentric squares, the temple covers a vast rectangular area, 843 feet by 787 feet (257 meters by 240 meters).

Built in three periods—the Pāṇḍya, Vijayanagara, and Madurai Nayaka—Pāṇḍya survivals of the temple's structures are few in number. The temple is a classic example of the Vijayanagara–Nayaka style. Its double shrine, large pillared halls, twelve towered gateways and large tank, and the layout and location of different deities are defined by a sacred architecture that is too complex to be described here. Under the Nayakas, it developed into a huge temple complex, especially under Tirumala Nayaka, the great builder, and Vīrappa Nayaka (r. 1572–1593), when significant additions were made.

The goddess Mīnākshi's special prominence is a later development of the fourteenth century, with Mīnākshi emerging as the chief deity, after the Muslim invasions of 1310; the temple's restoration changed the focus of the temple to the goddess. Yet Sundareshvara, the god of the main shrine in the first *prākāra*, is still the main deity, the sovereign at the center, represented as a *liṅga* in the shrine but as a Somāskanda image for procession. All ritual activity centers around the relationship between Mīnākshi and Sundara. The royalty of the deities is particularly striking, as they are identified as the Pāṇḍyan queen and king, with the city the microcosmic image of the kingdom and the universe, in a symbolic representation of Madurai as a sacred royal space.

The present extent of the temple is 720–729 feet north to south (219–222 m), and 834–852 feet (254–260 m) east to west. It has three major *prākāras* and a double shrine for the god and the goddess. The shrines are small Dravida style *vimānas* with the usual *mandapas* in alignment, but it is in the horizontal elaboration, through *mandapas* and *prākāras* with *gopuras*, that the architectural importance of the temple lies. The first *prākāra*, measuring 250 feet by 150 feet (76 m x 46 m), has the Sundaresvara shrine, called the Indra *vimāna*, followed by a *mahā mandapa* and *mukha mandapa*. Images of Shiva in various forms, along with eight *dikpāla* figures and stucco panels of the *Tiruviḷaiyāḍal Purāṇam* (divine sports of Shiva) on the *mahā mandapa* walls, are the decorative and iconographic features of the Shiva shrine.

The second *prākāra*, measuring 420 feet by 320 feet (128 m x 98 m), has the Mīnākshi shrine, with its *ardha mandapa* and Shakti images in the niches, datable to the first half of the fifteenth century. The most remarkable of the structures here is the Golden Lily (*poṟṟāmarai*) tank east of the Amman (goddess) shrine, with several *mandapas* around the tank and four *gopuras* in the outer walls. The north and east walls of the Chitra *mandapa* have murals, modern (post-seventeenth century) paintings of the sixty-four *lilas* of the *Tiruviḷaiyāḍal Purāṇam*. The most ornamental Kiḷikaṭṭi *mandapa*, in front of the *gopura* of the goddess shrine, is a single corridor with richly carved pillars, statues of various deities, and painted ceilings. The Mandapa Nayaka *mandapa*, a hundred-pillared hall, has a Sabhāpati (Naṭarāja) shrine. Stucco figuress of Tirumala Nāyaka and his queen are found in the northeast corner.

The second *prākāra* has several *mandapas*, including the Kalyāṇa, or Kolu *mandapa* for the Navaratri festival and a thousand-pillared hall. This hall, built under Vīrappa Nayakain 1572, is a huge edifice (240 ft. x 250 ft., or 73 m x 76 m) with a Sabhāpati (Naṭarāja) shrine and beautifully carved icons. The Kambattaḍi *mandapa* in front has a Nandi shrine of Vijayanagara style and monolithic pillars with icons. Images of the sixty-three Shaiva saints are found in the southeast corner. Other shrines include that of the Navagraha within the nave of the *mandapa*. In the Vijayanagara style *mandapas* of the sixteenth and seventeenth centuries, apart from a few "musical" pillars, the *yāḷi* and equestrian pillars are favored. The characteristic Vijayanagara pillars, with groups of slender columnettes, are absent in Madurai. Several shrines (Īshvarams) exist in the first two *prākāra*s, dedicated to Vigneshvara and to Kumāra or Subrahmaṇya. There are a number of subsidiary shrines to folk deities, such as Karuppaṇṇa Svāmi and Madurai Vīran, in the outer *prākāra*.

The Madurai temple has both styles of *gopura*s, the straight-edged pyramid and the more ornate style with a concave outline. The outer *gopura*s are of stone but with brick and stucco superstructures. All have nine stories, with a height of 150 feet (46 m) each. The high *gopura*s date from the late twelfth and early thirteenth centuries (east), fourteenth century (west), and latter half of the sixteenth century (south), with later Vijayanagara and Nayaka characteristics. The superstructures are straight-edged pyramids; the south *gopura* near the Golden Lily tank, however, has a concave sweeping curve, more elegant than the rest.

Axially in front of the east *gopura* is the Pudu *mandapa* (330 ft. x 105 ft., or 101 m x 32 m) built by Tirumala Nayaka (r. 1626–1633), and remains in an unfinished stage. The Rāya *gopura*, east of the Pudu *mandapa*, nearly twice the size of the east *gopura*, a stupendous structure, is the largest but is also incomplete. Its origin is dated to the time of Tirumala Nayaka, and it has monolithic lion-based pillars 50 feet (15 m) high. This *mandapa* is highly ornate, with massive carvings and large-scale ornamentation on the jambs. There are also reliefs of Tirumala Nayaka and his queen in the Madura style. There are several other *gopura*s, built in the period from the thirteenth to the sixteenth centuries, making a total of twelve *gopura*s in the Mīnākshi temple.

The twelve-day Chittirai festival celebrates Mīnākshi's conquest of the world, or Digvijaya, with her coronation on the eleventh day. On the ninth day, the defeat of the goddess by Sundara in battle and their subsequent wedding transforms a warrior queen into a gracious bride. Involvement of Vishnu as Kaḷḷaḷagar at Aḷagarkoyil and Subrahmaṇya from Tirupparankuṇṛam in the marriage in Madurai forms part of the festival. The city is ritually represented as being much more closely integrated with its surrounding area. The entire city and the region around it, between Alagarkoil to the northeast and Tirupparankuṇṛam in the southwest, become one vast sacred royal space, whose focal point is the Mīnākshi temple itself.

R. Champakalakshmi

See also **Chola Dynasty; Temple Types (Styles) of India**

BIBLIOGRAPHY

Devakunjari, D. *Madurai through the Ages.* Chennai: Society for Architecture, History and Archaeology, 1979.

Doshi, Sarayu, ed. *Homage to Sravana* Beḷgoḷa. Mumbai: Marg, 1981.

Foekemo, Genard. *Hoysaḷa Architecture: Medieval Temples of Southern Karnataka during Hoysaḷa Rule.* New Delhi: Books and Books, 1994.

Harle, James C. *Temple Gateways in South India. The Architecture and Iconography of the Chidambaram Gopuras.* Oxford: Bruno Cassirer, 1963.

Maity, S. K. *Masterpieces of Hoysaḷa Art.* Mumbai: Taraporevala, 1978.

Michell, George. *The Vijayanagara Courtly Style.* New Delhi: Manohar, 1992.

———. *Paṭṭadakal: Monumental Legacy.* New Delhi: Oxford University Press, 2002.

Michell, George, ed. *Temple Towns of Tamil Nadu.* Mumbai: Marg, 1993.

Natarajan, B. *The City of the Cosmic Dance.* New Delhi: Orient Longman, 1974.

Pichard, Pierre. *Tanjāvūr Bṛhadisvara: An Architectural Study.* New Delhi: Indira Gandhi National Centre for the Arts, 1995.

Settar, S. *Sravana* Beḷgoḷa. Dharwad: Ruvari, 1981.

Suresh, K. M. *Temples of Hampi and Its Environs.* Delhi: Bharatiya Kala Prakashan, 2003.

WESTERN INDIA

Gujarat and Rajasthan, which share a cultural and artistic identity, at the same time possess individual stylistic idioms. The combined geographical extent of the states is over 200,000 square miles (518, 000 sq. km).

Political History

Early Hindu kingdoms. The medieval period in western India witnessed the gradual disappearance of the early ruling dynasties and the emergence and consolidation of powerful new Hindu kingdoms. Some of these, like the Pratiharas, the Chaulukyas, and the Chahamanas, attained imperial status; other dynasties, such as the Grahapatis, the Mauryas, and the Guhilas, remained mere provincial potentates.

Harichandra, the progenitor of the Mandor branch of the Pratiharas, was a Brahman. His descendant Nagabhata, in the seventh century, shifted his capital to Medantaka-Merta. The Pratiharas ruled over northern Gujarat up to the first quarter of the tenth century, when the Rashtrakutas of the Deccan extended their political influence north.

Pratihara Vatsaraja (reigned c. 775–800) was a powerful monarch who conquered both Bhillamala in modern southwestern Rajasthan, and Malwa, in central and eastern Rajasthan. Vatsaraja was embroiled in the triangular struggles for power among the Pratiharas, the Deccani

Rashtrakutas, and the Bengali Palas. He lost power to the Rashtrakutas, but his son and successor Nagabhata II (r. c. 815–833) regained the lost fortunes of the dynasty.

Nagabhata II's powerful successor, Bhoja I (c. 836–c. 890), was a strong ruler. During his long reign of over fifty years, he regained control over Gujarat and central and eastern Rajasthan. His successors were Mahendrapala and Mahipala. The Pratiharas, all great patrons of the arts and architecture, disappeared after the third quarter of the tenth century.

The Chaulukyas. The Chaulukyas, also known as Solankis, of Gujarat, ruled in 941 over Anhilwad Patan, eventually rising to the status of an imperial power. The dynasty continued to rule over all of Gujarat until 1220. The dynasty's founder, Mularaja (r. 942–997), and his successors, Chamundaraja (r. 997–1010), Durlabharaja (r. 1010–1022), Bhimadeva I (r. 1022–1066), Karnadeva (r. 1066–1094), Siddharaja Jayasimha (r. 1094–1144), Kumarapala (r. 1144–1174) and Bhimadeva II (r. 1174–1242), had hundreds of enduring stone religious monuments, temples, monasteries, tanks, and reservoirs constructed. The temples at Modhera, Patan, Sidhpur, and Prabhas Patan, and the reservoirs or wells at Anhilwad Patan are all Chaulukya constructions.

The Chahamanas. In both Rajasthan and Gujarat, the eighth century saw powerful kings and prolific artistic activity, encouraged by the Guhilas of Mewar and the Pratiharas of Marwar, particularly Jabalipura or Jalor, but also those of Mandor and Medta. In Mewar the Grahapati king Manabhanga founded two imposing monuments on Chittor hill, now known under the names of the Kalikamata and Kumbhashyama.

In the tenth century, the Chahamanas, whose founder Vasudeva was a Brahman, succeeded the Pratiharas in the Marwar region. They encouraged and supported artistic enterprises, especially two of their maharajas, Simharaja (r. 944–971) and Vigraharaja II (r. 971–998). Another Chahamana dynasty was independently established at Nadol, under Lakshmanaraja, who also supported architectural projects throughout the region.

The Guhilas shifted their capital from Chittor to Ahar, a modern suburb of Udaipur, in the tenth century. Nagda, 15 miles (24 km) to the north, was also an important center of Chahamana art activity. The period between the rule of Allata (c. 950) and Shaktikumara (980) witnessed the construction of many stone monuments in Mewar.

Maha-Gurjara, Maha-Maru, Surashtra, and Maru-Gurjara Styles

The exact limits of the architectural and sculptural styles of Rajasthan and Gujarat are from Parnagar in district Barmer of Rajasthan in the north to Parol near Mumbai in the south, and from Osian and Kiradu in the west to Atru in the east.

Stone Sculpture, Vishnu. Stone relief of Vishnu (as the dwarf avatar of Vamana), dating to fifth-century Maharashtra. NATIONAL MUSEUM / FOTOMEDIA.

Medieval North Indian temple styles may be classified into four geographical varieties: the eastern, the central, the northern or upper India, and the western. Of these, the western variety was of the longest duration and was the most prolific; also called the Maru-Gujara, this style appeared around the beginning of the eleventh century.

The styles of western India that predate the appearance of the Maru-Gurjara style may be divided into the following three schools: the Maha-Maru, the style of Rajasthan; the Maha-Gurjara style of northern Gujarat, the northern part of the Saurashtra peninsula, Cutch, and southern Rajasthan; and the Surashtra style, which was limited to the southern part of the Saurashtra peninsula of Gujarat.

The Maha-Maru style was essentially a homogenous style, though it expressed itself through two schools, the Maru-Sapadalaksha in the north and the Medapata-Uparamala in the east. From the early eighth century—when the Maha-Maru began its independent course after the post-Gupta phase—to the end of the tenth century, when it merged into the Maru-Gurjara, three phases can be detected in its evolution.

The first phase lasted from the early eighth to the mid-ninth century; the second from mid-ninth to the mid-tenth; and the third phase can be placed in the second half of the tenth century.

The Maha-Maru school is reflected in many temples. The Kumbhashyama temple at Chittorgarh, built between 644 and 743 by the Grahapati dynasty's Raja Manabhanga, is the earliest example. Other securely dated monuments are the Mahavira temple at Osian, constructed during the reign of the Pratihara king Vatsaraja (r. 777–808), and the Vishnu temple at Buchkala, from the reign of his son Nagabhata II in 815. Similarly, an inscription dated between 956 and 973 provides the date for the Harshanatha temple at Sikar.

The temples of the early phase normally stand on a platform, and have a single projection. Their walls are decorated with sculptures of the divine regents of the quarters (Dikpalas) and other gods of the Hindu or Jain pantheon. The images are crowned by tall pediments. The superstructure (*shikhara*) has a meshwork of creepers, a distinguishing feature. The door frames are richly decorated, with motifs that include *naga* pairs (*nagashakha*), pilasters with vases, foliage above and carved panels below, and amorous couples embracing. On the walls and on the other parts of the structures a rich variety of figures and motifs are represented.

The Medapata-Uparamala branch of the Maha-Maru style saw the production of such large temples as the Kalikamata and Kumbhashyama at Chittorgarh (later renovated extensively in the fifteenth century). The Maha-Gurjara style, with its three branches of Anarta, Arbuda, and lower Medapata, enjoyed an almost unbroken continuity between the second half of the eighth century until about the end of the tenth. Among the securely dated temples are the Ambika temple at Jagat (961) and the Lakulisha temple at Eklingji (972).

The earliest shrines of the Maha-Gurjara style belong to its Anarta variety and are located at Roda. These early temples are rather plain when compared to contemporary Maha-Maru constructions. They have *shikhara*s with meshwork patterns. In contrast to Maha-Maru shrines, Maha-Gurjara monuments have plain walls and a solitary niche on the main offset, with a short pediment. Most often there is no hall in front but only a short wall on two pillars, and a roof of the stepped pyramid type known as *phamsana*. The door frames of Maha-Gurjara temples are lavishly decorated. They may have three or five jambs, with floral bands, jewel bands, *vyala*s (mythical animals) and decorated pilasters. The best examples of the Maha-Gurjara style are from the second half of the tenth century, and their walls display the full range of statuary, with divine images, *apsara*s (nymphs), *gandharva*s (heavenly musicians), *vidyadhara*s (supernatural beings possessing magical powers), and *vyala*s. Their *shikhara*s are arranged in multiples around the central spine, with excellent meshwork on the surface.

The merger of two of the three styles, Maha-Gurjara and Maha-Maru, in the eleventh century resulted in a new style whose sway extended over nearly all of Rajasthan and Gujarat up to the end of the thirteenth century. The form of the Maru-Gurjara temple is not very dissimilar to any other example of contemporary date from anywhere in North India. It is in the organization of its component elements and in the details of its decoration and sculpture that a Maru-Gurjara temple is distinctive.

Temples and Sculptures

The Shitaleshvara temple, Jhalrapatan. The Shiva temple of 689, known as the Shitaleshvara (Lord of Shitala, the goddess of smallpox), is the earliest securely dated standing temple in western India. An inscription recording the name of Raja Durggagana was found associated with the temple. Rather simple and heavy in form, the Shitaleshvara consists of a sanctum and a frontal chamber, to which a pillared hall was added in the tenth century. The walls of the sanctum have prominent projections and pilasters, elaborately carved with bold floral designs and other motifs. The superstructure is no longer preserved.

The Shitaleshvara is one of a small but significant group of monuments situated within a limited area in this part of Mewar-Rajasthan, the others being the Kalikamata and Kumbhashyama, two shrines at Menal, one at Joganiamata nearby, and an as yet unpublished ruined shrine at Khor, near Chittorgarh. All these shrines have the features of the styles of Malwa and Mewar, and all are datable to the late seventh or early eighth centuries. Some sculptures from the site have been preserved in the local museum. Images of seven goddesses from this site are housed in a small chamber near the Shitaleshvara. From their attributes—their total nudity, the winnowing fans, brooms and daggers in their hands, a donkey mount for at least some of them—they could be the images of Shitala, the goddess of smallpox. Since Shiva here is Shitaleshvara, or the "lord of the goddess of smallpox," the presence of her representations, of the same date as Shiva's temple, is not unusual.

Abhaneri. Ancient Abhanagari, "city of splendor," about 60 miles (96 km) to the east of Jaipur, has preserved two very significant monuments of the eighth century, of the

Chahamana period, even though both have suffered much damage. The Vishnu temple is now standing only up to the walls, as are parts of the vast terrace on which it stood. The plinth moldings have twelve panels with scenes of royalty—princes with beautiful female companions—in varied romantic situations, and the style of carving is among the most charming of all Indian art.

The large square-shaped stepped tank, known as the Chand Baodi, was also adorned with beautiful carvings. It was renovated during the Rajput period, when arched pavilions typical of the time were built. A large number of sculptures from the tank's shrine and the great Vishnu temple are stored in the compound of the tank.

Osian. Before the two styles of architecture, the Maha-Gurjara and the Maha-Maru, merged to form the pan-western Indian style of Maru-Gurjara in the early eleventh century, the two individual parent styles did occasionally encroach upon each other's territory. Osian was, however, one center where the Maha-Maru style retained its pristine purity.

The many temples at Osian, near Jodhpur, are datable to a period from the eighth to the eleventh century, and are scattered all around the small town. The two Harihara temples (numbers 1 and 2), the two Surya temples (numbers 2 and 3), and a tank for sacred water are the earliest monuments here, and are all datable to the eighth century. Fine sculptures of Hindu gods, such as Vishnu's Narasimha (Man-Lion) incarnation, in which he killed a demon king, and Trivikrama (Three-Strike) incarnations, in which he "measured" the entire universe in just three steps, adorn the walls of Harihara 2. Surya 3 has sculptures of Gaṇesha and the Sun god, Durgā, in its sanctum walls. Many of the temples have lost their superstructure, but where they are intact, they are the elegantly curving northern Indian *shikharas*.

To the Jains, Osian's importance rests in the fact that the prominent Ukeshvala sect originated here, and the earliest Jain temple of western India, dedicated to the Tīrthānkara Mahāvīra, was built here. The Mahāvīra temple, together with its adjuncts, was built during the reign of the Pratihara ruler Vatsaraja, while other structural parts were added in the tenth century.

Roda. Just as Osian possesses the perfect examples of early Maha-Maru architecture, and was never influenced by any Maha-Gurjara elements, Roda in Gujarat is the site that displays the Maha-Gurjara idiom in its clearest form, without any alloy from the Maru. The seven temples here are small, having only a sanctum fronted by a porch. The walls, sometimes with single central offsets, the columns, and the *shikhara* all exhibit the pure Maha-Gurjara elements. The temples, as well as a tank at the site, have been dated to the eighth century.

Harshagiri. The temple of Shiva Harshanatha (Lord of Joy) on the Harshagiri hill, is worth noting, especially for its sculptural art, even though it has suffered great damage. The site is a strikingly beautiful plateau, on a high hill some 8 miles (13 km) to the south of Sikar in northern Rajasthan. The temple possesses a sanctum, whose floor is about 2 feet (.6 m) lower than the floor of the hall, an antechamber, a hall, a porch, and a separate pavilion for a Nandi (Shiva's "bull" *vahana*) image. Parts of the temple were reerected haphazardly in the thirteenth century and later; its superstructure has vanished entirely. The surviving sculptures, however—one of Pārvatī performing her penance of the "five fires," flanked by a dozen young maidens, and a Lingodbhava Shiva preserved in the museum at Jaipur—testify to the high standards of the sculptural art. On the basis of an inscription of 956, the Harshanatha has been ascribed to the period of the Chahamana raja Simharaja I. The beautiful columns, architraves, and sculptures collected from the site have been transferred to the town of Sikar at the foot of the hill, where they form the nucleus of a local museum.

Baroli. A group of nine temples of the Maha-Maru style were built at Baroli, 30 miles (48 km) southwest of Kota in eastern Rajasthan, during the first half of the tenth century. They are all of modest size, and of a homogeneous style, with a shrine fronted by a narrow chamber, to which is attached a porch. They are dedicated to Shiva, Vishnu, the Devi Mahishasuramardini ("Mother Goddess, destroyer of the Buffalo demon"), and elephant-headed Gaṇesha. Only the Ghateshvara temple has large sculptures in the niches of its walls, the walls of all the other temples being quite plain.

The Maheshamurti aspect of Shiva in the temple dedicated to him is particularly interesting. Maheshamurti, or Shiva as "the Great Lord," is that aspect in which the totality of his being is revealed, including his tranquil central face, with a fierce demon (Aghora) face on one side, complemented by a female or Mother Goddess (Uma) face on the other. Shiva as the Great Lord was a favorite theme in southern Rajasthan's art. At Baroli his bust is 6 feet (1.8 m) high and equally wide; it is severely damaged, but even these mutilated Aghora and Uma faces are very expressive of Shiva's contrasting characters. What is equally interesting is that the sculpture is not independently carved and installed in the shrine; rather, the inner face of the slabs forming the back wall of the shrine is carved with Shiva's form, with the outer faces forming the wall's surface.

Shiva as Gajasurasamharamurti ("Slayer of the Elephant Demon") on the south wall of the Ghateshvara temple is an especially spirited image, standing diagonally in the rectangular niche. The human busts, complete with flailing arms, which form his garland, create a macabre effect. On the other hand, the *apsara* clinging to a column of the temple has an alluring look.

Jagat. The village of Jagat is situated 40 miles (64 km) to the south of Udaipur, where there is a well-preserved temple of goddess Ambika. The temple stands in a large enclosure with an entrance structure in the east, and consists of the sanctum, a closed hall, and also a small structure for collecting bathing water. On the three sides on the walls at the level of the plinth there are small but deep niches, which house the images of Devi Mahishamardini ("Mother Goddess destroyer of the Buffalo demon"). On either side on the walls, following a fixed pattern, are the regents of the four directions, celestial nymphs, and mythical animals. A multiturreted *shikhara* crowns the sanctum. An inscription helps to fix the date at 961.

Eklingji. About 15 miles (24 km) to the north of Udaipur is a group of temples at a site called Eklingji. The Guhila dynasty of Mewar held Shiva Lakulisha as especially sacred, and his temple at Eklingji is the one where Mewar's kings worshiped. This is a simple shrine of the third quarter of the tenth century, comprising a sanctum, a narrow chamber, and a hall. The sanctum has a superstructure with many turrets. On the walls of the sanctum are sculptures relevant to its Shaiva dedication.

Nagda. 15 miles (24 km) to the north of Udaipur, close to Eklingji, are the twin temples of Vishnu, with their own subshrines known as the Sas-Bahu, or "Mother-in-Law's" and "Daughter-in-Law's" temples. It is a late tenth century temple of the type known as *panchayatana*, with Vishnu enshrined in the main temple, and with four smaller corner shrines dedicated to four lesser Hindu divinities. The whole complex is built on a high platform, situated in the middle of much greenery, and is fronted by an ornamental arched entrance gateway. The name of the site derives from *nagadraha* (snake pool), inspired by the nearby lake.

Toos. About 20 miles (32 km) to the east of Udaipur on the road to Chittorgarh is a mid-tenth century temple of the Sun god Surya in the village of Toos. Built in the Mewar idiom of the Maha-Gurjara style, the temple has lost its original superstructure (the present one is much later); it has a sanctum fronted by a narrow passage and a hall with three entrances on the east, south, and north. The outer walls have a repertory of sculptures: seated figures of Surya in the wall niches, standing Surya on the outer walls of the passage in front of the sanctum, and the regents of the four directions, *apsaras*, and mythical animals in their allotted places on the offsets and recesses.

Modhera. Modhera in northern Gujarat can be said to occupy the same position in western India that Khajuraho does in central India. It is the finest example of a mature temple of the Maru-Gurjara style. The temple is part of a large complex comprising a tank with small shrines punctuating the landings on the steps, a dancing hall, and an ornate entrance archway. There are other shrines within the premises as well, as also an old stepped well to the northeast of the temple complex.

The temple, known since the nineteenth century as the Sun temple, consists of a closed hall in front and a shrine at the rear, connected by means of a narrow passage. Curiously, the floor of the shrine is no less than 12 feet (3.6 m) below the floor of the hall, a phenomenon that has never yet been satisfactorily understood. The statuary on the outer walls of the temple neatly divides itself into two groups: solar and Shaiva; on the walls of the shrine are the sculptures of the twelve Adityas, or solar gods, and on the hall's walls are twelve images of Gauris, or Shaiva goddesses. Inside the temple, however, the solar element predominates, but on the shrine doorway there is an image of Shiva presiding over the lintel. The Solanki kings under whose patronage the complex at Modhera was built were devotees of Shiva. Ancient Hinduism also has a syncretic god, who is a blend of Shiva and the Sun god Surya, called Martanda-Bhairava. It is more likely that the temple at Modhera was dedicated to this combined deity rather than to Surya alone.

Vimala Vasahi, Mount Abu. Jain temples were also erected during the reign of Bhima I. The beautiful Adinatha temple on Mount Abu was one of them. It was built by Vimala, a minister at the court of Bhima, and is therefore commonly known as the Vimala Vasahi. The original structure, founded in 1033, consists of a sanctum, a closed hall, and another hall known as the *trikamandapa*; to this nucleus other structural members were added in the twelfth century. The Vimala Vasahi is justly famous for its minutely carved columns and its ceilings, which are covered with semidivine female figures and other delicately carved decorative friezes.

The Mahavira temple, Sewadi. Temples of the style known as the Bhumija were principally built in Malwa, or central India. A variety of the North Indian Nagara style, the Bhumija is distinguished by the form of its *shikhara*, which has a central mesh running from base to finial on all its four sides, with a *chaitya* (decorative trifoliate dormer window) at the base. The quadrants between the tall mesh are filled with miniature *shikhara* models resting on columns, known as *kutastambhas* or *stambhakutas* of five to seven stories in three to five horizontal rows. The base of the frontal mesh always has a large antefix, which displays an image of the god enshrined within the sanctum. The Mahavira temple at Sewadi has a well-proportional *shikhara* of bricks with three vertical and six horizontal rows of miniature *stambhakutas*.

Menal. Other temples of this Bhumija class in Rajasthan are much later, of the Chahamana period. The

Mahanaleshvara ("Shiva the Lord of the Gorge") is so called because it is built facing a 100 (30.5 m)-foot-deep gorge and a waterfall. Its tall *shikhara* has four busts of Shiva at the top of its central *latas* (creepers). The walls of the *rangamandapa* (pillared hall) and the shrine have the usual complement of sculptures, regents of the four quarters, *apsaras*, and divinities of the Hindu pantheon, but they are rather stereotyped and lack the verve of earlier sculpture.

Bijolia. A few miles from Menal is another group of temples at Bijolia. The Undeshvara is so named because the *liṅga* of Shiva is here installed some 10 or 12 feet (3–3.6 m) below the floor of the hall; probably it was a *svayambhu liṅga* (self-manifested *liṅga*), over which the shrine was erected. The temple has a stellate plan; it has a *shikhara* that is *navabhauma* (having 9 stories). The *shukanasa* antefixes at the bases of the *latas* have sculptures of Shiva. It can be dated to the first half of the twelfth century.

Mahāvīra temple, Kumbhariya. If the Vimala Vasahi was built on Mount Abu in 1032, in the early years of the reign of Bhima I, the Mahāvīra temple at Kumbhariya was built toward its end, in 1062. It was planned on an ambitious scale, with a sanctum, a closed hall, several other halls, and several small nichelike shrines, all standing on a high platform. The interior columns, brackets, ceilings—indeed, all available surfaces—display carvings that have an almost lapidary quality, more intricate even than the Vimala Vasahi, which has rarely been equaled.

Ranakpur. The complex of Jain temples at Ranakpur built in the fifteenth century is a virtual temple town. Measuring over 300 feet by 300 feet (91.5 m x 91.5 m), it possesses four smaller shrines and several pillared halls surrounding the central shrine in honor of Adinatha, the first Jain Tīrthānkara. A high terrace with entrances on all four sides accommodates the central shrine of Adinatha, with a multiturreted tower and with pillared halls on the four sides. The corner shrines are smaller, with simpler superstructures. Hundreds of tall and slender columns and an infinite variety of delicately carved ceilings made this complex a marvel of architectural planning.

Shatrunjay. This temple town, situated on a high hill near Palitana in Gujarat's Saurashtra peninsula, has a large number of Jain temples datable from the sixteenth to the nineteenth centuries. Monuments of a still earlier period must have existed at one time; but no trace has survived. The Jains hold this entire hill in great reverence because of its associations with their first Tirthankara Adinatha, and it remains one of their most sacred pilgrimage centers. Its Adinatha temple of the sixteenth century, with its two-storied hall and complex superstructure, has a towering statue of Adinatha in its sanctum.

The Tower of Victory, Chittorgarh.

Maharana Kumbhakarna, better known as Kumbha, erected this monument on the Chittor hill in the second half of the fifteenth century. Conceived as a hollow column, the tower is about 120 feet (36.6 m) high and is divided into nine stories. Its surfaces are adorned with hundreds of sculptures from the Hindu pantheon; gods and goddesses, and characters from the epics and mythology are all identified with brief labels, a virtual handbook of Hindu iconography. Rana Kumbha is known in Indian artistic tradition for the renaissance of Indian culture that he attempted, documented by the Tower of Victory.

Reservoirs and Stepped Wells

No account of the art of western India can be complete without a reference to its hundreds of stepped wells and reservoirs. With its semidesert climate and scant rainfall, there was a constant need to create sources of water. Thousands of stepped wells, lakes, and drinking places have been excavated since early times, often in memory of dead relatives.

The grandest and most elaborate of all stepped wells, known as the Queen's Stepwell, was at Patan, capital of the Chaulukya, or Solanki, dynasty. It was built by Udayamati, queen of Bhimadeva I, after his death in 1064. It has seven underground stories, and its draw well attains a depth of more than 100 feet (30.5 m). The total length at ground level is 220 feet (67 m). The walls of the corridor and the well are adorned by sculptures of the Hindu pantheon. Vishnu, his incarnations, Shiva, Gaṇesha, Pārvatī performing penance for reunion with Shiva (an allusion perhaps to Udayamati's own aspirations after her separation from Bhimadeva), are all there, together with hundreds of other divine or semidivine beings.

The Sahasraliṅga reservoir. Bhimadeva was followed to the throne by his son Karnadeva. He created, at Patan, the Sahasraliṅga (Thousand *Liṅga*) reservoir in the later years of the eleventh century, by digging a channel from the Sarasvati River nearby. In the bed of this channel one thousand small shrines were erected, each housing a *liṅga* of Shiva, hence the reservoir's name.

The Adalaj Stepwell. The stepped well at Adalaj, about 10 miles (16 km) north of Ahmedabad, was built by Queen Ruda in memory of her deceased husband in 1499. In size, it is comparable to Udayamati's monument but, being a construction of the time when Muslim rule was firmly established in Gujarat, it is bereft of figure carvings, since Islam forbids figurative depictions. It is also a rare example of a stepped well with three entrances.

Kirit Mankodi

See also **Temple Types (Styles) of India**

BIBLIOGRAPHY

Burgess, James, and Henry Cousens. *The Architectural Antiquities of Northern Gujarat, More Especially of the Districts Included in the Baroda State.* Archaeological Survey of Western India, Vol. IX. London: Kegan Paul, Trench, Trubner, 1903.

Cousens, Henry. *Somanatha and Other Medieval Temples in Kathiawad.* Archaeological Survey of India, Vol. XLV, Imperial Series. Reprint, Delhi: Indological Book House, 1986.

Dhaky, M. A. "The Chronology of the Solanki Temples of Gujarat." *Journal of the Madhya Pradesh Itihas Parishad* 3 (1961).

———. "The Genesis and Development of Maru-Gurjara Temple Architecture." In *Studies in Indian Temple Architecture,* edited by Pramod Chandra. New Delhi: American Institute of Indian Studies, 1975.

Fergusson, James. *History of Indian Eastern Architecture.* 2 vols. 1876. Reprint, New Delhi: Munshiram Manoharlal, 1967.

Jain, K. C. *Ancient Cities and Towns of Rajasthan.* Delhi: Motilal Banarsidass, 1972.

Lobo, Wibke. *The Sun-Temple at Modhera.* Munchen: Verlag C. H. Beck, 1982.

Mankodi, Kirit. *The Queen's Stepwell at Patan.* Bombay: Franco-Indian Research, 1991.

Nanavati, J. M., and M. A. Dhaky. "The Ceilings in the Temples of Gujarat." In *Bulletin of the Baroda Museum and Picture Gallery* XVI–XVII (1963).

Tod, James. *Annals and Antiquities of Rajasthan; or, The Central and Western Rajpoot States of India.* 2 vols. London: Routledge and Kegan Paul, 1829 and 1832.

John Morley. Also an advocate of universal suffrage and Irish home rule, Morley implemented several important reforms within the Indian Constitution, but anti-partition forces within the National Congress only grew louder and more influential during his tenure as British Secretary of State for India. MICHAEL NICHOLSON / CORBIS.

MORLEY, JOHN ***(1838–1923), British Liberal secretary of state for India (1906–1910).*** John Morley launched a number of significant Constitutional reforms during his half decade at the helm of Whitehall's India Office. Liberal Prime Minister William Gladstone's biographer and his Irish secretary, strongly in favor of Home Rule, "Honest John" Morley's reputation as a man of courage and sterling principles raised nationalist India's hopes too high as soon as his appointment was announced. Unfortunately, the previous Tory government had so recently sent Conservative Lord Minto to India as viceroy that to recall him was hardly a viable option. A few months before Morley's appointment, moreover, Lord Curzon had inaugurated the ill-considered partition of Bengal.

Impact of Bengal's Partition

That partition divided Bengal's province into West Bengal and Eastern Bengal and Assam, provoking heated opposition from the Bengali-speaking leaders of India's National Congress, who viewed it as imperial "divide and rule" with a vengeance. The line divided the Bengali-speaking majority just east of Calcutta, the heart of long-united old Bengal, leaving its Hindu Bengali-speakers as a minority to Bihari- and Oriyya-speakers in West Bengal, while elevating its Muslim Bengali-speakers to majority control over their own province. British India's first Muslim-majority province thus emerged with its new capital of Dhaka, where the Muslim League was born in December 1906. When Morley was pressed by Congress leaders like Gopal Krishna Gokhale to reverse that "cruel partition," he refused, calling it "a settled fact." He hoped that would silence opposition, permitting him to move on to what he considered more important reforms. But Congress's antipartition forces only grew louder throughout Morley's tenure, its extremist "New Party," led by Bal Gangadhar Tilak, introducing bombs to add explosive emphasis to their petitions and pleas. Before leaving office in 1910, Morley drafted Bengal's reunification announcement made by King George at his Delhi Durbar in 1911.

India Council Reforms

Morley introduced several major reforms in British India's Constitution, enacted as the Indian Councils Act of 1909, less accurately termed "Morley–Minto Reforms," since Minto's role was primarily to delay and undermine the effectiveness of the original bill Morley had proposed. Great Liberal that he was, Morley pressed for and achieved the introduction of two Indian members, the first in 1907, to his own India Office Council in Whitehall, the second, Satyendra P. Sinha (1864–1928), to the Viceroy's Administrative Council of the Government of India in 1910. Expanded Legislative Councils under Morley's act all had many new directly elected Indian members, another principle doggedly opposed by Minto and his die-hard British civil servants. Another of Morley's gifts to India was to prevent the appointment of Lord Kitchener, whom he considered an arrogant racist, to the job Kitchener coveted: viceroy of India.

Stanley Wolpert

BIBLIOGRAPHY

Das, Manmath Nath. *India under Morley and Minto: Politics behind Revolution, Repression, and Reforms.* London: G. Allen and Unwin, 1964.

Knickerbocker, Francis W. *Free Minds: John Morley and His Friends.* Cambridge, Mass.: Harvard University Press, 1943.

Morgan, John H. *John, Viscount Morley: An Appreciation and Some Reminiscences.* Boston: Houghton Mifflin, 1924.

Sirdar, Ali Khan Syed. *Life of Lord Morley.* London: I. Pitman, 1923.

Staebler, Warren. *The Liberal Mind of John Morley.* Princeton, N.J.: Princeton University Press, 1943.

Wolpert, Stanley A. *Morley and India, 1906–1910.* Berkeley and Los Angeles: University of California Press, 1967.

MOUNTBATTEN, LORD *(1900–1979), last British viceroy of India.* Lord Louis (Dickie) Mountbatten was Britain's last viceroy of India (1947) and independent India's first governor-general (1947–1948). Queen Victoria's dashing great-grandson, Dickie, the son of First Sea Lord Prince Louis of Battenberg (obliged to Anglicize his German name at the start of World War I), initially followed his father's career at sea, becoming a naval officer. He first visited India with his cousin, the Prince of Wales, in 1922, hunting tigers and becoming engaged to wealthy Edwina Ashley, who was the house guest of Viceroy Lord Reading in Simla.

The Mountbattens first met and befriended India's National Congress leader, soon to become India's first prime minister, Jawaharlal Nehru, in Singapore in 1946. A year later, Britain's newly elected Labour Prime Minister Clement Attlee invited Mountbatten to replace wartime Field Marshal Lord Wavell as Britain's viceroy. The Labour Party was weary of wastefully exorbitant British imperial costs and martial commitments in South Asia, resolving to leave India no later than June 1948. Mountbatten flew to India in April 1947 with the blessings of cousin King George as well as Attlee's Cabinet.

Two months after he reached Delhi and met with Nehru, Mahatma Gandhi, M. A. Jinnah, and other leaders of British India's political parties, as well as his own officials and generals, Mountbatten decided that Hindus, Muslims, and Sikhs were too volatile and enraged to risk waiting as long as a year to withdraw British troops. He insisted instead that Attlee's government transfer all British power to two new dominions of India and Pakistan by mid-August 1947. He ignored the advice of much wiser men, including both Gandhi and Jinnah, who warned him that dividing Punjab and Bengal down the middle of those multicultural provinces would unleash disastrous forces of murder and mayhem. But Mountbatten raced ahead, so eager to protect his own troops and Britain's royal reputation and his own image that he left India naked to the slaughter of a million innocents during the desperate migration of more than 10 million Hindus, Muslims, and Sikhs across newly drawn "international borders" that a day earlier had been rural byways.

Mountbatten's royal birth helped him persuade all but three of India's 562 princes to accept pensions, agreeing to allow their states to be integrated into India's Union by signing instruments of accession. He failed, however, to persuade either the nizam of Hyderabad or the maharaja of Jammu and Kashmir, India's two largest states, to transfer their quasi-sovereign powers before the independent dominions of India and Pakistan were created. Mountbatten remained in Delhi as governor-general of the Dominion of India until June 1948, after which he returned to the Royal Navy, over which he presided seven years later as First Sea Lord. In 1979 he was assassinated by Irish revolutionaries, who blew up his yacht in Irish waters.

Stanley Wolpert

See also **Gandhi, Mahatma M. K.; Jinnah, Mohammad Ali; Nehru, Jawaharlal**

BIBLIOGRAPHY

Campbell-Johnson, Alan. *Mission with Mountbatten.* London: Robert Hale, 1951.

Collins, Larry, and Dominique Lapierre. *Freedom at Midnight.* New York: Simon and Schuster, 1975.

Hodson, H. V. *The Great Divide: Britain-India-Pakistan.* London: Hutchinson, 1969.

Menon, V. P. *The Transfer of Power in India.* Princeton, N.J.: Princeton University Press, 1957.

Moon, Penderel. *Divide and Quit.* Berkeley and Los Angeles: University of California Press, 1962.

Philips, C. H., and Mary Doreen Wainwright, eds. *The Partition of India.* London: George Allen and Unwin, 1970.

Wolpert, Stanley. *Shameful Flight: The Last Years of the British Empire in India.* New York: Oxford University Press, 2005.

MUGHAL EMPIRE. *See* **History and Historiography.**

MUGHAL PAINTING The Mughal dynasty was founded by Zahir al-Din Muhammad, called Babur (r. 1526–1530), a member of the princely Chagatai Turk clans of the Ferghana Valley in modern Uzbekistan, who claimed descent from the great conquerors Timur and Genghis Khan. Although no works of art can be attributed to Babur's patronage, his royal seal can be found in a number of extant manuscripts attesting to his bibliophilic interests. According to his own autobiography the *Baburnāma* (Story of Babur), he was a connoisseur well versed in the artistic works produced by contemporary Persian and Central Asian painters.

Humayun

Only two years after assuming rule in Delhi, Babur died and was succeeded by his son Humayun (r. 1530–1540; 1555–1556). Only a handful of paintings can be ascribed to Humayun's reign; however, two incidents noted posthumously in the *Akbarnāma* (Story of Akbar), a biography of his son and heir Akbar (r. 1556–1605), indicate that Humayun treasured rare books and kept them with him even while traveling. Included among the manuscripts mentioned is a copy of the history of Timur's rule, said to be illustrated by Bihzad, the highly esteemed Persian painter, and probably one of the many volumes he inherited from his father Babur. Early examples of painting from this period include illustrations to a manuscript of *Yusuf and Zulaykha* (New York Public Library), painted in a style resembling that of contemporary Bukharan works, made about 1530–1553 for Humayun's brother Kamran, governor of the fort at Kabul.

In 1540 Humayun and his court fled from Delhi after losing a battle to Shir Shah Suri, an Afghan chief, and was granted safe haven at the court of the Safavid Persian ruler Shah Tahmasp at Tabriz. After gathering financial and military resources, Humayun returned to the subcontinent via Kabul in 1555 and wrested Delhi from Shir Shah. Accompanying the returning Mughal entourage were two accomplished artists of the Safavid atelier, Mir Sayyid ʿAli and ʿAbd al-Samad, who had been given permission by the shah to leave. Other artists from the Persian court joined their colleagues in Delhi, including Mir Sayyid ʿAli's father, Mir Musavvir. These émigrés took their place at Humayun's court, and in concert with local painters, prepared works, such as a manuscript of the *Khamsa* (Five poems) of Nizami (Ahmedabad, private collection), that display the varied artistic influences of the newly formed atelier, including Bukharan, Safavid, indigenous Indic, and Indo-Persian styles. Historical manuscripts and depictions of court scenes were apparently favored by Humayun, as evidenced by a painting from about 1550, *Humayun and His Brothers in a Landscape* (Berlin, Staatsbibliothek Preussischer Kulturbesitz), attributed to the Persian painter Dost Mohammad. Not long after his return to Delhi, Humayun tumbled down a stairway as he was rising from his prayers. At Humayun's untimely death, his son Akbar ascended the throne at the age of thirteen.

Babur in the Chaharbagh. This sixteenth-century painting commemorates the first Mughal emperor's love of the garden. He later imported this concept of the formal garden from Persia to India with great success. Mughal miniatures similarly evolved from Persian painterly traditions. NATIONAL MUSEUM / FOTOMEDIA.

Akbar

Akbar inherited his father's library and his atelier of artists, calligraphers, and illuminators who produced manuscripts in the *karkhana*, or imperial workshop. Following Timurid and contemporary Safavid practices, the atelier was organized hierarchically, and duties were be assigned according to the experience and skill of the individual artist. Senior artists supervised the production of manuscript illustrations and would often lay out preliminary drawings, leaving space for the text to be added later by the calligrapher. One or more artists collaborated in the painting of the composition, with portraits and other detailed areas left to be completed by master artists.

Young apprentices (usually the sons or nephews of artists) would first learn how to prepare pigments and brushes. Pigments were made by grinding minerals such as lapis lazuli, resulting in a rich ultramarine, and other substances, such as gold in leaf and powdered form, which were then mixed with a liquid vehicle. Brushes were made from fine animal hair, such as that of a squirrel, and would be carefully arranged and tied to terminate in a sharp point. Preparation of the paper ground consisted of burnishing an individual sheet by placing it on a flat surface and repeatedly rubbing a smooth stone over the front and back surfaces. Between applications of pigment, the folio would be turned over and the back would be burnished to create a brilliant enamel-like surface on the front side. After the illustration was complete, it was inserted into an ornamented border and bound with other folios.

Akbar was an enthusiastic patron of the arts, and numerous marvelously colored and detailed manuscript paintings were produced at his capitals at Delhi, Agra, Fatehpur Sikri, and Lahore. One of the earliest challenges for the Mughal atelier was Akbar's request that a manuscript of the *Hamzanāma* (Story of Hamza) be produced. This epic story conflated the heroic exploits of Hamza, the uncle of the prophet Muhammad, with the fantastic tales of an adventurer by the same name. Mir Sayyid ʿAli and then ʿAbd al-Samad oversaw the production of the ambitious project, which took fourteen years to complete and resulted in fourteen volumes, each containing one hundred folios. The unusually large illustrations (averaging approximately 26.6 x 20.2 in., or 67.6 x 51.2 cm) were painted on cotton cloth, and the Persian text, written on paper, was affixed to the back of the cloth painting. The now dispersed manuscript took fourteen years to complete (c. 1562–1577), and featured unusually large folios (averaging approximately 26.6 x 20.2 in.) as compared with other manuscripts that could be easily held in the hands of a single person. The composition, coloration, and figural representations of the *Hamzanāma* exemplify an early stage of experimentation and synthesis in Akbar's atelier. An examination of the 140 or so extant folios now dispersed in public and private collections reveal the use of brilliant saturated colors influenced by traditional indigenous artistic sensibilities, combined with elegant Persianate patterned textiles and architectural elements.

Epic, historical, and poetic manuscripts were among the preferred subjects produced for Akbar, including illustrated copies of his grandfather's autobiography, the *Baburnāma*. The emperor's biography, the *Akbarnāma* (Story of Akbar), was commissioned in 1590–1591 and was written by Abu al-Fazl, Akbar's close friend and panegyrist. One of the earliest volumes produced enumerated the emperor's many activities and accomplishments between the years 1560 to 1578. In these richly embellished folios, he was often portrayed centrally in the composition, as shown in a folio painted about 1590–1595 by Basawan with Nand Gwaliari that documented Akbar's journey on foot from Agra to Ajmer in fulfillment of a vow following the birth of his son and heir Salim (London, Victoria and Albert Museum). Although some compositions may have been conceived in the mind of the painter, it was not unusual for one or more artists to accompany the emperor and his court on military campaigns, hunts, and other forays, where documentary sketches made on the spot would later be used as the basis of a fully realized folio. The identification of the hand of a specific artist during this period is aided by the occasional inclusion of signatures within the painting or noted on the border.

When the Mughal court was in residence at Lahore (1585–1598), a number of exquisitely rendered illustrated literary works were produced for Akbar. Among these are two poetic anthologies, painted with precision and jewel-like colors: the 1588 *Divan* (Collected poems) of Anvari (Cambridge, Mass., Harvard University Art Museums), and a 1595 copy of the *Khamsa* (Five poems) of Nizami (London, British Library and Baltimore, Walters Art Gallery). Diverging from an earlier tradition whereby one or more artists would collaborate in the production of a single folio, many of these paintings were completed by a single artist, a practice that would be further developed under the patronage of Jahangir.

The translation of Hindu texts from Sanskrit into Persian are evidence of Akbar's ecumenical nature and philosophical curiosity. A brilliantly delineated folio from a dispersed copy of the *Harivamsha* (Lineage of Hari [Krishna]) produced about 1585–1590, depicts the slaying of the demon king Samvara by the hero Pradyumna. Although this composition includes a fantastically colored landscape similar to those found in mid-sixteenth-century Safavid manuscript illustrations, there is also evidence of artistic influences from contact with European models. European artistic influences are manifest in the form of the representation of atmospheric perspective, a naturalistic depiction of forms receding in space, and the chiaroscuro modeling of figures.

The first documented gift of a European work to the Mughal court was in 1580, when a copy of the eight-volume

Royal Polyglot Bible printed in Antwerp between 1568 and 1573 by Christopher Plantin was presented to the emperor by a mission of Portuguese Jesuit priests who visited the Mughal court at Akbar's invitation. Subsequently, numerous religious publications and prints were sent as gifts to the emperor and his courtiers in the hope of influencing Akbar's conversion to Christianity and in order to negotiate trade agreements favorable to the Portuguese crown. These religious and allegorical prints, largely the works of northern European artists such as Georg Pencz and Albrecht Dürer, were studied closely by Mughal artists, who integrated European representational elements into their works and sometimes faithfully copied entire compositions.

Rochelle Kessler

See also **Akbar; Aurangzeb; Babur; Humayun; Jahangir; Shah Jahan**

BIBLIOGRAPHY

Beach, Milo C. *The Grand Mogul: Imperial Painting in India, 1600–1660.* Williamstown, Mass.: Sterling and Francine Clark Art Institute, 1978.

———. *The Imperial Image: Paintings for the Mughal Court.* Washington, D.C.: Smithsonian Institution, 1981.

———. *Early Mughal Painting.* Cambridge, Mass.: Harvard University Press, 1987.

Beach, Milo C., et al. *King of the World: The Padshahnama.* London: Thames and Hudson, 1997.

Dye, Joseph M., III. "Artists for the Emperor." In *Romance of the Taj Mahal,* edited by P. Pal, J. Leoshko, J. M. Dye III, and S. Markel. Los Angeles: Los Angeles County Museum of Art, 1989.

Leach, Linda York. *Mughal and Other Indian Paintings from the Chester Beatty Library.* 2 vols. London: Scorpion Cavendish, 1995.

Okada, Amina. *Indian Miniatures of the Mughal Court.* New York: H. N. Abrams, 1992.

Stronge, Susan. *Painting for the Mughal Emperor.* New York: H. N. Abrams, 2002.

Welch, Stuart Cary. *The Art of Mughal India.* New York: H. N. Abrams, 1964.

Welch, Stuart Cary, et al., *The Emperor's Album.* New York: H. N. Abrams, 1987.

MUGHAL PAINTING, LATER Although is was the Mughal emperor Akbar (r. 1556–1605) who, by virtue of prosperous and stable reign, contributed toward the blossoming and development of a Mughal school of painting distinct from the Persian models from which it originated, it was under the brilliant reigns of his successors, emperors Jahangir (r. 1605–1627) and Shah Jahan (r. 1628–1658), that Mughal art and painting reached their apogee.

Emperor Jahangir's interest in painting dates to his early years, when he avidly collected the European engravings brought to the Mughal court by Jesuit missionaries. He was attracted to the "exoticism" of these works from the Flemish and German schools. When the young prince, rebelling against his father, Akbar, established an independent and short-lived court in Allahabad between 1599 and 1604, he did not neglect to take with him a few of the painters from the imperial studio, such as Aqa Reza and his son, Abu al-Hasan, as well as Mirza Ghulam and Bishandas. When he acceded to the imperial throne, Jahangir quite naturally inherited painters from the royal studio founded by Akbar. His taste for painting grew and became more discerning through contact with the delicate and refined works produced by these experienced artists, who placed their talent in service of his reign. An aesthete and a demanding connoisseur, Jahangir took legitimate pride in his aptitude for distinguishing without the slightest hesitation the work of a particular artist from that of his colleagues. Hence he notes in his memoirs, the *Tūzuk-i-Jahāngīrī*: "As regard myself, my liking for painting and my practice in judging it have arrived at such a point that when any work is brought before me, either of deceased artists or those of the present day, without the names being told me, I say on the spur of the moment that it is the work of such and such a man. And if there be a picture containing many portraits, and each face be the work of a different master, I can discover which face is the work of each of them. If any other person has put in the eye and eyebrow of a face, I can perceive whose work the original face is, and who has painted the eye and eyebrow" (vol. 2, pp. 20–21). The emperor even went so far as to grant flattering and prestigious titles to some of the most eminent painters in the imperial studio. Hence the title of Nādir az-Zamān (wonder of the time) was bestowed on Abu al-Hasan in 1618, and Nādir al-ʿAsr (wonder of the age) on the animal painter Ustad Mansur.

The extensive illustration of historical, literary, and epic manuscripts characteristic of Akbar's reign declined rapidly under Jahangir. Whereas the earlier illustrations were the work of two or three artists collaborating on a single painting, the new emperor preferred miniatures executed by a single artist, whose talent and style could thereby be displayed more freely and brilliantly. These isolated miniatures were then mounted on album pages (*muraqqa*), where they alternated with brightly colored pages of text done by renowned calligraphers. The albums assembled during Jahangir's reign thus bear witness to the eclecticism of the sovereign's tastes. The dazzling calligraphies and Mughal miniatures executed by the masters of the imperial studio were complemented by European engravings and Persian and Deccani miniatures. The borders and margins surrounding these paintings and calligraphies were highlighted with floral motifs painted with extraordinary mastery and extreme delicacy and sometimes augmented with small human figures or delicate little scenes depicted with phenomenal intensity. They attest to the virtuosity that the painters in the imperial studio had achieved. Their art was no longer confined to miniatures alone but extended to the entire surface of the page.

Beginning with Jahangir's reign, Mughal painting was dominated by the art of the portrait. These were psychological and realistic portraits (no longer idealized, as in the Persian aesthetic tradition), in which the artist was sometimes unsparing in his endeavor to capture and express his model's personality. The greatest artists in the imperial studio were extraordinary portraitists, who gave the Mughal art of the portrait its pedigree: Abu al-Hasan, Bichitr, Hashim, Govardhan, and Bishandas, among others. Recall that in the last decades of the sixteenth century, Emperor Akbar had already expressed the desire to better know the dignitaries and nobles of his empire through individualized portraits. Abu-al-Fazl, the chronicler of Akbar's reign, mentions in *Āʾīn-i-Akbarī* the sovereign's original decision to put together a vast portrait album of the grandees in the kingdom: "His Majesty himself sat for his likeness, and also ordered the likenesses taken of all the grandees of the realm. An immense album was thus formed: those that have passed away have received a new life, and those who are still alive have immortality promised them" (vol. 1, p. 115). The albums assembled during Jahangir's reign were adorned with brilliant and penetrating portraits of emperors, princes, and major dignitaries. Based on a rigorously static conception of the human figure, Mughal portraits traditionally depict their subject with the face represented in profile (bodies are generally represented in three-quarters profile) to allow better definition and legibility of facial features. The human figures, fixed in sober and often hieratic poses, stand out sharply against the bare and light-colored ground of the page. There were both individual and group portraits. Nobles and dignitaries gathered together at formal royal audiences (*durbār*) were always captured in poses marked by stiffness and deference. Mughal portraits were hence also a brilliant reflection of the court, which was governed by strict etiquette and ceremonial, designed to glorify the sovereign and extol his power and majesty. Jahangir's interest in the individualized and intensely realistic portraits sometimes led him to ask his painters to observe the ravages of the human body caused by illness and then to reproduce them with complete fidelity in their pictorial works. Hence in 1618 the emperor commanded his painters to do a portrait of one of his dignitaries, Inayat Khan, who was dying from an illness and from the overconsumption of opium. A drawing and a painting depicting Inayat Khan a few hours before his death are known to us. In their poignant and morbid realism, they bear witness to the extraordinary degree of expressiveness and naturalism henceforth achieved by Mughal portraits. A similar propensity for naturalism also governed depictions of fauna and flora painted during Jahangir's reign. The monarch, captivated by the sight of the odd or unusual, readily assigned the great animal painter Ustad Mansur (Nādir al-ʿAsr) the task of representing all animal species whose presence at the Mughal court might seem out of the ordinary. For instance, in 1621 the talented Mansur did a striking portrait of the famous zebra brought back from Abyssinia by Mir Jaʿfar, which the emperor presented as a gift to Shah Abbas I of Persia. Jahangir's interest in the animal and plant world was inherited from Emperor Babur, whose memoirs are bursting with lively and detailed descriptions of the flora and fauna found in the recently conquered India. That interest was catered to by incomparable painters whose works were to achieve the same degree of realism and objectivity as the brilliant portraits of imperial dignitaries.

One of the most original contributions of Jahangir's painters to the history of imperial Mughal painting was unquestionably the extraordinary "allegorical portraits" commissioned by the sovereign in 1616–1620. The subtle and erudite iconography of these complex, ambitious works was derived in large part from European imagery discovered by the Mughals in Flemish and German engravings brought by the Jesuit missionaries in 1580. They show Emperor Jahangir illuminated by vast golden nimbi and shining like a star. Sometimes he is standing on a large globe, laden with gems or endowed with the attributes of royal power. In other works he is surrounded by putti, who fly through the clouds holding parasols, a symbol of dignity and sovereignty, or the sword or the Timurid crown. These brilliant and profoundly symbolic works show that a few of the greatest painters in the imperial studio, such as Abu al-Hasan and Bichitr, deliberately assimilated foreign motifs: the crown, the earthly globe, the hourglass, the shining nimbus, or putti brandishing the insignia of sovereignty. These motifs were subtly integrated into imperial iconography and were sometimes associated with ancient Islamic symbols that also celebrated royalty and dynastic legitimacy. These "allegorical portraits," which bear striking witness to the iconographical and pictorial eclecticism of Mughal art, continued to be produced—though in a less exalted and less grandiloquent form—during the reign of Emperor Shah Jahan. Among their iconographical sources were obviously the European paintings that Sir Thomas Roe, ambassador to King James I of England, brought to the Mughal court when he was received by Jahangir in 1615. In particular, the emissary to the king of England presented the Mughal emperor with portraits done by the famous English miniaturist Isaac Oliver, and with one or several portraits of the king himself.

These works obviously played a role in enriching the thematic and aesthetic repertoire of the Mughal painters charged with executing the famous "allegorical portraits" designed to exalt the majesty and omnipotence of the Great Mughal.

Emperor Akbar, obsessed with the majesty and legitimacy of the Mughal dynasty, had already commissioned imperial painters to illustrate important historical manuscripts that related the great feats of his ancestors Genghis Khan and Timur (*Chingīznāma*, *Ta'rīkh i-Khāndān i Tīmūriyya*). His successors Jahangir and Shah Jahan took upon themselves that desire to constantly define and remember the historical and political meaning of the Timurid line and the Mughal dynasty. Under their reigns, imperial painters created many "dynastic portraits," works that are brilliant at a symbolic level and yet sometimes repetitive and formulaic. On a single page, they show Timur offering the imperial crown to Babur, founder of the Mughal dynasty in 1526, in the presence of his son and successor Humayun; or they depict Akbar, seated between Jahangir and Shah Jahan, handing over the Timurid crown to the latter.

In 1605, the year of his coronation, Emperor Jahangir began to write his memoirs, the *Tūzuk-i-Jahāngīrī* (or *Jahāngīrnāma*), which covered the time between his accession to the throne and the nineteenth year of his reign (1624). Several pages of this manuscript are illustrated with remarkable paintings that bear the signatures of the greatest painters of the imperial studio. These illustrations are now dispersed, housed in various public and private collections. This was the only historical manuscript of importance to have been illustrated during the reign of Emperor Jahangir, who preferred superb albums of paintings (*muraqqa*) to the amply illustrated historical and literary manuscripts in vogue under the previous reign.

Hence it is from the reign of his successor, Emperor Shah Jahan, that the most sumptuous of the imperial Mughal manuscripts dates, the famous *Pādshāhnāma* housed in the Royal Library of Windsor Castle. This two-volume official chronicle of the reign of Shah Jahan, composed by ʿAbd ul-Hamid Lahori, relates the first twenty years of the imperial reign. The manuscript of the first volume includes forty-four illustrations of great beauty, done by the best imperial painters and depicting for the most part royal audiences (*durbār*), feasts, ceremonies, hunts, and military campaigns. In some sense, this splendid imperial manuscript with dazzling illustrations using a sumptuous palette constitutes the most accomplished synthesis of Mughal pictorial genius, the result of diverse influences and reminiscences subtly assimilated and transposed in a profoundly original style.

All the same, Emperor Shah Jahan displayed more interest in architecture than in painting. Hence the pictorial currents that emerged during his reign cannot be fundamentally distinguished from those seen during that of Jahangir. There was, however, a revival of interest in the theme of the prince visiting a Hindu or Muslim holy man at his retreat to benefit from his wisdom and teaching. (Painters in Akbar's studio had often illustrated this theme in the last decades of the sixteenth century.) These miniatures illustrating the "visit to a holy man" or a "gathering of ascetics" can no doubt be attributed to the patronage of Prince Dara Shikoh, Emperor Shah Jahan's eldest son and heir apparent, who was by nature inclined toward philosophy, spirituality, and the study of religions and who had a well-known penchant for mysticism. Some of the greatest imperial painters, such as Govardhan, produced superb and poignant studies of holy men depicted in solitude and contemplation at their woodland hermitages, happened upon by a prince or nobleman in quest of wisdom or spiritual truth. These profound and often moving works allowed the artist to evoke the opposition between spiritual power, incarnated by the holy man, and temporal power, incarnated by the prince, and to allude symbolically to the preeminence of the former over the latter.

The chief aesthetic characteristics of Mughal painting were maintained under the reign of Emperor Aurangzeb (r. 1658–1707), though the works produced in his imperial studios were usually marked by a less accomplished and less brilliant style than during the previous reign. That austere reign was clearly less favorable to the flourishing of the fine arts. (In 1659 Aurangzeb did not hesitate to condemn his brother, Prince Dara Shikoh, to death for impiety and apostasy toward Islam.) In 1665 Aurangzeb, whose interest in painting was on the decline, even went so far as to shut down the imperial studios. Artists, henceforth deprived of imperial favor and support, sought to place themselves in the service of new patrons, often chosen from among the nobles and major dignitaries. A brief pictorial revival characterized the turbulent and unhappy reign of Emperor Muhammad Shah (r. 1719–1748), which the sack of Delhi by the Persian Nadir Shah in 1739 would bring to a brutal and tragic end.

Amina Okada

See also **Akbar; Aurangzeb; Babur; Jahangir; Shah Jahan**

BIBLIOGRAPHY

Allami, Abu'l Fazl. *A'in-i-Akbarī*, translated by H. Blochmann. Kolkata: Royal Asiatic Society of Bengal, 1938–1939.

Jahangir. *The Tuzuk-i-Jahangiri; or Memoirs of Jahangir*, translated by A. Rogers and edited by H. Beveridge. Reprint, Delhi: Munshiram Manoharlal, 1968.

MUMBAI. *See* **Bombay.**

MUSIC

This entry consists of the following articles:

AN INTRODUCTION

The Sanskrit word for music, *saṅgīt(a)*, meaning "with song," refers to both vocal and instrumental music as well as music for the accompaniment of dance. Some reserve use of this term for the classical traditions of urban, elite India and for religious music, describing other forms of music as "folk music" (*lok gīt*, possibly following the European model) or, in the case of music for the cinema, *filmigīt* (film song).

Tabla and Sitar Players. Tabla and sitar players, c. 1948. Although hereditary musicians are still important in India, greater access to education and social mobility have also created musicians who have chosen their careers by avocation. HULTON-DEUTSCH COLLECTION / CORBIS.

Early India

Regional musical styles, both secular and sacred, have existed for millennia in India, though we have little documentation of their existence prior to Matanga's eighth/ninth-century A.D. text, *Bṛhaddesī* (which also includes the new, probably regional term, *rāga*).

One of the earliest descriptions of Indian musical ideas comes in the context of Vedic chant, particularly in reference to the musical intervals of the Sāma Veda's presentation. Portions of the *Nāradiyashikshā* (Narada's manual) date from about the fifth century, with other portions added later. The students for whom Narada intended this work learned about religious chant (Vedic chant), how to deal with the all-important issue of pronunciation, and, notably, issues of musical pitch. In this last context, the author links the musical scales used in sacred chant and in secular singing.

The approach of Narada's culture to deriving intonation may well have paralleled that of the Greeks. Given the contact between India of this era and Hellenistic culture (particularly in the aftermath of Alexander the Great's conquest of the Punjab), the similarities between those systems may have been more than mere chance. Narada spoke of two important pitch distinctions: *svara* and *shruti*. The former refers to the musical pitches of a musical scale, while the latter refers to the quality of a tone that the listener may hear but have difficulty distinguishing.

An even earlier text, Bharata's *Nātya Shāstra*, dates from the beginning of the first millennium of the common era and details many aspects of music in the context of dramatic presentation. Bharata describes the instruments and some of the musical forms of his era, along with details about musical scales, including an enigmatic description of the term *shruti* (heard). Notably, the *Nātya Shāstra* describes a musical system that is already highly developed, one that reflects a well-established musical heritage.

Later Development

Although the Indian subcontinent has been subject to many waves of migration and cultural change, the successive waves of Turks, Persians, and Mughals who invaded South Asia between the eighth and eleventh centuries A.D. brought with them dramatic infusions of Western and Central Asian musical ideas.

In North India, successive waves of migrants and rulers patronized Indian music as well as their own in their homes, communities, and courts. The music of the West and Central Asian Muslims, particularly that of Persian, enriched Indian music in the court setting. Eventually a blend of the two traditions emerged, with singers from Gwalior (India) joined by instrumentalists from Mashhad, Tabriz, and Herat (Persia and Afghanistan).

The court of Ala'-ud-Din Muhammad Khalji, sultan of Delhi (r. 1296–1326), was a particularly fertile ground for this exchange. By far the most notable musical figure in this context was Amir Khusrau, an expert in the music of both India and Persia. Many scholars credit him with inventing the sitar and tabla, many *rāg*s and *tāl*s, and several vocal forms.

Indian courts of the sixteenth and seventeenth centuries sponsored resident scholars who wrote numerous treatises describing the aesthetics of music, including the association of sentiments (*rasa*), colors, Hindu deities, and so forth, with particular *rāga*s. A particularly important era in the patronage of Indian music came during the reign of the Mughal emperors. Emperor Akbar (r. 1556–1605) had two outstanding musicians at his court, Miyañ Tansen and Baz Bahadur; Emperor Jahangir (1605–1627) had musician Bilas Khan; and Emperor Shah Jahan (1628–1658) patronized Lal Khan. Many modern hereditary musicians trace their lineage to these eminent musicians.

The treatises of the sixteenth and seventeenth centuries show an evolution from the tradition of the *Nātya Shāstra* and an increase in the importance of Arabic and Persian musical ideas. Toward the end of Mughal period (18th and early 19th centuries), court scholars translated early Sanskrit treatises into Persian, allowing them to learn about the music of ancient India and in some cases to attempt to reconcile differences between millennia-old treatises and contemporary practice.

The Mughal era also marked the ascendancy of the British Raj and a flourishing of Indian musical life in provincial capitals and courts. There, musicians worked in smaller and less affluent settings than Delhi for less powerful patrons, some of whom knew a great deal about the music, some who simply wanted to hear it and enjoyed the prestige.

British Orientalists took an active interest in India's music and culture. Sir William Jones, a linguist and translator, compiled his *On the Musical Modes of the Hindus* (1799) largely from Indian sources, but without much comment on current practice. However, Captain Augustus Willard, in his *Treatise on the Music of Hindustan* (1834), drew attention to the gap between theory and practice and observed that much contemporary musical practice in Indian courts was a mix of Indian, Persian, and Afghan musical ideas. Indian treatises of the period reveal continued shifts in musical thinking, with the "major" scale (*Bilāval thāt*) as the "natural" scale replacing the "minor" (Dorian) scale that had long been associated with Bharata's intonational root scale, *shadjagrāma*.

Perhaps the most important figure in twentieth-century Indian musical theory is V. N. Bhatkhande. In his *Hindusthāni Sangīt Paddhati* (1932) and *Kramik Pustak Mālikā* (1937), he attempted to derive theory from observations of practice, interviewing court musicians, collecting their music, and analyzing and cataloging contemporary *rāga*s. Many twentieth-century writers on Indian music continued this trend, attempting to reconcile ancient practice with contemporary musical practice and terminology. In general, however, scholarship has separated the study of ancient musical practice from examination of modern performance practice.

Until the twentieth century, musicianship in South Asia was a combination of hereditary legacy and cultural adaptation. For many Hindus, the *guru-shishya*, or teacher-pupil relationship, was the context for the transmission of traditional musical knowledge. The relationship was sometimes familial, but the artistic "lineage," or *parampara*, resulted from generations of teaching and learning. For Muslims, the *gharānā* (household) delineated the transmission of musical knowledge and the line of musical authority. The teacher-student relationship between an *ustād* (master) and his *shagird* (student) provided instruction in everything from musical performance to conduct in public. The ultimate official arbiter of disputes in these extended familial relationships was the senior male, the *qalīfā*. In the early twenty-first century, although hereditary musicians are still important, music schools fostered by Bhatkhande and others (e.g., Palushkar), along with an increased sense of social mobility, have created musicians who have chosen their careers by avocation.

Gordon Thompson

See also **Nātya Shāstra; Rāga; Sitar; Tabla; Tāla**

BIBLIOGRAPHY

Bhatkhande, Visnunarayan. *Hindustāni Sangīt-Paddhati.* Hathras: Sangeet Press, 1932.

——. *Kramik Pustak Mālikā.* 6 vols. Hathras: Sangeet Press, 1937.

——. *A Short Historical Survey of the Music of Upper India: With Special Reference to the United Provinces of Agra and Oudh.* 1943. Reprint, Baroda: Indian Musicological Society, 1974.

Jones, William, and N. Augustus Willard. *Music of India.* Kolkata: Anil Gupta, 1962.

Neuman, Daniel M. *The Life of Music in North India: The Organization of an Artistic Tradition.* Detroit: Wayne State University Press, 1980.

KARNĀTAK

During the twelfth and thirteenth centuries, the musical tradition of India divided into two main schools, that of the Hindustani tradition of North India, influenced by Persian music, and the Karnātak, or Carnatic, school of South India. The Karnātak school drew on Tamil and Telugu literary as well as Hindu devotional traditions. The earliest Karnātak music was devotional, performed in temples, but then royal families and prosperous landowners patronized musicians who would perform for them in their palaces and mansions. The royal courts at Tanjore, Pudukkottai, and Ettayapuram became renowned centers of Karnātak music with Tanjore at one time employing some 360 musicians in concerts known as *arangam*, *sabha*, or *sada*s. The kings of Vijayanagar and, after its fall in 1565, the Wodeyars of Mysore were also great patrons of Karnātak music. The music developed in *sampradaya*s (music schools), and although four types of improvization are the norm, these occur along well-defined and well-organized lines. Karnātak music is almost exclusively devotional, but there are also children's songs, humorous compositions, and film songs.

Karnātak music is performed by a small group of musicians consisting of a vocalist, a primary instrumentalist playing such instruments as the vina or violin, sometimes a wind instrument such as a flute, a drone instrumentalist perhaps playing a tamboura or *shruti* box, and a rhythm instrumentalist who might play a percussion instrument such as a *mridangam* or *ghatam*. The two main components of Karnātak music are the *rāga*, a melodic pattern, and the *tāla*, a rythmic pattern, where singers keep the beat by moving their hands in specific patterns. There are seventy-two primary or parent *rāga*s, and each one is associated with one of nine feelings: *shringara* (romance), *hasya* (humor), *karuna* (longing), *raudra* (anger), *veera* (heroism), *bhayanaka* (fright), *vibhatsa* (disgust), *adhbuta* (wonderment), or *shanta* (contentment). *Rāga*s are also associated with the seasons of the year or time of day. The songs usually eulogized the Hindu Gods, especially Vishnu and his incarnations. The songs usually consist of three verses: the *pallavi*, the refrain of two lines; the *anupallavi*, the second verse, also of two lines; and the *caranam*, the final verse, usually of three lines and one that borrows from the *anupallavi*.

One of the earliest composers was Purandara Dasa (1480–1564), who systematized the laws of teaching music and was reputed to have composed 475,000 songs in Kannada and Sanskrit, although only a hundred survive. He invented the *tāla* system and preached the virtues of a pious life in his songs, known as *pada*s. They were simple metrical devotional songs of the *bhāgavata* tradition, sung in a simple language, that also appealed to the illiterate. He sang the praises of the Hindu God Krisha, and his four compositions in praise of the Hindu God Gaṇesha are practiced today by students of the Karnātak tradition. He inspired the three greatest composers of the Karnātak tradition, Thyagaraja (c. 1759–1847), Mutusvāmi Dīkshitar (1776–1827), and Syami Sastri (1762–1827), who are considered to be the "Trinity" of Karnātak music. In the twentieth century, Semmangudi Srinivasa Iyer (1908–2003), a teacher of three generations of Karnātaka musicians, was acclaimed as the second Pitamaha (Great Father) after Purandara Dasa. One of his most famous pupils is the female singer Madurai Shanmukhavadivu Subbulakshmi (b. 1916), popularly known as M. S. or M. S. S., who completely charmed both Mahatma Gandhi and Jawaharlal Nehru. Damal Krishnaswamy Pattammal (b. 1919) is often referred to as the second of the "Female Trinity" of Karnātak music; M. L. Vasanthakumari is the third. Modern Karnātak music is sometimes played as a musical composition without singers.

Roger D. Long

See also **Dīkshitar, Muttusvāmi; Rāga; Subbulakshmi, M. S.**

BIBLIOGRAPHY

Ayyangar, R. Rangaramanuja. *History of South Indian (Carnatic) Music: From Vedic Times to the Present.* Mumbai: Vipanci Cultural Trust, 1993.

Bhagyalekshy, S. *Rāgas in Carnatic Music.* Trivandrum: CBH Publications, 1990.

Kuppuswami, T. V. *Carnatic Music and the Tamils.* Delhi: Kalinga Publications, 1992.

Rao, B. Dayananda, ed. *Carnatic Music Composers: A Collection of Biographical Essays.* Hyderabad: Triveni Foundation, 1994.

South India

The music of South India (Sanskrit, *Karnātaka Sangītam*) is referred to as Carnatic or Karnātak music in English. It has absorbed a number of traditions, theories, and stylistic features over a long period of time. Many of the features discernible in today's concerts, be it the lyrics of a song, an instrumental style, or a typical rhythm, can be traced to different parts of a vast area comprising Andhra Pradesh, Karnataka, Kerala, and Tamil Nadu. As the four southern states were created on the basis of linguistic considerations following India's independence in 1947, it is important to recall here that this music is not confined to Karnataka, nor can it be ascribed to any particular group on the basis of ethnic, linguistic, sectarian, or social categories.

History

Only in the last few centuries has "music" in the modern sense of the word become an art in its own right, and early Indian music was by definition subservient to the needs of drama, dance, public festivities, and religious rituals. Much of South India's musical evolution has therefore eluded the scrutiny of historians concerned with factual and biographical accounts rather than hagiography or the intricacies of current Karnātak music theory: "It is very difficult to make a purely chronological survey of musicological writing. . . . Many streams of musical systems existed; little is known about their time of origin and extinction. Some overlap others in time, some stay independent of one another, and some cross one another's path; sometimes the impact of one is seen on the other" (Ramanathan).

Inscriptions and evidence in Tamil literature, for instance the *Cilappadikāram*, leave no doubt that there has been a give and take between dance, temple and concert musicians since ancient times: "Provisions of endowments were made for the maintenance of professional dancers, singers and instrumentalists who were attached to temples. Available evidence makes it more than clear that they were expected not only to perform before the deities as part of divine services but also to entertain the visitors to the temples through public performances. As a matter of fact the *ranga-mandapa*, the theatre for performing arts, became an integral part of the architectural features of any temple worth the name" (Ramesh).

Rāmāmātya, a sixteenth-century scholar and minister who flourished at Vijayanagar, is regarded as the first writer who outlined a distinct South Indian music system in his treatise titled *Svara Mēla Kalānidhi*. Like other music scholars before and after him, he sought to reconcile the discrepancies between conventional music theory and established practice. With the defeat of the Vijayanagar empire in 1565 and the subsequent destruction of its splendid capital, the focus of Karnātak music shifted farther south. Patronage was available in plenty at Tanjāvûr (English, Tanjore), Thiruvananthapuram (Travancore), and Mysore. The Nayaka rulers, a Telugu-speaking dynasty flourishing in the seventeenth century, and their successors, the Marathas who ruled from the late seventeenth to the early nineteenth centuries, are regarded as the patrons under whom Karnātak music acquired its present characteristics. Since then, members of several erstwhile royal families of South India, most notably those of Travancore and Mysore, have continued to play an active role in every aspect of South Indian musical life, be it as patrons, scholars, composers, or performers.

Music Education

Formal education has never been the sole source of musical knowledge. Semmangudi Srinivasa Iyer (1908–2003), the most influential Karnātak teacher and vocalist of the twentieth century, leaves no room for doubt about the important role played by the community of hereditary temple musicians: "In the past, Carnatic music was nourished by the *nadaswaram* tradition. As a child I followed the pipers through the four streets round the temple in the procession of the deities. Now and then the pipers would stop and ruminatively elaborate a *raga*. The crowds would throng to worship the gods as well as to listen to the music." He continues to highlight the value of personalized music education: "Staying with the guru for years and absorbing music by listening as well as learning is no longer feasible. . . . I find that those who learn from classes held in the home of *vidwan*s show better results than government college students." The informal "family" environment (*gurukulavāsam*) in which most performers and teachers of the past were formed has thus been substituted by the courses offered by private and government institutions. Yet, as far as the family members of prominent musicians are concerned, it still plays as significant a role as it did several generations ago.

A distinct feature of South Indian music is the body of exercises and didactic compositions known as *abhyāsa gāna* (practice music). Many months are devoted to the lessons included in this basic curriculum, during which a teacher supervises the exact repetition of pitches, phrases, embellishments, and increasingly complex metric arrangements in several tempi. The skills acquired through these exercises, and also the ability to discern minute stylistic details, are needed by soloists and accompanists alike. The importance of this learning method lies in the common denominator it provides for all performers, thus enabling most experienced Karnātak musicians to perform together without any prior rehearsals.

Purandara Dāsa (1484–1564), the most prolific among the saint-composers, is credited with establishing the current curriculum of Karnātak music. His method was disseminated by his fellow members of the *Haridāsa* movement ("servants of Hari" or Vishnu). His songs provide students with colorful mental images and an appealing, endearing tone. In his most popular piece, the composer addresses Gananātha as the "big-bellied, elephant-faced Lord" (Gaṇesha) who has the "power to remove all obstacles," a gift for which he is "praised by the patron deities of the arts and sciences." This small composition, "Shrī Gananātha," belongs to a genre known as *gītam*, wherein the practice of musical skills is easily combined with involvement and expression (*bhāva*). The *lakshana gītam* is a variant containing lyrics that inform the learner about the special features (*lakshana*) of the underlying *rāga*.

Concert Repertoire

A Karnātak concert (*kachēri*) gives ample scope for spontaneity, precise ensemble work, and the rendition of compositions belonging to different genres that evolved quite independently from one another over several centuries. Ariyakkudi Ramanuja Ayyangar (1890–1967), a vocalist whose style has influenced many of his disciples and admirers, first introduced the concert format now followed on most occasions: artistically conceived études known as *tāna varnam* form the opening item; then follow several pieces belonging to the vast and varied repertoire of elaborate art and devotional songs (*kriti, kīrtana*); the *rāgam-tānam-pallavi* "suite" is sometimes performed as the main concert item. As an extension of this conventional concert format (*kachēri paddhati*), one or several compositions belonging to the traditional dance repertoire, are presented toward the end: the rhythmically conceived *tillāna* (the only song genre devoid of "meaning"), and a *padam* or a *jāvali*, based on lyrics with an erotic theme (*sringāra bhāva*). In addition, many performers present Tamil pieces such as the lively *Tiruppugal* or their own musical adaptations based on devotional lyrics in any Indian language (e.g., Sanskrit *shlōkam*, Tamil *viruttam*). Among the "minor" (*tukkadā*) items included in the final stage of a concert are popular versions of pilgrim songs (*kāvadi chindu*) and adaptations of North Indian genres set to hybrid (*dēshya*) *rāga*s.

During a concert, several compositions alternate with solo and group improvisations in the form of *rāga ālāpana* (unmetered *rāga* exposition), *tānam* (pulsating yet unmetered *rāga* exposition), *niraval* (sequences based on tonal variations of a given theme), *svara kalpana* ("imaginative" tone combinations), and *tani āvartana* (rhythmic interlude by one or several performers).

In view of the artistic freedom enjoyed by all South Indian performers, it is important to highlight their respect for a concept that connects them with the music of their ancestors, namely that of the learned composer whose task is to create elaborate pieces that have pride of place in a modern concert. In Lewis Rowell's translation of a passage in the thirteenth-century *Sangītaratnākara*, a *vāggēyakāra* (literally, "word singer") is "one who composes both music and text." This master composer is endowed with "a thorough knowledge of grammar, proficiency in lexicography, knowledge of prosody, proficiency in the use of figures of speech, comprehension of aesthetic delight (*rasa*) as related to emotive states of being (*bhāva*), intelligent familiarity with local custom, knowledge of many languages, proficiency in the scientific theories of fine arts, expert knowledge of the three musical arts, a lovely tone quality, good knowledge of tempo, *tāla*, and *kalā*, discrimination of different intonations, a versatile genius, a beautiful musical rendering, acquaintance with regional (*desi*) *rāgas*." These characteristics still account, in the view of most Karnātak musicians and critics, for the lasting appeal of the songs bequeathed by the "Trinity" of South Indian music (Tyāgarāja, Shyāma Shāstri, and M. Dīkshitar) and their musical heirs. The intricacies underlying their compositions has also opened floodgates to individual artistic expression. Following the advice given in the lyrics of these *vāggēyakāra*s, musicians now dare to express themselves for the sake of artistic and spiritual fulfillment.

Our understanding of the music prior to the "Trinity" is quite limited, however, as these three were evidently the first composers who succeeded in passing on many of their compositions to posterity by way of oral transmission: "In India composers till the beginning of this century did not notate their compositions. In other words, no original scores are available. Songs have come down only in the oral tradition" (Ramanathan).

Rāga

The melodic and rhythmic theories of Karnātak music are referred to as *rāga* and *tāla*, respectively. Although Hindustani music has similar concepts, and both systems have their roots in the same ancient theories, several major differences remain, both in the realms of theory and practice. The most obvious difference concerns the theory that prescribes either the day or night for the performance of North Indian *rāga*s. South Indian musicians and theorists, generally observant of traditional customs (*sampradāya*), regard such restrictions as obsolete and counterproductive from an artistic point of view. The sole reminders of similar restrictions are certain *rāga*s originally associated with temple rituals and therefore performed at certain hours of the day. Conversely, certain moods, such as those associated with loneliness at night or the excitement of spring, are often evoked by specific *rāga*s in the Karnātak music composed for *Bharata Natyam* dance and dance drama.

A musician is expected to portray the finer points of a *rāga* in a manner that discerning listeners (*rasika*) would recognize and relish. The "shape" of a *rāga* (*rāga rûpa*), traditionally regarded as a "personality" unlike any other, is largely defined by compositions. In the absence of detailed notation, most musicians rely on learning by hearing, particularly for the study of specimens belonging to the *gītam*, *varnam*, and *kriti* genres. These items provide the musical context for all the phrases included during the exposition (*ālāpana*) of a given *rāga*.

On similar lines, ornamentation (*gamaka*) depends on the melodic context of each note, either as part of an ascending or a descending series of notes, or within an oblique phrase. Auxiliary notes (*anusvara*) provide the contours and "colors" characteristic of Karnātak melody, and color is indeed implied by the Sanskrit word *rāga* (from the root *ranj*, "to color," or "to be attached to"). The rich texture achieved by the skillfull and appropriate application of embellishments helps a musician to endow a melodic line with continuity and expressiveness, even in a slow tempo.

An estimated two hundred to three hundred South Indian *rāga*s (recognizable melodic entities) are currently performed, more or less regularly, during concerts and in dance recitals. In theory, several thousand different *rāgas* could be formed by way of applying all the conceivable combinations of the basic seven notes (*sapta svara*), the twelve semitonal variants (*svarasthāna*), the enharmonic variants assigned to four out of the five "variable" notes (*vikrta svara*), and numerous microtonal shades (the proverbial 22 *shrutis*). On a more practical level, South Indian music is based on 72 scale types, from which 72 corresponding "parental" *rāgas* (*janaka rāga*) as well as their numerous "offspring" (*janya rāga*) are derived for the purpose of classification.

Tāla

The South Indian concept of *tāla* is based on a cyclic arrangement of units (*kriyā*, "gestures"), which helps all participants to coordinate the rhythmic flow (*laya*) of a concert in an appealing manner, either as part of a song or in any improvised concert item. Many distinct *tālas* and their innumerable variants enable Karnātak musicians to create an astonishing variety of intricate rhythmic figures and cross-rhythms.

Among the unique features of Karnātak rhythm are the different starting points (*eduppu* or *graha*), for the beginning of a song or theme, and the subdivisions (*nadai* or *gati*) of each "beat" within a given *tāla*, while maintaining the basic tempo (*kālapramānam*) throughout a concert item. Specialists in the rhythmic aspect (*laya*) of Karnātak music manage to increase or decrease the tension and density of rhythmic patterns with mathematical precision and at any given moment. Such flights of imagination may either be subjected to the rules of prosody, as in the case of items based on lyrics (e.g., *pallavi* or *kriti*), or may be meant only to heighten the aesthetic pleasure of listeners on the basis of abstract rhythmic patterns (*yati*) and pleasant combinations of sounds, as in the case of a drum solo.

The elaborate climax of a drum solo (*kōrvai*) consists of carefully constructed sequences of complex patterns in which all the aforementioned concepts are translated into practice. Ideally, this process should manifest itself in a spontaneous and effortless manner, making listeners forget that a drum solo is nowadays rarely, if ever, performed without some amount of calculation.

Later Developments

Music and dance. Since the middle of the nineteenth century, prominent dance masters (*nattuvanar*) and the musicians belonging to their dance ensembles (*chinna mēlam*) have assimilated as well as enriched the concepts and playing techniques now associated with Karnātak "art" music: melodic expressiveness (*rāga bhāva*), aesthetic appeal (*rasa*), and rhythmical variety (*tāla*). As a result, *bhāva* (bha), *rasa* (ra), and *tāla* (ta) are commonly said to be the very essence of the dance now called *Bharata Natyam* (bha-ra-ta dance), a dance style that was still known as *sadir* in the early twentieth century.

Women as performers. Until the beginning of the twentieth century, a "respectable" musician was understood to be male: "Another tremendous step forward is the emergence of women as equals of men in this male-dominated field" (Semmangudi Srinivasa Iyer). As the rich legacy of "artful" songs (*kriti*) permeated the educated classes of South Indian society, many women from different social backgrounds could, for the first time in history, pursue successful musical careers without being stigmatized. The list of prominent female singers includes pioneers like "Vīnā" Dhanammāl (1867–1938), "Bangalore" Nāgaratnammāl (1878–1952), Sarasvati Bai (1894–1974), T. Brinda (1912–1996), M. S. Subbulakshmi (b. 1916), D. K. Pattammal (b. 1919), and M. L. Vasanthakumari (1928–1990). They acquired the skills and knowledge to develop individual styles (*bāni*) of their own, and thereby encouraged their own disciples and other educated women to perform in concerts and broadcasts and to produce recordings.

Vocal and instrumental music. With the emergence of an affluent and cultured urban class from the late nineteenth century onward, and especially following the foundation of societies (*sabhā*) for the promotion of musical excellence, solo and ensemble performances by instrumentalists have ceased to be regarded as inferior to a vocal recital. Interestingly, though, there still exists no instrumental repertoire as such; all musicians have learned their music through singing, and the *gāyakī*, or "vocal" type of expression, continues to be regarded as superior to any style that emphasizes the technical possibilities of an instrument. Even a vina (long-necked lute) is meant to "sing," and the human body has been referred to as *gātra vīnā*, the human counterpart of the wooden lute mentioned in ancient texts.

For at least four centuries, the tamboura (a long-necked lute serving as a drone) has been the main support and common denominator for most traditions of Karnātak music. On the other end of the spectrum, there is the humble bamboo flute (Tamil, *pullankuzhal*; Sanskrit, *vēnu*), which was introduced into concert music by Sharabha Shāstrigal before the turn of the twentieth century. As evidenced by numerous sculptures in South Indian temples, as well as its mention in ancient Tamil literature, the transverse flute had been a leading instrument in dance music for most of the last two millennia. Along with the violin, the flute has since acquired the status of a full-fledged instrument. Several other melody and rhythm instruments, including the saxophone, mandolin, and *ghatam*, have either been newly introduced or have gained prestige. The prevalence of electronic amplification during concerts has also facilitated the formation of ensembles with instruments that would have been incompatible in the past.

The inclusion of at least one extensive drum solo (*tani* or *tani āvartanam*) is a conspicuous feature of contemporary Karnātak music. Palghat Mani Iyer (1913–1981), an exponent of the *mridangam* (double-faced drum), became a legend in his own lifetime as the musician who elevated the perfunctory *tani* to a highlight of all the concerts in which he participated. Most modern percussionists seek to emulate his precision, virtuosity, and imaginative treatment of any given *tāla*; his sense of self-restraint, so conducive to the aesthetic balance of a concert, is much harder to come by.

The future. Many South Indian performers are now in a position to interact with appreciative fellow musicians, composers, and audiences all over the world. In spite of the alarm periodically raised by experts and critics, the proven resilience of authentic Karnātak music, combined with a profound regard for classical standards (*sampradāya*) on the part of many young musicians, will ensure its survival.

Ludwig Pesch

See also **Dīkshitar, Muttusvāmi; Rāga; Shyāma Shāstri; Tāla; Tyāgarāja**

BIBLIOGRAPHY

Pesch, Ludwig. *The Illustrated Companion to South Indian Classical Music*. Delhi: Oxford University Press, 1999.

Ramanathan, N. "Musicology in India." *Sangeet Natak. Journal of the Sangeet Natak Akademi New Delhi* 110 (1993): 31–41.

Ramesh, K. V. *Inscriptions on Music from South India*. Mysore: Dept. of Epigraphy, Government of India, 1988 (unpublished paper).

Reck, David B. "India/South India." In *Worlds of Music: An Introduction to the Music of the World's Peoples*, edited by Jeff Todd Titon. 4th ed. Schirmer/Thomson Learning, 2002.

Rowell, Lewis. *Music and Musical Thought in Early India*. 1992. New Delhi: Munshiram Manoharlal, 1998.

Srinivasa Iyer, Semmangudi. "Music Then and Now." Interview and translation by Gowri Ramnarayan. *Frontline Magazine* 14, no. 16 (1997).

MUSLIM LAW AND JUDICIAL REFORM Family law, also called personal or customary law in contexts of legal pluralism, governs features of family life such as marriage, separation, divorce, the consequences of divorce (such as alimony and property division), maintenance for children and other dependents, inheritance, adoption, and guardianship. Distinct family laws govern most of India's major religious groups—Hindus, Muslims, Christians, Parsis, and Jews—as well as many so-called tribal groups. (Hindu law governs Sikhs, Jains, and Parsis.) Muslim leaders pressed for the retention of legal pluralism far more than did the leaders of other religious groups soon after Indian independence, especially during the debates of the Constituent Assembly. Concerns about the recognition of distinct religious identity were most strongly felt among Muslims in the aftermath of the formation of Pakistan, which was associated with considerable collective violence, and which substantially reduced the Muslim share in India's population, middle classes, and political elite. Some leaders of the Congress Party gave these concerns of Muslims considerable weight, as they had suggested through the 1940s that Muslim law would continue to govern Muslims in family matters, in return for the support of some Muslim religious elites. As demands for the retention of Muslim law crucially influenced the choice to retain legal pluralism, public debate about Indian family law gives considerable attention to Muslim law.

While the legislature introduced major changes in Hindu law in the 1950s, major policy makers claimed that they were leaving changes in the laws of the religious minorities to the initiative of unspecified representatives of these groups, who in practice were typically conservative religious and political elites. The conservatism of such elites made major changes in these laws seem unlikely. Nevertheless, some changes took place in Muslim law and in India's other family laws that potentially gave women greater rights, particularly over the last generation. The judiciary was the main agent of change, although legislatures and some religious leaders and religious institutions played secondary roles. Both formal courts and community courts adjudicate matrimonial disputes in India. The changes the judiciary introduced are relevant to adjudication in the formal courts. Change was slower in Muslim community courts, which included prayer groups (*jamaats*), popularly recognized judges (*qazis*), and courts established by Muslim religious institutions (*dar-ul quzats*).

Women's Rights

The limited codification of Muslim law gave the judiciary considerable autonomy in interpreting Muslim law. Of the three acts pertaining to Muslim law in India, the Dissolution of Muslim Marriages Act governed the grounds on which Muslim women could get judicially mediated divorce since its passage in 1939, and the Muslim Women (Protection of Rights on Divorce) Act primarily governed the rights of Muslim women to postdivorce maintenance after it was passed in 1986. The other act, the Muslim Personal Law (Shariat) Application Act of 1937, stated that the Shariʿa would apply to Muslims in family matters without specifying the rules it recognized, although the "Islamic laws" applied in different regions of the world vary considerably. This act's silences left much of the content of India's Muslim law to the judiciary's discretion.

Indian legislatures gave the content and implementation of Muslim law little attention after independence. Reflecting this, not one of the 182 official Law Commissions of the post-colonial period assessed the functioning of Muslim law or considered possible changes in Muslim law. Only a few legislative changes were introduced in Muslim law after independence: the passage of the Muslim Women (Protection of Rights on Divorce) Act, which is applicable throughout India, and amendments to the Muslim Personal Law (Shariat) Application Act in certain states, which made Muslim law rather than local custom applicable to succession to agricultural land. The amendments of the Shariat Application Act gave daughters the right to half the shares of sons in their parents' agricultural land (along with the half share they already had since 1937 in other forms of parental property), in contrast with most of the local customs, which gave daughters no share whatsoever in agricultural land. Legislative restraint was meant to give Muslim leaders the primary role in determining the future of Muslim law, but in effect gave the judiciary that much more control over shaping Muslim law.

Despite the autonomy it enjoyed, the Indian judiciary largely followed the precedents of the colonial period in Muslim law adjudication through the first post-colonial generation. Muslim law in the colonial courts was based largely on later commentaries and compendia of Hanafi law, the legal tradition taken to apply to the majority of South Asian Muslims, although local custom rather than earlier Islamic jurisprudential traditions determined many features of adjudication. Judges interpreted the provisions of Hanafi law in light of British common law traditions, and did not recognize some laws that they considered incompatible with "justice, equity and good conscience" (e.g., the recognition of slavery, the death penalty for adultery and apostasy), a standard they used in a rather unsystematic way. They rarely referred directly to Islam's founding texts, the Qur'an, the Hadis (the reputed sayings of the prophet Muhammad), and the Sunna (accounts of the Prophet's life). Colonial Indian Muslim law assumed a definite shape, somewhat resistant to change, from the late nineteenth century. It had rather conservative implications for gender relations, particularly in comparison with family law in countries that saw the extensive reform of Muslim law through the 1960s and 1970s, such as Tunisia, Libya, Jordan, Iraq, and Malaysia. For instance, Muslim men were allowed to have up to four wives, unilateral and irrevocable male divorce was recognized, and Muslim men were obliged to support their ex-wives only for three months after the pronouncement of divorce in India. Some features of Indian Muslim law were changed through infrequent legislation, mainly in the 1930s and 1940s, and judicial reform, especially from the 1970s.

Deepening of Democracy

The courts introduced only one major change in Muslim law in the first post-colonial generation: taking bigamy to create a presumption of cruelty toward a wife claiming divorce in the *Itwari v. Asghari* case of 1960, making the wife eligible for divorce on the ground of cruelty, although the Dissolution of Muslim Marriages Act did not recognize bigamy as a ground on which women could claim divorce. Some changes urged the judiciary toward greater activism, beginning in the 1970s, in many areas of law, including family law and Muslim law. Sections of the legal elite felt pressed to enable the deepening of democracy after the experience of the "National Emergency," when democratic institutions were suspended for eighteen months in the mid-1970s. This led to the growth of public interest litigation, to bring the attention of the judiciary to various concerns of underprivileged groups. Concerns about different forms of gender inequality were more prominently voiced in public debate, especially because the women's movement grew in strength and became more autonomous of political parties through this period. These concerns influenced the legal elite more than they did the political elite. Activist lawyers periodically contested the unequal provisions for the genders and the different laws governing the relevant religious and other cultural groups in family law.

While policy makers did not respond to all pressures to reduce gender inequality, ongoing political and social changes led more of them to prioritize state intervention to address some of the inequalities in family law and matrimonial life. Judges in particular became more willing to depart from precedent to provide women protection in matrimonial cases. Their activism was tempered by two concerns: the need to recognize cultural pluralism and the need for judicial restraint. However, a critical awareness grew among both judges and lawyers of the directions of family law reform elsewhere, especially of reforms in Muslim law that often involved the appropriation of earlier Islamic texts and traditions that recognized more rights for women. This context made more judges willing to initiate reform within the framework of legal pluralism by departing from precedent and by amending particular statutes. Judges justified reform through somewhat novel interpretations of statutory law and group normative tradition, as well as with reference to the fundamental rights recognized in the Indian constitution to life, liberty, dignity, and equality.

The two main reforms the judiciary introduced in Muslim law were in alimony rights and the conditions under which unilateral male divorce would be recognized. Until the 1970s, the courts restricted the obligation of Muslim men to maintain their ex-wives to the three-month *iddat* period after divorce is initially pronounced, a period during which the ex-wife is expected to remain in seclusion, leaving it up to the ex-wife's successors or local *wakf* boards (Muslim social service institutions funded largely through private donations) to provide for her if she is indigent. They did so although verses of the Qur'an suggest that the man provide for his ex-wife's future, or require such provision from the ex-husband according to some interpretations. The parliament amended Section 125 of the Criminal Procedure Code in 1973 so that a man's obligation to support a wife he deserted or from whom he is judicially separated was extended to ex-wives. The requirement of permanent alimony was meant to apply to all religious groups, but Section 127(3)(b) of the Criminal Procedure Code deducted any amount the ex-husband may have given his ex-wife following the customary or personal law governing the couple from the payment due from the husband. Most courts resolved this ambiguity in favor of women from 1973 to 1985, taking the legislative amendment of 1973 to apply to all Indians and referring for justification to a verse of the Qur'an that suggests the ex-husband provide for his ex-wife's future. A Constitution Bench of the apex court (the Supreme Court) did so in the *Mohammad Ahmed Khan v. Shah Bano Begum* case of 1985, sparking intense conservative Muslim opposition, led by the All-India Muslim Personal Law Board, the main organization demanding adherence to conservative precedent in Indian Muslim law.

The Indian Parliament passed the Muslim Women (Protection of Rights on Divorce) Act in 1986 to contain conservative Muslim mobilization, but some of the act's provisions did not clearly fit the conservative position that the obligation of Muslim husbands to provide for their ex-wives be limited to a three-month period. While Section 3 restricted the husband's maintenance obligations to the *iddat* period, Sections 3(1)(a) and 4 called for the husband to pay for his ex-wife's "fair and reasonable provision" (perhaps in addition to maintenance) for an unspecified length of time "within the *iddat* period." The courts resolved the resulting ambiguity about the period for which ex-husbands needed to provide alimony by decreeing alimony until the woman's remarriage or death in the majority of cases between 1986 and 2001, until the Supreme Court made this interpretation binding on all courts in the *Danial Latifi v. Union of India* case in 2001.

Until 1978 the courts recognized men's unilateral divorce of their wives in a single sitting through the so-called triple *talaq*, more formally called the *talaq-ul ba'in* (irrevocable divorce), through the oral or written statement "*talaq, talaq, talaq*" ("I divorce you," repeated thrice). They did so although there were many grounds on which this interpretation of Islamic law could be opposed: such pronouncements of unilateral divorce in one sitting were deemed revocable in the early Islamic community; some schools of Islamic law did not ever consider such divorces valid (including the Shafi'i, Ithna Ashari, Mustaʿlian Ismaʿili, and Ahl-e-Hadith schools, whose adherents account for a significant minority of India's Muslim population); and all schools of Islamic law considered other forms of divorce preferable, with the claim that such a method of divorce is "good in law, though bad in theology." Some courts ruled the triple *talaq* revocable from 1978 onward, and established two conditions for the validity of unilateral male divorce, based on verses of the Qur'an: the husband providing a reasonable cause, and spousal reconciliation being attempted through the mediation of relatives of both spouses. The Supreme Court made this the law binding on the lower courts in a case of 2002 (*Shamim Ara v. State of Uttar Pradesh*).

The judicial reform of Muslim alimony and divorce law effected partial convergence with Hindu law, the law governing about 78 percent of India's population. In the reform of both alimony and divorce law, the courts introduced only those changes that they felt could find justification in Islamic normative tradition, and resisted the efforts of activist lawyers to systematically remove the gender inequalities in family law with reference to the constitutional rights to life, liberty, dignity, and equality. For instance, they did not deem Muslim law irrelevant to divorce or alimony among Muslims, grant Muslim women rights to either unilaterally pronounce divorce or to shares in matrimonial property upon divorce, or give sons and daughters equal inheritance rights. The restrained nature of judicial reform contained conservative Muslim opposition, and so made the subsequent legislative overturning of these reforms unlikely. It suggests that the judiciary is unlikely to use the Indian constitution's egalitarian principles to systematically address the gender inequalities in Muslim law and in the other family laws.

The recent judicial reforms of Muslim law encouraged and drew indirect support from ongoing changes in matrimonial practices among Indian Muslims. Partly in response to these reforms, some conservative Muslim elites began attempts to reduce the incidence of the triple *talaq* and polygamy, to include in marriage contracts rights for women to initiate divorce and to get a substantial dower from their ex-husbands upon divorce, and to get community courts to recognize these rights.

As community courts consider the majority of Muslim matrimonial disputes, the future of Muslim law in India depends crucially on patterns of adjudication in these courts, over which all the branches of government exercise only limited influence.

Narendra Subramanian

See also **Family Law and Cultural Pluralism; Muslims**

BIBLIOGRAPHY

Agnes, Flavia. *Law and Gender Inequality: The Politics of Women's Rights in India*. Oxford University Press, 1999.

An-Na'im, Abdullahi. *Islamic Family Law in a Changing World: A Global Resource Book*. London: Zed Press, 2002.

Mahmood, Tahir. *Islamic Law in the Indian Courts since Independence: Fifty Years of Judicial Interpretation.* New Delhi: Institute of Objective Studies, 1997.

Menski, Werner F. *Modern Indian Family Law.* Richmond, U.K.: Curzon Press, 2001.

Parashar, Archana. *Women and Family Law Reform in India.* Sage Publications, 1992.

Sathe, S. P. *Judicial Activism in India: Transgressing Borders and Enforcing Limits.* New Delhi: Oxford University Press, 2002.

MUSLIM LEAGUE. *See* **All-India Muslim League.**

MUSLIMS There has been an ongoing controversy for many decades regarding the ways in which Islam entered Indian civilization and culture. This controversy has been largely connected to varying political characterizations of Indian Islam—its opponents seeing it as a fundamentally "foreign" imposition and "alien" presence in the subcontinent, and its advocates and believers viewing it as a brilliant and positive contribution to the heritage of Indian civilization. Historically, Islam came to be a religious, cultural, and political force in India in three different ways: through trade, conquest, and conversion. Its effects on Indian civilization then cannot be fairly seen from any one-dimensional perspective, but have from the beginning been multifaceted, diverse, and complex.

The Arrival of Islam in the South

It is generally believed that Islam first spread in South India with Arab traders passing through what is now Malabar. Commercial contacts were present between regions of the Arabian Peninsula and several western Indian coastal towns, which were conduits to centers of trade within southern India. Thus it is known that in the Malabar region (today part of Kerala) the presence of Arabs was quite common in pre-Islamic times. As Islam emerged in Arabia, these traders began to engage not only in trading goods but also in sharing their new faith with the people they encountered during their travels.

Namaz (Friday Prayers) at the Taj Mahal Mosque. In recent years, tensions between Muslims and Hindu nationalists have again mounted, with violence toward Muslims on the upswing. Many fear that this will soon result in a more militant brand of Islam in India. MARYAM RESHI / FOTOMEDIA.

According to most accounts, Islam received a warm welcome in the southern regions of India. Muslim traders constituted an important link to prosperous intercontinental trade that benefited local Indian merchants and consumers alike. In addition, early Muslim settlers in southern India were seasoned traders who were cognizant of their responsibilities and for the most part did not harbor any political ambitions. As they built mosques and community institutions, their religion, Islam, became known and attracted converts. As a different ethnic group, they were seen as having a distinct caste status, equivalent to the Hindu high caste, and thus were able to associate with Hindu nobles and other upper caste people of influence. They were also able to intermarry, which gave these non-Hindus greater status among the locals. The intermarriage between Arabs and South Indians and the raising of children in such marriages as distinctly Muslim in the Indian environment created a

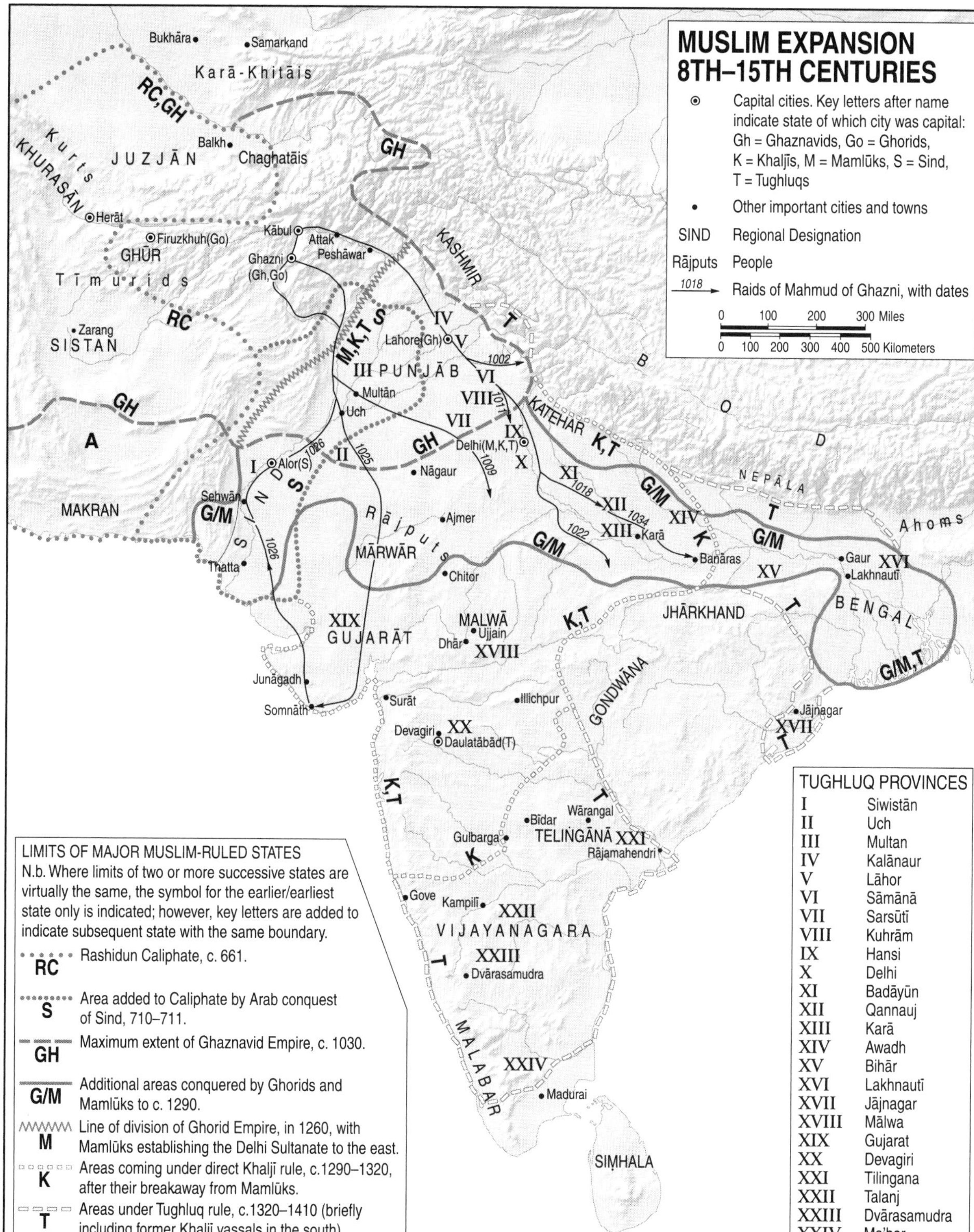

fusion of cultures and traditions at various levels. Since Arabic was fast becoming the dominant language of culture, scholarship, and commerce, these indigenous Muslims consciously retained their Arab heritage and used their Arabic language skills as a bridge between natives and Arabs in the pursuit of commercial gains. The Arabs and the native Indian rulers and traders benefited by complementing each other; the Arabs benefited from the trade of Indian goods, and the Indians learned the art of seafaring from the Arabs. Thus several examples of such mutual exchange and cooperation can be found during this period. Some are even found in legends and folklore.

Conquest and Alliance in the Northwest

In the northwestern region of the subcontinent, Islam arrived through various forms of conquest. In 711 when Muhammad bin Qasim arrived in Sind, he was not greeted with the same hospitality as the Arabs in the south. The reasons for the invasion of Sind by Qasim, who later became governor of the region in the Umayyad caliphate of Damascus, were—from the historical records we possess—retaliations for having his trading caravans attacked by local "bandits."

Muhammad bin Qasim made alliances in the region and declared Hindus (Brahmans) and Buddhists as *dhimmi*s (protected groups). They were allowed to practice their religion and maintain their religious institutions under Muslim rule in exchange for their services, which included the collection of revenues from subjects of the state. Religiously speaking, considering Hindus and Buddhists as *dhimmi*s was a remarkably "liberal" step, as they are not mentioned in the Qur'an or in the sayings of the Prophet as being such. This was an act of *ijtihad* (independent reasoning) on the part of Qasim, who was supported in his judgment by the ulama (Islamic religious scholars) of the Umayyad court, who had previously declared the Zoroastrians of Persia as deserving of *dhimmi* status.

The first major sultanate to emerge in North India was the Ghaznavid (997–1175), which marked the beginning of the rule of the "slave kings," so called because prior to their rule, they served as trained and compensated soldiers within the Abbasid dynasty (750–1258), guarding its outposts in the regions of Afghanistan and northwestern India. The most famous figure from this dynasty is Mahmud of Ghazni (971–1030), reputed to have championed temple destruction in many regions of northern and western India. He plundered the wealth from many of the famous temples, including the Somnath, and used this wealth to strengthen his hold on power. Mahmud staged more than a dozen invasions of Sind over a period of approximately fifteen years, though he was clearly less interested in establishing an outpost of the Abbasid empire in North India than he was in buttressing the wealth of his own empire and its center in Ghazni.

In the employ of Mahmud of Ghazni worked one of the most famous medieval scholars, Abu Rayhan al-Biruni (973–1048), the first to study and write extensively on Indian religions and intellectual traditions. His work on India, *Kitab al-Hind*, was a compendium of India's religious and philosophical traditions. Al-Biruni, though under Mahmud's patronage, was critical of the latter's destruction of the Hindu temple in Somnath.

Historically, growth in the numbers of practicing Muslims in India has been a subject of controversy. Muslim rulers were not interested in converting the masses to Islam as much as they desired to maintain political and economic control over their territories.

From the ninth through the twelfth centuries, the Muslim populace expanded due to multiple factors. Some emigrated from other Muslim lands in North Africa and Arabia through Central Asia and Afghanistan. There were also conversions to Islam from various Hindu castes and subcastes. The single largest factor in conversions seems to have been an egalitarian form of Islam displayed by the Sufis and others who seemed open to a wide variety of spiritual practices. Sufis were apolitical and sometimes antiestablishment. They were often critical of the institutional religious and political hierarchy; hence they were closer to the masses than to the Muslim elite. They established *khanqah*s (community centers) for spiritual guidance, which were open to all.

There were other factors that led to the growth of Muslim communities in India, notably political patronage by the Muslim rulers, which attracted artisans, scholars, landed gentry, and other high caste Hindus. Some historians in recent times have argued that there were also forcible mass conversions to Islam, but a general consensus of scholars opposes this view. There are several examples of the destruction of Hindu temples at the hands of some rulers, but these were exceptions to the norm. Rulers were often interested in increasing their political capital, and where it suited them they destroyed temples, while in other places they granted land and other resources for temple building. Indeed, indigenous Hindu groups were often militarily aligned with both centralizing and anticentralizing forces during the six successive dynasties of the Delhi Sultanate (1192–1526).

The Sultanate Period (1192–1526)

As Ghaznavid power declined, it gave way to the reign of other "slave kings," which included the dynastic succession of the Ghorids (1192–1290), the Khaljis (1290–1320), and the Tughluqs (1320–1398), culminating in the Lodi (1451–1526) dynasty. The Sultanate period, which lasted from the late twelfth to the early sixteenth centuries, began with the invasion of India by Muiz al-Din Ghori, who was of Turkish origin. Unlike Mahmud of Ghazni, who came to India simply to plunder and loot, Ghori and his descendants aimed to establish political control which manifested itself as the Delhi Sultanate.

The sultanates created a relatively stable political structure during this period, while the ultimate political

TOP: Covered with traditional veil and bejeweled in gold, a Bishnois woman smiles for the camera outside the city of Jodhpur, in Rajasthan. AMIT PASRICHA/ FOTOMEDIA

TOP: In Mysore, Karnataka, a worker applies final touches of white paint to a 5-foot elephant intricately carved from rosewood. V. MUTHURAMAN/FOTOMEDIA

BOTTOM LEFT: This vendor's eclectic selection of straw hats mirrors the rich ethnic heritage of the city of Kochi (or Cochin) in Kerala. V. MUTHURAMAN/FOTOMEDIA

BOTTOM RIGHT: Artisans sculpt miniature likenesses of legendary places from pith, a porous reed endemic to Eastern India with a pure white inner core. Their handiwork is astonishingly detailed and accurate. V. MUTHURAMAN/FOTOMEDIA

TOP LEFT: In Lucknow, Uttar Pradesh, a seamstress painstakingly stitches a sari with gold thread, embellishing its floral motifs. AMIT PASRICHA/FOTOMEDIA

TOP RIGHT: Detail of royal heirloom from Jaipur, emblematic of traditional *zari*, dense gold embroidery. ADITYA PATANKAR / FOTOMEDIA

BOTTOM: In Sualkuchi, Assam, spindles of vibrantly hued silk yarn. In this town, just about every household participates in the business of silk—from raising silk worms to weaving the final product. IPSHITA BARUA/FOTOMEDIA

TOP: With careful precision, an artisan creates a *mridangam*, a double-sided drum, from a single piece of wood and goatskin. V. MUTHURAMAN/ FOTOMEDIA

BOTTOM: In India's rural communities, the exteriors of homes are frequently painted in swirling floral patterns to welcome the gods and ward off evil spirits. Practiced by women, this art involves mixing mud and cow dung, which is then plastered to the walls and decorated with rice paste and brightly colored powders. ADITYA PATANKAR / FOTOMEDIA

TOP: In the hands of this craftsman in Kerala, a dancing Shiva ("Nataraj") emerges from wood. AMIT PASRICHA/FOTOMEDIA

BOTTOM LEFT: In rural Rajasthan, a young weaver deftly works her loom. AMITA PRASHAR GUPTA/FOTOMEDIA

BOTTOM RIGHT: Artisan crafts a long-necked *veena*, the traditional string instrument of South India that resembles a sitar. V. MUTHURAMAN/FOTOMEDIA

TOP: In Vishakapatnam, Andhra Pradesh, hand-woven grass mats and baskets for sale. DINESH KHANNA/FOTOMEDIA

BOTTOM: A fair-goer sports embroidered vest at Tarnetar in Gujarat. For centuries, Gujarat has been identified with such intricate handiwork, a craft still practiced by the semi-nomadic communities of Kutch. DINESH KHANNA/FOTOMEDIA

TOP: In preparation for the ten-day Durga Puja festival in Bengal, a member of the Kumartuli (the artisan caste) creates a life-size idol. AMIT PASRICHA/ FOTOMEDIA

BOTTOM: Before his painted and richly adorned chariot, revelers pay homage to Jagannath (Lord of the Universe). Photo taken at the Rath Yatra festival, held every June/July in Puri, Orissa. DINESH KHANNA/FOTOMEDIA

TOP: Two members of the Salawas, a Rajasthan community, weave a dhurrie rug. Dhurries are typically made of cotton or camel's hair and distinguished by bold geometric patterns. AMIT PASRICHA/ FOTOMEDIA

BOTTOM: Colorful cast of characters in Jaipur, Rajasthan. Puppet theater is a long-standing tradition and remains an important form of entertainment. DINESH KHANNA/FOTOMEDIA

authority rested with the Turkic sultans who, at least nominally, displayed Islam as their religious as well as political ideology. Among the populace, the religion of Islam meant something different. It was not synonymous with power or political dominance, and mostly grew among the poor. In fact, in the multifaceted social structure that developed in the midst of this complex period, it was generally acknowledged within the Muslim populace that the ulama held a religious authority that could not be subordinated or abrogated by the sultan, be he a local or imperial sultan. Instead, sultans generally attempted to legitimize their rule by acknowledging the authority of local ulama and particularly of Sufi saints.

It should be noted that during this period there was a creative cultural melding of traditions, which resulted in systems of military cooperation strong enough to head off the powerful Mongol advance, agrarian management systems that would survive well into the British colonial period, and an artistic and architectural synthesis so compelling that its creations still draw tourists to India today. Through the medieval period, Muslim intellectuals, Sufis, artisans, and travelers in general were attracted to South Asia from all parts of the Muslim world. This resulted in an administrative system resembling Islamic structures developed in the Muslim caliphates of Iraq and Syria.

The role of the Sufis was central to the growth of Islam, as they were generous in establishing their *khanqah*s. These centers also served as places for devotional and therapeutic needs. Sufis and religious leaders filled the need for education as well as spiritual fulfillment.

As the Delhi Sultanate became weak at the center, it resulted in the emergence of regional dynasties—in Bengal in the east and Gujarat in the west. The Bahmani kingdom in the south became independent of the Sultanate in 1347 and lasted for almost two hundred years before being split up into four smaller kingdoms. Its rulers, patrons of Sufi saints, also supported a variety of forms of Indo-Islamic art and the spread of Islamic tradition in South India.

In this regional arrangement of political power, Muslim culture developed in collaboration with local linguistic and social norms. This contributed to the increasing diversity of Islamic societies, cultures, and traditions. Muslim rulers and nobles formed alliances based on political and economic interests that went beyond religious and sectarian (Shiʿa-Sunni) affiliation. Hindu kings fought with Turkish rulers, Muslim rebels collaborated with Hindus to secede from the Sultanate's center, and so on.

The Mughal Empire (1526–1858)

The Mughals were heirs to the earlier Muslim dynasties that were sustained by their concentration of power within the Turkic ruling classes. By contrast, the Mughal empire thrived through power-sharing practice with Hindus and other Muslim elites. The Mughal rulers often had alliances that cut across religious and ethnic divides. The two major concentrations of power at the dawn of the Mughal period in India were with the Lodhi dynasty and the Rajputs.

As the Sultanate of Ibrahim Lodi became divided into many regional kingdoms, it was successfully invaded by Zahir al-Din Babur (1483–1530), who himself hailed from the central Asian region of Ferghana. There he laid the foundations for what became the most powerful and extensive Muslim empire in India. Babur also had to defeat the Hindu Rajput kingdom before consolidating his power. Babur's son Humayun ruled India from 1530 to 1556, except for a period of fifteen years (1540–1555), and eventually recaptured the throne by absorbing many regional kingdoms in the fold of the empire. He died a year later, in 1556, leaving behind a very young Akbar in charge.

Jalaluddin Muhammad Akbar (r. 1556–1605) has been credited for laying the foundations for the empire by initiating a number of innovations, such as a centralized political administration. His fiscal reforms were also effective. Akbar had the acumen to draw on his knowledge of both Persian and Turkic administrative practices on the one hand and those of the Rajputs and Indian Muslim dynastic rulers on the other. He was successfully able to fuse elements from these systems to construct his own administrative structure, which became the sustaining factor of the empire and continued to be implemented during the reigns of all the great Mughals until the beginning of the eighteenth century. Under Akbar, the Mughal empire continued to expand. This was possible because of alliances through marriage and royal patronage with other powers such as the Rajputs. Akbar was succeeded by his son, Jahangir (r. 1605–1627), and his grandson, Shah Jahan (r. 1628–1658).

The political expansion of the empire continued during the reign of Aurangzeb (r. 1658–1707). With a centralized power structure and an elaborate system of promotion of the nobles, the Mughals were successful in politically uniting most of the Indian subcontinent. But the wars of succession weakened the empire after Aurangzeb and eventually led to the British political takeover of parts of the empire. Rival Muslim rulers twice sacked Delhi, the seat of Mughal power, first in 1739 by Nadir Shah of Persia and again in 1761 by the Afghan ruler Ahmad Shah Abdali. In 1757 the British East India Company defeated the Muslim armies at Plassey, and by the beginning of the nineteenth century, Delhi, too, was effectively under the control of the British, although a figurehead Mughal emperor remained on the throne until after the "Mutiny" of 1857.

British Rule in India (1757–1947)

After the 1857 mutiny (also known as the "Sepoy rebellion") was crushed and Delhi was under the control of the British, the East India Company was no longer in charge, and the rule was administered directly by the British Crown.

Muslim power had been reduced to a few regions. Despite attempts to assert its legitimacy, Muslim rule had basically come to an end, and the British were firmly established throughout most of the Indian subcontinent. From their humble beginnings in the early eighteenth century as a trading company in Bengal, to a full-fledged empire with millions of Indian subjects, the British succeeded the Timurid Muslim (Mughal) power, which had constructed a unique cultural landscape in its three-hundred-year presence in India.

There were several attempts to reverse the course of British expansion during the three centuries of British presence in India. The Muslim loss of power meant that as a political minority they would stand to lose the most under non-Muslim rule. It was generally believed that Muslim rule was essential to the implementation of Shariʿa (Islamic law), which governs all aspects of Muslim life. Without Shariʿa Muslims would not be able to fully practice their faith.

There were calls for jihad, or armed resistance against the British, such as the one made by the Muslim scholar Sayyid Ahmad Barelwi (1786–1831). He argued that because of the loss of Muslim power, India was no longer *dar al-Islam* (house or land of Islam). India had fallen into opposite category—*dar al-harb* (territory open to war)—and thus it became incumbent for Muslims to wage war against the British establishment. Sayyid Ahmad led many of his followers into the movement and died in 1831 while fighting the Sikhs in the northwestern India. He is widely regarded as a *shahid* (martyr).

Muslim Modernist Reformers (Nineteenth and Twentieth Centuries)

Many Muslim scholars, Sufis, and political elite challenged the authority of the British on religious grounds. There were some, however, who chose the path of cooperation with the British. One such scholar, who later founded the Mohammadan Anglo-Oriental College in 1875 (later renamed Aligarh Muslim University), was Sayyid Ahmed Khan (1817–1898). Khan was primarily concerned with the welfare of Muslims in light of what he saw as the intellectual and scientific advancements made by the British. He wanted Muslims to learn from the British in order to improve their educational and social status. While Khan promoted British-style educational curriculum and called for Muslim women's education, other ulama (Muslim religious scholars) established the Dar-ul ʿUlum at Deoband, which became the center of Islamic learning and continues to enjoy an international reputation as such.

Sayyid Ahmed Khan inspired other reformers. Sayyid Ameer Ali (1849–1928) was a Western-educated Shiʿa scholar whose major contribution was his work on Islam for a Western audience. Muhammad Iqbal (1877–1938) was also trained and educated in the West and steeped in its philosophical tradition. Iqbal, the poet and the philosopher, inspired some Muslims to see in his thought an argument for a separate Muslim homeland, later translated into a demand for Pakistan in the mid-1940s.

Independence from the British in 1947

The idea of a Muslim homeland surfaced as the anti-British nationalist movement was about to witness the realization of its main objective, freedom from the British. The Indian National Congress (the Congress Party), which was established in 1885 as a political organization for and by the Indian elite, increasingly began to challenge the legitimacy of the British in India. In the early twentieth century, the Congress became the principal agency representing the aspirations of millions of Indians seeking to rid India of the British Raj. It coexisted and sometimes cooperated with other nationalist and religious movements, such as the All-India Muslim League (established in 1906), which worked toward similar objectives.

Muslims and Hindus both participated in the Congress's efforts to establish what they called "self-rule." Even though the British had tried and, to some extent, succeeded in creating separate communal identities for Hindus and Muslims, the two communities resisted such compartmentalization based solely on religious differences. Most Muslims and Hindus shared common cultural and ethnic backgrounds, their linguistic and social commonalities more significant than their religious differences. But the British, based on the Orientalist constructions of the two communities as two different peoples, continued their policy of treating them as such. Politically, this worked in favor of the British; by pitting one group against the other, they were able to continue their political and economic subjugation of India. Hindu-Muslim unity was a major threat to the existence of British power.

The key players in the Congress Party, Mohandas Gandhi (1869–1947), Jawaharlal Nehru (1889–1964), and Abul Kalam Azad (1888–1958), worked tirelessly to deconstruct the idea of Hindu and Muslim separateness. Other Muslims, such as the prominent leader of the

Muslim League, Mohammad Ali Jinnah (1876–1948), argued that Muslims in free India would not be able to receive just treatment as a minority and that their interests would not be protected. He and some others demanded special autonomous powers for the Muslim-majority regions as part of a federal system once India became free. The alternate solution was to partition India into two separate states. The new state, Pakistan, would be fashioned out of the territories in the northwest and the eastern half of Bengal (the latter was to become independent from Pakistan in 1971 as the separate nation of Bangladesh). Neither proposal was acceptable to the leaders of the Congress Party.

Among the Muslims who opposed the idea of partition were two influential community leaders, Abdul Ghaffar Khan (1890–1988) and Abul Kalam Azad. Ghaffar Khan was an admirer and follower of Gandhi who believed in and implemented the latter's principle of *ahimsa* (nonviolence) by forming what he called the Khudai Khidmatgar (servants of God) movement, in which members vowed to serve God by serving others, while utilizing nonviolence as their only weapon. He worked among his ethnic community of Pathans in the North-West Frontier province and was quite successful in mobilizing his people to engage in nonviolent social activism against British rule.

Azad, an erudite scholar of Islam and a colleague and admirer of Gandhi, was particularly distressed by the idea of a separate Muslim homeland causing a permanent rift between Hindus and Muslims. Unlike some other Muslim elite who dreamed of restoring Muslim rule in India, Azad focused on possible models in which Hindus and Muslims would be able to share power in a democratically governed India. Azad was a nationalist and a committed anti-British activist.

The early 1920s brought Indians of all stripes and vocations closer together. Even Muslim religious organizations such as the Jamiʿat ʿUlama-i Hind (Society of Indian Islamic Scholars) supported the nationalist struggle against the British and were opposed to partition. In fact, a vast majority of Muslims were not enthusiastic about the "two-nation" idea because of sheer practical concerns. Muslims were spread all over India and lived side by side with Hindus. The partition, as it was imagined in the minds of the handful of Muslim elite, was neither possible nor desirable.

Another major Muslim institution that came into being during this time, with the support of Gandhi and other nationalists, was the Jamia Millia Islamia (Muslim Nationalist University). Established in 1920 at Aligarh (later moved to New Delhi in 1925), it began as a reaction to the then famous Aligarh Muslim University, which had been founded on the principle of cooperation with the British and remained to some extent oriented toward British intellectual traditions. Many nationalist and secular-minded Muslims later became associated with the Jamia, and others emerged from its ranks as the institution developed into a full-fledged university in a democratic republic of India.

The Partition

The movement for Pakistan based its rationale on religious and cultural notions of self-preservation. Its proponents argued that Muslims must preserve their culture and religious way of life by implementing the Shariʿa. This would not be possible in a free India where Muslims, being a minority, would not have the power to ensure governance according to Islamic law. The main thrust of this movement was a desire to return India to Muslim rule, albeit with a twist of religious flavor. This was a classical Islamist proposition. Maulana Abu'l ʿAla Maududi (1903–1979), the founder of the religious organization Jamaʿat-i Islami (Islamic party, founded in 1941), who was at first against the partition of India, became the chief proponent of the idea of implementing Islamic law in a newly created Pakistan. There were others who had similar objectives on the grounds that Muslim cultural and economic interests would not be met in a Hindu-majority India. Jinnah, a secularist leader of the Muslim League, was in the forefront of this struggle. Earlier in the Congress's struggle for independence, he had worked with Gandhi, but toward the mid-1930s he parted ways and worked in competition with and against the Congress Party.

Eager to remove themselves from the subcontinent, the British, under the pretext of being concerned for minority rights in a Hindu-majority India, seemed willing to accept the Muslim League's proposal of a "two-nation" solution. Gandhi, Azad, and other leaders of the Congress Party were against the division of the country, but they reluctantly accepted it; the alternate solution, having a federal system with greater autonomy for the Muslim provinces, drew even more severe objections from the members of the Congress, including Nehru, who advocated a centralized power structure. Thus on 14 August 1947, the dominion of Pakistan was created and consisted of two noncontiguous territories, the northwestern region as well as the eastern half of Bengal. Jinnah became the new nation's first governor-general and president of its legislative assembly. However, he did not live long enough to see the struggle that ensued between Islamic and secular forces, each vying to move Pakistan toward their respective visions of a Muslim homeland. Hours later, just past midnight on the 15th, India was declared independent, dividing the Muslims of British

India into two roughly equal halves. Nehru became the first prime minister of independent India.

While celebrations for independence were underway, a tragedy of massive proportions unfolded. Thousands of Hindus and Sikhs had to leave their belongings and migrate from what had become Pakistan, the west Punjab, and Sind, while Muslims from various parts of India migrated toward Pakistan and eastern Bengal. The partition of India was a major tragedy for Indians in general. Members of the same family found themselves at opposite sides of the great political divide, afraid at times to even communicate with each other lest they become suspected of compromising their loyalty to the state in which they resided.

Indian Muslims since Independence

The partition caused a serious blow to Indian Muslims. Even though India became a secular and not a Hindu state, the blame for the division of the country (at least unofficially) was placed squarely on Muslims. Since independence, Muslims as a minority have experienced large-scale violent campaigns launched against them. Known as communal riots, many of these are deemed to be planned and well-organized "pogroms." The net result of the violence has been that, over fifty years after independence, there is little mutual trust between members of the two communities.

The recent rise of Hindu militant nationalist groups has once again raised the issue of Muslims' loyalty to India in light of their erroneous reading of Indian history. Since the reasons given for the partition were religious and communal, Muslims, as a religious community distinct from Hindus, were seen as misplaced and unwelcome in independent India. They suffered the most politically, by not being part of the Pakistan movement, but also in social, economic, and psychological terms. The wounds of the partition incurred by many Muslim families on both sides of the border took three decades to heal, since they found themselves divided physically as well as psychologically.

Hindu-Muslim riots, or what many have recognized as pogroms against Muslims, have become increasingly organized and coordinated over the years. Before the 1990s they were more sporadic, and while highly organized, the element of local initiative was crucial. But, during the height of the Babri Mosque controversy, the organized efforts to destroy and uproot Muslim communities received far greater national-level support from right-wing resources than was imagined before. The act of destruction of the historic mosque in Ayodhya was carried out locally, but it was planned, supported, and funded by the vast network of Hindu nationalist elements throughout India. It was a tragedy of international proportions, one that shook the secular foundations of the democratic Constitution of India. Even the central government was unsuccessful in preventing the destruction because, as Paul Brass in *The Production of Hindu-Muslim Violence in Contemporary India* rightly observes, anti-minority violence is coordinated in the sense that most of the time the police forces are found to be prejudiced against Muslims; therefore, despite its best intentions, the government is unable to act because this essential arm of the law becomes paralyzed.

Muslims in the Twenty-first Century

Even though the notion of "Indian Muslims" may appear somewhat reasonable given the unifying nature of the fundamentals of Islam, it is, in fact, a construction like its counterpart, "the Hindus." Muslims are a very dissimilar group with respect to their religious practices, ideological affiliations, and social, cultural, and political preferences. Such construction of identity is also problematic in dealing with issues of gender justice. The Muslim religio-cultural discourse tends to define women as well as their roles in homogenous terms, disallowing full realization of their potential. During Muslim rule between the twelfth and eighteenth centuries, however, Muslim women made significant contributions as poets, authors, mystics, and teachers. Princess Jahanara (1614–1681), the eldest daughter of Shah Jahan, was one such famous intellectual and mystic. Women were not completely absent from public life either; the Sultanate period had its first queen in Razia Sultana (r. 1236–1240). During the nineteenth and twentieth centuries the throne of Bhopal was occupied by women rulers; the last to be named was Abida Sultaan (d. 2002) who ruled the state from 1935 to 1949.

Within Muslim communities, Muslim women are among the most disadvantaged. Women's educational rights are only recently being recognized, while they remain politically marginalized for cultural and economic reasons. Despite these challenges, Muslim women have made and continue to make significant advances in promoting female education and in removing barriers preventing their economic independence.

Even though Muslims are a diverse people, both the right-wing Hindus and the politically motivated Muslim leaders continue to insist on identifying Muslims as a monolith block of people with one agenda, one culture, and one religion. Nothing could be further from the truth. In fact, as recent studies (by Peter van der Veer and Cynthia Talbot) have shown, individual identities were understood in flexible terms in the past, and they were not compartmentalized in a single characteristic form, such as Muslim, Hindu, or Christian. Rather they were perceived in terms of geography, culture, state, profession, and language. Thus in medieval India, one could not simply be identified as Muslim without also being recognized as, for example, a Bengali, an easterner, a trader, a speaker of Bengali, and so forth.

In the post–Babri Mosque era, steps have been taken in building bridges between Hindus and Muslims and highlighting their shared history and common objectives in a democratic India. Several Muslim leaders, such as Wahiduddin Khan (b. 1925) and Asghar Ali Engineer (b. 1939), have made significant intellectual and social contributions through their writings, dialogue, and personal examples.

The legacies of Islam in India are, despite the minority framework imposed during the colonial period, inextricably intertwined with the legacies of Indian society as a whole, and both of these continue to unfold in the present. In the entire millennium of its presence in India, from architecture to music, from language to community belonging, from history writing to history making, Muslims have joined with Hindus and other groups in constructing the edifice of a great civilization. It lies to Indians of the twenty-first century to find paths through their communal frameworks and to continue to build upon this edifice.

Irfan A. Omar

See also **Akbar; Aurangzeb; Ayodhya; Babur; British Crown Raj; Congress Party; Gandhi, Mahatma M. K.; Humayun; Iqbal, Muhammad; Islam; Jahangir; Jinnah, Mohammad Ali; Nehru, Jawaharlal; Sayyid Ahmed Khan and the Aligarh Movement; Shah Jahan**

BIBLIOGRAPHY

al-Biruni, Abu Rayhan. *Alberuni's India*, edited by Ainslee Embree. New York: Norton, 1971.

Ali, Azra Asghar. *The Emergence of Feminism among Indian Muslim Women, 1920–1947*. New York: Oxford University Press, 2000.

Bayly, Susan. *Saints, Goddesses and Kings: Muslims and Christians in South Indian Society, 1700–1900*. Cambridge, U.K.: Cambridge University Press, 2002.

Brass, Paul. *The Production of Hindu-Muslim Violence in Contemporary India*. Seattle: University of Washington Press, 2003.

Eaton, Richard M., ed. *India's Islamic Traditions, 711–1750*. New Delhi: Oxford University Press, 2003.

Gandhi, Rajmohan. *Eight Lives: A Study of the Hindu Muslim Encounter*. Albany: State University of New York Press, 1986.

Haq, Mushir-ul. *Muslim Politics in Modern India, 1857–1947*. Meerut: Meenakshi Prakasan, 1970.

Hardy, Peter. *The Muslims of British India*. Cambridge, U.K.: Cambridge University Press, 1972.

Ikram, S. M. *Muslim Civilization in India*. New York: Columbia University Press, 1993.

Jackson, Peter. *The Delhi Sultanate: A Political and Military History*. New York: Cambridge University Press, 1999.

Lelyveld, David. *Aligarh's First Generation: Muslim Solidarity in British India*. New Delhi: Oxford University Press, 1996.

Maclean, Derryl. *Religion and Society in Arab Sind*. Leiden: E. J. Brill, 1989.

Metcalf, Barbara Daly. *Islamic Revival in British India: Deoband, 1860–1900*. New Delhi: Oxford University Press, 2002.

Taher, Mohamed. *Muslim Political Thought in India*. New Delhi: Anmol Publications, 1998.

Talbot, Cynthia. "Inscribing the Other, Inscribing the Self: Hindu-Muslim Identities in Pre-colonial India." *Comparative Studies in Society and History* 37, no. 4 (1995): 692–722.

Veer, Peter van der. *Religious Nationalism: Hindus and Muslims in India*. New Delhi: Oxford University Press, 1996.

MUTUAL FUNDS, ROLE OF The foundation for the mutual fund industry in India was laid in 1963 with the passage of the Unit Trust of India (UTI) Act. The act entrusted the Reserve Bank of India (RBI) with the task of setting up an institution that could facilitate the mobilization of resources from investors across the country. The UTI then floated its maiden open-ended fund in 1964, Unit-Scheme 1964, popularly known as "US-64"; the UTI Act had provided for an initial capital of 50 million rupees to be invested in this first plan. Several insurance companies, finance institutions, and banks, including the RBI, contributed to this initial corpus.

The initial years of the UTI Act laid down the milestones of policies, standards of conduct and practices, and processes of management. The Board of Trustees initially decided to offer the sale of units at a nominal value of 10 rupees each at par for the entire month of July 1964, attracting of 175 million rupees from 125,000 investors. US-64 underwent many changes, with added features, including a reinvestment plan, under which the unit holders automatically reinvested dividend earnings, and a children's gift plan.

During the initial years of development, from 1964 to 1987, UTI was the lone mutual fund, managing five open-ended funds. The second phase started in 1987 with the arrival of new mutual funds, sponsored by nationalized banks and other public sector financial institutions. The State Bank of India (SBI) and Canara Bank set up an SBI Mutual Fund (SBI MF) and Canbank Mutual Fund (Canbank MF), respectively, in 1987. Subsequently, other public sector banks and insurance companies joined the race by the end of 1990. With the beginning of economic liberalization, the financial sector industry also witnessed liberalization, with new players, new regulations, and a new structure. In 1993 the Securities and Exchange Board of India (SEBI), the capital market regulator, for the first time issued mutual fund regulations, which permitted entry to private sector mutual funds.

The UTI Act of 1963 was repealed in February 2003, and consequently UTI bifurcated into two distinct organizations: Specified Undertaking of Unit Trust of India (popularly known as UTI I) and UTI Asset Management Company Limited (UTI AMC). The UTI I is under the supervision of the government of India, and UTI AMC is regulated by SEBI.

The first growth fund (mutual fund), Mastershare, was launched in 1986 by the UTI. The success of Mastershare provided impetus to float more growth-oriented funds. Consequently, new entrants to the industry, namely Canbank MF and SBI MF, joined the race. The year 1989 witnessed further product innovations: venture capital funds began operating for the first time, and tax saving funds also entered the market. SBI MF was the first to offer a tax saving fund, while UTI offered a venture capital fund. Assured return funds started functioning from 1990 with the launch of Candouble. With a view to meeting the objectives of different sectors, the industry has responded by introducing products such as regular income, capital appreciation, and a children's gift growth fund. The industry is in the process of introducing more new products, including a commodity mutual fund and a real estate mutual fund.

Growth and Status

By June 1974, investable funds under UTI's management reached 1,720 million rupees (unit capital 1,520 million rupees). There were 6 lakh (600,000 rupees) unit holding accounts under four plans. US-64 investors were rewarded well, with their investment consistently earning better returns than deposits in banks. It was during the 1980s that UTI grew in stature to emerge as one of India's large nationwide financial institutions. From 1981 to 1984, UTI introduced more than six new open-end and closed-end schemes; investable funds quadrupled from 5 billion rupees to 20 billion rupees; the number of unit holding accounts grew from 1 million to 1.7 million; and the number of branch offices increased to eleven. From 1986 to 1990, UTI launched a large number of innovative products, strengthened the marketing network, and promoted new organizations in the financial sector.

The industry has, however, experienced a sporadic expansion of late. The assets under management slowly grew from 32,180 million rupees in 1985–1986 to 1,396,160 million rupees in 2003–2004. The yearly resources mobilized also have had ups and downs. In the year 2003–2004, the industry mobilized 468,090 million rupees, the highest in its history. As of 31 March 2004 there were 403 different plans.

Consolidation in the Indian Mutual Fund Industry

India's mutual fund industry, under its new regulatory environment, is quite young. There was an initial exuberance, and many domestic as well as overseas professional and industrial houses sought regulatory licenses to set up asset management companies to manage mutual funds. Many of them have been granted licenses. A large number of mutual fund houses have been set up. Some mutual fund houses could not attain a critical mass for many years, and several foreign funds found it very expensive to operate in India.

Competition in the industry increased pressure on marketing expenses, and the relatively small investor base made it difficult for smaller players to survive. For all these reasons, consolidation of the Indian mutual fund industry began, and since 2000 some of the industrial houses have sold their assets to other mutual funds.

Challenges

Though the industry started with one lone player, in 1986 the government of India allowed others to enter, and now many public, private, joint, and foreign sector mutual fund houses operate in India. Yet the growth of the industry has not been very impressive. Unlike most countries, in which retail and small investors are the major investors in mutual funds, in India the share of retail investors has recently been coming down. Corporations and institutions accounted for about 57 percent of total investors as of 31 March 2003, and individuals accounted for only about 41 percent.

Close examination of the investment pattern of Indian mutual funds reveals that there is a heavy tilt toward fixed income products (government debt, money market instruments, and corporate debt). Mutual fund industry champions need to initiate mass level investor education about the mutual fund industry and its pros and cons. Many investors still believe that investments in mutual funds cannot give negative returns.

Frequent change in tax policy has caused aberrations in the functioning and performance of the funds. Incentives are extended, withdrawn, and reintroduced many times, without sufficient notice, causing disturbances to the industry in its assets and performance. The industry, after a long period of existence, is still confined to large cities and towns. Most investable funds come from urban areas. In order to grow and serve larger economic functions, the industry must spread its scope to other areas.

A very skewed interest rate environment exists in India. There are certain guaranteed return plans of the government of India that offer higher rates of fixed coupons, some of which provide tax breaks. For certain categories of investors, the effective rate of return is very high over time. Therefore, among small investors in semiurban and rural areas, there is a lack of interest in mutual funds. This is a major hurdle that has inhibited the development of a more vital mutual fund industry.

M. T. Raju

See also **Capital Market; Commodity Markets; Debt Markets; Securities Exchange Board of India (SEBI); Stock Exchange Markets**

BIBLIOGRAPHY

Association of Mutual Funds in India and UTI Institute of Capital Markets. *Mutual Fund Yearbook, 2000.* Mumbai: AMFI and UTI-ICM, 2001.

Bhatt, R. S. *Unit Trust of India and Mutual Funds: A Study.* Navi Mumbai: UTI Institute of Capital Markets, 1996.

National Stock Exchange. *Indian Securities Market: A Review*, vol. V. Mumbai: NSE, 2002.

Reserve Bank of India. *Annual Report, 2003–04.* Mumbai: RBI, 2004.

Sahadevan, K. G., and M. Thiripalraju. *Mutual Funds: Data, Interpretation and Analysis.* New Delhi: Prentice-Hall of India, 1997.

Securities and Exchange Board of India. *Annual Report 2002–03 and 2003–04.* Mumbai: SEBI, 2004.

Unit Trust of India. *Three Decades of Unit Trust of India.* Mumbai: Department of Research and Planning, UTI, 1995.

MYSORE A city in the state of Karnataka, Mysore had a population of 742,000 in 2001. It was the old capital of the maharajas of Mysore before they shifted their capital to Bangalore. The name Mysore is derived from the mythical buffalo demon, Mahisasura, who was slain by the goddess Durgā, who is worshiped in Mysore under the name Chamundeshwari. Her temple on the Chamundi Hills is placed high above the city. Mysore is located at the center of a high plateau surrounded by mountains. Thus it was well suited as a stronghold of regional rulers such as the Wadiyar dynasty that controlled Mysore after the power of the Vijayanagar empire declined. In the last decades of the eighteenth century, the Wadiyars were temporarily replaced by the usurper Hyder Ali and his son Tipu Sultan. Hyder Ali was a very competent general who imitated European methods of warfare and military organization. Hyder Ali and Tipu Sultan were fighting against the British and the Marathas. In the first Mysore War, the British were defeated, but in the second one, Governor-General Lord Cornwallis defeated Tipu Sultan, annexing a large part of his domain; wanting, however, to retain Tipu as a counterweight to the Marathas, Cornwallis let him rule the remnant. In the third Mysore War, Tipu Sultan died on the battlefield in 1799. The new governor-general, Lord Wellesley, had been eager to get rid of Tipu, who was in league with the French. Wellesley's brother Arthur, later known as Iron Duke of Wellington, defeated Tipu just as he vanquished Napoleon Bonaparte.

The Wadiyar dynasty was later reinstated by the British, and a legislative assembly was also established. In subsequent years, Mysore became a model state as its rulers took a personal interest in its industrial advancement. Oil and soap made from sandalwood became major products of Mysore. It was also known for its fine silks. Even a small steel mill was started in the 1920s. Hydroelectic power was generated at Krishnarajasagar near Mysore city, another successful ambitious project.

Dietmar Rothermund

BIBLIOGRAPHY

Isaar, T. P. *Mysore. The Royal City*. Bangalore: Marketing Consultants, 1991.

Mahadev, P. D. *People, Space and Economy of an Indian City: An Urban Morphology of Mysore City*. Mysore: Institute of Development Studies, University of Mysore, 1975.

Misra, P. K. *Cultural Profiles of Mysore City*. Kolkata: Anthropological Survey of India, 1978.

n

NABOB GAME The "Nabob Game" is a modern term to describe the early method of imperial expansion in India by agents of European trading companies, especially the British East India Company and the French East India Company (La Compagnie perpétuelle des Indes), usually with the support of their respective governments. The French governor-general Joseph François Dupleix and the Englishman Robert Clive were pioneers in the Nabob Game. The term itself, and the related "Nabobism," derive from the Persian *nawāb*, meaning governor. "Nabob" was a pejorative rubric for East India company agents, such as Clive, who had garnered power and wealth in India. Methods used ranged from negotiation and diplomacy to bribery, extortion, coercion, threats, and force. Their motives were often mixed, intended to gain commercial advantage, military supremacy, and influence and power over Indian rulers and territories, as well as personal aggrandizement. By the 1770s, Nabobs were mistrusted, even reviled, upon returning to Europe. Nonetheless, the Nabob Game laid the foundation of the British Empire in India, especially the system known as "indirect rule."

Nabobism filled the political vacuum in India following the death of the Mughal emperor Aurangzeb in 1707. Within a decade, the Mughal empire began to disintegrate, and the nizam of Hyderabad and the *nawāb*s of Arcot, Mysore, Oudh, and Bengal could govern autonomously. They nominated and appointed tax collectors, used revenues and resources as they wished, conducted diplomatic and military activities among themselves, minted coins locally, and selected their successors. They no longer maintained the fiction that they were courtiers, and paid little more than lip service to the Mughal who gave them legitimacy.

Among Europeans, the French East India Company was the first to gain from the Mughal disintegration. French success in the Nabob Game depended largely on Dupleix, but even before he became governor-general in 1742, the French company had obtained the Mughal title of *nawāb* and the rights to maintain an armed force, collect land revenue, and mint rupees in Pondicherry. Dupleix's diplomacy was instrumental in obtaining the title of *nawāb* for the French company while he was governor of the French trading colony in Chandarnagar (near Calcutta), where he had regular contact with the Mughal court in Delhi. Dupleix and Governor-General Benoit Dumas both insisted that the Mughal rank be bestowed upon the company, although the powers and honors of the title were to rest with the governor-general in Pondicherry. Governors-general were, of course, chosen by the company directors, not the Mughal authority, so the choice of successors belonged, in practice, to non-Indians. The company's private army, needed for protection, was legitimized, and the company negotiated the right to mint rupees from imported silver in order to reduce minting costs. The French also obtained grants to collect land revenue from specified territories. The direct collection of land revenue, ostensibly to support troops, meant that the European *nawāb*, just as its Indian counterparts, had neither to depend on the Mughal treasury nor account for the revenue collected. In the case of the French East India Company, their territories constituted a trade zone closed to competition and a buffer from the depredations of warlords, brigands, and armies. The British had also sought land grants for the same reasons some years earlier. The assumption of Mughal titles was primarily a commercial decision, and their political and military benefits were secondary, albeit substantial.

As Anglo-French rivalry intensified during the War of the Austrian Succession (1742–1748) and the Seven Years' War (1756–1763), the respective East Indian companies found themselves enemies by proxy. In 1746 the French East India Company took Fort St. George (Chennai) from the British and was challenged by the *nawāb* of Arcot, who had forbidden hostilities. A small detachment of French troops defeated the *nawāb*'s much larger army, demonstrating European military superiority. Henceforth, the threat or use of European military force against an Indian force was a hallmark of the Nabob Game. The struggle for the throne of Hyderabad, the most powerful post in the south, was a more convincing example of the uses of force in the Nabob Game. With the deaths in short order of the aged Nizām al-Mulk in 1748 and his immediate successor, Nasir Jang, late in 1750, the throne of the nizam of Hyderabad was contested by Muzaffar Jang. Dupleix, in league with Chanda Sahib, a claimant to the throne of Arcot, successfully backed Muzaffar, who in return confirmed Chanda Sahib as *nawāb* of Arcot and ceded large and valuable land grants to the French. It is doubtful Dupleix sought anything more than commercial and strategic advantage, because he did not try to make either Chanda Sahib or Muzaffar Jang instruments of French policy. Even when French interests alienated Chanda Sahib, Dupleix did little to undermine his protégé, leaving Chanda Sahib to rule until 1752, when the Marathas, with British connivance, deposed him. Unsurprisingly, his successor on the throne was more congenial to the British.

Before being recalled in 1752, Dupleix treated appeals from the nizam of Hyderabad for help against the Marathas, led by the *peshwa* Balaji Rao, as more of an annoyance than an offer to ally against a real threat. Dupleix sent only a protective force commanded by the Marquis de Bussy, thinking of them as profitable mercenaries. Upon the unexpected death of the nizam, Muzaffar Jang, de Bussy backed Salabat Jang, and the grateful new nizam rewarded de Bussy handsomely, and, for the next seven years, the Marquis de Bussy was his senior political adviser and the prototype for "political agents" in Indian courts. Under the British, such political agents were to make policy and create kings for nearly two centuries.

French policy was more focused on fortune than power, but the Englishman Robert "Bully" Clive turned that on its head. He had intrigued against the French, using rivals to the nizam of Hyderabad and *nawāb* of Arcot, but nothing in the French experience prepared him for the next step when he was ordered to Bengal. The British had held a grudge against Siraj-ud-Dawla, the young and impetuous *nawāb* of Bengal, ever since his capture of Calcutta had resulted in the atrocity dubbed the "Black Hole." Clive easily recaptured Calcutta and, using the Seven Years' War as an excuse, took the nearby French settlement at Chandarnagar for good measure. Clive's defeat of Siraj-ud-Dawla's army at the battle of Plassey in June 1757 was based on a small but well-trained European force, large bribes provided by a Hindu banker, and the perfidy of Siraj-ud-Dawla's Muslim nobles. In a mere six months, Clive established British commercial and military primacy in Bengal, placed a friendly ruler on the throne in Bengal, and, almost in passing, acquired a huge personal fortune. His success made him the stereotypical Nabob.

Although other Nabobs and the British East India Company profited greatly from the war in Bengal, Clive's wealth dwarfed theirs. In victory, he received an incredible sum in cash and land grants worth an annual fortune. When the newly retired thirty-two-year-old Clive triumphantly stepped off the gangplank in London, he was one of the richest men in England. Unfortunately for him, public discomfiture at the enormous wealth of Clive and other East India Company servants—and the manner in which they had acquired it—was so great that the term "Nabob" was used to mock them. This censure was based on accurate suspicions that the Nabobs had been greedy in pursuing wealth through fraud, extortion, and violence. Furthermore, the Nabobs were spending their wealth in ostentatious and socially disruptive ways and were tainted by "oriental" manners and morals. These last indictments reflected upper-class snobbery against parvenus from the commercial classes. Although Clive and the other Nabobs could buy the trappings of English gentry, they were not accepted by the titled elites.

The most serious charge against the Nabobs was, of course, the manner in which they had obtained their wealth. Whereas bribery, violence, and treachery to Indian interests might be overlooked, the defrauding of East India Company investors could not. Agents of European East India companies had always been allowed to supplement their pay by engaging in "country" or "private trade," usually by consigning them free portage in a company ship. The directors of the companies had, perforce, to recognize the entrepreneurial spirits of their servants and were never successful in banning private trade. Company directors even rationalized that privately developed "country trade" exposed new markets from which the company could also profit. Of course, the conflict of interests inherent in such country trade did drain company profits. Agents could coerce concessionary prices or rebates for themselves as they negotiated larger company purchases or deal only in goods with higher profit margins, leaving the company to transport the bulkier items, and could demand bribes and kickbacks from suppliers. Investors could suspect double-dealing, but even when company servants made fortunes from private trade, as did Dupleix, or profited from company-financed military actions, as in the case of Clive, the directors objected but did little. That benign official attitude changed between 1765, when Clive returned to India as governor-general, and 1772, the year that *The Nabob* opened on the London stage. *The Nabob* was a play by W. Foote skewering Nabobs returning from India with disproportionate wealth and airs of becoming titled gentlemen. While English society was comfortable with successful businessmen becoming country gentlemen, this new breed was more rapacious and ambitious.

The change in English attitudes rested on class consciousness and a residual suspicion of fraudulent conflicts of interest, but what perhaps tipped the scales against the Nabobs were events in Bengal. By the time Clive returned to Bengal, a British army had defeated an alliance of the Mughal emperor and the *nawāb* of Bengal at the battle of Baksar in 1764. The victory established the British East India Company as the strongest political force in eastern India. The Mughal emperor had to cede his enormous land revenues (known as the *divānī*) of Bengal, Bihar, and Orissa; in the years following, company servants extorted wealth and plundered the resources of eastern India with an unprecedented rapacity and corruption. Clive left after two years, railing against what he saw as Bengal's march to disaster. But he was ignored, as he had done nearly the same thing in his day. Then, in 1770, famine hit Bengal and an estimated one-third of its peasantry, already reduced to penury, starved to death. English opinion was outraged at the Nabobs, who were blamed for this inhumanity. Clive was held responsible for the disaster, even though he had condemned the way his countrymen were conducting themselves in Bengal. Parliament acted, in large part because the East India Company was unable to repay a loan to the Treasury. The resultant "reforms," introduced to India by Warren Hastings, led to a crackdown, and more of the wealth of eastern India reached company coffers, and not the pockets of company agents. Hastings's Bengal administration thus marked the beginning of the end of Nabobism. Nevertheless, Indian rulers were forced to follow the advice of their British political advisers, who served British interests first, and to underwrite the expenses of the British-led troops that protected and controlled them. Indirect rule thus continued as the predominant method of British rule in much of India until the integration of most of the princely states into India's union at independence in 1947.

J. Andrew Greig

See also **Clive, Robert; Dupleix, Joseph François; French East India Company; French Impact; Hastings, Warren**

BIBLIOGRAPHY

Barnett, Richard B. *North India between Empires: Awadh, the Mughals, and the British, 1720–1801.* Berkeley: University of California Press, 1980.

Chaudhuri, Nirad. *Clive of India: A Political and Psychological Essay*. London: Barrie & Jenkins, 1975.

Dodwell, Henry. *Dupleix and Clive: The Beginning of Empire.* London: Frank Cass, 1920.

Keay, John. *The Honourable Company: A History of the English East India Company*. London: HarperCollins, 1991.

Spear, Percival. *The Nabobs*. London: Curzon Press. 1963.

Wolpert, Stanley. *A New History of India*. 7th ed. New York: Oxford University Press, 2004.

NAGAS AND NAGALAND Nagaland became the sixteenth state of the Indian Union on 1 December 1963. It has a rapidly expanding population (about 2 million in 2004) and is divided into sixteen districts, with Kohima as the capital. Its official languages are English and six tribal languages. The literacy rate is nearly 70 percent. The Nagas are a tribal Indo-Mongoloid people who live in the Northeast region of India, the Himalayas, and Burma (Myanmar). More than a dozen tribes, including the Angamis, Aos, Chakhesangs, Changs, Khienmungans, Konyaks, Lothas, Phoms, Rengmas, Sangtams, Semas, Yimchangurs, and Zeliangs, make up the Naga tribes. The Nagas were a warlike people who engaged in head-hunting raids on each other, on Nagas across the border in Burma, and on the people of the lowlands. The *morung*, dormitories for young bachelors, served as training centers, barracks, and centers for ceremonial purposes, where skulls and other trophies of war were also displayed. Rice beer and meat such as beef and pork were the Nagas' favorite diet. Each of the Naga tribes enjoys elaborate festivals, some of which last several days. Although suspicious of outsiders, they have a highly developed sense of hospitality and generosity. The Naga tribesman was fiercely loyal to his family, his clan, his *khel* (the village), and his land, and he brooked no interference by outsiders in these or the village and tribal courts. Beginning in the 1840s, Christian missionaries converted many Nagas. The major Naga tribes each had representatives in the Naga Baptist Christian Convention. In 1881 the British established the Naga Hills District, with Kohima as the chief administrative center, and they initiated punitive expeditions to avenge head-hunting raids. After 1947 head-hunting raids continued and involved Naga tribes on both sides of the Indo-Burmese border.

In 1945 the Nagas had set up the Naga Hills District Tribal Council, which in 1946 became the Naga National Council (NNC), published the *Naga Nation*, and called for separation from India upon independence. In March 1956, the Nagas founded the Naga Federal Government with its own flag, and created the Naga Home Guards of five hundred men from each tribe. Eventually 15,000 men were under arms, attempting to achieve independence through a campaign of terror; throughout the struggle, however, the Nagas have been divided on whether to fight for independence or to accept statehood within the Indian Union. The Indian army was sent into the province in 1957. Accusations of atrocities by both sides were made. Moderate Nagas began to realize that secession was unrealistic, and they formed a Naga Peace Organising Committee. In 1957 they met in an All Tribes Naga Peoples' Convention. The "Naga Hills" was a district of the state of Assam, but the Naga Hills Tuensang Area was created on 1 December 1957. In 1963 the state of Nagaland was created. In spite of this, violence continued. On 23 May 1964 a cease-fire agreement was signed by both sides. On 31 August 1972 the underground NNC, the Naga Federal Government, and the Naga Federal Army were all banned, and the government ended the cease-fire. On 11 November 1975 the two sides signed the Shillong Accord, and the rebels surrendered large numbers of weapons, and many gave up the struggle. From the mid-1980s there were renewed bouts of violence, which led to the cease-fire agreement of 25 July 1997. An uneasy peace followed.

Roger D. Long

See also **Assam; Ethnic Conflict; Ethnic Peace Accords; Insurgency and Terrorism; Tribal Peoples of Eastern India; Tribal Politics**

BIBLIOGRAPHY

Gurudev, S. *Anatomy of Revolt in the North East India*. New Delhi: Lancers Books, 1996.

Pakem, B., ed. *Regionalism in India (With Special Reference to North-East India)*. New Delhi: Har-Anand Publications, 1993.

Vashum, R. *Nagas' Right to Self-Determination: An Anthropological-Historical Perspective*. New Delhi: Mittal Publications, 2000.

NAIDU, SAROJINI ***(1879–1949), Indian poet, feminist, and nationalist leader.*** Sarojini Naidu was born on 13 February 1879, the eldest child of Brahma Samajist parents: Varada Sundari Devi, who wrote Bengali lyrics, and Aghorenath Chattopadhyaya, scientist and founder of Nizam's College in Hyderabad. Sarojini Naidu's verses were published in four volumes: *Songs* (1895), *The Golden Threshold* (1905), *The Bird of Time* (1912), and *The Broken* Wing (1917), all highly acclaimed for their evocative and romantic descriptions of India.

Raised by liberal parents, her creative talents awoke in a home open to scholars and diverse visitors. Sarojini later made passionate speeches on the importance of women's education. In 1891, when she was twelve, she achieved the highest rank in the Madras presidency matriculation exams, and her literary talents impressed the nizam, who gave her a scholarship to study at Girton College, Cambridge. In England she cultivated the friendship of famous writers, and later briefly traveled in Europe. In 1898 Sarojini challenged caste by marrying Govindarajulu Naidu, a non-Brahman Telegu doctor and widower, with whom she had four children.

Sarojini Naidu's nationalism was underscored by feminism, and from 1904 onward, her oratory drew large crowds. At the Framji Cowasji Institute, where practical Ramabai Ranade urged affluent women to help their poorer sisters, Naidu recited "Ode to India," calling upon Mother India to "awaken from slumber." In 1906 she addressed the Indian National Congress (INC) session in Calcutta on women's education, and also spoke to the Indian Social Conference there. Awarded the colonial Kaiser-I-Hind in 1911 for flood relief work, Naidu remained a political activist.

She became a close associate of Gopal Krishna Gokhale and Mahatma Gandhi, and a friend of Rabindranath Tagore and Sarladevi Chaudhrani. In Madras in 1909 she met Muthulakshmi Reddi, her future colleague in the Women's Indian Association (WIA). On 18 December 1917 Naidu led the WIA delegation to Secretary of State Edwin Montagu, requesting equal female suffrage in the next elections. When appealing earlier for support from the INC, she argued that women voters and leaders would not usurp male authority, and that all Indians would be inspired by their nationalism and maternalism. As a founding member of the All-India Women's Conference in 1927, Naidu was considered one of India's feminist luminaries. She addressed women's groups on obstacles like child marriage, *pardah* seclusion, bigamy, and widow immolation (*sati*), while she fought for female suffrage. Yet, some modern feminists call her a "traditional feminist" because she praised women for being true *satis* for their self-sacrifice.

Naidu's speeches were marked by idealism, humor, and a cascade of poetry. At Lucknow and Patna, she urged a Muslim-Hindu dialogue based on shared Indian ethnicity and humanity. On 21 December 1917 she pleaded with the Madras Special Provincial Council to support the Lucknow Congress League Pact of the previous year. Between 1917 and 1919, Naidu joined Gandhi's *satyagraha* (nonviolent resistance) movement, actively participating in the 1920 campaign, and in 1925 she became the first Indian woman president of the INC. Tensions developed between Indian feminists and male nationalists in 1930, when Gandhi initially refused to include women *satyagrahi*s in the arduous Salt March. He

Patriotism is not a thing divorced from real life. It is the flame that burns within the soul, a gem like Flame that cannot be extinguished. . . . . . but if you are united, if you forget your community and think of the nation, if you forget your city and think of the province, if you forget you are a Hindu and remember the Musalman, if you forget the Brahmin and think of the Panchaman, then, and then alone will India progress.

Sarojini Naidu, *Speeches and Writings,* G. A. Natesan, 1919, p. 219.

later relented, however, after being persuaded by Naidu, Kamaladevi Chattopadhyaya (1903–1990), and Khurshed Naoroji (1894–1966). Naidu led the women marchers and, like countless others, she was jailed for manufacturing salt. Naidu was jailed by the British in 1932, and again in 1942 during the Quit India movement. In 1947 she was appointed the first governor of Uttar Pradesh in independent India. She died in 1949.

Sita Anantha Raman

See also **Congress Party; Nightingale, Florence; Women and Political Power; Women's Indian Association**

BIBLIOGRAPHY

Baig, Tara Ali. *Sarojini Naidu: Portrait of a Patriot.* New Delhi: Congress Centenary Celebration Committee, 1985.

Banerjee, Hasi. *Sarojini Naidu: The Traditional Feminist.* University of Calcutta monograph no. 16. Kolkata: K. P. Bagchi, 1998.

Basu, Aparna, and Bharati Ray. *Women's Struggle: A History of the All India Women's Conference, 1927–2002.* Delhi: Manohar, 2003.

Chandra, Bipin. *India's Struggle for Independence.* Delhi: Penguin, 1989.

Chatterjee, Partha. "The Nationalist Resolution of the Woman Question." In *Recasting Women: Essays in Colonial History,* edited by Kumkum Sangari and Sudesh Vaid. Delhi: Kali for Women, 1989.

Forbes, Geraldine. *Women in Modern India.* Cambridge, U.K.: Cambridge University Press, 1996.

Jag Mohan, Sarla. *Remembering Sarojini Naidu.* Delhi: Children's Book Trust, 1978.

Jain, Devaki. *Indian Women.* Delhi: Government of India Publication Division, 1976.

Kaur, Manmohan. *Role of Women in the Freedom Movement, 1857–1947.* Delhi: Sterling Publishers, 1968.

Kumar, Radha. *The History of Doing: An Illustrated Account of Movements for Women's Rights and Feminism in India, 1800–1990.* Delhi: Kali for Women, 1997.

Naidu, Sarojini. *Broken Wing: Songs of Love, Death, and Destiny.* London: William Heinemann, 1917.

———. *Speeches and Writings.* Chennai: G. A. Natesan, 1919.

———. *The Bird of Time: Songs of Life, Death, and the Spring.* 1912. Reprint, London: William Heinemann, 1926.

Navaratne, V. S. *Sarojini Naidu: Her Life, Work, and Poetry.* Delhi: Orient Longman, 1980.

Raman, Sita Anantha. "Crossing Cultural Boundaries: Indian Matriarchs and Sisters in Service." *Journal of Third World Studies* 18, no. 2 (Fall 2001): 131–147.

NAINSUKH ***(1710–1778), Pahari painter.*** The son of Pandit Seu of Guler, and younger brother of the celebrated Manaku, Nainsukh is the Pahari painter about whom we know the most. He must have started painting while still quite young, for an early work, almost certainly a self-portrait, datable to around 1730, shows him, brush held in right hand, poised to paint upon a sheet of paper. In another portrait, done some twenty years later, he appears standing behind his patron, hands folded and body bent at the waist, looking at a painting that his prince holds in his hand. But the most detailed information comes from an entry made in 1763 in his own hand, in the pilgrims' register of a priest at Haridwar, in which he speaks of his lineage at length. There is a remarkable self-awareness in this entry, and he prefaces the ten-line text with a delicate little drawing of Shiva and Pārvatī seated even as the river Gaṅgā emerges from Shiva's matted locks, while Bhagirath, the devotee, stands offering obeisance to the Lord.

Virtually nothing is known of Nainsukh's early training, presumably under his father, but about 1740 he seems to have left his hometown of Guler and moved to Jasrota, a little principality to the west, across the river Ravi. Nainsukh apparently worked first for some senior members of the Jasrota royal family, and then attached himself to the young prince, Balwant Singh, whose side he apparently never left for the next twenty years. In swift sketches or elaborate paintings, he captured his patrons in a range of moods and situations to which there are virtually no parallels outside the work of the Mughal ateliers. Nainsukh's work reflects his patrons' interests, their pursuits, even their dreamlike visions of grandeur. With Balwant Singh he appears to have developed a very special bond, for in these paintings and drawings we see him shadowing his patron everywhere and, with singular warmth, rendering him in what is truly an extraordinary range of situations: writing a letter, stalking a duck, watching a group of professional mimics, examining a painting, riding out in a litter for a hawking expedition, striking a lion down with his bared sword, having his beard trimmed, listening to petitioners, supervising a construction, standing in front of a fire before retiring, offering prayers, or simply smoking a *huqqa* in a camp bed, wrapped in a quilt and staring into space. Close to sixty such works have survived, some of them bearing inscriptions that make both patron and painter spring to life for the viewer.

After Balwant Singh's death around 1763, Nainsukh moved from Jasrota to the state of Basohli to take up work under its ruler, Amrit Pal. The work he did between 1763 and 1778, the year of his own death, has a different orientation, a distinctive flavor: an image of Vishnu seated in all his glory; the opening leaf of what might have been a series based on the celebrated poetic work of Bihari, the *Satsai*; and three paintings of what might have been a large *Rāgamālā* series bear witness to this change. Another possibility that can be entertained is that as he grew old, Nainsukh, following established practice among painters, occupied himself with planning rather than executing a series of paintings, preferring only to put down first thoughts in the form of sketches on paper or to create a body of drawings to leave to his sons. One of the series that Nainsukh made sketches for, and helped plan, is likely to have been the great *Gītā Govinda* series that is seen as a crowning achievement of Pahari painting.

Nainsukh's work is subtle, and its appeal lies not in surface skills, but in its deep humanity. Beginning with copying, or closely following, some late Mughal works that appear to have reached the hills at that time, Nainsukh swiftly began to alter them, bringing in fresh elements of observation and introducing little twists or surprises that infused them with lyricism. It is certain that even at a young age, Nainsukh was armed with prodigious skills: the ability to observe the tiniest, most casual of details with a clear eye; the use of a remarkable, supple line; the power to make clean, uncluttered paintings with a poetic air. His portraits are fine studies, well grasped, cleanly drawn, studded with the most appropriate details, conveying the true sense and presence of the person portrayed. But, interestingly, the more formal the portrait, the less interested he was in it. His interest lay apparently not in static or ceremonial studies, but in rendering, around his central figure, groups of related people over whom he trained a warm, mellow light. In his painting of the Jasrota prince Zorawar Singh watching the dancing girl Zafar (now in the Chandigarh Museum), for instance, the prince does appear closely observed, but the dancer and the musicians are animated and wonderfully depicted, their necks arched, fingers nimbly playing the instruments, their bodies utterly and totally absorbed in what they are doing. In the celebrated painting of Balwant Singh examining a painting with Nainsukh himself, the prince is naturally the center of attention, with his regal bearing and all signs of elegance, but the eye travels quickly, and with eagerness, to the minor characters in the work: a tall courtier respectfully seated, the man standing behind him with his hands folded across his waist and a box of implements tucked into his belt, and, above all, to the three musicians who are seen playing in one corner of the painting. Nainsukh lavished so much attention upon them—their gestures, the liveliness of their figures, the subtle differences in their complexions—that it is with effort that one's eye moves away from them back to the prince, or even to Nainsukh himself.

In the range of his work—close to a hundred works, now widely dispersed all over the world, can be attributed to him at present—Nainsukh conjures up stillness and tumult with equal ease, quiet moments melding seamlessly into situations astir with energetic action. But there is also discernible, under the surface, a certain playfulness, even open humor. Yet idioms do not dominate Nainsukh's work. What shines forth is his ability to seize a detail and exalt it, to grasp a moment and render it timeless.

B. N. Goswamy

BIBLIOGRAPHY

Archer, W. G. *Indian Painting in the Punjab Hills.* London: Her Majesty's Stationery Office, 1952.

Gangoly, Ordhendra C. "Pandit Nainsukh, a Kangra Artist." *Rupam* 37.

Goswamy, B. N. "The Problem of the Artist Nainsukh of Jasrota." *Artibus Asiae* 28 (1966): 205–210.

———. *Nainsukh of Guler: A Great Indian Painter from a Small Hill State.* Zürich: Museum Rietberg, 1997.

Goswamy, B. N., and Eberhard Fischer. *Pahari Masters: Court Painters of Northern India.* Zürich: Museum Rietberg, 1992.

NAOROJI, DADABHAI ***(1825–1917), Parsi politician from Mumbai, the "Grand Old Man of India."*** Dadabhai Naoroji graduated from Elphinstone College, Mumbai (Bombay), in 1845, and became a professor of mathematics in 1854. He was cofounder of the Students' Literary and Scientific Society and of the Bombay Association (1844). After the Mutiny of 1857—which shattered British self-confidence but also ended as a setback

Dadabhai Naoroji. As head of the Indian National Congress, Naoroji presided at its 1906 session in Calcutta, where Congress first called for *swaraj* (self-rule). K. L. KAMAT / KAMAT'S POTPOURRI.

to the precocious nationalism of India's Western-educated elite—Naoroji dared to launch the East India Association in 1866. He later became a cofounder of the All-India National Congress in 1885. Subsequently he sailed to England and was elected one of the first Indian members of the British Parliament, representing Finsbury in the House of Commons from 1892 to 1896 as a member of the Liberal Party.

In 1901 he published his most famous book, *Poverty and Un-British Rule in India*, in London. Assessing the British in terms of their own liberal standards, he found their colonial rule "un-British." He blamed them for the increasing poverty of India and expounded his theory of Britain's "drain of India's wealth." Checking the export and import data of British India, in the long run, he found out that lucrative gains from trade accrued to the British, whereas India did not receive adequate returns. His theory was an important contribution to India's economic nationalism, which gained more and more adherents over time.

Naoroji presided over two earlier sessions of the National Congress, but his most important presidency was in 1906 at the Kolkata (Calcutta) Congress, when Congress first called for *swaraj* (self-rule). The partition of Bengal in 1905 had fanned revolutionary radicalism in India, but in 1906 the Liberal Party won national elections in Great Britain, and the moderate wing of Congress hoped for major constitutional reform in India. Gopal Krishna Gokhale, the great moderate leader, implored Naoroji to keep the Congress united by presiding at this important annual session; at the age of eighty-one, Dadabhai traveled home and succeeded in preventing a split of the Congress, though it broke apart a year later, in 1907. Service to his country was the greatest principle of Naoroji's life, and he is still revered in India for that.

Dietmar Rothermund

BIBLIOGRAPHY

Besant, Annie. *How India Wrought for Freedom*. London: Theosophical Publishing House, 1915.

Ganguli, B. N. *Dadabhai Naoroji and the Drain Theory*. Mumbai: Asia Publishing House, 1965.

Naoroji, Dadabhai. *Poverty and Un-British Rule in India*. 1901. Reprint, New Delhi: Commonwealth, 1988.

Rothermund, Dietmar. *The Phases of Indian Nationalism and Other Essays*. Mumbai: Nachiketa Publications, 1970.

NARAYAN, JAYA PRAKASH ***(1902–1979), Indian political figure and nationalist leader.*** A prominent socialist leader in the Indian nationalist movement against British rule and in postindependence politics, Jaya Prakash Narayan was known popularly as "J. P." and was often referred to as Lok Nayak, the "people's leader." Narayan was born in the United Provinces (now Uttar Pradesh) in 1902. He studied at Patna College in Bihar and married in 1920. He thereafter went to the United States for graduate studies in sociology, leaving his wife behind at one of Mahatma Gandhi's ashrams. In the United States, Narayan worked part time in grape fields, factories, and restaurants to pay for his education. He changed universities a few times until settling at the University of Wisconsin for a doctoral degree in sociology; there, his paper "Social Variation" was described as one of the best papers of the year. He was influenced by Karl Marx's *Das Kapital*, which inspired much of his socialist ideology. He had to cut short his doctoral studies and return to India in 1929 when his mother became seriously ill.

On his return, Narayan joined the Indian National Congress at Jawaharlal Nehru's invitation, becoming part of the freedom movement. He declared, however, that freedom was more than freedom from British rule, but freedom from poverty, hunger, disease, and ignorance. In 1934 he founded the Congress Socialist Party, a socialist wing of the Congress Party. He was arrested several times by the British during the nationalist movement, and he served several years in jail for his nationalist activities.

Jaya Prakash Narayan. Here photographed in 1938, Narayan eventually broke with the Praja Socialist Party to pursue *lokniti* (politics of the people). In 1977 his Janata Party was voted into power, becoming the first non-Congress party to form a government at the center. K. L. KAMAT / KAMAT'S POTPOURRI.

The Congress Socialist Party after independence became the Praja (People's) Socialist Party. In the first national general elections of 1952, his socialist party lost badly to the Congress Party. Nehru nevertheless invited Narayan to join his Cabinet, though he could not promise to fulfill Narayan's fourteen-point plan to reform the Constitution, the administration, the judicial system, redistribute land to the landless, nationalize banks, revive "Swadeshi" (home-produced goods only), and set up village cooperatives. Narayan therefore declined to join Nehru's Cabinet. In 1954 Narayan joined Vinobha Bhave's Sarvodaya Movement to redistribute land to the landless in India's villages. He was also active in India's trade union movement. Narayan in 1976 established the People's Union for Civil Liberties and Democratic Rights, an organization that sought to draw people from various political parties together for the defense of civil liberties and human rights.

Narayan achieved national prominence during the Congress Party rule of Prime Minister Indira Gandhi. In 1974 India faced a severe economic crisis, with high inflation and unemployment and a shortage of basic necessities. Narayan was alleged by the Congress government to have called upon the armed forces to overthrow Indira Gandhi. A year later, in June 1975, following Indira Gandhi's conviction by the Allahabad High Court for the misuse of government vehicles in her election campaign, the prime minister declared a state of "National Emergency." Fundamental rights were suspended. Under that "National Emergency," Narayan was arrested and sent to prison.

In March 1977 the emergency was lifted, and Narayan spearheaded the opposition campaign in the subsequent elections, forging an alliance of almost all opposition parties (except the Communist parties) into a new party, the Janata Party. The Janata Party, led by Narayan, defeated the Congress Party in 1977, the first time that Congress had lost since independence. Narayan declined to lead the new Janata government as prime minister, or to accept any other public office, epitomizing the combination of Gandhi's philosophy with the practice of Western democracy. His book, *The Reconstruction of Indian Polity*, reflected this blend and won him the Ramon Magsaysay Award as Asian statesman of the year. J. P. Narayan died in 1979.

Raju G. C. Thomas

See also **Bhave, Vinoba; Congress Party; Nehru, Jawaharlal**

BIBLIOGRAPHY

Das Gupta, Nitis. *Social and Political Theory of Jaya Prakash Narayan*. New Delhi: South Asian Publishers, 1997.

Nath, Jyoti Bikash. *Socialist Leadership in India: A Tribute to Jaya Prakash Narayan and Rammanohar Lohia*. Delhi: Kaniksha Publishers, 2002.

Singh, Bhola. *Political Ideas of M. N. Roy and Jaya Prakash Narayan: A Comparative Study*. New Delhi: Ashish Publishing House, 1985.

Sinha, Renu. *Samagra Kranti: Jaya Prakash Narayan's Philosophy of Social Change*. Delhi: Siddharth Publications, 2002.

NARAYAN, R. K. ***(1906–2001), renowned author of novels, short stories, and essays.*** Regarded by many critics as India's greatest writer in English, R. K. Narayan's birth name, Rasipuram Krishnaswami Narayanaswami, was shortened at the suggestion of his first English publisher for the convenience of Western readers. Born on 10 October 1906 in Madras (Chennai), he was the third of eight children of Gnanambal Iyer and Rasipuram Iyer. His father was a well-educated school teacher in the education department in the princely state of Mysore, but Narayan was brought up in Madras by his maternal grandmother. In his memoir, *My Days* (1974), as well as in his last novel, *The Grandmother's Tale* (1992), he acknowledged his debt to her, not only for maternal care but also for a deep introduction to South Indian traditional culture. His knowledge of the wealth of Hindu legends and myths reflects her storytelling, but she also taught him Sanskrit, the classical language of religion and literature, as well as Tamil, the South Indian language rich in song and poetry. From her he learned to understand and enjoy classical Canatic music, one of the most complex of Indian musical systems. In his old age, he remarked that "We don't have that kind of granny nowadays."

While immersed in his grandmother's culture, at the same time he was also introduced to the greatest literature of the West, thanks to an uncle—a college student who lived in the family house—who was taking part in a production of William Shakespeare's *Tempest.* Narayan knew it, he said, before he knew anything else. Part of Narayan's greatness as a writer is explained by the "Indianness" of his early upbringing as well as his love of English literature, acquired from his father and his college teachers. No other Indian writer reflects so unselfconsciously the seamless inheritance of these two rich, but very different, cultures. Of the many Indian writers in English, none impresses readers as does Narayan, conveying an authentic voice of the unique historical experience of the making of modern India in the context of the modern West, mediated through the imposition of British rule on a traditional society. An interviewer once asked Narayan whether the creative writer is a free spirit or a spokesman of the community in which he lives. A writer, Narayan replied, must be a free spirit if he is to be a creative writer, but he is always a spokesman of the community in that he is a product of his society. So a writer must keep a tricky balance between the two.

Narayan's formal introduction to Western learning began in 1912, when he began attending kindergarten in Madras, at a school founded by Swedish Lutherans. Readers of his novels, as well as of his memoir and his collection of essays, conclude that he hated school, but his unhappiness appears to be the normal response of an intelligent child being taught by boring, unimaginative teachers. He hated arithmetic, dreaded exams, and, like the schoolboys in his novels, welcomed the freedom of summer holidays. "No child with red blood in his veins," he said in *A Writer's Nightmare* (1956), "could ever think of its school with unqualified enthusiasm." Narayan neatly summarized his views on childhood by saying that children are "existentialists," living in the moment, sometimes happy, sometimes miserable. He was, he insisted, the same person that he had been eighty years before: "Inside, the sense of awareness, of being, is the same throughout. The chap inside is the same, unchanged." When he graduated to the better-known Madras Christian College High School, the "chap inside" rejoiced in having nicer classrooms, a good library, and educated, reasonable teachers, but his father summoned him to Mysore to live with his siblings, one of whom, R. K. Laxman, was to become India's best-known political cartoonist and the illustrator of many of Narayan's books. In Mysore, where he was to live most of his life, he attended Maharajah's Collegiate High School, where his father was headmaster. The great bonus of being the headmaster's son was that he had free range of the library, and he read voraciously, including the romantic poets and the novels of Sir Walter Scott, Charles Dickens, and Leo Tolstoy, as well as those of contemporary writers like Rider Haggard and Marie Corelli, his favorite. Through English journals, he became familiar with all the literary greats of the era, including G. B. Shaw, H. G. Wells, and Thomas Hardy. He also learned about American writers through *Harper's* and the *Atlantic.* People unfamiliar with the fascination that England had for educated Indians of that time speak of the English language being "forced" on Indians, but nothing could be further from the truth. English was the key to another world, sought with eagerness by young Narayan. Despite his eclectic reading, for two years in succession he failed the university entrance examination, the first time in English, the second in Tamil literature. In *My Days,* he says his failure in English was due to concentrating on Dickens and poetry, while the questions were from the dull books he had left unread.

After managing to pass the exams, he attended Maharaja's College, got his bachelor of arts degree, and, when nothing else was available, took a job as a teacher. By his own account he was a disastrous failure, and after two attempts at maintaining discipline, gave it up and went home, deciding to devote himself full time to becoming what he always wanted to be—a writer. "I want to finish my novel," he announced, "and when it is published, it will solve all problems." Making a living from writing novels in India, especially in English, was virtually unknown, and the comment of an old friend expressed the almost universal reaction of his family and friends: "Unwisdom! Unwisdom! You could write as a hobby. . . . The notion is very unpractical" (*My Days,* p. 92). Making a living became an urgent necessity in 1934, however, when Narayan, defying the customs of his society, did not settle for a marriage arranged by his family; he fell in love with a beautiful girl, Rajam Iyer, and made the arrangements himself. Two years later, their daughter Hema was born. She became his lifelong companion.

The novel that he was writing was *Swami and Friends,* which drew very heavily upon his school experiences and was set in Malgudi, the imaginary South Indian town that figures in many of his later books. "As I sat in a room nibbling my pen, Malgudi with its little railway station swam into view, all ready made with a character called Swaminathan running down the platform" (*My Days*, p. 79). For most foreign readers, Malgudi is their entry into the complex world of India, in many ways physically chaotic but with a carefully articulated social order. There was little hope of a novel of this kind, written in English, being published in India, but in any case his dream was to find a publisher in England, and against all probability his dream came true. *Swami and Friends* was rejected by a number of publishers, but he had sent the manuscript in 1935 to a friend, Purna, who was studying at Oxford, who persuaded Graham Greene, already one of England's most famous authors, to read it. Greene was delighted with the novel and recommended it to Hamish Hamilton, the publisher. Purna was able to send Narayan a telegram: "Novel taken. Graham Greene responsible" (*My Days*, p. 115). This was the beginning of a friendship that was of great importance to Narayan, for it brought him into the literary and academic world of Great Britain and the United States. He and Greene corresponded regularly, and Greene read and commented on his manuscripts, though they met only once, in 1956.

Other novels followed regularly, all marked by kindly ironic wit as he observes the comic absurdities in the lives of many of his characters; at the same time, he conveys the disappointments and tragedies of their everyday lives as they confront the conflicts engendered by their ambitions, their weaknesses, their self-delusions, and society's demands. His second novel, *The Bachelor of Arts*, published in 1937, is also autobiographical, and in some ways is his most humorous book, ending with the central character falling in love and marrying, euphoric in his happiness. His next novel, *The Dark Room* (1938), explores new territory, perhaps less successfully, with the story of a woman who, against all conventions, leaves her bullying husband.

There was a long break before *The English Teacher* was published in 1945 (in the United States it was published under the title *Grateful for Life and Death*). It is the most somber of Narayan's novels, and the most autobiographical. The story of the death of the young wife of a struggling schoolteacher replicates the death of Narayan's wife in 1939, leaving him utterly bereft, with his small daughter. Unable to work, he turned to spiritualism, and he believed that a medium had put him in contact with her. The friendship of the English mystic Paul Brunton helped him to return to writing in 1945, and Narayan began editing a literary journal, *Indian Thought*. He gave this up, however, to become his own publisher. Narayan entered a new and fruitful period, publishing some of his work in both England and the United States, including *The Financial Expert* (1952); *The Guide* (1958), which many readers consider his best work; *The Man-Eater of Malgudi* (1961); *The Vendor of Sweets* (1967); and *The Painter of Signs* (1976). *The Guide* was made into a widely publicized but unsuccessful movie, which many reviewers, including Narayan himself, considered a serious distortion of the novel. In addition, he published collections of short stories, essays, and notable retellings of the great Sanskrit epics *The Mahābhārata* (1978) and *The Rāmāyaṇa* (1972).

In 1956 he made his first visit outside India, stopping in London, where for the first time he met Graham Greene, on his way to the United States. There he met many authors, film personalities, and intellectuals. In *My Dateless Diary* (1960) he gives a humorous but very penetrating account of American life, including delightful meetings with actress Greta Garbo, who wanted him to discuss mysticism, which he felt unable to do. He subsequently became fond of travel, traveling often to London and New York as well as to many cities in Europe and Asia. He received numerous literary honors in foreign countries, as well as one of India's highest national awards, the Padma Bhushan. In 1985 the president of India appointed him a member of the Rajya Sabha, the upper house of Parliament, as one the country's most distinguished citizens; there, he took a special interest in the welfare of children. This was in keeping with his literary work, which, as an obituary declared, expressed "a philosophic depth and a strikingly original moral analysis" (*Manchester Guardian*).

Ainslee T. Embree

BIBLIOGRAPHY

Only the dates of the first publication of Narayan's books are given above, because almost all of them were published by different publishers in India, Great Britain, and the United States, and often by more than one publisher in the same country. The best biographical study is Susan Ram and N. Ram, *R. K. Narayan* (New Delhi: Viking, 1996), which relates the novels to Narayan's life. John Updike wrote a sensitive appreciation of his work in "Books," in *The New Yorker*, 12 Sept. 1974, pp. 80–82. Narayan has been the subject of many critical studies. N. P. Nair, *Irony in the Novels of R. K. Narayan and V. S. Naipaul* (Trivandrum, Kerala: CBH Publications, 1993), offers interesting insights and has an almost complete listing of Narayan's many books. Michael Pousse, *R. K. Narayan: A Painter of Modern India* (New York: Peter Lang, 1995), stresses the value of his writings for their insights into Indian culture. Geoffrey Kain, editor, *R. K. Narayan, Contemporary Critical Perspectives* (East Lansing: Michigan State University Press, 1993), examines many of his works. While these are all useful, Narayan's artfully crafted autobiographical works give insights into his life and work. These include *My Day* (New York: Viking Press, 1974) and *My Dateless Diary* (Mysore: Indian Thought Publications, 1960), as well his collections of essays, including *A Writer's Nightmare* (New Delhi: Penguin, 1988). An early insightful American review is found in Glendy Dawedeit, *Washington Post*, 3 November 1956, E, p. 6). An affectionate obituary by Susan and N. Ram appeared in *The Guardian* (Manchester,

U. K.), on 14 May 2001. Narayan gave a selection of his private papers to Mugar Library at Boston University.

NARAYANAN, K. R. ***(1921–), president of India (1997–2002).*** Kocheril Raman Narayanan became vice president of India in 1992, and in 1997 he was elected the nation's president. Narayanan was born on 4 February 1921 into a poor Dalit (formerly called "untouchables") Hindu family in what was then the Indian princely state of Travancore and Cochin (now Kerala). The elevation of a former "untouchable" to the highest office in India was an indication of his remarkable intellectual and professional qualities, and demonstrated as well that a person born to the lowest caste could reach the highest pinnacle in India. Although an excellent student, he had to be pulled out school once because of his impoverished family's inability to pay his tuition fees. But his determination and dedication saw him graduate from school and college.

He obtained a master's degree in English literature from the University of Travancore in 1943. Thereafter, he worked as a journalist for the *Economic Weekly for Commerce* in Delhi. The Indian industrialist J. R. D. Tata was favorably impressed with his credentials, and Narayanan received a scholarship from the Tata foundation to study in England. He subsequently studied under the renowned scholar Harold Laski at the London School of Economics, graduating with a first class degree in economics and political science in 1948. He taught at the Delhi School of Economics in 1954 and 1955. He served as vice-chancellor of Jawaharlal Nehru University, and as chancellor of Delhi University, Punjab University, Pondicherry University, Assam University, North Eastern Hill University, and Gandhigram Rural Institute.

Narayanan successfully passed the Indian Foreign Service examinations in 1949 and was posted as second secretary at the Indian Embassy in Rangoon, Burma. There he met his Burmese-born wife, Ma Tint Tint, who changed her name to Usha Narayanan after their marriage. Subsequently, he served as the Indian ambassador to Thailand (1967–1969), Turkey (1973–1975), China (1976–1980), and the United States (1984–1988). He was a member of the Indian delegation to the United Nations General Assembly and the Security Council. During his ambassadorial tenure at Beijing and in Washington, Narayanan undertook the difficult tasks of seeking rapprochement with China after fourteen years of hostile relations following the 1962 Sino-Indian war, and of explaining India's continued close ties with the Soviet Union following the Soviet invasion of Afghanistan in 1979 and its continued military occupation there.

Thereafter, Narayanan left the Indian Foreign Service to enter Indian politics. He was elected to the Lok Sabha (the lower house of India's Parliament) from Kerala in 1984 on a Congress Party ticket, and was reelected in 1988. As Congress member of Parliament, he held the portfolios of minister of state for planning, minister of state for external Affairs, and finally, minister of state for science and technology.

Raju G. C. Thomas

See also **Presidents of India**

BIBLIOGRAPHY

Sharma, Sita Ram. *K. R. Narayana: Just the President of India*. New Delhi: Sublime Publications, 1998.

Singh, Darshan. *K. R. Narayanan: A Journey from Uzhavoor to Raisina Hills*. New Delhi: United Children's Movement, 1999.

NATARAJA. *See* **Shiva and Shaivism.**

NATIONAL CONGRESS. *See* **History and Historiography.**

NATIONALIST MOVEMENT. *See* **History and Historiography.**

NATIONAL SECURITY DECISION-MAKING When India won its independence in 1947, it had little experience in security policy making. Then, Field Marshal Kodandera Madappa Cariappa was the only Indian who had reached the highest rank of brigadier. British officers manned all higher echelons of the government's security establishment. Nor was the army always provided with everything necessary for an effective defense of the nation, as was evident in the border war with China in October 1962. Till then, India spent annually only 2.6 percent of its gross domestic product on defense. Prime Minister Jawaharlal Nehru distrusted armed forces and at times questioned their loyalty to a democratic India. He desired to prevent army chiefs from interacting directly with the civilian heads of the government. Hence, members of the Indian Administrative Service, successor to the British Indian Civil Service, occupied higher echelons of the defense department, preventing chiefs of the armed services from directly placing their ideas and plans before the defense minister or the prime minister.

The British had left the structure of Defence Committee of the Cabinet and a Defence Minister's Committee. On the first, chiefs of three armed forces were attending as advisors while the latter was the only institution that gave the armed forces a chance to place their views before civilian authorities. These institutions, however, fell into disuse after the 1950s. As a result, independent India national security policy decision-making has been controlled by a few civilians and is ad hoc, responding to crises rather than being proactive.

During India's formative years, the morale of ministers and civil servants declined because of a lack of coordination in the decision-making process. These defects were distinctly noticeable in the ministry of defense, where internal tensions, favoritism in promotion to the top military offices, reduction of power of the chiefs of staff, and lack of discipline among civilians and military personnel led to the early resignation of the army chief of staff, General Koodendera Subayya Thimmayya, in 1961. Instead of investigating the situation, Nehru congratulated the defense minister, Krishna Menon, and snubbed General Thimmayya. A year later, as General Thimmayya had warned, China invaded and Krishna Menon was forced to resign in the wake of a humiliating Indian defeat.

Yet, the Indian army had earlier performed well in 1947–1948, expelling from two-thirds of Kashmir the Pakistani so-called tribal invaders. Even then, Nehru accepted the advice of Governor-General Lord Mountbatten to take India's charge of Pakistan's aggression to the Security Council of the United Nations, which arranged for a cease-fire in Jammu and Kashmir on 1 January 1949.

Institutions Making Security Policy

Nehru's successors, Lal Bahadur Shastri and, especially, Indira Gandhi, appreciated the need for coordinated security policy making. Shastri established in 1965 the Joint Intelligence Committee (JIC) to coordinate intelligence with an additional Secretary in Cabinet secretariat as its chairman. The Intelligence Bureau (IB) and intelligence agencies of three services hitherto functioning independently of one another were placed under the chairman, JIC. Gandhi realizing the importance of integrated intelligence in the making of security policy created the Research and Analysis Wing, a new intelligence agency to gather external intelligence in 1968 after splitting the IB, which was restricted to the work of domestic intelligence gathering. There was an apex committee under the cabinet secretary as the chairman with secretaries of ministry of external affairs and defense as members. She also established a Joint Chiefs of Staff Committee, which considered a security matter before bringing it to the civilian authorities.

In spite of pragmatism exhibited by Prime Minister Gandhi in prosecuting the Bangladesh war in 1971, she was led to believe an "oral assurance" of Zulfikar Ali Bhutto to gradually initiate action to make the Line of Control between India and Pakistan in Kashmir into an international border. Her secretary, P. N. Dhar, wrote on 4 April 1995 that she did not wish "to appear to be dictating terms to a defeated adversary." Equally disastrous was Prime Minister Rajiv Gandhi's decision to send Indian troops to Sri Lanka in July 1987 to "keep the peace" between Sri Lankan troops and Liberation Tigers of Tamil Ealam (LTTE). This decision turned India into a party to the dispute, an unfortunate change from its earlier role as an honest broker of peace between Sri Lanka's government and its rebellious Tamil minorities. Prime Minister Rajiv Gandhi made his crucial decision to send Indian troops to Sri Lanka on peacekeeping mission without proper deliberation within the cabinet or proper staff work, confident that he would prevail upon LTTE leader Prabhakaran to force his cadre to lay down the arms. The absence of adequate deliberations in decision-making thus landed India into a state of perpetual crisis with Sri Lanka.

Much of Indian security policy making before 1962, however, concerned relations with Pakistan. Thereafter the border war with China created a triangular security problem between India, China, and Pakistan. It then became a pentagonal problem during the Bangladesh war of 1971, with the Soviet Union and India on one side, and the United States, China, and Pakistan on the other. The disappearance of the Soviet Union and the end of the cold war has changed the focus of Indian security policy.

This ad hoc approach to national security policy continued, however, under former Prime Minister Atal Bihari Vajpayee and the coalition government led by his Bharatiya Janata Party. During the Agra Summit in July 2000, India agreed with Pakistan's proposition that all references to previous summits at Simla and Lahore be "dropped" in return for a Pakistani promise "to discard reference to the United Nations resolutions on Kashmir." Ultimately the Agra Summit between Vajpayee and General Pervez Musharraf failed.

Even after fifty years of Indian independence, there has never been any structured interaction between the departments of defense, home, and external affairs, the three primary departments involved in security policy making. Modern national security policy, however, involves many other departments, including commerce, industry, petrochemicals, and finance. Coordination of policy took place, if at all, when the secretaries of these ministries met one another. J. N. Dixit, former foreign secretary noted that in the 1990s "an informal sort of National Security Advisory Group" existed in the cabinet secretariat.

National security coordination has assumed greater significance since the end of the cold war because security threats do not emanate from external conflicts alone but from internal issues as well, such as ethnic and religious conflicts, terrorism, the narcotics trade, illegal immigration, the criminal-terrorist nexus, and money laundering by the groups indulging in anti-national activities in league with international intelligence agencies inimical to India.

National Security Council

Should India establish a National Security Council (NSC) similar to that of the United States? Those who have opposed the idea argue that the NSC is a unique institution suitable for a presidential system of government, in which there is a concentration of powers in one individual. Hence, there is a dire need for advice in security policy making. However, in the parliamentary government, there is a collective body that works with the prime minister as its head; thus there is no need for another advisory or decision-making body. However, because India's Cabinet is so large a body, its political affairs subcommittee, consisting of the prime minister and the ministers for home, defense, and external affairs, considered issues of national security before any directions were given to officials.

Prime Minister Vishwanath Pratap Singh in 1989 promised to establish an NSC for effective national security decision-making; and though he did establish one by executive order in September 1990, his government went out of office the same year. When the Congress Party assumed power in 1991, Prime Minister Narasimha Rao emerged as a successful dodger of the idea even though he did not deny the need for an NSC, and he left office without establishing it.

Prime Minister Inder Kumar Gujral, who had initially been minister of external affairs, during the brief tenure of the United Front government in 1996-1998, was committed to the idea of establishing NSC. He proclaimed it as his first priority on the first day in office but instead established a Cabinet Committee on Security (CCS). The Bharatiya Janata Party led the National Democratic Alliance (NDA) government that came to power in 1998, also committed to the formation of NSC. Thus, all of India's main political parties were agreed on the creation of an NSC, which was established by executive order.

The NSC, constituted by Prime Minister Vajpayee during the NDA coalition government, has the prime minister as its chairman, and the ministers for external affairs, home, defense, finance, and the deputy chairman of the planning commission as its members. Below the NSC, there is a National Security Group consisting of the secretaries of departments represented in the council and the chiefs of Research and Analysis Wing and the three services. This is the principal body to plan, coordinate, and integrate policy at the middle level of India's policy-making process.

The secretariat can function to coordinate security policy if it has an independent official called either national security adviser or the executive secretary of the NSC. However, the Vajpayee government made the prime minister's principal secretary act as the part-time national security adviser. Because the principal secretary to the prime minister is always overloaded with work, making him national security adviser added too great a burden on him. The Congress-led United Progressive Alliance (UPA) government under Manmohan Singh, which came to office in May 2004, has continued the office of national security adviser, appointing J. N. Dixit to it without burdening him with a role of principal secretary to the prime minister. He died, however, of heart failure within a few months.

The NSC has also been given a National Security Advisory Board consisting of many retired officials and former leaders of the armed forces. But, since its establishment, the government has not used it effectively to coordinate policy. The government has made it a practice to use CCS as its policy-making mechanism.

Proliferation of Agencies in Security Decision-Making

The major problem that afflicts national security policy making is the proliferation of agencies involved in decision-making. The latest one is a Nuclear Command Authority with Political Council, with the prime minister at its head. An executive council, with the prime minister's national security adviser as its head, was created as part of India's national security doctrine. Nuclear weapons are under a Strategic Forces Command, headed by the chief of command. These collectively decide on the ultimate use of nuclear weapons and on issues like the deployment of short-range or long-range nuclear capable missiles.

Defense Minister George Fernandes revived the defense minister's committee after the Kargil crisis of 1999. As of 2005 there was a proposal before the government to create the post of chief of defense staff, which would rotate among the three service chiefs for a term of two years. Ongoing efforts to integrate the defense department with civilian authorities are designed to increase the accountability of India's defense forces.

P. M. Kamath

BIBLIOGRAPHY

Dhar, P. N. "LAC as Border: Bhutto's Deal with Mrs. Gandhi." *Times of India* (Mumbai) (4 April 1995).

Directorate General of Infantry, Field Marshal K. M. Cariappa Memorial Lectures, 1995–2000. New Delhi: Lancer Publishers, 2001.
Kamath, P. M. *Foreign Policy-Making and International Politics.* New Delhi: Radiant Publishers, 1990.
Kamath, P. M *National Security Council for India: Structure and Functions.* Mumbai: Rambhau Mhalgi Prabodhini, 1998.

NATYA. *See* **Dance Forms; Nātya Shāstra**

NĀTYA SHĀSTRA Nātya Shāstra (*nātya*, Sanskrit, "drama" + *shāstra*, Sanskrit, "treatise"), is one of the earliest Indian treatises on the varied aspects of drama, including important sections on dance and on music (particularly instrumental music) with passages on tuning, scales, modal patterns and functions, instrument types, performance techniques, and accompaniment styles. The core parts of the treatise are the work of the dramatist Bharata, who compiled them around the beginning of the first millennium of the common era. The work is probably a compendium of material by different authors, some of whom may predate Bharata, as he clearly describes a flourishing tradition that is already well developed. The *Nātya Shāstra* serves essentially as a manual on how to organize and to perform a drama, complete with passages on the characteristics of particular character types and their demeanor, how they move, and the music that should accompany them. As such, the work is perhaps the most important reference text on Indian musical practice in this era. The *Nātya Shāstra* continues to have importance today for musicians and scholars, some of whom reference contemporary practice with ancient models.

Musically, Bharata speaks of *dhruva* (Sanskrit, "fixed"), a category of song type that probably served both as a dramatic device to help establish and reinforce character and mood as well as a vehicle for commentary and diversion. *Dhruva* is one of the earliest Indian references to the notion that a listener might link sentiment and music. The principal melodic concept of this period of ancient Indian music was *jāti* (Sanskrit, "family"), a mode (that is, an identifiable pattern of notes in which some pitches are more important than others) set in a scale (*mūrcchana*). A *mūrcchana*, however, derives from either of two possible heptatonic and intonational parent scales: the *shadja-grāma* (a scale based on the note *shadja*) and the *madhyama-grāma* (a scale based on the note *madhyama*). The only difference between these two parent scales was the placement of a microtone, the *shruti*. The *shruti* (Sanskrit, *shru*, "to hear" or "that which is heard") is one of the most enigmatic ideas of this musical system. Bharata recognizes twenty-two possible microtonal divisions within an octave, although he does so in the context of *mūrcchana*. The distances between notes in a scale, consisting of intervals of three sizes—four, three, or two *shrutis*—formed the basis for ancient scales (most probably derived from the intonation patterns associated with Vedic chant). Later authors such as Venkatamakhi preserve the notion of *shrutis* in their systems, even if the implications of Bharata's musical system had not been in effect for well over a millennium. Modern musicians still use words such as *shruti* to describe their playing.

Gordon Thompson

See also **Bhajan; Music; Rāga**

BIBLIOGRAPHY

Bharata. *The Natyasastra: English Translation with Critical Notes.* Edited and translated by Adya Rangacharya. New Delhi: Munshiram Manoharlal Publishers, 1961.
Rowell, Lewis. *Music and Musical Thought in Early India.* Chicago: University of Chicago Press, 1992.

NEHRU, JAWAHARLAL ***(1889–1964), nationalist leader and first prime minister of India (1947–1964).*** Jawaharlal Nehru was born in Allahabad on 14 November 1889. The Nehrus originally came from the valley of Kashmir and had migrated to Delhi at the beginning of the eighteenth century. Jawaharlal's grandfather, Gangadhar, was a police officer in Delhi at the time of the Revolt of 1857. When the victorious British troops stormed their way into Delhi, he escaped with his family to Agra. Early in 1861, at the age of thirty-four, he passed away. Three months after his death, his wife gave birth to a son, who was named Motilal. He was brought up by his elder brother, Nandlal. Motilal Nehru, the father of Jawaharlal, forged his way to the forefront of the Allahabad Bar, where he built up an enormous practice; he was noted for his natural shrewdness, persuasive advocacy, and ready wit. Genial, fond of good food and good wine and good conversation, he was known among his friends—British and Indian—for his generous hospitality.

The Early Years

As a child, Jawaharlal was the recipient of much anxious solicitude from his parents. His mother, Swarup Rani, showered on him, as he wrote later, "indiscriminate and excessive love." Motilal decided that the schools in Allahabad were not good enough for his son, and arranged for his instruction at home by European tutors. Though he was spared the straitjacket of a conventional education, solitary instruction at home deepened the loneliness of the boy, who as the only child for eleven years had little opportunity to play with children of his own age. One of his tutors, Ferdinard T. Brooks, a young man of mixed Irish and French extraction, inspired in him a zest for reading and an interest in science.

From English tutors to an English public school must have seemed to Motilal Nehru a natural, perhaps a necessary step. In 1905 he took his son to England and had him admitted to Harrow public school. Jawaharlal entered the school routine of studies and sports, though he did not seem to leave any impression on his contemporaries, nor did they find his company intellectually stimulating. "My tastes and inclinations," he wrote to his father, "are quite different. Here boys older than me and in higher forms than me take great interest in things which appear to me childish."

In October 1907 Jawaharlal was admitted to Trinity College at Cambridge. His interest in science led him to take the Natural Science Tripos for his subjects. The three years he spent at Cambridge were, as he recalled later, "pleasant years with many friends . . . and a gradual widening of the intellectual horizon." The days were taken up with work and play, and the long winter evenings passed in interminable discussions on life, literature, politics, ethics, sex, and people, until long after midnight the dying fires sent Jawaharlal and his friends shivering to their beds. Cambridge also imparted a keen edge to Jawaharlal's political thinking. His letters from Harrow and Cambridge exuded nationalist fervor and aggressive anti-imperialism, which alarmed his father, though it was not uncommon for Indian students at British universities to pass through a phase of intellectual rebellion and political extremism.

Jawaharlal Nehru. Nehru's diplomatic style as India's first prime minister was distinctly his own. Often suggesting solutions in strong intellectual and moral terms, his candid comments on world events, especially in the early 1950s, evoked much resentment in the West. CORBIS.

A Political Calling

After graduating from Cambridge, Jawaharlal qualified as a barrister and returned to India in 1912 to practice at the Allahabad High Court as his father's junior. He was soon bored by what he called "the technicalities and trivialities of much of the legal lore." Deep down in him, there was a vacuum, which required filling with something more than personal and professional ambition. It was politics that seemed to strike a vital chord in him, but politics in Allahabad were too tepid for him. It was only in June 1917, when the arrest of Annie Besant, the leader of the Home Rule movement, created a political storm that he was drawn into the vortex of political agitation. However, soon afterward, a declaration by the British government affirming the British policy of "developing self-governing institutions" in India brought down the political temperature. The politics of Allahabad relapsed into their wonted torpor; the Nehrus fell back into domestic and professional grooves.

Advent of Gandhi. Meanwhile, Jawaharlal had married Kamala Kaul, the daughter of a Delhi businessman, in 1916. In November 1917 Indira, their only child, was born. Like many of his contemporaries, educated in British universities, young Nehru would have slid into the comfortable anonymity of a well-off up-country lawyer, were it not for the emergence of a new leader on the Indian scene. M. K. Gandhi had returned to his homeland in 1915 after twenty years' sojourn in South Africa, where he had led the small Indian immigrant community in its struggle against racial discrimination. In the course of this struggle, Gandhi had evolved *satyagraha*, a new method of rectifying injustice and resisting oppression nonviolently. Nehru first met Gandhi in 1916. He was somewhat puzzled and baffled by his political philosophy but attracted by his personality. Reports of an agrarian agitation that Gandhi led against European indigo planters in Bihar in 1917 impressed Nehru; they indicated that Gandhi possessed a keen political sense and an effective weapon of nonviolent resistance, which was a promising alternative to the armchair polemics and the sporadic acts of terrorism between which Indian politics had so far been oscillating.

Nehru's real initiation into militant politics came in the spring of 1919, when Gandhi launched a campaign against the Rowlatt Bills restricting civil liberties, one of which was passed by the Imperial Legislative Council in the teeth of the opposition of Indian members. Jawaharlal felt an irresistible call to follow Gandhi, but his father, a moderate and constitutionalist Congress leader, strongly disapproved of his twenty-nine-year-old son plunging into an unconstitutional agitation. Having failed to dissuade his son, Motilal Nehru sought Gandhi's intervention. Gandhi visited Allahabad and advised Jawaharlal to be patient. Soon afterward the British massacre in Amritsar and martial law in the Punjab alienated millions of Indians from the British Raj and brought both Nehrus, father and son, into political alignment with each other and with Gandhi. Motilal was the first front-rank leader of the Congress to cast his lot with Gandhi when the Mahatma launched a campaign of "nonviolent noncooperation" in September 1920. The call to nonviolent battle against British rule swept young Nehru off his feet. "I gave up," he was to write later in his autobiography, "all other associates and contacts, old friends, books, even newspapers, except insofar as they dealt with the work in hand. I almost forgot my family, my wife and my daughter."

In December 1921, Jawaharlal and his father were arrested and sentenced to six months' imprisonment. The noncooperation movement was fast gathering momentum when in February 1922, alarmed by a riot in a remote village in eastern India, Gandhi called it to a halt on the ground that the atmosphere in the country was not conducive to nonviolent mass civil disobedience. Not surprisingly, he was arrested soon afterward, and his campaign collapsed.

Visit to Europe. The sudden revocation of civil disobedience by Gandhi shocked Jawaharlal. During the next five years, nationalist politics were in the doldrums. Gandhi's followers in the Congress Party were themselves divided on the issue of entry into the legislatures. There was also a deterioration in Hindu-Muslim relations. Jawaharlal disliked factional and communal politics and kept out of them. In March 1926 he left for Europe for the treatment of his wife, who was suffering from tuberculosis. While she was convalescing in Switzerland, Nehru had time for reading, reflection, and travel. In February 1927 he attended the Congress against Colonial Oppression and Imperialism at Brussels, where he met radicals and revolutionaries from four continents. In November 1927 he paid a short visit to Moscow when the Soviet Union was celebrating the tenth anniversary of the Russian Revolution. What impressed him was the planned Soviet assault on poverty, disease, and illiteracy, and the tremendous push toward industrialization and away from customs that impeded social progress.

The European visit gave a radical edge to Jawaharlal Nehru's politics. His speeches and writings acquired a sharp anti-imperialist and pro-socialist slant. At the annual session of the Indian National Congress at Calcutta in December 1928, he clashed head-on with the "old guard" of the party on the issue of dominion status versus complete independence as the goal of the party. Thanks to Gandhi's ingenuity, a compromise was reached, and a split was averted. It was decided that if by 31 December 1929 dominion status was not conceded by the British government, the Congress would demand complete independence for India and fight for it by resorting to civil disobedience.

The Calcutta Congress stirred the stagnant pools of Indian politics. For Nehru, politics again acquired a sense of purpose, urgency, and adventure. All signs pointed to Gandhi's return to active leadership of the Congress. Gandhi was in fact elected president of the Congress session to be held in December 1929, but he declined the honor in favor of Jawaharlal. The fact that it fell to young Nehru to preside over the momentous session at Lahore, and to unfurl the flag of *purna swaraj* (complete independence), gave a tremendous boost to his popularity throughout the country.

Salt Satyagraha. As the new year dawned, Gandhi announced that he would launch his campaign by marching the 240 miles (388 kilometers) from Ahmedabad to Dandi, a village on the western coast, to break the salt tax law, which made the manufacture of salt a state monopoly. The first impulse of the government, as of the Congress intellectuals, was to ridicule the idea that there could be any connection between salt and *swaraj* (self-government). However, the political scene was quickly transformed under Gandhi's magic.

The Salt Satyagraha electrified the country. It drew the entire Nehru family into the political arena. Jawaharlal was the first to go to prison; he was followed by his father, his sister, and his wife. Jawaharlal was thrilled by the tremendous response of the people to Gandhi's call. More than 60,000 people courted imprisonment. But a year later, in March 1931, Jawaharlal was shocked, when after talks with Viceroy Lord Irwin, Gandhi agreed to call off civil disobedience and to attend a Round Table Conference in London to discuss constitutional reforms. A few days later, however, at the annual Congress session at Karachi, he piloted a resolution supporting the Gandhi-Irwin Pact.

Nehru and Gandhi. This was not the first, nor would it be the last, time that Nehru differed with Gandhi. There were numerous occasions when he was assailed by doubts about Gandhi's policies, but he did not press his differences to the breaking point. They were divided by twenty years of age as well as intellectual and temperamental differences. Contrary to the common impression, however, it was not always Nehru who gave in. Gandhi knew that young Nehru was not a blind disciple; he wanted to harness Nehru's talents and dynamism for the national cause, and was confident of containing his impetuous and rebellious spirit. It was not without much inner conflict that Jawaharlal was able to reconcile the conflict between his mind and his heart, between his own views and his loyalty to Gandhi. He knew that Gandhi was open to argument and compromise on important issues. There were several planks in the Congress program that Nehru sponsored and Gandhi accepted, such as the declaration of fundamental rights in 1931, the struggle for civil liberties in the princely states, and the unequivocal denunciation of Nazism and fascism in Europe.

Nehru and World War. In 1935, when Nehru's wife suffered a serious relapse of her pulmonary tuberculosis, he was released from prison—he had been arrested in February 1934—to take her to Switzerland. This visit increased his sensitivity to the currents and crosscurrents of international politics and his hatred of the totalitarian regimes that were casting the shadow of war over Europe. When World War II broke out in 1939, Nehru wanted the Indian National Congress to throw its weight on the side of the democracies, but he realized that the people of India could hardly be inspired to wholeheartedly participate in the war effort unless the British government gave India a real stake in the war. Nehru hated the totalitarian regimes and wanted India to strengthen the Allied cause but, to his dismay, the British government headed by Winston Churchill failed to make any imaginative gesture to nationalist India. In 1940–1941, after the fall of France and after the entry of Japan into the war, the Congress had offered to join a national government to resist the Axis powers. In March 1942 the British government sent a Cabinet minister, Sir Stafford Cripps, with proposals on the future constitution of India to enlist the support of Indian political parties, but no agreement could be reached.

Independence. In the aftermath of the failure of the Cripps mission, Gandhi's decision to embark on mass civil disobedience created a painful dilemma for Nehru, but he fell in line with the decision of the party. The government unleashed a massive repression. All Congress leaders, including Gandhi and Nehru, and more than 60,000 adherents of the party were imprisoned. This was Nehru's longest spell in jail; it was also his last. He was released in 1945, just in time to attend the abortive Simla conference convened by the viceroy, Lord Wavell, to break the political deadlock. Soon after, the Labour Government was voted into power in Britain, and it decided to concede self-government to India. Nehru played a prominent role in this conference as well as in the subsequent negotiations with the Cabinet mission in 1946, and later with Lord Mountbatten, for transfer of power from British to Indian hands. In these negotiations the most vexed question was the position of the Muslim community in India after the withdrawal of the British power.

Nehru was a rationalist and a humanist and was remarkably free from religious passions and prejudices. The communalism of India, he told Lord Lothian, a British Liberal politician, in 1936, "is essentially political, economic and middle class." He had observed upper-class politicians, both Hindu and Muslim, who had little contact with the masses, and were wrangling endlessly over the distribution of seats in legislatures and jobs under the government. The Muslim League had been the principal proponent of Muslim separatism since the beginning of the twentieth century. It was founded in 1906 with a two-fold program: loyalty to the British Raj, and provision of safeguards for Muslims against a Hindu majority in a future constitution. The League had met with an electoral disaster in 1937. But nine years later, in the general election of 1946, it won a landslide victory under the leadership of Mohammad Ali Jinnah, the president of the All-India Muslim League. He owed his victory to his undoubted tactical and polemical skills, but he was also able to exploit the antagonism between the Congress and the British government that prevailed throughout World War II. The vision he held forth of a separate Muslim state, reminiscent of the glory of the Mughal empire, struck the imagination of his coreligionists. Nehru has been blamed for underrating Jinnah, but in retrospect, it seems it was beyond the power of Nehru and the Congress Party to stem the tide of Muslim separatism, which had been rising since the beginning of the twentieth century, and which took the form of secession and nationalism in the 1940s. The stand taken by Nehru, and indeed by the Congress leadership, was that religion was not a satisfactory basis for nationality, and that the best course for multiracial and multireligious countries was to seek a solution within the framework of a federal constitution, as the United States and Canada had done. Such a proposition was, however, not acceptable to the leaders of the Muslim League; its truth was to dawn upon them much later, in 1971, after the breakup of Pakistan and the emergence of Bangladesh.

Nation Building

When Nehru assumed office as prime minister, he was fifty-eight. Although his entire working life had been spent in opposition to British rule—nine years actually spent in jail—he made a remarkably effortless transition from rebel to statesman. His political philosophy was eclectic. It drew upon nineteenth-century British liberalism, Fabian socialism, Marxist dialectics, Soviet economics, and Gandhian ethics. In spite of a penchant for political theory, Nehru's approach to critical issues was pragmatic. In 1949 he led India into the Commonwealth despite the long history of conflict with Britain and his own vehement opposition to dominion status twenty years earlier. Similarly, even though he had avowed his allegiance to the socialist ideal in the 1930s, he sought, after he assumed office, to reconcile socialism with economic growth and stability.

Immediately in 1947, Nehru's government was faced with formidable challenges: the restoration of order after the terrible upheaval caused by the partition of the subcontinent, the resettlement of the uprooted 5 million refugees from West Pakistan, and the rehabilitation of the transport system and the administrative machinery. The five-hundred-odd princely states, with the exception of Kashmir, were integrated into the Indian Union with remarkable speed and smoothness. Nehru took an active part in the Constituent Assembly in framing the constitution of the Indian Republic, which was inaugurated on 26 January 1950. He had to lay the foundations of a new political and economic order. He had never been a member of a legislative body, but he quickly became a great parliamentarian. Unlike many other leaders of newly liberated countries in Asia and Africa, he submitted himself to the verdict of three successive general elections, the fairness of which was never questioned. He nurtured institutions and traditions indispensable for the growth of parliamentary democracy, such as a free press, an independent judiciary, and the supremacy of the civil government.

Economic policy. Nehru had studied Marx and admired Soviet attempts at planned economic development, but his socialism was not of the doctrinaire variety. After he came to power, he sought to reduce economic disparities, but without hampering the growth of the economy. He knew India had been bypassed by the industrial revolution in the eighteenth century. His aim was "to convert India's economy into that of a modern state and to fit her into the nuclear age and do it quickly." He lifted Indian science from its small beginnings to a national effort. There was a tremendous expansion of higher education, especially in science and technology; the result was that the country was able to build a large reservoir of scientific manpower, second only to that of the United States and the Soviet Union.

The establishment of the Planning Commission in 1950 was a landmark in Nehru's economic policy. The commission fixed levels of investment, prescribed priorities, apportioned investment between agriculture and industry, and allocated resources between the state governments and the central government. Nehru envisioned economic planning as a long-term strategy. He used it not only to make the best use of available resources, but also to forge links of economic unity in the Indian federal system, and through public debate to make it an instrument of democratic education and peaceful social change. The results of the first fifteen years' efforts were substantial; the area under irrigation increased by 45 million acres, food production rose from 55 million to 89 million metric tons, installed power generating capacity increased from 23 million to 102 million kilowatts, and industrial production grew by 94 percent. Unfortunately, most of the gains of these years were offset by an unexpected and unprecedented increase in population.

Foreign policy. Nehru's entire term as prime minister was conterminous with the peak of the cold war between the United States and the Soviet Union, but he refused to ally India with either of them. Originally, this policy was an assertion of India's right, after attainment of independence, to conduct her international relations without being tied to the apron strings of Great Britain or any other great power. But it also became, in Nehru's hands, a calculated and sophisticated response to the postwar scene, dominated as it was by the rivalry of the two superpowers. Nehru, who, besides his lifelong association with Gandhi, had been trained as a scientist and was a self-taught historian, was quick to perceive that the two power blocs were poised for mutual destruction, which, in the post-Hiroshima era, posed a serious threat to the future of humankind. India's refusal to be stampeded into either bloc blazed a trail that most of the newly liberated countries of Asia and Africa followed. The organization of the nonaligned movement remained somewhat loosely knit and amorphous, but it nevertheless became a force to reckon with inside and outside the United Nations, and it acted as a vocal pressure group in the battle against neocolonialism and racism and in favor of world peace. At the Bandung (1956) and Belgrade (1961) conferences of nonaligned countries, Nehru's was on the whole a reassuring voice and a steadying hand on the leaders of the Afro-Asian bloc.

Nehru's diplomatic style was peculiarly his own; it owed much to his experience as a nationalist leader for three decades, when he was continually, and publicly, analyzing problems and suggesting solutions in intellectual and moral terms. His instant and candid comments on world events, especially in the early 1950s, evoked much resentment in the West. It was alleged that his criticisms of the actions (such as in Hungary) of the Soviet Union tended to be more cautious and modulated than his criticisms of the actions (such as over Suez) of the Western powers. The fact is that Nehru's sharp criticism of particular policies of the Western democracies was intended to bring to bear the pressure of public opinion in these countries on their governments. Since this method could not work in the case of the Soviet bloc (the media being controlled by the state), the use of the diplomatic channels was a better option for Nehru than was public criticism. Nehru's object was, as he once put it, "to bring about results rather than put up people's backs." On such issues as West Berlin and the independence of

Austria, his moderating influence through personal appeals to Soviet leaders, exercised behind the scenes, was much greater than what has been commonly assumed. Willy Brandt, the chancellor of the Federal Republic of Germany (West Germany) during the Berlin crisis, told the author of this article in 1971 that Nehru had used his influence with the Soviet Union to calm the crisis. Similarly, according to Chancellor Kreisky of Austria, Nehru had already before 1955 begun to mediate between Austria and the Soviet Union. "We asked Nehru," Kreisky recalled, "to tell the Soviets that if the Soviets were to sign a treaty, Austria would become a neutral country."

It was a great disappointment to Nehru that he failed to win and sustain the goodwill of India's two great neighbors, China and Pakistan, but it was not for lack of trying. "The root cause" with Pakistan, as Nehru explained to President Harry Truman in 1949 during his visit to the United States in 1949, was "the emotional climate of Pakistan whose people were being constantly encouraged by the government and leaders to pursue a policy of inspired fear and hatred towards India. Kashmir was thus not so much a cause as an illustration of tensions between the two countries."

India was one of the first countries to recognize Communist China. Nehru showed extraordinary restraint when Chinese troops marched into Tibet in 1950. He even incurred the displeasure of the Western bloc by supporting China's entry into the United Nations. But from 1959, India was faced with territorial claims and encroachments on the India-China border. Three years later came a surprise attack in full force. On the Indian side, there were doubtless lapses both in diplomacy and defense. The Indian positions on the mountainous terrain in the northeast were not well defended; India suffered a defeat that deeply hurt Nehru and perhaps hastened his death in May 1964.

Conclusion

Nehru was a writer of distinction. His major works, *Glimpses of World History* (1934), *Discovery of India* (1946), and *An Autobiography* (1936), were all written in prison. His *Autobiography* is considered his most important work. It is less a chronicle of his life than that of the nationalist movement. It was too much to hope that the British public would take to sharp criticisms of British rule in India from one of the most radical leaders of Indian nationalism, but the book became a best-seller in England. It had ten printings in 1936 and was translated into thirty-odd languages. Besides being an exercise of the author in introspection, it presented for the first time the case for Indian independence under Gandhi's leadership in an idiom that the West could understand.

No political leader, with the exception of Gandhi, stirred the minds and hearts of the Indian people for so long and so deeply as Nehru did. As one of the principal architects of Indian freedom, as a nation builder and as a champion of world peace, Jawaharlal Nehru was among the tallest figures of the twentieth century. He led his country during the difficult years of transition from colonialism to democracy, from traditionalism to modernity, and from a stagnant to a developing economy.

As prime minister of India, the task Nehru undertook was a formidable one: the simultaneous pursuit of national integration, political democracy, economic development, and social justice; in all these objectives he achieved a measure of success. But there were losses as well: the failure to foresee the population explosion, to strictly enforce land reforms, to accelerate universal elementary education, and to stem the slide in the standards of administration. These deficiencies and failures were partly attributable to Nehru's own limitations, partly to the actual working of his party and the political system. Unlike Gandhi, Nehru lacked the gift of identifying and harnessing political talent, and he failed to build up a second line of leadership. However, the charge that he sought to set up a political dynasty is untenable. It is true that he stubbornly refused to nominate a successor. A week before his death, he said, "If I nominate somebody, that is the surest way of his not becoming prime minister. People would be jealous of him, dislike him." However, during his last illness, when he recalled Lal Bahadur Shastri to join his Cabinet, it was taken as a hint that he favored him as his successor. As for his daughter, Indira Gandhi, her opportunity was to come seventeen months later, after Shastri's sudden and untimely death, when she was elected leader of the Congress Party in an open contest.

B. R. Nanda

See also **Congress Party; Gandhi, Indira; Gandhi, Mahatma M. K.; Gandhi, Rajiv; Nehru, Motilal; United States, Relations with**

BIBLIOGRAPHY

Brecher, M. *Nehru: A Political Biography.* London: Oxford University Press, 1959.

Brown, Judith. *Nehru: A Political Life.* New Haven, Conn.: Yale University Press, 2003.

Gopal, S. *Jawaharlal Nehru.* 3 vols. London: Jonathan Cape, 1973–1984.

Nanda, B. R. *The Nehrus: Motilal and Jawaharlal.* London: George Allen & Unwin, 1962.

———. *Jawaharlal Nehru: Rebel and Statesman.* New Delhi: Oxford University Press, 1995.

Nehru, Jawaharlal. *An Autobiography.* London: John Lane, 1936.

———. *The Discovery of India.* Mumbai: Asia Publishing House, 1946.
———. *Selected Works of Jawaharlal Nehru.* 1st series, edited by S. Gopal. New Delhi: Orient Longman, 1972–1982.
———. *Selected Works of Jawaharlal Nehru.* 2nd series, edited by S. Gopal. New Delhi: Oxford University Press, 1984–2002.
Pandey, B. N. *Nehru.* London: Macmillan, 1977.
Wolpert, Stanley. *Nehru: A Tryst with Destiny.* New York: Oxford University Press, 1996.

NEHRU, MOTILAL ***(1861–1931), attorney and political leader, president of Indian National Congress (1919 and 1928).*** Motilal Nehru was the father of India's first prime minister, Jawaharlal Nehru; the grandfather of the third prime minister, Indira Gandhi; and great-grandfather of her son, the fourth prime minister, Rajiv Gandhi. One of British India's wealthiest and wisest lawyers, Motilal abandoned his life of Western luxury in the aftermath of the Jallianwala Bagh Massacre at Amritsar in 1919 to follow Mahatma Gandhi's call for nonviolent noncooperation (*satyagraha*). That December, Motilal presided over India's National Congress, which met in Amritsar.

Motilal Nehru was less revolutionary, however, than either Gandhi or his own son, Jawaharlal, and he refused to boycott elections to India's new Legislative Councils following the enactment of Edwin Montagu's 1919 Government of India Act. Motilal joined forces with his Bengali barrister friend, Chitta Ranjan Das (1870–1925), to start their Swarajist (Freedom) Party in 1923, sponsoring Indian candidates to run for council seats in local elections, which Gandhi and his Congress disciples boycotted. The Swararjists did fairly well, but when their candidates won seats to provincial legislative councils, instead of supporting the British viceroy and his government, their strategy was to vote against and criticize every measure proposed by the government from within its own council chambers. Nehru and Das both knew the new viceroy Lord Reading, a jurist, well enough to argue with him personally, while Gandhi retreated to his rural ashram, spinning and weaving cotton, focusing his energies on village self-help as the best means of attaining self-rule (*swaraj*), or "freedom."

Soon after Das died in 1925, Nehru lost faith in the efficacy of the party they had founded, and before the end of his own life he returned to Gandhi's way. Together, they worked to revive Congress demands for changes leading to independence, too long ignored by British Tory indifference and arrogance. Nehru accepted for one last time the heavy burden of presiding over the Calcutta Congress in 1928. His own heart was weakening by then, but he went to Calcutta more to keep his only

Motilal Nehru. Shown here wih his wife Swarup Rani and son Jawaharlal c. 1899, Motilal Nehru, one of British India's wealthiest barristers, later abandoned his life of Western luxury to follow Mahatma Gandhi's call for nonviolent action. GETTY IMAGES.

son from leaving the Congress in disgust and frustration. He sponsored Jawaharlal, with Mahatma Gandhi's support, to preside over the next Congress in Lahore, which resolved to call in December of 1929 for *purna swaraj* (complete freedom) from the British Raj in one year.

Motilal and Jawaharlal would both be back in jail, however, long before India's freedom was finally won. Yet by securing for Jawaharlal the helm of the Congress when he did, Pandit Motilal assured his son the first premiership of independent India, sixteen long years after his own death.

Stanley Wolpert

BIBLIOGRAPHY

Nanda, B. R. *The Nehrus: Motilal and Jawaharlal.* New York: John Day, 1963.
Panikar, K. M., and A. Pershad, eds. *The Voice of Freedom: The Speeches of Pandit Motilal Nehru.* London: Asia, 1961.
Wolpert, Stanley. *Nehru: A Tryst with Destiny.* New York: Oxford University Press, 1996.

NEOLITHIC PERIOD A general term used by archaeologists, "Neolithic" (or New Stone Age) identifies cultural adaptations that involve the transition from mobile hunting-gathering strategies to sedentism and the domestication of plants and animals. Numerous different Neolithic transitions were taking place in South Asia, but there are only a few regions that have evidence for the initial processes that led to the domestication of animals and plants. In the northwestern subcontinent, the regions of Afghanistan and Baluchistan provide the earliest evidence for the use of domesticated sheep or goats, cattle (humped zebu), and wheat and barley between 9000 and 7000 B.C. In other regions, mobile hunter-gatherers continued to live by hunting and gathering a broad spectrum of animals and plants, but they began to settle down in large communities near these abundant resources. These Mesolithic (Middle Stone Age) communities continued quite late in some parts of the world, and in South Asia the evidence for long-term Mesolithic adaptations is seen in the Gangetic region. In the subsequent Gangetic Neolithic period, there is evidence for domesticated rice and possibly a separate episode of cattle domestication. The Southern Neolithic of peninsular India may represent the initial domestication of local millets and also of cattle, though there may be a connection between the cattle of the middle Ganga and those of South India. In Kashmir, the Neolithic sites of Burzahom and Gufkral may represent connections to a separate Neolithic transition linked to Tibet and China. Other regions that have yet to be fully explored are the Chotanagpur Plateau and the southern Gangetic Plain in Bihar and Bengal, as well as northeastern India in Assam, Nagaland, and Manipur.

Northwestern Neolithic

In the northwestern subcontinent, between 20,000 and 15,000 B.C., Upper Paleolithic communities in the Aq Kupruk area had begun to focus their hunting on wild sheep and goats as well as cattle, and they may have begun gathering wild grains such as wheat and barley. Between 9000 and 8000 B.C., the first evidence of domestic sheep or goats and possibly cattle has been found at the cave sites of Gar-i-Mar and Gar-i-Asp, Aq Kupruk, Afghanistan. These communities did not produce pottery and were still involved in hunting and probably gathered wild grains, but they provide important evidence that the processes leading to domestication were occurring in this region at about the same time as in the Near East.

The preceramic Neolithic sites of Afghanistan provide a clue to the importance of this region, but the site of Mehrgarh, in Pakistan, gives a much clearer picture of the complex processes leading to a sedentary lifestyle based on domestic plants and animals. The transition at Mehrgarh was part of a larger process occurring throughout Baluchistan and Afghanistan, and extending all the way to the Zagros Mountains and the Fertile Crescent region of the Near East. In Baluchistan the earliest agricultural settlements have not been located, but excavations at the site of Kili Gul Mohammad (4600–3900 B.C.), near Quetta, suggest that the earliest communities in the highlands may have harvested wild or cultivated cereal grains and possibly managed sheep, goat, and cattle herds. With the approach of winter, many communities would have moved through the passes with their herds and bags filled with grain to spend the winter next to the rivers or springs along the piedmont. Today, winters in the Kachi Plain are quite pleasant, with only occasional frost, but the summers are unbearably hot and dry. In the past, from 16,000 to 7000 B.C., there may have been a slightly stronger summer monsoon and more seasonal variation in temperature. Over time, communities began to cultivate grain crops on the plains. These crops were probably planted in October, at the end of the summer monsoon, and were watered by the winter rains in December and January. The annual migration back to the highlands would have taken place after the spring harvest in much the same pattern as we see today among agro-pastoral communities living in the Kachi Plain.

Mehrgarh is located at the foot of the Bolan Pass that connects the highland plateaus of Baluchistan to the Kachi Plain at the edge of the Indus Valley. From around 7000 B.C., the initial settlers used wild as well as cultivated barley and grew domestic wheat, but they relied primarily on hunted wild game, with only a few examples of domestic goat. Wild game included gazelle, deer, pigs, sheep, and goats, as well as larger animals such as wild cattle, water buffalo, and onagers. Even elephants may have been hunted; a large tusk was found in one of the early houses. An important wild fruit that was collected is the jujube, a plumlike fruit that ripens in the spring. This fruit can be dried or preserved as sweet chutney. Date seeds found at the site indicate the collection of summer crops, but it is not possible to determine if they are from wild or domestic plants. At first the site was inhabited seasonally, and through repeated flooding from the nearby Bolan River and subsequent rebuilding, the mound grew to a height of over 33 feet (10 m). By 5500 B.C. agriculture and animal husbandry became more important. The use of sheep, goats, and cattle increased, with the humped variety of cattle, *Bos indicus* being the most important. Although it is not clear if sheep and goats were domesticated indigenously or brought in from the Zagros to the west, the humped zebu was locally domesticated, and recent genetic studies show that it is distinct from the nonhumped cattle (*Bos taurus*) of the Near East.

The first inhabitants of Mehrgarh used stone blades, polished stone adzes, and bone tools, but no pottery was produced. Numerous ash layers filled with fire-cracked rock indicate that some foods, such as grain and stews, were cooked in skins or baskets with hot rocks. The earliest inhabitants were, however, familiar with the plastic properties of clay; they made small clay figurines and small unfired clay containers, as well as hand-formed mud bricks. Most of the evidence for early grains comes from impressions of wheat and barley preserved in the mud bricks. Mud-brick houses separated by refuse dumps and passageways were oriented in different directions and not as a planned settlement. The earliest houses were square or rectangular and were subdivided into four or more internal rooms. Later structures had larger rooms with numerous internal subdivisions set below the floor level for storage of grain and other valuable commodities.

Although the early inhabitants may have left the site for short periods, they buried their dead in open spaces between the houses and over time built new houses on top of earlier burials. The graves were made by digging a vertical shaft, then excavating a side chamber in which the corpse was placed, lying on its side in a flexed position. Funerary offerings were placed around the head or at the feet of the individual, and they often included a variety of ornaments. In many of the earliest burials, dating to about 6500 B.C., young goats were slaughtered and buried with the dead, a practice that has also been noted at other Neolithic sites in Baluchistan, Afghanistan, and Central Asia. Utilitarian objects were included with the dead, presumably for use in the afterlife. Men were often buried with polished stone adzes, blades, and blade cores, while some of the female burials had bone and antler tools, baskets coated with bitumen, lumps of red ochre, and grinding stones. Ornaments were included in the burials of men and women as well as children. The most common ornaments were necklaces, bracelets, and anklets made of various types of beads, using locally available yellow-brown limestone as well as exotic materials: azure blue lapis lazuli, blue-green turquoise, black unfired steatite, white fired steatite, red-orange carnelian, banded agate, and various colors of marine shell. A single copper or malachite bead was found in one of the burials, but no other precious metals were used at this time.

Wide shell bangles made from a single large conch shell (*Turbinella pyrum*) and worn by women on the forearm have also been found in the earliest burials. This species of shell was probably traded up the Indus Valley from the Makran coast near modern Karachi, some 310 miles (500 km) to the south. Many of the marine shells and pendants made from mother-of-pearl (*Pinctada*) may have come from areas farther to the west along the Makran coast, and possibly even from across the Persian Gulf in Oman. Copper and malachite, as well as banded agates, probably came from central and northern Afghanistan; lapis lazuli was brought from the far northern mountains of Afghanistan, and turquoise from northeastern Iran. These different varieties of ornaments indicate that long-distance trade networks had been established as early as 7000 B.C., linking the coastal regions of the Indus Valley with the interior plains and on into the highlands of Baluchistan and Afghanistan. Numerous sites like Mehrgarh were scattered along the edges of the Indus Valley, and by 5500 B.C. they had established the basic subsistence economy, the trade networks, and patterns of craft specialization that set the foundation for later Chalcolithic cultures.

Gangetic Neolithic

Settled agriculture in the central Gangetic Plain emerges from indigenous Mesolithic communities that appear to have settled in large villages, with a focus on the hunting of wild cattle and the collection of grains such as wild rice. At the site of Koldihwa, early evidence for cattle and domestic rice has been confirmed by the discovery of numerous other sites. At Mahagara, the earliest Neolithic village had circular huts made of reeds and mud plaster, with a large central pen for keeping cattle. The animal bones from the site include sheep or goats and cattle as well as wild animals. Because the remains of animal bones are fragmentary, it is possible that the sheep or goat bones could have come from gazelle or antelope, but there is no question that the cattle remains represent domestic animals because of the presence of a pen filled with cattle hoof prints. Stone blades and ground stone axes were used, along with bone and antler tools. Pottery, made with basket or cord impressions as decoration on the exterior, has impressions of rice grains in the clay. The earliest dates from Koldihwa suggest that rice and cattle were being domesticated around 6700 to 4500 B.C., but the charcoal used for dating may belong to a hearth from the earlier phase of occupation. Additional charcoal samples from both Koldihwa and Mahagara, combined with dates from other sites with similar material culture, place the occupation of Koldihwa and Mahagara between 2400 and 1700 B.C.

Southern Neolithic

Neolithic transitions in South India are the result of similar processes seen in other regions, but the plants and animals are somewhat different. There is also more variation in the material culture because the sites are located in a large area of the central Deccan Plateau (Karnataka, Andhra Pradesh, and Tamil Nadu), with some settlements scattered along the Andhra coast. The earliest date comes from the lowest levels of Watgal, Karnataka (2900–2600 B.C.). Two major types of sites have been identified. Ash mound sites such as Utnur and Kodekal are the result of repeated accumulations and burning of cattle dung. Some habitation areas are found alongside the ash mounds, but in other areas like Watgal, the site is not associated with an ash mound. Early scholars argued that the people who established these sites were seminomadic herders who migrated to the Deccan from northeastern Iran, but this view is no longer supported. In fact, the pottery and stone tool technology appears to be the result of local processes not at all related to the Indus Valley or Gujarat to the northwest. Urn burials of infants and some adults are also found in association with ash mounds and habitation sites.

While detailed studies have not been conducted on the cattle bones, some scholars suggest that the bones represent two different breeds, which may have been domesticated locally. Sheep and goat bones have been reported, but as mentioned for the Gangetic sites, these bones are easily confused with gazelle and antelope. The most convincing evidence for local domestication comes from the botanical remains of indigenous millets, grams, and pulses (edible seeds of certain bean and lentil crops). Earlier reports of African millets in the early Neolithic have proven to be unfounded. Tubers were also collected and processed at the sites.

In the later Neolithic and early Iron Age sites in South India, there is evidence for the introduction of African millets, wheat, and barley, as well as the horse, that would have come from Gujarat or farther north. This evidence of northern contacts may have begun quite early, based on the presence of copper tools that would also have been traded from the Aravalli region of Gujarat and Rajasthan. Overall, the Southern Neolithic represents a combination of indigenous subsistence strategies that eventually incorporated external subsistence practices and cultural traditions. One of the main questions that scholars need to address is the relationship between these early Neolithic communities and later Dravidian-speaking peoples.

Jonathan Mark Kenoyer

See also **Chalcolithic (Bronze) Age; Goddess Images; Indus Valley Civilization**

BIBLIOGRAPHY

Allchin, F. Raymond. *Neolithic Cattle Keepers of South India: A Study of the Deccan Ashmounds*. Cambridge, U.K.: Cambridge University Press, 1963.

Jarrige, Catherine, et al., eds. *Mehrgarh Field Reports, 1975 to 1985: From the Neolithic to the Indus Civilization*. Karachi: Dept. of Culture and Tourism, Government of Sindh, 1995.

Jarrige, Jean-François, and M. Lechevallier. "Excavations at Mehrgarh, Baluchistan: Their Significance in the Prehistoric Context of the Indo-Pakistan Borderlands." In *South Asian Archaeology 1977*, edited by Maurizio Taddei. Naples: Istituto Universitario Orientale, 1979.

Mandal, Dinesh. "Neolithic Culture of the Vindhyas: Excavations at Mahagara in the Belan Valley." In *Indian Prehistory: 1980*, edited by V. N. Misra and Jaga Nath Pal. Allahabad: University of Allahabad, 1997.

Meadow, Richard H. "The Origins and Spread of Agriculture and Pastoralism in South Asia." In *The Origins and Spread of Agriculture and Pastoralism in Eurasia*, edited by David R. Harris. Washington, D.C.: Smithsonian Institution Press, 1996.

Meadow, Richard H., and Ajita K. Patel. "From Mehrgarh to Harappa and Dholavira: Prehistoric Pastoralism in Northwestern South Asia through the Harappan Period." In *Indian Archaeology in Retrospect*, Vol. 2: *Protohistory: Archaeology of the Harappan Civilization*, edited by S. Settar and Ravi Korisettar. New Delhi: Indian Council of Historical Research, 2002.

Sharma, G. R. "From Hunting and Food Gathering to Domestication of Plants and Animals in the Belan and Ganga Valleys." In *Recent Advances in Indo-Pacific Prehistory*, edited by Virendra Nath Misra and Peter Bellwood. Delhi: Oxford and IBH Publishing, 1985.

Singh, P. "The Neolithic Cultures of Northern and Eastern India." In *Indian Archaeology in Retrospect*, Vol. 1: *Protohistory: Archaeology of South Asia*, edited by S. Settar and Ravi Korisettar. New Delhi: Indian Council of Historical Research, 2002.

NEPAL The kingdom of Nepal, centered in the Kathmandu Valley, has existed for more than fifteen hundred years. On the north, it is bounded by China and the Himalayas, including Mount Everest, and on the south, east and west it borders India. Modern Nepal dates from the founding of the Gurkha dynasty in the sixteenth century. At their apex, Gurkha conquests reached from Garhwal, India, in the west, through Sikkim in the east. The Anglo-Nepalese War (1814–1816) reduced the kingdom to its current, much smaller boundaries. Nepal is the world's only official Hindu state. It includes multiple ethnic and caste groups that include Brahman, Chetri, Newar, Gurung, Magar, Tamang, Rai, Limbu, Sherpa, and Tharu. The population in 2004 was 25.7 million, according to United Nations figures, while per capita annual income was about U.S.$240, according to the World Bank. About 80 percent of the population lives in rural areas.

The Ranas, the Panchayat System, and Democracy

From 1846 to 1950, Nepal was ruled by autocratic hereditary prime ministers, the Ranas, supported by the army. Their legal code institutionalized the caste system. Nepal remained isolated from the outside world. The monarchy regained executive powers in 1951, with the support of India and anti-Rana leading party, the Nepali Congress Party formed a government. In 1960, however, King Mahendra seized control, suspending Parliament, the Constitution, and party politics. In 1962 Nepal's king devised a multitier, partyless the political system known as *panchayat* for village, district, and national government. Although incorporating some democratic feature, the system remained firmly under the control of the monarch. Popular pressure from a democratic movement, established in 1980, led to the end of the *panchayat* system in 1990, the reestablishment of multiparty politics, and revision of the constitution. The Nepali Congress Party, which had collaborated with leftist groups in street protests against royal authoritarianism, won the country's first democratic elections in 1991. Democracy did not bring the desired degree of economic development or political stability, however.

Nepal's first political parties, the Nepali Congress Party and the Nepal Communist Party, though it has split and re-formed and been renamed many times, have remained the most important political parties. The Congress Party governed for most of the democratic period, while the Communist Party of Nepal/United Marxist-Leninist (CPN/UML) served as the main party of opposition. Elected governments were formed on average once a year, and corruption was rampant. Nepal remained one of the world's poorest countries, with profound economic, social, and educational inequalities, few roads or jobs, little electricity or health care, and with environmental degradation taking an increasing toll. Many young Nepalis left to work overseas or in India.

The People's War and Subsequent Instability

In 1994 a Communist Party government was elected, which lasted only a year. In February 1996, a small, left-wing faction of the UML renamed itself the Communist Party of Nepal (Maoist), or CPN-Maoist, and presented forty demands for political, social, and economic reform to the Congress-led coalition. When the government failed to respond, the CPN-Maoists declared a "People's War," centered in remote parts of the mid-western hill districts of Rukum and Rolpa. The government was slow to take notice. By 2001, when the army was ordered to counter the insurgency, the Maoist elements were present in nearly all of Nepal's seventy-two districts.

Further weakening the country's stability and the institution of the monarchy, in June 2001 almost a dozen members of the royal family, including King Birendra and Queen Aishwarya, were murdered by Crown Prince Dipendra, who then shot himself. Prince Gyanendra was crowned king. In October 2002, Gyanendra dismissed the prime minister and his cabinet. The king subsequently reinstated a multiparty government in June 2004, which he tasked with preparing for elections in the spring of 2005. Before they were held, however, the king seized power again.

The Maoists' key leaders, Chairman Pushpa Kamal Dahal (known as Prachanda) and Baburam Bhattarai, participated in parliamentary democracy but were disenchanted by its political squabbling and their party's inability to win more seats. They and others adopted Mao Zedong's belief in violent revolution, seeking to end Nepal's constitutional monarchy and the unequal treatment of lower castes. The Maoists also were inspired by Peru's Shining Path guerrillas. By 2005, various estimates put Maoist strength at between 10,000 to 15,000 fighters, in addition to tens of thousands of hard-core followers and perhaps several hundred thousand sympathizers. Up to 30 percent of the cadre and combatants may be women. Rounds of peace talks between the government and the Maoists in 2001 and 2003 failed.

Role of India in Nepal

Referring to their geographic location between their large neighbors, China to the north and India to the south, Nepalis sometimes compare their country's situation to that of a "yam between two boulders." Both countries have influenced Nepal's history and culture, but India has been the more prevalent force in trade, language, religion and custom. So dominant has India been that many Nepalis fear their country's cultural absorption if not annexation by India. For its part, India has viewed the Hamalyas as its northern strategic boundary, exacerbating Nepal's anxieties.

Nearly 8 million Nepalis reside in India. India is Nepal's largest trading partner, though Nepal imports almost three times as much from India as it exports there. Inhabitants of Indian descent are especially numerous in the Terai, Nepal's flat, fertile land near the southern border. Indians, many of whom come to visit the birthplace of the Buddha, are Nepal's most numerous tourists.

After China forcibly annexed Tibet in 1950, India sought to strengthen its security by signing a Treaty of Peace and Friendship and a trade and transit agreement with the Rana regime in Nepal. Indian advisers played key roles in reorganizing Nepal's armed forces, training the civil service and police force. In March 1989, in a dispute over the renewal of the agreement that began when Nepal purchased some military supplies from China, India effectively blockaded Nepal, cutting off most of landlocked Nepal's trade with the outside world. Other points of friction have been boundary disputes and the Mahakali Treaty with India of 1996 concerning the distribution of water and electricity. The government of Nepal has been looking to India for help in its conflict with the Maoists, believing that some of the insurgency's key leaders have taken refuge in India.

Jennifer Noyon

See also **China, Relations with; Pakistan and India**

BIBLIOGRAPHY

Gellner, David N., ed. *Nationalism and Ethnicity in a Hindu Kingdom.* Amsterdam: Harwood Academic Publishers, 1997.

Gregson, Jonathan. *Massacre at the Palace, the Doomed Royal Dynasty of Nepal.* New York: Hyperion Press, 2002.

Kumar, Dhruba, ed. *Domestic Conflict and Crisis of Governability in Nepal.* Kathmandu: Centre for Nepal and Asian Studies, 2000.

Mikesell, Stephen. *Class, State, and Struggle in Nepal: Writing 1989–1995.* New Delhi: Manohar Publishers, 1999.

Nepal and Bhutan: Country Studies/Area Handbook Series. Washington, D.C.: Library of Congress, 1993.

Singh, Nagendra Kumar. *Nepal.* New Delhi: APH Publishing, 1997.

NEPAL, RELATIONS WITH Nepal is a landlocked country adjacent to India, China, and Bangladesh. It lies in the foothills of the Himalayas, dominated by the Kathmandu Valley, where most Nepalis live. Nepal is the only Hindu monarchy in the world and one of a handful of Asian countries to have escaped European colonial conquest.

The foundations of modern Nepal were laid by its conquest by Gurkha ruler Prithvi Narayan Shan in 1768. China defined Nepal's northern boundary in 1792 by halting Nepal's territorial expansion toward Tibet. The Anglo-Nepalese War (1814–1816) culminated in a treaty that defined the southern territorial boundaries of modern Nepal. In 1846 the kingdom of Nepal came under the sway of hereditary chief ministers, known as Ranas, who isolated Nepal and wielded decisive influence over its fortunes late into the twentieth century.

The onset of armed rebellion, sponsored by the Nepali Congress Party (NCP), resulted in the end of almost one hundred years of Rana paramountcy in 1951 and restoration of the sovereignty of the crown. The anti-Rana Nepalese Congress Party (NCP), which had been operating from India, joined their Rana adversaries to form a government, though headed by a Rana. It collapsed shortly afterwards and the NCP itself split in bitter division. M. P. Koirala, heading a pro-Monarchist faction known as the RPP, became Prime Minister. Several palace nominees succeeded him until 1958. More political unrest led to Nepal's first parliamentary elections in 1959, which were won resoundingly by B. P. Koirala (brother of the more monarchical M. P. Koirala) and the adoption of a multiparty Constitution. But King Mahendra, who had succeeded his father, King Tribhuvan, in 1955, seized power in 1960, suspending Parliament. Another new constitution legitimated the exercise of absolute power by the monarch, and Nepal was still an absolute monarchy when King Birendra ascended the throne in 1972.

In 1980 King Birendra agreed to allow direct elections to Parliament again in response to agitation for reform, but the NCP rejected them because of the stipulation that elections should take place on a nonparty basis. A campaign of civil disobedience by the NCP, which enjoyed the support of India because of its espousal of pluralist politics, gathered momentum. King Birendra agreed to a new Constitution in 1990 in the face of widespread street protests, and G. P. Koirala of the NCP became the first prime minister of democratic Nepal in 1991.

Nepal, the home of the legendary Gurkha soldiers, who fought with great distinction for the British Empire and still provide important contingents for the Indian army, remains a largely illiterate and impoverished country. It has virtually no resources, except for the beauty of its mountainous environment, which attracts tourists, and a potential for generating hydroelectric power that could be destined for the Indian market beyond its southern borders. Remittances from migrant workers, including, until recent times, hard currency income from Gurkhas serving with the British armed forces, are an important source of national revenue. More than 70 percent of Nepal's national budget is funded by foreign aid.

Nepal's international trade is dominated by India and is governed by a Trade and Transit treaty signed in 1951. It is estimated that half of Nepal's population lives in India, which exercises no control over inward migration from Nepal. Nepal's highly asymmetric dependence on India has engendered severe mistrust between its elites, and popular Nepali sentiment displays overt hostility toward India. Specific Nepali grievances over trade relations, the sharing of water resources, and demarcation of the border have been worsened by acrimony over the use of Nepal as a base by Pakistani agencies for subversion against India. Nepal also occupies the strategic geographical position of a buffer between India and Tibet, which entails a difficult balancing act between the two giants of the region, India and China. An underlying cause of tension between influential opinion in Nepali society and India has been the latter's historic support for parliamentary politics in Nepal as well as its effective veto over unwelcome outcomes.

Political instability did not end in Nepal with the new democratic constitutional dispensation introduced in 1991, as various factions struggled for position. The NCP government was overthrown in 1994, and a Communist-led coalition came to power. The Communists themselves split, and a radical Maoist group, the Nepal Communist Party, began an armed insurrection, demanding an end to the monarchy and the establishment of a people's republic.

A succession of parliamentary governments, led by different political factions, failed to resolve the deepening political crisis provoked by the Maoist rebellion. Nor did they institute good governance, although Nepal's socioeconomic indices showed some improvement during the decade of parliamentary rule. King Birendra relinquished formal power, assuming the role of constitutional monarch. The army remained loyal to the palace, and despite abrupt administrative reforms, including the centralization of administrative power and wholesale retrenchment of the existing bureaucracy, the old Nepali elites retained considerable influence.

In June 2001 the monarchy almost came to an end when Crown Prince Dipendra Bikram Shah murdered King Birendra, his own immediate family, and other close relatives, fatally injuring himself as well. National grief and mourning followed, after which the sole surviving brother, Gyanendra Bikram Shah, ascended the throne.

The increasingly bloody Maoist rebellion continued, and the eleventh government in a decade of parliamentary rule seemed powerless to resolve the political crisis. A truce with the Maoists in July 2001 failed within months, and a state of emergency was declared, with the army launching a determined assault on Maoists strongholds. Controversy over extending the state of emergency led to the dissolution of Parliament in May 2002. A few months later King Gyanendra dismissed the caretaker government of Prime Minister Sher Bahadur Deuba when he sought to postpone parliamentary elections.

King Gyanendra assumed constitutional authority himself, and has nominated two interim prime ministers from the small pro-monarchical Rashytria Prajatantra Party. A fresh truce was agreed with the Maoists and peace talks commenced, but they also failed, and the bitter civil strife resumed in August 2003. The parliamentary parties, with the exception of the pro-monarchical group, were increasingly alienated from the monarchy, refusing all cooperation until the king restores parliament.

In the following year, the former elected premier, Sher Bahadur Deuba, was renominated as prime minister by King Gyanendra. But he dismissed him in February 2005 yet again, allegedly for failing to make headway in peace talks with the Maoists and schedule parliamentary elections that the end to the conflict was hoped would allow. The declaration of an emergency and assumption of power directly by King Gyanendra, suspending civil liberties and arresting leading politicians, was greeted with emphatic international disapproval. Nepal found itself isolated, with the king at odds with parliamentary politicians, a disrupted economy and no end in sight to the bloody conflict that had already claimed thousands of lives.

Gautam Sen

See also **China, Relations with; Pakistan and India**

BIBLIOGRAPHY

Hutt, Michael. *Nepal in the Nineties: Versions of the Past, Visions of the Future*. New Delhi: Oxford University Press, 2001.

Shaha, Rishikesh. *Modern Nepal: A Political History, 1769–1955*. Vols. 1–2. New Delhi: Manohar, 1990.

Thapa, Deepak, and Bandita Sijapati. *Kingdom under Siege: Nepal's Maoist Insurgency, 1996 to 2004*. Kathmandu: Printhouse, 2003.

Whelpton, John. *A History of Nepal*. New York: Cambridge University Press, 2005.

NEW DELHI Every conquering people of India used Delhi, because of its strategic location between the Indus and the Gangetic Plains, for the site of their capitals, from the ancient Hindu Indraprastha to the Turko-Afghan Sultanate of Tuglaqabad to the Mughal Shahjahanabad to the British Empire's New Delhi. And every ruler of India has manipulated architecture to leave his imprint on the city, giving the present city of Delhi the distinction of being the seventh capital. Following nearly a century and a half of struggling to tame "ungovernable" Calcutta, British India's premier city, the British shifted their capital to New Delhi after 1912. Their decision to employ an Indo-Saracenic visual language for the new capital's architecture was a demonstrated desire to encapsulate India's imperial past in its modern center of power, and to legitimize the Brtish Raj in India.

Delhi's ancient Hindu heritage no doubt remains remote and shrouded in mystery, although archaeological excavations (the most recent conducted in 1991 at Anangpur, near Suraj Kund) reveal human habitation dating back to the late Stone Age. Indraprastha, mentioned in the great Aryan epic Mahābhārata (c. 1000 B.C.), is believed to have been located on the western bank of the Yamuna River, near the Purana Qila (Old Fort), where the Afghan Sher Shah established his capital. Excavations at Indrapat (near Purana Qila) have yielded painted gray earthenware dating back to 1000 B.C. The Aryan residents of Indraprastha used clay to make pots, made ornaments from precious stones, and lived in houses built from mud bricks, wattle, and daub.

Delhi was destined to play an increasingly prominent role as the capital of Muslim conquerors from the thirteenth to the nineteenth centuries. The Islamization of Delhi commenced with its conquest by Muhammad of Ghur in A.D. 1193, followed by invasions by rival Turko-Afghans, until the Mughal emperor Babur captured the city in 1526. The Turko-Afghan period, remembered as the Delhi Sultanate, left several important monuments,

Shoppers in New Delhi. New Delhi in the twenty-first century is a capital under siege from its own population. Teeming shoppers on Chandni Chowk ("Silver Street"), a commercial district near the Red Fort (named for its red sandstone walls). LINDSAY HEBBERD / CORBIS.

including the Qutab Minar, the tomb of Ilutmish at Mehrauli, the Ferozshah Kotla, Nizzamuddin (named after a Sufi saint), Kotla Mubarakshah, the tomb of Sikander Lodi, and his fortress in the Lodi Gardens.

Mughal imperial Delhi enjoyed a cultural renaissance during the reign of Shah Jahan (1627–1658), known for his monumental architecture, with intricate designs of inlaid jewels and semiprecious stones. He envisioned a magnificent new capital in Delhi that would harken back to the splendor of his ancestral Persia, and in 1648 Delhi was renamed Shahjahanabad, serving as the twin Mughal capital along with Agra, about 110 miles (177 km) to the southwest. At Agra, Shah Jahan built the famous monument in white marble, the Taj Mahal, as a tomb for his beloved wife, Mumtaz Mahal; and at Delhi, he built the Red Fort in red sandstone and the Jama Masjid at Bhoja Pahadi. The Nahar-i-Bist (canal) linked the Red Fort with Chandni Chowk (Silver Street), a crowded commercial district that continues to offer goods to local residents and tourists alike.

The British understood the historical significance of Delhi when they shifted their capital from Calcutta. Among British India's officials, it was widely believed that Delhi's imperial associations would not only provide "a sense of historical continuity" but would also secure "permanency" for British rule in India. Viceroy Lord Hardinge kept the decision to build a new capital there top secret until the coronation durbar of King George V at Delhi's historic Red Fort on 12 December 1911. On that occasion the king himself made the announcement.

New Delhi's planning committee, appointed to determine the site for the new capital, selected municipal engineer John A. Brodie, Captain George Swinton, chairman of the London Country Council, Edwin Landseer Lutyens, a country house specialist, and Henry V. Lanchester, as a consulting architect. They decided to construct the new capital south of Old Delhi, in the area around Raisana Hill.

Covering an area of 3,200 acres (1,300 hectares), New Delhi was initially designed to accommodate a population of 65,000. British art critic Sir George Birdwood reminded the architects, "It is not a cantonment we have to lay out at Delhi, but an Imperial City—the symbol of the British Raj in India—and it must like Rome be built for eternity." Lutyens and his associate Herbert Baker initially called for a tightly knit, high-density city with broad boulevards and high-rise buildings reminiscent of the Champs Élysées or Bombay; but they were opposed by other British officials who felt that in hot and humid India they must have space, greenery, and low-density bungalows on spacious parcels of land, ensuring distance between the English and the Indians, which had become the objective of British urban policy since the Great Rebellion of 1857. In New Delhi, the British produced mixed architectural results in their efforts to reflect British "achievement" while incorporating Indian tradition. Still, by blending European classicism with Indo-Saracenic motifs, they attempted to provide historical continuity to the new imperial capital of India.

Although New Delhi was planned adjacent to Old Delhi, the two cities were separated by open spaces and a railway embankment. New Delhi was accessible from Old Delhi through only two underpasses: the Minto and Lady Hardinge Bridges. New Delhi was laid out in a geometric pattern over a triangular base formed by Connaught Place (the commercial district), the government complex (housing the two secretariat blocks and the viceroy's palace), and India Gate (that housed the statute of King George V, now removed). The centerpiece of the New Delhi plan is the use of a broad processional avenue, King's Way (now Rajpath), linking India Gate with the vicerory's palace (Rashtrapati Bhavan). The central secretariat complex is planned to dominate the skyline of New Delhi. The two secretariat blocks are separated by the viceroy's palace in the middle, the three buildings occupying the highest land of Raisina Hill. The residential areas for lower- and middle-income employees were placed to the north of King's Way; senior British officials were provided bungalows with generous land to the south. In contrast to the old high-density walled city, New Delhi had a density of only twenty-five persons per acre.

It would take the Indian government two decades to complete the new capital before finally shifting all its offices from Calcutta to New Delhi in 1931. The capital had been conceived in the pomp and circumstance of the coronation *durbār*; it would be inaugurated in the throes of Mahatma Gandhi's *satyagraha* campaigns; and it would serve as the capital of British India for a mere fifteen years. Jawaharlal Nehru, India's first prime minister, declared New Delhi "un-Indian." What Nehru objected to, and what other Indian leaders have dutifully objected to since, was the grandiose monumentality of its official buildings, created as the urban centerpiece of British rule of India.

In retrospect, the British had been correct in selecting the southern site around Raisana Hill, for New Delhi has expanded unabated since the 1980s, and the city's population in 2004 topped 10 million. New Delhi's rapid growth and the centralization of resources have served to induce the development of new towns on its periphery: Ghaziabad, Noida, Gurgeon, and Sonepat. New Delhi in the twenty-first century is a capital under siege from its own population, although its government has so far succeeded in protecting Lutyens's remarkable architectural vision.

Ravi Kalia

See also **Babur; Shah Jahan; Urbanism**

BIBLIOGRAPHY

Gupta, Narayani. *Delhi between Two Empires, 1803–1931: Society, Government and Urban Growth.* Delhi and New York: Oxford University Press, 1998.

Irving, Robert Grant. *Indian Summer: Lutyens, Baker and Imperial Delhi.* New Haven, Conn.: Yale University Press, 1981.

Kalia, Ravi. *Gandhinagar: Building National Identity in Postcolonial India.* Columbia: University of South Carolina Press; New Delhi: Oxford University Press, 2004.

Metcalf, Thomas. *An Imperial Vision: Indian Architecture and Britain's Raj.* Berkeley: University of California Press, 1989.

Florence Nightingale. In her final years, Nightingale feared that she had not done enough to further the cause of freedom in India, but took solace in the Bhagavad Gītā's reassurance that a soul was judged by its righteous action, not worldly results. HULTON-DEUTSCH COLLECTION / CORBIS.

NIGHTINGALE, FLORENCE ***(1820–1910), founder of modern nursing and champion of Indian reform.*** As a child, Florence Nightingale played upon the knee of Ram Mohan Roy, the "father of modern India," when he was a guest of her Unitarian parents in England. One of the first letters she penned as a young girl was filled with questions about the political status and social condition of women in India. In a natural extension of her interest in India and her work among the wounded during the Crimean War (1854–1856), Nightingale envisioned bringing a nursing corps to India during the War of 1857. Though this hope went unrealized, her interest in India thereafter deepened. She secured improvements in the health of the British army on the subcontinent through a Royal Commission (1859) and pressured the India Office into establishing a Sanitary Department in India (1868). She is credited with the founding of the modern nursing profession in India, dispatching ten qualified British army nurses for Indian service in 1888 and establishing a training scheme that benefited Indian nurses and midwives whose skills she admired.

As early as the 1870s, Florence Nightingale's Indian agenda began to expand beyond the army and immediate health matters to nation-building issues, including political education. Her closest friends then sought to dissuade her from "wasting" her time on Indian affairs, pointing out the dominant characteristics of British Indian policy at the time that would impede her. These factors did, in fact, combine to thwart her initial appeals for Indian reform at the India Office in London, though she subsequently outmaneuvered her opponents there by working through intermediaries drawn from her many friends in India, who included all of the viceroys of her day and many Indian civil servants.

Nightingale ultimately found, however, that even her most loyal supporters among Indian officials were reluctant to pursue her ideas to their ultimate conclusion: the creation of an Indian nation capable of making its own choices in the spirit of what Mahatma Gandhi was to call *sarvodaya*, or the uplift of all. In an effort to overcome these obstacles, Nightingale broke ranks with the prevailing imperial ethos, much as she had broken ranks with the prevailing class structure of England through the elevation of female nurses from servants to middle-class professionals. While fear of being dismissed as a "dangerous woman" forced her to act largely behind the scenes in the politics of British India, she publicly championed the efforts of the marquis of Ripon to promote Indian self-government. She also lent assistance to those Indian nationalists, such as Gopal Krishna Gokhale, who identified themselves with the interests of India's masses. Her long-standing friendship with several men who came to be presidents of the Indian National Congress heightened her awareness of that movement. She became one of its first and staunchest British supporters, publishing articles in its journal, *India*. She also met and inspired Cornelia Sorabji, who became known as the "Florence Nightingale of India" for her social activism. In her last years, Nightingale struggled to reconcile Western science and Indian tradition, but took solace in the Bhagavad Gītā's reassurance that a soul was judged on its performance of righteous action, not by worldly results. Though acutely aware of the cultural blinders worn by so many British "reformers" of India, this "Lady with the Lamp" strove to promote India's own unique light.

Marc Jason Gilbert

See also **Congress Party**

BIBLIOGRAPHY

Cook, Edward. *The Life of Florence Nightingale*. 2 vols. London: Macmillan, 1913.

Gilbert, Marc Jason. "Florence Nightingale and Indian Politics." *Charisma and Commitment in South Asian History: Essays Presented to Stanley Wolpert*, edited by Roger Long. Delhi: Orient Longman, 2004.

NIZAM OF HYDERABAD The first nizam, Qamaruddin, of Hyderabad traced his ancestry to Central Asia, while serving the Mughal emperor in southern India as the viceroy of the Deccan in 1724. He commanded the six Deccan provinces of Bidar, Berar, Bijapur, Adilabad, Golkonda, and Hyderabad. With later annexations of Khuldapur and Burhanpur and with access to the Bay of Bengal through Masulipatam, Hyderabad became the largest and wealthiest part of Mughal India. In subsequent times, though a process of reversal occurred with gradual reductions of its territory, the state survived.

The first nizam exemplified the virtues of common sense, pragmatism, balance, and restraint in his personal conduct—qualities that the last nizam, Mir Osman Ali Khan, sought to practice, not always with success. Indeed, the last nizam was frequently bizarre in his behavior, yet also able to solemnly direct the daily affairs of his court, remaining an enigma. He had the means to buy several banks, but he kept in his personal quarters a huge collection of dust-covered cartons containing hard cash and a fabulous range of jewels and precious metals, never cataloged during his lifetime.

A similar anomaly marked Hyderabad state. With a preponderantly Hindu population, its rulers were Muslim. Medieval, feudal patterns coexisted with some progressive modernist trends. Relations between Hyderabad and the new nation of Pakistan ranged from the explicit to the covert, from great expectations to reversed fortunes. There was empathy and understanding at the nizam's court and among the Muslim population of Hyderabad for the Pakistan movement. At the same time, the sheer distance between both wings of Pakistan and Hyderabad precluded any possibility of major co-operation without India's permission, which was not forthcoming.

Through his delegation, which met the founding father of Pakistan, M. A. Jinnah, on 4 August 1947, the nizam had inquired about the extent to which Pakistan—to be established ten days later—could provide economic, military, and political support to Hyderabad. Jinnah politely declined to make any precise commitments. Just six months later, on 10 January 1948, it was the nizam who extended emergency financial support to Pakistan.

The most crucial support by the last nizam remained the least acknowledged. Both giver and recipient had vital reasons to maintain secrecy and, indeed, to deny its occurrence. Soon after Pakistan became independent on 14 August 1947, its due share from the resource pool of the undivided British assets of India was not remitted to Karachi on schedule. A similar delay marked the transfer of military equipment. Mahatma Gandhi launched his last "fast unto death" in January 1948 to persuade the Indian government to release the frozen assets.

The new Pakistani state experienced formidable difficulties, rushed into premature birth at ten weeks' notice by Lord Mountbatten's arbitrary deadline for South Asia's partition, given on 2 June 1947. Resources were urgently required to manage an unprecedented structure, comprising two wings separated by a thousand miles of unfriendly Indian territory. Cash was desperately needed to pay salaries to Pakistan's government staff and to meet basic expenses. Hundreds of thousands of refugees had begun to migrate across newly drawn borders of Punjab and Bengal to towns without adequate infrastructure.

At this critical time, the nizam provided lifesaving support. One part of the aid was official and publicly announced: a transfer of securities valued at about 1 million pounds (200 million rupees, or 20 crores). Announcing the country's first budget on 28 February 1948, Pakistan's finance minister included this amount in his calculations, ensuring a minor surplus, even in those extraordinary conditions. However, that loan could not be encashed because the Indian government immediately termed it a violation of the Standstill Agreement: New Delhi's prior consent had not been obtained. The securities were thus frozen and eventually returned unused to Hyderabad.

But, according to several reliable sources, substantial sums of hard cash and gold bullion were secretly transferred by the nizam to Pakistan between August 1947 and September 1948. This secret and substantial aid was never openly announced or formally documented. One method of transfer used the exploits of a daring Australian entrepreneur-aviator named Sydney Cotton, who assembled a small fleet of Royal Lancaster planes and plucky pilots in Karachi to help break the Indian blockade of Hyderabad. Cotton's team flew numerous missions by night between Karachi and Hyderabad, ferrying in vital supplies, including arms and ammunition. They sometimes brought back stacks of cash and gold.

By one account, the last flight by Cotton from a Hyderabad airfield to Karachi was on 17 September 1948, literally minutes before the Indian army took complete control of Hyderabad state. That flight carried a large wooden box stashed with four and a half million pounds sterling in currency notes. The nizam later confirmed to his outgoing prime minister that he had destroyed all "sensitive" documents in his possession: some of these must surely have recorded amounts secretly transferred. Within seven days of that final flight, Quaid-i-Azam (Great Leader) Jinnah died. Jinnah's steel-like determination had perhaps inspired the last nizam's refusal—over a period of about 400 days—to accede to India despite suffering stiff sanctions.

Less than forty-eight hours after Jinnah's death on 11 September 1948, no longer inhibited by his presence, the Indian government sent its armed forces into Hyderabad state. For a royal realm that had survived for well over two centuries through turbulent change, the collapse was cruelly rapid and complete, taking less than four days.

Thereafter, the paths of Pakistan, of Hyderabad state, and of Nizam Osman Ali Khan diverged completely. Pakistan explored its turbulent future. Though the last nizam retained his title, all his powers of governance were surrendered, as he became a loyal, royal citizen of India. On Republic Day, 26 January 1950, the nizam read the proclamation declaring India to be a "sovereign democratic republic" while being sworn in to his new office of *rajpramuk* (president) of Hyderabad state, a purely ceremonial position. Hyderabad state and the Asaf Jah dynasty thus reached a cul-de-sac, formed by the convergence of unchanging geography and unfolding history.

Javed Jabbar

See also **Hyderabad; Jinnah, Mohammad Ali**

BIBLIOGRAPHY

Ali, Mir Laik. *Tragedy of Hyderabad.* Karachi: Pakistan Co-operative Book Society Limited, 1962.

Austin, Ian. *City of Legends: The Story of Hyderabad.* New Delhi and New York: Penguin, 1992.

Bawa, V. K. *The Last Nizam: The Life and Times of Mir Osman Ali Khan.* New Delhi and New York: Viking, 1992.

Fukazawa, Hiroshi. *The Medieval Deccan.* Delhi and New York: Oxford University Press, 1991.

Government of Pakistan, Ministry of Information and Media Development. *Pakistan's Chronology, 1947–1997.* Islamabad: Government of Pakistan, 1998.

Hasan, Mushirul, ed. *India's Partition: Process, Strategy and Mobilization.* Delhi and New York: Oxford University Press, 1993.

Jeffrey, Robin, ed. *People, Princes and Paramount Power: Society and Politics in the Indian Princely States.* Delhi: Oxford University Press, 1978.

Razvi, Aziz. *Betrayal: A Political Study of British Relations with the Nizams' Hyderabad.* Karachi: South Asia Publications, 1998.

Yazdani, Zubaida, with Mary Chrystal. *The Seventh Nizam: The Fallen Empire.* Cambridge, U.K.: Cambridge University Press, 1985.

Wolpert, Stanley. *Jinnah of Pakistan.* New York: Oxford University Press, 1984.

NOBILI, ROBERT DE ***(1577–1656), Jesuit missionary to India.*** Robert de Nobili was born in 1577 of noble Italian parents with impressive connections to the Vatican. He was intelligent, zealous, and a Jesuit. He arrived in India in 1606 to discover that nothing significant had occurred in the Roman Catholic Church since the days of Francis Xavier. He made the strategic decision of settling in Madura, an influential center of Hinduism. De Nobili believed that Christianity, while retaining its essential core of doctrine, should be divested of its European cultural trappings in order to flourish in India. He assumed the dress and lifestyle of a Brahman *sanyasi*, learned Sanskrit, and studied the Vedas. Within a couple of years, a number of converts had been baptized. De Nobili did not insist that they break caste, change their dress or even their customs, save idolatry. Thus began the work of the Madura Mission.

Several of de Nobili's colleagues among the Roman Catholic community disapproved of his tactics. In 1610 letters were sent to Rome asserting that de Nobili was corrupting Christianity by compromising on Hindu practices, especially with regard to caste. De Nobili defended his methods as accommodation. In 1619 de Nobili's methods were condemned by a council that met in Goa. The council's decision was that the Brahmans and caste converts might retain their high caste appearance, but that they must forsake Hindu ceremonies.

Armed with Pope Gregory's approval, however, de Nobili wandered from town to town in the style of a Brahman guru. Many among the lower castes converted and were baptized. De Nobili lived extremely simply and sacrificially, often facing considerable humiliation; his health deteriorated and eventually he became totally blind. He died in Mylapore, 16 February 1656.

Many priests remained concerned over what was perceived to be the downright deception on which the work of the Madura Mission was founded. Only a remote resemblence of biblical identity remained among those the mission claimed were Christian. The Vatican commissioned the patriarch of Antioch to visit India in 1703 to conduct an inquiry. Once he understood the situation, he issued a decree that condemned de Nobili's system. At first the Jesuits refused to obey, but when Pope Benedict XIV issued a bull that described the Jesuits as "perverse," "rebellious," and "lost," they had to accept defeat, and in 1759 their order was required to leave India.

Graham Houghton

See also **Christian Impact on India, History of**

BIBLIOGRAPHY

Amaladoss, Anand, ed. *Jesuit Presence in Indian History*. Anand: Gujarat Sahitya Prakash, 1988.

Firth, C. B. *An Introduction to Indian Church History*. Chennai: CLS, 1961.

Ogilvie, J. N. *An Apostle of India*. London: Hodder and Stoughton, 1915.

Robinson, Charles. *History of Christian Missions*. Edinburgh: T & T Clark, 1915.

NON-BANKING FINANCIAL INSTITUTIONS, GROWTH OF India's financial system contains many institutions other than banks, including: corporations set up by legislatures; cooperative societies; companies and unincorporated bodies; government-owned entities; nongovernment public limited and private limited companies; foreign companies; joint ventures among different types of owners; Hindu Undivided Families; clubs; unincorporated associations; and partnership firms. Many of the smaller entities are also engaged in financial services and nonfinancial activities.

Despite the unavailability of insurance for non-banking deposits, the higher rates of return, though marginal, have drawn large numbers of small savers to them. The gradual integration of domestic and external markets have also contributed significantly to the growth of this sector. With innovative market strategies, the non-banking financial institutions have mopped up public savings and command large resources.

Government-owned corporations and companies are governed by specific provisions in their respective statutes and state policies; cooperative societies function within a limited geographical area or particular business activity. The companies are permitted to operate in any part of the country, subject to compliance with the relevant regulations. Many of them are family-owned businesses, with financial support from a closely knit group of friends and relatives. With the liberalization and globalization of the economy, the role of private sector operators in the financial system has increased dramatically.

The small companies in towns and villages cater to the needs of local people, particularly for transport vehicles, and as such they supplement the role of banks. Entities engaged in leasing and purchase finance activities deserve special mention for their role in promoting capital investment in different sectors of the economy. They serve as the link between savers and users of money, mobilizing dormant savings into productive economic activities.

Linkages between Banks and Non-Banks

Non-bank and informal credit institutions are competitive as well as complementary to banks. The distinction between banks and non-banks has been blurred, since both engage in similar types of activities. Non-bank institutions supplement the role of banks in meeting the credit needs of traders and other businesses. Banks can perform the function of a wholesale credit institution; in recognition of this role, the ceiling on bank credit to non-banks was abolished. There is thus cohesion and working synergy between banks and non-banks, inasmuch as banks can function as wholesale credit providers, with the non-banks serving as their retail arm.

The government of India has permitted foreign direct investments in lease and finance, housing finance, and microcredit and rural credit activities. Any company incorporated under the Indian Companies Act of 1956 and engaged, as its principal business, in finance is identified as a non-bank financial company (NBFC). While the Reserve Bank of India (RBI) is vested with powers to supervise the deposit-taking activities of all NBFCs, various authorities, like the Securities Exchange Board of India (SEBI), the National Housing Bank, and the Insurance Regulatory and Development Authority, have been set up for closer regulation of the diverse functions of the companies such as capital market intermediaries, housing finance, and insurance.

The Reserve Bank of India Act, as amended in 1997, introduced comprehensive changes, vesting more powers with the RBI. The act now stipulates: a minimum entry point norm (Rs. 20 million); that all NBFCs obtain certificates of registration from the RBI; that the RBI may give directions to the NBFCs and their auditors and may file petitions and impose penalties against erring NBFCs; the maintenance of liquid assets as a percentage of deposit liabilities; the creation of a reserve fund and the transfer of at least 20 percent of their net profits to such reserve fund to strengthen their fund's base. Unincorporated entities engaged in financial business have been entirely banned from taking deposits from the public. Other entities engaged in nonfinancial activities have, however, been permitted to take deposits without any restriction or limitation. As such, the unincorporated bodies engaged in financial business have been marginalized.

A new RBI regulatory framework was devised in January 1998 to ensure that the NBFCs function on economically sound lines and strengthen the financial system of the country, while affording protection to depositors. A comprehensive supervisory and monitoring mechanism was put in place, encompassing ceilings on the quantum of public deposits (subject to the minimum investment grade credit ratings and capital adequacy ratios), interest rate on deposits, brokerage, period of deposits, methodology of accessing such deposits, maintenance of liquid assets as a percentage (currently 15%) of public deposits, and disclosure norms and requirement to furnish periodic returns. Investment patterns and the nature of securities in which the liabilities to depositors are to be invested has also been stipulated for non-banking companies. The prudential regulations on income recognition, accounting standards, asset classification, provisioning for doubtful debts, capital adequacy, exposure norms, and restrictions on investment in real estate and unquoted shares have been prescribed on lines similar to those applicable to commercial banks. The prudential standards relating to transparency in balance sheets and disclosure of the true and fair financial health of the company in the nature of income recognition norms, asset classification, and provisioning against nonperforming assets are also extended to non-banks.

The RBI has instituted a four-pronged supervisory mechanism over NBFCs. On-site examination is structured on the RBI's own CAMEL (capital, assets, management, earnings, liquidity) system. Off-site surveillance helps the RBI pick up warning signals, which can result in prompt supervisory intervention.

Status of Registration of NBFCs

The RBI received 37,318 applications from existing and new companies seeking grants of certificate registration under the new act to function as non-bank financial companies. All these applications were assessed, and by the end of August 2003, some 725 were registered for "public deposit"; 13,136 were registered as "nonpublic deposit" companies; and 23,434 were rejected for various reasons, including serious irregularities and violations of RBI regulations, weak financials, or poor track records of management.

With the prescription of prudential norms, sound guidelines, comprehensive regulations and supervision, and weeding out the weak as well as the unscrupulous players, the non-banks should regain their credibility. The share of institutional credit to the total resources available to non-banks accepting public deposits has risen steadily. The unauthorized acceptance of public deposits may soon become a recognizable offense. There are certain other measures that the government of India is considering, including tax parity for non-banks, extension of the facility of Debt Recovery Tribunals, and special recovery mechanisms to help them recover their dues from defaulting borrowers as speedily as do banks. Private sector companies have strong survival instincts and should emerge as strong and vibrant partners with public banks in India's fast-growing financial system.

Mohinder Kumar

See also **Bank and Non-Bank Supervision; Economic Development, Importance of Institutions in and Social Aspects of**

BIBLIOGRAPHY

Annual Reports of the Reserve Bank of India, 1998–2002. Mumbai: Reserve Bank of India.

Irani, Farouk. *Inside Leasing.* New Delhi: Tata McGraw-Hill, 1994.

Kapila, Raj, and Uma Kapila, eds. *A Decade of Economic Reforms in India.* Ghaziabad: Academy Foundation, 2002.

Khan, M. Y. *Indian Financial System: Theories and Practices.* New Delhi: Vikas Publishing House, 1980.

Shah, Mahesh. *NBFCs, Procedures and Regulations*. Kolkata: Book Corporation, 1997.

NORTHEAST STATES, THE India's northeastern corner faces insurgencies or separatist movements from over fifty groups. Although each conflict has its own roots and history, the issues they raise include language and ethnicity, tribal rivalry, migration, control over local resources, access to water, and a widespread sense of exploitation and alienation from the Indian state. From the Indian government's perspective, these movements represent not just domestic discontent, but the danger of destabilization and possible interference by Chinese or Pakistani intelligence activities. People from India's smaller northeastern neighbors, Nepal and Bangladesh, as well as economic migrants from the rest of India, have swelled the destabilizing migrations at the root of some of these insurgencies, and dissident groups have used these countries, as well as Bhutan and Myanmar (Burma), for sanctuary.

The seven states (also known as the Seven Sisters) that make up India's Northeast—Assam, Nagaland, Mizoram, Manipur, Tripura, Meghalaya, and Arunachal Pradesh—cover a total area of 98,470 square miles (255,037 square kilometers) and are linked to the rest of India by a narrow arm (the 13 mile–wide [21 kilometer] Siliguri corridor). The region borders on China, Burma, Bhutan, and Bangladesh. Except for Assam, which has substantial plains areas, this is a region of high mountains and dramatic rivers. It is home to over two hundred tribal groups and subgroups, many of whose historic rivalries continue today. Christianity is the majority religion in Meghalaya, Mizoram, and Nagaland, and there are substantial Christian minorities in the rest of the region.

The energy-rich Northeast has substantial oil, natural gas, and coal resources, much of it unexploited because of political violence. Its rivers move enormous amounts of water, and could generate far more electricity than they now do, but harnessing them raises environmental issues as well as political and international ones. The area also has abundant forest resources. It is nonetheless one of India's most economically backward areas. As is the case with many areas of entrenched instability, the insurgencies have spawned extortion and violence, as well as high unemployment in a rapidly growing population. Despite the announcement of development packages for the area by the central government, insurgency and trade in small arms and narcotics remain attractive options for young people.

The Northeast region has complex historical roots. The Ahoms, from whom the term "Assam" derives, were a people of Shan origin who came from Burma in the early thirteenth century but adopted Hinduism and the culture of the land they conquered. The Kingdom of Ahom, which included the entire present-day Northeast, remained independent of any Indian power, and withstood a dozen Mughal raids. An attack by another Burmese tribe in 1817 left it weakened, and the British were able to annex the kingdom in 1826. The Northeast has historically felt that modern India had no claim to its territories, and many of the tribes asserted their independence early on.

At various times since India's independence, the states of Meghalaya, Nagaland, Mizoram, Manipur, Tripura, and Arunachal Pradesh were carved out of the territorial boundaries of the old Ahom kingdom to strengthen the administrative structure of the Indian state and to appease tribal demands for independence. During the 1947 partition of the subcontinent, parts of Assam, including the district of Sylhet, went to East Pakistan, present-day Bangladesh. These partitions did not pay sufficient attention to tribal groupings, with the result that considerable tribal populations were divided between states and nations. Assam remains the largest and most important state in the region.

The Principal Insurgencies

A complete account of the numerous insurgencies in the northeastern states is outside the scope of this entry. The most violent and destabilizing insurgencies in the region in the past few decades have been in Nagaland and Assam.

Nagaland. This area boasts the region's oldest insurgency, which served as a model for several of the others. The Naga tribes are divided by state and national boundaries. The principal Naga militant group today, the National Socialist Council of Nagalim (Isak-Muivah; NSCN[I-M]), demands a united homeland, Nagalim, and claims a territory six times the size of present-day Nagaland, including most of Manipur, as well as parts of Assam, Arunachal Pradesh, and Burma. Angami Phizo, the founder of the Naga insurgency, opened the Burma front to the insurgency in the 1950s. Phizo's group established links with Chinese leadership at the same time, and later with Pakistan. Tribal divisions within the Naga insurgency surfaced in the 1960s and continue to plague the movement today.

In 1997 the Indian government signed a cease-fire agreement with the NSCN (I-M), extending it in June 2001 to cover predominantly Naga areas outside Nagaland as well. The extension was greeted with widespread protests and rioting in the adjoining state of Manipur, which was put under president's rule. The northeastern states saw this action by the central government as the first step toward redefining state boundaries and threatening the political status quo. Prime Minister Atal Bihari Vajpayee and Home Minister L. K. Advani somewhat belatedly announced that the central government would never consider changing state boundaries, and the ceasefire agreement was revised to apply only to Nagaland.

Assam. Assamese nationalism was first articulated in 1979 as a protest against the influx of large numbers of economic migrants from the state of West Bengal, as well as from Bangladesh and Nepal. The first non-Congress party to come to power in Assam, the Asom Gana Parishad, did so on the "foreign nationals" issue in 1985. The most prominent insurgent group in Assam has been the United Liberation Front for Asom (ULFA), which demands secession from the Indian state, citing the economic exploitation of Assam. It represents Assamese-speaking Hindu descendants of the Ahoms, but has also made overtures to other groups. At the height of its power, ULFA exercised complete control over parts of the state, running a parallel de facto government. In the initial stages of the insurgency, ULFA enjoyed widespread support in Assam, but the violence of their tactics and extortion of local businesses, notably the tea estates, have done more harm than good for the local population. While ULFA has lost much of its power and popularity, it continues to be a source of violence and instability. Bitter resentment of "outsiders," and of New Delhi, is keenly felt in Assam, and continues to be a useful rallying point for political parties as well. Attacks against minority migrant groups have persisted in the past two decades. As recently as November 2003, the state was rocked by attacks against Hindi-speaking settlers from Bihar. The Indian government's political efforts to settle the problem, notably the Assam Accord of 1985, have been unsuccessful, and the state governments have been ineffective in negotiating with insurgent groups.

Mompa Tribal Couple in Tawang, Arunachal Pradesh. Arunachal Pradesh is Northeast India's largest and most remote state, with an amazing diversity of tribes (some 60 tribal languages are spoken in the state). Here, a Mompa couple in Tawang. The culture of the Mompa shares much with that of nearby Tibet. IPSHITA BARUA.

The Bodos. The Bodos are the largest plains tribe of Assam, and their movement is a quest for indigenous rights and tribal empowerment in a majority nontribal state. They mobilized in 1987 to demand the creation of a separate state of "Bodoland," based on the historical precedent of forming new states out of Assam. India's response to their insurgency has been predominantly military.

Indian military operations against insurgent groups in Assam resulted in the gradual move of the insurgents' military training bases to the neighboring kingdom of Bhutan. In December 2003 the Royal Bhutan Army and the Royal Bhutan Guards launched a military operation against ULFA, the National Democratic Front of Bodoland, and the Kamatapur Liberation Organization training camps. Thirty such camps have been operating inside Bhutan since 1992. Press statements from Thimphu have stated that at the time its army launched the military offensive, the rebel strength was in excess of 3,000 heavily armed fighters. The military operations have been quick and successful, resulting in the dismantling of all thirty camps. Having confronted the militant groups, both Bhutan and India will need to remain vigilant against future infiltration along the thickly forested and highly porous borders between Assam and Bhutan.

Mizoram. Launched in 1966, the Mizo insurgency lasted for two decades of fighting from bases in Burma, and maintained active links with China and Pakistan. The leader of the Mizo insurgent group (the Mizo National Front), Laldenga, signed an accord with the central government in 1986, effectively ending the insurgency through dialogue and emerging as the chief minister in the newly pacified state. In the latest development

Monoliths in an Ancient Khasi (tribe) Graveyard. In the rugged terrain of the Khasi Hills (in the state of Meghalaya, literally "abode of the clouds"), a number of ancient monoliths—almost Celtic in appearance—commemorate the dead. IPSHITA BARUA.

package to the Northeast, Mizoram has been given a U.S.$38 million "peace bonus."

Meghalaya, Manipur, Tripura, and Arunachal Pradesh. These areas have not been free from violence either. Manipur's insurgencies have focused on different issues at different times: an ideological struggle based on Marxism and Maoism, a campaign to protect Vaishnava Hindu rights, and an ethnic struggle launched by the Meiteis, plains dwellers from the Imphal Valley. Tripura, like the state of Sikkim, has seen a complete demographic transformation since the 1950s. The nineteen indigenous tribes of the state, a mixture of Christians, Buddhists, and nature worshipers, are now a minority in a state dominated by migrants from the plains of West Bengal and Bangladesh. The tribes of Tripura share ethnic linkages with those of Myanmar (Burma) and the Chittagong Hill Tracts (CHT) of Bangladesh, and tribal insurgents have based themselves out of the CHT. Soon after the Mizo peace accords, the leading Tripura insurgent group, the Tripura National Volunteers Force, also signed a peace agreement with the Indian government in 1988. While sporadic violence against Bengalis continues, the insurgency has lost its revolutionary force.

Meghalaya and Arunachal Pradesh are the only two states in the Northeast that have not seen a full-fledged insurgency. The state of Meghalaya was carved out of Assam to meet the political demands of the Khasi, Garo, and Jaintia tribes, who felt that the Assam government did not represent their needs. Despite periodic attacks against Bengalis and Nepalis that paralyze the capital of Shillong, it is relatively better off than its neighbors. Arunachal Pradesh, along with Mizoram, became a separate state from Assam in 1987. The most remote of the northeastern states, the area was known as the Tribal Areas and, later, the North East Frontier Agency until 1972. Much of Arunachal has been a contested area between India and China since independence, and the two share the longest disputed border in the world. Much of India's failed war against China in 1962 was fought in Arunachal, and China has had de facto control over parts of Arunachal's territory since then.

Motivated by a range of issues, such as anti-immigration, ethnic separatism, intertribe tensions, or Marxism and Maoism in the case of Manipur, violence has taken a heavy toll on these states, leaving them underdeveloped and socially fragmented. There is widespread unemployment across the northeastern states, with a rising number of social problems as a result of protracted conflict. The prevalence of drug use in this region is the highest in India. Insurgency has curtailed political development in the region, with many political leaders rendered either ineffective or complicit vis-à-vis the insurgent groups, and corruption is endemic.

Sikkim. While Sikkim is not one of the "Seven Sister" states that make up the Northeast, it is an integral part of the northeastern region, and serves as a cautionary tale to India's smaller neighbors such as Bhutan and Nepal. Sikkim was incorporated into the Indian state in 1975. India justified its action by citing misrule by the Chogyal (king) of Sikkim. However, the underlying cause of India's move was an influx of Nepali migrants, which changed the demographics of the country, outnumbering the native Sikkimese. The demographic change and the demands of the Nepali population posed an insurmountable challenge to the monarchy, and India stepped in. Ultimately, fear of compromising their sovereignty underlies the resentment smaller neighbors feel toward India.

Regional Issues

The Indian approach. Indian scholars cite Mizoram as the model for a successful anti-insurgency policy, and attribute its good results to the Indian government's willingness to allow an insurgent leader to emerge as an officially recognized leader within the political system. The Indian government appears to be trying the same approach in Nagaland, and has been willing to accept the NSCN (I-M) as its exclusive negotiating partner there. The Nagas' territorial ambitions have complicated the picture, however, as has the fact that the NSCN (I-M) does not represent all the Naga tribes. Over time, the development of other entrenched interests makes it difficult to put together a "Mizo solution." New Delhi's intensive counterinsurgency operations and the militarization of daily life in the region have compounded the problem. The local population is trapped between a coercive government and intolerant militants, and the democratic process is in shambles. Governors appointed by Delhi in the Northeast play a dominant role in local political life, further fueling local leaders' alienation from Delhi.

Agreements to resolve political unrest in tribal areas often restrict land ownership to local citizens and limit movement of people into the area. However, population growth in the nearby Indian, Nepali, and Bangladeshi plains continues to push people off the land, generating a continuing source of conflict and difficulty in maintaining this type of restriction. Political parties, most notably the Congress Party, exacerbated the problem in earlier decades by actively assisting illegal Hindu and Muslim migrants from Bangladesh and the Indian plains in an effort to cultivate critical pools of voters in the states.

"The foreign hand." The Indian government has always been quick to see Pakistani and Chinese intelligence activities, with the goal of encircling and destabilizing India, at the root of insurgencies in the Northeast. Many insurgent groups, including ULFA and the Nagas, have traveled to training camps in China and in Pakistan, and this connection has exacerbated New Delhi's suspicions. The Indian government believes that the Northeast is a hotbed of Pakistan's Inter-Services Intelligence (ISI) activity, and that ISI also uses Nepalese soil for activities directed against India. This attention to foreign intervention tends to ignore the domestic realities in which the insurgencies are grounded.

The northeastern neighbors. One of the main difficulties in understanding unrest in the Northeast is the fact that insurgencies overrun not just state, but national boundaries. Thus, any discussion of the northeastern states must factor in India's northeastern neighbors. Nepal, Bhutan, and Bangladesh all share porous borders with India and will be part of the solution or the exacerbation of the problems facing the region. India's relationship with Myanmar (Burma) was nonexistent since the 1960s, but has undergone a dramatic change since 2000. India is acutely sensitive to any indication of Pakistani or Chinese intelligence activity in these countries. In an attempt to keep China out of its "sphere of influence," India poured development and infrastructure aid into Nepal, Bhutan, and Sikkim (prior to its incorporation into the Indian state). Illegal migration is a recurring bilateral problem with Nepal and Bangladesh, as is the insurgent groups' use of territories of the three nations. The importance of India's northeastern states in larger geopolitical calculations concerning China and regional security has influenced Indian response to the politics of the region. This geopolitical insecurity has encouraged military intervention in the region rather than more measured political initiatives. In fact, for some decades since independence, India's policy for the Northeast states was formulated by the Ministry of External Affairs in Delhi, not the Home Ministry.

Myanmar (Burma). After a quarter century of little political contact, India has reestablished a relationship with Myanmar, motivated primarily by security considerations. Myanmar borders four of India's northeastern states (Mizoram, Manipur, Nagaland, and Arunachal Pradesh), and the border between the two countries is a gateway for insurgents trying to destabilize both. A nexus between Naga and ULFA militants operating in India, and Chin and Karen rebels operating in Myanmar, has proved to be a challenge that the two nations can curb only through bilateral counterinsurgency measures. Indian fears of a growing Chinese naval presence in Myanmar, with dire implications for the security of the Bay of Bengal, was a further catalyst for building ties with its military junta, in spite of considerable domestic opposition. India also sees Myanmar as its gateway to Southeast Asia, which has become a major priority in India's "looking East" foreign policy. During a February 2001 trip to Myanmar, then Indian foreign minister Jaswant Singh inaugurated a highway connecting Manipur and Myanmar, a road that is expected to strengthen economic and security links between the two countries.

Bhutan. Bhutan's basic relationship with India is set by the India-Bhutan Treaty of 1949, which commits Bhutan to taking India's advice on defense and foreign affairs. Within these limits, India has respected Bhutan's sovereignty and has not meddled in its internal affairs. In return, Bhutan has steered clear of China, and has limited its foreign relations to avoid raising suspicions in New Delhi. The presence of ULFA and Bodo militants in Bhutan's densely forested foothills raised fears that India would upset the agreed balance of Indo-Bhutan relations and compromise Bhutan's sovereignty and strong national pride, which could in turn affect the institution of the monarchy. Successful operations to oust the insurgents from Bhutanese soil have stabilized the issue, but there is a real fear that this could unleash a backlash from the insurgent groups, embroiling Bhutan in a protracted conflict.

Bangladesh. Relations between India and Bangladesh have been fairly good on the surface, but Bangladesh is suspicious of India's overweening presence in the region. Cordial Bangladeshi political and defense ties with China and Myanmar have also aroused Indian suspicions. Illegal Bangladeshi immigration into India is a leading cause of insurgencies in the Northeast, as is the somewhat paradoxical fact that some of these insurgent groups have taken refuge in Bangladesh.

With India's cooperation, Bangladesh signed an agreement settling its tribal insurgency in the Chittagong Hill Tracts (CHT) in 1997. Implementation has been somewhat uncertain, however, and the basic population pressures at the root of the insurgency remain strong. This dispute is intertwined with several of those in northeastern India. The Chakmas, the principal indigenous tribe of the CHT, are Buddhists of Tibeto-Burmese origin. The Bangladeshi government for years encouraged Muslim migration to the relatively sparsely populated CHT, as the Indian government had done in Assam. The Chakmas mobilized in 1972 and attacked Bangladeshi installations under their armed wing, the Shanti Bahini. Army operations against the Shanti Bahini and displacement of people after the construction of a major dam led some 250,000 Chakmas to settle in nearby areas of India, including Tripura, Mizoram, and Arunachal Pradesh.

Nepal. Millions of illegal migrants from Nepal have contributed to the insurgencies in the Northeast. Bhutan too alleges that illegal Nepalese immigration is widespread, and the two countries are in a deadlock over Bhutan's decision to repatriate 100,000 illegal Nepali immigrants from Bhutan. The immigrants themselves claim Bhutanese citizenship and accuse Bhutan of deporting them for ethnic reasons, citing Bhutan's fear that its Drukpa national identity would be threatened and would be unable to cope with the impact of the Nepali minority on its system of government and sovereignty. Nepal's political instability, and the violent Maoist insurgency that it is struggling to deal with, will continue to be a problem for the region. Nepal's economy is in disarray, and its growing population pressures make migration a natural choice for some of its people.

India has intermittently tried to redress the imbalance in its bilateral relations with Bangladesh, Bhutan, and Nepal by finding areas of common interest and mutual cooperation. The only forum for multilateral cooperation in the region, the South Asian Association for Regional Cooperation, is at best a weak organization whose mandate explicitly excludes any role in bilateral disputes, and which has been further debilitated by the conflict between India and Pakistan. Partly as a result, India has focused more on bilateral or other subregional mechanisms for cooperation. India has a hefty trade surplus with each of these neighbors. Energy trade could shift this balance and benefit everyone. Bhutan already exports hydropower to India and will be expanding this trade. A similar agreement with Nepal has been under discussion for decades, but faces both political and environmental obstacles. The export of natural gas from Bangladesh could also be beneficial to both states, but has been political dynamite within Bangladesh.

China. China is at the root of India's security concerns about the Northeast. The established Chinese relationship with Pakistan is already a major concern for India, as is the newer Chinese link to the military government in Myanmar. Any indication of active Chinese involvement in India's insurgencies or a serious move to undermine India's primacy in Nepal and Bhutan could send the uneasy relationship between the two dominant regional powers into a sharp decline.

The two countries have strikingly similar concerns about one another's roles in their Himalayan border region. In China's case, the issue is Tibet, two of whose most prominent leaders, the Dalai Lama and the Karmappa, have taken asylum in India. In addition, China has always challenged India's sovereignty over Sikkim, as well as over parts of Arunachal Pradesh. India claims the Chinese-controlled area of Aksai Chin in Kashmir. The two countries have, however, reactivated their border talks and are trying to put their relations on a friendlier and firmer footing. The most positive sign of change in entrenched attitudes, and one that holds a key to addressing change in the Northeast, is the July 2003 bilateral decision to institute a border trade regime in Sikkim, creating a vital economic hub for the landlocked Northeast.

Creating a more stable future. India's preoccupation with the law-and-order aspects of its troubles in the northeastern states has tended to deepen those states' alienation from Delhi. The key to a more stable future lies in a better mix of Indian policies. The key ingredients in future stability are economic development, focusing especially on the region's energy resources; greater tolerance for local control; willingness to work with local leaders; and strengthening democracy and civil society.

Similarly, India's stress on maintaining and expanding its current primacy with its smaller northeastern neighbors has amplified their sensitivity about dealing with an overbearing India. Some adjustments in Delhi's operating style could ease this problem, and could lead to more cooperative policies to address both domestic problems in the Northeast, as well as bilateral issues in the region. Dealing with the problems of the northeastern states requires a twofold approach—one that addresses the domestic causes and consequences of the insurgencies, and another that works toward an integrated solution that involves the Northeast's surrounding states, creating opportunities for all.

Mandavi Mehta

See also **Arunachal Pradesh; Assam; Bangladesh; Burma; China, Relations with; Ethnic Conflict; Geography; Insurgency and Terrorism; Manipur; Meghalaya; Mizoram; Nagas and Nagaland; Nepal, Relations with; Pakistan and India; Paramilitary Forces and Internal Security**

BIBLIOGRAPHY

Ao, Lanunungsang A. *From Phizo to Muivah: The Naga National Question in North-East India*. New Delhi: Mittal Publications, 2002.

Banerjee, Dipankar. *Myanmar and Northeast India*. New Delhi: Delhi Policy Group, 1997.

Barooah, Nirode. *Gopinath Bardoloi: Indian Constitution and Centre-Assam Relations*. Guwahati: Publications Board, 1990.

Bhattacharyya, Bhubaneshwar. *The Troubled Border: Some Facts about Boundary Disputes between Assam-Nagaland, Assam-Arunachal Pradesh, Assam-Meghalaya, and Assam-Mizoram*. Guwahati, Assam: Lawyer's Book Stall, 1995.

Elwin, Verrier. *India's North-East Frontier in the Nineteenth Century*. London: Oxford University Press, 1959.

Hazarika, Sanjoy. *Strangers of the Mist: Tales of War and Peace from India's Northeast*. New Delhi: Viking, Penguin Books India, 1994.

———. *Rites of Passage: Border Crossings, Imagined Homelands, India's East and Bangladesh*. New Delhi and New York: Penguin Books, 2000.

Rustomji, Nari. *Imperilled Frontiers: India's Northeastern Borderlands*. Delhi: Oxford University Press, 1983.

Sharma, Suresh. *Tribal Identity and the Modern World*. Tokyo and New York: United Nations Press; New Delhi and Thousand Oaks, Calif.: Sage Publications, 1994.

Singh, B. P. *The Problems of Change*. Delhi: Vikas Publishing, 1989.

Verghese, B. G. *India's Northeast Resurgent: Ethnicity, Insurgency, Governance, Development*. Delhi: Konark, 1996.

Weiner, Myron. *Sons of the Soil: Migration and Ethnic Conflict in India*. Princeton, N.J.: Princeton University Press, 1978.

NORTH-WEST FRONTIER. *See* **Baluchistan and the North-West Frontier.**

NUCLEAR PROGRAMS AND POLICIES India took the world by surprise when it tested five nuclear explosive devices on 11 and 13 May 1998. Its capability to produce nuclear weapons had been well known within governmental circles even before 1974, when it conducted its first nuclear explosive test. At that time, however, the Indian government labeled the event a "peaceful nuclear experiment" (PNE) and refrained from producing nuclear weapons. After decades of hesitation and delay by successive governments in New Delhi, India's sudden willingness to defy the international proponents of the nuclear nonproliferation regime struck both the Indian public and foreign observers as an uncharacteristically brazen act of resolve. In subsequent years, however, India again appears to have slipped back into a relaxed nuclear policy. It has been slow to turn its nuclear weapons capability into an operational nuclear deterrent, although it has issued a nuclear doctrine and announced the basic outlines of a strategic command and control structure.

India's interest in mastering the technology to build nuclear weapons dates back six decades. Over this period, its nuclear programs and policies can be divided into four distinct phases. The first phase began when India initiated a modest nuclear research effort in June 1944, more than one year before the U.S. nuclear attack on Japan and three years prior to winning its independence from Great

Britain. In fact, India was one of the first nations to realize the economic and military importance of nuclear energy. Although India's initial nuclear program had no military orientation, India's first prime minister, Jawaharlal Nehru, and his chief nuclear adviser, Homi Jehangir Bhabha, built into the program from the very outset the technical, political, and legal features that would enable India to begin serious work on nuclear explosives in 1964, to conduct a nuclear test ten years later, and to become an acknowledged nuclear weapons power at the turn of the twenty-first century.

The second phase of India's nuclear program began in 1954, when Bhabha seized upon new opportunities for nuclear imports enabled by the U.S. Atoms for Peace program. Before this period ended, with the deaths of Nehru in May 1964 and Bhabha nineteen months later, India had nearly the entire infrastructure needed to produce nuclear weapons. However, in the next phase of the program, which began in 1966, Nehru's successors refused to allow the nuclear establishment to build the bomb. Nehru's daughter, Prime Minister Indira Gandhi, authorized the 1974 PNE, but this period of hesitation continued until 1998, when India conducted its next round of nuclear tests, this time boldly declaring itself a nuclear-weapon state. The fourth phase of India's nuclear program and policy began in May 1998 and is characterized by a surprisingly lenient effort to field an operational nuclear deterrent—an endeavor that to this day is far from complete.

Phase 1: Initiating India's Nuclear Program

India's path to nuclear weapons acquisition was neither direct nor quick. The Indian government initiated its nuclear research and development program in the mid-1940s not as a response to an immediate military threat to its security, but rather because of the power of certain ideas about the scientific, political, and possibly long-term military utility of nuclear energy. Many of these ideas originated in the West, but Jawaharlal Nehru embraced them and fashioned them into official policy.

Nehru's vision. Nehru thought and spoke extensively about the military and economic utility of nuclear energy. When a reporter asked in August 1945 whether soon-to-be-independent India would seek nuclear arms, Nehru said that India would use atomic energy for peaceful ends, but if threatened militarily, the government "will inevitably try to defend itself by all means at its disposal" (Gopal, vol. 14, pp. 192–193). Despite India's poor scientific and industrial infrastructure, Nehru often asserted that India must obtain the latest military technology.

Nehru specified the role that nuclear energy should play in Indian defense in a key report of 3 February 1947 on "Defense Policy and National Development." First Nehru explained why science and technology must underpin India's defense industry: "Modern defence as well as modern industry require scientific research, both on a broad basis and in highly specialized ways. Even more than before, war is controlled by the latest scientific inventions and devices. If India has not got highly qualified scientists and up-to-date scientific institutions in large numbers, it must remain a weak country incapable of playing a primary part in a war." Calling India an emerging "major power in the military sense," Nehru declared: "The probable use of atomic energy in warfare is likely to revolutionise all our concepts of war and defence. For the moment we may leave that out of consideration except that it makes it absolutely necessary for us to develop the methods of using atomic energy for both civil and military purposes" (Gopal, vol. 2, p. 364).

The defense policy report concluded with an important directive: "An Atomic Energy Commission should be appointed for research work in the proper utilization of atomic energy for civil and other uses." Under Nehru's leadership, independent India embarked on a quest to become proficient in military as well as scientific and industrial uses of nuclear energy. Hardly warranted by India's relatively peaceful security environment, India's early nuclear policy was shaped by Nehru's worldview and his faith in the ability of science and technology to transform India's long-term security and economic welfare.

Bhabha's plan. Nehru's dream for India to become a nuclear power would have gone unrealized had it not been for the achievements of a handful of Indian scientists, most notably Homi Bhabha. Nehru popularized the belief that nuclear energy would enhance India's security and influence, but Bhabha was responsible for establishing the technical and economic feasibility of starting a nuclear research program, building and operating nuclear reactors, and later, developing nuclear weapons. Bhabha's stature as a physicist and his vision for using nuclear energy to pull India out of poverty and backwardness enabled him to establish the credibility of India's nuclear program at home and abroad, which in turn helped Bhabha obtain a very large share of the Indian government's scarce resources and considerable foreign nuclear technology, training, and materials.

Bhabha initiated India's nuclear program in March 1944, when he appealed to the Indian philanthropist Sir Sorab Saklatvala for financial support to develop nuclear energy for power production—several years before a nuclear reactor produced electricity anywhere in the world. Undeterred by the skepticism voiced by his Indian colleagues about obtaining usable energy from the atom, Bhabha was convinced of the possibility of producing nuclear energy on an industrial scale by the proliferation of promising scientific literature on the subject before wartime secrecy terminated all public mention of nuclear energy.

Saklatvala and the government of India agreed to support Bhabha's plan, and in June 1945 Bhabha created the Tata Institute of Fundamental Research (TIFR). Initially consisting of a laboratory for work in cosmic rays and theoretical physics, the scientific areas in which Bhabha was most interested, TIFR expanded soon after independence into a broad-based center for training and research on all aspects of nuclear physics.

The Atomic Energy Act. After its independence, India took decisive steps to improve the internal organization of India's nuclear program, the most important of which was the enactment of the Atomic Energy Act, which provided sweeping authority over all nuclear matters to Nehru and Bhabha. Drafted on 15 August 1948 along the lines of the 1946 atomic energy acts of the United States and the United Kingdom, the legislation gave the Indian government exclusive authority to survey and exploit nuclear-related materials and to conduct research on the scientific and technical problems associated with the development of atomic energy. The act also established the Indian Atomic Energy Commission (IAEC) to manage all nuclear activities for the government.

Nehru always maintained close control over India's nuclear program. He set up the IAEC as his chief policy-making body for nuclear matters, and mandated it to: survey the country for atomic minerals; collect and develop such minerals on an industrial scale; set up a nuclear research reactor and, more generally, conduct research on the scientific and technical problems associated with the peaceful exploitation of atomic energy; recruit and train the scientific and technical personnel required for this undertaking; and direct fundamental research in nuclear sciences in its own laboratories and in India's other research institutions and universities. He also gave the commission sweeping authority to take such steps as may be necessary to protect the interests of the country in connection with atomic energy. Predictably, Nehru appointed Bhabha as the first chair of the IAEC, a post he held until his death in January 1966.

Right from the start, there was a small but significant domestic opposition to the idea of creating an independent atomic energy agency in India. Political activist Krishnamurthy Rao and India's nuclear physicist-turned-politician, Meghnad Saha, contended that the plan would remove fundamental research from India's universities. Saha opposed the IAEC, refused to be associated in any way with the nuclear establishment, and by 1954 became the country's leading voice of dissent on the general structure and orientation of India's nuclear program.

Saha especially detested the strict secrecy with which Indian atomic activities were shrouded, and he also opposed plans for close collaboration between the Indian government, private industry, and foreign firms. Nehru understood Saha's objections, but insisted that nuclear research had unique requirements. When he introduced the atomic energy bill, Nehru stated, "atomic energy research, if it is to be effective and successful, must be on a big scale" (Gopal, vol. 4, p. 422). Nehru added that the government's unusual secrecy was needed to protect the findings of India's scientific research and to attract the cooperation of other countries which themselves insisted on conducting nuclear affairs under strict secrecy.

What Nehru did not reveal may have been his main motivation for creating a highly centralized and secret nuclear establishment—his abiding desire to develop a military nuclear option. After India achieved its independence, Nehru rarely talked about developing nuclear weapons, in contrast to his pre-independence musings on the necessity of military nuclear research for India. On more than one occasion, however, the prime minister implied that the development of nuclear energy for scientific and industrial purposes would provide India with a significant capability for pursuing military applications. On 29 February 1948, Nehru urged Defence Minister Baldev Singh to appoint a scientific adviser for the Defence Ministry to consider the defense aspects of nuclear energy:

> Dr. Homi Bhabha . . . has given me a long report about atomic energy research. I am very much interested in this and I am sure that we should seriously start taking steps in this direction. I think this is important from many points of view. It will not, of course, bring immediate results. But the future belongs to those who produce atomic energy. . . . Of course, Defence is intimately concerned with this. Even the political consequences are worthwhile. (Gopal, 2nd series, vol. 5, p. 420)

Nehru then told the Lok Sabha (the lower house of India's Parliament) that Indian scientists must create a nuclear program to serve military as well as industrial ends:

> The point I should like the House to consider is that if we are to remain abreast in the world as a nation which keeps ahead of things, we must develop this atomic energy quite apart from war—indeed, I think we must develop it for the purpose of using it for peaceful purposes. It is in that hope that we should develop this. Of course, if we are

compelled as a nation to use it for other purposes, possibly no pious sentiments of any of us will stop the nation from using it that way. (ibid., p. 427)

Nehru always declared that India would use nuclear technology for peaceful ends. On several occasions, however, he revealed his interest in exploiting the military potential of nuclear energy—an option that he and Bhabha had created in the initial design of India's nuclear program. Apart from the establishment of government control over all nuclear materials, facilities, and scientific activities, extreme secrecy was the most important feature built into the program for potential military uses. When Krishnamurthy Rao asked why secrecy was required for the entire program when the British insisted upon secrecy "only for defense purposes," Nehru replied: "I do not know how you are to distinguish between the two" (ibid., p. 426). Nehru could not have been more honest. He ensured that the nuclear weapons option was an integral part of the nuclear program from its beginning until his death in 1964. And even after Nehru's death, his legacy continued. Every subsequent prime minister secretly protected this option until Atal Bihari Vajpayee exercised it in May 1998.

Phase 2: Developing the Nuclear Infrastructure

While Saha and other Indian politicians, scientists, and bureaucrats were wondering whether India's costly nuclear practices would ever lead to the operation of a nuclear reactor, Nehru and Bhabha took decisive steps to move the program back on course. Recognizing that the pace and scope of further growth was restricted by the nuclear program's outdated administrative structure, Nehru decided in August 1954 to fund a new nuclear laboratory at Trombay, near Bombay, and to create a Department of Atomic Energy (DAE) to give the Atomic Energy Commission more resources and improved access to Nehru and the growing executive branch of the government.

Bhabha lobbied Nehru to locate the DAE headquarters in Bombay—close to the new atomic energy establishment at Trombay, but over 700 miles (1,126 km) away from the capital, where all other governmental departments were located. (After Bhabha's death, Prime Minister Indira Gandhi renamed this facility the Bhabha Atomic Research Centre.) The DAE was endowed with executive authority to carry out policies formulated by the Atomic Energy Commission. Nehru made himself the first minister of the department and appointed Bhabha as his secretary. With Bhabha serving simultaneously as DAE secretary, IAEC chairman, and TIFR director, and answerable in each of these positions only to the prime minister, he gained nearly absolute authority over India's nuclear program.

At this point, Bhabha's concept for India's nuclear future was fairly vague. He wanted to set up an electricity-generating reactor, but in 1954, no power reactor had gone into operation anywhere in the world (the first small-scale power reactor, Britain's 37-megawatt Calder Hall plant, did not produce electricity until 1956). So Bhabha decided to construct a small laboratory reactor as a research facility and then work on acquiring a larger reactor when the opportunity arose. Bhabha traveled to England to meet with the Nobel Prize–winning physicist Sir John Cockroft, then director of the United Kingdom Atomic Research Establishment. Perhaps because Bhabha and Cockroft had worked together at Cambridge, Cockroft offered enriched-uranium fuel elements and the technical support that India needed to build a research reactor.

This still left the matter of obtaining a power reactor. Nuclear reactor technology was not widely understood at the time, but Bhabha knew that three varieties of power reactors were under development in the West: light-water (ordinary water) moderated reactors, heavy-water (deuterium oxide) moderated reactors, and graphite moderated reactors. American scientists were working on light-water reactors, but these facilities were fueled by enriched uranium, which India would have to import. In contrast, heavy-water reactors were fueled by natural uranium, which India already possessed. Apart from mining and milling the uranium and fabricating it into fuel rods, Bhabha's key challenge would be to produce heavy water to moderate the facility, but this appeared to be a manageable task (in fact it turned out to be very challenging). India soon started construction on a small facility in the north Indian state of Punjab to produce heavy water.

Foreign assistance. India's next task was to develop a complete nuclear fuel cycle. From the mid-1950s to the mid-1960s, Bhabha took steps to produce, or import if necessary, all the facilities needed both to supply fuel for nuclear reactors and to make use of the reactor products for commercial and scientific purposes. His plan called for the acquisition of unsafeguarded plutonium-producing reactors (reactors for which there are no foreign inspection arrangements or other controls to ensure that the reactor products are not diverted to weapons uses) and then the construction of a reprocessing facility to separate plutonium from the other elements in the spent reactor fuel (uranium and radioactive wastes). He claimed that the plutonium produced at the "back end" of the fuel cycle would be returned someday to the "front end" as fuel for a sophisticated energy-producing fast-breeder reactor. What Bhabha did not advertise was his intention to create an abundant stockpile of plutonium for the possible production of nuclear explosives.

India was not the only country to assemble a complete nuclear fuel cycle during the relatively permissive Atoms for Peace era, but its ability to avoid the strict safeguards that the United States and other nuclear exporters generally required was unique. This was a remarkable achievement considering the problematic relationship India had with the United States from the mid-1950s to the early 1960s, when India opposed Western interests on nearly every vital world issue: nuclear disarmament, the Korean War, the Suez crisis, U.S. regional security alliances, Vietnam, and China. U.S. officials accepted New Delhi as an imperfect partner because they feared that if India or Pakistan came under communist influence, chain reaction effects, going as far as Western Europe, would result. With India positioned as a mainstay in their cold war struggle against communism, therefore, Washington and its allies took pains to enhance India's security, internal stability, and economic development. Especially during the Eisenhower administration, the peaceful uses of atomic energy played an important role in the American strategy to make India strong and to keep communism out of South Asia. What U.S. policy and intelligence experts failed to understand, however, was that Nehru and Bhabha secretly planned to use imported nuclear technology to produce nuclear weapons.

India's first plutonium production reactor. The plutonium India used to detonate its 1974 "peaceful nuclear experiment" came from the spent fuel of Cirus, a 40-megawatt research reactor supplied by Canada in the late 1950s. Canadian and U.S. officials knew that if Indian scientists reprocessed the spent fuel from this reactor, they could separate about 22 pounds (10 kg) of bomb-grade plutonium annually. However, Ottawa curiously did not insist on intrusive inspections or other control mechanisms to prevent the reactor from being employed for military ends. Because of India's stubborn refusal to accept safeguards, the bilateral reactor agreement simply contained a clause committing India to employ Cirus and its by-products for "peaceful purposes only." With uncharacteristic disregard for the proliferation potential of its exports, Canada provided India with its only unsafeguarded source of fissile material until the locally built Dhruva reactor went into operation in 1985.

U.S. assistance and safeguards. After the Canadian Cirus deal, Washington agreed to lend India the money it required to construct two American power reactors at Tarapur, but only with strict safeguards as a condition of the deal. U.S. officials had become worried that India might be toying with the idea of producing nuclear explosives. In April 1961, India began construction on a plant at Trombay, named Phoenix, to extract plutonium from the spent fuel produced in the Cirus reactor. Nehru had authorized this secret project in July 1958. The unsafeguarded facility, which was based on the Purex (plutonium-uranium extraction) reprocessing technology developed and declassified by the United States, could provide India with a stockpile of bomb-grade plutonium. U.S. officials still believed that Nehru would not sacrifice his reputation as a crusader against nuclear weapons, and they accepted Bhabha's claim to use plutonium to fuel breeder reactors, though a growing body of evidence suggested that India was trying to keep its options open.

Then, in January 1961, Prime Minister Nehru told the Indian National Development Council: "We are approaching a stage when it is possible for us . . . to make atomic weapons" (Beaton and Maddox, p. 144). This statement came shortly after Cirus went into operation. The following month, Bhabha declared that India could build a nuclear bomb in two years or so if it wanted to.

U.S. officials became even more concerned when, on 31 August 1961, an Indian government spokesman declared: "We are against all tests and explosions of nuclear material except for peaceful purposes under controlled conditions." The implication was that Indian officials were now considering the use of peaceful nuclear explosives, which were becoming the fascination of scientists all over the world. Despite mounting Western concerns, Bhabha was able to negotiate amazing deals for the Cirus research reactor, the heavy water needed to moderate it, and the uranium required to fuel it, all at bargain-basement rates and without the provision of strict safeguards to prevent diversion to military uses. As a result, India was able to assemble in a period of ten years a complete nuclear fuel cycle, which produced a substantial supply of plutonium to fuel advanced power-production reactors and possibly to build nuclear bombs.

U.S. security assurances. The victory of Chinese forces over India in the 1962 Himalayan border war and Beijing's race for its own nuclear bomb created a serious security predicament for India. Although Nehru rejected a U.S. military plan for a semipermanent U.S. air and naval presence on Indian territory, he did believe that U.S. military threats helped deter China from both widening the 1962 war and launching subsequent incursions into India. The fact that these threats included a nuclear component strengthened Nehru's interest in a covert nuclear weapons capability. After 1962 it became difficult for Nehru, Bhabha, and a widening group of other senior politicians and bureaucrats to think about India's security without a nuclear weapons capability.

India's liveliest nuclear debate was sparked by China's nuclear explosive test in October 1964. Even before the detonation, Homi Bhabha had established the technical and economic feasibility of building nuclear bombs in India, and then he lobbied to persuade key political elites to approve the development of a limited nuclear deterrent capability. Prime Minister Lal Bahadur Shastri, the humble politician who succeeded Nehru, initially rejected the bomb option, preferring a diplomatic solution to counter China's nuclear threat. But Bhabha lobbied him to reconsider the nuclear option. Finally giving in to the wellspring of political opinion favoring the bomb, in early 1965 Shastri authorized Bhabha to start work on the Subterranean Nuclear Explosion Project, a top-secret program to design and develop nuclear explosives. The project slowed after Shastri died of a heart attack in January 1966. When Bhabha perished two weeks later in an airplane crash in the Swiss Alps, the bomb program came to a virtual standstill. If Bhabha had survived, he might have persuaded Prime Minister Indira Gandhi, Nehru's daughter and Shastri's successor, to authorize a nuclear explosive test well before 1974.

Phase 3: Delay and Hesitation

Homi Bhabha died just one day after Indira Gandhi became the prime minister of India. Under her leadership, three key developments transpired to shape Indian nuclear policy for many years to come. The first was her controversial decision in the late 1960s not to sign the newly negotiated nuclear nonproliferation treaty (NPT), which would have bound India to the legal status of a nonnuclear weapons state in perpetuity. The second was India's perception of a U.S. nuclear threat during the Indo-Pakistani war, which created Bangladesh as an independent country in 1971. And third, because of the cumulative impact of the first two developments, Indira Gandhi ordered the detonation of the India's first nuclear explosive test, which she called a peaceful nuclear experiment, in May 1974. Although diverse political, economic, and military factors affected all of these issues, Prime Minister Gandhi's NPT and PNE decisions were shaped heavily by the domestic political legitimacy that the nuclear program had acquired as a result of Bhabha's assiduous efforts a decade earlier.

India's PNE turned out to be a landmark event for the world as much as for India. It represented the first case of a country developing and detonating a nuclear explosive from an ostensibly peaceful nuclear effort. Stung by this experience, the world's leading nuclear suppliers, many of whom unwittingly had assisted the Indian program in one fashion or another, resolved not to make the same mistake again—in India or elsewhere. The explosion beneath the sands of Pokhran, therefore, fundamentally altered the manner in which the international community would henceforth handle the export, and even the indigenous development, of nuclear technology and materials. The present-day nuclear nonproliferation regime owes its present composition more to India's 1974 nuclear blast than to any other event or condition.

While not ruling out further experiments with nuclear explosives, Prime Minister Gandhi declared that a second Indian nuclear explosion would be held only "when the need for a peaceful experiment is established." Whether because of the lack of an acute security threat, continued international pressures, severe domestic resource constraints, or possibly the lack of a proponent of Bhabha's stature, no subsequent Indian leader established the "need" for a second nuclear detonation—until May 1998, when Prime Minister Atal Bihari Vajpayee ordered another series of nuclear tests and openly proclaimed India a nuclear weapons power.

From the mid-1970s until the late 1990s, India's leadership was unwilling to defy the United States and other powerful proponents of international nuclear nonproliferation by testing another nuclear device. But the Indian nuclear establishment was not idle. They continued Bhabha's two-track plan of setting up numerous power production reactors across the country while at the same time secretly assembling the components to manufacture, test, and ultimately deploy—if the need ever arose—several nuclear weapons. The nuclear bomb program actually was accelerated in the mid-1980s after India learned that its chief rival, Pakistan, had also acquired the means to make nuclear weapons. It was also during this period that India put significant resources behind two ballistic missile systems—the short-range Prithvi and the intermediate-range Agni—the latter of which would become India's primary nuclear delivery system.

Phase 4: Building an Operational Nuclear Deterrent

After India conducted five nuclear explosive tests in May 1998, Prime Minister Vajpayee declared that India would pursue a "minimum but credible" nuclear deterrent and would not use nuclear weapons first in a conflict. A government-appointed panel formulated the draft of a nuclear doctrine in August 1999, calling for India to ensure the effectiveness and survivability of its nuclear deterrent by developing a triad of air-, sea- and land-based nuclear forces, a robust command and control system, and the ability to shift rapidly from peacetime deployments to full operability. In January 2003 New Delhi formally reiterated its "credible minimum deterrent" doctrine and announced the creation of a National Command Authority, in which a political council, chaired by the prime minister, would be responsible for authorizing the use of nuclear weapons, and a Strategic Forces Command would manage India's nuclear weapons and delivery systems.

In keeping with India's long tradition of civil-military relations in which democratically elected civilians control the military, India's nuclear weapons program has always been under the firm control of the prime minister and his carefully selected confidants. Largely because of the system Nehru had established in the late 1940s and early 1950s, the prime minister continues to deal directly with scientists from the Atomic Energy Commission and the Defence Research and Development Organization, whereas the armed forces generally have been kept out of the nuclear decision-making and advisory loop. Despite the creation of the Strategic Forces Command and other organizational changes implemented since the 1998 Pokhran tests, the Indian government's reluctance to more fully integrate the military into the strategic planning process has slowed the development of an operationally usable nuclear deterrent capability, especially compared to the state of affairs across the border, where the armed forces control all elements of Pakistan's nuclear program and policy.

Leaders of India's longtime rival, Pakistan, believe that they might have to use nuclear weapons first in a conflict. If Islamabad were unable to deter a conventional attack, it might feel compelled to employ nuclear arms to prevent India from destroying Pakistan's armed forces or occupying large portions of its territory. Lieutenant General Khalid Kidwai, director of Pakistan's Strategic Plans Division, said in 2002: "Nuclear weapons are aimed solely at India. In case that deterrence fails, they will be used if India attacks Pakistan and conquers a large part of its territory; India destroys a large part either of its land or air forces; India proceeds to the economic strangling of Pakistan; or India pushes Pakistan into political destabilization or creates a large-scale internal subversion in Pakistan."

Today each rival is increasing its stockpile of nuclear weapon components and could assemble and deploy a few nuclear weapons within a few days to a week. Because neither has signed the 1968 Treaty on the Non-Proliferation of Nuclear Weapons, which limits ownership of nuclear explosives to the first five nuclear powers, Indian and Pakistani nuclear policies are not illegal. However, many countries viewed their nuclear tests as a challenge to the norm of nuclear nonproliferation, which underpins the NPT regime. Even today, the international community has not managed to integrate India and Pakistan into the NPT-based nuclear order.

The size, composition, and operational status of the Indian nuclear arsenal are closely guarded secrets. According to published sources, India produces approximately 55 to 88 pounds (25–44 kg) of weapon-grade plutonium each year. It probably has accumulated between 617 to 1,323 pounds (280–600 kg) of plutonium from the operation of its Cirus and Dhruva plutonium-production reactors. Based on these assessments, it could possess enough fissile material to manufacture between 40 and 120 weapons.

India has several aircraft and missiles that could deliver nuclear weapons to their targets. In 2001 the U.S. Defense Department speculated that India would most likely use fighter-bomber aircraft—Jaguar, Mirage-2000, MiG-27, or Su-30—for nuclear delivery because its ballistic missiles probably were not yet ready for this role and because its superior air force could be expected to penetrate Pakistani air defenses. India's Prithvi missile can carry a 2,200 pound (1,000-kg) warhead, but because of its short 93 mile (150-km) range, India most likely will turn to its newer solid-propellant Agni 1 and Agni 2 missiles. The Agni 1 has a 435–560 mile (700–900 km) range and was rushed into development after the 1999 Kargil conflict. The Agni 2 has a 1,243–1,864 mile (2,000–3,000 km) range but is not yet operational.

The nuclear deterrent capability that India now possesses owes much to the pioneering decisions and activities of Jawaharlal Nehru and Homi Bhabha some fifty years ago, when they set about developing a secret nuclear weapons option. Subsequent political and scientific leaders have perpetuated the nuclear policies and programs created by Nehru and Bhabha, albeit on many occasions with hesitation and restraint. Since 1998 India's political leadership has demonstrated much more boldness and resolve, but even today, because of lingering concerns about radically revamping long-standing civil-military relationships, India remains several steps away from fielding a truly operational nuclear deterrent. Therefore, in many important respects, India's original policy of creating a nuclear deterrent option remains in place today, even though the capabilities of the nuclear program are much more sophisticated and somewhat less secret.

Peter R. Lavoy

See also **China, Relations with; Nuclear Weapons Testing and Development; Pakistan and India; Strategic Thought; United States, Relations with; Wars, Modern.**

BIBLIOGRAPHY

Beaton, Leonard, and John Maddox. *The Spread of Nuclear Weapons.* New York: Praeger, 1962.

Gopal, Sarvepalli, ed. *Selected Works of Jawaharlal Nehru.* 1st and 2nd series. New Delhi: Orient Longman, 1982.

Lavoy, Peter R. "Fighting Terrorism, Avoiding War: The Indo-Pakistani Situation." *Joint Forces Quarterly* 32 (Autumn 2002): 27–34.

"Nuclear Safety, Nuclear Stability and Nuclear Strategy in Pakistan." *Concise Report of a Visit by Landau Network-Centro*

Volta (January 2002). Available at <http://lxmi.mi. infn.it/ ~landnet>

U.S. Department of Defense. *Proliferation: Threat and Response*. Washington, D.C.: Department of Defense, January 2001.

NUCLEAR WEAPONS TESTING AND DEVELOPMENT In 1945, when the first atomic bomb destroyed Hiroshima, Mahatma Gandhi predicted that "unless now the world adopts nonviolence, it will spell certain suicide for mankind." Following India's independence in 1947, the Tata Institute of Fundamental Research (TIFR) and Bhabha Atomic Research Centre (BARC) were founded by Homi Bhabha with encouragement from Prime Minister Jawaharlal Nehru, who also served as science minister. TIFR's function was solely to conduct pure research; BARC's explicit role was to harness nuclear energy to help provide for the electric power needs of a post-independence industrial India. India in the early days managed to acquire nuclear reactor technology from a number of Western countries, primarily Canada (CANDU reactors) and the United States (Tarapur). Gandhi's warnings against the use of nuclear energy for military ends may have helped to prevent the development of the Indian bomb well into the 1960s. It was only after the Bangladesh War of 1971 that India, under Indira Gandhi, was sufficiently emboldened by its military victory against Pakistan to test a nuclear device of its own. In 1971 Prime Minister Gandhi gave the order to go ahead with the test. It took two years to prepare for the test, which was reportedly beset with problems with electronic detonators. In 1974 India conducted its first test of a "peaceful nuclear device," the underground "Smiling Buddha" detonation (on the Buddha's birthday in May) in the Rajasthan desert at Pokharan. Estimates of the yield vary, but it is thought to have been around 12 kilotons of trinitrotoluene (TNT), somewhat smaller than the Nagasaki bomb of 20 kilotons.

China, on the other hand, had already made progress in the development of nuclear weapons. In a thirty-two-month period, China successfully exploded its first atomic bomb (16 October 1964), launched its first nuclear missile (25 October 1966), and detonated its first hydrogen bomb (14 June 1967).

On 11 May 1998 (again on the Buddha's birthday), India conducted three underground nuclear tests of a 12 kiloton conventional fission bomb (an improved version of its 1974 device), a 43 kiloton thermonuclear device, and a device smaller than a kiloton. Enriched plutonium is the suspected fuel, although for the small devices, enriched uranium may have been used. These tests were followed days later by two small devices at a different site. In both cases, the devices concerned were exploded simultaneously. P. K. Iyengar, former chairman of the Indian Atomic Energy Commission (IAEC) and a key player in the development of the 1974 device, said in an interview that the tests show that India has three categories of nuclear weapon design: a low-yield tactical weapon, a full-size fission weapon, and a thermonuclear weapon. He added that these three options should satisfy the military's interests.

Seismic test analysts have disputed India's claim of the strength of the devices, but a report in the journal *New Scientist* (Mackenzie, p. 2138) supports the Indian claim, citing a University of Leeds seismic expert, Roger Clark, whose calculations tend to buttress the Indian claims of the yield. Debate continued over the strengths of the Indian tests and the ability of seismic monitoring to verify the Comprehensive Test Ban Treaty (CTBT). India continues to maintain that it exploded a hydrogen bomb. R. Chidambaram, then IAEC chairman, has said that India can explode a 200 kiloton device if it chooses to do so. Some Western scientists have cast doubt on this claim, speculating that what was exploded was a fusion-boosted fission device, which is technologically less challenging.

India has developed missiles—the Prithvi, with a range of 155 miles (250 kilometers), and the Agni, with a range of 932 miles (1,500 kilometers)—that are capable of delivering nuclear weapons. These could already be mass-produced and are capable of reaching the Chinese cities of Beijing and Shanghai. India is thus capable of conducting retaliatory strikes against nations that threaten it with nuclear power, although the Indian government has foresworn any first use of nuclear weapons.

According to the publication *Jane's Defence Weekly* (May 1999), Indian scientists are reportedly developing a longer version of their intermediate range ballistic missile Agni III, which will have a range of 2,175 miles (3,500 kilometers). Together with its 1,243 miles (2,000-kilometer) range Agni II (designed to carry a nuclear warhead) and its Agni I (already test-fired three times), and its short range surface-to-surface missiles Prithvi I and II and surface-to-air Akash and Trishul missiles, the Agni III will give India its minimum nuclear deterrent (MND). India is also on the threshold of deploying a submarine-launched ballistic missile, Dhanush, which could later be deployed on surface warships.

One factor that impelled the Indian government toward nuclearization was the preferential treatment that successive U.S. governments gave to the Communist government of Beijing. Since U.S. president Richard M. Nixon's visit to China in 1972, U.S. governments largely ignored abuses of human rights in China, awarding the nation most favored nation status and a permanent seat in the United Nations Security Council. It is no coincidence that the permanent members of the United Nations Security Council are also the nations that constitute the "nuclear club," namely Great Britain, France, Russia, China, and the United States. U.S. overtures to China even include cooperative scientific ventures. The U.S position was that the only way to "wean" China away from its Communist political system was to teach it capitalist economics and to engage it constructively. The Indian defense minister at the time of the 1998 nuclear tests, George Fernandes, announced that it was China, not Pakistan, that was India's "main threat," perhaps thus signaling the imminent nuclear tests by seeking to clarify India's defense concerns.

The harsh U.S. reactions to the tests (sanctions, suspension of scientific collaborations, repatriation of Indian scientists visiting the United States, denial of visas to scientists wishing to visit the United States, and preventing U.S. scientists from attending conferences held in India) contrasted sharply with Washington's lack of reaction when China and France last conducted nuclear tests (1995), in violation of the CTBT, which neither have as yet signed.

An unfortunate and perhaps unforeseen effect of the tests by India and Pakistan is that the Kashmir issue, which was languishing on a bilateral backburner, suddenly found "legs" and was elevated to a high profile in the international list of "problems to be solved." This clearly was not beneficial to the Indian position and may be seen as an unfortunate outcome of India's nuclear tests.

On 13 May 1998 the U.S. government imposed sanctions on India, "in accordance with Section 102 of the Arms Export Control Act, also known as the Glenn amendment," involving "termination of assistance under the Foreign Assistance Act of 1961, except for humanitarian assistance for food or other agricultural commodities; termination of sales of defense articles, defense services, or design and construction services under the Arms Export Control Act . . . termination of all foreign military financing under the Arms Export Control Act" and "denial of any credit, credit guarantees, or other financial assistance by any department, agency or instrumentality of the United States Government."

On 28 May Pakistan conducted tests, and equal U.S. sanctions were applied to Pakistan. In July 1998, seven Indian scientists were expelled from the United States, and a "blacklist" of sixty-three Indian and five Pakistani institutions was announced. TIFR and BARC were on that list.

It was only with the visit of U.S. president Bill Clinton to India in 2000 that the U.S. government relented. India has joined the United States as a "strategic partner," though neither India nor the United States has signed the CTBT, though India has announced a voluntary moratorium on further testing.

Nuclear tensions in the subcontinent have eased somewhat since the peace overtures made between India and Pakistan at the South Asian Association for Regional Cooperation meeting in Islamabad in January 2004. Further easing of tensions may result with improved economic ties between the two nations and with India's reaffirmation of the Gandhian principle of nonviolence.

Rajendran Raja

See also **Ballistic and Cruise Missile Development; Ballistic Missile Defenses; Nuclear Programs and Policies**

BIBLIOGRAPHY

Mackenzie, Debora. "Making Waves." *New Scientist* (13 June 1998): 2138.

Perkovich, George. *India's Nuclear Bomb: The Impact on Global Proliferation*. Berkeley: University of California Press, 2001.

SarDesai, D. R. and Raju G. C. Thomas, eds. *Nuclear India in the Twenty-First Century*. New York: Palgrave-Macmillan, 2002.

NYĀYA *Nyāya* philosophy is also called *pramāna shāstra*, or the science of correct knowledge. The objective of the *Nyāya* is *ānvīkshikī*, or critical inquiry. Its beginnings go back to the Vedic period, but its first systematic elucidation is Akshapāda Gotama's *Nyāya Sūtra*, dated to the third century B.C. This text consists of five books. After an overview, the text begins with the nature of doubt and the means of proof. Next it considers the nature of self, body, senses and their objects, cognition and mind.

The *Nyāya* system supposes that we are so constituted as to seek truth. Our minds are not empty slates; the very constitution of the mind provides some knowledge of the nature of the world. The four *pramānas* through which correct knowledge is acquired are: *pratyaksha*, or direct perception; *anumāna*, or inference; *upamāna*, or analogy; and *shabda*, or verbal testimony.

Gotama mentions that four factors are involved in direct perception: the senses (*indriyas*), their objects (*artha*), the contact of the senses and the objects (*sannikarsha*), and the cognition produced by this contact (*jnāna*). *Manas*, or mind, mediates between the self and the senses. When the *manas* is in contact with one sensory organ, it cannot be so with another. It is therefore said to be atomic in dimension. It is because of the nature of the mind that our experiences are essentially linear, although quick succession of impressions may give the appearance of simultaneity.

Dharmakīrti, a later *Nyāya* philosopher, recognizes four kinds of perception: sense perception, mental perception, self-consciousness, and yogic perception. Self-consciousness is a perception of the self through its states of pleasure and pain. In yogic perception, one is able to comprehend the universe in fullness and harmony.

Anumāna (inference) is knowledge from the perceived about the unperceived. The element to be inferred may be the cause or the effect of the element perceived, or the two may be the joint effects of something else.

The *Nyāya* syllogism is expressed in five parts: (1) *pratijnā*, or the proposition: the house is on fire; (2) *hetu*, or the reason: smoke; (3) *udāharana*, the example: fire is accompanied by smoke, as in the kitchen; (4) *upanaya*, the application: as in the kitchen, so too in the house; (5) *nigamana*, the conclusion: therefore, the house is on fire. This recognizes that the inference derives from the knowledge of the universal relation (*vyāpti*) and its application to the specific case (*paksha-dharmatā*). There can be no inference unless there is expectation (*ākānkshā*) about the hypothesis, which is expressed in terms of the proposition.

The *Nyāya* attacks the Buddhist idea that no knowledge is certain by pointing out that this statement itself contradicts the claim by its certainty. Whether cognitions apply to reality must be checked by determining if they lead to successful action. *Pramā*, or valid knowledge, leads to successful action, unlike erroneous knowledge (*viparyāya*).

In the twelfth century, the *Navya-Nyāya* system was founded by Gangesha Upadhyaya. It developed a highly technical language to formulate and solve problems in logic and epistemology.

Subhash Kak

BIBLIOGRAPHY

Matilal, B. K. *Nyāya-Vaisesika*. Wiesbaden, Germany: Otto Harrassowitz, 1977.

Vidyābhusan, Satisa Chandra. *History of Indian Logic.* Kolkata: Calcutta University, 1921.

Vidyābhusana, Satisa Chandra.. *The Nyāya Sūtras of Gotama.* Revised and edited by Nandalal Sinha. Delhi: Motilal Banarsidass, 1990.

O

OM. *See* **Upanishadic Philosophy.**

ORISSA. *See* **Geography.**

OUTCASTES. *See* **Dalits.**

P

PAITHANI The oldest weaving technique for the creation of multicolored woven patterns was the tapestry technique, using noncontinuous weft threads. Known in India as Paithani, after the city of Paithan, the technique uses multicolored silk weft threads to create intricate patterns on a gold background. The overall effect is similar to that of *meenakari*, enameling on gold jewelry. This ancient weaving technique was used throughout the world, in the Coptic textiles of Egypt, in the pre-Columbian textiles of Latin America, and in China's intricate silk hangings (*ko'sseu*). Central Asia's nomadic weavers created *gelims* with this technique on simple mobile looms from ancient times. The technique was possibly brought to India by migrations from Central Asia in the ancient past. Examples can be seen in the cotton *gelims* of North India, as well as in the intricately woven Navalgund *jamkhans* of Karnataka in South India. It is possible that the technique was adapted for the weaving of intricate borders and cross borders of saris for royalty.

Paithani weaving was centered in the western region of Maharashtra, where women wore long 9-yard (8.2 m) saris. The technique was named after the ancient city of Paithan, the capital of the powerful Satavahanas (c. 300 B.C.–A.D. 230).

Stylistic Variations

Chanderi in Madhya Pradesh produced fine-quality cotton saris with borders woven in Paithani technique. Saris from the collections of royal houses reveal intricate Paithani borders and cross borders in silk and gold thread. They carry complex patterns of *shikar-gah* (hunting), as well as the tree of life, shrubs, and curvilinear flowering creepers, often woven separately and attached. The royal families who patronized these saris extended from Madhya Pradesh to Gujarat, Maharashtra, and Andhra Pradesh. Men wore the *patka*, a Paithani sash tied at the waist, and the ends of their turbans were adorned with gold and silk Paithani borders.

The Paithani saris were woven in heavy silk with borders carrying extra warp patterns; only the cross border was worked in gold using the Paithani technique of multiple weft silks, in interlocking tapestry. The design of the cross border had a rich gold surface, enclosed by borders woven in the tapestry technique; sometimes the central section had extra weft silk patterns of mango or shrub motifs.

Paithani textiles were later patronized by the Golconda court and by the ruling house of Hyderabad. These used a heavier silk and were renowned for the excellent quality of their *kalabatun*, or gold thread. Old examples of Paithani saris and *patkas* have gold threads that still shine like a mirror.

Other centers where Paithani technique was used were Yeola in Maharashtra and Gadwal in Andhra Pradesh. Yeola saris were woven in silk, but they were not as complex in their patterning as those of Hyderabad. The Gadwal saris were woven in cotton, often with intricate check patterns, with a silk border having extra warp gold thread patterns; the cross borders were in some cases woven in the Paithani technique.

Technique

The technique of weaving was simple, but the process painstaking, laborious, and complex. The main loom was a pit loom; the weave was a plain weave and was warp faced, so that the multiple weft threads would be dominant on the face of the fabric. When the borders were woven separately, the loom had no heddles. The multiple threads were wound on fine bamboo needles, which were

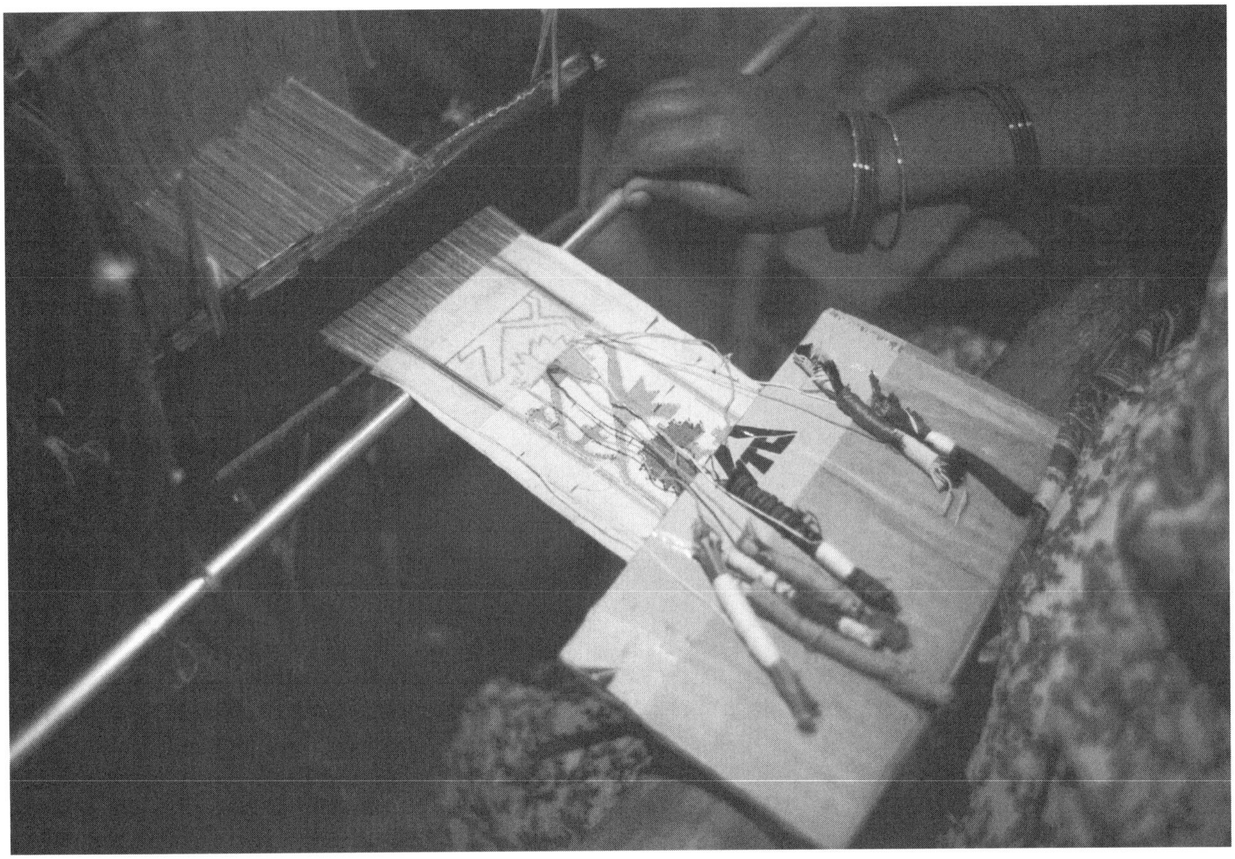

Weaver Works a Paithani Loom in Hyderabad. This ancient process is painstaking, laborious, and complex, requiring great skill. DAVID H. WELLS / CORBIS.

inserted by hand and interlocked with the next thread, and the thread was then reversed. Hundreds of bobbins rested on the woven section, and the weavers created the pattern by following a graph design on paper. This process required great skill, and only seasoned masters could weave these patterns.

The colonial influences in the late nineteenth and early twentieth centuries changed the demands of the royal houses. Women of the royal households began to wear imported chiffon and georgette saris, lowering demand for the heavy cotton and silk 9-yard saris. Most centers weaving in the Paithani technique discontinued the practice. The only place where it survived was in Paithan. The Nizam of Hyderabad patronized the technique himself, setting up a center for weaving saris, veils, turbans, and sashes at Paithan. It was also mandatory for his courtiers to wear Paithani turbans when presenting themselves at court. Paithani weavers also copied floral patterns painted inside the Buddhist caves at Ajanta. The curvilinear motifs of lotus flower and bird were well suited to the Paithani technique and were woven into borders, which were stitched to georgette saris, creating a new fashion. European visitors to the Ajanta caves also were happy to buy the intricately woven panels as souvenirs.

In the early 1950s, when Kamaladevi Chattopadhya initiated India's movement for the revival of traditional handicraft skills, she visited Paithan with the author. The old craftsmen, who were weaving panels, were encouraged to weave saris in silk with traditional patterns. An exhibition was arranged to promote the saris, and it was probably then that the term *Paithani* came to be applied to the technique. Later traditional examples of Hyderabad and Gadwal saris were also revived through a government center at Wanaparti, in Andhra Pradesh, and elaborate saris with rich tapestry cross borders were once again brought back into the market. The government of Maharashtra began a program for reviving the Yeola tradition at the encouragement of Shilpi Kendra, a non-government organization in Mumbai. By 1970 Yeola saris with Paithani cross borders had returned to the market.

Chanderi, where the finest examples were once woven, could not revive the Paithani technique, as none of its surviving weavers knew the technique. A private center, near Hyderabad, run by Suraiya Hasan Bose, brought two of the best workers from Paithan and reproduced some of the Chanderi border designs, weaving cotton saris with traditional tapestry borders and cross borders. They also trained young women from the village in the Paithani weave, which had earlier been the domain of men. Meera Mehta, a former student of the National Institute of Design in Ahmedabad, began work on improving the Yeola saris, and thanks to her intervention, weavers there are producing extremely refined Paithanis.

Jasleen Dhamija

BIBLIOGRAPHY

Chattopadhya, Kamaladevi. *Handicrafts of India*. New Delhi: Indian Council for Cultural Relations, 1975.

Dhamija, Jasleen. *Indian Folk Arts and Crafts*. New Delhi: National Book Trust, 1970.

———. "Paithani Weaves: An Ancient Tapestry Art." In *The Woven Silks of India*, edited by Jasleen Dhamija. Mumbai: Marg Publications, 1995.

Morwanchikar, R. S. *Paithani: A Romance in Brocade*. Delhi: Bharatiya, 1993.

PAKISTAN Pakistan came into existence as a homeland for Muslims on 14 August 1947, carved out of Muslim majority regions of British India. Partition accompanied the British grant of independence and the transfer of power to leaders of the Indian and Pakistani national movements, respectively. Approximately 14 million people moved from both sides of the border, Muslims to Pakistan, and Hindus and Sikhs to India, in an exchange that left at least a half million people dead in communal violence.

Pakistan owes its existence above all to the leadership and vision of Mohammad Ali Jinnah, who headed the Pakistan national movement and was known to his followers as Quaid-i-Azam (Great Leader). As Pakistan's first head of state, he inherited a county beset with problems of identity and limited resources. Jinnah's death, only thirteen months after independence, followed by the assassination of his successor Liaquat Ali Khan three years later, left the country without clear direction on unresolved constitutional issues, including the balance of state and religion.

Pakistan is bounded on the west by Iran, to the north by Afghanistan, to the northeast by China, to the east and southeast by India, and to the south by the Arabian Sea. It has an area (excluding the Pakistani-held part of Jammu and Kashmir) of 307,374 square miles (796,095 sq. km). Pakistan's population in 2003 was nearly 150 million, and its growth rate was officially estimated at 2.5 percent per annum.

The country is comprised of four provinces, each with a distinctive language: Punjab, the most populated and agriculturally rich; Sind, which has important tracts of irrigated farmland but also large barren areas, and which contains several major urban centers, led by Karachi, the country's largest city and original capital; Balochistan, primarily desert and sparsely populated by Balochi tribes; and the North-West Frontier province (NWFP), which has large mountainous areas, is mainly Pashto speaking, and shares several Pashtun tribes with eastern Afghanistan. A Pashtun-inhabited Federally Administered Tribal Area, which hugs the border with Afghanistan, is outside any province and is vested with considerable political autonomy. Islamabad, the country's capital since 1960, is located in a designated federal area in northern Punjab.

Until 1971 Pakistan had an East and West Wing, separated by about 1,000 miles (1,609 km) of Indian territory. Dominance of the political system by West Pakistani elites resulted in economic exploitation and disparities favoring West over East, generating Bengali resentment and separatism. Bengalis, the country's ethnic majority, believed they were intentionally underrepresented in the government and the military. In a civil war that succeeded with Indian military intervention, the East Wing broke away to form Bangladesh.

Muslims constitute 97 percent of Pakistan's population, mostly divided between Sunnis, who make up 77 percent of Muslims, and nearly 20 percent who are Shiʿa. Hindus, Buddhists, and Christians comprise the remaining 3 percent. The country's principal ethno-linguistic groups are Punjabis, Sindis, Pathans (or Pashtuns), Baluchis, and a significant, largely urban population of Muhajirs, Urdu-speaking refugees (who migrated to Pakistan from India following independence) and their descendants. Pakistan's official language is Urdu, but the dominant spoken language is Punjabi, the first language of 65 percent of the population, followed by Sindi (11 percent), Pashto (8 percent), and Urdu (9 percent). English is widely used in educational institutions, business circles, and in the government.

The task of national integration has been made difficult by deep fault lines that have formed over the contending aspirations and grievances of the country's provincially concentrated ethno-linguistic groups, the vesting of political power, and the appropriate role of Islam in public life. Social class disparities, economic instability and deprivation, and tribal and linguistic populations that overlap with India and Afghanistan have aggravated these differences. Divisions among Pakistanis have occasioned bitter ideological debates and have subjected the country to periodic political instability. Serious implications exist, moreover, for Pakistan's economic development and foreign policies.

There is contention among and within Pakistan's provinces, and between provinces and the federal government, over how the resources of the state should be equitably allocated. Most resentment today is directed against the politically ascendant Punjab. The NWFP, Sind, and Baluchistan all have had nationalist movements seeking greater political autonomy and larger representation in the country's civil bureaucracy, military, and key sectors of the economy. Sindis accuse Punjab of an unfair distribution of Indus River waters through major canal and dam diversions. Muhajirs concentrated in Karachi bitterly object to their lack of political influence in Sind province and complain about a system of federally legislated quotas for government jobs and college entrance. Rural Sindis, along with Pathans who have settled in the province's major cities, are discontented with past Muhajir and new Punjabi domination of commercial and industrial activities in Karachi and other urban centers.

An insurrection in Baluchistan against the federal government was put down militarily under the government of Zulfikar Ali Bhutto in the 1970s, but grievances continue to simmer. Pashtun nationalism in the NWFP has been periodically at odds with the central government on foreign policy issues, and with the province's religious parties over the implementation of Islamic social and economic principles.

Pakistan has also been unable to settle on the kind of political system that promotes effective governance, needed social and economic development, and national identity to counter regional and ethnic diversity. It remains uncertain whether the country requires a more authoritarian, centralized state, primarily run by the military and bureaucracy, or is better served by greater federalism and democratic institutions. Nor has Pakistan been able to resolve whether it should be simply a homeland for the subcontinent's Muslims or instead seek to realize the ideals of an Islamic state, with laws and practices that adhere to strict Islamic precepts.

At the time of independence, Pakistan was an agrarian society with very little industrial capacity. A small number of powerful landowners with large land holdings dominated the country politically and economically. Much of the country continues to have a land tenure system that is feudal, in which tenant farmers cultivate land owned by usually absentee landlords. Agriculture remains the nation's major source of income, employing almost half of the country's population, and accounting for roughly 25 percent of its gross national product. Wheat, cotton, rice, barley, sugarcane, maize, and fodder are the main crops.

The industrial sector has played an increasingly critical role in the country's economic development. Pakistan now has in place a broad industrial base, producing a wide range of consumer and industrial products in such key industries as textiles, construction materials, sugar, food processing, paper products, and rubber. However, the industrial sector, which employs over 20 percent of the formal workforce, has failed to create jobs for an increasingly younger population. Neither has it succeeded in training and retaining a highly educated workforce. Importantly, political instability, corruption, and the threat of conflict with India have affected Pakistan's ability to attract domestic and foreign investment.

While domestic economic growth rates have averaged about 5 percent, economic disparities have increased, in both rural and urban areas. The poorest 20 percent of the people, or those with the lowest income, have a share of 6.2 percent of the income of the nation, while the richest 20 percent have an estimated 50 percent share. There is only a minimal safety net for the poor. The proportion of Pakistanis living below the poverty line is estimated to have risen in recent years, from about 26 percent in 1990–1991, to nearly 40 percent in 2003. In a global measure of health, education, and income, Pakistan's human development has been slipping year after year; by 2003 it stood behind that of many African countries. The country's literacy rate is only 36 percent.

Pakistan's leaders have relied heavily on foreign aid, remittances from workers in the oil-producing states, and international credit. Over the years, the United States has been the major provider of bilateral aid and was particularly generous during the 1980s, when Pakistan was a frontline state against Soviet forces in Afghanistan. U.S. economic and military aid was cut off in 1990, the year following the Soviet withdrawal, with Washington's decision to no longer ignore Pakistan's nuclear weapons program. Economic and military support for Pakistan was resumed in 2002, as Pakistan won U.S. favor for its willingness to cooperate in the "war on terrorism," specifically U.S. operations in Afghanistan. The country has also been able to reattract greatly increased financial assistance from the international creditor community. However, despite rescheduling and some debt write-offs, Pakistan remains burdened in servicing its heavy external debt.

Pakistan confronted numerous social, political, and security problems as a consequence of the Afghan war to oust the Soviets and their Communist allies, and the subsequent civil strife in Afghanistan during the 1990s. Hosting millions of Afghan refugees and giving sanctuary to fighters turned urban areas in Pakistan into thriving markets for small arms and illicit drugs. The growth of Islamic religious schools through the 1980s and 1990s spawned volunteers for the conflicts in Afghanistan and Kashmir and also contributed to making the country's interethnic and sectarian politics more violent and intolerant.

Pakistanis have lived under military rule for more than half their history. The failure of Pakistan's elected politicians

Islamabad Market, Pakistan. Merchants sell their wares on a busy Islamabad street. In Pakistan, the number of Islamic fundamentalists continues to grow. INDIA TODAY.

to provide stable, honest, and effective government has repeatedly been used to justify the military's intervention to remove civilian leadership. Differences among political figures over regional and ethnic distribution of power delayed approval of a constitution until 1956. By October 1958 the army had suspended a collapsing parliamentary system. A year later, army chief General Mohammad Ayub Khan assumed full control of the military government. He introduced an indirect election system known as "Basic Democracies" that also provided the framework for local government and development. In 1962 a new constitution created a strong presidency, to which Ayub was elected in 1965. Ayub aligned Pakistan with the United States in military and economic agreements, and also reached out to China. Ayub was weakened politically, however, by Pakistan's failure to make gains against India in the 1965 war over Kashmir. Popular dissatisfaction with corruption and inflation, together with Ayub's ill health, led to his removal in 1969 by General Yahya Khan.

Following the disastrous war with India that resulted in the loss of the East Wing in December 1971, Zulfikar Ali Bhutto assumed the presidency. Bhutto's populist Pakistan People's Party had run strongest in the West Wing in Pakistan's 1970 election, the first under universal suffrage. With the passage of a new constitution in 1973, Bhutto assumed the office of prime minister. He proceeded to forge closer relations with the Arab and nonaligned world than had his predecessors, and he undertook a controversial program of nationalization. Popular agitation in the wake of a discredited national election in March 1977 led General Mohammad Zia ul-Haq to depose Bhutto in July and, two years later, to have him executed.

General Zia's rule was defined most by his cooperation with the United States in supporting the insurgency against the Soviet occupation of Afghanistan, which began in December 1979. He is also remembered for fostering the Islamization of Pakistan's politics. In 1985 he ended his martial law regime, allowing for the election of a nonparty government, over which he nevertheless remained in command as president. Zia was killed in a still mysterious explosion of his plane in September 1988, ushering in the restoration that November of democratic government with the election of Benazir Bhutto, daughter of the executed leader, as prime minister.

Over the course of the next eleven years, Bhutto's People's Party and the Muslim League headed by Nawaz Sharif, both essentially secular parties, alternated in power. During this time, no elected government completed its term of office. On three separate occasions, the prime ministers—Bhutto in 1990 and 1996, and Sharif in 1993—were dismissed on the grounds of corruption and incompetence by the country's presidents, acting on behalf of the military. In a direct civilian-military clash, General Pervez Musharraf ousted Nawaz Sharif in an October 1999 coup. Musharraf assumed the office of chief executive and then president. Civilian government was ostensibly restored with the election of a National Assembly in October 2002. But whether formally in charge or not, the military has remained the final arbiter of Pakistan's politics.

Internal disorder and continuing concerns for Pakistan's security have helped to institutionalize the military's pivotal political role and assure its popular esteem. The large, highly professional standing army makes strong claims on the national budget and is heavily invested in key industries through wealthy and privileged foundations. An amply rewarded officer corps ensures internal cohesion and loyalty. For both foreign ventures and domestic security, the military employs a pervasive and powerful intelligence service, the Inter-Services Intelligence Division.

Pakistan's dispute with India over Kashmir remains a national obsession and largely shapes its defense policies and domestic priorities. Successive Pakistani governments have sought, both through diplomacy and assistance to militants, to undo the 1947 accession of the most prized half of the once princely state of Jammu and Kashmir to India. India has accused Pakistan of fostering infiltration and terrorism, while Pakistan has justified its resistance by citing the human and political rights violations suffered by the Indian state's Muslim majority. At a conventional military disadvantage, Pakistan considers nuclear weapons its most effective deterrent against a large-scale Indian attack. Concerns about nuclear proliferation from Pakistan and over the possible escalation of a conflict with India to a nuclear confrontation have heightened international attention to the region.

Marvin G. Weinbaum

See also **Afghanistan; Jinnah, Mohammad Ali; Kashmir; Pakistan and India**

BIBLIOGRAPHY

Blood, Peter R., ed. *Pakistan: A Country Study*. Washington, D.C.: Library of Congress, 1994. A valuable reference guide.

Jalal, Aysha. *The State of Martial Rule*. Lahore: Vanguard, 1991. A deeply analytic, perceptive study of military rule.

Jones, Owen Bennett. *Pakistan: Eye of the Storm*. New Haven, Conn.: Yale University Press, 2002. A highly readable, broad examination of events, institutions, and personalities.

Kux, Dennis. *The United States and Pakistan, 1947–2000*. Washington, D.C.: Woodrow Wilson Center Press, 2001. The definitive study of U.S.–Pakistan relations.

Stephens, Ian. *Pakistan*. New York: Fredrick A. Praeger, 1967. One of the best descriptions available of Pakistan's first two political decades.

Wirsing, Robert G. *India, Pakistan, and the Kashmir Dispute*. Kolkata: Rupa, 1995. An objective, informative examination of the unresolved dispute.

Wolpert, Stanley. *Jinnah of Pakistan*. New York: Oxford University Press, 1984. An insightful, comprehensive study of Pakistan's founding father.

Ziring, Lawrence. *Pakistan: At the Crosscurrent of History*. Oxford: Oneworld Publications, 2003. An excellent survey of Pakistan's troubled history from a veteran observer of Pakistani politics.

PAKISTAN AND INDIA After decades of unfulfilled promise, India now seems to be moving ahead, with more rapid economic growth, a more assertive foreign policy, better relations with the United States and China, and a modest nuclear arsenal. Adding these developments to India's traditional strengths—a unique and persistent democracy and an ancient, influential culture—it is no wonder that many predict the emergence of India as a major Asian power, or even a world-class state. However, this remains problematic as long as India's comprehensive and debilitating rivalry with Pakistan continues. If India cannot "solve" or better manage its relationship with Pakistan, which has become increasingly dangerous in recent years, then its wider strategic role is likely to remain circumscribed.

The origins of the India-Pakistan conflict have been traced to many sources: the cupidity of the British in their failed management of the partition; the cold war; the deeply rooted antagonisms between the subcontinent's major religious communities, Hindus and Muslims; the struggle for control over Kashmir; that province's importance to the national identities of both states; and the greed or personal shortsightedness of leaders on both sides of the border. These and other factors all play a role, but the conflict is greater than the sum of its parts.

Like many seemingly intractable disputes, the India-Pakistan conflict is a psychological, paired-minority conflict. Such conflicts are rooted in perceptions held by important groups on both sides—even those that are not a numerical minority and may even be a majority—that they are the threatened, weaker party, under attack from the other side. Paired-minority conflicts are most often found within states, but some occur at the state level, such as that between Israel and some of its Arab neighbors. These extremely persistent conflicts seem to draw their energy from an inexhaustible supply of distrust, and are remarkably resistant to compromise or the good offices of third parties.

Indian Insecurity

In the case of India-Pakistan relations, one of the puzzles is not why the smaller Pakistan feels encircled and threatened, but why the larger India does. It would seem that India, seven times more populous than Pakistan and five times larger, would be more secure, especially since it defeated Pakistan in 1971. This, however, is not the case, and historical, strategic, ideological, and domestic reasons all play a role in India's obsession with Pakistan, and in Pakistan's concern with India.

Generations and chosen grievances. The first generation of leaders in both states was devoted to achieving independence and building new states and nations. With the exception of Mahatma Gandhi, they did not believe that partition would lead to conflict between India and Pakistan. On the Indian side, some expected Pakistan to collapse, but did not see the need to hasten that collapse through war. On the Pakistani side, Mohammad Ali Jinnah hoped that the two countries would have good relations; he expected a multireligious Pakistan to be counterpoised against a predominantly Hindu India, with both possessing significant minorities whose presence would serve as hostage to good relations.

India's Prime Minister I. K. Gujral Meets Nawaz Sharif, Prime Minister of Pakistan. In September 1997, concurrent with the 52nd session of the United Nations General Assembly in NYC, Gujral (left) meets Sharif. The two premiers failed to break the impasse over stalled talks on Kashmir. PRESS INFORMATION BUREAU / FOTOMEDIA.

A second generation of Indian and Pakistani leaders was unprepared to solve the problems created by partition. Nothing in their experience had led them to place reconciliation ahead of their own political advantage. They reached a number of agreements that cleaned up the debris of partition, and there were trade and transit treaties, hot lines, and other confidence-building measures as early as the 1950s. India and Pakistan seemed to be headed toward an uneasy accommodation.

For India, what set the second generation apart from its predecessors was the defeat by China in 1962; for Pakistan, it was the division of their country by India in 1971. The ten-year difference is important: Indians have had longer to reconsider their great humiliation than the Pakistanis, and even the prospect of economic competition with China was met with equanimity by an economically resurgent India. In each case, the other side denies the seriousness of the other's grievances, and doubts the sincerity of the other's claim. In 1962 Mohammad Ayub Khan stated his skepticism that there was a real India-China conflict, and Pakistanis still belittle Indian obsessions with Beijing. Indians seemed to assume that Pakistanis have more or less forgotten the events of 1971 and cannot understand why Pakistani officials remain suspicious when New Delhi professes its good intentions. These two conflicts had profound domestic consequences, not a small matter in a democracy. No Indian politicians have admitted publicly that the Indian case against China is flawed or have suggested that there should be a territorial exchange. Until recently, no Pakistani could publicly talk about a settlement of Kashmir short of a plebiscite and accession, lest he or she be attacked as pro-Indian and anti-Islamic.

Each trauma led directly to the consideration of nuclear weapons and further militarization. In India's case, the lesson of 1962 was that only military power counts and that Jawaharlal Nehru's faith in diplomacy without the backing of firepower was disastrously naive. The link between the shock of 1971 and the nuclear option is even tighter in Pakistan, and for Zulfikar Ali Bhutto a nuclear weapon had the added attraction of enabling him to reduce the power of the army. Ironically, Pakistan has wound up with both a nuclear program and a politically powerful army.

Hindus Migrate during Riots. Hindus flee to safety during the riots preceding the 1947 partition of India. Thousands upon thousands were driven to make such a journey. PRESS INFORMATION BUREAU / FOTOMEDIA.

Traditions: New and invented. While many Hindu and Islamic traditions suggest ways of reducing differences and ameliorating conflict, each also has elements that contribute to the idea of what historian Elias Canetti terms a "war-crowd." Indians and Pakistanis draw selectively from their own traditions, pointing to those on the other side that seem to "prove" the other intends to conquer and dominate. For example, Pakistanis cite the *Artha Shāstra* as "proof" that the Indian/Hindu approach to statecraft emphasizes subversion, espionage, and deceit. For their part, Indian strategists, especially at the Hindu nationalist end of the spectrum, emphasize those aspects of Islamic teachings that portray a world divided between believers and unbelievers, and suggest the former are obliged to convert the latter. Additionally, while Pakistani ideologues see the spread of Islam to South Asia as having purged and reformed the unbelievers, Indians read this history as reinforcing the notion of a comprehensive civilizational and cultural threat to India.

Indians also see Pakistan as an important example of neo-imperialism, meaning that when neighbors (that is, Pakistan) are allied to powerful intruders (such as Britain, the United States, or China), their domestic politics and their foreign policies become distorted. The U.S.–Pakistan alliance is widely believed to have militarized Pakistani politics and foreign policy, making it impossible for Delhi to come to an accommodation with Islamabad over Kashmir. Most Indians also believe that Pakistan compounded the error by allowing its territory to be used for the objectives of the cold war alliance, introducing a superpower into the region. The American tie is also seen as encouraging Pakistan to challenge the rightfully dominant regional power by providing the advanced weapons that enabled Pakistan to attack India in 1965. The preferred Indian solution to such a distortion of the natural regional power structure is for the international community to recognize regional dominant powers that are benign, accommodating, and liberal, rather than allowing either a global hegemon or adjacent powers to meddle in South Asia.

Pakistan is seen as an essential element in a shifting alliance against New Delhi composed of the West, Islam, China, and other hostile states. Another focus of attention in recent years has been the extremist Islamic forces led by Pakistan, with China as a silent partner. Like the political scientist Samuel P. Huntington, many in the strategic community see a grand alliance between Islamic and "Confucian" civilization. The ring of states around India provides a ready-made image of encirclement. India has threats from the north, east, west, and over the horizon; naval theoreticians eagerly point out the threat from the sea, from whence both the Arabs and the Europeans came, and—thirty years ago—the USS *Enterprise.*

The threat from Pakistan, Islam, China, and the West is attributed to jealousy of India: outsiders wanting to cut it down to size. India's sense of weakness, of vulnerability, is contrasted with its "proper" status as a great power, stemming from its unique civilization and history. It is India's very diversity, long regarded as a virtue, that offers a tempting target for Pakistan, the Islamic world, and others. In the views of some of India's Hindu hawks, even the minorities (tribals, Sikhs, Christians, and Muslims) are a potential fifth column, awaiting foreign exploitation.

Pakistan as an incomplete state. The very nature of the Pakistani state is said to pose a threat to India. According to a 1982–1983 survey of India's security problems, the "Pakistan factor" looms large for reasons related to Pakistan's many shortcomings. These include Pakistan's limited cultural and civilizational inheritance, its military dictatorship, theocratic identity, unworkable unitary system of government (as opposed to India's flexible federalism), the imposition of Urdu on an unwilling population, the alienation of Pakistan's rulers from their people, Islamabad's support of "reactionary" regimes in West Asia (India identified its interests with the "progressive" segments of Arab nationalism, such as Saddam Hussein's Iraq), its dependency on foreign aid, and the failure to develop a strong economic base. This perspective has enjoyed a renaissance in the twelve years since Pakistan began to openly support the separatist and terrorist movements that emerged in Indian-administered Kashmir.

Pakistan is considered a threat also because it still claims that partition was imperfectly carried out; it harbors some revanchist notions toward India's Muslim population; and it falsely accuses India of wanting to undo Pakistan. Thus Pakistan still wishes to claim Kashmir, and even to upset the integrity and unity of India itself. More recently, Pakistan has served as the base for Islamic "jihadists" who seek not only the liberation of Kashmir, but also the liberation of all of India's Muslims.

The Pakistani Perspective

Pakistani leaders see themselves as even more threatened than their Indian counterparts but still more able to withstand the challenge than the larger, more powerful India. Its leaders have a profound distrust of New Delhi, and the latter's reassurances that India "accepts" the existence of Pakistan are not taken seriously. The dominant explanation of regional conflict held by Pakistan's strategic community is that, from the first day of independence, there has been a concerted Indian attempt to crush their state. This original trauma was refreshed and deepened by the loss of East Pakistan in 1971. Many Pakistanis now see their state as threatened by an increasingly Hindu, extremist India, motivated by a desire for religious revenge and a missionary-like zeal to extend its influence to the furthest reaches of South Asia. There is also a strand of Pakistani thinking that draws on the army's tradition of geopolitics, rather than the two-nation theory, to explain the conflict between India and Pakistan.

Like Israel, Pakistan was founded by a people who felt persecuted when living as a minority; even though they possess their own states (based on religious identity), both remain under threat from powerful enemies. In both cases, an original partition demonstrated the hostility of neighbors, and subsequent wars showed that these neighbors remained hostile. Pakistan and Israel have also followed parallel strategic policies. Both sought an entangling alliance with various outside powers (at various times, Britain, France, China, and the United States). Both ultimately concluded that outsiders could not be trusted in a moment of extreme crisis, which led them to develop nuclear weapons.

Further complicating India-Pakistan relations is the 1971 defeat, a great blow to the Pakistan army, which has governed Pakistan for more than half of its existence. Thus to achieve a normal relationship with Pakistan, India must not only influence Pakistan's public opinion; it must also change the institutionalized distrust of India found in the army. The chances of this happening are slim.

Another source of Pakistani hostility is the Indian claim that Pakistan needs the Indian threat to maintain its own unity. This argument has an element of truth: distrust of India and the Kashmir conflict do serve as a national rallying cry for Pakistanis, and thus as a device for smoothing over differences between Pakistan's dominant province, Punjab, and the smaller provinces of Baluchistan, Sind, and the North-West Frontier. "India as enemy" is also useful to distract the Pakistani public from other concerns, such as social inequality, sectarian (Sunni-Shiʿa) conflict, and the distinct absence of social progress in many sectors of Pakistani society.

Strategies in a Paired-Minority Conflict

States or groups that see themselves as threatened minorities have at least eight coping strategies. In the abstract, these include: fleeing the relationship, either physically or psychologically; demonizing the opponent; assimilation; accommodation; changing the behavior or perception of the enemy state; using outsiders to redress the balance of power; and finally, changing the balance of power by war or other means (such as increasing one's economy or population faster than the other side). Over the past fifty years, India and Pakistan, not to mention third parties, have contemplated each of these strategies.

Flight. India and Pakistan have tried to flee their relationship several times. The first instance was literally a physical escape; the others constitute symbolic, psychological, and strategic flight. Even though its founders had no interest in creating a theocratic state, Pakistan was created as a "homeland" for Indian Muslims, and most of its subsequent leaders left India to establish the new state of Pakistan. The key West Pakistani leaders were from Uttar Pradesh, Delhi, and Bombay; the key East Pakistani leaders were Bengali Muslims. Intermittently, India has pursued a policy of psychologically escaping the relationship with Pakistan by the "look East" policy, or by ignoring Pakistan, simply refusing to engage in serious negotiations with it.

Demonization. Demonization is another way of escaping a relationship. If the leaders of the other country are evil, misguided, or corrupt, then dialogue with them is immoral and dangerous. For many Indians, Mohammad Ali Jinnah, the founder of Pakistan, has long personified the misguided, evil leader who challenged India's civilizational unity with his two-nation theory, began the militarization of Pakistan by seeking arms from the West, and in a cold, undemocratic, and jealous spirit whipped up hatred and fear of India. His successors, largely military officers, are thought to lack even Jinnah's leadership qualities and the moral authority to place their country on a solid footing.

Pakistan's image of the Indian leadership is no less hostile. An important component of Pakistan's founding ideology was that Muslims could not trust the "crafty" Hindus, who still suffered from an inferiority complex. While Gandhi and Jinnah were once respected rivals, their successors in both states lacked even professional respect for each other.

Assimilation. Although many on both sides would like to flee the relationship, some Indians hope that Pakistan will someday rejoin India. Indeed, most of India's past leaders assumed that the Pakistan experiment would fail and that the state would come back to the fold. However, Pakistan's leaders have never contemplated assimilation. Indians no longer talk of reintegrating Pakistan into India, but there are widespread (if generally private) discussions about how India might establish friendly relations with successor states to present-day Pakistan. Like Bangladesh today, these states might not like or love India, but they may fear and respect Indian power and would not dream of challenging New Delhi as Pakistan has.

Accommodation. If Pakistan did not rejoin India, many Indians expected it to accommodate Indian power. However, Pakistani strategists view the accommodation of Nepal, Sri Lanka, Bhutan, and even Bangladesh as precisely the wrong model for Islamabad. These states have lost their freedom of action, they have been penetrated by Indian culture, and New Delhi has undue influence on their domestic politics, even intervening by force where necessary. For example, India absorbed Sikkim, intervened in Sri Lanka, and has a military presence in Bhutan. Because Pakistan is larger and more powerful than any of these states, many of its strategists contend, it does not need to accommodate India. This resistance to accommodation or compromise with India is especially powerful in the armed forces. Pakistan, its officers argue, may be smaller, but it is not weaker. United by religion and a martial spirit, it need not lower its demands of India, especially regarding Kashmir.

Altering perceptions. From time to time, there have been attempts to change perceptions of Indians and Pakistanis to promote better understanding between the two. Several nonregional states and organizations have tried to promote India-Pakistan cooperation or dialogue. In the 1950s and 1960s, the United States wanted to broker a détente between the two states so that they might join in a common alliance against threats from the Soviet Union and China. Considerable diplomatic energy was expended on these efforts, but the only result was to provide each with enhanced diplomatic leverage against the other.

Within South Asia the regional organization, the South Asian Association for Regional Cooperation (SAARC), has provided a venue for meetings between Indian and Pakistani leaders and sponsors some cooperative projects on regional issues. However, SAARC cannot deal with bilateral issues, and the smaller members are vulnerable to Indian pressure concerning the focus of SAARC initiatives. India has twice been able to force a postponement of its annual meetings when it was displeased with developments in Pakistan.

Most of the India-Pakistan dialogues, intended to promote understanding, wind up rehearsing old arguments, often for the sake of the non–South Asian participants present. History is used—and abused—to emphasize the legitimacy of one's own side and the misguided policies of the other. For years, meetings between Indians and Pakistanis rarely lasted long enough to systematically discuss

India's Prime Minister A. B. Vajpayee (left) with Pakistan President Pervez Musharraf. At Musharraf's presidential palace, the two men met (for an hour) on 5 January 2004, before an upcoming SAARC summit, declaring their wish for normalized relations between both countries. INDIA TODAY.

the differences between the two sides and how those differences might be ameliorated or accommodated.

Proposals that emerge from the two countries were often not serious, their purpose usually being to convince outside powers of Indian (or Pakistani) sincerity. Much the same can be said of recent proposals for the institution of confidence-building measures (hot lines, summits, dialogues, and various technical verification proposals) between the two countries. Since the 1990s, there have also been at least one hundred programs to bring together students, journalists, politicians, strategists, artists, intellectuals, and retired generals from both countries. Much of the goodwill created by such efforts, however, was washed away by the 1999 Kargil conflict, an Indian Airlines hijacking, the attack on the Indian Parliament in 2001, and an extended military crisis that lasted well into 2002. A new round of dialogues, begun in late 2003, shows promise but has yet to yield concrete results.

The Indian and Pakistani governments have also tried to influence deeper perceptions across the border. Several Indian governments—including those of Morarji Desai, Inder Kumar Gujral, and Atal Bihari Vajpayee—have undertaken major initiatives in an attempt to win over Pakistani opinion. Most efforts seem to have failed dramatically, with the Lahore meeting between Vajpayee and Prime Minister Nawaz Sharif in the spring of the 1999 discredited by the subsequent Kargil conflict, and the Nawaz linkage destroyed by the army coup of October 1999. The Indian proponents of a conciliatory line toward Pakistan came under strong attack from both the opposition parties and more hawkish elements of the Bharatiya Janata Party, although the new (2004) Congress-led government seems to be showing more flexibility. On Pakistan's part, President Zia's "cricket diplomacy" of the late 1980s and President Musharraf's participation in the Agra Summit in July 2001 raised the prospect of a more forthcoming Pakistani policy. Nevertheless, Pakistan's two democratically elected prime ministers, Benazir Bhutto and Nawaz Sharif, fearful of the army, both assumed a very hawkish stance toward India.

Seeking outside allies. The most consistent policy in both states for over fifty years has been to seek outside allies against each other. Pakistan has enlisted several Arab states, Iran, the United States, China, and North Korea in its attempt to balance Indian power, but Washington, uncomfortable shouldering such a role, has resisted Pakistan's efforts to extend the security umbrella to cover an attack by India. The Reagan administration drew the line at calling India a communist state, which would have invoked the 1959 agreement to take measures to defend Pakistan against communist aggression.

The Chinese have been less restrained, and while no known treaty binds Pakistan and China together, Beijing has provided more military assistance to Pakistan than it has to any other state. Beijing saw its support for Pakistan as serving a dual purpose, since a stronger Pakistan could counter the Soviet Union and resist Indian pressure. Yet, China has moderated its support for Pakistan's claims to Kashmir, and has gradually normalized its relationship with India. After 1988 New Delhi itself saw an opportunity to weaken the Beijing-Islamabad tie by moving closer to China and lately has been circumspect in its criticism of Chinese policies in Tibet and elsewhere. This trend has continued through 2004 with the reinvigoration of commercial trade, investment, and border talks between China and India.

India also saw the former Soviet Union as a major ally in its competition with Pakistan. The Soviet Union provided a veto in the United Nations, massive arms supplies, and general sympathy for New Delhi. However, this support was not directed so much against Pakistan as it was against China; when the Gorbachev government began to normalize relations with Beijing, its support for India gradually declined. This trend is likely to continue indefinitely, with India and Pakistan both seeking outside support against the other.

Changing the balance of power. Both India and Pakistan have also attempted to use their armed forces to change their balance of power. The closest the two have come to a decisive turning point was in 1971, when the Indian army secured the surrender of the Pakistan army in East Pakistan. However, rather than pressing on to a decisive victory in the West—which would have been very costly and might have brought other states into the contest—India settled for a negotiated peace and the Simla agreement. Both the United States and China provided verbal support for Pakistan in 1970 and 1971, but neither seemed prepared to take any direct action that would have prevented India from defeating the Pakistanis in East Pakistan. A second opportunity came in 1987 during the Brasstacks crisis, when India had conventional superiority and Pakistan had not yet acquired a nuclear weapon.

By 1990 both India and Pakistan had covertly exercised their nuclear options and seemed to have concluded that the risk of escalation had reached a point where the fundamental balance between the two could not be achieved by force of arms. This did not prevent the discrete use of force, and Pakistan adopted a strategy of hitting at India through the support of separatist and terrorist forces and, in 1999, a low-level war in Kargil. Now this raises the prospect of escalation to nuclear war, but so far there has been no Indian or Pakistani advocacy of a decisive nuclear war.

Resolution or Permanent Hostility?

A paired-minority conflict does not lend itself to the kind of sustained dialogue that leads to regional peace. Neither does it imply that war is likely. Other paired-minority conflicts have been moderated or appear to be on the road to resolution, or at least manageability. On the one hand, it is possible to envision a peace process that could resolve or ameliorate the core conflicts between India and Pakistan, though such a process would require major policy changes on the part of India, Pakistan, and the most likely "facilitator" of such a process, the United States. A regional peace now seems improbable, however, given Washington's reluctance (since 1964) to become deeply engaged in South Asian conflicts and the difficulty of arriving at political acceptance in both countries at the same time.

A more likely development is that steps will be taken to encourage India and Pakistan to accommodate one another and reduce their conflict. Such measures have already been gaining support since the early 1990s and in some quarters are seen as a prelude to a real peace agreement. The uprising in Kashmir and the nuclearization of India and Pakistan have stimulated this interest, as reflected in the expansion of "Track II" diplomacy as well as increasing research on ways to stabilize the India-Pakistan relationship and various confidence-building measures. The goal of all of these efforts is to increase regional cooperation and trust, and to moderate, if not transform, a relationship that seems to be based on fear, hatred, and distrust. These suggestions emphasize the gains and benefits that each side may reap from cooperation.

Finally, the possibility that the India-Pakistan relationship might undergo a major transformation cannot be ruled out. Several scenarios suggest themselves, and though some of these seem far-fetched at the moment, all merit at least a brief mention.

Pakistan could collapse under the weight of its own contradictions and cease to exist in its present form, perhaps splitting into several states.

India could cause Pakistan to change its identity or cease to exist in its present form, instead emerging as a state less able or willing to challenge India in any significant way.

Some Hindu nationalists believe that India's "civilizational pull" will triumph over the idea of Pakistan, and that Pakistanis will simply succumb to India's greater cultural and social power (though not necessarily merge with India).

India may underestimate Pakistani nationalism and power and take some action that would lead Islamabad to actually use its nuclear weapons in a final attempt to defend Pakistan and, if that fails, to bring India down with it by attacking India's cities.

Pakistan might change its priorities, putting development ahead of Kashmir—at least for a while. This seems to be the strategy adopted by Pakistan's president Pervez Musharraf in 2003–2004.

India could accept Pakistan's identity as an Islamic state and move toward cooperating with it on a range of shared interests. Or, it could declare that it disagreed with this identity and point to the accomplishments of a secular democracy, but also acknowledge that on this irreconcilable point Pakistanis have the right to choose a different path.

None of these extreme outcomes seem likely, but together they add up to a possibility that the India-Pakistan relationship could take a dramatic and even dangerous turn. Without some fundamental changes in India and Pakistan, the most likely future of this dispute will be a continuing stalemate, one of hesitant movements toward dialogue, punctuated by attempts on both sides to unilaterally press their advantage in Kashmir and in international forums. This is a conflict that Pakistan cannot win and India cannot lose, a true "hurting stalemate."

India's dilemma. A state of stalemate is seen to be more attractive to each side than finding solutions. From the perspective of the Pakistan military, which has an absolute veto over any policy initiative regarding Kashmir, the ability to tie Indian forces down in Kashmir is an important consequence of the dispute; cynically, it could be said that Pakistan is willing to fight India to the last Kashmiri. For India, Kashmir has so many links to India's secular political order—especially the place of Muslims—that any settlement that appears to compromise this order is unacceptable.

Until a few years ago, the prospect of a "failed" Pakistan did not greatly disturb India. In the face of Islamic extremism, Pakistan's acquisition of nuclear weapons, and the state's economic collapse, however, the thought of a failed Pakistan is worrying India more and more. Pakistan could spew out millions of refugees, it might accelerate the spread of nuclear weapons to hostile states and terrorist groups, and it could serve as a base for radical Islamic movements that target Indian Muslims. Strategically, a failed Pakistan might draw outside powers into the subcontinent. Conversely, a more normal India-Pakistan relationship could help India assume a place among the major Asian and even global powers. It would not be a question, as it is now, of Indian power minus Pakistani power, but of an India free to exercise its influence over a much wider range, without the distraction—and the cost—of a conflict with a still-powerful Pakistan.

India's strained relationship with Pakistan resembles a chronic ailment. It has not prevented the Indian economy from forging ahead, India has been able to pursue its great democratic experiment, and it is now recognized as one of Asia's major powers—with its sights set on a wider arena. Yet, Pakistan remains an obsession for a sector of the Indian elite, and Islamabad's new nuclear capabilities, plus its willingness to tolerate if not support separatist and terrorist groups operating in India and Kashmir cannot be ignored. Indians (and perhaps even more so, Pakistanis) need to come to grips with the relationship. The problem is that events may outrun the process of accommodation. In recent years there has been a summit, a miniwar, a coup in Pakistan, and a major crisis (in 2002). India, as of early 2005, appears to be searching for a stable relationship with Pakistan, but the most important question one can ask of the relationship is not whether Indians or Pakistanis can be trusted to fulfill obligations incurred in agreements where they had little incentive to comply, but whether, under the influence of a pessimistic vision of the region's destiny, they can be trusted in cases where it is in their self-interest to comply.

Stephen P. Cohen

See also **China, Relations with; Kashmir; Nuclear Programs and Policies; Nuclear Weapons Testing and Development; Pakistan; United States, Relations with**

BIBLIOGRAPHY

Behera, Navnita Chadha, Paul M. Evans, and Gowher Rizvi. *Beyond Boundaries: A Report on the State of Non-Official Dialogues on Peace, Security and Cooperation in South Asia.* Toronto: University of Toronto, 1997.

Canetti, Elias. *Crowds and Power.* New York: Seabury Press, 1978.

Cohen, Stephen Philip. *India: Emerging Power.* Washington, D.C.: Brookings Institution Press, 2001.

———. *The Idea of Pakistan.* Washington, D.C.: Brookings Institution Press, 2004.

Das, Gurcharan. *India Unbound: The Social and Economic Revolution from Independence to the Global Information Age.* New York: Anchor, 2003.

Ganguly, Sumit, ed. *India as an Emerging Power.* London: Frank Cass, 2003.

Nayak, Polly. "Reducing Collateral Damage to Indo-Pakistani Relations from the War on Terrorism." Brookings Institution Policy Brief no. 107 (September 2002). Available at <http://www.brookings.edu/comm/policybriefs/ pb107.htm>

PALA DYNASTY. *See* **Bengal.**

PALAEOLITHIC PERIOD A general term used by archaeologists, *Palaeolithic* refers to the earliest period of human cultural development when the primary cultural remains are stone tools and occasional fossil bones of either early hominids or the animals that they butchered for food. The discovery of early Miocene hominoids such as *Sivapithecus* (14 to 7 million years ago, or M.Y.A.) and *Ramapithecus* (13 to 9 M.Y.A.) in the Siwalik deposits of northern Pakistan and India provide evidence for early primate evolution. Unfortunately, the crucial Pliocene deposits dating from 4 to 1 million years ago are badly eroded and contain none of the fossils that are needed to identify the presence of hominids that were ancestral to humans. Early scholars proposed that the roughly flaked tools of the Pre-Soan and Soan traditions belonged to a very early period of human evolution, but their discovery in eroded deposits made it impossible to accurately date them. Improvements in palaeomagnetic and other chronometric dating techniques have now confirmed very early stone tools in deposits at Riwat (+2 M.Y.A.) in the Potwar Plateau, Pakistan, and at Uttarbani (+2.8 M.Y.A.) in Jammu, India. These new discoveries have extended the Lower Palaeolithic in northern South Asia to more than 2 million years ago, during the late Pliocene Epoch. No fossil hominids have been found from this early period in South Asia, but early *Homo* fossils, possibly *Homo erectus*, have been found in China and date to approximately this same time period, while in Africa the main tool-using hominid was *Homo ergaster*. Considerably more evidence for tool-using hominids is found from sites throughout most of the northern and peninsular regions, dating from 700,000 to 500,000 years ago. While the earliest stone tools were made by irregular flaking on pebbles or large blocklets, the later forms demonstrate more refined bifacial flaking to produce bilaterally symmetrical hand axes and cleavers that fall within the Acheulian tool tradition. These early Acheulian stone tools were probably used to dig tubers, butcher animals, and make wooden tools. The Lower Palaeolithic period continues until around 100,000 years ago, when changes in tool technologies indicate the emergence of new subsistence strategies that may also be associated with more evolved species, such as archaic *Homo sapiens*.

The Middle Palaeolithic period extends from around 100,000 to 30,000 years ago, though it may end earlier or later in different regions of the subcontinent. The earliest hominid fossil to be discovered in South Asia comes from the site of Hathnora, in Maharashtra, on the Narmada River in central India. This fossil skull (frontal) fragment was initially identified as belonging to *Homo erectus* (1.5 M.Y.A. to 500,000 Y.A.), but more recent studies have confirmed that it should be classified as archaic *Homo sapiens* (400,000 to 100,000 Y.A.). The Hathnora fossil was found in eroded gravels along with late Acheulian tools that could date anywhere from 700,000 to 125,000 year ago, but most scholars place the fossil at around 125,000 years ago. The only other Middle Palaeolithic fossil is a temporal bone from the skull of an archaic *Homo sapiens*, similar to Neanderthal skulls from Skhul cave in the Levant. This important fossil was found at the site of Darra-i-Kur, Afghanistan, and is dated by the radiocarbon technique to around 30,000 years ago, using charcoal from an associated hearth. Numerous Mousterian-style tools, scrapers, a Levallois point, and small hand axes are comparable to tools from Neanderthal sites in the Near East and Europe. Faunal remains at the site indicate the people were hunting wild goats or sheep and possibly cattle. Many more cave sites and open air sites of the Middle Palaeolithic have been found throughout South Asia, and they demonstrate that archaic *Homo sapiens* populations were adapting to all of the varied environments, from the glacial highlands in the north to the rich alluvial plains near Rohri, Pakistan, to the deserts of Rajasthan and the tropical jungles of peninsular India.

The Upper Palaeolithic period dates from around 30,000 to 12,000 years ago and corresponds to the period of maximum glaciation in northern latitudes. The peninsular environment changed from moist to semiarid, resulting in a change in fauna from large Late Pleistocene mammals to smaller modern forms. Periodic interglacial episodes allowed human communities to expand into the mountainous regions, such as Kashmir and northern Afghanistan. The stone tool technology gradually became more specialized, with many backed blades and some burins, scrapers, ring stones, and geometric microliths. Few bone tools have been recovered, except from Kurnool Cave in South India. One of the important cave sites is Bhimbetka (III F-23), in Maharashtra, that has early levels dating to around 100,000 years ago in the Late Acheulian. The Upper Palaeolithic occupation at the cave dates from 30,000 to around 10,000 years ago. Near Bhimbetka are hundreds of caves and rock shelters with rock art. Some of the earliest geometric paintings made with red pigments and others that depict large pigs and bison may date to the end of the Upper Palaeolithic period, or Epi-Palaeolithic, but most of the caves belong to the subsequent Mesolithic period. Very little movable

FIGURE 1

Time Line

PLEISTOCENE (10,000 TO 2 M.Y.A.)

Upper Pleistocene	Mesolithic	8,000–9,000 Y.A.
10,000 to 100,000	Epi-Palaeolithic	10,000 Y.A.
(127,000)	Upper Palaeolithic	10,000–30,000 Y.A.
(100,000)	Middle Palaeolithic	30,000–70,000 Y.A.
Middle Pleistocene	Lower Palaeolithic	100,000–500,000 Y.A.
100,000 to 1 M.Y.A. (.7)	Archaic *Homo sapiens*	
	Late Acheulian	
Lower Pleistocene	Lower Palaeolithic	to 1.9 or 2 M.Y.A.
1 to 2 M.Y.A.	Early Hominids,	
(1.9, 1.7)	Soan, Acheulian	
Pliocene	Lower Palaeolithic	2 to 4.5 M.Y.A.
2 to 5 M.Y.A.	Early Hominids and Pre-Soan, origins of tool making	
Miocene	Higher Primates	
5 to 25 M.Y.A.		

SOURCE: Courtesy of author.

art has been discovered so far except for a carved pebble and notched stone from the site of Gar-i-Asp (Horse cave), in Aq Kupruk, Afghanistan.

In central India, the site of Baghor I, in Madhya Pradesh, is an important Epi-Palaeolithic site dated to around 11,000 years ago. This open-air campsite was located next to an oxbow lake on the Son River and contained rubble floors for huts, hearths, and large quantities of manufacturing waste from heat treatment of chert nodules and stone tool manufacture. Many broken backed blades and geometric microliths indicate that hunting weapons were being hafted and repaired at the site; used stone tools indicate the processing of hides and woodworking. Ring stones that may have been used with digging sticks suggest that the people were also collecting tubers, and grinding stones indicate that they were processing wild plant foods. A small rubble platform with a unique triangular stone in the center is thought to represent the earliest ritual structure or shrine in the subcontinent. The ancient triangular stone is identical to modern stones used in local shrines to represent the Mother Goddess and female energy, or *shakti.*

Jonathan Mark Kenoyer

See also **Chalcolithic (Bronze) Age; Indus Valley Civilization; Neolithic Period; Rock Art**

BIBLIOGRAPHY

Allchin, Bridget, and Raymond Allchin. *The Rise of Civilization in India and Pakistan.* Cambridge, U.K., and New York: Cambridge University Press, 1982.

Dennell, Robin W. "The Indian Palaeolithic since Independence: An Outsider's Assessment." In *Recent Studies in Indian Archaeology*, edited by K. Paddayya. New Delhi: Munshiram Manoharlal, 2002.

Dupree, Louis, ed. *Prehistoric Research in Afghanistan, 1959–1966.* Transactions of the American Philosophical Society. Philadelphia: American Philosophical Society, 1972.

Kennedy, Kenneth A. R. "The Fossil Hominid Skull from the Narmada Valley: *Homo erectus* or *Homo sapiens*?" In *South Asian Archaeology 1989*, edited by Catherine Jarrige. Madison, Wis.: Prehistory Press, 1992.

Kenoyer, Jonathan Mark, J. Desmond Clark, Jaga Nath Pal, and G. R. Sharma. "An Upper Palaeolithic Shrine in India?" *Antiquity* 57 (1983): 88–94.

Korisettar, Ravi. "The Archaeology of the South Asian Lower Palaeolithic: History and Current Status." In *Indian Archaeology in Retrospect*, vol. 1: *Protohistory: Archaeology of*

South Asia, edited by S. Settar and Ravi Korisettar. New Delhi: Indian Council of Historical Research, 2002.

Pal, Jaga Nath. "The Middle Palaeolithic Culture of South Asia." In *Indian Archaeology in Retrospect*, vol. 1: *Protohistory: Archaeology of South Asia*, edited by S. Settar and Ravi Korisettar. New Delhi: Indian Council of Historical Research, 2002.

Raju, D. R., and P. C. Venkatasubbiah. "The Archaeology of the Upper Palaeolithic Phase in India." In *Indian Archaeology in Retrospect*, vol. 1: *Protohistory: Archaeology of South Asia*, edited by S. Settar and Ravi Korisettar. New Delhi: Indian Council of Historical Research, 2002.

PALLAVAS. *See* **History and Historiography.**

PANCHAMAS ("FIFTHS"). *See* **Dalits.**

PANCH SHILA (FIVE PRINCIPLES). *See* **Nehru, Jawaharlal.**

PANDAVAS. *See* **Mahābhārata.**

PANDIT, VIJAYA LAKSHMI *(1900–1990), Indian political leader and diplomat.* Vijaya Lakshmi Pandit was born on 18 August 1900, the daughter of Motilal Nehru, a wealthy lawyer, and his wife Swarup. (She too was given the name Swarup at birth; Vijaya Lakshmi, the name by which she became known in public life, was given to her when she married.) Her older brother, Jawaharlal, served as prime minister when India became independent in 1947 until his death in 1964. Her younger sister, Krishna (later, Hutheesingh), in her memoirs described her famous sister as docile, obedient, tactful, and eminently suited to high office. She was also beautiful, highly intelligent, at ease with people of all classes, witty, and, on occasion, sharp-tongued. She was educated entirely at home by tutors under the supervision of her English governess, Jane Hooper.

The family became involved in nationalist politics when Motilal Nehru gave his support to Mohandas Gandhi, leader of the Indian National Congress, in its opposition to British rule. In 1921 Vijaya married Ranjit S. Pandit, a lawyer and Sanskrit scholar, and they had three daughters. Both she and her husband were active in the freedom movement, and they were imprisoned at various times. He died in 1944 after a prison term. Elected in 1937 to the provincial legislature of the United Provinces, she became minister in charge of local self-government, medicine, and public health.

Vijaya Lakshmi Pandit. At the United Nations, Vijaya Pandit poised to take charge of the General Assembly as its president. September 1953. TIME LIFE PICTURES / GETTY IMAGES.

Vijaya Pandit made her first visit to the United States in 1944 to see her daughters, Nayantara and Chandralekha, who were students at Wellesley College. She lectured widely on India, befriending influential Americans, including Eleanor Roosevelt. She represented India at the initial meeting of the United Nations in 1946 at San Francisco. When India became independent, she was appointed ambassador to the Soviet Union (1947–1949) and then to the United States (1949–1951). From 1952 to 1954, she was a member of Parliament, and from 1953 to 1954, she led India's delegation to the United Nations, where she became president of the General Assembly. From 1954 to 1961, she was India's high commissioner to Great Britain. Governor of the province of Maharashtra from 1962 to 1964, she was a member of Parliament from 1964 to 1969.

Her niece, Indira Gandhi, daughter of Jawaharlal, had become prime minister in 1964, but there were increasing strains between them as the Gandhi administration became more authoritarian, culminating in the suspension of civil rights. Pandit joined the opposition party and in 1978 won a seat in Parliament in the election that defeated Indira Gandhi. On her retirement from parliament, she wrote her memoirs, *The Scope of Happiness.*

When she died on 1 December 1990, newspapers cited her as one of the most outstanding women of the century.

Ainslie T. Embree

See also **Nehru, Jawaharlal; Nehru, Motilal; Women and Political Power**

BIBLIOGRAPHY

The best source for her life is her autobiography, *The Scope of Happiness: A Personal Memoir* (New York: Crown, 1979). Anne Guthrie, *Madame Ambassador: The Life of Vijaya Lakshmi Pandit* (New York: Harcourt, Brace, 1962), gives additional details on her family, as does the autobiography of her sister, Krishna Nehru Hutheesingh, *With No Regrets* (New York: John Day, 1945). Her relationship with her niece is discussed by her daughter, Nayantara Sahgal, in *Indira Gandhi: The Road to Power* (New York: Frederick Ungar, 1982).

PANDITA RAMABAI ***(1858–1922), social activist, proponent of women's rights in India.*** Pandita Ramabai was born in Mangalore District in 1858. Her father was a Chitpavan Brahman scholar, who taught her Sanskrit and refused to arrange her marriage. The family traveled from one pilgrimage site to another; her father supporting them by giving recitations of the Purāṇas. The famine of 1874 reduced the family to starvation. In the forest near Tirupathi, her father, mother, and elder sister died. She and her brother wandered all over India, mostly on foot, for the next six years, in an effort to attain to the forgiveness of sins. What they found was "insincerity and fraud" (Macnicol, p. 16). But Ramabai and her brother were not deceived. "We knew we were sinners," she confessed, "though we did not acknowledge it." Still it was in those years that Ramabai became profoundly aware of the sufferings of women. In Calcutta, her intellect and charisma while expounding the scriptures captivated the Sanskrit scholars of Bengal, who bestowed on her the title *Pandita* (mistress of learning). However, Ramabai eventually became disillusioned with Hinduism.

Pandita Ramabai became a champion of the oppressed, particularly women. In 1880 she married a Bengali lawyer; he died within two years, leaving her with a baby daughter, Monorama. Ramabai began an aggressive crusade in favor of female education and a higher marriage age for girls, rousing the opposition of orthodox Hindus.

In 1882 Ramabai published her first book in Marathi, *Shree Dharma Neety* (Morals for women), which drew attention to the plight of child widows and married and unmarried women. Pandita Ramabai spoke out on women's rights long before Mahatma Gandhi did. In 1883 she was called before the Education Commission, chaired by Sir William Hunter. "The educated men of this country are opposed to female education and the proper position of women," she told them. "It is evident that women, being one half of the people of this country, are oppressed and cruelly treated by the other half." She also appealed to the government to open medical schools to women.

In Britain, in September 1883, Ramabai and her daughter were baptized. Before returning to Poona in 1889, she wrote *The High Caste Hindu Woman, 1887.* It was the first book ever published in English by an Indian woman. A few months later she became the first woman to address the Indian National Congress.

The famines of 1896 and 1897 were a watershed in Ramabai's life. She saw people dying, especially girls, and knew she must save some. She acquired a 500-acre property in Kedgaon, near Poona. It was dedicated in September 1898 and came to be known as the Mukti (Salvation) Mission. The residents were abandoned and abused women and girls. All were taught skills to earn their own living. Before the end of her life, the community had grown to two thousand residents. She was awarded the Kaiser-i-Hind gold medal in 1919 for her social contributions. She died peacefully on 5 April 1922.

Graham Houghton

BIBLIOGRAPHY

Batley, Dorothea S. *Devotees of Christ*. London: Church of England Zenana Missionary Society, 1937.

Kosambi, Meera, ed. *Pandita Ramabai through Her Own Words*. New Delhi: Oxford University Press, 2000.

Macnicol, Nicol. *Pandita Ramabai*. Kolkata: Associated Press, 1930.

PANDITS. *See* **Jammu and Kashmir.**

PĀNINI, ***fifth-century-*B.C. *grammarian.*** Dākshīputra Pānini, author of India's greatest grammar, *Ashtādhyāyī* (Eight chapters), was born in Shalātura in northwest India. According to tradition, he became a friend of Raja Mahānanda of Magadha (fifth century B.C.). Pānini's grammar described, in four thousand *sūtras*, the rules to generate all Sanskrit sentences.

The Dakshas were a northern clan organized into a republican *sangha*. The Chinese Buddhist pilgrim Hsieun Tsang visited Shalatura in the seventh century and found that the grammatical tradition was continued there, and that Pānini had been honored with a statue. The *Kathā-sarit-sāgara* (Ocean of verse) of Somadeva (eleventh century) mentions that Pānini's teacher was Varsha and his rival was Kātyāyana.

Pānini's *Ashtādhyāyī* is the greatest ancient masterpiece of the Sanskrit grammatical tradition. It took the earlier Pratishākhya rules on converting the word-for-word recitation of the Veda into a continuous recitation and created an abstract grammar of unsurpassed power. Pānini's grammar, along with its word lists, presents invaluable incidental information about life and society in fifth-century-B.C. India. It preserves the names of cities, towns, villages, and cultural and political entities called *Janapadas* (states), as well as details regarding social life, economic conditions, education and learning, religion, and political conditions. The Janapada states had different types of government; some were republics, others were monarchies. We learn that the king did not have absolute power and that he shared authority with his minister.

Pānini's references shed important light on the way religion was practiced. We find that images were used to represent deities in temples and open shrines. There were images in the possession of the custodian of shrines.

Pānini is aware of the Vedic literature and the Upanishads. He also knows the Mahābhārata. Pānini's work is thus invaluable in the dating of the texts of the Vedic period. Pānini describes coins that came prior to the period of Kautilya's *Artha Shāstra* (Textbook on material gain; 4th century B.C.).

Pānini appears to have traveled to Pātaliputra to participate in a great annual meeting of scholars.

Subhash Kak

See also **Ashtādhyāyī; Vedic Aryan India**

BIBLIOGRAPHY

Agrawala, V. S. *India as Known to Pānini*. Lucknow: University of Lucknow, 1953.

Cardona, G. *Panini: His Work and Its Traditions: Background and Introduction*. Delhi: Motilal Banarsidass, 1997.

Sharma, R. N. *Astādhyāyī of Pānini*. New Delhi: Munshiram Manoharlal, 2001.

PANT, GOVIND BALLABH *(1887–1961), Indian politician, home minister (1954–1960).* Born at Khunt, near Almora, United Provinces, in the Himalayas on 30 August 1887, Govind Ballabh Pant became India's "greatest parliamentarian," serving for ten years as chief minister of the United Provinces (Uttar Pradesh) and for six years as home minister of the Indian government. He grew up in Almora and was known as a *pahari* or, as Jawaharlal Nehru put it, "a son of the mountains." His father was a *naib tahsildar* (deputy collector of revenue). Pant was educated at home and was sent to school at the age of ten. In 1905 he enrolled in Muir Central College in Allahabad and between 1907 and 1909 studied law. A serious student of politics, he kept a notebook and diary of contemporary events and modeled himself on the Congress moderate Gopal Krishna Gokhale (1866–1915). Pant began a law practice in Almora but moved his practice to Kashipur, which, although a political backwater, became the center of his legal and political life. In 1914 he established Prem Sabha, a literary and social organization, and became the secretary of the Uday Raj Hindu School. In 1916 he founded the Kumaun Parishad to voice the demands of the Kumaun people. In 1916 he attended the renowned Congress session at Lucknow. He fought his first election to the United Provinces Legislative Council in 1920 but lost by thirty-three votes.

In 1922 he gave up his legal practice to follow Mahatma Gandhi. In 1923 Pant was elected to the United Provinces Legislative Council on the Swarajist ticket and headed the party in the assembly. He was reelected in 1926 but resigned in 1930. Between 1929 and 1934 he served time in prison for his noncooperation activities, shared a cell with Nehru, and they became close friends. In 1934 he was elected unopposed on the Congress ticket to the Legislative Assembly of India. In 1937 and again in 1946 he was elected to the United Provinces Legislative Assembly, serving as chief minister between 1937 and 1939. Between 1946 and 1950 he represented Uttar Pradesh in the Constituent Assembly of India. From 1946 to 1954 he returned as the chief minister of Uttar Pradesh before finally accepting Nehru's offer to serve in the central government. He was the home minister until 1960. He had a prodigious capacity for work, and as a first-class administrator he was a master for details. Govind B. Pant died on 7 March 1961.

Roger D. Long

See also **Gandhi, Mahatma M. K.; Nehru, Jawaharlal**

BIBLIOGRAPHY

Chalapathi Rau, M. *Govind Ballabh Pant: His Life and Times*. New Delhi: Allied Publishers, 1981.

Nanda, B. R., ed. *Selected Works of Govind Ballabh Pant*. 18 vols. New Delhi: Oxford University Press, 1994–2002.

PANTH. *See* **Sikhism.**

PAPERMAKING In India, paper came into use relatively late. In the Hindu tradition, from the ancient Aryan Brahmanic oral transmission of the Vedas, nothing was written until about the sixth century B.C. In South India, the earliest portable writing materials were *tadpatra* (palm leaves), *bhurja patra* (beaten birch bark), and cotton cloth. Perhaps for religious reasons, parchment, made

A Woman Making Rice Paper from Rags and Scraps. In the state of Sikkim, situated in the eastern Himalayas, a woman sifts through cotton rags and scraps of paper. This technique of using recycled goods to make new paper was introduced in contemporary India to revive a stagnating industry. EARL & NAZIMA KOWALL / CORBIS.

from the inner lining of the stomach of a calf, which was commonly in use in the Christian and Arab world, was not used in India.

The earliest mention of paper in India is in the records of the Cairo *Genizah*, a repository of Jewish manuscripts that cover the period from A.D. 1000 to 1250 These documents note that many Jewish traders were closely linked to Western India and that paper was sent as a present from Aden to India. It seems clear that paper first came to India through trade and was used long before it was actually made there. It appears to have been brought as a commodity into Gujarat by Arab merchants who sailed along the west coast of India. Inscriptional references of the thirteenth century attest to settlement by Arab traders in the ports of Cambay, Prabhas Patan (Somnath), Junagadh, and Anahilvad (Patan).

The earliest use of paper was to record religious scriptures, particularly in the Jain tradition. The Jain kings of the Chalukya period (10th–13th century) were great patrons of learning who established libraries. Commoners also gained merit by commissioning copies of sacred texts. After the Muslim conquest of Gujarat in the early fourteenth century, the number of manuscripts increased. Palm leaf was no longer in use in western India by the latter half of the fourteenth century. In other regions, it was used well into the sixteenth century, and in Orissa as late as the nineteenth century for religious texts. Abu Hamid al Gharnati in his *Tuhfat ul Albab*, written in 1162, notes that "Indian paper" compared favorably with that made in Iraq and Khorasan.

In Kashmir, however, the craft of papermaking is believed to have been introduced by Zain ul-Ab-ud-Din in the fifteenth century upon his return from Samarqand, where he had been taken hostage by Timur. The emperor appears to have brought back craftsmen trained in the Persian tradition. From Nowshera, papermaking spread south to Sialkot and into North India.

Local lore in Khuldabad claims that Chinese craftsmen, among them papermakers, who were at the court of Sultan Muhammad ibn Tughluq (r. 1325–1351), moved with the court when the capital moved south from Delhi to Daulatabad, renamed Deogiri. The paper made there, possibly already in the fourteenth century, appears to have followed the Chinese tradition, with some local differences.

The first recorded use of paper is in Barani's *Tarikh I Firuzshahi*, where he refers to a *firman* that Sultan Balban (r. 1266–1286) ordered to be washed in order to annul a decree. This indicates that paper was not only strong but also valuable.

Raw Materials and Technique

The raw materials used for paper were never fresh fibers. Paper was made from discarded items of everyday use, for example, ropes, fishing nets, and gunny sacks, all made from *sunn* hemp (*crotolaria juncea*).

The rags would be chopped into small pieces with a hatchet and soaked in water for three to four days. They would then be washed, preferably in river water, by two men standing in the water with a cloth tied around their waists like a hammock. The rags would be scrubbed vigorously to release dirt. The washed rags would then be placed in a clay pot embedded in the ground and retted in a mixture of six parts crude carbonate of soda and seven parts quicklime. This system of cold retting broke down the fibers. After eight to ten days, the rags would be washed again and macerated either by rubbing on a roughened surface or by stamping underfoot. In the nineteenth century the *dhenki* was developed; a wooden stamper with a long horizontal beam, it could be operated by two men. The rags were then left out to dry in the sun. The entire laborious process would be repeated again three times to achieve the required whiteness. A small quantity of fiber was put into a clay pot, mixed with water, and shaken vigorously to check for an even dispersion of fibers, which was essential to the process. Country soap was added to serve as a bleaching agent, and then the pulp was made into cakes and dried in the sun.

When ready for use, the pulp was soaked in a small cylindrical vat, or *kundi*, and was trodden with bare feet to make a gruel. This was put into the main vat and left to soak overnight. The next morning the papermaker, or *kagzi*, squatted facing the vat and stirred the pulp vigorously with a bamboo pole to evenly disperse the fibers. He would lay the pole across the vat and place the *sacha*, a rectangular wooden frame with triangular ribs, on top of it. He would then spread the *chhapri*, a grass mat woven using hair from the tail of a horse, over the *sacha*, keeping it taut with two deckle sticks. The *kagzi* would hold the *sacha* with the deckle sticks loosely in his thumb and forefingers and dip the frame almost vertically into the vat; turning it horizontally in the water, he would lift out some pulp, shaking it gently to and fro. This shaking in all directions ensured a biaxial interlocking of the fibers, which made the paper strong. The *sacha* would be lifted out of the water and placed back on the bamboo pole; the excess water was allowed to drain away, and then the deckle sticks were removed. The *chhapri* with the thin film of pulp would be lifted carefully and couched on a cloth stretched on a wooden board. For each sheet he made, the *kagzi* put a small stone in a clay dish to keep tally. After 50 sheets, another cloth was spread on the pile. Between 150 to 200 sheets were made in a day. The piles were then pressed between two boards and left to stand overnight. The next day, the sheets were peeled apart and pasted onto a wall plastered with lime mortar, using a brush.

When the paper was dry, it was scraped with a pumice stone to remove grit and was sized using either rice or wheat starch. This not only rendered the paper impervious but also strengthened it. Finally, the paper was burnished on a concave wooden board with an agate embedded in clay, a marble roller, or even a conch shell.

The best-known papers of the sixteenth century were the *Sahebkhani* of Ahmedabad, the *Khash I Jahangiri* of Sialkot, the *Daulatabadi*, and the *Kashmiri*, which was famous for its soft, silken texture, reputed to come from waste silk cocoons beaten into the pulp.

Papermaking in the Modern Era

With industrialization, a horizontal mechanical beater called the Hollander beater took some of the labor out of the process, which otherwise remained largely unchanged into the early years of the nineteenth century. In 1825 a Mr. Marsham of Serampore imported a papermaking machine. In 1850 Charles Wood, secretary of state for India, passed an order requiring all paper for the government if India to be supplied from Great Britain.

This edict was a great blow to the craft of papermaking. Waste paper was added to make the process easier, and the quality rapidly deteriorated. Mahatma Gandhi attempted in the early years of the twentieth century to revitalize the craft. Paper was made using waste cotton fiber rags, and orders were issued requiring government files to use only handmade paper. But there was little concern for quality.

Sanganer, Kalpi, Wardha, Ahmedabad, Junnar, Daulatabad, Gosunda, and Pondicherry, all centers long reputed for their fine paper, declined rapidly. In the last decade of the twentieth century, the Indian government redefined handmade paper, permitting paper that was made entirely by machine using waste cotton fiber, but that was cut by hand, to be sold as handmade paper. This immediately improved sales as prices dropped, but as there was no regard for quality, the craft was still threatened. An attempt is being made in Daulatabad to revive the original tradition, but it has yet to prove sustainable.

Neeta Premchand

BIBLIOGRAPHY

Ghori, S. A. K., and A. Rahman. *Paper Technology in Medieval India*. New Delhi: National Institute of Sciences of India, 1966.

Hunter, Dard. *Papermaking by Hand in India*. New York: Pynson Printers, 1939.

Jaggi, O. P. *Science and Technology in Medieval India*. Delhi: Atma Ram, 1977.

Joshi, K. B. *Paper Making (as a Cottage Industry)*. Wardha: All India Village Industries Association, 1938.

Mehta, Makrand. *Indian Merchants and Entrepreneurs in Historical Perspective*. Delhi: Academic Foundation, 1991.

PARAMILITARY FORCES AND INTERNAL SECURITY India has undergone one of the fastest expansions of paramilitary internal security forces in the world. Though estimates vary, India's paramilitary strength is widely believed to be over 1 million, representing some 50 percent of the country's total armed forces, making India's the second-largest (after China) paramilitary force in the world.

The growth of India's paramilitary forces has been as diverse as it has been dramatic. The most remarkable rise has been that of the central paramilitary forces, light-infantry troops for service in border security, riot control, counterinsurgency, and close protection. The national government maintains six such forces, comprising half a million troops. Most of the remaining forces are organized by the states, in armed police units used for riot control and public order. The states have also raised special operations groups and special task forces to pursue specific criminal or rebel targets. In rebellious states, militias called village defense committees have been raised from among loyal elements. The national government's Intelligence Bureau is also actively involved in countering political unrest. The large paramilitary growth was meant to relieve the Indian army, but 30 to 40 percent of the regular army continues to be engaged in maintaining internal security, and the army has been forced to assign regular troops to counterinsurgency operations.

Growth

Under British rule, internal security had been maintained by Britain's colonial army. Though sparingly used in the twentieth century, the British Indian army's system of city garrisons supported its constabulary role, even when both world wars demanded overseas expeditionary duties. The British also had a practice of maintaining paramilitaries, such as the Cachar Levy (later Assam Rifles) and Punjab Irregular Frontier Force, but these were never quite separate from the army. Free India inherited paramilitary provincial constabularies in its largest states and a mounted infantry battalion, the Crown's Representative Police Force, later renamed the Central Reserve Police Force (CRPF).

The first spurt of post-independence growth of paramilitary forces occurred in the 1960s in response to external, rather than internal, threats. The threat from China led to the founding of the Indo-Tibetan Border Police (ITBP) in 1962. The force was intended for surveillance and special operations along the northern border and inside Chinese territory. The ITBP was recruited from acclimatized Himalayan communities and Tibetan refugees and received significant but short-lived U.S. assistance. The force was placed under the Ministry of Home Affairs, rather than the Indian army, to facilitate coordination with the Intelligence Bureau. India's largest paramilitary, the Border Security Force (BSF), was similarly raised after the 1965 war with Pakistan, which had begun with Pakistani border incursions in Kashmir.

The BSF and the ITBP were subsequently engaged in internal security, mostly focusing on counterinsurgency and counterterrorism in the border states. In Jammu and Kashmir, the BSF served as the leading paramilitary agency until 2003. The ITBP mostly provided close protection to political leaders and government officials targeted by rebels. The ITBP's select recruitment procedures made it less susceptible to infiltration and a natural choice for this duty.

The CRPF, which was established for internal security, expanded riot and crowd control and counterinsurgency capabilities. Through the 1980s and 1990s, the CRPF became a more mobile force, reconstituting its riot control squads into Rapid Action Force. In Punjab, the CRPF served effectively at the height of the Sikh rebellion. After the successful end of that insurgency in Punjab, the CRPF reverted to riot and crowd control, while continuing limited counterinsurgency in the Northeastern region. In 2004 the Indian government proposed to replace the BSF units in Jammu and Kashmir with new CRPF units, but held back the changeover following murderous suicide attacks on CRPF camps in the state that raised doubts about the force's capacity to fight effectively. This has led to some rethinking about the utility of paramilitary growth that has accompanied increased political efforts to resolve the dispute in Jammu and Kashmir.

In 2002 the central paramilitary forces consisted of over half a million troops. The BSF stood at 191,000, divided about evenly between border management and counterinsurgency. The force had gone from its initial 37 battalions to 56 in 1980 and 157 in 2002. The CRPF, the second largest, was 167,000, up from 15,000 in 1965. The ITBP went from a few battalions of special forces to 52,000 in 2002. The paramilitaries grew six times faster

India Border Security Force. Members of India's largest paramilitary group, the Border Security Force (BSF), patrolling the India-Pakistan divide. INDIA TODAY.

than the regular military between 1965 and 2002. Their budgets also increased dramatically: the BSF went from 3.5 billion Indian rupees in 1987–1988 to 11.8 billion in 1996–1997; the CRPF budget grew from 1.9 billion rupees in 1985–1986 to 12.5 billion rupees in 1997–1998.

Despite the fast growth, the central paramilitary forces have been overstretched. A CRPF unit, for example, was ordered to move thirty-three times in 1987. In the riot-prone city of Moradabad, in Uttar Pradesh, a single deployment of the force lasted four years, from 1980 to 1984. Between 1981 and 1992, the number of CRPF companies employed in the state of Uttar Pradesh alone rose from 50 to 208 (approximately 12 battalions, or 12,000 troops, to 50 battalions, or 50,000 troops). In the early 1990s as much as 45 percent of the CRPF was deployed in Punjab alone. Though the CRPF was the worst hit, other paramilitary forces were also extended beyond their limits.

A second tier of internal security forces, the provincial constabularies, passed into the hands of the state governments following independence. The bulk of the state forces for the most part became unreliable and were practically abandoned. Uttar Pradesh's Provincial Armed Constabulary and Bihar's Armed Police, for example, committed some truly horrific human rights offenses. The security reorganization in the states, therefore, concentrated on using task forces for the most grievous threats. The first widely publicized special task force was established in the early 1980s by the states of Tamil Nadu and Karnataka against the infamous ivory poacher, Veerappan, who ruled the jungles between the two states and was finally killed in 2004. In the late 1980s in Punjab, CRPF officers and troops seconded the state police and formed the core of special teams (described as India's death squads) that targeted Sikh militants. In Jammu and Kashmir, the special operations group, comprising select provincial constabulary and central paramilitary troops, has fought effectively against the insurgents. Special teams have also been used by states such as Uttar Pradesh, Maharashtra, and Gujarat to fight organized crime. The choice of special teams reflects an effort to concentrate resources on small, uncompromising teams operating with some impunity.

The third tier of internal security forces constitute the village defense committee (VDC). The VDC is a militia constituting state-supporting elements armed, trained, and paid for by the government. They provide intelligence to central and state forces, and in some cases hold off insurgent attacks while calling in reinforcements. VDCs are usually organized in sections of six to ten men, but there are larger and more organized militias as well. The Ikhwan-e-Muslimoon in southern Kashmir, for example, comprised former rebels who worked with government forces against the rebels. In Manipur the government has similarly used ethnic Kuki groups to fight the Naga insurgency. The special police officer (SPO) innovation emerged most publicly from the suppression of the armed peasant and student rebellion in West Bengal in 1969–1970. The SPO was usually an undercover agent, often a former rebel, who gathered intelligence and helped apprehend other rebels. In Punjab some 10,000 men were organized in VDCs and as SPOs.

Legality

Despite the preponderance of central paramilitary forces, law and order is a state subject under the Constitution of India. The states must request help from the central government before military or paramilitary troops may be used. In most cases, the use of force occurs under the authority of the state government working through local administration officers, usually the district revenue collector, who doubles as a magistrate. The combination of executive and judicial authority is a colonial legacy that has enabled the internal use of force in free India as well. The Constitution also allows the national government to dismiss state governments that fail to preserve law and order and to impose emergency central rule. While these powers have been misused for partisan politics, the most serious interventions occurred as a result of rebellion.

The actual deployment and behavior of India's armed forces is governed by specific laws. The Armed Forces Special Powers Act passed in 1958 to aid in the pacification of rebels in Nagaland and Mizoram, has been extended to other areas as required, and allows military personnel to enter and search, make arrests, and use lethal force. Other laws mimic these provisions for the central paramilitary forces. A series of "disturbed areas" laws further allow the national government to deploy security forces without the direct supervision of a magistrate, as is otherwise required for "aid to the civil" operations.

In 2002 the Bharatiya Janata Party (BJP) government pushed through Parliament the Prevention of Terrorism Act, which gave the police and security agencies broad authority to suspend civil liberties and due process. The new Congress government in 2004 allowed the law to lapse and has been trying to push through a more lenient version as replacement. The previous two decades were marked by controversy over the Terrorists and Disruptive Activities (Prevention) Act of 1987, which gave similar powers to security agencies. A news report in April 1992 found that 13,225 persons had been detained under the law in the previous seven years, but only 78 were convicted, despite easy rules of evidence. As many as 65,000 persons, including opposition politicians, lawyers, and journalists, had been detained under the law in 1993. Not surprisingly, the number of complaints filed with the National Human Rights Commission have also increased rapidly, from 496 in 1993–1994, when it was founded, to 6,947 in 1994–1995 and 20,514 in 1996–1997.

Command and Control

The Internal Security Division of the Ministry of Home Affairs (MHA) controls the central paramilitary forces. The forces receive their own budgets and are commanded by a powerful officer corps that safeguards their institutional interests. Only the Assam Rifles, a paramilitary force in the Northeastern region, serves under the command of the Indian army. The separation of command between the military and the paramilitary, going up through the Ministries of Defence and Home Affairs, is an important feature of post-independence institution building in India. By most accounts, the divided command arrangement has hurt the government's ability to fight internal security threats, but it continues to thrive, presumably, as an instrument of civil supremacy over the armed forces. Only during wartime can the military assert command over India's paramilitary forces.

The Indian army raised its own counterinsurgency force, the Rashtriya Rifles (National Rifles), by reconstituting two army corps (about 75,000 troops) for service in the rebellious state of Jammu and Kashmir. In 1993 a former Indian army chief appointed as governor to the state created a united headquarters to coordinate the various forces, but the arrangement did not quite work until the Kargil war in 1999, when the paramilitary forces were expressly placed under army command as part of wartime regulations.

Political leaders have supported paramilitary separation from the military in the hope of being able to better control the use of force, since the army's structure and institutional norms shut out state politicians from internal security campaigns. Army officers report directly to the national government through their own chain of command, and generally view state government officials as meddlesome and counterproductive to their military goals. Paramilitary forces, on the other hand, are more amenable to political control because they are part of the policing structure over which states enjoy constitutional authority. A system of common officership between paramilitary and police forces consolidates civil political control over paramilitary forces. Key command positions in the paramilitary forces are occupied by members of the Indian Police Service (IPS), an elite civil service. IPS officers also occupy positions in the Home Ministry's Internal Security Division.

Causes and Consequences

The rise of paramilitary forces in India is the result of worsening internal security propelled by several governance failures since the mid-1970s. Punjab, the Northeast states, and Jammu and Kashmir have been torn by rebellion because of the inability of the national and state governments to accommodate the political and economic aspirations of important social groups in those states. Political violence also increased in the "mainland" states of Bihar and Uttar Pradesh, and even in the political and commercial capitals of New Delhi and Mumbai, as a result of new aspirants claiming political power and the ruling elite seeking ways to prevent it. A gathering Hindu movement since the 1980s further added the possibility of Hindu-Muslim rioting. Disaffected groups have had increasing access to assault rifles and plastic explosives. Between 1990 and 1998, Indian security forces in Kashmir alone recovered around 18,000 AK series rifles, 7,000 pistols and revolvers, and 500 rocket launchers. In Punjab, an estimated 10,000 AK series rifles were captured between 1988 and 1994.

The Indian Institute of Public Administration lists 210 major incidents of communal violence—mostly caste and religious rioting—in the period 1951–1985; of these, 58 occurred in 1951–1970, and 152 in 1971–1985. The trend has since intensified. India's Ministry of Home Affairs reports that in Jammu and Kashmir in 1988–2000 there were 45,500 incidents of political violence, including 16,800 attacks on security forces, 13,000 incidents of explosion and arson, and 10,000 attacks on civilians by rebels. As many as 8,300 civilians and 2,200 security personnel (most of them paramilitary) died, and 11,479 rebels were killed. Militancy in Punjab in 1983–1992 caused about 12,000 deaths, including 1,400 police, 300 paramilitary, and 50 army troops. During more than a decade of deployment in Punjab, the CRPF alone killed 2,551 rebels and captured 12,977.

This massive use of force by the government has eroded the quality of Indian democracy. The long periods of quasi-martial law in the Northeast states and in Kashmir have led some observers to suggest that significant numbers of Indians actually live under authoritarian rule, belying the country's pride in being the world's largest democracy. What is most worrisome is the majoritarian sanction for the growing use of force in the country, the logic of which has already led to increased civil violence, most notably in Gujarat and in Mumbai. The general willingness to allow the state to use force as a primary instrument of policy means that when leaders feel politically and materially constrained, they will use majority anger to fill the coercion gap. The police and paramilitary forces in these circumstances stand back to allow majority groups to commit violence, further politicizing their ranks and spirit. The fast growth of the paramilitary forces has already led to training and control problems that affect their performance. Though India's political institutions continue to show an ability to accommodate new interests, changes in the character of the coercive apparatus, combined with a greater willingness to use force, constitute a significant departure from the past, when the majority of Indians believed that politics was the best mechanism for conflict resolution in their deeply divided country.

Sunil Dasgupta

See also **Ethnic Conflict; Insurgency and Terrorism; Jammu and Kashmir**

BIBLIOGRAPHY

Arya, D. C., and R. C. Sharma, eds. *Management Issues and Operational Planning for India's Borders.* New Delhi: Scholars Publishing Forum, 1991.

Brass, Paul R. *Theft of an Idol: Text and Context in the Representation of Collective Violence.* Princeton, N.J.: Princeton University Press, 1997.

Cohen, Stephen P. "The Military and Indian Democracy." In *India's Democracy: An Analysis of Changing State-Society Relations,* edited by Atul Kohli. Princeton, N.J.: Princeton University Press, 1988.

Collier, Kit. *The Armed Forces and Internal Security in Asia: Preventing the Abuse of Power.* Politics and Security Series Occasional Papers no. 2. Hawaii: East-West Center, 1999.

Dasgupta, Sunil. "India: New Militaries." In *Coercion and Governance,* edited by Muthiah Alagappa. Stanford, Calif.: Stanford University Press, 2001.

———. *Internal Security and Military Reorganization: The Rise of Paramilitaries in Developing Societies.* Ph.D. diss., University of Illinois, 2003.

Ghosh, S. K. *Communal Riots in India.* New Delhi: Ashish, 1987.

Grossman, Patricia. "India's Secret Armies." In *Death Squads in Global Perspective: Murder with Deniability,* edited by Bruce B. Campbell and Arthur D. Brenner. New York: St. Martin's Press, 2000.

Gupta, Shekhar. "The Tired Trouble Shooters." *India Today,* international ed., 15 February 1988: 82–84.

Hardgrave, Robert, Jr. "The Northeast, the Punjab, and the Regionalization of Indian Politics." *Asian Survey* 23, no. 10 (November 1983): 1171–1181.

Karan, Vijay. *War by Stealth: Terrorism in India.* New Delhi: Viking, 1997.

Kasturi, Bhashyam. "Review of Four Books." *Seminar* 479 (July 1999): 51–54.
Kochanek, Stanley A. *Politics of Democracy and Human Rights in South Asia.* Paper prepared for conference "Politics of Human Rights and Democratization," University of Illinois at Urbana-Champaign, 31 March–2 April 2000.
Kumar Jha, Sanjay. *Internal Security in a Third World Democracy: The Role of Paramilitary Force in India.* Ph.D. diss., Jawaharlal Nehru University, Center for International Politics, Organization, and Disarmament, School of International Studies, 2000.
Lal, Chaman. "Terrorism and Insurgency." *Seminar* 483 (November 1999): 18–24.
Nirmal, Anjali. *Role and Functioning of Central Police Organisations.* New Delhi: Uppal Publishing House, 1992.
Saha, B. P. *Growing Violence in Rural Areas: A Sociological, Political, and Economic Analysis.* New Delhi: Vikas, 1994.
Rajgopal, P. R. *Communal Violence in India.* New Delhi: Uppal, 1987.
Rao, B. V. P. "Small Weapons and National Security." *Seminar* 479 (July 1999): 36–41.
Rustamji, Khusro F. "The Paramilitary-Army Interface." In *Indian Defence Review Digest*, vol. 3, pp. 80–84 edited by Matthew Thomas. New Delhi: Lancer, 1992.
Shukla, K. S. *Collective Violence: Genesis and Response.* New Delhi: Indian Institute of Public Administration, 1988.
Vinayak, Ramesh. "A Law without Claws." *India Today*, international ed., 15 April 1992: 92.

PARASHURAMA. *See* **Vishnu and Avatāras.**

PARLIAMENT. *See* **Political System.**

Madame Bhikaji Cama, 1861–1936. Portrait of Madame Bhikaji Cama in her most celebrated act as Parsi nationalist: unfurling the first Indian national flag at the International Socialist Conference in Stuttgart, Germany, 1907. PRESS INFORMATION BUREAU / FOTOMEDIA.

PARSIS The Parsis are among India's smallest minorities. They comprise less than 0.01 percent of India's population but have nevertheless made significant contributions to Indian society, economy, and politics. For example, India's largest industrial empire, the Tata group, is headed by a Parsi, as is Godrej, India's largest privately owned conglomerate, and Bombay Dyeing, one of the largest textile groups in India. The number of Parsis is, however, declining. The Indian census counted the Parsi population to be 85,000 in 1881, 115,000 in 1941, 76,000 in 1991, and 69,600 in 2001.

Parsis came to India from Iran (Persia), hence the name "Parsi." Fleeing religious persecution, they first arrived in Gujarat in the seventh century. Many settled in the port of Surat, where, in the fifteenth century, Portuguese, British, and Dutch merchants had been given permission by the Mughals to establish trading factories. In Surat, Parsis soon became prosperous traders and chief native agents, as well as shipbuilders. A few Parsis left Surat, moving south to Bombay, where they acted as brokers between Indians and Portuguese. When Bombay was ceded by Portugal to England's crown in 1665, and, three years later, handed over to the East India Company, Parsis were already a presence in the region.

The East India Company sought to make Bombay its leading commercial center and it needed Indian traders, merchants, and craftsmen to settle there. Parsis were quick to seize the opportunity. Parsi entrepreneurs became prominent in small and large business enterprises in Bombay. They also laid the foundation for India's textile and cotton mill industry from the 1850s onward. Parsi industrialist Naoroji Wadia and his sons controlled the textile mills Bombay Dyeing and Century Mills. The Lowjee Wadia family dominated ship construction.

Accomplishments

Parsi entrepreneurs not only developed business empires but were also philanthropists who contributed to national development. The Tata Group was founded by Jamsetji Nusserwanji Tata, who initially established textile mills and later concentrated on the iron and steel industry, electrical power generation, and technical education.

Tata believed that India's political independence would be meaningless without economic self-sufficiency. His vision for creating national educational and industrial instititutions, such as the Institute of Science in Bangalore, a steel plant in Jamshedpur (Bihar), and a hydroelectric company, was brought to fruition by his successor, Jamsetji R. D. Tata, who guided the Tata Group for over half a century. He headed Tata Sons in 1938, Tata Chemicals in 1939, and the Tata Engineering and Locomotive Company in 1945. He also promoted civil aviation in the Indian subcontinent and founded Tata Airlines (which was later nationalized as Air India). Further, he funded the Tata Institute of Fundamental Research, which was the cradle of India's atomic energy program; started the Family Planning Foundation in 1970; established Asia's first cancer hospital (the Tata Memorial Hospital in Bombay); and in 1992 was awarded India's highest civilian honor, the Bharat Ratna, as well as the United Nations Population Award.

In politics, Parsis contributed to the Indian independence movement, and have been prominent in areas such as law, military affairs, and public service. Dadabhai Naoroji was a leading early Parsi nationalist who fought for the Indianization of the Indian Civil Service. In 1892 he narrowly won election to the British House of Commons as a Liberal from London's Central Finsbury. He was elected president of the Indian National Congress three times: in 1886, 1893, and 1906. The Congress's demand for *swaraj* (independence) was first expressed publicly in Naoroji's 1906 presidential address. Another Parsi, Madame Bhikaji Cama (1861–1936), who was exiled from India and Britain and lived in France, was a tireless propagandist for Indian independence. Pherozeshah Mehta (1845–1915) was known as the "father of municipal government in Bombay." He drafted the Bombay Municipal Act of 1872, served as municipal commissioner in 1873, and was elected president of the Indian National Congress in 1890.

A full list of Parsis in public service would run many pages long. Parsi scientists were instrumental in developing India's nuclear program. Homi Bhabha established the nuclear program and also served as the president of the United Nations conference on peaceful uses of atomic energy in 1955 and as president of the International Union of Pure and Applied Physics from 1960 to 1963. Homi Sethna was chairman of India's atomic energy commission in the 1970s and 1980s. General Sam Maneckshaw was the Indian army's first field marshal, leading the Indian army to victory over Pakistan in the Bangladesh War in 1971. In the 2000s, two Parsis were on India's Supreme Court (Chief Justice Sam Bharucha and Justice Sam Variava), and one was India's attorney general (Soli Sorabjee). An earlier legal luminary, Nani Palkhivala, served briefly as India's ambassador to the United States. Feroze Gandhi, a Parsi, was the husband of prime minister Indira Gandhi and the father of Rajiv Gandhi.

Parsis have established and headed dozens of hospitals, educational institutions, and research centers, including the Tata Cancer Hospitals, Sir J. J. School of Arts, the Institute of Social Sciences, and the Institute of Fundamental Research. Parsis also established the first Indian newspaper and the first Indian-owned bank. In the arts, prominent Parsis include singer Freddie Mercury, of the British rock group Queen, and Zubin Mehta, conductor of the Israel Philharmonic since 1981, the New York Philharmonic (1978–1991), the Los Angeles Philharmonic (1962–1978), and the Montreal Symphony (1961–1967). Many Parsis have excelled in sports and in various professions at the national and international level.

Religious and Cultural Practices

Parsis are Zoroastrians. Zoroastrianism was founded on the teachings of the prophet Zoroaster, who lived around 1500 B.C. in Iran (then Persia). Parsis are the Zoroastrians of India, descendants of the Zoroastrians who fled Iran and came to India in the seventh century A.D. Another group of Zoroastrians continued to live in Iran. The World Zoroastrian population in 2004 was estimated at 124,000–190,000: 69,600 in India, 24,000–90,000 in Iran, 10,000 in the United States, 6,000 in Canada, 5,000 in the U.K., and some 2,000 each in Australia, the Gulf, and Pakistan.

In terms of customs, Parsis have been incorrectly called "fire worshipers." They do not worship fire, but fire has special significance to Zoroastrians. It is regarded as giving light, warmth, and energy, and therefore as vital to life. Zoroastrian temples have altars with fire within, and are thus called fire-temples. Eight large fire-temples in India include four in Mumbai and four in the state of Gujarat (two in Surat, one in Udwada, one in Navsari). There are no caste divisions among Parsis, and no religious restrictions concerning food.

One major controversy within the Parsi community is intermarriage, and this has implications for the dwindling Parsi population. The Parsi Marriage and Divorce Act of 1936 and its amendments state that children born to a Parsi man and non-Parsi woman can be admitted into the religion. But children of a Parsi woman and a non-Parsi man would not be admitted. However, over the past decades, a section of the community has been accepting such children, provided that the mother had continued to be a practicing Zoroastrian after her marriage. A new edict discarded these progressive changes. In this situation, especially because perhaps one in three

Parsis marries a non-Parsi, the number of Parsis in each successive generation will drastically decline. Partly to stem the decline in numbers, reformists argue that children of mixed marriages should be accepted as Zoroastrians.

Even if the intermarriage issue is resolved, declining numbers will still be a concern. A large proportion of Parsis do not marry, or marry late and have few children, aspiring to complete their education and establish themselves in a profession before considering marriage. The average age of marriage for Parsis is the early thirties for men and the mid- to late twenties for women. In India's 1991 census, over 70 percent of Parsi males and over 40 percent of females in the high-fertility age group of 25 to 29 were "never married"; in the age group of 45 to 49, about 20 percent of males and 10 percent of females fell in the "never married" group. In this situation, some reformists suggest allowing children of non-Zoroastrian parents (both male and female) to be initiated into the Zoroastrian religion, but this remedy has not been seriously considered.

Parsis have been and will continue to be prominent in Indian business and society. Yet their numbers are declining. India's 2001 census counted 69,600 Parsis, including 46,600 in Mumbai and 8,000 elsewhere in the state of Maharashtra. Their numbers in India could decline to perhaps 20,000 to 30,000 by the year 2020. This decline will stem from natural reasons—larger death rates than birth rates (India's 2001 census noted a Parsi death rate of 16–18 per 1,000 persons and a birth rate of 6–7 per 1,000 persons; other statistics for Mumbai's Parsis indicate some 367 births and 936 deaths in 1995, and 300 births and 858 deaths in 2002)—and from migration. Like other Indians, a large number of younger Parsis migrate to the West. Thus, while their numbers in India may fall, their numbers in the West could increase in the twenty-first century.

Dinshaw Mistry

See also **Naoroji, Dadabhai; Tata, Jamsetji N.; Zoroastrianism**

BIBLIOGRAPHY

Boyce, Mary. *Zoroastrians: Their Religious Beliefs and Practices.* London: Routledge, 1979.

Boyce, Mary, and Frantz Grenet. *A Persian Stronghold of Zoroastrianism.* Oxford: Oxford University Press, 1977.

———. *A History of Zoroastrianism.* Leiden and New York: E. J. Brill, 1996.

Hinnells, John. *Zoroastrianism and the Parsis.* London: Ward Lock Educational, 1981.

Irani, Kaizad. "A Brief History of an Ancient Faith." *India Abroad*, 16 April 1993: 30–35.

Mehr, Farhang. *The Zoroastrian Tradition: An Introduction to the Ancient Wisdom of Zarathushtra.* Rockport, Mass.: Element Press, 1991.

Mistree, K. P. *Zoroastrianism: An Ethnic Perspective.* Mumbai: Zoroastrian Studies, 1982.

Nigosian, S. A. *The Zoroastrian Faith: Tradition and Modern Research.* Montreal: McGill-Queen's University Press, 1993.

Rivetna, Roshan. "The Zarathushti World Demographic Picture." *Fezana Journal* 17 (Winter 2004): 22–25.

Writer, Rashna. *Contemporary Zoroastrians: An Unconstructed Nation.* Lanham, Md.: University Press of America, 1993.

Zoroastrian Association of Greater New York. *The Good Life: An Introduction to the Religion of Zarathushtra.* New Rochelle, N.Y.: Zoroastrian Association of Greater New York, 1994.

PARTITION OF BENGAL. *See* **Bengal.**

PARTITION OF BRITISH INDIA. *See* **History and Historiography.**

PARVATI. *See* **Devī.**

PATALIPUTRA. *See* **Patna.**

PATANJALI, ***second-century-*B.C.*, Indian scholar and grammarian.*** There is an old Indian tradition, accepted by ancient scholars such as Bhartrihari (who lived only a few centuries after Patanjali) that Patanjali contributed to yoga through the Yoga Sūtra, to grammar by his *Mahābhāshya*, and to Āyurveda through the *Charaka Samhitā.* Modern scholarship has discounted the authorship of the *Charaka Samhitā* by Patanjali, although he may have edited it. There is much evidence that the *Mahābhāshya* and the Yoga Sūtra were written by the same person. This article will consider only the contributions of Patanjali to grammar.

It is believed that Patanjali's mother was named Gorika and that he was born in Gonarda in Kashmir. He was educated in Takshashila, and he taught in Pataliputra. From the textual references in his works, it can be inferred that he lived during the second century B.C.

Patanjali's *Mahābhāshya* is a commentary on Pānini's *Ashtādhyāyī*. Although it comments on only 1,228 of the 4,000 rules of Pānini, it remains the most authoritative text on Sanskrit grammar. The *Mahābhāshya* is a most important text for Indian history, containing over 700 brilliant quotations from the Vedic texts, epics, and the Sūtra literature.

The *Mahābhāshya* calls itself the "science of words." It has three goals: to defend Pānini where Kātyāyana's emendations appear unreasonable; to examine the rules of Pānini that were not discussed by Kātyāyana; to make additions to Pānini's rules where they cannot account for the usage in Patanjali's time.

The *Mahābhāshya* is written as a dialogue among three speakers: Purvapakshin (who raises doubts), Siddhāntaikadeshin (who refutes the objections and provides partial answers), and Siddhāntin (who gives the final verdict). The pattern of argument follows an alternating process of questions and answers until a resolution is reached. Patanjali deals with three important subjects: formation of words, determination of sense, and the relation between a word and its sense.

The *Mahābhāshya* consists of 85 chapters. In the very first chapter, Patanjali's ideas on grammar and philosophy are summarized in his approach to his commentary. He speaks of the following tasks: (1) definition and nature of *shabda*, word; (2) methods of teaching words and their meanings; (3) meaning of grammar; (4) the uses of grammar; (5) knowledge of correct words and their uses; (6) the teaching of speech sounds; (7) whether words are permanent (*nitya*) or impermanent (*karya*); and so on.

Subhash Kak

See also **Ashtādhyāyī; Pānini; Vedic Aryan India; Yoga**

BIBLIOGRAPHY

Pande, G. C., ed. *Life, Thought and Culture in India (from c. 600 BC to c. AD 300).* New Delhi: Centre for Studies in Civilizations, 2001.

Scharfe, H. *Grammatical Literature.* Wiesbaden, Germany: Otto Harrassowitz, 1977.

PATEL, MANIBEN. *See* **Patel, Sardar Vallabhbhai.**

PATEL, SARDAR VALLABHBHAI ***(1875–1950), Indian nationalist leader.*** Along with Mahatma Gandhi and Jawaharlal Nehru, Sardar Vallabhbhai Patel was one of the three foremost leaders of modern India, who inspired and awakened the nation during its arduous freedom struggle and in the precarious early years of independence. As India's first deputy prime minister, Sardar Patel unified the country and helped it survive its first harshest trials. Patel alone dealt with the complex problem of integrating over 560 princely states into India's federal union, achieving this monumental objective in little more than a year. Only three such states refused to join the Indian union initially: Jammu and Kashmir, Hyderabad, and Junagadh, the latter integrated by martial pressure on orders from Patel.

Vallabhbhai Jhaverbhai Patel was born on 31 October 1875 to a poor rural family of Nadiad in the Kheda district of Gujarat. His father, Jhaverbhai, was a small farmer with 10 to 12 acres (4–5 hectares) of land in Karamsad village, near Nadiad. Jhaverbhai was a sturdy, upright, and straightforward man of independent nature to whom the villagers flocked for advice in times of distress. Vallabhbhai inherited from his father the skill to organize and plan a political movement at the oppurtune moment.

Vallabhbhai Patel (1875–1950). Shortly after this photo was taken, Patel was imprisoned by British authorities for three years. Upon his release in 1945, he declared, "My path is clear before me. I want freedom, I am going to get it." HULTON-DEUTSCH COLLECTION / CORBIS.

Hardworking and conscientious from childhood, Vallabhbhai helped his father in the fields while still a student at the local primary school in Karamsad. For his secondary education he had to walk 9 miles (nearly 14 kilometers) from his village. He was an outspoken leader from his early school days. As a young pupil, Vallabhbhai clashed with a teacher who was in the habit of using his rod too frequently and punishing the students too harshly, imposing heavy fines on students who could barely afford to pay. Vallabhbhai was so outraged that he persuaded all the students of that class to abstain from attending. The strike went on into its third day, at which time the principal relented, sending for Vallabhbhai, recognized as the student leader, to assure him that the students would never again be punished so severely.

Unlike some of his contemporaries, especially the wealthy Motilal Nehru and his son Jawaharlal, Patel was obliged to work for his education. He was twenty-two years old when he passed his matriculation examination. Having witnessed rural poverty and suffering, he was determined to fight for justice for the poor. He decided to study law, passing the District Pleader examination at the age of twenty-five. He then launched his career at Godhara, where his elder brother, Vithalbhai, had already made a name for himself. He later moved his practice to Borsad.

Vallabhbhai Patel was an excellent criminal lawyer, and he soon became well respected in Borsad. His common sense, courage, temperament, and understanding of human psychology proved to be assets in his chosen profession. He was not content, however, with his lot as a local lawyer. He wanted to go to England to become a barrister, but his father did not have the means to allow him to fulfill that ambition. With hard work and frugal habits, Vallabhbhai was able to save enough money within three years of setting up his practice at Borsad. He then applied for admission to London's Middle Temple in 1905. He wrote to the travel agency Thomas Cooke and Sons for arranging his travel to London. By a quirk of fate, when all the formalities were nearly complete, the company's last letter containing his travel documents, addressed to him quite properly as Mr. V. J. Patel, Pleader Borsad, was delivered to his elder brother Vithalbhai, who had the same initials. Vithalbhai was himself eager to go to London, and pleaded with his younger brother to let him go, suggesting that Vallabhbhai could go later. Vallabhbhai so respected his older brother that without hesitation he acceded to his request.

Fate dealt Vallabhbhai a harsher blow soon after. His wife Zaverbai died in Cama Hospital, where she had been admitted for surgery to relieve severe intestinal pain. Vallabhbhai was in Anand defending a client accused of murder. He was in court, cross-examining a witness, when he was handed the telegram informing him of his wife's death. He opened the telegram, read the tragic news, and silently put it in his pocket. He continued his cross-examination and did not disclose the contents of the telegram until court was adjourned. His client was acquitted, but never knew the price Patel had paid to defend him. He was left with a six-year-old daughter, Maniben, and a four-year-old son, Dahyabhai. Vallabhbhai, only thirty-eight years old at the time, resolved not to marry, first for the sake of his children, and later for the liberation of his country.

After the return of his brother Vithalbhai to India, Vallabhbhai left for London in 1910 and joined the Middle Temple Inn, as London's law colleges were called. That same year, Jawaharlal Nehru, fourteen years younger than Patel, was admitted to the Inner Temple. No record has been found of Patel and Nehru meeting in London at that time, though their paths may well have crossed near London's courts.

Patel had to work hard in London due to his meager resources. He would walk daily to the library in the Middle Temple and rarely finished his reading until the library closed. His studious habits helped him to complete his course a year early, winning a first class in his finals and a prize of fifty pounds. He returned home to India elated.

After his return, Patel was offered a professorship at the Government Law School (College) by the chief justice of Bombay, but he preferred to live in Ahmedabad. Now completely Westernized, Patel built himself a reputation as a "smart young man," always well dressed, and his Ahmedabad practice prospered.

As G. V. Mavalankar, his lawyer friend, later to become speaker of the Lok Sabha (the lower house of India's Parliament), noted: "His conduct of cases always exhibited thorough mastery of facts, a proper and correct estimate of the opponents case and line of attack." He was fearless as well, and it was this quality, Mavalankar felt, that assured his success in the legal profession as well as in politics. By 1916 Patel's fees were the highest in Ahmedabad. A year later, he contested a seat and was elected to serve as a municipal councillor of Ahmedabad.

Barrister Mohandas Karamchand Gandhi had also moved back to Ahmedabad in 1915, after spending over twenty years in South Africa, where he led the struggle for the equality and human rights of Indians. Soon after establishing his first Indian ashram on the outskirts of Ahmedabad in 1915, Gandhi became a familiar figure at the Gujarat Club, dressed in his Kathiawadi turban, *kurta* (a loose shirt), and dhoti (loincloth). Vallabhbhai reportedly brushed aside any idea of listening to Gandhi speak at the Gujarat Club. He would also comment sarcastically on Gandhi's faith in the nonviolent resistance movement called *satyagraha* (hold fast to the truth) for securing liberty from British rule.

Gandhi's heroic stand on behalf of exploited indigo workers in Bihar's district of Champaran changed Patel's outlook toward the Mahatma, who soon became his political guru and remained his leader. Gandhi, when ordered to leave Bihar by the district magistrate, refused to obey the order, welcoming imprisonment, as he had in South Africa. The news of Gandhi's stand against the Raj inspired Patel and many others. Brave as Patel was, Gandhi's courage found a ready response in the Sardar, who left his highly lucrative practice and dedicated himself to India's liberation, under Gandhi's leadership. When they differed, Patel would give his frank and independent opinion but ultimately did whatever Gandhi directed. In his humorous way, Patel would say that he had locked his own brain and had given the key to Gandhi.

Patel began his own experiments in *satyagraha* from his position on Ahmedabad's Municipal Committee, inspired by what Gandhi had declared in 1917 at the first meeting of their Gujarat Political Conference: "Local Government has the key to *swarajya* ('freedom')." As chairman of Ahmedabad's Sanitary Committee, Patel remained in the city when the bubonic plague hit in 1917, refusing to move out for his personal safety. He became a familiar figure in the streets of Ahmedabad, urging workers to clean out the sewers and disinfect the plague-stricken areas.

Patel's first great *satyagraha* movement was the agrarian struggle he led in the Kheda district of Gujarat. The poor farmers of the district had pleaded with the government to lower the land revenues, as their crops had rotted due to excessive rains, requesting the suspension of revenue collection for some time. The government rejected their plea, adamantly insisting upon complete revenue collection. Gandhi asked him to take up the cause, and Patel toured every village, listening to the farmers and advising them not to pay any taxes despite the repressive measures of the government, which auctioned many houses and crops and threatened long terms of imprisonment. Most of the farmers stood firm, and the *satyagraha* continued for six months. Ultimately the government relented, and a decision was reached, with Gandhi and Patel, that only 8 percent of the land revenue was to be recovered.

On 1 August 1920 Gandhi launched his first national *satyagraha*, a nationwide boycott of British goods, promising "*swaraj* within a year." In Ahmedabad, people made huge bonfires and burned their foreign clothes. Vallabhbhai's barrister robes, imported suits, neckties, and many pairs of shoes were all consigned to those flames. Gandhi also exhorted students to boycott British schools and government colleges. He asked lawyers to withdraw from the courts, asked parents to remove their children from English schools, and urged everyone to wear *khadi*, the hand-spun and handwoven cloth that Gandhi himself wore until his death. Patel withdrew his daughter Maniben from her British school. His decision to give up his legal practice brought hardship to his family, as this was their only source of livelihood.

Patel was aware of the grave economic implications of the national boycott of British cotton cloth and other goods. On 6 December 1923 he informed his followers that "Englishmen import cotton worth five crores of rupees from India and send us textiles made from that cotton which are worth sixty crores of rupees. The money which they get from you is utilized to appoint Commissioners and Collectors, to buy guns which are utilized to keep you under their heels." He also moved a resolution in the Ahmedabad Municipality to remove government control over primary education.

After Gandhi's arrest in 1922, Patel devoted all his energies to the propagation of his political guru's ideals. In 1928 Patel electrified the country by leading the poor farmers of Bardoli in an epic struggle against increased land revenues, the famous Bardoli *satyagraha*. The farmers were incensed by the unjust increase in land taxes, and Patel went from village to village advising them to turn their dismay into action. At the same time, he advised then to remain peaceful, even when tax collectors came to attach their property. The government came down with a heavy hand on the farmers, selling their attached land and movable property. Patel appealed to the governor, calling for an impartial tribunal to examine the excessive increase in land taxes, warning that otherwise the peasants would continue their noncooperation. The government finally had to relent. The tribunal found an error in the earlier assessment and recommended an increase of 7 percent rather than the 22 percent previously assessed, thus vindicating Patel's stand. It was indeed an inspiring *satyagraha*, in which not a single life was lost and a great victory won. Thereafter, Patel was hailed as "Sardar" (village leader), the title of respect by which he came to be known throughout India.

In March 1931 Sardar Patel presided over the annual Indian National Congress session at Karachi, where he stressed the need for *purna swaraj*, or complete independence, and for Hindu-Muslim Unity. It was during his presidency that India's national flag was adopted. The flag was to have three colors in equal horizontal stripes: saffron, white, and green, from top to bottom, with Gandhi's spinning wheel in the center of the white stripe. Saffron represented courage, white peace and truth, and green faith and chivalry; the spinning wheel symbolized national unity and the hope of the masses.

Under the Government of India Act of 1935, provincial elections were held, bringing Congress candidates to power in eight of eleven provinces of British India. Sardar Patel, because of his organizational skills and integrity, supervised and coordinated all the Congress provincial ministeries.

In September 1939, when Great Britain declared war against Germany, Viceroy Linlithgow announced that India had also joined the Allies in that war, without consulting any Indian leaders. Patel was outraged at Linlithgow's announcement that "a country having one-fifth of the population of the world" could be made to join a war without its consent. He added that "Congress wants independence for . . . the whole of India." Linlithgow opted, however, for "divide and rule," frankly informing Patel that the "Raj would turn to the Muslims if Congress did not cooperate."

The years from May 1940 to December 1943 were very significant in India's struggle for freedom. The Cripps Mission reached India in March 1942, but failed to work out a political settlement. Gandhi, hitherto averse to launching a mass movement, sounded the call of "Quit India" on 8 August 1942 at the historic session of the All-India Congress Committee in Bombay. He declared as his mantra "do or die"—either India must win its freedom or die in the attempt. Though Nehru had reservations about launching the movement, Sardar Patel supported Gandhi completely and told his countrymen that it would be better to die than to be "completely ruined." He advised railway and postal employees, government servants, and police to leave their jobs and thus not allow the machinery of the government to function. Then the "Quit India" slogan would become a reality.

Sardar Patel was arrested and imprisoned in Ahmednagar Fort from 1942 until April 1945 and was subsequently held in Yeravade prison in Poona until June 1945. On his release, Patel returned to active political life, declaring "I want freedom."

After the end of World War II, national elections in United Kingdom brought the Labour Party to power, with Clement Attlee replacing Winston Churchill as prime minister. The Labour goverment ordered India's general elections for September 1945, testing the relative strength of India's political parties. Sardar Patel resolved to run in the election, which resulted in a sweeping victory for the Congress Party, which won most of the general seats, while the Muslim League won an overwhelming majority of separate seats reserved for Muslims. The British government then decided to send three Cabinet ministers, among them Stafford Cripps, to negotiate a final settlement for the transfer of British power to a single Indian government, if possible. The Cabinet Mission proposal for a Constituent Assembly and an interim government was favored by Sardar Patel, who felt that the Muslim League would then lose its power to veto Congress legislation, and the Indian states would have to enter into treaties with the interim government. He also insisted that the single Constituent Assembly would soon draft a constitution for a unified India, which the British government would have to accept.

The Muslim League also accepted the interim government, despite their demand for a separate nation of Pakistan. However, Patel's apprehension that the Muslim League's entry into the interim government was to get a foothold to fight for Pakistan proved correct, as the violence in the Noakhali district of West Bengal, under Chief Minister H. S. Suhrawardy of the Muslim League, seemed to indicate. Soon after M.A. Jinnah called for "direct action" to help propagate his theory of "two nations," riots in Calcutta left Hindu temples destroyed, some three hundred Hindus murdered, and many others converted to Islam. There was immediate retaliation by Hindus in Bihar, where seven hundred Muslims were massacred. Despite Gandhi's strong opposition, both Nehru and Patel agreed to India's partition, hoping to free the country from more violent and disruptive politics by the Muslim League. Patel told Gandhi, that it was a question of civil war or partition. He viewed the loss of Pakistan as "like our agreeing to a have a diseased limb shorn off so that the remaining part may live in sound condition." Sardar Patel felt satisfied, moreover, that "we have 80 percent of the country with us which is a compact unit with great potentialities." He was not prepared for the holocaust that followed in the wake of partition. He had believed that it would be an amicable division and did not expect bloodshed, nor did Nehru.

Sardar Patel became the home minister in British India's interim government, and after 15 August 1947, when India became an independent nation, he was also appointed Nehru's deputy prime minister. In addition to remaining in charge of the Home Ministry, he was also put in charge of the Ministry of Information and Broadcasting. He continued to serve as minister of the States, a most difficult job, which he held from 5 July 1947. Sardar Patel, for all practical purposes, was supreme in all the departments he directed, fully trusted by Prime Minister Nehru to act as he saw fit, during the painful and trouble-filled first three years of India's independence. In many ways, Sardar Patel was the true architect of a viable Indian state, which without his steady control might not have survived the violence, uncertainty, disorder, and terror that followed partition.

It was indeed remarkable that the Sardar managed to achieve the peaceful merger of 562 princely states, comprising one-third of the total area of India, into the Indian union within the short span of less than two years. Within two years, with the exception of Hyderabad, Junagadh, and Kashmir, all the princely states contiguous to India acceded to the Indian union. Junagadh was integrated, with some support by the Indian army, by the people of the state, who voted overwhelmingly to join the Indian union. In Hyderabad, the Sardar felt he had no alternative but to order his troops to take over Hyderabad by force after other avenues had failed to convince the nizam to join India. Jammu and Kashmir was a strategic state with common borders with Pakistan as well as India, and the Sardar and Pandit Nehru were both determined that it should accede to India. Though Jammu and Kashmir should have been under Sardar's ministry of states, Prime Minister Nehru insisted on taking personal charge of Kashmir, which he always called his "ancestral home," as his great-grandparents had been born there.

Patel was eager for India to take its proper place as a world power by raising its international status and military strength. He disagreed with Gandhi's opposition to atomic energy and its use, if necessary, to protect India from any attacks. Sardar Patel also wanted a strong central government and a modern army, navy, and air force, ultimately subordinate, however, to the civil central government. He felt that India's industrial development was absolutely essential for the production of all necessary military matériel for a strong modern army. He therefore insisted on accelerating the production of Indian iron and steel, cement, and other essential articles both for the civil population and for defense. He was, however, against the nationalization of industries, though he died before Nehru's Five-Year Plans were fully launched.

Partition had also divided British India's civil service, comprising some 1,500 officers, who had kept India's administration together; all the British and Muslim officers had left before mid-August 1947. In April 1948 Sardar Patel informed Nehru that he had established two new services to take the place of the Indian civil service and the Indian police: the Indian Administrative Service (IAS) and the Indian Police Service, for which he drafted special recruitment, discipline, and control rules. Patel was determined that IAS officers set high standards of discipline, urging probationers "to maintain the utmost impartiality and inoorrupubility of administration." They should "not take part in politics" and keep in view "the achievement of the highest standard of integrity."

While the unification of the states was succesfully achieved, the evacuation and rehabilitation of refugees, another of Patel's urgent postpartition responsibilities, proved difficult to accomplish. He attempted to give all help and protection to Muslims migrating to Pakistan. To India's Muslim minority, Patel said, "as a friend of Muslims . . . it is the duty of a good friend to speak frankly. It is your duty now to sail in the same boat and sink [or] swim together." Strong Hindu though he was, Patel was a stronger nationalist, insisting that every Muslim who chose to stay in India must first resolve to remain a loyal Indian. Patel invited every Indian citizen of every province to help him in the task of safe rehabilitation of all Hindu and Sikh refugees from Pakistan. He worked for a safe, prosperous, united India until his death on 15 December 1950. The entire nation mourned his death and the loss of his courageous leadership.

P. N. Chopra
Prabha Chopra

See also **Congress Party; Gandhi, Mahatma M. K.; Nehru, Jawaharlal; Princely States**

BIBLIOGRAPHY

Chopra, P. N. *The Sardar of India*. New Delhi: Allied Publishers, 1995.

Chopra, P. N., and Prabha Chopra, eds. *The Collected Works of Sardar Patel*. 15 vols. New Delhi: Konark Publishers, 1990–1999.

———. *The Inside Story of Sardar Patel Manibeh Patel's Diary (1936–1950)*. New Delhi: Vision Books, 2001.

———. *Sardar Patel: Kashmir and Hyderabad*. New Delhi: Konark Publishers, 2002.

———. *Sardar Patel, Nehru, Gandhi, and Subhas Bose*. New Delhi: Konark Publishers, 2003.

Gandhi, Raj Mohan. *Patel: A Life*. Ahmedabad: Navjivan Publishing House, 1990.

Kulkarni, V. B. *The Indian Triumvirate: A Political Biography of Gandhi, Patel, Nehru*. Mumbai: Bhartiya Vidya Bhavan, 1969.

Shankar, V., ed. *Sardar Patel: Select Correspondence, 1945–1950*, vols. I–II. Ahmedabad: Navajivan Press, 1976.

PATNA Patna (Pataliputra), the capital of Bihar state, is a historic city located at the confluence of three rivers, the Ganga, the Gandak, and the Sone. The Ganga flows all along its northern boundary. The area in the south is generally low-lying and as such is prone to floods from the rivers Punpun and Sone. The city has a mean elevation of 173 feet (53 m) above sea level and is situated at 28°37′ north latitude and 85°10′ east longitude. It has been a center of learning, religion, and art since time immemorial. Hinduism, Buddhism, Jainism, and Sikhism are deeply connected to this city. It is one of the longest and the narrowest among the largest cities of the country, with a population of over a million and a half spread over an area of about 30 square miles (77.7 sq. km).

The ancient city of Pataliputra was a mere village—Pataligram—in the time of the Buddha in the sixth century B.C. However, Ajatasatru realized its great strategic value for the growing kingdom of Magadha, facing the rival Licchavis republic of Vaisali on the northern bank (other side) of the Ganga, and erected a military outpost there. The natural advantage of the site made it commercially important and also helped its growth. The Magadhan king Udai transferred his capital from Rajgriha to Pataliputra. It remained the imperial capital under the Nandas, the Mauryas, and the Guptas. It was a prosperous and populous city when Megasthenes, the Greek ambassador to the court of Chandragupta Maurya, visited it twice.

Pataliputra acquired the status of a capital city during the reign of Emperor Ashoka (ruled c. 268–231 B.C.). However, it later faced Indo-Greek invasion, and the city was sacked in A.D. 185. But its glory again revived under the Guptas. Fahsien, the Chinese pilgrim who studied there for three years during the reign of Chandragupta I in the early fifth century A.D., not only considered it a famous center of learning but also the most beautiful and largest city of the world. The city again suffered destruction, and when Hsieun Tsang visited the city in A.D. 637, it had become desolate and deserted.

Pataliputra emerged from its political obscurity when Sher Shah, the great Pathan ruler, built a fort there in 1541, transferred the provincial capital from Bihar Sharif, and gave it the new name of Patna. It became an important commercial center during the seventeenth century. Mughal emperors further extended the city in 1704. Prince Azimusshan, the grandson of Aurangzeb, the new governor (*subedar*) of Bihar, renamed Patna as Azimabad. With the coming of the Europeans, the city had expanded beyond its fortified walls and became famous in Southeast Asia as a source of sugar and saltpeter. The importance of Patna was further enhanced when it was made the capital of the newly created province of Bihar in 1912. It also contributed significantly to India's freedom struggle against British imperial rule. More recently, Jaya Prakash (J. P) Narayan launched his "Total Revolution" against corruption from Patna in 1974.

Yuvaraj Prasad

BIBLIOGRAPHY

Ahmad, Qeyamuddin, ed. *Patna through the Ages: Glimpses of History, Society, and Economy.* Patna: Janaki Prakashan, 1988.

Salvi Patola Weavers. Here, a 1992 photograph of members of the Salvi community in Patan who continue to weave the rare double *ikat* fabric. The Salvi are one of the few remaining communities of *patola* weavers in India: Their spindles of silk thread rest in the foreground. LINDSAY HUBBARD / CORBIS.

PATOLA One of the most complex techniques for creating multicolored patterning is the double *ikat*, in which warp and weft are tied and dyed in three to four colors, then woven so that the weft pattern is synchronized perfectly with the warp. There are only two countries where double *ikat* is woven: India and Indonesia. The finest double *ikat* is woven in Patan, Gujarat, by the Salvi community and is known as Patan *patola;* the others are the Vachitrapuri *saktapar* pattern in Orissa, known as *bandha*, and rare examples of Tilia *Rumal* in Andhra Pradesh. In Indonesia it appears as the sacred *gringsing*, woven in Tenganan in Bali.

From a study of ancient murals, it may be concluded that *ikat* was practiced throughout southern India. Sarongs with *ikat* technique were found in the Ajanta cave murals (6th–7th century A.D.) and later noted in the temple murals of Kerala. The murals of Mattancheri Palace in Cochin (16th century) depict *patola*. Literary references to double *ikat* do not occur prior to the fourteenth century, when Ibn Batuta mentions that Sultan Ala'-ud-Din Muhammad Khalji (r. 1296–1326) received a *patola* from Deogiri. Malayan Annals refer to *cendai*, a Malayan word for Indian *patola* from an earlier date. The oral tradition of the Salvis implies that the technique had evolved in the Deccan. The Salvis were Jains originally belonging to the Digambara sect, which dominated in southern India. They traveled with their family Trithankara. After moving to Patan they converted to the Swetambara tradition and covered the Trithankara with a brass sheet. Another factor that supports this assumption is that Patan is the only center in north India where *ikat* was practiced, while single *ikat* was widely used throughout the Deccan, specially for ritual purposes.

Technique

The complex technique of tying is carried out by masters by first degumming the silk and preparing the warp thread. The warp is divided into bunches, then stretched in preparation for tying. A grid is prepared, using coal dust, and the border and cross border are demarcated. The outline of the pattern is tied down, along with those areas that are to be dyed a specific color. First the lightest color, generally yellow, is dyed. The areas that are to remain yellow and green are tied and those areas that are to be blue are opened and immersed in blue dye. The ties in areas that are to be green are opened when the threads are dyed with blue. In fact, when a pure color is to be obtained without any hues of the previous dye, the original ties are opened. Using a highly complex system of tying, dyeing, reopening, dyeing, and retying, the complete design is achieved.

After completing the dyeing of the warp and weft, the warp is stretched on the loom, where the warp beam is placed at an angle. The warp is approximately 49 to 59 feet (15 to 18 m) in length for weaving three saris. The tie-dyed weft is reeled into bobbins and placed in the shuttle. The fabric is a simple plain weave; two people, often husband and wife, sit and weave the sari. The weft thread is thrown across, and the weavers check both ends to see that the threads have matched the end border of colored stripes, as it is not possible to create patterns at the end. Further adjustments of the weft are made with a long needle, so that it lies exactly on the matching color of the warp. The weavers' aim is to create as perfect a line as possible and to prevent blurring of the outline. The weavers of Patan are known for their meticulous precision.

Ceremonial Use

The use of *patola* was essential in the ceremonies of well-to-do communities, supposedly providing magical powers of protection against evil. Except for Surat's Bora community, it was not used by the bride, but was worn by the mother of the bride at the most important part of the wedding, *kanya-dan* (bestowing of the virgin). *Patola* was worn by an expectant mother at the *simanth* ceremony, for the seventh month of pregnancy, to protect the mother and the unborn child. In some cases, the bridegroom wore a sash of *patola* as protection against the evil eye.

The *patola* was never discarded. Worn-out saris were used to make a quilted wrapper for a newborn baby; rags of old *patola* were tucked into the cradle for protection. The lamp wick for the newborn baby was made from old pieces of *patola*, so that the child's vision would be pure.

The use of *patola* in India outside Gujarat is found only in Kerala. Known as *virali pattu*, it was used by priests in the worship of the Mother Goddess Badrakali, and it was painted as a powerful symbol on temple murals, as well as at Cochin's Mattancheri palace. Cochin, the entrepôt of India's spice trade, was the center from which *patola*s traveled to Southeast Asia, where they became an important part of ceremonies and rituals. Known in Malaysia and Java as *cendai*, it was an essential part of the dress of royal couples and was used as hangings for rituals and as canopies for processions. An extraordinary *patola* made for the Indonesian market has a repeat of two pairs of juxtaposed large elephants, with foot soldiers, horseback riders, lions, and chariot. In the covered howdah (seat), the elephant's *mahout* (driver) is seated in the front, holding an *ankush*, or elephant ear hook. Behind him is the seated king with a flower in his hand and possibly a *huqa* (smoking pipe), a typical portrayal of royalty. These ceremonial cloths, which were found at Toraja, have been carbon-dated to the fifteenth or sixteenth century.

A popular pattern for export was a circle of lotus flowers, buds, and leaves. Known in Gujarat as *chabardi bhat* (basket design), it was associated with fertility and was used in the wedding ceremony. This pattern was copied in single *ikat* and *batik* throughout Indonesia. *Patola*s in Southeast Asia were considered the "wealth" of women. In some areas, particularly in Sumba, the burial of a head of a family could take place only when the body was covered with a number of *patola*s.

The Patan *patola* has a market as a speciality sari throughout India. Three families of Salvis continue this work, which remains distinctive; though the *ikat* weavers of Poochampalli imitate the Patan *patola*, to the discerning viewer their work remains a pale copy of the original.

Jasleen Dhamija

See also **Textiles: Early Painted and Printed**

BIBLIOGRAPHY

Bühler, Alfred. "Patola Influences in South East Asia." *Journal of Indian Textile History* 4 (1959): 1–46.

Bühler, Alfred, and Eberhard Fischer. *The Patola of Gujarat: Double Ikat in India*. Basle: Krebs, 1979.

De Bone, Mary Golden. "Patolu and Its Technique." *Textile Museum Journal* 4, no. 3 (1976).

Desai, Chelna. *Ikat Textiles of India*. San Francisco: Chronicle Books, 1988.

Dhamija, Jasleen. *Indian Folk Arts and Crafts*. New Delhi: National Book Trust, 1970.

———. *Woven Magic*. Jakarta: Dina Rakyat, 2002.

Gulati, A. N. *The Patolu of Gujarat*. Mumbai: Museums Association of India, 1951.

Guy, John. "Sarasa and Patola: Indian Textiles in Indonesia." *Orientations* 20, no. 1 (1989).

Ibn Batuta. *Travels in Asia and Africa, 1325–1354*. Translated by H. A. R. Gibb. 1929. Reprint, New York: A. M. Kelley, 1969.

Maxwell, Robyn. *Textiles of South East Asia: Tradition, Trade, and Transformation*. New York: Oxford University Press, 1990.

Nambiar, Balan, and Eberhard Fischer. "Patola/Virali Pattu from Gujarat to Kerala: New Information on Double *Ikat* Textiles in South India." *Asialische Studien, Zeitschrift der schweizerischen Gesellschaft fur Asiakunde* 41 (1987).

PAUL, K. T. ***(1876–1931), cofounder of the National Missionary Society (1905).*** Kanakarayan Tiruselvam Paul was the first Christian statesman in India. Born in Salem, Tamil Nadu, of Christian parents, he studied in the London Mission High School, where one of his friends was Chakravarti Rajagopalachari, who became South India's greatest nationalist leader. In 1892 K. T. went to Madras Christian College; after graduating, he took an appointment with the Government Secretariat, studying law at night.

In December 1905 K. T. Paul and V. S. Azariah established the National Missionary Society, the first indigenous missionary society, organized to represent all Protestant denominations Azariah was elected general secretary and Paul the treasurer. Paul also contributed to the formation in 1908 of the South India United Church, a union of Presbyterian and Congregational churches. He longed for a truly Indian church.

In 1912 Paul accepted an invitation to become a national secretary of the Young Men's Christian Association (YMCA). Extensive travel on behalf of the YMCA and the National Missionary Society made Paul deeply conscious of the economic plight of rural Christians. In 1905 the government had passed the Cooperative Securities Act, with the aim of providing credit for poor village farmers. K. T. Paul realized that the most sensible way to liberate village Christians and others from poverty was to extend the work and effectiveness of Cooperative Credit Societies.

Paul's plan was to foster habits of prudence and thrift, to increase the earning power of villagers, to enrich the pleasure of village social life by means of festivals and excursions, and to provide facilities for healthy and cheap Indian sports and gymnastics. To help finance his dream, Paul set up a Christian Central Cooperative Bank in 1916; its object was to provide loans for Christians and the rural poor. In the 1920s Paul coined the phrase "rural reconstruction."

K. T. Paul was involved in India's nationalist movement from its earliest phase, following the lead of Gopal Krishna Gokhale and Mahatma Gandhi. He often met with Viceroy Lord Irwin, an ardent Christian. He deeply regretted the Christian community's aloofness from the freedom struggle. In March 1920 he resigned his offices with the National Missionary Society and the YMCA to allow himself the freedom to speak on matters of political concern. He was invited to the first Round Table Conference held in London, representing Indian Christians.

The conference began on 12 November 1930, but Paul was generally exasperated over the outcome, and the stress proved too much for him. He returned to India early, only to arrive in Salem completely broken in health. He died on Saturday, 11 April 1931, aged fifty five. Mahatma Gandhi wrote, "I had the privilege of knowing K. T. Paul. The nearer I came to him the more I respected him." It would always be remembered to his credit, Gandhi went on, "that he stoutly opposed the demand for any special concessions for Indian Christians in the forthcoming constitution, believing . . . that character and merit would always command not only proper treatment, but respectful attention" (Eddy, p. 175).

Graham Houghton

BIBLIOGRAPHY

Eddy, Sherwood. *Pathfinders of the World Missionary Crusade.* New York: Abingdon-Cokesbury, 1945.

"Indian Christian Leadership." *Harvest Field,* March 1913: 94–104.

Popley, Herbert A. *K. T. Paul.* 1938. Reprint, Chennai: Christian Literature Society, 1987.

PENSION FUNDS AND SOCIAL SECURITY

India does not have a comprehensive old-age income security system. The vast majority of Indians continue to rely on support from their children as their main income in old age. Two important mandatory, albeit narrow, pension systems exist, however: the civil servants' defined benefit pension and the organized sector system run by the Employee Provident Fund Organisation (EPFO), which is an arm of the Ministry of Labour.

Traditional Civil Servants' Pension

The phrase "traditional civil servants pension" (TCSP) connotes the pension program that existed for employees of the central government who were recruited prior to January 2004. With small variations, the TCSP applies to most employees of state governments as well. The TCSP for central government employees is administered by the Department of Pensions and Personnel Welfare. The TCSP is a defined benefit pension. It was an integral part of the employment contract for government employees. There is a minimum requirement of ten years of service before a worker is entitled to this pension. There is no attempt at having contributions or building up pension assets—in other words, it is unfunded. The benefit promised by the TCSP is a pension that is roughly half of the wage level of the last ten months of employment. The benefit rate is computed as 1/60 for each year of service, subject to a cap of a 50 percent benefit rate. In case of death after retirement, the spouse gets the full pension for seven years, after which the benefit rate drops to 30 percent until the death of the spouse.

There is a commutation provision, under which the pensioner can choose to forgo up to 40 percent of the pension payout for fifteen years, taking instead a lump sum. The TCSP is indexed to wages. There is a "one rank, one wage" principle, whereby all retired persons of a certain rank get the same pension, steadily revised to reflect growth in wages. Hence, the growth in pension payout in old age is typically higher than inflation.

The standard information released as part of the budgeting process only reveals information for the flow of annual pension payouts by both the central government and the states. Estimates of unfunded liabilities, that is, the implied pension debt, associated with workers and pensions under the TCSP are not computed or disseminated by the government. Over the period from 1987–1988 to 2003–2004, while nominal gross domestic product (GDP) grew by a compound rate of 14.5 percent, central pension payments grew at a compound rate of 17.8 percent and state pension payments grew at a compound rate of 21 percent. These magnitudes—with a fast-growing expense that is already at 1.64 percent of GDP—highlight the fiscal ramifications of pension reforms.

The Employee Provident Fund Organisation

The EPFO runs two programs: the Employee Provident Fund (EPF) and the Employee Pension Scheme (EPS). Both plans are mandatory for workers earning below 6,500 rupees a month, in establishments with over 20 workers in 177 defined industries. As of 31 March 2003, there were 344,508 such establishments, and 39.5 million members.

The EPF is an individual account contribution system, using a contribution rate of 16 percent. The flow of contributions in 2002–2003 was 114 billion rupees, and the stock of assets was 1.03 trillion rupees. There are several provisions for premature withdrawal of balances under EPF, which are routinely exploited by most members, leading to small balances at the time of retirement and consequently limited old-age income security.

The EPS is a defined benefit system, based on a contribution rate of 8.33 percent. The government contributes an additional 1.16 percent. EPS was created in 1995, and it applies only to workers who entered the labor force after 1995. In 2002–2003, the flow of contributions that came into EPS was 48 billion rupees, and the stock of assets was 450 billion rupees. The EPS provides a defined benefit at a rate of 1/70 of the salary drawn in the last twelve months preceding the date of exit, for each year of service, subject to a maximum of 50 percent. Upon death, the EPS provides a pension to the spouse for life or until remarriage.

Establishments covered under the EPF can seek an exemption from the EPFO for fund management and set up their own self-administered fund. These "exempt funds" are required to use identical investment regulations to those of the EPFO. There were 341,944 establishments with exempt funds as of March 2003, covering 3.75 million members.

Other Elements of the Pension System

"Gratuity" is a mandatory lump sum benefit, up to a maximum limit of 350,000 rupees, paid to the employee at the time of exit, under the Payment of Gratuity Act 1972. It is applicable to establishments with 10 or more people. The National Old Age Pension Scheme is a part of the National Social Assistance Program, which came into effect 15 August 1995. It is funded by the central government but administered by the state governments. It pays a benefit of 75 rupees per month to "destitutes" above the age of 65.

The most basic problem of India's pension plans is that of coverage. Two systems, the TCSP and the EPFO, cover just 11 percent of the workforce. Hence, the majority of the workforce has no formal pension system. In the case of the TCSP, the major problem has been that of fiscal stress. The pension payout of the central government and states has risen at a compound average annual growth rate of 20 percent over the period from 1987 to 2004. The TCSP was designed in a world where most workers who retired at age sixty were likely to be dead by seventy. The value of the annuity embedded in the TCSP has gone up dramatically, owing to the elongation of mortality in recent decades. The fiscal stress has been particularly acute at the state level. Some states are reported to have delayed pension payments. In 2003 the state of Tamil Nadu chose to cut pension benefits by reversing recent increases in pensions that followed as a consequence of wage hikes to existing employees.

The EPFO has several shortcomings that undermine its service provision, financial stability, and hence effectiveness as a pension system. Its accounting systems and policies have certain weaknesses. The lack of computerized databases spanning information from the entire country has led to difficulties in reconciliation. More importantly, the valuation framework used is one in which all bonds are valued at 100 rupees, regardless of market price. The "interest rate" on EPF that is announced every year is the average coupon rate on the bond portfolio. It is announced at the start of the year, which necessitates a difficult effort in forecasting interest rates during the year. There is an explicit subsidy in the form of assets of roughly 0.5 trillion rupees, which have been deposited with the government at an above-market rate of return.

A difficulty that runs across both the TCSP and the programs of the EPFO is that of taxation. Fiscal subsidies underlie EPFO, and these subsidies constitute a regressive transfer from the exchequer to the members of the EPFO, who are likely to fall into the top quartile by income. Further, even among EPFO customers, recently released distributional data has shown that only 7 percent of the accounts have an account balance of above 50,000 rupees, so that the bulk of the subsidy that EPFO members are enjoying is being captured by the richest among them.

Recent Initiatives in Reforms

Meeting the challenges of old-age poverty requires fresh efforts in many areas. Modern information technology needs to be implemented across the country, in order to deliver high quality customer service with low administrative costs. Members need portability that enables migration across multiple geographical locations, across different employers, and across multiple fund managers. Modern investment regulation needs to be in place, so that professional pension fund managers can produce the best risk/reward combinations for their members, using globally diversified portfolios and giving members the choice of exposing themselves to systematic risk factors. Clear separation is required between policy making, regulation, and service provision.

In recent years, EPFO has embarked on efforts to introduce computer technology and improve customer service. At the same time, there has been no progress in terms of the deeper policy problems. While there has been considerable public criticism and awareness of the deficiencies, significant progress in terms of EPFO reforms is likely to be infeasible without broad-based support in Parliament.

On the other hand, major progress has been made in recent years in civil servants' pensions and the problem of extending coverage into the unorganized sector. This progress flowed mainly from the recommendations of the Old Age Social and Income Security Committee, chaired by S. A. Dave, which was constituted by the Ministry of Social Justice in 1999. Through a multiyear process of debate and discussion, decisions have been made on the introduction of a New Pension System (NPS). The key elements of the NPS include the following: it will be an individual account system with defined contributions; there will be competition between multiple pension fund managers; and each pension fund manager will offer roughly three standardized products. The three product types will differ in their exposure to equity. Individuals will be free to spread their pension wealth among all the available products. The selection of pension fund managers is likely to be based on an auction, focusing on the sum of fees and expenses.

There will be a centralized record-keeping agency, which will give customers a single account balance statement covering all products in the system. The agency will also reduce transactions costs. As befits a pension system, withdrawals prior to age sixty will be disallowed. There will be a network of banks, post offices, and other "points of presence" across the country, where consumers will be able to access the pension system. The focus of the NPS is on building pension wealth. Upon retirement, it is expected that there will be a minimum mandatory annuitization of 40 percent of terminal pension assets.

All new recruits into the central government (excluding the armed forces) who joined after 1 January 2004 have been placed in the NPS, using a contribution rate of 20 percent. Many states have also chosen to join the NPS. Once the institutional structure stabilizes, it will be opened to voluntary participation by anyone in the country. A new regulatory agency, the Pension Fund Regulatory and Development Agency (PFRDA), is expected to come into existence once suitable legislation is passed by Parliament. PFRDA will closely coordinate its activities with other modern Indian financial regulators.

Ajay Shah
Urjit R. Patel

See also **Economic Development, Importance of Institutions in and Social Aspects of; Economy since the 1991 Economic Reforms**

BIBLIOGRAPHY

Asher, Mukul G. "Case for a Provident and Pension Funds Authority." *Economic and Political Weekly* 37, no. 8 (2002): 688–689.

Bordia, Anand, and Gautam Bhardwaj, eds. "Rethinking Pension Provision for India." New Delhi: Tata McGraw Hill, 2003.

Patel, Urjit R. "Aspects of Pension Fund Reform: Lessons for India." *Economic and Political Weekly* 32, no. 38 (1997): 2395–2402.

Srinivas, P. S., and Susan Thomas. "Institutional Mechanisms in Pension Fund Management: Lessons from Three Indian Case Studies." *Economic and Political Weekly* 38, no. 8 (2003): 706–719.

PESHWAI AND PENTARCHY The power and polity that Shivaji established flourished far beyond the limits of his *swarajya* into North India under the brilliant *peshwa*s, whose office was invested with tremendous authority and made hereditary by Shivaji's grandson, Shahu. The period of the expansion of Maratha power under successive *peshwa*s, with Pune as the seat of their power for nearly a century (1713–1818), is often called the Peshwai. There were two important political "arrangements" that helped the extension of Maratha polity, which exercised tremendous authority over the ruins of the fast declining Mughal empire.

During that period, the *peshwa*s encouraged and supported some of their sirdars, notably the Shindes centered in Gwalior, Holkars in Indore, Gaikwads in Baroda, and Bhosles in Nagpur, to establish and maintain their own extensive semiautonomous fiefdoms, constituting, together with the *peshwa*, a pentarchy under the overall control of the *peshwa*s. The second "arrangement" was between the *peshwa*s and the *chhatrapati*s, or kings, of Shivajis's line in Satara: Shahu and his successors. It resembled the position of the hereditary shogun vis-à-vis the Japanese emperor, with separate capitals for the Maratha king and the *peshwa*, with the latter receiving the robes of investiture from the king. Although the *peshwa*s lived virtually like kings in Pune with most of the royal accoutrements, they displayed the respect owed to their royal masters when visiting Satara. There, before entering the capital, the *peshwa* stopped the marching strains of his troops, dismounted from his elephant, and walked to the *chhatrapati*'s palace, sitting on an ordinary low *baithak* (seat) in his presence. All grants of titles, honors, and lands to the sirdars were made on the recommendation of the *peshwa* but with the knowledge and seal of the *chhatrapati*. All treaties and important documents were explained, in most cases, personally by the *peshwa* to the *chhatrapat*i before the latter's seal was affixed to make them final and legal documents.

The founder of the line of the *peshwa*s was Balaji Vishvanath (r. 1713–1720), a Chitpavan Brahman who came from the Bhat family of Shrivardhan in Konkan. The crucial help he gave Shahu in rallying important sirdars and administrators from Tarabai's camp dramatically strengthened Shahu's position, and Shahu showed his appreciation by appointing Balaji his *peshwa* (prime minister). Balaji expanded his power far beyond the territorial limits of Shivaji's kingdom or that of his successors, far beyond Maharashtra, the home of the Marathas, to the capital of the Mughal empire in Delhi, where instability and weakness among Aurangzeb's successors afforded opportunities for someone with ambition and ability. In 1719 Peshwa Balaji Vishvanath marched on Delhi and secured not only Shahu's family from Mughal captivity but, importantly for the future of the Maratha polity, the Mughal court's recognition of the Maratha *swarajya* and additional *sanad*s (deeds)—*chauthai* and *sardeshmukh* (the rights, respectively, to collect and keep 25 percent and 10 percent of the revenues)—over six *subha*s (provinces) of the Deccan.

The origin of the *peshwa*'s authority lay in two *yadya* (plural for *yadi*), or lists drawn up in a handwritten document by Shahu himself in 1714, stipulating the duties and obligations of the *peshwa* and making that office hereditary in the family of Balaji Vishvanath. After the childless Shahu's death in 1749, Ramaraja, then twenty-five years old, from the Kolhapur branch of the Bhosle family, was adopted and crowned as *chhatrapati* in the following year. Not trained to be a king and having little or no administrative abilities, he readily signed a second *yadi*, most likely drawn up by Peshwa Balaji Baji Rao, giving the *peshwa*s additional authority to act on behalf of the *chhatrapati* in all matters. The new *yadi* also validated the total authority of the *peshwa* over all Maratha domains.

Baji Rao I (r. 1720–1740)

Balaji Vishvanath's elder son, Baji Rao I, broke the traditional limits of the Bhosle kingdom as he adopted a forward policy that would extend the Maratha dominion into the north. In 1734 he captured the Malwa territory, and in 1739 his brother Chimnaji drove out the Portuguese from almost all their possessions in the northern Konkan, notably Salsette and Bassein. Baji Rao himself attacked the nizam of Hyderabad four times because he would not let the *peshwa*s collect the *chauthai-sardeshmukhi*, which were the *peshwa*'s due under the terms of the *sanad*s (deeds) from the Mughal emperor. At the time of Baji Rao's early death on 27 April 1740, the *peshwa*'s writ ran over all of Maharashtra and over large chunks of territory in central and northern India, through his new, loyal Maratha sirdars. Later, they would develop into a pentarchy: Gujarat under the Gaikwads of Baroda; Shindes (Scindia) in Gwalior; Holkars in Indore; and Bhosles in Nagpur—all under the overall authority of the *peshwa* or his council in Pune.

Balaji Baji Rao (r. 1740–1761)

Known as Nanasaheb Peshwa, Balaji Baji Rao succeeded Baji Rao I. He had two brothers, Raghunath Rao, who later betrayed the Marathas and joined hands with the British, and Janardan, who died in his early youth. Nanasaheb was talented in the arts of war, diplomacy, and administration. Soon after assuming the position of *peshwa*, he spent a year improving the civil administration of Pune. The period from 1741 to 1745 was of comparative calm in the Deccan, which enabled Nanasaheb to reorganize agriculture and introduce effective measures for protecting the villagers and their produce. There was a general improvement in Maharashtra in terms of revenue collection, services, and law and order. A major flaw in

Nanasaheb's policies was the destruction in 1756 of the Maratha navy, so farsightedly built by Shivaji under the Angres. Because Tulaji Angre would not toe his line, Nanasaheb accepted the help of the British East India Company in Bombay to attack the Angre navy and destroy it, thus leaving the field open for the English to establish their maritime supremacy on the west coast.

In 1761 the Marathas were dismally defeated at the third battle of Panipat against Shah Abdali, an invader from Afghanistan. He raided the Mughal capital, Delhi, several times in the 1750s. To save his capital, the effete Mughal emperor asked his vizier, Safdarjung, to sign an agreement (called the Ahmednama) with the Marathas, whereby the *peshwa* agreed to defend the Mughal emperor against his domestic and foreign foes. The nizam of Hyderabad, not too happy with the Ahmednama and the prominence it gave the Marathas, attacked them. The *peshwa* defeated the nizam's forces at Sindkhed in 1757 and Udgir in 1760. The Marathas also successfully drove out Abdali's forces from the Punjab, raising their own flag at Attock in 1756. When Abdali heard the news, he led a major force, which would end in challenging the very large force sent by Peshwa Nanasaheb under his own brother Sadashiv Rao and son Vishwas Rao.

On 14 January 1761 the third Battle of Panipat took place, which dealt a major setback to the Marathas in the north. They lost more than 100,000 men and dozens of important sirdars in the battle, in addition to elephants and countless horses, heavy equipment, and treasure. Both Sadashiv Rao and Vishwas Rao died in the battle. The news shattered Nanasaheb, who died shortly afterward on 23 June 1761. Panipat drew a dividing line in the fortunes of the Marathas; Nanasaheb's reign marked the highest and the lowest points of Maratha power.

Madhav Rao I (r. 1761–1772)

The second son of Nanasaheb and his wife Gopikabai, Madhav Rao became the *peshwa* because his elder brother, Vishwas Rao, lost his life at Panipat. This fourth *peshwa* was only sixteen years old and held office for only eleven years, but he was notable for reestablishing Maratha authority on almost all the lands that had been theirs before 1761.

Historians give much credit for the childhood education of Madhav Rao to his mother Gopikabai, who continued to guide him, particularly in handling his uncle Ragunath Rao. When Madhav Rao assumed the reins of power, he was besieged by many enemies, who wanted to take advantage of the post-Panipat weakness of the Marathas, whose power in the north had been devastated by loss of so many important members of prestigious sirdar families. Nearer home, the nizam took advantage of the dissensions within the *peshwa* household, as the *peshwa's* warrior-uncle Raghunath Rao, in the early years of Madhav Rao's rule, did not hesitate to use the nizam's assistance to buttress his own ambitions. Very soon, Madhav Rao divided the work of dealing with the regime's external enemies: he took on the nizam and Hyder Ali himself, sending his recalcitrant uncle, Raghunath Rao, to the distant north to deal with the Bundelas, Jats, and Rohillas, who had challenged Maratha positions there. When the nizam, with the help of some Maratha dissenters, attacked Pune in 1763, young Madhav Rao led his regular as well as guerrilla forces against Hyderabad, looted the treasury there, and faced the divided forces of the nizam at Rakshasbhuvan on the banks of the Godavari, inflicting a defeat of such magnitude on 10 August 1763 that the nizam did not seriously attack the Marathas for the next twenty-two years. Madhav Rao maintained the new initiative by marching south in the following year against Hyder Ali, defeating his forces at three different locations in Karnataka and compelling him to return all Maratha territories north of the Tungabhadra in addition to a large tribute of 3.2 million rupees.

As for the north, Madhavrao reestablished Maratha authority there through the exertions of Raghunath Rao, Tukoji Holkar, and Mahadji Shinde (Scindia), who not only defeated the rebellious Bundelas, Jats, and the Rohillas, but also wrested control over Delhi from Najib Khan's son, Zabit Khan, and brought back Emperor Shah Alam from his refuge with the English in Allahabad, restoring him to the throne on 6 January 1772. They also recovered considerable portions of the loot Abdali's forces had hidden. The Maratha ascendancy in Delhi was continued for the remainder of the century, thanks to the leadership of Mahadji Shinde and Tukoji Holkar.

By 1772 Madhav Rao had largely made up for the defeat and losses suffered at Panipat. Additionally, he had shown impressive gains in administration, in the steady collection of revenues, the introduction of a number of programs for the welfare of the common man, and, above all, in the establishment of respect for the Maratha judicial system. Just when stability had returned to Pune as the center of power and administration, the young *peshwa* died of tuberculosis on 18 November 1772. His untimely death proved a great destabilizer of Maratha power, causing the noted English administrator-historian Grant Duff to comment: "The plains of Panipat were not more fatal to the Maratha empire than the early end of this excellent prince."

Ineffective Peshwai and the Rise of the Pentarchy (1772–1800)

Dissensions in the *peshwa* line largely arose from the ambitions of Raghunath Rao and led to the assassination of Narayan Rao Peshwa (r. 1772–1773). Raghunath Rao's usurpation of the position of *peshwa* was not only opposed by the elite of Pune but was declared illegal by an upright judge, Ramashastri Prabhune, whose name has been ever since synonymous with integrity, courage, and justice in Maharashtra. When Narayan Rao's widow gave birth on 18 April 1774 to a son, Sawai Madhav Rao (1774–1795), he was recognized as the new *peshwa* by a council of twelve (Barbhai, or twelve brothers), which included Nana Phadnavis, Holkar, Phadke, and Shinde, who declared Sawai Madhav Rao, the posthumous child of the murdered *peshwa*, as the next *peshwa*. The arrangement lasted over a quarter century, until Nana's death in 1800. Appealing to the Maratha "destiny" and the importance of unity in the context of the fast disappearing, nominal Mughal "empire" and the rapidly rising empire of the East India Company, the frail but tenacious Nana virtually presided over the Maratha polity by judiciously giving adequate prominence and credit to the Pentarchy's constituents.

Early in this new phase of the Peshwai, Raghunath Rao sought refuge with the East India Company in Bombay, whose forces joined his in a march toward Pune in 1774. The Barbhai defeated them in what is known as the First Anglo-Maratha War. The company's headquarters in Calcutta, allergic to wars at that time, compelled the Bombay Council to sign a treaty with the Marathas in March 1776. The disgruntled Bombay Council took up Raghunath Rao's cause again, and the British forces were defeated again; the Barbhais demanded the British hand over Raghunath Rao. This time, it was Governor-General Warren Hastings's turn to disagree. He asked General Goddard to attack the Maratha positions in Konkan and Gujarat. For the third time in a decade, the Marathas prevailed, so the company was forced to sign the Treaty of Salbai in May 1782, by which they handed over Raghunath Rao to the Barbhais. He was confined thereafter at Kopargaon, where he died on 11 December 1786.

The Maratha triumphs in the north by the pentarchy, and nearer to Pune against the British, were all carried on in the name of Peshwa Sawai Madhav Rao. On 25 October 1795, in a delirious state induced by high fever, he jumped down from his quarters and died two days later. After Nana's death, Raghunath Rao's incompetent but ambitious son, Peshwa Baji Rao II (r. 1795–1818), following his father's example, signed with the British the Treaty of Bassein in 1802. This essentially ended the Peshwai. In 1804 General Wellesley proclaimed the Deccan in a state of chaos, established British military rule, and the *peshwa*s remained rulers only in name. In 1818 Baji Rao II was removed from his position as the *peshwa* and exiled to far-off Bithur in Uttar Pradesh, where the last of his line, the adopted son Nanasaheb, was not recognized by the British governor-general Dalhousie. Nanasaheb became a crucial leader of the 1857 uprising. He eluded capture and possibly disappeared in the wilds of Nepal.

The Marathas, particularly during the Peshwai, were India's major Hindu power prior to the British conquest of the subcontinent, and came closest to replacing the Mughals; with their indigenous pentarchy, the Marathas ruled from Pune a vast territory, extending at its mightiest peak from Delhi to the outskirts of Madras, from Bombay to the environs of Calcutta.

D. R. SarDesai

See also **British East India Company Raj; Maharashtra**

BIBLIOGRAPHY

Banerjee, A. C. *Peshwa Madhav Rao I.* Kolkata: Mukherjee, 1943.

Choksi, R. D. *History of British Diplomacy at the Court of the Peshwas, 1786–1818.* Poona: R. D. Choksey, 1951.

Desai, Sudha V. *Social life in Maharashtra under the Peshwas.* Mumbai: Popular Prakashan, 1980.

Duff, James Grant. *A History of the Marathas.* 1826. Reprint, New Delhi: Associated Publishing House, 1971.

Gokhale, Balkrishna G. *Poona in the Eighteenth Century: An Urban History.* Delhi: Oxford University Press, 1988.

Gune, Vithal T. *The Judicial System of the Marathas.* Poona: Deccan College, 1953.

Gupta, P. C. *Baji Rao II and the East India Company, 1798–1818.* 2nd ed. Mumbai and New York: Allied Publishers, 1964.

Kincaid, Charles A., and Rao Bahadur D. B. Parasnis. *A History of the Maratha People.* 3 vols. Delhi: S. Chand, 1968.

Majumdar, R. C., and V. G. Dighe. *The Maratha Supremacy*, vol. 8 of *The History and Culture of the Indian People.* Mumbai: Bharatiya Vidya Bhavan, 1977.

Patwardhan, R. P., and H. G. Rawlinson. *Source Book of Maratha History.* 1928. Reprint, Kolkata: K. P. Bagchi, 1978.

SarDesai, G. S. *The Main Currents in the Maratha History.* Patna: M. C. Sircar & Sons, 1926.

———. *New History of the Marathas.* 3 vols. Mumbai: Phoenix Publishers, 1946–1948.

SarDesai, G. S., ed. *Selections from the Peshwa Daftar.* 45 vols. Mumbai: Department of Archives, 1930–1934.

Sen, Surendra Nath. *Military System of the Marathas.* 2nd ed. Kolkata: K. P. Bagchi, 1958.

———. *Administrative System of the Marathas.* 3rd ed. Kolkata: University of Calcutta, 1976.

Shejwalkar, T. S. *Panipat, 1761.* Poona: Deccan College, 1946.

Vaidya, Suman G. *Peshwa Bajirao II and the Downfall of Maratha Power.* Nagpur: Pragati Prakashan, 1976.

Varma, Shanti P. *A Study in Maratha Diplomacy.* Agra: Shiva Lal Agrawala, 1956.

Wink, Andre. *Land and Sovereignty in India: Agrarian Society and Politics under the Eighteenth Century Maratha Swarajya.* Cambridge, U.K.: Cambridge University Press, 1986.

PILLAI, SAMUEL VEDANAYAKAM *(1826–1889), Tamil author and proponent of women's rights.* Samuel Vedanayakam Pillai was a Tamil humanist who used his literary talents to promote women's rights and Tamil cultural unity. He revitalized his mother tongue by his use of elegant, simple prose devoid of archaic Tamil embellishments. He is best known for writing *Pratapa Mudaliyar Charitram* (Pratapa Mudaliyar's story), his first novel in Tamil, in 1879. Set in an idyllic, pristine era when Tamil society was relatively untouched by colonial encroachment, the novel relates the adventures of a heroine wiser and braver than her hero, a sage matriarch, and other romantic characters. It was highly popular, and it was soon adopted as a school text in Madras presidency.

A Christian of upper caste *vellala* ancestry from Kallatur near Tiruchirapalli town, Vedanayakam was raised by his educated mother Mariammal, and he was educated in Tamil and English at a missionary school. In 1868 Vedanayakam first discussed the importance of girls' education in a Tamil tract, *Penmathimalai* (Women's knowledge). In 1870 he elaborated on this subject in another tract titled *Pen Kalvi* (Women' education), which he dedicated to his mother and daughters. To anchor his ideas on equality and nonsectarianism within the Indian context, Vedanayakam Pillai drew upon earlier Tamil texts such as the *Tirukkural*, a classic of aphorisms by the Tamil Jain sage Tiruvalluvar, and the hymns of medieval *bhakti* saints whose spiritual visions transcended caste. Pillai also drew inspiration from the works of Voltaire and Jean-Jacques Rousseau, his Western models of reason and equality. His second novel, *Suguna Sundari* (1887), challenged upper caste Hindu customs of early marriage and widow celibacy.

His other works included original essays, marriage songs based on folk models, and a translation of the legal codes into Tamil. He wrote popular nonsectarian hymns, such as *Sarva Samaya Samarasa Kirtannai* (Perennial pleasing hymns for all); *Satyavedaka Kirtannai* (Songs of the true Veda); *Tiruvarulmalai* (Garland of God's grace); *Tevastottiramalai* (Verses in praise of God); and two poems in the *antati* genre, *Tiruvarul Antati* (God's grace) and *Tevamata Antati* (Mother Goddess). He frequently signed his name simply as Vedanayakam Pillai, although in 1870 he may have edited the Christian journal *Narbodhakam* (Virtuous knowledge) under his full name. Vedanayakam Pillai argued that Tamil unity was based on a common language and on an ethical system transcending sectarian boundaries, so that all Tamils refer to an Unmanifest God as *katavul.* His nonsectarian hymns inspired later Tamil reformers A. Madhaviah and C. Subramania Bharati. At one time, when Vedanayakam Pillai served as a district official near Tiruvatuturai Saiva monastery, he came to admire the work of Meenakshisundaram Pillai and U. V. Swaminatha Iyer, who were then editing and translating archaic Tamil palm-leaf manuscripts. Swaminatha Iyer wrote the preface to *Pen Kalvi*, in which he warmly praised Vedanayakam for spreading the message on how to cherish the girl child.

Sita Anantha Raman

See also **Literature: Tamil**

BIBLIOGRAPHY

Pakiamuthu, D., ed. *Nutrandu Tamil Novel Tharum Chaiydi.* Chennai: Christian Literature Society, 1979.

Pillai, Vedanayakam. *Pen Kalvi.* 1870. Reprint, Tirunelveli: Saiva Siddhanta Publishing Society, 1950.

———. *Pratapa Mudaliyar Charitram.* 1879. Reprint, Chennai: Vanavil Press, 1984.

———. *Suguna Sundari.* 1887. Reprint, Nagapattinam: Himaya, 1992.

Pullavar, E. Ramaswamy Pullavar, ed. *Ithazha Vilakka Virisai.* Tirunelveli: Saiva Siddhanta Society, 1961.

Raman, Sita Anantha. *Getting Girls to School.* Kolkata: Stree, 1996.

———. "Old Norms in New Bottles: Constructions of Gender and Ethnicity in the Early Tamil Novel." *Journal of Women's History* 12, no. 3 (Autumn 2000): 93–119.

Swaminatha Iyer, U. V. *The Story of My Life*, translated by S. K. Guruswamy. Tirunmiyur: U. V. Swaminatha Iyer Library, 1980.

Varadarajan, M. *A History of Tamil Literature.* Delhi: Sahitya Akademi, 1988.

PINGALA, *c. fifth century* B.C., *Indian mathematician.* Binary numbers were known at the time of Pingala's *Chhandah-shāstra* to classify Vedic meters. According to an old Indian tradition, Pingala was the younger brother of Pānini. This is so stated by Shadgurushishya in his *Vedārtha Dīpikā*. If this tradition is correct, he should be assigned to the fifth century B.C., the most likely period of Pānini's life. The fact that the *Chhandah-shāstra* is in the early unversified *sūtra* style makes this conclusion quite plausible. In Europe, a rediscovery of the binary notation, in a slightly different form, was made by Gottfried Leibniz (1646–1716) at the end of the seventeenth century.

Most Vedic hymns are in stanzas of four quarters (*pāda*), though there are some with three or five divisions. The most popular meters have quarters that have 8, 11, or 12 syllables. The usual way to classify meters is by counting the number of syllables in each line. Thus the *gāyatrī* consists of 8 syllables in 3 lines (8 x 3), *anushtubh* is 8 x 4, *trishtubh* and *indravajra* (Indra's thunderbolt) is 11 x 4, *indravamsha* (Indra's family) is 12 x 4, *vasantatilakā* (the ornament of spring) is 14 x 4, *mālinī* (the girl wearing a garland) is 15 x 4, *prithivī* (the earth) is 17 x 4, *mandākrāntā* (the slow stepper) and *harinī* (the doe) are 17 x 4, *shārdūla-vikrīdita* (the tiger's sport) is 19 x 4, and the sragdharā (the girl with a garland) is 21 x 4. The meters *gāyatrī* (24), *ushnik* (28), *atishakkarī* (30 for half), *anushtup* (32), *brihatī* (36), *pankti* (40), *trishtup* (44), and *jagatī* (48) were used most frequently in the Vedic texts.

The syllables are prosodically either short (*laghu*) or long (*guru*). A *laghu* syllable is a short vowel followed by at most one consonant; any other syllable is a *guru*. Within each quarter verse, a sequence of *laghu*s and *guru*s defines the meter; this is much like the representation of a number by a succession of 0s and 1s used in the binary arithmetic of computers.

Pingala presented a method where all the binary *laghu-guru* sequences were shown as a matrix, *prastāra*. Given a specific sequence, he showed how it could be converted into an equivalent decimal number; he also showed how a given decimal number could be expanded into the sequence of *laghu*s and *guru*s. This suggests that an understanding of the basis of the representation of numbers existed. The Pingala octal assignment has much similarity with the Katapayādi notation for representing numerals as words.

Subhash Kak

See also **Pānini; Vedic Aryan India**

BIBLIOGRAPHY

Kak, Subhash. "Indian Binary Numbers and the Katapayadi Notation."*Annals of the Bhandarkar Oriental Research Institute* 81 (2000): 269–272.

Nooten, Barend van. "Binary Numbers in Indian Antiquity." In *Computing Science in Ancient India*, edited by T. R. Rao and S. Kak. New Delhi: Munshiram Manoharlal, 2000.

PLANNING COMMISSION The Planning Commission was established in 1950 by the government of India. Thus it does not have statutory status by virtue either of a provision in the Constitution or an Act of Parliament. Yet over the years it acquired the status of more than a ministry and at times gave the impression of being a parallel government. The prime minister has always been its chairman, but the deputy chairman has in practice been in charge planning. The finance minister is an ex-officio member of the commission, and from time to time other ministers have been appointed members, depending on the contemporary significance of their departments. The commission's original, primary function was to prepare a five-year plan of development. Planning was in fashion during the early years of India's independence, influenced by the Soviet Union's experiment. Pandit Nehru, prime minister of India, was fascinated by the five-year plans, as was India's business community. The first "plan" of development was a rudimentary effort by the business community—the so-called Bombay Plan—to restore worn-out railway and industrial infrastructure.

Centralized Planning

The first five-year plan (1951–1956) was essentially a listing of development projects already in the pipeline (from the late war years, when the British regime had set in motion a process of postwar development). But it also provided a brilliant exposition of the state of the economy, the nature and magnitude of the development task, and an analytical basis for future effort.

The second five-year plan created a four-sector model for Indian development: large-scale industries for the production of capital goods; large-scale industries for the production of consumer goods; agriculture; small and household industries; and services. Accelerated growth, it was argued, required public investment in the production of heavy capital machinery, while investment for the production of consumer goods would be mostly in the private sector, some of which would follow labor-intensive techniques, securing additional employment. The machines-to-build-machines strategy, however, soon ran to ground as the marginal rate of saving proved insufficient to sustain it. Balance of payments problems forced a hiatus in planning, but by the late sixties, planning resumed with emphasis on poverty alleviation. As of 2002, India had implemented nine five-year plans. The current tenth plan (2002–2007) has a target of 8 percent growth rate.

The plans embraced the public and the private sectors. The plan for the private sector was intended to be merely indicative, though attempts were soon made to enforce targets through the elaborate mechanism of industrial licensing. The Industries Development and Regulation Act of 1956 defined those sectors reserved for the public; other sectors were open for private investment, governed by the targets of the plan. The mixed economy model, well-defined in theory, led to serious problems in practice. The marriage of planning to licensing proved disastrous and eventually necessitated liberalization in the mid-1980s and more prominently since 1991.

The Economic Affairs Department of the Ministry of Finance, which was responsible for the annual government budgets, and thus for raising tax and nontax revenues, argued that the size of the plan was constrained by the saving propensity of the economy and the possibility of mobilizing private savings through taxation and borrowing. The debate over financial planning, and between the virtues of a big plan as opposed to a moderate-sized

Prime Minister Dr. Manmohan Singh Chairs a Meeting of the Planning Commission. Shortly after assuming office in 2004, Singh requested that the commission determine whether India's economic programs were, in fact, serving the segments of the population they were intended to help. INDIA TODAY.

plan, continued throughout the late 1950s and early 1960s.

The Planning Commission is organized both territorially and functionally. Apart from the members, who constitute the decision-making body, the commission uses a number of advisers, drawn from the Indian Administrative Service, primarily economists and scientists. Each adviser looks after one or more sectors (e.g., rural development, energy, or transport) and also one or more states. Macroeconomic work is done by the Economic and Resources Division and the Perspective Planning Division, in close association with the Ministry of Finance and the Reserve Bank of India.

A draft plan is submitted for approval to the central cabinet and the National Development Council, including central ministers and the state chief ministers. The entire five-year plan is implemented through annual plans, which are formulated by the central and state governments and approved by the Planning Commission. A Programme Evaluation Organization generates periodic evaluations of the plan's schemes and programs.

Center-State Relations

The Planning Commission plays a major role in managing the economic relations between the central government and the states, approving the plans of the states after discussions with them. In addition, the center allocates some 25 percent of the assistance it receives from abroad to various states. The percentage has gone up over time, and all foreign aid that specifically pertains to projects in designated states is now passed on to them.

States also receive central funds for specific programs sponsored by the center, such as malaria eradication. The Planning Commission tries to use the leverage of resource transfers to introduce reforms and better practices in the states, for example power sector reforms and fiscal management reforms. The Finance Commission, which is a statutory body under the Constitution, appointed every five years, also tries to encourage reforms, though its basic task is to decide on the central transfers, by way of tax sharing and grants to fund non-plan revenue expenditures of states. The Finance Commission's work thus overlaps with that of the Planning

Commission. Most states seem to favor dealing with the Finance Commission, since whatever they receive from it is treated as their statutory right. Though the two commissions never meet, one member of the Planning Commission has usually been appointed to the Finance Commission to facilitate the coordination of their tasks.

The commission lost much of its power and glory during the economic crises in the 1960s. Rajiv Gandhi made no secret of his contempt for it by describing its members as jokers.

In the post-1991 liberalized economy, which relies more on the free market than governmental controls, the Planning Commission has had to redefine its role, adapting to India's new economic realities. Its focus is now on defining broad infrastructure and social sector goals. Nonetheless, it continues to play a role in managing center-state financial relations, seeking to improve fiscal discipline in the states and to provide general guidance on health, education, and poverty alleviation programs.

Manu Shroff

See also **Economic Reforms of 1991; Economy since the 1991 Economic Reforms**

BIBLIOGRAPHY

Domar, Evsey D. *Essays in the Theory of Economic Growth.* New York: Oxford University Press, 1957.

Government of India, Planning Commission. *Planning Process.* Delhi: Controller of Publications, 1975.

Mahalanobis, P. C. "The Approach of Operational Research to Planning in India." *Sankhya, the Indian Journal of Statistics* 16, parts 1 and 2 (December 1955): 3–130.

Myrdal, Gunnar. *Asian Drama: An Inquiry into the Poverty of Nations*, vol. II. New York: Pantheon, 1968.

PLASSEY, BATTLE OF. *See* **Bengal; British East India Company Raj; Clive, Robert.**

POLICE ATROCITIES. *See* **Human Rights.**

POLITICAL SYSTEM

This entry consists of the following articles:

CABINET

CONSTITUTION

PARLIAMENT

PRESIDENT

PRIME MINISTER

CABINET

Parliamentary democracies, including India, are more accurately described as cabinet governments. While the council of ministers has constitutional status in India, the cabinet does not get a mention in India's Constitution. Its powers are defined instead by convention and usage. The council of ministers consists, in order of precedence, of: cabinet ministers; ministers of state; deputy ministers; and parliamentary secretaries.

The full executive is the council of ministers, with the cabinet being but one of its four components. In reality, though, the cabinet is much more important, influential, and powerful than the full council. While the latter meets rarely, the cabinet meets frequently. In some respects, ministers of state and deputy ministers are closer to being departmental heads than cabinet ministers. With coalition governments and the resulting need to accommodate various political parties, their numbers have increased dramatically. In November 2003, there were 29 cabinet ministers (of whom 2 were women) in addition to the prime minister and deputy prime minister, and 49 ministers of state (5 women). Every minister must be a member of parliament (MP) of either the lower house (Lok Sabha) or upper house (Rajya Sabha). If this is not the case upon appointment to the cabinet, he or she must become an MP within six months of appointment, either through nomination or by election. A minister may take part in the proceedings of either house of parliament, but voting rights are restricted to the house to which he or she belongs.

The cabinet of India serves three principal functions: to determine government policy for presentation to Parliament; to implement government policy; and to carry out interdepartmental coordination and cooperation. Interestingly, the cabinet as a whole does not consider the budget, the responsibility for which rests with the finance minister, the prime minister, and one or more other related ministers.

What is the power and influence of the cabinet collectively, or of cabinet ministers individually? The answer depends not only on the personality of the prime minister of the day—whether he or she is assertive and domineering or more of the delegating type—but also on how powerful and independent-minded the cabinet ministers themselves are. On the one hand, they are rival centers of political gravity within the ruling party, and therefore a potential threat to the continuing position of the prime minister as head of government. On the other hand, they are of immense help to the prime minister in articulating and defending government policy in Parliament and in the nation at large, to both party faithful and political opponents alike. And the knowledge that the government is not a one-person band can be greatly reassuring to the people and to business and investor confidence. In the 1998–2003 period, when Lal Krishna Advani served as deputy prime minister and home minister, the Vajpayee government had one of the most powerful deputy prime ministers in decades of Indian politics. For all his commanding stature in the country, even Jawaharlal Nehru (prime minister 1947–1964) had to contend with Sardar Vallabhbhai Patel, who was second only to Nehru in influence in the cabinet and the party. Patel was considered to be Nehru's equal in many respects.

In contrast to her father, Indira Gandhi (prime minister 1966–1977, 1980–1984) established a more personalized and centralized form of prime ministerial government. Efforts by the Janata government (1977–1980) to restore the principle and substance of collective responsibility fell victim to internecine conflict within the cabinet. Prime Minister Gandhi's dominant role in her cabinet was reflected in the expanded size and enhanced status of the prime minister's secretariat, compared to that of the far more humble Lal Bahadur Shastri (prime minister 1964–1966).

"Responsible government" ensures that the head of state acts only on the advice of responsible advisers. As in other parliamentary governments, the Indian cabinet operates on the basis of the two further working principles: "cabinet responsibility" and "ministerial responsibility." While cabinet responsibility places individual ministers under the cabinet as a collective entity, ministerial responsibility puts them in charge of government departments. Thus the former is more political and the latter more bureaucratic in nature.

All cabinet ministers must accept the principle of collective responsibility. That is, under collective leadership each minister accepts and agrees to share responsibility for all decisions of the cabinet. Doubts and disagreements may be expressed either diplomatically or forcefully, but they must be confined to the privacy of the cabinet room. Cabinet decisions are rarely taken by formal vote. Instead, the cabinet proceeds by a sense of the meeting after the discussion has taken place. If any member of the cabinet is unable to support government policy in public, in Parliament, or in the country at large, then that member is morally bound to resign. Foreign Minister M. C. Chagla resigned from the cabinet in 1967 because he believed that the government's educational policy, which obviously did not fall within his ministerial jurisdiction, was likely to endanger and undermine national unity. A dissenting minister may neither vote against government policy in Parliament, nor speak against it in public. Minister of State Mohan Dharia was dismissed from the council of ministers in 1975 because of public dissent from government policy on how to handle Loknayak (People's Leader) Jaya Prakash Narayan's people's movement. Open bickering between members of the Janata government on matters of public policy proved to be the prelude to the collapse of the government in 1979. For more than two years the Janata cabinet was less a forum for reaching collective decisions than an arena for factional conflict. During 1998–2003, the problems for the Bharatiya Janata Party (BJP)–led government came from coalition allies rather than BJP members. But the numerical dominance of the BJP and the personal popularity of Prime Minister Atal Bihari Vajpayee sufficed to overcome any dissidence within the coalition.

Each member of the cabinet accepts full political responsibility for all acts of commission and omission by officials of the department that falls under her or his portfolio. Officials are there to advise the minister and implement the minister's decisions. The minister, rather than her or his officials, reaps the rewards of the ministry's policy successes, and has to be prepared to pay the political price for its failures. Thus Defence Minister V. K. Krishna Menon was forced to resign by Prime Minister Nehru after the disastrous performance of the Indian military in the war with China in 1962. Serious railway accidents have led to calls for the resignation of railway ministers. When Foreign Minister Jaswant Singh accompanied alleged terrorists whose release from Indian detention was demanded by the hijackers of an Indian Airlines plane that had been taken to Afghanistan in 1999, the shame and ignominy was not transferred to the shoulders of his civil servants and advisers.

Ministerial responsibility is the doctrinal assertion of the supremacy of politicians over the entire machinery of government. Cabinet ministers accept responsibility for departmental acts because in the system of cabinet government they are expected and required to exercise firm control over the bureaucracy. One reason why Prime Minister Nehru did not abandon the bureaucratic structure inherited from the British colonial administration was that he and his ministers provided crisp and clear policy guidance to their civil servants. Furthermore, they also asserted and established the supremacy of political control over the military.

The cabinet is assisted in its many tasks by several committees. The most important of these deal with parliamentary, political, foreign, defense, and economic affairs. The key cabinet committees are always dominated by the senior ministers, starting with the prime minister. Important issues are usually examined in committee before being taken to the cabinet as a whole for debate and approval or rejection. The committee system can be used by a prime minister or an "inner cabinet" (sometimes referred to as the "kitchen cabinet") to preempt decisions, using the full cabinet chiefly for ratification of the policy already agreed to by a powerful small clique.

In principle, nevertheless, the cabinet is the chief governing authority in the country. Its central role in government also makes it the focus of most interest group activity and lobbying, which in turn makes it one of the chief mediators and conciliators of sectarian and sectoral interests. It is the cabinet that tenders advice to the president for the exercise of all his or her functions, and that provides legislative leadership in Parliament, political leadership in the country, and administrative leadership of government departments. The cabinet is also the final arbiter of India's external relations, from declaration of general principles of foreign policy to decisions of war and peace and negotiations of trade agreements and military alliances. In 2003, for example, India was urged by the second Bush administration in Washington to contribute a division of troops (over 15,000) to Iraq. There was a split within the government ranks on how to respond, taking into consideration the government's wish to consolidate relations with the United States against the backdrop of the dominant public sentiment against the U.S. war. Some ministers wanted to agree to the U.S. request; others were initially sympathetic but changed their minds; and some stayed opposed from start to finish. In the crucial meeting of the cabinet committee on security on 14 July 2003, Prime Minister Vajpayee sided with the opponents, and the matter was thus settled. The cabinet committee on security was the crucial body in which the decision was made.

Ramesh Thakur

See also **Federalism and Center-State Relations**

BIBLIOGRAPHY

Brady, Chris. "Collective Responsibility of the Cabinet: An Ethical, Constitutional or Managerial Tool?" *Parliamentary Affairs* 52, no. 2 (April 1999): 214–229.

Burch, Martin, and Ian Holliday. "Prime Minister's and Cabinet Offices: An Executive Office in All but Name." *Parliamentary Affairs* 52:1 (January 1999): 32–45.

Limaye, Madhu. *Cabinet Government in India*. New Delhi: Radiant Publishers, 1989.

Panandikar, V. A. Pai, and Ajay K. Mehra. *The Indian Cabinet*. Delhi: Konark, 1996.

CONSTITUTION

Constitutionalism is the technique of striking the proper balance between establishing a system of government that has sufficient enabling authority and power to permit it to perform the necessary tasks, and restricting the government with a system of restraints to preclude the creation of a tyranny. If a country has a written constitution that does not act as an effective restraint on the exercise of arbitrary power by the government of the day, it cannot be said to serve as the backbone of constitutional government.

As the highest law in its land, the constitution sets out the rules to ensure fair competition between official contenders, vying for the authoritative allocation of scarce resources through control of political office. It establishes the framework within which competing individuals and groups can pursue their struggles for power in a stable, orderly manner. Every political system needs clearly understood rules to make, interpret, implement, and enforce public policy. The constitution does this by specifying the organs of government; their powers and limits in relation to one another and to citizens; procedures for formulating and executing laws and resolving conflicts among units and members of the political community; and the conditions under which a polity may be defended against internal and foreign foes. The constitutional relationship between the state and its citizens—a government elected by and accountable to the people, both government and citizens being subject to the rule of law—contains the key to the organizing principle of every political system.

The Constitution of India tries to strike a balance between the liberty of citizens, the authority of the state, and the cohesiveness of society. The key to the successful establishment of constitutional democracy in India may lie in the quality and gradualism of British tutelage. Prior to independence, India went through a fairly long gestation period of parliamentary democratic institutions. The principle of gradualism guided the widening of suffrage to new classes of citizens, the extension of the principles of elective government from local to national levels, and the deepening of power-sharing arrangements between elected representatives and appointed officials.

India inherited its basic organizational structure of government from the British Raj, including a unitary system of government, albeit with strong federal features. The Morley-Minto reforms of 1909 extended the elective principle to the provincial (state) legislative councils, extended a limited central legislative council suffrage, and introduced communal electorates. They also initiated a far-reaching debate on three constitutional issues: a further broadening of the suffrage, and if so, the principles on which this was to be done; the further extension of the elective principle to all members of legislative bodies; and the appropriate power-sharing arrangements between provincial and national governments. The Montagu-Chelmsford reforms of 1919 divided authority between central and state governments and legislative functions between two chambers. The suffrage was still limited, however, to property taxpayers, landholders, and men with educational qualifications, who together accounted for under 4 percent of the population in rural areas and 14 percent in municipal areas. The Government of India Act (1935) of the British Parliament provided the

Supreme Court, New Delhi. Domed home to India's Supreme Court, arbiter of the Constitution. On Talak Marg, New Delhi, not far from the banks of the Yamuna River. INDIA TODAY.

structural link from the 1919 reforms under British rule to the 1950 Constitution adopted after independence. Independent India also inherited some of the actual institutions of the British Raj, including central and provincial legislatures, the bureaucracy, the judiciary and the security services; and the conventions of parliamentary democracy, for example the requirement for the prime minister to be a member of the lower house of Parliament, and for his cabinet to resign if ever it loses a vote of "confidence" in that house.

The new Constitution of independent India, drafted by a specially convened Constituent Assembly, completed the democratization of politics begun by the British. Reflecting the Congress Party triumphs in the provincial elections of 1945, the Constituent Assembly was dominated by the Congress, which had led the struggle for independence. The president of the assembly was Rajendra Prasad, who later became the first president of India. The drafting committee was chaired by B. R. Ambedkar. Other influential personalities in the Constituent Assembly were Jawaharlal Nehru, Sardar Vallabhbhai Patel, and Maulana Abul Kalam Azad. Elected indirectly by the provincial assemblies in 1946, the Constituent Assembly aimed to set up a system of government that would facilitate social change and economic development within a democratic structure. The debates in the Constituent Assembly are a rich mine of information on the thinking and philosophy, the fears and hopes underlying the Constitution of India.

Divided into twenty-two parts of 395 articles, plus another eight schedules (since expanded to over 400 articles and a dozen schedules), the Constitution of India is among the longest in the world. It came into effect on 26 January 1950 and established a republic, with no hereditary rulers. The date of 26 January is celebrated every year with due pomp and ceremony as Republic Day. Under the terms of the Constitution, India is democratic, secular, federal, and republican. India has a representative and parliamentary system of government formed on the basis of elections held at prescribed intervals under the auspices of an independent electoral commission. Every adult citizen may vote in elections and seek public

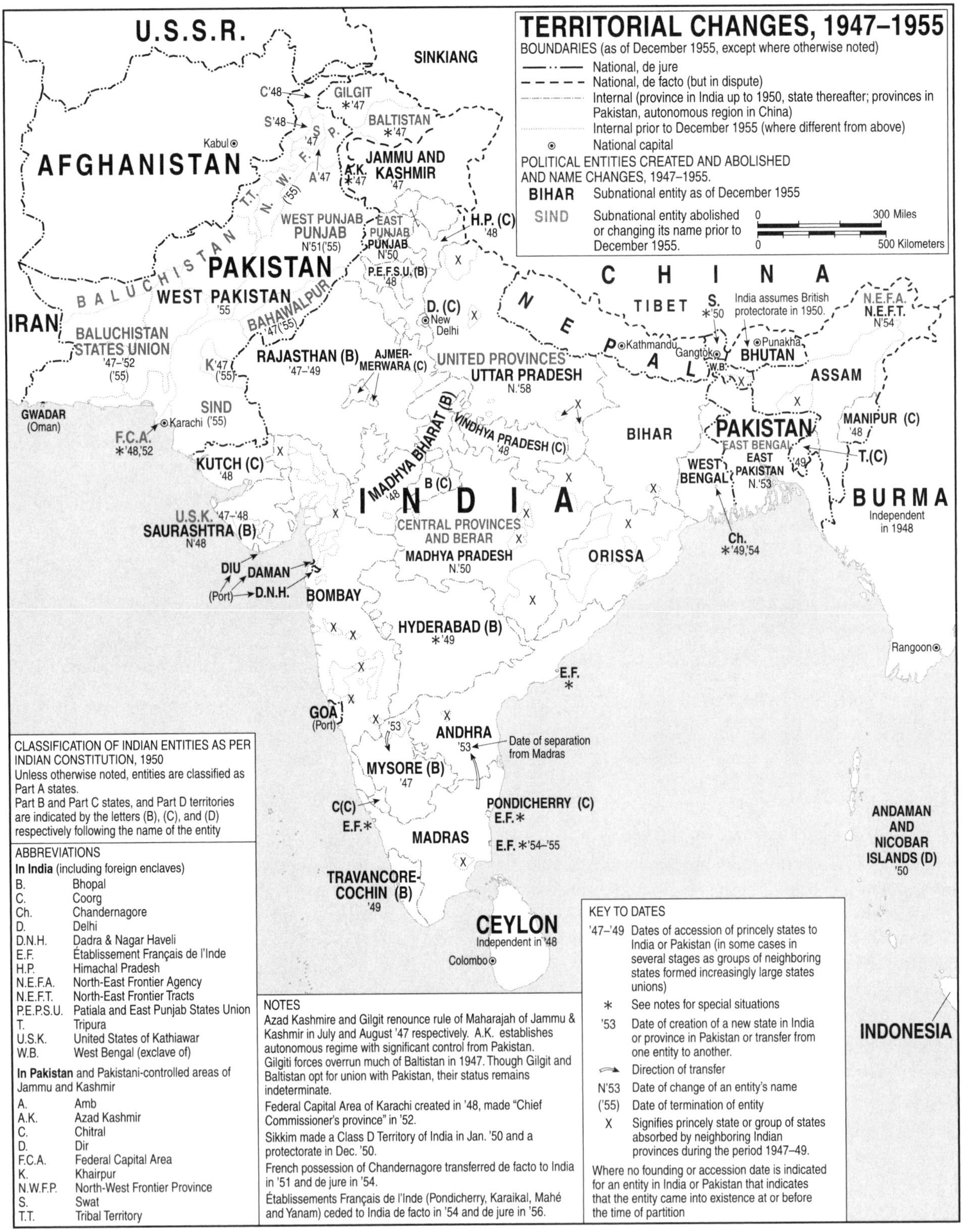

office. While some drafters of the Constitution had wanted a decentralized Gandhian state, most felt comfortable with the system of parliamentary democracy bequeathed by Britain. A distribution of powers between a federal center and component states, equally familiar from the colonial heritage, was regarded as the best institutional means of accommodating India's need for unity-in-diversity through appropriate power sharing on

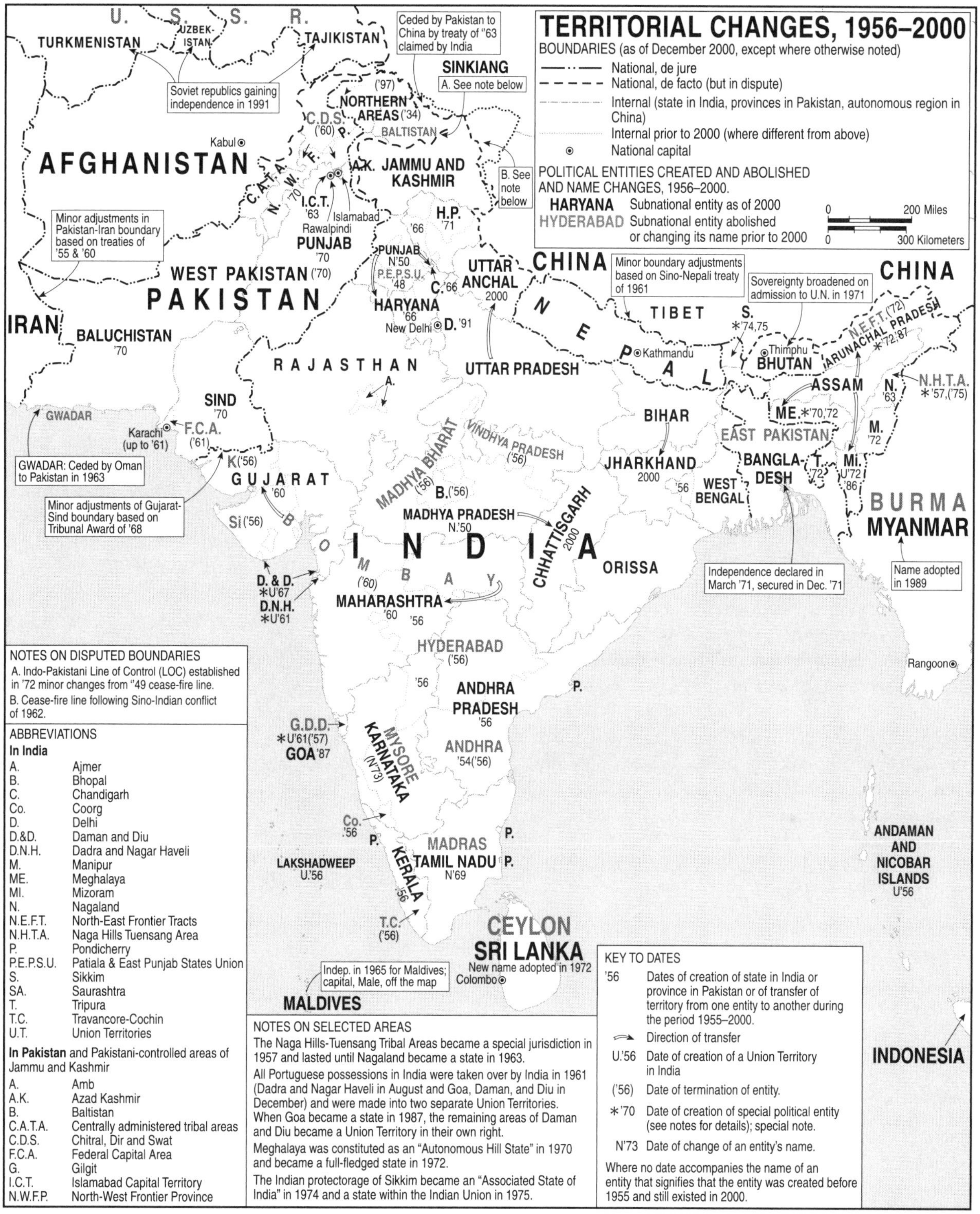

a geographical basis. The history of difficulties in neighboring Pakistan, which broke apart in 1971, and Sri Lanka, which has struggled with demands for greater autonomy by the Tamils, has vindicated the formula adopted by the Indian Constitution. Secularism was a logical corollary of the Congress Party's passionate rejection of the two-nation theory, by which Pakistan had been severed from India through partition-at-birth. The decision to become a republic was an assertion of freedom and independence from the British Crown. Nevertheless, India was allowed to remain a full member of the Commonwealth of Nations, through the creative formula of accepting the British "Crown" as a symbol of the free association of Commonwealth member-nations, and as such the head of the Commonwealth.

The Constitution prescribes four methods for its own amendment (Part XX). Some clauses may be amended by a simple majority of Parliament, in consultation with or at the request of the states. A second category of clauses may be amended by a simple majority in Parliament. A third group requires a majority of the total membership of each house plus a two-thirds majority of members of Parliament present and voting in each house. The final class of clauses, pertaining to state borders and rights, requires, in addition to the preceding, ratification by half the number of state legislatures. The Constitution has been amended around one hundred times, but without altering the "basic structure" of the system of government established in 1950, whose custodian is the Supreme Court of India.

The philosophy underlying the Constitution of India reflects attractions and aversion to aspects of Western liberal democracy and Soviet-style Marxism. During the struggle for independence, many leading personalities in the Congress Party, although Western-educated, had flirted with communist ideals. India's Constitution reflects this dual attraction and ambivalence. The Preamble declares India to be a sovereign democratic republic and proclaims the following goals: social, economic, and political justice; liberty of thought, expression, belief, faith, and worship; equality of status and opportunity; dignity of the individual; and unity of the nation. The simultaneous attraction of Western democracy and Soviet socialism is particularly apparent in the chapters on Fundamental Rights (Part III) and Directive Principles of State Policy (Part IV), respectively.

In some respects the Indian framers borrowed ideas from the U.S. Constitution, starting with the need for a written constitution. The functions of rule making, rule enforcement, and rule interpretation are separated into the three institutions of the legislature, the executive, and the judiciary. The U.S. influence is strikingly evident in the institution of the judiciary, including a Supreme Court as the final court, and the principle of judicial review. If constitutional government is to have practical and not merely theoretical meaning, then there must be an independent judiciary that can act as a check on the arbitrary exercise of legislative and executive power. If independent India was going to give meaning to the fine sentiments expressed in its Constitution—to protect minorities, to give practical content to the principles of equality of opportunity and equality under the law, to establish that democracy means that all votes have equal value and all officials as well as citizens are answerable for their actions in court—then the judiciary, led by the Supreme Court of India, would have to provide firm guidance. By and large it has done so. For the rule of law to prevail, the judiciary must be seen to be universal, impartial, and impersonal. Its task is to expand individual rights and state power simultaneously. The judiciary is also the final arbiter on what the Constitution itself means. Though the Constitution of India lacks the longevity of its U.S. counterpart, and reverence for it is perhaps diminished by the ease and frequency of its amendments. it nevertheless has proven to be remarkably resilient.

Ramesh Thakur

See also **Federalism and Center-State Relations**

BIBLIOGRAPHY

Austin, Granville. *Working a Democratic Constitution: The Indian Experience*. Delhi: South Asia Books, 2000.

Basu, Durga Das. *Constitutional Law of India*. 6th ed. Delhi: Prentice-Hall of India, 1991.

Chaube, Shibanikinkar. *Constituent Assembly of India: Springboard of Revolution*. Delhi: Manohar Publishers, 2000.

Grover, V. *The Constitution of India*. Delhi: Deep and Deep, 2002.

Hasan, Zoya, E. Sridharan, and R. Sudharshan, eds. *India's Living Constitution: Ideas, Practices, Controversies*. Bangalore: Orient Longman, 2002.

Joshi, Ram. *The Indian Constitution and Its Working*. Mumbai: Orient Longman, 1979.

Misra, Surya N., Subhas C. Hazary, and Amareshwar Mishra. *Constitution and Constitutionalism in India*. New Delhi: A.P.H. Publishing, 1999.

Palekar, S. A. *Constitution and Parliamentary Democracy in Contemporary India*. Jaipur: A.B.D. Publishers, 2002.

Saharay, H. K. *The Constitution of India: An Analytical Approach*. 3rd ed. Kolkata: Eastern Law House, 2002.

PARLIAMENT

In India both the prime minister and the cabinet are subject, or "responsible," to control by Parliament. Indians were introduced to the institution of responsible parliamentary government by the British. The lineage of the Parliament of India created by the Constitution in 1950 includes the Indian Councils Act (1861), the Morley-Minto reforms (1909), the Montagu-Chelmsford reforms (1919), and the Government of India Act (1935). These various reforms each represented a gradual increase in the democratization and indigenization of responsible rule in India by the transfer of British imperial power to elected representatives of India, completed with independence and the adoption of parliamentary government modeled on that of Westminster.

The powers of the Indian parliament may be divided into legislative, financial, procedural, governmental, constitution-amending, and constitutive. Parliament

Parliament Building, New Delhi. On December 13, 2001, five terrorists firing AK-47 rifles breached the security perimeter around the Parliament House, but failed to enter it. In the gun battle that ensued, the terrorists, six security officers, and a gardener were killed. PREM KAPOOR / FOTOMEDIA.

enacts the law of the land, at least in theory. In reality, the legislative agenda is controlled by the government and usually rubber stamped by Parliament with the help of tightly maintained party discipline. If it chooses to act with the government, as is almost always the case, Parliament is all-powerful; if it chose to act independently of the government, Parliament would create confusion and unpredictability in the affairs of state; and by voting to act against the executive, Parliament indicates that a government has lost its confidence, bringing the business of that government to a standstill until new elections can be held.

The financial powers of Parliament empower it to raise and spend money as it sees fit, including discussion and approval of the annual budget, which is usually introduced in mid-February. Only Parliament has the authority to levy taxes and spend money from the consolidated fund. Its procedural powers are those that permit Parliament to make rules for the conduct of its own business. Parliament formally controls the reins of government in that the cabinet is required to have the confidence of the lower house, Lok Sabha, and is collectively responsible to Parliament. Under Article 368, Parliament is the main body for amending the Constitution of India. Under its constitutive powers, Parliament can legislate to admit or create new states into the union of India; to create a high court for a union territory, and to extend the jurisdiction of a high court to or restrict it from a union territory; and to create or abolish the upper house for a state of the union, with the consent of its lower house.

The Lok Sabha

The Parliament of India is bicameral. The lower house is the Lok Sabha, or the "House of the People." Its members are elected on the basis of universal adult suffrage. The distribution of seats among the states is roughly in proportion to their population. Thus Uttar Pradesh and Bihar, the two most populous states, have 85 and 54 members of Parliament (MPs) respectively, while the smallest states and union territories have only one MP each. Of the 543 elective seats in the thirteenth Lok Sabha (1999–2004), 413 MPs were in the general category, 81 were from scheduled castes (formerly known as "untouchables"), and 49 were from scheduled tribes. Any citizen of India who is at least twenty-five years old may seek election to the Lok Sabha from a constituency in which he or she has resided for a minimum of 180 days. In a reserved constituency, only members of the scheduled castes and tribes may run for office, but all adults within the constituency may vote. The two nominated seats are filled by the president with representatives of the Anglo-Indian community.

The system of voting is the single-member constituency. Each constituency is represented by only one MP in the Lok Sabha. Of those contesting from any constituency, the candidate with the highest number of votes is declared elected, even if the total is well short of a majority. The plurality rather than majority system of voting can produce, and generally has done so, governments that have substantial majorities in Parliament but lack endorsement from a majority of the voters. In 1984, for example, the Congress Party captured 77 percent of seats in Parliament but won only 48 percent of the votes. Conversely, in 1996, a drop of 8.4 percent in the popular vote saw the party's parliamentary representation halved. A proportional representation system would be more representative in a mathematically defined version of democracy. However, under Indian conditions (size, diversity, and complexity), it would almost certainly produce chaos in each general election.

The conduct of elections is entrusted by the Constitution itself to an election commission. The chief election commissioner is an independent official appointed by the president under conditions of service resembling those of senior judges. The tasks of the election commission include designing voting forms suitable for Indian conditions, determining the best dates for holding elections, whether the elections should be held simultaneously, on consecutive days, or at staggered intervals, and so on.

By and large, Parliament is fairly chosen. While individual seats may have been determined by musclemen or bribes, no general election in India has produced an overall result that was not a fair reflection of voter preferences. As with all political systems, the party in government has all the advantages of incumbency when contesting elections. These have not been sufficient to prevent spectacular electoral reverses for the party in power in several elections since 1967, including the elections of 2004. Indeed, in some ways, a notable trend in Indian elections is the anti-incumbency factor: voters seem to punish those in office for their shortcomings and failures as much as they reward newcomers for fresh promises.

In the early years after 1950, many MPs came from a background of activism in the struggle for independence. The first Parliament (1952–1957) was dominated by professionals, especially lawyers. In the thirteenth Lok Sabha (1999–2004), 419 MPs were university graduates, including 30 with Ph.D. degrees. Over 70 percent were between 41 and 65 years old. (The oldest was born in 1913, the youngest in 1968.) In terms of castes, Brahmans are still overrepresented and the lower castes remain underrepresented. But the general trend is toward greater democratization. Such is not the case with regard to gender balance: only 44 of the 543 elected members of the thirteenth Lok Sabha were women.

The term of the Lok Sabha is five years, although in an emergency this may be extended for one year at a time. This has happened only once, after the 1975 "emergency." While Parliament may be dissolved and fresh elections held because a government has lost the confidence of the Lok Sabha, the more common occurrence is for a prime minister to call for new elections when he or she deems it possible to maximize personal or party political gains. For this reason, the exact date for new elections is usually uncertain.

Required to convene at least twice a year, the Lok Sabha normally meets in three sessions each year. In 2002 the budget session met from 15 April to 17 May, the monsoon session from 15 July to 12 August, and the winter session from 18 November to 20 December. The language of parliamentary business is mostly Hindi or English, although a member may use any of the recognized official languages. The official records of parliamentary debates are printed in both English and Hindi.

The legislative process involves three stages, corresponding to the British three readings of bills: a bill's introduction, its consideration, and its enactment into law. At its first reading, the bill is introduced, along with an explanation of its aims and purposes. After the second reading, a bill may be referred to a select committee, circulated for public response, or taken up for immediate consideration. The most substantial consideration of any bill takes place in committee. The Lok Sabha operates with the aid of about a dozen committees of between twenty and twenty-five members. The composition of the committees is determined by the speaker and the chief whip with due regard to respective party strengths in the house. No minister who is in charge of a bill being considered by committee is permitted to participate in the deliberations of that committee, which helps to insulate the committee proceedings from undue executive influence.

The select committee reports back either unanimously or with a majority recommendation and a minority note of dissent. The bill is then considered in the house clause by clause, with members allowed to introduce amendments. Once all clauses have been dealt with, the bill has successfully crossed the report stage, and is listed for its third and final reading. At this stage, only tidying-up amendments are permitted, and the bill is put to a vote. If approved, and when formally authenticated as such by the Speaker of the Lok Sabha, the bill is sent to the second house, where the entire procedure is repeated. When both houses of Parliament have passed an identical version of a bill, it is presented to the president for formal assent, and becomes law upon receiving his assent.

"Ordinary" bills can be introduced in either house, the Lok Sabha or the Rajya Sabha. They must be passed by both houses before they can be sent to the president, and they only become law once they have been signed by the president. "Money" bills can be introduced only in the Lok Sabha ("no taxation without representation!"). While they may be taken up for discussion in the Rajya Sabha, the upper house cannot refuse assent to money bills. Nor may it frustrate the passage of a money bill by the simple expedient of procrastination: the bill is deemed to have passed if not returned by the Rajya Sabha within fourteen days.

The daily and sessional business of government is decided by the cabinet and its parliamentary affairs committee under the chairmanship of the chief whip. In parliamentary systems, party discipline in the legislature is far tighter than in presidential systems, and is maintained by "whips" for each party. A senior MP is chosen as the chief whip and is assisted by other whips. Their function is to maintain party discipline in the house, especially when it comes to voting on issues that are important to the party. Failure to obey instructions can lead to expulsion from the party.

Although any individual member of Parliament may introduce a private member's bill, most of the Lok Sabha's time is in fact devoted to dealing with government business. Individual members of Parliament can exert influence more in party forums than in Parliament itself. A private bill will have little prospect of enactment, but does help an MP to reassure, appease, or deflect criticism from constituents. Its main purpose often is, indeed, to play to the gallery.

Like the speech from the throne, each session of the Lok Sabha is opened with a presidential address. The quorum for the Lok Sabha to be able to meet is one-tenth of its membership. The daily session opens at 11:00 A.M. with a question hour, which is strongly reminiscent of the British tradition. Some twenty to twenty-five questions are asked, answered, parried, or successfully evaded each day. The form of the initial question is tightly disciplined, but supplementary questions are generally given fairly wide latitude by the Speaker. As in all parliamentary systems, question hour can break or make a minister. An opposition backbencher can make her or his mark by displaying grasp of detail and mastery of debating skills, and might then be made a minister with a change of government; a serving minister can perform so poorly as to become a liability for the government in Parliament and the nation at large, and may be dropped from the cabinet.

The conduct of the house is in the hands of the Speaker. Selected by the governing party for formal election by the house and expected to conduct parliamentary business with fairness and impartiality, the Speaker recognizes members, keeps order, and has other duties that are required of presiding officers. The Speaker may not vote on an issue before the Lok Sabha, but can exercise a casting vote in the event of a tie on any motion being put to the vote.

Rajya Sabha

The Rajya Sabha (Council of States), the upper house, has 250 members, of whom 238 represent each of India's states and union territories; the remaining 12 are nominated by the president, acting on the advice of cabinet. The latter are chosen on the basis of their special knowledge or skills in the arts and sciences, or in order to rectify a serious underrepresentation in parliament of any particular group, or in an exercise of political patronage to reward the party faithful or major financial donors. The distribution of Rajya Sabha seats among states is roughly in proportion to their populations, with some effort at equalization. Bihar, for example, has 54 seats in the Lok Sabha and 22 in the Rajya Sabha; Himachal Pradesh has 4 seats in the lower house and 3 in the upper. Members of state legislative assemblies elect Rajya Sabha representatives for their states on a proportional representation system.

Members of India's upper house, as well as its lower house, are called members of Parliament (MPs). Rajya Sabha MPs are elected for six-year terms, with a biennial turnover of one-third of the house. Unlike the Lok Sabha, the upper house is not subject to dissolution. The quorum of the Rajya Sabha is 25 (one-tenth of the total membership), with decisions being made by a majority of members actually present and voting. The presiding officer of the Rajya Sabha is the vice-president of India.

There were three sets of reasons behind adopting a bicameral legislature for the union of India. First, the Rajya Sabha, as its name implies, was to be the custodian of states' rights in a federal polity. Second, it provides an opportunity and a forum for second thoughts and wiser counsel, even after the passage of a bill by the Lok Sabha. And third, it enables a bill (other than financial bills) to be introduced in Parliament even when the Lok Sabha is not in session. As a result of this sensible procedure, much of the preliminary debate and work on the bill can be completed by the time the Lok Sabha reconvenes.

In theory, the Rajya Sabha provides the opportunity to bring into Parliament competent, skilled personnel who may not be prepared to face the uncertain rigors of political campaigns. They can be appointed to the Rajya Sabha and be inducted into cabinet without having to go through an election. In practice, however, the Rajya Sabha can provide a backdoor entry into Parliament for unelectable or defeated candidates whose loyalty to the party is believed sufficient for access to power.

The Opposition

The opposition in a parliamentary democracy is expected to play the role of an alternative government, complete with a "shadow" prime minister- and cabinet-in-waiting. Because of the large number of political parties in India, the status of the leader of the opposition can be conferred only on the leader of a party that has at least fifty seats in the Lok Sabha. The leader of the opposition in the thirteenth parliament was Congress Party leader Sonia Gandhi, widow of the assassinated former prime minister Rajiv Gandhi and the heir apparent of the Nehru-Gandhi political dynasty. Following the success of the Congress Party in the 2004 elections, she would have become prime minister had she been willing to do so. (A naturalized citizen, her foreign birth would not have barred her from office.)

Opposition parties may not have many MPs in the house, and their claims to be a government-in-waiting may be utter fiction. Nonetheless, by their existence and their voice in parliament they express the diversity of opinions in a country as large and varied as India. Party discipline ensures that the opposition loses when the votes on any motion are tallied, but statements in Parliament are heard in the country at large and are often listened to within the ranks of the ruling party. This is particularly relevant in a country like India, where the major parties are not sharply distinguished by ideological differences. This has been especially noticeable with the proliferation of the increasingly influential independent electronic media during the 1990s. Although the debate in Parliament is ostensibly between the government and the opposition, it can also serve to structure the internal debates within an omnibus ruling party. This has been a distinctive feature of Indian politics.

Ramesh Thakur

See also **Federalism and Center-State Relations**

BIBLIOGRAPHY

Biju, M. R. *Parliamentary Democracy and Political Change in India*. New Delhi: Kanishka Publishers, 1999.

Handbook for Lok Sabha Members. New Delhi: Lok Sabha Secretariat, 1998.

Handbook for Members of Rajya Sabha. New Delhi: Rajya Sabha Secretariat, 1996.

Hatchard, John, ed. *Parliamentary Supremacy and Judicial Independence: A Commonwealth Approach*. London: Cavendish Publishing, 1999.

Kashyap, Subhash C. *History of the Parliament of India*. New Delhi: Konark Publishers, 2000.

———. *Parliamentary Procedure: The Law, Privileges, Practice, and Precedents*. Delhi: Universal Law Publishing, 2000.

Kurian, George Thomas, ed. *World Encyclopedia of Parliaments and Legislatures*. Chicago: Fitzroy Dearborn, 1998.

Palekar, S. A. *Constitution and Parliamentary Democracy in India*. Jaipur: A.B.D. Publishers, 2000.

Pandya, B. P. *Parliamentary Government in India*. Delhi: B. R. Publishing, 1999.

Parliament of India web site. Available at <http://parliamentofindia.nic.in>

PRESIDENT

The president of India nominally stands at the apex of the country's political system. The executive power of government is vested in the president as both the formal head of state and as a symbol of the nation. In reality, the office of president confers status more than power. The president has symbolic authority and dignity but little power, except in times of emergency, and performs an essentially ceremonial role. The actual functions of government are carried out by the president only with the aid and advice of the prime minister and the cabinet.

The president is elected to office for five-year terms. Reelection is permitted, but to date only the first president of India, Rajendra Prasad, was given a second term. Any Indian citizen who is at least thirty-five years old and qualified for election to the Lok Sabha (the lower house of Parliament) is eligible to seek the presidency. The president is not directly elected by the people. Instead, in order to avoid creating a parallel center of authority in a parliamentary system of government, the president is chosen by an electoral college, consisting of both houses of Parliament and the state legislative assemblies. This method of election helps to keep in check presidential ambitions: chosen by legislators, presidents may not challenge those who have been directly elected by the people. The twin principles, of uniformity among states and parity between the central government and the states, are meant to ensure the election of a truly national candidate.

The weight assigned to each state elector's vote reflects population ratios: one-thousandth of the total population of each state is divided by the number of elected legislators in the state assembly. (The quotient is rounded to the nearest whole number.) This ensures uniformity among states. The aggregate value of the votes of the electors of all states (say 500,000) is then divided by

Vladimir Putin, A. P. J. Abdul Kalam, and A. B. Vajpayee. Russia's President Vladimir Putin being welcomed by India's President A. P. J. Abdul Kalam and Prime Minister A. B. Vajpayee. INDIA TODAY.

the number of members of the Lok Sabha and the Rajya Sabha (say 750 altogether) to determine the value of the vote of each member of Parliament (which in this case would be 667). Using this method, the aggregate vote of the Lok and Rajya Sabhas combined necessarily equals the aggregate vote of all the state assemblies combined, thus satisfying the principle of parity between the center and the states.

In order to be elected president, a candidate must receive an absolute majority of the votes cast by the electoral college. The method of voting is the single transferable vote, with electors casting first and second preferences. As the lowest polling candidate is eliminated in each round, his or her preferences are transferred to other remaining candidates as per the electors' wishes, until such time as one candidate crosses the threshold of 50 percent of the votes cast. The lack of popular participation robs the choice of the excitement normally associated with elections in India, but it does serve to underline the dignity of the office.

The president is not answerable to any court for actions taken in the course of performing official duties, but is subject to impeachment by Parliament for violating the constitution. A serving president can also resign, for example, for reasons of personal health.

The vice-president is elected for a five-year term by both houses of Parliament in a joint session, not by an electoral college. Responsibilities include presiding over the sessions of the Rajya Sabha (the upper house), deputizing for the president as necessary and succeeding the president if the office should fall vacant for any reason until new elections can be held. There is no necessary expectation that the vice-president should become the next president.

The choice of president and vice-president requires political judgment and balance, especially over a period of time. The offices must be rotated among India's major regions and among the major components of the Indian population (especially Hindu and Muslim, but also other minority groups, such as the Sikhs). The one balance that has not been struck so far is that of gender: no woman has yet been elected president of India. The professional background of India's presidents has mostly been political.

Powers

The powers of the president of India are normally ornamental, comprising appointive, dismissive, legislative, and symbolic functions. The president appoints the prime minister and also, on the advice of the latter, the cabinet; the justices of the Supreme Court and state high courts; the attorney general and the comptroller and auditor general of India; members of special commissions and other high public officials; and the governors of states. The choice of prime minister is not a discretionary prerogative to be exercised by the president, but is usually dictated by the party commanding a majority in the Lok Sabha. In most cases, the power to appoint is matched by the power to dismiss. The prime minister formally holds office at the pleasure of the president; in reality, the prime minister retains office as long as he or she can demonstrate majority support in the Lok Sabha.

The president calls Parliament into session, nominates twelve members of the Rajya Sabha, has the right to address both houses of Parliament, and the power to dissolve the lower house. A bill that has been passed by Parliament must be presented to the president for formal assent in order for it to become law. The president may withhold assent and return a bill—unless it is a financial bill—for clarification, reconsideration, or possible amendment by Parliament. However, such a presidential "veto" can be overridden if both houses of Parliament simply pass the bill again. Some types of bill, for example those seeking to alter state boundaries, can be introduced in Parliament only on the president's recommendation.

Another legislative power is in the form of ordinances. When Parliament is not in session but immediate action is deemed necessary, the president is empowered by the Constitution (Article 123) to issue ordinances on the advice of the government. Although ordinances have the same force and effect as acts of Parliament, they must be laid before Parliament for formal enactment within six weeks of Parliament reconvening.

The president is the commander-in-chief of India's armed services, receives ambassadors from other countries, represents India on state visits abroad, and presides in New Delhi's Parliament or Old Delhi's Red Fort on the great national occasions. The president has the power to grant pardons. However, in almost all cases, presidential powers are exercised only on the advice of the prime minister and the Cabinet.

Controversies and Debates

Sometimes the election of the president can itself become the arena for a power struggle between rival political factions. When President Zakir Hussain died in office in 1969, Vice-President V. V. Giri took over as acting president until the election of a new president, which was required to be held within six months. The official Congress Party candidate was N. Sanjiva Reddy, a politician from within the party. Prime Minister Indira Gandhi, who was locked in a struggle for power within her own ruling party, let it be known that her preferred candidate was V. V. Giri. His election underscored Gandhi's power in Parliament over older Congress stalwarts who had long dominated the party organization.

Another debate that exercised an earlier generation but has become less salient in recent times is whether a president could abuse emergency powers granted under the Constitution in order to capture real power. The more interesting debate in recent times has been whether a presidential system of government might be better suited to Indian conditions and needs. A presidential system like that of the United States separates the executive from the legislature and places a directly elected president at the head of the executive branch. In a parliamentary system, the government is headed by a prime minister who is a member of the party or coalition commanding a majority in the legislature. The president has no equal; the prime minister is first among equals.

The debate on the relative merits and suitability of parliamentary and presidential systems is rooted in the belief that the performance of parliamentary government has been unsatisfactory. The desire for presidential government betrays a frustration among some Indians with the weakening of the central government under challenge from a number of states. A presidential type of government, its proponents believe, would help to restore order to a troubled country, dilute the corruption of the political system, and accelerate the pace of India's economic development.

Most Indian analysts reject this view. Parliamentary democracy can be more stable, especially in societies riven by deep social and political cleavages. Under such conditions, parliamentary regimes have built-in mechanisms for power sharing, for example through coalition governments, whereas presidential elections are winner-take-all affairs that effectively disenfranchise the losing minority until the next election. Parliamentary governments also have the greater ability to rule in multiparty settings. A presidential system takes a zero-sum game approach to political power, with one winner and one or more losers for the entire term of presidential office. Parliamentary regimes place a higher premium on the political skills of bargaining and consensus building than do presidential counterparts. Coalitions can offer effective and continuous representation to a variety of interests that would be excluded from the administration in a presidential government.

The discretionary latitude available to a president depends less on the office or the incumbent and more on the state of party politics in Parliament or the Cabinet. If a prime minister commands the loyalty of the cabinet and the confidence of Parliament, and if the government in power is stable, there is little scope for independent presidential initiatives. Even within this limitation, nevertheless, when the Rajiv Gandhi government tried to enact a bill in 1987 giving the government new powers to spy on private correspondence, President Zail Singh withheld assent from a bill already passed by both houses of Parliament. With public opinion strongly on the side of the president, the government backed down. If the government is a coalition of different parties based in different ideologies, interests, states, or regions, then the president can play an interesting mediating role in center-state relations. For example, the prime minister and cabinet may recommend the replacement of an elected state government by direct "presidential" rule from the center, but the president may demur and seek further "clarifications." This happened in Bihar in the 1990s, and the Bharatiya Janata Party (BJP)–led coalition government in New Delhi backed off from dismissing the non-BJP government in the state.

Ramesh Thakur

See also **Federalism and Center-State Relations**

BIBLIOGRAPHY

Butler, David, and D. A. Low, eds. *Sovereigns and Surrogates: Constitutional Heads of State in the Commonwealth*. London: Macmillan, 1991.

Jai, Janak Raj. *Presidents of India*. New Delhi: Regency Publications, 2000.

Noorani, A. G. *Constitutional Questions in India: The President, Parliament, and the States*. Delhi: Oxford University Press, 2000.

Riggs, Fred W. "Presidentialism versus Parliamentarism: Implications for Representativeness and Legitimacy." *International Political Science Review* 18, no. 3 (1997): 253–278.

Jawaharlal Nehru (prime minister 1947–1964). A complex man and perhaps India's greatest prime minister, he once stated: "Peace is not a relationship of nations. . . . Peace is not merely the absence of war. . . . It is a condition of mind brought about by a serenity of soul." NEHRU MEMORIAL TRUST / FOTOMEDIA.

PRIME MINISTER

The prime minister of India, as in London's Westminster, is the linchpin of India's system of government. In Britain, the convention is firmly established that the prime minister must be a member of the lower house of Parliament. By contrast, at the time of her selection as prime minister in 1966, Indira Gandhi was a member of the upper house of India's parliament, the Rajya Sabha. In order to deflect criticism and to consolidate her family's political power base, Gandhi was subsequently elected to the Lok Sabha from Rae Bareilly, which had been her father's constituency in the state of Uttar Pradesh. Rajiv Gandhi maintained the Nehru-Gandhi family tradition of representing Rae Bareilly in the Lok Sabha, as would his widow Sonia Gandhi.

India's Constitution defines the duties of the prime minister in Article 78. Sources of prime ministerial power include: leadership of the council of ministers, leadership of party, control of parliamentary activities, control of intelligence agencies, control of the bureaucracy, control of foreign policy, emergency powers, and personal charisma.

The prime minister has almost total freedom in appointing members of Parliament (MPs) to ministerial posts. In making the selections, nevertheless, the party leader must ensure adequate representation to India's regional and sectarian interests, and also to the various factions within the ruling party. For example, in 1977, regardless of personal likes and dislikes, Prime Minister Morarji Desai had to include Charan Singh and Jagjivan Ram in his Cabinet and give them powerful portfolios (finance and defense, respectively). Sometimes public

Three Generations of the Nehru Family. Jawaharlal (who served as India's first prime minister from 1947–1964), daughter Indira Gandhi (who served as prime minister from 1966–1977 and from 1980 until her assassination in 1984), and her sons Rajiv (who directly succeeded his mother, serving until 1989, and was later assassinated while mounting a political comeback) and Sanjay (who it was assumed would enter politics until a plane crash took his life in 1981). NEHRU MEMORIAL TRUST / FOTOMEDIA.

opinion may force certain changes even on the most powerful prime ministers. After the debacle of the war with China in 1962, for example, Prime Minister Jawaharlal Nehru had to remove Defence Minister V. K. Krishna Menon from the cabinet, since Krishna Menon had become identified in the public mind with the disasters of India's China policy. India has learned to live with coalition governments ruling in New Delhi for over two decades, and its prime ministers have had to manage fractious coalition allies with large egos. Former prime minister Atal Bihari Vajpayee sometimes used the threat of resignation to force recalcitrant allies to fall in line behind government policy. At other times he allowed some members of the coalition to resign from his Cabinet rather than meet their demands.

Still, in general a prime minister can exercise considerable influence on parliamentary colleagues, and therefore on the destiny of the country, by constituting, reconstituting, and reshuffling the cabinet and chairing cabinet meetings. Prime Minister Gandhi began to assert herself against party elders almost from the start by inducting her own people into the cabinet, such as Ashoka Mehta, G. S. Pathak, and Fakhruddin Ali Ahmed.

In parliamentary governments in the West, there is a tendency to leave particular individuals in charge of particular portfolios for a period of time so that they may develop and use specialized expertise. Confident of his stature in the country and his authority over his Cabinet, Prime Minister Jawaharlal Nehru kept some Cabinet colleagues in charge of the same ministry for considerable lengths of time, allowing them to acquire expertise in their respective fields. Prime Minister Gandhi, on the other hand, was notorious for the continual reshuffling of the ministries. She did this in part to demonstrate her power, and in part to prevent potential rivals from developing independent power bases by keeping them all off balance. The net result was to disrupt the efficient functioning of government. Rajiv Gandhi maintained his mother's tradition of frequent reassignment of Cabinet posts.

Shifting Cabinet portfolios enlarges the room for maneuver of a prime minister who wishes to control the agenda of government. The prime minister is the head of government by virtue of being the leader of the majority party in parliament. A party is elected to office on the basis of a policy platform spelled out in an election manifesto. The party leader is exceptionally well placed to influence and shape the translation of the party manifesto into government policy. The extreme example of prime ministerial control of parliamentary activities was probably the period of "National Emergency" rule by Indira Gandhi (1975–1977), when Parliament was in effect converted into her personal rubber stamp. All constitutional fetters were removed from the de facto exercise of power by the prime minister, and opposition leaders were, for the most part, in jail.

In parliamentary systems in the West, the functions and the functionaries of the leader of the party as an organization and the leader of the party in Parliament are usually separate. India is unusual among mature parliamentary democracies in having largely fused the offices of head of party organization and leader of the parliamentary wing of a political party; that was not the case after the 2004 elections, however, when Sonia Gandhi led the Congress Party and Manhohan Singh led Parliament as prime minister. In the early years after independence, Prime Minister Nehru had to learn to live with another person as Congress Party president—Purushottam Das Tandon. But Tandon, the protégé of the powerful Home Minister Sardar Vallabhbhai Patel, was outmaneuvered by Nehru soon after Patel's death. Nehru became Congress Party president in September 1951, thereby ending the so-called duumvirate, even though in later years he was to relinquish the party post, first to a weak and relatively unknown U. N. Dhebar, and then to his daughter, Indira Gandhi. The latter also acted as Nehru's social hostess, often accompanying him on many of his travels around India and abroad.

Indira Gandhi was minister of information and broadcasting under Nehru's successor, Prime Minister Lal Bahadur Shastri. When Shastri died after India and Pakistan signed a peace treaty in Tashkent in 1966, she was catapulted into power by the Congress Party bosses, who considered her a pliant woman, young in years and lacking in political experience. Her fierce independence was quickly demonstrated by her devaluation of the rupee in June 1966, a decision taken without prior consultation with such senior party colleagues as Morarji Desai and Congress Party president Kamaraj Nadar. The 1967 general election saw the defeat of many of the old party stalwarts, including Kamaraj, Atulya Ghosh, S. Nijalingappa, and S. K. Patil. When the ruling Congress Party split in 1969, Indira Gandhi turned to the many small parties of India's left wing for her political survival.

Indira Gandhi's fortunes revived with the general election of 1971 and the state elections of 1972, which together gave her a commanding position in New Delhi, with 352 seats for the Congress Paty in the Lok Sabha, and with Congress majorities in fifteen states and one union territory. Thereafter, she began to dominate every party organ: the All-India Congress Committee (AICC), the Congress Working Committee (CWC), the Congress Parliamentary Board (CPB), and the Central Election Committee. Even in defeat in 1977, when the organizational sections of the Congress Party deserted her, she abandoned them and effectively took the Congress Party majority with her, as was only too vividly demonstrated by her electoral triumph in 1980. It may not have been entirely accurate to say, as her many sycophants did, that "India is Indira, and Indira is India," but she certainly proved that "Indira is Congress, and Congress is Indira."

Prime Minister Rajiv Gandhi was the final arbiter in the choice of Congress Party candidates for election from all constituencies throughout India. The party organization became an instrument for the prime minister of India to control, and thus to dominate state politics as well. In 1975, for example, in the context of factional infighting within the state unit of the Congress Party, Uttar Pradesh chief minister H. N. Bahuguna declared that "Mrs. Gandhi is our Supreme Court."

Heads of government can also abuse their control of intelligence services for personal and party political purposes. Intelligence agencies traditionally come under prime ministerial oversight, not least because heads of government would mistrust potential rivals in charge of such key operations. The size and complexity of India, as well as its colonial past, account for the emergence of several intelligence agencies, the most important of which are: the Intelligence Bureau, including a Research and Analysis Wing (RAW); the Central Bureau of Investigation; the Criminal Investigation Department (Special Branch); and the Directorate of Revenue Intelligence.

Established in 1968 as an external intelligence agency, RAW was separated from the Intelligence Bureau in 1969 and placed under the cabinet secretariat, with the prime minister in the chair. Indira Gandhi expanded the powers and activities of RAW during the 1975–1977 "emergency" period and gave it an internal surveillance role, with the director of RAW reporting directly to her. The Shah

Commission report (withdrawn from sale and circulation by government order on 7 March 1980 after Gandhi's return to power) documented how the various branches of intelligence succumbed to political pressure and were used to harass, intimidate, and imprison political opponents during the two years of "emergency" rule. RAW was stripped of its internal surveillance functions by the Janata government (1977–1979). But Indira Gandhi was not the first nor the last prime minister of India to use the intelligence agencies to keep abreast of moves and countermoves by potential challengers and to harass political opponents. Similar allegations were also leveled against the Vajpayee government.

In addition to using intelligence agencies for maintaining a watching brief over opponents and potential rivals, the prime minister can exercise political control through the regular channels of bureaucracy (including the police). This is especially so in India, where the centralization of the elite administrative and police services facilitates vertical control of their activities. Early in her tenure, Indira Gandhi introduced such phrases as "committed bureaucracy" into her political vocabulary. Personal loyalty to the prime minister became the most important criterion in determining promotions and assignments of senior officials.

The greatest opportunity for a prime minister of India to exercise total power within the constitution comes during the declaration of a national emergency. It is not an exaggeration to say that the 1975–1977 experience was a period of prime ministerial dictatorship. The period of "emergency" rule was an aberration, even by Indian standards. Increasingly in the modern world, heads of governments of all countries have begun to play the most visible role in determining their countries' foreign policies. India is no exception to the rule. Nehru was a founding father of nonalignment and the chief architect of independent India's foreign policy. Prime ministerial dominance of foreign policy did not diminish under his successors. No one in India or abroad was in any doubt that the country's foreign policy during Indira Gandhi's premiership was determined first and foremost by her, regardless of who may have been foreign minister. The same remained true of Rajiv Gandhi. The chief spokesman for India's place in the world since the nuclear test of 1998 has been the prime minister.

An international role in turn enhances the domestic status and stature of the prime minister. Nehru profited from his image as a world statesman, and Rajiv Gandhi tried to carve out a niche by such means as the Gandhi-Gorbachev Delhi Declaration of 27 November 1986. All major international conferences, for example the Commonwealth Heads of Governments Meeting, are attended by the prime minister personally. Visits abroad to other countries and to such forums as the United Nations are treated as major political events, where the prime minister is on show. Prime Minister Vajpayee was a regular participant in the annual opening of the United Nations General Assembly, and he used the sidelines of the event to meet with any number of counterparts from around the world (as well as to interact with the increasingly influential expatriate Indian community in the United States).

Prime Minister of India, Dr. Manmohan Singh. Sworn in on May 22, 2004, the low-key Manmohan Singh, India's first non-Hindu prime minister. In the mid-1990s, the course of economic liberalization he charted as finance minister helped to save India from the brink of bankruptcy. INDIA TODAY.

The final source of prime ministerial authority is the individual attributes and charisma of the person occupying the office. As one would expect, some are more charismatic than others.

Ramesh Thakur

See also **Gandhi, Indira; Gandhi, Rajiv; Nehru, Jawaharlal; Vajpayee, Atal Bihari**

BIBLIOGRAPHY

Manor, James, ed. *Nehru to the Nineties: The Changing Office of Prime Minister in India.* London: C. Hurst, 1995.

Thakur, Janardhan. *Prime Ministers: Nehru to Vajpayee.* New Delhi: BPI, 2002.

PONDICHERRY. *See* **French Impact.**

POPULATION, GENDER RATIO OF India's gender ratio (females per 1,000 males, or FMR)—933 in 2001—is strikingly low compared to both developed and developing countries (about 1,050 in Europe, 960 in North Africa, and 940 in China). Moreover, the FMR has declined monotonically since 1901 (from 972), reaching its lowest level in 1991 (927) with small improvements in 1981 (934) and 2001. This secular decline has prompted estimates of "missing women," based on standard census benchmarks. P. N. Mari Bhat (2002) estimates that the number of women "missing" in 1951, relative to 1901 age-specific FMRs, was 5 million; based on 1951 benchmarks, the number "missing" in 1991 was 9 million.

Though FMR declines in Indian states from 1901 to 1991 were diverse, they traced regional patterns that cut across state and district boundaries. Since antifemale bias in northern India is well documented, demographers initially focused on a north-south divide with a notional boundary at the Narmada River. In 2001, however, the Narmada boundary was breached. FMRs were low (below 925) not only in the north, but also in the west and center, and high (above 975) in the south and east.

The real causes of India's low and declining FMRs are hard to determine. Explanations have centered on spatial and demographic patterns, cultural phenomena, socioeconomic determinants, and the impact of poverty and growth.

Spatial and Demographic Patterns

State and regional patterns. Jean Drèze and Amartya Sen (1995) identified declines in state-specific FMRs as proximate causes of India's falling gender ratio, noting that six states (Bihar, Madhya Pradesh, Maharashtra, Orissa, Tamil Nadu, and Uttar Pradesh) were largely responsible. Bhat's regional analysis (2002) revealed that though FMRs declined across all regions during 1901–1951, the east (Assam, West Bengal) and center (Madhya Pradesh, Bihar, Orissa) led the fall; however, during 1951–1991, the central region clearly spearheaded the decline. The north (Haryana, Himachal Pradesh, Punjab, Rajasthan, Uttar Pradesh), with the lowest FMR in 1901, was still at the bottom of the ladder in 2001. Though FMRs in the south (Andhra Pradesh, Karnataka, Kerala, Tamil Nadu) declined throughout the last century, the region ended up in 2001 with the highest gender ratio. By 2001, FMRs for the center, east, and west (Maharashtra, Gujarat), which had started out at very different levels, had converged to a range of 920–935.

Three fallacies. An early explanation of low Indian FMRs, the underenumeration of females, buckled under scrutiny. Though occasional census undercounts (for censuses before 1931 and for 1971 and 1991) cannot be ruled out, a sustained and increasing underenumeration is implausible. Another explanation, the migration of males in search of economic opportunities, clearly cannot explain the secular decline in national FMRs. A third rationale, exceptionally high masculinity at birth in India, is spurious as Asok Mitra (1979) pointed out; India's sex ratio at birth has varied in the normal range of 104–107 male births per 100 female births (FMRs of 935–960) during 1901–1981.

Fertility. M. Das Gupta and Bhat (1997) demonstrated that in India where son-preference is strong, fertility decline itself could worsen child sex ratios. Even if son-preference falls with fertility decline, access to sex-abortion technology could exacerbate gender bias. However, fertility decline in India clearly reduced adult female mortality because childbearing declined.

Mortality. Pravin M. Visaria (1969) firmly established that India's low FMRs were due to sex differentials in mortality. Others suggested that a small sex differential in infant and childhood mortality persisting over a period might have caused India's high masculinity, but the decomposition of India's FMRs by Bhat and Drèze and Sen suggested greater complexity.

Adult FMRs. Drèze and Sen's analysis revealed that the overall FMR was driven by a sustained decline in the FMR of the thirty plus age group during 1901–1971. Bhat corroborated their conclusion for adults aged fifteen plus, surmising that the substantial survival advantage that women aged fifteen plus enjoyed over men in 1901 quickly eroded as mortality levels fell during the last century. Bhat also found that of the 5 million women estimated missing in 1951, all were aged fifteen and over. The central region had the sharpest decline in adult FMRs during 1951–1991, and contributed nearly half the women estimated missing in 1991 (using 1901 benchmarks).

Juvenile FMRs. Bhat found that the age structure of missing women changed dramatically after 1951: almost half the 9 million women missing in 1991 were children aged fourteen and under. This dramatic change justifies an in-depth focus on juvenile FMRs, but the definition of "juvenile" has varied.

Bhat argued that age misreporting could distort juvenile FMRs, because in societies with son preference, censuses tend to overestimate the age of males and underestimate female ages beginning from early childhood. Such misreporting exaggerates early childhood FMRs, like FMR aged 0–4, and lowers FMRs in later juvenile age groups; however, as age reporting improves with increased literacy and birth registration, FMR 0–4 falls, and older juvenile FMRs rise. Bhat claimed that more accurate age reporting was therefore partly responsible for the observed fall in FMR 0–4 and the rise in FMRs for children aged 5–9, 10–14, and 0–14 during 1901–1951. On the other hand, the subsequent fall in FMR 0–4 (38 points) during 1951–1991 and the significant associated declines in FMR 5–9, FMR 10–14, and FMR 0–14 (27 points) indicated that these declines in childhood FMRs were largely real.

Satish B. Agnihotri's classic analysis (2003) of recent juvenile gender ratios was built on his insights that gender gaps in mortality affect FMRs more strongly than mortality levels; gender differentials in infant mortality rates affect FMR 0–4 most acutely, while gender differentials in mortality in the 1–4 age group affect FMR 5–9 most severely. Thus, since FMR 0–4 and FMR 5–9 levels and gaps are good indicators of gender differentials in mortality, Agnihotri focused on these FMRs. In the 1981 Census, low values of FMR 5–9s and large gaps between FMR 0–4 and FMR 5–9 in numerous districts indicated significant excess female child mortality and confirmed a north-south divide; low FMR 0–4s (<910) in Punjab, Haryana, and western Uttar Pradesh suggested excess female infant mortality. The picture darkened in 1991. Districts with FMR 0–4 of less than 910 increased, pointing to the prevalence of female infanticide and (possibly) sex-selective abortions, while the startling rise in districts with FMR 0–4 of less than 960 suggested that increased girl mortality in the post neonatal and 1–4 age groups was "pushing further and deeper into the south."

The rural-urban divide and sex-selective abortions. Census and survey data confirmed that the rural FMR 0–14 fell continuously during 1951–1991, while the urban ratio fell precipitately after 1981. In 2001 the 18-point drop in the overall FMR 0–6 and the sharp plunge in the mean urban FMR 0–6 relative to the rural confirmed that the "northernization" of gender ratios was taking an urban route, thanks possibly to greater urban access to technologies for sex-selective abortion. Microresearch and S. Sudha and S. Irudaya Rajan's (2003) estimates of sex ratios at birth supported the hypothesis that the increased masculinity at birth over the last two decades was manmade, and confirmed that the pattern had extended beyond the north-northwest and had penetrated deeply into the four southern states.

Cultural Phenomena

Ethnicity. In 1961 FMRs of scheduled tribes (STs) and scheduled castes (SCs), which now constitute about 8 and 16 percent of India's population respectively, were higher than for the "rest of the population" (987, 957, and 934 respectively). Though FMRs of all groups declined during 1961–1991, the SC decline was so dramatic that the FMRs of the SCs and the "rest of the population" converged at about 922. Bhat found that almost two-fifths of the women missing between 1961–1991 were from SCs.

Proximity to Muslim influence is alleged to have lowered northwestern FMRs, but the notion is spurious: in both 1981 and 1991, Muslims were associated with less risk of excess female child mortality.

Kinship. Conventionally, the north-south divide in FMRs has been associated with different kinship systems. Northern women generally have low status associated with relatively high fertility and mortality, strong son preference, limited female property rights, low female labor participation, female seclusion, neglect of female children, and endogamous marriage; southern women enjoy stronger female agency. Agnihotri matched linguistic and kinship systems to arrive at a new binary classification of 1981 Census districts: a male-centered, Indo-Aryan "core" of 164 districts (primarily in the north and west, but including pockets in the south) with significantly low FMRs; and a "periphery" of the remaining 202 districts (including some female-friendly northern districts), combining Indo-Aryan, Dravidian, and Munda kinship and language systems, with high FMRs. Agnihotri found that in 1981 the "core" was associated with both excess female infant mortality and excess female mortality under the age of five.

Socioeconomic Determinants

Female labor participation (FLP). Demographers have long recognized that work affects FMRs by enhancing women's worth and their access to basic household resources. In 1981 FLP was highest among STs, lower for SCs, and lowest for the rest of the population. Agnihotri found that the relationship between FLPs and FMR 5–9s was strong in the "core" in 1961 and 1981, both for SCs and the "rest of the population." However, Agnihotri found that kinship explained a larger part of the variance in FMR 5–9s than FLPs.

Multivariate analysis of other socioeconomic correlates of female disadvantage in child mortality revealed that the association between male literacy and female disadvantage was either positive or not significant, and that between female literacy and female disadvantage was negative but not consistently significant between 1981 and 1991.

Poverty and Growth

Both the literature and cross-section data indicate that poverty and gender inequality are negatively associated.

If so, are economic growth and poverty reduction likely to induce greater gender inequality and lower the FMR over time, or is a U-shaped Kuznets curve likely (whereby the FMR initially decreases, bottoms out, and then rises as income increases)? Analyzing National Sample Survey Organization data (for 1987–1988, 1992–1993, and 1999–2000), Agnihotri found a negative association between FMRs and per capita expenditures for the total, adult, and juvenile populations, and urban and rural areas. The results therefore appear to negate the prosperity optimism of proponents of the Kuznets curve. Thus, despite five decades of growth, declining FMRs persist as a symptom of gender inequality and female deprivation, which Drèze and Sen characterize as "among India's most serious social failures."

Jayati Datta-Mitra

See also **Economic Development, Importance of Institutions in and Social Aspects of; Poverty and Inequality**

BIBLIOGRAPHY

Agnihotri, Satish B. *Sex Ratio Patterns in the Indian Population: A Fresh Exploration.* New Delhi: Sage Publications India, 2000. A classic work on the importance and determinants of disaggregated juvenile sex ratios using post-1961 census and survey data.

———. "Survival of the Girl Child: Tunnelling Out of the Chakravyuha." *Economic and Political Weekly* 38, no. 41 (11 October 2003): 4351–4360. An excellent exploration of the urban spread of the declining sex ratio for children aged 0–6 years during 1991–2001, and the possible role of sex-selective abortion.

Bhat, P. N. Mari. "On the Trail of Missing Indian Females." *Economic and Political Weekly* 37, no. 51, 37, no. 52 (December 2002): 5105–5118, 5244–5263. A solid exploration of the conundrum of India's falling gender ratio during 1901–1991, from a demographic, regional, and social perspective.

Das Gupta, M., and P. N. Mari Bhat. "Fertility Decline and Increased Manifestation of Sex Bias in India." *Population Studies* 51, no. 3 (1997): 307–315. A signal contribution to the literature on the impact of fertility decline on sex bias in India in the context of other Asian societies with strong son-preference, estimates of "missing" women between 1981 and 1991, and the emerging evidence on sex-selective abortion.

Drèze, Jean, and Amartya Sen. *India: Economic Development and Social Opportunity.* Delhi: Oxford University Press, 1995. Chapter 7 provides one of the best introductions to gender ratio issues in the broader context of gender inequality, socioeconomic indicators, and women's agency.

Mazumdar, Veena, and N. Krishnaji, eds. *Enduring Conundrum: India's Sex Ratio: Essays in Honour of Asok Mitra.* Delhi: Rainbow Publishers, 2001. Contains valuable reviews and analysis of the issues as well as a glimpse into the role played by the Committee on the Status of Women in India in insinuating gender concerns into public policy.

Mitra, Asok. *Implications of the Sex Ratio in India's Population.* New Delhi: Allied Publishers, 1979. Mitra, a pioneer in promoting women's studies in India, was one of the first to direct public attention to the country's declining gender ratio.

Sudha, S., and S. Irudaya Rajan. "Persistent Daughter Disadvantage: What Do Estimated Sex Ratios at Birth and Sex Ratios of Child Mortality Risk Reveal?" *Economic and Political Weekly* 38, no. 41 (11 October 2003): 4361–4369. The authors present an insightful perspective on increasing (manmade) masculinity at birth during 1981–1991, based on estimated sex-ratios at birth and multivariate analysis of socioeconomic and cultural variables.

Visaria, Pravin M. *The Sex Ratio of the Population of India.* Census of India 1961, vol. 1, monograph no. 10. New Delhi: Office of the Registrar General, 1969. Recognized by demographers as one of the first landmark studies in the field.

POPULATION PRESSURE. *See* **Demographic Trends since 1757.**

PORTUGUESE IN INDIA The Portuguese were the first Europeans to arrive in India by sea, thus securing a monopoly of Asia-Europe maritime trade for a century until the advent of the Dutch, English, and French in the region. Vasco da Gama's "discovery" of the sea route to India inaugurated the Age of Colonialism, which brought revolutionary changes to economic, political, and cultural spheres in most of Asia.

The Portuguese exploratory enterprise vigorously supported by Prince Henry the Navigator in the mid-fifteenth century may be seen in the context of a major event—the discovery of the sea route—that affected both trade and religion. Thus, after the fall of Constantinople to the Turks in 1453, the Italian city-states that were trading in spices, sugar, and other Eastern goods demanded astronomical prices from their European customers on the pretext that it was much harder to get such goods through the Arab- and Persian-controlled Middle East. There was much profit in bypassing the traditional route and reaching the source of these products directly by sea.

Second, concerned with the threat of Muslims advancing toward Europe, Pope Alexander VI encouraged finding a route to India, which was then, albeit erroneously, believed to be Christian thanks to the exertions of Apostle Thomas in the first century A.D. The pope hoped that with the help of "Christian" India, it would be possible to attack the Muslims in a pincer movement.

The Papal Bull of 1492 specifically authorized the Portuguese with such a mission, which brought Vasco da Gama and his four ships to Calicut in present-day Kerala on 18 May 1498. Asked by two Muslim merchants of Tunis, who happened to be in Calicut, "What the devil

Statue of a Portuguese Nobleman in Diu. Diu is a former Portuguese colony on the western coast of India with a strategic location on the idyllic Gulf of Cambay. Along with Daman and Goa, it remained a territory of Portugal until liberation by Indian forces in 1961, when all three became the Indian state of Goa (since then each has been granted separate status). CHRISTINE PEMBERTON / FOTOMEDIA.

has brought you here? In search of what have you come from such a long distance?" a man in Vasco da Gama's party promptly replied, "We have come in search of Christians and spices." The Portuguese thought that the people of Calicut were Christians and that their temples were chapels. Vasco da Gama and his men offered prayers in a "chapel" before the image of "Mary" in what was, in fact, a Hindu temple. The mistake was not discovered until the second Portuguese visit, led by Pedro Álvars Cabral in 1500; the king of Portugal subsequently ordered conversions of as many Indians as possible to the Catholic faith. Profits from trade and the spread of Christianity remained the twin Portuguese goals, though relatively modest success crowned their prodigious efforts over the 450 years of their presence in the East.

The importance of da Gama's discovery was recognized by the Portuguese king, Manuel I, who made Vasco da Gama "admiral of the Indian Ocean" and assumed for himself, in 1499, the pompous title—reflecting more a hope than reality—"lord of the Conquest, Navigation and Commerce of Ethiopia, Arabia, Persia and of India." Conquest, Commerce, and Christianity were closely intertwined as the intrepid Portuguese worked for God, gold, and glory for their king.

The Portuguese were very fortunate in the timing of their arrival in South India. The Bahamani kingdom in the Deccan had split into five entities, none of which had a significant navy. Historically, although India had distinguished itself in maritime trade, no Indian ruler (with the exception of Rajendra Chola in the eleventh century) had built a navy, for offense or defense, because no enemy had ever attacked India from across the seas. The rulers of Calicut, Cochin, and Cannanore, to mention only a few coastal states dependent on the substantial revenues coming from coastal and oceanic trade, were accustomed to large numbers of merchants from China, Malacca, Java, Arabia, and North Africa who came as peaceful traders and exchanged merchandise; some of them even left representatives behind to look after their trading interests, which included warehouses.

Initially, the *samuri* (*zamorin* in Portuguese parlance) of Calicut was friendly and hospitable to the Portuguese.

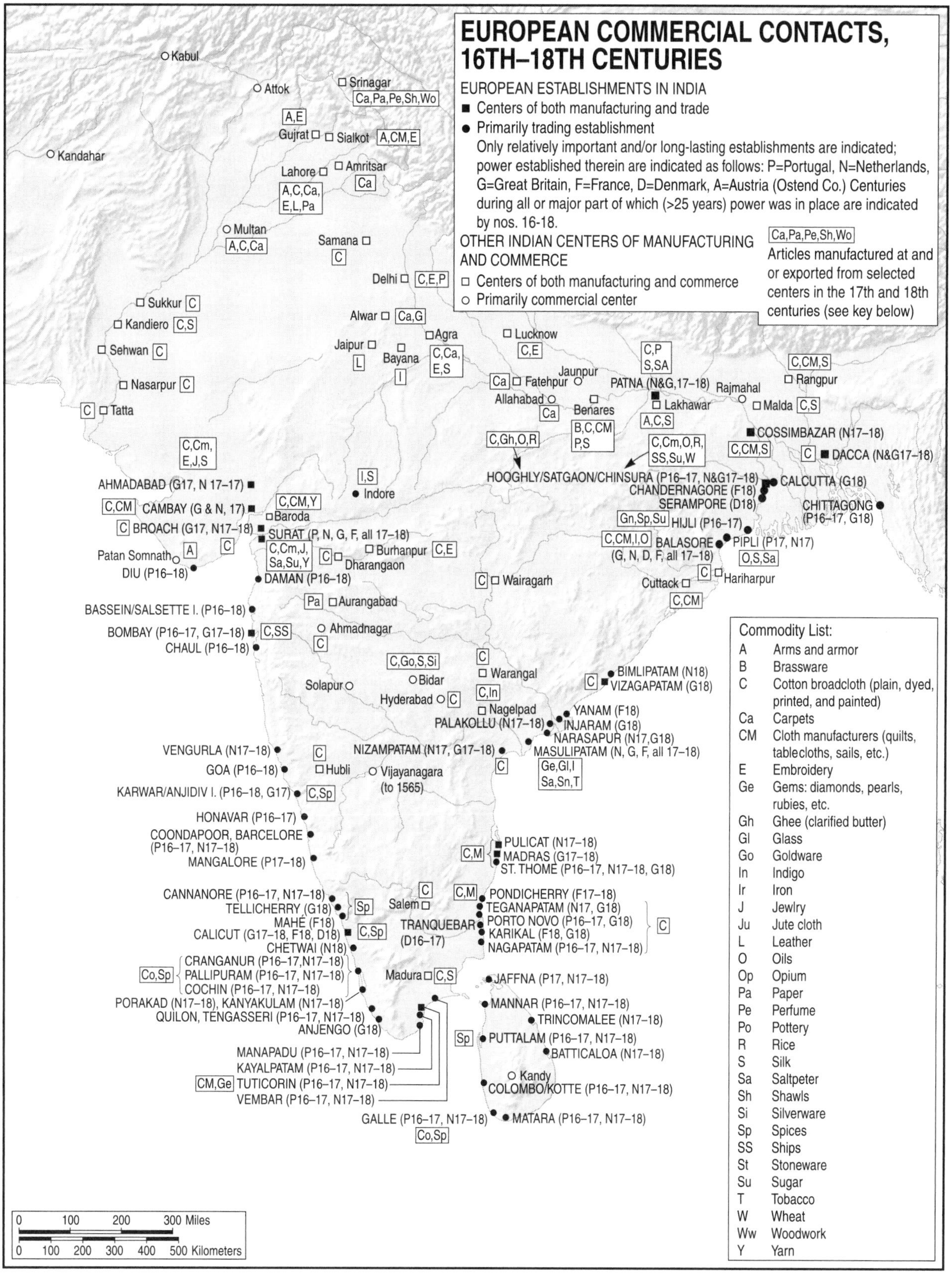
EUROPEAN COMMERCIAL CONTACTS, 16TH–18TH CENTURIES
EUROPEAN ESTABLISHMENTS IN INDIA
■ Centers of both manufacturing and trade
● Primarily trading establishment
Only relatively important and/or long-lasting establishments are indicated; power established therein are indicated as follows: P=Portugal, N=Netherlands, G=Great Britain, F=France, D=Denmark, A=Austria (Ostend Co.) Centuries during all or major part of which (>25 years) power was in place are indicated by nos. 16-18.
OTHER INDIAN CENTERS OF MANUFACTURING AND COMMERCE
□ Centers of both manufacturing and commerce
○ Primarily commercial center
Ca,Pa,Pe,Sh,Wo
Articles manufactured at and or exported from selected centers in the 17th and 18th centuries (see key below)
Kabul
Attok
Srinagar
Ca,Pa,Pe,Sh,Wo
A,E
Gujrat
Sialkot
A,CM,E
Kandahar
Lahore
Amritsar
A,C,Ca,
E,L,Pa
Ca
Multan
A,C,Ca
Samana
C
Delhi
C,E,P
Sukkur
C
Kandiero
C,S
Alwar
Ca,G
Agra
Lucknow
Jaipur
Bayana
C,Ca,
E,S
C,E
Sehwan
C
L
I
C,P
S,SA
C,CM,S
Jaunpur
Nasarpur
C
Ca
Fatehpur
PATNA (N&G,17–18)
Rajmahal
Rangpur
Allahabad
Benares
Lakhawar
Malda
C,S
C
Tatta
Ca
B,C,CM
P,S
A,C,S
COSSIMBAZAR (N17–18)
C,Cm,
E,J,S
C,Gh,O,R
C,Cm,O,R,
SS,Su,W
C,CM,S
C
DACCA (N&G17–18)
I,S
HOOGHLY/SATGAON/CHINSURA (P16–17, N&G17–18)
AHMADABAD (G17, N 17–17)
Indore
CHANDERNAGORE (F18)
CALCUTTA (G18)
C,CM
CAMBAY (G & N, 17)
C,CM,Y
SERAMPORE (D18)
CHITTAGONG
(P16–17, G18)
Baroda
Gn,Sp,Su
HIJLI (P16–17)
C
BROACH (G17, N17–18)
SURAT (P, N, G, F, all 17–18)
C,CM,I,O
BALASORE
PIPLI (P17, N17)
C
C,Cm,J,
Sa,Su,Y
C
Burhanpur
C,E
(G, N, D, F, all 17–18)
O,S,Sa
Patan Somnath
A
Dharangaon
C
Hariharpur
DIU (P16–18)
DAMAN (P16–18)
C
Wairagarh
Cuttack
C,CM
Pa
Aurangabad
BASSEIN/SALSETTE I. (P16–18)
BOMBAY (P16–17, G17–18)
C,SS
Ahmadnagar
CHAUL (P16–18)
C
C
C,Go,S,Si
Warangal
BIMLIPATAM (N18)
C
VIZAGAPATAM (G18)
Solapur
Bidar
Hyderabad
C
C,In
Nagelpad
YANAM (F18)
PALAKOLLU (N17–18)
INJARAM (G18)
NARASAPUR (N17,G18)
VENGURLA (N17–18)
C
NIZAMPATAM (N17, G17–18)
MASULIPATAM (N, G, F, all 17–18)
GOA (P16–18)
Hubli
Vijayanagara
(to 1565)
C
Ge,Gl,I
Sa,Sn,T
KARWAR/ANJIDIV I. (P16–18, G17)
C,Sp
HONAVAR (P16–17)
COONDAPOOR, BARCELORE
(P16–17, N17–18)
PULICAT (N17–18)
C,M
MADRAS (G17–18)
MANGALORE (P17–18)
ST. THOME (P16–17, N17–18, G18)
CANNANORE (P16–17, N17–18)
C
C,M
PONDICHERRY (F17–18)
TELLICHERRY (G18)
Sp
Salem
TEGANAPATAM (N17, G18)
MAHÉ (F18)
TRANQUEBAR
PORTO NOVO (P16–17, G18)
C
CALICUT (G17–18, F18, D18)
C,Sp
(D16–17)
KARIKAL (F18, G18)
CHETWAI (N18)
NAGAPATAM (P16–17, N17–18)
CRANGANUR (P16–17,N17–18)
Co,Sp
PALLIPURAM (P16–17, N17–18)
Madura
C,S
JAFFNA (P17, N17–18)
COCHIN (P16–17, N17–18)
PORAKAD (N17–18), KANYAKULAM (N17–18)
MANNAR (P16–17, N17–18)
QUILON, TENGASSERI (P16–17, N17–18)
TRINCOMALEE (N17–18)
ANJENGO (G18)
Sp
PUTTALAM (P16–17, N17–18)
MANAPADU (P16–17, N17–18)
BATTICALOA (N17–18)
KAYALPATAM (P16–17, N17–18)
Kandy
CM,Ge
TUTICORIN (P16–17, N17–18)
COLOMBO/KOTTE (P16–17, N17–18)
VEMBAR (P16–17, N17–18)
GALLE (P16–17, N17–18)
MATARA (P16–17, N17–18)
Co,Sp
Commodity List:
A Arms and armor
B Brassware
C Cotton broadcloth (plain, dyed, printed, and painted)
Ca Carpets
CM Cloth manufacturers (quilts, tablecloths, sails, etc.)
E Embroidery
Ge Gems: diamonds, pearls, rubies, etc.
Gh Ghee (clarified butter)
Gl Glass
Go Goldware
In Indigo
Ir Iron
J Jewlry
Ju Jute cloth
L Leather
O Oils
Op Opium
Pa Paper
Pe Perfume
Po Pottery
R Rice
S Silk
Sa Saltpeter
Sh Shawls
Si Silverware
Sp Spices
SS Ships
St Stoneware
Su Sugar
T Tobacco
W Wheat
Ww Woodwork
Y Yarn
0 100 200 300 Miles
0 100 200 300 400 500 Kilometers

His attitude changed with pressures from both the anti-Portuguese Arab merchants as well as from Vasco da Gama himself, who demanded that the *samuri* abandon all trade with the Muslims and, in addition, grant the Portuguese exemption from customs duties.

In the first decade of contact with the Portuguese, the horrendous atrocities of both da Gama and Afonso de Albuquerque—including burning Arab ships carrying cargo and pilgrims (men, women, and children enroute to Mecca for *hajj*, or religious pilgrimage), wanton bombardment of port cities in Malabar and the Persian Gulf, chopping off the noses and ears of unarmed fishermen, forcing conversion of the widows and daughters of the defeated to Catholicism, and converting temples and mosques into churches—affected the attitude of the Hindu rulers of these coastal kingdoms. They approached the sultan of Gujarat, who in turn sought the help of Egypt and Ottoman Turkey to launch a combined naval attack on the Portuguese at Chaul in 1507 and 1508. To avenge the defeat, the Portuguese viceroy, Francisco d'Almeida, mobilized a large fleet and wrested a spectacular victory in 1509, defeating the combined Muslim fleets at Diu, a strategic location at the entrance to the Gulf of Cambay.

The Portuguese were not the best ambassadors of Christianity or of European culture. Their lack of personal hygiene, going unbathed for months, and their wild behavior under the influence of alcohol at all times of the day left an unsavory impression of Europeans among many Indians. And if the religion they professed was given by the "Prince of Peace," there was no hint of it in the Portuguese propensity to violence even against unarmed people, including women and children. Far from being the harbingers of a respectable civilization, the Portuguese left impressions of unmitigated and wanton barbarism, no different from the uncivilized marauders who had destroyed civilizations in the past. Indeed, the Portuguese were, by and large, still medieval in their thinking, their religious fanaticism being typical of new converts from Islam to Catholicism. European renaissance had not yet touched Portugal to any significant degree.

The vision and foundation of the Portuguese thalassocracy in the East are appropriately attributed to Afonso de Albuquerque. With a view to secure and enforce a monopoly in the Asia-Europe trade, Albuquerque envisioned an empire of ports and forts at key points on the trade routes between South Asia, Southeast Asia, and the Persian Gulf. His conquest of Goa in 1510 (making it the headquarters of the Portuguese possessions in the East), Malacca (the major mart for spice trade in Southeast Asia) in 1511, and Ormuz (the key port in the Persian Gulf) in 1515 provided the beginnings of an empire that would, by the middle of the sixteenth century, extend from Sofala in Southeast Africa to numerous islands and ports in the Indonesian Archipelago and Macau off the China coast.

In India, the Portuguese held almost complete maritime supremacy over the west coast and some limited control over the east coast and the Bay of Bengal. It was based on three cornerstones of policy: First, the Portuguese gained control over the high seas, disallowing Arab shipping, seizing it, either confiscating the cargo (and at times the ship itself) or setting it on fire. Such piratical acts were, indeed, aimed at dissuading non-Portuguese shipping in what had been for centuries, true to its name, the Arabian Sea. Second, the Portuguese built forts, equipping them with powerful cannon, at all major ports on the west coast from Cochin to Diu for the protection of the traffic and goods there. The Portuguese centered their trade on three great factories at Malacca, Calicut, and Ormuz, which made it possible for the Portuguese to purchase and store spices and other products at low prices during the season until ships arrived to take the goods to Portugal. Third, and most important, the Portuguese controlled trade traffic in and around India by requiring all non-Portuguese seacraft to carry a *cartaz* (pass), issued by the Portuguese for a fee. That "simple system," as Portuguese economic historian Vitorino Magalhaes Godinho outlined it, was enforced by a fleet of two squadrons, supported in an emergency by naval units under the governor-general in Goa, and seven fortresses in other principal ports. Of the two squadrons, one was used to block the Red Sea and the other to patrol the west coast of India, stopping non-Portuguese craft.

In tune with the rise of religious bigotry in Europe and the establishment of the Jesuits and the Inquisition by the middle of the sixteenth century, and following the resolutions of the Council of Trent, the Portuguese banned the exercise of all religions other than Catholicism in their territories in Asia and Africa.

They destroyed Hindu and Buddhist temples in western India and Sri Lanka, burned their sacred books, and banned the public observance of non-Catholic religious rites associated with birth, marriage, and death. In the void thus created, large-scale conversions were carried out by the official use of force and direct threats to life and property. In the eyes of the Jesuits, "God's purpose" in assisting the Portuguese in their seaborne trade with India was to increase "the harvest of souls." The Portuguese monarchs were active partners in this religious enterprise by dint of their *padroado real*, or crown patronage, of the church.

The period following the arrival of Vasco da Gama in 1498 and of the Dutch in 1595, followed by the English and the French, is aptly called "the Portuguese century" in Asia. Portuguese fortunes in the East first suffered when the crowns of Portugal and Spain were combined from 1580 to 1640. Their enterprise was, in any case, too overextended for a nation with a meager population of less than a million. In contrast to the Portuguese enterprise, the British East India Company and the Dutch East India Company focused on trade and profit and stayed away from the propagation of religion.

Their success in India and Indonesia was at the cost of the Portuguese, whose once extensive empire shrank by the end of the seventeenth century to a few far-flung, poorly administered, hardly profitable territorial niches. By that time, they had lost their monopoly of the Asia-Europe maritime trade and the supremacy of the sea to their English, French, and Dutch competitors. After the loss of the relatively valuable Bassein in North Konkan to the Marathas in 1739, the Portuguese in India were limited to Goa, Daman, and Diu.

The Portuguese possession in India, miniscule in comparison to the vast British Indian empire, remained with them because of their special relationship with Britain as its "oldest ally." Although Portugal professed to being neutral in the two world wars, it tilted toward Britain and was, therefore, able to keep its Estado da India (State of India).

Goa, Daman, and Diu survived economically because of the educational and economic opportunities in British India, notably Bombay, where one-fifth of the Goans lived and sent remittances to their families back home. Coincidentally, a year before India attained independence from the British, manganese and iron ore were discovered in Goa, which made the territory not only economically viable but earned valuable foreign exchange for Portugal. The leaders of the freedom movement in India, who had expected the Portuguese and the French to relinquish their possessions when the British would quit the subcontinent, were shocked when the Portuguese dictator Antonio Salazar passed legislation altering the status of all Portuguese possessions into "overseas provinces," entitled to protection from the North Atlantic Treaty Organization (NATO), of which Portugal was a valuable member thanks to the valuable NATO military base of Portuguese Azores in the Atlantic.

Under orders from Salazar, the Goa government shot down the peaceful, unarmed Goan and non-Goan Indian *satyagrahis* attempting to cross the border into Goa to demand independence for the territory. Unlike the French, who negotiated the transfer of their possession to the Indian government, the Portuguese refused to talk. On 19 December 1961, Goa was rid of the 450-year Portuguese rule after a thirty-six-hour Indian military operation. Ironically, the Indian takeover began with the aerial disablement of the only Portuguese frigate in Goa, the SS *Albuquerque*, named for the conqueror of Goa, founder of the Portuguese Estado da India.

D. R. SarDesai

See also **Albuquerque, Afonso de; British East India Company Raj; Christian Impact on India, History of; Gama, Vasco da; Goa**

BIBLIOGRAPHY

Boxer, C. R. *Portuguese India in the Mid-Seventeenth Century.* Delhi: Oxford University Press, 1980.

Chaudhuri, K. N. *Trade and Civilization in the Indian Ocean: An Economic History from the Rise of Islam to 1750.* Cambridge, U.K., and New York: Cambridge University Press, 1990.

Danvers, F. C. *The Portuguese in India.* 2 vols. 1894. Reprint, London: Cass, 1966.

Godinho, Vitorino Magalhaes. *L'Économie de l'empire portugais aux XVe at XVIe siècles.* Paris: SEVPEN, 1969.

Panikkar, K. M. *Asia and Western Dominance: A Survey of the Vasco da Gama Epoch of Asian History, 1498–1945.* London: Allen & Unwin, 1953.

Pearson, Michael N. *The Portuguese in India.* Cambridge, U.K.: Cambridge University Press, 1987.

———. "Conversions in South Asia: Evidence from the Portuguese Records." *Portuguese Studies* 6 (1990): 53–70.

———. *Port Cities and Intruders: The Swahili Coast, India and Portugal in the Early Modern Era.* Baltimore: Johns Hopkins University Press, 1997.

Ptak, Roderich, ed. *Portuguese Asia: Aspects of History and Economic History (Sixteenth and Seventeenth Centuries).* Stuttgart and Weisbaden, Germany: Steiner Verlag, 1987.

Subrahmanyam, Sanjay. *The Portuguese Empire in Asia, 1500–1700: A Political and Economic History.* London and New York: Longman, 1992.

Whiteway, R. S. *The Rise of Portuguese Power in India, 1497–1550.* 1899. Reprint, London: Susil Gupta, 1967.

POVERTY AND INEQUALITY An attempt to examine the intertwined issues of poverty, inequality, and growth in India in the 1990s involves an exploration of all three topics. The conventional view of what happened in the Indian economy in the 1980s and the 1990s is that economic growth averaged around 5.5 percent per annum; population growth was around 2 percent, so per capita growth averaged 3.5 percent. This rate of growth was a major acceleration from the past, and both the agricultural and the nonagricultural sectors of the economy shared in it. Agriculture grew at a robust 3.7 percent per annum, and nonagriculture grew at 6.6 percent. Rural India, where most of the poor reside, benefited enormously, and absolute poverty declined at a fast pace in the 1980s. The head-count ratio of poverty (the proportion of people below the poverty line, compared to the total

Poverty in the District of Madhubani, Bihar. The prevailing socioeconomic situation there (the second most populous state in India) is so alarming that Bihar is often described as the "state without hope," a graveyard for the economic development projects that have achieved success elsewhere in the country. AMAR TALWAR / FOTOMEDIA.

population) declined from 45 percent in 1983 to 37 percent in 1993–1994. This decline is remarkable because both in the 1950s and in the 1960s, the poverty ratio had, in some year or another, hovered around 45 percent. (For the same poverty line, poverty in 1951 was 45.3, and in 1961, it was 46.5 percent.)

In the early 1990s, the Indian economy ran into a balance of payments crisis, a situation that forced India to return for help to the World Bank and the International Monetary Fund. The government of India then instituted major economic reforms from 1991 to 1993. The reforms were primarily oriented toward industry and external trade (the rupee was devalued by 20 percent in two quick steps, over two days, and tariffs were reduced from outright bans and astronomical levels to open imports, and lower levels).

These reforms led to an acceleration of growth for a few years (particularly from 1994 to 1997, when growth of the gross domestic product [GDP] averaged over 7 percent). However, except for these years, GDP growth for the eleven years following the reforms (1992 to 2002) was exactly the same as ten years prior (5.7% per annum) to the reforms. Some have argued that the reforms were oriented toward the rich, urban sectors of the economy, that these sectors benefited disproportionately, and income inequality worsened.

According to this interpretation, four important pieces of evidence were cited. First, the rate of agricultural growth collapsed in the 1990s—from 3.7 percent per annum to only 2.6 percent. Second, and perhaps even reflecting this slowdown, the rate of growth of real wages in agriculture collapsed to less than half the robust rate of the 1980s—from about 5.0 to 5.5 percent per annum to only 2.5 percent. For considerations of poverty, this is significant, since agricultural households constitute the poorest of the poor. Third, the gap between urban per capita expenditure and rural per capita expenditure increased significantly. Fourth, the poorest states lagged behind the growth of richer states. The surveys of the National Sample Surveys Organization (NSSO) also showed that the rate of poverty decline was definitely slower in the 1990s. The critics of reforms further argue that in the 1980s the head-count ratio of poverty declined by eight percentage points, while in the 1990s poverty declined by only five percentage points. This slower decline in poverty is all the more shocking, according to the critics, because it occurred with considerably faster economic growth.

The critics of the economic reforms further argued that the four factors mentioned above conclusively demonstrate that prior to 1990 India performed better than China, where inequality worsened by more than 30 percent in the short span of six years. India, in contrast, at least until 1993–1994, had witnessed generally declining inequality. Even more importantly, the skewed nature of growth in the 1990s represented a period of (relatively) jobless growth. Organized sector employment, after registering an annual growth of 1.6 percent in the 1980s, barely grew in the 1990s (0.4 percent per annum).

Some of the above conclusions are controversial. For instance, the estimates of poverty and inequality by Angus Deaton and Jean Drèze (2002) are biased downward if a more acceptable real measure of equality is used. Changes in inequality are more accurately measured by changes in inequality measured at constant prices. Furthermore, the trends in real consumption cited above are contradicted by the trends in growth in real wages, which almost doubled between the 1980s and 1990s. Whether taken separately or together, the evidence provided by the increase in real wages of the poor and/or the change in real inequality, is indicative of a very minor change in inequality, rather than the "pervasive increase" postulated by Deaton and Drèze.

Growth and Inequality

Poverty and inequality are generally ideological and emotive issues. Often, the discussion assumes that changes in the level of poverty are independent from economic growth and inequality. As for the latter, it is not overall inequality, but rather inequality around the poverty line and changes therein that are most important for the determination of poverty decline.

Part of the reason for varying estimates of poverty decline in India in the since the 1970s is the fact that there are several different estimates of what happened to growth. According to national accounts data, the estimate used by most analysts and policy makers, income (GDP) growth has averaged about 5.6 percent per annum for the last twenty-four years. Per capita growth, the one relevant for poverty calculations, has accelerated to 4.5 percent per annum in 2004 from 3 percent per annum in the early 1980s. India's growth performance for the twenty-two-year period from 1980 to 2002 was bettered by only a handful of countries, led by China and Korea.

In cumulative terms, per capita income growth, if translated into consumption growth (i.e., no increase in the rate of savings), would result in a per capita consumption level in 1999–2000 that would be about 80 percent higher than that which prevailed in the early 1980s. However, there has been an increase in the savings rate, so the appropriate measure of growth is that revealed by the growth in per capita consumption. This estimate of growth is an average of 2.4 percent per annum, or a per capita consumption level in 1999–2000 that is 48 percent higher than the 1983 level. With no inequality change, this would mean that the head-count ratio of poverty in India was in the low teens in 1999–2000, or about half the level indicated by official data.

Poverty, however, is not calculated on the basis of growth in national accounts data, but rather on the basis of growth as revealed by consumption as reported in household surveys. And the growth as revealed by household surveys has been considerably less than the growth revealed by national accounts. The most widely used forms of survey data, and indeed the official source for measurement of poverty, are the consumer expenditure (CE) surveys conducted by the NSSO, which conducted the first household surveys as far back as 1950–1951. The NSSO large-sample surveys indicate a ten-and-a-half-year growth rate from 1983 to 1993–1994 (hereafter the 1980s) of only 1.2 percent per annum, followed by the mildest of accelerations to 1.3 percent per annum growth rate in the six-year period from 1993–1994 to 1999–2000 (hereafter the 1990s). Accordingly, for the entire period from 1983 to 1999, the average growth rate stands at only 1.25 percent per annum. With this growth rate, the cumulative increase in per capita consumption is only 23 percent, and it is this estimate of growth that results in a poverty decline from 43 percent in 1983 to 26 percent in 1999–2000.

This is a gross relationship and one which incorporates all inequality changes that may have taken place. Over this sixteen-and-a-half-year period, inequality thus diminished in India, as indicated by both the Gini (marginal change) and the share in total expenditures of the poor (bottom 40 percent). Thus, what is causing a huge divergence in the poverty estimates for India are not measures of changes in inequality, but rather the widely diverging estimates of growth in per capita consumption, as indicated by national accounts and household survey data.

It is difficult to identify which of the two estimates of growth is more accurate, though this divergence is a common phenomenon, observed in most parts of the world. For India, however, there is another NSSO survey–based estimate of growth for the period 1983 to 2000. For 1983 and 1993–1994, the NSSO surveyed the same households in each year, as canvassed by the CE survey. In 1999–2000, the same sampling frame was used. These

NSSO Employment and Unemployment (E&U) surveys also recorded, in great detail, the employment in different activities and the wages of each member of the household. Nonwage income was not recorded. Since the poor gain their incomes mostly from labor, the E&U survey data can be used to estimate the income growth of poor households. And this income growth is considerably higher than the consumption growth estimated for the same households (1983 and 1993–1994).

Rather than the 1.25 percent average for sixteen and a half years, per capita income growth averaged almost three times higher, at 3.2 percent per annum. But this is for all wage earners, including rich, educated urbanites. For rural India, where a large proportion of the poor reside, the average growth rate was only marginally lower, at 3.1 percent per annum. For the poorest of the poor, the agricultural labor households, the average growth rate was still 2.5 percent per annum. Thus, consumption growth of such households was at least twice the rate indicated by consumer expenditure surveys.

So we have three estimates of consumption and income growth in India: first, per capita consumption growth, national accounts, at 2.4 percent per annum; second, per capita consumption growth, NSSO CE survey, 1.25 percent per annum; and third, growth in incomes of the poorest of the poor, the agricultural labor households, 2.5 percent per annum. All other sources of income growth (e.g., surveys conducted by other survey organizations like the National Council of Applied Economic Research) are closer to the NSSO income growth estimate. There is no evidence, direct or indirect, that supports the NSSO CE low growth estimate of only 1.25 percent. A safe conclusion is that consumption growth of the poorest in India was at least 2.5 percent. Given the fact that average consumption growth was also at this level, consumption inequality could not have changed much for these years.

The question of which consumption growth estimate (NSSO consumer expenditure data supported by NSSO wage income data, or non-NSSO survey data) is correct has an obvious and large effect on conclusions about poverty levels and poverty decline. An overwhelming amount of recent poverty literature in India has been devoted to establishing the percentage by which the NSSO CE survey of 1999–2000 overstated the cumulative six-year growth between 1993–1994 and 1999–2000. The "error" being talked about is only 1 to 2 percent, and this will have a very small effect on aggregate growth. However, the different cumulative NSSO survey estimates of growth (consumption and income based) diverge by about ten to twenty times this amount. Thus, the significant "growth gap" between per worker wage growth and per capita consumption growth during both the 1980s and 1990s dwarfs any calculations of the overestimate or underestimate of mean per capita expenditures in 1999–2000.

It was generally believed that inequality worsened significantly in the 1990s, but to accurately assess trends in inequality, it is more appropriate to consider changes in real inequality (i.e., per capita expenditures deflated by an appropriate price index) rather than changes in nominal inequality (expenditures not deflated by any price index). Unfortunately, the latter has been used by those economists who contend that inequality worsened significantly.

If inequality change is estimated separately for the 1980s and the 1990s, the following results emerge: inequality either stayed flat, or its level improved slightly between 1983 and 1993–1994, both in absolute terms and in comparative terms (with other countries). Since overall inequality improved slightly between 1983 and the terminal year, 1999–2000, if inequality did worsen in the 1990s, it could not have worsened by a significant amount. But this result is contrary to the result of either a "pervasive" increase in inequality reached by Deaton and Drèze, or an increase comparable to that of China (Sen and Himanshu, 2004) or a trend increase in inequality (Ravallion, 2000). How is it possible that the official data yield such little change, yet experts document large changes?

This divergence is possible because in 1999–2000, the NSSO survey authorities changed the definition of per capita consumption from that which prevailed in 1993–1994 (and earlier) concerning different recall periods and different consumption items. Official data inequality levels were reported under the assumption that there was no bias concerning food expenditures and that the 1999–2000 consumption data are comparable to the 1993–1994 data. Given that the raw official estimate of inequality was biased upward, the measured Gini increase of 6 percent can be considered a likely upper bound to inequality change in the 1990s.

This increase was for nominal per capita expenditures. For real per capita expenditures (nominal data deflated by the Planning Commission poverty line deflator) the increase in the Gini was from .28 to 0.29, only a 3 percent increase.

Pooling all the results, a fair conclusion appears to be a mild V-shaped pattern of inequality change in India, meaning that inequality improved by about 2 to 8 percent in the 1980s, and deteriorated between 0 and 10 percent in the 1990s. For consistent definitions and estimation methods, a mild improvement was observed between 1983 and 1999–2000. Whatever worsening in inequality which occurred in the 1990s was small, mild, and less than the small improvement in the 1980s.

Poverty in India, 1983 to 1999–2000

The likely estimate of growth in the 1980s and 1990s was somewhere between 23 and 51 percent. The former is the estimate of per capita expenditures, NSSO surveys, and the latter is a lower-bound estimate of income growth of landless, agricultural laborers (also NSSO surveys). Inequality change, as documented in the previous section, is shown to have either stayed the same, or most likely improved slightly, since 1983. The juxtaposition of these two "facts" indicates that what matters for a realistic poverty decline estimate for India is a judgment of what happened to growth in India, and not what happened to inequality.

What level of poverty in 1999–2000 is suggested by growth in rural wages from 1983 to 1999–2000? If the distribution of consumption did not change between 1983 and 1999 (and all indications are that it did not worsen), then the 1983 distribution, along with growth in the wages of the poorest agricultural workers, can be used to estimate the poverty level in 1999–2000. This method allocates consumption growth to each household, the income growth of the poorest that is, a conservative, upper-bound estimate of poverty in 1999–2000. Thus, if real incomes are assumed to grow at 2.5 percent annum real for sixteen and a half years, the average real consumption in 1999–2000 would be 51 percent higher than that observed in 1983. Recall that 23 percent growth resulted in a decline of 17 percentage points in the head-count ratio (official data). So 51 percent growth would result in a reduction in poverty of approximately 38 percentage points, or a 5 percent level of the head-count ratio (HCR) in 1999–2000.

However, it is the case that often, and especially when the HCR is in the low teens or lower, more and more growth is needed to bring about the same decline in poverty. Calculations suggest that 51 percent growth would have reduced poverty by 30 and not 38 percentage points, that is, the level of poverty in India in 1999–2000 was close to 13 percent, rather than the 26 percent stated by the official data, or even higher estimates by some authors.

The 1990s was the beginning of several transitions in the Indian economy—a decline in fertility rates, population growth, labor force growth, and potential labor force growth. These transitions have not been emphasized by authors who emphasize that the 1990s were characterized by slow growth in jobs, or "jobless growth." The "shortfall" in jobs is mostly explained by examination of a little emphasized statistic: the potential labor force (people between the ages of 15 and 59). This grew by only 1.9 percent per annum in the 1990s, a steep decline from the 2.7 percent growth rate of the 1980s. What this simple statistic implies is that the much-hyped jobless growth was much more about the supply of labor bottlenecks in the 1990s rather than about jobless growth. This is the case because total output growth (GDP growth) stayed the same or was higher in the 1990s. With a declining rate of growth of the labor force, labor tightening was to be expected, even with the same rate of growth, let alone with sharply accelerating growth. Rural wages grew at 2.3 percent in the 1980s, somewhat ahead of urban wages, which increased at 1.4 percent. In the 1990s there was a significant across-the-board acceleration, a doubling in average growth rates. As a result, wage growth in rural areas jumped to a rate of 4.3 percent per annum, and in urban areas to 4.8 percent.

Surjit Bhalla

See also **Development Politics; Economic Reforms of 1991**

BIBLIOGRAPHY

Bhalla, Surjit S. "Growth and Poverty in India: Myth and Reality." In *Development, Poverty and Fiscal Policy: Decentralization of Institutions*, edited by Govinda Rao. New Delhi and New York: Oxford University Press, 2002.

———. "Recounting the Poor: 1983–99." *Economic and Political Weekly* 38, no. 4 (25–31 January 2003): 338–349.

———. "Poor Results and Poorer Policy: A Comparative Analysis of Estimates of Global Inequality and Poverty." *CESifo Economic Studies* 50 (2004): 85–132.

Datt, Gaurav, and Martin Ravallion. "Is India's Economic Growth Leaving the Poor Behind?" *Journal of Economic Perspectives* 16, no. 3 (Summer 2002): 89–108.

Deaton, Angus, and Jean Drèze. "Poverty and Inequality in India: A Re-examination." *Economic and Political Weekly* 37, no. 36 (7 September 2002): 3729–3748.

Drèze, Jean, and Amartya Sen. *India: Development and Participation*. New Delhi and New York: Oxford University Press, 2002.

Kakwani, Nanak. "Poverty and Economics Growth with Application to Côte d' Ivoire." *Review of Income and Wealth* 39 (1993): 121–139.

Ravallion, Martin. "Should Poverty Measures Be Anchored to the National Accounts." *Economic and Political Weekly* (26 August–2 September 2000): 3245–3252.

Sen, Abhijit, and Himanshu. "Poverty and Inequality in India: I." *Economic and Political Weekly* 39, no. 38 (18 September 2004): 4247–4263.

———. "Poverty and Inequality in India II: Widening Disparities during the 1990s." *Economic and Political Weekly* 39, no. 39 (25 September 2004): 4361–4375.

Sundaram, K. "Employment-Unemployment Situation in the Nineties: Some Results from NSS 55th Round Survey." *Economic and Political Weekly* (17 March 2001): 931–940.

———. "Employment and Poverty in the 1990s: Further Results from NSS 55th Round Employment-Unemployment Survey 1990–2000." *Economic and Political Weekly* (11–17 August 2001): 3039–3049.

Sundaram, K., and D. Tendulkar Suresh. "Poverty in India in the 1900s: Revised Results for All-India and Fifteen Major States for 1993–94." *Economic and Political Weekly* (15–22 January 2003).

———. "Poverty Has Declined in the 1990s: A Resolution of Comparability Problems in NSS Consumer Expenditure Data." *Economic and Political Weekly* (25–31 January 2003).

———. "Poverty in India in the 1990s: An Analysis of Changes in Fifteen Major States." *Economic and Political Weekly* (5–11 April 2003).

PRAJĀPATI. *See* **Vedic Aryan India.**

PRAJA SOCIALIST PARTY. *See* **Political System.**

PRASAD, RAJENDRA ***(1884–1963), first president of India, one of Mahatma Gandhi's closest lieutenants.*** Rajendra Prasad was born on 3 December 1884 at Zeradai village in Bihar. An outstanding student, an erudite scholar, a true humanist, and a deeply religious person, he committed himself to the cause of his country and remained in the vanguard of India's freedom struggle, guiding the destiny of the new nation after independence. President of the Indian National Congress in 1934, 1939, and 1947, Prasad chaired India's Constituent Assembly and was chosen as first president of the republic when the Constitution came into force on 26 January 1950. He left a permanent mark on the polity of independent India, as his career continues to inspire the nation's citizens.

Rajendra Prasad. Both men in almost military-like formation, U.S. President Dwight Eisenhower and Prasad meet in New Delhi, 1959. In fact, as India's first president, Prasad exercised a moderating influence and molded national policies unobtrusively, never appearing to rule authoritatively. BETTMANN / CORBIS.

Early Years

Rajendra Prasad's Bihar village was cosmopolitan enough to ensure communal harmony and self-sufficiency, allowing its people a comfortable life. He was married at the age of twelve to Rajvanshi Devi. He received his elementary education at the village and then studied at Chapra District School, where he excelled. Prasad stood first in the Entrance Examination of the University of Kolkata (Calcutta), whose jurisdiction in 1902 still extended over Bengal, Bihar, Orissa, and Assam. He then joined the prestigious Presidency College in Kolkata. He continued his academic career there, winning the admiration of his teachers and fellow students. As a third year student, he won the first election for the post of secretary of the College Union. Though he continued to excel in his studies, this was also the time—following the first British partition of Bengal in 1905—of a new political awakening. The antipartition movement greatly agitated young Prasad, and the popular Swadeshi and boycott movements inspired him to enter public life. He was instrumental in the formation of the Bihari Students' Conference in 1908, an organization that provided political leadership to Bihar in the ensuing decades.

Rajendra Prasad impressed Sir Ashutosh Mukherjee, vice-chancellor of Kolkata University, so deeply that the latter offered him a lecturership in the Presidency Law College. At the same time, he started practicing law under the apprenticeship of Khan Bahadur Shamsul Huda. Swayed by the nationalist movement, Prasad joined the Indian National Congress and was elected to the All-India Congress Committee. Gopal Krishna Gokhale had started his Servants of India Society in Pune in 1905; Prasad hoped to join the society, and Gokhale personally invited him to be a part of the movement. Prasad was deterred, however, by opposition from his elder brother, Mahendra Prasad. The economic needs of the family compelled him to pursue his legal profession, so he refused Gokhale's invitation. He later recalled his feeling of "helplessness" in doing so. About that time, his mother had died and his only sister, Bhagwati Devi, had become a widow at the age of nineteen, coming back to her parents' home.

Bihar became a separate British Indian province, following the reunification of Bengal, in 1912. The High Court was established at Patna in 1916, and Rajendra Parasad moved there to practice, swiftly making his mark as a lawyer. His incisive intellect and phenomenal memory were his great assets. His integrity and character impressed not only his clients and colleagues but the judges of the High Court as well. Often when an adversary failed to cite a legal precedent, judges asked Prasad to cite a precedent against himself.

Ardent Freedom Fighter

Rajendra Prasad first met Mahatma Gandhi in 1915 at Kolkata. In the December 1916 session of the Congress held at Lucknow, they met again. In that session, Brajkishore Prasad, a veteran Congress leader of Bihar, moved a resolution denouncing the exploitation of Champaran peasant by Bihar's cruel indigo planters, requesting that Gandhi visit Champaran. Gandhi could not turn down Rajkumar Shukla's appeal. En route from his Gujarat ashram to launch his fact-finding mission to Champaran, Gandhi first stopped at Patna to visit Rajendra Prasad. Mahatma Gandhi soon called Prasad to assist him in Champaran. Prasad rushed to Champaran and accompanied Gandhi wherever he went to interrogate the indigo workers. This proved a turning point in Prasad's life. Gandhi asked him to prepare a list of peasants who had been exploited by the planters. He undertook the task with enthusiasm and conducted the inquiry most effectively. Gandhi was arrested but was quickly released after the government agreed to appoint a committee to investigate the matter. Rajendra Prasad's contribution would not be forgotten by Gandhi, who later supported him to become president of the National Congress.

Rajendra Prasad was so shocked by the Jallianwala Bagh Massacre in Amritsar in 1919 that he endorsed Gandhi's call for a noncooperation movement against British Raj. The special session of India's National Congress held in Kolkata in 1920 passed a noncooperation resolution, confirmed by the Nagpur Congress session that December. Rajendra Prasad played an important role in helping to pass the resolution. He left his lucrative legal practice at the call of Mahatma Gandhi, ceased serving as a senator of Patna University, and withdrew his sons, Dhananjay and Mrityunjay, from their British educational institutions. He started writing articles for *Searchlight* and *Desh*. He traveled all over the country, exhorting people to make the supreme sacrifice for their country. A number of new "national" schools were opened under his patronage in Bihar. Gandhi felt the need to start a *vidyapeeth* (seminary) at Patna for those students who had boycotted government educational institutions. Rajendra Prasad became the principal of this institution. After the tragic murder of police by *satyagrahi*s in Chauri Chara on 4 February 1922, Gandhi immediately called a halt to his noncooperation movement. Rajendra Prasad remained with him wholeheartedly, agreeing that appropriate change could never be brought about by violent means.

Constructive programs. Rajendra Prasad now helped Gandhi to launch his constructive program of *khadi* (hand-spinning of cotton) and village industries in the rural areas of Bihar. Like Gandhi, Prasad realized that without reviving India's traditional handicrafts, primarily cotton spinning and weaving, Indians could not recapture their former prosperity and self-reliance. He felt, as Gandhi did, the urgent need of transforming Indian villages. The Khadi and Village Industries program was to help India's rural people, including women, acquire greater self-confidence. The generation of self-confidence would stimulate political consciousness and prepare people for sacrifice for the sake of the country.

Disaster manager. Bihar was devastated by a terrible earthquake on 15 January 1934, after which Prasad immediately organized a massive relief campaign, raising a fund of 38 lakh (3.8 million) rupees. Prasad was widely admired for his selfless devotion to the relief effort. The same year he was elected president of the Indian National Congress in Bombay (Mumbai).

Congress presidency and other offices. The Government of India Act of 1935 awarded provincial autonomy to the people of India. Under the provisions of the Act, elections were to be held in the provinces in 1937. Congress won a majority in most of the provinces of British India, including Bihar. Rajendra Prasad was a member of the Parliamentary Board and played a key role in choosing candidates for election. When Subhash Chandra Bose resigned from the presidency of the Congress in 1939, Gandhi persuaded Rajendra Prasad to accept the difficult job, having the full support of his Working Committee. Congress was again faced with a similar crisis in 1947 when Acharya Kriplani resigned, and Prasad again took on the presidency, always trusted by his colleagues. Just prior to independence, Rajendra Prasad was invited to join the viceroy's Indian government in 1946. He was put in charge of Food and Agriculture, and he created the popular national slogan "Grow More Food." Prasad was then elected chairman of the Constituent Assembly, an important and challenging job, from which he guided, regulated, and controlled the drafting and adoption of India's Constitution from August 1947 until 26 January 1950.

First president of India. When the Constitution of India came into force on 26 January 1950, Rajendra Prasad was elected to serve as India's first president, retaining that high office for twelve years. He exercised his moderating influence and molded national policies unobtrusively, leading many to think that, unlike any other head of state, he never reigned or ruled. In 1960 Prasad announced his decision to retire. After retirement, he returned to Patna, living in Sadaqat Ashram, the headquarters of the Congress Party in Bihar. Within months of his retirement, his wife Rajvanshi Devi died, in September 1962. He himself had been suffering from acute asthmatic disease and breathed his last in Patna on 28 February 1963.

Legacy and Contribution

Rajendra Prasad left a rich legacy of inspiration for generations to come. He shared Gandhi's great vision of peace and rural development, and to realize this goal, he argued for the need for a fundamental change in the prevailing system of education. He lamented the lack of character building or moral training of students in the prevailing system of British education. He believed that education would be useful only if it was integrated into the whole life of an individual. "Education today," he once observed, "is getting more and more divorced from actual life and its requirements. This, in turn, is responsible for the ever-increasing unemployment among the educated classes." (Datta 1970, p. 315) Prasad supported the establishment of new type of "rural university." He advocated the comprehensive development of the student as a person, the growth of close and meaningful contact between teachers and students, and the role of the teacher as a "man with capacity to communicate something good." He recognized the value of scientific research and the application of the results for amelioration of the conditions of India's masses. At the same time, he considered India's past to be a great source of inspiration for the present and the future, since it helped in meeting the challenges of modern times created by the technical achievements of science. He argued that India needed a true history of its glorious past, which should be not only an account of the wars and conquests of kings and emperors, but also one of how great religious, cultural, and literary movements have arisen and influenced hundreds of millions of people, and how art and science, industry and commerce have developed. He held the view that there should be a change in the medium of instruction and that it should be imparted through the "language of the people." He favored Hindi as the Indian national language, since it was "the most common and most widely understood" of all the Indian languages. However, he was opposed to any attempt to impose the study of Hindi on non-Hindi speaking people. He also attached great importance to the freedom and education of women for a healthy national reconstruction, economic development, and social uplift.

Village-based economy. Rajendra Prasad totally agreed with Gandhian values with regard to rural economic development. In his scheme of things, human needs and acquisitiveness were to be regulated through self-discipline, agricultural production should be maximized, village industries resuscitated and expanded, the old sense of community recaptured. He well understood that industrialism disrupted the web of village life, woven and integrated for millennia. He therefore advocated the revival of old village industries and widespread use of the *charkha* (spinning-wheel) and *khadi* as efficacious means for rehabilitating India's village economy. It not only provided employment to agriculturists during their leisure time but also helped them in augmenting their income. He wanted cottage industries to play an important role in the economic growth of the country, and he recommended that government departments propagate and use *khadi* for official uniforms and clothes.

Social reform. A true humanist with an instinctive love for humankind, Rajendra Prasad helped ameliorate the living conditions of the despised and downtrodden Dalits ("untouchables"). He contributed significantly to important social changes to modern Indian society by the uplift those Gandhi called Harijans (children of God) and the removal of untouchability. He was also greatly concerned for improvement in the social and economic conditions of the Adivasis (Tribals). He believed that if the Adivasis remained backward for ages, it was not their fault. In free India, every citizen, including the Adivasis and Dalits, had equal rights. Rajendra Prasad wanted people to develop sympathetic attitudes toward the downtrodden, appreciating their customs and traditions in order to help bring them into India's mainstream of development.

World vision. Gandhi conceived of a human society based on love (*ahinsa*). Rajendra Prasad, as a true disciple, also advocated the efficacy of Mahatma Gandhi's method of true nonviolence for the eradication of hatred and all conflicts between nations and within nations. He strongly pleaded for the cessation of nuclear tests, the banning of nuclear weapons, and total disarmament, and for abjuring the use of force altogether. It is no wonder that his views on world peace and harmony have great significance in the strife-torn world of today.

Rajendra Prasad's life is a saga of the self-sacrificing struggles of an idealist who possessed a combination of sterling qualities. He was a true representative of Indian culture, with deep admiration for its ancient noble traits. His gentleness, simplicity, and modesty made him the darling of the masses. He remains one of modern India's most revered leaders, honored for his patriotism, honesty, and selfless service to his motherland.

Yuvaraj Prasad

See also **Congress Party; Gandhi, Mahatma M. K.**

BIBLIOGRAPHY

Datta, Kali Kinkar. *History of Freedom Movement in Bihar.* 3 vols. Patna: Government of Bihar, 1952, 1957, 1958.

———. *Rajendra Prasad.* Delhi: Government of India, 1970.

Prasad, Rajendra. *India Divided.* Mumbai: Hind Kitabs, 1947.

———. *Satyagraha in Champaran.* Ahmedabad: Navajivan Publishing, 1949.
———. *Autobiography.* Mumbai: Asia Publishing House, 1957.
———. *At the Feet of Mahatma Gandhi.* Mumbai: Asia Publishing House, 1961.
Punjabi, Kewal L. *Rajendra Prasad: First President of India.* London: Macmillan, 1960.

PRE-ARYANS. *See* **Indus Valley Civilization.**

PREMCHAND ***(1880–1936), prominent Hindi-Urdu author.*** Dhanpat Rai Srivastava, better known as Premchand, is widely regarded as the most important Hindi-Urdu author of the twentieth century. He has to his credit fourteen published novels, three hundred short stories, plays, film scripts, translations from English, and a vast number of editorials and essays. Born in Lamhi, a village near Benares (Varanasi), the son of a poor village postmaster, he acquired education by dint of his own efforts. His first career was as a primary school teacher, and he later became an educational administrator. He wrote first in Urdu but switched later to Hindi at the suggestion of his publishers. He remained important in both literary streams, and would continue to be claimed by both as a master storyteller.

Srivastava began writing under the pseudonym Premchand when early in his career he aroused the ire of the British government for writings that were considered inflammatory and seditious. He resigned from government service in 1921 in answer to Mahatma Gandhi's call for noncooperation and remained ideologically indebted to him, though his later politics were also clearly colored by socialist thought. His writings reflected this confluence of thought. He considered it important to portray noble and ideal aspirations, and to provide some ground for activism and optimism; his social realism was deliberately peppered with idealized figures and Gandhian resolutions to conflict. He himself participated actively in the political and social reform debates of his day; he wrote short stories not only for the premier journals of his times, *Saraswati* and *Naya Zamana*, he was editor of the important Hindi journal *Madhuri* (1927–1931) and of his own journals, *Hans* (1930–) and *Jagaran* (1932–), which he continued to publish until the end of his life, though plagued by government restrictions and dogged by heavy debts.

Premchand's novels and short stories drew from his own vast experience of the conflicts of village life, caste tensions, excessive revenue demands, and the never-ending chain of debts entailed by these. If these were grim tales, they were both deepened and lightened by psychological insight, irony, and humor, and the broad canvas on which they were drawn, which came to link country and city in a manner previously unknown in Hindi-Urdu fictional literature. Women's issues, particularly in the urban sphere, occupied a large amount of space in his writing. He wrote women-centered stories for the radical women's journal *Chand.* Two well-known novels, *Sevasadan* (House of service; 1918), his first success, and *Nirmala* (1927), focused on the plight of attractive young women, yoked to older men for lack of dowry. In the one case, the young woman took to prostitution, where she achieved a measure of independence, only to be cast into fetters of another kind by the efforts of social reformers. In the later novel, the ending was much more tragic. Suspected of a liaison with her stepson, Nirmala experienced psychological pain and loss of almost unbearable intensity. Of his peasant novels, *Godaan, the Gift of a Cow* (1936) is considered a classic of modern Hindi-Urdu literature. Written at the end of his life, it is set within two overlapping narrative frames, one provided by the social codes of village life on the North Indian plains and the other by the wider network of colonial and nationalist politics in the city of Lucknow. *Godaan* is Premchand's most mature novel; it presents a clear-eyed vision of pre-independence politics with little utopian relief provided for the memorable peasant characters, Hori, Dhania, and Gobar.

Premchand was elected president of the newly formed Progressive Writers Association in 1936. His view of the aim of literature, as presented in his address to the first meeting of the association in Lucknow, has remained formative for succeeding generations of radical writers in Hindi-Urdu: "Now literature does not view the individual as separate from society, on the contrary, it sees the individual as an indissoluble part of society! Not so that the individual should rule over society and make literature a means for pursuing his self-interests, as if eternal enmity existed between him and society, but because the individual's existence is dependent on the existence of society, outside of which his value is next to nothing." (*The Oxford India Premchand*)

Vasudha Dalmia

BIBLIOGRAPHY

Premchand. *Godaan, the Gift of a Cow*, translated by Gordon C. Roadarmel, with a new introduction by Vasudha Dalmia. Bloomington: Indiana University Press, 2002.
———. *The Oxford India Premchand* (42 short stories and the novels *Nirmala*, translated by Alok Rai and *Gaban, the Stolen Jewels*, translated by David Ruben, with an introduction by Francesca Orsini). Delhi: Oxford University Press, 2004.
Rai, Amrit. *Premchand. His Life and Times*, translated from the Hindi by Harish Trivedi, with an introduction by Alok Rai. Delhi: Oxford University Press, 2002.

PRESIDENT. *See* **Political System.**

PRESIDENTS OF INDIA Article 52 of the Constitution of India defines India's president as the formal head of state and the supreme commander of the armed forces. Since the Indian parliamentary system is modeled along the lines of the British parliamentary system, the role of India's president parallels that of the crown in Britain. An unusual aspect of the Indian Constitution, however, is Article 53, whereby Parliament has the authority to confer the powers and functions exercised by the president upon any other authority.

The president must be a citizen of India but, unlike the U.S. president, he or she does not have to be born in India. Unlike the hereditary king or queen of Britain, the president of India is elected indirectly by a complex electoral college system consisting of single and multiple votes assigned to members of both houses of India's Parliament (MPs), and members of the lower houses of the state legislative assemblies (MLAs), with the proviso that total votes cast by MLAs do not exceed the total multiple votes cast by MPs. The president is elected to serve a five-year term, with the possibility of several renewals, although no president has served more than two five-year terms. In case of the president's death or incapacitation, the vice-president serves as acting president until a new president is elected. Political rivalries among the parties tend to determine new nominations.

While the Indian president is the nominal executive head of the state and commander of the armed forces, actual executive power is exercised by the prime minister of India and his or her appointed council of ministers. According to Article 74 of the Constitution, the prime minister and council of ministers will "aid and advise the President who shall, in exercise of his functions, act in accordance with such advice."

However, the power of the Indian presidency rises when no political party is able to form a government in national elections, and there is no consensus among them in forming a coalition government, or when there are rival coalition groups seeking to form the government. This problem has been more acute in the politically unstable Indian states. Under these circumstances, "President's Rule" is imposed on the state by the president, acting on the advice of the prime minister. Under similar circumstances at the central level, when no prime minister and cabinet exist to advise him, the president must make independent judgments in forming the government. Such a situation usually occurs just after a general election in which no party gained a majority, or following a parliamentary vote of no-confidence in the government.

Dr. Shankar Dayal Sharma and Dr. Narayanan Two former presidents of India: Sharma (left, an activist in the earlier struggle for freedom from British colonial rule who served from 1992–1997) and Narayanan (born to an "untouchable" family, he served from 1997–2002). INDIA TODAY.

The nomination of the president follows certain norms that allow for the presidency to shift between the linguistic Indo-Aryan northern states and the Dravidian southern states, with a preference for the southern minority. This is interspersed by the periodic nomination of minority religious and low caste groups. As of 2005, India has had four presidents from the North, including two Muslims and one Sikh, and seven presidents from the South, including one Muslim and one member of the Dalits (formerly called "untouchables"). There has been no Christian president, although Christians are the third-largest religious group after Hindus and Muslims.

The unwritten practice, until the nomination and election of A. P. J. Abdul Kalam to the presidency in 2002, has been for the ruling vice president to be proposed as the next president, especially if the president died in office or has completed his five-year term. All the presidents of India except Zail Singh, Fakhruddin Ali Ahmed, and Abdul Kalam, were vice presidents before becoming presidents. Note that all three non–vice presidential

GOVERNOR-GENERALS AND PRESIDENTS OF INDEPENDENT INDIA

Governor-Generals	
Lord Louis Mountbatten (last British Viceroy)	1947–1948
Chakravarthi Rajagopalachari (South; Hindu)	1948–1950
Presidents	
1. Rajendra Prasad (North; Hindu)	1950–1962
2. Sarvepalli Radhakrishnan (South; Hindu)	1962–1967
3. Zakir Hussain (North; Muslim)	1967–1969 (died in office)
3a. Mohammed Hidayatullah (acting president; North; Muslim)	July–August 1969
4. Varahagiri Venkata Giri (South; Hindu)	1969–1974
5. Fakhruddin Ali Ahmed (North; Muslim)	1974–1977 (died in office)
5a. B. D. Jatti (acting president; South; Hindu)	February–July 1977
6. Neelam Sanjiva Reddy (South; Hindu)	1977–1982
7. Giani Zail Singh (North; Sikh)	1982–1987
8. Raman Venkataraman (South; Hindu)	1987–1992
9. Shankar Dayal Sharma (North; Hindu)	1992–1997
10. Kocheril Raman Narayanan (South; Hindu)	1997–2002
11. Avul Pakir Jainulabdeen Abdul Kalam (South; Muslim)	2002–

nominations were from religious minorities. The first two were brought in by the Congress governments to accommodate Muslim and Sikh political sentiments. The reasons underlying the appointment of Abdul Kalam instead of Vice President Krishan Kant, a long-time Congress Party member, were political. During the intense rivalry between the Bharatiya Janata Party (BJP) and Congress in 2002, the ruling BJP coalition chose to depart from this usual practice, since the ruling vice president had been nominated and elected by the previously ruling Congress Party.

In 2002 the Christian governor of Maharashtra, P. C. Alexander, a native of Kerala, was proposed by the Hindu nationalist BJP and other nationalist parties as the next president to follow K. R. Narayanan, a Dalit who was also from Kerala. But this candidate was ruled out in favor of Abdul Kalam, a Tamil Muslim, when the secular Congress Party, led by Sonia Gandhi, refused to support Governor Alexander's nomination. Reportedly, the Congress Party feared that a Christian was being nominated by Hindu nationalists for the presidency as a strategic move in order to rule out the prospect of Sonia Gandhi, the Christian leader of the Congress Party, from becoming prime minister. A concurrent Christian president and Christian prime minister in Hindu-majority India would have been politically unacceptable. Given the precedent set in 2002, presumably the vice president will not automatically become the president following the president's death or retirement.

Following the rule of the first non-Congress government between 1977 and 1979, and the new era of changing coalition governments led by the Congress or the BJP since 1989, there have been some demands that the president in office should reflect the party of the government in power, even if this meant that the term of the ruling president had to be curtailed. But this idea has not found favor, since the president is expected to be the impartial representative of the people of India, and in particular, to follow the advice of the prime minister and his Cabinet. Indian presidents have been of distinguished backgrounds, and have maintained the dignity and the impartiality of India's highest office.

In the period between Indian independence on 15 August 1947 and the promulgation of the Constitution of the Indian republic on 26 January 1950, there were two interim governor-generals of India: the last viceroy, Lord Louis Mountbatten, and the distinguished Tamil Congress leader, Chakravarti Rajagopalachari. Including Rajagopalachari and the Dalit president K. R. Narayanan, nine Indian heads of state have been Hindus, of which two were acting presidents. As of 2005, there have been three Muslim presidents, one Sikh, and one Dalit. The two acting presidents following the deaths in office of the president, were a Muslim from the North and a Hindu from the South. Thus, while the majority linguistic Hindu North has dominated elected political representation in Parliament, the nominal and formal presidency of India has been dominated by the minority linguistic South, and by religious minorities.

The Presidents

Rajendra Prasad (1950–1962). Born in 1884, Prasad was selected as the first president of India following the adoption of the Indian Constitution in January 1950. He was a follower of Mahatma Gandhi and a believer in nonviolence. He had briefly held the portfolio of the ministry for food in 1947 in the interim government of Jawaharlal Nehru. He was awarded the Bharat Ratna in 1962. Dr. Prasad died in 1963.

Sarvepalli Radhakrishnan (1962–1967). Born in 1888, Radhakrishnan was a scholar, philosopher, writer, and statesman. He served as the first vice president of India (1952–1962). Dr. Radhakrishnan taught at Oxford University for sixteen years and served as chairman of the United Nations Educational, Scientific, and Cultural Organization in the late 1940s. His books include *Indian Philosophy* (1923) and *The Hindu View of Life* (1942). He was awarded the Bharat Ratna in 1954. Dr. Radhakrishnan died in 1975.

Zakir Hussain (1967–1969). Hussain was born in 1897 and died in 1969 while in office. A great patriot, educator, and social worker, he previously served as chancellor of Aligarh Muslim University. Dr. Hussain received the Bharat Ratna in 1963.

Mohammed Hidayatullah (acting, July–August 1969). Born in 1905, Justice Hidayatullah was a judge of the High Court and served as chief commissioner of Scouts and Guides. He died in 1992.

Varahagiri Venkata Giri (1969–1974). Born in 1884, Giri was a lawyer by profession and a veteran trade unionist. He received the Bharat Ratna in 1975 and died in 1980.

Fakhruddin Ali Ahmed (1974–1977). Ahmed, born in 1905, was active in the freedom movement. He served as a union minister from 1966 before becoming president. He died in 1977.

B. D. Jatti (acting, February–July 1977). Born in 1913, Jatti was a lawyer who had previously served as chief minister of Karnataka and as governor of Orissa.

Neelam Sanjiva Reddy (1977–1982). Reddy was born in 1913. He served as chief minister of Andhra Pradesh, union minister, and Speaker of the Lok Sabha (Parliament's lower house). He had been a freedom fighter and president of Indian National Congress. He died in 1996.

Giani Zail Singh (1982–1987). Born in 1916, Zail Singh's public life was long and varied. He was a freedom fighter, social reformer, state congress leader, successful chief minister, and union home minister. He died in 1994.

Raman Venkataraman (1987–1992). Venkataraman was born in 1910. He was elected to India's First Parliament (1952–1957), and reelected in 1957. However, he resigned his seat to join the State Government of Madras as a Minister. In 1980, Venkataraman was reelected to the Lok Sabha and was appointed minister of finance and later minister of defense in the government headed by Indira Gandhi. He was elected vice president of India in August 1984, then was elevated to the office of president after Zail Singh completed his five-year term in office.

Shankar Dayal Sharma (1992–1997). Born in 1918, he had served as vice president and was elevated to president after Venkataraman completed his five-year term. Dr. Sharma was a scholar and freedom fighter and had served as chief minister of Madhya Pradesh, president of the Congress Party, and cabinet minister. He died in 1999.

Kocheril Raman Narayanan (1997–2002). Born in 1920, Narayanan was born into a Dalit family in the village of Uzhavoor in the Kottayam district of Kerala. He was educated at the London School of Economics, and served as Indian ambassador to the United States from 1980 to 1984. On his return to India, he entered politics and won three successive General Elections in 1984, 1989, and 1991 from his constituency in Kerala. During this time, he was minister of state for planning, for external affairs, and for science and technology. He was elected vice president of India in August 1992 and assumed the presidency after President S. D. Sharma completed his five-year term.

Avul Pakir Jainulabdeen Abdul Kalam (25 July 2002–). Abdul Kalam was born in 1931 into a poor Tamil Muslim family in Dhanushkodi in the Rameshwaram district of Tamil Nadu. Having headed and directed the Indian missile program in India, Kalam has been recognized as the father of India's missile technology and is often called the "missile man" of India. Dr. Abdul Kalam formerly served as the scientific adviser to the government of India.

Raju G. C. Thomas

See also **Abdul Kalam, Avul Pakir Jainulabdeen (A. P. J.); Narayanan, K. R.; Political System; Radhakrishnan, Sarvepalli**

VICE PRESIDENTS OF INDIA

S. Radhakrishnan	1952–1962
Zakir Hussain	1962–1967
Varahagiri Venkata Giri	1967–1969
G. S. Pathak	1969–1974
B. D. Jatti	1974–1979
M. Hidayatullah	1979–1984
R. Venkataraman	1984–1987
S. D. Sharma	1987–1992
K. R. Narayanan	1992–1997
Krishan Kant	1997–2002
B. Shekhawat	2002–

BIBLIOGRAPHY

Ahuja, M. L. *The Presidents of India and Their Constitutional Portrayal.* New Delhi: Om Publications, 1997.

Goswami, Prashanta. *Presidents of India: 50 Years.* New Delhi: B. R. Publishing Corporation, 1999.

Jal, Janak Raj. *Presidents of India, 1950-2000.* New Delhi: Regency Publications, 2002.

Noorani, A. G. *Constitutional Questions in India: The President, Parliament and the States.* New Delhi: Oxford University Press, 2000.

PRICE MOVEMENTS AND FLUCTUATIONS SINCE 1860 Prior to the mid-nineteenth century, price statistics for British India were fragmentary, pertaining to very few markets and commodities. In the first half of the nineteenth century, prices saw several cycles of steady fall or rise, over a span of six to seven years each. In the absence of other data on economic activity, historians have sometimes relied too heavily on these price cycles, which do not necessarily infer cycles in production.

By 1875, however, an unmistakable trend does emerge; prices rose for the next fifty years. The price of wheat at the end of period in 1925 was about three times what it had been at the beginning. The expansion of the world economy, with buoyant demand for primary commodities, played an obvious role in stimulating more rapid rises in the prices of exportable commodities rather than those of imports. Monetary policy also played a role, via devaluation of the rupee between 1873 and 1893. From the mid-1920s, however, world commodity prices began to be depressed. The monetary policy of the British colonial government was faulted, this time for its determined defense of an overvalued rupee in the interest of British stabilization.

Fluctuations

The longer trends and cycles were broken frequently by sharp short-term fluctuations. Prices in colonial India fluctuated rather more than either post-independence Indian or contemporary global prices. Between 1900 and 1935, for example, severe inflation of 20 to 30 percent was not uncommon, often as part of a price-cycle. On the other hand, during the Great Depression, prices fell by a factor of four or more.

Agricultural production, of course, depended too heavily on rainfall, which could change without warning. However, in the early twentieth century, unpredictable weather alone does not fully explain price movements. The correlation between prices and rainfall was mediated by other variables, such as addition to the money supply, and changing demand for nonmonetary gold. India functioned under currency regimes that left its money supply sensitive to balance of payments, and perhaps as a result, more volatile than one would expect under a central bank. The central bank began operation in 1935, but for a long time after that date, there was no explicit stabilization policy at work. Real incomes, on the other hand, depended primarily on harvests, which were more weather-sensitive in the early twentieth century than a hundred years later. These features led to an inherent maladjustment between money supply and transactions demand for money, which J. M. Keynes considered a major weakness of the Indian monetary system.

For example, in a year that had seen a bad harvest, domestic income and consumption might fall. And yet, a buoyant world trade could lead to monetary expansion, adding fuel to an ongoing price-rise. The real effects of monetary expansion were relatively weak because of undeveloped asset markets. A bad harvest normally led to a contraction in the demand for nonmonetary gold import, further adding to currency growth. If inflation eventually depressed exports, a countercyclical mechanism could work. In the interwar period, harvest fluctuations were milder. Still, the Great Depression was an example of the same kind of maladjustment. A trade-induced monetary contraction coincided with normal, even unusually good, agricultural seasons, leading to a large fall in prices. The microeconomics of price formation might also contribute to fluctuations, depending on how quickly and easily information about harvests traveled from the production site to the wholesale markets, and finally to the retail market. Traders were known to collaborate to try to control this information as much as possible.

Episodes

In the early twentieth century, a conjunction of monetary and real pressures led to price instability. Each of the three major inflations—1903–1908, 1913–1914, and 1919–1920—was preceded by a major harvest failure. Real agricultural output declined by 7 percent in 1902–1904, by 15 percent in 1906–1907, by 14 percent in 1910–1913, and by nearly 30 percent in 1917–1918. Prices began to rise due to the shortage of agricultural goods. In each case, buoyant export demand led to expansion in money supply. These two factors combined to generate a very rapid rise in prices.

The intensity and duration of the inflations varied. Prices increased by 33 percent in 1905–1907; the average annual rates were about 6 to 10 percent in the second episode; whereas in 1919 prices increased by more than 50 percent over the previous year. This variation can be attributed to the extent of currency expansion. In the first of these three episodes, gold imports fell much more than agricultural exports, so that money supply expanded. In the second case, the effect of inflation on commodity trade was more pronounced than the effect on gold, dampening monetary growth. In 1919 private gold transactions were suspended, as the government needed gold for currency reserve.

During both world wars, expanding world demand for war-related goods coincided with supply constraints, resulting in rapid inflation. In World War II, however, monetary policy complicated the picture. The government had to spend much larger sums and proportions of the budget on defense. Fiscal measures were insufficient to cover the deficit. In 1939, however, unlike 1914, India had a central bank and substantial monetary autonomy. Consequently, money supply increased to finance the deficit as never before.

In the interwar period generally, harvest fluctuations were milder. As a result, price and currency fluctuations in the interwar period were entirely due to trade shocks. While the exchange rate partially bore the impact of trade shocks until the mid-1920s, thereafter the exchange was effectively fixed again, so that a gradual decline in export demand induced steady deflation. From 1926, currency growth, and all prices, began a seven-year downward course, the climax coming in 1931, when a sharp fall in exports caused prices to crash.

India shared two conditions with nearly all other open economies that suffered the depression. First, there was a contraction in exports. Second, the gold exchange standard compelled a deflation. Whereas the threat of deflation forced Britain, like several other economies, to leave the gold standard and devalue, India could not devalue. British authorities determining Indian policy feared that devaluation would render the government unable to pay its foreign debt. The result was a steady and severe deflation, worsened by cuts in government expenditure and a series of good harvests. Rise in real interest rates crowded out private investment. Private debts and rents ballooned. As time went on, land and gold began to be sold. A great deal of rural unrest began, crystallized around debt and rent relief. The really effective counterdeflationary measures did not come from the government. These were the export of gold that reflated the economy to some extent, and widespread cuts in money wages that restored profitability.

Prices and Production

Price trends have often been cited, and misused, as a link between politics and economic change under British rule. The earliest episode illustrating this is a price depression in the second quarter of the nineteenth century, which has been read widely as a sign of rural economic crisis, at some neglect of the fact that the prices of major consumer goods like cotton textiles in this period were falling worldwide. In the period of the essay, the two particularly controversial episodes were the mild inflation of 1870 to 1890 and the Great Depression. Both episodes involved a monetary policy driven by British imperial interests rather than Indian ones.

Tirthankar Roy

See also **Agricultural Prices and Production, 1757–1947**

BIBLIOGRAPHY

McAlpin, Michelle. "Price Movements and Economic Fluctuations." In *The Cambridge Economic History of India*, vol. 2: *C. 1757–1970*, edited by Dharma Kumar. Cambridge, U.K., and New York: Cambridge University Press, 1983.

Roy, Tirthankar. "Price Movements in Early Twentieth Century India." *Economic History Review* 55 (1995): 118–133.

PRIME MINISTER. *See* **Political System.**

PRIME MINISTERS OF INDIA The prime minister is the leader of the ruling party in the national Parliament and the effective political head of the government of India, in contrast to the president of India, who is the constitutional head of state exercising the formal duties of government. The parallels are that of the prime minister and the crown in the British parliamentary system, which served as the model for the Indian political system. The prime minister, who oversees the functions of government, is assisted in this task by a Council of Ministers comprising cabinet ministers, ministers of state with independent charge, ministers of state who work with cabinet ministers, and deputy ministers. The Council of Ministers is appointed by the president on the advice of the prime minister.

By constitutional arrangements, the president of India appoints as prime minister the leader of the party or alliance that enjoys majority support in the Lok Sabha (the lower house of the Indian Parliament). If no single party or alliance has secured a majority of seats, the leader of the largest single party or alliance group is appointed prime minister. In these unclear circumstances, the appointed prime minister must demonstrate the party or coalition's ability to govern by securing a vote of confidence in the Lok Sabha, that is, a majority of votes cast on the issue of governability.

The prime minister can be a member of either the Rajya Sabha (the upper house of Parliament) or the Lok Sabha. As prime minister, he or she is the leader of the house to which he or she belongs. The prime minister is

PRIME MINISTERS OF INDIA

Prime Minister	Party	Dates in Office
Jawaharlal Nehru (North/Hindu)	Congress	August 1947–May 1964 (died)
Lal Bahadur Shastri (North/Hindu)	Congress	June 1964–January 1966 (died)
Indira Gandhi (North/Hindu)	Congress	January 1966–March 1977 (defeated)
Morarji Desai (North/Hindu)	Janata	March 1977–July 1979 (defeated)
Charan Singh (North/Hindu)	Janata	July 1979–January 1980 (defeated)
Indira Gandhi (North/Hindu)	Congress	January 1980–October 1984 (died)
Rajiv Gandhi (North/Hindu)*	Congress	October 1984–December 1989 (defeated)
Vishwanath P. Singh (North/Hindu)	National Front Coalition	December 1989–November 1990 (defeated)
Chandra Shekhar Samavadi (North/Hindu)	Janata	November 1990–June 1991 (defeated)
P. V. Narasimha Rao (South/Hindu)	Congress	January 1991–June 1996 (defeated)
H. D. Deve Gowda (South/Hindu)	United Front Coalition	June 1996–April 1997 (replaced)
Inder K. Gujral (North/Hindu)	United Front Coalition	April 1997–December 1997 (defeated)
Atal B. Vajpayee (North/Hindu)	BJP-led Coalition	March 1998–April 1999 (lost vote of no confidence)
Atal B. Vajpayee (North/Hindu)	BJP-led Coalition	October 1999–2004 (defeated)
Manmohan Singh (North/Sikh)	Congress-led Coalition	May 2004–

Defeated = ruling party or coalition defeated in elections Died = died in office Note: Gulzarilal Nanda was interim caretaker prime minister for a few weeks following the deaths of Jawaharlal Nehru in May 1964 and Lal Bahadur Shashtri in January 1966. *Rajiv Gandhi's father was a Parsi Zorastrian although his religion is identified by that of his mother, Indira Gandhi.

also the chairman of the Planning Commission of India. As head of the Council of Ministers, the prime minister oversees the work of all the ministries. He or she presides over Cabinet meetings, which are normally held in the Cabinet room of the prime minister's office. The Union Cabinet functions on the principle of "collective responsibility."

The prime minister's office (PMO) is located at South Block, Raisina Hill, in New Delhi. South Block is one of the two secretariat blocks (the other is known as North Block) that flank Rashtrapati Bhavan, the residence of the president of India. The PMO staff provides secretarial assistance to the prime minister. It is headed by the principal secretary to the prime minister and is staffed by other civil service officers and clerical staff. The PMO also includes the anticorruption unit and the public wing, which deals with grievances.

The range of subjects that the prime minister examines directly depends on the ministerial portfolios that the prime minister has chosen to keep under his responsibility. Other subjects are the responsibility of the cabinet minister or minister of state (independent charge) in charge of the ministry. Most subjects and issues are dealt with by the cabinet minister or minister of state-in-charge. All important policy issues that the minister in charge feels require the attention of the prime minister are sent to the PMO. The prime minister has traditionally been the minister-in-charge of the Departments of Space, Atomic Energy, and Ministry of Personnel, Public Grievances and Pensions. The prime minister has traditionally been the chairman of the Planning Commission as well.

Important issues that usually require the Prime Minister's personal attention include the following:

1. Important defense-related issues;
2. Decorations, both civilian and defense, where presidential approval is required;
3. All important policy issues;
4. Proposals for appointment of Indian heads of missions abroad and requests for grant of agreement for foreign heads of missions posted to India;
5. All important decisions relating to the Cabinet Secretariat;
6. Appointments to State Administrative Tribunals and the Central Administrative Tribunal, Union Public Service Commission (UPSC), Election Commission, appointment of members of statutory/constitutional committees, commissions attached to various ministries;
7. All policy matters relating to the administration of the civil services and administrative reforms;
8. Special packages announced by the prime minister for states are monitored in the PMO and periodical reports submitted to the prime minister; and
9. All judicial appointments for which presidential approval is required.

Parliament questions relating to the ministries and departments of which the prime minister is the minister-in-charge are first examined and answered by his civil service staff of experts, then submitted to the prime minister for his judgments and views, and then presented to Parliament by the prime minister himself.

Prime Ministers since 1947

Jawaharlal Nehru (1947–1964). The first prime minister of independent India, Jawaharlal Nehru held office for seventeen years, the longest thus far of any Indian prime minister. He was born in 1889. An intellectual, he laid the foundations of India's secular democracy and is the author of the monumental *The Discovery of India*, a personal interpretation of Indian history and politics, much of which was written while he was jailed during the freedom struggle against the British. He died in office in 1964.

Gulzari Lal Nanda (May–June 1964, acting; 11–24 January 1966, acting). A follower of Mahatma Gandhi's movement, Gulzari Lal Nanda was born in 1898. A veteran labor leader, he was a long-time Congress Party member, and he held several portfolios in the Union Cabinet. He died in 1998.

Lal Bahadur Shastri (1964–1966). Known for showing resolve during the Indo-Pakistan war of 1965, Lal Bahadur Shastri negotiated the subsequent Indo-Pakistani agreement at Tashkent with Pakistani president General Ayub Khan. He was born in 1904 and died in 1966.

Indira Gandhi (1966–1977; 1980–1984). The daughter and only child of Jawaharlal Nehru, Indira Gandhi was born in 1917. The second-longest ruling prime minister after her father, she held office for fifteen years in two separate terms. Her son Rajiv Gandhi became prime minister following her assassination in 1984. A strong, outspoken leader with an independent mind, she negotiated the Indo-Soviet Treaty of Peace and Friendship in August 1971, and then led India to victory in the December 1971 war against Pakistan.

Morarji Desai (1977–1979). The first non-Congress Party prime minister of India, Morarji Desai was born in 1896. He was a member of the Congress Party for decades, serving as finance minister and deputy prime minister, until he defected from the Congress under the leadership of Indira Gandhi. He served as chief minister of Maharashtra from 1952 to 1956. A staunch Gandhian and naturalist, he died in 1995.

Charan Singh (1979–1980). Born in 1902, Charan Singh occupied the position of president of the Lok Dal for many years. He was the deputy prime minister during the Janata regime from 1977 to 1979. He died in 1987.

Rajiv Gandhi (1984–1989). The son of Prime Minister Indira Gandhi, Rajiv Gandhi was born in 1944. A commercial pilot turned politician, he was assassinated during an election campaign in Tamil Nadu in 1991.

Vishwanath Prathap Singh (1989–1990). A Union minister in the Janata Party government from 1977 to 1980, Vishwanath Prathap Singh was a senior leader of Janata Dal. Born in 1931 into a North Indian princely family, Singh was a renowned painter. He served as prime minister of a coalition government from 1989 to 1990.

Chandra Shekhar Samavadi (1990–1991). Born in 1927, Chandra Shekhar Samavadi was a parliamentarian and a socialist. He served as president of the socialist Janata Party from 1977.

P. V. Narasimha Rao (1991–1996). Born in 1921, P. V. Narasimha Rao served as chief minister of Andhra Pradesh from 1971 to 1973, external affairs minister, defense minister, and human resources minister in the Congress government from 1980 onward, then as prime minister.

H. D. Deve Gowda (1996–1997). Born in 1933, H. D. Deve Gowda was the former chief minister of Karnataka and a Janata Dal leader.

Inder K. Gujral (1997–1998). Born in 1919, Inder K. Gujral was formerly a minister in the Union Cabinet from 1967 to 1976 and from 1989 to 1990, minister of external affairs (1989–1990, 1996–1997), and ambassador to the Soviet Union (1976–1980).

Atal B. Vajpayee (1998–1999, 1999–2004). A long-time Jana Sangh and later Bharatiya Janata Party (BJP) member of Parliament, Atal Bihari Vajpayee was born in 1924. A poet, journalist, and social worker with the Rashtriya Swayamsevak Sangh, he was a founding member of the Hindu nationalist party, the Jan Sangh, and the former president of the BJP. He was the leader of opposition in the Lok Sabha in 1993 as a member of the BJP.

Dr. Manmohan Singh (22 May 2004–). Born in 1932, Manmohan Singh is best known as the "father of Indian reforms" for his role in the economic reforms of 1991, when he served as finance minister of the Congress Party government. An academician by profession, he has taught in several universities and also has held various positions in government service.

Raju G. C. Thomas

See also **Gandhi, Indira; Gandhi, Rajiv; Nehru, Jawaharlal; Political System; Singh, Manmohan; Vajpayee, Atal Bihari**

BIBLIOGRAPHY

Gupta, M. G. *The Prime Ministers of India.* New Delhi: M. G. Publishers, 1989.

Hardgrave, Robert, Jr., and Stanley A. Kochanek. *India: Government and Politics in a Developing Nation.* Orlando, Fla.: Harcourt College Publishers, 2000.

Manor, James, ed. *Nehru to the Nineties: The Changing Office of Prime Minister in India.* Vancouver: University of British Columbia Press, 1994.

Mehta, Ved. *Family Affair: India under Three Prime Ministers.* New York: Oxford University Press, 1982.

Seshan, N. K. *With Three Prime Ministers: Nehru, Indira and Rajiv.* New Delhi: Wiley Eastern Ltd., 1993.

Thakur, Janardhan. *Prime Ministers.* New Delhi: BPI (India) Ltd., 2002.

PRINCELY STATES The princely states of India and their rulers have been the subject of romantic novels and films, paintings, Orientalist and nationalist exposés, and advertising campaigns in which maharajas are synonymous with luxury, yet they have received relatively little scholarly attention. These political units reflected the political, cultural, and geographical diversity of the Indian subcontinent; their number varied according to different accounts that used varying criteria to define a princely state. The *Imperial Gazetteer of India* (1909) recorded 693 states, but that figure included the Shan states in Burma as well as Nepal. The Report of the Indian States Committee, issued in 1929, claimed 562 states. These statistics are deceptive, since many political entities included in these documents were small estates belonging to landholders who might exercise some magisterial powers. Over 360 such small states were concentrated in western India alone. The princely states that had sovereign powers of collecting taxes and distributing justice numbered less than a hundred.

When most sources refer to the princely states of India, they focus on those political units whose rulers had secured some type of quasi-legal relationship with the British colonial government in India from the late 1700s onward and then formally survived until the late 1940s. Many of these princely states had existed in India for centuries before the British emergence as a colonial political power in the late eighteenth century. Indeed, Hindu princes had been called various titles, such as *raja*, *rana*, and *rao*, that were more appropriately translated as "king" (or "great king" for those designated as *maharaja*, *maharana*, or *maharao*), but the British translated the titles of these rulers as "prince" to indicate their subordinate status to the British monarch as their suzerain. Thus the British did not create many of the princely states, but once the states entered into treaty relations, the British significantly controlled their external relations and communications networks and gradually extended their symbolic suzerainty over the princes and their states. Still, during the colonial period, the rulers of eighty to one hundred states exercised considerable internal autonomy, collecting taxes, administering justice, and in some cases launching impressive economic developments and some social reforms.

Origins

Antique states. Princely states may be grouped in three categories according to their origins. The states ruled by the Rajputs may be labeled antique, since many were founded before the arrival of the British and some even before the establishment of the Mughal empire in 1526. Rajputs, whose name comes from the Sanskrit *rajaputra*, or "sons of kings," migrated from Central Asia into the Indian subcontinent from around A.D. 200 onward. They spread in a broad arc from the western coast of Gujarat through the Thar desert, a region that came to be known either as Rajputana or Rajasthan, across the Indo-Gangetic Plain into the foothills of the western Himalayas. The major princely states of Rajputana include Mewar (or later Udaipur, after its capital); Marwar (or Jodhpur, after its capital); Amber (known as Jaipur, after its capital built in the early 1700s by Jai Singh); and Bikaner. The rulers of these states legitimated themselves by their military control, elaborate genealogies claiming divine descent or sanction, and assiduous maintenance of their *izzat*, or "honor." The rulers of Mewar claimed primacy among the Rajputs for their defense of *izzat* when confronted with defeat in battle and their refusal to offer their daughters in marriage to the Mughal emperors. Other Rajput rulers, most notably those of Amber, Marwar, and Bikaner, provided daughters to the Mughal emperors, accepted ranks in the Mughal *mansabdari*, or administrative system, led Mughal armies in battle, governed Mughal provinces, and retained internal autonomy within their states. Their entry into the Mughal imperial structure prefigured their subsequent accommodation with the British Empire.

Successor states. The second major category were provinces of the Mughal empire, whose Mughal governors gradually asserted a quasi-independent status during the mid-eighteenth century, just when the British East India Company began its initial political expansion in Bengal. Labeled successor states, they were Awadh (Oudh), Bengal, and Hyderabad. By 1856 the British ruled both Awadh and Bengal directly, but Hyderabad would survive until 1948 as the premier princely state of India, with the largest population and revenues of any princely state. Its Muslim ruler, with the title of nizam, governed a political unit in which Hindus constituted 87 percent of the population and spoke Telugu (43%), Marathi (26%), and Kannada (13%), while Urdu-speaking

View of City Palace, Udaipur. This is the largest palace in Rajasthan (covering an area of 5 acres), in fact a complex of several palaces extended by twenty-two different Maharanas or kings between the sixteenth and twentieth centuries. It is now home to a museum and several luxury hotels. ADITYA PATANKAR / FOTOMEDIA.

Muslims were a distinct minority at 10 percent of the population by 1911 (Census of India, 1921, XXI, 74, 192).

Warrior states. During the eighteenth century, the third category of warrior states arose with the decline of the centralized power of the Mughals. In return for their protection of cultivating peasants and local merchants, ambitious, enterprising, venturesome men with military resources gained political control. This group was the most disparate and ranged from Sikh-ruled states in Punjab, such as Patiala, to the Maratha-ruled states of central India, scattered from Gwalior near Agra to Baroda in Gujarat, Mysore in the center, and Travancore on the western coast of peninsular South India. Jammu and Kashmir, with the largest territory (85,885 sq. mi., or 222,442 sq. km) of any princely state, is the prime example of a warrior state created by imperial imperatives. Gulab Singh, a Dogra military ally of the kingdom of Punjab, parlayed his control over Jammu to acquire Kashmir for 75 lakhs of rupees (7,500,000 rupees) paid to the British after their victory in the first Anglo-Sikh war in 1846. At the other end of the size and geographical spectrum is the state of Pudukkottai (1,179 sq. mi., or 3,054 sq. km) near Madras (Chennai). In return for timely military service against the French and Mysore state, in 1806 the British acknowledged the Tondaimans as rulers of the internally autonomous state of Pudukkottai, which would survive until 1948. Most other rulers of such little kingdoms in South India were transformed into landlords.

Power and authority. The Rajput rulers and those of successor and warrior states owed their power to control of military forces that were in turn commanded by kinsmen, military entrepreneurs, or petty local magnates who were willing to ally with a stronger rival rather than suffer defeat and possible extinction. The successor states claimed their authority to rule from their appointments by the Mughal emperor. Rajput and warrior rulers frequently based their authority to rule on divine sanction. Thus some Rajputs traced their lineages back to the Hindu gods of the sun (Surya) or moon (Chandra). While the maharanas of Udaipur claimed to be the servants of Shiva in his form as Eklinga (an iconic pillar with one

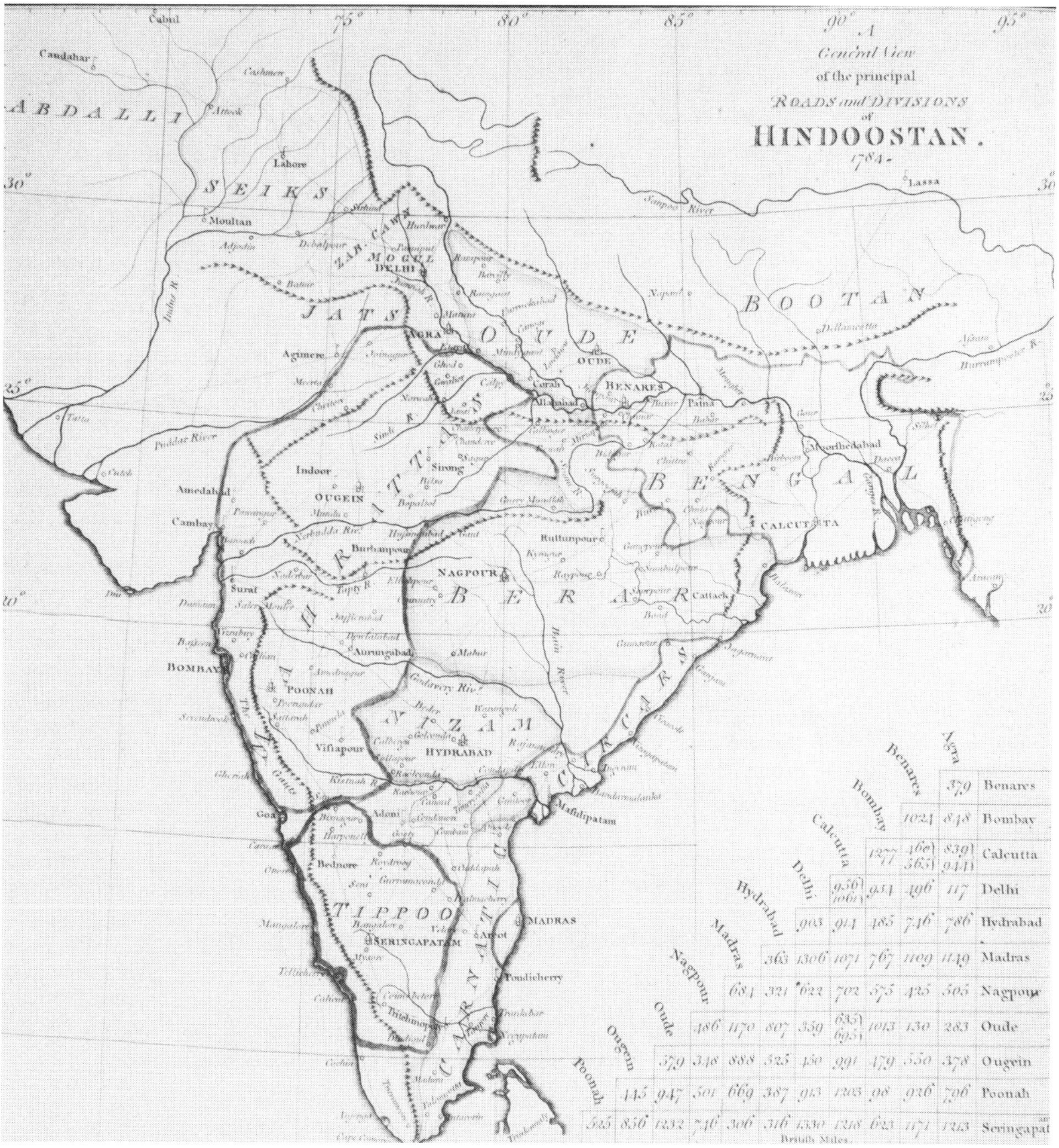

Road and Division Map of India, 1784. Map of "Hindooland" as divided into princely states and recognized by colonial Britain, late eighteenth century. At India's independence in 1947, nearly 680 such states or feudal monarchies existed, all led by hereditary rulers. SURVEY OF INDIA / AKHIL BAKSHI.

face), the maharajas of Bikaner proclaimed themselves to be the prime ministers of an incarnation of Vishnu. Maharaja Martanda Varma (r. 1729–1758) of Travancore dedicated his state to an incarnation of Vishnu, and his successors claimed to rule as servants of this god. Muslim rulers, including the nizam of Hyderabad, sought to legitimate their political power by tracing their descent from Muslim holy men and patronizing pan-Islamic institutions, including the holy cities of Mecca and Medina.

Indirect Rule

Subsidiary alliance system. As European politics began to affect the activities of European trading companies in

India, the British East India Company obtained the *diwani*, or the right to collect land revenue, in Bengal, inaugurating its metamorphosis from a trading company into a regional Indian political entity. By the end of the eighteenth century, the company had waged several wars against the Maratha and Mysore states, its two main competitors for political domination. Upon his arrival as governor-general in 1798, Lord Wellesley embarked on a resolute policy of imperial expansion. Relying upon an increasingly effective military force of British officers and mixed other ranks of Britons and Indians, he constructed a subsidiary alliance system incorporating earlier treaties with Indian states. These new alliances extended British control, exterminated some Indian states, and ensured the continued existence of other Indian states. In return for British protection from external enemies and internal dynastic rivals and a guarantee of their internal autonomy, Indian rulers who concluded subsidiary alliances with the British achieved some security in exchange for accommodation. The Indian rulers had to relinquish the power to wage war, the right of direct relations with other princes and external countries, and their control of communications networks, and sometimes were required to pay an annual monetary subsidy or to support contingents of troops for British use.

The state of Mysore is one example of how this system worked. In 1799 Arthur Wellesley defeated Tipu Sultan, the Muslim ruler whose father had usurped the Mysore *gadi* (throne) from its Hindu rulers, the Wadiyars. The East India Company annexed the western coastal districts, attached them to its Madras presidency, gave some Mysore territory to Hyderabad, which had entered into a subsidiary alliance in 1798, and restored the Wadiyar family to its *gadi* in return for the largest subsidy that the British would demand of any princely state.

British officials—termed "residents" if they were posted to important states such as Hyderabad, or "agents to the governor-general" or "political agents" if in charge of several smaller states—conducted relations between the company and the princes. Replacing the *vakil*s, the agents that states used to maintain at Mughal and other princely courts, the British political officers were to implement British policy in the states but also to represent the interests of the princes and activities within their states to the British official hierarchy. These company servants could intervene dramatically in the state administrations, especially when the heir was a minor and a council of regency governed.

Ambivalent British policies toward princely states. After Wellesley was recalled to London in 1805 because company directors deemed his expansionist policies too costly, despite the use of Indian allies, there was a temporary lull but not a total cessation of the expansion of this system of indirect rule. Lord Moira, later Lord Hastings, governor-general from 1813 to 1823, offered treaties to the Rajput states in Rajputana. He sanctioned military campaigns that further reduced the territories of key Maratha rulers—Gaekwad of Baroda, Scindia of Gwalior, Holkar of Indore, and Bhonsle of Nagpur—and integrated them more firmly into the subsidiary alliance system. Lord Dalhousie, governor-general from 1848 to 1856, orchestrated the last major extension of British direct rule on the basis of three criteria. Defeat in war occasioned the final annexation of the kingdom of Punjab; the lack of an heir, the so-called doctrine of lapse, led to the annexation of the Maratha-ruled states of Satara, Jhansi, and Nagpur; and charges of maladministration were used to justify the annexation of Awadh (Oudh), an early entrant to the subsidiary alliance system.

Political Structure

During the early 1800s, most princely states had autocratic, relatively simple administrative structures. The prince was the source of political authority and power, combining the roles of policy maker, chief judge, and sometimes commander in chief of state forces or military units dedicated to British service. A council of ministers, sometimes with a *diwan* or chief administrator, supervised departments such as home (internal order), finance, justice, and household. In many states, princes had granted or confirmed the right to collect revenue from specificd tracts within their states to relatives, military allies, or indigenous hereditary aristocrats in return for services rendered during the establishment of the state and for

DESPATCH OF LORD WELLESLEY DATED 4 FEBRUARY 1804 TO RESIDENT AT HYDERABAD

"The fundamental principle of His Excellency the Governor-General's policy in establishing subsidiary alliances with the principal states of India is to place those states in such a degree of dependence on the British power as may deprive them of the means of prosecuting any measures or of forming any confederacy hazardous to the security of the British empire, and may enable us to reserve the tranquility of India by exercising a general control over those states, calculated to prevent the operation of that restless spirit of ambition and violence which is the characteristic of every Asiatic government, and which from the earliest period of Eastern history has rendered the peninsula of India the scene of perpetual warfare, turbulence and disorder."

Tupper, *Indian Protectorate*, pp. 40–41.

RUDYARD KIPLING, "A LEGEND OF THE FOREIGN OFFICE"

Rustum Beg of Kolazai
slightly backward Native State
Lusted for a C.S.I.
So he began to sanitate.

Built a Goal and Hospital
nearly built a City drain
Till his faithful subjects all
thought their ruler was insane.

Rudyard Kipling, *Verse: Definitive Edition.* Garden City, N.J.: 1940, p. 8. First published in *Departmental Ditties*, 1885.

continued loyalty. By the middle of the nineteenth century, some Indian princes on their own initiative, along with some British officials, sought to centralize the administrations of princely states to enhance the power of the princes as well as that of the British at the expense of intermediate landholders. Their measures, frequently termed "reforms," tended to alienate the hereditary aristocracy, who would be losing both financial resources through new land revenue settlements and political influence at the princely *durbārs*, or courts, with the introduction of administrators recruited from outside the state, frequently men with education and bureaucratic experience in British India. A few British officials favored maintaining the nobility as a check on the autocracy of the princes, but increasingly the British supported more rationalized administrations. As late as 1938, Raja Rao Kalyan Singh, the *thikanadar* (holder of a small state or estate) of Sikar in Jaipur state, challenged the efforts of the Jaipur state to intervene in his internal affairs. A combination of British officials, Indian nationalists, and popular peasant leaders assisted the state administration in squashing his revolt.

Legitimation of British Suzerainity

By the end of 1856, the East India Company directly ruled three-fifths of the territory of the Indian subcontinent, and the Indian princes indirectly ruled two-fifths of the territory and one-third of the population. To reward the loyal support of most princes during the "Mutiny" or Revolt of 1857, the British Crown, which assumed the governance of India with the liquidation of the company, announced an end to any further annexation and extended treaties or *sanads* (letters of agreement) to many states, recognizing their right to adopt heirs. With minor variations, the map of princely states was set until the late 1940s. Although a few princely states, such as Hyderabad with prime cotton-growing tracts and some coal reserves, Mysore with the Kolar gold fields, and Patiala with fertile soil, were centrally located and had valuable natural resources, most princely states were concentrated in areas more remote and less economically productive than the British Indian provinces. The latter category ranged from Jammu and Kashmir, strategically important on the northern borders of India but dominated by inhospitable mountains, to states such as Bikaner and Jodhpur in the desert tracts of Rajputana, those in the salt marshes and dry lands of western Gujarat, and those in the ravines of central India and jungle tracts of Orissa.

During the second half of the nineteenth century, the British articulated rhetorical and legal rationales for their system of indirect rule. The princes were declared the natural leaders of their people, in contrast to the ever more vocal Western-educated middle-class critics of colonial rule. To integrate the princes into an imperial hierarchy, the British granted various honorary titles to the princes and regularized a table of salute, with Queen Victoria accorded 101 guns, and the princes deemed most significant given salutes ranging from 21 guns (Baroda, Gwalior, Hyderabad, Mysore, and later Jammu and Kashmir) down to 9 guns. Princes could earn an increase in their salutes by notable contributions to British military ventures or by undertaking internal reforms that modernized their administrations. By 1945 the table of salutes embraced 117 princes. Schedules of personal and local salutes enjoyed by princes within their lifetimes or states were developed to assuage princely anxiety over their *izzat.*

The British as paramount power. The British claimed suzerainty over the princes because of the British self-proclaimed status as the paramount power in India. Their assertion of paramountcy was based on precedence that was cobbled together from earlier official correspondence and treaties. The elastic concept of usage was invoked to justify changing British policies. Political officers, such Charles U. Aitchison (1832–1896) and William Lee-Warner (1846–1914), who usually had more experience at the provincial and central secretariats than in the princely states as political agents and residents, compiled procedural manuals and theoretical works to guide policy makers and political officers in the field. Lee-Warner averred that usage "amends and adapts to circumstances duties that are embodied in treaties of ancient date, and it supplies numerous omissions from the category of duties so recorded" (*Native States*, p. 204). Thus the British could demand new duties from their princely clients in order to adapt to changing circumstances. In other words, treaties and *sanads* were not written in stone.

In January 1877 Lord Lytton, the governor-general and viceroy from 1876 to 1880, presided at an Imperial Assemblage in Delhi at which Queen Victoria was declared the Kaiser-i-Hind, or Empress of India. Sixty-three princes paraded as loyal feudatories who received banners with newly created coats of arms from the representative of their empress. As late as 1893, Charles Tupper reiterated this interpretation when he declared that the British relationship with the princes was a feudal one since "the Indian Protectorate rests on ideas which are fundamentally indigenous. . . . There were many tendencies making for feudalism in the India of our predecessors; and . . . our protection has been sought in India as vassals sought the protection of their lords" (*Indian Protectorate*, p. 240).

The Twentieth Century

Twilight of empire and internal autonomy. Major challenges confronted both British power and princely rule by 1900. During the late nineteenth century, a few princes launched substantial administrative, economic, and social reforms and consequently acquired the reputation of being "progressive" rulers who were modernizing their states. Maharaja Sayaji Rao Gaekwad (1863–1939) of Baroda inaugurated universal compulsory primary education and mobile public libraries to help his subjects maintain their literacy, founded the Bank of Baroda, and fostered textile and chemical industries. Maharaja Krishnaraja (1884–1940) of Mysore undertook an ambitious program of industrial development and established both a university and an institute of technology. The rulers of Travancore and Cochin promoted education at all levels and extensive public works programs that fostered internal trade. By the 1930s all four states and about twenty others had representative assemblies and later legislative bodies with limited powers. Still, princes remained benevolent autocrats who retained much of their power and tried to contain or dampen popular political activity. In many states, reforms of revenue systems sought to increase state revenues and to eliminate intermediaries who might divert revenue and squeeze peasant taxpayers. Police departments were reconstituted to ensure more effective control over not only criminals but also popular political leaders critical of state policies.

Old and new roles for princely clients. Confronting defiance from Indian nationalist leaders and the burdens of World War I, the British government of India initially affirmed the role of the Indian princes and their states as military allies. Princely contributions included military contingents, money, and war matériel, and princely rulers in Punjab permitted extensive recruiting for the British Indian army within state territories. When urging his subjects to enlist, Maharaja Bhupinder Singh (1891–1938) of Patiala argued that it was far better to meet the angel of death on the battlefield than in bed. Nizām Osman Ali Khan (1886–1967) of Hyderabad issued a *firman*, or decree, declaring that the war was not a jihad but a war over politics; Indian Muslims could therefore legitimately fight with British forces against the Ottoman Empire, whose sultan was also the caliph of Islam.

Simultaneously, the princes began to function as political allies for their imperial patron or as representatives of their religious communities. In India the nizam of Hyderabad was strongly opposed to the Khilafat movement, and several Hindu princes intervened in a controversy over the construction of irrigation works on the Ganges near the sacred city of Hardwar. Abroad, princes began to attend imperial and international conferences as representatives of India. Maharaja Ganga Singh (1880–1943) of Bikaner was at the Imperial War Conference in 1917 and was a signatory of the peace treaty of Versailles.

Constitutional efforts to integrate the states. Among the British rewards to the princes for their support during World War I was the inauguration of a Chamber of Princes, an advisory body, in 1921. Dominated by a small group of princes from middle-sized states in North India and with the viceroy as presiding officer, the Chamber's resolutions ultimately had relatively little impact on British policy. The Chamber was more significant for bringing together a group of contentious princes who began to debate common issues, to develop some contacts with moderate British Indian nationalists and conservative British politicians, and to lobby with British officials for a definition of paramountcy

SPEECH BY MAHARAJA BHUPINDER SINGH OF PATIALA ON 3 FEBRUARY 1930 AT PATIALA CITY ON OCCASION OF BASANT PANCHAMI DURBAR (CELEBRATION OF SPRING)

"[T]he new attitude towards us is that the States are interpolated pages, apocryphal additions, in this history of India. I need not point out to you how wrong this view is, how fundamentally opposed to the evolution of our history. To forget the persistent regionalism of our people which finds expression in the Indian states is an error which as from time to time spelt disaster for Indian in the past. If the nationalist movement in its desire for a symmetric pattern of Indian political life decides to act as if the States did not exist, the prospects before the whole country are gloomy indeed."

Punjab State Archives at Patiala, Chamber Section, Case No. II (a) 34 of 1930, Vol. 2.

CABINET MISSION'S "MEMORANDUM ON STATES' TREATIES AND PARAMOUNTCY" PUBLISHED 22 MAY 1947

"When a new fully self-governing or independent Government or Governments come into being in British India . . . the rights of the States which flow from their relationship to the Crown will no longer exist and . . . all the rights surrendered by the States to the paramount power will return to the states. . . . The void will have to be filled either by the States entering into a federal relationship with the successor Government or Governments in British India, or, failing this, entering into particular political arrangements with it or them."

V. P. Menon, *The Story of the Integration of the Princely States*, Appendix II, 475–476.

that would reduce British intervention in the internal affairs of states.

Threatened with the Indian National Congress's demands for *swaraj*, or self-rule, and the possibility of a renewed civil disobedience campaign by Mahatma Gandhi, in 1930 the British invited the princes as well as a wide spectrum of Indian and British politicians to attend what became a series of three Round Table Conferences in London to discuss possible constitutional reforms. In 1935 a Government of India Act envisioned a constitutional federation of British Indian provinces and princely states in which the states would balance the British Indian provincial governments now to be formed from the majority parties in the provincial legislatures. Princely desires to reduce British intervention in their internal affairs, reluctance to concede essential powers to a federal legislature, and concern about any additional financial demands to support the federal institutions, as well as opposition from Conservative forces in Britain, stymied negotiations over federation. Upon the outbreak of World War II in 1939, the government of India suspended these negotiations.

Popular political activity. During the 1920s embryonic state's people's groups emerged to challenge princely autocracy and to demand certain civil rights, such as the freedoms of speech, of the press, and to assemble. These groups generally did not deny the authority of the princes to rule but frequently blamed corrupt or overbearing administrators for tyrannical policies. The Indian National Congress, under the direction of Mahatma Gandhi, did not formally become involved in the internal politics of the princely states until the late 1930s. Initially neither Gandhi nor other Congress politicians were particularly successful in either organizing a mass base or achieving changes in state policies. By the 1940s, however, the Congress was able to develop effective organizations in a few states such as Mysore.

Integration. As the process of decolonization in India unraveled, the increasing demand for the creation of Pakistan and escalating communal violence overshadowed the situation of the princely states. Although the princes clung to the forlorn hope that their treaties with the British Crown would ensure their future existence, their fate was sealed once Lord Louis Mountbatten and the British government decided on the partition of the British Indian empire into two independent states. Governor-general and viceroy from 1946 to 1948, Mountbatten advised the princes that their future involved accession to either India or Pakistan. Sardar Vallabhbhai Patel (1875–1950), the home and states minister in the interim government of India, and V. P. Menon (1894–1960), secretary of the states ministry, used a carrot-and-stick approach in their negotiations with the princes. Mollified with boons such as privy purses and various honorific concessions and threatened with possible deposition, most princes gradually agreed.

Three notable holdouts were Nawāb Mahabat Rasulkhanji, who sought to accede to Pakistan even though his state of Junagadh did not share a contiguous border with Pakistan, and the rulers of Hyderabad and Jammu and Kashmir, who wanted to remain independent. Jawaharlal Nehru launched a police action in 1948 that brought Hyderabad into the Indian union, and Maharaja Hari Singh (1895–1961) of Kashmir signed a letter of accession as Muslim tribesmen invading from Pakistan threatened his capital of Srinagar. In 2005 Pakistan controlled two-fifths of the former princely state as Azad (Free) Kashmir, and India had the other three-fifths.

The dispute over Kashmir has triggered three wars and several other military campaigns and remains the major impediment to normal relations between India and Pakistan. Smaller princely states that acceded to India were either integrated into new states created from British Indian provinces or were formed into unions of princely states. Hyderabad and Mysore were the only princely states to remain distinct political units, until 1956 when they were incorporated into the new states of Andhra Pradesh and Karnataka, respectively.

Princes in independent India. The most important rulers were appointed as governors or deputy governors of these unions or other states and occasionally as ambassadors. A few princes or their consorts entered electoral politics. Most notable were Maharani Gayatri Devi of Jaipur, who won a seat in the Lok Sabha (the lower house of India's Parliament) in 1962 with a plurality of 175,000 votes, and Rajmata Vijayaraje Scindia (d. 2001) of Gwalior, who moved from the Congress Party to a leadership role in the Bharatiya Janata Party. In 1971 Prime Minister Indira Gandhi secured a constitutional amendment that terminated the privy purses and other personal concessions to the princes. At the beginning of the new millennium some scions of former princely families enjoyed success in electoral politics. In 2005 Amarinder Singh from Patiala was serving as the Congress chief minister of Punjab state, and Vasundhara Raje (b. 1953), the daughter of Vijayaraje Scindia, was the Bharatiya Janata Party chief minister of Rajasthan.

Barbara N. Ramusack

See also **Baroda; Hyderabad; Jammu and Kashmir; Pakistan and India; Patel, Sardar Vallabhbhai; Punjab**

BIBLIOGRAPHY

Lee-Warner, William. *The Native States of India*. Rev. ed. London: Macmillan, 1910.

Menon, V. P. *The Story of the Integration of the Princely States*. Kolkata: Orient-Longmans, 1956.

Punjab State Archives at Patiala. Chamber Section, Case No. II (a) 34 of 1930, vol. 2.

Tupper, Charles Lewis. *Our Indian Protectorate: An Introduction to the Study of the Relations between the British Government and Its Indian Feudatories*. London: Longmans, Green, 1893.

SECONDARY SOURCES

Balzani, Marzia. *Modern Indian Kingship: Tradition, Legitimacy and Power in Rajasthan*. Oxford: James Currey, 2003.

Copland, Ian. *The British Raj and the Indian Princes: Paramountcy in Western India 1857–1930*. Mumbai: Orient Longman, 1982.

———. *The Princes of India in the Endgame of Empire, 1917–1947*. Cambridge, U.K.: Cambridge University Press, 1997.

Jeffrey, Robin. *The Decline of Nayar Dominance*. London: Chatto and Windus, 1976.

Jeffrey, Robin, ed. *People, Princes and Paramount Power: Society and Politics in the Indian Princely States, 1857–1947*. Delhi: Oxford University Press, 1978.

Kooiman, Dick. *Communalism and Indian Princely States: Travancore, Baroda, and Hyderabad in the 1930s*. New Delhi: Manohar, 2003.

Leonard, Karen. *Social History of an Indian Caste: The Kayasths of Hyderabad*. Berkeley and Los Angeles: University of California Press, 1978.

McLeod, John. *Sovereignty, Power, Control: Politics in the States of Western India, 1916–1947*. Leiden: Brill, 1999.

Nair, Janaki. *Miners and Millhands: Work, Culture and Politics in Princely Mysore*. Walnut Creek, Calif.: AltaMira, 1998.

Rai, Mirdu. *Hindu Rulers, Muslim Subjects: Islam, Community, and the History of Kashmir*. Princeton, N.J.: Princeton University Press, 2004.

Ramusack, Barbara N. *The Indian Princes and Their States*, vol. III, part 6 in *The New Cambridge History of India*. Cambridge, U.K.: Cambridge University Press, 2004.

Rudolph, Susanne Hoeber, and Lloyd I. Rudolph. *Essays on Rajputana*. New Delhi: Concept, 1984.

Thompson, Edward J. *The Making of the Indian Princes*. London: Oxford University Press, 1943.

Zutshi, Chitralekha. *Languages of Belonging: Islam, Regional Identity and the Making of Kashmir*. New York: Oxford University Press, 2004.

PRIVATE INDUSTRIAL SECTOR, ROLE OF

India faced a severe balance of payments crisis in 1990–1991. Thanks to this crisis, fairly substantive economic reforms have been introduced since 1991 to stimulate India's economy, especially its industrial sector. Import duties have been slashed, dropping from 47 percent in 1990–1991 to 16 percent in 2001–2002. Since this average duty of 16 percent is for all products, if one excludes agricultural products, the average import duty is lower still. By 2006–2007 the peak import duty is likely to be 20 percent for consumer durables and no more than 10 percent or lower for all other manufactured products. Most quantitative restrictions on imports have, moreover, disappeared, and income tax exemptions on export profits are being phased out. Barring a few strategic sectors reserved exclusively for the public sector, foreign direct investment in all other manufacturing activities is permitted, with no equity caps. However, equity caps continue in many services sectors, and foreign investment remains prohibited in agriculture. The Reserve Bank of India no longer administers the exchange rate, which is now market-determined, and India's rupee is already convertible on the current account, some steps having recently been taken toward capital account convertibility.

Historically, protected markets at home had led to inefficiencies and outdated technology for costly Indian industry, scant attention being paid to customer needs. Since such inefficient industry could not compete in the global market, export incentive "crutches" supported it. Now these are gone, or are in the process of being scrapped. Modern India's market-determined exchange rate no longer cushions the Indian economy from foreign exchange fluctuations. Simultaneously, with exchange controls eased, it has now become easier for Indians to borrow and invest abroad.

Private industry legitimately complains, however, that domestic reforms have not kept pace with external sector reforms, making it difficult for private investors to compete, even though industrial licensing has ended. Historically, such licenses had long been required for expansion, or for setting up fresh capacity. Additional licenses were required by companies that were under the purview of India's Monopolies and Restrictive Trade Practices Act or the Foreign Exchange Regulation Act. Such licensing is

Thermal Power Station, Tata Iron & Steel Works, in Jamshedpur, c. 1950. The Tatas were among India's first entrepreneurial families and have remained an industrial giant, with the recent economic boom having transformed their various holdings into a large multinational corporation. PRESS INFORMATION BUREAU / FOTOMEDIA.

over, and in that sense, the so-called license raj has ended. There has also been a spate of reforms in the financial sector.

Nonetheless, other vital domestic reforms still remain to be implemented, starting with needed infrastructure improvements in power transmission, as well as repairs to roads, ports, and telecommunications systems. Proper targeting of subsidies and levy of right-user charges has not generally been possible. Because of high fiscal deficits, central and state governments were in no position to invest adequately in physical and social infrastructure. Downsizing of government expenditure has not as yet occurred. Because governments borrow, often at artificially high interest rates, interest rates for industry remain high. Indirect tax reforms are required, since—with a multiplicity of taxes—that structure is nontransparent and leads to costly cascading effects. An integrated value-added tax has been talked about for quite some time, but its implementation keeps getting postponed. Nor have necessary agricultural reforms occurred. These are urgently required to stimulate income and consumption growth and to dispel the myth that reforms are pro-rich and anti-poor. In the absence of agricultural reforms, industry has neither the requisite demand nor the inputs required for industrial production. Thus, the evolution of India's food-processing industry has been totally inhibited. In India, "small-scale" industry is still defined by investments in plant and machinery being below a certain threshold, as elsewhere, not in terms of employment. Reservations of certain sectors for production by small-scale industries hence prevent those sectors from improving their technology or reducing costs. India's legal framework also needs reform. Some of this is statutory, such as the Industrial Disputes Act, which prevents retrenchment, lockouts, or closure without government permission, discouraging the use of labor-intensive techniques. Other laws are not statutory, but executive, leading to an "inspector raj," characterizing all three steps of private industrial entry, functioning and exit. The old licensing raj may be dead, but the inspector raj is still alive, and leads to deterrent procedures, bribery, and rent seeking. Finally, dispute resolution does not work fast enough, although a new Arbitration and Conciliation Act was passed in 1996 and a new Civil Procedure Code was amended in 2002.

The private industrial sector needs to be defined, since it is not a uniform or heterogeneous category. A broad distinction is sometimes drawn between the "organized" and the "unorganized" sectors. However, this definition is ambiguous, and there are at least three definitions of organized versus unorganized. First, any factory that employs ten or more workers and uses power (or twenty or more workers but does not use power) comes under the coverage of the Factories Act. This is the first definition of organized. Thus defined, around 8 percent of the labor force works in the organized sector, while 92 percent works in the unorganized sector, which of course includes all self-employment and agriculture. Second, there is a definition of small-scale industry, defined through investments in plant and machinery, and there is a similar definition for *khadi* (hand-spun cotton) and village industries. These are therefore equated with unorganized industry, and all other industry is organized. Such unorganized industry is exempt from some labor laws. Data for organized sector industry are obtained through the Annual Survey of Industries. Subject to this data, around 45 percent of industrial output (with similar figures for exports) is estimated to originate in the small-scale sector. Third, depending on threshold levels of turnover, some units do not have to pay indirect taxes. Those outside the ambit of indirect taxation are referred to as the unorganized sector. There is strong correlation between these three different definitions of organized and unorganized, but the definitions are not identical. Also, to avoid paying indirect taxes or to circumvent labor laws, units deliberately stay small by fragmenting production.

There are some 140,000 factories, of which India's factories employ fewer than one hundred workers. In number, most factories are in sectors like food products and small machinery, but in terms of value of products, most are in sectors like basic chemicals, heavy machinery, and electricity. Some factories are in the public sector, run by the central, state, and local governments. There are a few that are jointly public-private. However, 92 percent of all factories are completely private, more than 3,500,000 begin small-scale units. More than 250,000 units are estimated to be "sick," their loans overdue to banks and financial institutions that cannot enforce claims on collateral. But a new Securitisation, Reconstruction of Financial Assets and Enforcement of Security Interest Act—enacted in 2003—should make that much easier.

India's labor force in 1999–2000 was around 365 million. Because of unemployment, the working force was slightly lower, around 335 million. Of this 335 million, 59 million worked in industry, which does not mean only manufacturing but also includes mining, quarrying, construction, electricity, gas and water supply. Of the 59 million who worked for industry, 41 million worked in manufacturing; 28 million worked in the organized sector (19 million of those in the public sector and 9 million in the private sector). Because of reforms and a reduced role for government, growth in the public sector has stagnated.

There are significant differences across the Indian states. The pre-1990 industrial licensing policy sought to ensure that jobs were created where there was adequate workforce. Since the onset of reforms, however, the public sector has much declined in importance, and many "sick" units are in the eastern states, which have had little private sector employment. Faster growing, richer states are usually in the north and the west.

India's manufacturing sector began to recover in 1992–1993 and through 1995–1996 enjoyed a heady annual average growth rate of almost 12 percent. A deceleration began in 1996–1997, however, and from that fiscal year to 2002–2003, annual growth averaged less than 6 percent. This deceleration may finally be over in 2003–2004, but it is uncertain whether this recovery is sufficiently broad-based and robust.

The reasons for the manufacturing (and industrial) deceleration were that initial growth in the immediate wake of reforms was sustained through demand for consumer goods and cheaper consumer credit. Once this demand was satisfied, growth ran out of steam. Government capital investments then declined, triggering a negative effect. The initial boom led, moreover, to greatly expanded capacity, and once the boom was over, investments flagged. Increasing real interest rates and a slump in India's capital market from 1995–1996 made the situation worse, especially for new investments in the unorganized sector. Manufacturing growth was sustained through a very high rate of export growth, which slowed down from 1996–1997, thanks to the crisis in Asia, a global slowdown, and a real appreciation in the value of the rupee.

Deceleration was also attributed by some to a widespread scare that Indian manufacturing would be swamped by cheaper Chinese products. Chinese costs of production were half or even one-third the costs of comparable Indian products. Two-thirds of Indian antidumping investigations (and actual antidumping duties imposed) were then levied against Chinese products, including chemicals, pharmaceuticals, toys, athletic shoes, and batteries. Though the Chinese paranoia has dissipated, the Chinese competitive advantage still remains, partly due to lower infrastructure costs of power and transportation in China, nontransparent input prices, and labor market flexibility combined with lower interest rates. Chinese advantages are no different from those articulated in global competitiveness yearbooks, but the Chinese also have better technology and economies of scale. This underlines the lack of adequate private sector investments in India. India missed the export bus in exports of low-tech consumer goods. Indian manufacturing often sought to relocate to China, especially in sectors like services and pharmaceuticals. India's official targeted annual real gross domestic product (GDP) growth figure is 8 percent. By the twenty-first century, industry accounted for 25 percent of Indian GDP, services accounted for 50 percent and agriculture for the remaining 25 percent. Industry is thus on the low side, especially when compared to East Asia. Industry's contribution to Indian GDP ought to be around 35 percent, if not higher.

Without domestic reforms, such an increase is hard to imagine, because the industrial sector (which increasingly means the private industrial sector) is still constrained. However, individual private companies have become much more competitive and efficient, although no remarkable productivity increases are detected for industry as a whole. There are now globally competitive Indian companies, not just in information technology, biotechnology and pharmaceuticals, but also in garments, jewelry, auto parts, bicycles, and electrical machinery. Competition consequent to reforms triggered such efficiency, one of the reasons since 2002 that Indian exports have tended to do so well, despite the rupee appreciating somewhat. Investments undertaken now are more efficient than investments undertaken before the mid-1990s, at least in the organized private industrial sector.

Bibek Debroy

See also **Industrial Growth and Diversification; Industrial Policy since 1956**

BIBLIOGRAPHY

Acharya, Shankar. *India's Economy: Some Issues and Answers.* New Delhi: Academic Foundation, 2003.

Ahluwalia, Isher, and I. M. D. Little, eds. *India's Economic Reforms and Development: Essays for Manmohan Singh.* New Delhi and New York: Oxford University Press, 1998.

Government of India. *India Infrastructure Report.* New Delhi, 1996.

Government of India. *Recommendations of Prime Minister's Economic Advisory Council on Economic Reforms: A Medium-Term Perspective.* New Delhi, 2001.

Government of India. *Budget Speeches of the Union Finance Minister, 1990–1991 to 2003–2004.* New Delhi, 2003.

Jalan, Bimal. *India's Economic Policy.* Delhi: Viking, 1996.

Joshi, Vijay, and I. M. D. Little. *India's Economic Reforms: 1991–2001.* Oxford: Clarendon Press, 1996.

Krueger, Anne O., ed. *Economic Policy Reforms and the Indian Economy.* New Delhi and Chicago: University of Chicago Press, 2002.

National Council of Applied Economic Research. *The Impact of India's Economic Reforms on Industrial Productivity, Efficiency and Competitiveness: A Panel Study of Indian Companies, 1980–1997.* New Delhi, 2001.

Parikh, Kirit S., and R. Radhakrishna, eds. *India Development Report.* Mumbai: Indira Gandhi Institute of Development Research and Oxford University Press, 2002.

PUBLIC DEBT OF STATES SINCE 1950 The steady accumulation of debt and the growing interest burden feeding back into its accumulation raises serious questions about debt sustainability at the state level in India and constrains the ability of the central government in its macroeconomic management of the economy. Growing debt-servicing burdens reduce the resources available for the provision of public services by state governments.

Article 293 of India's Constitution empowers the states to borrow within India upon the security of the consolidated fund of the state and to extend guarantees within the limits fixed by the state legislature. Thus, the states can borrow from the central government, and the latter can extend guarantees of loans raised by any state. The states can also borrow from the market within India, but if a state is indebted to the central government, it must seek the latter's consent. All the states are indebted to the central government, and therefore, states' market borrowing each year is determined by Ministry of Finance in consultation with Delhi's Planning Commission and the Reserve Bank of India.

Loans from the central government have increased mostly in order to finance five-year plans. In the plan assistance given by the central government to the states, until 2004–2005, 70 percent was given as loans and the remaining amount as grants. From 2005–2006, the central government has stopped giving loans the states based on the recommendations of the Twelfth Finance Commission (India, 2004). From 2005–2006, the states are required to access funds for their plans mainly from the market. The states also get temporary accommodation from the Reserve Bank of India as ways and means advances. Before 1985 the states accumulated loans in this category as well, and the central government converted the overdrafts into medium-term loans. Since 1985, however, the overdraft regulation program was established, in which the central government disallowed continuous overdraft facilities for more than seven working days, the violation of which could invite dishonoring the states' checks. The present overdraft regulation limit is fourteen continuous working days, and a total of thirty six days in a quarter.

Thus, the Constitution envisages a hard budget constraint at the state level. However, the states have adopted a variety of means to soften the constraint. An important means used for this is to increase the liability in public accounts, particularly provident funds and small savings collections. Until 1998–1999, this was considered part of the loan from the central government. However, in 1999–2000, the National Small Savings Fund was created, and any loan from the fund is now treated as part of a state's internal debt. Since this source is uncapped and the central government has no control over it, the states have expanded their borrowing from this source.

In recent years, loans from banks and financial institutions have become an important source of state borrowing. These loans include borrowing from the Life Insurance Corporation of India, the General Insurance Corporation, the National Bank for Agriculture and Rural Development, the Rural Electrification Corporation, the Housing and Urban Development Corporation, the Industrial Development Bank of India, and other financial institutions. With the erosion of resources available for capital investment, these institutions have emerged as supplementary sources to finance infrastructure.

In recent years, off-budget borrowing also has become an important source of state liabilities. Many states resorted to borrowing through the public enterprises under their control, enabling them to float bonds by providing guarantees. Some states have floated special purpose vehicles to finance infrastructure projects, such as irrigation. These are contingent liabilities, and although they do not form an integral part of the states' debts, they carry a high degree of fiscal risk.

The aggregate indebtedness of India's states increased from a mere 3.8 billion rupees in 1950–1951 to nearly 7 trillion rupees in 2001–2002, or about 1,765 times. As a percentage of gross domestic product (GDP), states' indebtedness increased from a mere 3.9 percent in 1950–1951 to over 25 percent in 2001–2002. The increase in states' indebtedness in the initial years of independence was a concomitant of India's planned development strategy, but later increases in indebtedness were mainly to finance current expenditures.

Recent Developments

An important development in recent years has been the emergence of multilateral lending to the states. Though state governments cannot have direct access to loans from multilateral institutions, in recent years they have been allowed to negotiate loans contracted by the central government and passed on to the respective states as additional central assistance, by recasting the original terms of the loans. However, even after taking into account these multilateral loans, the share of central loans in total indebtedness of states has shown a steady decline, from 67 percent in 1990–1991 to 45 percent in 2000–2001, and this reflects the central government's own resource constraint.

Considering that there are constraints on all the states' borrowing powers, increase in their indebtedness during the 1990s mainly came about through borrowing from financial institutions and banks on the one hand, and increasing small saving loans on the other. Outstanding loans from banks and financial institutions increased from just about 2.6 percent of total loans in 1990–1991 to 6.5 percent in 2000–2001. Similarly, loans from small savings and provident funds increased from 15.4 percent to 18.5 percent during the same period. In absolute terms, outstanding loans from banks and financial institutions increased from 29 billion rupees in 1990–1991 to 322 billion rupees in 2000–2001, and liabilities from public account (small savings, provident funds, etc.) increased from 170 billion rupees to 920 billion rupees during the period. The increase in loans has been particularly sharp after 1997–1998, as many of the states impounded part of the additional emoluments and arrears in salaries in their provident funds or small savings certificates. In these sources, the central government cannot exercise any control over borrowing, and thus the states find an easy way to overcome hard budget controls.

Another important means adopted by the state governments to soften their budget constraints is to borrow through public enterprises under their control by enabling them to float bonds against state government guarantees. The contingent liabilities of the states are not fully recorded, and the available information shows that they have shown a sharp increase from 526 billion rupees in 1995–1996 to 1,687 billion rupees in 2000–2001. As a percentage of GDP, the contingent liabilities of the states increased from 5.7 percent in 1990–1991 to 7.2 percent in 2001–2002.

The attempt by the states to soften budget constraints by borrowing from sources not capped and controlled by the central government has steadily increased the average effective interest rate. The average interest rate on states' borrowing increased from 3.8 percent in 1960–1961 to 9.2 percent in 1990–1991, and increased further to 13.2 percent in 1999–2000 before tapering off at 12.5 percent in 2000–2001. The interest rate on small savings also reached a peak of 14 percent in 1998–1999, but was subsequently reduced to 9.5 percent by 2004. The rate of interest on central loans increased from 7.5 percent in 1984–1985 to 15 percent in 1995–1996, and thereafter was reduced to 10.5 percent by 2004. The interest rate on market borrowings is the lowest. Until the beginning of the 1980s, the rate of interest was kept artificially low. As part of the financial sector reforms, interest rates on government loans was aligned to the market rate, gradually reaching a peak of 14.2 percent in 1995–1996, and declining thereafter to 6.2 percent by March 2003.

The sharp increases in the indebtedness of India's states as well as increases in average rates of interest have increased the debt service burden and have raised serious questions concerning debt sustainability. The fact that the proportions of loans in plan assistance is much higher than the proportion of capital expenditures indicates a lack of viability in the system of central loans to the states. Furthermore, the attempt by the states to soften budget constraints by contracting loans bearing high interest rates only adds to the problem. In fact, the debt to gross state domestic product (GSDP) ratio in some states, notably Punjab, Uttar Pradesh, and Orissa, is in excess of 25 percent, and more than 30 percent of those states' revenues are spent on interest payments. Similarly, the debt-GSDP ratio in Rajasthan and West Bengal is more than 25 percent, and their interest payments are in excess of 20 percent of their own revenues. The problem is equally severe in the state of Bihar and the special category states of Arunachal Pradesh, Himachal Pradesh, Jammu and Kashmir, Mizoram, Nagaland, and Sikkim, where more than 50 percent of their own revenues are spent in debt servicing.

Concerned at this serious problem of debt in so many of the states, the central government initiated a debt swap policy in 2004, under which high-interest borrowing of the past is repaid by borrowing at prevailing lower interest rates, thereby reducing the overall interest burden on the states. This will bring some relief, but the long-term solution to the problem of increasing state indebtedness will require changing the structural nature of state finances.

Another important development in the states' borrowing scene is the discontinuation of the practice of central government's lending to states. Based on the recommendation of the Finance Commission, the central government has discontinued the practice of lending to states for financing plans and instead the states have been asked to access the markets. This is likely to create transitional problems in the coming years as the primary debt market is still in its infancy. In addition, many states do not have the credit worthiness and the Reserve Bank of India and the central government will have to persuade the banking system to subscribe to the papers of these states.

M. Govinda Rao

See also **State Finances since 1952**

BIBLIOGRAPHY

Favaro, Edgardo M., and Ashok Lahiri, eds. *Fiscal Policies and Sustainable Growth in India.* New Delhi: Oxford University Press, 2004.

Rao, M. Govinda, and Raja Chelliah. *Fiscal Federalism in India.* New Delhi: Indian Council of Social Science Research, 1996.

Rao, M. Govinda, and Nirvikar Singh. *Political Economy of Federalism in India.* New Delhi: Oxford University Press, 2005.

Report of the Twelfth Finance Commission (2005–10). Ministry of Finance, Government of India, 2004.

Srivastava, D. K., ed. *Fiscal Federalism in India—Contemporary Challenges: Issues before the Eleventh Finance Commission.* New Delhi: Har Anand Publications, 2000.

PUBLIC EXPENDITURES The Indian constitution, which came into force in 1950, set forth expenditure responsibilities and spheres for the central and state governments in lists of subjects that are the exclusive domain of each, as well as a concurrent list of subjects that are dealt with by both levels of government. Local governments at the village, district, or county level received special recognition through the 73rd and 74th Amendments to the Constitution. These amendments specified the range of expenditures that could be incurred by local administrative bodies, and the financial nexus between the state and local governments, to enable the latter to finance those activities. These amendments came into effect in 1992.

Activities financed by public expenditures are now carried out by New Delhi's central government, twenty-eight state governments, and nearly a quarter of a million local bodies, ranging from village councils and local urban bodies to district councils. The central and state governments are by far the largest spending agencies in India, their combined expenditure totaling about 28 percent of gross domestic product (GDP) in fiscal year (FY) 2001–2002. (India's FY is from 1 April to 31 March of the following year.) Within the total expenditure of these two levels, the share of the central government was 49 percent, while the total of state expenditures was 51 percent in 2001–2002. The expenditure of local governments is still very small, amounting to little more than 1 percent of GDP, or less than 5 percent of the total expenditure of all governments. Slow progress has thus, as yet, been made in implementation of the goal of financial decentralization envisioned in the above noted constitutional amendments. Within the existing resource structure, the flexibility and the range of administrative decision making at local levels is limited to about 3 percent of total operations; most transfers from the central and state governments continue to be made in the form of specific or conditional grants.

Government expenditures are incurred through a large network of government departments, autonomous agencies owned and controlled by the respective governments, state-owned enterprises, public-private partnerships, and several nongovernmental organizations (NGOs). The NGOs, which include parochial and faith-based organizations, form an important link in the delivery of services, particularly in education and health. They receive the bulk of their revenues in the form of grants-in-aid, mostly conditional, from both levels of government, but retain a major degree of autonomy in their operations. In some states, they play a crucial role, with approximately half of the educational budgets incurred through them.

The pursuit of a common fiscal policy by both the central and state governments is facilitated by several unifying features, arrangements for regular consultation between the two levels, and the monitoring of state finances on a regular basis by the central government and its agencies, such as the Reserve Bank of India (the central bank). A unique feature of the Indian budgetary system is that the budgets of both central and state governments follow the same budgetary classification and approaches toward the compilation of accounts. State government accounts are maintained by the Indian Audit and Accounts department, headed by an independent comptroller and auditor general. Fiscal policy and the determination of its associated annual objectives, which govern the formulation and implementation of budgets, are undertaken as a part of five-year and annual development plans. The broad aggregates of expenditure, as well as sectoral allocations, in particular for major investment expenditures, are determined as part of development plans, and state governments play an extensive role in this process. The compilation of development plans affords numerous opportunities for both levels to have extended consultations and to pursue coordinated fiscal policies. Although the share of plan expenditures is less than a quarter of the annual budgets, the rest reflects the continuing share of previously completed plans that becomes maintenance expenditure.

Federal financial arrangements also reflect the growing dependence of state and local governments on the central government and on market borrowing, which is coordinated by the Reserve Bank of India. State revenues as a ratio to aggregate expenditures declined during the 1990s from 43.5 percent to 41.5 percent. The transfers from the central government take several forms: shares in the devolution of total tax revenues, which is determined for every five-year period; grants for the pursuit of various development objectives; and loans extended by the central government. Of these transfers, more than 60 percent is at the discretion of the central government. Part of the uncertainty about the availability of money generally associated with discretionary action is mitigated by the fact that there are jointly agreed upon formulas governing the determination of these transfers.

The central and state governments broadly use the same set of instruments to pursue the objectives of expenditure policies. These include direct-expenditures, tax expenditures and subsidies, trading activities, loans to government and nongovernment institutions, and provision of guarantees when governmental agencies engage in borrowing from the market. During the first two decades after India's independence (1947–1967), the central government also used quasi-fiscal accounts maintained at the central bank. Nonbudgetary accounts, such as the oil coordination account, have since been abolished. The overall structure of the expenditure management machinery implies a major role for the central government as exemplar and as lead "thinker," but in practice neither role has been completely fulfilled.

Objectives, Policies, and Portfolios

The objectives of expenditure policies have changed over the years, reflecting the needs of each era. Immediately after independence, the focus was on postwar reconstruction, refugee rehabilitation, moderate build-up in defense (reflecting the conflict with Pakistan), and problems of dislocation stemming from partition. This was followed until 1963, when the emphasis shifted to economic development; as a part of this effort, there were greater expenditures on multipurpose river valley projects, establishment of essential infrastructure facilities, formation of a chain of national laboratories devoted to science and technology, and industrial development. Expansion took place through state-owned enterprises both at the center and in the states, which grew in number, size, and capital base. Most of their financial requirements were met through investment in their equity and through loans. There was a steady bonding between the central government and the states, as the latter began to receive extensive transfers of central loans and grants to finance regional development.

The war with China in 1962 contributed to a major change, with more development focused on expanding military defense. Heavy expenditure came to be incurred on defense production and on the acquisition of modern weaponry and technologies. To ensure food security, outlays on agriculture were stepped up, contributing to India's "Green Revolution." A new set of subsidies were aimed at providing, on the one hand, fertilizers to peasant producers at a subsidized rate, and on the other, cushioning the impact on urban consumers through subsidized public distribution of food. This was followed, in the early 1970s, by more intense efforts to alleviate poverty. Several affirmative actions were taken, measures aimed at providing free food, housing, water supply, electricity, and medical care. Education was generally provided free up to matriculation, while fees for college and technical education were kept very low. Many states began also to provide electricity free of charge to the agriculturalists, and the loans previously given to them for various development purposes were written off. New arrangements were made to address the problems of educated unemployment. Meanwhile, as food production grew, governments spent more on buying food grains at a price higher than the market price, and on maintaining buffer stocks of grain. The steady growth in subsidies and social transfers, as well as maintenance of capital expenditures at more or less previous levels, contributed, in the absence of revenue mobilization efforts, to more borrowing by the central government and the states, in turn leading to a situation in which interest payments, which hitherto were low, began to rise. A national economic crises ensued in the early 1990s when India recognized that expenditures had to be severely restricted to be sustainable. A slew of measures aimed at moderating expenditure were introduced during the middle of the decade, and provisional relief has been gained through severe compression of capital outlays. These broad trends are illustrated in Table 1. The composition of expenditures at the central government and in the states during 1990–1991 and during 2001–2002 is shown in Tables 2, 3, 4, and 5.

As noted, there has been significant growth in interest payments, reflecting excessive reliance on borrowing as a means of financing budget deficits. Nearly a third of the total expenditure of the central government is devoted to the payment of interest. There has also been significant growth in salaries and pension payments both by central and state governments, reflecting the implementation of the Pay Commission's recommendations. Other central government revenue or current expenditure has gone up from a little more than a quarter of total expenditures, to more than one-third of total expenditures at the beginning of 2000. To contain total expenditure within reasonable limits, outlays on subsidies, capital, and loans and advances have been reduced, reflecting India's new policy to reduce subsidies on fertilizers.

TABLE 1

Consolidated cultural state expenditure (as percent of GDP)

Category	1950–1951	1960–1961	1990–1991	2001–2002
Revenue (current) expenditure	7.36	9.82	21.62	24.47
Capital expenditure	1.70	5.69	5.31	3.80
Total expenditure	9.06	15.51	26.93	28.27
Interest payments	0.71	1.27	4.40	6.30

SOURCE: Adapted from *Long Term Fiscal Trends in India, 1950–1951 to 2000–2001,* National Institute of Public Finance and Policy, Delhi, 2002. (The table has been updated for this study.)

TABLE 2

Central government: Expenditure pattern (as percent of total)

Category	1990–1991	2001–2002
Interest	20.4	29.6
Defense	10.3	10.5
Subsidies	11.5	8.6
Other current expenditures	27.6	34.5
Loans and advances	18.7	9.5
Capital outlay	11.5	7.3
	100.0	100.0

SOURCE: Data and growth calculations have been provided by the Reserve Bank of India, Mumbai.

TABLE 3

Central government: Functional categories of expenditure (as percent of total)

Category	1990–1991	2001–2002
General services	42.3	54.9
Social services	3.0	4.0
Economic services	22.8	21.6
Unallocable expenditure	31.9	19.5
	100.0	100.0

SOURCE: Data and growth calculations have been provided by the Reserve Bank of India, Mumbai.

Problems and Solutions

The adverse impact of growing expenditures on interest rates, macroeconomic stability, and the general sustainability of public finances was recognized by both the central and state governments, as well as by international financial institutions such as the Asian Development and the World Bank, which have begun to extend loans to subnational governments. The broad range of problems and the remedial measures have aimed at moderating the growth of expenditures, at improving delivery of services, transparency, and accountability.

The central government appointed an expenditure commission to inquire into the activities of each agency and to make recommendations for possible reduction in

TABLE 4

States: Functional categories of expenditure (as percent of total)[1]

Category	1990–1991	2001–2002
Social services	32.9	31.0
Economic services	36.7	26.4
Interest payments	9.5	16.6
Administrative services	7.7	7.2
Pensions	3.4	7.5
Other	9.8	11.3
	100.0	100.0

(1) At the local level (both in urban and rural areas), a significant part is devoted to the provision and maintenance of core services.

SOURCE: Data and growth calculations have been provided by the Reserve Bank of India, Mumbai.

TABLE 5

States: Expenditure pattern (as percent of total)

Category	1990–1991	2001–2002
Interest payments	9.5	16.6
Pensions	3.4	7.4
Other current expenditure	12.2	13.4
Development expenditure	53.6	46.0
Loans and advances	6.3	3.3
Capital outlay	10.2	8.5
Other capital expenditure	4.8	4.8
	100.0	100.0

SOURCE: Data and the growth calculations have been provided by the Reserve Bank of India, Mumbai.

TABLE 6

Growth of expenditure: Central government (percent)

Category	1990–1991 to 2001–2002 (annual compound rates)
Interest payments	15.8
Defense revenue expenditure	12.1
Subsidies	8.9
Other revenue expenditure	14.2
Loans and advances	5.2
Capital outlay	7.4
Total expenditure	11.9

SOURCE: Compiled by the Reserve Bank of India from the budget documents of the central and state governments.

TABLE 7

Growth of expenditure: States (percent)

Category	1990–1991 to 2001–2002
Interest payments	19.7
Pensions	22.1
Other nondevelopment expenditure	14.8
Development revenue expenditure	12.2
Loans and advances	7.2
Capital outlay	12.0
Other capital expenditure	13.9
Total expenditure	13.8

SOURCE: Compiled by the Reserve Bank of India from the budget documents of the central and state governments.

expenditures. As a result of the work of the commission, subsidies on fertilizers were reduced, and a voluntary retirement scheme for government personnel was announced. Moreover, recruitment to government was effectively stopped, and personnel positions that long remained unfilled were abolished. The range of measures taken at the state level was more extensive. Most have restricted creation of new positions, abolished unfilled posts, selectively moderated subsidies through efforts at higher cost recovery, and introduced voluntary retirement schemes as well as new pension schemes. Several state governments introduced fiscal responsibility, using restrictive legislation to limit amounts of guarantees, and introducing sinking funds to arrange for orderly repayment of public debt.

The limited impact of these measures is reflected in a slight change in total expenditure of central and state governments, moving up by only 1.59 points as a ratio of GDP from 1999 to 2002.

Structurally, expenditures by the central and state governments reveal a good deal of rigidity, reflecting in turn the share of interest payments, and other supply side factors that have steadily contributed to expenditure increases. Most personnel positions are formula-based and to that extent supply-driven. As a result of the application of these formulas and associated norms, there has been a grade inflation, particularly at senior levels. Moreover, at the end of each five-year plan, the bulk of maintenance expenditures moves from the capital to the current side of the budget, contributing in turn to a steady increase in expenditures. In some sectors, such as defense, the cost of modern equipment (mostly imported) has also gone up. The steady increase in personnel, as well as grade inflation, has contributed to higher costs of all services, which was further exacerbated by growing reliance on borrowing as an important instrument of financing government. Regular adjustment of wages and pensions to the cost of living index has had its own impact. The net result of these factors is seen in Table 6 and 7, dealing, respectively, with central and state governments.

Data on public employment also show that, while relative to 1997 there has been a decline in the overall public employment, reflecting in part the efforts at retrenchment (primarily in quasi-government), the overall effect on expenditures has not been significant, as the wage bill itself has risen due to the implementation of the Pay Commission's recommendations.

Liquidity problems are more apparent at state government levels. Many of them are in arrears of payments to contractors, and delays in the payment of salaries are common. Many run overdrafts with the Reserve Bank of India, and appear to have little margin in their financial arrangements. Late release of central assistance in turn contributes to slow implementation of projects and programs and to carrying over of funds, through irregular channels, to future years.

Most delivery of services, particularly in the educational and health sectors, takes place at the level of state governments, and frequently at lower levels. In most cases, links between the allocation of resources and final delivery of services are nebulous, and there are no performance norms against which actual progress can be measured. For the most part, it is the financial performance that is measured. Although an initiative has recently been taken in introducing performance measurement and evaluation, progress in uneven. There has also been a disconcerting increase in the bureaucracy required to undertake inspections. As a result, transaction costs have escalated, more than half of every rupee spent going to cover administrative costs alone. Also, corruption experienced in daily life appears to confirm the general perception of extended leakage in the system and failure of controls.

In a curious variation of laws on information, the greater the amount of information provided, the less comprehension seems to exist in the community. In part, arcane language used in budget documents helps to create, rather than lessen, an information gap. A greater part of the central government's budget was of late approved by the legislature during the "guillotine hour." At the state level, many public accounts committees have rarely met regularly, and as a result there has been an enormous increase in expenditures regularized on an ex-post basis. Legislators do not have an effective say in financial management, and for the most part, there has been a dramatic shift of power from the legislative to the executive branch of government.

The outlook for Indian public expenditures is critical. There are many growing demands (even as the government contemplates sending a man to the moon, there remain countless unmet daily pleas for potable water). Major changes are required in the way in which resources are allocated and utilized. The need of immediate expenditure increases can only be met by abandoning wasteful expenditures, and through major reductions in existing manpower. With a view to reducing costs of services, less reliance must be placed on borrowing as a means of financing expenditure. Innovative alternatives must be found for the delivery of services. Progress remains to be made in the decentralization of expenditure. More and effective improvements are required for fiscal transparency and accountability. These add up to a considerable improvement in policies of expenditure and management. The imperatives of reform are such that they can no longer be postponed or ignored.

A. Premchand

See also **Federalism and Center-State Relations; Fiscal System and Policy since 1952; State Finances since 1952**

BIBLIOGRAPHY

Premchand, A. *Control of Public Money*. New Delhi and New York: Oxford University Press, 2000.

Premchand, A., and Saumen Chattopadhyay. "Fiscal Adjustment and Expenditure Management." World Bank Conference Paper. New Delhi: National Institute of Public Finance and Policy, 2001.

Reserve Bank of India. *Report on Currency and Finance*. Mumbai: Reserve Bank of India, annual.

———. *State Finances: A Study of Budgets*. Mumbai: Reserve Bank of India, annual.

PUJA. *See* **Hinduism (Dharma).**

PUNJAB Its name derived from a Sanskrit word meaning "five rivers," Punjab is a culturally and physically distinct region, part of which now constitutes one of Pakistan's four provinces, and part that forms a state in the Indian Union. It is named for five major rivers—the Jhelum, Chanab, Ravi, Sutlaj and Beas—all originating in the Himalayas, that cross a large plain in the northwest corner of the Indian subcontinent.

Punjab served as the juncture of a number of the world's great civilizations. Historically, the area west of Punjab fell within the sphere of influence of the Persians, Arabs held sway to the south, and the north was subject to Turko-Mongolian influence. To the east lay the heartland of the Indian civilization. Several religious movements that found wide appeal took root in Punjab, including Buddhism, Sikhism, and several schools of Sufi Islamic thought. Ethnic diversity is also reflected in the cultural mosaic of contemporary Punjab. Its strategic location and fertile lands attracted waves of migrants to

Sikh Farmer and Wife Survey Their Mustard Field. Beginning in the mid-1960s, Punjab (together with Haryana) became the centerpiece of India's "Green Revolution," which introduced high-yielding varieties of grain on irrigated lands. DINESH KHANNA.

the area so that, although originally of the Aryan stock, the people of Punjab are today descendants of the Iranians, Turks, Afghans, and Arabs.

Punjab has long been a battleground fought over by competing empires, After Mughal authority declined in the subcontinent, the Persians under Nadir Shah invaded from the northwest in 1737–1738 to sack Lahore and Delhi, and to carry off such Mughal treasures as the Peacock Throne and Koh-e-Noor diamond. The Afghans also launched a series of invasions of Punjab to loot and dominate the area. Beginning in the early nineteenth century, the British vigorously accelerated their territorial aggrandizement at the expense of India's Hindu and Muslims rulers, expanding their paramountcy to northwest India at mid-century.

A large and powerful Sikh state, which included all of the Punjab, was put together by Ranjit Singh (1780–1839), who in 1798 embarked on ambitious plans to expand his territory and to unite all Sikhs under his rule. He succeeded in creating a powerful Sikh state through clever diplomacy as well as the numerous wars he waged against rival Sikh princes, Muslim rulers, and Afghan invaders. Throughout his long and successful rule, he avoided conflict with the expanding British Empire. Following his death, however, civil strife among rival claimants to the throne and corruption brought on political chaos. When a Sikh army went to attack British territory in 1845, the British in a series of hard-fought battles defeated it. The British began direct rule of the Punjab after again defeating Sikh forces in a second war in 1848–1849.

The political boundaries of the Punjab were far less expansive when, in the partition of 1947, the territory was basically divided along religious lines. The predominantly Muslim western districts acceded to Pakistan, and nearly all Hindus and Sikhs fled to India in a massive population exchange. Indian East Punjab retained only a small portion of its once sizable Muslim community when an estimated 4.35 million Muslims left for Pakistan.

Partitioning the Punjab resulted in a humanitarian catastrophe, with an estimated half a million people killed overall. The deep-rooted communal beliefs gave vent to violence that engulfed village after village and did not spare women and children. Some of the worst atrocities occurred in East Punjab during August 1947.

Pakistan's Punjab

Pakistani Punjab covers 97,192 square miles (251,726 sq. km), 28.5 percent of the total area of Pakistan. Its population, according to a 1998 estimate, was 72.6 million, or approximately 56 percent of the country's total. Punjab is surrounded on the north by the North-West Frontier province (NWFP) and the Federal capital area of Islamabad. To the northeast is Azad Kashmir. To the east and south are India's Punjab and Rajasthan states. On the southeast is Pakistan's Sind province, and to the west lie Baluchistan province and the Federally Administrated Tribal Areas.

Post-independence Punjab ceased to exist as an administrative and political unit when a Constituent Assembly in 1955 combined it with Sind and the NWFP West provinces. This One-Unit Plan, designed to balance politically Pakistan's West and East (Bengali) Wings, was dissolved in 1970. The restoration of federalism occasioned Pakistan's first election on the basis of one person, one vote for national and provincial assemblies. Under the 1973 Constitution, Punjab and the other provinces also acquired the right to elect their own chief ministers, instead of having them appointed by provincial governors representing the federal government.

Punjab is often referred to as Pakistan's "heartland." Though the idea of Pakistan was initially not as warmly received among West Punjab's Muslims as in central India and Bengal, Punjab's major city, Lahore, was the site of the famous Pakistan Resolution in March 1940. Today, Lahore is considered the country's cultural and intellectual capital, as it had been under Mughal and British rule. Together with Punjab's urban centers of Faisalabad, Multan, and Rawalpindi, Lahore ranks also among Pakistan's most important commercial hubs.

Agriculture contributes the largest part of Pakistan's economy, and Punjab, known as the country's granary, makes by far the largest contribution to agricultural production and export income. Summer and winter rains can deposit 15 to 20 inches (38–50 cm) of rain across areas of the Punjab. Even so, the province's agriculture is mostly dependent on irrigation, which makes possible major crops in wheat, rice, cotton, and sugarcane. The Tarbella Dam on the Indus and the Mangala Dam on the Jhelum Canal, along with numerous barrages and canals, are key components in a system of irrigation and flood control. Canal irrigation has its downside, however. Poor water management and seepage, along with drainage problems, have resulted in severe waste and waterlogging, creating accumulated salts that make the soil uncultivable. Additionally, the southeast section of the province remains undeveloped and is extremely hot and dry.

During the British Raj, Punjab alone provided more than a quarter of army recruits, mostly Sikh and Muslim Indians. The disproportionate recruitment of Sikhs and Muslims reflected the notion that they were among the "martial races." With the creation of Pakistan, Punjabis came to dominate its army, and the other provinces were helpless to prevent Punjabis' ascendance in the country's higher civil service.

Resentment against the Punjab takes other forms as well. Sind is engaged in a virtual water war with Punjab. Sindis believe that the reason for an often dry Indus River is excessive use of water by Punjab. Baluchistan claims that it provides 50 percent of Pakistan's natural gas resources but is not given a fair share in jobs or in the allocation of funds in a federal government dominated by Punjab. Punjab is also accused of delaying a census in Pakistan for fear that it could change the distribution of resources and political power among the four provinces. Many non-Punjabi politicians, intellectuals, and journalists believe that Pakistan's periodic military interventions are taken on behalf of Punjabi interests. The transfer of the nation's capital from Karachi to northern Punjab in 1960 and the 1979 execution of Prime Minister Zulfikar Ali Bhutto, a champion of Sindi regionalism, are seen through this prism.

There have also been intraprovincial tensions. Though 90 percent of the population speaks Punjabi, Seraiki-speaking people in Multan and central Punjab have serious issues with Punjabi speakers, and Seraikis feel isolated and politically underrepresented. Punjab's 1953 anti-Ahmadiyya religious riots, which were carried out with local government officials' complicity, required military intervention. Violence between Muslim Sunni and Shiʿa militants erupted beginning in the mid-1990s. A provincial landed elite, in control of the most productive land, is held largely responsible for keeping peasants uneducated and poor.

Even then, Punjab outranks Pakistan's other provinces on a United Nations Human Development Index. Punjab has the best performance in school enrollment and educational attainment. It closely matches the NWFP for highest rank in a health index and Sind for adjusted real gross domestic product per capita. Punjab's Jhelum district stands first among all of Pakistan's districts in a composite of education, health, and wealth indexes. In overall human development, Punjab also has the lowest disparity between urban and rural districts.

Punjab has mostly given its political allegiance to the Pakistan Muslim League (PML). The party, whose origins lay in a pre-independence political organization, has relied heavily on the mobilizing strength and financial support of Punjab's major landlords and industrialists. But the PML did poorly in the 1970 elections against Bhutto's Pakistan People's Party (PPP), and lost out to the PPP in Pakistan's discredited 1977 elections. In the four national and provincial elections between 1988 and 1997, the PML could count on all but the province's southern pro-PPP districts, and PML candidates led by Punjab's once chief minister Nawaz Sharif scored a decisive victory nationwide in 1997. A breakaway faction of PML members backing President Pervez Musharraf captured the largest share of seats for the national and provincial assembles in the 2002 elections.

Indian Punjab

Punjab occupies an area of 20,254 square miles (52,458 sq. km), 1.7 percent of India's total land area. The state's population in the 2001 census was 24.3 million, of which about a third are urban dwellers. Over 60 percent of Punjab's population is literate. Sikhs constitute upward of 60 percent of the state, with about 35 percent Hindu and 2 percent Muslim. In 1966 East Punjab was divided into three parts to form, along with a Punjabi-speaking Punjab state, the states of Haryana and Himachal Pradesh, both with greater than 90 percent Hindu populations. Punjab and Haryana share a state capital at Chandigarh.

Punjab is one the most prosperous states in India. Together with Haryana, it became, beginning in 1965, the centerpiece of India's "Green Revolution," featuring the introduction on irrigated lands of high-yielding varieties of food grains. By 1980, overall crop production rose sixfold from the years following partition. Productivity gains through an input-intensive strategy have also depended on the province's adroit, independent farmers, and the incentives provided for larger producers. Newly introduced agricultural universities have offered highly valued extension services to farmers.

Punjab's Sikhs have been a restive population. Serious agitation for greater linguistic and religious separatism, political autonomy, and economic opportunities began in 1973. As a religious and ethnic group, Sikhs asked for greater recognition of their language, Punjabi, including the territorial incorporation of additional Punjabi-speaking areas from neighboring states. The leading Sikh party, Akali Dal (Eternal Party), demanded the transfer of Chandigarh, the state capital, from a union territory to Punjab. Among more symbolic demands, this nationalist, paramilitary party called for Amritsar, site of the religion's revered Golden Temple, to be designated a holy city, and for the sale of liquor and tobacco to be banned in the vicinity of the holy shrine. Punjab's farmers were deeply upset over the division of Beas and Sutlej river waters with Haryana, while a new generation of better-educated, younger Sikhs complained about their under-representation in most urban and modern occupations, and the need for larger investment of central government funds in Punjab's industrialization.

Bitterness toward central authorities led to separatist and terrorist activities in what was called the Khalistani insurgency. Murder, arson, and looting were common occurrences, claiming both Hindu and Sikh victims as interfactional violence also engulfed the Sikh community. The Indian government insisted that arms and drugs from Pakistan encouraged the unrest. The conflict came to a head in May 1984 with the New Delhi government's order for troops to storm the Golden Temple complex to flush out extremists. At least 750 insurgents and army personnel were killed. Legislated mass detentions and secret tribunals to combat Sikh terrorism from a number of organizations further fueled the community's anger. In time, however, the insurgency waned with strong repressive measures by security forces and the capture of leading militants. Sikhs have shunned terrorism since the early 1990s, but many still harbor grievances, despite some concessions from the central government.

Before the division of India's Punjab, the Congress Party consistently outpolled the Akali Dal in state elections. During the 1950s, Akali Dal entered into alliances with Congress at the national level. In Punjab's first post-division state elections in 1967, an Akali-led opposition front was able to defeat Congress. Although Prime Minister Indira Gandhi's party retook the state assembly in the 1972 elections with a substantial majority, Akali Dal remained in strong competition with Congress. In 1972, defections from Congress to the Akali Dal brought the state government's fall and the imposition of President's Rule. But Congress again prevailed in elections the following year. An Akali-Janata Party alliance overwhelmed Congress in 1977, taking power in the state assembly as well as in New Delhi. Instability within the state government and increased violence led in 1984 to Punjab being placed under direct rule by the central government. When President's Rule was lifted in 1992 and the assembly restored, the Congress emerged victorious in state elections. Though by the late 1990s a moderate faction of the Akali Dal led a governing coalition, the Congress returned to power in the state in April 2002.

For almost two decades after partition, Punjabis continue to provide a preponderance of those in the army's officer corps, in the mid-1950s, as much as a third. In August–September 1965, after Pakistan tried to foment a rebellion in Indian Kashmir and penetrated the state with armored units, the Indian army responded by attacking across the international border toward Lahore. Despite the desire for greater autonomy among many Sikhs, those in the military as well as within the civilian community remained overwhelmingly loyal to India. Sikhs were rewarded by New Delhi with a Punjabi-speaking state, but the 1965 war prompted changes in recruitment patterns, leading over time to a more geographically representative Indian military.

Marvin G. Weinbaum

See also **Geography; Pakistan**

BIBLIOGRAPHY

Blood, Peter, ed. *Pakistan: A Country Study*. Washington, D.C.: Library of Congress, 1995. A collection of essays and leading handbook on Pakistan's history, society and environment, government and politics, and national security.

Burki, Shahid Javed. *Pakistan: A Nation in the Making*. Boulder, Colo.: Westview Press, 1986. An excellent overview of Pakistan's formative years.

Chopra, V. D., R. K. Mishra, and Nirmal Singh, eds. *Agony of Punjab*. New Delhi: Patriot, 1984. A comprehensive account of the insurgency.

Cohen, Stephen P. *The Pakistan Army*. Berkeley: University of California Press, 1984. The foremost study of the Pakistan military.

Heitzman, James, and Robert L. Worden, eds. *India: A Country Study*. Washington, D.C.: Library of Congress, 1995. A useful handbook on the country's history and political institutions.

Hussain, Akmal. *Pakistan: National Human Development Report, 2003*. Karachi: Oxford University Press. A UNDP–sponsored report on poverty, growth, and governance, with references to specific provinces.

Weiss, Anita. *Culture, Class, and Development in Pakistan*. Boulder, Colo.: Westview Press, 1991.

Wriggins, Howard H., ed. *Pakistan in Transition*. Islamabad: University of Islamabad Press, 1975.

PURĀṆAS. *See* **Hinduism (Dharma); Shiva and Shaivism; Vishnu and Avatāras.**

PURNA SWARAJ. *See* **Nehru, Jawaharlal.**

PURUSHA. *See* **Caste System; Vedic Aryan India.**

PURVA-MIMANSAKA. *See* **Brāhmaṇas.**

q

QAWWĀLĪ A form of ecstatic Sufi Muslim worship in which a soloist leads a group of singers, *qawwālī* (Arabic, *qawwāl*, "one who speaks well") possibly derives its name from a community of performers. *Qawwālī* refers to both a nonliturgical religious musical gathering associated with the Chishti sect of Sufi Muslims, as well as the repertoire sung at these gatherings. The poetry of *qawwālī* draws upon the traditions of Urdu and Persian poetry, although folk genres such as *qawl* and *rang* are a historic part of this worship. The most common musico-poetic forms of *qawwālī* are *gazal* (expressions of divine mystical love or praises of God), *hamd* (praises of God), *na't* (praises of the Prophet, Muhammad), and *manqabat* (praises of saints or imams).

*Qawwal*s are religious musicians and, more specifically, the community that performs Sufi religious song. Many *qawwāl*s trace their performing tradition to Amir Khusrau (1253–1325) and to his ties with the Chishti sect of Sufism probably founded by Mu'inuddin during the twelfth century. Professional *qawwāl*s and dedicated amateurs perform *qawwālī* at shrines and private homes, and increasingly in concerts, often on the death anniversaries (*urs*) of famous Sufi saints, as well as in informal weekly contexts. Today, *qawwālī* is also a popular form of entertainment for wedding ceremonies and other auspicious occasions; performers appear in films and on television, and tapes and records are widely available in the marketplace.

The performance model for a *qawwālī* ensemble is that of the *murshīid* (director/guide) *murīd* (aspirant) relationship of Sufism in which a knowledgeable guide assists a disciple in the pursuit of divine knowledge. The principle singer (*mohrī*) of a performance leads the ensemble of responding singers (*awāziya*, "voices") and instrumentalists, as well as other listeners in the pursuit of *hāl*, an ecstatic divine experience and personal knowledge of God (*ma'rifa*) through the musical performance. The services of the *mohrī* are essential both to performers and audience members who wish to transform the self (*fana'*).

A *qawwālī* performance psychologically attempts to bring willing individuals from a state of passive observation to full involvement. The music often begins with an instrumental prelude (*naghmā*) and/or an *ālāp* (sometimes known as *mahfil-i samā*, "gathering for listening") and gradually builds in intensity. The responsorial structure of the music, while requiring a knowledgeable professional, allows for the easy involvement of those present.

The accompanying ensemble of performers, like the Sabri Brothers, commonly consists of drums (tabla and/or *dholak*) and harmonium; however, *qawwālī* performers are, if anything, eclectic. Today, *qawwālī* performances include instruments such as the mandolin, violin, *sārangī*, and *dilrūba*, and, perhaps, electric guitars and synthesizers. Notably, performers such as Nasrat Fateh Ali Khan demonstrated that not only can one incorporate new musical instruments into *qawwālī*, one can merge Western pop idioms (for example, a drum-and-bass groove/ostinato) with a traditional song, such as "Mast Qalandar" (a *manqabat* in praise of the Sufi saint, Lal Qalandar).

The musical materials are fundamentally simple. The *qawwālī* repertoire consists of both existing songs and new creations based on classical *rāg*s, *rāg*-like melodies peculiar to the *qawwālī* tradition, and folk melodies. Generally, *qawwālī* performances have featured only two short *tāl*s: the four-beat *qawwālī tāl* and six-beat *dādra tāl*. Contemporary performances build on these immediately

***Qawwāli* Singer, Nusrat Fateh Ali Khan.** *Qawwāli's* devotional themes of peace and love date back some 700 years. Recording artist Nusrat Fateh Ali Khan, shown here before his death in 1997, helped make it a force within the popular culture. GETTY IMAGES.

perceivable meters, combining predictable cycles with internal syncopations. These catchy repetitive time cycles can have a hypnotic effect on performers and audiences alike.

Gordon Thompson

BIBLIOGRAPHY

Qureshi, Regula. "Indo-Muslim Religious Music: An Overview." *Asian Music* 3, no. 2 (1972): 15–22.

———. "Islamic Music in an Indian Environment." *Ethnomusicology* 25, no. 1 (1981): 47–71.

———. *Sufi Music of India and Pakistan.* Cambridge, U.K.: Cambridge University Press, 1986.

See also **Music.**

QUR'AN. *See* **Islam.**

RABBAN, JOSEPH, *one of the founders of the Jewish community in South India.* Joseph Rabban (Issuppu Irappan), also known as Rabbani, is revered by the Jews of Cochin, Kerala, as a prince among the founders of their community in India. He is the recipient of the famous copper plate grant from the region's ruler, Bhaskara Ravi Varma, allotting him and his descendants specific rights and privileges. Very little is known about the identity of this early Jew of South India. Even the approximate date of his arrival is obscure. Estimates of the period of the copper plate grant range from the fourth to the eleventh century A.D. The earliest memory of the Kerala Jews is related to the ancient port of Cranganore (which the document refers to as Muyirikkodu), also known as Shingly, about 20 miles (32 km) north of Cochin. The southern coastal ports of India, along the eastern edge of the Arabian Sea, were often visited in ancient times by traders seeking spices, particularly pepper, so it is possible that Jewish merchants were aboard the ships that docked along the Malabar Coast. These Jews might have been the founders of the Kerala communities. The exact reference of the term "Anjuvannam" from the grant is in dispute; although it has been understood as meaning Cranganore, more recent scholarship translates it as a town guild or corporation.

In the fourteenth century the port of Cranganore silted up, forcing the Jewish community to move to other towns, among them Cochin. According to oral tradition, the king of Cochin welcomed the refugees, granting them an area in which to settle. Perhaps as a result of the move, the Jewish community became divided into distinct groups: indigenous and "foreign" (*paradesi*), the latter group consisting of newcomers from Spain and Arab lands. Nonetheless, Joseph Rabban plays a very prominent role in the folklore of the Cochin Jewish community. He was the first in a line of Jewish "kings," men of power and privilege who were recognized as such by the surrounding population. A Jewish visitor from Spain in the fourteenth century wrote a poem, preserved in a Cochin song book, that is sung in the synagogue: "I had heard of the city of Shingly, / I longed to see an Israeli king / Him, I saw with my own eyes" (Katz and Goldberg, p. 40). A Cochin Jewish wedding song in Malayalam, referring to the groom, contains the following verse: "Conches and drums are beautifully echoing in the palace. / When he comes in such splendor / Let us sing of Joseph Rabban" (Johnson, p. 165).

Brenda Ness

BIBLIOGRAPHY

Johnson, Barbara Cottle. "The Emperor's Welcome: Reconsideration of an Origin Theme in Cochin Jewish Folklore." In *Jews in India*, edited by Thomas A. Timberg. New Delhi: Vikas, 1986.

Katz, Nathan, and Ellen S. Goldberg. *The Last Jews of Cochin: Jewish Identity in Hindu India.* Columbia: University of South Carolina Press, 1993.

Segal, J. B. *The History of the Jews of Cochin.* London: Vallentine Mitchell, 1993.

RADHAKRISHNAN, SARVEPALLI *(1888–1975), philosopher, president of India (1962–1967).* Dr. Sarvepalli Radhakrishnan was independent India's second president, serving from 1962 to 1967. From 1952 to 1962, he had served as vice president under India's first president, Dr. Rajendra Prasad. Radhakrishnan was the leader of the Indian delegation to the United Nations Educational, Scientific, and Cultural Organization from 1946 to 1952, becoming president of that organization during his last two years there. He served as India's ambassador to the Soviet Union from 1949 to 1952.

Radhakrishnan, a Tamil Brahman born just outside Madras in 1888, was one of India's most distinguished philosopher-statesmen, and a world-renowned exponent of Hindu philosophy. His brilliant master's thesis at the University of Madras was titled "The Ethics of the Vedanta and Its Metaphysical Presuppositions." Between 1909 and 1929, Radhakrishnan held professorial positions at the universities of Madras, Mysore, and Calcutta. During this time, he received international attention for his flawless speeches when he represented Indian universities at the Congress of the Universities of the British Empire in June 1926, and at the International Congress of Philosophy at Harvard University in September 1926. At Harvard, he bemoaned the lack of spiritualism in modern civilization.

In 1929 Radhakrishnan became the principal of Manchester College, Oxford University. From 1936 to 1939, he held the chair of Spalding Professor of Eastern Religions and Ethics, and was elected Royal Fellow of the British Academy. He returned to India in 1939 and, until 1949, served as vice-chancellor of Benares Hindu University. Thereafter, during his vice presidency from 1952 to 1962, he was also chancellor of Delhi University. With the spread of his reputation for eloquence and brilliance, he was invited frequently to give lectures on Hinduism and eastern philosophy in the West.

Aldous Huxley observed that Dr. Radhakrishnan's mastery of the English language was beyond excellence and that Radhakrishnan was "the master of words and no words." American scholar George P. Conger noted: "Among the philosophers of our time, no one has achieved so much in so many fields as has Sarvepalli Radhakrishnan of India. . . . William James was influential in religion, and John Dewey has been a force in politics. One or two American philosophers have been legislators. Jacques Maritain has been an ambassador. Radhakrishnan, in a little more than thirty years of work, has done all these things and more. . . . Never in the history of philosophy has there been quite such a world figure. With his unique appointment at Banaras [University] and Oxford, like a weaver's shuttle, he has gone to and fro between the East and West, carrying a thread of understanding, weaving it into the fabric of civilization." Radhakrishnan died in 1975.

Raju G. C. Thomas

BIBLIOGRAPHY

Gopal, Sarvepalli. *Radhakrishnan: A Biography*. Oxford and New Delhi: Oxford University Press, 1989.

Minor, Robert N. *Radhakrishnan: A Religious Biography*. Albany: State University of New York Press, 1987.

Parthasarathi, G., and D. P. Chattopadhyaya, eds. *Radhakrishnan: Centenary Volume*. Oxford and New Delhi: Oxford University Press, 1990.

Radhakrishnan, Sarvepalli, and Charles A. Moore. *A Source Book in Indian Philosophy*. Princeton, N.J.: Princeton University Press, 1967.

Rama Rao Pappu, S. S., ed. *New Essays in the Philosophy of Sarvepalli Radhakrishnan*. New Delhi: South Asia Books, 1995.

Rodrigues, Clarissa. *The Social and Political Thought of Dr. S. Radhakrishnan: An Evaluation*. New Delhi: Sterling Publishers, 1992.

RĀGA Rāga (Sanskrit, *ranj*, "color"), in the classical music tradition of India, is the combined concept of melody and scale. To the listener, a *rāga* is a category of melodies all sharing key melodic features and inflections as well as scalar relationships, not to mention psychological associations. To the musician-composer, *rāga* is a resource of melodic ideas upon which he or she can draw to create music that is at once unique and familiar. In the northern and southern traditions, multiple performances or compositions of any particular common *rāga* will yield realized melodies that share a general scale type, an emphasis on particular pitches, and characteristic ways of engaging these pitches; yet they can be unique utterances.

However, while North and South India share this melodic concept, their approaches to *rāga* are subtly different. No term is as fundamentally important to contemporary Indian classical music yet as descriptively elusive as *rāga*.

Pitch

Underlying India's *rāga*s is a sense of pitch that is fundamentally similar to that found in the West and that indeed may have common ancient historical roots. As in many cultures, the physics of pitch production seem to generate the primary underlying structures, while cultural practices have defined specific pitch relationships; that is, the primary overtones of pitch production (the unison, the octave, and the fifth representing the open string and string divisions of one-half and one-third) result in a generalized conception of the octave being divided into seven principal steps and twelve incremental steps.

Musician-scholars of ancient India—probably reflecting practices historically deriving from the intonational relationships of Vedic chant—recognized an even smaller pitch increment: the *shruti*. The scholar Bharata describes how to derive twenty-two of these microtonal intervals in the *Nātya Shāstra* (c. 200 B.C.–A.D. 200), demonstrating that he clearly could hear the pitch relationship but generating many questions and interpretations. However, even for Bharata, the *shruti* was never a functionally separate entity, but rather an intonational difference between two intervals. Subsequent treatises show that the concept was increasingly vague, although in typical Indian fashion, scholars continue to reference the concept in their own works (particularly in the South).

The primary term relating to pitch is *svara* (Sanskrit/Vedic, *sur,* "sun, heaven"; Hindi, "voice, sound, note"). As in the West, South Asian music recognizes seven scale steps (see Table 1): *shadja* (Sanskrit, *sasa*, "of six"; *shadja*, "six-born"), the principal note from which the other six derive, the tonic; *rishabha* (Sanskrit, "bull"), the second note of the gamut; *gandhāra* (Sanskrit, "the name of a people"), the third note of the gamut; *madhyama* (Sanskrit, "the middle"), the fourth note of the gamut; *pañcama* (Sanskrit, *pañcha*, "the fifth"), the fifth note of the gamut; *dhaivata* (Sanskrit, *dhi*, "to think, perceive [?]"), the sixth note of the gamut; and *nishāda* (Sanskrit, *nishāda*, "to sink or go down"), the seventh note of the gamut. Musicians commonly abbreviate these note names as *sā*, *ri/re*, *gā*, *mā*, *pā*, *dhā*, and *ni*. (South Indian musicians use the abbreviation *ri* for the second scale degree, whereas North Indian musicians use *re*.)

TABLE 1

Scale steps in South Asian music

Solfeggio	Svara Name	Abbreviation
Doh	*Shadja*	Sā
Ti	*Nishāda*	Ni
La	*Dhaivata*	Dhā
Sol	*Pañcama*	Pā
Fa	*Madhyama*	Mā
Mi	*Gandhāra*	Gā
Re	*Rishabha*	Ri/Re
Doh	*Shadja*	Sā

SOURCE: Courtesy of author.

South India

The *Karnātak Sangīt Paddhati* (South Indian musical tradition) emphasizes *rāga* as an organization of scale and pitch hierarchy. Moreover, various treatises demonstrate how the South's systemic approach to *rāga* developed. *Rāga* in the South involves the concepts of *melā* (Sanskrit, "group," or "scale"), *melākārta* (Sanskrit, "scale matrix"), and *svarasthāna* (Sanskrit, "note placement").

Ramamatya, a minister of Rama Raja of Vijayanagar, finished the *Svara-melā-kalānidhi* (1550) fifteen years before that city fell to northerners. Remarkably, the treatise shows either relatively little influence from the Islamic north or steadfast resistance to the growing importance of western Asia's music culture. Notable is Ramamatya's description and grouping of *rāga*s according to the number of scale types necessary to accommodate the varying intervallic structure of *rāga*s in current practice. This grouping of *rāga*s by scale type probably dates from the fourteenth century, but most musicians today know Ramamatya's sixteenth-century interpretation. Somanatha's *Rāgavibodha* (1609) shows the court traditions of South India to be cosmopolitan and connected to other cultures around the Indian Ocean (e.g., *rāga* Arabhi).

The scholar Venkatamakhi in his *Caturdandī-prakāsika* (1661) features a classification of *rāga*s into seventy-two basic scales (*melās*) derived from a note placement (*svarasthāna*) of twelve available semitones in which some notes have enharmonic equivalents (i.e., the same pitch can have a different name, depending on context). This system still prevails in South Indian classical music. His ingenious system makes maximum use of the available twelve semitones with the following premises:

1. Scales have a maximum of seven possible pitches.
2. These seven pitches occur in order (*sā*, *ri*, *gā*, *mā*, *pā*, *dhā*, *ni*).
3. The octave repeats (a named pitch in one octave is synonymous with a pitch of the same name in a different octave).
4. Some notes can enharmonically overlap in different scales.
5. Scales consist of two conjunct tetrachords: *sā-mā* and *pā-sā* (octave).
6. The natural (*shuddha*) position for every note is the lowest position.

Venkatamakhi describes three positions each for *nishāda*, *dhaivata*, *gandhāra*, and *rishabha*, and two positions for *madhyama*. *Shadja* and *pañcama* have fixed positions. The logic behind this lies partly in the physics of sound. *Shadja* and *pañcama* are the most prominent overtones produced by a vibrating string or column of air. *Madhyama* is at once the inverse of the *shadja-pañcama* interval (i.e., the distance from the upper *shadja* to *madhyama* is the same as from the lower *sadja* to *pañcama*) and the defining upper limit to the lower tetrachord. *Nishāda*, *dhaivata*, *gandhāra*, and *rishabha* lie in acoustically unstable areas. That is, the seventh, sixth, third, and second scale degrees have no strong harmonic overtones to support them. Interestingly, the concept of *shruti* remains in the names for the variants of *rishabha* and *dhaivata* in the modifiers *sat-shruti* (seven *shrutis*) and *catus-shruti* (four *shrutis*).

In Table 2, each of the twelve discrete semitones has an assigned number from 0 to 11. Note that *nishāda* and *dhaivata*, as well as *gandhāra* and *rishabha*, share two note positions each. Also note that the examples in this entry

TABLE 2

South Indian *svarasthāna* (note placement)

Shadja	sā	0	sā	*shadja*	
kakali nishāda	ni##	11			
kaishiki nishāda	ni#	10	dhā##	*sat-shruti dhaivata*	
shuddha nishāda	ni	9	dhā#	*catus-shruti dhaivata*	***uttarānga***
		8	dhā	*shuddha dhaivata*	
pañcama	pā	7	pā	*pañcama*	
prati madhyama	mā#	6			
shuddha madhyama	mā	5			
		4	gā##	*antara gandhāra*	
sat-shruti rishabh	ri##	3	gā#	*sadharāna gandhāra*	***purvānga***
catus-shruti rishabh	ri#	2	gā	*shuddha gandhāra*	
shuddha rishabh	ri	1			
Shadja	sā	0	sā	*shadja*	

SOURCE: Courtesy of author.

use the Western musical symbols of # (indicating a note is in a raised position by a semitone), ♮ (indicating a note is in a lowered position by a semitone), or, as in this particular example, ## to indicate that a note is two semitones higher than the natural position. Similarly, the use of the numerals 0 to 11 is consistent with Western pitch-class analysis and is not generally a part of South Asian musical dialogue. Nevertheless, that both Western and Indian musical practices have enough commonalities to allow both the use of the concept of semitone and raised and lowered positions, not to mention seven note identities, is possibly indicative of cultural links over the centuries.

The principles underlying Venkatamakhi's system are as follows:

1. *Sā* and *pā*, as the most important notes in the harmonic series, are fixed in their positions. That is, the overtones produced by the fundamental *sā* include first its octave equivalent and the fifth (*pā*). In melodic contexts, these notes can be omitted, but they are inherent in the scale.
2. *Mā*, as the next most important note in the harmonic series, has two positions: *shuddha* (pure) *mā* and *prati* (raised) *mā*.
3. The second (*ri*), third (*gā*), sixth (*dhā*), and seventh (*ni*) of the scale have three variations, each beginning with a *shuddha* (pure or natural) position and two raised positions above. *Ri* and *dhā*, as the notes immediately above the immovable notes of *sā* and *pā*, borrow from ancient terminology with the indication that they are four (*catus*) and seven (*sat*) *shrutis* above their respective notes. Thus, *ri* has a natural position (*suddha rishabh*) with two raised positions above (*catus-shruti rishabh* and *sat-shruti rishabh*). The third and the seventh employ a different nomenclature, but their *shuddh* positions are also the points above which their alternates are placed. In practice, these intervals are roughly equivalent to modern semitones, although Venkatamakhi would have used something closer to just intonation (with note positions based on string ratios).

Mughal Painting, c. 1590. This painting honors the legendary singer Tansen. Believed by some to work miracles with his *rāgas*, he was regarded as one of the "Nine Jewels" of Akbar's court. NATIONAL MUSEUM / FOTOMEDIA.

4. When constructing a scale, the notes must always appear in the order *sā*, *ri*, *gā*, *mā*, *pā*, *dhā*, *ni*, *sā*, no matter which position they are in.
5. Venkatamakhi divides his scale into lower (*purvānga*) and upper (*uttarānga*) tetrachords (groups of four notes), reflecting the importance of stringed lutes in the definition of these scales. The *purvānga* consists of the notes *sā*, *ri*, *gā*, and *mā*. The *uttarānga* consists of the notes *pā*, *dhā*, *ni*, and *sā*.
6. The first *cakra* (cycle) has *sā* and *mā* fixed in the *purvānga*. *Ri* and *gā* are in their *shuddh* or lowest positions. Thus, the first *melā* (scale) of the first *cakra* has *sā*, *suddha ri* (one semitone above *sā*), *suddha gā* (one semitone above *suddha ri* and a whole tone above *sā*) and *mā* (a perfect fourth above *sā*). The second *melā* of the first *cakra* has *sā*, *ri*, and *mā* in the same positions as the first *melā*, but raises *gā* one semitone. The third *melā* follows the same pattern with *gā* now two semitones above *ri*. The fourth *melā* starts with *sā* and *mā* in the same position, but raises *ri* to the *catu-sruti* position, two semitones or one whole tone above *sā*. This leaves only two positions for *gā* (*sadhārana* and *antara*). Finally, with *sā* and *mā* still fixed, *ri* raises to its highest position (*sat-sruti*) leaving only one position for *gā* (*antara*) so that the first *cakra* has six *melā*s.
7. The *uttarānga* (upper tetrachord) functions the same way, except that now *pā* and *sā* are the fixed notes and *dhā* and *ni* move. More important, the six parallel changes in note position take place once for each *cakra*. Thus, in the first *cakra*, *dhā* and *ni* begin in their *suddh* positions (*dhā* one semitone above *pā* and *ni* one semitone above *dhā*) and remain in those positions while *ri* and *gā* go through their mutations in the lower tetrachord. When the second *cakra* begins, *ni* raises one semitone to its first raised position (*kaisiki*) and remains there until the third *cakra*, when it rises to its highest position (*kākili*). Again, the upper tetrachord parallels the lower tetrachord in note changes, matching one change for every *cakra* (or set of changes in the lower tetrachord).
8. Matching the six positions of the lower tetrachord with the six positions of the upper tetrachord yields thirty-six different scales. Venkatamakhi then derives an additional thirty-six *melā*s by repeating the process with *mā* in the *prati* position.

Performance practice places a number of qualifications on *rāga*. First, a *rāga* may use some or all of the notes available in a *melā*. A *sampurna rāga* (Sanskrit, "complete") is a *rāga* having a heptatonic or seven-note scale. A *shadava rāga* (Sanskrit, "sweetmeats") is a *rāga* having a hexatonic or six-note scale. An *audava rāga* (the name of a constellation) has a pentatonic scale. And a *rāga* that introduces notes from other *melā*s, or mixes *melā*s, is a *janya rāga* (Sanskrit, *janya*, "derivative").

Ustad Asad Ali Khan. In 2005 he remains one of the few active modern masters of the *rudraveena* (or *been*), the premier instrument of Indian classical music. His musical roots date back some seven generations to the eighteenth century, when his ancestors served as musicians to the princes of Jaipur. INDIA TODAY.

In describing a *rāga* and in defining its melodic characteristics, musicians and scholars employ a variety of terms. Among the most important are those describing a *rāga*'s ascending (*ārohana*) and descending (*avarohana*) scalar movement. Such movements commonly omit a note in one direction, only to include it in another. This movement may also be *vakra* (crooked) such that a momentary ascent may interrupt a descent and vice versa. Perhaps even more important are the notions of *jīva-svara* (Sanskrit, "life-note") and *pitippu* (Telegu, "catch"). The former is the most important note of a *rāga*, the note that stands out and contributes to the melodic dynamics of the *rāga*. The latter is a characteristic melodic phrase commonly generated by the *jīva-svara* and which stands out as a principal way to identify the *rāga*. Scholars sometimes project this last idea into a *rāga-chāyā-sañcāra* (Sanskrit, "*rāga*-image-phrase"), an extended notion of characteristic melodic phrase. Another important component is the treatment (*gamaka*) that individual notes receive, of which there are numerous kinds of shakes, vibratos, and slides.

North India

While North and South Indian classical music systems hold many fundamental concepts in common, at the same time there is much that is different. The names of the seven notes of the scale are nearly identical (with some minor variations) and the word for melody is essentially the same, *rāga* (*rāg* in common Hindustani speech).

The word for scale in the north is *thāt* (Hindi, "framework," or "skeleton"). Instead of the complicated and comprehensive system espoused by Venkatamakhi, North Indian musicians and scholars use a set of scales derived largely from practice, not theory. Furthermore, the North Indian *svarasthāna* is a straightforward approach with the five movable notes having only two positions each (rather than three). A *svar*'s position is either *shuddh* (natural) or one of two *vikrit* (altered) positions: *tīvra* ("strong," "intense," or "raised") or *komal* ("soft," or "lowered"). As in South Indian musical practice, *shadja* and *pañcama* are in fixed positions. The other notes—*nishāda*, *dhaivata*, *madhyama*, *gandhāra*, and *rishabha*—have two possible positions each (see Table 3).

TABLE 3

North Indian *svarasthāna* (note placement)

Shadja	**sā**	**0**	**sā**	***shadja***	
		11	ni	*shuddha nishāda*	***uttarānga***
		10	ni♭	*komal nishāda*	
shuddha dhaivata	dhā	9			
komal dhaivata	dhā♭	8			
pañcama	pā	7	pā	*pañcama*	
tivra madhyama	mā♯	6			
Shuddha madhyama	mā	5			
		4	gā	*shuddha gandhāra*	***purvānga***
		3	gā♭	*komal gandhāra*	
shuddha rishabha	ri	2			
komal rishabha	ri♭	1			
Shadja	sā	0	sā	*shadja*	

SOURCE: Courtesy of author.

The scholar V. N. Bhatkhande (1860–1936) collected and organized North Indian *rāgas* according to scale, describing *rāgas* in terms of ten *thāts*. Bhatkhande's beginning scale, or *shuddh thāt*, is Bilāval *that*, which is parallel to the Western major scale. He describes the other *thāts* in terms of the ways in which they vary from Bilāval (see Table 4).

Melody is by far the most important defining aspect of *rāga* in the Hindustani *sangīt paddhati* (North Indian classical music tradition). In most *rāgas*, only one version of a *svar* occurs (either the *shuddh* or the *tīvra/komal* position of any one note). However, in some *rāgas* (especially the so-called light *rāgs* or in the Lalit group of *rāgas*), more than one note may appear. N. A. Jairazbhoy (1971) has commented on the historical mutation of *rāgas* and has proposed both an explanation for this evolution (in tetrachordal symmetry) and a thirty-two-*thāt* system to include all—not just ten—possible combinations.

As in South Indian practice, some North Indian *rāgas* use only some of the notes available in a *thāt*, which—while confounding classification by scale—contributes to the diversity of musical possibilities. Scholars recognize three such *jātī* (Sanskrit, "species"): *sampurn* ("complete"; heptatonic scales, i.e., those with seven notes), *shadav/khadav* (hexatonic scales, i.e., those with six notes), and *audav* (pentatonic scales, i.e., those with five notes).

Indian music does not generally make use of equal temperament, but rather something closer to just intonation; that is, Indian musicians tend to tune their instruments to pure acoustic intervals. Individual musicians will further fine tune specific notes, for the most part, according to their prerogatives, paying particular interest to fine shades of intonation. Musicians commonly highlight particular notes with several "intonational" ornaments: *mīnd* (slides), *andolan* (exaggerated vibrato), and *gamak* (a quick shake). The word musicians commonly use to describe these fine discriminations in intonation is *shruti* (that which is heard), which, while referencing the ancient microtone of Bharata's time, has no specific or measurably consistent equivalent today.

Scholars and musicians in northern Indian practice describe the melodic movement of *rāgs* with a number of terms. They recognize *rāgs* by their characteristic melodic movement or *varn* (Sanskrit, "kind" or "class"). The terms *āroh* (or *ārohi varn*) and *avroh* (or *avrohi varn*) describe the ascending and descending aspects of the *rāga* in abstraction. Three other terms also find their way into contemporary usage: *sthāyī varn* ("steady" or "unchangeable" form, i.e., the *rāg* has characteristically straight ascents or descents), *sañcārī varn* ("wandering," i.e., a mixture of *āroh* and *avroh*), and *vakr varn* ("crooked" or "oblique"). This last term describes the characteristic passages of some *rāgs*, which demand a deviation from the straight scale. The note from which a *vakr varn* must begin is the *vakr svar*.

One of the most important ways of identifying a *rāg* is through its *pakad*, or characteristic phrase. An even more

TABLE 4

Bhatkhande's *thāts*

		Bilāval	Kalyān	Kamāj	Kāfī	Āsāvarī	Bhairavī	Bhairav	Todī	Purvī	Mārwa
shadja	0	sā	sā	sā	sā	sā	sā	sā	sā	sā	sā
shuddha nishāda	11	ni	ni					ni	ni	ni	ni
komal nishāda	10			ni♭	ni♭	ni♭	ni♭				
shuddha dhaivata	9	dhā	dhā	dhā	dhā						dhā
komal dhaivata	8					dhā♭	dhā♭	dhā♭	dhā♭	dhā♭	
pañcama	7	pā	pā	pā	pā	pā	pā	pā	pā	pā	pā
tīvra madhyama	6		mā♯						mā♯	mā♯	mā♯
madhyama	5	mā		mā	mā	mā	mā	mā			
gandhāra	4	gā	gā	gā				gā		gā	gā
komal gandhāra	3				gā♭	gā♭	gā♭		gā♭		
shuddha rishabha	2	re	re	re	re	re					
komal rishabha	1						re♭	re♭	re♭	re♭	re♭
shadja	0	sā	sā	sā	sā	sā	sā	sā	sā	sā	sā

SOURCE: Courtesy of author.

elaborate description of a *rāg* is a *svar vistār*, a series of phrases illustrating the characteristic shapes of a *rāg* in a variety of registers.

Most *rāg*s have two notes of particular importance: the *vādī* and *samvādī*. The *vādī* (Sanskrit, "sonant") or *amsha* is the most important note, often approached via the *sam vādī* (consonant), the second-most important note. Historically, scholars have used the terms *visranti svar* or *maqām sthān* to describe the terminal or resting notes, sometimes equating these with *vādī*. Modern musicians are more likely to use the term *vādī*. Two terms that are used often (but that are more commonly defined by what they are not) are *vivādī* (a dissonant note to be avoided, sometimes also described as the *varji svar*, "omitted note") and *anuvādī* (an assonant note that is perceived neither as consonant nor as dissonant to the *vādī*).

According to Bhatkhande, musicians should perform between noon and midnight those *rāg*s that have their *vādī* in the *purvāng* or that emphasize the lower tetrachord. *Rāg*s that have their *vādī* in the *uttrāng* or that emphasize the upper tetrachord should be performed between midnight and noon.

Gordon Thompson

See also **Music; Tāla**

BIBLIOGRAPHY

Bhatkhande, V. N. *Kramik Pustak Malika*. 6 vols. Hathras: Sangeet Press, 1937.

Jairazbhoy, N. A. *The Rāgs of North Indian Music: Their Structure and Evolution*. Middletown, Conn.: Wesleyan University Press, 1971.

Rowell, Lewis. *Music and Musical Thought in Early India*. Chicago: University of Chicago Press, 1992.

RĀGAMĀLĀ Literally meaning "a garland of melodies," *Rāgamālā* paintings illustrate Indian melodic forms, or *rāga*s and *Rāginī*s. Indian musicians also use this term while playing several melodies in a continuous sequence. An Indian melody, or *rāga*, is a composition of musical modes having a sequence or structure with a specific mood or significance. *Rāgamālā* paintings visualize such melodies in pictorial forms.

The source of *Rāgamālā* illustrations lies in the descriptions of melodies, using vivid verbal imagery, by the Indian musicologists of the late medieval period. The *Sangeeta Ratnākara* of Sharangadeva, an important treatise from the twelfth century A.D., for the first time mentions the presiding deity of each *rāga*, associating the *rāga*s and *rāginī*s with certain gods. The growing number of *rāga*s and their increasing variety created the need for analytical study and classification into relative groups. The earliest systematic exposition of such classification divides them into eight major "male" *rāga*s and three derivative "female" *rāginī*s, each listed in the *Rāga Sāgara*, written around 1440. That work also gives the iconographic description of *rāga*s such as Bhairava, Bhupāla, Patamañjarī, Mālava, Rāmapriyā, Gurjarī, Todī,

***Rāgamālā* Painting Portraying Hindola.** Though the mood of such a painting was inspired by the sound of the corresponding *rāgā*, the musician relies on it as a kind of guidebook, suggesting nuances of interpretation and clarifying the sentiment his performance should evoke. BURSTEIN COLLECTION / CORBIS.

and Madhumādhavī, in the chapter titled *Rāgadhyāna Vidhānam*. Treatises on musicology of this period suggest that the names of the melodies have contextual origins, and it is possible that this context is reflected in the iconography of each *rāga*. This context includes: the structure of the *rāga*, its geographical area of origin, the festivals and seasons associated with each, and the tunes used by the people of certain professions while at work or engaged in religious celebrations. For instance, *Rāgini Āsavarī* is connected with the music of the *saperā*, or people belonging to a snake-charmer community, who entice snakes with the music of their special instrument, known as *bin*. *Rāgini Āsavarī*, therefore depicts a girl who, having lured snakes to her, is holding them in her hands. *Rāga Vasanta*, meaning the spring season, depicts the festival of colors celebrated at the advent of the spring; *Rāga Megha-malhār* (*megha* meaning "cloud") illustrates the monsoon season. *Rāga Māru* (*maru* meaning "desert") has a geographical context and is illustrated by depicting camel riders or camels. This *rāga* must have its origin in the desert areas of Rajasthan. Melodies also relate to the moods of heros and heroines. *Rāga Bibhāsa* (twilight), for instance, depicts a couple in a romantic mood, aiming an arrow at a rooster as he announces the advent of morning.

The art of miniature painting on paper was also gaining patronage during the seventeenth century, and the Rajput royal families and patrons also began commissioning secular paintings including the *rāgamālā*. The earliest visual depiction of melodies found to date is in a *Kalpasūtra* of about 1475, initially published by Sarabhai Nawab, in which the *rāgas* and *rāginīs* are shown in purely iconic form, as the forms of gods and goddesses. *Rāgamālā* acquired the importance of an independent theme during the Delhi Sultanate and Mughal rule, when secular themes were in demand. The earliest set of *rāgamālā* was painted in what is known as the Chaurapanchashika style of the Delhi Jaunpur area, in the mid-sixteenth century. It splendidly depicts the main iconographic features of each *rāga*, the literary description of which is inscribed on the reverse.

However, the real precursor of the Rajasthani *Rāgamālā* of the later period is the famous Chawand *Rāgamālā* painting by the artist Nisardi in Chawand (Chanda), Mewar, in 1605. Set against a red lacquer background, a dark sky, and a variety of floral decorative plants, the *rāga*s and *rāginī*s are depicted with bold draftsmanship. During the same period, the *Rāgamālā* theme found patronage from circles more influenced by the Mughal idiom. A *Rāgamālā* dated 1605, painted in the popular Mughal style, offers an interesting companion to the set Chawand *Rāgamālā*. The paintings have much more realistic renderings, while the iconography remains the same.

The cultural climate of the Deccan was particularly vibrant during the late sixteenth and early seventeenth centuries under the reign of Sultan Ibrahim Adil Shah II (r. 1580–1627), who was a lover of painting and a fine musician himself. A few folios from several *Rāgamālā* sets, painted in Bijapur and Ahmednagar styles and dating from the late sixteenth century, are dispersed in various collections.

Later treatises on *Rāgamālā* were written in Hindi. Many more *Rāgamālā* were added to the original set of thirty-six, and the artists began to take more liberties in the iconography of the *Rāgamālā* of the later periods. From the seventeenth century onward, *Rāgamālā* paintings were commonly depicted by the painters of all schools of miniature painting in India. Though generally the iconographic details are the same, the northern and the southern versions vary considerably. In the north the literary version of *Rāgamālā* used by the artists of the Kangra Valley or the Basohli differs from that used in Rajasthan.

A number of sets from Sirohi, Bundi, Kotah, Marwar, Kangra, and Hyderabad have come to light. *Rāgamālā* paintings were also painted in the women's quarters of the Havelis. It is possible that the visual form of these paintings was easily understood by many people, or they may have been created only for the enjoyment of the connoisseur.

Kalpana Desai

See also **Miniatures; Rāga**

BIBLIOGRAPHY

Ebeling, Klaus. *Ragamala Painting.* Basil: Ravi Kumar, 1973.

Sarangadev. *Sangitaratnakar of Sarangadeva.* New Delhi: Munshiram Manoharlal, 1991.

Waldschmidt, Ernst, and R. L. Waldschmidt. *Miniatures of Musical Inspiration in the Collection of the Berlin Museums of Indian Art, Parts I and II.* Berlin: Museums für Indische Kunst, 1975.

RAHMAN, SHEIKH MUJIBUR ***(1920–1975), first president and prime minister of Bangladesh (1971–1975).*** Adored and loved as Bangabandhu ("Bengal's Friend"), Sheikh Mujibur Rahman was a charismatic, crowd-inspiring leader. The birth of Bangladesh was bloody; it passed through a nine-month gestation of massacre unleashed by the Pakistanis, and the intervention of the Indian army helped deliver it. The end of the Bangabandhu's colorful and constructive career was equally bloody.

Sheikh Mujib, as he was popularly called, was born in 1920 in the Faridpur district of present-day Bangladesh. The son of a civil court official, Mujib graduated from a local missionary school in Faridpur in 1942, and from the Islamic College in Kolkata (Calcutta) in 1947. While attending high school, Mujib emerged as a student activist. In January 1938 he confronted Chief Minister A. K. Fazlul Haq when he came to Gopalganj, Mujib's town, on an official visit. He asked the chief minister to provide funds for upgrading the school and its hostel, and Haq agreed to release funds for the school projects. Mujib was hailed as a local hero. This event marked the beginning of Mujib's increasing entwinement with Bengal politics and with its Muslim leadership. It also marked the beginning of his intermittent run-ins with the police and, later, long spells of imprisonment: he was arrested twice at the age of eighteen for inciting fellow students to protest, and for unruly behavior.

Mujib Rahman joined the Muslim Students' Federation of India in 1940. He was elected a member of the Bengal Muslim League Council in 1943. Soon he found himself in the front ranks of progressive Muslim student leaders who were enjoined by their leaders to oppose the communalists in the Indian Muslim League. Mujib joined with Shahid Suhrawardy against Kwaja Najimuddin. In June 1947 the British announcement of their plan to partition India into two sovereign nations, India and Pakistan, led Mujib to mobilize young Muslim leaders in a secret conclave at the Islamic College in Kolkata to work on a political organization in opposition to the Muslim League. Some consider this development to be the seed of Mujib Rahman's Awami League, which would later lead to the movement for the creation of Bangladesh and the breakup of Pakistan in 1971.

Toward the end of 1947, Rahman left Kolkata for Dhaka and joined the Law College there as a student. He was expelled from the University of Dhaka for "inciting the fourth class employees." In 1948 he helped establish the East Pakistan Muslim Student League, which was enlarged into the East Pakistan Awami Muslim League in 1949. In 1953 he was elected general secretary of the Awami Muslim League and later became its president in 1966. After the 1954 general elections, he joined Fazlul Haq's government, and when it was dismissed by the Pakistani government after two months, he was arrested along with the others in his party, which was renamed the East Pakistan Awami League. The word "Muslim" was dropped to suggest its secular character.

In more ways than one, the genesis of Bangladesh lies in the language movement in which Mujib and his cohorts in the Awami League took an active part, and for which they received prison sentences in the 1950s and 1960s. The demand to make Bengali the official language of the people of Bangladesh was first presented by Dhirendranath Datta in the Pakistan Legislative Council in 1948. He asked for the acceptance of Bengali as a national language, along with Urdu and English. Mohammad Ali Jinnah, governor-general of Pakistan, summarily rejected this demand, declaring Urdu the sole national language of all of Pakistan. The firm rejection only hardened the determination of students, intellectuals, and secular political activists to seek and establish Bengali identity in language rather than religion.

The movement to make Bengali a state language in Pakistan, and the only language of East Pakistan, gained in momentum and quickly enveloped the entire region. Field Marshal Ayub Khan, who had seized power in 1958, ruling all of Pakistan with an iron hand, responded with more repression. He was supported by the Islamists, who saw in Rahman, the language movement, and the Awami League the seeds of the destruction of Pakistan as an Islamic republic. In 1966 Rahman issued a six-point program to reconstitute Pakistan as a parliamentary democracy, leaving the central government with only defense and foreign policy in its jurisdiction, with the rest of the powers to be vested in the states. He asked for a separate currency and armed forces for East Pakistan. Ayub Khan, convinced that Rahman was, in so many words, calling for independence, arrested him on a trumped-up charge. Ayub faced a populist upsurge in West Pakistan and decided to abdicate, handing over the presidency to Yahya Khan, the commander-in-chief of the army. Mujib Rahman was released from prison, and President Yahya Khan called for a general election.

The results surprised Khan. Rahman's party, the Awami League, swept the polls in the East, and Zulfikar Ali Bhutto's Pakistan People's Party won a majority of the seats in the West. With the plurality of seats in his favor, Rahman now expected an invitation from Yahya Khan to lead and form the new government in Pakistan. Khan decided to call the National Assembly to session on 25 March 1971. Neither Khan nor Bhutto was willing to hand the position of prime minister to Rahman. They invited him to talks, which failed. At midnight on 25 March, the army opened fire on students and faculty at Dhaka University's dormitories and faculty housing complexes. Mujib Rahman was arrested. The die was cast. In his parting message to his people, Rahman declared them citizens of a free country—Bangladesh. The army crackdown continued, causing some 10 million refugees to flee to neighboring West Bengal in India. An inestimable number of men, women, and children were killed and women raped. Prime Minister Indira Gandhi, after signing a friendship treaty with the Soviet Union, sent the Indian army into Pakistan on 23 November; on 15 December 1971, India's chief-of-staff Sam Manekshaw formally accepted Pakistani General Niazi's offer of surrender.

Soon after the army crackdown of 25 March, the Mukti Bahini (Freedom Fighters) had launched a war of liberation and had formed a provisional government, declaring Mujib Rahman as its president. On 10 January 1972, Mujib returned to Dhaka after being released from prison in Pakistan. He became the first prime minister of independent and sovereign Bangladesh.

The birth pangs were, however, extreme. Mujib and his government faced gargantuan tasks of reconstruction and rehabilitation, attempting as well to stem the tide of mass revenge against those who had supported Pakistan. Mujib, the charismatic leader, was not a competent administrator. On 15 August 1975, disaffected members of the Bangladesh army assassinated Mujib Rahman and members of his family at the presidential palace.

Dilip K. Basu

See also **Bangladesh**

BIBLIOGRAPHY

Ahmad, Kamruddin. *A Socio-Political History of Bengal and the Birth of Bangladesh.* Dhaka: Zhiruddin Library, 1975.

Islam, Sirajul, ed. *Banglapedia: National Encyclopedia of Bangladesh.* Dhaka: Asiatic Society of Bangladesh, 2003.

RAILROADS. *See* **British Impact.**

RAJAGOPALACHARI, CHAKRAVARTI ***(1878–1972), writer and statesman, prominent in India's independence movement; last governor-general of India (1948–1950).*** Chakravarti Rajagopalachari (often called C. R. or Rajaji) was born on 10 December 1878 to a family of poor Iyengar Brahmans in Thorapalli, near Hosur, in the Tamil country. The first Indian to serve as free India's head of state, he was ninety-four when he died in Chennai (formerly Madras) on 25 December 1972.

Early Life

As the headman first of Thorapalli and later of the larger settlement of Hosur, Rajagopalachari's father, Chakravarti Iyengar, earned a monthly salary of around five rupees (about one U.S. dollar at the time). The youngest of three brothers, Rajagopalachari saw the blackboard as a blur in Hosur's government school, but at the age of thirteen, when he obtained spectacles, he understood, as he put it, "what green was" and that stars were not "just a vague mist of light" but "had points, and corners, and colours" (Gandhi, p. 5).

By this time he was studying in the British-run Central College in Bangalore, the city closest to Hosur. Graduation from Central College was followed by a course and degree in law in Madras and the start of a practice as a criminal lawyer in Salem, headquarters of the district to which Thorapalli and Hosur belonged and the seat of the district's British Collector.

Politics—Salem's civic affairs as well as the cause of Indian self-government—pulled Rajagopalachari, the more so following the illness and early death (at the age of twenty-six) of his wife Alarmelu Mangammal, or Manga, who bore him five children. He entered the municipal council, chaired it to much acclaim, took some steps, despite sharp opposition from orthodox Hindus, that reduced discrimination against "untouchables," followed events in the Indian National Congress, which had been founded in 1885, preferred the Congress's extremists to its moderates, and briefly day-dreamed about bombs and assassinations ending British rule.

Satyagraha. The possibility of another route to independence was suggested by press accounts of the nonviolent disobedience that Mohandas Gandhi and numerous Indians were practicing in South Africa from 1906, accounts confirmed to Rajagopalachari by relatives (in India) of Tamils indentured in South Africa. Sending Gandhi money for the South African effort, Rajagopalachari argued in a 1916 article that Gandhi's technique of *satyagraha* ("clinging to the truth"), pitting "soul force" against "the force of arms," was "a great question" for those wanting independence in India (Gandhi, p. 26).

Though by this time Gandhi was back in India, most Congress politicians considered him impractical; Rajagopalachari was probably the first to suggest that *satyagraha* might succeed in India. When, early in 1919, Gandhi proposed nonviolent resistance to the newly announced Rowlatt Bills that sought to curb free speech, Rajagopalachari, moving at this juncture from Salem to the city of Madras, at once offered his support. Gandhi's stay as Rajagopalachari's houseguest in Madras in March 1919 marked the end of his legal practice. Henceforth he would be a full-time, unpaid worker for independence, Gandhi's close colleague, and the commander of nonviolent battles in the south.

The British jailed him five times, for several months at a time, between 1921 and 1941. After independence, an entry in a diary that Rajagopalachari kept in Vellore—where, tormented by solitary confinement, filthy food, and sickness, he spent the first of these terms—would be recalled for its foresight:

> *Swaraj* (independence) will not at once or, I think, even for a long time to come, be better government or greater happiness for the people. Elections and their corruptions, injustice, and the power and tyranny of wealth and inefficiency of administration will make a hell of life as soon as freedom is given to us. . . . The only thing gained will be that as a race we will be saved from dishonour and subordination. (Gandhi, pp. 72–73)

Leader of the Congress. From 1919 to 1942, Rajagopalachari was on anyone's list of five or six leading figures of the Indian National Congress. Referring to a Congress plenary held, while Gandhi was in prison, in Gaya in Bihar in 1922, where Rajagopalachari's debating skills turned the tables on numerous opponents of *satyagraha*,

Rajagopalachari, Portrait of India's Last Governor-General. A life long student of Hinduism, Rajagopalachari published a highly regarded edition of the Mahābhārata in his later years. His political writing spanned many decades and forms. K. L. KAMAT / KAMAT'S POTPOURRI.

Prafulla Chandra Ghosh, later a chief minister of West Bengal, would say, "Mr. Rajagopalachari became the leader of the Congress at Gaya" (Gandhi, p. 80).

Responding in 1927 to a question asked in Karaikudi in Madras province, Gandhi observed that Rajagopalachari was his "only possible successor" (Gandhi, p. 103). In 1930 Rajagopalachari led a defiant and strictly nonviolent "salt march" to Vedaranyam on South India's east coast that wiped out, as the Raj privately acknowledged, any "sense of devotion to the Government" in the Tamil country (Gandhi, p. 123). This was followed by a fresh *satyagraha* campaign in 1932 and another in 1933, the year in which Rajagopalachari's link with Gandhi was buttressed by the marriage of his youngest daughter, Lakshmi, to Gandhi's youngest son, Devadas.

In the mid-1930s, Rajagopalachari played a major role in a switch in Congress strategy from *satyagraha* to measured cooperation with the Raj's political reforms. After elections held in the first half of 1937, Congress ministries took office in eight provinces, and Rajagopalachari found himself prime minister of the extensive Madras presidency, stretching from the Bay of Bengal to the Arabian Sea.

British civilian and police officers who had earlier monitored, curbed, or jailed Rajagopalachari were now his subordinates, though the British governor of Madras, Lord Erskine, held reserve powers and could block or even remove his premier. Rajagopalachari charmed the officers and also the governor, who, however, thought that his premier, radical in some areas but conservative in others, was "an odd mixture" whose "main object in life" seemed to be to "get India back to what it was in the days of King Asoka" (Gandhi, p. 179).

Rajagopalachari's Madras ministry was doing very well and had entered its third year in office when Adolf Hitler attacked Poland in September 1939 and the viceroy, Lord Linlithgow, declared that India too was at war with Germany. When Congress's plea for a commitment of Indian independence at the end of the war was turned down, all its ministries, including Rajagopalachari's, resigned.

The Postwar Years: Nationalism and Independence

The war had strengthened nationalist urges among the British and in the Congress, and also in the Muslim League, which, in March 1940, demanded the separation, as Pakistan, of the subcontinent's Muslim-majority areas. After Japan's sweep in 1941 and 1942 in the Pacific and Southeast Asia, Rajagopalachari concluded that the Congress could not fight the British, the League, and the Japanese at the same time.

He did not join the Gandhi-led Quit India stir of 1942. Inviting the League to stand alongside the Congress in its bid for independence, he asked the Congress, on its part, to concede that contiguous Muslim-majority districts in India's Northwest and East could separate after independence, if opting out was desired by their populations.

In the nationalistic heat of 1942, when Rajagopalachari's Pakistan "formula" was first aired, it was dismissed as traitorous by many in the Congress and rejected as "moth-eaten" by Mohammad Ali Jinnah, the League president. Yet that formula formed the basis of the partition to which, five years later, the Congress, the League, and the British would agree.

Well before Rajagopalachari took his stand over Quit India, popular opinion and Gandhi himself had determined the question of "succession" in favor of Jawaharlal Nehru. Yet the Congress needed his talents. In the summer of 1946, the party summoned him for negotiations with the Cabinet Mission that had arrived from London; in September of that year he became a Congress minister in the interim government formed as a prelude to a transfer of power to Indian hands.

Governor-general. When, on 15 August 1947, independence arrived, preceded the previous day by the creation of Pakistan, Rajagopalachari became the governor of Bengal's western half; East Bengal had gone to Pakistan. The following summer, he succeeded Lord Mountbatten as free India's governor-general; his is the last—and the only Indian—name in a line of governors-general starting in the eighteenth century with Warren Hastings. It was only in protocol, and not in political power, that Rajagopalachari ranked above Prime Minister Nehru and Deputy Prime Minister Sardar Vallabhbhai Patel. Yet he wielded significant influence as a head of state who was also a founding figure of the Gandhi-led independence movement.

Closer, on questions involving India's Muslims, to Nehru than to Patel, who was also the home or interior minister, yet closer to Patel on economic issues, Rajagopalachari seemed to be the preference of both Nehru and Patel for selection as India's first president when, in January 1950, India became a republic. But rivalry in the Nehru-Patel relationship as well as lingering grievance inside the Congress over Rajagopalachari's 1942 stand came in the way, and it was Rajendra Prasad, a lawyer and veteran congressman from Bihar, who became India's first president. Rajagopalachari returned to Madras. In less than six months, however, invited by both Nehru and Patel—each of whom saw Rajagopalachari as a counterweight against the other—he was in the Indian capital again, as minister without portfolio. After Patel's death in December 1950, Nehru asked Rajagopalachari to take over the key department of Home.

Dealing with a Communist insurgency in some of South India's Telugu districts was one of Rajagopalachari's major tasks as home minister, but Patel's death had reduced Nehru's need for Rajagopalachari, who retired to Madras in November 1951. However, a political crisis in the southern province following elections held in early 1952 brought Rajagopalachari back as the chief minister of Madras. Refusing to contest an election, he ran the state government from a nominated seat in the upper house of the Madras legislature.

The arrangement was hardly democratic, yet Rajagopalachari seemed again to be doing very well as chief minister when, two years later, his educational policy forced him out of office. To double the number of pupils in the state's schools, and also in the belief that parents would impart skills in rural crafts to their children, he proposed a halving of school hours and an emphasis on learning crafts. Political opponents portrayed the policy as a Brahman's device to perpetuate the caste system, and Congress legislators asked for its abandonment, but Rajagopalachari, who never denied charges of stubbornness, preferred to leave. Within a few weeks, Kumaraswami Kamaraj, the new chief minister, withdrew the policy. By this time, Rajagopalachari was immersed in his writings. (His *Mahābhārata*, written in the 1940s, had been published in 1951.)

The 1950s and Beyond

In the late 1950s, after a socialist agenda had added to Nehru's continuing popularity, Rajagopalachari declared that bureaucrats would be disastrous in running businesses, and he attacked a proposal for joint ownership of cropland as being "as bad for the farm as polygamy is for the family" (*Swarajya*, Madras, 14 February 1959). It was "not an idea born of experience or thought" and tried only in countries "where personal liberty is absent and forced labour is commandeered" (*Hindu*, Madras, 6 January 1959).

In the summer of 1959—supported by, among others, Minoo Masani, a former socialist from Bombay, and N. G. Ranga, a peasants' leader from Andhra—Rajagopalachari, who had turned eighty some months earlier, launched a new political party, Swatantra (Freedom). He also coined, for a state-controlled economy, the pejorative expression, "Licence-Permit Raj." While enthusing many with its platform of an open economy and individual rights, Swatantra faced long odds in a land where the vast majority were poor, and where Nehru (and later his daughter Indira Gandhi, who championed socialism for much of her career as prime minister) enjoyed a large and seemingly unquestioning following. Confident, however, of his understanding of economics and of human nature, Rajagopalachari asserted in 1971, within six weeks of a bitter electoral defeat at the hands of Indira Gandhi, that Swatantra's policies were "bound to become the government's policies and programs, if not now, some years hence" (*Swarajya*, Madras, 1 May 1971). This prediction was offered twenty years before India's embrace of liberalization.

One of the first Indians to be publicly troubled by China's policies regarding Tibet and by what he saw as China's hopes of dominance in Asia, Rajagopalachari would nonetheless write in 1969, long before China's economy showed signs of booming, that "the industriousness of the Chinese people, their piety and their adherence to the rules of conduct laid down by Confucius have not ceased to be on account of the black shadow of Communism now upon them. These will shine again." (*Swarajya*, Madras, 24 May 1969).

Opposing nuclear weapons. From the end of 1954, when the *New York Times* published in full a 1,300-word letter from him on the subject, Rajagopalachari became known as one of the world's leading opponents of the nuclear weaponry, as well as its chief Indian foe. Asking for the initiation of nuclear disarmament, his *Times* piece said: "Let either America or Russia begin. . . . Indeed, she who has committed the mistake first is duty bound to begin now, not as a penalty but as a noble privilege" (Gandhi, p. 359).

Meeting visiting Soviet leaders Nikita Krushchev and Nikolai Bulganin at the end of 1955, Rajagopalachari asked them to give up nuclear weapons unilaterally. They said they could not, but added that the Soviet Union would accept a joint renunciation. Six years later, when the Soviet Union exploded a 50-megaton bomb, Rajagopalachari asked Premier Nehru to "ostracize" the Soviet Union. When the United States scheduled retaliatory tests in a portion of the Pacific, Rajagopalachari went a step further, endorsing the suggestion of Bertrand Russell that in protest India should send a ship to the designated waters. Rajagopalachari told Nehru that he would go himself on any Indian ship as a "resister." Nehru was unresponsive.

In 1962, when he was eighty-four, Rajagopalachari made his first trip outside South Asia, flying to the United States in a bid to persuade President John F. Kennedy to abandon nuclear testing. The meeting in the White House went beyond the allotted twenty-five minutes to about an hour and was preceded by an eighty-minute meeting with a team led by William Foster, head of the U.S. Disarmament Agency. On his way back to India, Rajagopalachari met with Pope John XXIII in

Rome, urging him to make a formal plea against further testing.

Whether or not at Rajagopalachari's urging, the next papal encyclical included just such a plea, and at the end of July 1963, the United States, the Soviet Union, and Great Britain agreed on a test ban treaty. In a letter that he wrote to Rajagopalachari on 9 August 1963, Chester Bowles, the U.S. ambassador to India, said that the administration would defend the treaty in the Senate, a "persistence," added Bowles, that was "in no small measure due to your eloquent plea for just such a step as this . . . during your visit" (Gandhi, p. 400).

India-Pakistan relations. During the twenty-five years following the gory birth of free India and Pakistan, and the related beginning of the India-Pakistan dispute over Kashmir, no one strove harder than Rajagopalachari to normalize relations between the two South Asian neighbors. In private letters and public statements, he asked successive Indian prime ministers and their Pakistani counterparts to find a rapprochement; he tried ceaselessly to influence Indian public opinion along similar lines; and three weeks before his death, in the last piece he ever wrote, he called for a fresh "summit meeting as soon as possible" to take the accord that Indira Gandhi and Pakistan's leader, Zulfikar Ali Bhutto, had earlier reached in Simla "to its true fulfillment" (*Swarajya*, 9 December 1972).

The Later Years

A politician who both enjoyed and scorned power, Rajagopalachari seemed to embody other contradictions as well. Thus, while dismissing theories of nuclear deterrence, he defended capital punishment; while keeping an austere, almost bare, home for himself and his children, he called for free enterprise to banish Indian poverty. In some ways the inconsistencies added to his appeal.

Whether written or spoken, his words sparkled. Lionel Fielden, an English friend whose cousins had called on Rajagopalachari in 1962, wrote to him that "they—like me—thought you by far the most interesting and lively man in all India," much more so, Fielden added, than Nehru. Rajagopalachari answered that if Fielden's cousins "found me worthy of the time they gave me," it was perhaps because unlike Nehru, "who is big and too conscious and anxious about it, I don't care and let go" (Gandhi, p. 388).

The sparkle (some of it captured in Monica Felton's *I Meet Rajaji*) was joined to an attractive modesty. When, in 1950, Nehru as well as New Delhi–based diplomats referred to his success, Rajagopalachari, who was about to leave as governor-general, replied: "The Prime Minister says I have done very well and many of you, my friends of the diplomatic corps, have been saying the same thing, before me at any rate—I do not know what you have said in my absence. What is the secret? I am a simple fellow. I do not hate anybody" (*Hindustan Times*, 26 January 1950).

A lifelong student of religion in general and Hinduism in particular, Rajagopalachari claimed in 1966 that "as long as there is suffering in the world, as long as there is the great curiosity to unravel truth, as long as men and women have some intense desire to be fulfilled, as long as there is wisdom in this world, the future of religion is assured" (Gandhi, p. 429).

His understanding of Hinduism, offered in his studies of the Gītā and the Upanishads and in his comment-laden renderings of the Rāmāyaṇa and the Mahābhārata, was of an ancient perspective that remained valid for modern times, and he felt that "the children of the rishis (sages) of the Upanishads have a mission for the world" (*Swarajya*, 2 December 1972). Yet he disavowed any wish "to plead that the Gita is better or fuller than any other scriptures" (Gandhi, p. 429), and his respect for other religions and their followers was striking.

Writings

Apart from the prose renderings of the epics, Rajagopalachari's body of work includes, among other texts, commentaries on the Bhagavad Gītā and the Upanishads, a translation in English verse of the Tamil Rāmāyaṇa of Kamban, about three dozen short stories, and articles (in English and Tamil) published during a period of nearly six decades. All his short stories were written first in Tamil; all their characters are from rural South India. Basing his opinion largely on the short stories, the scholar K. R. Srinivasa Iyengar places Rajagopalachari among "the masters and makers of modern Tamil prose" (Gandhi, p. 431). The Sahitya Akademi (India's Academy of Letters) chose his version of the Rāmāyaṇa as "the best work in Tamil in 1955–1957" (Gandhi, p. 386).

A stream of political writing, often pungent and always trenchant, also flowed from his pen, both before and after independence—much of it in Gandhi's journals, which he at times edited (*Young India* and *Harijan*), and later in the weeklies that his associates published in Madras, *Swarajya* (English) and *Kalki* (Tamil). Often, however, his columns looked at a world beyond politics and at events outside India, offering urbane reflection and acute observation. They also included insightful, concise, and graceful obituaries of political and non-political contemporaries; because of his long life, Rajagopalachari would write many.

Rajmohan Gandhi

See also **Gandhi, Mahatma M. K.; Nehru, Jawaharlal; Patel, Sardar Vallabhbhai**

BIBLIOGRAPHY

Chatterjee, Bimanesh. *Thousand Days with Rajaji.* New Delhi: Affiliated East-West, 1973.

Felton, Monica. *I Meet Rajaji.* London: Macmillan, 1962.

Gandhi, Rajmohan. *Rajaji: A Life.* New Delhi: Penguin, 1997.

Iyengar, Masti V. *Rajaji.* Mumbai: Bharatiya Vidya Bhavan, 1975.

Rajagopalachari, Chakravarti. *Upanishads.* New Delhi: Hindustan Times, 1937. An overview of early Hindu doctrines.

———. *A Jail Diary.* Chennai: Rochouse, 1941. A 1921–1922 diary written in Vellore Jail.

———. *Ambedkar Refuted.* Mumbai: Hind Kitabs, 1946. A defense of the Congress's stand on the "untouchables."

———. *Mankind Protests.* New Delhi: All India Peace Council, 1957. On nuclear disarmament.

———. *Rajaji's Speeches.* Mumbai: Bharatiya Vidya Bhavan, 1958.

Sitaramayya, Pattabhi. *History of the Indian National Congress.* Mumbai: Padma, 1947.

RAJASTHAN. *See* **Geography.**

RAJ, BRITISH, PRE-BRITISH, AND PRINCELY. *See* **History and Historiography.**

RAJNEESH, OSHO *(1931–1990), controversial spiritual leader.* Born to Jain parents in the small town of Kuchwara in central India, Rajneesh's original name was Chandra Mohan; he changed it to Osho toward the end of his life, referring to "oceanic experience," a term used by William James. He became a professor of philosophy early in life and claimed to have attained enlightenment on 21 March 1953. He regarded himself as a follower of no particular religion. Initially he delivered lectures in Mumbai (Bombay), but then moved to Pune in 1974, where he established an ashram at Koregaon Park. Many European and American disciples were attracted by him. His message of sexual liberation was praised by them but criticized by conservative Indians. In 1981 he left India for the United States for medical treatment. He then also transplanted his ashram, and his devotees acquired Big Muddy Ranch at Antelope, Oregon. Rajneesh settled there, and the place became known as Rajneeshpuram. He now remained silent for most of the time; most of the talking was done for him by his ardent disciple Sheela Silverman, who predicted in 1983 that the world would be destroyed sometime between 1988 and 1999. Her autocratic behavior annoyed the neighbors of Rajneeshpuram, and the numerous complaints finally drove him to resettle in North Carolina in 1986. He was imprisoned there, charged with transgression of the immigration laws. His sentence was suspended on the condition that he leave the United States. In 1987 he returned to India, once more settling in Pune, where he died in 1990.

Osho Rajneesh. Here photographed in the 1980s, during the height of his popularity when his cult numbered some 200,000 members worldwide, Rajneesh lived—without compunction—a lavish life in the United States. JP LAFFONT / SYGMA / CORBIS.

Rajneesh was a controversial figure throughout his public life. His disciples led frugal lives, giving him all their money, but he and his secretaries lived in luxury. The twenty-seven Rolls-Royces donated to him by rich followers were only the most visible signs of his luxurious lifestyle. Most of his disciples came from Western countries, and he catered to their spiritual needs. Western thought and religion no longer helped them to overcome feelings of emptiness and frustration, so they turned to this self-confident guru, who told them how to conduct their lives.

Dietmar Rothermund

BIBLIOGRAPHY

Aveling, Harry, ed. *Osho Rajneesh and His Disciples: Some Western Perceptions.* Delhi: Motilal Banarsidass, 1999.

Carter, Lewis F. *Charisma and Control in Rajneeshpuram: The Role of Shared Values in the Creation of a Community.* Cambridge, U.K.: Cambridge University Press, 1990.

Prasad, Ram Chandra. *Rajneesh, the Mystic of Feeling: A Study in Rajneesh's Religion of Experience.* Delhi: Motilal Banarsidass, 1978.

Strelley, Kate. *The Ultimate Game: The Rise and Fall of Bhagwan Shree Rajneesh.* San Francisco: Harper & Row, 1987.

RAJPUT (WESTERN, CENTRAL, AND HILL) PAINTING The history of painting in the Indian subcontinent has ancient origins with the first expressions of artistic creativity found in scenes depicted on prehistoric caves. In the early historic period, excavated Buddhist caves were embellished with beautiful murals. The first manuscripts in the region were produced on prepared palm leaves and years later on paper. Among the most vibrantly expressive and numerous paintings were those produced for the Rajput rulers of western, central, and northern India. These works consisted of illustrated manuscripts and poetic sets, as well as elaborate wall paintings on palace walls.

Cave Paintings: Early Artistic Expressions in South Asia

Due to their ephemeral nature, ancient narrative or ritual scenes painted on prepared animal or vegetal media would have little chance of survival; consequently, for the pre- and early historic periods, paintings found in rock shelters or excavated caves provide rare and invaluable information about the formative period of two-dimensional artistic representation in South Asia. Among the earliest examples are those found within rock shelters at Bhimbetka in Madhya Pradesh, where excavations revealed paintings ranging from the Upper Paleolithic (40,000–15,000 B.P.) to the Mesolithic (15,000 B.P.–8,500 B.C.) periods. The Upper Paleolithic paintings, tentatively dated to circa 40,000 B.C., contain scenes portraying humans dancing or hunting quadrupeds, delineated in green and red mineral pigments. By the Mesolithic period, the Bhimbetka paintings display expanded compositions that may represent more complex societal developments. Humans were now depicted as engaging in multiple aspects of the life cycle, such as pregnancy, childbirth, and funereal ceremonies. Ritual performances and allusions to mother and animal cults are indicated by depictions of costumed male and female dancers, numerous female figures, and monumentally drawn naturalistic or composite animals.

The caves at Ajanta in Maharashtra provide the most extensive evidence of artistic production in the early historic period. Scholars date the first excavations at Ajanta to about 50 B.C. to A.D. 100, culminating in the twenty or more marvelously carved and painted rock-cut Buddhist shrines produced particularly under patronage of the Vakataka ruler Harisena (reigned c. 460–477). Only traces remain of the very earliest paintings, as they were either damaged or obscured by subsequent paint layers. The Ajanta artists produced beautifully colored wall and ceiling decorations in an apparent cohesive visual program that included geometrical designs and a profusion of naturalistically rendered figural and vegetal decoration. To prepare the rock surface for painting, layers of cow dung, mud, straw, and a final coating of lime plaster were applied. Pigments, primarily from mineral sources, were adhered with a binding material and applied with animal-hair brushes. When the composition was complete, artists burnished the surface to yield a lustrous surface. Among the most fascinating and gracefully rendered works were illustrations representing episodes of the Buddha's previous lives (*jātaka*). Aside from their inherent high aesthetic and narrative qualities, the *jātaka* compositions provide a veritable compendium of information about contemporary costumes, textiles, and architecture. There is a gap of many centuries in the artistic record after the magnificent Ajanta paintings, and only fragments, such as those found in the sixth-century caves at Badami in Karnataka and the mid-eighth-century paintings on the Kailasha Temple at Ellora in Maharashtra, give evidence of continued artistic activity through the centuries.

Painting on Palm Leaf and Paper: A.D. 1000–1550

Very few early manuscripts have survived from the Indian subcontinent, with the exception of a few examples, which include a cache of sixth- to tenth-century birch bark, palm leaf, and paper manuscripts found during excavations of a Buddhist site at Gilgit, Pakistan (now in New Delhi's National Archives and other collections). However, palm-leaf manuscripts with elaborately painted wooden covers datable to the early eleventh century to the thirteenth century survive from the eastern part of the subcontinent (particularly Bihar and Bengal); they were apparently produced for pious Buddhist patrons and donated to monastic libraries.

Illustrations of the Buddha, *bodhisattva*s, and Tantric Buddhist deities used a limited palette that featured tones of yellow, red, blue, green, and white. These compositions were delineated in a stylized and linear fashion, with flatly rendered as well as naturalistically modeled figural types that varied in execution between individual manuscripts. As the depiction of Buddhist teachers and deities was of primary importance, architecture and foliage appear in these compositions predominantly as framing devices or as decorative embellishment. The only incidence of narrative subjects is found in *Ashtasahasrika Prajnaparamita* manuscripts, which include depictions of episodes in the Buddha's life. As exemplified in folio (c. 1150) from a copy of the manuscript produced in Bihar (Los Angeles County Museum of Art), in the hand of an accomplished artist, these subjects could be transformed into elegantly portrayed vignettes in miniature.

There is evidence that paper was manufactured as early as the sixth century in the northwest Himalayan regions, and from the twelfth century in Nepal; however, it was not used as the primary medium for manuscript production until the early thirteenth century, when Turkic and Afghan Muslim rulers gained suzerainty over northern regions of the subcontinent. Paper was imported to western India from the Middle East as early as the eleventh century, and records attest to the establishment of a paper mill in Kashmir in the fifteenth century. Some of the earliest examples of paper used as a medium for manuscript production are found in mid-fourteenth-century copies of Jain religious texts, such as the Kalpa Sūtra (Book of Ritual) and the Kalakacharyakatha (Story of the monk Kalaka), produced in western India. Emulating the format of earlier palm-leaf manuscripts, these folios were rectangular, and, perhaps to allow for larger and more complex compositions, the shape was modified by increasing the folio height. Further developments included an abandonment of pierced holes that were replaced by red or gold circles, or ornamented medallions. Instead of binding a text with a cord threaded through the folios, as was the tradition with earlier palm-leaf manuscripts, loose manuscript pages were gathered together and placed between cardboard and cloth covers.

All elements of these narrative compositions were rendered in a flat, linear manner using a palette of brilliant primary colors, particularly crimson and ultramarine, enlivened by white and gold accents. Figures were highly stylized and display purposefully distorted or idiosyncratic features. One of the most distinct features of this type is the representation of a projecting, or "farther," eye in three-quarter profiles, an artistic convention that continued in some western Indian paintings through the sixteenth century. An interesting exception to this mode of representation is seen in Kalakacharyakatha manuscripts, in which foreigners were differentiated by the absence of a farther eye and by a different skin tonality, and were clothed in distinctive regional costume. Both figural types are shown within the same illustration in a folio dated to about 1400 from western India, depicting the Jain monk Kalaka discussing the abduction of his sister with the Central Asian Sahi king and a retainer (Mumbai, Chhatrapati Shivaji Maharaj Vastu Sangrahalaya). These illustrations are historically important, as they provide visual evidence of cultural contacts between indigenous populations and foreigners during a period when much of the northern and central regions of the subcontinent had come under the rule of Turco-Afghan sultans. Elements of artistic exchange during this period can also be seen in the similar use of coloration and vegetal or geometric motifs to embellish manuscript folios for Jain and Muslim patrons, as exemplified in a mid-fifteenth-century Qur'an from the library of Mahmud Shah I Bigarha, the sultan of Gujarat (r. 1459–1511). Although naturalism is eclipsed in favor of representations in which gestures and symbols convey the narrative, these paintings reveal a brilliant use of decorative ornamentation (particularly evident in the representation of textiles), which visually enlivens the folios.

The format, figural, and decorative elements of these manuscripts were not restricted solely to Jain manuscripts, as evidenced in a folio of about 1450 from a copy of the Hindu text, Balagopalastuti (Eulogy of the Child Cowherd [Krishna]), made in Gujarat or Rajasthan, which depicts Krishna dancing with the *gopi*s in Vrindavan (Los Angeles County Museum or Art), and in a fifteenth-century folio from a Durgāsaptashati (Seven hundred verses in praise of Durgā) portraying the multi-armed Durgā on her leonine mount battling demons (Cambridge, Mass., Harvard University Art Museums).

One of the classic Sanskrit Hindu texts most often illustrated was the tenth chapter of the Bhāgavata Purāṇa (Story of the great lord [Vishnu]) which recounts the life of Krishna, the most beloved of Vishnu's *avatāra*s. Among the earliest extant examples of the text is a now dispersed copy that may have been produced around 1520–1530 in the Delhi-Agra region. Illustrated folios from this text belong to a group of religious and secular texts produced for Hindu, Jain, and Muslim patrons described as the *Chaurapanchasika* group, as they are stylistically related to a 1550–1560 copy of the *Chaurapanchashika* (Fifty stanzas of a love thief) by the early twelfth-century poet Bilhana (Gujarat, Ahmedabad, Culture Centre). This group of works is related to the traditional western Indian paintings described above, and they were typically rendered with a limited palette of strong, brilliant colors applied in flat, unmodulated areas. Figures were often rendered in exaggerated, angular poses with faces rendered in profile with large almond-shaped eyes. Costume details often included a distinctive turban (*kulah*), and garments that terminate in spiky points or with fan-tailed flourishes. As illustrating the narrative elements of the story was of utmost importance, representations of architecture and foliage were highly stylized and served primarily to enhance the narrative and provide a visual setting. Illustrated works belonging to this group provide an insight into the dominant painting style in North India in the early to mid-sixteenth century. The prevalence of the *Chaurapanchashika* stylistic elements is evident in folios from a Mughal copy of the *Tutinama* (Stories of a parrot, c. 1560–1565, Cleveland Museum of Art) and indicates the importance of indigenous artistic traditions in the formation and spread of the early Mughal style.

The Rajputs

For centuries, the Rajputs (*raja putra*, or "son of a king"), said to be descendants of warrior clans, ruled much of the northern and central parts of the Indian subcontinent. Although the origins of these clans are unknown, some scholars believe that they may have migrated from Central Asia in the sixth and seventh centuries, over time adopting the status of the warrior class to legitimize their place within the Hindu social system. By the ninth and tenth centuries, the Rajput clans had risen to political prominence and had proclaimed independent dynasties. Renowned for chivalry and valor on the battlefield, their combative spirit often led to internecine warfare, which undermined Rajput solidarity and ultimately made them vulnerable to invasions of various Turkic and Afghan groups who had begun to encroach upon Rajput territories in the thirteenth century. The most significant of these foreign intruders were the Central Asian Mughals, who established themselves as a dominant power under the leadership of Zahir al-Din Muhammad, Babur (r. 1526–1530). By the time of the emperor Akbar's death (r. 1556–1605), most of the Rajput rulers had submitted to Mughal rule either voluntarily or by force, many making political and marital alliances to ensure Mughal beneficence.

Subjects for Illustration

Paintings and manuscripts produced in the Rajput courts before the seventeenth century depicted religious subjects such as the epic Mahābhārata (The great descendants of Bharata), the Rāmāyaṇa (Story of Rāma), and as noted above, the Bhāgavata Purāṇa. Stimulated by periodic upsurges in the devotional (*bhakti*) strand of the Hindu religion, texts and poems in Sanskrit and vernacular languages gained popularity, such as the Gītā Govinda (Song of the Herdsman) composed in Sanskrit by the twelfth-century poet Jayadeva, which describes the love of Krishna and Rādhā as a metaphor for the union of the individual with the divine.

A vast corpus of love literature inspired Rajput artistic interpretation, including the *Rasikapriya* (Connoisseur's delight), a sixteenth-century Hindi poem by Keshavdas that analyzes the stages of love using the analogy of the love between Krishna and Rādhā. Keshavdas also wrote the *Kavipriya* (Poet's favorite), based on the *Baramasa* (twelve months) genre of poetry that describes the interrelationship of human love through the changing seasons. Other poetic works favored for illustration were those in which gods and mortals were characterized as personifications of various romantic situations or embodiments of heroic behavior. The *Rasamanjari* (Bouquet of delight) by the fourteenth-century poet Bhanudatta, one of the best-known Sanskrit works in this genre, categorizes and describes the various types of romantic heroes (*nayaka*) and heroines (*nayika*) according to their age, personalities, and circumstances. Numerous *Rāgāmalā* (Garland of melodies) series were produced for both Rajput and Mughal patrons. These visualizations of classical Indian musical modes (*rāgas*), accompanied by poetic verse, combined aspects of religion, love, and music. Each *rāga* is associated with a specific season and time of day, and personifies characteristics of love or heroic behavior.

With the increasing influence of Mughal artistic techniques and subjects during the seventeenth century, including naturalistic shading, subtly modulated colors, and secular subject matter, many Rajput artists incorporated these new elements into their works. Emulating Mughal royal portraiture, Rajput rulers were often depicted in hierarchical compositions depicting court gatherings or equestrian scenes. Blending ancient Indic and Mughal concepts of kingship, painters included halos around the heads of rulers, a symbol of their role as regents of the gods.

By the late eighteenth century, the need for extensive military campaigns had diminished, and elaborate hunts became an important outlet for the vital martial Rajput spirit. Perhaps another reflection of this time of relative peace and stability are the humorous and bawdy scenes of Rajput rulers presiding over drunken parties or dallying in lush gardens and pavilions with beautiful ladies of the court. With the increasing presence of the British, the influence of photography and European modes of artistic representation added yet another facet to the ever responsive and adaptive Rajput painters and their works.

Rajput Painting in Central and Western India

Malwa. Works from the Malwa, a region that roughly corresponds to the modern state of Madhya Pradesh, can be characterized as the most artistically conservative of the Rajput styles. Early paintings associated with the region, from about the first decade of the sixteenth century, include works painted in the Indo-Persian style prevalent in the Sultanate period. During the second quarter of the seventeenth century, a style emerged that blended elements of indigenous western Indian and *Chaurapanchashika* paintings. The earliest dated paintings from this period, from a dispersed 1634 *Rasikapriya* series, feature unmodulated flat expanses of color and the use of a strong outline to delineate figural, architectural, and foliate elements. In many of these works, the artists used a brilliant juxtaposition of red, green, blue, yellow, and black coloration to enhance the dramatic visual impact of a composition. Women were usually portrayed wearing gaily colored skirts (particularly with horizontal stripes), and representations of architecture and foliage scenes, though highly schematized, were enlivened by the inclusion of preening peacocks or scampering monkeys.

About the mid-seventeenth century, a modified and more refined Malwa style was introduced, perhaps influenced by Mughal works, that included a more subtle palette with mauve and pink tones blended with other hues. This style is most clearly evident in two dispersed manuscripts of the *Amarushataka* (One hundred verses of Amaru), dated 1652 and about 1680, a text that features the romantic exploits of heroes and heroines. Distinctive to both sets is a decorative floral scroll placed at the bottom of the illustrated folios. By the eighteenth century, the distinctive Malwa artistic tradition appears to have all but disappeared, perhaps replaced by other styles, or perhaps due to a lack of patronage during a time of political turbulence. Traces of Malwa style can be observed in works produced at Datia and other central Indian centers, where aspects of Malwa-type compositions and format were apparently appropriated and combined with other artistic elements.

Mewar. With the increasingly close interaction of the Rajput clans with the Mughals, many Rajput rulers emulated Mughal court fashions, customs, and institutions such as in Bikaner, Amber, and Bundi. Others rulers, however, resisted Mughal political and cultural hegemony, as exemplified by the Mewar kings, who did not succumb to the Mughals until 1615. Although the Mewar *rana*s were patrons of the arts, the earliest dated example of royal patronage is a *Rāgāmalā* series made at Chawand, the temporary Mewar capital during the reign of Rana Amar Singh I (r. 1597–1620). The now-dispersed set was made by Nasir al-Din, a Muslim artist working in a lively style with elements reminiscent of *Chaurapanchashika* works.

After the capitulation of Mewar to the Mughals, Karan Singh (r. 1620–1628), then prince, was required to spend time in residence at the Mughal court, was accorded great respect and privileges, and became a close friend of Shah Jahan (r. 1628–1658), the future Mughal emperor. There are no works that can be specifically ascribed to Karan Singh's patronage, and so the relationship of Mughal and Mewar painting remains unclear during this period. During the reign of Maharana Jagat Singh I (r. 1628–1655), a number of extant works indicate a flourishing of artistic production at the Mewar court at Udaipur. Of particular interest are the works of Sahib al-Din, Jagat Singh's senior artist, including a 1628 *Rāgāmalā* series and manuscripts with Vaishnavite themes, such as a 1629 Gītā Govinda manuscript, a 1648 Bhāgavata Purāṇa, and his collaborative work on a magnificent multivolume illustrated Rāmāyaṇa in 1650–1652. Sahib al-Din's paintings indicate that at some point he was trained in the popular Mughal style prevalent in many Rajput centers, but the specific method of transmission of these techniques is unknown. Some of his early works present an innovative use of elements borrowed from Mughal works, including a taller page format, a subtle outlining of figural elements that are rendered more naturalistically, and a softer palette. In later works attributed to Sahib al-Din, such as a *Rasikapriya* series painted about 1630–1635 (Udaipur, Government Museum), there is a return to more traditional brighter coloration, now interpreted with fresh and brilliant tones, and compositional schemes using both synoptic and framing elements to portray narrative episodes.

Works produced during the late seventeenth century were primarily reformulations or copies of earlier paintings, following the style of Sahib al-Din, but without his inventiveness in color and composition. In emulation of Mughal court compositions, royal portraiture was a new innovation added to the Mewar artistic repertoire. These works included depictions of maharanas riding horses, accompanied by attendants hurriedly shuffling along on foot, in formal meetings with courtiers or clansfolk, and enthroned, observing elephant fights and other amusements.

Under Maharana Amar Singh II (r. 1698–1710), a number of portrait scenes were produced by an anonymous artist who experimented with a stippled treatment similar to the *nim qalam* (half-brush) technique sometimes employed by early seventeenth century Mughal and Deccani artists to produce a grisaille effect that emulated the appearance of European engravings. During this time, a larger format was introduced, providing more room for complex compositions that afforded bird's eye or topographic views, such as the portrayal of Amar Singh celebrating the spring festival of Holi with his nobles within the lush vegetation of the royal Sarvaritu Vilas garden (c. 1708–1710, Melbourne, National Gallery of Victoria).

Other paintings document the multifarious activities of rulers such as Maharanas Sangram Singh II (r. 1710–1734) and Jagat Singh II (r. 1734–1751). These large compositions were filled with vignettes of the maharana and his companions, portrayed in consecutive narrative, as exemplified in a 1749 painting by the artist Jiva depicting Jagat Singh in sequences of a lakeside tiger shoot (San Diego Museum of Art). The verso side of these works often include inscriptions detailing the artists' names, the date and place of the activity portrayed, and the participants.

By the early eighteenth century, a decline in patronage at Udaipur resulted in the departure of a number of artists, who sought employment at the courts of Mewar nobles. At Deogarh, the artist Bakhta and his son Chokha, and Chokha's son Baijnath, continued to produce works of the highest quality, surpassing those done in Udaipur itself. Chokha worked for both Maharana Bhim Singh (r. 1778–1828) at Udaipur and Gokul Das, the *rawat* of Deogarh, and interpreted court promenades, meetings, and intimate moments with observational insight, creating an atmosphere of dreamy sensuality.

During this period, the increased presence of foreigners is indicated in many Rajput paintings, as in the 1817 portrait (attributed to Chokha) of Lieutenant-Colonel James Tod, the British political agent, riding an elephant (London, Victoria and Albert Museum) and an 1825 painting (attributed to Ghasi) representing Maharana Bhim Singh formally receiving Sir Charles Metcalf and his entourage (Udaipur, City Palace Museum). Other compositions included fanciful portraits of Europeans that may have been inspired by imported prints. With the arrival of professional and amateur British watercolor artists, such as William Carpenter, who arrived at the court of Maharana Sarup Singh (r. 1842–1861) in Udaipur in 1851, Mewar artists were exposed to new techniques and modes of representation. From this period to the reign of Maharana Fateh Singh (r. 1885–1930), the last of the great Mewar rulers, two styles continued to be produced for the royal court: a modified version of the earlier court reportage genre, and European-style portraits in oil on canvas. With the advent of photography, a new form of expression for royal portraiture was introduced. Although some artists introduced photographic realism into their portraits, others abandoned their brushes and pigments entirely to take up the new medium.

Marwar. The Marwar region occupies much of the western part of the modern state of Rajasthan, and was ruled for centuries by the Rathor Rajput clan from their capital at Jodhpur. One of the only pre-Mughal works from Marwar that has come to light is a *Rāgāmalā* series dated 1623, produced by Pandit Virji in the provincial town of Pali. Its horizontal format and illustrative style indicates that the artist may have been influenced by earlier Jain and other western Indian models. Throughout the early to mid-seventeenth century, works from Marwar are distinguished by varied but conservative styles related to the earlier traditions, as well as those of contemporary Mewar and Malwa. Influences from Malwa-style painting is particularly evident in the introduction of a vertical page format and a palette that juxtaposes somber green and brown tones with earthy and brilliant reds.

By the middle of the seventeenth century, the close relationship between the Marwar and Mughal courts is particularly evident in paintings that display Mughalizing subjects and compositions. A number of portraits of Maharaja Gaj Singh (r. 1620–1638) painted by his Mughal-trained artists were based on portraits of Gaj Singh produced by artists at the Mughal court. He is depicted in an idealizing profile, wearing an elegant ensemble, and holding a long sword, befitting a Rajput ruler. Mughal-influenced court scenes continued to be produced under Gaj Singh's son Maharaja Jaswant Singh (r. 1638–1678). Toward the end of his rule, a few works suggest that there were attempts to experiment with stylistic elements, including a resurgence of certain Rajput-style elements combined with Deccani artistic modes, presumably influenced by Jaswant Singh's posting to the Deccan in 1667. This beautiful synthesis of traditions is exemplified in a painting from about 1667–1670, which depicts the maharaja listening to female musicians in a palatial garden within a verdant landscape inspired by Rajput prototypes. Deccani elements appear in the form of a visual play between the boldly patterned carpets and the garden's brilliantly colored flowers.

During the first quarter of the eighteenth century, equestrian portraits, processions, and hunt scenes were added to the repertoire of Jodhpur court painting. The most accomplished artist to emerge from this period was Dalchand, a Mughal-trained artist who worked for Maharaja Abhai Singh (r. 1724–1749). His training in the Mughal court at Delhi is evident in an exquisitely composed and rendered portrait of the enthroned Abhai Singh watching a dance performance (c. 1725, Jodhpur, Mehrangarh Museum Trust). Under Maharaja Ram Singh (r. 1749–1751, 1753–1772), Mughal-type court scenes were still popular; however, human and animal forms were increasingly depicted in a more flat, schematic, and idealized manner. This style was also emulated by artists working at Ghanerao, Nagaur, and other districts, or *thikana*, of Marwar that were ruled by Rathor nobles swearing allegiance and paying tribute to Jodhpur. Characteristic of these compositions are depictions of a maharaja or a senior noble surrounded by members of his court, each man wearing lofty and elaborately wrapped colorful turbans that distinguished their specific clan affiliation.

The tendency toward idealized portraiture was taken to new heights under the enthusiastic patronage of Maharaja Man Singh (r. 1803–1843). Additionally, Man Singh was shown participating in a variety of court activities, including festive ceremonies and in playful dalliance with the women of his court, as in a painting from about

1840 depicting the maharaja riding on a Ferris wheel in the company of his ladies. Man Singh's piety was also documented in numerous paintings in which he is shown meeting with his guru Devnath or members of the Nath sect. These works display an idiosyncratic style developed by Dana Batiram, Bulaki Das, Amar Das, and other senior artists in Man Singh's employ. Characteristic of works from this period is the use of vibrant and rich colors, embellished with a generous application of gold to highlight details. Dramatic landscapes were created with hills and mountains represented by turbulent ripples and fantastic surging forms. Overall, there is a tendency toward using repeated curve or swirling patterns throughout paintings to delineate distinctive scrolling cloud formations, stylized palm fronds, banana trees leaves, the swelling chests of prancing horses and camels in procession, the upturned swing of hems in costumes for both genders, and the representation of arched eyebrows and exaggeratedly elongated and upswept eyes in portraits of men and women.

Under Maharaja Takhat Singh's (r. 1843–1873) patronage, the same style continued to be executed by many of the same artists that had previously worked for Man Singh. Toward the end of Takhat Singh's rule, Eugene Impey, an amateur English photographer, visited Jodhpur and took the first photographic portraits of the maharaja. During the rule of his successor, Maharaja Jaswant Singh II (r. 1873–1895), court painting severely declined in the name of modernity, as the maharaja increasingly preferred the medium of photography to document court life at the Marwar capital.

Amber and Jaipur. Maharaja Prithvi Raj (r. 1503–1527), of the Kachchhwaha Rajput clan ruling at Amber, was a member of the confederacy of Rajputs formed by Rana Sanga of Mewar to fight the Mughal emperor Babur. Years later, his son Maharaja Bharmal (r. 1548–1574) was introduced to Akbar, the young Mughal emperor, and a strong personal and political alliance was forged between the Amber rulers and the Mughals, which lasted for two centuries. The earliest mention of artworks commissioned at Amber is found in biographies of Raja Man Singh I (r. 1589–1614), who was also a senior member of the Mughal court under Akbar and his son Jahangir. These contemporary accounts mention that the walls of Man Singh's palace were painted with folk-story vignettes, *Rāgāmalā* compositions, and depictions of flora and fauna, traces of which still remain.

Maharaja Sawai Jai Singh (r. 1699–1743) continued to maintain close relations with the Mughals and was an enthusiastic patron of art and architecture. Folios from a now dispersed *Rāgāmalā* set, painted about 1709, display static compositions typical of local, more conservative Rajput artistic traditions, but include figural types influenced by Mughal models. In 1727 Sawai Jai Singh moved his capital from Amber to Jaipur and established a large atelier of artists, papermakers, and bookbinders who were recruited locally and from the Mughal centers at Delhi and Agra. During his reign, the maharaja amassed a large collection of Mughal, Deccani, and Rajasthani illustrated manuscripts and single folios. The use of Mughal paintings as models for Amber works is evidenced by a nearly identical pair of portraits in the collection of the Los Angeles County Museum of Art. The earlier of the two paintings is a portrait of Maharaja Jai Singh of Amber and Maharana Gaj Singh of Marwar (c. 1638), attributed to the Mughal painter Bichitr. Both rulers share a splendid gold throne set upon an elaborately patterned carpet. Two angels float above and carry an embellished canopy. The later work, made in Amber around 1710, is a portrait of Maharaja Sawai Jai Singh of Amber, seated with Maharana Sangram Singh of Mewar. The compositions of both paintings are the same, although there are differences in execution, as the later Amber work implements a more subdued and dull palette and there is a lack of delicacy and accomplishment in the figural details. The blue and gold border decoration added to both folios matches works that were mounted together in a codex album format in the Amber atelier, and indeed these two folios may have been mounted facing each other in that album.

Painting at Jaipur continued, enthusiastically encouraged by Maharaja Sawai Madho Singh I (r. 1750–1768), and came to full flourish during the reign of Maharaja Sawai Pratap Singh (r. 1778–1803) when his painting workshop grew to include as many as twenty-five painters. Sawai Pratap Singh was a pious devotee of Krishna and must have looked favorably upon a magnificent large painting made in about 1790, depicting Krishna and Rādhā surrounded by concentric circles of *gopi*s who sway in unison to the movements of the great *Rasa lila* dance (Jaipur, Maharaja Sawai Man Singh II Museum). A decline in Jaipur painting occurred during the rule of Maharaja Sawai Ram Singh II (r. 1835–1880) when works were done in a stiff and formulaic manner or were influenced or eclipsed altogether by the medium of photography. An fascinating portrait of Sawai Ram Singh II (c. 1870) depicts the ruler at worship within his private quarters, and is clearly influenced by the type of photographic realism that was practiced in many late nineteenth-century Rajput royal ateliers.

Bundi and Kota. The origins of the Bundi and Kota rulers, members of the Hara Rajput clan, are based on ancient tales of a fantastic weapon-bearing warrior who emerged from a gigantic fire pit. The Bundi ruler Rao Surjan (r. 1554–1585) surrendered the fort at Ranthambhor to the Mughal emperor Akbar in 1569, and thereafter Bundi rulers were accorded special status by the

Mughals. One of the earliest works attributed to Bundi patronage was a *Rāgāmalā* set produced at Chunar, near Varanasi, in 1591. Rao Surjan had been posted as commander of the Chunar fortress in 1575, and his son Rao Bhoj Singh (r. 1585–1606) spent some years there before being assigned to Agra. According to a colophon, the set was made by artists trained in the Mughal atelier, and although no specific patron is named, it has been surmised that the set was made for Bhoj Singh. This set is highly important to the understanding of the influence of Mughal painting on works created at Bundi, and it also indicates the close artistic relationship between Bundi and Kota. A consistency can be observed in the compositional format and stylistic elements used in the Chunar *Rāgāmalā* folios and the seventeenth-century *Rāgāmalā* sets made in Bundi, and later in eighteenth-century Kota *Rāgāmalās*. This continuity, with variations in coloration and details of ornamentation, is quite remarkable when a comparison is made between a folio from the dispersed Chunar set depicting *Vilaval Ragini* (Varanasi, Banaras Hindu University, Bharat Kala Bhavan) and an illustration of the same *ragini* made around 1760 in the Kota workshop (Boston, Museum of Fine Arts).

Wall paintings in the palace of Rao Ratan (r. 1607–1631) at Bundi vividly document the vitality of artworks produced during this period, which include richly colored depictions of Hindu gods and goddesses, and animal combat and hunting scenes set within lush landscapes. During the rule of Bundi by one of Rao Ratan's son, Rao Shatru Sal (r. 1631–1658), the evolution of a more distinct Bundi style emerged, as is particularly evident in portraits of the period, which often depicted figures in full profile, with large oval-shaped heads and pointy noses. In slightly later works, facial features became softened, more refined, and more delicately rendered. Typically, figures were placed against a monochrome background, as in one of the most beautiful works produced in the late eighteenth century at Bundi, which depicts a sympathetic lady-in-waiting attending to a lovesick lady yearning for her lover (Cambridge, Mass., Harvard University Art Museums). The two women are placed against a stark white background where the edges of the palace terrace and the sky almost seamlessly meet. At the very top of the composition, a glowing silver moon illuminates the sky, and a pair of Sarus cranes, said to mate for life, frolic as if to remind the damsel of her lonely status.

In 1631 Rao Madho Singh (r. 1631–1648 at Kota), the second of Rao Ratan's sons, was awarded the territory of Kota by Emperor Shah Jahan for his continued aid to the Mughals. Unfortunately, only a few posthumous portraits of Madho Singh remain, and so his contribution to the early history of Kota painting remains a mystery. Under Rao Jagat Singh (r. 1658–1684), painting at Kota flourished, as indicated by a number of his portraits executed with great subtlety in modeling and coloration. A portrait of Jagat Singh in a garden, surrounded by female attendants (c. 1670), exemplifies Kota works inspired by contemporary Mughal portraiture; it also includes an abundance of floral patterning and varied colors that are evocative of landscapes portrayed by Deccani painters. The inclusion of Deccan-derived artistic elements here should not come as a surprise, as Jagat Singh and many other Rajput nobles spent considerable time waging campaigns against the Deccan sultans in the employ of the Mughals. Some Rajput rulers may have returned home with paintings acquired in the Deccan, or may have brought back Deccani artists (eager for employment after the vanquishment of their sovereigns) to work in the Rajput ateliers. During this time, Kota artists began to produce carefully observed and beautifully delineated studies of animals, particularly elephants, that were shown at play and at combat. These depictions sharply contrast the representation of humans, who are increasingly shown in a formulaic manner, with distinctively rendered large eyes that are ringed by an oval line representing the outer perimeter of the eyelids.

Beginning in the eighteenth century, both Bundi and Kota were subjected to internal intrigues and external turmoil, which included the threat of Maratha raids and interventions by the British. Paintings from both courts during this period convey a sense of escapism and the reluctance of the rulers to face their positions of political vulnerability. One might expect to find, during this period, scenes depicting strategic planning or military drills, but the paintings depict playful vignettes of court activities in which the rulers are shown hunting, gaming, and participating in ceremonies. The most spectacular of these works may represent visualizations of Rajput prowess in the form of magnificent and complex large-scale hunting scenes from Kota. Similar to contemporary works noted above at Mewar, these paintings were often inscribed on the verso with the names of the participants, the date, and the names of the master artists of that period, including Shaykh Taju, Hansraj Joshi, and Chateri Gumani, who produced a portrait in 1784 documenting a lion hunt attended by Maharao Umed Singh I of Kota (r. 1771–1819) and his minister Zalim Singh Jhala (Rajasthan, Rao Madho Singh Trust Museum, Fort Kota).

The last phase of artistic brilliance at Kota was under the patronage of Maharao Ram Singh (r. 1827–1866). Ram Singh was portrayed more often that any other Kota ruler and was shown in all manner of daily activities, including meeting with visiting dignitaries and playing polo with courtiers. One of the most humorous events documented by the eccentric ruler's court artists occurred in 1851, when Ram Singh rode his horse up a ramp to the roof of the Kota palace. The painting is attributed to the artist Namaram and faithfully depicts those present at the event, including courtiers, dancing girls, musicians, and the local British agent, who is shown wearing a blue suit and a top hat (Philadelphia Museum of Art).

Bikaner. Bikaner paintings are among the most lyrical and refined of the Rajput styles and were the product of a synthesis of Rajput, Mughal, and Deccan artistic traditions. Maharaja Karan Singh (r. 1631–1669) is the first documented royal patron of Bikaner painting, and among his atelier were some of the early masters, such as Rukn al-Din and Natthu, who played important roles in the early evolution of the court style. One of the most beautiful of these works was done by ʿAli Raza, a painter originally from Delhi, who produced *Vaikuntha Darshana* (Vision of Vishnu, c. 1650), a painting based on a dream that Karan Singh had of Vishnu and Lakshmī enthroned in their heavenly palace (Varanasi, Banaras Hindu University, Bharat Kala Bhavan). Karan Singh's successor, Maharaja Anup Singh (r. 1669–1698), was a connoisseur who gave great impetus to the creation of artworks, as exemplified in the production of a Bhāgavata Purāṇa manuscript (now dispersed, c. 1675–1700), which presents episodes from Krishna's life in continuous narrative vignettes with delicately rendered figures that appear to float upon the softly toned landscape.

During the reign of Maharaja Sujan Singh (r. 1700–1736), more intimate compositions were produced, rendered in dreamlike tones of pink, purple, and pastel greens, influenced by Sujan Singh's posting to the Deccan, or by artists that may have accompanied him back to Bikaner in 1707. Many of these works can be attributed to the artist Ustad Murad, including a jewel-like painting dated to 1710 depicting a princely youth (perhaps Sujan Singh) and his ladies shooting heron from a terrace (Cambridge, Mass., Harvard University Art Museums). Another work by Ustad Murad was the production of a now dispersed *Baramasa* set painted around 1725. In a folio depicting the month of Jyestha (May–June), Ustad Murad carefully selected a palette of vibrant, glowing colors to evoke the intense heat of this season (Cambridge, Mass., Harvard University Art Museums).

During the mid- to late eighteenth century, Bikaner painting was increasingly influenced by works of art from Jodhpur and Jaipur, and the migration of artists from those courts to Bikaner, as a result of marital alliances between the rulers of Jodhpur, Jaipur, and Bikaner. The sensual refinement of earlier Bikaner works was discarded in favor of more conventional, stiff representations.

Kishangarh. Kishangarh was founded in 1609 by Maharaja Kishan Singh (r. 1609–1615), a son of the Jodhpur raja, who had close ties to the Mughal court. This amicable affiliation continued through the eighteenth century and is represented artistically by the flourishing of a Mughalized Kishangarh style. Bhavani Das was among three artists working at Delhi who joined the Kishangarh atelier during the reign of Maharaja Raj Singh (r. 1706–1748). Bhavani Das was highly esteemed by the Kishangarh royalty, and numerous works depicting members of the court and distinguished guests from other principalities can be attributed to him, such as the technically refined portrait (c. 1725) of Prince Padam Singh of Bikaner seated with his bard on a terrace (New York, The Metropolitan Museum of Art).

The pinnacle of Kishangarh painting occurred under the patronage of Maharaja Sawant Singh (r. 1748–1757; d. 1764), an ardent follower of Krishna, who wrote romantic poems recounting the love of Krishna and Rādhā under the pen name Nagari Das. Although courtly subjects were also portrayed, the most distinctive and beautifully conceived paintings were those inspired by Sawant Singh's devotional tendencies. Krishna and Rādhā, the divine lovers, were portrayed trysting in a multitude of dark and lush romantic landscapes. One of the most exquisite examples of this genre, *The Boat of Love*, was made about 1750 or 1760 by Sawant Singh's primary artist, Nihal Chand. The painting presents an elaborate fantasy-landscape containing two vignettes of Krishna and Rādhā: in the foreground, Krishna tempts Rādhā to kiss him; in the midground, the two lovers are shown seated in a boat floating on a river dotted with lotuses (Delhi, National Museum). Facial features become a distinguishing feature of this mature Kishangarh style, characterized by the representation of attenuated heads, long noses, and prominent elongated almond-shaped eyes framed with arched eyebrows. It is thought that many of the Krishna-Rādhā paintings represent idealized portraits of Sawant Singh and his beloved, the poetess Bani Thani, with whom he went into self-imposed exile at Vrindavan. Artists continued to paint works for the Kishangarh rulers well into the nineteenth century in a style that was based upon the works of Nihal Chand but devoid of his complex subtlety and magnificent delicacy of execution; instead they presented overly exaggerated facial features and stylized, flat figural forms.

Rajput Painting in the Punjab Hills

Paintings produced for the rulers of the many small kingdoms found in regions that now consist of the modern states of Himachal Pradesh and Jammu and Kashmir are frequently referred to as "Pahari" (hill) or Punjab Hill paintings. One of the earliest manuscripts found in that region is an illustrated copy of the *Devī Mahatmya*, dated 1552, that establishes the existence of a pre-Mughal style in the Punjab Hills closely related to the *Chaurapanchashika*-type paintings produced in northern India (Himachal Pradesh State Museum, Simla). Beginning in the seventeenth century, two distinct styles appeared in neighboring Punjab Hill states. The first style implemented a bold palette of saturated brilliant colors applied in unmodulated, flat zones, as exemplified in the paintings at Basohli and Mankot (and other areas such as Nurpur, Kulu, and Chamba). Mughal-influenced details are included, but appear discreetly in the form of touches of color applied to the faces to indicate modeling, and in the depiction of richly patterned textiles. A second style, predominant in the works produced in Guler and Kangra, exhibits a strong relationship to Mughal works in the use of a subtle, varied palette, and the portrayal of naturalistically rendered landscapes.

Basohli and Mankot. One of the earliest group of paintings associated with Basohli is a seventeenth-century series of square-format paintings, each depicting Devī the great goddess in one of her Tantric forms. As if to match the divine subject matter presented, these works glow with a ferocious beauty. Embellishments distinctive to Basohli paintings are exhibited in this set: thickly applied dots of white pigment representing pearl ornaments, and iridescent green beetle-wing carapaces, applied to emulate emerald gemstones. Although no inscription identifies the patron or artist of the series, it has been stylistically associated with an illustrated copy of Bhanudatta's *Rasamanjari*, produced about 1660 or 1670. As Raja Sangram Pal (r. 1635–1673) adopted the worship of Vishnu, or Vaishnavism, it has been suggested that he may have been the patron of this vibrantly rendered version of the *Rasamanjari*. A folio from the set illustrates *Guru Mana*, or the "intense pride of the *nayika*," as identified by an inscription in *takri* script at the top margin. After a night spent with another woman, the *nayaka* (visualized in this series as the amorous god Krishna) sheepishly approaches the *nayika* (Rādhā) with a strand of pearls in his hand, the gift of a guilty lover (Cambridge, Mass., Harvard University Art Museums). Here we see quite clearly elements typcially associated with Basohli works: flat juxtapositions of colors; figural, architectural, and foliate forms delineated by a strong almost calligraphic line; and idiosyncratically presented physiognomies, all contained within a wide, brilliant red border.

Another beautiful *Rasamanjari* series was produced in 1694–1695 for Raja Kripal Pal (reigned c. 1678–c. 1693) by an artist named Devidasa, a member of a family of painters originally from the nearby state of Nurpur. A folio illustrating a spirited exchange between Shiva and Pārvatī during a game of *chaupar* depicts the pair seated on an upturned tiger skin that seemingly floats between two schematically rendered curving trees (New York, The Metropolitan Museum of Art).

Works from Mankot are stylistically related to contemporary paintings produced at Basohli, as illustrated by a Bhāgavata Purāṇa series produced about 1700 (Chandigarh, Government Museum and Art Gallery). The destruction of the evil King Kansa at Krishna's hand is depicted in a beautifully composed frame that conveys the chaotic scene just before Krishna lands the fatal blow.

Royal portraiture inspired by Mughal models produced for Emperor Shah Jahan was introduced in Basohli and Mankot during the seventeenth century. A portrait of Shah Jahan, attributed to either Basohli or Mankot, was painted in about 1690 and depicts the emperor in a manner similar to the way he would have been portrayed by his own artists (Los Angeles County Museum of Art). However, in this work, Shah Jahan is positioned against a flat bright orange ground, his figure is devoid of naturalistic shading, and his head is disproportionally large—stylistic elements that distinguish this hill painting from imperial Mughal portraits. A slightly later Mankot painting of Raja Ajmat Dev (reigned c. 1730–c. 1760), painted about 1730, is even more schematically composed and depicts the elegant ruler seated while smoking a *huqqa* (London, Victoria and Albert Museum). The artist's virtuosity is especially displayed in the rendering of the raja's form, which is composed of sweeping lines that are paralleled in the shape of his *huqqa's* hose and the curve of his sword.

Portraiture at Basohli underwent a dramatic transformation beginning with works produced for Amrit Pal (r. 1757–1776), which were rendered in a naturalistic style. It is possible that this change may have been influenced by the presence of the artist Nainsukh of Guler, who moved to Basohli sometime after the death in 1763 of his patron, prince Balwant Singh of Jammu.

Guler, Jasrota, and Kangra. Nainsukh was a member of one of the most renowned families of Rajput artists; his father Pandit Seu and his elder brother Manaku also worked for the rajas of Guler. Raja Rup Chand (reigned c. 1610–c. 1635) of Guler and his descendants were closely affiliated with the Mughal emperors and went on military campaigns on their behalf. Although later artistic works from Guler appear to have been strongly influenced by the Mughal idiom, there is no evidence that yet explains this process of transmission.

Among the earliest works at Guler are those attributed to Pandit Seu while in the employ of Raja Dalip Singh (r. 1695–1741), such as a Rāmāyaṇa set painted about 1720, and a series of royal portraits. A wonderful painting attributed to the artist from about 1730 depicts the gyrations of men dancing to the accompaniment of four musicians (Los Angeles County Museum of Art). Although the men are placed against a rich, solid-red ground reminiscent of compositions from Basohli, Mankot, and Nurpur, their delicately modeled and individualized portraits prefigure the works of his son Nainsukh.

Pandit Seu's elder son Manaku was also very active at Guler, and his early works, which include a Gītā Govinda series (c. 1730, Chandigarh, Government Museum and Art Gallery), are rendered in a more conservative style. A large-scale "Siege of Lanka" series, from about 1725–1730, was left unfinished, and the now dispersed folios provide an interesting study of artistic process in the Rajput atelier, as they display varied stages of execution from preliminary underdrawings to finished folios. A painting by Manaku (c. 1750–1755) illustrating an episode from the Bhāgavata Purāṇa (in which the youthful Krishna and his brother Balarama play blindman's bluff with cowherd boys) displays the idealized beauty and naturalistic representation of landscape and figures that distinguish Kangra and later Guler.

Manaku's younger brother Nainsukh found patronage for many years at the small principality of Jasrota under Raja Balwant Singh, a prince of the Jammu family, until Balwant Singh's death in 1723. He arrived at Jasrota from Guler in about 1740, working first for Raja Mian Zorawar Singh, Balwant Singh's father. Nainsukh's many marvelous portraits of Balwant Singh provide the viewer with a compendium of the raja's activities and events. Nainsukh apparently accompanied his patron everywhere, making sketches and paintings of the prince, depicting him in quiet, intimate moments, as in a painting of Balwant Singh writing in his camp tent (c. 1750, Mumbai, Chhatrapati Shivaji Maharaj Vastu Sangrahalaya). The works also include lively compositions, such as a painting dated 1752 that depicts Balwant Singh perched in a howdah on top of an elephant, slashing at an attacking lioness with his sword (Cambridge, Mass., Harvard University Art Museums). The superb delicacy of line and color with which Nainsukh rendered his works is matched only by his ability to transmit the emotional aspects of the people and events that he documented.

Kangra was a center of artistic production from the eighteenth through early twentieth century. Although there were many families of artists working in Kangra, the primary creative impetus came from the grandsons of Pandit Seu of Guler. One of the most important patrons of art in the region was Maharaja Sansar Chand (r. 1775–1823) of Kangra. One of the most beautiful sets, of which about 140 folios survive, made during the early part of Sansar Chand's reign, was a Gītā Govinda series painted around 1775–1780. This set is attributed to a member of the Pandit Seu family, a generation after Nainsukh. An illustration depicting Rādhā and Krishna's tryst in a grove exemplifies the lyrical beauty and delicacy of line of early Kangra painting (London, Victoria and Albert Museum). Among other extant works from Kangra are numerous paintings from dispersed sets, including folios from a *Bihari Satsai* (c. 1780–1790) and illustrations that feature romantic and heroic *nayaka* and *nayika* themes. The refinement of Kangra paintings produced during the eighteenth and early nineteenth centuries was eventually lost in favor of overly sentimental and repetitious compositions. In the beginning of the nineteenth century, the Sikh ruler Maharaja Ranjit Singh (r. 1801–1839) occupied the Kangra fort, and Gurkha troops triumphed in battle over Sansar Chand, and so for some years life was disrupted at Kangra. Many artists, including those from Pandit Seu's family lineage, moved to other villages, where they worked for patrons from nearby small hill principalities.

Rochelle Kessler

See also **Ajanta; Mahābhārata; Mughal Painting; Rāmāyaṇa**

BIBLIOGRAPHY

Archer, W. G. *Indian Painting in the Punjab Hills*. Victoria and Albert Museum, Museum Monograph no. 3. London: H. M. Stationery Office, 1952.

———. *Indian Painting at Bundi and Kotah*. Victoria and Albert Museum, Museum Monograph no. 13. London: H. M. Stationery Office, 1959.

———. *Indian Paintings from the Punjab Hills: A Survey and History of Pahari Miniature Painting*. 2 vols. London: Sotheby Parke Bernet, 1973.

Barrett, Douglas, and Basil Gray. *Painting of India*. Geneva: Editions d'Art Albert Skira, 1963.

Beach, Milo Cleveland. *Rajput Paintings at Bundi and Kota*. Ascona: Artibus Asiae, 1974.

———. *Mughal and Rajput Painting*. New York: Cambridge University Press, 1992.

Brown, Percy. *Indian Painting*. Heritage of India series. Kolkata: Association Press, 1918.

Brown, W. Norman. *A Descriptive and Illustrated Catalogue of Miniature Paintings of the Jaina Kalpasutra as Executed in the Early Western Style*. Washington, D.C.: Smithsonian Institution, Freer Gallery of Art, 1934.

Chandra, Moti. *Mewar Painting in the Seventeenth Century*. New Delhi: Lalit Kala Akademi, 1957.

———. *Studies in Early Indian Painting*. New York: Asia Publishing House, 1970.

Coomaraswamy, Ananda K. *Rajput Painting*. 2 vols. London: Oxford University Press, 1916.

Crill, Rosemary. *Marwar Painting: A History of the Jodhpur Style*. Mumbai: India Book House, 1999.

Desai, Vishakha. *Life at Court: Art for India's Rulers: 16th–19th Centuries*. Boston: Museum of Fine Arts, 1985.

Dickinson, Eric, and Karl Khandalavala. *Kishangarh Painting*. New Delhi: Lalit Kala Akademi, 1959.

Doshi, Saryu. *Masterpieces of Jain Painting*. Mumbai: Marg Publications, 1985.
Ehnbom, Daniel J. *Indian Miniatures: The Ehrenfeld Collection*. New York: Hudson Hills, 1985.
Goetz, Hermann. *The Art and Architecture of Bikaner State*. Oxford: B. Cassirer, 1950.
Goswamy, B. N. *Nainsukh of Guler: A Great Indian Painter from a Small Hill-State*. Zürich: Artibus Asiae Publishers and Museum Rietberg, 1997.
Goswamy, B. N., and Eberhard Fischer. *Pahari Masters: Court Painters of Northern India*. Delhi: Oxford University Press, 1997.
Gray, Basil. *Rajput Painting*. New York: Pittman, 1949.
Guy, John, and Deborah Swallow, eds. *Arts of India: 1550–1900*. London: Victoria and Albert Museum, 1990.
Khandalavala, Karl. *Pahari Miniature Painting*. Mumbai: New Book Company, 1958.
Kossak, Steven. *Indian Court Painting, 16th–19th Century*. New York: Metropolitan Museum of Art, 1997.
Krishna, Anand. *Malwa Painting*. Varanasi: Bharat Kala Bhavan, 1963.
Leach, Linda L. *Mughal and Other Indian Paintings from the Chester Beatty Library*, vol. II. London: Scorpion Cavendish, 1995.
Losty, J. P. *The Art of the Book in India*. London: British Library, 1982.
Mason, Darielle, et al. *Intimate Worlds: Indian Paintings from the Alvin O. Bellak Collection*. Philadelphia: Philadelphia Museum of Art, 2001.
Pal, Pratapaditya. *The Classical Tradition in Rajput Painting from the Paul F. Walter Collection*. New York: Pierpont Morgan Library, 1978.
Poster, Amy G., et al. *Realms of Heroism: Indian Paintings at the Brooklyn Museum*. New York: Brooklyn Museum and Hudson Hills Press 1994.
Randhawa, M. S. *Kangra Painting on Love*. New Delhi: National Museum, 1962.
———. *Kangra Paintings of the Bihari Sat Sai*. New Delhi: National Museum, 1966.
Randhawa, Mohinder Singh, and John Kenneth Galbraith. *Indian Painting: The Scene, Themes and Legends*. Boston: Houghton Mifflin, 1968.
Shiveshkar, Leela. *The Pictures of the Chaurapancasika: A Sanskrit Love Lyric*. New Delhi: National Museum, 1967.
Spink, Walter. *Krishnamandala*. Ann Arbor: University of Michigan, 1971.
Topsfield, Andrew. *The City Palace Museum Udaipur*. Ahmedabad: Mapin Publishing Pvt., 1990.
———. *Court Painting at Udaipur: Art under the Patronage of the Maharanas of Mewar*. Zürich: Artibus Asiae Publishers and Museum Rietberg, 2002.
Welch, Stuart Cary. *A Flower from Every Meadow*. With contributions by Mark Zebrowski. New York: Asia Society, 1973.
———. *India: Art and Culture, 1300–1900*. New York: Metropolitan Museum of Art, 1985.
Welch, Stuart Cary, and Milo Cleveland Beach. *Gods, Thrones, and Peacocks: Northern Indian Paintings from Two Traditions, Fifteenth to Nineteenth Centuries*. New York: Asia House, 1965.
Welch, Stuart Cary, et al. *Gods, Kings and Tigers: The Art of Kotah*. New York: Prestel, 1997.

RĀMA. *See* **Rāmāyaṇa.**

RAMAKRISHNA MISSION. *See* **Vivekananda, Swami.**

RAMANANDA ***(1400–1470), Hindu religious teacher.*** The founder of the Rāmanandis, a sect of Vaishnava Hinduism, Ramananda was part of the medieval Hindu devotional movement (thirteenth to seventeenth centuries) in North India, when focus moved from polytheism to the worship of one God and his avatars, especially Krishna and Rāma. Devotees did this through an emotional, passionate devotion or love of God, *bhakti*. In his youth Ramananda resided in South India and on his return was a follower of his great, great-grandfather Rāmānuja's Srivaishnava sect. Ramananda settled in Benaras (Varanasi) and developed his ideas of egalitarianism, preaching in a local dialect. He called for the love of God in as intense a manner as possible. He saw humanity as one large family, in which all men were brothers, and caste and creed were irrelevant. Accordingly, he preached to everyone, no matter how high on the social and ritual scale they were. His twelve personal disciples included women, an outcaste, and a Muslim. Ritual was unimportant, only personal love of God was meaningful. He also believed in "service to man," following the beliefs of Vaishnavite and Shaivite saints of the first millenium. He advocated devotion to Rāma and his *shakti*, Sītā, but a devotion devoid of eroticism. Accordingly, the devotee's attitude should be that of servant to master, rather than that of a lover, as epitomized by the service given by Hanuman to his master Rāma.

Ramananda's sect is of great historical significance because its followers started a number of other sects and movements in North India and inspired the Sikhs and Kabirpanthis, who adopted their social concerns. The Rāmanandis base their theology on the writings of Tulsidas (1532–1623), the author of *Rāmacaritmanasa* (The sacred lake of Rāma's deeds), in which Rāma is the supreme lord and the other deities are subordinate to him. It is composed in Hindi rather than Sanskrit and is derived from Valmiki's Rāmāyaṇa. The Rāmanadis are ascetically minded, and while all castes were welcome in the sect, including "untouchables," and caste duties were abolished, with devotion to Rāma replacing all obligations, the contemporary practice is to impose caste resrictions in Rāmanandi temples, where only Brahmans can be priests. Likewise, both sexes were originally initiated into the sect, but there are now very few nuns. Their most popular festival is Rāmlila, which is celebrated throughout North India. The *Rāmacaritmanasa* is recited, and the story of Rāma and Sītā is enacted, from Rāma's birth to the establishment of his *Rāmrajya* ("Rama's Rule," i.e., paradise).

Roger D. Long

See also **Bhakti**

BIBLIOGRAPHY

Basham, A. L., ed. *A Cultural History of India*. Oxford: Clarendon Press, 1975.

Flood, Gavin, ed. *The Blackwell Companion to Hinduism*. Oxford: Blackwell Publishing, 2003.

RĀMĀNUJA ***(1017–1137), Hindu Vaishnava teacher and philosopher.*** A South Indian Brahman, Rāmānuja has a dual importance, as a thinker within the tradition of Vedantic philosophy and as a religious figure within the Sri Vaishnava community. Even though he is acknowledged today as a great expositor of the Vedāntic tradition, the many accounts of his life revere him more for his pious life and religious leadership than for his intellectual prowess. Rāmānuja lived at a time when Hinduism was firmly established in India, with Buddhism having almost disappeared and Jainism being confined to a few pockets of western India. Within the Hinduism of his time, Rāmānuja's self-perceived role was to preserve the integrity of the ancient Vedantic tradition and to explicate it in a new context. This inevitably generated conflicts, both with other schools of thought and with some contemporary forms of religious practice. In particular, Rāmānuja saw his main opponents as the Shaivites in religion and the Advaitins in philosophy. This conflict accounts in part for the polemical tone of much of his writing.

Within the Sri Vaishnava community, Rāmānuja was acknowledged as the sixth great guru in their line of gurus. There is a well-known story that illustrates both his character and the impact he had on subsequent Hinduism. Rāmānuja was initiated into the community of the *ācārya* (authoritative teacher) Yāmuna by the latter's disciples. When it came time to impart the all-important secret formula (mantra) of the community, they swore Rāmānuja to secrecy. The day after receiving the mantra, however, Rāmānuja shouted the mantra out loud to his fellow devotees from the temple top. Acknowledging that he might well go to hell for this radical act of disobedience, he justified himself thus: "But because of their connection with you [his teachers] these souls will be saved." This concern for the spiritual welfare of others marked the active religious ministry of Rāmānuja. He became the head of the main Sri Vaishnava temple at Srirangam in South India and loosened the caste restrictions so as to honor both his own lower caste teacher and to open the doors of worship to non-Brahmans. For this he suffered the persecution of the reigning Shaiva-oriented king in the South and had to flee to the Hoysala kingdom of the North, where he spent the last part of his life. As a result of his efforts, Brahmanic Hinduism was transformed: the quality of *bhakti* (religious devotion) rather than caste-based ritual purity was, at least in principle, made the criterion of authentic religious life.

Rāmānuja's philosophy was of one piece with his religious practice. The three most important of the nine texts conventionally attributed to him are his commentaries on the Vedānta Sūtra: his famous *Shrībhāsya* and the shorter *Vedāntadīpa* and *Vedāntasāra*. In them he provided his own exposition of the Vedānta, which in contemporary terms may be characterized as a version of *pantheism*. God and the world are both real and internally related in the way a human self is related to its body. God may be distinguished but not separated from the world, and just as the self transcends the body, so also God transcends the world. In laying out his own views, Rāmānuja severely criticized what he saw as the errors of Shankara. Rāmānuja moved Vedānta in a firmly theistic direction in contrast to the impersonal nondualism of Shankara. Īshvara as the lord of creation is the highest God, the *saguṇa* ("with qualities") Brahman, above whom there is none. He disagreed, therefore, with Shankara's hierarachy of *nirguṇa* ("without qualities") and *saguṇa* Brahman. He likewise qualified Shankara's nondualism—hence the name of the Vedāntic school with which Rāmānuja is associated, Vishiṣṭadvaita, or "qualified nondualism." The reality of God is internally differentiated to create the space within the godhead for selves and matter. Unlike Shankara, for whom the primary religious act is that of right knowledge (*jnāna*), whereby one sees through and beyond the illusory nature of the world, Rāmānuja emphasized *bhakti*, or devotion. Being grounded in God, the religious acts of devotion and surrender are a form of ontological homage—the return of the creature to his or her source.

Joseph Prabhu

See also **Shankara; Upanishadic Philosophy**

BIBLIOGRAPHY

Carman, J. B. *The Theology of Ramanuja*. New Haven, Conn.: Yale University Press, 1974.

Lipner, J. J. *The Face of Truth*. Albany: State University of New York Press, 1986.

Lott, E. J. *God and the Universe in the Vedantic Theology of Ramanuja*. Chennai: Ramanuja Research Society, 1976.

Radhakrishnan, S. *The Vedanta according to Sankara and Ramanuja*. London: George Allen & Unwin, 1928.

RĀMĀYAṆA Traditional Rāmāyaṇa scholarship has been marked by what Robert Goldman calls a "zeal" (1984, p. 63) to demonstrate that most or all of this epic's first book is late. Books 2–6 are taken to supply most or all of the poem's "'genuine' portions," and the closing Book 7 is taken as axiomatically late. For such scholars, Books 2–6 have presented the possibility that they narrate a largely consecutive heroic story of a man who is for the most part not yet "divinized."

This view has been challenged over the last several decades. Pivotal to this rethinking has been the completion of the Baroda Critical Edition of the Rāmāyaṇa (1960–1975), which this article will use for its synopsis. Most of the key passages that speak of Rāma as an incarnation of Vishnu make the Critical Edition's cut. Sheldon Pollock (1986, pp. 38–42) and Madeleine Biardeau (1997, pp. 77–119) have also introduced a consideration based on comparison with the Mahābhārata and the fruits of its Pune Critical Edition. Up to Book 2, each epic follows a similar archetypal design, with each Book 1 introducing the frame stories, origins, and youth of the heroes, and each Book 2 describing a pivotal court intrigue. This approach can be carried further: Book 3, Forest (in the title of both epics' third books); Book 4, Inversions (the Pāṇḍava's topsy-turvy disguises in Virāṭa's kingdom of Matsya (Fish); Rāma's engagement with the topsy-turvy world of the monkeys' capital, Kishkindhā, in which the lead monkeys play out a reverse image of Rāma's own story); Book 5, "Effort" (*udyoga*; see *Rām* 5.10.24; 33.66) made in Preparation for War (by both sides in the Mahābhārata; by Hanumān and all the monkeys in the Rāmāyaṇa) with Krishna and Hanumān going as divine messengers into the enemy camp, where there are attempts to capture them; War Books (Rāmāyaṇa 6; Mahābhārata 6–11), and denouements (Rāmāyaṇa 7; Mahābhārata 12–18). The Rāmāyaṇa's term for its Books is *kāṇḍa*, meaning a "section" of a stalk of a plant, such as bamboo, between its joints; the Mahābhārata's is *parvan*, which can mean the joints themselves of such a plant. Together they could describe a complete stalk of a noded plant. Such closeness of design cannot be accidental. This article favors the priority of the Mahābhārata and will be presented from that standpoint, with the corollaries that Rāmāyaṇa Books 1 and 7 are integral to its earliest design and that the Rāmāyaṇa poet is not only familiar with the Mahābhārata's design but intent upon refining it.

Such a relation can be exemplified by the two epics' frame stories, which are opened at the beginning of the first Books and left pending into the denouements. Unlike the Mahābhārata's three frame stories, which present a serial layering of the first three recitals of supposedly the same text that are scattered over its first fifty-six chapters and resumed in late portions of its twelfth Book, the Rāmāyaṇa frame, in only its first four chapters (known as the *upodghāta* or preamble), presents two progressive unfoldings of the story—the first by the sage Nārada to the hermit Vālmīki; the second by Vālmīki himself, now a poet—that trace its ripening into the third full unfolding, the Vālmīki Rāmāyaṇa itself.

In the first, in answer to Vālmīki's opening question of whether there is an ideal man in the world today (1.1.2–5), Nārada satisfies the question with a brief and entirely laudatory account of Rāma's virtues and adult life, presumably to date (1.1.7–76). Saying the minimum about Rāma's killing of the monkey Vālin (1.1.49, 55), Nārada hardly hints at anything problematic in Rāma's life and omits both Sītā's fire ordeal and her banishment. Among the great *rishi*s, or seers, that Rāma encounters, he mentions only Vasishtha (29) and Agastya (33–34).

In the second *sarga*, once Nārada has left, Vālmīki witnesses the cries of grief of a female krauñca bird (probably the large monogamous sarus crane) over the slaying of her mate by a "cruel hunter," and is provoked into the spontaneous utterance that creates "verse" (and thus poetry) out of "grief" (*shloka* out of *shoka*; 1.2.9–15). As this verse is said to mark the origins of poetry, the Rāmāyaṇa is called the *ādikāvya*, or "first poem"—a term that does not occur in the Critical Edition, though it probably should since it occurs in a universally attested *sarga* where, after Sītā has vanished into the earth, the god Brahmā encourages Rāma to hear the rest of this *ādikāvya* (7, Appendix I, No. 13, lines 31–39). Now, however, the same Brahmā appears (22–36) to prompt Vālmīki to tell the story he has just heard from Nārada, and gives him the insight to see what he did not know and what is still yet to happen—confirming that his poem will all be true (1.2.33–35). Brahmā thus assures Vālmīki that he will know things omitted from Nārada's encomium. When Brahmā leaves, Vālmīki conceives the idea of composing "the entire Rāmāyaṇa poem (*kāvya*)" in *shloka*s (1.2.40cd).

In the third *sarga*, Vālmīki meditatively enters into this project for the first time and has a sort of preview of the story (1.3.3-28): not a retrospective table of contents like the Mahābhārata's *Parvasaṃgraha*, but a kind of first glimpse of what his poem will contain. Here he provides the first reference to some of Rāma's encounters with important *rishi*s (Vishvāmitra [4], Rāma Jāmadagnya [5], Bharadvāja [8]). Most important, he closes with Sītā's banishment (28).

Then, looking back upon the poem's completion, the fourth *sarga* hints at the context in which Vālmīki's Rāmāyaṇa will finally be told by the twins Kusha and Lava to their father, Rāma. Just as information on the Mahābhārata's frame is resumed with further revelations in Book 12, the Rāmāyaṇa's frame will be picked up in

Book 7, when Kusha and Lava do just that. The main difference is that when the Rāmāyaṇa frame is reentered in Book 7, it is not just a matter of further revelations about the composition that are difficult to relate to the main story. Vālmīki's dramatic entry into the main story presents the occasion to reveal the poetic heart of the whole poem through its effects on its hero and its heroine.

Vālmīki thus gets a triple inspiration—from Nārada, the *krauñcī*, and Brahmā. Yet the *upodghāta* leaves us in suspense as to when Sītā came to his ashram. Was it before or after the *krauñca* bird incident? The poem never tells whether Vālmīki's response to the female bird comes before or after his familiarity with Sītā's grief at her banishment. But in either case, now that Vālmīki knows the whole story from Brahmā, he could connect Sītā's banishment with the *krauñcī*'s cry whenever she arrived. What we do know is that, having had pity (*karuṇa*) for the female bird, Vālmīki will compose his poem with pity as its predominant aesthetic flavor (*aṅgī rasa*) in relation to grief (*shoka*) as its underlying *sthāyibhāva* or "stable aesthetic emotion." Vyāsa, the Mahābhārata's author, provides no such developmental inspiration story. The Rāmāyaṇa frame is thus shorter, more focused, and more poetically traceable into the main narrative and the whole poem.

Although the *upodghāta* concludes with Rāma, as chief-auditor-to-be, inviting his brothers to join him in listening to the boys he is yet to recognize, he interrupts their narration to question them only once: when he asks them who authored this poem (*kāvya*; 7.85.19). Otherwise he is the rapt and silent listener. He launches their recital in the penultimate verse of the *upodghāta*: "Moreover, it is said that the profound adventure (*mahānubhāvaṃ caritam*) they tell is highly beneficial even for me. Listen to it" (1.4.26d). Who says this? Why beneficial to Rāma? The preamble leaves us with such implicit and subtle questions. In these passages, we see two of the three leading terms by which the Rāmāyaṇa describes itself: *kāvya* (poem) and *carita* (adventure), the third being *ākhyāna* (tale, narrative). *Kathā* (story) is also used, but with less specificity. These four terms are woven through the *upodghāta*. It is noteworthy that *itihāsa* (history), which along with *ākhyāna* is one of the two main terms to describe the Mahābhārata, is not only unused to describe the Rāmāyaṇa but is absent from the latter's entire Critical Edition. In this, it is like the absence of *kāvya* in the Mahābhārata's Critical Edition; as if the two texts were in early agreement to yield one of these terms to the other. Neither does *purāṇa* (ancient lore) describe the Rāmāyaṇa, which evidently places itself outside the *itihāsa-purāṇa* tradition that Chāndogya Upanishad 7.1.2 links with Nārada as a fifth Veda. Similarly, *upākhyāna* (subtale) is used only in the Mahābhārata, although there is an interpolated verse in the *ashvamedha* recital scene in which the twins begin singing the poem and tell Rāma that the Rāmāyaṇa has twenty-four thousand verses and a hundred *upākhyānas* (7.1328*, following 7.85.20)—suggesting Mahābhārata influence.

Kāvya is used only at the Rāmāyaṇa's two framing points: nine times in the *upodghāta*, four in the *ashvamedha* recital scene. It thus has a kind of bookend function of describing the work as poetry, most notably that "it is replete with" all the "poetic sentiments" or *rasas* (1.4.8). In contrast to *kāvya*, *carita* implies the "movement" of the main narrative. Of its four usages in the *upodghāta* to characterize the Rāmāyaṇa, two present a juxtaposition. The first has Brahmā enjoin Vālmīki to "compose the whole adventure of Rāma" (1.2.30cd). The second, once it is implied that Vālmīki has composed it, calls "the whole Rāmāyaṇa poem (*kāvya*) the great adventure of Sītā" (1.4.6). This suggests that, although Rāma's adventure is Vālmīki's starting point, the complete poem is also about Sītā's. The "profound adventure" that Rāma prepares himself to hear at the end of the *upodghāta* would thus include the two adventures intertwined (4.26). *Carita* is also the main word to describe the Rāmāyaṇa when these adventures are in course (2.54.18; 6.114.4)—and even in the course of hearing it. When the twins begin reciting the poem and Rāma asks who composed it, they reply, "The blessed Vālmīki, who has reached the presence of the sacrifice, is the author by whom this adventure is disclosed to you without remainder" (7.85.19).

Meanwhile, *ākhyāna* is used four times in the *upodghāta*. It describes the benefits of hearing the tale's recital (1.1.78), that it is "unsurpassed" as a "tale exemplary of righteousness" (1.4.11), that it is a "wondrous tale told by the sage" that he "completed in perfect sequence" as "the great source of inspiration for poets (*kavīnām*)" (1.4.20), and that Rāma urged his brothers to "listen to this tale whose words and meanings alike are wonderful as it is sweetly sung by these two godlike men" (1.4.25). It is also the first term to describe the Rāmāyaṇa when the recital of its main story begins: "Of these kings of illustrious lineage, the Ikhvākus, this great tale is known as the Rāmāyaṇa. I will recite it from the beginning in its entirety, omitting nothing. It is in keeping with the goals of righteousness, profit, and pleasure and should be listened to with faith" (1.5.3-4). *Ākhyāna* can also be used for tales told in course, most notably for the "glad tidings" that Hanumān brings at various points to others (5.57.1, 59.6, 6.101.17, 113.40). Complementary to both *kāvya* and *carita*, it links the narrative to the inspiration of poets while also bringing listeners into the poem's double adventure.

The Rāmāyaṇa thus makes very selective use of limited terms. In contrast to the Mahābhārata, they are used strategically rather than as definitions, and they are not used to emphasize the interplay between the Rāmāyaṇa's parts and its whole. Emerging from and flowing back into the passages that frame the Rāmāyaṇa (the *upodghāta* and the *ashvamedha* recital scene), side-stories fall within a single poetic narrative that is portrayed as being addressed uninterruptedly (the one exception noted) to Rāma. It does not have multiple audiences in a threefold stacking of dialogical frames (Shulman 2001, pp. 28–33).

Synopsis

Book 1, the *Bālakāṇḍa.* or "Book of the Boy[s]," begins with the *upodhghāta* (*sargas* 1–4), which leads directly to the main narrative, starting with the origins of the Ikshvāku dynasty and quickly narrowing to the one defect in the long reign of the current monarch, Dasharatha: he is sonless. At this time the gods and *rishis* (seers) are alarmed by the Rākshasa Rāvaṇa, who harasses the seers in their hermitages. With the help of a descendant of the sage Kashyapa, named Rishyashriṅga (whose story is told in the Mahābhārata's *Rishyashriṅga-Upākhyāna* [Mbh 3.110–113]), Dasharatha's three wives bear four sons, all partial incarnations of Vishnu: Rāma, Bharata, and the twins Lakshmaṇa and Shatrughna. Meanwhile Brahmā directs other gods to take birth as monkeys. Once the boys start their Vedic education, the sage Vishvāmitra (whose story is told in the Mahābhārata's *Vasishtha-* and *Vishvāmitra-Upākhyānas* [Mbh 1.264–273, 13.3–4]) arrives (*sargas* 5–17). He demands that Dasharatha allow Rāma and Lakshmaṇa to accompany him into the forest, and is supported by the sage Vasishtha. Once Dasharatha releases the boys, Vishvāmitra teaches them divine weapons and prepares them for a Rākshasa encounter. They kill Tātakā (a female) and Subāhu, but Mārīca escapes. Vishvāmitra then mentions that King Janaka of Mithilā will be performing a sacrifice at which a great bow will be presented as a test of strength (*sargas* 18–31).

Along the way to Mithilā, Vishvāmitra tells stories: the last of them about Ahalyā. Cursed by her husband, the sage Gautama, for being seduced by Indra (this story is told in the Mahābhārata's *Cirakāri–Upākhyāna* [12.258] and alluded to in its *Indravijaya-Upākhyāna* [5.12.6]), she is redeemed by Rāma's arrival at their hermitage—a cautionary tale about marriage and sexuality (Sutherland Goldman, p. 72)—before Rāma learns more about Janaka's sacrifice. Janaka's minister Shatñanda then tells Rāma the story of Vishvāmitra's former rivalry with Vasishtha (a topic, again, of the Mahābhārata's *Vasishtha-Upākhāyana* [Mbh 1.64–73]; *sargas* 32–65).

Janaka's sacrifice turns out to be Sītā's "self-choice" of a husband, where Rāma wins Sītā by breaking the great bow of Shiva. To unite the houses further, Janaka provides wives for Rāma's brothers. Vishvāmitra departs, and on the way back to Ayodhya, Rāma is confronted by Rāma Jāmadagnya (who appears repeatedly in the Mahābhārata, notably in the *Kārtavīrya-* [Mbh 3.115–117], [*Bhārgava-*] *Rāma-* [12.48–49], and *Vishvāmitra-Upākhyānas* [13.3–4]). This older Brahman Rāma blocks the new Kshatriya Rāma's path and demands that he break a bow of Vishnu—which Rāma does, making the older Rāma yield. The young couples then return to Ayodhya for happy honeymoons. But Dasharatha sends Bharata and Shatrughna with Bharata's maternal uncle back to Kekaya, the country of Bharata's mother Kaikeyī (*sargas* 66–77).

Rishyashriṅga's contribution to the four brothers' births, the stories told along the way by and about Vishvāmitra, and the encounter with Bhārgava Rāma have often been viewed as "digressions" or "interpolations" because they depart from a straightforward Rāma saga. But this view overlooks an emerging pattern. The sequence of *rishis*—Rishyashriṅga (a descendant of Kashyapa), Vasishtha, Vishvāmitra, Gautama (with Ahalyā), and Rāma Jāmadagnya (son of Jamadagni)—has linked Rāma's early years to sages from five of the eight great Brahman *gotras*, or lineages, whose eponymous ancestors are connected with the composition of the Rig Veda and are regarded as the main *pravara rishis*—the ones to whom all Brahman families make invocation (*pravara*) when they give their line of descent.

At the beginning of Book 2, the *Ayodhyā Kānda*, or "Book of Ayodhyā," Dasharatha—with the whiff of a scheme—announces his intention to make Rāma his heir-apparent with Bharata away. Kaikeyī's maidservant Mantharā arouses Kaikeyī's jealousy and reminds her that Dasharatha once granted her two boons, which she has yet to claim (2.9.9–13). In a wrenching scene that launches the Rāmāyaṇa's unending skein of pity and grief, the aged Dasharatha hears her two demands: Rāma's fourteen-year banishment and Bharata's installment as heir-apparent (10.28–29). At the news, Rāma calmly says he will honor his father's word, and does so even when Dasharatha urges him to ignore it. Sītā demands to accompany Rāma, who then approves Lakshmaṇa's offer to attend them. Nearing their departure, Kaikeyī contemptuously gives Sītā bark to wear over her sari, and when Rāma has to help Sītā put it on, Dasharatha gives Sītā garments and jewels to cover the bark (*sargas* 1–34).

The departure is then a long scene of grief from the principals down to Ayodhya's citizens. Crossing the Gaṅgā, the trio heads toward their first destination, the hermitage of the *rishi* Bharadvāja. When Rāma asks Bharadvāja to "think of some good site for an ashram in a secluded place," the seer directs them to Mount Citrakūṭa, "a meritorious place frequented by the great *rishis*" (2.48.25). Meanwhile, back at Ayodhya, Dasharatha dies after tortured recollections, leaving a widowed city, and messengers are sent to Bharata (*sargas* 35–65).

Bharata learns of Dasharatha's death at Ayodhya and grieves, denouncing Kaikeyī. Affirming the Ikshvākus' custom of primogeniture, he tells his deputies that he rather than Rāma will fulfill the terms of exile and orders them to prepare an army to help him bring Rāma back. Following the same route, Bharata reaches Bharadvāja's ashram. Bharadvāja tests him, conjuring up a feast for the army and a royal palace for him. Bharata rejects the royal seat, foreshadowing how he will steward Rāma's throne. Having seen Bharata's worthiness, Bharadvāja again gives directions to Citrakūta (*sargas* 66–86).

Descrying Bharata's approach with an army, Lakshmaṇa fears that he wants to kill them. Rāma attests to Bharata's trustworthiness. Bharata reaches Rāma alone, leaving the army camped below. Upon meeting, they embrace, and Rāma learns of Dasharatha's death. After long discussion, Bharata agrees to be regent for the exile's duration, and Rāma gives him his sandals. Having worn these on his head all the way back, Bharata leaves Rāma's throne empty and takes up residence in a village outside Ayodhya, where he consecrates the sandals and apprises them before giving any order (*sargas* 87–107).

Soon sensing disquiet among the Citrakūṭa *rishis*, Rāma learns that Rāvaṇa's younger brother, Khara, has been cannibalizing ascetics in nearby Janasthāna. The sages retreat to a safer ashram and Rāma moves on to the ashram of Atri, where Atri's wife Anasūyā tells Sītā the duties of a faithful wife and gives her more apparel and jewels. Rāma gets his next directions from the ascetics there, who recommend, all other routes being treacherous, "the path through the forest that the great *rishis* use when they go to gather fruits" (111.19; *sargas* 108–111).

With this close of Book 2, Rāma has now been linked with seven of the eight *pravara rishis*—Vasishtha, Kashyapa, Vishvāmitra, Gautama, Jamadagni, Bharadvāja, and Atri—or their descendants. These original seven, who together constitute the northern constellation of the Seven Rishis (Big Dipper), have pointed Rāma south.

The first line of Book 3, the *Araṇya Kānda*, or "Book of the Forest," finds the trio entering the "vast wilderness" of Daṇḍaka. As they move on from a circle of ashrams, a Rākshasa named Virādha ("one who thwarts") looms before them and seizes Sītā. Pained by seeing her touched, Rāma fills Virādha with arrows, and the brothers each break off an arm to release her. Virādha realizes he has been slain by Rāma, which relieves him from a curse. Before going to heaven, he tells Rāma that the great *rishi* Sharabhaṅga "will see to your welfare" (3.3.22–23). Sharabhaṅga relays Rāma to the hermitage of Sutīkshṇa, who offers his ashram as a residence; but Rāma says he might kill the local game. The trio lives happily for ten years in another circle of hermitages before returning to Sutīkshṇa (10.21–26). Storytellers have now told Rāma about Agastya's ashram and he asks Sutīkshṇa how to find it in so vast a forest (29–30). Sutīkshṇa heads him due south, and along the way Rāma tells Lakshmaṇa stories told about Agastya that also occur in the Mahābhārata's *Agastya-Upākhyāna* (Mbh 3.94–108). Rāma intends to live out the remainder of his exile with Agastya (Rām 3.10.86), but Agastya, after meditating a moment, says that he knows Rāma's true desire and directs him to a lovely forest called Pancavaṭī near the Godāvarī River, where Sītā will be comfortable and Rāma can protect her while safeguarding the ascetics (12.12–20). These words of the eighth, last, and southernmost of the great *pravara rishis* resound with forebodings, as does the trio's meeting on the way to Pancavaṭī with the vulture Jaṭāyus, who offers to keep watch over Sītā whenever they are away (*sargas* 1–13). However kindly, a vulture is normally a bad omen (3.22.4).

At their Pancavaṭī ashram, the trio is soon visited by Rāvaṇa's sister Shūrpaṇakhā. Motivated by her rejection by both brothers to devour Sītā, she provokes Rāma to order Lakshmaṇa to mutilate her, and Lakshmaṇa cuts off her ears and nose. She rushes to her brother Khara in Janasthāna, where he heads a Rākshasa outpost in Daṇḍaka Forest. Khara and fourteen thousand Rākshasas are annihilated by Rāma. Shūrpaṇakhā then goes to Laṅkā and, with talk of Sītā's beauty, inspires Rāvaṇa to make her his wife. Rāvaṇa engages Mārīca to disguise himself as a golden deer, anticipating that Sītā will send Rāma and Lakshmaṇa to capture it. Mārīca knows Rāma from Book 1, and tries to warn Rāvaṇa against this plan. But unable to avoid Rāvaṇa's threats, he boards his celestial chariot. Sītā is enchanted by the golden deer. Rāma chases it. Its dying words convince her she hears Rāma crying for help, and she goads Lakshmaṇa to aide Rāma by accusing him of desiring her. Rāvaṇa comes disguised as a mendicant, sprouts ten heads, carries her off by her hair and thighs onto his chariot, and flies away. Sītā calls to Jaṭāyus, imploring him to tell Rāma and Lakshmaṇa all that has happened (47.36). Having slept through her abduction, Jaṭāyus flies up to challenge Rāvaṇa, destroys his chariot, and forces him to the ground. But Rāvaṇa severs his wings. Able to fly without a chariot, Rāvaṇa grabs Sītā to continue his journey. When she sees five monkeys on a mountain, Sītā drops some of her jewels and a garment, hoping they will mark her route. Once in Laṅkā, Rāvaṇa leaves her in a grove of *ashoka* trees outside his palace, giving her twelve months to yield or be chopped into minced meat for his breakfast (*sargas* 14–54).

Rāma goes mad looking for Sītā until the brothers come upon Jaṭāyus, who, before he dies, tells them of her abduction by Rāvaṇa and that he headed south. They head south on an "untrodden path" (65.2), passing into the Krauñca Forest, still hoping to find Sītā. Instead they run into a Dānava-turned-Rākshasa, Kabandha ("headless trunk" but also a name for a sacrificial post). He guards the way past him as Virādha did for the Daṇḍaka Forest at the beginning of Book 3 (and as Kirmīra and the Yaksha do at the beginning and end of the Mahābhārata's Book 3). Kabandha is a headless torso with a single-eyed face in his stomach, a huge devouring mouth, and long grabbing arms that suddenly seize the brothers, who quickly sever them. Realizing that this amputation by Rāma ends a long curse, Kabandha tells his story, and after Rāma has asked if he knows anything about Rāvaṇa and has cremated him, Kabandha rises lustrously from his pyre to say that Rāvaṇa's abode may be found if Rāma allies with the monkey Sugrīva, whom Rāma should quickly make a "comrade" or "commiserator" (*vayasya*), sealing their pact before fire (68.13). Kabandha then directs them to Sugrīva's haunt on Mount Rishyamūka. This path takes them through Mataṅga's Wood to Mataṅga's ashram, where all the *rishis* have passed away except the "mendicant woman" Shabarī ("the Tribal Woman"). As Shabarī soon corroborates, Mataṅga and his disciples ascended to heaven just when Rāma reached Citrakūṭa, but Shabarī has awaited Rāma's arrival so that she can go to heaven after seeing him. For this, Rāma permits her to enter fire (70.26)—indexing an association between fire-entry and purification that will also apply to Sītā. Rāma now sees Mount Rishyamūka (*sargas* 55–71).

Painting Depicts Srī Rāma, the Loyal and Chaste Sītā, and Hanumān. The centuries-old *Rāmāyaṇa*, the Hindu epic recounting Rāma's struggles and victories, remains an intellectual and artistic force in the Indian world and beyond. DAVID CUMMING; EYE UBIQUITOUS / CORBIS.

Book 4, the *Kishkindhā Kāṇḍa*, or "Book of Kishkindhā," the monkey capital, begins with Rāma exploring Rishyamūka. Sugrīva, thinking the brothers could be his brother Vālin's spies, sends his minister Hanumān to scout out their intentions. Learning of the similarities between Rāma and Sugrīva's situations (forest exile; stolen wife), Hanumān says Sugrīva will help Rāma's search, and Lakshmaṇa remarks that this help will come with Sugrīva's own purpose. Hanumān brings the brothers to Sugrīva and tells him that they desire his friendship. As advised by Kabandha, "Sugrīva and Rāghava (Rāma) entered into *vayasya* by reverently circling the blazing fire" (5.16). Sugrīva tells Rāma he will recover his wife, like the lost Vedas, whether she is in the underworld or the heavens. He further recalls that he saw a woman drop her shawl and jewels when she saw him and four other monkeys on the mountain. She was crying "Rāma, Rāma! Lakshmaṇa!" while being carried off by Rāvaṇa. Rāma weeps, recognizing the articles as Sītā's (6.1–19).

Sugrīva now tells his account of how Vālin wronged him, which is only his side of the story. Rāma accepts it, even before fully hearing it, and promises to kill Vālin (8.23–26). Once Vālin was fighting the *asura* Māyāvin in a cave outside Kishkindhā and had stationed Sugrīva outside the entrance. After a year Sugrīva noticed signs of what he thought was Vālin's death, so he blocked the cave to prevent the demon's exit. Back at Kishkindhā, he replaced Vālin as king. But it was Māyāvin who had died, and when Vālin got out, he reclaimed the throne, took Sugrīva's wife, and drove Sugrīva away. Rāma accepts that Sugrīva is innocent, assures him that Vālin sinned in taking his wife, and repeats that he will kill him (9–10). But behind this story lies another, in which Sugrīva discloses why Mount Rishyamūka provides him asylum. Māyāvin opposed Vālin because he had killed Māyāvin's older brother, "a buffalo named Dundubhi" (4.11.7). Dundubhi terrorized Kishkindhā with his horns; roaring like a kettle drum (*dundubhi*), he lured Vālin from his drunken amours. Grabbing Dundubhi's horns, Vālin crushed him until blood oozed from his ears and hurled away the carcass. But "blood drops from the wounds fell out from its mouth and were lifted by the wind toward Mataṅga's hermitage" (41). Mataṅga then cursed Vālin to be unable to enter his Wood on pain of death. Sugrīva now points to Dundubhi's bones, which Rāma kicks off to a great distance with just his big toe.

Mataṅga's departure thus defines his hermitage, along with Mount Rishyamūka, as a place cursed for its pollution. Though Mataṅga is a *rishi*, he is not a Vedic *rishi* or even a Brahman. Rather, his name denotes the "untouchable" just as Shabarī's denotes the tribal. Dundubhi's killing has behind it a buffalo sacrifice—a quite archaic one, with death by wrestling rather than the sword—in which this "untouchable *rishi*" takes on the pollution of this non-Vedic village rite. Rāma thus forges his "friendship" with Sugrīva in a place that is both cursed and beyond the range of the Vedic *rishi*s, who up to now have marked his trail. In entering this topsy-turvy monkey world, where Vedic practices are distorted at the advice of Kabandha, a speaking sacrificial post, Rāma is all the while being drawn into a sequence of non-Vedic killings of questionable *dharma* in which he himself is to make Vālin the next victim. Rāma tells Sugrīva to challenge Vālin to single combat and Rāma shoots Vālin from ambush. Against Vālin's complaints that Rāma is a *dharma*-hypocrite (4.17.18), Rāma has only dubious replies: he acts as Bharata's proxy; princes go about the world guarding *dharma*, which is subtle; Vālin is only a monkey and cannot understand *dharma*, yet deserves this punishment for the sin of taking his brother's wife; Rāma had promised Sugrīva to kill Vālin and his truth is unexceptionable (*sarga*s 1–18).

Sugrīva is reconsecrated, and Vālin's son Aṅgada is made heir apparent. With these events the main story enters the monkeys' cave capital Kishkindhā. But Rāma does not. In keeping with his minimal contact with Mataṅga and Dundubhi, and on the pretext of having promised Dasharatha he would not enter any village or city during his exile (4.25.8), he lives outside Kishkindhā with Lakshmaṇa in a cave on Mount Prashravaṇa to await the end of the rainy season, when Sugrīva will summon the world's monkeys to begin searching for Sītā. But when Sugrīva extends his debaucheries, Rāma grows angry and sends Lakshmaṇa to threaten him into action. Sugrīva says he has not forgotten, and summons the monkeys (*sarga*s 19–38).

Sugrīva orders monkey squads to search each direction and return after a month. Noticing that Sugrīva pays special attention to the southern party, which includes Hanumān, Rāma gives Hanumān a "ring engraved with his name" (43.11) to show to Sītā so that she will know whose message Hanumān bears and not fear him. A month later, all parties have returned but this southern one, which now emerges from a magical cave near the ocean. Dejected over their failure, they start fasting to death but are observed by a wingless vulture, Jaṭāyus's older brother Sampāti, who thinks better of eating them and says that he and his son saw Rāvaṇa taking Sītā to Laṅkā, adding that the fierce *rishi* Nishākara told him to wait in this spot until Rāma's monkey helpers should arrive. Mission accomplished, Sampāti sprouts new wings and flies away. The monkeys then decide that one of them must leap to Laṅkā, and decide it is a job only for Hanumān (*sargas* 39–66).

Sundara Kāṇḍa, "The Beautiful Book" (Book 5), then begins with Hanumān's leap to Laṅkā. Landing and determined to search for Sītā, he makes his way at night to Rāvaṇa's palace where he sees, sleeping after their carousals, Rāvaṇa, his harem, and a most beautiful woman—Rāvaṇa's queen Mandodarī—whom Hanumān joyfully mistakes for Sītā, until he thinks through the implications, and soon recovers his propriety after taking such fascination at another man's boudoir. Satisfying himself that there was nowhere else to begin looking for a woman, he goes to a nearby *ashoka* grove and finds a woman surrounded by *rākshasīs*, looking gaunt from fasting, unornamented and dirty, whom he barely makes out to be Sītā—as if faced with "some Vedic text once learned by heart but now nearly lost through lack of recitation," or "as one might make out the sense of a word whose meaning had been changed through want of proper usage" (13.36–37; *sarga*s 1–15).

As Hanumān looks on, Rāvaṇa pays another visit. Again, once Sītā defies him, his words turn to threats: before she becomes his breakfast she now has only two months to come to his bed. He orders the Rākshasīs to bend her will to his and walks off with one of them, who has begun seducing him. The browbeating goes on until an elderly Rākshasī named Trijaṭā recounts a dream that portends Rāma's reunion with Sītā, Rāvaṇa's death, and Laṅkā's destruction. Trijaṭā observes that certain auspicious bodily signs indicate that her dream has encouraged Sītā, and these signs intensify even after Sītā has spoken of hanging herself while "holding the fillet for her hair" (26.17; *sarga*s 16–27).

Hanumān, whose presence these omens register, now reflects that he must comfort Sītā lest she take her life. Not to alarm her, he starts a short "sweet" account of Rāma and Sītā's story, down to her being found by the unknown voice she is hearing (29.3–9). When Sītā sees a monkey above her, she faints and first thinks it is a dream—in which monkeys, she says, are inauspicious according to the *shāstras* (30.1–4). But verifying that she is Sītā, they intertwine stories until Hanumān shows her Rāma's signet ring. Sītā tells Hanumān to tell Rāma to make haste; she has only two months (35.7). As tokens for Rāma, Sītā tells an intimate story that only she and Rāma could know and, saying she has now but one month left, gives Hanumān a precious hair ornament that she has kept carefully concealed. Leaving Sītā, Hanumān rampages through the palace grounds, killing Rākshasa warriors sent to capture him until Rāvaṇa's son Indrajit immobilizes him with divine weapons. Brought before Rāvaṇa, Hanumān tells him he faces the worst if he does not return Sītā. Rāvaṇa sets Hanumān's tail afire and has him marched through Laṅkā. Making himself small, Hanumān slips his bonds; leaping from house to house, he torches Laṅkā with his tail. Then, thinking of Sītā, he reassures himself that she will survive since "fire cannot prevail against fire" (53.18; *sargas* 28–53).

Hanumān then recrosses the ocean to join his companions and bring them up to date. Nearing Kishkindhā, they break into Sugrīva's honey grove to get drunk. The guardian reports to Sugrīva that they have destroyed the grove, but Sugrīva joyfully senses that this can only mean their mission's success. Sobered and told that Sugrīva excuses their exuberance, the southern party reports back to him and the brothers. Hanumān tells Rāma the confirmatory story, gives him Sītā's jewel, tells him she has but one month left, and poses the challenge of devising a way to cross the ocean.

Rāma clasps the jewel to his heart. Sītā had described it as "born from the sea" (63.22)—perhaps a pearl. Confirming these origins, Rāma adds that Janaka gave it to her at their wedding when it was "fastened to her head" (64.4). When Hanumān presents a fuller account of the jewel's transfer, he says that when Sītā released it from her garment, she "gave me this jewel fit for being fastened (or, for the fillet) around her braid (*veṇyudgrathanam*)" (65.30). That compound also described the fillet when she thought of hanging herself. She thus seems to send the jewel that she would fasten to this fillet without sending the fillet, which would still be keeping her hair back in an *ekaveṇī* or "single braid"—a kind of ponytail that signals a woman's separation in anticipation of her husband's return, and in Sītā's case is once said to be "matted" (55.27; *sargas* 54–66). Left pending, as it were, is the symbolism of fully loosened hair that could denote a woman's widowhood or mourning—or, if one thinks of Draupadī, her Kālī-like anger.

The *Yuddha Kāṇḍa*, or "Book of the War" (Book 6), begins with prewar consultations on both sides, out of which Rāvaṇa's younger brother Vibhīshaṇa emerges as a righteous, but rejected, adviser. Once the brothers and monkeys reach the seashore, Vibhīshaṇa receives asylum from Rāma. Helped by his advice to call on Rāma's ancestor Sāgara (Ocean), the latter grants permission for a bridge to Laṅkā, which the monkeys then construct. Rāvaṇa seems unable to focus on Rāma or the war until his wise maternal grandfather Mālyavān, counseling peace with Rāma and Sītā's return, says the gods and *rishi*s desire Rāma's victory, differentiates *dharma* and *adharma* as divine and demonic, alludes to the (Mahābhārata) idea that the king defines the age (*yuga*), says that throughout the regions the *rishi*s are performing fiery Vedic rites and austerities that are damaging the Rākshasas, foresees the Rākshasas' destruction, notes the sinister omens surrounding Laṅkā, and concludes, "I think Rāma is Vishṇu abiding in a human body" (26.31). Mālyavān not only gets it right but provides analogs to features of the Bhagavad Gītā: a theology for the war about to happen; a prediction of its outcome; and a disclosure of the hidden divinity behind it—in this case, hidden so far mainly from himself. Rāvaṇa will hear none of this (*sargas* 1–30).

Rāvaṇa orders his warriors into action. Most just go through a routine of boasting, ignoring omens, and getting killed. Exceptions are his gigantic brother Kumbhakarṇa, who must be wakened from his half-year sleep, fed, and toppled, and Rāvaṇa's magician son Indrajit, who immobilized Hanumān. Indrajit figures in the two main episodes that threaten Rāma's side: he nearly kills the brothers with snake arrows until the celestial bird Garuḍa rescues them by routing the snakes; and he lays low nearly all the monkeys until Hanumān returns from the Himalayas carrying a whole peak, capped with healing herbs. The fighting is also interrupted by reminders that Sītā is at stake. Finally, Rāma kills Rāvaṇa and consecrates Vibhīshaṇa as Laṅkā's king (*sargas* 31–100).

Now Sītā, who hears from Hanumān of Rāma's victory and rejoices at her deliverance, is brought to Rāma by Vibhīshaṇa—who relays Rāma's directive that she appear adorned with divine unguents and jewels and a washed head (102.7). She would rather see her husband unbathed, but takes this advice and wears (seems to choose) a white garment (13)—soon a symbol of what troubles Rāma: her purity, one supposes, though white is also worn in widowhood. When Vibhīshaṇa announces her, Rāma is filled with "joy, misery, and anger" (16). As she advances, an "unseemly commotion" (Shulman 1991, p. 91) breaks out as Vibhīshaṇa's servants aggressively clear her way among the monkeys, bears, and Rākshasas struggling to see her. Rāma censures Vibhīshaṇa for injuring "my own people (*svajano mama*)" (25); since women can be seen in public during disasters, wars, and weddings, there is no reason to shield Sītā "in my presence (*mat samīpe*)" (28). As she stands anxiously before him, beginning to weep, Rāma gives "utterance to the anger in his heart" (103.1). Barely mentioning her misfortune, he insists on how he fulfilled his honor, acting as a man should. Seeing more tears and hearing Sītā reply that such words are rather less than manly, Rāma's mood further darkens: he fought not for her sake but to remove insults; she is now free to choose Lakshmaṇa, Bharata, Sugrīva, or Vibhīshaṇa! Rāvaṇa would not have left her alone in his own house (103.22–24). Meeting only Rāma's silence after a last appeal, Sītā tells Lakshmaṇa to light a pyre; stricken by these false charges, she cannot live (104.18). Rāma gestures consent. Sītā takes Agni as witness that her heart has never strayed, asks his protection, circumambulates the fire and enters it—as the Rākshasas and monkeys scream (20–27). And all at once Rāma is beset by deities who have come to ask him, their hands cupped in adoration, "O Creator of the entire world and the very best of enlightened beings, how do you ignore Sītā as she is falling into fire? How do you not know yourself to be the best of the host of gods!" (105.5). Rāma replies, "I think myself a man, Dasharatha's son Rāma. Who am I? From whom and whence do I come? Let the blessed one (Brahmā) tell" (10). Whereupon Brahmā names Nārāyaṇa, Purushottama, and Krishna as identities by which Rāma can now know himself as Vishnu; you have "entered a human body for the sake of killing Rāvaṇa" (26). Agni now restores Sītā unscathed (her garment now red) and attests to her fidelity and purity. Speaking in her presence for the first time since his insults, Rāma seems to seize on the outcome to offer excuses: had he taken Sītā back unpurified (*avishodhya*; 106.12) the good would have considered him foolish and driven by desire; he knew her fidelity all along; he could no more abandon her than his own fame (18)! Shiva now tells Rāma to return to Ayodhya to perform a horse sacrifice (107.6), and announces Dasharatha, now redeemed (*tārita*) by Rāma, who has come from Indra's heaven. Dasharatha embraces Rāma, and in the embrace of his two sons says, "I am now freed from misery (*duhkhād*)" (107.15); he now understands that Rāma is none other than the supreme being ordained (*purushottamam vihitam*) by the gods to have come to earth to kill Rāvaṇa (17); Rāma should see that everyone is reconciled back at Ayodhya. Rāma then gets Indra to resurrect the slain monkeys, and Vibhīshaṇa arranges for the trio to fly to Ayodhya in the Pushpaka chariot—most recently Rāvaṇa's. The monkeys and Rākshasas then persuade Rāma to let them accompany him (110.16–20). Before they arrive, they stop at Bharadvāja's ashram and learn that Bharata has continued to honor Rāma's sandals. Bharadvāja recounts the trio's whole adventure, which he knows by his penances (112.14). From there, Rāma sends Hanumān to Nandigrāma (Bharata's village residence outside the capitol), to tell Bharata their story and to assess his expressions. At last Rāma is enthroned in the presence not only of his rejoicing family and people but the monkeys, Rākshasas, and *rishi*s. Twice it is said that Rāma ruled for ten thousand years (82, 90), the second time in this Book's very last words (*sarga*s 101–16)—surely sounding like a happy ending, as many Western scholars and some Indian vernaculars have taken Book 6 to be.

But the *Uttara Kāṇḍa*, or "The Final Book" (Book 7), opens with Rāma just consecrated and a series of departures and dismissals. First, the *rishi*s come to his palace—Agastya and the original Seven among them (17.1.3–4). Rāma asks about the Rākshasas he conquered, launching their former near-neighbor Agastya on a lengthy Rākshasa genealogy, with tales of Rāvaṇa's boon and his violations of women. These lead to stories about Indrajit and end with others about Hanumān and the monkeys. Rāma is repeatedly filled with wonder. Then "all the rishis went as they came" (36.46). Rāma also dispatches a hundred kings, and the Rākshasas, monkeys, and bears—Hanumān parting with the famous words: "As long as I hear *Rāma-kathā* on the face of the earth, so long will my breaths reside in my body" (39.16). Next Rāma dismisses the Pushpaka chariot while keeping it on call (*sarga*s 1–40). And next he dismisses Sītā, who will not remain on call. All these dismissals subtract down to a great unraveling.

There is a time of felicity between Rāma and Sītā, but at news that Ayodhya's citizens gossip about Sītā's chastity in Rāvaṇa's house, Rāma banishes her to protect his royal reputation. Sītā has just announced that she is pregnant and would like to visit some pilgrimage spots, so Rāma orders Lakshmaṇa to take her to the forest on that pretext and abandon her. Painfully, Lakshmaṇa leaves her at Vālmīki's hermitage. Next Rāma hears that there are still some ascetics who live in fear of a Rākshasa named Lavaṇa. Shatrughna goes to tackle Lavaṇa, and stops over in Vālmīki's leafy hut on the night Sītā gives birth to the twins. Vālmīki goes to bless and name the infants, and at midnight Shatrughna hears the good news and comes to bless Sītā and the boys. At dawn he resumes his journey, kills Lavaṇa, and establishes a kingdom at Mathura. Twelve years later he decides to visit Ayodhya. On the way, in a passage rejected by the Critical Edition even though it appears in all the manuscripts collated, he stops at Vālmīki's hermitage, overhears the twins' elegant recitals, and promises that he and his army will keep their birth secret (7, Appendix 1, no. 9; Shah, pp. 26–27). When Bharata sees Rāma, he mentions nothing about Vālmīki, Sītā, or the twins (*sarga*s 41–63).

A Brahman now comes to Rāma's palace gate with his dead son in his arms, announcing that Rāma must have committed some great fault for a child to die in his kingdom (64.9). The narrative thread seems to suggest that Rāma's fault could be his abandonment of Sītā, for which, in order to keep ignoring it, he would have to find a scapegoat. If so, the always clever Nārada provides a fitting cue: Rāma should look for someone unlawfully performing *tapas* (austerities), a Shūdra who would only be able to do this in the Kaliyuga (65.22), an age yet to come. Nārada knows of a Shudra doing *tapas* somewhere and recommends that Rāma tour his kingdom. Recalling the Pushpaka chariot, Rāma finds the Shūdra Shambūka, who announces his intent to become divine. Rāma beheads him, reviving the Brahman's son and delighting the gods. Following the latter to Agastya's hermitage, Rāma stays there to listen to more of Agastya's stories before returning to Ayodhya and again dismissing the Pushpaka (*sargas* 64–73).

Rāma now tells Bharata and Lakshmaṇa he wishes to perform a Rājasūya sacrifice, but Bharata tells him a horse sacrifice is less destructive and Lakshmaṇa adds that the *ashvamedha* removes all sins and purifies (75.2). Rāma approves the *ashvamedha*. He orders Lakshmaṇa to make invitations to Sugrīva and Vibhīshaṇa to bring their parties, and to the regional *rishis* and their wives, and to prepare a vast sacrificial enclosure in the Naimisha Forest. Bharata is to lead a procession trailed by all the mothers from the inner apartments and "my golden wife (*kāñcanīm mama patnīm*) worthy of consecration (*dīkshā*) in sacrificial rites" (19). Sītā thus has a replacement-statue even while still alive. With the sacrifice proceeding, Vālmīki suddenly arrives with his disciples (84.1) and directs the twins to sing "the whole Rāmāyaṇa poem at the gate of Rāma's dwelling" (3–5)—twenty *sargas* a day (9). Rāma hears the boys sing the first twenty *sargas* beginning "from the sight of Nārada (*nāradadarshanāt*)" (11)—that is, from the beginning of the *upodghāta* on. Once the twins tell Rāma who authored this poem that contains his whole adventure (19), they offer to continue singing it at intervals in the rite (21). After many days, Rāma recognizes them, misses Sītā, and summons her to attest to her purity by oath in the midst of the great *rishis*, Rākshasas, and monkeys, plus unnamed kings and the four castes in thousands (87.6–7). But when Vālmīki brings Sītā, he attests to her purity himself (19), and tells Rāma only that "she will give proof of her fidelity" (15, 20). No longer demanding the oath just announced, Rāma accepts Vālmīki's word as tantamount to being Sītā's: "Surely I have proof of fidelity in your stainless words. Surely Vaidehī gave proof of fidelity formerly in the presence of the gods" (88.2–3)—who by now have also come to witness (5–7). Indeed, in a phrase that occurs nowhere else in either epic, this conclave occurs "in the middle of the universe (*jagato madhye*)" (1, 4). Though not demanded to make an oath, Sītā nonetheless makes one implicitly in her only and last words: "If I have thought with my mind of none other than Rāma, let the goddess Mādhavī [Earth] give me an opening." (10). Rāma, who had hoped for "affection" (*prīti*) from Sītā (4), has thus accepted the author's word as Sītā's, only to be overwhelmed with grief and horror by what her word—and the poet's—actually is. This is the moment at which he comes to realize what it means to be caught up in his own story, which, if he heard it from the frame on, as we are told, he would know it to have also been Sītā's story and to have been inspired by the grief of a female bird. Rāma now threatens to destroy Earth unless she returns Sītā intact (7, Appendix I, No. 13, lines 18–20) until Brahmā repeats what he told him after Sītā's fire ordeal, that he is Vishnu, and invites him to listen with the great *rishis* to the rest of this "first poem," which will now tell what is yet to happen (21–40). Once Brahmā returns to heaven, the *rishis* in Brahmaloka obtain his permission to return for the rest as well (43–49; *sargas* 74–88). Though the Critical Edition rejects this *sarga*, it is universally attested. For Rāma, the relation between Sītā's two ordeals seems to be that whereas his first self-recognition as Vishnu emerges out of a human identity crossed with uncertainty and confusion as to his all-too-human emotions, his second comes after he has learned of his divinity and has repeatedly pared his life down to a perfect rule through his dismissals of others, yet without consideration of what this has cost him since the banishment of his wife—not to mention what it has cost her. If so, the poem could be saying that Vālmīki's initial question to Nārada—whether there is an ideal man today—was not really convincingly answered.

Once the *ashvamedha* ends, Rāma finds the universe empty without Sītā and again dismisses the kings, bears, monkeys, and Rākshasas (89.1). He never remarries, but at all his sacrifices there is a golden Sītā (*jānakī kāñcanī*; 4). For ten thousand years he rules a harmonious kingdom. Finally Death or Time (Kāla) comes to him as a messenger from Brahmā and tells him they must meet alone; anyone hearing them must be killed. While Rāma posts Lakshmaṇa at the door, "Time who destroys all" (94.2) tells Rāma it is time to return to heaven as Vishnu. As the two converse, the congenitally ravenous sage Durvāsas tries to barge in, threatening to curse the kingdom if he is prevented. Lakshmaṇa chooses his own death rather than allowing that of others and admits him. Durvāsas wants only something to eat after a thousand-year fast, which Rāma happily provides. At Vasishtha's advice, Rāma then banishes Lakshmaṇa as equivalent to death, and Lakshmaṇa, meditating by the Sarayū River, is taken up to heaven. Bharata then advises Rāma to divide Kosala into two kingdoms to be ruled by Kusha and Lava. Bharata and Shatrughna then follow Rāma, who enters the Sarayū and resumes his divine form (*sargas* 89–100).

The Rāmāyaṇa and the *Rāmopākhyāna*

The relation between the Rāmāyaṇa and the Mahābhārata's *Rāmopākhyāna* is usually posed as one between just these two Sanskrit Rāma stories, and as a question of whether there is a genetic relation between them. Which came first? Or do both rely on some prior *Rāmakathā*? On these questions, this article's position is twofold. First, the primary relation is not between the Rāmāyaṇa and the *Rāmopākhyāna*, but between the Rāmāyaṇa and the Mahābhārata, which it views as the slightly earlier of the two epics. On this point, it was noted that their similar designs could not be accidental. It is easier to imagine Vālmīki refining *kāvya* out of a multigenre Mahābhārata than to imagine Vyāsa overlooking this achievement to spread disarticulation. In this vein, the *Rāmopākhyāna* opens with material about Rāvaṇa that the Rāmāyaṇa saves for Book 7. It thus cannot be explained as an epitome of the Rāmāyaṇa, since it lacks the structure that the Rāmāyaṇa shares with the Mahābhārata.

Second, this article holds that it is helpful to reflect on how *upākhyāna* material is used in both epics. As observed, the Rāmāyaṇa uses this term only in an interpolation. Rather than having stand-out "subtales," the Rāmāyaṇa folds all its secondary narratives into one consecutively unfolding poem. This is especially noteworthy in its stories about the eight great *rishi*s encounterd by Rāma, many of which include material that the Mahābhārata relates in its *upākhyāna*s. Other than Vasishtha, a fixture in the Ikshvāku house, the *Rāmopākhyāna* does not know these *rishi*s. It has no Vishvāmitra, Gautama and Ahalyā, Rāma Jāmadagnya, or for that matter, Vasishtha involved in the stories from youth through marriage; just this: "In the course of time [Dasharatha's] sons grew up very vigorous, and became fledged in the Vedas and their mysteries and in the art of archery. They completed their student years, and took wives" (Mbh 3.261.4-5). It has no Bharadvāja; just this of Bharata: "He found Rāma and Lakshmaṇa on Mount Citrakūṭa" (216.63). And from Citrakūṭa on, there is not a peep from Atri and Anasūyā or Agastya. There is also no Vālmīki, Mataṅga, or Nishākara. It is improbable that the *Rāmopākhyāna* would have strained out all these figures and episodes if it were a Rāmāyaṇa epitome. Vālmīki would seem to have worked such *upākhyāna* material into something he claims to be new: *kāvya*, "the first poem." And this would seem to be the best way to think about what he did with the *Rāmopākhyāna:* go beyond it to author a poem in which Rāma and Sītā move through their double adventure along paths signposted by *rishi*s who impart Vedic authority as *dharma*, who represent "all the *rishi*s," high and low, who motivate the divine incarnations to cleanse the world of noxious Rākshasas, and who in turn are represented by Vālmīki himself, who frames all the paths that Rāma and Sītā take as ones that begin with his inspiration to tell their adventures in a poem that will lead them ultimately to him.

Alf Hiltebeitel

See also **Brāhmaṇas; Hinduism (Dharma); Mahābhārata; Rāmāyaṇa and Mahābhārata Paintings**

BIBLIOGRAPHY

Biardeau, Madeleine. "Some Remarks on the Links between the Epics, the Purāṇas and Their Vedic Sources." In *Studies in Hinduism: Vedism and Hinduism*, edited by Gerhard Oberhammer. Vienna: Verlag der Österreichischen Akademie der Wissenschaften, 1997.

———. *Le Rāmāyaṇa de Vālmīki*. Paris: Gallimard, 1999.

Goldman, Robert P., trans. and ed. *The Rāmāyaṇa of Vālmīki*, vol. 1: *Bālakāṇḍa*. Princeton, N.J.: Princeton University Press, 1984.

Goldman, Robert P., and Sally Sutherland Goldman, trans. and eds. *The Rāmāyaṇa of Vālmīki*, vol. 5: *Sundarkāṇḍa*. Princeton, N.J.: Princeton University Press, 1996.

Hiltebeitel, Alf. "Sītā Vibhūitā: The Jewels for Her Journey." *Ludwik Sternbach Commemoration Volume. Indologica Taurinensia* 8–9 (1980–1981): 193–200.

Leslie, Julia. "A Bird Bereaved: The Identity and Significance of Vālmīki's *Krauñca*." *Journal of Indian Philosophy* 26 (1998): 455–487.

Pollock, Sheldon I. "Ātmānam mānuha manye: Dharmākūtam on the Divinity of Rāma." *Journal of the Oriental Institute of Baroda* 33 (1984): 505–528.

Pollock, Sheldon I., trans. *The Rāmāyaṇa of Vālmīki*, vol. 2: *Ayodhyākāṇḍa*, edited by Robert P. Goldman. Princeton, N.J.: Princeton University Press, 1986.

Shah, U. P., ed. *The Uttarakāṇḍa: The 45 Vālmīki Rāmāyaṇa*, vol. 7: *The Vālmīki Rāmāyaṇa: Critical Edition.* G. H. Bhatt and U. P. Shah, general editors. Baroda: University of Baroda, 1975.

Shulman, David. "Fire and Flood: The Testing of Sītā in Kampa's *Irāmāvatāram*." In *Many Rāmāyaṇas. The Diversity of a Narrative Tradition in South Asia*, edited by Paula Richman. Berkeley: University of California Press, 1991.

———. *The Wisdom of Poets: Studies in Tamil, Telugu, and Sanskrit.* Delhi: Oxford University Press, 2001.

Sutherland Goldman, Sally. "Gendered Narratives: Gender, Space and Narrative Structures in Vālmīki's *Bālakāṇḍa*." In *The Rāmāyaṇa Revisited*, edited by Mandakranta Bose. Oxford: Oxford University Press, 2004.

RĀMĀYAṆA AND MAHĀBHĀRATA PAINTINGS Stone and terra-cotta relief sculptures depicting participants and episodes from the two great ancient Indian epics, the Rāmāyaṇa (Adventures of Rama) and the Mahābhārata ([War of the] Great Bharatas), were made as early as the fifth century for use in the iconographic programs of Hindu temples. However, the earliest surviving painted illustrations of the epics (apart perhaps from no longer extant murals) are in a manuscript on paper of the Āraṇyakaparvan (Forest book) of the Mahābhārata, which according to its colophon was created at Kacchauva near Agra in 1516 (VS 1573) during the reign of Sultan Sikandar Lodi (1489–1517). Now in the Asiatic Society, Mumbai (MS.B.245), this profusely illustrated manuscript owes much of its artistic inspiration to slightly earlier Jain illustrated texts, such as the Jaunpur Kalpasūtra (Book of sacred precepts) of 1465, and it shares several stylistic characteristics with the renowned *Caurapañchāśikā* (Fifty stanzas of secret love) series of paintings dating from 1525–1575, now in the Lalbhai Dalpatbhai Institute of Indology, Ahmedabad. Following the seminal Kacchauva Mahābhārata of 1516, many illustrated manuscripts of the great epics were produced, especially of the Rāmāyaṇa.

Early Mughal

Several important illustrated manuscripts of the great epics were produced under the enlightened patronage of the liberal Mughal emperor Akbar (r. 1556–1605). In 1582 Akbar commissioned a Persian translation of the Mahābhārata, titled the Razmnāma (Book of wars), which was created in 1584–1586. It was followed by a translation of the Rāmāyaṇa made in 1588–1591. Both of Akbar's imperial presentation copies are now in the Maharaja Sawai Man Singh II Museum, Jaipur (MS. AG. 1683–1850 and MS. AG. 1851–2026 respectively). Akbar also ordered that his leading Muslim nobles have their own copies made of the two imperial manuscripts in order to promote a greater understanding of Hinduism. The extant copies of the Razmnāma, now dispersed, are dated 1598 and 1616 (another known copy dated 1605 is now missing). A Rāmāyaṇa manuscript dated 1587–1598 that was directly inspired by Akbar's imperial manuscript was commissioned by a leading patron of painting, the Mughal courtier ʿAbd al-Rahīm, the Khān-i Khānān (commander-in-chief). The manuscript, classified as subimperial because of its nonimperial patron, contains 130 paintings and is now in the Freer Gallery of Art, Washington, D.C. (07.271). Another subimperial Rāmāyaṇa manuscript, now dispersed, is attributed to about 1595. A number of folios from these subimperial manuscripts survive in various museum and private collections, including the Chhatrapati Shivaji Maharaj Vastu Sangrahalaya (formerly called the Prince of Wales Museum of Western India), Mumbai; Indian Museum, Kolkata; British Library, London; National Museum, New Delhi; Victoria and Albert Museum, London; Chester Beatty Library, Dublin; Museum Rietberg, Zürich; Arthur M. Sackler Museum, Harvard University, Cambridge, Mass.; Cincinnati Art Museum; Cleveland Museum of Art; Freer Gallery of Art, Washington, D.C.; Los Angeles County Museum of Art; Metropolitan Museum of Art, New York; Museum of Fine Arts, Boston; Philadelphia Museum of Art; San Diego Museum of Art; and Virginia Museum of Fine Arts, Richmond.

Rajput

Presumably stimulated in part by the splendor and success of the imperial and subimperial Mughal manuscripts, illustrated Rāmāyaṇa manuscripts soon began to be created for the rulers and high nobles of the various Hindu Rajput (princely) courts in Rajasthan and central India that were encompassed within the greater Mughal empire. They were perhaps made for certain wealthy Hindu merchants as well. These manuscripts displayed varying degrees of Mughal-influenced naturalism, a stylistic feature that Rajput artists encountered due to their patrons' participation in the Mughal political world. One of the earliest surviving Rajput Rāmāyaṇa manuscripts features a bold palette, lively expression, and scant if any Mughal stylistic influence. The manuscript is generally ascribed to the central Indian regions of Malwa and Bundelkhand in modern Madhya Pradesh, although its exact place of origin remains a matter of scholarly dispute and is dependent upon the interpretation of two important later colophons. According to the manuscript's colophon on a folio in the Bharat Kala Bhavan, Banaras Hindu University, Varanasi (6756-6815), it was made for Hira Rani, who can be identified as Hirade, the queen of Pahar Singh of Orchha (r. 1641–1653). The manuscript is attributed to about 1640, as its sophisticated compositions represent a slightly later stage of artistic evolution than those of a dispersed Malwa Rasikapriyā dated 1634, folios of which are now primarily in the National Museum, New Delhi. Other paintings from the 1640 Malwa Rāmāyaṇa manuscript are in the Kanoria Collection, Patna; Arthur M. Sackler Museum, Harvard University, Cambridge, Mass.; Brooklyn Museum of Art; and Los Angeles County Museum of Art. It is relevant to note here that a newly published inscription on a Soratha Rāgiṇī dated 1687 (VS 1744) in the Collections of Basant Kumar and Sarladevi Birla, Kolkata, records that the painting was made in the city of Lalitapura near Jhansi in Bundelkhand, thus providing at least one definite place of creation for central Indian paintings during the seventeenth century.

One of the largest and most accomplished Rāmāyaṇa manuscripts is a now dispersed compendium of over 450 full-page paintings made between 1649 and 1653 for Maharana Jagat Singh I of Mewar (r. 1628–1652). Three master artists directed the production of different sections of the seven-book manuscript: Sahibdin (active c. 1628–1655), Manohar (active beginning c. 1640), and an unnamed Deccani artist. The first book, the Bālakāṇḍa (Book of childhood), was completed in 1649 and painted by Manohar. It contained seventy-nine illustrated folios, twenty of which are now in the Chhatrapati Shivaji Maharaj Vastu Sangrahalaya, Mumbai; two in the Baroda Museum; and approximately fifty-five folios in the family collection of the late Sir Cowasji Jehangir, Mumbai. The second book, the Ayodhyākāṇḍa (Book of Ayodhya), has sixty-eight paintings attributed to Sahibdin. It was finished in 1650 and is now in the British Library. The third book, Āranyakāṇḍa (Book of the forest), has thirty-six paintings executed in the style of Manohar. It was completed in 1651 and is now in the Rajasthan Oriental Research Institute, Udaipur. The fourth book, the Kishkindhākāṇḍa (Book of Kishkindhā), has thirty-four paintings primarily attributed to the Deccani artist and his assistants. It was finished in 1653 after the death of Jagat Singh I at the beginning of the succeeding rule of Maharana Raj Singh I (r. 1652–1680). It is now in the British Library. The fifth book, the Sundarakāṇḍa (Beautiful book), may have never been completed. However, eighteen paintings attributed to the Deccani artist and his assistants that are presumably from the fifth book have survived. They were probably executed early in Raj Singh I's reign, and are now in the India Office Library collection of the British Library. The sixth book, the Yuddhakāṇḍa (Book of the battle), has eighty-eight paintings by Sahibdin. These superlative works represent the mature phase of Sahibdin's production and are among the finest paintings ever produced during India's long and rich artistic heritage. The sixth book was finished in 1652 and is now in the British Library. The seventh book, the Uttarakāṇḍa (Final book), contains ninety-two paintings attributed to a follower of Manohar. It was completed in 1653 and is now in the British Library. Another notable Mewar Rāmāyaṇa containing 201 paintings was produced during the early rule of Maharana Sangram Singh II (r. 1710–1738). It was finished in 1712 and is now in the British Library.

Pahari

Illustrated manuscripts of the great epics were also produced by families of artists working in association with various courts located in the Himalayan foothills known as the Pahari region, primarily in present-day Himachal Pradesh but also in neighboring Jammu and Kashmir and the Punjab. Although only five folios may have survived, perhaps the earliest Pahari Rāmāyaṇa was created at Mandi around 1630–1645, during the late rule of Raja Hari Sen (r. 1604 or 1623–1637) or during the early rule of his successor Raja Suraj Sen (r. 1637–1664).

One of the finest and best known, but until recently improperly understood, Pahari Rāmāyaṇas is known as the "Shangri" Rāmāyaṇa because it was once in the ancestral collection of the Shangri branch of the royal family of Kulu in Himachal Pradesh. Accordingly, most of the manuscript of at least three hundred paintings was once attributed to Kulu, with some later sections thought perhaps to have been finished in Mandi or even Bikaner in Rajasthan. However, more current research indicates that the beginning portions of the manuscript were painted by an unknown master artist working about 1690–1710 at the Bahu branch of the Jammu court in the modern state of Jammu and Kashmir during the reigns of Raja Kripal Dev (reigned c. 1660–1690) and his son Raja Anand Dev (r. 1690–1730). The "Shangri" Rāmāyaṇa manuscript is now dispersed, with 168 folios now in the National Museum, New Delhi. Additional pages are in the Bharat Kala Bhavan, Varanasi; British Museum, London; Victoria and Albert Museum, London; Museum Rietberg, Zürich; Brooklyn Museum of Art; Los Angeles County Museum of Art; Metropolitan Museum of Art, New York; Philadelphia Museum of Art; San Diego Museum of Art; Virginia Museum of Fine Arts, Richmond; and various private collections.

Other significant Pahari Rāmāyaṇas, all now dispersed, include a Mankot manuscript of about 1700–1710, the Guler manuscript of about 1720 attributed to the master artist Pandit Seu (c. 1680–c. 1740), the Kangra manuscript of about 1775–1780 attributed to a first-generation descendant of Pandit Seu's son Nainsukh (c. 1710–1778), and the "Nadaun" Rāmāyaṇa done in Kangra around 1820. Although the Mahābhārata was apparently not as favored as the Rāmāyaṇa in the Pahari artistic traditions, there is also a Kangra manuscript of the Mahābhārata attributed to about 1775–1800.

Deccan

Although three South Indian Jain manuscripts survive from as early as the twelfth century, very few illustrated manuscripts from South India predate the eighteenth century. One of the earliest and most important such works is a dispersed *Mahābhārata* manuscript made for the Brahman Timaji Pandit in the Mysore region, probably at Seringapatam. The colophon records the manuscript's completion date of 1670 (VS 1592) and the name of its scribe, Govind Sharma from the village of Chalitgram. Folios from the manuscript survive in the collections of the Jagdish and Kamla Mittal Museum of Indian Art, Hyderabad; Salar Jang Museum, Hyderabad; National Museum, New Delhi; Freer Gallery of Art, Washington, D.C.; Los Angeles County Museum of Art; and Virginia Museum of Fine Arts, Richmond. There is also a mid-eighteenth-century Rāmāyaṇa manuscript from southern Andhra Pradesh, now in the State Museum, Hyderabad.

Vernacular Renditions

Finally, mention should be made of the numerous Rāmāyaṇa and Mahābhārata manuscripts and individual illustrations created by folk artists across India in the eighteenth through twentieth centuries, such as the so-called Paithan paintings of Maharashtra, northern Karnataka, and Andhra Pradesh; the "Kalighat" paintings of Kolkata (Calcutta) in West Bengal; and the "Mithila" or "Madhubani" paintings of Bihar. These works form a rich corpus of epic imagery. Moreover, they are distinct from the Rajput and Pahari traditions in that they are often based on vernacular renditions of the Rāmāyaṇa and Mahābhārata rather than the revered Sanskrit originals of Valmiki and Vyasa, respectively.

Stephen Markel

See also **Miniatures; Mughal Painting**

BIBLIOGRAPHY

The Arts of India and Nepal: The Nasli and Alice Heeramaneck Collection. Exhibition catalog. Boston: Museum of Fine Arts, 1966.

Beach, Milo Cleveland. *The Imperial Image: Paintings for the Mughal Court*. Washington, D.C.: Freer Gallery of Art, Smithsonian Institution, 1981.

———. *Mughal and Rajput Painting. The New Cambridge History of India* I:3. Cambridge, U.K.: Cambridge University Press, 1992.

Chandra, Pramod. "Notes on Malwa Painting," In *The Ananda-Vana of Indian Art: Dr. Anand Krishna Felicitation Volume*, edited by Naval and Manu Krishna. Varanasi: Indica Books and Abhidha Prakashan, 2004.

Craven, Roy C., Jr., ed. *Ramayana Pahari Paintings*. Mumbai: Marg Publications, 1990.

Dehejia, Vidya, ed. *The Legend of Rama: Artistic Visions*. Mumbai: Marg Publications, 1994.

Dye, Joseph M., III. *The Arts of India: Virginia Museum of Fine Arts*. Richmond: Virginia Museum of Fine Arts, 2001.

Ehnbom, Daniel J., with essays by Robert Skelton and Pramod Chandra. *Indian Miniatures: The Ehrenfeld Collection*. New York: Hudson Hills Press, 1985.

Glynn, Catherine. "Early Painting in Mandi." *Artibus Asiae* 44, no. 1 (1983): 21–64.

Goswamy, B. N., and Eberhard Fischer. *Pahari Masters: Court Painters of Northern India*. Artibus Asiae Supplementum 38. Zürich: Artibus Asiae Publishers and Museum Rietberg, 1992.

Khandalavala, Karl, and Moti Chandra. *An Illustrated* Āraṇyaka Parvan *in the Asiatic Society of Bombay*. Mumbai: Asiatic Society of Bombay, 1974.

Krishna, Anand. *Malwa Painting*. Varanasi: Bharat Kala Bhavan, Banaras Hindu University, 1963.

Losty, Jeremiah P. *The Art of the Book in India*. London: British Library, 1982.

———. "Aurangabad or Mewar? The Influence of the Deccan on Rana Jagat Singh's *Ramayana* of 1649–53." In *Indian Painting: Essays in Honour of Karl J. Khandalavala*, edited by B. N. Goswamy in association with Usha Bhatia. New Delhi: Lalit Kala Akademi, 1995.

Markel, Stephen. "Images from a Changing World: Kalighat Paintings of Calcutta." *Arts of Asia* 29, no. 4 (1999): 58–71.

Mittal, Jagdish. *Andhra Paintings of the Ramayana*. Hyderabad: Andhra Pradesh Lalit Kala Akademi, 1969.

Pal, Pratapaditya. *Indian Painting*, vol. I: *1000–1700*. Los Angeles: Los Angeles County Museum of Art, 1993.

Richman, Paula, ed. *Many Rāmāyaṇas: The Diversity of a Narrative Tradition in South Asia*. Delhi: Oxford University Press, 1992.

Stronge, Susan. *Painting for the Mughal Emperor: The Art of the Book 1560–1660*. London: V&A Publications, 2002.

Topsfield, Andrew. *Court Painting at Udaipur: Art under the Patronage of the Maharanas of Mewar*. Artibus Asiae Supplementum 44. Zürich: Artibus Asiae Publishers and Museum Rietberg, 2001.

RAM RAJYA. *See* **Gandhi, Mahatma M. K.**

RANADE, MAHADEV GOVIND ***(1842–1901), Indian jurist and reformer.*** One of India's most brilliant jurists, social reformers, and early nationalist leaders, Mahadev Govind Ranade inspired Gopal Krishna Gokhale and entire generations of young Maharashtrians to follow in his path of national service. Born to the Chitpavan Brahman community of Pune's ruling Peshwas, Ranade graduated from the first class of Bombay University in 1862, receiving highest honors, then went on to study law; he was appointed a subordinate judge in Pune in 1871, the youngest Indian jurist of Bombay State.

Social and Religious Reformer

Ranade recognized the cruel and archaic inequities of Hinduism, especially its harsh household laws dealing with women, child marriages, widow immolation, and the treatment of "untouchables." He resolved to start a society in Western India, similar to earlier reform groups that had been founded in Bengal, starting with Ram Mohan Roy's enlightened "Brahmo Samaj." Ranade called his organization Prarthana Samaj (Prayer Society), bringing several like-minded reformers together for its first meeting in 1869 in Bombay (Mumbai). They focused first on educational reforms and later on legislative widow-remarriage reforms, encouraging young Hindu widows, whose lives would otherwise have remained wasted in dismal neglect and total isolation, to improve their minds and to remarry. Ranade himself helped to arrange the first widow remarriage in Bombay. On 2 April 1870 Ranade took charge of Pune's Sarvajanik Sabha (Public Society), which Gokhale later joined and helped him run, petitioning the governor, the viceroy, and the British House of Commons for various legal as well as sociopolitical reforms. In 1887 Ranade founded the National Social Conference, which met each year just after India's National Congress, since Bal Gangadhar Tilak and other devout Hindus threatened to riot if social reform issues were ever raised in the annual meetings of the nation's largest political association.

Political Reforms

As a justice of the High Court, Ranade could not become an official delegate to India's National Congress, but he was instrumental in inviting all seventy-three initial delegates to Bombay in December 1885 for the inaugural meeting of what was soon to become India's leading political association. In 1895, when the Congress and Social Conference both held meetings in Pune, Tilak protested against Ranade and Gokhale's desire to hold their Social Conference in the tent for which he had collected funds as "joint secretary" of the Congress. Bitter factionalism ensued and continued to divide the liberal Ranade-Gokhale mainstream of moderate political and social reform from Tilak's reactionary Hindu cultural traditionalism and radical anti-British political demands. "Sweet reasonable" Ranade died, however, before that conflict tore Congress apart in 1907.

Stanley Wolpert

See also **Congress Party; Gokhale, Gopal Krishna; Maharashtra; Tilak, Bal Gangadhar**

BIBLIOGRAPHY

Karve, D. G. *Ranade: The Prophet of Liberated India.* Poona: Aryabushan Press, 1942.

Kellock, J. *Mahadev Govind Ranade: Patriot and Social Servant.* Kolkata: Association Press, 1926.

Mankar, G. A. *A Sketch of the Life and Works of the Late Mr. Justice M. G. Ranade.* 2 vols. Mumbai: Caxton, 1902.

McLane, John R. *Indian Nationalism and the Early Congress.* Princeton, N.J.: Princeton University Press, 1977.

Parvate, T. V. *Mahadev Govind Ranade.* New York: Asia Publishing House, 1963.

Ranade, M. G. *Religious and Social Reform. A Collection of Essays and Speeches.* Mumbai: 1902.

———. *The Miscellaneous Writings of the Late Hon'ble Mr. Justice M. G. Ranade.* 1915. Reprint, New Delhi: Sahitya Akademi, 1992.

Wolpert, Stanley A. *Tilak and Gokhale: Revolution and Reform in the Making of Modern India.* Berkeley and Los Angeles: University of California Press, 1953 and 1961.

RANGŌLI *Rangōli* in Sanskrit means "colored creepers"; as such, it describes an art form that was created in ancient India to decorate the mud-covered walls and the mud floors of homes with attractive and colorful floral designs. *Rangōli* initially referred to this art as practiced in Maharashtra, Gujarat, and Rajasthan, but the term is now used to refer to any form of art drawn on the floor. Other types of floor art include *kōlam* and *alpana*. The former confined to the southern states, the latter to the eastern states.

Rangōli

Popular *Rangōli* designs, made with rice powder, charcoal, or chalk, are usually mythological figures, such as the elephant-headed god Gaṇesa, Lord Krishna playing his flute, Goddess Sarasvatī playing the vina (a stringed musical instrument), and Goddess Lakshmī sitting on a large lotus flower. Designs drawn from nature are also popular, particularly those that are mentioned in Hindu mythology, such as peacocks, swans, and the leaves of the pipal tree.

Traditionally, the materials used were powders made from natural ingredients such as rice (white), turmeric (yellow), turmeric mixed with alum (red), and indigo (blue). Today one can find fillers made from cereals and pulses (legumes), flower petals in myriad hues, and even synthetic dyes. The effect, when completed, is breathtaking. Although more accomplished artists will always manage to achieve the right proportions, balance of colors, and overall effect, even an amateur can produce delightful designs.

Rangōli artists have become more and more creative in modern times. The traditional floor designs were always flat on the floor, since very fine powders were used to fill the design. Nowadays, texture is added through the use of roughly ground and whole grains as well as tiny rocks, stones, and even bricks, giving the work a three-dimensional effect.

Rangōli designs are very popular during India's festive seasons. One of the most popular Hindu festivals is *Navarāthri* (the doll festival), a celebration of nine nights, in September and/or October. A beautiful *rangōli* is created outside the front doors of the house or in front of the family's display of dolls. Some families may even create a different design each day to symbolize the Hindu deity being worshiped on that particular night. These designs are usually small and simple, in proportion to the floor space available, but that is not necessarily the case, and large designs with highly intricate compositions have also been created. While smaller motifs may be drawn freehand, the large ones are often executed with the help of grid lines drawn on the floor in chalk. *Rangōli* motifs not only decorate homes and wedding and festival venues, but are also created in hotels and at receptions for dignitaries.

Kōlam

Kōlam designs, on the other hand, are composed of line drawings and are more geometric in pattern. Though less spectacular because they are often drawn with white rice powder, they are the pride of every South Indian home. A common sight in every village, town, and city in the early hours of the morning is that of the woman of the house bending over, deftly drawing the *kōlam* on the front porch or street. As the sun rises and fills the streets with light, the *kōlam* creations come to

In Tamil Nadu, *Rangōli* Adorns the Ground, Marking the Festival of Pongal. The ancient coloring technique has evolved over the centuries, with texture now often part of the traditional floor designs, yielding an almost three-dimensional effect. CHRISTINE PEMBERTON / FOTOMEDIA.

life. During the month of Margazhi (mid-December to mid-January), the center of the *kōlam* is decorated with a bright orange-yellow pumpkin flower to enhance the design, the contrast of the single yellow flower against the whiteness of the rice powder imparting an understated elegance.

In contrast to *rangōli*, which is created mainly on festive occasions, the *kōlam* is drawn every day of the year, except when there has been a death in the family or when there a family member is seriously ill with an infectious disease. The latter communicates to the neighborhood that one should avoid visiting the family until the *kōlam* reappears.

The rice powder that is used for *kōlam* performs the added humane function of feeding insects and birds, giving the family the satisfaction of doing a good deed for the day. One disadvantage, however, of using dry rice powder is that it is easily blown away when there is a gust of wind, leaving a rather untidy mess on the floor. A windswept *kōlam* could also be interpreted as a bad omen. Therefore, for special and auspicious occasions, a more permanent mixture is made by grinding soaked rice into a smooth paste. Using a wad of cotton cloth, dipped in the thick paste and held between the thumb and two fingers, designs are drawn by hand all over and around the entry and on the front porch. Once dry, there is no danger of it being wiped off. To make it even prettier, a paste of a special red brick, called *kāvi*, is used to outline the design, creating a pleasing contrast of red and white.

The *kōlam* is easier to draw than the *rangōli*, as it comprises lines joined to produce intricate designs with less effort. To enable even a novice to create well-executed designs, several devices are available to the modern practitioner. For example, there are numerous instruction books that show how dots drawn at regular intervals within an overall shape can be used effectively. By joining the dots, a beautiful mango bouquet or a temple with four *gôpurams* (steeples) can be drawn in minutes. Innovative shops sell templates for a variety of *kōlam* designs: slotted steel plates or rollers allow fine rice powder to flow through, resulting in pretty motifs. Also available these days are sticky plastic sheets with a *kōlam* design printed on them, ready to be peeled off and placed on the floor in front of the altar or the front door.

Modern Variations

Artists now use their imaginations to produce newer designs in both *rangōli* and *kōlam*. It is even possible to use water to make a *rangōli*, as demonstrated by one artist who filled a tub with water and spread a handful of powdered charcoal on top, creating a floating layer on the surface of the water. Next a variety of colored powders were deftly sprinkled over the charcoal layer, and a magnificent design was created. A well-known Indian dancer spread a sheet of cloth, which had the underside covered in red paint, on the stage and danced over it for some time; when the dance was over, she pulled away the cloth to reveal a *rangōli* in red of the elephant-headed god, Lord Gaṇesa.

Another unique floor art, a hybrid of *rangōli* and *kōlam*, is the *malar kōlam* (flower *kōlam*) of Kerala. Whole flowers, petals, and leaves may be used for this. The artist must first visualize the whole design and decide what colored flowers to use for the border, the center, and the fillers. Then, the artist draws the design on the floor or on a plastic sheet. Sometimes, moist sand is spread on the sheet and the floral decoration is made on the sand, filling it thoroughly so that no sand is visible at the end, creating the effect of a thick carpet. The beauty of the *malar kōlam* comes from the natural textures and hues contributed by the flowers. A common sight at receptions for important guests is the *malar kōlam*, created around the base of a large brass lamp, which the guest of honor lights to open the occasion.

Rohini Rajagopalan

See also **Folk Art**

BIBLIOGRAPHY

Cartwright Jones, Catherine. *Rangoli.* Stow, Ohio: Tap Dancing Lizard, 2002.

Kamat, Jyotsna. "Rangoli: The Painted Prayers of India." Kamat's Potpourri. Available at <http://www.kamat.com/kalranga/rangoli>

Maravanthe, Bharathi. *Rangoli.* Basrur Udupi, India: Samsevini, 2000.

RASHTRAKUTAS. *See* **History and Historiography.**

RĀVAṆA. *See* **Rāmāyaṇa**

RAY, SATYAJIT ***(1921–1992), renowned Indian filmmaker.*** In 1955, with the release of his first feature film, *Pather Panchali*, Satyajit Ray became an internationally acclaimed filmmaker. His reputation further surged with the completion of the *Apu Trilogy* (1959), considered by some critics to be the greatest cinematic suite ever made. By the time of his death in 1992, Ray had made twenty-nine features and seven documentaries and shorts. Working with simple tools, he fashioned tales, both visual and literary, that were straightforward in their presentation yet richly complex in their capacity to suggest multiple meanings and interpretations. He wrote his own screenplays, handled the camera, and did his own editing work as well. After 1962, he began scoring the music for all his films. Trained as a graphic artist, he sketched out each scene before shooting and designed the posters that publicized his new releases.

Ray worked under two severe constraints: all his films, made for relatively small Bengali-speaking audiences in India, had to be modestly budgeted, and he had to rely on stories and themes that he found filmable in modern Bengali fiction. These included some of his own; he is Bengal's best-selling adventure and science-fiction writer to this day. During his life and filmmaking career, Ray received many honors. In addition to the Honorary Academy Award for Lifetime Achievement, which he received in 1992 in his hospital room, a few weeks before he passed away, he was presented with the Bharat Ratna, India's highest civilian honor. Oxford University conferred on him an honorary doctorate; the University of California, Berkeley, awarded him the Berkeley Medal. President François Mitterrand of France went to Kolkata (Calcutta) to personally award him the Légion d'Honneur.

Satyajit Ray was born on 2 May 1921 in Kolkata to Sukumar and Suprabha Ray. He was born into a distinguished family of artists, writers, musicians, scientists, and physicians. His grandfather, Upendra Kishore, was an innovator, a writer of children's storybooks (popular to this day), an illustrator, printer, and musician. Ray's father, Sukumar, trained as a printing technologist in England, was Bengal's most beloved nonsense rhyme writer, illustrator, and cartoonist. He died when Satyajit was only two and a half years old.

Ray's mother, Suprabha, was a singer. After his father's death, they lived with Suprabha's brother's family and with Ray's paternal uncles. The extended family had many talented uncles, aunts, and cousins, including artists and musicians. One of the uncles was a cameraman, who later became a director of films. As a youngster, Ray developed two significant interests. The first was music, especially Western Classical music. He learned to read music, collected albums, and started to attend concerts. The second was movies. He saw silent films as well as "talkies," and began to compile scrapbooks with clippings from newspapers and magazines on Hollywood stars. As a young man, Ray developed an avid interest in the craft of cinema. He read books on filmmaking and theoretical works on cinema, and wrote screenplays for his own amusement.

Upon graduating from Presidency College, Kolkata, majoring in economics, he joined the art school Kala Bhavan, founded by Rabindranath Tagore, at Visva Bharati University in Santiniketan, at Tagore's personal encouragement. Tagore had been close to both Upendra Kishore and Sukumar Ray. At Santiniketan, Ray learned to draw from the great master teachers, Nandalal Bose and Binode Behari Mukherjee. Bose and Mukherjee were pioneers of what became known as the Bengal School, innovating and inventing an art form that emphasized an Asian style, combining Chinese and Japanese calligraphy with traditional Indian elements. Ray later developed this style in his illustrations and graphic designs.

While in Santiniketan, Ray was exposed to film theory and read books on cinema. He discovered that his two passions—music and film—actually convergenced. After returning to Kolkata, he began the habit of going to the theater with a notebook. He was not just watching, he was studying as well. His apprenticeship in filmmaking thus began.

Ray joined the British advertising agency D. J. Keymer in Kolkata in 1943 as a junior designer. The job helped him bloom into a graphic artist, typographer, book-jacket designer, and illustrator. He went to London

Satyajit Ray. From 1955 to 1964, Ray directed, arguably, his greatest films. This period coincided with the first flush of India's independence and Nehru's experiments with a secular democracy based on internationalism, and humanist and modernist principles. ASIT PODDAR / FOTOMEDIA.

in 1950 on a commission from the company. While there, he saw many films, including Vittorio De Sica's *Ladri di biciclette* (*The Bicycle Thief*, 1948) and Jean Renoir's *La Règle du jeu* (*Rules of the Game*, 1939), which made abiding impressions on him.

While returning from London by sea, Ray illustrated a children's edition of *Pather Panchali*, a semi-autobiographical novel by noted Bengali author Bibhuti Bhushan Banerjee. The sketches became storyboard elements when he elected to make a film from the novel. He managed somehow to make the film, using mostly amateur actors, shooting outdoors in natural light, financing it by pawning his rare music albums and his wife's jewelry, and calling on his mother's connections in government circles in Kolkata. This became typical of his mode of independent filmmaking—an endless search for the elusive producer who would agree to his nonnegotiable artistic terms.

The release of *Pather Panchali* in 1955 brought Satyajit Ray instant international as well as national recognition. It was first screened without subtitles at the Museum of Modern Art in New York in 1955 to critical acclaim. It was shown the following year at the Cannes Film Festival, where it won the Best Human Document award. The die was cast: Ray resigned from his post at D. J. Keymer, and he became a full-time filmmaker, directing one or more films every year until 1983, when he suffered a massive heart attack. He remained an acute heart patient, which drastically reduced his ability to make films, though he continued to produce provocative work.

Ray earned very modest amounts from directing his small-budget films, not sufficient to support his small family. He started writing and illustrating stories for *Sandesh*, the children's magazine that his grandfather had founded, and which Ray revived in 1961. In 1968 the editor of *Desh*, a popular Bengali literary magazine, persuaded Ray to write a novella for its annual edition. Ray, the writer of mysteries, adventure stories, and science fiction, all appropriately illustrated by him, thus made his debut on Bengal's literary scene. This was the beginning of his prolific literary output of some seventy novellas, stories, and translations, each of which became a bestseller in Bengali.

One can identify three major compositional periods in Ray's life. The first period (1955–1964) was remarkable for its robust optimism, celebration of the human spirit, and creative satisfaction. Ray was not only directing and scripting, but also scoring the music and taking charge of the cinematography. During this period, he directed, arguably, his greatest films. This period coincided with India's early years of independence and Jawaharlal Nehru's experiments with secular democracy based on humanism, internationalism, and modernism.

The second period (1965–1977) saw India come under a dark spell. There was the war with China (1962), during Nehru's last years, and a war with Pakistan (1965). Growing urban unemployment and an agricultural crisis brought about by a command economy created near-famine conditions in parts of the country. The war in Vietnam and the Cultural Revolution in China had radicalized Kolkata's youth, artists, writers, and intellectuals. Revolutionary and counterrevolutionary violence gripped the city. Kolkata, once known as a friendly and safe city, became a dangerous place to live. The Bangladesh War (1971) caused an influx of millions of refugees fleeing the Pakistani army, filling Kolkata and its outskirts. Prime Minister Indira Gandhi, battling a massive opposition to her government, imposed "National Emergency" rule on the country. India came under draconian control, but there were few signs of serious protests: people followed orders, the streets looked cleaner, the economy showed growth, and the trains were running on time.

Ray was troubled. The films he made during this period clearly projected a troubled vision of India. The Calcutta Trilogy—*The Adversary*, *Company Limited*, and *The Middleman*—created powerful portraits of alienation, waywardness, and moral collapse. *Days and Nights in the Forest* and *Distant Thunder*, made during the Bangladesh

War on the subject of the Bengal famine of 1943, showed rape and violence in a straightforward manner. *The Chess Players*, made during the Emergency, used the metaphor of a chess game to show how the king of Oudh, more a poet and composer than a ruler, submitted to the British takeover of his kingdom in 1856 as his people fled their villages. The two short films *Pikoo* and *Deliverance* raised the issues of adultery and untouchability. Even his so-called escapist films—the Goopy and Bagha musicals and the detective film *Golden Fortress*—carried messages against wars, criminality, and greed. In midlife, at the height of his creative powers, Ray seemed to have adopted a dark worldview. Socially, he became increasingly isolated.

In the third and last phase (1977–1992), Ray's worldview came full circle. In the 1980s he became even more isolated and distant. In the films he made during this period, he related his messages in definitive terms: unlike his early work, his films became didactic and frank. Gone were the carefully crafted shades of gray. *Home and the World* (1984), based on a Tagore novel, is a diatribe against nationalism, the mix of religion and politics, and political opportunism and dishonesty. Although the theme is the Swadeshi movement of 1905, *Home and the World* addressed issues of critical concern in the 1980s. Stricken by two heart attacks, Ray was not able to make films with his characteristic rigor. He made modest family dramas, shot indoors under the watchful eyes of his doctors. He made three films, all based on his own stories, in 1988, 1989, and 1990. The first, *Enemy of the People*, an adaptation of the Henrik Ibsen play to Bengali in 1988, addressed questions of capitalist corruption and manipulation of religion, people, politics, and environment. *Branches of a Tree* (1989) also addressed issues of capitalism as it impacts family values and ethics. The protagonist, a heart patient like Ray, is obsessed with honesty, mediated by mood swings of music and madness. The third film, *The Stranger* (1990), literally carries Ray's own voice in three places, where he sings. The protagonist is clearly Ray himself. His global concerns are articulated locally. Who is an artist? Who is civilized and who is primitive? The protagonist is against narrowness of all sorts, against boundaries and borders. "Don't be a frog in the well," he tells his grandnephew as the film comes to an end.

Ray was a product of the Anglo-Bengali encounter of the nineteenth century. His cultural, intellectual, and ideological roots can be traced to what is known as the "Bengali Renaissance." As a powerfully creative artist, his craft was influenced as much by the West as by the Bengal School. One can argue that, in the final analysis, he was more than a product of the "Calcutta modern"—a synthesis of the East and the West. His creativity, he once remarked, remained grounded both in what is uniquely Bengali and in what is universal.

Ray's mother had taken him to visit Rabindranath Tagore when he was five years old. Young Ray extended his autograph book to Tagore. Tagore wrote in it in verse:

> For a long time, over many miles,
> I've been to many countries.
> I've spent a lot of money.
> I've seen the highest peaks;
> I've seen the greatest oceans.
> But I still have yet to open my eyes,
> glance over at the field next to my house,
> and see a dewdrop on a blade of grass.

Tagore then told Ray, "When you grow up, you'll understand what I've written for you here."

Years later, while filming *Pather Panchali*, Ray realized that all his theoretical knowledge and study of film proved inadequate to the challenge he faced. He wrote, "One day's work with camera and actors taught me more than all the dozen books [I read on film making]. [I found out for myself] how to catch the hushed stillness of dusk in a Bengali village, when the wind drops and turns the ponds into sheets of glass, and the smoke from the ovens settles in wispy trails over the landscape, and plaintive blows on conch shells from homes far and near are joined by the chorus of crickets which rise as the light falls, until all one sees are stars in the sky, and the fireflies that blink and swirl in the thickets" (*Satyajit Ray: An Anthology of Statements on Ray and by Ray*, pp. 23–24).

Satyajit Ray died on 23 April 1992. A million mourners marched in the funeral procession, the greatest outpouring of public grief in Kolkata since Tagore's death fifty years earlier.

Dilip K. Basu

See also **Tagore, Rabindranath**

BIBLIOGRAPHY

Dasgupta, Chidananda. *The Cinema of Satyajit Ray*. New Delhi: Vikas, 1980.

Robonson, Andrew. *Satyajit Ray: The Inner Eye*. London: Andrew Deutsch, 1989.

Satyajit Ray: An Anthology of Statements on Ray and by Ray. Delhi: Film India, 1981.

Seton, Marie. *Portrait of a Director: Satyajit Ray*. London: Dennis Dobson, 1971.

READING, LORD ***(1860–1935), viceroy of India (1921–1926).*** Lord Reading (Rufus Isaacs) was Britain's Lord Chief Justice in David Lloyd George's Liberal Cabinet prior to his appointment as viceroy of

India in 1921. Reading was one of the most distinguished jurists of his time, the only person of Jewish faith appointed viceroy of India. Arriving so soon after Amritsar's Jallianwala Bagh Massacre, in the midst of Mahatma Gandhi's first nationwide *satyagraha*, Reading ruled India during one of its most revolutionary half decades. His judicious temperament and calm patience helped keep India's body politic from further chaos during his era, when constitutional reforms inaugurated under the Government of India Act of 1919 were introduced.

Reading held six lengthy interviews with Gandhi, whose deep religious convictions and "sincerity" he "liked," but with whom he could reach no political agreement on any issue. Concerned about a possible Afghan invasion at the time, Reading asked Gandhi how he would deal with it, to which the Mahatma replied that he would go personally to "meet" the invaders and "conquer them by love." The viceroy tried his best to dissuade Gandhi from his boycott of the reforms and elections, insisting that they were honestly designed to help Indians enjoy a more representative form of government than had ever been possible before. But since the 1919 massacre in Jallianwala Bagh, and its aftermath of brutal martial "laws" (including crawling orders inflicted on Indians residing in Amritsar), Gandhi mistrusted British officialdom, even their most seemingly selfless acts, which he viewed as wily tactics of "divide and rule," designed only to keep all Indians permanently enslaved.

Reading also met with Mohammad Ali Jinnah, finding him less radical than Gandhi, but "rather extremist," nonetheless, and forthright in demanding the dismissal of Punjab officers who had committed the grossest violations of human rights. He rightly recognized barrister Jinnah's "acute sensibility and subtlety of mind," but failed to take advantage of Jinnah's willingness to serve as honest "broker" between himself and Gandhi, possibly helping to avert the tragedy of South Asia's partition two decades later.

Lord Reading hosted Edwina Ashley, granddaughter of his wealthy banker friend, Sir Ernest Cassel, on the eve of her engagement to Lord Louis Mountbatten, who first visited India as aide to his cousin Edward, Prince of Wales, in 1921–1922. The Mountbattens would return to India a quarter century later to preside over the British transfer of power and the partition.

In 1923 Reading's government introduced civil service examinations in New Delhi, held simultaneously with those in London, thus making it possible for young Indians to sit for those prestigious administrative tests without having to embark on a long expensive voyage to England. He also created a popular Tariff Board in New Delhi, which soon abolished cotton excise taxes, allowing Indian cotton mill owners, including the Birlas and Tatas, to compete fairly with Manchester imports. But to compensate for the resulting annual loss of revenue, Reading doubled the salt tax, which was to become the prime target of Gandhi's most successful *satyagraha* campaign in 1930.

Stanley Wolpert

See also **British Crown Raj; Gandhi, Mahatma M. K.; Government of India Act of 1919; Satyagraha**

BIBLIOGRAPHY

Hyde, H. Montgomery. *Lord Reading: The Life of Rufus Isaacs, First Marquess of Reading*. London: Heinemann, 1967.

Judd, Denis. *Lord Reading: Rufus Isaacs, First Marquess of Reading, Lord Chief Justice and Viceroy of India, 1860–1935*. London: Weidenfeld and Nicolson, 1982.

Khan, Syed Sirdar Ali. *The Earl of Reading*. London and New York: Pitman, 1924.

Reading, Second Marquess of. *Rufus Isaacs: First Marquess of Reading*. 2 vols. London: Hutchinson, 1943–1945.

REDDI, MUTHULAKSHMI ***(1886–1968), first female Hindu doctor in Madras; educator, legislator, and feminist.*** Muthulakshmi Reddi was a pioneering feminist, doctor, educator, and legislator in colonial Madras presidency. Born in 1886, she was raised in the princely state of Pudukōttai by her upper caste father, who was a college professor, and her mother, whose ancestors were *dēvadāsi* musician-dancers. Her upbringing led her to dislike caste and sectarian divisions, and as a rationalist, she fought against superstitions and misogynistic traditions that hindered modernization. She was sent to school to learn reading and arithmetic for household accounts. However, her father soon supported her entry into a local college. In 1912 Muthulakshmi graduated at the top of an all male class from Madras Medical College, the first Hindu woman doctor in this presidency.

She began working at a government hospital, treating women and children and the urban poor. In 1913 she became the resident doctor for R. S. Subbalakshmi Ammāl's Brahmin Hostel for Widows. In 1914 she married Dr. Sundara Reddi, who shared Muthulakshmi's interests in medicine and social welfare. The couple established girls' orphanages and rehabilitation centers for destitute women. When treating vagrant children at the Dr. Varadappa Naidu Home in 1919, Muthulakshmi perceived the connections between women's low status, neglect, illiteracy, early marriage, childbirth death, prostitution, and disease, and she became politically active in the struggle for women's rights.

In 1917 Muthulakshmi Reddi cofounded the Women's Indian Association (WIA), and in 1928 the Muslim

Women's Association. As a member of nonsectarian organizations like the Madras Seva Sadan, Madras Vigilance Society, and Indian Ladies' Samaj, she worked with women of many communities, including Hindus (Pārvati Ammāl Chandrasēkharan and Mangalāmmal Sadāsivier), Muslims (Dr. Rahamatunīssa Bēgam and Shafia Mazeruddīn), Christians (Swarnam Appāsamy and Poonen Lukhose), Parsis (Hirābai Tātā), and Anglo-Irish women (Annie Besant and Margaret Cousins). She joined the 1917 All India Women's Delegation to Secretary of State Edwin Montagu, requesting provincial female suffrage under the Government of India Act of 1919. In 1926 she represented India at the International Suffrage Conference of Women in Paris, and in 1933 at the Congress of Women in Chicago.

In 1927 Reddi became the first woman legislator in colonial India, and she was chosen as the deputy president of the Madras Legislative Assembly. Reddi and her colleagues campaigned for the Sarda Act in 1930, which raised the age of marriage for girls to fourteen. She campaigned for increased state funding for girls' schools and occupational centers, low caste Ādi Dravida (aboriginal) girls' teacher training programs, and Muslim girls' education. She was a member of the Hartog Committee on education in 1928. Although she believed that the *purdah*, or veil, promoted female ill-health, as a pragmatist, she passed an Assembly resolution for separate wards and doctors for Muslim women in *purdah*. In 1929 she helped pass Act V of the Madras Hindu Religious Endowments Act, which severed the cultural tradition of *dēvadāsi* (slaves of the god) dedication to temples from its economic link to shrine properties. She supported Mahatma Gandhi's ideals of moral purity and the emancipation of women. Muthulakshmi Reddi was awarded the prestigious Padma Bhushan award for her services to Indian women before her death in 1968.

Sita Anantha Raman

See also **Feminism and Indian Nationalists; Women's Indian Association**

BIBLIOGRAPHY

Government of India. *Review of the Growth of Education in British India by the Auxiliary Committee Appointed by the Indian Statutory Commission, September 1929.* Kolkata: Central Publication Branch, 1929.

Kumar, Radha. *The History of Doing.* Delhi: Kali for Women, 1993.

Raman, Sita Anantha. "Crossing Cultural Boundaries: Indian Matriarchs and Sisters in Service." *Journal of Third World Studies* 18, no. 2 (Fall 2001): 131–148.

Reddi, Muthulakshmi. *My Experience as a Legislator.* Triplicane: Current Thought Press, 1930.

———. *Autobiography.* Adyar: Avvai Home, 1964.

Sattianadhan, Kamala. "The Society for the Protection of Children." *Indian Ladies' Magazine* 2, no. 7 (February 1929): 355–357.

Srinivasan, Amrita. "Reform or Conformity? Temple 'Prostitution' and the Community in the Madras Presidency." In *Structures of Patriarchy*, edited by Bina Agarwal. Delhi: Kali for Women, 1988.

Vishwanatha Sastri, C. V. "The Child Marriage Bill." *Indian Social Reformer* 38, no. 26 (February 1928): 407.

REINCARNATION. *See* **Upanishadic Philosophy.**

RESERVE BANK OF INDIA, EVOLUTION OF

The shape of the Reserve Bank of India (RBI) which was set up in 1935 during British rule, was influenced by two different attitudes, though with agreement that it should be independent of government. The British rulers were swayed by the prevailing monetary orthodoxy, of keeping the functions of raising and using money separate from that of creating money, while the nationalists wanted independence for the RBI in order to insulate it from the interference of the alien power. Despite this general agreement, the act establishing the RBI was so drafted that it left several gray areas for interpretation of the RBI-government relationship. As a result, the executive started, from the beginning, to encroach on the autonomy of the RBI, as evidenced by the finance member of the government of India selecting the composition of the RBI Board, and also by a virtual dismissal of its first governor, Sir Osborne Smith, on the ostensible grounds of disagreement on the issue of fixing the bank rate. During World War II, the authority of the RBI was further clipped in regard to its monetary policy, when it was forced to pursue a government-initiated low interest rate policy to keep the cost of financing the war low and to expand money supply through accumulation of sterling (foreign exchange) balances.

After a brief interlude of relative autonomy experienced after independence in 1947, the RBI's monetary policy domain shriveled rapidly when planning dominated India's overall economic policy. Since 1951, the government aimed at a mixture of public and private sectors, but much greater weight was assigned to the former. This had serious consequences for the RBI's functioning, organization, and the use of its policy instruments. Its main policy instruments, such as open market operations, and cash reserve and statutory liquid assets ratios, took the character of fiscal instruments directed more toward raising resources for the government than facilitating the financing of private sector investment—the main area for the exercise of monetary policy. Even more significantly,

Y. V. Reddy, Governor of the Reserve Bank of India. Y. V. Reddy at a 2003 press conference in Mumbai, prepared to face his challenges as newly appointed governor of the Reserve Bank of India. A key player in the economic turnaround of the 1990s and former executive director of the IMF, Reddy has thus far responded creatively to the core issues facing the RBI, implementing a number of important reforms. INDIA TODAY.

the RBI was obliged to extend credit to government, which fueled inflationary pressures in the economy.

The erosion of the RBI's power was also reflected in its other two collateral functions, that is, the exchange rate management, and the supervision and prudential control of the banking system. Because of ill-defined provisions of the RBI and the Banking Companies Act, and the ideological dispensation of the government, the RBI was unable to efficiently discharge these functions. The five-year plans, implicitly based on the assumption of constant prices, took as axiomatic that the exchange rate—the price of Indian currency in terms of gold or other foreign currencies—should remain unchanged. As it turned out, however, the government had to devalue the rupee by force majeure in 1966—a decision in which the RBI played only a technical role. There was, however, some change in 1976, when the RBI was given greater leeway in regard to exchange rate determination. It adopted a multicurrency basket of exchange rate under which the rupee value was determined with reference to the exchange rate movements of a select number of currencies of India's trading partners.

In the area of bank supervision and inspection, the RBI's record was marred by government decree. In the beginning, the RBI discharged its prudential control policies efficiently, but with the advent of Indian official intervention, this function was increasingly politicized. In the case of Palai Central Bank of Kerala State, where the government disregarded the RBI's advice, a serious banking crisis emerged a few years later. The RBI's prudential responsibilities were further downgraded in 1969 when banks were nationalized, the government of India assuming more direct and tighter control of banks.

Back to the Basics of Central Banking

The economic context in which the RBI functioned was radically transformed in 1991, when economic rationality was given precedence over ideology and politics. The private sector was liberalized from the straight jacket of industrial licensing, trade barriers were lowered, the foreign exchange control regime was gradually transformed into a market-oriented foreign exchange management system and, most important, the financial sector was liberalized from the earlier restrictive regime, which had substantially erased the distinction between the monetary policy of the RBI and the fiscal policy of the government. Those economic and financial reforms gave primacy to markets, incentives, and prices, thereby creating ideal conditions so essential for the unhampered exercise of the RBI's monetary policy instruments.

The RBI's freedom to exercise its policies was facilitated by two important developments. First, India liberalized its current balance of payment account, almost totally by 1995, and followed that up by selectively eliminating some restrictions on the capital balance of payments account. This led to a large movement of capital across India's borders, requiring the RBI to remain alert to both the exchange rate and interest rate movements, since both of these affected capital flows. The second development was the deregulation of domestic interest rates, thereby giving greater leverage to the RBI to influence them through its various policy instruments.

The RBI regulates the cost and availability of aggregate money by controlling the determinants of reserve money, that is, currency in circulation and banks' cash on hand and bank deposits held with the RBI. The determinants of reserve money are net bank credit to the government and to banks, and its holding of net foreign exchange assets. Prior to 1991, the RBI regulated reserve money by changing the quantity of its credit to government and banks, and varying its cash reserve requirements ratio, but currently, the RBI relies more on open market operations, that is, the purchase and sale of government securities held by it, varying its lending rates on credit extended to banks as well as to the central and state governments.

Since 1994 and 1995, a concordat was entered into between the RBI and the government of India under which automatic financing of government deficit by the RBI (called monetization) was capped. Only short-term credit to government was extended, which was required to be cleared at the end of the fiscal year. Any credit beyond the limit was treated as an overdraft, permissible for not more than ten consecutive days and on which interest rate was charged at bank rate plus two percentage points. This landmark decision has strengthened the RBI as a monetary authority. In regard to the net credit to banks, the RBI made its bank rate and other refinancing rates more effective. It instituted a Liquidity Adjustment Facility for banks for meeting temporary liquidity shortages, the rates on which were linked to the bank rate, thereby reviving the bank rate as a reference rate as in many central banks.

The RBI's role in regulating net foreign exchange assets has become dominant. It now intervenes in the foreign exchange market by the purchase and sale of foreign exchange and offsets the impact of these transactions on money supply by countervailing sale and purchase of securities. During 1992 to 1993 and 1998 to 1999, when there was a large inflow of private capital in India, the RBI bought foreign exchange to maintain a stable exchange rate, but at the same time, it sold securities to absorb liquidity so as not to weaken its restrictive monetary policy.

Though the RBI has moved in the right direction of greater independence and power in formulating its policies, it has considerable ground to cover. To emerge as a central bank of truly modern mold, it has to shift, as Anand Chandavarkar (1996) emphasized, "from independent to effective central banking based on the highest professionalism and integrity."

Deena Khatkhate

See also **Monetary Policy from 1952 to 1991; Monetary Policy since 1991; Money and Credit, 1858–1947**

BIBLIOGRAPHY

Balachandran, G. *Reserve Bank of India, 1951–1967.* Delhi and New York: Oxford University Press, 1998.

Chandavarkar, Anand G. *Central Banking in Developing Countries.* New York: St. Martin's Press, 1996.

Deshmukh, Chintaman D. *Central Banking in India: A Retrospect.* Poona: Gokhale Institute of Politics and Economics, 1948.

Joshi, V., and I. M. D. Little. *India: Macroeconomics and Political Economy, 1964–1991.* Washington, D.C.: World Bank, 1994.

Reserve Bank of India. *History of the Reserve Bank of India, 1935–1951.* Mumbai: Reserve Bank of India, 1970.

RIGHTS, FUNDAMENTAL. *See* **Human Rights; Judicial System, Modern; Political System.**

RIG VEDA. *See* **Vedic Aryan India.**

RIPON, LORD ***(1827–1909), British politician, viceroy of India (1880–1884).*** Lord Ripon was one of British India's most liberal and popular viceroys. The first marquis and second earl of Ripon, George Frederick Samuel Robinson was elected to Parliament from Hull in 1852 and served as undersecretary of state for India from 1861 to 1863, then as secretary of state for India in 1866. Eight years later, he converted to Catholicism, and six years afterward became the only Roman Catholic British viceroy of India, presiding over the Raj from 1880 to 1884.

A peace-loving, wise, and kindhearted aristocrat, Ripon was sent to India as Prime Minister William Gladstone's Liberal reflection. He swiftly ended the Second Anglo-Afghan War, which his predecessor, Tory Lord Lytton, Prime Minister Benjamin Disraeli's imperial reflection, had started, recognizing Amir Abdur Rahman Khan as Afghanistan's king, and withdrawing all British troops in 1881. He also liberated India's press, repealing the hated Vernacular Press Act of 1878 that Lytton had imposed to silence Indian editorials critical of his autocratic martial imperial rule. Ripon's bravest policy was to appoint and fearlessly support Sir Courtney Ilbert as law member of his council. Brilliant jurist and humanitarian that Ilbert was, he immediately sought to rectify the gross racial inequity of British India's criminal system of jurisprudence, discriminating as it did against all high court judges of Indian birth, who were automatically "disqualified" from trying any criminal case that charged a "European" with unlawful action against an Indian. Ilbert's Criminal Jurisdiction Bill, which would have removed such racial prejudice from the system, was introduced to Lord Ripon's council in February 1883. The viceroy strongly backed his law member. But as soon as the new bill's proposed change was emblazoned in boldest type on the front page of every Anglo-Indian newspaper in Bengal, the British community, civil and judicial, most violently protested. Ilbert and Ripon were tarred as "traitors" to their "race" and nation, and images of both were burned in effigy in Calcutta (Kolkata). Mass meetings filled every hall in the capital, denouncing the Ilbert Bill as "unconstitutional" and demanding its emasculation by requiring that any trial of an Englishman in a "native's" courtroom should be judged by a jury, at least half of whom were of "European blood." The intensity of those anti-Ilbert protests taught generations of Indian nationalists how best to protest against government policies and officials, including the very viceroy. Leaders of India's

National Congress, born but two years after Ilbert's Bill was enacted in its disgracefully emasculated form, never forgot those powerful lessons in public protest.

Ripon was so dispirited by the narrow-mindedness of his countrymen that he resigned his office a year before his term would have expired. When he traveled by train from Calcutta across the full breadth of India to Bombay (Mumbai), where a P & O vessel waited to take him home, tens of thousands of bareheaded Indians lined the tracks, bowing to offer silent thanks to the British viceroy who had fought so hard for them that he incurred the enmity of his own people.

Stanley Wolpert

See also **British Crown Raj**

BIBLIOGRAPHY

Gopal, S. *The Viceroyalty of Lord Ripon, 1880–1884.* London: Oxford University Press, 1953.

Seal, Anil. *The Emergence of Indian Nationalism.* London: Cambridge University Press, 1968.

Sisson, Richard, and Stanley Wolpert, eds. *Congress and Indian Nationalism.* Berkeley: University of California Press, 1988.

RISHI A sage or seer, a *rishi* (*ṛṣi*) is a semidivine being gifted with insight, sacred knowledge, and special powers. Most famous are the seven *rishi*s (*saptārshayaḥ*), the Brahmans to whom the Vedas were revealed. The entire corpus of sacred texts, beginning with the Rig Veda, was orally passed on to humans and even today is recited by Vaidika Brahmans who consider the original seven as role models. Both the idea of seven and several individuals called *rishi*s were known in the Rig Veda and Atharva Veda, but the generally accepted list of seven names did not occur until centuries later in the Brihadāraṇyaka Upanishad and the Sūtras: Vishvāmitra, Jamadagni, Bharadvāja, Gotama, Atri, Vasishṭhaṭha, and Kashyapa. An eighth, Agastya, was added, associated with South India rather than the Gangā-Yamunā region usually given as the location of *rishi* ashramas. Bhrigu, Aṅgiras, and others were considered *rishi*s as well. The core seven endured as a mythic nucleus, each one a progenitor of a distinct family. In modern times, if a person is asked to name a *gotra* (lineage) by a priest in a Hindu temple, for example, ancestry is declared by naming a specific *rishi*. And in the *pravara* included in personal prayers, an extended list of *rishi* ancestors is affirmed.

The signal features of the *rishi* were the gift of spiritual insight and his conduct of extraordinary asceticism. By means of *tapas*, powerful austerities, the *rishi* attained superhuman status rivaling the gods. Miraculous feats (*siddhi*s) were accomplished, including the ability to change shape, become invisible, or fly through the air. Various *siddhi*s and the role of *rishi* continued to be important later in traditions of Yoga, Buddhism, and Jainism. By the seventh century B.C., however, early Upanishads directed spiritual insight and power beyond the results of sacrifice (*yajña*) on one hand, or miracle working on the other, toward liberation through a new definition of existence as *saṃsāra*, and this by means of the *ātman-brahman* identity. In other words, the *rishi* of the early Upanishads became a being with esoteric knowledge not of the Vedas or of the rituals but of the cosmic identity that conquers death. These Upanishads also elaborated earlier identifications of the seven *rishi*s with the seven life-breaths (*prāṇa*) of the body.

Many additional *rishi* names appeared in the Mahābhārata, Rāmāyaṇa, and the Purāṇas. Some groups were called the Seven Prajāpatis or Seven Mind-Born Sons of Brahmā. By virtue of *tapas*, the *rishi*s achieved heaven (*svarga*). Myths note them in the night sky as the constellation Ursa Major, the Great Bear (or Big Dipper), first known in the Rig Veda as seven bears, later as seven *rishi*s. Arundhatī was rewarded with the eternal company of her husband, *rishi* Vasishṭhaḥa; she is the tiny star Alcor immediately next to him, pointed out to the bride in marriage rites as a symbol of fidelity. Their enduring presence also resides in topography—in rivers, for example. *Rishi*s are said to have made seven channels of the Ganga at Hardwar, and channels of the Godavari in its delta bear their seven names. The *rishi*s belong to an ancient past, yet even today some village folk relate a lucky moment, a glimpse of the seven through the mist as they bathe in the river before dawn.

David M. Knipe

See also ***Tapas*; Upanishadic Philosophy; Vedic Aryan India; Yajña**

BIBLIOGRAPHY

Eliade, Mircea. *Yoga: Immortality and Freedom.* 2nd ed. Princeton, N.J.: Princeton University, 1970. Lucid on the Upanishads, Yoga, the *siddhi*s.

Elizarenkova, Tatyana J. *Language and Style of the Vedic Ṛsis.* Albany: State University of New York Press, 1995. Philological and literary analysis of mystical exchanges between *rishi*s and Vedic gods.

Mitchiner, John E. *Traditions of the Seven Ṛsis.* Delhi: Motilal Banarsidass, 1982. Detailed examination of *rishi*s from Vedic Saṃhitās to epics, Purāṇas and beyond.

Rahurkar, V. G. *The Seers of the Ṛgveda.* Poona: University of Poona, 1964. Genealogical study of each family of rishis.

ROCK ART Found in many different regions of South Asia, evidence for rock art dates back to the late Upper Paleolithic period (c. 15,000 B.C. and continues through the Mesolithic (c. 8000 B.C.) and Neolithic (c. 7000 B.C.) up through the Historic period. While some rock art is painted or engraved on the walls of rock shelters and caves, movable rock art is found on smaller pieces of stone that could be set in special locations for rituals and then carried away. A carved stone pebble with what may be the face of a human and a slab of stone with incised lines that may be calendrical notations were found in the Upper Paleolithic cave site of Gar-i-Asp, Afghanistan. Recent research in the Zhob and Loralai valleys of Baluchistan have reported what may be Upper Paleolithic paintings and Chalcolithic engravings. More than thirty thousand rock carvings dating from the Upper Paleolithic to the Early Historic period have been reported along the upper Indus Valley and its tributaries in the mountains of northern Pakistan and Afghanistan. Engraved rock slabs have been found in the Neolithic levels at Burzahom in Kashmir, and a Mesolithic/Chalcolithic chert blade core with an engraved geometric motif was found at Chandravati, Rajasthan. More than five thousand painted rock shelters have been reported in the hills of peninsular India, the most famous in the region around Bhimbetka, Madhya Pradesh.

Rock-Cut Jain Sculptures in Gwalior Fort. Near the southern entrance to Gwalior Fort (in the northern part of Madhya Pradesh), these imposing Jain sculptures rise from the cliffs. They were originally cut in the mid-fifteenth century, defaced by the marauding armies of Babur in 1527, but later restored. ADITYA PATANKAR / FOTOMEDIA.

Rock Art of Central India

Many different techniques were probably used to create graphic symbols and naturalistic representations on rock surfaces, but the only ones preserved are paintings made with permanent mineral pigments or engravings that physically modified the surface of the rock. Prehistoric rock art was usually executed on easily accessible surfaces in caves or rock shelters, but in some regions the paintings were clearly made with the help of elaborate scaffolds or ladders. The colors used for rock art are the commonly available iron minerals that come in red, orange, brown, and black (hematite) or yellow (limonite). White pigments were made using limestone, natural chalk, white kaolin clay, or scintered calcium carbonate (*kankar*) nodules. Occasionally, green pigments were made from glauconite (*terra verde*) or the greenish weathered surfaces of chalcedony nodules.

The simplest technique of application was to use the colored nodule as a crayon. Faceted nodules of hematite have been found in the Lower Paleolithic levels at Bhimbetka Cave, but the only modifications to the walls dating from this time are two depressions that may be the earliest evidence for cup-shaped petroglyphs. Faceted hematite nodules have also been found in the Upper Paleolithic levels of Bhimbetka and can be associated with the earliest prefigurative geometric designs. Green anthropomorphic figures often overlap the geometric designs and have been dated to the Upper Paleolithic, but some scholars believe that they may belong to later periods. The most complex forms of painting would have involved the preparation of pigments by grinding and mixing with water or organic solutions derived from plants or animal fat. Complex paintings of large animals that may represent deified bison or deer at Bhimbetka and other sites may have been produced with specially prepared pigments and brushes made from twigs or animal hair. Many of these large deified animal paintings are thought to belong to the end of the Upper Paleolithic or the subsequent Mesolithic period. Other techniques of application involve handprints or fine incising with sharp stone tools and filling the lines with color.

The major themes of rock paintings vary from region to region and change over time. The earliest Upper Paleolithic paintings appear to be geometric designs; these are followed by the introduction of depictions of humans and large-scale animals filled with cross-hatching and concentric designs. Mesolithic rock paintings follow some of these same trends, but there is more emphasis on narrative scenes depicting the hunting of game with barbed spears or groups of animals and humans. The Neolithic paintings tend to focus on various everyday activities like hunting, gathering, collecting honey, and feeding pigs. The types of animals depicted in the paintings include all of the major animals seen in tropical jungles, from elephants and tigers to rabbits and lizards. Hunting is sometimes associated with male figures defined by clearly visible genitalia, while some figures of women with prominent breasts and large hips are associated with gathering activities. Most anthropomorphic figures are not distinguished by sex, unless that is the subject of the painting. Prehistoric rock art in peninsular India is followed by depictions of warriors with what appear to be classic iron weapons, riding horses or driving wheeled chariots. These paintings date to the early Iron Age, around 1000 B.C., and continue throughout the Historic period.

Rock Art in Northern Pakistan

Three of the great mountain ranges of South Asia come together in the northern regions of Pakistan: the Hindu Kush on the west, the Karakorum in the center, and the Himalayas, which extend east across India and Nepal to the edges of Myanmar (Burma). The Indus River and its tributaries emerge from the glacial lakes and snow fields of these mountains. Beginning in the Upper Paleolithic, some 20,000 to 10,000 years ago, people began moving up these rivers in pursuit of game during interglacial periods. The earliest anthropomorphic figures and animal petroglyphs of large horned goats, sheep, ibex, and snow leopards probably date to this time period. Petroglyphs, or rock engravings, are made by pecking or bruising the surface of large flat boulders using smaller hammer stones. Due to the heavy brown weathered surface or patina on the rock surface, the freshly produced lines reveal the light colored stone and show up very clearly. Over thousands of years, these engraved lines themselves become weathered, and later petroglyphs can be identified by the different color of the patina and by their superposition on earlier engravings.

Large engravings of humped zebu cattle indicate the presence of herders who would have begun to frequent the region during the Neolithic and Chalcolithic periods, moving up from the Indus plain and then returning with trade goods from regions farther north. Anthropomorphic masks carved on some boulders have parallels with Chalcolithic cultures of southern Siberia, providing evidence for early contacts with Central Asia in the third millennium B.C.

During the first millennium B.C., nomads from the Eurasian steppes began to move down these valleys, and their carvings of stags and ibex with large backward curving horns can be linked to Scythian artistic traditions dating to the eighth century B.C. and even earlier animal-style art from Siberia that dates from the eleventh to the ninth centuries B.C. Later carvings of people, gods, temples, and ritual symbols can be attributed to the ebb and flow of pilgrims, traders, and armies along this major trade route. Achaemenid Persians, Sogdians, Hindu pilgrims who worshiped either Shiva or Vishnu, and Zoroastrian fire worshipers all contributed to the rock art of this region.

Jonathan Mark Kenoyer

See also **Neolithic Period; Palaeolithic Period**

BIBLIOGRAPHY

Bandini-König, D., M. Bemmann, and H. Hauptmann. "Rock Art in the Upper Indus Valley." In *The Indus: Cradle and Crossroads of Civilizations*, edited by H. Hauptmann. Islamabad: Embassy of the Federal Republic of Germany, 1997.

Brooks, R. R. R., and V. S. Wakankar. *Stone Age Painting in India*. New Haven, Conn.: Yale University Press, 1976.

Jettmar, K. "The Main Buddhist Period as Represented in the Petroglyphs at Chilas and Thalpan." In *South Asian Archaeology, 1985*, edited by K. Frifelt and P. Sørensen. London: Curzon Press, 1989.

———. "The Art of the Northern Nomads in the Upper Indus Valley." *South Asian Studies* 7 (1991): 1–20.

———. "Rock Carvings in a Stratified and Multi-ethnic Society." In *South Asian Archaeology, 1995*, edited by B. Allchin and R. Allchin. New Delhi: Oxford & IBH, 1997.

Marshack, A. "Aq Kupruk: Art and Symbols." In *Prehistoric Research in Afghanistan (1959–66)*, edited by L. Dupree. Philadelphia: American Philosophical Society, 1972.

Sonawane, V. H. "Rock Art of India." In *Recent Studies in Indian Archaeology*, edited by K. Paddayya. New Delhi: Munshiram Manoharlal, 2002.

Wakankar, V. S. "Rock Art of India." In *Archaeology and History: Essays in Memory of Shri A. Ghosh*, edited by B. M. Pande and B. D. Chattopadhyaya. Delhi: Agam Kala Prakashan, 1987.

ROY, RAM MOHAN ***(1772–1833), leading figure of the Hindu Renaissance, founder of the Brahmo Samaj.*** Ram Mohan Roy was born to a Bengali Hindu family with a history of service to Muslim rulers. He studied Persian and Arabic, as well as Bengali and Sanskrit, in preparation for a similar career. In 1797 Ram Mohan moved to Calcutta (Kolkata) and became wealthy through investments with the British East India Company and in rural estates. From 1803 to 1815 he was intermittently in the service of company officials stationed in rural Bengal; during this period he mastered the English language and culture and absorbed Western religious radicalism. About 1815 he settled permanently in Calcutta, mixing with Europeans and studying Vedānta.

During the next fifteen years Roy earned his fame as a key figure in the Hindu Renaissance. He was initially prominent in the religious arena. Drawing upon Hindu, Muslim, and Christian rationalist traditions, he championed the unity of God and challenged established doctrines and customary practices. His rationalist views drew him into heated public debates with both Hindu pandits and Christian missionaries: the former objected to his egalitarian reading of Vedānta texts, while the missionaries resented his embrace of Unitarian doctrines. His criticism of image worship and his campaign against *sati* (the immolation of Hindu widows on their husbands' funeral pyres) earned him further enmity among more orthodox Hindus. He enjoyed support from Western-educated Hindus, including those who joined the Brahmo Samaj, the influential religious reform society he established in Calcutta in 1828.

Roy was also active in other areas. A pioneer of Bengali journalism, he founded, or supported, some of the first vernacular newspapers in Bengal and wrote brilliant defenses of freedom of the press. He encouraged Western education, helped establish English-language schools, and opposed the 1823 establishment of Sanskrit College, Calcutta, because he believed the British were obligated to introduce modern Western knowledge. He remained committed, however, to Sanskritic education and founded Vedanta College in 1826, while his many vernarcular publications—including grammars, translations from Sanskrit, and Vedānta commentaries—have drawn comparisons to Martin Luther for their influence on the evolution of modern Bengali. His campaign against *sati* led Governor-General William Bentinck to seek Roy's advice before abolishing the practice in 1829. During the ensuing public outcry, Roy stood forth as a champion of *sati*'s abolition.

In late 1830 Roy left for Britain. One of the first Brahmans to cross the "dark waters," he traveled as the emissary of the Mughal emperor, who granted Roy the title of "raja" (king) to enhance his diplomatic status. Roy's private agenda included opposing the Dharma Sabha's petition to Britain that protested the abolition of *sati*. He was lionized in Britain by religious and political reformers, seated among the foreign ambassadors at King William IV's coronation, and encouraged by radicals to stand for Parliament. Largely unsuccessful in securing redress of the emperor's complaints against the East India Company, he was nevertheless present when the privy council upheld the abolition of *sati*, and he presented written testimony to Parliament regarding Indian affairs. He traveled briefly to France, where his republican sympathies were strengthened. Ram Mohan Roy died of pneumonia and was buried in Bristol on September 1833. His gravesite later became a place of pilgrimage for Indians in Great Britain.

Lynn Zastoupil

Ram Mohan Roy. Drawing on Hindu, Muslim, and Christian rationalist traditions, Roy challenged long-established religious doctrines and customary practices. K. L. KAMAT / KAMAT'S POTPOURRI.

See also **Brahmo Samaj**

BIBLIOGRAPHY

Biswas, Dilip Kumar. *The Correspondence of Raja Rammohun Roy*. 2 vols. Kolkata: Saraswat, 1992, 1997.

Collet, Sophia Dobson. *The Life and Letters of Raja Rammohun Roy*, edited by Dilip Kumar Biswas and Prabhat Chandra Ganguli. 1900. Reprint, Kolkata: Sadharan Brahmo Samaj, 1962.

Robertson, Bruce Carlisle. *Raja Rammohan Ray: The Father of Modern India*. Oxford: Oxford University Press, 1999.

RURAL CREDIT, EVOLUTION OF SINCE 1952 India's rural credit system is divided into two segments: an unorganized or informal system of moneylenders, traders, and input suppliers; and a formal, organized segment constituted by cooperative banks, regional rural banks, commercial banks, and nonbanking financial companies. In recent years, the move to strengthen formal credit institutions was justified by not only the demands of modern inputs but also usurious moneylending practices that could not otherwise be countered effectively. India's ideological commitment to encouraging a "cooperative commonwealth" also played a role, especially in strengthening cooperative credit institutions at all levels.

Structure of Rural Financial Institutions

Rural credit needs in India are met by an elaborate structure of rural financial institutions (RFIs). The National Bank for Agriculture and Rural Development (NABARD) acts as the apex institution and also as the principal refinancing agency for the RFIs. The Reserve Bank of India, as the principal monetary authority of the country, has retained some powers of regulating and directing agricultural credit, though most of its developmental functions in this area have been ceded to NABARD. Cooperative banks, scheduled commercial banks, and regional rural banks are the three principal rural financial agencies. Numerous state-sponsored institutions and nongovernmental organizations established for development of special sections of the population or particular regions in the country also advance credit to the rural population.

Cooperative banks cater to the short-term as well as long-term requirements of credit in rural and semiurban areas. The short-term credit structure is a three-tier structure, with state-level cooperative banks, or SCBs (numbering 30), at the apex, district-level credit cooperative banks, or DCCBs (numbering 368) constituting the middle tier, and over 98,000 village-level primary societies. Each higher tier largely relies on the lower tier for credit dispersal and, to an extent, on deposit mobilization. State- as well as district-level cooperative institutions also operate, to a limited extent, through their branches. There are 847 branches of the SCBs and over 12,000 branches of the DCCBs. Long-term credit structure is also a tiered structure. There are 20 state-level cooperative agricultural and rural development banks. Some of these banks, mainly in the smaller states, operate directly through their branches. Others, especially those located in the larger states, operate through an intermediary level called primary cooperative agricultural rural development banks, the latter numbering nearly 800, with a branch network of nearly 1,100.

Ninety-eight scheduled commercial banks operate through more than 66,400 branches, of which nearly 32,000 are located in rural areas. The rural and the semiurban branches of the commercial banks are controlled at the regional level by their regional offices, and the regional offices are coordinated at the zonal level by zonal offices, with the headquarters of the banks responsible for overall control and supervision. The commercial banks have also sponsored, in collaboration with the central and state governments, local district level banks, known as regional rural banks (RRBs). The RRBs number 196, and have a network of over 14,000 branches, which are located preponderantly in rural areas.

There are more than 157,000 credit outlets serving India's rural population of nearly 742 million people. By the end of the financial year (April–March) 2001–2002, the flow of credit for agriculture and allied activities was estimated at 6204.5 billion rupees, of which 4050.9 billion rupees were disbursed as production credit and 2153.6 billion rupees as investment credit. A progressively larger share of ground-level credit in agriculture is accounted for by commercial banks. During the period 1994–1995 to 2001–2002, the share of the commercial banks in the total credit, short term and long term, increased from 44 percent to 54 percent. The share of the cooperatives declined to that extent.

A remarkable feature of the RFIs is their comprehensive coverage of different segments of rural society, including the small and marginal farmers. With the organization of self-help groups of poor farmers and artisans, now numbering over 780,000, and their coordination with the banking institutions, the RFIs now cover a large number of households among the disadvantaged sections of rural society.

Evolution of State Policies

Three distinct phases can be identified in the evolution of the RFIs. The first phase began in 1954, when the recommendations of the Rural Credit Survey Report were largely accepted and efforts made to encourage formal credit institutions, particularly cooperatives. The beginning of the second phase coincided with bank nationalization in 1969, when credit was considered an important instrument of eradicating poverty. The third phase began in 1991, when the RFIs sought to be reformed in consonance with the overall policy of economic reforms.

Serious efforts to revamp the rural credit system began with the publication, in 1954, of the Report of the Rural Credit Survey (RCS) sponsored by the Reserve Bank of India. The recommendations of the RCS made a profound impact on the rural credit structure. State policy was directed to provide a comprehensive and viable alternative to nonformal credit agencies such as moneylenders and traders. Among the formal credit institutions, it emphasized the importance of cooperatives. The

RCS was aware of the weaknesses of the cooperative movement, but considered it the best organizational form to meet the requirements of the rural population. It inspired the now famous slogan "cooperation has failed, but cooperation must succeed." The committee was equally eager to make cooperatives financially viable, suggesting large-sized credit cooperatives, and rejecting the "one village, one society" norm.

An equally important recommendation of the RCS was state partnership in the cooperative structure at all levels. Two funds were created in the Reserve Bank of India: the National Agricultural Credit (Long-Term Operations) Fund for advancing loans to the state governments to subscribe to the cooperative institutions and to assist land mortgage banks; and a National Agricultural (Stabilization) Fund to help cooperatives convert short-term loans of members to medium-term loans during periods of natural calamity. Some attention was also given to bringing commercial banks into the rural credit arena. The RCS's recommendation of nationalization of the Imperial Bank of India, enjoining the new State Bank of India to open a large number of branches in rural areas, heralded the entry of commercial banks as important players on the rural credit scene.

Some of these recommendations generated heated controversy. There were serious reservations in a section of cooperators, and also in some government quarters, but, by and large, the recommendations were accepted and were acted upon. Reforms in the credit institutions resulted, though not to the extent expected, in the desired direction, that is, the substitution of the formal sector in place of the informal sector. The proportion of credit from the formal sector increased from 3 percent in 1952 to nearly 30 percent in 1969. Similarly, the land mortgage banks, which had mainly financed redemption of old loans, changed into institutions for long-term funding for productive purposes. However, the major objective of strengthening cooperatives was not achieved. Neither the large-size cooperatives nor the state partnership helped in rejuvenating the credit cooperatives.

Meanwhile, the deepening agricultural crisis of the 1950s and the early 1960s led to greater attention being given to raising agricultural productivity, first by concentrating on a few potentially favorable districts under the Intensive Agricultural District Programme, popularly known as the Package Programme, and later, by spreading this program to a large area. The approach was based on the application of a package of modern inputs and improved practices. To implement such packages, the producers, obviously, needed credit. As efforts to develop agriculture intensified, the need for a higher scale of credit became obvious. The era of exclusive reliance on cooperatives was over, and a multiagency approach to rural credit was initiated. The Agricultural Review Committee noted the need for a multiagency approach in its report in 1969, coinciding with the nationalization of fourteen major commercial banks, a measure that completely changed the character of the banking industry in India. Prime Minister Indira Gandhi felt threatened by her political opponents and had to garner support form the general public with the slogan "*garibi hatao*" (eradicate poverty). Subsequently, six more banks were added to this list of banks obliged to lend 40 percent of their advances to "priority" sectors, 18 percent of which were in agriculture. The banks were compelled to open branches in the rural areas. They came to be heavily involved in funding the beneficiaries of the poverty alleviation programs, such as the Integrated Rural Development Programme. Other measures in the same direction included the lead bank plan, under which the principal commercial bank operating in a district was given responsibility for coordinating the efforts of all the banks of the area for funding rural development and poverty alleviation.

These measures had an important bearing on the rural credit system. First and foremost was the extension of the credit delivery system to every part of the country. The number of credit outlets of commercial banks in the rural and semi-urban areas, for example, witnessed a phenomenal increase, from 8,262 in 1969–1970 to 60,220 by 1990–1991. The regional imbalances in the number of credit outlets did continue, however, the northeastern states receiving a much smaller number of credit outlets than some of the more advanced states. The absence of proper infrastructure of roads and communications did not inhibit the spread of formal credit institutions in rural areas. In coverage of India's rural population, the objectives of bank nationalization were thus largely fulfilled. Major weaknesses also crept in, reflected in a growing share of overdue and nonperforming assets (NPAs). By the beginning of the 1990s, the percentage of recovery to demand had fallen to 41 percent in the case of RRBs, 54 percent for commercial banks, and 57 percent for primary cooperative societies. The accumulated NPA crippled the financial health of the RFIs.

Since the beginning of the 1990s, the pace of economic reforms, that is, measures to liberalize the domestic economy and to achieve greater integration with the global economy, were accelerated. As a part of these reforms, far-reaching changes were introduced in the financial sector. These included:

- freeing larger resources of the commercial banks, which had previously been preempted by the government as cash reserve ratio and statutory liquidity ratio;
- interest rate deregulation;

- introduction of prudential norms with increase in capital adequacy ratio, risk weighting of assets, stricter norms for income recognition and asset classification;
- adequate provisioning for nonproductive assets, adherence to prudential norms, especially in income recognition, provisioning for sticky accounts and capital adequacy; and
- transparency in financial dealings.

The reforms were accompanied with many structural, legal, and procedural changes. Sick regional rural banks, as well as a few commercial banks, that had the potential for revival were recapitalized, after promising to stick to the norms suggested by the Reserve Bank of India and NABARD. A Multi-State Cooperative Act was passed by Parliament to free part of the cooperative credit system from the stranglehold of state bureaucracies.

Major initiatives were taken during the postreform period to bring down the transaction costs in rural lending and to extend the reach of the RFIs to the poor. One of these is the organization and development of self-help groups of poor people, and connecting them to the banking system. Nearly 800,000 groups, each comprising ten to twenty poor households, generally headed by women, have already been organized. They have encouraged savings among the members, reduced the transaction costs of the lending institutions, and ensured a high (more than 80%) rate of recovery. The self-help group movement of India is the largest, and arguably the most successful, micro-credit program of its kind. Another innovative measure is the introduction of the Kisan (Farmers') Credit Card, which enables cardholders timely and flexible availability of credit.

Another important change that took place during this period was the creation of a Rural Infrastructure Development Fund (RIDF). It was observed that very few commercial banks were able to fulfill the mandatory requirement of advancing 18 percent of their total lending to agriculture. At the same time, there was a crying need to invest in rural infrastructure to strengthen the production base of agriculture. A fund was created, to which the banks had to contribute to cover the shortfall. The Expert Committee on Rural Credit recommended the introduction of an element of penalty in terms of lower interest rates on the amount falling short of the mandatory requirement for advances to agriculture, deposited in RIDF.

Almost every medium-sized village in the country now has a credit outlet, cooperative or commercial. A substantial part of agricultural operations are financed by financial institutions. There is a wide variety of products offered to borrowers. At the same time, there are many unresolved issues. The most important are the organizational problems facing the cooperative sector. As a delivery system, it is in a state of disarray. A large number of DCCBs are defunct, and the malady has spread to the state-level institutions. The long-term credit agencies, known as agricultural and rural development cooperative banks, are in a worse plight. Duality of control and supervision, by the registrars of the Cooperative Societies in the states and by the Reserve Bank of India and NABARD in the central government, has not helped matters. The role of the apex and secondary institutions in strengthening the primary units is proving ineffective. The ground level institutions, the cooperative credit societies, are proving to be high-cost credit-dispensing outlets, rather than genuine cooperatives of the members.

Regional rural banks have failed to prove themselves as low-cost, rural-oriented credit institutions, and have largely become deposit-mobilizing institutions for their sponsoring banks. Their cost for dispersing credit is high, and their reach is limited. Their present status and performance do not inspire much confidence. The commercial banks are reluctant to expand their lending to the agricultural sector beyond the statutory requirements, and even there, they fail by a substantial margin. Newer agencies—non-banking financial institutions, local area banks, input suppliers, and a few non-governmental organizations—are now coming into the picture.

At the policy level, the main debatable issue is the mandatory lending targets, for the priority sector in general, and agriculture in particular. As agricultural production is becoming diversified to more value-added products and enterprises, it is becoming much more expensive and capital intensive. If India's small farm sector, which accounts for not only a large number of holdings but also a progressively increasing area of cultivated land, is to participate in this second "Green Revolution," access to timely and low-cost credit will be required. Credit has an important developmental role in a poor country like India. The challenge before the country is to adapt its vast credit system to meet the legitimate demands of the population in India's vast rural areas, without impairing the viability of its financial institutions.

Vijay Vyas

See also **Bank and Non-bank Supervision; Banking Sector Reform since 1991; Development of Commercial Banking 1950–1990; Non-banking Financial Institutions, Growth of**

BIBLIOGRAPHY

National Bank for Agricultural and Rural Development. *Expert Committee on Rural Credit.* Mumbai: NABARD, 2001.

———. *Rural Credit and NABARD.* Mumbai: NABARD, 2003.

Reserve Bank of India. *All India Rural Credit Survey: Report of the Committee of Direction.* Vol. II: *General Report.* Mumbai: RBI, 1954.

———. *Report of the Agricultural Credit Review Committee.* Mumbai: RBI, 1989.

———. *Report of the Committee on Financial Systems.* Mumbai: RBI, 1991.

———. *Handbook of Statistics on Indian Economy, 2002–2003.* Mumbai: RBI, 2003.

RUSSIA, RELATIONS WITH Russia (and its predecessor, the Soviet Union) is the only great power with which India's relationship has been one of mutual trust, cooperation, and strategic partnership, bolstered by ideological convergence and cultural exchange, especially throughout the cold war. Though the post–cold war dominance of the United States in all fields of international affairs has transformed the dynamics of Indo-Russian relations, the basic foundation of the relationship remains intact.

Relations between India and Russia can be broadly categorized in four distinct phases. Relations with the erstwhile Soviet Union prior to India's independence in August 1947 form the first phase of the relationship. The post-independence era can be bifurcated into three distinct phases, with the Indio-China conflict of 1962 and the end of cold war and subsequent disintegration of the Soviet Union acting as the demarcating episodes.

Pre-Independence Era

The leaders of India's freedom struggle drew ideological support from the Soviet Union in their fight against British imperial power. The ideals espoused by India's Communist parties and Nehruvian socialism were inspired by the Russian Communist Party and its revolution. Being a communist power with strong anti-imperial leanings, Russia supported the decolonization efforts of many Afro-Asian nations, including India. This support formed the foundational basis on which the edifice of a mutually beneficial, long-term relationship was laid. The Indian National Congress, which led India's mass struggle to oust the British from India, had established a small foreign department in 1925 to publicize its freedom struggle and garner support. Jawaharlal Nehru and his father, Motilal Nehru, visited Russia two years later, on the tenth anniversary of the Bolshevik Revolution. The youthful Nehru was personally fascinated by the socialist ideology of the Soviet Union, and he taught his daughter, Indira, to admire it as well.

1947–1962

India established diplomatic relations with the Soviet Union on 13 April 1947. Prime Minister Jawaharlal Nehru, who served as his own foreign minister, was determined to win the support of Moscow in helping India to achieve strategic security and economic independence from the West. Nehru sent his sister, Vijaya Lakshmi Pandit, as the first Indian ambassador to Moscow. Thanks to Nehru, India adopted the Russian model of centralized planning, in the form of five-year plans, as its major approach to development.

The Soviet Union, however, was initially hesitant to embrace India, considering it a "tool of Anglo-American imperialism." Only after Josef Stalin's death in 1953 did the situation improve, and the Soviet Union expressed its hopes for "friendly cooperation." Russian fears were dispelled when India refused to be influenced by Washington's power bloc during the cold war era. India's anti-imperialist, anticapitalist Nehruvian policies tilted it toward the Communist bloc headed by Moscow, and Russia soon responded by providing direct as well as indirect assistance to India in economic, technological, and strategic fields.

On 7 June 1955, Prime Minister Nehru himself made an official state visit to Moscow. That event was reciprocated by the visit of Soviet leaders Premier Nikolai Bulganin and Communist Party General Secretary Nikita Khrushchev in November 1955. Pakistan's alliance with the United States throughout the cold war spurred India to establish closer relations with the Soviet Union. The relationship paid off rich dividends. Russia supported India's stance concerning Kashmir in the United Nations Security Council, where Russia exercised its veto power many times in favor of India. In 1956, during their visit to India, Russian leaders Bulganin and Aleksey Kosygin referred to Kashmir as an "integral part" of India. Russia's support proved crucial as well for India's integration of Goa in 1961. In addition to this vital strategic help, Russia's tacit support to India during the brief 1962 India-China conflict firmly established Russia as a dependable Indian ally.

China's invasion across India's northern border in 1962 was a rude awakening to Nehru's last government, and revealed the ill-prepared state of India's military establishment. New Delhi's determination to equip its forces with more advanced weaponry spurred India toward Russia, opening a new chapter in Indo-Russian relations, with sustained engagement between the two countries, primarily based on military cooperation.

1963–1990

Formal Indo-Russian cooperation began in 1962, when the two countries agreed to a program of military-technical cooperation. Indian acquisition of Soviet military equipment was significant militarily as well as economically, as the purchases were made against deferred rupee payments, a major concession to India's chronic shortage of foreign exchange. India received extensive cooperation from the Soviet Union in developing its space project, setting up the Thumba Equatorial Rocket Launching Station, launching Indian remote sensing satellites, and sending the first Indian astronaut into space. On the economic front, the Soviet Union was by 1965 the second-largest national contributor to India's development, primarily to the public sector. On the diplomatic front, the Soviet Union played the role of peacemaker between India and Pakistan, brokering the Tashkent Agreement after the 1965 Indo-Pak War. Soviet premier Kosygin offered his services to help reach a settlement, which was embodied in the Tashkent Agreement on 10 January 1966.

The high point of Indo-Soviet friendship was reached with Indira Gandhi's signing of the historic twenty-year Treaty of Peace, Friendship, and Cooperation in August 1971. That treaty gave India the superpower support it needed to launch its army into East Pakistan in December 1971, led by Russian tanks and heavy artillery, defeating Pakistan's army in a few weeks and bringing about the new state of Bangladesh. Articles 8, 9, and 10 of the treaty committed both signatories "to abstain from providing any assistance to any third party that engages in armed conflict with the other." This acted as a deterrent against China. Because of this strategic partnership, India could comfortably make its decisive move of intervention in East Pakistan. During that war, Russia played a significant role in support of India in the United Nations. India in return turned a diplomatic blind eye to the Soviet intervention in Afghanistan in 1979.

In the subsequent years, the leaders of both countries exchanged visits and made serious efforts to promote greater bilateral cooperation in various fields. The first state visit of a Soviet president came about in 1973, when Leonid Brezhnev visited India amid much fanfare. That year, India and the Soviet Union signed a fifteen-year Economic and Trade Agreement, which facilitated cooperation in industry and agriculture. The following year, the Soviet Union demonstrated its support of India's nuclear policy by refusing to condemn either India's first underground plutonium explosion or India's refusal to sign the Non-Proliferation Treaty (NPT). Russia launched India's first satellite, *Aryabhatta*, on 19 April 1975 in keeping with their 1971 agreement, by which both countries agreed to expand cooperation in the exploration and use of outer space. In December 1976 the Soviet Union agreed to supply 5.5 million tons of crude oil to India over a period of four years. Indo-Russian cultural exchanges, including film festivals and visits of cultural groups, were also features of this phase of increased friendship. By the end of the 1970s, the Soviet Union had become India's largest trading partner.

In 1977, soon after the Janata government was elected in the aftermath of Indira Gandhi's "National Emergency," Soviet foreign minister Andrey Gromyko paid a visit to India. With growing Sino-Pakistan strategic cooperation, New Delhi's government was well aware of the importance of friendly relations with Soviet Union. In October 1977, Indian prime minister Morarji Desai visited Moscow, affirming his faith in the 1971 Indo-Soviet friendship treaty. The return of Indira Gandhi to power in January 1980 brought even greater Indian reliance on the Soviet Union. After her assassination in 1984, Rajiv Gandhi continued his mother's policy of close relations with Russia. During his tenure, many high-level visits took place. Rajiv Gandhi visited the Soviet Union in 1985, 1986, 1987, and 1989, while Soviet president Mikhail Gorbachev visited India in 1986 and 1989. India and Russia signed agreements covering such important sectors of India's economy as power, steel, mining, coal, and oil. The Integrated Long Term Programme of Cooperation in Science and Technology (ILTP) was signed in July 1987. Despite some serious irritants, like the Soviet decision to supply arms and military hardware to Pakistan and the publication of Soviet maps showing parts of northern India as part of China, the cordial and warm bilateral relationship continued.

Post–Cold War Era (1990 Onward)

During the cold war the Soviet-Indian relationship rested on twin pillars of mutual interest: containment of a common threat, China; and the reduction of Western influence in Asia. With the end of the cold war, new challenges surfaced for both India and Russia. Coping with the post–cold war international order diverted their energies from bilateral relations to more urgent domestic issues. As a result, Indo-Russian relations saw a marked downtrend in the early 1990s.

The disintegration of the Soviet Union led to the loss of Russia's status as a superpower, and caused a major setback to its economy and ideology. The collapse of the economy and loss of strategic power meant that the Russian federation could no longer continue to favor India in international politics. The collapse of the Soviet Union highlighted the shortcomings of a socialist planned economy, inspiring India to strengthen its resolve to liberalize its own economy and enter the era of globalization.

The emergence of the United States as the world's only superpower compelled both India and Russia to rethink their strategic relations. Both the countries started reestablishing their equations with the United

States, China, and Pakistan. India now realized the potential of closer economic, technological, and strategic cooperation with Washington, while Russia's worldview became more Eurocentric. After withdrawing from Afghanistan, moreover, Russia embarked on repairing its relations with Pakistan, which was unacceptable to India.

In the new global strategic environment, Russia realized that it could no longer match American superiority in any sphere, so it made a decisive strategic shift toward China, which also perceived the United States as a potential threat. India, on the contrary, no longer viewed the United States as a threat but as a potential strategic partner. Many Russian thinkers have proposed the formation of a Russian-Chinese-Indian triangle to counter U.S. global hegemony. The idea was supported by some Indian scholars as well. Yevgeny Primakov's visit to India in 1996 as foreign minister and in 1998 as premier of Russia was viewed as significant in this regard. During his visit to New Delhi in 1998, Primakov suggested the possibility of building a "strategic triangle" between Russia, India, and China as a "viable opposition to American supremacy." But in view of growing Sino-Russian military cooperation, with reportedly more than four thousand Russian scientists and technicians currently working in Chinese defense production facilities, India can hardly trust such potential strategic "cooperation." China appears neither ready to treat India at par nor to abandon its primary strategic nexus with Pakistan.

India no longer depends solely on Russia for strategic or economic assistance. India's defense purchases from Russia are no longer made on rupee payments but in hard currency. India's excessive reliance on Russian weapon systems left India vulnerable to coercive Russian pressure. India now realizes the need to diversify its strategic and economic relations in the new global environment. With that intention, it explored new channels of military support with the United States and the European Union.

The very cornerstone of the Indo-Russian strategic partnership, the 1971 Treaty of Peace, Friendship, and Cooperation, was, moreover, questioned by the Russians themselves as early as 1992. All these reasons depict that the imperatives which shaped the India-Russia strategic partnership in the cold war era have either withered away or stand significantly changed.

Nonetheless, there remained continuity and congruency of interest. Russia declared itself to be the "state-continuator" of the erstwhile Soviet Union and India on its part recognized Russia as the successor-state to the former Soviet Union. Indo-Soviet relations moved seamlessly into Indo-Russian relations. In this transitory phase, an Indian delegation led by Prime Minister V. P. Singh visited Moscow in 1990. The joint statement issued by the leaders of the delegations affirmed their commitment to a more equitable world order. In March 1992 there was another setback to bilateral relations, however, with Russia's decision to apply "full-scope safeguards" to future nuclear supply agreements with India. Though the move was a result of U.S. pressure, it caused a fair amount of resentment among India's leadership. To counter the downward trend in the relationship, in May 1992 an Indo-Russian Commission on Trade, Economic, Scientific, Technological and Cultural Cooperation was established. Within the framework of the commission, twelve working groups, covering different spheres, were established. But the credit for reviving Indo-Russian relations goes to Russian president Boris Yeltsin's visit to India in January 1993. A new Treaty of Friendship and Cooperation was then signed; the only change to the 1971 treaty was the dropping of the security clause and a new emphasis on economic cooperation. Russia was made India's Technical and Economic Cooperation partner country. The long-standing issue of the rupee-ruble exchange rate was also resolved during that visit. President Yeltsin committed to the delivery of cryogenic engines and space technology for the smooth progress of India's space program under a $350 million deal between the Indian Space Research Organisation and the Russian space agency, Glavkosmos.

Positive developments, including the signing of the Moscow Declaration of 30 June 1994 between the two countries (on the protection of interests of pluralistic states and in the interest of mutual security, development, and prosperity of its citizens), put the bilateral relationship back on track. In March 1995, India and Russia signed agreements aimed at suppressing illegal weapons smuggling and drug trafficking. In October 1996, India and Russia agreed to exchange information on military interests and to hold joint military exercises. Indian prime minister H. D. Deve Gowda's visit in March 1997 was another landmark in Indo-Russian relations because many agreements were signed during that visit, including accords concerning extradition, mutual cooperation in customs-related matters, sports, and culture, and the avoidance of double taxation. India's testing of nuclear weapons in 1998 led to a slight downswing in the relationship, as Anglo-American members of the nonproliferation nations wanted Russia to put pressure on India to sign the NPT. But President Vladimir Putin's state visit to India in October 2000 put Indo-Russian relations back in high gear. Seventeen bilateral agreements were signed during Putin's visit, among which the establishment of an Inter-Governmental Commission for Military Technical Cooperation was of prime importance. The ILTP, which was signed between the former Soviet Union and India in July 1987, was extended until 2010. A Declaration on Strategic Partnership was signed by President Putin and Prime Minister Atal B. Vajpayee. This was in tune with the new Foreign Policy Concept released by Russian Federation on 10 July 2002, which stated that one of the crucial directions in the Russian policy in Asia will be to develop friendly relations with the leading Asian states including India. Though the post–cold war era has seen many ups and downs in the relations, mutual interest and politico-strategic compulsions kept them together. A testimony to the depth and enormity of the relationship is the eighty odd bilateral documents that have been concluded between India and the Russian Federation in this period alone.

Contemporary Concerns and Future Prospects

Russia and India have real problems of a similar nature. Economic problems related to increasing poverty and growing economic disparity among various sections of their citizenry, a rise in religious extremism and aggressive nationalism, growing regional imbalance and sectarian violence, weakening rule of law and increasing law and order problems, are causing domestic unrest, while externally aided terrorism and illegal activities like smuggling, drug trafficking, and money laundering are exacerbating the difficulties. Terrorism is now plaguing India as well as Russia, in Kashmir and Chechnya, respectively. Their Strategic Partnership Declaration allows India and Russia to share information, to mount international pressure, and to make joint decisions on international terrorism. Substantial efforts have been made by both countries to suppress illegal weapons smuggling and drug trafficking. Both the countries see many of these problems as ones not only impacting respective national and regional security but international peace, security and stability and hence advocate the need to combat them at all levels.

The common concerns have provided added impetus to bilateral relations. Russia still supplies India with military hardware in sizable quantities, including SU-27 fighter aircraft, TU-22 backfire bombers, SU-27 SK fighter aircraft, MI-17 helicopters, SU-30 MI multipurpose combat aircraft, nuclear-powered submarines (Typhoon class), KILO class submarines, S-300 antimissile systems, and T-72 and T-80 tanks. Russia, to this day, remains India's most reliable defense partner. This was proved during the Kargil crisis of 1999, when Russia stripped its own army of spares to supplement Indian demands. Bilateral defense cooperation between India and Russia goes beyond procurement or a buyer-seller relationship to cover critical aspects of joint research, development, manufacture, and service.

On the economic front, bilateral trade between the two countries has remained sluggish since the breakup of the Soviet Union. It has stagnated at about $1.5 billion. In order to better that, the two countries have revamped the Indo-Russia Inter-Governmental Commission for trade, economic, scientific, and technological cooperation, a crucial agency for facilitating trade and commerce. There is also a shift in the areas of economic interaction from coal, steel, pharmaceuticals, and consumer edibles to cutting-edge areas like space, information technology, robotics, and oil exploration. Russia's entry into the World Trade Organization will provide another common platform for the two countries to work on.

There are some real benefits in bettering India's relationship with Russia. Russia holds the world's biggest reservoir of natural gas, a potentially useful source of energy to the rapidly growing India. Aligning with Russia will also ensure Soviet veto power in India's favor on the Kashmir issue at the United Nations. India will receive Russia's unqualified support for its membership in the expanded United Nations Security Council, which it has been hoping to secure. Finally and most importantly, India will have a strong, vocal partner in striving for a multipolar international system and the strengthening of United Nations.

India's Ministry of External Affairs web site aptly terms the Indo-Russian relationship as "civilisational and time-tested," transcending party lines and political vicissitudes. The relationship is based on mutual respect, trust, understanding, and complementarity of interests. Consistent military cooperation and support for each other's strategic concerns and aspirations, moreover, form the basis of an enduring relationship.

Sultanat Aisha Khan

See also **China, Relations with; Kashmir; National Security Decision-Making; Pakistan and India; Strategic Thought; United States, Relations with; Wars**

BIBLIOGRAPHY

Bakshi, Jyotsna. "Russian Policy towards South Asia." *Strategic Analysis* 23, no. 8 (November 1999): 1367–1398.

Basu, Baidya Bikash. "Putin's Visit and Future of India-Russia Defence Cooperation." *Strategic Analysis* 24, no. 9 (December 2000): 1763–1769.

Cherian, John. "Arms Deals with Russia." *Frontline* 17, no. 16 (18 August 2000): 127–128.

Chopra, V. D., ed. *New Trends in Indo-Russian Relations.* New Delhi: Kalpaz Publications, 2003.

Chufrin, Gennady, ed. *Russia and Asia: The Emerging Security Agenda.* Oxford: Oxford University Press, 1999.

Gidadhubli, R. G. "India-Russia Economic Relations: Issues and Prospects." *Economic and Political Weekly* 34, no. 20 (15 May 1999): 1215–1219.

Kapila, Subhash. "India-Russia Strategic Cooperation: Time to Move Away." Available at <http://www.saag.org/papers2/paper144.html>

Radyuhin, Vladimir. "Rebuilding Russia's Global Role." *Hindu*, 26 July 2003.

Raja Mohan, C. *Crossing the Rubicon: The Shaping of India's New Foreign Policy*. New Delhi: Penguin Books, 2003.

Shams-ud-din, ed. *India and Russia, towards Strategic Partnership*. New Delhi: Lancer Books, 2001.

Tamilin, Alexei. "Does Indo-US Rapprochement Spell Trouble for Russia?" *Journal of Peace Studies* 7, no. 3 (May–June 2000): 66–69.

Unnikrishnan, Nandan. "Indo-Russian Relations." *World Focus* 16, no. 4 (1995): 22.

Yuralov, Felix N. "Russia: Problems of Security in Post Cold War World." *World Affairs* 4, no. 2 (April–June 2000): 51–55.

Zwick, Peter. *Soviet Foreign Relations: Process and Policy*. Englewood Cliffs, N.J.: Prentice Hall, 1990.